TO
IMPROVE
LEARNING

volume II

TO IMPROVE LEARNING

An Evaluation Of Instructional Technology

volume II

PART THREE
Instructional Technology:
Theories and General Applications

PART FOUR
Instructional Technology:
Practical Considerations

PART FIVE
Instructional Technology:
Implications for Business and Industry

PART SIX
Instructional Technology:
Economic Evaluations

EDITED BY
SIDNEY G. TICKTON

with the Staff of
the Academy for Educational Development, Inc.

R. R. BOWKER COMPANY, NEW YORK & LONDON 1971

Published by R. R. Bowker Co. (A XEROX COMPANY)
1180 Avenue of the Americas, New York, N.Y. 10036

International Standard Book Number: 0-8352-0463-4
Library of Congress Catalog Card Number: 79-126018

Printed and bound in the United States of America.

Contents

PART FOUR
Instructional Technology: Practical Considerations

Selected Papers:

PART FIVE
Instructional Technology: Implications for Business and Industry

Selected Papers:

PART SIX
Instructional Technology: Economic Evaluations

Selected Papers:

Introductory Paper

MEMBERS OF THE COMMISSION
ON INSTRUCTIONAL TECHNOLOGY

STERLING M. McMURRIN *Chairman* Dean of the Graduate School,
University of Utah

DAVID E. BELL, executive vice president, the Ford Foundation.

ROALD F. CAMPBELL, dean of the Graduate School of Education,
University of Chicago.

C. RAY CARPENTER, research professor of psychology and anthropology,
Pennsylvania State University and University of Georgia.

NELL P. EURICH, dean of the faculty, Vassar College.

HAROLD B. GORES, president, Educational Facilities Laboratories, Inc.

A. LEON HIGGINBOTHAM, judge, U.S. District Court, Eastern District of
Pennsylvania.

KERMIT C. MORRISSEY, president, Community College of Allegheny
County, Pa.

KENNETH E. OBERHOLTZER, former superintendent of schools,
Denver, Colo.

Commission Staff Provided By
The Academy For Educational Development

EXECUTIVE DIRECTOR OF THE STUDY: Sidney G. Tickton.

ASSOCIATE DIRECTORS: Ronald Gross and Judith Murphy.

SPECIAL CONSULTANT TO THE EXECUTIVE DIRECTOR: Richard Hooper,
Harkness fellow studying instructional technology throughout the
United States, 1967-69.

STAFF CONSULTANTS: Frederick Breitenfeld, Jr., Maryland Center for Public
Broadcasting. Howard B. Hitchens, Lieutenant colonel, U.S. Air Force, U.S.
Air Force Academy. Robert C. Snider, Division of Educational Technology,
National Education Association. Richard E. Speagle, Drexel Institute of
Technology.

RESEARCH ASSISTANTS: Louise Abrahams, Lane Carpenter, Patricia Wagner,
and Nikki Zapol.

ADMINISTRATIVE ASSISTANT: Lonna Jones.

Technology and Education

STERLING M. McMURRIN

Dean of the Graduate School
University of Utah

Chairman
Comm. on Instructional Technology

The Commission on Instructional Technology

The 90th Congress enacted the Public Broadcasting Act of 1967 to develop the potential of noncommercial television and radio. The first two titles provided for the extension to June 30, 1970 of federal grants for the construction of educational broadcasting facilities, and for the establishment of the Public Broadcasting Corporation. Title III of the act authorized "a comprehensive study of school uses of TV, radio, and allied instructional media." On the basis of Title III, plus an administration proposal, a nine-member Commission on Instructional Technology was appointed by the Secretary of Health, Education, and Welfare and the Commissioner of Education in March, 1968 to conduct this study. Under the Congressional act, the Commission is required to submit its report to the President for transmittal to the Congress not later than June 30, 1969.

Most of the commissioners are laymen in the matter of instructional technology; only a minority have expert knowledge in the field. All, however, are vitally interested in education and most of them are actively engaged in educational professions. By profession they represent the public schools, universities, foundations, and community colleges. In addition, the membership includes a federal judge. The Commissioners are Dr. David Bell, Ford Foundation; Dr. Roald Campbell, Dean, Graduate School of Education, University of Chicago; Dr. C. Ray Carpenter, Professor of Psychology, Pennsylvania State University; Dr. Nell Eurich, Dean of the Faculty, Vassar College; Dr. Harold B. Gores, President, Educational Facilities Laboratories, Inc.; the Honorable A. Leon Higginbotham, Jr., Judge, Eastern District of Pennsylvania; Mr. Kermit Morrissey, President, Community College of Allegheny County; Dr. Kenneth Oberholtzer, Denver, Colorado, former Superintendent of Schools; and Dr. McMurrin, Chairman.

The Act which directed the establishment of the Commission described its purposes primarily in terms of the instructional uses of television and radio. It authorized the Secretary of Health, Education, and Welfare to

> conduct a comprehensive study, in consultation with other interested federal agencies, of instructional television and radio (including broadcast, closed circuit, community antenna television, and instructional television fixed services, and two-way communication of data links and computers) and their relation to each other and to instructional materials such as videotapes, films, discs, computers, and other educational materials or devices, and such other aspects thereof as may be of

assistance in determining whether and what Federal aid should be provided for instructional radio and television.

When the Commission was constituted, however, the United States Commissioner of Education directed it to study the entire field of instructional technology without giving special emphasis to any particular medium. Accordingly, the work of the Commission has been concerned with the whole gamut of instructional techniques—old, new, and future; printed, mechanical, and electronic; automated and cybernated; from books to computers, from classrooms to learning centers, from overhead projectors to satellite transmission, from pre-school to graduate school. However, I would like to assure those who are especially interested in the instructional uses of radio and television that the Commission and its staff are fully conscious of the emphasis of the congressional act and there will be no neglect of these media. On the contrary, the Commission intends to fully explore the great values which the arts of radio and television have for education to assure appropriate support for their future development and use. I am pleased to report here that the National Association of Educational Broadcasters and individual members of that Association are currently working closely with the Commission in its studies.

In an address before the National Audio-Visual Association on July 13, 1968, Mr. Howe, the Commissioner of Education, briefly described the purposes of the Commission on Instructional Technology:

> We have reached the point where we have to find an approach to the development and use of educational technology that is at least superior to the process of sink-or-swim selection or of random, accidental experiment. We have got to come up with a more orderly, informed way of taking advantage of all that the new technology has to offer. . . .
>
> I think we have every reason to expect that the report of this Commission will give us the kind of authoritative, independent, and expert assessment of instructional technology that we have long lacked. It will suggest priorities for the purchase and use of the new technology. It will give our school officials better guidelines and grounds for deciding how much to spend for what devices in what combination. Equally important, it will help elected and other government officials determine levels of funding—both locally and nationally.
>
> The report of this Commission will be relevant no matter who occupies the White House or the office of the U.S. Commissioner of Education. It will represent the common and considered judgment of a distinguished group of men with very broad backgrounds in education and related fields. It will reflect the vast amount of research already done on educational technology but never really put in a total perspective. It will give full weight to the views and experience of all interested parties—in education, in industry, in government.

With this charge in mind, the Commission is looking at "instructional technology" as a whole, as a system greater than the sum of the various media. It is concerned with the status and potential of each medium and of the media combined, with prospective developments, with attitudes and obstacles, and with the most significant questions raised by the introduction of technical means in education. Throughout, the focus is on the most urgent and imminent problems facing America's determination to equalize educational opportunity and individualize the processes of instruction.

The first meeting of the Commission was held on April 22, 1968. By this time the Office of Education had selected the Academy for Educational Development to act as staff for the Commission, with the Academy's executive vice president, Sydney G. Tickton, as study director. Under the Commission's direction, the staff promptly began to assemble ideas and information. Letters were sent to over 2,000 persons representing a broad sampling of the educational community as well as other interested institutions, individuals, government agencies, associations, and private enterprises involved with instructional technology. In addition, in order to ensure the widest range of response, announcements were placed in trade, professional, and other publications inviting communications to the Commission.

Simultaneously, an extensive set of questions probing broad policy matters as well as technical details and specific uses of instructional technology has been developed. The staff has sought expert information and opinion on every phase of the Commission's mandate—from establishment representatives and mavericks alike. As a result, between 150 and 200 research and information papers have been commissioned, and numerous interviews have been arranged. The Commission has also retained expert consultants to work with its staff.

Most meetings of the Commission are combined with field investigations to give the Commissioners a close look at technology at work in all levels and areas of education (public schools, universities, the armed services, industry, the Job Corps, etc.), in order to observe at first hand the various ways "instructional technology" is currently employed. They also are exposed to theorists and researchers at the frontiers of the field.

Besides regular meetings of the Commission, seminars bring together groups of knowledgeable, experienced specialists in specific media fields. In the meantime, staff members are making field trips and preparing memoranda on organizations and projects recommended to the Commission's attention because of their quality, special promise, or cautionary import.

The staff has also been searching out and cataloguing a library of relevant materials, published and unpublished. This includes studies and projections supported by the Office of Education and other government and private agencies. Selections of this material are sent, week by week, to Commission members along with the reports prepared especially for the Commission. To date, upwards of fifty notebooks have been received by each Commission member.

Finally, it should be mentioned that cooperation has been established with the several administrative departments and other agencies of the federal government which have an interest in instructional technology and which are competent to contribute importantly to the study.

The Commission members have been gratified by the interest manifested in their work, and by the calibre of the dozens of distinguished persons—scholars, technicians, practicing schoolmen and others—who have agreed to prepare papers or grant interviews. Hundreds of thoughtful replies have come in response to the Commission's original invitation and announcement. They have come, and continue to come, from all quarters—from industry, from superintendents of big school systems like Detroit, Chicago, and New York, and from dozens of smaller places; from nearly every state commissioner of education and state office of education.

We have received valuable input, for instance, from such professional groups as the American Library Association, Association of Classroom Teachers, American Association of School Administrators, National Association of Educational Broadcasters, American Association of University Professors, and from the Boy Scouts, YWCA, Institute of Electrical and Electronic Engineers, and the American Bankers Association.

There have been answers from approximately two hundred colleges and universities— from the Chairman of the Corporation at M.I.T. and the President of Princeton; from the deans of education of numerous leading universities throughout the nation; from deans and department heads in the fields of computer science, behavioral research, medicine, engineering, instructional resources, communications, instructional television.

In television alone, respondents include heads of educational networks and independent stations, university stations, school TV systems, and state systems.

The response directly from the schools has been of immeasurable value.

The August Commission meeting was held in the Denver area with visits to the Air Force Academy and to Lowry Field. The Commission was briefed on overall Air Force involvement with instructional technology and its applications in the Lowry training program and in the regular academic work of the Air Force Academy.

In October, the Commission met in San Francisco and in addition to its deliberations visited the Ampex laboratories, the Job Corps Center at Pleasanton, San Jose State College, the IBM Education Center at Los Gatos, and the Palo Alto Unified School District.

Within the past few days the Commission met at Detroit and combined its meeting with observations of the uses of instructional media in advanced industrial establishments of that area.

A seminar to explore communications satellites and their implications for instructional technology was held in September. Participating were representatives of the National Aeronautics and Space Administration, National Association of Educational Broadcasters, Federal Communications Commission, National Educational Television, United States Office of Education, the President's Task Force on Communication Policy, and the Joint Council on Educational Telecommunications.

Early in November, a seminar was held with a representative group of ITV practitioners to brief the Commission on unique problems of ITV and to acquaint the profession with the Commission's purposes. Later to provide a forum for the discussion of instructional television, the Commission held a seminar in Washington which was attended by a group of 19 national leaders in the field. Participants included network, station, administrative and school people as well as delegates from such associations as the National Association of Educational Broadcasters, the Joint Council on Educational Telecommunications, and the National Education Association.

Staff members have already inspected many projects, attended many conferences, visited many organizations. They will pursue these investigations at an accelerated pace in the months ahead. Organizations visited include the American Association for Colleges of Teacher Education, the American Association for the Advancement of Science, the American Vocational Association, the National School Boards Association. Conferences attended include a Leadership Seminar on Teaching the Film, sponsored by the American Film Institute; the Second Annual Los Angeles Film Study Conference, sponsored by Fordham University and the American Film Institute; the Conference on Computer Assisted Instruction sponsored by IBM, the National Council of Teachers of Mathematics, and Pennsylvania State University; Curriculum and Training Strategies, and Managing the Creation and Adaptation of CAI Instructional Programs, sponsored by the Institute for Computer-Assisted Instruction. Some of the institutions visited thus far are Miami-Dade Junior College (Learning Resources Center); Michigan State University (closed circuit television); Oklahoma Christian College (dial access); New York Institute of Technology (computerized management of the educational process); NDEA Summer Institute for Teachers of the Disadvantaged at the University of Southern California; U.S. Penitentiary, Leavenworth, Kansas.

The questions which the Commission on Instructional Technology is examining are not limited to educational problems that are currently urgent or to the uses of equipment which is presently available. In assigning papers and interviewing experts, the Commission has attempted to avoid undue emphasis on equipment per se or on the particular medium, but has attempted instead to probe the value of technology employed in systems of instruction. I cannot overstate the Commission's interest in the instructional possibilities of technical instruments when these are employed in instructional systems which relate them effectively to one another and to the purposes and total activities of the instructional staff.

The papers that are now being received range from such broad topics as: "The most pressing educational needs that face the country today and how new technology can help to meet those needs" to such specific applications as the use of the 8mm camera.

Following are examples of the questions to which the study seeks answers:

What changes may be necessary in the organizational patterns and administrative procedures of schools and colleges in order for new technologies to effectively improve instruction?

What effect would the extensive use of instructional technology have on the teaching profession?

What are the costs of selected programs and technical systems? What can we learn from past costs and results? How can hypothetical cost studies establish guidelines and rules for the future? How can cost-benefit analyses be made of present activities and future activities?

How can instructional technology be employed to improve the quality of teaching and learning in ghetto schools and in schools in other poverty areas?

In addition to such across-the-board questions, state-of-the-art papers on individual media are under preparation. The Commission is seeking insight into outstanding successes, failures, problems of utilization and attitude, and informed projections of the likely and/or desirable future.

The report will in no sense be a technical manual nor a chapter-by-chapter handbook on each individual technology or medium. Instead, we propose to present findings under such tentative headings as "Educational Needs and Instructional Technology," "The Present State and Future Possibilities of the Art," "New Goals and Possibilities of Instruction," "Administration, Management and Policy-Making," "Costs and Financing."

The shape and scope of the prospective report will be formulated by the Commission at its next few meetings. At these sessions, the Commission will come to grips with the information and recommendations then at its disposal. It will then hammer out the conclusion and recommendations that will constitute its final report. The report may be presented in other forms as well as print, utilizing one or another of the media which are under consideration.

The Commission's report will provide information and explicit recommendations. It will be directed primarily to the federal government—to the administration and the Congress—but it will be of special interest and value to all leaders in education, local, state, and national, to teachers and students, to decision makers in civic affairs, and to the general public.

Technology in Education and Education in a Technological Society

To turn to the role of technology in education and the task of education in a society where technology is rapidly becoming the chief determinant of the culture: It is now commonplace to say that we are at the beginning of a revolution in education. Certainly all the ingredients for revolution are at hand and the signs are promising. But we cannot yet say for sure whether the revolution will be productive or abortive. And if it is productive, we do not know for sure just what it will produce.

What we do know is that while the tasks of education are becoming more complex and more difficult, great possibilities seem to be opening up before us. And that in the months and years immediately ahead the schools must make a series of decisions which will importantly affect the character and quality of education and have a determining impact upon the total life of our society for a long time to come. Genuine openness to innovation, readiness for experiment, commitment to a continuing assessment of ends and of the most effective ways of achieving them—these are the decisions which must be made now and can be made now.

It is here, of course, where technology enters the picture. There are at least two kinds of

schoolmen who are likely to short-change their schools in the future; those ultraconserva-
tives who refuse to believe that the new developments in educational technology have
something genuinely important to bring to the improvement of instruction, and those
ultras at the other extreme who plunge too hastily into expensive investments without
reliable knowledge of their value and without adequate competence to employ the equipment effectively.

It is entirely obvious that the discussion of the processes of instruction becomes inevitably involved with problems of the substance of education. It is clearly impossible to
answer the question of *how* without at the same time coming to grips with the question of
what. But judging from the energy expended on these matters, it apparently is not equally
clear that neither of these questions can be properly pursued without including the question of *why,* the question of the large aims and purposes of education and their relation
to the goals of instruction. In recent decades much attention has been given to methods.
Fortunately over the past decade and a half the substance of education has begun to find
its proper place in research and development. And effective techniques are being developed for the conception and production of improved instructional materials. We appear to
be on the threshold of a major breakthrough in instructional processes. Moreover, the close
relation between substance and method is receiving more respect. But the serious discussion
of educational purposes and goals and their relation to the substance and techniques of
instruction still lags far behind.

The importance of this predicament is immediately seen when we consider the possibilities of the new instructional technology, possibilities for a more effective individualization of instruction and for a generally larger return on the investment in the schools, a
return in the form of increased knowledge, improved skills, and cultivated talent. But here
also are the dangers which many fear, the possible depersonalization of instruction, the
breakdown of the human relationships which, ideally at least, have traditionally characterized the schoolroom. These relationships are often assumed to have an important relevance to the effectiveness of instruction in addition to their obvious intrinsic worth and
their value in the personal and social cultivation of the individual. At least the dangers of
dehumanization are real for the schools, as they are for all our social institutions, if they
fall prey to a technological order in which ends are dominated and determined by means.
And such is the power of our rapidly developing technology that such an order is a real
possibility if we fail to contend intelligently with the question of purposes and goals. The
means of instruction will inevitably influence the shape of both the ends and substance of
education, but the ends of education, the purposes for which we establish and maintain
our schools, must be continually defined and redefined on the basis of genuinely humane
considerations.

This is not to deny the close relationship that should obtain between ends and means.
It is not a proposal to abstract the determination of ends from involvement with specific
and practical means. Professor Dewey's case against the separation of ends and means is
probably the most important insight contributed to moral philosophy in modern times and
it demands respect here as elsewhere if our ends are to avoid the risk of vain abstraction
or absolutistic dogma. In the determination of educational purpose, to ignore the actual
and possible concrete means of instruction, ranging from the uses of books, laboratories,
television, or computers to the deployment of teaching personnel or the patterns of school
architecture, would not be unlike ignoring the social facts of ghetto life or the realities of
race prejudice while designing the curriculum for educating urban teachers. That means
will inevitably become a force in shaping ends is clearly evident from a glance at the obvious impact of modern industrial and transportation technology on the common values
of our society.

But this, of course, comes directly to the crux of the problem. How can the means of
instruction play a proper role in fashioning ends, both the large purposes of education and

the proximate goals of instruction, without becoming the dominant factor in the mixture? The ends we seek must be genuinely relevant to the means which we can competently and effectively employ, and we should leave no corner unturned in our exploration for more effective means. Yet if our means, our methods and techniques, become the chief force that shapes our ends we will already have sacrificed the personal and humane to the dictature of technology. This is the great problem we face as we survey the future of educational technology. Success here will surely require a larger investment of talent and energy in the investigation and determination of educational purposes than we are accustomed to make.

The purposes of education cannot be deduced from cosmic principles, nor are they established as a body of absolute values laid up eternally in some platonic heaven. They are not irrelevant to metaphysical considerations, and they certainly are intimately involved with, and in some instances identical with elements of moral philosophy and value theory. But attempts to derive educational purposes from philosophical theory, as has so often been done by educational scholars in the past, will fail to produce anything genuinely viable and relevant as a body of principles unless that theory is brought into some meaningful relationship with the facts of personal and social experience, with the needs, interests, and aspirations of individuals, with the failures, successes, and goals of society, with the established personal and social values and the criticism of those values.

When the question is asked, what is the purpose of education, what are its ends, to what are the commitment and energies of our schools properly directed, the answer must be sought across the total spectrum of human interest, experience, and value. In our society, education concerns first the well-being of the individual pupil and student, his capabilities for a productive and happy life in which he can pursue an interesting and satisfying vocation and in which his potentialities as a person are enlarged and fulfilled. But it concerns as well the strength of the Nation, its social solidarity, its industrial and commercial power, its economic integrity, political wisdom, and military competence, its total strength for security and survival. And it concerns the quality of the culture, the substance of its values, the intellectual, artistic, and spiritual norms by which we live and by which our judgments are made and our purposes defined. The meaning of education for our society is found in the all important question of how we are to achieve and preserve a genuinely free society in which men are authentic persons who are masters rather than slaves of the forces which shape their world.

Now to think on these large matters can be useful in seeking perspective, motivation, and direction for the work of the schools. But the schools must shape their instructional programs to fit more immediate goals, the proximate ends which lie within the near reach of the child. These goals are tied to the basic types of personal experience: the *cognitive,* the *affective,* and the *volitional.* The worth of the various instructional instruments and techniques must be judged in terms of their effectiveness in achieving these goals.

School education is essentially an intellectual enterprise and the *cognitive* function of instruction lies at its center. The cognitive task is not only the achievement and communication of knowledge. It is discipline in the habits of reason, in the ways of knowing; a discipline in perception, in the inductive, deductive, and intuitive processes, and in the techniques of analysis and generalization. It involves both sensory knowledge and abstract thought. And for the lower schools, it entails especially the cultivation of the skills of literacy—the capacity for reading, writing, oral expression, and computation—which make the acquisition of knowledge possible.

The *affective* function of instruction, concerning which we now know far too little but which relates to much that is most precious in the experience of the child, is concerned with the dispositions of the practical life—motives, passions, the esthetic and moral sensitivities, the feelings of concern, appreciation, sympathy, and attachment.

Between the *affective* and *volitional* functions and goals of instruction no clear line can be drawn. Volitional goals have to do with will, decision, and action, with commitment, struggling, and striving. These cannot be divorced from the passions and sentiments or from knowledge and the processes of rational thought.

At the present time we know far more about the processes of learning that are geared to cognitive instructional goals than we know of those relating to emotional and volitional experience. My point in mentioning this matter is that far more adequate knowledge in these latter areas is quite desperately needed if we are to intelligently evaluate the new technology. Here we are in danger of serious error. Cognition and its related functions are not the whole story of instructional goals, and as we move toward new techniques of instruction, often employing automated and electronic instruments, we must develop methods of evaluating those techniques, not only for their effectiveness in communicating factual information or in cultivating the various knowledge skills, but also for their impact on the emotions, the imaginative and creative powers, the artistic and moral sensibilities. It is important to know, for instance, not only whether individualized instruction through the use of video-tapes or computers will importantly facilitate the learning of historical or scientific data, but also whether it will have an effect on the student's intellectual initiative, his independence of mind, or his artistic responsiveness.

We are sometimes in danger of seriously neglecting the non-cognitive facets of life, not only in the schools but in social life generally. Occidental culture has a long tradition of preoccupation with knowledge, reason, and abstraction, a habit of mind that has produced a verbal-conceptual type of education that relies heavily on language and language skills. The ability to use words and mathematical symbols and to engage in logical discourse with complex ideas is for us the chief mark of educational achievement. The inner life of feeling and appreciation and the countless moral, aesthetic, and spiritual values associated with that life deserve far more attention than they commonly receive. How will the new technology serve us in these areas of learning? What mix of media, of teacher and machine, should be used, and when—if any?

At any rate, we must be ready to ask a few pointed questions of our automated and cybernated machines:

> Can the proposed technique be effectively employed in the cultivation of an open, inquiring mind? Or does it tend to produce conformity, dogmatism, and regimentation of thought?

> Is it capable of communicating and facilitating an understanding of complex concepts? Or is its usefulness limited to the management and manipulation of simple ideas?

> Is it capable of cultivating sensitive insight, originality, analytical facility, and creative intellectual skills?

> Can it be employed to induce and deepen artistic and moral sensitivity and appreciation?*

It is not my intention here to labor the specific issues with which the decision makers must contend in matters pertaining to educational technology, but a few miscellaneous guidelines may be in order.

> 1. The concern for speed, efficiency, accuracy, and economy must be balanced by the concern for educational quality and humane values. The new technology, like any other method, is justified only where it produces education of higher quality.

> 2. The diversity of the curriculum and the multiple purposes of education require variety in teaching methods. The instructional uses of television, programs,

*I wrote these questions for Innovation in Education: New Directions for the American School, a policy statement of the Committee for Economic Development, published in 1968. (S.McM.)

or computers have limitations, as do the more conventional techniques. Those limits must be carefully established by achievement testing and experimentation. Both the uses and abuses of the new technology must be clearly known by both teachers and administrators.

3. For most purposes a mixture of techniques has proved more desirable than concentration on a single method. Particular techniques should be evaluated in relation to specific tasks. They may not be applicable to the whole process of instruction.

4. The values of the new technology must in every case be carefully weighed against the values of conventional methods and new non-technological methods before judgments and decisions are made effecting large changes in instructional patterns. The comparison of methods is a complex task involving differences in instructional goals as well as in subject matter and techniques.

5. Judgment and decision on the new technology must be made on the basis of extensive experience and expert analysis, not on the persuasion of rhetoric and the desire for institutional status. It involves an understanding of whole complex of human values, side effects, etc. Research and experimentation in this area are expensive and difficult. They must be done at a high level of competence to avoid eventual waste in money and effort and they inevitably entail risk and the possibility of failure. This is a national task that reaches beyond the resources of the vast majority of individual school districts.

6. An adequate design for the effective employment of mechanical or electronic audiovisual techniques in our instructional system cannot be made apart from considerations involving the pre-service and in-service preparation of teachers, the structure and deployment of professional and paraprofessional personnel, technical assistance, and methods of storage, retrieval, and maintenance.

7. Always, this question should be asked: Do the benefits gained justify the costs incurred?

To add a final note, two things should never be forgotten: first, that there is a point at which the student needs a teacher rather than a machine to confer with and relate to. The personal relationship between student and teacher should never be neglected. And second, that the values that accrue from the intellectual interactions and social relationships with other students should not be lost.

The problem of educational purposes and instructional goals and the means for achieving them has far-reaching implications for our society beyond its immediate bearing on the quality of instruction. The central issue of our time is the question of ends and means. It asks whether in the future we will live in a humane society or in a technological order. Will we live in a society in which ends are established by consideration of the human values which we associate with intellectual, moral, and spiritual freedom, with individuality, uniqueness, and spontaneity, a society of persons in which the autonomous personality is both the sovereign and sacred end? Or will it be an order whose ends are determined by our means—by our techniques, our ways of effective manipulation, our mass actions and rituals, our automated and cybernated technology, our need and demand for efficiency and organization; an order in which individualism yields to collectivism, diversity to sameness, freedom to regimentation; and where persons are transformed into things.

Now this is an overstatement of the alternative worlds which we face. Such simple and extreme descriptions distort the utter complexity of the historical process and the social structure.

But we do, in fact, face two worlds—a world of "boundless hopes" and a world of "deep menace." And the hopes and the menace do not lie entirely in the future. They are already with us and are profoundly true of us.

It is in education more than in any department of our civic and cultural life where we must face these promises and threats—first because they are basic to the quality and character of education itself—but even more because where education goes, there go the foundations of our culture.

Already we are affected in some degree by the tyranny of our technical means over our humane ends and we may expect that this condition will become increasingly grave as we refine and expand our techniques, whether they are techniques of human organization and social manipulation or the techniques of our remarkably sophisticated technology, the automated machines which extend our physical capabilities and the cybernated electronic devices which extend our mental powers. This condition will become increasingly grave, that is, unless in some way we reverse the trend and climb on top of the vast and difficult problem which our own genius has created. The same creative effort, energy, and inventiveness which have produced our material technology must be invested in defining the goals of our culture and civilization and exploring the ways for insuring that our purposes will rule our techniques and will not be simply determined by them.

This is the great task of education—to guarantee the progress that assures us the full benefits of an advancing technology and yet to preserve and enhance the humane quality of a civilization whose humanity is threatened by that technology. To fully succeed in this task, our schools must effectively employ the instruments of instruction which the technology provides—but employ them always as means only, and never as ends or as the chief determiners of ends.

Instructional Technology: Theories and General Applications

23.
Teleinstruction
And Individualized Learning*

C. R. CARPENTER
Research Prof. of
Psychology and Anthropology
Penn. State Univ.
Univ. of Georgia

Approaches to the Subject

The purpose of this paper is to contribute to the tasks of clarifying and extending design strategies and practices for effectively using available and emerging telecommunication technologies for instigating the formal learning of college students.

The new cryptic term, *teleinstruction,* conveys the concept of the use of equipment, processes and procedures which provide instruction or the stimulation of learning at a distance from the original source of the stimulus materials. The operations can be simultaneous or sequential and involve recordings and time schedules.

The Multi-Media Approach

Closed circuit television (CCTV) is only one type of a very wide array of equipment, apparatus, instrumentation and procedures for providing communications for the instruction of individuals at remote points. Radio and broadcast television, on-line and shared-time computer arrangements, dial access materials and telephones can be used for purposes of teleinstruction. This extended concept should make a useful contribution to this important seminar on *Using Educational Media to Individualize Instruction* and to the design and use of instructional systems.

The problem that confronts us, and which we shall attempt to resolve, is to show how the so-called "mass media" and other associated and complemental technologies can be used in new patterns and varied configurations to provide some of the required conditions for formal instruction and the educational development of college students.

Rapidly advancing thinking holds that the designing of optimum conditions and general systems of information for learning by students in colleges and universities requires the use of planned and tested *combinations of media.* The correct instructional uses of closed circuit television, for example, currently may require books and periodicals, audio communication, tutorials, seminars and direct lectures, laboratory "experiments" and field experiences. This

This paper was prepared for faculty seminars sponsored by Bucknell University and the U.S. Office of Education, November 1967, on using educational media to individualize college instruction.

list does not exhaust the possible means and methods that may be needed for designing the complex requirements for optimally stimulating academic learning.

The multi-media system of instruction is widely accepted, and wise, knowledgeable people have long since ceased to display the pathological syndrome of single medium fixation which was so characteristic of educational media innovators of the 1940s, 1950s and the early 1960s. Nevertheless there are still, at this late hour, fashions of media. The current one can probably be labeled "computer aided instruction" (CAI). Programmed instruction and teaching machines was CAI's immediate predecessor and closed circuit and broadcast television were previous fashions. We are becoming rapidly more perceptive than formerly about media fads and fashions, and we calmly understand that as each medium is proposed as the solution to learning strategies that "this, too, shall pass away."

Redefinition of the Problem

There is an advance also of conceptual thinking about the media. They are carriers of information. They are empty channels and raw tapes, films and paper. The basic, complex problem is to select the most appropriate modes of communication for learning strategies and put these into combinations. What kinds and proportions of modes are most effective for insuring specified learning results and performance changes for specified content units and for learners with known characteristics? When and where do we use print, spoken language (directly or recorded), graphic modes of communications, animation, art forms, and photography (both still and motion)? What kinds of print in what formats best fit the requirements for optimizing the learning conditions? The same question can be asked about the other modes of communication. How do we use combinations of these modes in both simultaneous or sequential configurations? For what reasons or learning objectives should different modes and *combinations of modes* be used to provide high quality instruction? When do different modes summate, extend learning, increase generalization and when do different modes produce interference with learning?

When we become more specific in the task of design strategies, the problem becomes that of selecting modes and mode configurations which summate, reinforce and strengthen the stimulus impact on students and which shape their conceptual skills and intellectual competencies. Those media and modes should be selected and used to *broaden* and *vary* stimulus conditions to enhance the interests of students, and, to increase the possibilities for the retention and generalization of learned performances. It is most difficult to select mode combinations which do not have internal interferences or do not overload the neuro-sensory channels with information or exceed the optimum rate of stimulus presentations.

What are the relations of all of these questions to the problem of individualizing instruction?

This line of thinking points to some of the most fundamental problems of instructional communications, and indeed of the nature of knowledge, its origin and order, its growth and organization.

Teleinstruction and individualized learning would seem to pose a dilemma, a clash of ideas and a conflict of concepts—How can the media and modes of modern technology be appropriately employed in learning strategies?

Education has many shrines where educators worship, and one of these modern shrines is individualized instruction. There is no inter-individual nerve net. Let us agree once and for all time that only individuals learn. Classes, groups, seminars, families, audiences and populations do not learn. Individuals alone learn, but most frequently they learn in classes, groups, seminars, families, audiences and populations. These groupings constitute important if not essential conditions which affect in many ways the learning of individuals.

Furthermore, it should be observed that there are factors in social conditions that affect learning positively by reinforcing the learning, and there are other factors that affect learning negatively by interfering with or inhibiting learning.

Surely individuals do talk audibly or subvocally with themselves to good effect; they think, solve problems, test for better words or phrases, imagine new concept structures, create art objects and dream about the future. Surely, too, individuals do listen to others and learn; they engage in intensive and revealing dialogues, contend in debate and try their wings of logic in disputations. They observe models of intellectual performances and reject them or emulate them. In brief, learning is individualized and socialized. Only individuals learn but social factors provide positive and negative conditions which importantly affect the kind and rate of learning.

There are four practical guidelines that may be useful in the planning and execution of learning strategies.

1. Design and provide varied and balanced patterns of conditions for learning. Vary sizes and composition of learning groups. Vary schedules. Balance study in splendid isolation for depth with discussions in groups for brightness and interest.

2. Design and provide conditions for learning which are like or which simulate the future conditions under which the individuals under consideration will continue to learn during their whole life cycle. There is, pertinent to our topic of *teleinstruction,* little prospect that the radio, the telephone, television, and motion picture films will disappear as sources of information, instruction and entertainment.

3. Whatever the conditions of learning and learning technology, students need training in the strategies and skills for learning under the *special conditions* arranged or provided for formal learning. This proposition applies especially to individualizing learning and to planning for students to study independently.

4. Students should be taught in ways which lead them to become autonomous learners who are weaned both from their parents and teachers. The autonomous learner is freed from school requirements and restraints. He sets his own learning tasks, selects his own materials and methods, he achieves his own goals and reaps his own rewards.

With these approaches now made explicit, let us turn directly to the question of how to use *teleinstruction media* and how at the same time to individualize optimally the learning conditions. The question could be stated to read: How to individualize learning optimally while using teleinstructional principles, means, and methods.

Let us be very clear about the kinds of equipment, methods and content or messages that we are discussing and from which we can select patterns and combinations. The roll call is as follows: printed materials; recordings on film or tape, both audio and video; live transmissions ranging from telephone lines to multi-channel cables and on-line computers to laser beams; and broadcast diffusions ranging from radio to continent-spanning communication satellites. It is proposed, furthermore, that many patterns of these phenotypically different but functionally similar media can be used to solve the design problems of maximizing the efficacy of instruction for learning. The design may include the special case of precisely adapted instruction for individualized learning.

Analysis of the Problem of Individualization of Learning

Essentially the general problem is to arrange for and adapt mediated instruction and conditions of media-mode uses to accommodate within the tolerance limits of individual differences which are essential and integral to learning. We are not to be concerned here with individual differences which are not highly contingent to learning operations. We are especially concerned with those adaptations and sets of conditions which affect learning to a degree of practical significance as well as statistical significance.

Ideally and theoretically we should include the settings or conditions for learning as well as the displays of materials for learning whether mediated by a teacher or through technologies. Individual requirements for learning are not unlimited. Tolerance limits can be found, it is assumed, and levels of difficulty, pacing rates and progression rates can be adjusted within these limits.

Managing Instruction

In addition to individual differences of students, there are other major components of the problem of individualized learning. Some of these are the following:

1. Arranging for optimized interactions of instructional materials with the personalized goals, values, interests and activated motives of students.

2. Determining the general and specific educational competency levels of students and adjusting the levels of possible interactions with the right *kinds* and *levels* of instructional materials and methods.

3. Designing and arranging the *places* where learning interactions are to occur between students and the stimulus materials, students and teachers and students with students.

4. Scheduling, programming and pacing the patterns of interactions with the selected and designed instructional materials.

5. Programming the gradual transition from external control to self-regulated learning activities.

The regulation of interactions over time involves two main operations; scheduling or programming, and timing or pacing. Programming a student through a curriculum or course is a gross operation extending over years, months, days and hours. Pacing is the rate at which an individual processes information provided by the instruction; the rate of perceiving, speed of reading, the rates of learning and understanding stimulus materials are processes that are included in pacing or fine timing. Pacing requires fine timing which may have an optimum rate range extending from microseconds for some kinds of foreign language learning, which involves matching and modeling phrases and sentences, to minutes for some kinds of problem solving or the mastery of complex concepts. Furthermore, scheduling like pacing can be self-regulated or externally controlled.

Learner Adaptations

The designing of instructional strategies includes another problem; namely, apportioning the kinds and amounts of adaptation demands or requirements between the *instructional materials and associated media* on the one hand and *the student* on the other hand. Effective instruction involves, among many other things, making appropriate and increasing demands on the student for increasing efforts to learn. When this is done, the student has many options of his own for accommodating to these demands. He can accept, reject or accommodate to them. Involved here are many styles of gamesmanship that is both understood and misunderstood by teachers and students. Students are not merely response mechanisms; they are persons who take action.

There is a problem here that we believe we discovered at Penn State. We had been mystified over and over again by the finding that regardless of the attempts to improve the instruction of courses, at least by greatly increasing the instructional energy input and by the elaboration of instructional materials and methods, grades and test scores remained relatively constant. The results were reflected both in measurements of means and variances.

A condition that prevailed in our experiments was that we usually attempted to develop only one, and never more than two, of the four or five semester courses of the student full course load.

It is known that students establish for themselves levels of performance expectancies, and these same expectancies are established for grades. Serious students also differentiate grade level expectancies for different courses in relation to their importance to him. It is more important for students to achieve good grades, for example, in their majors than in their elective courses.

There is an additional set of factors which seems to be operating. *Poor instruction may be compensated for by good learning.* A condition for this to occur is strong interest on the part of students in a subject.

Now we are ready for the paradox and hypothesis: when instruction is importantly improved in one of a set of courses and learning is made easier for the student, the demands on the student are reduced in that course and the grade level expectancy can be achieved with less effort, then the student channels his energies into the other courses of his total program, consequently grades and test measures in the improved experimental course remain as they were before the course was developed.

The most important conclusion that can be formulated, assuming that the hypothesis is correct, is that good experimentation in an operational educational context requires that the *total demand system* which operates on students be brought under control or included in the experimental design strategies.

It is interesting to observe that our definition of an adequate sampling of content has changed from lesson or instructional units in 1948 to full courses in 1958 and now the entire work load of students in 1968!

Patterns of Use of Teleinstruction

The patterns of use of telecommunications equipment and technology for instruction in colleges and universities is only part of the full strategies of instruction. From 1954 to 1964 we planned, developed, used and generally evaluated about twenty-five permutations and variations of patterns of use of telecommunications.

These studies have been reported in four major reports and a sound picture.* I propose to review some of the main developments and suggest how some of these patterns can be used to accommodate to the goals and interests of students and their individual differences and also used to provide flexibility of instruction. Other patterns of use require adaptations that students themselves can make. There are patterns of production and patterns of use that cannot be recommended. There are those that remain to be developed, perfected and accepted by educators.

Initially we used the basic and primitive method of originating instruction from a large classroom with fixed cameras connected by means of cable to a series of small and moderate-sized classrooms. The instructors lectured, performed demonstrations, asked and answered

---

*First closed circuit TV report, The Pennsylvania State University. Carpenter, C. R., Greenhill, L. P. Project Number One: An Investigation of Closed Circuit Television for Teaching University Courses, July 1955. Carpenter, C. R., Greenhill, L. P. An Investigation of Closed Circuit Television for Teaching University Courses, Report Number Two. Carpenter, C. R., Greenhill, L. P. Comparative Research on Methods and Media for Presenting Programmed Courses in Mathematics and English. USOE, Instructional TV at The Pennsylvania State University: 1954-1963. A documentary sound film 38 min. 16mm.

questions and otherwise conducted the class as they would have done before the introduction of television. The television equipment and operating personnel were intentionally made inconspicuous and unobtrusive.

This basic feasibility study that was done for the Fund for the Advancement of Education provided comparisons between (1) *direct instruction* in a class of several hundred students with fixed cameras and (2) *transmitted and cathode-tube displayed instruction* in classes ranging in size from about 35 to 60 students.

The classes with television receivers were monitored first by faculty members, then by graduate students and later by undergraduate proctors. Finally monitoring in classrooms was reduced in most courses and discontinued entirely in some courses. We made every effort to encourage each student to *accept increasing amounts of responsibility for managing his own learning and other classroom behavior.*

Otherwise there was no more or less individualization of learning for students than in traditional college courses of instruction even though the students were on a TV cable length removed from the instructor. Here a teacherless classroom was a new learning condition for many students.

It was clear from these early experiments that the fields of perception and information displays were importantly selected by the camera operations. Objects and processes were enlarged or magnified, and the view of the instructor and what he displayed, including blackboard work, was improved for students seated from the center to the back of large classrooms. Thus, demands in students to select and react to instructional elements may have been reduced while viewing conditions were improved. Interferences of the large classes were reduced in the classrooms with television receivers.

The next set of variations which we introduced was the renovation of a classroom and remodeling it to serve as a place where instruction could be originated. In this "origination room" or studio there were several variations which differed from the pattern just described. The instructor could have with him in the studio small groups of students who could give immediate reactions to his lecture or questions, or raise representative questions that might have been asked in larger sections or by students not in the origination room. Then the instructor could lecture in the studio without students but direct his instruction to the movable cameras and the camera operators. This pattern made it possible to have more and better instructional materials such as charts, titles and graphics, as a result of more space and maneuverability of the television cameras. Later when slide and film chains were added to our equipment these media could be used also by the instructor.

On the reception side we used a wide range of classroom sizes and solved many problems of arrangements of television receivers and speakers in classrooms that were not designed for the uses of 'new' media. The objective was to have good viewing and listening conditions in all of the varied classrooms. Television was used as a justification for renovating old classrooms.

It was in developing a third set of conditions of learning that we gave the most attention to providing for adaptations and *variations of conditions* for student learning. The first step was to determine that the whole course of instruction need not be channeled over television and that the academic *time-credit accounting system could and should be changed.* Scheduling of segments of some courses was changed to provide time for lectures, both straight verbal and illustrated, lecture-demonstrations, proctor-led discussions, practicum sessions (e.g., in accounting), and regular and special laboratory work in sciences. In addition, of course, there were the regular assignments of text materials, reference sources, library work and other study. What we began to realize at this stage was that closed circuit television could be made flexible and varied across courses and curriculums and within a course of study.

Flexibility and variations of instructional technology, methods and even goals and levels of attainment are very important even if they are not ideal conditions for individualized learning.

The instructors in originating studios without students expressed the need for means of talking with students. Realizing the problem of passivity of television viewing and the need for active responses and "feedback" to the instructors, we developed the "Telequest" means for studio-classroom and classroom-studio intercommunication. With the "Telequest" sub-system, either the instructor or a student in any of the classrooms, and there could be 14 of these, could initiate a question. The question or comment could be heard by students in all 14 interconnected classrooms. Then, there could follow a discussion between the instructor and an individual student or several students in any of the classrooms.

The "Telequest" arrangement provided a means for the instructor to query individual students, and thus to introduce an element into his instruction which increased the alertness of students in television classrooms. This had a beneficial effect on class attendance even when rolls were not checked.

Some instructors provided times when students could see them but students themselves infrequently used these periods set aside for them. This problem raises a cluster of questions about how "feedback" on learning can be provided and used to improve instruction and the conditions for student learning.

Stephens College has very successfully adapted the telephone for mediating the "Tele-lecture." We tested this method for reaching out long distances for information that is current and for outstanding people who could not have been otherwise brought to students in formal class instruction. Thus, two further developments followed.

The closed circuit television and "Telequest" systems were interconnected with the telephone systems so that up to 400 or 500 students located in 14 classrooms could listen to conversations and discussions by leaders in relevant fields and by specialists in subjects of interest. Students on signals could query the guest telelecturer. Conference telephone arrangements made available to students in a course in economics the opportunity to hear management and labor leaders at a state capitol in a strike situation and in a legislative debate on proposals for new labor laws. In political science, leaders of contesting parties were invited into the closed circuit course by means of telelecture discussions.

The second major development during the early stages of experimentation was on the distribution side of the television operation. We reasoned that if it were practical to transmit instruction from one campus building to another then why not reach out to the expanding number of Commonwealth campuses. This we did as a test case by installing a microwave link between University Park and the Altoona campus.

In the pre-videotape era we also experimented with kinescopic recordings of instruction. We undertook to produce two core-of-course sets of instruction for the Air Force. We helped the DageBell Company perfect an inexpensive kinescopic recorder and used a strategy that opens up television instruction to many and varied patterns of use and flexibility for individualized learning or study in small groups. The strategy is that of recording the *central* and most important parts of courses, those parts that are appropriate for the medium, and those that have the "longest help-life" or slowest rate of antiquation, along with the greatest consensus of experts about both the content and methods.

The recorded core-of-course development provides flexibility of scheduling and actually requires planned supplementary work on the parts of students and teachers in the learning situations.

The effects of these developments can be to provide specified places and roles for both students and teachers. Thus, the *displacement effects* of the televised "master teacher" can be greatly reduced or perhaps entirely eliminated.

The next development which became possible by linkage with Channel 10 Altoona was to simultaneously broadcast courses of instruction while the same instruction was being given to formally organized classes at University Park and at the Altoona campus. Here we challenged the course-credit-fee structure of higher education. Courses in philosophy, sociology, economics, history and meteorology were distributed by both closed circuit arrangements and by broadcast methods.

We determined by a well-conducted telephone survey of population of people of the broadcast area that about 35,000 people viewed and listened fairly regularly to the course in sociology. However, less than 25 persons were interested in credit for the course. Most of the 35,000 were *individual* viewers. Thus, we opened up the formal classrooms of the University and invited the public to see and learn what transpires at the very heart of the University's instructional program. Sensitive administrators viewed as delicate public relations issues instruction in such subjects as comparisons of religious, political issues, comparative economic systems, and instruction of the physiology of reproduction. Actually there was less than one tenth of one percent of negative comments. The economics professor received almost a thousand letters of appreciation.

Agreements were proposed to the colleges of the broadcast area that they use the teleinstruction without cost during the experiment and keep records of the results. There were few professors who would accept instruction originated by another in another university. This reaction deserves further discussion and constitutes one of the main barriers to the development of levels of utilization that justify the costs of producing high quality programs of instruction.

What did this development show? That we could move instruction of some kinds to people rather than transport people to already crowded campuses. They showed that a very small percentage of an adult population is interested in courses for *credit*. Finally, it was shown that it is difficult to share or exchange instruction among institutions.

There is much to be done and much promise in instructional broadcasting that can lead to individualized learning. Neither management strategies for instructional broadcasts nor those for use in homes have been as fully developed as they might be. There are needs for an instrument development in the home which will do the following: provide the means for informing viewers immediately of the correctness or incorrectness of their responses to questions, problems and issues; make permanent records of the learners' responses which can be transmitted to the origination of the instruction; make on pre-scheduled timing a record of a unit of instruction that can be studied when this is best and most practical for the learner.

In addition, there need to be developments in producing and testing printed materials for coordinated study with televised instruction. There are no real technical barriers to the use of telephones for feedback from home-viewed instruction to points of origination. And finally, the Albany Medical School has made successful demonstrations of two-way radio, which could also involve television components. Radio and television can be harnessed together.

We at Penn State demonstrated two other adaptations of televised instruction before attempting to apply programming procedures to courses for use over the media. First, we developed a variation of the Pyramid Plan for use with large television-instructed sections in sociology. This involved the organization of several hundred students in a closed circuit television course into small groups of 12-15 individuals. The group discussions were led by selected and coached undergraduate students. The focus of the group's dialogues was on the issues and problems raised by the professor over television and on those that were of interest to students themselves.

The other adaptation of television during this phase was to install receivers in dormitories. This method of use was at a later date tested thoroughly at the University of Illinois and found to be acceptable. The next step, obviously, is to provide television sets for student dormitory rooms which make some of the best carrel spaces available on university campuses. Further advances in dormitory design using individual rooms in the same manner as is now done in modern hospitals, will make it possible to *individualize learning* by having in the living-study room arrays of equipment which include sound systems, small television receivers and dial access capabilities for sound tape and film clips. In the building but not in the individual rooms, there could be on-line terminals for accesses to Computer Regulated Instruction (CRI).

In summary, we have in this section traced one exploratory development of *teleinstruction,* and thus we have described how technology has progressively become more varied and flexible, and therefore, more useful in *individualizing instruction.* By developing patterns of distribution of instruction over space, by scheduling and time-sequencing, by creating new patterns of course arrangements, the instruction has become more pliable and adaptable for both instructors and students. What remains is to deal with advances in providing pacing rates that are optimized for the differences in learning rates of individuals and to demonstrate how branching and differential leveling may be accomplished.

Pacing Rates of Media

There is a pervasive belief in educational circles that pacing rates should be adjusted to each individual learner. When it is said that the student should be allowed to proceed at his own rate, two very different conditions may be involved: (1) the rate or schedule at which a student progresses through a course in terms of hours, weeks or months, and (2) the rate of learning which may include speeds of perceiving, reading, conceptualizing, choosing, solving problems and responding.

The independent study plan at Bucknell University releases the student from regular class attendance and permits him to regulate his own rate of progression through the course. The more microscopic pacing rate is not controlled. The Bucknell condition provides, however, possibilities of great economics. The problem would seem to be that of preparing students for accepting the unusual responsibilities for managing their own study time. It should be observed that after instructional materials are prepared and made available the students may need to make little demand on their instructors for his time and help.

We at Penn State have conducted research and development work in an attempt to apply programming principles with the 'new' media, including, closed circuit television (CCTV). The critical problem to be solved was that of the rate of presentation and the rate of development of the instructional materials, lessons and courses. We solved this problem by determining the normal rate of work of samples of the target audience of students using preliminary versions of programmed instruction in Algebra and Grammar. After these empirical tests pacing was adjusted to the several formats used in the project. Experiments were conducted with different pacing rates both slower and faster than the learner-based norms. Students adjusted their work rates to the controlled rates. There were no significant differences in test scores among the -80, -90, *100* +110 rates.

Two concepts resulted from these studies. First, it became doubtful whether or not the self-pacing rates of students are the optimum rates. Second, pacing that is slightly faster than an individual's normal rate may improve his speed of response.

Results of the studies and analyses of pacing rates of instructional displays gave us confidence to proceed with programming materials for film strips, motion picture films, film loops and for closed circuit television.

Programmed instruction was originated 'live' in studios by especially planned mirror techniques, precisely paced on the basis of information collected from sample groups of students and distributed to classrooms where experimental groups randomly assigned, observed and responded to the frame by frame materials. Student responses were made on "response schedule sheets" which paralleled the televised instruction. Reinforcement was given in either the written or the verbal mode at a time estimated to be after students had made their responses. Thus administered, the test scores for students who were instructed over closed circuit television were not significantly different from the scores made by students who were instructed by the programmed book, film strip and teacher-presented versions of the course.

There was an incidental finding which relates to individualized instruction. It is generally known that some programmed books may not maintain the interest and motivation of students. This was found to be true with the Penn State programmed Grammar course. Student assistants and observers proctored the evening sessions, and the students complained about the lack of availability of instructors and the lack of appeal, or dullness, of the course material. Reacting to these opinions and attitudes, we *paired students* randomly and required each pair to use the same programmed booklet, and to complete one answer sheet. The pairs of students were asked to agree about the responses to frames or answers to problems and to accept the same unit test score. Complaints about the lack of attention from instructors ceased as did complaints about dullness of rather finely programmed material.

It will be observed that programmed courses administered by media permitted the instruction of classes and multi-sectioned courses. Also, it is proposed that these feasibility demonstrations present the very real possibility that the procedures can be adapted and developed for uses with the broadcast media.

Individualized Instruction by Multi-Versions of Instructional Materials

Instructional film research led to the development of production procedures for making multiple film versions. The experimental films differed with respect to defined variables either in the commentary and sound or in pictorial characteristics. All materials for the versions were "shot" or processed on a planned schedule and then edited together to meet the requirements of experimental designs.

This development demonstrated a means for producing instructional units for target audiences of trainees and students who differed in significant learning characteristics. Versions could be produced at low, medium and high levels of difficulty or in rates of context development. Thus, it was suggested that instructional film units could be adapted so as to be accommodated to limited ranges of individual differences.

An extension of this methodology involves the production and use of "single concept" films either 8mm or 16mm which presents, usually in silent form, the core-of-a-unit or the core-of-a-course of instruction, and then provides varied opportunities for individualized adaptations to be made in the situations of use. This arrangement has the advantage at some levels of instruction of schools and colleges of providing for essential and defined roles for teachers and instructors. They are not as clearly displaced with core-of-unit or core-of-course materials as they are by full courses of media-presented instruction.

Dial access tapes and films are yet other adaptations of mediated instruction for different individuals. It should be observed that pacing rates are fixed in most dial access materials but that the rate of progression through a course of study, the selection of what units to study when and the amount of repetition and review are under the control and judgment of individual students.

In conclusion, the theme that has been developed is (1) that individualized instruction has both limitations and advantages, (2) that the varied characteristics of individualized instruction such as pacing rates and rates of progression through courses of study, or the levels of relative difficulty, need to be defined, and (3) that many adaptations can be made in media programs to provide new and significant means for *Teleinstruction and Individualized Learning.*

24.
Systems Analysis and The Introduction of Educational Technology In Schools

by EUGENE A. COGAN
Dir., Research Design and Reporting
Human Resources Research Organization
Alexandria, Virginia

The defense establishment and industry have made extensive use of a set of techniques, procedures, and attitudes that, taken together, are called Systems Analysis, Operations Research, Cost Benefit Analysis, Cost Effectiveness Analysis, and so on. The concepts embodied in these techniques—often defined as the application of the scientific method to practical problems—have proven to be a powerful means for approaching, clarifying, and solving problems in industry and defense. Can these concepts and techniques be adapted to the field of education? More particularly, can these concepts and techniques be used to help introduce "space age" technology in a fashion that would help solve the problems of modern education?

Quite clearly, the only answer we can accept is "yes" because sophisticated problem solving techniques are needed for education.

The systems approach to using—or developing—new technology works well when:

1. Problems in a system are many and complex—present-day education feels the impact of *all* of society's major general problems plus many that are peculiarly its own.

2. The scope of activity is large—estimates place the national cost of education at 60 billion dollars per annum, second only to defense as a national effort.

3. The functions being served are important—education counts job preparation, acculturation to societal values, preparation for citizenship, enriching the lives of the people among its missions.

4. There is readiness to innovate, to improve and to develop more effective modern approaches to activities—the "readiness quotient" of a society cannot easily be measured, but increasing federal expenditures, increasing interest by industry, increasing numbers of study groups, and vocal public interest in improvement suggest readiness.

5. Functions are being performed in "time-honored" ways—while some intrusion of modern technology into education has occurred, education is conducted essentially as it was 50 or 100 years ago. New devices such as computers, television, tape recorders, motion pictures, and so on are very little used or used only as minor adjuncts to traditional ways; the fundamental pattern of a teacher-class instructional unit is as it has been for generations.

Although there are strong forces for educational innovation, and thus, for using whatever aid the systems approach can provide, there are special characteristics of education that produce obstacles to applying the techniques as they have been developed for the defense department and industry. First, the kinds of large-scale and very expensive development programs for which systems analysis has played an important role are practical and fruitful in an orderly, hierarchical setting under unitary management. The American education complex, however, consists of about 26,000 distinctive school districts, many private and parochial schools below the college level, a large number of individual private colleges and universities, public community and four-year colleges and universities at the level of the 50 separate states, similar public higher education facilities at city or county levels, nursery and other pre-school elements, commercial trade schools, and so on. This is far from single hierarchical management.

Second, innovation for the educational community has acquired a poor reputation, and deservedly so. "Innovative" experience of educators has mainly been with gadgets of one sort or another for which supporting software was nonexistent or poor in quality, or gadgets that fell far short of promised performance. Still other frustrations for educators who might have been prone to innovation came from no real attention by innovators to just how a new method or curriculum or whatever may have been proposed could be put into operation in a school. What, if any, special provisions for training existing personnel were needed or provided? What, if any, adjustments in the rest of the educational setting needed to be made to use the innovation properly? How should the educator go about making accommodations needed?

Third, with few exceptions, funding for education is made available to educational systems on a hand-to-mouth basis, with almost all raises in funding committed to increases in payroll, needed additional school buildings, and the like. Very little has been made available to support innovative efforts, or long-range projects extending beyond an operational year.

Fourth, systems analysts and associated research and development specialists, with experience and background appropriate to help fill the needs of American education for modern educational technology, have only very recently begun to appear on the scene—and they are in very short supply. Without the people qualified to devise and implement innovations, the best intentions and heaviest investments are unlikely to be fruitful.

Systems analysis—the "kind of approach" that has been so useful for innovation in industry and the defense department—is needed for education. While education has special features that must be taken into account in order for systems analysis to be useful, there are many problems that are common across major segments of the 60 billion dollar education complex. Solutions, therefore, have the potential of massive application—the condition necessary for large-scale systems analysis and design to be a worthwhile undertaking. What must be recognized is the need for special effort to devise new techniques of analysis and new kinds of solutions to accommodate to the fact of tens of thousands of distinctive, independent elements, each with its own management and decision makers and each with its own peculiar set of constraints, problems, and resources.

Further, education is fundamentally a "soft" human and social phenomenon and experience developed with electronic, mechanical, weapons and even economic systems must be tempered gingerly with new and different factors and approaches to enable "the scientific approach to practical problems" to bear fruit. There is a serious risk in uncritical transfer of systems analysis and analysts from "hard" applications to education. First efforts in a new domain are likely to be based on successful experiences and solutions in an old domain; for education, this might mean inappropriately distorting "soft" problems into distantly related "hard" vague analogs, to the disservice of education and the discipline of systems analysis.

Only in the last decade, have any of the systems analysts and cost benefit analysts begun to shift their attention to education. The earliest efforts and literature are interesting in that they seemed oriented mostly to developing and arguing for the proposition that such applications were sorely needed and clearly indicated. Exactly what might be done, however, and actually doing it seemed to be another matter, with the sole exceptions of gross, broad economic analysis of the value of education and manpower and facility projections of what would be needed by a given year.

On the heels of these early evidences of interest came the beginnings of small efforts for more direct impact on education. These efforts were mostly under the leadership of psychologists with background and experience in military training research and development. These people had both background in depth in the instructional process and direct experience with systems analysts, systems engineers, and the products of modern "hard" technology, such as computers, since military training research and development is part of overall weapon system design. However, some of their earliest efforts floundered on inexpert shifting from the special case of training within an explicit mission-oriented institution to the much "softer" context of education within society at large.

To date, the examples of modern systems design approach to education have been small and are few in number—but with exciting potential nonetheless. The remainder of this paper will be devoted to characterizing the kinds of systems approach activities that are now going on, and what needs to be done to extend and increase the impact of these efforts to make headway on the massive problems facing education now and for the foreseeable future.

While applications to date are interesting and promising, it cannot be overemphasized that the societal resources so far invested in trying to deal with the problems of education have been incommensurately small in relation to both the magnitude and complexity of the problems, and the size and complexity of education. Solutions and approaches to solutions to date are bare scratches towards "beginning to begin" serious attention to modern system approaches to bring education into the "space age".

Applications of Analysis and Innovation to Education

Although applications of the systems approach to education are recent and on a small scale, the pace of increase in attention is rapid, so rapid that any attempt to provide a comprehensive inventory of applications would be obsolete before it could be produced. It is more useful, for the present, to try to identify varieties of application than to record all of them. The risk of "undesirable duplication", which might be warded off by an inventory of efforts completed or in progress, is unlikely to require attention for at least a decade, since so much needs to be done. The main purpose will be to illustrate the kinds of problems in education to which systems analysis approaches have been directed. The nature of systems analysis as a general tool—applying the scientific method of practical problems—makes such a review no more than an indication of the problems thus far approached; it should *not* be taken to imply other problems are beyond the purview of the scientific method.

Application to "Ordinary" Problems

Whatever else may be said about education, it is clear that a university, or a large high school, or a large school district shares many functions with any administrative bodies. These include purchasing, transportation (school bus systems), personnel management, scheduling elements to resources (e.g., students to classes or classes to rooms), data collection and management (e.g., registration), and so on. These are direct parallels to, or identical with, many industry and government problems that have long since been solved using esoteric algorithms such as linear programming, queueing theory, computer data processing systems, and the like.

These "ordinary" solutions are greatly in evidence in present-day education, mainly in universities offering instruction in operations research and systems analysis *and* those with their own computing facilities. These applications of "ordinary" solutions are useful and increase the efficiency of the schools using them, sometimes by decreasing costs but more often by making effective resources more available.

Applications of this sort are, of course, tangential to the *main* functioning of a school—conducting instruction—and are of importance to the main problems of schools only indirectly. First, for the universities, they suggest a peculiarly rare and recent phenomenon—universities applying the work of their own people to the university's operations! Second, they provide a beginning for schools to become accustomed to innovation and more prone to accept products of educational technology for instruction.

While considerable benefits and improved efficiency can come from applying ready-made solutions to "ordinary" problems of schools, by far the more important product of these efforts rests in improving the readiness of schools to adopt innovations in educational technology for their main functions.

Application to Functions Ancillary to Instruction

One step removed from "ordinary" functions of a school system are activities that are not directly instructional in nature but are intimately related to the instructional process and to the instructional mission of a school. Normally, such functions are performed by specialized personnel in a school system or else managed as additional duties for all or a portion of the instructional staff.

The System Development Corporation became interested in "space age" approaches to ancillary functions, at least in part as a step (following one on "ordinary" applications) towards bringing the computer into the operating matrix of a school. In furtherance of this objective and as a sample of modern means for ancillary functions for schools, SDC devised a computer-based student counselling system. This system, based on detailed analysis of the counselling process as conducted by experienced counsellors, allows a student to "interact" with a computer and obtain guidance information related to courses he should take, possible vocational directions for him, further schooling, and so on. Automating student counselling was SDC's second step towards introducing modern educational technology for instruction into the schools, and further developments are under way by SDC for instruction itself (such as with computer-administered instruction).

It must be emphasized that automated approaches to ancillary (or even instructional) functions normally performed by teachers or specialized personnel is *not* conceived as "replacing the person". It is, for example, neither possible nor practical to prepare a program to cope with all of the possible counselling problems a student might have. The counsellor "replaced" remains in the system but with a more challenging role because the ordinary and routine questions and answers involved in counselling are "automatically" taken care of. This leaves the counsellor free for counselling in depth with students who have problems beyond the ordinary or beyond the automated program.

The automated student counselling system deals with only one of the ancillary functions in a school, and it is based only upon the amount and kind of information normally available to a person counselling the student. Obvious directions for further development are being explored by SDC and others, to include dealing with additional ancillary functions and using the complete store of administrative and academic date regarding the student in an overall computer-based information system to provide a data bank serving many different functions. As for "ordinary" applications, practical, operating "space age" versions of systems for ancillary functions will improve the readiness of a school for innovation in the main stream of their activities, instruction.

Systems Analysis and Design Applied to Instruction

The more exciting—and very recent—intrusions of technology into education consist of systems designed to *individualize* the instructional process in order to gear the instruction given to a student to precisely what *he* needs. A number of different systems of this nature are in varying degrees of development or try-out.

The most avant garde of these approaches is computer-administered instruction (CAI), with many development or operational efforts under way. These are sponsored by the military (e.g., SDC's work and HumRRO's Project IMPACT), by industry (Westinghouse and IBM, among others), the universities (most notably Stanford, Harvard, and Florida State University), and even efforts by local school systems (e.g., Montgomery County, Maryland, and a large joint project by Philco and the Philadelphia School System). The full impact, possible value, and probable costs for such systems have yet to be established; however, it is important to note that the concept of computer-administered instruction has passed the stage of a dream for tomorrow and is going through explicit system development phases, including some pilot and actual operations.

Other, more immediate, systems for individualizing instruction have been devised. Perhaps the best known is one by the University of Pittsburgh Learning Research and Development Center—Individually Prescribed Instruction (IPI). IPI mainly represents an extensive system of self-instructional modules, together with extensive assessment instruments arranged so that a student's short-term achievement (after modules of self-instructional material) can be measured and the measures processed to select and prescribe the next set of instructional modules for him. The critical ingredients are specific instructional modules, assessment of achievement, and individually prescribed "next steps". The main innovative feature of IPI consists of special mechanisms for detailed self-correcting *individual management* of a student's schedule of learning experiences. Other approaches to the same end are the Duluth (Minnesota) system for individualizing instruction and computer-managed instructional systems devised by New York Institute of Technology, American Institutes for Research, and System Development Corporation.

Still another development effort is under way at the Naval Academy in Annapolis. This effort—referred to as the Multi-Media Project—is a joint Office of Education-Navy project with considerable emphasis on behavioral training objectives, assessment devices, and multiple alternative media, including programmed instruction, computer-administered instruction, and instructional television. This project, as is true for the IPI and CAI projects, is oriented towards pushing the present state of the art as far as possible into a concerted system development phase.

Feasibility-Possibility Studies

In industry or defense, feasibility studies are geared to choosing among explicit alternative approaches to performing a mission or else evaluating the cost aspects of a candidate system. In classical form, such studies do not fit present-day educational problems. First, they don't fit because educators rarely have available alternate proposals for new systems that might be developed. Second, costs and budgeting for education are normally hand-to-mouth projections to be "fought through" reluctant local legislative bodies. Newer concepts such as the Defense Department or federal Planning-Programming-Budgeting system (PPB) have yet to filter to states and smaller governmental levels.

For these reasons, a more general kind of analysis is needed, and this general kind of analysis is, perhaps, more appropriate for research and development groups or for study commissions than for educational units themselves. Perhaps, the variant on normal feasibility or cost-effectiveness analysis might be called "conceivability or possibility" analysis.

Some efforts have been made towards such analyses, mainly with regard to very major innovations. An early example was for educational TV which received major impetus (and funding!) from the Ford Foundation. Here, major parameters of cost include matters of public policy such as use of COMSAT and allied facilities.

Another study that initially was mainly concerned with costs was a HumRRO analysis of computer-administered instruction. While the beginning of that study dealt with cost per se (and a reasonable basis for projecting costs was developed), the most interesting outcome of analysis were implications for adaptations in education that would be called into being by computer-administered instruction. Strong economic arguments were adduced for reducing the idle time of computer-administered instruction facilities by extending the operating period for a school beyond the traditional five-hour day (by scheduling several sessions and evening or night sessions to keep equipment operating as much as possible, and by keeping facilities operating twelve months per year), for developing arrangements whereby instructional material—each unit of which would be very expensive—can be used widely throughout the nation, and for developing new specialized personnel to prepare instructional material for computer-administered instruction and also perform needed programming for such systems. The overall conclusion was that computer-administered instruction could be cost effective, and very much so, but that it would require major modification in the personnel and operating spectra of present-day school systems in order to exploit the benefits of this instructional system.

Manpower-Facility Planning Studies

The studies by economists and econometricians have played an important role for both industry and government by helping decision makers and planners cope with economic aspects of society, to anticipate and plan for markets, sales, needed facilities, supply, demand, resources and so on. Many of the models and methods used for these purposes can be applied quite directly to education since, for some purposes, the product of education in the form of a school's graduate can be considered to be a commodity, students can *also* be considered the market, schools can be considered production facilities, and projection of future population size is important for education as are trends of escalation in demand factors that can be projected.

While normally not specifically thought of as part of systems analysis per se, the methods and purposes of manpower analysts and econometricians are very reasonably viewed as "cut from the same cloth". This commonality is more than an accident or coincidence since many of the important contributions to present-day systems analysis and design have come from people who trained as economists and econometricians, including those with special interests in manpower.

More than any other application of systems analysis, manpower and facility projections have a history of useful contribution to planning in the educational community. Most of the effective studies have been for local consumption rather than for broad use, since the planners and decision makers have generally been concerned with formulating projections of the needs of a particular institution or system such as, for example, a particular multi-university in a large state or "10-year building plans" for a school district.

There are also evidences of generalized materials in the literature. One of the more interesting is international in scope—both as to participants and as to problems addressed—and appears in the form of a Technical Report published in 1967 by the Organization for Economic Co-operation and Development. This report deals with mathematical models in educational planning and is a record of the proceedings of an international symposium.

Another report on manpower-facility planning was published by the Academy for Educational Development and records a study completed in 1966 for the state of Maine to project that state's requirements for higher education. Of course, the particulars and details of the projections emerging have direct relevance only to Maine, but the methods and general conclusions have much broader applicability.

Studies, both broad and specific, for manpower and facility projections provide an invaluable background for other analysis oriented towards the instruction process, since they help define the magnitude of tomorrow's problems. Also, instruction-process systems analysis and development projects need to be taken into account as input to manpower and facility studies since exactly how instruction is to be conducted "tomorrow" is far from a negligible factor in considering what projections can be made.

Without doubt, manpower and facility projections are needed in ever-increasing numbers and with ever-increasing precision so that good educational planning can become commonplace rather than exceptional. Such studies, however, need to become closely integrated with other, more "traditional" systems analysis and development studies so that each can gain in power and relevance from the contributions of the other. The magnitude of tomorrow's needs cannot be considered out of the context of tomorrow's methods, nor can tomorrow's methods be considered without reference to the magnitude of tomorrow's needs.

Studies in Economics of Education

Preparation of students for an occupation is among the missions of education. While this is often explicit for vocational schools, with the possible partial exception of "culture" courses in adult education centers of high schools, universities, colleges, and community colleges, some part of all education is relevant to an individual in his role as an economic unit earning (or preparing to earn) his living.

Viewed from a different economic perspective, a modern technological society needs an ever-increasing supply of trained and educated people in order to conduct its economic activities. From still another point of view, the costs and expenses of government services for all purposes and at all levels are derived from "surplus values" created by the economic activities manned by trained and educated people. These factors of gain to the individual (his salary), to the society (the gross national product), and to the government (the tax dollar) can be and are being related to costs, the costs of education.

From a broader social-economic perspective, based on the costs to the government of nonproductive (or less productive) people (as, for example, welfare costs), education and training to prepare people for occupational activities can be related to "savings" of what would otherwise be societal costs.

There are many complex issues for which analysis of economic factors provides useful data. But, rarely have results of economic analyses for education been clearly definitive. Some work has been done to estimate economic factors such as the return on a dollar of educational investment to the individual. Studies have also been done to estimate net savings to society from investments in educational programs which would reduce the likelihood or magnitude of eventual expensive social delinquency.

Studies of the cost, gain, and needs for education in relation to the economy or in relation to the costs and savings in other societal programs can be very valuable and can help guide policies regarding educational facilities, special educational-social programs, and matters such as tuition rates or public underwriting of education.

There is, however, need for considerable caution in how the results of economics studies are used, even where conclusions are completely definitive. Dollars gained and dollars spent provide a simple and orderly paradigm for decision making; therefore, it is tempting (and all too common) to dismiss as imaginary or not important, or "not relevant for this analysis", human and social motives and values aside from the economic. The propensity for ascribing a primal status to economic factors is probably a tribute to the residue of "The Great Depression" of 30 to 35 years ago. While education does—and should—serve important economic functions for the individual, for the economy, and for the society, viewing the educational process solely from an economic perspective can lead to unsound action. Human and social values and motives are—and always have been—broader than the purely economic. Furthermore, the present and future students in our educational systems do not share Depression scars; their motive and value guidelines for decisions— in which the economic is not predominant—must be considered in planning viable and workable educational systems, facilities, and policies.

Half a dozen varieties of the systems approach to analysis and design for education have been identified. An attempt has been made to describe major kinds but the listing is far from exhaustive and, for each variety, only sample instances have been indicated. The list of varieties could easily be extended to include, at the least, a large miscellaneous category—such as educator personnel and training systems (usually done as part of instructional system development), new kinds of instructional specialists for preparing programmed instruction, preparing computer-administered instruction, using instructional media, teacher aides (evolving as part of team teaching experiments), and evaluation. Studies of building design for education could be described, both those that are parts of instruction-process systems and others concentrating on the effects of room, hallway and other physical arrangements on patterns of interactions for students and between students and staff. However, rather than attempting to expand or exhaust the listing of varieties, it appears more useful simply to point to the range of those systems analysis and design varieties that have been presented—it is large!

Experience in industry and the defense department suggests the systems analysis approach is powerful. A seemingly unlimited scope for its relevance is not at all unreasonable if one refers to the basic definition for the systems approach—the application of the scientific method to practical problems. The scientific method has already been well established as a mighty tool for the classical sciences ranging from nuclear physics through the social sciences and to astronomy. Therefore, it is likely to have few, if any, bounds for education beyond those intrinsic to available resources, trained people, existing knowledge, and imaginative and flexible application or development of techniques.

Directions for Systems Analysis Effort

This paper is based on the premise that the American society is on the brink of extensive effort to improve education. Further, this improvement will come about by the application of rapidly evolving educational technology, and the repertoire of tools called systems analysis can and will play an important role in this endeavor, just as they have for innovation and new system development for defense and industry.

Although there is clear indication that systems analysis is being applied to education problems at this time, the total effort has barely begun. What are the ways in which systems analysis and systems design should be directed for most rapid and most efficient introduction of "space age" technology into education? What are the first steps needed in support of explosive and rapidly evolving innovation for education?

Objectives, Evaluation, and Criteria

Carefully defined system objectives are the first step and the main essential for a systems analysis. Objectives pinpoint the "mission" so that a set or sets of functions and their arrangements into an operating pattern can be directed to doing exactly what the system is supposed to do. Objectives also provide the basis for planning evaluation of a system or alternate systems, and they are used to generate the criteria which can be measured for system output to be considered in terms of cost, mission accomplishment, or both. For education as for any other realm of systems activity, effective innovation and design must begin with objectives.

A great deal has been written in the educational literature about objectives. Special commissions have been formed to formulate the purposes, missions, and objectives of education. But, the definitions available are either very general—so "fuzzy" as to be worthless for analysis or design—or very narrow and lacking authentication. Education is a key instrument of society to serve both long-term and relatively unchanging purposes, and it also is an instrument for use in coping with immediate societal problems. Clearly, among the missions of education are occupational preparation, influence on attitudes and values, teaching basic skills and knowledges, helping people to "get more out of life", and so on. All of these seem valid and appropriate as objectives, but a systems analyst or systems designer needs much more specific, detailed, and complex specifications for his work.

In addition to identifying the objectives, since the time, energy, and resources of an educational system are limited, *relative* importance must be ascribed to each objective. It is not the province of a systems analyst to define objectives nor their importance relative to one another, since the objectives are society's objectives. The analyst can assist "society" by clarifying "draft" objectives, or exploring consistency of objectives or posing questions about priorities or values, but the fundamental definition and decision must be made by societal planners and decision makers, or at least under their direction.

The most useful and important single step to further improvement in education would be an authoritative system of educational objectives, carefully prepared in clear, specific, and *measurable* terms and with indices of relative importance together with notation of whatever conditional contingencies are important.

The idealist would prefer to "stop the world" until the objectives are available; however, the pragmatist must proceed with the conduct of business—both society and systems analysts are pragmatic. Lacking a usable set of definitive ultimate output objectives, there are, nonetheless, objectives and goals that "seem right" for education. Generally, these are either process objectives or things that seem unlikely to be omitted from an authoritative set of objectives.

Of the process-type objectives, foremost is individualization of instruction. It is clear that mass and uniform education, forced by old methods and applied without regard to individual characteristics, can match the needs of students only very imprecisely.

Another set of process objectives is scholastic achievement of the "normal" knowledges and skills that are part of present-day educational curricula. The knowledges and skills seem to have the character of general tools a person can use for many purposes. While an ultimate output criterion remains undefined, some aspects of education system effectiveness seem reasonably measured by the learning of the three Rs and the present-day additions to that list.

Still a third set of process objectives consists of continuing education or preventing "drop out". This objective follows from the reasonable proposition that education is good for many things, including occupational preparation and economic and other needs of the nation.

In addition to process objectives—only some of which have been described—are a set of probable "partial ultimate output" objectives.

One set of these are occupational objectives. Such objectives include rather explicit, particular job preparation objectives such as printer, or physician or lawyer, but these are only part of the range. Occupational preparation also includes more abstract matters such as working with people and developing good work habits. Another output-type class of objectives concerns values and attitudes. These cover a very wide range of matters including citizenship, acculturation, socialization and, in general, development of "standard" American values and attitudes. Still a third group of "partial ultimate output objectives" is a set that are preventive in nature—discouraging criminal activities, discouraging unhealthful practices (e.g., smoking), discouraging dangerous activities (e.g., unsafe driving). At this time in American society a very major set of "partial ultimate output objectives" are those encouraging socioeconomic mobility by providing interest, motivation, and opportunity for members of culturally deprived subgroups in society.

The categories of "probably valid" educational objectives described above are a very bare beginning to a possible list. Further, the category level is not sufficient since the categories must be analyzed carefully into their constituent objectives, each one of which must be described with sufficient specificity to allow educational systems to be developed to meet them and also to allow measurement of the extent to which they are achieved.

The important work for a definitive and authoritative definition of educational objectives can only be performed by a formally constituted body with a charge from society to set and define societal objectives for education.

Models and Data Base

The chief instrument of systems analysts consists of a model of the phenomena being dealt with and of the functions that must be performed in order to achieve a desired output. Models are, in one way or another, mathematical or quasi-mathematical representations of "cause and effect" relationships between things at a beginning state, operations performed with these things in a particular sequence and pattern, and the consequences as output characteristics.

Models are neither more nor less than theories or systems of natural laws governing phenomena. Just as with classical sciences, systems analysts devise their models through successive approximation cycles going between observed data to ideas, back to data, back to ideas, and so on with ever more refined models and ever more focused collections of data.

Despite the fact that much research has gone on in the psychology of learning and much educational research has accumulated in the literature over centuries, very little is really known and understood about the instructional process as it takes place in educational institutions. There are, of course, theories and there are, of course, data but these all fall short of the robustness and breadth needed for effective systems analysis and design in education.

It is very difficult to say whether the greater present need is for thinking (i.e., formulating models) or for the raw material to use in thinking (i.e., banks of fundamental data). And, in fact, an either/or approach would be doomed to failure since both kinds of things are needed in continuing interaction.

As to data there is a very long tradition for developing data regarding education—the Office of Education has consistently collected, analyzed, and published educational statistics. However, these statistics have mainly concerned administrative rather than process-oriented matters and for that reason have been only partially useful in devising useable models.

Two recent large-scale efforts to develop more and better data for understanding education are available to the research community. The first data bank was produced in Project Talent, an activity of the American Institutes for Research sponsored by the Office of Education and the Department of Defense. This large and careful study included data collected throughout the country using càreful sampling and measuring devices. While not yet thoroughly exploited, it has proven invaluable to guide modeling and research on the educational process.

Another data bank, more recent than Project Talent, is that developed for the so-called

Coleman Study on equality of educational opportunity. This effort, drawing upon the experiences of Project Talent and further developments in thinking about education since the inception of Project Talent, was mainly oriented to the civil rights aspects of education. At the same time it provides an excellent general purpose data bank which covers the entire country and consists of information on more than one-half million students at the public school level. The equality of educational opportunity bank is also being explored in a vigorous fashion towards a better understanding of factors important in educational achievement.

The data so far available on the educational process have led to better theories and the beginnings of usable models of the instructional process. In turn, these improved theories and steps towards models have created the need for still more data on new aspects of the process not considered very important earlier.

Models are normally developed when they are needed—to explore, to analyze, or to design something. At any time a model is needed, analysts use whatever information and data banks exist, with whatever limitations they may have. The limiting feature for rapid progress is the availability of sufficient data on the right parameters. Second in priority only to definitions of objectives for education, more, and more refined data banks must be created to provide raw material for systems analysts and innovators to work with. It would be useful to establish a system for continuing data accumulation, one with sufficient flexibility so that new kinds of data collection could be added to an on-going system to fill needs for data as particular questions become evident.

Techniques—Personnel—Teams

As was indicated earlier, the framework of education differs from that of the Department of Defense or an industrial setting, because, although "education" is very large, it is dispersed in a great many relatively small, independent and very heterogeneous units. Also, it was suggested that the nature of the "soft" phenomena of education make *direct* application of "hard" experience of systems analysts and systems design people not quite right for the problems of education. These factors have an important bearing on both the kinds of techniques that are needed for education systems analysis and the kinds of people who can perform effectively in that role.

From a purely methodological standpoint, there is clearly a need to broaden and generalize traditional systems analysis decision paradigms to accommodate to the nature and organization (or un-organization) existing in education. Where unitary, hierarchical management exists, many *variables* that are relevant to a decision can be set as fixed values, by applying "readings" from the operating context of the decision maker. For education, this won't do because there are tens of thousands of decision makers, each of whom needs a basis for making his own choice among alternate courses of action. Hence, considerable and important developmental work is needed to "parameterize" decision paradigms, to provide *generalized* algorithms for choice and a clear method for identifying and measuring the *critical variables* that must be specified in order to tailor the decision to the conditions and constraints of an individual manager.

There are, of course, general models for decision algorithms and in even larger numbers there are algorithms for making particular decisions. The need in education, however, is somewhere between the "so general that it provides only the beginning point" and the specific that provides a solution that may not fit a set of particular local conditions. Striking the proper balance for a general and yet readily usable model is a methodological challenge for systems analysts that should not be underestimated.

In addition to the need for generalized—but not too generalized—decision paradigms are those needs for placing all products of systems analysis and design into "put in your own parameter" form. While it is sufficient to conclude that thus and such weapon system would fill the needs of the Army in Air Defense, thus and such system in education must be analyzed and characterized for the set of conditions—modeled into an algorithm—that each manager must consider to determine relevance or cost effectiveness for his local needs.

A decade or so ago, the systems approach was typically characterized as the inter-disciplinary approach to problems and teams of different kinds of specialists were assembled to approach problems. The inter-disciplinary concept, perhaps as a consequence of increasing subject matter sophistication on the part of those who are systems analysts per se, has recently received much less attention. It is worthwhile to think of education today in terms of the Department of Defense and industry of a couple of decades ago and to reconstitute the concept of the inter-disciplinary team for exactly the reason it was so useful in the early days of industrial and defense systems analysis. The needed combination of experience, knowledge, and technique sophistication for useful and important work in education, only rarely exists in the "head" of a single individual. Systems analysis approaches in education are far too new for educators to have learned the analysis techniques or for systems analysts to have developed the subject matter sophistication. The closest approximation to the needed spectrum of skills consists of the specialists in military training research and development, but even they are unprepared for spanning the gap from military training to education.

In order to provide a cadre to begin systems analysis and design in education-type activities, it is essential to reinstitute emphasis on the concept of inter-disciplinary teams. Such teams should consist of combinations of educators (both administrators and teachers), military training research and development personnel, and operations research-systems analysis personnel together with economists, computer specialists and mathematicians as needed. All of the problems traditionally associated with inter-disciplinary teams would, of course, descend upon the team approach to education. Nevertheless, sharing, inter-mingling and articulating the special backgrounds of the diverse specialists are needed in order that the right problems be approached in the most fruitful fashion for the greatest gains.

Development Goals for Systems Analysts and Innovators

Emphasis on "fundamentals" for systems analysis or innovation should not be at the expense of actually going about innovating and designing systems. It is only through the moving inertia of on-going and future new projects that "big" solutions can possibly develop. There are, however, some guidelines that can be useful in selecting the kinds of developmental goals that would make interim efforts most likely to be useful in their own right and also most likely to provide building material for subsequent developments.

The key to effective educational technology rests in software. New audiovisual or even more modern-day exotic devices such as computers or CRTs are very useful as vehicles to implement software, and can even make possible kinds of software not previously dreamed about. But it is in the software—the instructional material, concepts of instruction sequencing, feedback for student and instructor—that the heart of an educational technology endeavor rests. No matter how "space age" an instruction device or system may be, it will be of only marginal value unless the software—the instructional material itself—is of good quality.

Together with the software must come strong emphasis upon evaluation. A very refreshing and laudatory emphasis currently exists in Office of Education sponsored activities; firm requirements for evaluation are established and resources for evaluation are being provided.

An orientation toward evaluation accomplishes two things: First, the worth (or lack of worth) of a new system can be established to provide a basis for decisions. Second, diagnosis for system modification or information for next generation or other systems is made available to guide design and redesign.

Iterative strategies for development are a special case of using evaluation. Iteration is actually used very rarely for instructional system design, for some not very clear reasons. Perhaps out of misplaced self-confidence, the approach taken by designers of instructional systems has usually been to get it done in one fell swoop and *then* evaluate it. The pattern for electronic system development with its "breadboard" and other intermediate development states and constant adjustment by cut-and-fit methods or redesign, should come into common use by instructional system designers. It would, in the long run, accelerate the pace of major and effective innovation.

Finally, attention must be paid to designing systems for use and for the user. It is traditional to speak sneeringly about the hardened resistance to innovation of the educational community and to point to lags of 50 years between educational invention and complete diffusion. It may be more to the point to scowl at the innovators for typical failure to complete development work and produce total package systems that can be adopted readily. Defense department concepts of total system development and procurement—which include not only the hardware but training programs, "spare parts", maintenance procedures and aids, training devices and so on—provide a model that should be adopted by educational technology innovators. It is neither attractive to nor efficient for many, many educators throughout the country to be wondering "How do you get this kind of thing going? What other things will we need to go with it? What does my staff need to learn in order to use it? How can I train them?"

Should experience show that total package system innovations that have been thoroughly evaluated and found to be cost effective exhibit hitherto characteristic diffusion lags, we may fairly dust off notions about innovation-resistance and re-use them with confidence. But, until system designers consistently take preparation for implementation as part of the system specification, the educator's countering scowl is valid.

In this paper, the question of whether systems analysis can be made appropriate to introducing educational technology into education has been addressed. The question has been approached by discussing systems analysis, education, and the general relevance of systems analysis tools to education, by discussing a variety of kinds of application that have been made and are being made, and by discussing steps needed and directions for effort to hurry and improve the use of systems analysis tools for education. It seems clear that education problems can be approached and the introduction of educational technology can be aided by systems analysis. However, total solutions will not be achieved overnight, nor will they be achieved without the investment of resources commensurate with the magnitude of the problems of and challenges to the educational complex.

25.
Sketching a Context
For Instructional Technology

by RICHARD H. de LONE*
A. N. Whitehead Fellow
School of Education
Harvard Univ.

An Overview

The historians will have to tell us what the age of the computer (and its technological compatriot, TV) means. But if the future will have the last word, we have to try to guess now. At least we have to keep in mind the alternatives. In no instance is this truer than in the technologizing of education.

To start with sweeping generalities, there seem to be at least three possible societal outcomes of the computer age. Each has tremendous implications for education.

The most uncomfortable thought is that the computer will simply clinch the industrial revolution—and thus escalate the crises in dehumanization which poets and (now particularly) young people, have been decrying since Goldsmith wrote "The Deserted Village." Thus it is that some perceive the prophets of the "technetronic age" as devils surrounded by demons of quantification, reductio ad statistic, and amorality. The end product would be programmed man—men who can't be folded, spindled or mutilated and who can't love either. This would be the most frightening kind of totalitarianism. Presumably this is where the pervasive if unsophisticated fretting about the computer "taking the place of the teacher" gets its strength.

There is a more optimistic view, typified by the McLuhanists, that the computer and other media are harbingers of revolutionary new ways of relating, perceiving and being in the world. A less romantic way to put it is to borrow the notion of paradigms from T. S. Kuhns, and suggest that computer technology, in ways not yet actively clear to us, will provide a new way of structuring reality and hence a new reality.[1] George Leonard, in his book *Education and Ecstasy,* seizes on these possibilities in portraying the school of the future as an electronic phantasmagoria. (It is our view that there is a lot more of educational value in Leonard's fantasy than in the drudgery of, say, Individually Prescribed Instruction which might be called the pedagogic equivalent of shredded wheat: knowledge broken into easily digestible bits.) But there is comparatively little thinking, and there are comparatively few dollars, being invested to permit instructional technology to match Leonard's enthusiasm.

A third possibility is that the computer revolution should not be judged in either quantitative and qualitative terms. Rather, it may render such categories useless, or, if not useless, produce quantitative changes which ultimately become qualitative. Quite simply, this

*At the time this paper was written (February 1968) he was assistant to the superintendent, Philadelphia public schools.

means that the computer as a "mind expander" (in the non-psychedelic sense) be vastly improving memory and speed of logic will enable understandings and problem solvings and discoveries and operations in minutes that the human brain by itself takes years to do. As a result, the sense of time itself will be changed, and life, inevitably, with it.

Call the Impacts A, B, and C. Let them sit for a minute and come back to here, now and instructional technology as it exists. Or rather, instructional technology as its present state can be characterized.

The first thing to be said is that precious little effort is being made to establish any cosmic context for the development of an educational technology. Rather, we are, to crib from McLuhan, looking through the rear view mirror and taking definitions, goals, and assumptions about education from the factory-world in which, for which, and in the image of which public schools were created.

Computer applications to instruction seem particularly geared to making the old ways more efficient, to improving the assembly line. Computer Assisted Instruction becomes the ne plus ultra of remedial education. And remedial education, too often, can be defined as an effort to pour into a student in concentrate what he has already rejected in diluted form. Most efforts at programmed learning, and their refinement into CAI, seem to adopt wholesale this pernicious assumption.[2]

This approach to computerized instruction has its parallel in the pervasive use (or misuse) of TV as a medium for presenting lectures. The assumption that seems to underly most instructional TV is that a jazzy packaged lecture is better than a dull live lecture. There are three big problems with this assumption. First is that TV may be unsuited, as a medium with peculiar characteristics of its own, to the presentation of lectures at all. Secondly, instructional lectures are rarely jazzy. Neither the talent or the money needed are there to do a lecture as well as, say, a commercial (which, it might be added, seems to be the form which best exploits the nature of the medium). And thirdly, lectures are perhaps the least useful and least effective vehicles for educating anyone about anything. But that kind of truism we shrug off easily.

Both instructional TV and CAI, then, as they are usually practiced, perpetuate without serious examination (and at considerable cost) anachronistic notions and processes of education. They accord the student a passive role; they arbitrate content for him (assuring that it is mere accident when the content is useful or relevant in *his* eyes). The student is restricted to absorbing data. He does not generate it; nor does he generate and explore issues, ways of being, or ways of thinking. It is doubtful that anyone ever *learned* much this way. But it is becoming increasingly clear that education which consists primarily of transferring data from one receptacle to another is useless. It is useless in part because there is too much data around, and it grows obsolete too quickly. And it is useless because it does not help the student learn how to process data, or help him learn how to learn.

If it is true, as Kenneth Boulding has suggested, that we have entered the era of operations overload, then information no longer is power. It is a swamp. But pattern recognition, as a way to handle information, is essential. Patterning becomes power. Electronic media all rely on patterning. And this should be taught, rather than using media to further overload students.

Indeed, most efforts at instructional technology have ignored the growing body of evidence and theory which points to the importance of *process,* as opposed to content, in learning. All John Holt is saying in *How Children Fail* is that, in schools, the medium really is the message. In an authoritarian classroom, or school, or system of schools, grades, rote learning and pleasing the teacher are the real "curriculum". Kids learn in varying degrees how to get good grades, how to parrot the teacher or how to ingratiate themselves. (Or else, they turn off.) They certainly don't learn how to think, cope, feel, express or analyze.

Is it not equally possible that a generation raised on the current varieties of CAI, ITV and all those other acronyms will grow up thinking that knowledge comes in small bits? And will only be able to think in small bits?

A visitor to Philadelphia's CAI biology project in its early days observed the following:

Six high school pupils sat before six consoles, scratching away with their styli. They were obviously absorbed in their work. Suddenly, all the screens went blank. "Mr. _____," they chorused. "It's gone off again." The teacher, with some embarrassment, explained something about bugs in the system and the program not being adequately pre-tested. He disappeared into a back room to consult with a technician. A few moments later, the consoles flickered back on. The kids resumed scratching away with their styli. Minutes passed. The consoles went blank again. "Mr. __," came the chorus. "It's gone off again." The teacher disappeared into the back room. In a few moments, the consoles flickered on. The kids resumed scratching . . .

Precisely *because* the process was not working, it was obvious that the process was the source of fascination to the students. They did not discuss biology during the breakdowns. Rather, they stared blankly at the blank screens, reduced to utter passivity. ("Godammit, Martha, will you fix the picture.")

The challenge for instructional technology, as for education in general, is to devise and institutionalize an anti-institutional approach to education: an educational program that aims at the growth of students, not of test scores; growth in their ability to explore, to discover both themselves and the world around them and make connections between the two. This means making students active participants in education; it means changing the one-way authoritarian relationship which prevails in most classrooms between instructor (whether teacher or programmed instruction or machine) and student. It means making the teacher's role catalytic, not prescriptive. It means changing those structures in school systems and bureaucracies which force teachers into rigid, non-growing roles, and shut parents out of their children's classrooms. It means changing both the content and process of most curriculum. It means taking seriously cliches about the complex, fluid, constantly changing, constantly shrinking world we increasingly inhabit, and doing something to relate the process of education to that reality.

Marshall McLuhan suggests that the new technologies are themselves instrumental in defining to today's youngsters what is real and what is relevant. Describing the effects of weaning on TV, McLuhan suggests:

"The young today reject goals. They want roles. R-O-L-E-S. That is, total involvement. They do not want fragmented or specialized goals or jobs. We now experience simultaneously the drop-out and the teach-in. The two forms are correlative. They belong together. The teach-in represents an attempt to shift from instruction to discovery, from brainwashing students to brainwashing instructors. It is a big, dramatic reversal. The drop-out represents a rejection of nineteenth century technology as manifested in our educational establishments. The teach-in represents a creative effort, switching the educational process from package to discovery."[3]

Certainly if one accepts McLuhan's notion that it is the nature of television that "the viewer is the screen" (as opposed to movies in which "the viewer is the camera,") and accepts the pervasive influence of TV, then this basic challenge to educational assumptions is an important starting point in any consideration of instruction.

It is not enough, however, to challenge assumptions; the structures which tend to codify, rigidify and support anachronistic assumptions must be challenged as well. Joseph Grannis does just this while making some points not so far from McLuhan's in a recent issue of the Harvard Graduate School of Education Bulletin.

"Individuals," Grannis states, "find meaning and control in modern life, as in the life of any society, by participating in its social institutions—political, economic, artistic, and so on—or by rebelling against institutions which they understand are stupid or inequitable. Our, problem, in essence, is that effective entry into most of the institutions of modern society is a great deal more complex than was entry into the institutions of pre-industrial society." (Or, one might add, pretechnetronic society.)

Grannis proceeds to argue that the current disconnection between schools and community, which is most marked in urban settings, must be altered. He suggests this means "community control" of schools, but not simply in the sense in which New York is embarking on community control. Rather, he argues that "community control of the schools should be conceived of in terms of a plurality of communities of interest, each having relatively greater control over that part of the school's program which it is competent to, and cares to, participate in."

Another way of saying the same thing is that the community (or communities) must be brought into the classroom—or must become the classroom—if the classroom is to connect with the real world; if it is to be relevant.

In terms, say, of vocational education, this has obvious ramifications. The laboratory approach has been too long restricted primarily to science. But a factory is a lab; a data processing center is a lab; a television studio is a lab if it is viewed as one and if it becomes available to students for learning. Indeed, to simply maintain the hardware which permits students to learn vocationally much useful about technology is too great a financial burden for schools. But the hardware is all around them in business and industry. Business and industry, if they want something as comparatively simple as a well-trained labor force, are going to have to get in the business of vocational-technical education for secondary school children. (This is exactly what is happening in Philadelphia's Parkway Program, which is described below.)

But first and foremost, the institutions of education, particularly in big cities where scale and bureaucratization have made them so remote, must connect to the realities of people's lives.

This means reexamining the institutional context in which education takes place; a context established by a variety of relationships—between pupil and pupil, pupil and teacher, teacher and administrator—and a variety of processes—political, administrative, and educative. It also means examining the relationship of that context to both the world around it and the world that will be. To make such a reexamination, one does not simply call in experts.

Rather, expertise is gained through a process which itself becomes instrumental in recreating school systems. Philadelphia's superintendent, Mark R. Shedd, has suggested that there are at least four steps to this process:

"1. Listening to the students and their parents to discover what felt and/or perceived needs are not being met.

2. Joining with those students and parents to redefine education and develop programmatic responses to those needs.

3. Relating such responses directly to the reality of the students, which is to say the reality of American society, and particularly urban society.

4. Adopting an approach to instruction which is based on the above steps and which reflects full awareness of individual schools (and school systems) as social organisms in themselves."

The so-called Coleman Report, and other data, tell us that there is a direct relationship between a student's feeling of his ability to control his own destiny and his achievement. Certainly students are not going to have that feeling unless their parents feel they can have some impact on the school, and unless teachers feel they have some impact. Yet, we insist on maintaining bureaucratic, centralized structures which by their very nature perpetuate authoritarianism, severely restrict participation of parents, teachers and students, and teach the lesson that somebody "up there" makes all the decisions. The process Shedd has described is both a step towards, and an outcome of, decentralizing the policy-making and the administrative decision-making of school systems; it is decentralization conceived of primarily not as a management tool, but as a way to free up the prime participants in education (pupil, parent, and teacher) and strike a blow at an authoritarian value structure which in itself is anti-educational. At its simplest, it means making education a democratic process.

Indeed, all these statements are cliches. They have been for some time. But they are cliches more honored in the breach, alas, than the observance. And to try to spell them out in any more detail would take more space than this paper permits.

The point is, that educators and capitalists alike will be delinquent if they plunge into the technologizing of instruction without first taking a hard look at where they are going, what their assumptions are, and what basic changes in the education system must be made if technology is going to make any real impact, any real difference for the students.

Big city school systems today are like old automobiles once the parts start to break down. It costs more to keep them going than to buy a new model. Tacking on a few innovations, getting a few new parts, adding some gimmicks won't do.

If the present system of education, with its anti-intellectual, anti-learning, anti-growth biases remains intact, and if instructional technology is simply used to buttress that system and its assumptions, then education is on the verge of its greatest boondoggle. Money poured into the sieve will accomplish nothing, just as the money poured into compensatory education—which tinkers with but does not alter the machine—has accomplished nothing.

There is real cause to suspect that exactly this may happen. The cost of computer systems is de-escalating rapidly. The sophistication of instructional approaches to technology gives little indication of rising as fast. As CAI, for instance, becomes economically feasible on a large scale, education may find itself locked once again into a new, technological self-perpetuating tradition of mediocrity. The basic blame will rest with the pedagogues who accept current mediocrities and are often hired to develop software. Corporations willing to turn all responsibility for content, process and educational assumptions over to the educators so they can make a buck on hardware, however, will have to assume some of the collective guilt.

At some point, there must be matrices in which the nature of relevant education and the nature of technology intersect, and this returns to Impacts A, B, and C. It is not within my competency to pinpoint these matrices. Rather, hoping to be suggestive and at risk of being vague, I would like to suggest some of the kinds of tests, paradoxes, approaches and questions that would have to be faced in such a process.

Suppose we decide the impact of technology on human life will be Impact A. Then, it becomes obvious that—if humanism has any life left in it—it is important students understand, and learn to manipulate, the basic principles and operations by which the computer will manipulate them. Before anyone gets exposed to programmed instruction, a thorough appreciation of memory, time and perhaps set theory would be essential. The first use of the computer in education should be the study of the ways in which computers handle the reality. Certainly, if geometry and even calculus can be taught to elementary school children through new math, then they can learn how computers think. They should be able to write programs and design systems, however simple. This suggests a first paradoxical law of technologized instruction: learning starts before the hardware is turned on.

It would be equally important to understand the limits of the computer. If the linear model of the computer which characterizes the first three generations is presumed to be the model which will continue to be most pervasive—in which case the computer simply will lock in the industrial age—students should learn the great deficiency of programmed instruction. That is, someone who has a brilliant reason why two and two make five gets the same treatment as someone who makes a dull error. Both get branched back to one plus one. Educators should learn the corrollary: computers only half-individualize instruction; they can tailor instruction to pace, but not to style.

Or, to give another example, let us envision a computer assisted course in rhetoric, and a particular lesson in making of metaphor. The program might assume that certain basic principles go into an effective metaphor for, say, a flower. To simplify, it may be determined that all good metaphors for flowers contain two elements: an animal and a color, which seem unrelated to flowers (thus having the element of surprise), but which in combination (according to some principle of association) definitely connect and expand on the idea of flower. All possible animals and all possible colors become part of the program. Selections are made, according to the principles just described. The machine produces several metaphors. Some are better than others, but probably none will be any good. The question is "why?" At that point learning begins.

From such an example, one might extract a paradoxical law of CAI: learning begins when the computer stops.

If Impact B is determined the likely outcome, then computers themselves (or other media) should become the direct object of study as media. For if we are going to create the new paradigm that creates us, then we should understand that paradigm. (It's probably fair to say that the average high school graduate has never had a chance to study the Newtonian paradigm—as opposed to memorizing it—and is hence unable to articulate how it affects his life.)

Similarly, if we believe in Impact B, educators, before plunging into instructional technology, should at least play with some rather difficult questions. For instance;

—Are non-linear models of the computer (such as the parallel systems model) potentially more important to instruction than linear models?

—Where is the quest for new models of the computer? And where is it going?

—Will the computers reliance on the past be supplanted, through some new model, with reliance on the future? (i.e., what will a computer be like which relies on foresight rather than memory?)

—There is a curious kind of distance between the excitement implied by the language of computers (feedback, simulation, associative addressing, etc.), and the reality of the operation's these terms describe. What inhabits that distance?

Or if Impact C is the choice, a major effort would be to have students learn about information systems: how to build them and how to use them (in a way they never learn how to use libraries). In this, (and in the other alternatives as well), the key characteristic is *engagement*—making the student an active learner, not a passive tutee. The hardware is not the master; the student is.

Whatever the impact of technology on education, the possibility of its diminishing human interaction and contact is obvious and real. Similarly, it will diminish opportunities to experience interdependence (as distinguished from dependence or independence). This is paradoxical because the rarest feats of the new technology—space flights or heart transplants, for example—are extraordinary examples of interdependent group accomplishments, just as communications media are increasingly creating a world community in which interdependence among nations is vital to survival. It is the more unfortunate because the style of American public education has generally prohibited any chance for students to learn how to function in groups. (The exception is, of course, the highly formalized group work of athletics.) The growing role of technology in instruction simply makes it more imperative that schools stop ignoring group behavior and individual behavior in groups. The technology, to stretch a word, of human behavior should itself be a key part of the curriculum. Certainly this means a growing emphasis on affective, as opposed to cognitive, development. It may mean tackling the issues of behavior head on in T-groups. Or tackling them indirectly through games. Stanley Kubrick has wryly warned us, in his movie, *2001,* what happens in situations requiring interdependence when the group cannot function as a whole. That Kubrick makes the neurotic a computer, rather than a person, is perhaps no more than an amusing way to suggest that technology does not relieve us, but only intensifies for us, this basic issue.

Anyone who looks at the behavioural assumptions embodied in school organizational structure, or who has attended a few education conferences, or administrative meetings, knows that the place to start in this endeavor may well be with some education for the educators.

It should be stressed that underlying the entire impact of technology on education—and particularly the impact of the computer—is the development of a new, sophisticated symbolic language, with both its own logic and its own relationship to "reality." In schools, we are just getting around to acknowledging in the curriculum that mathematics is a symbolic language. That English or any language is also a symbolic system is still generally obscured. (Perhaps because the teachers don't know it).

Again, the growth of technology in education dramatized the need to address another shortcoming of the system as its exists.

The remedy for one problem often produces a new one. The question must be asked, what would be in the impact on students of dealing with a curriculum that is highly symbolic? Extensive symbolic manipulation can produce anxiety. Should there then be therapy in the schools? Or should, at the least, such subjects as art, music and writing be used as personal, creative ways of expressing and dealing with feelings and/or the environment. After all, this is what art is all about (although again that is not usually recognized in schools).

An equally basic question is, will it take longer than the existing 12-year period of schooling for students to acquire the kind of sophistication—so far beyond what schools offer now—suggested in this paper? And what sort of sequence, what articulation, what continuity, should develop for the K-12 or K-? curriculum? It certainly does seem foolish to proceed with a dash of computer biology in the eighth grade, a little simulated economics in the fifth grade, some ITV in kindergarten and a little film-making in summer school— which is the kind of slapdash, patchwork way instructional media are being introduced now. Tacking on gimmicks, the traditional approach to "innovations" in schools, won't create a revolution. Planning for systems change just might.

The kinds of questions posed here have been posed primarily in terms of computers. But they can, and should be, posed in terms of all forms of technology which impact on education.

Moreover, it should be acknowledged squarely by anyone facing the problems of technology and instruction that the grip of dead tradition on school systems is strong indeed. Perhaps instructional technology can be used to help break that grip—although there is very little evidence to make one believe it is helping so far. Certainly it would be irresponsible to push for heavy investments into instructional technology without first addressing squarely not only the nature of those investments, but also the process by which systemic change will occur that make pay-off possible.

This is a tall order. It may seem rather Utopian, and rather beyond the purview of a study of instructional technology. But considerable experience and certainly the opinion of top leadership in the Philadelphia schools reinforce the gloomy opinion that nothing less than total overhaul will "save" education, particularly education in urban areas. And that should be everyone's business.

The following section of this paper switches gears, and no pretense at a graceful transition is made. From the general and the abstract, it will attempt to suggest some glimmerings, based on Philadelphia programs, of how instructional technology may make a difference in the future. There is a disparity between the cosmic task which has been sketched above, and the modest beginnings which will be described below. A disparity, but not, it is hoped, glaring inconsistency.

Some Uses of Technology in Philadelphia

Education needs new metaphors—new ways of looking at itself and organizing itself. Technology, or media, which technology becomes in instruction, can provide some of those new ways and can serve as a vehicle for changing not only the content of instruction, but the process, or behavior of those involved in teaching-learning.

Media in the classroom may range from a simple object (say a bag of beans used in a math laboratory) to a complex piece of hardware (a videotape machine, a computer). The Madison Math program is a good example of an instructional approach which uses its own technology to teach math, to provide different methods (manipulation of materials; playing games) of learning and, in the process, to change the relationship between teacher and student. Most simply put, Madison Math forces a teacher to stop meddling with the students and let them meddle with the materials. The students learn through meddling. (The teacher primarily assists and sets up possibilities for instruction; the student does the learning himself.) The teachers learn a new way—a non-authoritarian way—of operating a classroom. And the latter is really the "hidden agenda" of the Madison Math program.

This is to suggest that technology can be a change agent by its mere use. It can also be a metaphor, an organizing principle, a message, an environment, a catalyst, and, as McLuhan suggests, an extension of man.

In varying degrees, media is all these things in the Parkway Program—a rather radical departure in secondary education which has just begun in Philadelphia.

The mile-long Benjamin Franklin Parkway is a broad, tree-lined mall that runs between City Hall and the Museum of Art. Along it are clustered many of the primary cultural institutions of the city—the Franklin Institute (physical sciences) and its research laboratory; the Academy of Natural Sciences; the Rodin Museum; the Free Library. Nearby are the Zoo and Fairmount Park. And within the radius of a half-mile or so of its center are the main institutions of government in the city (City Hall, County Court, the Board of Education); two penal institutions (one for youth, one for adults); the major transportation centers; several major corporate headquarters; some industry, a hospital, two colleges of art and a college of music, newspaper plants, television studios, and every kind of urban living condition, from townhouse to tenement to high-rise apartment.

This area is Philadelphia's newest high school. One hundred twenty students, chosen at random from over 2000 applicants, and representing a broad range of backgrounds, interests and scholastic achievement and aptitude, currently attend it. They are receiving their total educational program in the massive learning laboratory that the Parkway area has become, and they are helping plan the program that up to 2,400 students will receive there as the project expands in the next few years.

Available to them, chosen with the aid, but not at the direction, of the faculty, are courses offered by businesses, by the various institutions and by the faculty, in a broad range of subjects from vocational to traditional academic areas in the humanities, social studies and sciences, to offerings in urban affairs, multi-media journalism, and so forth. A student's own goals and projects are the organizing principle around which he or she selects among the offerings granted. There is a high degree of reliance on independent study. But group experiences (in seminar and counseling sessions) are built in. Time is allocated according to the needs of a particular course or a particular project—not according to the arbitrary rigors of a roster. Indeed, the "technological tyrannies" of the average high school program—time and space—are replaced by near total flexibility. And the tyranny of the teacher is eliminated by permitting students to plan their own program. If they don't like a course, they don't take it. But they learn at the same time that the world has some givens, and there are certain things they must do to meet their own life goals.

In the Parkway Program, the city and its people quite literally become media. They are the object of study and the means of study and source of information. Students learn from, learn about and learn through them. The metaphor is media; the objective correlative is man. Technologies are studied, used and learned from primarily insofar as they contribute to this understanding of a society, its institutions and it workings.

John Bremer, director of the Parkway Program, argues strongly that the project is an idea, not a place. He maintains that almost any strip of the city, a mile long and a half mile wide, has within it the full array of technologies, the potential to become a laboratory in which a full educational program can be executed.

Nonetheless, Philadelphia continues to build schools, and no doubt will. (The Parkway Program has a small headquarters in rented space, but no facility of its own.) The same concern for physical environment as a medium which not only helps shape instruction but should itself be an object of study is explicit in the North Philadelphia School Facilities Study, performed for the Board of Education by David Crane.

The Crane study accomplishes three major aims. First, it is a systemic analysis of the components of school buildings. Secondly, it suggests alternative ways to design, provide or construct those components which permit the school building itself to be "decentralized" so it blends into the contours and the overall physical development of a neighborhood (from transportation to business, to recreation, to health and other facilities); and thirdly, through reduction of a facility to its components and by simulating the process of design, it provides a workable way for community groups to engage in the complexities of designing a school for their neighborhood.

The Crane Study assumes that open and flexible space to permit a flexible instructional program is not enough. Rather, the technology of school design and construction must itself connect and be integrated into the total community environment. The technology of school construction thus can and should be viewed as inseparable from the instructional program itself and from its relationship to particular communities. The technology of environment is a part of the instructional program.

The Film/Media Center which operates in District Two, one of the city's eight Sub-districts, is an example of a decentralized curriculum service unit which has as its explicit concern technology.

The media center is a resource for teachers, a resource for staff development and co-ordinates curriculum developed by teachers. Its program includes an emphasis on media (primarily film and television, although not exclusively) as a "content" area and a valid activity (student film-making, slide tapes, radio programs) in and of itself. But it also is developing an approach to media as an organizing principle for an educational program. The September, 1968 issue of "Media and Methods" describes one such approach developed at the media center in an article entitled "The Wheel: A Model for Multi-Media Learning."[4]

A "media wheel" can be used to teach almost any subject. It is based on the assumption that learning takes place in at least two phases—an active phase in which the student produces, makes, shapes or processes information, and a reactive phase, in which the student receives information. A "media wheel" provides a progression of media for approaching the same topic for each phase. A typical wheel, for instance, uses six different media: the body (the senses, mime, improvisational drama); design (art graphics, constructions); sound (speech, noise, music); photography and the moving image, and print. All are media which people use everyday to learn. For some students, moreover, the pervasive learning medium in schools—print—is not by itself an adequate medium of instruction. It is a technology which requires a fairly high tolerance and appreciation of abstraction. The media wheel is a device to enable different perspectives on a given lesson. It seeks to utilize and approximate the full range of methods available and natural to learning. And, again, stress is placed on student involvement (through media).

The development of the 12th and Oxford Street Gang from a street-corner gang to a diverse, if fledgling, corporation, illustrates the utility of media as a catalyst—a point of entry—into learning. The School District can take no credit for the evolution of this group, but its relevance as an educational model is undeniable.

A few years ago, an enterprising youth worker began to work with about thirty members of this gang—a group of kids with police records, a history of gang killings, and un-satisfactory school performance, if they still happened to be in school—typical of much gang youth.

The worker got the idea of putting a movie camera in their hands. They began to play around with it. After a while they decided to make a film. With the assistance of a television cameraman from a local TV station, they did. The film produced, "The Jungle," has since been shown on television; has won an award at a New York Film Festival; and has been shown in this country and abroad. The gang is at work now on its second and third films, under contract and for money.

In the process, some remarkable metamorphoses took place within the gang itself. The 12th and Oxford Street Gang has become the 12th and Oxford Street Corporation. They are legally incorporated. And in the process of forming a film company, several things hap-pened to the gang members:

First of all, they wanted to do it themselves. So, they found out that there were some very basic steps they had to take. They needed to understand law, and this meant reading and learning something about the legal structures of our society. They needed to be able to handle accounts. This meant math. They needed to develop high level competencies within the group in a variety of fields connected with film-making: script writing, film editing and processing, sound effects, lighting effects, equipment repair and the like. A number of them went back to school to sharpen up on these very skills. Others came in contact with lawyers, with accountants, and with a variety of professionals from the com-munications industry, and they learned first hand, from real professionals doing the real thing.

Not surprisingly, some of the gang members began to develop other interests, particularly in small businesses, such as laundromats, and in housing renewal and rehabilitation. The idea of the corporation expanded, and a federal grant of $170,000 gave impetus to this broader range of projects, which the gang is now undertaking, and for which various members are acquiring the necessary skills. As an end result, the 12th and Oxford Film-Making Company is now a subsidiary of the 12th and Oxford Corporation.

This narrative condenses substantially the development of the 12th and Oxford group, but it should suggest several basic principles about an approach to education that is organic, that starts with the student and provides him a chance to grow and explore and learn in ways relevant to himself.

Moreover, it may suggest one of the virtues of at least one technology. Archimedes declared that given a place to stand on, he could move the world (with a lever, of course). The camera and the medium of film gave the 12th and Oxford group "a place to stand on," something which quite literally enable them to put their lives in focus. Perhaps this was just luck. But perhaps it is no accident that the camera provides a concrete way of ordering and, in a sense, controlling one's environment. Moreover, making a movie about themselves gave the members of the group a chance to analyze their own behavior, their own values, and come to some conclusions about it. Without this chance, they might still be on the streets.

The 12th and Oxford "model" does present an anti-institutional approach to education. Its spontaneity may be more than one can reasonably expect in schools. But the area of gaming and simulation can be very useful in approximating the same sort of process. Games are, of course, a kind of technology themselves. And other technologies can be helpful in either the presentation of the game or in deepening the understanding of the game.

At the Pennsylvania Advancement School, gaming is a major strategy for reaching under-achievers—such games as the Life Careers Game or the Consumer Game developed at

John Hopkins, or the "race game" of Western Behavioural Sciences, Inc. The Advancement School has concluded that games sharpen cognitive development in a variety of ways: they provide frames of reference which enable students to pull together pieces of information that otherwise were floating—perhaps semiforgotten—and not apparently relevant to the student. In other words, they help a student make knowledge useful. New (or renewed content) becomes arresting because it is related to an experience. Games develop the ability to make strategic decisions, comprehend relationships (cause-effect or interrelation of components of a system), and they demand planning. Moreover, a good game strongly involves even "unreachables" and involves them actively.

Finally, games like the "race game" provide a powerful series of experiences which teach them about power, group behaviour and individual behaviour as it is affected by group membership.[5]

Some work, here and elsewhere, has of course gone into the programming of these and similar games. Extremely sophisticated simulations, of course, become possible through the use of computers, and there is enthusiasm in Philadelphia for their instructional role. Closed circuit television has been used at P.A.S. and elsewhere in the system, particularly to record games which emphasize behavior, and, here as elsewhere, has been found an effective way to give students feedback and a chance to study in depth both themselves and the group. Similar use of closed circuit television has been made in improvisational dramatics and role-playing, as developed by the Advancement School and the Philadelphia Research Project in Affective Development, to get at issues of human behaviour in the classroom.

Finally, it should be noted that Philadelphia has invested several million dollars in computer assisted instruction of the sort disparaged in the first section of this paper. But even CAI has its place in the galaxy of instructional technology. It is merely that it should be recognized as performing the most menial function of education and should have a place only if it has its proper place in a redefined educational context.

REFERENCES

1. Cf. Kuhns. *The Structure of Scientific Revolutions.* University of Chicago.

2. The author of this paper was once horrified when the teacher of a CAI Biology course said, "This is fine for my bright students. But I don't use it with my slow ones. What they need is more drill in the old method." On second thought, however, he may be right, for CAI has many of the earmarks of fast drill.

3. *Understanding Media.* New Directions.

4. Suid, Murry, Roberta Suid, and James Morrow.

5. These games are both well-known and easily available. It would require too much space to describe their workings.

26.

Relationships Between The Restructuring of Schools And Communications Technology

by REV. MICHAEL J. DEMPSEY
Asst. Superintendent, Catholic Schools
Diocese of Brooklyn
Brooklyn, N.Y.

> I wot well clerks will say, as them leste
> By arguments, that all is for the best.
> Chaucer: *The Frankeleyns Tale.* (14th Cent.)

Crises are opportunities for constructive and imaginative change. It would take the most obdurate optimist not to quail before the mounting destructive pressures in American educational systems. Yet, to this writer, it seems as equally narrow-minded to fail to appreciate and attempt to seize the opportunity to reformulate the organization of our instructional systems, given the unique capability for successful change which instructional technology presents to schools for the first time.

Schools are one of the few human businesslike enterprises which annually decrease in system productivity and yet are maintained relatively unchanged. Each year, the input of education increases substantially; each year the output, in terms of number of students taught effectively per teacher, or per school, or per dollar spent, decreases. It has generally been accepted that a qualitative jump in quality of education required smaller class sizes, more materials, more audiovisual equipment, additional school specialists and so forth. Whatever be the case for the practice of the past, there seems little justification now for equating quality in education merely or even basically with greater per student expenditures. It is time to redesign instructional relationships.

Technology has been part of Western life now for several centuries. Its applications naturally tended to center about the areas of business and profit-making enterprises. One new factor today is the willingness of many insightful people to consider the application of technology to concerns much more intimate with human life. The field of education is one humanistic endeavor that has not until recently considered itself addressed by the surging tide of technology. The basic process of teaching and learning seemed too interpersonal, too defined by the need for human contact, to be substantially assisted by "industrialization." Books, buildings and mechanical devices were introduced into the teaching-learning process as they were needed and became available, but never fundamentally altered the prevailing concept. They were accidental and accessory to the process; they enabled the school to function better, but without suggesting that perhaps they should be considered a structural component of the process itself.

The formidable pressures upon school systems today are compounding at least one unexpected dividend, the need to innovate simply to survive. Now, this by no means guarantees that innovation will be worthwhile or that it will be related to the basic problems of the schools. It is quite possible that new structures, whether organizational, interpersonal, or physical, will be, as they have tended to be in the past, mainly experimental, temporary and out of the mainstream of educational practice. Nevertheless, the problems themselves are now so great and apparently so impervious to solution by any combination of regular procedures that educators, for the first time, are tending to consider alternatives. I am reflecting these views from a background rooted in the Catholic School System of this country. School system problems are often surprisingly similar in both public and non-public schools despite the fact that, to the uncritical public eye, the systems seem so dissimilar. The startling increase in the proportion of lay teachers, the geometrically increasing curricular demands, the multiplying roles of the schools, the haziness of educational objectives, the skyrocketing fiscal imbalance between costs and resources, the chorus of questioning concerning the effectiveness of and need for value-oriented, and especially regarding religious values, education and many more frustrating dilemmas are the daily fare of Diocesan Superintendents, their assistants and the host of religious sub-agencies associated with the operation of a Diocesan school system. Yet the point can, I believe, be made even more strongly here, that the pressures themselves are creating a climate favorable to the substantive alteration of our school systems that has not been present in the past. It is possible that the flexibility of parochial school systems, referred to by Commissioner Howe at the 1968 National Convention of the N.C.E.A. in San Francisco, combined with a presently very substantial and growing technological involvement, may be able to evolve a unique and viable model for the educators of the future.

The remainder of this paper will concentrate upon communications technology, especially in parochial school systems, its potential, its present level of implementation, and a number of avenues upon which some of us have already or are planning to embark. Let us begin with a brief outline of the implosion of television into Catholic school systems.

In early 1965, except for the Archdiocese of Boston's UHF Channel 38, no parochial school system in the United States operated a television system for its schools. Today, eight major Dioceses and Archdioceses operate very extensive 2500 megahertz instructional television systems that reach a potential elementary and secondary audience of 24,154,291. Another ten diocesan school systems are in various stages of planning for such systems. The statistics are impressive enough; what is more significant is the fact that none of these systems was inaugurated with a basic mentality such as, "We would like television in order to add an extra measure of equality to our educational system" or even, "A television system will permit us to experiment with new instructional techniques" and certainly not, "We have a little extra money, so let's try this promising new educational tool." These are all worthwhile motives; indeed, the negative findings of the Ford and Carnegie Foundation reports on instructional uses of television would likely never have resulted if educators had been influenced by such thinking as they approved or pressed for such projects. It is easy to generalize ebulliently concerning the underlying support for diocesan decisions and to gloss over the false starts, the mistakes in planning, the false, often subconscious expectations raised by too lyrical speeches and articles. Nevertheless, it is a fact that these systems were built to attack, for good or evil, the spectral problems facing Catholic education. Because, by intent even if not yet in fact, they are to be integral to the educative process, and not peripheral, they offer a genuine basis for confidence that these school systems will make significant contribution to American education in the area of restructuring through technology.

Two embryonic corporate structures have been established to provide two different levels of service to the Dioceses now operating ITFS systems. One organization will coordinate cooperative services needed for routine functioning. These would include the dissemination of information, the cooperative production and distribution of programs, the cooperative purchasing of materials and equipment, the development of sources of funding and so forth. The other provides a legal structure for a large scale cooperative venture into experimentation involving a combination of technologies, television, computer and satellite, in such a way as to open an approach to the reconstituting of the relationships between the elements of an instructional system, namely, students, teachers, materials and technology. Substantive experimentation along these lines has been carried on in the Diocese of Brooklyn over the past two years. It represents an effort to move from theoretic constructions to the concrete packaging of a viable instructional system intended to test out the promise of lower per unit cost for education. It assumes the absolute need for education to integrate innovative instructional techniques and hardware with a flexible new organization of the school system itself.

Most, perhaps all, new approaches to education have been unable to overcome the obstacles presented by traditional school organization. Each new technique, whether it be team teaching, instructional television, ungraded primaries, tutorial systems and so forth, is inserted into a traditional school organization and the process of organic rejection of the transplant seems to occur with dismaying regularity. It is not a question simply of the relative merits of the traditional and the new; quite possibly the former in a particular case is superior. The difficulty lies in the fact that the new makes demands on the old and vice versa. The participants in a team teaching system must have their schedules considerably altered from that required of fellow teachers. The ungraded primary raises questions by fourth grade teachers who are accustomed to a chronologically homogeneous group and presents often a problem for administrators to find instructional spaces different from the number and/or size ordinarily provided for the graded primary classes. Required high school class schedules make a shambles of the most ingeniously contrived television schedule. The list could be extended, but the point is not particularly controverted; the introduction of new curricular approaches and school organizations create frequently unavoidable abrasive planes of contact with the predominant system. Frequently these problems cannot be contained sufficiently to maintain the innovation.

The introduction of technology into education generates the additional awkwardness of seeming to challenge the accepted position of the human person in the process of instruction. How often is the charge made that the teacher is in danger of being replaced by the television set or the computer or some other mechanical monster. The presiding mind-set will accept these technologies only if they do not disturb the status quo; the teacher, the student, the book, the classroom must continue to do what they have always done. Of course, such a departmentalized superimposition of technology can happen; indeed this is precisely the reason why multi-million dollar television, computer and other systems of hardware are held to performing such peripheral functions for most of American education. It is not that American education does not use these instrumentalities, but that their utilization is rendered unimportant and ineffectual in relation to the problems of education. Nevertheless, it would be a mistake, in my opinion, to rail against this dominant attitude which is basically self-defensive in the face of suggestions and pressures that do not approach the question of education and schools organically and, as a result, often do not present acceptable alternatives to the persons threatened.

Technology must become involved in education in such a way that it is tied to the substantive core of the educative process and not left to dabble on the periphery. This cannot happen without major structural reorganization of the schools. Up to this period, there was no other way to improve the quality of education, or extend its reach, than to multiply the elements of education, namely, teachers, buildings and materials. This is no longer feasible nor, in a sense, is it necessary. It is simply not possible for school systems to find, train and pay the school staffs that would be required to meet modern educational demands; it is no longer possible for schools, as presently organized, to cope with the volume, complexity, and significance of the data modern life presents to education for digestion, reformulation and presentation to students. It is ordinarily stated in terms of money, but the problem is not simply a lack of money. It is more true to say that the function that instructional systems are required to perform today are beyond their designed capabilities. Even the suburban school, spending $1,600.00 annually per child without serious strain, and providing every service ordinarily available to teachers and students, still inadequately handles the minds and persons of its children when one considers the gap existing between the potential for and the actuality of learning.

Anyone can increase the quality of instruction or extend its benefits to more students by doubling the per unit expenditure. But, experimental schools that designedly exceed the normal annual per student cost very substantially are not capable of being replicated on a large scale. What good does it do to discover that the introduction of instructional television, or computer-assisted instruction, or massive doses of films or modular scheduling, or team teaching or any other worthwhile hardware or software, raises achievement levels if at the same time it is clear that nothing reasonably analogous to the experiment can be employed throughout the school district or diocese. In one sense, we are swimming in a sea of experiments with technologies that so far have not been related to the mainstream of education. We have made the point, over and over again, that the educational process can be substantially assisted, and improved by, even profitably reconstituted around, one or many of these new approaches and technologies; as yet, we have not actually done so in any large scale believable way.

Suppose we were to do the following. Let us take a school or an entire school system and accept as given the enrolled number of students, the physical plant, the present size of the staff and the actual operating cost. Within these parameters, considered flexibly, and apart from local or state requirements, set as the educational objectives only a level of education at least equal to that presently achieved in terms of quality or quantity. Then permit the school and system staff, with whatever resources of consultation is needed, to rethink the entire school or school system structure, governed only by the results. Why, for example, must a high school student be in the school building from 9:00 A. M. to 2:30 P. M.? Why should there be classes? Why should not most of the student's time be spent in independent study? Very few, if any, ideas would be likely to surface that have not been part of the vocabulary of visionary educators for the last many years. But the freedom would be present to reorganize totally the structure of the school so as to take advantage of any technique or technology that offers a practical and better alternative to traditional teaching and learning. It is my belief that, within such an operational design, we would be able to structure schools and school systems that are capable of educating more students better at a lower per unit expenditure than is the case today or is possible so long as we insist on the present structuring of schools.

Such a project must not be viewed as "tentative" in the sense that term ordinarily has when used of experiments. We know that these individual new educational approaches (team teaching, television, computers, individualized instruction etc.) work; they do not have to be validated. What is at question is the context into which they are inserted. The idea is to create a flexible environment already committed to the use of all these techniques in whatever combination, or relationship is required to effectuate better and more efficient learning. There is a kind of tentativeness present about the particular formulation that may arise at the beginning of such a procedure. But the basic structure is the conferral of a degree of professional freedom, not the initial outcome of the exercise of that freedom. We should decide at the outset that this is not an experiment in the sense that it can be dispensed with if subsequent events are not satisfactory. In my conception, we often fail in education for lack of decisiveness in recognizing what is known to be worthwhile and insisting that it be utilized successfully. We would commit ourselves to a process of change, of accommodation to known values, within a context of the unchallenged objectives of quality and efficiency. The firmness of the commitment would be critical to success.

The Diocese of Brooklyn is edging toward a procedure of this nature. Circumstances of finances and teacher shortages, together with the continuing pressure for religion-oriented education insist that we consider alternatives to the present routine of school operation. We envision that one high school and/or one elementary would be selected as prototypes on the basis of the ease with which this new approach might be applied. It would be most important that the schools selected be reasonably typical of the school system since the prime consideration is the ultimate replication of the process in the remainder of the schools. It might be possible to begin without the necessity of *re*-constructing a school organization if a situation were chosen where the school structure was as yet fluid. But in such a case we would be simply postponing the inevitable necessity of applying lessons learned here to already structured institutions and learning, in turn, how a going organization moves into this radically different manner of functioning.

One of the constant mistakes of would-be educational revolutionaries is the apparently automatic denunciation of educators in general for their allegedly "obstructionist" reaction to attempted change. Usually the charge neglects the required conditions that make change possible. The fact is that any system will resist a kind of process that is imposed from without or one that offers little else but apparent professional suicide. Much of the well-intended pressure is ignored because it is seen as intemperate, unfeeling or self-seeking, as in the case of educational broadcasters who on one occasion were told by one of their number to ". . . drag American education, kicking and screaming, into the 20th century." The intent of this project is to permit education to have the degree of freedom it needs to rethink its own function and implement worthwhile new approaches in such a manner not so much to threaten as to challenge its ingenuity.

Technology remains the key new "tool" element in the equation of evolutionary education. All the other factors are relatively "known;" this one is not. We have simply not tied it to the problems education faces. Yet, enough is known to determine that the need for individualization in instruction and simultaneous substantial reduction in the per-unit cost of education are simply not possible without it. It is altogether possible that the hope of such results from the application of technology to schools, particularly the second, are simply not realizable. But there is only one way to settle the question and besides no alternative is presently available.

Communications technology, of which instructional television is part, has a particularly significant role to play in this concept of a restructuring of schools and school systems. People familiar with the problems of reaching audiences, of moving sometimes hostile viewers, of designing messages in appealing ways, have something very important to contribute to educators. Sometimes the worthwhileness of broadcasters' contributions has been romanticized out of all proportion to the realities of learning situations. Nevertheless, one of the prime hopes in our Diocesan school system is the development of a cadre of educators themselves trained in the skills of broadcasting and able to apply that know-how to the substantive challenges of teaching real students.

The television operation in Brooklyn is by no means self-satisfied. For the past two and one-half years it had scrupulously avoided the trap of attempting to restructure our schools with tools that themselves had to be validated to teachers and students. We have spent this time doing what instructional television systems anywhere have professed to accomplish, namely, the production and transmission of typical televised instructional programs. We feel we have done this despite predictable technical, organizational and educational difficulties.

The result of the effort is interesting in terms of personnel. About seventy-five professional teachers have undergone intensive production workshops designed to give them a first hand experience of television production. Some of these continued in longer training programs and some eventually became staff members of the Television Center. Another roughly 200 teachers serve as television coordinators for their schools and receive some minimal level of training for their work. The Television Center's staff now numbers 22, including production, technical, administrative and secretarial personnel. All of this means that a total of several hundred professional teachers have been exposed to a real experience of television in education to varying degrees, apart from the continuing general program of education we offer annually to all principals, supervisors and teachers in the school system, now about 5,700 persons. There is a general positive conditioning toward an openness to communications technology inevitable in such an effort.

Now however, it is time for and conceivable that this sophisticated television system, still working out the most basic problems of any I.T.V. operation, become the leading edge of a general rethinking of the structuring of the school system itself. Until now, television served the needs of our schools in the traditional manner. Now, it should perform a more creative role, one that is made more believable by reason of the new skills and insights available to the school system through the numbers of trained professional teacher-communicators, the professional staff broadcasters, the utilization-oriented school television coordinators and so forth. The field of communications is not a foreign element in this school system; it is not administratively or instructionally segregated from the everyday routine of the schools. I believe the time has come for this television facility to project itself into the center of educational evolution as a point of creativity, intuition and cat-alystic activity.

A dream is stimulating, but will it work? Well, why not? The problem is not: "Can we design technical systems adequate to accomplish instructional objectives". We have been doing that for years, however uneconomically and lacking in pragmatism. The problem is much more: "What objectives do schools seek?" and "How can we integrate communications systems so as to reach identifiable goals at minimum cost?" Now that our own television operation is relatively stable and growing and communications satellites, computers, broad-cast facsimile devices, and the gradual emergence of the television tube as a potential universal display for all visual media are all realistic educational developments within the next few years, we are interested in taking the next necessary steps beyond the traditional stereotypes of both education and communications toward a hazy, but achievable new design for Catholic education in America.

27.

Proposal for a Department Of Education, a Council of Educational Advisers, And an Education Report To Congress to be Received By a Joint Congressional Committee

by *ALVIN C. EURICH and REXFORD G. MOON, JR.*
President   *V.P. & Director*
of Studies

Academy for Educational Development

Summary

For a number of years there have been proposals to transform the Office of Education into a Department of Education which would provide:

A. Greater influence for the federal educational arm within the hierarchy of other federal programs;

B. The possibility of pulling together some of the federal programs in support of education that are now in other departments.

This memorandum proposes the establishment of such a Department as one step in a series of decisive actions by the President and the Congress which would give education the priority it needs to meet the urgent needs of today. The proposal is that Congress establish:

1. A declaration of policy which explicitly states the federal government's responsibility for extending and improving educational opportunity.

2. Authorization for an annual Education Report by the President of the Congress, setting forth:

    The extent of educational opportunities in the United States, their quality, and the improvements needed to carry out national policy.

    Current and foreseeable trends in education.

    A review and assessment of federal education programs during the preceding year.

A program for carrying out policy more effectively, plus recommendations for appropriate legislation.

3. A Department of Education, headed by a Secretary of Cabinet rank who would have *specifically designated responsibility for coordinating all federal activities in the support of education.*

4. A Council of Educational Advisers, reporting to the Secretary of Education, and charged with helping him evaluate educational trends, appraise federal programs, and formulate others in line with national policy.

5. A Joint Committee of the Congress on Education, composed of the senior members of the Senate and House committees concerned with education, and charged with:

Receiving and studying the President's annual Education Report.

Submitting each year to the Senate and the House its own findings and recommendations on the main points of the President's report.

Conducting studies of important educational issues.

There actions could well be embodied in an *Education Act of 1970.* They could also be enacted in separate pieces of legislation although probably with a substantial diminution of force.

Further Details

1. Declaration of Policy

The purpose would be for Congress to declare in formal fashion that it has a broad national policy with respect to education. Despite much education legislation, a broad national policy has not yet been established.

The declaration might begin with the recognition that the nation's general well-being, its economic growth, its strength and freedom, and the quality of every citizen's life are inextricably bound up with the quality and extent of the education the nation provides. Education is, in short, a major national resource. Therefore, the declaration might continue, the Congress conceives it to be the continuing policy and responsibility of the federal government, consistent with the constitutional rights, the privileges, and the duties of the states, to create and maintain conditions which will provide appropriate opportunities, including self-education, for those able and wanting to learn; and to encourage the development of such conditions by assisting federal, state, local, and institutional planning agencies in their efforts toward this end.

2. Education Report

Having declared a national policy, the Congress should then require an annual *Education Report by the President of the United States.* This report, prepared in consultation with appropriate officers of the Executive and Legislative branches, would be transmitted to Congress shortly after the beginning of each regular session. It would set forth:

A. The extent of educational opportunities in the United States, their quality, and improvements needed to carry out the national policy as declared by Congress;

B. Current and foreseeable trends in education;

C. Review of the education program of the federal government during the preceding year and its effect upon educational opportunities in this country;

D. A program for carrying out the declaration of policy, together with such recommendations for legislation as were deemed necessary or desirable. The President could also transmit supplementary reports to the Congress from time to time, covering any additional or revised recommendations.

3. Department of Education Headed by a Secretary of Cabinet Rank

A Secretary of Education sitting with the Cabinet could forcefully project the educational needs of the nation and the requisite role therein of the federal government. The elevation of education to a seat in the Cabinet would strengthen the advocacy within the federal government of education's needs, and by ensuring better coordination, would help to encourage more effective planning for educational development throughout the country; specifically, the Secretary would be the federal government official who would:

1. Act as the principal federal officer responsible for the coordination of all federal programs in support of education, especially in his role as chairman of the Federal Interagency Committee on Education.

2. Assist and advise the President in the preparation of the Education Report.

3. Gather timely and authoritative information on developments and trends in education, establishing indicators that would measure these trends and developments against needs, analyzing and interpreting such information in the light of national policy, and conducting appropriate studies.

4. Develop and recommend to the President national policies which will foster additional educational opportunities for the people of this country.

5. Furnish such studies, reports, and recommendations on matters of federal educational policy and legislation as the President may request.

6. Encourage the development of common guidelines and standards for data collection and reporting, and for institutional and statewide planning to be followed by educational institutions and by state and federal government agencies concerned with education.

4. Council of Educational Advisers

In order for the Department of Education to bring the country's great diversity of educational effort into a scheme of national activity, the Congress should include in the legislation establishing a Department of Education the creation of a *Council of Educational Advisers,* to report to the Secretary of Education.

The Council should be composed of from three to seven members appointed by the Secretary, to serve full time, at a salary sufficient to attract highly qualified people. Ideally they should be educational statesmen of the first rank (not all professional educators), beholden to no constituency whether institutional or organizational. Each council member should, by virtue of his experience and attainments, be exceptionally equipped to analyze and interpret developments in education, to appraise federal programs in the light of national policy, and to formulate and recommend programs and policies to the Secretary.

5. Joint Committee

To ensure that Congress acquires a full and balanced picture of educational conditions and needs, a Joint Committee on Education should be created composed of the senior members of the Senate and House committees concerned with education. The chief function of this Joint Committee would be to make a continuing study of issues raised by the proposed Education Report by the President of the United States, to file an annual report with the Senate and House of Representatives of its findings and recommendations with respect to the main points of the President's report, and to make such other educational reports and recommendations as it deems advisable.

Conclusion

The proposal for the creation of a Department of Education, a Council of Educational Advisers, and a Joint Education Committee, is based on the conviction that only such major steps will give education the strength and status it requires in the federal structure. Education tomorrow will be bigger in every way. We can, with present methods, chart the rate of growth of our institutions in a number of areas, but simply encouraging growth along present lines will not be enough. We must encourage new ways of looking at a future that will be not only bigger but different. And having encouraged innovation, we must create the means through which innovative ideas can make their way into the mainstream of our educational systems.

28.
Learning Theory, Educational Media, And Individualized Instruction*

ROBERT M. GAGNÉ
Prof., Dept. of Educational Research
College of Education
Florida State Univ.

Instruction of college and university students is an activity not customarily derived in a deliberate fashion from theories about learning. Most college instructors set about their initial task of teaching courses by using a model derived from their own college experiences; in other words, they try to emulate their own professors. The new instructor may spend many hours in selecting a text and other references, in planning what he will say to his class of students, in seeing how certain topics will "fit" a semester of so many weeks. But the question of just what the students are going to be doing during these weeks, and how their activities are going to affect their capabilities, is not likely to be given a great deal of thought.

In proceeding in this manner to face the task of college instruction, it is obvious that the new instructor is perpetuating many traditions. He is planning his work in terms of the content of knowledge to which students will be exposed, the kinds of communication he will make to them in lectures. He is selecting for students a minimal set of readings and oral communications to which they will be "exposed." He is thinking in terms of how much reading material and orally-presented material his students may be expected to "absorb" during a given period of weeks. All of these activities are traditional in the sense that they are the same ones he himself was subjected to; they resulted in the framework for instruction as he experienced it.

It is also true that this traditional system may be said to "work." The young instructor knows that, because it has worked for him and for most of his fellow students. Why does it work? Under what circumstances does it work? One suspects that it works within the confines of two major conditions: (1) that students attending college are highly selected to accomplish learning in just this fashion; and (2) that what they are expected to accomplish represents a limited set of educational goals.

To treat these questions fully, and to deal with all of their implications would require a different direction than the one this paper is supposed to take. I shall therefore have to be content to suggest the lines of questioning that seem to me to be opened up by identifying these limiting conditions of traditional college instruction. Do we want to select just those students for college who are most able to learn by traditional means? By our selection

*This paper was prepared for faculty seminars sponsored by Bucknell University and the U.S. Office of Education on using educational media to individualize college instruction, November 16-17, 1967.

procedures, are we simply perpetuating patterns of thought and learning that are first laid down in high school and earlier? Are we in danger of screening out by such procedures many individuals whose potential contributions to our culture are the most unusual? Are traditional methods of instruction best adapted to prepare the student for the activities of graduate school, where greater independence of thought is expected? Are these methods, in fact, preparing the student to be both an independent thinker and a continuing learner?

If one admits these kinds of questions into his thinking about the nature of college instruction, one faces the problem of understanding the nature of instruction itself, and in particular, what instruction has to do with human learning. One is led to examine the ways in which things, events, and ideas about them are presented to the human learner; in fact, the ways in which relevant stimulation impinges upon the learner from his environment. Further, one is led to a consideration of what happens to this stimulation when it reaches the nervous system of the learner—in other words, what kinds of transformations it undergoes. For we know that this environmental stimulation is processed in at least several different ways: this is the kind of inference we make when we say that the human individual has changed in the sense that he has learned something.

Media   The first of these problems of stimulating the human learner, represents the area of media of communication. Generally, we tend to describe media in terms of the material things that provide the vehicles for the "messages"—as, textbooks, newspapers, blackboards, motion picture projectors, television systems. However, for the purposes of considering their effects on learning, there are advantages to attending instead to the kinds of channels they offer. Considered in this way, one may conveniently describe media in several major categories as follows:

1. actual objects and events

2. veridical pictures (static and moving)

3. diagrammatic pictures

4. printed language

5. auditory language

These are the different ways in which the learner is affected by media. He may be stimulated by actual objects and events, and a reasonable portion of his learning results from such stimulation. Once he has learned how, in his early years, the learner may be stimulated with apparently equal effect by pictures, whether he sees them in a textbook, on a movie or television screen. Again, following some early learning, he responds to diagrammatic pictures, which are of several varieties. He responds to a two-dimensional representation of a cube as if it were a cube, for example; and in a more abstract way, he comes to understand the communication of a bar chart or line graph. As schooling proceeds, learning comes to depend increasingly on the stimulation provided by printed language. There is surely much truth in the definition of a university as a collection of books; even though one recognizes this to be an ironically partial truth nowadays. Auditory language has always been another major source of information for use in learning, whether presented by itself as in a lecture, or combined with the pictorial mode as in a motion picture or television program.

Learning Theory   These are the ways, then, that stimulation is presented to the human learner. The second part of the problem to be considered concerns what happens to this stimulation when it reaches the learner. How is it transformed in such as way as to change his capabilities from one state to another? What kind of processing does it undergo in leading his professors to conclude that he has learned?

Obviously, this is the area of learning theory. Psychologists have studied, experimented upon, speculated about, and generally tried to understand learning for many years. Progress has not been rapid, but it surely appears to have been speeded by the application of experimental methods in use for about the last sixty years. As is not unusual with phenomena of living things, learning is a complicated process, occurring in many varieties, forms, and situations. It is necessary first, therefore, to recognize that learning theory as it exists today is a highly inelegant and unfinished entity. Nevertheless, there do appear to be some fairly fundamental and stable principles which serve to tell us what learning is not like, and to suggest the outlines of what it is like.

Sorting out the general principles from the more specific ones in learning theory is by no means an easy task. Similarly, selecting those principles of learning which are most highly relevant to the practical problem of instruction is not a self-evident procedure. The reason for this is that modern learning investigators have chosen different models to study, and they are intent on accounting for these models. Sometimes, these models resemble the learning of the school child, or the college student, and sometimes they do not. For example, the prototype learning situations represented in a recent influential book on *Categories of Human Learning,* (Melton, 1964), are approximately as follows:

1. Conditioning: learning to blink the eye to a signal
2. Rote learning: learning to memorize pairs and lists of words
3. Probability learning: learning to choose a correct alternative from a set of words or objects
4. Short-term memory: initial reception and storage of information, usually a syllable or word
5. Concepts: learning of simple object properties by young children
6. Perceptual-motor skill: learning to make continuous tracking movements
7. Problem solving: discovering a principle which achieves a stated goal

Obviously, not many of these prototype learning situations, in and of themselves, sound much like "learning the facts of history from a textbook," or like "learning to demonstrate Coulomb's Law in the laboratory." Nevertheless, at some level of generality, these models all contribute to learning theory. For example, short-term memory, the initial reception of information, is an important part of every learning act. In considering how such principles apply to practical learning situations, it is mainly a matter of deciding what can be assumed to be going on without a hitch, as contrasted with what requires critical planning and arrangement.

The design of effective instruction, then, has these two areas of knowledge to call upon. Instruction needs to be arranged so that it will bring about the kind of change in a student which is called learning, and this requires a consideration of learning theory. In attempting to bring about such a change, the act of instruction is a matter of stimulating the student in certain ways—and here one has a choice of media to work with. Putting ideas together from these two domains of knowledge can yield some techniques and procedures of instruction which should make the process of learning an optimally effective one.

Suggestions from Learning Theory

What specific suggestions about instruction can be derived from learning theory? As I have already noted, these are not self-evident. There are many learning theories, and most of them are micro-theories, designed to provide models of some relatively specific kinds of learning. Accordingly, a selection must be made among them, keeping in mind the purpose of orientation toward the learning of young adults, or college students, and with an awareness of the variety of media available.

I believe there are four different learning theorists who have presented ideas of major importance to the design of instruction. These are Neal Miller, Skinner, Gagné, and Ausubel. I intend to describe these ideas briefly here, before going on to elaborate on their implications. It will be apparent that the suggestions of these theorists vary in their specificity, and I have ordered them along this dimension. Miller's ideas are the most general, applying to a great variety of learning situations. The specificity of suggestions increases progressively through the theory of Ausubel, who attempts to deal in a highly concentrated manner with the problem of acquiring meaningful, organized knowledge.

N. E. Miller Miller's views regarding the implications of learning theory for instruction are presented in a volume of the *Audio-Visual Communication Review,* entitled *Graphic Communication and the Crisis in Education* (1957). The four principles he describes are suggested by the words: motivation, cue, response, reward. It is Miller's contention that an effective sequence of instruction, in any medium, must include provision for these four conditions.

First, motivation: the student must want something. The motivational effects of a "lesson" depend upon motivation which has already been learned. To be most effective, the motivations aroused by instructional materials must build upon those that are already in the life experiences of the student. In other words, instructional materials cannot in themselves be expected to generate brand-new sources of motivation; but what they can and should do is to capitalize upon, and add to, the kinds of motivations that are already there. Various kinds of motivation may be called upon, including some presumably fundamental ones such as intellectual curiosity and the desire to achieve. For students in college, learned motivations which form a part of the individual's life goals, and which may exhibit themselves as identification with admired people, as well as with choices leading to social approval, are possibly of special importance.

Second, there must be a cue: the student must notice something. Materials for instruction, whether verbal or pictorial, need to distinguish the relevant cues. Instructional materials are better to the extent that they facilitate the discrimination of cues. Printed materials may do this in a variety of ways—by varying type, by the use of color, but particularly by means of their organization. Lecturers have a variety of ways of distinguishing cues in auditory language—by differences in loudness and emphasis, and again by the organization of material. Pictorial presentations obviously have used a variety of ingenious techniques of distinguishing cues—by simplification, by the addition of pointers and markers, by the use of color and contrast. The general point is that instruction will be enhanced when the stimuli relevant to learning are readily discriminated by the student.

Third, response: the student must do something. Many studies of learning have indicated the importance of student participation. Of course, the doing may be a matter of internally conducted thinking or rehearsal. But whatever form they may take, responses to instructional materials are an essential element in learning. Instructional effectiveness will be increased to the extent that the materials involve the student in doing something with his just-acquired knowledge—transforming it, applying it, using it.

Fourth, reward: the student must get something he wants. Various techniques may be used to bring about satisfaction of this sort. Immediate rewards are presumably more effective than delayed ones. Instruction needs to reinforce the rewards learned in real life. For the student who is motivated to solve problems and to achieve some learning goal, finding out that he has done well is an important reward. Instruction will be improved in effectiveness to the extent that some desired aim can be achieved, and that knowledge of this achievement is given.

Obviously, these four principles described by Miller are considered to have highly general applicability to the design of instruction. They are relevant to the learning of all kinds of students, and presumably to all kinds of learning tasks. These principles may be put to work regardless of whether one is considering the task of a first-grader in learning to print letters, or to the task of a graduate student in understanding a scholarly article on Roman architecture.

The generality of these principles is also the key to their limitations in practical useful-ness. To the skilled teacher or designer of instruction, they seem obvious, and such a person would likely aver that he always uses such principles. Most instruction, in fact, could prob-ably be shown to incorporate these four principles in some degree. Even when one or another is not strongly exhibited by instructional materials, it may be expected that an experienced learner (like a college student) will often arrange his own learning conditions to include these principles. He comes with his own motivation, he makes responses to what he reads, sees, or hears, and he arranges his studying objectives so that some achievement will be noticeable. Miller's principles are surely important to instruction, but it is question-able whether they are often violated even in the most traditional instruction.

Skinner The views of Skinner on instruction are contained in a variety of articles, particularly those on teaching machines (Skinner, 1957, 1958, 1965). Valuable analyses are also contained in books and articles by his students (Gilbert, 1962; Green, 1962). At the most general level, it may be said that no great disagreement can be found with the principles of Miller. Skinner's analysis of instruction assumes that motivation must be present, that the student must make a response, and that this response needs to be reward-ed, or "reinforced." The increased specificity of Skinner's suggestions center around the principle of *stimulus control,* or the ways in which reinforcement may be used to establish both more precise and more elaborate learnings by manipulation of the stimuli impinging on the learner. In this sense, Skinner's views are most highly related to Miller's principle about the importance of the *cue* in learning. It is possible to interpret Skinnerian principles of instruction as a more extensive account of what must be done to present cues (or stimuli) in such a way as to optimize learning.

Several relatively specific ways of controlling the learning process by suitable sequencing of stimuli and reinforcement are suggested by Skinner's theory. One is the principle of *shaping,* applicable to the learning of motor acts. As the individual practices a motor re-sponse of some sort, reinforcement is given selectively so that the response which is originally only a crude copy of what is acceptable comes by a gradual process to be more and more exact. Such a principle applies, for example, to learning to pronounce an un-familiar language sound, such as the German umlauted u, or the French uvular r. A second principle, somewhat similar, is that of *successive approximation* of stimulus control, in which a response which is originally "prompted" comes to be given properly even when the prompt has been progressively "faded." Initially, a student may need many contextual prompts, for example, to remember what the Constitution says about the powers of the President, but as he continues to practice recounting these powers, he can do it without these extra cues. A third Skinnerian principle is *chaining,* which describes the conditions of reinforce-ment by means of which a lengthy procedure is learned. Essentially, the steps in the pro-cedure, which might be a computational procedure in mathematics, for example, are put together in a step-by-step fashion, insuring that the final step is always connected with the others which precede it (cf. Gilbert, 1962).

Thus it may be seen that the learning theory of Skinner leads to some relatively specific suggestions about the design of instruction. It gives us practical procedures for shaping motor responses, for establishing discriminations by successive approximations of stimuli, and for chaining together the steps in complex procedures. For certain kinds of learning tasks, these procedures are indeed specific and undoubtedly successful.

In my view, these principles are still only of general applicability to the learning of certain other kinds of tasks, particularly concepts and principles. For example, if one is concerned that a student acquire an understanding of the principle of separation of powers as defined by the Constitution, or an understanding of the principle of centrifugal force, the notion of successive approximation provides only a very general prescription for instruction. It says one must bring such behavior under finer stimulus control, but it does not specify how to do this. It does not say how to select the stimuli which will accomplish this purpose. It seems to me, therefore, that although some specificity about instruction in certain tasks is definitely gained from Skinnerian theory, for certain others of particular importance in college-level instruction, the suggestions remain highly general.

Gagné The ideas of this theorist regarding the learning process are contained in a book entitled *The Conditions of Learning* (1965), and their applicability to instructional practice is discussed in a chapter of another recent book, *Instruction: Some Contemporary Viewpoints* (Siegel, 1967). The suggestions to be derived from this view of learning are more specific for instruction than are those previously described.

The first principle deserving emphasis is that of *distinctive conditions* for different kinds of learning. Gagné distinguishes seven major kinds of mental processing which are called learning, each of which has a different set of conditions for its optimal occurrence. The seven kinds are called signal learning (classical conditioning), S-R learning, motor and verbal chain learning, multiple discrimination, concept learning, principle learning, and problem solving. He considers that the typical learning of young adults, high-school and college students, may partake of any or all of these types of learning, but that some are much more frequent than others in the school environment. For example, certain motor and verbal chains may need to be learned in tackling a new foreign language, but these types of learning would probably never be encountered in courses in history, government, or English composition. Most subjects in high school and college include primarily the kinds of learning described as concept learning, principle learning, and problem solving.

Although all types of learning may require certain general conditions for their establishment, such as those of contiguity, repetition, and reinforcement, emphasized by most learning theorists, the specific conditions for establishment of concepts, principles, and rules are in addition to these. Furthermore, they are distinguishable for each type: learning complex principles through problem solving demands a different set of conditions than does learning a new concept like "cell," "neuron," or "central nervous system." The external conditions for each particular type of learning form the basis for instruction. The internal conditions are retained capabilities of the student which have been established by previous learning.

The second principle of importance for instruction may be called *cumulative learning*. This is the principle that the learning of any new capability builds upon prior learning. According to this theory, there is a specifiable minimal prerequisite for each new learning task. Unless the learner can recall this prerequisite capability (or some other which can serve the same purpose), he cannot learn the new task. As a very simple example, unless a learner can recall how to factor numbers, how to divide, and how to multiply, he cannot learn to find a lowest common denominator, and thus to add fractions. This principle has a deceptive simplicity about it, and may readily be dismissed as either obvious or trivial. In actuality, it is neither. It does not say, before the learner undertakes to learn how to add fractions, he must have "had" or "been through" the factoring of numbers. Instead, it says he must have *mastered* and must *be able to recall* the factoring of numbers in order for the desired learning to take place at all. This principle is considered to have broad applicability to the learning of principles, whether they be the origins of the American Revolution, the generation of induced electric current, or the constancy of perceived size. In all of these instances, there are specific minimal prerequisite learnings, before the new learning task is undertaken.

Ausubel The views of this learning investigator may be sampled in *The Psychology of Meaningful Verbal Learning* (1963), and also in an informative chapter in the book *Instruction: Some Contemporary Viewpoints* (Siegel, 1967).

Ausubel insists, first of all, that school learning is meaningful learning and that this process is distinctly different from what is usually called rote learning. Thus he comes to grips directly and specifically with the learning of facts and principles, and is not particularly concerned with other forms of learning such as motor and verbal chains. In this theory, the most important principle is called *subsumption*. Meaningful learning takes place, according to this theory, when a new idea is subsumed into a related structure of already existing knowledge. The result of this process is the acquisition of a set of new meanings.

There are a number of implications of this view for instructional practice. For example, one is the importance of providing the learner with a meaningful structure before he attempts to learn a new principle—an *organizer,* which bears a logically superordinate relation to what will be learned. Putting this in a somewhat oversimplified form, it means that if the learner is expected to learn about coal and oil and gas, one must tell him ahead of time that he is going to learn about "the different forms of fuel." A second principle is that any subject should be presented by *progressive differentiation* of content, the most general and inclusive ideas first, and then the more detailed and specific ones. Ausubel states that although this seems a self-evident principle, it is rarely followed in actual teaching procedures or in textbooks.

Still a third principle of importance is called *consolidation.* This means the insistence on mastery of ongoing lessons before new material is introduced. This proposition is at least highly similar, if not the same, as Gagné's principle of cumulative learning. Another Ausubel principle of great importance would seem to be *integrative reconciliation.* By this he means that new ideas, once introduced, need to be deliberately related to old ideas, significant similarities and differences pointed out, real or apparent inconsistencies reconciled. Again, Ausubel finds this a practice followed scarcely at all by textbook writers.

These principles add up to a pretty strong specification of how instructional materials should be organized and presented for most effective learning. While one finds only very general guidance for the construction of programs of instruction, texts, or educational films by following such principles as Miller's, it is evident that Ausubel's principles are pretty specific. They tell an instructional designer what to do first, what sequence of ideas to follow, what to do to insure remembering, and what kind of outcome to expect. Note that I do not maintain that Ausubel's theory is entirely correct—only a good deal more experimentation will determine that. But his ideas lead to very concrete suggestions about how to conduct instruction.

Here then we have four theories of learning, each of which has something to say about how to design instruction. Virtually no instructional materials, texts, or films in existence today have deliberately been prepared on the basis of these principles. Today's instruction simply does not reflect these principles, but appears instead to be based upon an older set of principles derived from quite different considerations. Could instructional materials be designed to take these principles into account? I see no reason why this could not be done. It would be an expensive undertaking, even to design a single course this way. I am unable to estimate cost effectiveness—indeed this may not even be possible until someone has tried to do it once.

Otherwise, the kinds of principles I have been talking about can even now be put into effect in at least a partial fashion by, first, the instructor, and second, the student. For example, the instructor can use the principle of organizers, and the principle of integrative reconciliation, even though he may not be able in any immediate sense to rewrite the textbook or redesign the television lesson. The student is also able to put many of these principles into effect himself. In fact, it seems probable that what is meant by a sophisticated learner, as opposed to a novice, is one who imposes his own organizations on presentations of material, arranges his own distinctive conditions for learning different kinds of tasks, carries out his own integrative reconciliation of new and old ideas. Learning to do these kinds of intellectual activities, to carry out these kinds of strategies, may represent an educational goal of more fundamental importance than the learning of any particular set of facts, rules, or principles.

Learning and the Individual

This possibility of the learner's contribution to his own learning suggests an even broader theme than any which has been specifically defined by learning theories. Perhaps it may become the most general principle of all. It may be said, surely, that the great majority of modern studies of learning, of a variety of types, provide an accumulating body of evidence for this principle: Learning and remembering require the imposition of an active intellectual process by the learner on the material presented to his senses. One simply cannot account for learning by specifying only what is presented and the level of "intelligence" of the learner. Apparently, some specific sort of processing is always contributed by the learner himself. This kind of processing is given various names, in various experimental settings. For example:

1. In studies of rote verbal learning, it is typically called *mediation* (cf. Jenkins, 1963). Learning to associate a nonsense syllable like DEP with a nonsense syllable like RIV has been shown typically to involve the contribution of a linking mediator by the learner. (In this particular instance, it might be a word like "deprive," or two words like "deep river.")

2. In still other studies of memory, the process may be referred to as *coding* (cf. Melton, 1963). Investigations of short-term retention of small verbal units are generally considered to reveal important facts about the "intake" portion of the learning process. Here, it is found that a single syllable like XQR is not retained as well after one presentation as a syllable like NER, nor as well as a word like TOP. In fact, the single syllable XQR is retained no better than *three* short words. The suggestion is that something is done to these units before they are stored. They are first coded.

3. Investigations of the learning of concepts by children (cf. Kendler, 1964) provide other sources of mediational processes. It is found that children of four years of age cannot shift readily from one concept (like "black") to its opposite, whereas seven-year olds can. By inference, this is because the older children have a greater store of "mediators" to apply to this reversal situation.

4. Many studies of problem solving in young adults (cf. Gagné, 1964), using a variety of tasks, have emphasized the importance of prior knowledge, or an organization based upon prior knowledge (cf. Katona, 1940), to the successful solution of problems. Problems are solved when the learner is able to bring such an organization, which is already available to him, to bear upon the task at hand.

5. Studies by Rothkopf and his associates (cf. Rothkopf, 1966), have shown the important effects on learning and retention resulting from the introduction of questions into textual passages, even when the questions are irrelevant to what is ultimately tested as having been learned. In other words, the inference is that the learner applies to the learning task a complex set of behaviors which may be approximately summarized as a "set to remember."

These are only a few of the many lines of evidence showing that new learning cannot be adequately accounted for in terms of what is presented to the learner. In addition to these external stimuli, a very important part of the process is contributed by the learner himself, or more specifically by what is stored in his central nervous system. Furthermore, it is fairly clear that the coding or mediation done by the learner depends upon his particular store of past experience. The particular way the learner codes a presentation is peculiar to him, and not shared by other individuals. *The mediation of learning is idiosyncratic.*

The implication of these findings is quite clear. So far as theories of the learning process are concerned, the learning of any set of materials depends importantly upon individual contributions from the learner himself. Learning is an individual matter. In a fundamental sense, it is determined by what the learner does, and not by what the material does or what the teacher does. One can even go a step farther, in drawing implications for education. If one is concerned about how to make learning efficient, the focus of emphasis must be the student. The design of efficient conditions for learning demands that learning be conceived as an individual matter.

Now, there are conflicting views on this question. Some psychologists, looking at the educative process as typically involving a teacher and a class, have emphasized the teacher-student interaction, or what is sometimes called the teaching-learning process. Jackson (1966), for example, distinguishes between teacher-student dialogues which are private (as in a tutoring situation), those which are public (as in a classroom), and those which might be called semi-private, in which the teacher works with a single student while others engage in some other activity. He correctly notes that learning theorists have seldom if ever contributed to an understanding of the public teaching situation. Another theorist about teaching is Thelen (1967), who has carried out a series of most interesting studies of teacher-student interactions, seeking ways of finding a "fit" between teachers and groups of students. The absence of change in the school's output resulting from changes in administrative procedures such as class size, team teaching, ability grouping, as well as instructional procedures like discussions vs. lectures, leads Stephens (1967), to the conclusion that as long as a teacher has a strong interest in his subject, what he does is relatively unimportant.

For many legitimate purposes, there is surely much to be gained by studying the activities of the teacher, and theorizing about how he interacts or should interact with a learner. But such studies can tell us little about how learning occurs, or how to make it efficient. If we wish to find out about learning, we must begin and end with the human individual who is the learner. We must, in other words, find out what the learner is like, what he needs to know to begin the learning process, and what he needs to do to carry it out. The site of learning is not in a group, nor is it in a relationship between instructor and student. The site of learning is the individual's central nervous system. For this fundamental and unarguable reason, learning is individual. Efficient instruction is designed for the individual learner.

The recognition of the individual character of learning need not blind us to some of the necessities of public communication, with both teachers and other students. Schools and colleges are concerned with the transmission of public knowledge. There is, of course, such a thing as strictly private knowledge, as for example that exhibited in artistic accomplishment. But the schools cannot transmit this private experience, by definition. The communications of knowledge become refined, sharpened, and clarified by public discussion. In schools, therefore, public discussion serves the same highly essential purpose as it serves in other settings in the larger community. In a university setting, there is a great deal of public discussion, and it is highly important for the clarification and refinement of the "messages" that are to be transmitted. Often, discussion takes place in a classroom, among students, and between students and teachers. Much discussion takes place among faculty members. And obviously, a great deal takes place outside of class among students. I believe discussion is a highly important part of school learning. Unfortunately, it must be said that we have no theory as yet of the role of discussion in learning. Such a theory, it may be expected, will not be opposed to a theory of individual learning, but will supplement it.

Instruction and the Individual Learner

It is possible, then, to bring to bear upon the design of instruction some principles of learning theory. These principles range from those which are quite generally applicable to all forms of learning to those which apply specifically to the learning of concepts and principles of the sort which characterize the bulk of knowledge taught in the schools. In addition, modern studies of learning suggest the clear implication that some idiosyncratic processing of information is done by the learner. This provides a fundamental reason for viewing learning as an individual process, and strongly suggests that individualized instruction represents the route of efficient learning. If arrangements for individual learning are not deliberately made by the system, they presumably will be made by the learner himself. In doing this, he will presumably use whatever media are available, although some may be better adapted for some purposes than are others.

The "arrangements" of the external environment for purposes of efficient learning are what constitute the events of instruction. One should not lose sight of the fact, though, that learning in the sense used here also includes remembering and transfer of learning, since it is these less immediate outcomes that are the true concerns of an educational system. Assuming that these are included, what are the events of instruction that must take place in order for learning to occur?

In framing an answer to this question, I should first point out that according to Gagné's (1967) conception, the conditions of instruction differ with the type of learning being undertaken. Thus one does not design instruction on using a key-punch machine to be the same in its formal characteristics as instruction on how the mechanism of a key-punch machine operates. Or, in learning a foreign language, one does not design instruction on pronouncing words to be the same as instruction on understanding spoken sentences. There are some important distinctions here which should not be overlooked. However, for purposes of the present paper, I shall not elaborate them further. Instead, I shall speak only about the events of instruction applicable to the learning of principles, including facts, generalizations, and rules.

What appear to be the most important events of instruction are the following:

1. Gaining and maintaining attention. Obviously, in order for learning to occur, attention must be attracted in the first place, and then maintained. Many of the stimulation conditions that attract attention have been known for a long time, including such things as change, novelty, appeal to dominant interests. Concerning the maintenance of attention, we know somewhat less. Some clarification has surely been gained by Travers's (1964) demonstration that we only attend to one thing at a time, regardless of how many media channels may be bombarding us. Presumably, maintaining attention is a matter of achieving a set, related to one or more individual goals, which makes the learner return again and again to the task at hand. Manipulating external stimuli is probably ineffective over the long pull, and one must instead seek ways of reinforcing the motivational state of the learner.

2. Insuring recall of previously acquired knowledge is another important function of instruction. We have seen that recall of prior knowledge is considered an essential condition of learning by both Gagné and Ausubel. When the learner undertakes to learn something new, he must first be reminded of what he already knows which is relevant to that learning.

3. Guiding the learning is done in instruction by verbal or pictorial material that provides "cues" or "hints" to new principles, usually without stating them fully in verbal form. In part, the "organizers" mentioned by Ausubel perform this instructional function. In part, it is done by questions, as Rothkopf's work illustrates. The skilled self-learner, of course, provides his own questions.

4. Providing feedback to the learner on his accomplishments is another function of instruction. One of the surest ways, it seems to me, is by defining the objectives of

instruction clearly to the learner, so that he will become aware immediately when he has attained each specific goal. Again, the skilled learner may usually do this himself. Textbooks and other media often seem to neglect badly this essential instructional function.

5. Establishing conditions for remembering and transfer of learning would surely be counted as one of the essential functions of instruction. For purposes of transfer, there need to be a carefully designed series of problems to which application of the newly learned principle is made. Probably also having this function is the process Ausubel calls "integrative reconciliation," in which new ideas are compared and contrasted to related ones previously learned. For remembering, there needs to be provision for spaced review, which has often been shown to be an effective technique (cf. Davis, 1966, pp. 55-71).

6. Finally, there should be mentioned still another instructional function, often neglected. This is the assessment of outcomes. The outcomes of learning and remembering need to be assessed frequently. The administration of a final test or examination for purposes of determining a grade seems often to be a way of consolidating an onerous task which because of its unmanageable scope ends up avoiding the very assessment that should be done. Learning of the specifics needs to be assessed, perhaps more so than learning of the generalities. The five-minute daily or weekly quiz has much to recommend it. For the skilled learner, this function can often be performed with some success by himself. But to test oneself is indeed a highly sophisticated thing to do, and instructional materials should provide as much help as possible in this function.

There are, then, these six major functions that take place in instruction. It may be noted that learning theory does not, in and of itself, say exactly how these are to be put together in the great variety of specific instances to which they are applicable. What learning theory tells us is that when certain of these conditions are present, learning will occur, and when certain ones are not present, learning is improbable. Beyond such theory there must of course be both technology and artistry, whether this be exhibited by the textbook writer, the film-maker, or the master teacher. And to a considerable extent, at least, we should expect effective techniques of self-instruction to be present in the young adult.

What Can Media Accomplish?

It can readily be seen that most media of communication can readily perform most of these instructional functions. They can be performed by pictures, by printed language, by auditory language, or by a combination of media. So far as learning is concerned, the medium is not the message. No single medium possesses properties which are uniquely adapted to perform one or a combination of instructional functions. Instead, they all perform some of these functions well, and some not so well. The arrangement of instructional conditions is still the key to effective instruction, regardless of the medium or media employed.

One key to the question of which media is to be found by considering the learning task, that is, the objectives of the learning. A properly defined set of objectives provides information on the nature of stimuli to which the learner is expected to respond, after he has learned. Consider a few examples:

1. An objective in a course in physics might be, "demonstrating Ohm's Law." If one expects the student to show how resistance in an electric circuit varies with the current and voltage, there would seem to be considerable justification for using actual objects and events as the medium for instruction. In other words, one might set up

instruction in a laboratory. If the student has sufficient prior acquaintance with such actual objects and events, a pictorial presentation may perform the same functions.

2. An objective in a course in English might be, "editing composed written paragraphs for correctness of structure and optimal clarity of expression." Obviously, what has to be presented here initially are incorrect and non-optimal paragraphs. Printed language has to be the medium. However, it may be considerable importance in such an instance to arrange for frequent and prompt feedback to the learner as he makes his corrections. Thus one might choose to have a teacher convey this feedback in the presence of printed language given in a text or projected on a screen.

3. In a foreign language course, an objective might be, "making appropriate responses containing personal biographical information to questions asked by a speaker in the foreign language." Here again, the medium required is quite evident—it is auditory language. The learner must be presented with these questions in an auditory form, and the printed form will not be an adequate substitute.

Consideration of these examples, and others like them, leads to the following generalizations concerning the use of media for instruction. These seem to me to be more or less self-evident principles with which one must begin to think about media. They are not "the answers," but merely the basis for further investigation of the uses of media.

1. First, no single medium is likely to have properties that make it best for all purposes. There is, so far as we know, no special magic in any particular medium.

2. Second, the most important single criterion for a choice of medium is often the nature of the learning task itself—that is, the objective of the instruction. If the learner is going to respond to real objects, these need to be used at some point in instruction. If he is going to respond to auditory language, then this form of communication needs to be used at some point in his instruction. However, it should be noted that this criterion doesn't solve the whole problem, by any means. The reason is that for many objectives, one medium is as appropriate to the task as another. For example, the principle relating the sides and hypotenuse of a right triangle can be presented in printed words, in mathematical symbols, or in diagrammatic pictures. Or, the events leading up to the Boston Massacre can be described in a printed text or shown in dramatized pictorial form. In these instances, nothing in the instructional objective itself provides a clue as to which medium will be best.

3. Third, when one considers the six functions of instruction (controlling attention, stimulating recall, etc.) previously mentioned, it is evident that any given medium may perform one of these functions best at a given time during a period of instructing, while another medium may perform an instructional function best at another time. That is to say, the precise answer to the question of "which medium" is not to be found by matching courses with media, or even topics with media, but rather in matching *specific instructional functions* with media. Within a given topic, for example, attention might best be maintained by the introduction of pictures, whereas guiding learning might best be accomplished by printed verbal instructions, and feedback might be best performed by auditory language. This line of reasoning is developed more fully by Briggs *et al* (1967), in a monograph on *Instructional Media*. When one chooses a particular medium for a whole course, or even for the development of an entire topic, one is usually making a judgement that such a medium will be best suited "on the average" for the various instructional functions it must perform.

4. Finally, there is another suggestion to be derived from these considerations about the instructional functions of media. It may be that the most striking effects of in-

structional planning are to be sought in various combinations of media, where each may perform a particular function best. This does not mean reverting to the idea which Travers's (1964) work calls into question, that simultaneous auditory and visual presentations are superior to either alone. What it means instead is that any given medium might be used alternately with others over relatively short periods of instructional time.

Consider, for example, an instructional situation in which the student reads from a printed text and responds to it by writing problem answers. When the occasion demands, pictures or diagrams are presented to perform the functions of stimulating recall and guiding the learning. Now, as the student works along in this fashion, every so often, when a new subtopic is to be introduced, or special emphasis is to be given, a taped auditory message is introduced, having the primary purpose of controlling attention. Frequent questions are included in the printed text for self-assessment, and feedback is also provided in an auditory form. What would be the effectiveness of this kind of combination of media?

I do not know the answer to this question, and there is no research to provide it. Yet this kind of instructional arrangement, only roughly described in this example, may hold the key to effective instruction, particularly the sort of instruction which depends upon the individual to do a large part of the establishment of learning conditions for himself. Obviously, a good deal of testing of practical alternatives is needed before we can feel confident about the outcome of such plans for instruction.

I have been led in this paper to consider first how learning theory relates to the practical events of instruction. There is little doubt that this relationship can be demonstrated. Depending upon what learning theory one chooses, the suggestions for practical application to instruction are more or less specific. And running through all theories is the theme that learning is, after all, an individual matter, in which essential idiosyncratic elements must be supplied by the learner himself.

As a practical matter, the events of instruction encompass more processes than are included in learning theories themselves. Instruction involves gaining and controlling attention, stimulating recall, guiding the learning, providing feedback, arranging for remembering, and assessing outcomes. It is these functions that are performed by various media of instruction, and to a considerable degree by the learner himself. One should not expect, I think, to find that a single medium is best fitted to do all of these things. Instead, it seems likely that carefully designed combinations of media may be required to achieve the kind of instruction that is most effective, and which at the same time exploits the properties of media to fullest advantage.

BIBLIOGRAPHY

Ausubel, D. P. *The Psychology of Meaningful Verbal Learning.* New York: Grune and Stratton, 1963.

Ausubel, D. P. "A cognitive-structure theory of school learning." In L. Siegel (Ed.), *Instruction: Some Contemporary Viewpoints.* San Francisco: Chandler, 1967, pp. 207-257.

Briggs, L. J., P. L. Campeau, R. M. Gagne, and M. A. May. *Instructional Media.* Pittsburgh: American Institutes for Research, 1967. (Monograph No. 2).

Davis, R. A. *Learning in the Schools.* Belmont: Wadsworth, 1966.

Gagné, R. M. *The Conditions of Learning.* New York: Holt, Rinehart, and Winston, 1965.

Gagné, R. M. "Problem solving." In A. W. Melton (Ed.), *Categories of Human Learning.* New York: Academic Press, 1964.

Gagné, R. M. "Instruction and the conditions of learning." In L. Siegel (Ed.), *Instruction: Some Contemporary Viewpoints.* San Francisco: Chandler, 1967, pp. 291-313.

Gilbert, T. F. "Mathetics: the technology of education." *Journal of Mathetics,* 1962, *1,* 7-73.

Green, E. J. *The Learning Process and Programmed Instruction.* New York: Holt, Rinehart and Winston, 1962.

Jackson, P. W. "The way teaching is." In *The Way Teaching Is: Report of the Seminar on Teaching.* Washington, D.C.: National Education Association, 1966, pp. 7-27.

Jenkins, J. J. "Mediated association: paradigms and situations." In C. N. Cofer and B. S. Musgrave (Eds.), *Verbal Behavior and Learning.* New York: McGraw-Hill, 1963.

Katona, G. *Organizing and Memorizing.* New York: Columbia University Press, 1940.

Kendler, H. H. "The concept of the concept." In A. W. Melton (Ed.), *Categories of Human Learning.* New York: Academic Press, 1964.

Melton, A. W. "Implications of short-term memory for a general theory of memory." *Journal of Verbal Learning and Verbal Behavior,* 1963, *2,* 1-21.

Melton, A. W. *Categories of Human Learning.* New York: Academic Press, 1964.

Miller, N. E., et. al. *Graphic Communication and the Crisis in Education.* Washington, D.C.: Department of Audiovisual Instruction, National Education Association, 1957. (Audiovisual Communication Review, Vol. 5, No. 3).

Rothkopf, E. Z. "Some theoretical and experimental approaches to problems in written instruction." In J. D. Krumboltz (Ed.), *Learning and the Educational Process.* Chicago: Rand-McNally, 1965, pp. 193-221.

Siegel, L. (Ed.), *Instruction: Some Contemporary Viewpoints.* San Francisco: Chandler, 1967.

Skinner, B. F. *Verbal Behavior.* New York: Appleton-Century-Crofts, 1957.

Skinner, B. F. "Teaching machines." *Science,* 1958, *128,* 969-977.

Skinner, B. F. "Reflections on a decade of teaching machines." In R. Glaser (Ed.), *Teaching Machines and Programmed Learning: II. Data and Directions.* Washington, D.C.: National Education Association, 1965, pp. 5-20.

Stephens, J. M. *The Process of Schooling.* New York: Holt, Rinehart, and Winston, 1967.

Thelen, H. A. *Classroom Grouping for Teachability.* New York: Wiley, 1967.

Travers, R. M. W., *et al. Research and Theory Related to Audiovisual Information Transmission.* Salt Lake City: Bureau of Educational Research, University of Utah, 1964.

29.
Technology, Philosophy And Education

by JOHN R. GINTHER
Assoc. prof., Dept. of Education
Research assoc., Inst. for Computer Research
Univ. of Chicago

Consideration of each of the terms in the title is undertaken in most sections of this paper. However, technology is discussed first so that a particular view of it can be used throughout. The limited amount of educational philosophy incorporated is treated in a different fashion. Examples and suggestions of tendencies toward philosophic positions are sprinkled throughout the paper in an effort to build a basis for a major generalization. In this paper education refers to various concrete meanings for the concepts content, method and purpose. Schooling, on the other hand, is reserved to indicate that standard patterns of activities stemming from the meanings are conventionally carried out in special buildings. However, conventional phrases make it difficult to maintain this distinction throughout.

No Educational Technology

Possibly the most striking feature of technology in education is that it has failed to establish a watershed. The telescope replaced astrology with astronomy and altered irrevocably the history of man. The internal combustion engine forever changed transportation and the world of work. The assembly line revolutionized traditional ideas concerning the availability of goods to the population. The list of illustrations could be endless. Technology seems to change forever the style of that phase of man's life which is touched by it. But education and schooling remain relatively unchange even though there is much said about "educational technology."

Educational Problems Not Addressed

The topic of Congressional hearings in 1966, "Technology in Education" [1], provides a clue to the mysterious immunity the process of educating our nation's children has had to change from the impact of technology. Historically technology has been viewed as the application of science to the problems of some area such as production, housekeeping, or transportation. The Congressional sub-committee avoided the error of suggesting there might be an "educational technology" by the wording of their topic. Not all the witnesses followed suit, and the usual list of devices and objects were eventually suggested as being or representing educational technology. Such so-called educational technology typically fails the test of being addressed to an educational problem. Further, it beguiles the public which believes some educational problems have been addressed by "educational technology."

Miles of unused coaxial cable in school buildings, seldom-used language laboratories, malfunctioning tape recorders, and motion picture projection equipment in various states of disrepair belie the belief that technology has been brought to bear on educational problems. If all the equipment alluded to were serving to alleviate serious educational problems there would be a storm of protest until the gadgetry were restored to full capability. But equipment, materials or gadgets bought in a faddish atmosphere seldom address an educational problem. Thus it seems ludicrous to even imagine that technology has been applied to education.

Stumbling Blocks

William James once wrote:

> You make a great, a very great mistake, if you think that psychology, being the science of the mind's laws, is something from which you can deduce definite programs and schemes and methods of instruction for immediate schoolroom use. Psychology is a science, and teaching is an art; and sciences never generate arts directly out of themselves. An intermediary inventive mind must make the application, by using its originality.[2]

Professor James suggests the fundamental reason for the failure to apply technology to education, for it would seem just as true in technology as in psychology that "an intermediary inventive mind must make the application." A recent report states that "the bearded intellectuals of the education companies and the button-down organization men of industry just aren't getting along" in "The Learning Business" and that business acumen "has proved not so easily transferred to the subtleties of education."[3] Perhaps the words of William James are appropriate even for the industries that would serve education today.

Peter Drucker has a slightly different view of the matter. It is his thesis that

> it is *technologists* who do not transfer, technologists who do not realize that they possess a discipline and a way of looking at work and tools. It is technologists who neglect to project their vision and their approach on the redesign of the tools and equipment mankind uses in its everyday pursuit.[4]

Let us attempt to transfer that idea to the culture of educational institutions. This would seem to suggest that it is not the teachers and administrators of educational institutions who reject technology; rather it is the technologist, failing to adapt his technology to the everyday work of this culture, who keeps the technology from having a massive impact on the culture. To some extent this is certainly true. For example, at one major institution of higher learning which prepares a complete range of educational personnel from nursery school teachers through college presidents, it been impossible to interest the department of education in using the computer to carry out routines such as student record keeping, bookkeeping, or storing mailing lists, and computer-assisted instructional procedures are beyond mention. This is not entirely because the faculty and staff are disinterested in or afraid of computers. Rather it stems from the fact that every time one of them is enticed to examine the use of computers he is frustrated by the necessity for learning a computer language; furthermore, he is typically confronted by a renegade mathematician whose presentation of the potential uses of computer terminals is both terse and abstract. After each of these encounters the faculty or staff involved quickly turns away from further consideration of the use of this particular tool. So far as these educators are concerned the technologists are saying "if you wish to use the technology, become a technologist." The educators seem to be thinking "when this gadget is easy to learn to use and when it is readily available to me, I may try it." And so, Drucker's hypothesis may have validity in the subculture of education. However, perhaps the problem posed permits more than one approach to solution. Perhaps an occasional technologist can be persuaded to adapt equipment to address some of the everyday problems of educators. In addition, perhaps an occasional educator can be moved to develop a usable level of competence with the new tools and thus enable his profession to deal with the everyday problems via the technology. Either movement might help, but both would fall short of the approach suggested by Professor James's original contention.

The fact that there is no educational technology becomes more apparent as you consider the uses or applications of technology in other fields. Consider the queen of the arts, opera. There is no operatic technology, but certainly technology is applied in the production of opera. For example, at Lyric in Chicago radio replaces the familiar knock on the door to announce time until cue; hydraulic lifts in the basement are used by the stage crew to create basic floor designs for sets; closed circuit television is used to improve coordination of off-stage musicians with the pit orchestra and principals. In each instance it should be noted that Lyric overcame or alleviated some problem by the application of technology; for example, it is difficult to coordinate calls for "places" when dressing rooms are spread over several floors, halls tend to get congested, and two elevators service forty or fifty persons; radio, in this instance, simply cuts through the morass of difficulties.

Perhaps it is understandable that modern technology has failed to generate significant changes in education or schooling; it has not been addressed to educational problems. The suggested explanations for this state of affairs reveal obstacles. Unfortunately these are not the only difficulties ahead.

One Limited Use

A review of the limited uses made of technology in education suggests that if any purpose has been put forward to be served it has been the transmission or conveyance of information. By far and away the most typical use of technology has been to provide students with information which they are not necessarily to use in any way but which they are to remember. Research journals are filled with endless studies from which one concludes that there are several equally useful ways to convey information for this purpose. Of course, the term "education" is used to cover a multitude of operations which have little to do with the instructional act, and technology has been put to somewhat more use on problems of scheduling and bookkeeping than on the problems of teaching and learning.

The point is that when we look upon the teaching-learning sector of "education" we find that technology has been applied to a limited extent to the problem of transmitting information which is to be learned and remembered. Since it has been established that there are several equally effective ways to carry out this process it is understandable that a large group in the educational world raises their eyebrows when it is suggested that electronic computers be introduced into the educational scene; they feel that this is a very expensive way to move information to students who can apparently learn just as effectively from the lecture, and do it in larger groups. So as we explore technology applied to education, or perhaps technology not applied to education, we begin to see the underlying, prevailing view of the nature of method which, in turn, suggests a particular view of the nature of knowledge, if not the nature of mind. Later we will deal more directly with philosophic positions which touch on the nature of mind, method, and knowledge. Such views have direct implications for the problem of developing or applying technology to education.

Deterrents to Educational Technology

If the difficulty forecast by Messrs. James and Drucker were to be overcome, the development of an educational technology might still be in doubt. There are feelings and attitudes abroad which suggest a tacky road for technology in education. The thrust of this effect is motivated by fear of dehumanization and is aimed at mechanization of instruction as well as at infra-human views of the student in the educational process. These concerns will now be considered with rejoinders offered occasionally. The topics, in order, will be: mechanization including automation and isolation from other humans; infra-human ideas, including mechanistic psychology in both instruction and testing.

Dehumanization: Mechanization

When a person is made to operate as though he were part of a machine it can be said that he has been automated, a form of mechanization. Being automated means that one loses degrees of freedom; for example, one is denied the opportunity to pace himself and is bound so closely to other operations that objections or deviations from the restricted pattern of performance raise risk, perhaps even peril. In an educational system a student can be locked into a course of study or an instructional program which is moved forward without regard for his feelings, comfort, understanding, interest, or anything else which might be called a human attribute. If this suggests classrooms with none of the hardware of technology, be dismayed but not surprised, for this kind of system is readily found in classrooms, particularly where it is believed that "we have to cover the material" or where mastery of verbal material is the goal. But the great fear is that in the near future ideas like multi-media approaches to instruction would serve to automate the student by treating him as a cog which would move when a machine moved or a system dictated. However, the experience in Professor Postlethwait's multi-media learning laboratory for individualized instruction in biology at Purdue University suggests that large numbers of students do no resist or dislike their limited automated role in this learning situation.[5]

A different kind of concern is expressed by some who fear mechanization, especially by the computer, although their fear does extend to some extent to the whole range of technology. This fear is that the student will be dehumanized by additional, extended contact with technology because it will deprive him of that amount of interaction with human beings. To the extent that interaction with humans is humanizing, the argument is unassailable. But the question arises: to what extent is interaction with teachers humanizing? Professor Flanders has developed the following rule based on extensive observations of classrooms:

> In the average classroom, someone is talking two-thirds of the time. Two-thirds of the time the person who is talking is the teacher. Two-thirds of the time the teacher is talking he is using direct influence.[6]

"Direct influence" consists of: 1) Lecturing, 2) Giving directions, or 3) Criticizing or justifying authority. If this kind of activity is humanizing then the argument is still unassailable. If this approximately one-third of the classroom time which is spent in one-way communication is not necessarily humanizing, then perhaps the argument could be made that only part of this one-third of class time might be given over to the use of technology and we would not thereby be further dehumanizing students.

Another study raises some question about the firmness of the premise from which it is argued that technology removes students from the humanizing influence of teachers. Reporting on thirty taped hour sessions taken over ten day-long visitations another investigator came to the following conclusions:

1. These teachers dominated the oral activity, and were doing most of the work themselves.

2. By their methods of asking questions, the teachers encouraged guessing and slovenly habits of thought.

3. So many of the questions required only the use of memory to answer them, it indicates that memorization is of major significance, and could be the main goal of the instruction.

4. Teachers were acting as cross-examiners, relatively uninterested in the needs, interests, and capabilities of their pupils.

5. These teachers seemed unaware of the psychology of oral questioning. Not only were they unskilled in the use of questions as an instructional instrument, they did not even seem to realize such a skill could be developed.[7]

If the above conclusions suggest humanizing activities, then the argument is still unassailable.

Study after study indicates that the encouragement of student verbal participation is the exception rather than the rule. When it is encouraged, the teacher either ignores or does not know how to use the student contributions as the basis for a conversation which might be used as part of the instructional act.

Those easily frightened by the hardware of technology might wish to examine the suggestion that normal, or ordinary classrooms harbor in an unorganized state certain phenomena suggestive of witch-hunts. In one out of twelve classrooms observed by Jules Henry the "witch-hunt syndrome was in full panoply." In the interest of further softening the charge that technology might dehumanize students by removing them from human interaction we should note:

> We see in the organization of the components of the witch-hunt syndrome an important phase in the formation of American national character, for tendencies to docility, competitiveness, confession, intra-group aggression, and feelings of vulnerability the children may bring with them to school, are reinforced in the classroom. This means that independence and courage to challenge are observably played *down* in these classrooms.[8]

We are, nevertheless, clearly and well advised to resist borrowing from time spent in beneficial human interaction and using it for the potentially mechanizing, thus dehumanizing act of automating students, and to resist isolating them via the use of technology. Meanwhile it would be useful for someone to investigate more thoroughly the humanizing effects of current school situations.

Sub-Human Students

As opposed to the mechanized view of dehumanization, there is the infra-human view. Those holding the latter view suggest that students are going to be taught more and more, and treated more and more as though they were subhuman. Although technology is probably not responsible for the appearance of mechanistic psychology or for the idea that a small corner of reinforcement theory ought to be applied to the process of education, it is true that mechanical devices and self-instructional materials do tend to be based on such a sub-human view of the student.[9] Part of the great anxiety about using B. F. Skinner's fraction of reinforcement theory[10] is that it is a powerful, potent tool likely to succeed in the goals set by persons who follow Skinner. In other words it is the power of this simple-minded approach which is so frightening. Clearly some process like that suggested by mechanistic psychology does indeed operate in the human as well as in lower forms of animal life and it operates very effectively. In fact, exclusive attention to this level of human operation could lead to the point where other human potential would atrophy from disuse. Again, the concern expressed is that increased use of technology will lead to increased use of an infra-human view of learning theory as the basis for instructional practice.

The other point made by those who view education as dehumanizing because of the sub-human psychology used, is that the measurement of the outcomes of education are becoming more and more restrictive. We seem to be moving closer and closer to a measurement process which reflects the same kind of infra-human psychology which is reflected in the teaching-learning situation. Again, it is a little unfair to call this simply infra-human, for it does reflect a human potential although it is only a fraction of the potential that the human possesses. But the tests in courses tend to suggest not only what matter is important, but whether use is to be made of it. As a constricting measurement program is imposed, students restrict their efforts to fit the system.

Up to this point current cries of distress concerning the dehumanization of students have been suggested. As these are extrapolated, the technology, and especially the computer, loom large as bogeymen to be avoided if not destroyed. These fears will now be addressed; first the fear that students will be so automated, so much a part of a system, that they will not have an opportunity to alter what is going on. Neither will they have, it is said, access to human teachers. Two countervailing examples are offered, examples of well established operations which suggest that the fears are based on a narrow view of what is happening and what might happen.

Hopeful Signs

The first example is a laboratory section of a linguistics course. In this laboratory students learn to use a string language for manipulating linguistic material in computers. At each meeting students receive a set of mimeographed information and a set of problems to be solved by using the new language in a computer program actually run in a computer. A stored program, which included a variety of errors made by students, points out those errors actually committed by a particular student. These can then be corrected and the problem resubmitted. At each meeting the instructor asks whether or not students had difficulties they wish to discuss or questions to ask. When students initiate a discussion it is continued as long as necessary. The discussion concluded, or on days when there are neither questions nor difficulties, a new set of materials is distributed and the routine cycled. Although this procedure automates students and reduces interaction with the teacher to zero some weeks, there seems to be no anxiety driving students to open pointless discussions just to interact, and many students seem to like the style of instruction provided. The fact is that individual students seem to have gained options under this kind of regime; a student needing help can obtain it, and a student successfully completing the standard tasks can simply drop by at the end of each meeting and pick up the new materials. Postlethwait's work, mentioned earlier, also suggests that students operate with success and satisfaction in an environment characterizable as dehumanizing on the criteria of automation and isolation from human interaction.

The fact is that a useful range of educational environments, some under control of a live teacher, others directed entirely by instructional materials, has been hypothesized.[11] The resulting model for developing instructional environments has proved valuable in organizing massive amounts of research on instruction[12]; it has also led to a controlled study indicating that students of different personality types seem to prefer different styles of instruction.[13]

A few words are in order with regard to the belief that infra-human learning theory will dominate the educational materials and procedures issuing from the application of technology to educational problems. Here we speak primarily of computers and systems dependent on computers, for this is the area usually singled-out for abuse.

Men doing advanced research on computers are using models developed or suggested by the writings of well known psychologists, psychiatrists, biologists and physiologists. For example the last chapter of Freud's *Interpretation of Dreams* as well as some of Piaget's work on the developing intelligence of children are among the works which suggest to students of artificial intelligence that the use of models inside the system is a useful concept. Such a concept has already been used in studies of stabilizing perception, adaptive control systems to produce simple motor responses, in chess games to avoid extensive search of a very large tree of possible moves, and elsewhere.[14] All of these suggest to Professor Greene that perception involves a synthesizing out of your elements. This could hardly stem from the same view of mind as that apparently held by persons who were ecstatic about using linear programs for instructional purposes. The black box of stimulus-response psychology has been invaded[15] and the result is the development of theories about cognitive operations. As in so many other areas of technology, the greatest steps forward in pattern recognition by machine are being made on the basis of theories about human pattern recognition, theories which are plausible but obviously too simple-minded to account for more than a facet of the process carried on by the human. It is difficult to believe that anyone familiar with current work in cognitive psychology or on pattern recognition and artificial intelligence would be led to impose linear programming on students.

There are, then, formidable bases for objections and obstructions to the development of educational technology. Some of these can be dealt with by extending the information available to the objectors. Others need to be subjected to investigation and contrasted with situations dominated by human teachers. Only then will we have a clear, sound basis for making decisions about the development of educational technology.

Philosophy and Technology

The review of reasons for our failure to apply technology to the problems of education has only touched on philosophic problems. Now we turn to a fuller view of what seem to be the educational issues reflecting philosophic positions; issues brought into focus by recent discussions of the potential of technology in education.

Variable Intellectual Initiative

As one reads the report of the Carnegie Commission on Educational Television,[16] it seems clear that this Commission had a static view of the learner or the recipient of television broadcasting in mind. There are to be more stations, an attempt to improve the quality of television, and an attempt to provide wider educational programming, etc., but the Commission seems to have failed to consider the student in educational television as a dynamic person who might want to participate in the educational programming. In terms of the Ginther model,[11] there is to be no opportunity for the student to become involved in the programming to the extent of altering the progress of instruction as it is presented or unfolded; his degrees of freedom are severely limited. Fortunately, among the supplementary papers in the Carnegie volume is one by J. C. R. Licklider writing on "Tele-vistas: Looking Ahead Through Side Windows." Mr. Licklider deals with what he refers to as "interactive" and "selective" television as well as "narrowcast" as contrasted with the more conventional term "broadcast." Although Mr. Licklider purports to agree with B. F. Skinner's position about learning, his insistence upon interaction which permits the viewer or student to ask questions and otherwise participate in the selection and arrangement of materials to be used in the learning, belies his addiction to Skinner's views and suggests a somewhat broader use of the concepts available in reinforcement theory. When one considers Mr. Licklider's views of the possible activities of the typical television viewer who is about to watch the evening news at home, one sees that the future of technology is, in part, to extend our concept of educational method.

This forward look at the uses and forms of technology, a look which promises that the student will have undreamed of opportunities to become involved in the creation of his own learning situations, strikes a familiar chord. A report from the Center for the Study of Democratic Institutions suggests the general concept applicable here to technology in education.

> . . . if the building trades were to be automated, it would not mean inventing machines to do the various tasks now done by men; rather, buildings would be redesigned so that they could be built by machines. One might invent an automatic bricklayer, but it is more likely that housing would be designed so that bricks would not be layed.[17]

If new technology can suggest new methods, how short-sighted to use it merely to routinize old methods; and how fruitless to bring routinized old methods to bear on new problems and challenges, particularly when doing so clouds the real potential of technology. Students at all levels of our educational system are different today than they were even ten years ago because of the impact of technology in conveying information rapidly to the general public. We indeed live in the electric age. To the extent that this suggests that students need a different approach in the teaching-learning situation, we ought to be prepared to use technology to create something different. For example, one should be willing to try manipulating the richness of the environment for the learner so that the easily overwhelmed student might receive a low amount of potential stimulation while some students might be placed in a saturated educational environment. It may be that such diverse kinds of situations would be appropriate at different times for the same individual student. Mr. Michael reminds us that the use of technology should enable us to deal with current educational problems and difficulties in new rather than old ways, and Mr. Licklider provides concrete images of exciting possibilities. It does seem disappointing to read in 1968 that nearly one-and-a-half million dollars is spent by a high school to install an "automated library" which consists primarily of audio-tapes of printed material and which "features" the opportunity for teachers to record their lectures so they will be available to students for "individual instruction."[18]

One thing the computer phase of technology makes potentially feasible is the application of John Dewey's notion that thinking always starts with some kind of difficulty or problem or unresolved situation. It was his contention that education therefore started in such situations. Aside from the fact that some people did not like his brand of philosophy, this idea didn't get moving because of the fact that when students dealt with problems they sooner or later were confronted with situations which involved skills which took time to develop; or the situation required them to use information which they did not have at their command. The amount of time required to develop the skill or to command the information was usually sufficient so that the motivating force of the original situation would be dissipated before the skill or the command of information could be accomplished. The current technology, especially that which is assisted by the computer, makes it seem reasonable to reconsider Dewey's proposition. We now seem to be approaching the time when the necessary information could be made available in such short order that the student would be able to make use of it before motivation sagged. Depending upon the nature of the skill required, the student might also be in a better position today to develop the skill. To date a highly successful application of technology has been in skill training. Substitution for some skills is also possible today. For example, mathematical calculation need present no difficulty at all these days, for almost anyone can turn to a computer and have nearly any kind of mathematical calculation done as quickly as he can enter the data. The entire problem of dissipating interest while standing still to develop skill or to command information has not evaporated, but it has become much more manageable so that it would now be possible to reconsider Dewey's notions particularly as they bear on motivation and method.

Turning to the ideas of Whitehead, one might profitably heed Harold Dunkel's suggestion that "Whitehead's greatest contribution to modern education possibly lies in the number of points at which he can serve as a needed corrective to certain tendencies in current American education and in contemporary American society." [19] In a sharply focused article Professor Dunkel suggests that one improvement would consist of reintroducing the romance phase of the learning cycle into schooling.[20] There would be a revolution in American education if just this idea were to be followed. For example, if computer technology could be used simply to advise students of a range of books, pictures, magazine articles, film strips, recordings, or motion pictures which were readily available on some topic, we would be able to enhance exploration in depth during self-motivated study or investigation. The potential of the computer as a component in the instructional situation is also to be considered. For example, a computer program would permit the student to make an ecological study of colonies of bacteria in the human body. Via simulation he might suggest the numbers of bacteria, white blood cells, and chemical agents, as well as the conditions. Perhaps this suggests how an expanding array of potentially exciting situations might be used to develop understanding of difficult concepts at Whitehead's "precision" level. But the focus and the kind of change of emphasis which technology could help us create and which is badly needed on the American educational scene is the emphasis on the romance phase of Whitehead's rhythms of learnings.

Conceptualism

The usefulness of technology in conveying information would enable us to develop a new philosophic framework at least as an alternative to if not a protagonist of realism. The reference is to conceptualism as a point of view which is, on the one hand, not widely held formally by educators in this country and, on the other hand, is a philosophic position which is extremely difficult to translate into an educational program. The problem seems to be that no matter how you devise methodology or materials of instruction, the view of the world and matter and knowledge turns out to sound like it was based on realism. Perhaps the speed with which sets of alternatives could be provided via the computer would be useful in developing a corrective or an alternative to this situation. Perhaps this phase of technology would enable us to create situations in which the learner was not led to believe that realism was the only position available. There are some suggestions that this kind of major shift in emphasis on philosophic positions is near because of the availability of computer technology which might be turned to the problems of education.

Another suggestion basic to the application of technology to education is that the computer be thought of as a concept rather than a thing. Elsewhere I have attempted to persuade that "library" is a concept which has held and still holds a variety of meanings for teachers and librarians, and consequently takes a variety of forms and serves a range of functions, [21, 22] Similarly a computer can be thought of as a concept. The sooner this is done the sooner we may develop creative and useful ideas based on educational problems and capable of challenging the potential of computers in the educational process. The educator's conception of the computer will mold the uses made of it. It has already been suggested that technology has been viewed primarily as a means for transporting or presenting information to students, and this view has been extended to the computer. By way of contrast let us examine some recent applications of computers to instructional problems, imaginative applications stemming from consideration of the computer as a concept.

Starting with the complex problem of arranging for students to gain experience in the design of electrical circuitry or complex electrical jobs, two investigators devised a computer program which enables students to engage in creative design. The program also permits thorough testing of the designs. With this particular use of the computer "in the nine weeks session fifteen different designs, some of considerable sophistication, were built, modified, and tested."[23] Games have become a method for instructing in business management where intangible concepts such as planning and control and organization are deemed important.[24] The valid sorting of essays into "good," "poor," and those in between by means of a computer program has been demonstrated.[25] At the medical school at Case Western Reserve University a computer program, capable of bringing new pages of an interview schedule or stored data almost instantly at the touch of a hand on a cathode ray tube, is revolutionizing beliefs about the amount of information which can be summarized and used in developing an understanding of a patient's condition. Application of this idea to the problem of daily, if not continuous evaluation of the progress of students seems highly promising. These examples remind one of the statement that "speed-up of information ideally permits education to proceed by discovery and by pattern recognition rather than by instruction in classified data."[26] But note that the specific programs and uses are directed toward the solution of particular problems, and require that the authors have a relatively unfettered notion of the computer as a concept. This seems to free the imagination to give meaning to the computer.

Compelling Considerations

There are a number of activities abroad in the land which suggest that there may be compelling reasons for thinking seriously about using the potentials of technology in our educational system. These will be considered here with full sensitivity to the suggested dangers of dehumanizing students mentioned earlier. There is no conscious attempt to order these in any particular way.

One observable movement is the tendency for Americans to create an ever enlarging body of ideas classifiable as believable rather than really true. Even church groups are shifting many teachings into a contingent, bound-by-circumstances category, teachings which formerly were believed to be true absolutely and without qualification. This suggests that even if the schools are to play their historic role of supporting the belief system of the culture they will have to change. And perhaps it is worth repeating the contention that one of the most difficult tasks in teaching is to avoid the illusion that everything is based on a philosophic system of realism; difficult, that is, if undertaken. Yet we are urged to consider operating from a conceptualistic base.

> . . . the child's conception of reality or meaning, however deviant it may be from the adult educator's, must be respected. The child should not be told he is "wrong," for this will suggest to him that there is a "right." On the other hand, the child must not be left to himself to think that his way of thinking is the only one, or that he has ever achieved the most fruitful conception he can reach. It will be the task of a sensitive teacher to strike a balance between these by guiding the child through and to those experiences which the adult, from his own greater range of experiences combined with his empathy with the child, can select as potentially profitable for the child's development. This will demand more individualized instruction, and less concern with standardized achievement of prescriptive what-is-to-be-known.[27]

Simulations providing study of phenomena under shifting circumstances and the presentation of differing points of view through high speed delivery of relevant information are two potentials of technology which could serve the need to suggest a conceptualistic approach to some instruction.

A second noticeable phenomenon in American society is the demand for an increasing opportunity for participation in the development of decisions. This phenomenon yields two avenues of thought regarding technology, and particularly the computer. One avenue leads to the fact that citizens will have to learn how to make use of information which can be made available. Since nothing short of our new technology will approximate it in power and speed, we are obligated to use the technology simply to prepare citizens to use it. Such preparation surely will involve a range of established scholarship such as external and internal criticism of documents, although perhaps in modern dress since a document might now be a message on a cathode ray tube. The second avenue leads to the realization that citizens are not prepared emotionally to participate in discussions basic to decisions responsive to social demands. This suggests that the efforts of social psychologists to train students for and habituate them to the use of group processes be redoubled—surely an unexpected outcome of the impact of technology.

Still another set of activities in American society which compels thoughtful consideration of technology in education is that set consisting of disruptions of schooling. It is a clearly established fact that students, teachers and parents can, have, and apparently will continue to close schools for essentially non-educational reasons. Perhaps we should be prepared for the abolishment of schools or for significant alterations in them to accommodate essentially community-problem-oriented activities. Either contingency might be accompanied by the shifting of some form of conventional studies to a technologically based operation.

Some who believe that we are moving to a society based on a sophisticated technology also fear that the world cannot, under the attendant circumstances, exist as a coherent society unless a number of basic problems are solved. As has been suggested, life is simply different in the electric age. If the problems are to be solved we "will have to generate beliefs, behavior, and goals far different from those which we have held until now and which are driving us more and more inexorably into a contradictory world."[17]

We should not be surprised that compelling reasons have arisen for reconsidering our educational patterns and the place of technology in them.

> Electric speeds of information movement of themselves act as the new structuring forces as much in science and the arts as in politics and in entertainment . . . Co-existence in space assumes a different character when it is also coexistent in time. Many of the arrangements made for spacial coexistence become embarrassing and irrelevant when instantaneous information exchange intrudes. That is to say that almost all of the existing arrangements in the educational establishment, for example, must seem bizarre to any young person today. Growing up in a world where all data and events appear integrally related, the student enters the educational establishment where instruction is in the main provided by means of classified data and separate subjects.[26]

Unfortunately, compelling reasons are on an elastic scale which often permits us to wait for entirely too much data before taking corrective action. It seems always that several persons must be killed before barriers are erected at railroad crossings; numerous accidents must occur before a highway is straightened or a curve banked; murders must be committed before usury is investigated in business transactions; lives must be lost before health and safety codes are enforced in rental properties. Certainly there is reason to believe that compelling reasons for planning how to use the potential of technology in education will be ignored for the present. Perhaps the excitement of entertaining new methods of instruction or of developing conceptualism as a viable alternative to realism or of reintroducing romance in education will motivate continued thought for the time being.

The Charge: Challenge Technology

If we are to develop an educational technology, that is if we are to examine the range of problems which teachers confront, consider the potential of present technology and attempt to apply this potential to the problems in imaginative ways, we will probably have to move in unconsciously familiar yet "new" ways. Unconsciously, while a student, one who later becomes a teacher accepts or rejects instructional methods, materials and routines and in a very real sense learns to teach as he is taught. Unfortunately we standardize a particular subset of these variables and try to have all prospective teachers learn this same subset consciously. We need to recognize the unconscious element in the development of teaching style and use it in efforts to promote, develop and test the application of technology to education. We need to provide opportunities for teachers in training as well as established teachers to use technology in their own education, training or retraining. In other words we need to create one or more places where learning theory beyond a mechanistic level would be used in the education of teachers, not only to guide the application of technology, but also to suggest appropriate limits to the use of such technology; where Whitehead's romance and precision levels might be used as the basis for part of the education of teachers, that is, as guides to the developing technology which they, as students, commanded; where technology would be tested, by teachers-become-students, to determine its potential for providing instruction based on conceptualism as an alternative to realism. In short, our charge must be to challenge technology taking account of William James' warning of the need for creative minds to intervene. But we must also test the results issuing from the challenge, designing the applications for use first with teachers in their own developing pattern of education and training. And we must be sensitive to the cautions from humanists as well as alert to the beckonings of scientists who suggest ever more about the magnificent workings of both conscious and unconscious mind.

Finally, we must consider the possibility that we are in an era characterized by a new perspective on the nature of reality and, consequently, the nature and purpose of schooling and education. We must, then, extend our notion of the parameter of problems to which technology might be applied. There are several forces, some rational, which suggest that schools will one day be recognized as a concept with yet unimagined meanings. Technology is such a force; at the same time it is a tool which may be advantageously used to deal with currently unmanageable educational problems as well as with the dreams of those who believe that an extended view of the nature of mind, method, motivation and reality should be considered and tested in our educational system.

REFERENCES

1. *Technology in Education:* Hearings before the Sub-committee on Economic Progress of the Joint Economic Committee, Eighty-Ninth Congress, Second Session, June 6, 10 and 13, 1966. (Washington: U.S. Government Printing Office, 1966).

2. James, William. *Talks to Teachers on Psychology.* New York: Henry Holt, 1899.

3. "The Learning Business." *Newsweek,* September 30, 1968.

4. Drucker, Peter. "Modern Technology and Ancient Jobs." *Technology and Culture,* 4, 3, Summer. Detroit: Society for the History of Technology, 1963.

5. Postlethwait, S. N., J. Novak, and H. Murray. *An Integrated Experience Approach to Learning.* Minneapolis: Burgess Publishing Company, 1964.

6. Amidon, Edmund J. and Ned A. Flanders, *The Role of the Teacher in the Classroom.* Minneapolis: Paul S. Amidon and Associates, 1963.

7. Floyd, William D. "Do Teachers Talk Too Much?". *The Instructor,* 78, 3, October. 1968.

8. Henry, Jules. "Attitude Organization in Elementary School Classrooms." *American Journal of Orthopsychiatry,* 27, January, 1957.

9. Ginther, John R. "A Model for Analyzing Programmed Materials." *Administrator's Notebook,* 10, 5, January, 1962.

10. Skinner, Burrhus F. *The Technology of Teaching.* New York: Appleton-Century-Crofts, 1968.

11. Ginther, John R. "A Conceptual Model for Analyzing Instruction." *Programmed Instruction in Medical Education.* Jerome P. Lysaught (ed.). The University of Rochester: The Rochester Clearinghouse, 1965.

12. Rippey, Robert M. "Fitting Research on Instruction into Ginther's Conceptual Model." A paper presented at the meetings of the American Psychological Association. Chicago, 1965.

13. Berlin, Barney. *Learning Experiences of Students.* Unpublished Ph.D. dissertation, Department of Education, The University of Chicago, 1965.

14. Greene, Peter H. "Models for Perception and Action." *Proceedings of the First Annual Princeton Symposium on Information Systems and Science.* Princeton University: Department of Electrical Engineering, 1967.

15. Neisser, Ulric. *Cognitive Psychology.* New York: Appleton-Century-Crofts, 1967.

16. Carnegie Commission on Educational Television, *Public Television.* New York: Bantam Books, 1967.

17. Michael, Donald N. *Cybernation: The Silent Conquest.* Santa Barbara, California: The Fund for the Republic, Inc., 1962.

18. Haas, Joseph. "The Super Library" in "Panorama," *The Chicago Daily News,* October 5, 1968.

19. Dunkel, Harold B. "Whitehead on Education," *Studies in Educational Theory of the John Dewey Society, No. 3.* Columbus: Ohio State University Press, 1965.

20. Dunkel, Harold B. "Free Romance!", *The Elementary School Journal,* 68, 2, November, 1967.

21. Ginther, John R. "Computers in the Elementary School." *Illinois Elementary Principal,* May, 1967.

22. Ginther, John R. "Let's Challenge Technology." *Educational Leadership,* 25, 8, May, 1968.

23. Entwisle, Doris R., and W. H. Huggins, "Simulated Environments in Higher Education." *The School Review,* 75, 4, Winter, 1967.

24. Babb, E. M., and L. M. Eisgruber, *Management Games for Teaching and Research.* Chicago: Educational Methods, Inc., 1966.

25. Bhushan, Vidya and John R. Ginther, "Discriminating Between A Good and A Poor Essay." *Behavioral Science,* 13, 5, September, 1968.

26. "The Electric Message Came," *Times Literary Supplement,* March 10, 1966.

27. Satterlee, Barbara. "Conceptualist Curriculum: Problems of Implementation." Dittoed, Industrial Relations Center, The University of Chicago, March, 1967.

30.
Education and Technology

by *JOHN I. GOODLAD*
Dean, Grad. School of Education
Univ. of California, Los Angeles

Introduction

Some components of "modern" educational technology have been with us for some time: films, film strips, records, radio and television. One might expect that these components would be in wide-spread use, *circa* 1968. Surprisingly, they are not.

In visits to approximately 250 elementary school classrooms in 1967, we found little evidence of a technological explosion in the classroom. In fact, there was little evidence that "the golden age of instructional materials" is here. For instruction, teachers depend heavily on telling and questioning, with the primary exchange being between teacher and child, child and teacher—not among groups of children with the teacher as observer and occasional participant. The textbook dominates as the prime medium of instruction. There are striking classroom examples to the contrary. Nonetheless, the predominant tone is one of traditional teaching techniques and traditional textbooks, both long with us.

One is forced to ask, "why?" Undoubtedly, much of the quality is poor. Many educational films are pedantic, precious, and "holier than thou." They tend to talk at or to children and down to them. They do not grip the viewer. Increasingly, however, a first-rate film library is developing.

It is surprising that teachers do not make more use of the tape recorder, a highly flexible device. Also, records constitute one of the most efficient storage devices and could bring rich learning into the classroom if teachers were aware of their potentiality.

Quality does not fully explain the fact that teachers have eschewed audiovisual aids, however. No doubt, teacher training and tradition are enormously restraining influences. But it is clear that audiovisual aids almost always have been advocated as extensions of the teacher. The cant in audiovisual education is that the audiovisual presentation must be built into or made an extension of whatever the conventional teaching procedures may be. It is rarely assumed that youngsters are free to use such materials on their own initiative: to record tapes, to make records, to prepare films, or to use any of these which are available. Invariably the teacher intervenes in some way between student and the learning device. Herein, I think, lies the heart of the problem.

So long as the interface is not a direct one between student and material and so long as the teacher somehow must extend himself in order to make the material available, the audiovisual device enters in as a fifth wheel. We must shift to the notion that a substantial part of the educational process can be and should be a direct interface between student and stimulus, with the teacher acting only as a guide. Use of the material or device must lie completely within the ken and freedom of the individual learner.

We are now entering into a new phase of instructional technology made possible by the advent of the computer. The unique contribution of the computer is that it clearly needs little, if any, intervention on the part of the teacher. The computer marches on in its relentless way; students are plugged in; and the teacher is free to stand back from and appraise the learning under way. In fact, if the teacher seeks to monitor the computer as a teaching aid, in the conventional sense, the teacher's actions are dehumanized. The teacher becomes a human robot, always outstripped by the mechanical one which is indefatigable and, for most purposes, more efficient. The central problem, then, in the use of the computer in instruction is to develop a team teaching situation, with human and electronic teacher performing the roles most appropriate for each.

Classifications of Computer Role in Education

The computer lends itself to at least three sets of educational functions;

1. The management of masses of educational data. Large school systems, in particular, are confronted with formidable problems of storing and retrieving data pertaining to pupil records, teacher records, payroll, test results, and so on. These data can be managed much more efficiently by computers than by humans. A single third- or fourth-generation computer, programmed for storing and retrieving such data, has an enormous appetite—too large an appetite, usually, for small and intermediate school systems. Therefore, this aspect of computer use in education lends itself well to cooperative endeavor among several neighboring school systems, sharing a common computer. School systems are surprisingly stubborn and individualistic, however, in regard to the way in which such data are classified and otherwise identified. There are no strong arguments for one system of classification over another. Nonetheless, neighboring school systems stick stubbornly to their own methods when a little "giving" could result in collaborative effort and both savings and improved efficiency in regard to data control.

In a large school system, the option is to use the computer not only for these more mundane tasks, but also for various, somewhat more experimental endeavors. The office of research, for example, is able to conduct broad-scale research and evaluative activities which otherwise would not be possible. The City of Chicago represents an early example of this dual use. The computer is available to persons who have various individualistic concerns during the daytime hours and is devoted to the handling of routine matters at night. The possibilities of putting the computer to work at night is too little recognized by educational personnel. Most major universities run their computer facilities twenty-four hours a day, with students and faculty members gaining access to the facilities around the clock.

2. The second function might be described as management of the educational enterprise. There are several types of activities under this rubric but two of them, in particular, should be mentioned. First, increasingly the computer is entering into the management of students' programs. A well-known system is that generated by Stanford University which, using a module of time, individually schedules students located many miles away. Printouts from the computer tell each student where he is supposed to be and what he is supposed to be doing at any time during an instructional week.

But a much more sophisticated management activity lies just around the corner in education. It already has been extensively used in other fields and, particularly, for research purposes. This is a process of feeding data to decision-making processes. Administrators and teachers make hosts of decisions during a given day, most of them not based on data but on hunches and intuition. Human intuition needs to be enriched by the availability of data. For example, when teachers move into nongrading and team teaching, decisions which were formerly not theirs to make now lie before them. Unfortunately, however, modern management techniques have not caught up with these new decision-making processes and so teachers become frustrated because of the unavailability of the data they need. What is called for here is a conceptualization of the educational decisions involved in any aspect of the enterprise; the identification of the kinds of data needed for these decisions; the classification and storage of these data for easy recall; and the recall of the data at the point of decision-making. Thus, an instructional team considering the group placement of a given youngster for the following term should have at its disposal salient data pertaining to that child: adjustment to the previous group, learning accomplishments in various fields, difficulties with peers and adults, and so on. These data are then taken into account in making the appropriate educational placement. Even more sophisticated management techniques, using the computer, are on the horizon.

3. The educational function appropriate for computers which has attracted most attention is that of instruction. The computer is a tireless, relentless, evaluating teacher which has several modes of instruction at its disposal: sound, sight, and touch. A properly programmed computer is able to present words to be spelled, sounds to be made, instructions to be followed, and so on. It is able to present images and symbols to be responded to by touch. It is able to evaluate pupil performance and to direct the student backwards, forwards, sideways, for appropriate learning activity. Almost all of the computer-assisted instruction currently under way is experimental in character. Significant are the experiments in the teaching of spelling, reading, arithmetic, and so on, at the University of Pittsburgh, the University of Texas, Stanford University and other centers. The program in computer-assisted instruction at Stanford is, in most instances, based upon carefully worked out "software" in basic instructional areas. Programs are those using both "on site" computers and remote terminals. There are technical problems still to be resolved in computer-assisted instruction; the development of computers which can handle a large number of terminals; the refinement of communication to remote terminals; and more. Two other problems are more significant at this point in time. The first is cost. But rapid gains are being made here. The second is the human variable. There needs to be developed an enormous readiness on the part of the educational profession to build the computer into the instructional process.

Computer-Assisted Learning

The two key characteristics of computers which promise to change education in schools and society are *efficiency* and *availability*. The most dramatic changes in the conduct of education are likely to be more the product of the availability characteristic. The computer is ready, willing, and able; twenty-four hours a day, seven days a week, 365¼ days a year.

Before turning to these characteristics of efficiency and availability, let me say a little about the prognosis for early, wide-spread use of computers in the lower schools. First, there is likely to be relatively little use of computers for teaching and learning in these schools during the next decade. This view is in contrast to many of the wide-eyed claims for computer use in instruction. The reasons for my conservatism are those usually cited. The costs of computers and computer terminals already has been identified. A major cost item, whenever terminals are remote, is that of the telephone communication system. It is in this realm that breakthroughs are anticipated and it is likely that costs will be reduced markedly in the relatively near future. Nonetheless, costs in general and, in particular, the cost of transmission from computers to terminals will continue to be restraining factors, if only because the image of cost will continue to exist. And, of course, the real cost factors will continue to be formidable for some time. This problem is compounded by the fact that estimates of real costs are most difficult to come by and vary enormously with respect to any given cost factor.

In a second category explaining delayed use there are more subtle and, perhaps, more significant reasons. It must be remembered that school (and university) budgets are relatively inflexible. In California, for example, 80 per cent of the budget in a local school system is locked in to mandated specifications. For example, 60 per cent of the total outlay in elementary education must go to teacher salaries. It must be remembered that many of the potential savings in the use of computers occur only *after* computers have been installed. Consequently, there is a period of time during which a school system must suffer under dual budget outlays. It is difficult to amortize this kind of financial outlay. No matter what the computer may replace in the future it is laid on over whatever cost exists at the outset.

But the most subtle difficulty lies in simultaneously changing and maintaining the educational system. Innovation is difficult, not just because this is its character but because the existing system must be maintained while the new one is being introduced. The educational ship is not brought into dry dock but must remain on the high seas while repairs are effected. It is not surprising, then, that educators tend to tinker with the rigging, lowering the sails and raising the sails, polishing the brightwork and swabbing the decks. Meanwhile, it is the hull that really needs changing but it dare not be tampered with for fear that the ship will sink. Consequently, most educational change is at the periphery and, as a result, is inconsequential. To introduce a real change into the system is to change the whole system. The introduction of computers for instruction changes the system and, consequently, is threatening. This psychological difficulty will remain for some time as the least penetrable.

In part from the foregoing, therefore, one can conclude that the computer will enter into the schools at those points and in those ways that require a minimum of mediation by the teacher. This brings me back to where I started with respect to audiovisual aids in general. Almost all audiovisual aids used to date require maximum mediation by the teacher. It is not at all surprising, then, that they have not been extensively embraced. Skillful administrators who wish to see the computer used increasingly in the schools should devote some of their attention to how the computer can be introduced so as to require only a minimum of new behavior on the part of the teacher. Thus, we may expect to see the computer used as a teaching device in segments of the curriculum where there are rather well agreed upon skills or bodies of content which can be programmed for direct computer-student interface and little or no teacher participation. Already we see this to be the case in the teaching of reading, mathematics, and spelling. Where teachers are involved in rather close communication with the computer, one is depressed to note that the teacher tends to be robotized. He engages very often in perfunctory handling of printouts which might just as well be handled directly by the student. It is when the student encounters problems which are not programmed that a more sensitive kind of relationship is called for and the human teacher should be sought.

In brief summary, then, I am saying that the use of the computer in schools will be delayed primarily by the subtle difficulties of simultaneously changing and maintaining the educational system. To the extent that teachers do not have to carry the double burden, the computer is more likely to be welcomed than rejected.

Now, let me return to the efficiency characteristic of computers. These have been summarized in many places. First, the computer is capable of presenting an unvarying sequence of learning opportunities, uncontaminated by nuances of speech or by mannerisms characteristic of the varying human teacher. Second, it prevents the repetition of errors and provides for the reinforcement of correct responses. Third, it provides for individual rates of speed, with students usually able to control the rate of presentation and of response. Of course, there are situations in which both of these factors are controlled. Fourth, the computer provides individualized schedules, permitting students to exercise idiosyncratic behavior without having to get in the way of the limited energy restraints of the human teacher. Fifth, the computer eliminates or holds the potentiality for eliminating a host of routine pupil-teacher contacts which add little or nothing to the learning process. It is doubtful that meaningless, routinized human interactions are better than no human interactions at all. And it must be remembered that it is difficult for most human beings to be truly human in the best sense, hour after hour, all day long, with a passing parade of students.

But the efficiency characteristic of computers poses some problems which are rarely identified in the literature. The first is for theory and research. There are conceptual problems to be checked out empirically pertaining to the parts of the curriculum which should be allocated to computers and the parts which should be allocated to human beings. It is quite likely that there are certain kinds of processes which should remain in the exclusive domain of human beings. But we are not at all clear on what these might be. It is a kind of research in conceptualization which has rarely been popular in education but which must be carried on. The efficiency characteristic poses certain problems with respect to teacher self-respect. The computer is more efficient in most of what teachers now do. Research has shown that, even in classrooms rated as superior with respect to instruction, an enormous amount of teacher time is devoted to the purely routine. But this is not at all surprising. Human beings seem to need a considerable amount of routine to span out the time between less frequent, more creative efforts. What will the teacher do if not directing routine? Articles and books on computer-assisted instruction end with the captivating notion that the computer will enable human teachers to do those truly human things. What are they? And will teachers be able to do them all day long? Our divorce rate suggests that it is exceedingly difficult even for two people to establish a productive human relationship. How, then, is the human teacher to establish and maintain a productive relationship with thirty other human beings and maintain it throughout five or six hours of an instructional day? Most teachers would be in a state of collapse at the end of such days. Clearly, if teachers, given computers, are to move to more intensely human instructional activities, the nature of the instructional day must be completely rethought. The kind of teaching day in elementary and secondary schools probably ought to resemble the kind of teaching day in institutions of higher learning. A forty-hour work week for teachers may very well include only twelve to fifteen hours of instructional time. This will not be easily understood by the lay community.

Quite apart from the theoretical, research and affective problems involved under the efficiency rubric, there are problems of logistics and of politics. Teachers and computers must learn to work productively side by side in the school environment. We have not been outstandingly successful, however, in developing teams of human teachers. Ahead of us lies the logistical problem of developing teaching teams which will include the computer as one component of the team, with the electronic teacher performing the tasks of efficiency which are so appropriate to it and the human teachers engaged in other kinds of activities, one of which is only rarely the monitoring of the computer itself. In all of this lie implications for school building design, teacher allocation and utilization, and so on. Is the cost of adding a computer to be absorbed by reducing the size of the human teaching staff? The computer is not likely to add to the efficiency of education, since efficiency includes economics, if what it does efficiently is merely added to what human beings do inefficiently. Inherent in all of this, too, are implications for the role of teacher unions. Will we arrive at the day when teachers teaching only twelve or fifteen hours a week are paid by union contract a full week's wages for whatever they may do in their remaining hours? Might this mean that the potential additional time for planning, for preparing more effective lessons, for counseling with students, and so on, will go by the board? There are many intangibles here which cannot be predicted and which might very well change the nature of the teaching profession, as we know it.

While the efficiency characteristic of computers offers promise of performing conventional educational tasks better, the availability characteristic offers a promise of fundamentally changing or eliminating conventional educational tasks. The possibilities here begin to come into view when we realize how much of the conduct of schooling is geared to, or dependent upon, the limited availability of human energy.

It is possible to think of many specifics of school practice which depend, perhaps implicitly, on our awareness of the limits of human energy in a schooling situation; for example, entrance age has nothing to do with children's readiness to learn. It is now becoming clear that children are ready and, indeed, do learn for many years before coming to school. Entrance age, then, whatever it may be, has no real educational justification. It simply is difficult for teachers to look after 20 or 25 youngsters who are not toilet-trained, who are very little socialized, who need to eat relatively often, and who intend to carry on many of their pursuits in short bursts of energy. No, leave them home, we say, during this potentially troublesome period. Similarly, there is no educational justification for a nine to three school day. Such a period roughly coincides with the time when most human beings go to work and return. Why should school be any different? It is not easy for it to be any different so long as instruction is tied to human beings and their conventional, conforming utilization of energy. Similarly, children are placed in a grade because this, supposedly, limits teacher need to have high ceilings and low floors of expectancy and provision for learning within any class group. Of course, the grade is not really like this but we can pretend. Likewise, the eggcrate school building with its 30 to 1 ratio of children to teachers and the continuous interaction process suggested thereby, are related to notions of how many children can be handled at once and how many children can be within hearing and seeing range of the teacher. High school faculties are put together in order to provide for a balanced faculty at any one time. Is it possible that balance in the curriculum has more to do with the availability of human energy than educational rationality? Likewise, there is an orderly progression from elementary to secondary school, with the former tending not to tread on the domain of the latter. None of these accepted conditions of schooling is necessary when one introduces the concept of energy available at any time of the day or night, to any age group throughout the year. The learning stimulus is always there; one needs only to tap it. This is not the case with human teachers.

Perhaps the most significant aspect of the computer with respect to education, then, is that an altogether new kind of energy is injected into the educational process. It is energy which has nothing to do with the night before, with viruses, with unmanageable children, or any of the rest. Subjects missed this year can be picked up next year. Single subjects can be pursued intensively for periods of time related only to the whim of the learner. The fifty-year-old need not humble himself by going back to school with twelve-year-olds in order to get what he needs and wants. He may go directly to the energy system which is insensitive to age, color, or origin of birth.

The moment that we make teaching energy available throughout the 24-hour span of day to all individuals in any place, most of the conventions of schooling explode, school need no longer be what we have known it to be. And so it is the characteristic of *availability* of the computer which holds the potentiality for fundamentally restructuring, if not eliminating, school as we know and have known it.

It is quite reasonable, of course, to conceive of a school which is unnecessary for the purposes it has served traditionally as being necessary for latent functions which we have not, up to now, chosen to recognize. Consequently, school may be thought of as a place where children are located, where parents and guardians can locate them at will. They are accounted for, so to speak. It could be a place where students fulfill certain social functions, testing their peer relationships with members of both sexes. It could become a place where human beings are brought together not because they have to be brought together for the formalities of learning but where they begin to learn the higher literacy going far beyond reading, writing, and arithmetic. Such thinking certainly returns us to John Dewey's notions of education and life being one. But, clearly, unless schooling is rethought, it is unlikely that students, particularly at high school levels, will see school life as the kind of life that is most meaningful for them. And this brings us to another potentiality of the computer.

If terminal and transmission costs are brought down to a reasonable point so that the purchase of computer time and terminals is not unrealistic for schools, and if the production of software is vastly enhanced, then one major obstacle to computer-assisted instruction in schools is removed. But this economic factor applies also to homes. Consequently, the reduction of computer terminal costs for school use is equally applicable to home use. In fact, there are many more purchasers and it is likely that home potentiality for computer terminals will have a greater effect on cost reduction. All that remains, then, for computer terminals to be installed in homes is the availability of endless series of programs or software. The home becomes a most promising potential market for computer companies and the large, commercial education complexes.

We have not begun to tap the potentiality of the home as the locus of a much wider array of human activity. Thousands of commuters suffer through traffic jams in order to get to offices in which they operate in cells, with only occasional interaction with other human beings. A substantial part of the work force spends much of its time and does much of its business on the telephone. All of this might as readily be done by remaining at home and foregoing the traffic problems. Similarly, with learning.

The only thing standing in the way now of an enormous amount of productive learning occurring on television is the quality of programs. Envision a computer terminal, with a wider variety of instructional resources, available in the home in the same way a television set is available now. Given the rapid advancement and rapid outmoding of knowledge, age is a poor criterion for knowing or for needing to know. Consequently, one can envision families comprised of many age levels learning together from computer terminals in the home. This does not mean that members of the family will refrain from going outside for other kinds of learning activities, but it does suggest that both basic learning and updating, as appropriate, might very well be effected through home communication with a central learning unit generating to many computer terminals. Home budgets are more flexible than school budgets and, therefore, can be adjusted to take care of additional expense. And the social system is a relatively simple one. There are few problems of getting through it or into it. The door-to-door salesman is highly successful in this regard.

Now, let us put together the storage and retrieving capabilities, the management capabilities, and the instructional capabilities of computers. It is now possible to conceive of a computer programmed to provide instantly, at a home terminal, continuously updated information about the total educational resources of a community. In some sections of the country these resources already are staggering, but the communication system regarding them is bad. A member of a family might very well secure a printout of what is coming up in the way of art shows, museum displays, athletic events, plays, lectures, and so on, and where and how these educational and cultural resources might be reached. Clearly, some of them would come directly into the home via computer terminal. Included in this repertoire of cultural resources would be a library of educational programs spanning the whole gamut of human interest. Envision a cultural community generating center in which the totality of learning resources available is "programmed." Envision, also, an individual record-keeping system by means of which the segments of this, uniquely assembled for any given individual, are managed. Envision, also, human teachers located in various centers and with special skills available to those who need or call for them. Finally, envision guidance centers staffed with individuals uniquely equipped to counsel on individual learning interests and problems. Within this complex, "teachers" would play a diversified set of roles. Some would spend hours and hours in preparing a single lesson, to be viewed within the lifetime of that lesson by thousands, or even millions of individuals, over a wide age span. Others would be engaging in those group interaction processes which we might label intellectual dialogue. Others would staff the counseling centers referred to previously. Still others would engage in presentations viewed on home and "community" computer terminal screens. Others would evaluate the computer output of given learners in order to determine the effectiveness of instructional programs.

The above is not "education 1980." But it very well could be "education 2010."

But we cannot envision or bring about very much of this if we fail to realize that the changes potentially inherent in modern technology will change systems as we know them. Change is not just a matter of tacking on something new. If a change is significant—and computers hold the potentiality for significant change—then it will affect the entire organism. The system will enter into disequilibrium and all of its parts become subject to change. Consequently, all of its parts can be redesigned. It is the availability of new energy—energy which can be held stable over long periods of time; energy which is unfaltering; energy which stores and retrieves; energy which responds to and sustains the input of human energy—that promises to change the school as we have known it. It is this energy which promises to eliminate the unfortunate alienation of much of schooling from education, and to make the boundaries between the two indistinguishable.

31.
Effects of the Technological Mystique on Schooling

by *EDGAR Z. FRIEDENBERG*
Prof., Educational Studies
Dept. of Social Foundations
State Univ. of New York at Buffalo

In responding to the question addressed to me, "What are the educational needs of young people in America today, and what relevance might instructional technology have for meeting these needs?", my first responsibility, I believe, is to avoid entrapment in the assumptions on which the question is based. For the crucial questions facing education in America are ethical, not methodological; and there is nothing more American than the practice of concentrating attention on problems of technique in order to evade moral issues. This is what we have done throughout the Vietnam war; it is what we continue to do with reference to most of our difficulties, from air pollution to the character of American political campaigns. We seek devices—procedural, mechanical, electronic—that will help us do what we wish to do, without asking who is using those devices to do what to whom, and by what authority. Our answer to the questions *"Cui bono?"* and *"Quo warranto?"* is merely "The impossible may take a little while!"; which, except in a gung-ho television drama, is no answer at all.

Educators, especially, evade these questions for which society itself provides official answers that, as its agents, they accept as they cheerfully work toward a final solution of the youth question. *"Cui bono?"* The schools are assumed to exist for the benefit of their pupils and of the society that supports them. The question before us, then, is how they can do a better job than they admittedly do now; and this is precisely why an improved instructional technology is sought. *"Quo warranto!"* Society provides the warrant, and will issue one for the apprehension of any youth under 16 who commits the offense of existing—out of school. It is precisely in order to make this constraint more supportable and even profitable to him that we seek to improve instructional technology.

By the mere act of submitting a report to this Commission, one contributes to this evasion unless these questions are examined explicitly. Technology for what, and in whose service—these are surely questions that educators are less free to ignore than generals. Yet, we do ignore them—and, I suspect, for the same reasons that generals do. Not simply because Americans are, as is sometimes said, a practical people impatient of theorizing. Our military policies like our educational system, have not proved very practical judged in terms of results—and that is the only way a practical matter can be judged. Rather, we ignore questions whose answers might undermine our own social roles and undercut our authority. Questions about what devices to use to do our job better cannot do that. Questions about whether our job is worth doing, and for whom; or about who hired us to do it, by what right, and with whose consent; or about the alternatives to doing it at all and what happened to them—such questions as these are more disquieting. To ignore them, however, is to accept the answers to them implicit in existing social practice, and to accept complicity with existing social institutions. Like Bartleby the scrivener, I prefer not to.

The question *"Cui bono?"*, when applied to the schools, is remarkably difficult to answer. There are, of course, many conventional answers which are seldom challenged. But none of these I think, will survive the kind of rigorous test of causality which is applied in an empirical investigation of, say, the effectiveness of a pharmaceutical agent in combating a particular disease. Do the schools contribute to economic opportunity? It can certainly be demonstrated that the longer one stays in school, up to 20 years at least, the higher one's income is likely to be. But whether this is due to capacities actually developed through instruction, or the effect on character and personality of decades of submission to school routines, or merely the consequence of a complex, interlocking series of credentials which restrict opportunities to those who have satisfied the authorities at an earlier stage is not clear. All these processes are involved and are interrelated. But I have listed them, I think, in ascending order of their influence, though apologists for the educational system would prefer, I believe, that the order be reversed. Nevertheless, most of what is intentionally taught in secondary school is too bland, puerile, and inconsequential to be of any value; and in a society which refuses to accord people even the meager autonomy permitted adults until they are about 25, it is likely to be outdated as well. People simply do not turn back to what they have been taught in high school in order to live more sensibly in later life, and they seldom do so even to pursue more advanced study. They are more likely to have to unlearn it if it made any impression at all.

The character and personality traits developed through 12 to 20 years of submission to school routines do certainly play a part in making people marketable, and in developing in them what Fromm calls a "marketing orientation," so much so as to have become a widespread source of embarrassment. The official program of educational leaders now usually includes something about encouraging responsible dissent and the creativity of mavericks. But this, too, is directed toward making the personality more marketable, in an age said to demand greater flexibility—and betokens no greater respect for individuality as such. Moreover, since the school is still interested in turning out a product, it remains practical about problems that occur on its production lines. No doubt it would like to turn out a more sophisticated model this year; but if the teachers or the community rebel because the kids are getting too much freedom, the school administration cracks down on their hair or their speech or their invited speaker or their peace buttons, and calls this democracy in action—which, indeed, is just what it is. Democracy in action notes that the disfranchised, being powerless, have no rights and may be treated like things when the clutch comes and holds that any protest they might make is illegitimate per se. This is precisely the position of the Superintendent of Schools in sophisticated San Francisco, where all protest demonstrations in the public schools have been forbidden under threat of criminal prosecution, according to a headline story in the San Francisco Chronicle for Tuesday, October 29, 1968.

In view of the kinds of personality structure that facilitate the behaviors schools reward as "high achievement" and the interlocking system of credentials which impede the access of young people who respond in ways the schools condemn to better colleges, it is certainly clear that the schools channel students toward the levels of economic opportunity its staff deem appropriate. Aaron Cicourel and John I. Kitzuse, in their classic study of *The Educational Decision-Makers**, detail this process in action, with many quotations to show what it sounds and feels like. But again, *"Cui bono?"* Who benefits from this? The students who fail certainly do not. Those who succeed gain a competitive advantage, but at great cost to other potentials which the school stultifies as it moulds them into its ap-

*Indianapolis, Bobbs-Merrill. 1963

proved patterns. It has seemed very odd to me for some years now that adults who seem to enjoy worrying about the possible, if undemonstrated, damage that marijuana may do to the mind show no corresponding concern about the demonstrable damage that the schools do; the destruction of the capacity for intimacy in favor of defining relationships to peers as casual and competitive; the loss of capacity to entertain the idea that any economic system other than capitalism and any form of government other than representative democracy might have certain advantages—even moral advantages; the petty cowardice and cheerful surrender of any claim to privacy or dignity when faced by the demands of an intrusive and often vulgar-minded administration. Schools don't do all these things to every student, of course; but they do enough of them to most to make the total damage to the mind attributable to their action greater than marijuana, or even LSD, could conceivably do. But the damage pot does, if any, is antisocial; the damage schools do is the very stuff of socialization.

The question of whom the schools benefit becomes, then, a very complex one. They may be said to benefit society; they benefit students by preparing them to fill the roles available in society and even inducing them to want to fill them and to forget that other roles, and a different kind of society might be possible. But these are rather ambiguous benefits. Society, moreover, is not a unitary organism with particular needs of its own, but an arena in which genuinely conflicting interests contend. A major social function of the school—I believe the major social function of the school—is to take the edge off this conflict by supporting the more populist, anti-intellectual forces of the society and shaking the confidence and breaking the spirit of the more exuberant—which is usually also the more privileged—minority of youth. In this way, certain atavistic, elitist components of our society are rendered ineffective. One must teach the Constitution, but 12 years in school are usually enough to teach young people not to rely on the Bill of Rights; one must "transmit our cultural heritage;" but the minds of the staff and the routines of the school deprive it in transit of authority or power to sustain life.

In this way, the schools have played a very significant role in delaying the kind of polarization which has now occurred in our society, but they have done so by undermining the confidence of our more civilized and nobler youth in their right to their own moral choices or to be guided by their own experience of the values of their social class. Into each child, black or white, rich or poor, schooling implants a chill and permanent automatic reminder that in many respects, for all practical purposes Governor Wallace has already won; his victory over the human spirit has been woven into the social fabric of America, whether he or anyone like him succeeds in claiming that victory or not. It is present in the smug racism of the urban schools; in their dress regulations and preoccupation with sexuality and pornography, their inability to leave anybody alone. The schools, in short, have been the instrumentality through which the middle-classes have thrown their children to the common man as hostages against the possibility that they might become presumptuous. This is a clever means of insuring social stability; for the schools have also been made the custodians of the cultural instruments by which the young might have delivered themselves. To give the police MACE and put schoolteachers in charge of athletics, poetry and literature is a pretty effective way of preventing the emergence of a responsible elite, especially if the young are prevented by law from seeking the meaning of their lives outside the school, and mistrust and social sanctions deny them contact with adults who might respect them on their own terms.

As a system of socialization and control this worked remarkably well as long as the schools' ultimate sanction—the denial of access to economic opportunity through credential control—worked; and it still does for most youth and especially for petit-bourgeois youth. But it has failed for black youth, to whom the school system has not delivered the promised rewards; and it has failed for the most sensitive and creative of the more affluent youth, who are not growing up with a sufficient fear of failure to insure that their self-esteem is totally linked to being defined by school and society as successful. Crash programs to induce black people to accept the school as the instrument of their incorporation into the society and to induce schools to change their technics of instruction to make them more acceptable to black students will, I think, probably succeed. Black people, after all, perceive themselves as excluded and deprived; and will accept inclusion into society if this is offered on terms that are not insulting to them. This, incidentally, is one of the areas in which applications of new instructional technology to bypass the bias of existing school personnel are likely to prove most effective. But it is less likely that the schools can recapture their dissenting or hippy clientele, except by a series of search-and-destroy missions. Not only do these youth reject the rewards and resist the punishments administered by the schools; their humiliation in school is, I am convinced, a part of the public spectacle which the schools are expected to provide the vast and malevolent public which most enthusiastically supports them. It is asking a great deal of liberals—of which, presumably, this Commission is largely composed—to admit that any large group of people is hateful; but it is perfectly obvious—popular response to police action at the Chicago Democratic Convention would have made it so, if it had not been already—that most American adults loathe and fear young people, and get a great deal of satisfaction out of seeing them kept in line and beaten—figuratively or literally—if they get out of line. This is one of the things the schools are hired to do, and efforts to make schools more humane or educationally effective fail for the same reason that efforts to make prisons more humane and rehabilitative fail. It isn't that nobody knows how; we know how very well. It is that this is not what the people who support them really want—or would tolerate—and the people who run the prisons know this full well, and knew it when they chose their profession. Such humaneness as is found in prisons and in schools results less from either enlightened policy or genuine good will than from the empirical fact/that above a certain very high level, constraint and punishment make the place unmanageable. The level of authoritarian constraint that comes to prevail is that thought optimal to control the inmates, satisfy the public, and preserve the self-image of a staff which is at once sentimental, brutal, and insecure. The formal goals of the institution, whether reform or education, have very little to do with the matter at all.

But the parallel between schools and prisons breaks down in one very crucial respect. Society does not really expect prisons to rehabilitate anyone; and is prepared to support a high level of recidivism; it does not expect to recruit any of its leaders from the ranks of former convicts; and when it nevertheless does, as in the case of Eldridge Cleaver or Malcolm X, it is thrown into paroxysms of hostile confusion. One gathers that the prisons failed in not destroying these men. But the business and industrial leadership of the country, though it does not, I think, care very much about educational failure as such— the failure of the schools to educate black children did not, after all, become a serious issue till their parents made it one—does care about preserving the basic institutions of the country and also about preserving the succession. Even today, only a minority of youth are disaffected with society, and with the schools as the official instrument of that society. But that minority includes many—perhaps most—of the kind of young people who would normally come to occupy positions of leadership in this country. Their defection is serious, and is coming to be taken seriously. Schooling may or may not have benefitted them in the past; but it certainly played a major part in setting them off along the path most traveled by. Today, its practices and social climate are among the factors that lead to their defection. And that has made all the difference.

A partial answer to the question, Who benefits from the schools?, is therefore: (1) Persons who seek economic opportunity by acquiring marketable characteristics; (2) Employers who want to hire the kinds of people the schools find acceptable and give desirable credentials to; (3) Those who wish to minimize social conflict by indoctrinating young people from the beginning with the necessity of acquiescing to the demands of "common-man" standards of taste, behavior, and self-expression, regardless of their putative rights and the violence this may do their inner-life and spirit; (4) Parents who do not want their children around the house or cannot afford to have them there, but want to know where they are; and who want to be sure that they will not come to accidental physical harm and that if any adult touches them, it will not be in the act of loving—an occasional formal beating is, under the law of most states, quite acceptable; (5) The vast number of what William Burroughs has called "control addicts" in our society, who want to be sure youth is being kept in line and off the street and taught to respect authority. These, of course, are social functions of education; and since I have not so far taken account of economic factors as such, I have neglected two primarily economic functions of schooling which are probably even more fundamental to the maintenance of our present society than those I have noted.*

One of the most important, and least stressed consequences of compulsory school attendance is that it both keeps young people off the labor market—and the unemployment rate for those under 25 in America is about three times as high as for those over 25— and totally preempts their time in prescribed, unremunerated, labor. Ideologically, this is justified by the presumption that youth is "investing in its future" and that the school is contributing to this investment in lieu of payment. Whether one accepts this explanation as satisfactory is largely a value, rather than an empirical question. In any case, it is clear that, under our kind of capitalist economy, the schools and the armed services, expensive as they are, provide a relatively inexpensive way of disposing of young people and controlling them, as well as of denying them access to ordinary due process for their grievances.

The second of these economic functions has to do with the enormity of the educational enterprise itself. When we ask of the schools *"Cui bono?"* we sometimes forget to include the personnel of the schools themselves in our answer. Yet the educational system is, among other things, an enormous vested interest, as the New York City teachers' strike should have reminded us. On any given day nearly a third of the nation's population is required by law to attend school. There are now some 12,000,000 students in public high schools; and about a million and a half in private, including church-affiliated, secondary schools. There are more than a million elementary school teachers, backed by myriad bureaucracies and sustained by active service staffs. Total public school expenditures for the fiscal year ending June 30, 1967 were 28 billion dollars—about five times as much as in 1950, when enrollments were already a little over half their present size. It is also about twice as much as Vice President Humphrey's estimate of what it would cost to maintain a totally volunteer army and eliminate the draft. He concluded we couldn't afford it.

Liberal democracy is so firmly committed to the idea that public education is unquestionably good for the individual and society that this enormous expansion of the education industry is assumed to be a notable national achievement and an unalloyed blessing. Education does not share with the military its access to unlimited funding—bond issues and tax increases for educational purposes are often quite strongly resisted—but it does share, as no other public venture does, its immunity to popular radical criticism. There is constant complaint, certainly, that the schools are not doing as good a job as they might—and this, presumably, is why this Commission has been appointed. But except—again as with the military—from intellectuals, there is hardly ever a voice raised to suggest that what the schools are doing may be not only poorly done but undesirable, and may violate the interests of quite legitimate minorities in the society—especially those of youth itself—while it serves others; and that increased efficiency and indefinite expansion of the educational enterprise may result in a further loss of diversity and encroachment on civil liberty. Yet, I believe that this is so; and that in exploring the question *"Cui bono?"* I have dealt sufficiently with *"Quo warranto?"* as well. For the mandate under which the schools operate is essentially a conservative mandate; a mandate to keep the place of youth—our last disfranchised minority—in society defined and limited as it is. And what is expected of new instructional technology, surely, is primarily that it keeps them happy enough to prevent

*The economic functions of the school system are fully and insightfully discussed in a recent article by John and Margaret Rowntree, "The Political Economy of American Youth" in OUR GENERATION, 6, 1-2, 1968 (pp. 155-186).

trouble, but not so happy as to arouse the envy and suspicion of their elders; and, above all, that it reach and involve "disadvantaged" children before they abandon the educational system altogether as a proper channel for their aspirations and begin, instead, to aspire toward goals which the educational system does not accept and to develop extramural and possibly antisocial means of achieving them.

There are, it seems to me, many ways in which improved instructional technology might help the Commission to discharge this mandate. But I think it is a bad, or at least a highly suspect mandate. Nevertheless, there are also consequences of the use of improved instructional technology that will, I believe, contribute on balance to making education freer, more humane, and less bound to shabby-genteel norms. These consequences are not sought for their own sake and would not arouse the enthusiasm of school personnel if they were fully anticipated. They are rather in the nature of side-effects. But the side-effects of communications technology, as McLuhan has stressed, are often far more significant than the intended consequences; and this is likely to be as true in school as out. Some of these will, I think, be very desirable. I only hope that it is not unwise to call them explicitly to the attention of so respectable, and liberal, a Commission.

The first of these desirable effects is a greater centralization of resources for curriculum construction, which is likely to have several beneficial consequences—as well as some not so beneficial which in most situations will, I think, be less important. Obviously, the take-over of the preparation of curricular materials by the mass-media from smaller and more parochial publishing firms which are less able to resist the parochialism of the school-systems themselves, will permit a more costly production-job to be done. This will make the new materials slicker, and the new technologies more elaborate—which is not good. But it will also permit the hiring of more skilled people with a higher level of scholarship and ingenuity to work on their preparation in the first place; and these people, though they must ultimately appeal to their institutional clients, are surely less exposed to local but often violent community pressures to narrow or emasculate their materials.

As the newer instructional technologies prevail more and more, the effect on instruction will probably be comparable to the spread of Howard Johnson's restaurants and motels on the general quality of food and lodging available in the country; or of the establishment of flight kitchens for airlines in major airports. The results will never be either as good or as responsive as a first-rate chef or inn-keeper would provide; local variation will be superficial and whimsical if, indeed, it occurs at all; there can be considerable built-in flexibility in what is offered, but no spontaneity. Nevertheless, in most towns with a Ho-Jo's, the food and accommodation are better than could be obtained anywhere else for miles around; and it would usually be unwise for a first-class passenger in a transcontinental airliner to seek equally good food and service—poor as he may be getting aloft—in the drive-in immediately beneath him, even if it *is* very popular with truck-drivers. Ho-Jo's and the airliner have better equipment to work with, both in food preparation and distribution and in cost-accounting; they can deliver a better product per unit of cost. Moreover, they are much less ignorant and slightly less contemptuous of the tradition they work in: Howard Johnson's Beef Bourguignon won't make anybody think of Dijon, but the food technologists who devised it did, I think, have a fair Platonic conception of the real thing and were influenced by it in a civilized direction. You should only have anything as good in a school cafeteria; you better believe it.

The same thing will, I believe, happen with books, films, tapes, extra-sensory irradiations— whatever the medium, the message should be a bit richer; just as network TV, ghastly as it is, is better than what comes on local option time. This will seem a curious statement from a person who favors, as I do, school decentralization. But that is necessary in order to protect the autonomy of the client, which is the first consideration. Decentralization would not, certainly, contribute in the same way to the improvement of the curricular devices and services offered him.

Will this reduce the teacher to the status of a plastic *geisha,* as it has airline stewardesses—

who initially were qualified R.N.s with a quite different conception of their role? It will surely tend in that direction; but is this not also on balance a good thing? Airline stewardesses today come from about the same social class as schoolteachers; they are not notably less well educated; and they do not behave altogether differently. Notice how they handle passengers—especially in the more crowded Y-class section—who don't want to watch the movie on transcontinental flights; observe how readily they summon an officer from the cockpit to deal with a drunken passenger, and how unenthusiastically they greet the demands of an occasional passenger for a little unscheduled diversion, as of the aircraft to Havana—surely one of the most interesting cities in North America at the present time and one which, in the ordinary course of business, they would never get to visit. What keeps stewardesses from becoming oppressive is neither their *elan vital* or their devotion to their clients—both are often obviously limited—but the mutual understanding between the stewardess and her client that her role is actually carefully defined and largely limited to supplying him with pre-processed comforts and services to which his ticket, as a contract, entitles him. Granted a minimal civility, then, her personality really doesn't matter very much; and the occasions when one feels that one is thereby missing something are fewer than those on which one is grateful to be spared. Similarly, if centralized technology limits the scope of the dedicated teacher, it will also limit the effective lethal range of the vulgar-minded martinet.

There is already evidence, indeed, that "teaching machines" prove particularly effective with schizophrenic children who, in the ethnocentric language of the institutions that classify them "cannot relate to other people;" but who must, themselves, surely experience these other people as unbearably threatening or intrusive. We must, to be sure, beware of expecting too much on the strength of observations which may reflect nothing more than the primitive quality of present equipment. It would hardly challenge the art to devise a machine which would respond to wrong answers not by a neutral message but by a painful shock; the unit might even include a photo-electric cell to determine whether or not its pupil was black so that the shock could be diminished or intensified according to the political climate of the school district. Since the introduction of impunitive devices might seriously disrupt the routines of control and lead to the breakdown of law and order, it would perhaps be fruitless even to attempt to sell machines to major urban school districts until these refinements could be incorporated within them. Nevertheless, as of now, seriously disturbed children are less frightened of the machines than they are of teachers; and there must be many more children who, while not so disturbed but that they can relate to school personnel, would find machines more humane and easier to get along with.

The advantages I have attributed to improved educational technology in my discussion so far have been related to the quality of communication which it will help to supply to pupils. But there will be, I think, administrative advantages as well. The engines of contemporary technology are much better at keeping accurate, neat records, than people are; and while such record-keeping adds to their operating costs it does not add to their operating time. For this reason, their widespread introduction into schools will either tend to relieve teachers of their horrible present burden of paperwork or, according to Parkinson's law, require a new rationale for its expansion. While, in any social situation, status factors tend to prevail over technological innovation so that administrators might merely find new kinds of busywork for their staffs, the possibility of eliminating this tedium is still worth taking. A more fundamental administrative advantage of shifting some of the curricular load from teaching staff to programmed devices may be derived from the very casual attitude of Americans to machinery of all kinds. We expect equipment to be quickly obsolescent, and design it for replacement rather than repair. We do not, in short, give it tenure; and can scrap it when it becomes a drag on the enterprise. This is not an irrelevant attraction to a school system.

Most of the arguments I have read for the adoption of advanced instructional technology rest primarily on the expectation that the new media will permit the curriculum to be enriched by bringing a wider range of phenomena into the classroom and help the school to transcend its boundaries and its students to transcend their provincialism and limited social and geographical mobility—especially if they are "culturally disadvantaged." The new technology is expected, that is, to give them broader and higher horizons. I doubt this very much. It is more likely to add to their passivity by making even more of their experience of life either into a show that one watches or a game that one plays with a friendly computer. The life of the American masses is like that already in relation to the events that affect it; there must be very widespread resentment that the sponsor of our political assassinations, if there is one, has not managed to schedule these events more regularly, and on prime evening time; so that one might plan one's viewing. Moreover, McLuhan is right; the medium, not its content, is the message. There is no such thing as being present at an event through the medium of TV though there are many events to which TV gives an observer more intimate access than he could gain by being present. What one learns, instead, is that intimacy can be—and is at best—vicarious. One of the many comforts that Truman Capote must have afforded to poor Richard Hickok and Perry Smith during their last hours was the implication—inescapable from the very nature of his participation in social reality—that what they were really doing was working on a script for a movie the young men had begun, which they would all see together later.

There are severe limits, moreover—though educators are, as a profession, reluctant to acknowledge them—on the degree to which education, however technically ingenious, can impinge on the experience of persons who find it cognitively dissonant, whether because its idiom or its format is inappropriate to persons of their social class, or for more idiosyncratic reasons. Reality, itself, does not work much better. Foreign travel, notoriously, does not broaden the horizons of soldiers; it usually antagonizes them by showing them that the world is even more full of gooks than they had supposed, all of whom, in President Johnson's deathless phrase, "want what we've got; and we aren't gonna give it to 'em!" So I am not going to rest any claim for the desirability of improved instructional technology on the imputation that it offers wider communication. I'm not so sure; and, in any case, the curriculum of the school has always seemed to me largely the pretext on which students were obliged to submit to its routines, which are the real educative experience; and their function is not benign. The fundamental function of the schools is not to liberate, but to extinguish alternatives to socialization; and a lively, vital, probing curriculum would do this less effectively. From the point of view of a conservative, mass society, the ideal school functions like a domineering and unattractive wife who *derives* her authority from her stupidity; who would never acknowledge that she even comprehended that she might be abandoned if she did not become more loving—or at least more tactful; and who punished infidelity by suspension of the dubious privileges of the bedchamber but never—no, never—by divorce. Its relationship to the evolving potential of its students is, roughly, that of Lucy to the evolving potential of Charlie Brown.

Technological improvement in education cannot induce school authorities to do a better job than they want to do, though it may enable them to do their present job more effectively, for it is concerned with means, not ends. For this reason, it is to be feared. Yet, it is also a source of hope for administrative and structural change which will alter the locus of decision and simply by-pass the dingiest and most pettily provincial forces that affect curriculum.

32.
Educational Philosophy
And Educational Technology

by GLEN HEATHERS
Prof. of Educational Research
Learning Research & Development
Center
University of Pittsburgh

Educational philosophy is concerned mainly with the values education has, could have, or ought to have, for individuals and for society. Educational technology is concerned chiefly with the rational means whereby valued educational outcomes are, or could be, achieved. Viewed this simply, philosophy and technology have an essential relationship; the former specifies the goals education can strive toward while the latter provides means for reaching them. In practice, this statement of relationship is over-simple. Technology (in the form of research methodologies) can be useful in selecting educational values and even in evaluating values through searching out their interrelationships. Also, educational technology can determine in part the values toward which education is directed through making possible the accomplishment of certain goals. As Broudy states it, ". . . scientifically based technology is the most dynamic single factor in determining the scope of our possible duty . . . because it changes the domain of what we *can* do, out of which emerges the domain of what we *ought* to do."[1] He holds that "the abatement of ignorance" is our obligation today since we now have the power to accomplish it. A final sort of relationship between philosophy and technology in education is that they can proceed independently. This very often is the case, technology being put to use without examining even the potential it holds for realizing designated educational outcomes.

Most educators identify "the new educational technology" with machines and machine-linked learning programs. Many spokesmen on education distrust bringing machines into the schools, believing that their greatest effects will be to dehumanize instruction in the interest of efficiency. They hold this belief despite daily evidences that technological developments bear no fixed relationships to valued outcomes and that it is the uses made of technologies that determine their value relevancies. A laser beam can become a death ray or a surgical tool. Television can be used to advertise cigarettes and extol violence or to fight pollution and model racial tolerance. It is not machines that merit distrust, but the people who use machines, whether in the schools or elsewhere. A worthy aim is for educators to learn to use instructional machines to good purpose, and to teach their students to control and exploit machines in ways that benefit them and their fellows.

The most fundamental components of "the new educational technology" do not have to do with machines. Rather, they involve applications of basic scientific-technological methodologies to education. It is the impact of these methodologies, assisted by electronic computers, that seems certain to revolutionize education. These methods have developed largely outside education. Presently they are being put to use in devising, producing, and evaluating educational innovations. The methodologies we refer to include scientific methods of inquiry; research-and-development strategies and procedures; systems approaches; operations research; training research; cost/efficiency accounting; and policy research. It is significant that these powerful intellectual tools are being adapted for use in education mainly by persons trained in the behavioral or social sciences, rather than by professional educators. For example, the important volume, *Training Research and Education,* was edited by a psychologist, Robert Glaser, and nearly all of its chapter authors received their training and experience outside the field of education.[2]

Scientific-technological methods, as employed within education, promise to transform virtually every aspect of instruction. We can look to policy research for powerful analyses of educational aims as they relate to the nature and purposes of individuals and society. We can expect from behavioral and social science the development of a theory of instruction based on research in individual development involving learning, perceiving, thinking, feeling, motivation, personality, and social behavior. Research-and-development strategies, systems approaches, and training research can provide instructional programs, materials, equipment, and staff that implement a research-derived theory of instruction and guide students toward goals that have been identified and justified by educational philosophers, policy researchers, and others.

Scientific-Technological Society: A Challenge to Educators

Interpreters and evaluators of today's society are in general agreement on its salient features and their probable projections into the future. The slogan terms all are familiar: mass production, mass communications, automation, efficiency, impersonality, bureaucracy, complexity, rapid change, and unpredictability. The dynamic basis for creating this society has been the systematic and pervasive use of scientific rationalism. James E. Russell summarizes the process in these words: "There is a change in the role of the mind in human affairs, in the role of the rational . . . The processes involved are those of rational inquiry and empirical validation, the harnessing through logic and evidence of the abilities to recall and imagine, to classify and generalize, to evaluate and compare, to analyze and synthesize, to deduce and infer." [3]

Archibald MacLeish finds the essential value commitment of scientific society in the initial application of nuclear power. "After Hiroshima it was obvious that the loyalty of science was not to humanity but to truth—its own truth—and that the law of science was not the law of the good—what humanity thinks of as good, meaning moral, decent, human—but the law of the possible." [4]

C. Wright Mills is equally dubious about the human implications of science and technology. "Science, it turns out, is not a technological Second Coming. That its techniques and its rationality are given a central place in a society does not mean that men live reasonably and without myth, fraud, and superstition . . . The mass distribution of historic culture may not lift the level of cultural sensibility, but rather merely banalize it—and compete mightily with the chance for creative innovation. A high level of bureaucratic rationality and of technology does not mean a high level of either individual or social intelligence." [5]

I. A. Richards identifies the computer as the greatest force for good or evil in technology's armamentarium. "All the foregoing epochal steps may be regarded as extensions of familiar specific capabilities; steam replaced and transcended men's and horses' muscular energy as photography and telephony surpassed and extended the range of our distance receptors. So, more widely, did radio and television. But the offerings of the computer go beyond all such services; they extend the resources of the central nervous system itself. The computer can supply an inexhaustible slave service for whatever we have the wits to instruct it to do. Suddenly, we have a Caliban-Ariel executive that will achieve for us all that we, in our wisdom or folly, can contrive to tell it how to handle."

Richards further points the moral: "Someone will reply that computers by taking immense intellectual burdens off our shoulders, will free us for precisely these tasks of ultimate choice, these legislative acts. We may hope so, while fearing that they will not. Almost all of us are products of the assistance we can accept. Equally, we are potential victims of those who, for whatever motives, would like to run things for us. Like all power sources, the computer is not going to lessen our responsibilities but to increase them." [6]

The massive and rapid changes in knowledge, technologies, and social forms that characterize society today have vital implications for the individual as a worker, citizen, and person. With respect to vocational requirements, the point made by nearly every commentator is the paradoxical one that increasing automation tends to eliminate routine jobs and to retain or create jobs requiring communication skills, planning ability, and problem-solving competencies. Further, technological advances occasion frequent changes in job requirements, placing demands on the worker to keep his knowledge of his job up-to-date or to undertake training for a new type of job. Gow and co-authors sum it up: "The premium is, therefore, not on skills per se, but on the capacity to acquire skills, to modify them, and perhaps to begin again. Adaptability and flexibility are the key qualities demanded of today's worker." [7]

Broudy is one social analyst who questions whether, in the main, automation will place higher intellectual demands on the worker. He reasons that "although it has been argued that automation will necessitate large numbers of trained personnel within the labor force, it is not inconceivable that by splitting up jobs that now require a fairly high order of formal training, the amount of such training will be so reduced that it can be learned by apprenticeship or in relatively short periods of guided practice. In any event, there seems to be no foreseeable future when a substantial proportion of our population cannot get by quite well with relatively little effort of body, mind, or will." [8]

Very likely both viewpoints—Broudy's and the more usual one—share the truth concerning automation and job requirements. In this connection, it is of interest that Prime Minister Trudeau of Canada finds political capital in a presumed relationship between changing society and changing job requirements at top governmental levels. In a recent interview, he reported himself to be future-oriented. "It's one of the arguments I used in the leadership campaign, when they said, 'You don't have experience, how can you aspire to be a Prime Minister?' My answer was, Well, in the rapidly changing world, the experience isn't always very useful. The data are so different from one year to the next that what you learned in a previous context can hamstring you." [9]

Komoski proposes that there has very recently occurred in America a "radical *shift . . . from a primarily goods-producing economy* to the first *predominantly service-rendering economy.*" One indication of this is what Komoski terms a change from standardization to "optionization." He notes that "technology is able to provide seemingly endless arrays of goods and services that cater to individual needs and tastes of every variety." [10] This aspect of a service-rendering economy does not directly imply any changes in job requirements since it is automation that permits the great variety of products. A more fundamental point is that, as more jobs in the production and distribution of goods become automated, an increasing proportion of workers will find themselves engaged in service occupations. Komoski notes that, among such occupations, education is the largest. The clear implication is that skills in human relations and communication will become increasingly important in our economy.

An aspect of employment in bureaucratic organizations concerns job satisfaction and morale. As Luther Evans has pointed out, automation rather precisely regulates the individual by preplanning in detail what he does on the job and what human relationships are permissible there.[11] Broudy, however, offers a safety valve to this predicament. "The very system that has reduced the individual's freedom occupationally may help to free him from it psychologically. With automation and new forms of power, earning a living may well become a peripheral rather than a central principle of life and one's key significance may not be sought there." He goes on to suggest that the critical question with a 20-hour work week is whether the worker is prepared to spend the other 20 hours as "an authentic individual." [12]

A major product of science and technology has been a revolution in agriculture that has been the chief factor in the migration of millions from rural areas into the cities. The fact that most of these migrants lack the education and training required to obtain employment in urban society has imposed severe strains on the economic, political, and social components of our society. Frank Jennings doubts that these strains can be relieved except by bringing all of our resources to bear on them. "The forces that are roiling in our cities cannot be harnessed by education alone . . . It is possible that the new critical mass will blow down all the school walls and let the whole of urban society into the classroom. Perhaps the cities themselves must be re-created as giant learning centers." [13]

The effects of the scientific-technological revolution are as pervasive and powerful in the political and social aspects of society as in the economic. These areas too are characterized by mass organization, intense pressures toward conformity to group norms, rapid change, and great uncertainty. Under these circumstances, individuality tends to be stifled and choices reduced to a few group-sanctioned alternatives. Yet, if people are to retain, or regain, control of society, this must occur through the exercise of social influence and political power. Broudy has stated well what must occur if citizens are to control modern society: "The alternatives to tyranny by experts or mindless nose counting in such a society is political education for the masses. Such education requires certain kinds of knowledge, learning skills, and skills of deliberation and imagination." [14]

The impact of modern society on the individual goes beyond the changes it imposes on his economic, political, and social roles. It profoundly influences his view of his world and of himself. Alvin Toffler has sought to express the effect of cataclysmic change on the individual with the term "future shock." He writes: "We have encountered the future so rapidly and with such violent changes in the ordered and familiar patterns of our way of life that we are suffering . . . the dizzying disorientation brought on by the premature arrival of the future." [15] Today's future in America is the stalemated war in Vietnam; the imminence of racial warfare; civil disobedience and police brutality; the struggle of cities for economic and social survival; inflation coupled with rapidly-rising taxes; strikes by students, teachers, firemen, and policemen; and the ever-present monsters and bugaboos of the Cold War. In such a world, there looks to be no counter against onrushing events, and no hiding place from them. One becomes an observer of instant history and asks, not what he can or should do, but merely, "What happens next?"

Gow, Holzner, and Pendleton offer a telling analysis of the thinking man's predicament today. He must accept change as the rule while surrendering the belief that progress is the natural trend of human society. He "feels that progress, if it is to occur, has to be fashioned—and that it is, at best, precarious. . . . He orients himself to probabilities, not certainties, thus facing up to the fact that man is compelled to make responsible decisions in the face of uncertainty. . . . He requires a high level of tolerance for uncertainty and the ability to overcome through action the anxiety arising in situations of crises; and he is often fearful lest these demands prove too much for him and his fellow-men."

These analysts see modern man as highly reflective, trying to cope with uncertainty through searching out the motives underlying his and others' actions. They find some positive features of the view man is taking of himself and his world. A "new individualism has emerged through the concern for the responsibility of society to its members and of the citizen to his state. . . . This view of individualism is reflected in the movement to provide equal opportunities for all children, to overcome discrimination, and to build a new conception of the state as the protector of the individual." [16]

The most telling evidence today for individualism linked with social purpose is found in the world-wide revolt of youth against the impositions of adult society coupled with the readiness young people are showing to commit themselves to the welfare of people less fortunate than themselves. While many youths have joined the hippies, others have joined the Peace Corps, fought for civil rights for Negroes, and campaigned with Eugene Mc-Carthy for what they and he believe to be a better world.

In sum, what challenges to educators does the automated society present? *In the economic realm,* there is an increasing demand for workers possessing competencies in problem solving and human relations, and for people who are ready to relearn their jobs or prepare for different jobs. Also, education must reach the millions in our Appalachias and Harlems who presently are not being equipped to hold jobs in urban, industrial society.

In the political sphere, general education is needed to equip all our citizens for responsible decision-making. The alternative is the abrogation of democracy through permitting control of our society by whatever special-interest group can seize power—Fascists, technocrats, generals, unions, or corporations. Citizens in a democracy must have the autonomy and wisdom to persuade themselves while resisting the persuaders.

In the social realm, the increasing need is for the attitudes and skills required for effective interpersonal and intergroup relations. Our society is split into warring camps that are both unprepared and disinclined to find common purposes through negotiation. Ways must be found to break through the communication barriers separating young and old, Black and White, affluent and poor. Basic education for social living is needed by children, youth, and adults equally.

In the personal sphere, education needs to foster the development of individuality that can withstand societal pressures toward becoming what Mills has labeled The Cheerful Robot. The individual needs to be able to tolerate or cope with the complexities, contradictions, and uncertainties of mass society. He should be enabled to achieve personal satisfactions and develop meaningful human relationships despite the impersonal qualities of automation. And, since personal man provides the foundation for social man, the individual needs to learn empathy, tolerance, and the will to serve others as well as himself. The increased leisure individuals will have as a product of automation offers the opportunity, as Broudy puts it, to choose between "self-cultivation" and "distraction or boredom." Education for productive and enjoyable uses of leisure becomes a critical requirement since few people spontaneously learn such things.

Educational Aims for Today's World

Spokesmen within and outside education have brought forward a set of educational aims—or themes—that reflect their conceptions of modern society and of the education required for membership within it. These themes, on the face of them, do not bear the stamp of technology. Indeed, they appear to be a revival, a re-assertion, a rethinking of the philosophy of education presented by John Dewey. They mirror his scientific rationalism, his pragmatism, his emphasis on learning as experiencing and reflecting on one's experiences, and his stress on education for social living. These aims focus on the development of the individual learner, emphasizing his individuality, autonomy, and competence. They speak for the free, inner-directed person whose qualities and powers express adaptability rather than adaptation, decision-making rather than passive accommodation, openness to new learnings rather than rigid, unthinking adherence to accustomed views and familiar ways. In this section, these educational aims will be listed and characterized. In the following section, they will be viewed as they relate to the new educational technology. The reader should note that, while each of the themes presented below has numerous exponents in the literature, this list of eight is the writer's own and reflects his perceptions and biases.

Theme 1: Ideas   Today's curriculum innovators are generally agreed that instruction in the schools and colleges must shift from a predominant concern with teaching information within the subject-matter disciplines to a focus on teaching a command of powerful, general ideas that provide the bases for ordering, interpreting, and predicting phenomena within the domain covered by a discipline. Schwab has labeled this orientation as that of teaching the "structure" of a discipline.[17] Learning the structure of ideas within a discipline— concepts, principles, theoretical models—is an economical and therefore practical approach, considering that the student cannot possibly "cover the facts" of any field of knowledge, and considering that facts have little use—other than in information-please programs— except as they are employed in developing or applying ideas. This is true in regard to all students in all curricular areas. Slow learners even more than gifted students need to be taken off a factual diet since, unlike the gifted, they have very limited powers themselves to organize facts and draw ideas from them.

Theme 2: Inquiry   It is the fashion today among curriculum writers in the areas of natural science and social science to place emphasis above all on teaching the "methods of inquiry" employed by scientists and scholars in the respective disciplines. In the area of mathematics, the fashion is to speak of "learning by discovery." In the humanities and the arts, the favored term is "creativity." It is this writer's preference to use inquiry as the general term for competencies in problem-solving or creative production. In this usage, inquiry covers the intellectual operations and procedures a person uses in working toward the solution of any sort of academic or practical problem. By "problem" is meant more than a difficulty to be overcome. Also, it refers to any purpose or task calling upon the individual to work out a solution.

As was true of John Dewey, many educational leaders today believe that the most important function of education is to develop the individual's capabilities in inquiry toward the purpose of enabling him to function as an autonomous problem-solver in his various life roles, or to be an effective participant in group problem-solving. Clearly, inquiry-centered education is relevant to a society where knowledge and the uses of knowledge are changing with great rapidity. (Prime Minister Trudeau might better have claimed competencies in inquiry than professing as he did the lack of knowledge that might hamstring him.) If education is to prepare the individual adequately to confront life's problems, it must enable him to inquire about the consequences of actions and events—their values— since many decisions he makes in his roles as student, worker, citizen, community member, family member, or private person involve questions of value.

Theme 3: Independent Learning   Closely related to inquiry is student self-direction in acquiring and using knowledge or skills. The most fundamental reason for teaching the student to learn independently is that, throughout his life, his capabilities of expressing individuality in his choices and actions will be measured by his competencies in self-directed uses of his mind. A second reason for stressing self-direction in the school program is that individualized instruction on a grand scale becomes possible only when the majority of students, most of the time at school, can proceed with their studies without immediate help from their teachers.

There are two distinct ways in which student self-direction can occur within the school program. One involves the use of learning programs that provide the student with sufficient directions that he can proceed without the teacher's help. The second, and educationally the more fundamental, involves the student in planning and conducting his learning activities, that is, in programming his own learning.

A dramatic and important new viewpoint is that all students, not merely "the gifted," can acquire and use competencies in self-directed learning. This is a bold extension of the democratic faith. It is supported by mounting evidence that nearly all students can learn to guide their learning, and prefer to do so, when assigned tasks are made appropriate and vital.

Theme 4: Individualized Instruction   Individualizing instruction is the most nearly universal watchword and rallying cry among those who favor innovations in the schools. Programs offering new approaches to individualization are viewed with the most wide-spread interest. The priority assigned to this theme has several reasons. Child development research has increasingly stressed the magnitude and importance of individual differences. Various new programs have made it appear feasible to adapt instruction to the individual student better than previously. The "new humanism" previously mentioned encourages greater attention to the individual. Also, reactions of intellectuals against automation have favored devoting special attention to enhancing individuality.

The prevailing conception of individualization is that it consists either of independent study or a tutorial relation between the student and his teacher. A more general definition is needed, such as the following: *Individualized instruction consists of designing and conducting with each student programs of studies that are tailor-made to fit his learning needs and his characteristics as a learner.* Note that this definition requires starting with the individual, not the group, in planning what to teach. Group teaching is not ruled out since it is proper and desirable to assemble and teach students as a group whenever, at the same time, two or more students are ready to study the same task together with group presentation or discussion.

Theme 5: Education for Excellence   The view is gaining currency that instruction with each student should be conducted on the working assumption that he will master what he studies. The traditional view, aided and abetted by psychologists and test-makers, was that the quality of students' performance on any task should range according to the normal distribution curve. The emerging view is that mastery is a feasible standard with all students provided that each student is assigned tasks he is capable of accomplishing, and provided that he is offered the materials, the time, and the help he needs for success. Obviously, employing the mastery criterion throughout the school depends on individualized instruction that permits adapting the learning task, materials and methods, and rate of advancement to the student.

The value bases for employing a mastery criterion universally in education are readily found. John Gardner in *Excellence* has presented a forceful account of why individual well-being and the general welfare depend on everyone's doing his job well.[18] Bloom has outlined in considerable detail the implications mastery has for the student's progress at school and for his self-concept.[19] Effectively employed, a mastery criterion would largely eliminate the need for remedial instruction. Employed with "slow learners" and "the educationally disadvantaged," it would prepare these millions to achieve much greater effectiveness as workers, citizens, and persons. Employed universally, it would provide that the rank and file of citizens possessed greater competencies for making and implementing responsible decisions in their various life roles. The result should be a much higher probability than now that our citizenry would be able to cope successfully with the problems and challenges of technological society.

Theme 6: Educating Children of Poverty   The crises in the cities and the civil rights movement have given rise to vigorous programs designed to overcome the educational disadvantages suffered by ghetto children, children in poverty areas such as Appalachia and the rural South, and Negro children generally. Representative programs are Head Start, Follow Through, Higher Horizons, and the Job Corps. A conceptual basis for these programs is the working assumption that the educational deficits associated with an unfavorable environment can be removed by instruction that is especially designed to overcome "perceptual deficit," limited vocabulary, and low motivation to learn.

Theme 7: Education for Personal Development   This theme is clearly implied in the writings of many analysts of educational needs for today's world. Francis Chase, for example, gives major attention to this theme in a discussion entitled "The Ends of Education Reconsidered." Thus, he proposes that ". . . openness to self, openness to new experience, and autonomy rooted in this dual openness claim a place among the ends of education for reasons of self-fulfilment as well as because they underlie the capacity to make intelligent choices and assume responsibility in situations in which knowledge is incomplete and the consequences of choices are unclear." [20] Chase gives attention also to such aims as choosing one's life purposes, developing a personal style of behavior, and gaining capacities to respond to phenomena and relationships with understanding, appreciation, and appropriate action. Writers also have stressed the importance of developing tolerance for ambiguity, flexibility, and the willingness to take psychic risks. Recently, increased attention has been given to the development of a positive self-concept, a sense of adequacy and personal worth.

Despite the evident importance of education for personal growth, the school program usually has made few provisions for it. Instruction has been focused predominantly on cognitive learning. The recent publication of a taxonomy of educational goals in "the affective domain" has encouraged educators to give greater attention to the development of attitudes, interests, and values. In the main, however, today's educational reformers are inclined to reason that sound personal growth can best be fostered at school through developing the student's competencies in inquiry and self-direction, and through calling upon him to master his learning tasks. Individualized instruction also is seen as a way of fostering the development of individuality. Indeed, some educators use the term "personalized instruction" to give emphasis to their concern for personal growth at school.

Theme 8: Education for Social Living   This theme, like the preceding one, has received strong emphasis in the analyses made of the education required for living in modern society. It usually has not held a prominent place in the school's curriculum. A reason for expecting it to receive more attention in the near future is the fact that schools in the cities are coming into closer relations with their communities. Steps taken to decentralize the public school system of New York City offer a dramatic example of this trend. Another reason for expecting increased attention to social education is the sharpened concern about racial prejudice and intergroup relations brought about by the civil rights movement.

These eight sorts of educational values by no means exhaust the list of educational aims that have been recommended as important in preparing the student for his world. They do, however, appear to this writer to include the major purposes that have been advanced by educational spokesmen. We turn now to examine how these themes are related to the capacities and uses of educational technology.

Educational Technology and Educational Values

If education were a fully rational enterprise, one would find educators taking the initiative in searching out ways to use new technologies and technological devices to foster, directly or indirectly, the realization of designated educational aims. What usually happens, though, is that the initiative comes from someone representing the new technology who asks how one can put this device, or this methodology, to work in the schools. Frequently the adapter of the technology to education does a good job of relating means to chosen ends, but most often his concern is only directed toward those ends that can most readily be served by the technology at hand. And most often some important educational aims go begging because neither the schoolman nor the technologist has them in mind.

In this examination of relations between technological means and educational ends, we shall consider both what uses are now being made of technology and what further uses lie within the capabilities of the available technologies. It is convenient to organize this means-ends analysis according to the eight themes considered in the previous section, beginning with individualized instruction.

Technology and Individualization Individualized instruction is the educational aim that today is receiving more attention from both educators and laymen than any other. The chief reason is that a number of advanced programs in individualized instruction are test- ing the potentialities of recent developments in technology. Many people are optimistic about the practicality of individualization on a grand scale, having seen the progress made in these new programs. Suppes, the director of one of the individualized programs employing an electronic computer, expressed this judgment: "It is not too much to claim that for the first time since public education for everyone became a major goal of our society, individualized instruction at a genuinely deep level is now a feasible goal." [21]

Suppes's judgment may well be correct, even though he realizes that it will be some years before computer-assisted instruction can engage the student in a true dialogue rather than merely offering drill-and-practice, or tutoring, in skills, concepts, and principles. The most important question is not whether some instruction can be tailor-made for the learner, but *what* instruction can be individualized in this way. To date, individualized programs usually have not gone beyond the skill learnings in reading, spelling, and arith- metic. These learnings are important and individualizing them to the degree already realized is a major achievement.

Programmed instruction and computerized instruction appear to have some inherent limitations that will prevent them from being used to individualize education "at a gen- uinely deep level." True, as Hovland has explained, computer programs can simulate some varieties of thinking. [22] But Broudy observes that the computer is unable to simulate "molar problem solving" that involves "the recognition of problems, making judgments of relevance, formulating and assaying hypotheses, and choosing some form of com- mitment. . . ." [23] And Chase has noted that no one has been able to program such qualities as "psychic risk-taking," "openness to new learnings," or "deferment of im- mediate gratification for long-range benefits." [24] Obviously, computers have limitations with respect to learning personal and social qualities. Further, they cannot accommodate a high degree of student self-direction, nor can they teach the student to apply what he has learned in situations away from the computer terminal.

It is probable that the most critical contribution of the computer for individualization will be its uses in the management of learning. Computers have immense capacities for recording, storing, analyzing, and delivering data. Individualized instruction, whereby each student works on tasks that are designed especially for him, demands uses of data in diagnosing, planning, and assessing that far exceed the capacities of the unaided teacher who ordinarily is responsible for 25 or more students at one time. When we learn what data are needed, and how to gather, interpret, and use these data, computerized manage- ment systems can permit truly individualized instruction on a massive scale.

Aside from programmed instruction and computers, numerous advances in educational technology facilitate individualization through offering the student a greater variety of routes toward gaining knowledge or skills. This means that a student is more apt to find an avenue to learning that is both effective and suited to his "learning style." Audiotapes, videotapes, film loops, and dial selection systems illustrate such technological resources. Closed circuit TV, on the other hand, tends to work against individualization since it usually is employed for group teaching.

Technology and Independent Learning Programmed instruction, with or without the use of machines, enables the rank and file of students to proceed with learning tasks on an independent basis and thereby makes individualized instruction feasible. However, programmed instruction does not teach competencies in self-direction and succeeds with most students only because it provides very explicit directions for each step in the learning task. The more fundamental basis for independent learning, hence for individualization, is for the student to learn and use competencies in programming his own learning. This requires that he break free from student-proof learning programs. Such programs, however, are of great value in teaching reading and other skills that provide the student access to the knowledge he requires. One problem area with programmed instruction is that, while you can lead the student to a learning situation, you can't make him think while he is there. Many students, low on motivation or lacking habits of following directions closely, are not successful with programmed instruction.

Technology in Teaching Ideas and Inquiry   There is no question that educational technology can be used effectively to present models of theory and inquiry, and to practice the student in theorizing or in planning, conducting, and assessing certain forms of inquiry. Television has been used to stimulate inquiry and to provide the student with data needed to conduct inquiries. Computer simulation can be employed to individualize learning of theory and inquiry methods. One of the most imaginative uses of programmed instruction is Crutchfield's approach to teaching competencies in productive thinking to children in elementary school. He has developed a sequence of 16 programmed booklets, each working out the solution to a mystery. Students working through the booklets on an individual basis are led to participate actively in solving the mysteries through framing their own hypotheses and testing them against the evidence.[25]

Instructional technology involving programmed learning obviously has its limitations for teaching theory and inquiry. To think creatively and to behave as an effective inquirer, the student must become independent of programs prepared by others. Of course, it often will happen that a student will need to use a computer or other technological aids in conducting problem-solving tasks.

Achieving Excellence Through Technology   Programmed instruction has shown that it is possible for nearly all students to master learning tasks—provided the student has the prerequisite knowledge and provided the learning program is carefully constructed to lead the student step-by-step through the task while offering knowledge of results immediately after each step. Such learning programs in the basic skill areas, when they have become fully developed and widely disseminated, can result in a level of literacy much above that yet achieved. They can produce a nation of people who possess the fundamental competencies in language and mathematics that are required for many types of decision making in modern societies. Certainly this is an essential starting point for bringing science and technology under the control of our citizens and for ensuring that technology is used in their interest.

Mastery of basic intellectual skills is only one area of education where excellence is needed. There is the danger that more complex forms of intellectual activity, since they are hard to program and their attainment hard to measure, will not be brought under sufficient instructional control to employ mastery criteria. What is needed is to go beyond present technologies and develop educational counseling to a level where each student is guided toward excellence in the conduct of various sorts of problem solving, and toward achieving personal-social effectiveness in performing his several life roles.

Technology in Educating the Poor   While technology has been accused of dehumanizing education, some of its evidently human uses have been made in programs for children who come from unfavorable environments. Ghetto children have responded frequently to instruction in reading that employs the "talking typewriter" when other approaches have failed to reach them. Programs of early-childhood education have been designed to establish basic perceptual and cognitive skills that underlie reading and mathematics. "Contingency management" has been employed with ghetto children to reinforce behaviors that help them adjust to school and to learn at school. In short, technology has proven of notable value in gaining educational access to children who were unresponsive to usual instructional approaches. Programmed instruction, including that offered via computer, promises also to provide basic education to many millions of youth and adults in our country who otherwise would not have access to such schooling.

Technology in Education for Personal and Social Living   It should occasion no surprise that technology has had little application in the schools toward fostering personal and social growth. The curriculum in elementary and secondary schools, and in colleges likewise, gives little systematic attention to these areas of development. Most educators would say that instructional technology has relatively limited applicability to these educational aims, though they probably would concede that instructional television can be useful in modeling desired personal characteristics and social behaviors.

It was noted earlier that technology as applied in individualizing or "personalizing" instruction, in fostering self-direction and inquiry, and in promoting the mastery of learning tasks, has important implications for personal growth. Recently, academic games such as those described by Coleman have been used in simulating economic, political, and social problems, teaching students singly or in groups to inquire within these areas. The implications of these games for developing social role behaviors and attitudes are evident.[26]

Probably the most significant uses of educational technology in respect to developing personal and social behavior will occur through the uses of computers in educational counseling, following perhaps the approach outlined by Cogswell in which the computer program simulates actual counseling interviews.[27] Another use of computers for this sort of purpose is that of storing, analyzing, and retrieving data that the student's educational counselors can employ in planning, conducting, and assessing learning activities directed toward personal-social growth. In this type of usage, it is reasonable to expect that computer management can permit effective individualized instruction in an important area that has resisted definition and control within educational programs up to this point.

Summary Assessment on Values and Technology in Education   In perspective, what educational values are being promoted through uses of the new educational technology? The answer must be in terms of directions, trends, and implications since technological developments presently are having only scattered influences on teaching in elementary and secondary schools, and virtually no influences on college teaching.

The most general uses of technology in education concern what Broudy terms "the abatement of ignorance." Programmed instruction generally, and computer-assisted instruction particularly, have the potential for achieving universal literacy in our society, reaching people of all ages and circumstances, in and out of school, with individualized instruction that ensures mastery of the basic skills in language and mathematics. Further research-and-development is needed to provide the required methods, materials, and equipment, and massive dissemination approaches are needed to give everyone access to the new instructional programs. The critical point is that technology in the forms of new media and methodologies is making universal literacy within our reach.

Thus far, the uses of technology in education have given only limited attention to developing students' competencies in independent learning and inquiry, or to developing those personal-social qualities and competencies that characterize the inner-directed yet socially-responsible individual. In other words, the applications of technology in education are mainly directed toward providing everyone with basic intellectual tools without offering instruction in how to use them.

Probably this focus on tools rather than their uses is due to the preference today's educational technologists have shown for the precise control of learning through programmed instruction. For this, behavioral objectives—the more specific and concrete, the better—are required. We need other technologists, oriented toward fostering inquiry and personal-social growth, who will give their attention to developing instruction in these directions. Such instruction would include educational guidance and probably would employ computer management of the extensive data required about each student. Also, this instruction probably would use television, films, and computer simulation to present issues, provide data, and model solutions. Its emphasis, as with counseling generally, would be on developing the student's competencies in choosing ends and means, and in acting upon those choices.

Is instructional technology now changing the educational values that are expressed in school programs? The general answer to this question is "No," since technology is focusing on the same learning goals that schools usually have emphasized, that is, concepts and skills.

Thus far, developments in educational technology have given little attention to the humanities, the arts, and the sciences, and instruction in these areas usually is conducted without significant change even in schools where new technology is being used in teaching reading and mathematics. If today's educational technologists were to move into these other areas, they might try to shift the emphasis more strongly toward teaching concepts and skills in these subjects since they know best how to program these types of goals. The greater probability, however, is that efforts to engineer instruction in an area such as social science will begin with identifying as goals the teaching of theory, inquiry methods, and social attitudes and values. The problem then will be to develop and employ technological approaches that are relevant to these goals. Television, films, academic games, and computer simulation of inquiry about social issues are examples of approaches that already have been applied on occasion to instruction in social science. In sum, we can expect that instructional technology will be addressed to the same types of learning goals that educators long have espoused. The difference will be that technology can greatly improve their accomplishment and make their attainment more nearly universal.

Strategies for Optimizing the Uses of Technology in Education

The technological capabilities are at hand to create a genuine revolution in instruction. To accomplish this, there must be a more effective and better coordinated application of scientific-technological methods together with use of computers and other media. A total "systems approach" is required that begins with decisions about the educational aims that should be pursued, continues with research-and-development procedures for designing, producing, and assessing instructional programs directed toward the designated aims, and follows through with massive approaches to implementing the innovative programs. Supporting this total approach and coordinated with it must be strategic research in behavioral and social science, projects to engineer applications of new media to education, and programs to enlist public support for the full effort. Since we can assume that this country will not choose to establish a Manhattan Project encompassing all components of the approach, a major determinant of its success must be a high degree of communication among those who are responsible for the various components in order that they can coordinate their efforts.

Research on Educational Values Usually it is assumed that the aims of education are identified, studied, and justified by educational philosophers, while state departments of education, local school boards, and administrators of school systems decide which educational aims a school system shall pursue. These routes toward determining educational aims are too casual, too unsystematic, to ensure that education will be suited to the needs of individuals and society, today and in the future. Henry Dyer believes that most philosophers have contributed little since World War II to the value question, concentrating instead on "analyzing the absurdity of trying to specify educational goals." [28] Certainly school board members and local school administrators have little expertise in determining relationships between educational aims and individual or societal welfare in today's world.

Marvin Adelson points up the great importance today of making the right decisions about educational aims. He writes: "Many educators agree that *education is experiencing a value crisis from which it may emerge as a very different institution.* Since it is such a central, formative influence on the *character of the society, much of the future of the country and of the world depends upon the outcome.*" [29] MacLeish quotes Rene Dubos on a similar point: "We must not ask where science and technology are taking us, but rather how we can manage science and technology so that they can help us get where we want to go." [30] John Fritz urges that we must ". . . harness the machine and emerging electronic technology to the legitimate aims and tasks of the school . . ." and warns of the danger that decision-making and control in education will be assumed by the developers and distributors of new instructional systems.[31]

In a democracy, decisions about the purposes and aims of public schools should be made by the citizens those schools serve. The task for those who are experts on educational values is to offer citizens the data they need for making sound decisions about what the schools should accomplish. Quite recently, as part of the technological thrust within education, policy research has begun to address itself to the study of educational aims in their relationships with the future of man and society. As Willis Harmon indicates, policy research is a technology rooted in systems analysis and in such approaches as the forecasting of alternative futures. Harmon offers examples of what educational policy research includes: "Analysis of the *basic issues* involved in the choice of desired outcomes . . . Descriptions of feasible *alternative future states* of education and of society, and identification of the policy positions which would tend to lead toward each. . . . Comparison of *alternative means* for aiming toward chosen goals. . . . Analysis of the basic *dynamics of implementation,* including studies of anticipated interactions of various groups with different stakes in the policy choice, different perceptions of the problem, different goals, etc." [32] Harmon goes on to offer an analysis of four distinct policy positions respecting educational goals that concern whether motivation to learn is largely extrinsic or intrinsic, and whether the school should focus on cognitive learnings, or on a combination of cognitive and affective learnings.

In Harmon's view, the introduction of modern technology within educational policy-making is changing our whole way of thinking about the ends of education. He points out that we are coming to regard "educational outcomes as products to be evaluated" as is the case with industrial production. He says further: "More ambitiously, *we are beginning to think in terms of consciously choosing the kind of future we wish to have, and of education as a primary tool for shaping that future.*[33]

Policy studies clearly have great potential for showing the relations between various educational outcomes and various individual and societal values. Also, they can contribute by analyzing and assessing how different educational outcomes relate to the concerns of different groups in society. Findings of policy studies, however, cannot be used effectively in educational decision-making until our citizens possess the political education called for by Broudy. Policy research, therefore, must tie in with general public education for using the findings of such research.

Educational Values in the Design of New Instructional Programs   How effectively are research-and-development methods being employed to build different educational aims into the new instructional programs? Do these programs provide for inquiry, individualized instruction, independent learning, mastery, and personal-social growth? It is this writer's judgment that not one instructional program has yet been designed—either for the elementary, the secondary, or the college level—with the systematic purpose of providing instruction that implements a set of themes such as those listed in the sentence above. When programmed instruction is the predominant approach, individualized instruction and mastery are stressed in the teaching of concepts and skills, but there is neglect of inquiry, of competencies in self-direction, and of learning objectives in the personal-social realm. Curriculum projects in natural science, mathematics, and social science tend to emphasize the teaching of theory and inquiry, but do not provide for individualization, self-direction, or mastery. New plans for organizing schools, notably nongraded programs and team teaching, offer only unsystematic provisions for individualization, independent learning, and inquiry. Computerized scheduling programs tend to be quite neutral with respect to any educational aims.

The best that one can say about the design of new instructional programs is that, when they are systematic, this quality applies to one or more sub-systems within the total program. Perhaps this is all one can reasonably expect at this early stage of applying research-and-development strategies, or the systems approach, to education. In any event, the new educational technologies—methodologies and media—have only begun to find application toward realizing in instruction a full set of educational values.

Educational Values and Technology in the Education of Educators   Probably nowhere in the educational reform movement have educational values received so little attention as in the new programs of teacher education. There are signs that this situation will shortly begin to change; but, during the past decade, beginning with the Master of Arts in Teaching (MAT) and continuing through interaction analysis and micro-teaching, it has been as though the designers of these programs had no awareness of the educational aims characterizing today's efforts to transform instruction. With almost no exceptions up to the last year or two, the new teacher education programs have been employing the new methods and media to train teachers to teach in conventional instructional programs directed toward conventional educational goals. Micro-teaching, for example, has been using video-taping to assist in training teachers to conduct whole-class instruction via lecture and discussion. The training has ignored individualization, self-direction, mastery, and inquiry. Interaction analysis has been used to train teachers to analyze whole-class teaching with no attention to the educational values/involved aside from such matters as the amount of teacher-talk or pupil-talk, or the methods the teacher used to encourage or discourage different sorts of pupil participation in whole-class discussion.

Technology in the schools will have profound effects on teachers' roles, hence on teacher education. One possibility receiving attention is that the teacher can be by-passed through computerizing the planning, conduct, and assessment of instruction. This means that the instructional program would become both "teacher-proof" and "student-proof" in the sense that neither teacher nor student, despite inadequacies, could derail instruction. This would amount to what Alvin Weinberg has termed a "Quick Technological Fix," that is, solving an essentially-educational problem by fool-proofing the machine.[34] An illustration of the Technological Fix is to increase highway safety through making cars more nearly fool-proof rather than through improving the selection, training, and control of drivers. The sensible answer to this man-machine dilemma seems obvious: for increased traffic safety, improve both cars and drivers; for better instruction, strengthen both the school's instructional program and the competencies of its staff.

During the past couple of years, some experimental teacher education programs that focus on training teachers to individualize or personalize instruction have been initiated at a number of institutions including Bucknell University, Brigham Young University, University of Texas, and Research for Better Schools in Philadelphia. We have yet to see teacher education programs that offer systematic preparation for teaching competencies in self-instruction or inquiry, though some experimental programs—at the University of Chicago and Carnegie-Mellon University, for example—are exploring this area.

A systems approach to teacher education would require that teachers (or "instructional managers") receive formal training in specifying different sorts of educational goals within the areas they teach in measuring the attainment of those goals, in planning and conducting lessons directed toward those goals, and in managing individualized instruction. In short, teachers require training in operationizing educational values through the conduct of the instruction they offer their students. Until teachers have such training, the set of educational values under consideration in this paper has little chance of governing instruction in the schools.

What has been said about the education of teachers applies also to the education of school administrators and supervisors, of education professors, and of specialists in educational technology. For the educational system to work in terms of a given set of educational values, *all essential components of the system, personnel as well as materials and media,* must contribute in coordinated ways toward the attainment of those values.

Educational Values, Media, and Public Education From the foregoing analysis, it appears that one critical need is for the attention of systems technologists, policy researchers, and other specialists to turn toward developing ways to educate the public on ends and means in education. How, for example, can the thinking citizen learn the whys and hows of individualized instruction? How can he learn the nature and importance of problem-solving thinking (inquiry) as an educational aim? How can he come to learn the reasons for teaching every student competencies in independent learning? The need is for broad public education that provides a conceptual grasp of educational aims and of ways to attain them. This is what the citizen should have as a basis for decision-making in relation to his own education, that of his children, and that of his neighbors.

Various approaches to public education of this sort can be devised and tested by educational technologists. Giving members of the community a greater role in planning and conducting the school's program is one possibility. Conducting orientation programs for parents and other community members at school during evenings is another way. But the approach that appears most promising is to offer television courses on educational values that are designed to interest and inform the public. The challenge for program designers is to find an instructional approach that will capture the imagination and fancy of television audiences, not to amuse but to stimulate, to concern, and to teach. Probably the entertainment models for TV programs would not work for this purpose. The problem is that of being honestly didactic yet compelling and gratifying, and this on a massive basis. Is the technology of TV programming sufficiently advanced that it can develop serious educational programs that will capture and hold today's audiences? If the Public Broadcasting Act can help achieve public literacy on educational ends and means, it will have performed a high service in the national interest.

REFERENCES

1. Broudy, Harry S. "Art, Science, and New Values." *Phi Delta Kappan.* November 1967, p. 116.

2. Glaser, Robert, ed. *Training Research and Education.* New York: Wiley, 1965.

3. Russell, James E. *Change and Challenge in American Education.* Boston: Houghton-Mifflin, 1965, p. 17.

4. MacLeish, Archibald. "The Great American Frustration." *Saturday Review.* July 13, 1968, p. 14.

5. Mills, C. Wright. *The Sociological Imagination.* New York: Oxford, 1959, p. 168.

6. Richards, I. A. "The Creative Aim of Instruction." in Don D. Bushnell and Dwight W. Allen, *The Computer in American Education.* New York: Wiley, 1967, p. xviii.

7. Gow, J. Steele, Jr., Burkart Holzner, and William C. Pendleton. "Economic, Social, and Political Forces." Chapter VII in John I. Goodlad, ed., *The Changing American School.* 66th Yearbook of the NSSE, Part II, Chicago: University of Chicago Press, 1967, p. 185.

8. Broudy, Harry S. "To Regain Educational Leadership." *Studies in Philosophy and Education,* 1962, vol. 2, p. 156.

9. *New York Times.* November 29, 1968.

10. Komoski, P. Kenneth. "Opportunities and Hazards of the New Technological Thrust in Education." In Edgar L. Morphet and David L. Jesser, eds., *Planning for Effective Utilization of Technology in Education.* Denver, Colorado: Eight-State Project on Designing Education for the Future, 1968, p. 120.

11. Evans, Luther H. "Challenge of Automation to Education." *American Behavioral Scientist.* November 1962, p. 17.

12. Broudy. *op. cit.,* p. 139.

13. Jennings, Frank G. "It Didn't Start with Sputnik." *Saturday Review.* September 16, 1967, p. 97.

14. Broudy. *op. cit.,* p. 157.

15. Toffler, Alvin. "The Future as a Way of Life." *Horizons.* Summer 1965, p. 109.

16. Gow, et al. *op. cit.,* p. 164.

17. Schwab, Joseph J. "Structure of the Disciplines: Meanings and Significances." In G. W. Ford and Lawrence Pugno, *Structure of Knowledge and the Curriculum.* Chicago: Rand McNally, 1964, pp. 6-30.

18. Gardner, John W. *Excellence.* New York, Harper & Brothers, 1961.

19. Bloom, Benjamin S. "Learning for Mastery." *Evaluation Comment* (UCLA Center for the Study of Evaluation of Instructional Programs), May, 1968.

20. Chase, Francis S. "School Change in Perspective." Chapter II in John I. Goodlad, ed., *op. cit.,* p. 290.

21. Suppes, Patrick. "On Using Computers to Individualize Instruction." Chapter 2 in Bushnell and Allen, *op. cit.,* p. 24.

22. Hovland, Carl I. "Computer Simulation of Thinking." *American Psychologist.* 1960, vol. 15, p. 693.

23. Broudy, Harry S. "Some Potentials and Hazards of Educational Technology." In Morphet and Jesser, eds., *op. cit.,* p. 99.

24. Chase. *op. cit.,* p. 305.

25. Crutchfield, Richard S. "Instructing the Individual in Creative Thinking." *New Approaches to Individualizing Instruction,* Princeton, New Jersey: Educational Testing Service, 1965, p. 13-25.

26. Coleman, James S. "Academic Games and Learning." *Proceedings of the 1967 Invitational Conference on Testing.* Princeton, New Jersey: Educational Testing Service, p. 67-75.

27. Cogswell, John F. "Computers in Student Appraisal and Educational Planning." Chapter 11 in John W. Loughary and others, *Man-Machine Systems in Education.* New York: Harper & Row, 1966, p. 157-167.

28. Dyer, Henry S. "The Discovery and Development of Educational Goals." *Proceedings of the 1966 Invitational Conference on Testing Problems,* Princeton, New Jersey: Educational Testing Service, p. 12.

29. Adelson, Marvin. "Decisions, Decisions: Is Education Important Enough?" In Morphet and Jesser, eds., *op. cit.,* p. 232.

30. MacLeish. *op. cit.,* p. 16.

31. Fritz, John O. "The Emergence of Instructional Systems—The Educationist's Predicament." *Canadian Education and Research Digest.* June 1968, p. 119.

32. Harmon, Willis W. "Technology and Educational Policy Research." In Morphet and Jesser, eds., *op. cit.,* p. 251.

33. *Ibid.,* p. 261.

34. Weinberg, Alvin M. "Can Technology Replace Social Engineering?" *University of Chicago Magazine.* October 1966, p. 6-10.

33.
The Psychological Heuristics
Of Learning*

ERNEST R. HILGARD
Prof. of Psychology
Stanford University

Because we are discussing the teaching process today, rather than the finer structure of what goes on in the brain when you learn, my paper has been given the title of the "heuristics of learning," which means that I am to discuss what generalizations have come out of the laboratory studies of learning that bear upon the practical problems of encouraging someone to learn, and of helping him to do so. In the present-day language of science, we are somewhat out of the basic science area into the applied science or R&D portions of the spectrum.

Most of us agree, on the one hand, that the motivation of the basic scientist should be to direct his search for understanding and ordering natural phenomena wherever his discoveries or hypotheses may lead him. On the other hand, most of us take some satisfaction in the ultimate payoff of science through its applications; we are pleased about scientific medicine, no matter how worried we may be about other aspects of technology. What Robert Merton has aptly called "the potentials of relevance" are there in basic science, whether or not the scientist is himself concerned about them. This is doubtless true when he chooses to work on a topical field such as learning; surely the understanding of the basic problems of learning is potentially relevant to such practical problems as the acquiring of skills and of knowledge, and learning how to solve problems.

Until recently, the payoff from the basic study of learning to the applied areas has been quite limited, to the embarrassment of some of us who have worked on learning for many years. The topic has been one of high prestige within experimental psychology, perhaps the favorite topic for laboratory study over the last 30 years. Yet when it comes to teaching reading, writing, and arithmetic, the advances owing to this enormous investment in the science of learning have had but slight consequences. We know a great deal about how a white rat learns a maze, but when we teach a boy to ride a bicycle, we give him the bicycle and let him teach himself, without worrying about our carefully studied principles of task analysis, distributed practice, or prompt reinforcement. When we attend to the heuristics of learning we are more interested in how the boy learns to ride his bicycle than how the rat learns to thread his way through the maze.

This paper was prepared for a symposium of the National Academy of Sciences at California Institute of Technology, October 28, 1968, and was included in the July 1969 issue of the Proceedings of the National Academy of Sciences.

If I call attention first to the failures of the psychology of learning, I do not wish to give the impression that all is lost, for I believe that some of the contemporary developments are very promising. But let me first call attention to these failures.

Many of us are college or university teachers, and most of us have participated from time to time in discussions on what makes a good teacher, and what arrangements are best for instruction. Higher education is big business, and there is no reason we should not introduce economies in it through some sort of cost-benefit analysis of different kinds of teaching. One obvious candidate for study is class-size. Despite the fact that the teachers most of us remember best from our undergraduate days are the brilliant lecturers, there is a lingering feeling that there are advantages in small class-size, ideally Mark Hopkins on one end of the log and a single student on the other end. Careful analysis of nearly 100 studies over the past 40 years leads inescapably to one conclusion: there are no demonstrable differences in results (judged by final examinations) of small classes versus large ones, of individual study without a supervisor compared with supervised individual study (Dubin and Taveggia, 1969). If we trust these investigations, which have been done with great care because the investigators knew the stakes were large, we would accept either the very large lecture or the non-instructor method, as the economical ways of teaching, just as satisfactory as any of the other methods we typically use. This is really a rather shocking conclusion. Doubtless the most costly and wasteful method of all is the large undergraduate teaching laboratory. These results strike right at the heart of cherished beliefs, so that most of the authors of the studies themselves back off from accepting the conclusions of their own studies. They think maybe the examinations are at fault (but they continue to use them) or that there are subtle aspects of human contagion that they do not know how to measure which would be sacrificed if we gave up small classes.

The same kind of negative result holds for studies of elementary education. There are no consistent differences to be found between teaching reading by the whole-word method or the phonetic method, we don't really know whether or not there would be advantages in using a different initial alphabet in English with beginners, or in postponing the acquiring of reading until a little later, as practiced in Scandinavian countries and in Russia (Chall, 1967). We are so eager to start early that there is some pressure to go the other way, and to push reading instruction into the kindergarten. The point is that an established science of the psychology of learning is of very little help to us on these issues. This is a serious matter, and somewhere along the line suggests a failure of psychologists, in collaboration with educators, to develop a responsible applied psychology of learning.

Let me summarize the "state of the art" as of about 10 years ago.

1. There were thousands of experimental investigations of reading, but they had not led to agreement on the preferred methods of teaching.

2. There were upwards of one hundred quantitative studies of college teaching, with the verdict that one method was no better than another.

3. There were thousands of laboratory studies of conditioned responses, motor skills learning, nonsense syllable memorizing, with animals and human subjects, largely irrelevant to the solution of the practical problems, or at least lacking the in-between experiments to make relevancy explicit.

The obvious need was not for more of the same, but for something different. There is no reason to expect new studies of the old kind to lead to anything more definitive than the old studies. The temptation is to continue, which is, I suppose, a common disease in what Kuhn (1962) has called "normal" science.

Some efforts were indeed made over the years to break out a little from the standard patterns. As the motion picture became cheaper and easier for the teacher to project, visual aids were hoped to provide new dimensions to teaching, and then the tape-recorder added the audio-dimension, so we had audiovisual aids (e.g., Brown and Thornton, 1963). Count-less studies of these led to the same old conclusion: one method is as good as another (Schramm, 1960). Yes, people can learn from films, perhaps a little better than from a very poor instructor, but no better than from an average instructor. The hopeful thing in all of this is that people gathered together (or working alone) who want to learn, given some learning materials, can be shown to learn. The only problem is one of efficiency, and through the years notebooks, workbooks, laboratories, films, tapes, lectures, discussions, textbooks, have all helped people to learn, but never with any dramatic changes owing to the new technology.

Two new hopeful processes have come along which may indeed break this log-jam. The first of these is *programmed learning* in general, and the second is *computer-assisted instruc-tion,* a special derivative of programmed instruction.

Although there had been earlier teaching machines (Pressey, 1926, 1927), programmed learning took off from the work of B. F. Skinner (1954, 1958). He had done authoritative work on what has come to be called *operant conditioning,* chiefly with rats and pigeons, but developed a few simple principles that could be applied to any kind of training procedure. He and his students have turned out to be remarkably effective applied psychologists of learning, despite the basic-science attitudes inculcated over some 30 years of precise studies of animal learning in the laboratory. Here, then, is the kind of payoff that a science of learning might have hoped for.

The applications have extended to animal training, a curious lack on the part of others who have through the years worked on animal learning. It is Skinner's products which train the dolphins and other performers in the various Marine Worlds which are now so popular. His methods are used in drug-testing in pharmaceutical houses, in psychotherapy with autistic children and with schizophrenics, and in many other areas of application outside the schools. The advantage of his particular kind of formulation is that it tells you what to look for and what to do, and these are the marks of a science on the way to becoming a technology.

Let me summarize the Skinner system of operant conditioning to indicate what I mean by its technological simplicity.

First, the learner comes to a given learning problem with something he can already do. Thus he may know how to count before he tries to learn how to add or subtract, he knows how to talk before he learns how to read, and so on. This is described as the *operant level* at the time a new task is undertaken. Operant level is, in fact, a very complex matter of prior training, of memory, of individual differences, of motivation, but it reveals itself by the responses that the learner makes when he begins the new task, and from the point of view of the teacher it is just a matter of beginning to teach on the basis of what the learner already knows and can do.

Second, because of this operant level the learner does *something* in the presence of the new task. He characteristically varies his responses somewhat, in accordance with what has tradi-tionally been called trial-and-error. In any case, when he does something that approximates a desired performance he is given some sort of reward or *reinforcement* as it is called within this system. A reinforcement is anything which tends to increase the probability that when next exposed to the same opportunities for response he will tend to do what he last did; it may be a piece of candy, a pat on the back, or a verbal OK.

Third, absence of reinforcement leads to *extinction,* so that if behavior is non-reinforced its probability of occurring will be reduced, thus giving the opportunity for more appropriate behavior to appear and to be reinforced.

Fourth, by skilled use of selective reinforcement and extinction, behavior can be made to move from a crude approximation to a more refined and acceptable performance. This process of directing the behavior in desirable directions is called *shaping,* and represents the essence of the new technology.

A trainer or a teacher who knows about operant level, reinforcement, extinction, and their appropriate patterning in shaping, is ready to roll up his sleeves and go ahead. There are subtleties within the shaping process, such as the timing of reinforcements, the use of various schedules of reinforcement, and so on, but these are accessory principles, like learning how to tune the carburetor after you know how an internal combustion engine works.

While giving full credit to Skinner and his followers for the applied consequences both of his theory and of his inventiveness, let me point out that the theoretical support for his technology can come from sources other than his own theory.

Reduced to simplest terms, there are three major learning viewpoints which for some years have competed for attention in this country. (1) The first of these, for which Skinner is here the representative, is *operant reinforcement.* For the present I am letting this stand for some alternative but related interpretations of trial-and-error learning followed by reward, as espoused by Thorndike, Hull, Spence, Neal E. Miller. (2) The second, equally behavioristic, holds to *contiguous association,* without stress upon reinforcement. It is associated with Guthrie, and in the context of today's discussion, his disciples Lumsdaine and Sheffield. (3) The third and final view, called *cognitive theory,* is associated with Gestalt psychology, and Piaget, with Tolman, Bruner, and others.

An important set of developments in learning theory, known as mathematical models, with which the next speaker is identified are relatively neutral with respect to these global viewpoints, and I shall pass over any attempt to relate them.

I wish to point out that programmed learning, and its variants in computer-based instruction, derive some support from each of the three major views toward learning.

Operant Reinforcement In keeping with his conception that a response to be learned should be *emitted* rather than *elicited,* Skinner has commonly insisted that the learner in programmed instruction should be responsible for his own responses, which in practice means that he should write out his answer, rather than selecting in cafeteria style from a set of answers someone else has provided. Then his teaching machine or programmed book displays the right answer for comparison with the one he has produced; if they are alike he has been symbolically *reinforced.*

Another aspect of programming, deriving from the animal experiments, is the *shaping* of responses. A learner will learn to give more precise answers if at first approximate answers are rewarded, so that he knows he is on the right track and keeps working. In the laboratory, the rewards are gradually withheld for the inappropriate approximations, so that only the desired behavior is rewarded. Thus a rat can be made to press a lever with a limited amount of force, or to hold it in a prescribed position, in order to receive the pellet of food that is his reward. In the program the shaping tends to be done by *prompting,* that is by some sort of hint that makes it easier for the correct response to be emitted.

Contiguous Association Guthrie's theory of learning was also a beautifully simple one, which told you where to look and what to do, so that it was suitable to become a technology in the hands of its followers. According to him, the learner tends to do what he last did in the presence of stimuli, and new or associated stimuli come to elicit the response merely by being present (and attended to) when the response occurs. An associative shift can occur so that the old stimuli drop out and the new stimuli remain attached to the response. This is the heart of what we mean by learning. According to his supporters, the shaping that goes on through prompting is better understood in Guthrie's terms than in Skinner's. Fading is a technique lending itself to this interpretation. A word is first presented in skeleton form, with a few letters missing, to make it easy for the learner to produce the correct response. Later all letters can be omitted, for by this time enough new stimuli have become attached to the desired response that the old supports can be withdrawn. Lumsdaine takes the position that most of the efforts of the programmer is directed to having responses occur without error (a feature that is stressed by Skinner also); in that case he believes that we are really talking about *elicited* rather than about *emitted* responses.

Cognitive Theory   The cognitive theorist is impatient with a theory of learning that limits itself to talking about *small steps, responding,* and *reinforcement.* Surely any significant subject-matter has some kind of organization within itself that a learner must comprehend or understand if he has really mastered it. The cognitive theorist looks for the effect of the organization or structure of knowledge upon the learner.

Because the program constructor is likely to be talking the language of his technology, he may well fail to communicate all that he himself believes. Thus in stressing the reinforcement of responses he may in fact be neglecting to say anything about what is being learned.

The little responses that fill in the blanks at the end of a program, or the words that the student points out on the television screen with his electronic pencil are not what is being learned, although they may be *indicators* of what is learned. Suppose that in learning to extract the square root of 25 you get the answer 5, and write it down. The "5" then gets reinforced, because it is correct. Did you learn the response "5", or did you learn to extract the square root? When a rat runs a maze, and gets to the end-box, and eats the food there that serves as a reinforcement, is he learning to eat? Obviously the response at the end is merely a special output that shows that the essential responses along the way have been made, or, in cognitive terms, that the essential relationships have been understood. A program could be written that would have all the answers either the word "right" or the word "wrong", as in a true-false examination. Obviously more would be learned than to write the words "right" and "wrong". The point here is that cognitive learning can be taking place under arrangements of operant conditioning.

I believe that the advances made in programmed learning, while catalyzed by learning theory, have not in fact been based very much on strict applications of specific learning theories. However, one should be careful not to disregard the technological approaches suggested by the theories. In this respect, the reinforcement and contiguous association theories have been dominant because of their insistence on stimulus control, identifiable response, and prompt feedback, so that the programmer has instructions as to what he must do in order to help the learner. The cognitive theorist has been somewhat less successful in his technologies, although the lack of success is not owing to any necessary deficiency in the theory. For example, the cognitive theorist also has some technological suggestions such as beginning with less differentiated wholes before going to more differentiated ones, practicing on examples illustrating common principles within changing content (in order to encourage "transposition"), and so on. In fact, many of these principles become incorporated into the technological practices of those whose commitments are to the other theories. An interesting illustration of this is provided by the work of Sheffield and Maccoby (1961) who, while accepting Guthrie's contiguous association theory, when working within the context of producing a teaching film on how to assemble complex equipment, found it necessary to "rediscover" cognitive psychology, as in their insistence that the arrangement of learning had to be coherent with the *inherent organization* of the task if the learning were to be efficient.

Thus far I have talked about programmed learning, essentially as conceived in its earlier form, progressing by small steps from where the learner is to where the teacher wants him to go. The early teaching machines and programmed books tended to incorporate such procedures. These evolved from the laboratory experiments, which had usually set rather fixed tasks, such as learning a maze or memorizing a list of items in consecutive order.

Another kind of program developed very early, however, known as the branching program. All learners did not follow the same path through the program, but the next steps were contingent upon the earlier ones, and sometimes based upon the learner's preferences.

It is out of such programs that computer-assisted learning evolved. The computer provides maximum flexibility, and as the next speaker will doubtless indicate, the computer is neutral in respect to the theories you wish to test. It is highly flexible, will do what it is told, and does not forget its instructions.

One early advantage of programmed learning and the teaching machine, to which I have not referred, is that one has a record of progress, of errors made, of amount learned per time unit. This is in some respects the most significant advance over ordinary teaching methods. Most teachers really do not know what the learners are doing; they trust to a student's occasional smile or a nod of the head to assure that the student is listening; the questions that come up often as not show not that the student was listening, but that he really didn't hear what had gone before. When examination time comes teachers are often disappointed because of their students' failure to learn, and pleased with what the brighter ones know—but they have little idea what their own teaching had to do with it. In programmed learning you know where the student is and what he is doing; if he progresses through the program both he and the teacher have the satisfaction in knowing that he learned from it. Now computer-assisted instruction has not only this same advantage of keeping a record, but it has the further advantage that the computer can make *computations* so that an analyzed record is available for each student at any time. The details I leave to the others, but this advantage, if capitalized on, can prove enormously useful in preventing wasteful procedures.

I wish to address the rest of my remarks to the problem of the proper place I see for computer-assisted instruction in the total educational process, and what I see as its limitations.

Let me first acknowledge the promise that I believe such instruction holds for the efficient teaching of all manner of skills, information, and appreciation. I see no limitation inherent in subject matter as such; that is, such instruction is not limited to subject matter with fixed answers, such as mathematics, grammar, map-reading, historical chronology, or foreign-language vocabulary. It is possible to teach poetry or creativity as well.

Now a few propositions regarding to relationship of such instruction to the total educational enterprise:

1. Computer-assisted instruction, even when fully developed, must be *combined* with other learning activities, and not displace them. To the extent that learning goes on in the library, or in the laboratory, or in the studio, it will and should continue to go on there. It should not be taken for granted that time in the library, or craft shop, or music-listening room is well spent; criteria that we have learned to use in studying computer-assisted instruction may well be applied there also, but the chances that something can be done that cannot be done sitting at the computer terminal seems good.

2. Computer-assisted instruction is likely to be largely *sedentary,* for it is wasteful to monopolize a terminal while you are elsewhere. Much learning takes place on the hoof, or in conversation with a more capricious responder than the computer. If we are to encourage the spirit of inquiry, we want students to go to the library, to putter about the shop; to prepare them for responsibility we want them to meet together to make plans for group activity, to take part in plays and in team games. That is, learning by doing is not dead, and there are some "doings" that the terminal is unsuited for.

3. Teacher training will doubtless be greatly affected by the computer, because *the things the teacher now spends most time on may very well be the tasks for which the teacher is least needed.* We may therefore consider some of the things that a wise teacher might do better than a computer.

a. The teacher can take responsibility to see that the student learns to *initiate* inquiry on his own. While the computer can provide a range of opportunities, and can even engage in individual guidance, I doubt if it will ever do as well as a skilled teacher in fanning a faint spark into a glowing interest. Recent work on social learning theory (Bandura and Walters, 1963) has shown that *imitation* is one of the neglected areas in the psychology of learning, and the imitation of a teacher as an adult model may have great influence upon what is learned.

b. The teacher can help the student to gain *a favorable image of himself* as a learner and as a creative person. While the reinforcements of the computer will help, direct social approbation is an even more powerful reinforcer. I was greatly impressed by something that happened many years ago when working with young chimpanzees along with Professor Yerkes at the then Yale Laboratories of Primate Biology in Florida. So as not to introduce experimenter bias into the session, we were concealed behind a screen while the chimpanzee went about his puzzle-solving. He solved the problem, all right, and a banana appeared as a welcome reinforcer. He picked up the banana, but sought out the screen and peered behind it to show *us* the banana and get our commendation before he sat down to eat it. The "computer" had delivered his reinforcement, but he wanted ours in person. I suspect children are like that, too.

One way in which to engender creative expression is to modify excessive negative self-criticism through teaching the learner to take credit for and satisfaction in small evidences of creativity. We do not have to have distinguished products in order to be creative. This is something that a skilled teacher can have a share in, through adapting the critical appraisal to the stage of development of the learner. My guess is that not many teachers do this well, but that's why a different kind of teacher training may be necessary.

c. The teacher also has a role in directing the student toward *effective participation with others.* While I am against making everybody into extroverts, human life is inescapably social, and an effective person has to learn to cooperate with others in solving problems, in making plans, or in carrying out a cooperative enterprise, whether at home, at school, at work, or in the community. The skills of social participation, of leadership and of followership, of tolerance of opposition and of frustration, of social conflict resolution, can be learned only through exercising them. The discriminations are too difficult, the response interchanges too rapid, for them to be well programmed. Even after social skills and practices have been studied through a program they have to be exercised or they will not persist.

What this amounts to, then, from what we know about how an individual learns, and how he can be aided by those who wish to aid his learning, is that computer-assisted instruction is soundly grounded in what we know about learning, although its usefulness does not arise exclusively from any one of the prevailing theories; it will not make the teacher dispensable, but will alter the teacher's functions in such a way as to require the usual teacher to do what only the exceptional teacher now does well. This is itself an important challenge to teacher-training institutions, as they prepare teachers for the schools of the future.

BIBLIOGRAPHY

Bandura, A., and R. H. Walters. *Social Learning and Personality Development.* New York: Holt, Rinehart, and Winston, 1963.

Brown, J. W., and J. W. Thornton, Jr. (Eds.) *New Media in Higher Education.* Washington, D.C.: National Education Association, 1963.

Chall, Jeanne. *Learning to Read: The Great Debate.* New York: McGraw-Hill, 1967.

Dubin, R., and T. C. Taveggia. *The Teaching-learning Paradox: Comparative analysis of college teaching.* University of Oregon: Center for Advanced Study of Educational Administration, 1969. (To appear).

Kuhn, T. S. *The Structure of Scientific Revolutions.* Chicago: Univ. of Chicago Press, 1962.

Pressey, S. L. "A simple apparatus which gives tests and scores—and teaches." *School and Society,* 1926, *23,* 373-376.

Pressey, S. L. "A machine for automatic teaching of drill material." *School and Society,* 1927, *25,* 549-552.

Schramm, W. (Ed.) *New Teaching Aids in the American Classroom.* Stanford, Calif.: Institute for Communication Research, 1960.

Sheffield, F. D., and N. Maccoby. Summary and interpretation of organization principles in constructing filmed demonstrations. In Lumsdaine, A. A. (Ed.) *Student Response in Programmed Instruction.* Washington, D.C.: National Academy of Science, 1961, 107-116.

Skinner, B. F. "The science of learning and the art of teaching." *Harvard Education Review,* 1954, *24,* 86-97.

Skinner, B. F. "Teaching machines." *Science,* 1958, *128,* 969-977.

34.
Instruction as
A Systematic Approach
To Instructional Technology

by CHARLES F. HOBAN
Prof. and Dir. of Instruction
Annenberg School of Communications
Univ. of Pennsylvania

Contingencies of the Commission's Mission

Commissioner Howe's imperative to his Commission on Instructional Technology that "It must consider every aspect of instructional technology and every problem which may arise in its development" implies either a prescience of the Commission and its facilities which is unrealistic, or a life span of deliberation which is incongruous with the prevailing national demand for instant plans, insights, and R & D mappings complete to the last coordinate.

Given its task, however, the Commission's assignment is complicated by a posture of pessimism of the new power structure of instructional technology, or "learning systems," particularly among those involved in adapting computers to direct instruction or to the management of instruction. This posture appears to be based on the half-truths that all major instructional technological devices (motion pictures, ITV, etc.) have been oversold in the past, that they have not lived up to overstated performance promises when adopted by the schools. Consequently all technological innovations, including those in various stages of R & D, are viewed as vulnerable to the dreadful disclosure of fraud when submitted to the pragmatic test of trial and adoption in school instruction.

Factors Underlying Pessimism in the Establishment

Underlying this currently fashionable attitude of pessimism or defeatism are several major readily identifiable factors, which lie deep in the educational system as first causes of problems of all instruction. The relationship of these underlying factors are well known to those who over the years have (a) participated directly in technological innovation in public school systems, colleges, and mass military training; (b) done both contextual and evaluation research on what hitherto have been known as "new media in education"; and (c) have tried to develop viable theories dealing with the "new media in instruction." Among these major factors which impede instructional technology and inhibit optimization of its effectiveness are the following:

1. An overexpectation of effects from any given gadget or process, simple or complex, adapted to instruction from some other area, such as entertainment

(motion pictures, television), automated industrial processes and commercial transactions (computers); weapons systems research and development (programmed instruction, systems analysis).

2. "Measurement of effects" (evaluation) of the "new media" by instruments and techniques which are non-metric in the mathematical sense of measurement and insensitive to dimensions of human response that may be of much greater importance than the "behavioral objectives" they are designed to "measure."

3. A scientistic outlook among learning psychologists, instructional systems analysts and designers, programmed instruction developers, etc., which (a) ignores the importance and operation of intuition in classroom interaction, and (b) prescribes narrow behavioral objectives and their criterial "measures" (See 2 above).

4. An inertial property of educational and adjunct institutions which makes them resistant to change, slow to innovate, and methodologically non-adaptive when innovation is tried.

5. An irrelevance of much of learning psychology to classroom teaching situations as they exist in reality, rather than in psychology laboratories.

6. A curriculum which is frequently misphased, overintellectualized, and irrelevant to the individual needs and social milieu of large numbers of students, and consequently operative at best among bright and/or docile students responsive to pressures for compliance from both parents and teachers.

7. An overextended period of packaged preparatory education which induces boredom and maintains the status quo in a seller's market in formal education, and an underdeveloped program of continuing education which, incidentally, is particularly open and adaptable to instructional technology.

8. A narrow exclusiveness in the educational establishment, including the U.S. Office of Education and professional organizations of educational institutions and institutional teachers, which equates education and instruction with public (and private) school systems and colleges, and ignores the educational and training programs of business, industry, the military services, etc.

This list of factors can easily be extended. The eight listed above are sufficient to indicate that many problems of instructional technology are not unique to instructional technology as such, but are embedded in the broader and more universal problems of institutionalized school instruction and of old and new academic desciplines and professional bureaucracies which aspire to sovereignty over the instructional process.

The Concept of Instructional Technology

It seems the better part of valor in the present state of national puzzlement and confusion for the Commission to adopt a moderate view of the scope of instructional technology. Otherwise, it will become involved in a range of concerns from team teaching to underground, windowless schools, with great attention given to depth-psychology of color selection.

Essentially, instructional technology involves the management of ideas, procedures, machines, and people in the instructional process. As such, it involves:

(1) a physical device(s) which mediates information transmission;

(2) a system of instruction of which this device(s) is one of several components; and

(3) a range of mediating options involving progression in

    (a) requirements for physical alteration of the "classroom";

    (b) remoteness in time and space between the tutor-planner and the student;

    (c) sophistication of design of programmed information exchange between "tutor" and student;

    (d) complexity and cost of hardware;

    (e) level of technical skills required for equipment construction, installation, "debugging," operation, and maintenance;

    (f) independence of classroom teacher control or continuous monitoring in the operation of the device-centered "teaching";

    (g) additional manpower required by way of para-professional personnel for use of the instructional technology; and

    (h) role changes and new skills required of "classroom" teachers in (I) management of the technology, and (II) other and/or new non-structured, non-mediated teaching activities essential to personality development, humanistic growth, and cultivation of values, all of which lie outside the present and foreseeable potential of instructional technology as herein considered.

While the progression in technological devices in (3) above is not deliberately sequenced in order of increasing resistance to technological innovations in education, it is apparent that such a heuristic resistance sequence is implicit. There is presumably much less teacher resistance, for instance, to adoption of the overhead projector operated under complete control of the classroom teacher and requiring only easily manageable control of room illumination than to a purchased set of programmed instruction in which the classroom teacher does not even have control over the checking of correct and incorrect student responses.

Classroom Teacher Rituals

The current and historical role of the classroom teacher is highly ritualized. Any major change in ritual is likely to be resisted as an invasion of the sanctuary by the barbarians.

Ritualization in teaching is flexible enough to permit idiosyncrasies of personal style, arrangement of the daily schedule, police methods, pacing, etc., but major characteristics of ritual tend to be invariant.

Two of the great invariants are (1) complete control (within institutional limits of courses of study, textbooks, films, etc.) of the teaching-testing-grading-reward-punishment processes, and (2) face-to-face interaction with students. These two invariants of ritualization of teaching are very likely to be important determinants in the trial and adoption of technological innovation and in its effectiveness in either event at the classroom level.

Any *sudden* or *substantial reduction* of dominance status and/or domain of activities of the classroom teacher, any *major* change in the interpersonal teacher-student communication situation, or any *systematic* attempt to scientize and rationalize the intuitively determined interaction patterns of the teacher is likely to elicit at least some teacher hostility and resistance.

The attitude of the classroom teacher toward any instructional innovation—technological or otherwise—is of paramount importance, even when unintentionally expressed, as will be discussed immediately below. While trial or adoption of innovation may be formalized at the federal, state levels, or community levels of control, it is in the individual school and individual classroom that the transaction occurs functionally (or disfunctionally).

Indeed, it may be that the more or less generally accepted theory of instructional innovation as (a) originating from the outside (the supra system), and (b) proceeding from the top down in the hierarchical structure, carries within it the seeds of its own failures or imperfections by omitting participation of classroom teachers in adaptation and adoption decisions at the local implementation level.

Some remarkable research findings with direct bearing on the effects of teacher attitudes on student behavior are currently being spelled out by Robert Rosenthal and his associates using the concept of communication of expectancy.

It will be recalled that in widely reported studies of the introduction of programmed instruction in both Manhasset, Long Island, and Denver, Colorado, it was reported that students performed better under teachers favorable to programmed instruction *even when the sole function of the teacher was to maintain order.* Put another way, better results were obtained from students under programmed instruction when the expectancy of teachers was in a favorable direction, and this expectancy effect occurred independent of the participational activity role of the teachers in the instructional process.

Apparently, human beings are highly sensitive to both intended and unintended expectancy cueing behavior of other human beings in dominant roles. Rosenthal reports that in an experiment on perception of people, subjects were asked to rate experimenters on the "honesty" variable. This variable could be operative only *after* the experiment, and could occur in tabulating and summing the results. Errors in tabulation could be random or in the direction of confirming the hypothesis held by the experimenter, and tabulation and computational errors could be large or small.

Both tabulation and computational errors occurred. Among those who erred in the direction of the expectancy of their hypotheses, both tabulation and computational errors were larger.

The experimental result expecially relevant here is that, whereas all experimenters were rated by their subjects as honest, mean ratings by subjects on the honesty scale were significantly lower (moderately to highly honest vs. extremely honest) for those experimenters who made computational errors in the direction of their hypothesis. This suggests that subjects in the experiment were able to detect some cues in the behavior of experimenters which predicted beyond chance the subsequent "honest" and "dishonest" (or "less honest") errors in tabulation and computation of experimental data.

This apparent sensitivity of subjects (mostly students) to unitentional and perhaps non-formally coded cues to expectancy of results manifested by authority figures in an authority-structured social situation can, without straining the powers of reason to the point of collapse, be related to teacher influence on student performance in the direction of their expectancy hypothesis in the Manhasset and Denver trials of programmed instruction—especially when monitoring teachers exercised only the police function of preserving order in the classroom.

Even more remarkable results of teacher expectancy on student development of competencies are reported in a forthcoming (September, 1968) book, *Pygmalion in the Classroom,* by Robert Rosenthal and Lenore Jacobson. Teachers were told that 20 percent of the students in each class included in the reported experiment had been identified through extensive testing as having unusual potential for intellectual gains during the next year. No such extensive testing had been done. The names of the 20 percent identified as having this unusual potential were selected randomly.

The experiments were conducted in poverty area schools and involved no special programs, tutoring activities, or enrichment activities. The only new element was that of favorable teacher expectation—teacher attitude toward the "unusual" pupils—and presumably consequent verbal and non-verbal expression by the teachers of this attitude toward these students.

After eight months, the "unusual" students made significantly greater gains in IQ than the non-unusuals, and the non-unusuals made greater gains than did those in classes not included in the experiment.

The implications of these findings are difficult to overestimate. They clearly suggest that (a) teacher expectancy, often operating at the unintentional level, is a variable of major importance in the instructional and developmental processes; (b) students are highly sensitive and responsive to teacher expectancy along several dimensions of perception and growth; and (c) the effects of "host-specific" expectation are infectious.

It is reasonable to assume teacher expectancy operates negatively as well as positively, as suggested by the Manhasset and Denver findings. That is, negative teacher expectancy can have a depressing, or leveling, or inhibiting, or hostility-arousing effect on student development. Yet, as far as I know, teacher selection and certification procedures do not ordinarily include the criterion of the *true believer* in the "unusual" growth potential of students.

It may be hypothesized that all innovators and agents of change tend to be what Hoffer calls "true believers," oriented toward a better future of mankind, an improvement of the human condition of everyone, and that one of the most important aspects of instructional technology is the inherent expectancy of educational improvement shared by its advocates. The corollary is that instructional technology fails or disappoints when its implementation falls into the hands of skeptics and infidels whose habituated classroom rituals have attained doctrinal significance, and consequently whose expectancy of ritualistic change is negative.

Crystallization of the Argument

To crystallize the argument, it should be borne in mind that

    a. many of the troublesome problems of instructional technology are essentially further manifestations of the troublesome problems and properties of instruction in the American educational system;

    b. the fashionable attitude of pessimism and pooh-pooh toward instructional technology is particularly evident among an elite of the supra-educational establishment for whom the world of instructional technology originated last year or the year before and consists largely of promised but undelivered computer regulation of the process of individualized, multi-track instructional programs, task assignments, and performance monitoring;

    c. at least some, if not many, of the significant variables of in-school growth and development of students lie beyond the cognizance of learning psychology, and the consequences of these variables escape the narrowly prescribed "first order," behaviorally operationalized objectives of instruction and their criterial "measures";

    c. the process of innovation has been studied on the normative rather than the explanatory, i.e., theoretical, level and consequently the literature on innovation provides few cues for acceleration and adoption of desirable changes in the system of instruction; and

    d. the classroom teacher is by training and institutional control a prisoner of the orthodox ritualization of the educational system, negatively disposed to automation, and less of a gatekeeper than a positive or negative expectancy radiator.

Guidelines for the Commission

The Institutional Context of Instructional Technology

It follows that substantial, difficult, and not-clearly-defined changes must be made in the educational system both for its own effective survival and in order to accelerate the rate of development, adoption, and optimum use of instructional technology, assuming that instructional technology can be justified in the first place. This reconstruction is beyond the ken of the Commission on Instructional Technology, but recognition of its necessity is not.

A clear implication for the Commission is that it articulate its concern that instructional technology center on those areas of education that, by general concensus, are in greatest need of attention, e.g., the three R's—reading, 'rithmetic, and relevance. Parenthetically, the "new math," particularly in the elementary school, may not enjoy consensual approval at any level of expertise, and the linguistics approach to the teaching of language is regarded as premature and error prone by at least some with impressive credentials in both linguistics and education.

Justification of Instructional Technology

Instructional technology is more justified by its own logic than by empirical studies of its effectiveness in facilitating "learning." As already indicated, such empirical (evaluative) studies unfortunately ignore critical variables, and typically "measure" only those results which are easiest to operationalize within the state of the art of criterial specification and educational testing. The notion of "unobtrusive measures" has scarcely penetrated educational research, and at least some of the vigorously promoted techniques of multivariate analysis are too often used as a substitute for thinking or to elegantly demonstrate the obvious. This is not to say that empirical research has no place in uncovering important relationships or evaluating procedures and progress in instruction, but only that too often it is overburdened by techniques and designed with impoverished insight and imagination.

The development, use, and improvement of instructional technology, as defined in this memorandum, is justified in a broad general way by the fact that American schools operate as a formative institution of a highly technological society and should therefore incorporate, as appropriate, this characteristic of the larger society as well as its idealized values. In a sense, this principle of justification is aesthetic and can rest at that without decisive challenge.

However, since aesthetics generates much subjectivity and little objectivity, stimulates lofty dialogue at the philosophical level and restless, insistent controversy in relation to specific events, it is desirable to get down to tangible criteria in justifying instructional technology.

For what it is worth, it may be said reflectively that instructional technology is justified if and when it:

1. makes available, discreetly or continuously, a mode or multimodes of representation of any of several levels of reality, culturally recognizable as such, and without constraints of geography or of real time, and hitherto not available for instruction or non-tutorial education;

2. provides a model of behavior otherwise unavailable, or in scarce supply, or lacking authenticity or correctness of definition, and preferably when it provides opportunity for the student to compare his imitative behavior with that of the model;

3. sequences and, within reasonable limits and without undue restraints, manages stimulus inputs and response outputs on an individualized and structured basis otherwise difficult or impossible to achieve;

4. stores, retrieves, and rapidly processes a large amount of relevant information not otherwise readily available, or, if available, too time-consuming to process manually;

5. involves latent functions of a critical nature in the instructional process or system which, because they are not directly and immediately related to improved and "measured" student progress, may escape proper assessment or even official observation.

None of these five criteria is necessarily independent of the other four. All can be combined in complex hardware and electronic components. Also, it goes without saying that this brief list of criteria is not intended to be either definitive or exhaustive.

Minimizing Contingencies of Instructional Technology

Again, for what it is worth, it may be said reflectively, and with some empirical evidence, that the effectiveness of instructional technology will be less than optimum if and when it:

1. incorporates the format of other modes of instruction known to be relatively inefficient and ineffective instructionally, i.e., when McLuhan's "rearview mirror" effect occurs;

2. fails to challenge or slows down the natural pace of progression of students and thus induces student boredom and/or resentment;

3. rapidly reaches a point of diminishing returns and thus becomes monotonous and unrewarding.

4. severely and continuously reduces the *social* process of education, i.e., face-to-face interpersonal interactions, group participation, etc.;

5. requires logistical support beyond the capacity of the system to provide in proper time-phase and matching characteristics, and without heavy encumbrance of hardware, additional personnel, or hard-to-find dollars.

Priorities and Emphases

It may reasonably be expected that the Commission on Instructional Technology will come to some decisions on priorities. A set of questions such as the following should be considered and priorities of emphasis recommended:

1.1. Should motion pictures, film strips, radio, and other media, which are currently not considered as technological innovations but as adoptions, be taken for granted, or should they be re-examined for: currency of content, state of the art such as employment of more involving and perhaps less isomorphic symbolism, extent of adoption, logistical adequacy, etc.?

1.2. Should emphasis now placed on the newer technologies, such as ITV and PTV, Individually Prescribed Instruction, Computer Regulated Instruction, etc., be intensified, or should they undergo more extensive feasibility, operational suitability, and effectiveness testing, bearing in mind the kinds of variables already discussed, and the present limitations and necessary modifications of research procedures and techniques?

2.1. Should efforts to diffuse instructional technology and increase its effectiveness be time-phased from the elementary school, which is more open to innovation, and progressively to the high school and college which are discriminably more conservative and less open to changes in teacher role and ritual?

2.2. Should the efforts to diffuse instructional technology and increase its effectiveness be more emphasized among formally certified "systems" of education, such as public schools and colleges, which defy systems analysis simply because they are systematically chaotic, or should they be more emphasized on the para-formal educational institutions of industry, commerce, and the military services which are well systematized and more definitively goal oriented?

3.1. Within the formally structured and certified educational "systems," should emphases on the employment of instructional technology be directed to use among those schools serving the "culturally deprived" student population, or should it be directed to use among those schools serving the family reinforced, docile, complaint and thus more "teachable" student population?

3.2. Again within the formally structured and certified educational "systems," should emphasis on instructional technology be placed on the full-time day student population, or on the continuing education population among whom the struggle is greater, the need more acute, and the motivation possibly stronger?

As previously, this list of questions is not exhaustive, and their either-or formulation does not exclude the middle from consideration. Omitted from the list are questions dealing with the very important issues of teacher education, strategies of innovation, and research methodologies. Such questions are implicit in various foregoing sections. Also omitted are questions of use of technology in public relations, class scheduling, library controls, etc., not because they are unimportant but because they do not deal directly with instruction. However, the Commission would be in error if it were to ignore these areas of application.

The Systems Approach

Throughout the above discussion, the systems concept is embedded in various points. Like cost effectiveness, operations research, the affective domain and other terms on current display in the best company, the systems concept is being flogged mercilessly in educational discourse; nevertheless it is imperative that the Commission on Instructional Technology approach its task within a central concept of instruction as a system, and not as the installations of appliances, or the design of school buildings in the round. A system is an arrangement in which everything is related to everything else so that the malfunctioning of any part affects the output or outcome. It was, among other things, to emphasize this interrelationship that the preceding discussion of the role of authority expectancy and subject behavior was introduced and discussed.

The systems concept is not fully explicated or articulated in its educational applications and implications but its seminal ideas are clear and simple and need not await the master blueprint to be accepted and acted upon. Perhaps those simple little flow charts with boxes, circles, and arrows, that appear so elegantly professional and slightly awesome in the new educational literature, are a necessary and useful way of beginning to take a fresh look at instructional technology.

35.

A Framework
For Studying
Instructional Technology

by RICHARD HOOPER*

Where Is the Beginning?

The strength of educational technology will depend ultimately on the quality of the educational philosophy and the validity of the science of learning that undergird it. A study of "instructional television and radio . . . and their relationship to each other and to instructional materials such as videotapes, films, discs, computers, and other educational materials or devices"** cannot begin with discussions of machinery. The study must start with the totality, and not any specialized parts. There seems to be an increasingly powerful consensus amongst thinkers in many different, and previously unconnected, areas of life that any really basic advance in the future will come as a result of global rather than separatist patterns of thought. Whether it be the regional planners, the conservationists' concern about ecology, McNamara in the Defense Department, Michael Harrington talking about the war against poverty, John Cage on contemporary music, the trend is towards the comprehensive approach and away from the piecemeal.

The complexity of the comprehensive approach must be acknowledged at the outset. It is easy to use words such as "multi-levelled," "multi-faceted," "multi-phasic," and extremely difficult to use the thought processes they are trying to describe. A study of educational technology that is to be truly dynamic cannot shy away from the web of interrelationships which make up the educational process. Curriculum development, teacher training, school architecture, selection of textbooks, production of television lessons, scheduling arrangements, budgeting techniques are intimately connected despite national associations, jargon, and the traditional piecemeal thinking that have for years kept them apart. The Carnegie Commission on Educational Television emphasized this when it said: ". . . instructional television must be studied in the *full context* of education. . . ." (emphasis supplied). The finest plans for instructional television and radio will still founder if colleges of education across the USA continue to pay the most minimal attention to these media.

The instructional television producer daily makes decisions which involve—however unconsciously—educational philosophy and the science of human learning. If his program turns out to be effective, he will probably attribute its success to "good intuition." Unfortunately, good intuition is a rare commodity. There is an analogy here with teacher train-

*Richard Hooper was on leave of absence from the British Broadcasting Company as a Harkness Fellow spending two years studying the state of educational technology in the United States when this paper was prepared (May 1968).

**Title III of the Public Broadcasting Act of 1967.

ing. Educational reformers talk nonstop about the need for more good teachers, but are unable to describe the processes by which a teacher is good. Therefore, it is difficult to replicate them. The problem is not with the good teachers. But how do you consciously influence the teaching techniques of the majority whose intuition is not so good? The science of learning has to begin where the art of teaching and communication—unfortunately —ends.

It is difficult to treat educational philosophy and the science of learning separately. They interact on each other the whole time. Increased research into the nature of creativity has led to increased emphasis on fostering creativity in school. Evidence about the importance of different thought processes has led to educational objectives being made less content-oriented. Educational philosophy is, in simple terms, the *what* of education: what is education for, what should students learn, what sort of adults should they become, what sort of society are we building? The science of learning is the *how:* how do people learn, how do we organize the classroom to attain optimal learning, how do people think, how does the presence of color influence learning by television? Most people would agree that *what* students learn is *how* to think!

Educational technology's success will be in direct proportion to the amount of attention it pays to the whats and hows of education. The educational film-maker who says "Don't bore me with discussion of educational objectives" is putting his long-term head in the long-term sand. On a slightly different level, too many people working in school broadcasting dismiss any responsibility for educational philosophy. A member of WQED (Pittsburgh) schools television staff said to me: "We are broadcasters—not educators. We should do exactly what they tell us." This categorization of broadcasters and educators, which is very popular in ITV circles, is dangerous. What is more, it is an illusion.

Whats First

Education is notorious for stating its goals in vague and ambiguous terms. This seems an unsatisfactory environment for educational technology to operate in, and would account for much of its failure to date. If there are no reasonably clear-cut objectives, selection of one medium over another is arbitrary and worthwhile measurement is impossible. One of the great roles that the newer media can play is that of a catalyst. Instructional television can demand a statement of *whats* because, unlike the textbook, it is a newcomer. It is breaking fresh into the circle (often vicious) of curriculum development. It is not yet locked into the cycle.

The whats of education come in all shapes and sizes. There are significant questions to be asked about rural poverty, college student unrest, the small Negro colleges, drop-out statistics, the "psychological" drop-outs, continuing professional education for doctors, adult training and retraining programs, the finances of private colleges, quality and equality in the inner city, massive surge in student population, massive growth in information, the credibility gap between the world of the classroom and the world outside, the new industrial revolution of computers, automation, and leisure. Before technology rushes off to help individualize the whole curriculum we must ask: doesn't a technological society of such complexity require a redefinition of the individual as he works more and more in teams? These questions must preface any in-depth study of educational technology. Otherwise, after much labor and many almighty dollars, we discover we have not been asking the right questions. How does it affect our conventional telelessons on *Silas Marner* and *Mill on the Floss* if we know that the average child watching them will by the age of 18 have spent more time in front of the television and in the movies than any other single activity (including going to school itself!) except sleeping? What relevance have detailed behavioral specifications in an American History course 1776-1861 to students who are burning the building down?

These questions must not just preface a study of educational technology. It is easy to pay lip service to rural poverty at the beginning, and end up installing instructional television in the prosperous white suburbs (which probably don't really want it). Educational technology will only come to mean anything if it identifies and then gets involved with *real* educational needs. Harvard and Stanford are not the places to implement educational technology. They do not think they have that sort of problem. But what about the small colleges away from major population centers? What about the decentralized campuses of state universities and junior colleges?

Far too much of educational technology, such as television, has in the past avoided the main educational problem areas. How many ETV stations have done anything for the inner-city kids? The main aim (often unconscious) of instructional television staffs has been simply to get television used. How many sets do you have? How many programs do your children watch? Will you continue membership in the school television service next year? No further questions. In 1963 Dr. C. R. Carpenter of Pennsylvania State University estimated that only about one percent of the total formal educational activity in the United States involves in any way the use of the newer media.[1] A portion of the blame for the miserable failure must be attributed to this media nationalism which causes television to ask the wrong questions.

It seems clear that if education—and therefore educational technology—does not make a real effort to identify the whats first, then American society will continue to be torn apart by Watts first.

Which Way Is West?

The Carnegie Commission stated: ". . . further major investments in instructional television must benefit from the discovery of ways in which television can best contribute to the educational process." The word "process" implies change, movement. The second question, following the whats, must be: how is education proceeding? In which directions is it developing?

There seem to be two major educational wagon trails. What is not so clear is whether they are both leading westwards, or in opposite directions. The first trail could be labeled *Unstructured* and pioneering names along the way might be A. S. Neill, Jerome Bruner, Paul Goodman, R. F. Mackenzie in Scotland,[2] John Holt. The second trail—*Structured*—has people like Skinner, Pressey, Ofiesh, and Lloyd Homme.

UNSTRUCTURED	STRUCTURED
Education is internal growth, discovery, and development without fixed goals in a changing and changeable environment.	Education is change from less desirable to more desirable behavior, which is fixed in advance and is externally measurable.
1st step—questioning whether education should be goal-oriented at all. Here the student is more likely to define his own objectives with adult assistance. Non-predictive, "discovery" type of learning.	1st step—definition of objective behavioral goals. Adult fixes objectives and, by controlling environment, tries to predict behavior.
Move away from exams and measurement altogether.	Measurement (objective if possible) to see whether student has reached agreed-on performance level.
Openendedness, diversity, problem-finding.	Clearcut endedness, definition, problem-solving.

Students select amongst wide range of different materials (if only because we do not know enough about learning).	Materials and sequence pre-selected for students (we know enough about human learning to control conditions).
Students manipulate and change environment.	Students work inside fixed environments.
More self-direction, more freedom.	More external control of behavior and conditions of learning.
"Education."	Training.

This dualism may turn out to be false when, and if, the conflicting camps ever get to talking to each other. I am beginning to think it is not so much a matter of opposing strategies as of different points along a continuum stretching from TOTAL FREEDOM to TOTAL CONTROL. The exact point on the continuum depends on such things as the particular student, the type and training of the teacher, the nature of the educational materials available, the specific subject matter or skill to be taught, degree of parental and legislative intervention. Clearly A. S. Neill's Summerhill would be hard to justify in an underdeveloped country which has immediate specific manpower needs. On the other hand, training people to rather narrow specifications may be just as dangerous in an advanced technological society like the USA.

There are other trends in education where there is perhaps more consensus. Identification of these is important if educational technology is going to jump on the right bandwagon. Clearly, broadcast television and radio for schools have some awkward questions to face if the move towards nongraded, individualized systems continues. Must instructional broadcasting is firmly based on lock-step group-prescribed lessons. At the moment the move away from this traditional means of organizing education is mainly at elementary level, but it is spreading upwards. The following trends can be identified:

FROM	TO
Group-paced and group-prescribed instruction for all subjects.	Individually paced and individually prescribed instruction for certain subjects, e.g. math, reading.
30-to-a-class graded schools.	1-5-20-100 to a group in nongraded, continuous-progress schools.
900 sq. ft. egg-box classrooms with poor acoustics.	Flexible areas of learning, clusters of space, acoustic treatment.
Scheduling 40 minute periods, musical chairs.	Modular scheduling, self-scheduling flexibility of time.

FROM	TO
Teacher as presenter of information.	Teacher as manager of classroom, consultant/tutor, diagnostician.
Emphasis on teaching.	Emphasis on learning.
Teacher/textbook/chalkboard do 99 percent of all information-transmission.	Wider range of media allowed in the classroom—including films, television and radio, discs and audiotapes, games.

Learning information; emphasis on facts/memory.	Applying information; emphasis on thinking skills.
Passive learning and regurgitation predigested conclusions and secondary source material.	Active learning and participation; inquiry/discovery and primary source material.
Book libraries and film libraries.	Instructional resource centers serving both teachers and students.
Categorization by subject-matter disciplines.	"Seamless web of learning" (Whitehead).
Education ends at 18/22.	Education—a lifelong process.

Although most people would generally agree that these trends exist, there is disagreement as to how much the newer ideas have been implemented (as opposed to just talked about), and also as to how these newer ideas should be implemented. Terms like "media," "individualization," "nongraded" have not settled down into any consistent meaning.

Trickling into these currents of educational movement in a haphazard way are odd bits of data welling up from basic research. A study of educational technology must take this basic research into consideration. The links between researchers and the teachers and television producers need strengthening if the science of learning is ever to get out of the laboratory. The basic research into learning and into audiovisual communication[3] should be treated with the same amount of seriousness that medical research is used to. Advances in medicine have not come about because of good doctors alone. They have occurred as a result of the painstaking accumulation of valid data about the human organism. Medicine is made up of three components—doctors (some of them good), hospitals and machinery, and a fund of scientific principles which guide the behavior of the doctors and the design of the hospitals/machinery. In education the third component is more often than not missing. It is replaced by hunches disguised as substantiated theory, and by something loosely called experience. Hunches and experience are vital to the doctor, but he has more formal supports as well. It is clear that educational technology, of all things, cannot progress very far without that third component.

A Matter of Definition

Concern with philosophy and science does not end here, but at this point goes underground, to pop up again continually throughout the study. It must serve as a backdrop for any endeavors concerned with educational technology. This entails the sort of "multi-levelled" thinking mentioned at the start, the sort of thinking which après McLuhan is difficult to express at all satisfactorily in linear-sequential one-word-after-another typewriter print.

An important first step in discussing educational technology itself is definition. What do we mean by it? The subject is surrounded by great semantic confusion. There is, of course, a danger of being too dogmatic at such an early stage. If the definition is too tight, it may inhibit further discovery.

To limit the definition of educational technology to machinery—e.g., films, coaxial cable, teaching machines, antennae—would make the task easier. But a study using this definition would quickly find itself up a blind alley. It would lead to the kind of infertile questions which were found in the original Title III draft of the Public Broadcasting Act, such as "the advantages and disadvantages of closed circuit television." Educational technology must essentially be an *idea* of which a closed circuit TV system is one (but not the only) concrete example. Fascination with the tangible machine to the exclusion of the intangible idea behind the machine has in fact led to stereotyped and impoverished uses of television and to a race of gadgeteers disguised as educational technologists.

The essence of television is not x monitors, y image orthicons, z feet of cable. Television is the capability of transmitting live or recorded, over distances ranging from a few yards to thousands of miles, chunks of reality in sound and vision. It is the instant replay of what happened ten seconds ago. It is instant distribution, to an infinite number of places and an infinite number of people, of the same event. It is the computer's mouthpiece, an extension of the police, a modern version of the psychiatrist's couch, and an electronic bathroom mirror for the student teacher.

Much of the trouble with instructional television is that it has taken over all the paraphernalia of commercial and public television without stopping to think. Educational technology is not a *thing*. John Diebold, a most persuasive illuminator of modern cybernetic society, makes the same point in relation to automation: ". . . Automation . . . implies a basic change in our attitude towards the manner of performing work. Perhaps because we see things more easily than ideas, this meaning of automation as a way of thinking has been obscured by a fascination with the machines of automation . . . Automation is more than a series of new machines and more basic than any particular hardware. It is a way of thinking as much as it is a way of doing. It is a new way of organizing and analyzing production, a concern with the production process as a system, and a consideration of each element as part of the system."[4]

We could plagiarize John Diebold to get a useful working definition of educational technology:

> Educational technology is a way of thinking as much as it is a way of doing. It is a new way of organizing and analyzing education, a concern with the education process as a system, and a consideration of each element as part of the system.

All Media Are Equal . . .

Some of the main elements that make up this system need identifying. The ones most relevant to this study are the media by which information transmission takes place and the student interacts with the subject matter. The traditional media for these tasks are the teacher and the textbook. *It is vital that a study of educational technology does not engage in media apartheid,* treating some media to the exclusion of others. There are obvious pressures to avoid the teacher and textbook media when discussing television. But they are intimately connected.

Just because in the past textbook selection procedures have been cut off from selection of relevant audiovisual media, there is no need to continue this irrational fragmentation. It is either all or nothing, and the categorizations such as "newer media," "electronic media," "self-instructional media," "nonprint media" have only limited uses. Otherwise the study of educational technology will only serve to prolong the basic tenet of today's classroom: "All media are equal, but some media are more equal than others." By perpetuating this deeply entrenched attitude the study would be in the ironical position of tightening the noose around educational technology's neck.

It would be useful to compile a list of available educational media. Just putting them all together will help the cause of media equality. Such a list reveals the rich resources which more and more classrooms can call on:

TEACHER	Teacher/tutor (1-2 students)
	Teacher/seminar (8-10)
	Teacher/class (30-35)
	Teacher/lecture (40 upwards)
	Teacher/multi-media lecture hall

PRINT   Textbook
          workbook
          programmed text
      Reference books
      Library (traditional)

VISION   Television
          open circuit
              local/regional
              national
          closed circuit
              one-room system
              more than one room
          dial access/video
          Electronic Video Recording (CBS, coming soon)
      Film
          16mm
          8mm single concept
                  with sound
                  without sound
      Filmstrip
      Slides
          slide/tape
      Overhead transparencies
      Opaque projector
      Chalkboard
      Stills, charts
      Maps

SOUND   Radio
          two-way radio
          educasting radio
          sub carrier authorization
          radiovision (radio + filmstrip,
              very popular with
              BBC schools radio)
      Telephone
          telelecture
          telelecture with electronic blackboard
      Audiotape
          language laboratory
          self-instructional multi-media laboratory
      Phonograph discs
      Dial access/audio

TEACHING MACHINES   Teaching machines (not computerized)
      Computer-assisted instruction
              teletype
              teletype/audio/video

THREE DIMENSIONAL
EQUIPMENT   Laboratory equipment
      3-D manipulative materials, toys
      Educational games, e.g., EDC's social studies
          game *Empire*
      Simulation equipment, e.g., Navy's Anti-submarine
          Warfare Attack Trainer

OUTSIDE CLASSROOM   Field trips
    museums
    historical sites
    nature sites
    Correspondence courses

Is this sort of list useful? If so, how can it be developed so that more of the known characteristics of each medium come out? Four types of data could begin to be collected for each medium:

1. *Logistical*
Questions of cost, ease of accessibility and use.
Technical limitations. Availability of software, libraries, etc.

2. *Message characteristics*
What sensory modes? Television—auditory/visual
    3-D materials—tactile/visual/olfactory
    Simulation equipment—kinaesthetic, etc.
Modes of representation
    Radio—verbal, nonverbal sounds
    Textbook—verbal, print, still photos, maps
Feedback characteristics, branching potential, response modes
What new capabilities does it give teacher/student?
What are peculiar qualities of medium? How does it influence content?

3. *Attitudes towards medium*—Faculty, administration, students

4. *Research data on effectiveness*

No comprehensive data are available for any medium. Much that could be said about television would have to be subjective. But it might serve as a useful superstructure on which to build in the future. Evidence of costs and technical limitations would be useful immediately. For example, despite some ardent claims, there are limitations on what CAI can and cannot do at the moment. It is important when discussing media characteristics to draw a careful line between what is now possible and what is only potential. This line has been glossed over by dial-access enthusiasts. They use words like "random" which are misleading. In fact, students can have random access to only those tapes which have been set up on the hundred or so channels available, and even then they may come into a program half-way through. The present high cost of true random access makes its introduction seem remote (as with random access for computerized information retrieval).

These media and various combinations of them are the building blocks which can be manipulated by the educational technologist. Educational technology is the orchestration of available classroom media through the dimensions of time/space/dollars to achieve agreed-on objectives with a given student population.

Media Orchestration

If educational technology is a way of thinking about education, that way of thinking should be valid and useful in the analysis of any size unit from the events in one 45-minute period, the design of a closed circuit system, to the full operation of a university. This way of thinking should be valid and useful to a system which has little extra money and no great inventory of equipment. It should be able to provide creative answers for a distraught teacher who wants help *now* and cannot wait until the system is comprehensively reformed. It should lead to the fullest exploitation of television equipment that has already been purchased, whether or not new equipment can be added. It should be valid in the analysis of procedures in both the *Structured* and *Unstructured* systems.

Educational technology has four main components. The words "stages" and "steps" might be best avoided because the process is not strictly sequential:

Objectives formulation

Identification of types of learning involved

Manipulation of conditions of learning

Measurement

Objectives Formulation

Question A: Who Should Select Educational Objectives?

The answer to this—which is too often taken for granted—will vastly influence the rest of the process. In the more *Unstructured* system the students will play an important part right here. "We cannot have real learning in school," writes John Holt in *How Children Fail* (page 179), "if we think it is our duty and our right to tell children what they must learn. We cannot know, at any moment, what particular bit of knowledge or understanding a child needs most, will most strengthen and best fit his model of reality. Only he can do this. He may not do it very well, but he can do it a hundred times better than we can. The most we can do is try to help by letting him know roughly what is available and where he can look for it. Choosing what he wants to learn and what he does not is something he must do for himself."

The question of who selects objectives is equally vital in the production of a television lesson. At present, for example at Hagerstown, the television professional is thoroughly subordinate to the educator—usually a classroom teacher with minimal experience of the medium who has been chosen as TV teacher by other educators on the basis of classroom abilities. The result is Big Talking Face and a use of television to do what was already being done in the classroom. This is undeniably part of television's role but the medium should also open up new paths, not just retrace familiar ones. If it is agreed that the media of television and radio have special qualities and that it takes experience to feel them (it is much more than just an intellectual/conscious process), then there must be more equality at this point. Too often the television people are consulted after the major decisions have been made by highly print-oriented people who are unaware of their biases.

The medium *affects* the message and this is often forgotten in curriculum development. Too often, especially from the new "systems analysts" of education, the design of conditions of learning is overly sequential. First you define objectives and then you select the right media. This is a neat arrangement but, like so many neat arrangements, it is oversimplified. Form and content—as we know from poetry—cannot be so easily separated. This sort of thinking leads Hagerstown to state: "Television is a conveyor of ideas, not a creator."[5] Thus the creativity of the newer media is gently syringed out, and the members of the inner sanctuary continue to refuse entry to television and film people while the important objectives are being formulated.

Question B: Should There Be Objectives at all?

The all too easily accepted assumption "You must first state your objectives" must itself be scrutinized. Lack of objectives may turn out to be very fruitful in certain areas, despite what behaviorists say. It may actually inhibit a lot of art, literary appreciation, younger children's play to demand detailed objectives. These detailed objectives will be very useful when the student has decided he really does want to learn to speak Spanish. Marshall McLuhan points to this problem with objectives in an anecdote: "When people approached T. S. Eliot and said: 'Mr. Eliot, when you were writing "Sweeney among the Nightingales" in that passage XYZ did you mean . . .' he would wait patiently and say, 'Yes. I must have meant that, if that's what you got out of it.' "[6]

One of the problems that television and radio in education encounter is attracting creative people. Too often creative directors are confronted with lists of objectives and curriculum committees, also demands that they have a teaching certificate and/or Ph.D. in mass communications which may be irrelevant qualifications. By the time the list of objectives has been read out, they have probably left. It is worrying to think that imaginative television people get more freedom (not just financial) on Madison Avenue than they do in instructional television. Education—and educational technology—should be BIG enough to say to a radio wizard: "We want some ten-fifteen minute programs on Imagination for 10, 11 year olds," and leave him to it. The greatest works of art—in any medium—are those where each member of the audience comes away with something different.

Question C: What Input Data Should Be Collected To Assist in Formulation of Objectives?

Objectives are radically influenced by the kind of people who select them. They are equally affected by the amount and quality of the data that is collected and fed into the discussion. Too many of the variables which make up the conditions of learning are treated as constants and thus are not even questioned when objectives are being formulated. Which data are relevant depends upon the subject under analysis:

Category I

STUDENTS	Number; age; individual differences; prior knowledge; styles of learning; motivation; pace; interests; reading level.
INSTRUCTIONAL MEDIA	Teachers: number; competencies and experience; attitudes to change; costs per teaching hour. Textbooks; availability of xerox copier; projectors; availability of films, slides, tapes; number of television monitors; museum proximity; costs.
SPACE	Number and size of classrooms, lecture halls; library space, carrels; number of power points; acoustics; lighting arrangements; costs of space usage.
TIME	Maximum and minimum time available.
DOLLARS	Any spare dollars not tied up in buildings, teacher salaries.

Category II

SOCIETY'S, INSTITUTION'S OBJECTIVES	
LEGISLATIVE COMMITMENTS	Local state history, for example
MANPOWER NEEDS OF NATION	
REQUIREMENTS OF TECHNOLOGICAL SOCIETY	
SUBJECT MATTER	Structure of the disciplines (Bruner); old or new math; relationship between discipline as taught and discipline as practiced outside: analysis of engineers, historians, doctors to identify possible objectives; content or process approach.
LEARNING THEORIES	Assistance with correct sequencing of objectives; analysis of creativity in engineers.

Note: Category II will be more important during objectives formulation, whereas Category I's importance lies more with the design of instructional strategies.

Most analyses of education are suboptimizations. "Analyses . . . confined to lower level contexts, which assume decisions given at higher and collateral levels, are called 'suboptimizations.' They attempt to find optimal (or near optimal) solutions, but to subproblems rather than to the whole problem of the organization in whose welfare or utility we are interested. If a consumer tries to solve his transportation problem (Cadillac v. Chevrolet) more or less in isolation, taking other major decisions affecting his income and expenditure as given, he is suboptimizing."[7] The art teacher who wants to reform her procedures within the three 40-minute periods she has each week with class x is suboptimizing. The television producer is suboptimizing when he is given the task of producing thirty 20-minute lessons on Climate to go with y textbook.

The aim should be to take as much input data into consideration and as few "assumed decisions" as possible. Clearly the more input data and the less assumed decisions, the nearer you are to dealing with the totality of the system, and vice versa. How often can the television producer ask: why thirty lessons? Why twenty minutes long? Why this particular bit of geography? Why this textbook? And even, why television? Schools, television and radio are faced with the eternal problem of "not alienating the system," but as much as possible they should try and question assumed decisions taken at higher and collateral levels. Without this relentless questioning, television will continue to talk off the point and be used on the periphery.

The collection and organization *in manipulable form* of all relevant input data for a given set of objectives is a major task for the educational technologist. The high-speed data-processing capabilities of the computer will come to the rescue as input data from major systems such as school districts comes flooding in.

Question D: What Constitutes a 'Good' Objective?

There is no one criterion for judging objectives. It depends on the orientation of the people involved (more, or less, behaviorist), and most important on the subject matter. A good objective in the training of hard-core unemployed many differ greatly from a good objective in college-level physics. Possible criteria for judging the value of objectives are: degree of objectivity and measurability; degree to which it does not state the "means" by which the objective will be reached; degree to which its attainment is administerable; degree to which it does not select content; degree to which it stresses the intellectual skills and processes in relation to content; degree to which it is not a test item; degree to which it tells the student what he has to perform, under what conditions, and with what criterion of acceptable performance; degree to which objectives are sequenced in valid hierarchies and taxonomies; degree to which objectives have been externally validated (x behavior desired in medical course relating to x behavior displayed by successful practising doctor).

The development of techniques which can accelerate the formulation of good objectives is another major task for the educational technologist. Present procedures with behavioral objectives are time-consuming, thus arousing much faculty antipathy.

Identification of Types of Learning Involved

This component of educational technology is still closer to the researcher's laboratory than to the classroom or television control room. Given the objectives, what types of learning do they involve? Robert Gagné has described eight types in his well-known book *The Conditions of Learning:* signal learning; stimulus-response learning; chaining; verbal association; multiple discrimination; concepts; principles; problem-solving. Gagné stresses the provisional nature of this list and is sure that there exist higher-order cognitive processes which have not yet been identified. Knowledge of the types of learning should feed directly into the manipulation of the conditions of learning.

Manipulation of Conditions of Learning

Question A: What Are the Constraints Within Which Strategies Must Be Devised To Reach the Objectives?

This makes use again of the input data already collected (specifically Category I) and also the more detailed lists of media characteristics discussed on pp. 144-146. The formula for the actual manipulation looks like this:

STUDENTS
interacting with
SUBJECT MATTER
transmitted by
INSTRUCTIONAL MEDIA
in various combinations, dictated by:
SPACE
+
TIME
+
DOLLARS
+
TYPES OF LEARNING IDENTIFIED

This formula could, for example, lead the producer of a series of telelessons in a school district closed circuit system to ask the following questions:

STUDENTS — How many? What previous knowledge? Age and grade? Any common features, e.g., motivation level, academic/nonacademic?

SUBJECT MATTER — Which content to select? Does the content dovetail with objectives? What additional content could be introduced to heighten interest and broaden relevance? Does the presentation of content require more than just factual recall and recognition?

INSTRUCTIONAL MEDIA — What media are available?
Closed circuit television: Is there a TV course already produced that might be suitable? Live or recorded? Studio or classroom origination? What opportunity for student participation during lesson? Provision of worksheets to accompany lesson? Who should present lesson? What films, slides, stills are available/can be made? What music/sound effects? How should lesson end? What is role of television in relation to:

Classroom teachers: What preparation before lesson suggested? Follow-up activities? What content/skills will teachers handle which television does not? What visuals do teachers have to reinforce visuals in telelessons?

Textbook: What information does the textbook carry? Is it to be duplicated by television? Is it basically for reference and independent study? What visuals from book can be used in television lessons?

TIME — How much time is allotted to course overall? How much should be via classroom teachers, television, independent study? Is more time available? What about scheduling problems, repeat broadcasts? Has teacher time for previews?

SPACE — Should telelessons be watched in large group? In classroom groups? If in large group, how much teacher time is saved? Could some of the classroom follow-up be done in large-group lecture? Could some of classroom work be reinforced with independent study? If so, what are facilities for independent study? Is there space in instructional resources center for student review of videotapes?

DOLLARS — Are there any loose dollars? If so, could they pay for a set of overheads for classroom teachers? Can dollars be saved via large-group lecture/independent study? How efficient is space usage? What is cost of finding films and stills already produced, versus cost of producing them?

This type of thinking may not reveal anything very helpful. But it can be a useful device for getting people to see the wider implications and possibilities. It will help to get better mileage out of available resources. Many of the questions may not have answers, but this in itself will suggest further courses of action. This sort of questioning might in a small way stop television systems from sliding into ruts without realizing it. Time, space, teachers, television are called variables. They should vary.

Question B: Who Should Manipulate the Conditions of Learning?

This is as important as who selects educational objectives. In many places the same group do both. Where this is not the case, it is necessary to ensure that the collection of input data is not duplicated. From the *Structured* point of view the manipulation is done by the behavioral technologist. The John Holts would give much more power to the students themselves.

One of the real problems here is that students do seem to learn in different ways. It is probably only economics and tradition that make us think there is one solution for all the class. There is evidence that some students learn better from books, other from tapes; some are more methodical, others more intuitive. The John Holts are saying that, because of these individual differences, the best guide is the student himself. He will tend to gravitate, given a diverse enough environment, to the means that best suit him. The cafeteria studies with young children seem to support this. Given a varied diet to choose from and complete freedom, young children end up eating a good balance even though they may eat nothing but ice cream for two days! The great challenge to the new media in the *Unstructured* system is to make this diversity and richness possible. Books and live teachers cannot do it alone.

Under whatever system, the question of who manipulates the instructional strategies is very important for television. Television people must identify these manipulators and get with them. It affects the whole nature of their power to create, rather than just follow instructions. If television is to mean anything in education, its creators must be amongst the doctors writing the prescriptions, and not—as happens with audiovisual people—remain with the pharmacists filling those prescriptions. Television people do not question enough their role of service agency. Technology—whether it likes it or not—must struggle for power in education. Gas stations do not affect the design of new cars.

What is the optimal team for manipulating the conditions of learning? In the hypothetical example above of the closed circuit television producer, the success of the series will depend on the quality of the relationship he can establish with the TV teacher (if there is one—TV teachers should not be assumed) and also the classroom teachers. Teamwork between producer and classroom teachers is clearly easier in the highly localized Chicago cluster-school TV system (e.g., Richard Byrd Elementary School) than in WNYE which programs for all New York City schools. The real complexity of the problems facing the educational technologist is caused by the highly fragmented, highly decentralized nature of decision-making in education. The manipulators of the same conditions of learning may be separated by miles and never meet at all. The problem is discussed more fully under MEDIA ORGANIZATION. One thing is certain: a creative relationship has to evolve between the artist, who is traditionally individualistic, and other members of the team such as classroom teachers, behavioral psychologists, and measurement experts. For really dynamic television, form and content must be born together. The challenge of instructional television is that for many subjects, especially at college level, form and content have to be two different people.

It is too often assumed that there is only one way of combining the variables—the various media, time, space, etc.—to reach the objectives. Systems analysis in education promises experimentation with different combinations to achieve the same objective. *The essence of systems analysis is generating alternative models.* Education is strongly resistant to this kind of competition. ETV stations have carefully avoided competing with the educational establishment. When, and if, the financial base of the stations is strengthened, today's necessary political attitude may not prove quite so necessary.

One of the more tedious aspects of educational technology's confrontation with the traditional classroom is the amount of time and print devoted to assuring all concerned that "Nothing will ever replace the teacher." If this is true, then educational technology may as well surrender. The whole point of the newer media is to do things which the live teacher (for a number of reasons) is unable to do. In industry there is something called offensive research—research oriented towards making existing company products obsolete. Education and educational technology could do with some offensive research plus an admixture of competition which is so lauded in the rest of American society.

Measurement

Question A: Is Measurement Necessary?

Technology in its industrial application is tightly bound up with measurement. Measurement is at the heart of systems analysis. But educational technology may reject measurement in certain areas or, at least, make a much more sensitive use of it. There is a real danger when applying industrial techniques to education that we rush headlong into measurement and quantification without asking why. Measurement in education should be scrutinized and not assumed. As we know from Heisenberg in physics, the act of measurement disturbs the subject being measured. This disturbance may, especially on the arts and humanities side, prove to be unacceptable. Measurement is clearly involved in the educational process but it should not be allowed to dominate. Under the impact of an aggressive educational technology, this might happen. The trend away from exams amongst the *Unstructured* pioneers and the intense frustration of teachers and students with the grades system should not be lightly dismissed. Some educational technologists are so infatuated with the possibilities of measurement that the system they envisage turns out to be more authoritarian, more linear, more tedious, than the worst system is today:

> "As the student enters the school and takes the achievement and aptitude tests, the tests are scored and then the school psychologist examines the results and makes his recommendations as to the degree of reinforcement and the orientation or instructional methodology most apt to be successful with the particular individual. These test results and the psychometrist's recommendations are immediately acted upon by the school psychologist who specifies the student's counselor, subject matter teachers, carrel and initial program(s). The materials center and teaching staff (administrative heads at this point) operating within the guidelines provided by the administration and societal needs allow the school counselor to make this initial schedule."[8]

This "analysis" should be shown to anyone who cannot understand why faculty remain more than skeptical about the applications of technology to the educational process.

Measurement has a big function in education as it is today, and the discovery of really creative measurement people should have high priority. Educational measurement tends to be gross and insensitive. It reveals little or nothing about which instructional strategy is better, about how different sorts of audience participation improve learning by television. Measurement basically says that this student is "better" than that one but we are not sure why. Gross comparisons between television and conventional instruction have not yielded any very valuable data to help us with the following questions:

Why and when to use television as opposed to live teachers?

Which students gain more from TV than live instruction and vice versa?

What way can telelessons be improved to make for more effective communication?

Media orchestration is going to depend on this sort of evidence. Otherwise choice of medium will continue to have more to do with the bias of persons concerned than with any requirements stemming from the conditions of learning and the students themselves.

Some television people talk loud and long about each medium's having its own special qualities. This is true but it camouflages the fact that media are far more interchangeable than has been imagined. It would have been nice and comfortable if there was no overlap between the media and thus no cause for media hostilities. What has to be established by measurement is the amount of uniqueness and the amount of overlap each of the media possesses. Faced with the fact that both medium *a* and medium *x* are equally suited to performing this instructional task, then the choice may end up being an economic one—which is cheaper? If such a stage as this could ever be reached, radio would blossom again!

Question B: What Sorts of Measurement?

Pre-testing and Evaluation This measurement is important *before* the full implementation of an instructional strategy. How do we know that our manipulation of the conditions of learning is going to work? Will this radio series as designed be effective in teaching nurses principles of old-age care?

There has been very little pre-testing of any of the new media, except for some programmed texts. Television people are resistant to "wasting" any money on anything other than production. Pre-testing is expensive and will demand more cooperative regional production if it is to be feasible. Pre-testing must be used selectively. It will not be needed with a series of lectures by Hermann Bondi on gravitation. It should be used in a course for policeman on knowledge of the law. This kind of measurement has the great value of putting hunches and intuition periodically to the test. Broadcasters can become very isolated from their audience without knowing it. Pre-testing makes you question that audience, think about vocabulary and reading level, pace and sequencing decisions.

The television mistake is to rely on colleagues' evaluation. It can be taken for granted that those colleagues are only rarely a representative sample of the target audience. Pre-testing techniques for the newer media need more development. At the moment they resemble Stone Age Man's big club. Instructional television must question whether the production techniques and studio design which have been taken over without hesitation from commercial television are suited to the requirements of pre-testing.

Diagnostic Testing Diagnostic testing is playing a prominent part in the move towards individualization of teaching strategies. The Oakleaf School in Pittsburgh uses an individualized math course consisting of over 400 sequential objectives; it is vital to know where the student is, to start him at the right point. This problem is not so urgent with group-prescribed instruction. Diagnostic testing will help the teacher, in her new role as classroom manager, in putting the right child in contact with the right materials at the right time. To the educational technologist, diagnostic testing is important for the collecting of Category I data on students' characteristics. Communication starts with an awareness of the audience. Too often this stage is left out.

Criterion-Referenced Testing   Here instructional materials and strategies are internally, as opposed to externally, validated: What percentage of all the objectives set up for the particular course were reached by the students? Instructional materials are here judged by the degree to which they attain *their own* objectives. This may be a more fruitful sort of measurement than the usual normative testing.

It is a reaction against the rather sterile comparisons between television and conventional instruction which, as was said above, have not revealed much useful data. A French course is measured against x,y,z objectives which are its own stated goals, and not against another French course which, more than likely, does not have the same ones. One of the problems with media comparison′studies is that the live teacher does some things better, television other things. By comparing them, these cancel each other out and reveal no significant difference. But if we measure the live teacher by his ability to achieve those objectives which may be unique to the teacher medium, then progress is being made.

Unobtrusive Tests   The ideal testing situation would presumably be reached when testing and learning merge into each other. This is happening with CAI where complete records of the student's interaction are kept for analysis. In the freer learning environment, materials would be measured by their degree of popularity. People such as Richard Spencer at Illinois are developing course-evaluation questionnaires which are for student use. There are hopeful signs that the subjective comments of the students are quite a good (unobtrusive) measure of the actual course effectiveness.

Cost Measurement   There are two types of cost measurement: cost measurement pure and simple, and cost measurement in relation to effectiveness. The cost of music education for 5th graders in x school district can be measured even though there may be no desire to measure effectiveness. Cost-effectiveness should not be used indiscriminately in education.

Cost analyses would help to focus educational technology. When IBM says it can provide CAI for $1.00 per student-contact hour, it is talking a language almost totally foreign to education. Costing in education has tended to be as gross as many other forms of measurement. But it would be a great step forward if some elementary costing came into the classroom: what are the costs of teaching reading in 2nd grade? What are the costs of a freshman general science course? Such costing is complex because it requires splitting up teachers' salaries, materials costs, heating and electricity, space usage, and—at college level—separating out the closely knit strands of teaching and research. At the moment the real cost of television instruction is lost in the fog. Yet without this costing, it seems difficult to know how a university administration can make any rational decisions about its future.

Another advantage of costing is that it will make technologists and educators in general much more committed to getting mileage out of existing equipment and space. NBC can tell you how many dollars it costs to have studios unused. What university closed circuit systems could do the same? Schools already have, tucked away in parts of the building, many pieces of equipment which are under-utilized. Yet they complain that they do not have the media available to individualize as they would like to. The transmission powers of ETV stations remain unused two-thirds of the week[9] at a time when society needs more and more information movement.

Machinery in any form is money. Educational technologists cannot afford to be sloppy about costing procedures. Television people complain bitterly about shortage of money. But much money has been spent on television and is sitting around the country in the form of unused or underused cameras, studios, coaxial cable (see for example Indiana University, Great Neck Public Schools, Oral Roberts University, etc.). It is not so much shortage of money as very poor allocation of resources. As we move into the era of computer-assisted instruction, dial access, and computerized information retrieval, cost analyses must become part of the process.

The Programming-Planning-Budgeting System (PPBS) which rose to fame under Mac-Namara and Hitch in the Defense Department has potential application for education. Big-city school systems like Washington, D.C. are already thinking about it. It involves a deep analysis of decision-making procedures to see what information needs collecting in what form to facilitate that decision-making. PPBS is a systematic way of relating resources available (e.g., dollars) to objectives desired. It is a way of getting maximum competition of ideas in the search for the best solution to a problem.

Traditionally, the budgeting aspects of a system have been isolated. PPBS bring the budgeting problem back on stage. Traditional budgets list *objects* of expenditure—television maintenance, teachers' salaries, telephone bills. Under PPBS the aim is to list *objectives* of expenditure—remedial reading, 11th grade Chemistry, beginner's French. It is then possible to see what resources are going where, whether the right balance is being achieved, and—in the long term—generating more efficient ways of teaching reading (cost/effectiveness). This sort of budgeting will be a direct help to the television and radio enthusiasts. It will be possible to demonstrate what particular contribution and at what cost per student the radio series is making to any designated program objective. At the moment this cannot be done with much objectivity.

PPBS is the kind of technique that makes it possible to look at the total system. It is one of the best examples of the global thinking described at the beginning of the paper. Because of its complexity, the introduction of PPBS into education lies in the future. But the way of thinking it embodies can permeate the approach of the educational technologist now.

Media Organization

The ultimate success of the four-part process called educational technology will depend on the types of organization that are created to implement it. How can the necessary cohesion be given to the varied problems of production, storage, access to resources, evaluation, distribution, and utilization? For example, the high quality *production* of a schools radio series does not automatically ensure its *utilization*. How can we integrate the traditionally isolated decisions made by curriculum supervisors, librarians, film-makers, textbook selectors, school architects, audiovisual coordinators, and budget managers? In the past these decisions have been made by separate and semi-autonomous units without much attention being paid to the wider context or other units whose decisions overlap/duplicate.

The problem of media organization is encountered in the arrangement of a university, the administration of the school library, the storage and retrieval of nonprint materials, the size of materials-production centers, state and regional networks. The type of administrative structure radically affects the decisions and actions made within it. For example, the unpleasant question needs asking: is the present pattern of local stations compatible with good quality ITV production? The Carnegie Commission envisages in ten years 380 local ETV stations, of which over 200 will have production facilities of varying kinds. Are there 200 film editors available—given the call of commercial TV and films, and also the closed circuit systems? Is not the present poor quality of ITV programs related to the lack of shared and centralized resources? Why has EEN, the model regional network, produced only one series for schools on a regional/cooperative basis? Are local stations compatible with the move towards regional production centers for newer media, advocated by people like C. R. Carpenter?

At university level many of the problems of closed circuit television can be traced to a weak organizational structure. Television grew up by itself—cut off from the audiovisual services, the behaviorists interested in programmed instruction, the measurement people, and, of course, the library. The closed circuit system had one aim: to get closed circuit used. If a professor wanted help, that help was predetermined to take the form of closed circuit television. It is not therefore a surprise that television has not grown beyond rather elementary uses in a small percentage of courses. The educational process is far too complex to be adjusted by one medium, however valiant.

Today there is a trend to remedy the unhelpful categorizations of the past by moving towards some kind of integrated media structure. Michigan State University, Northeastern University in Boston, University of Illinois, University of Wisconsin are front-runners in this move. The new structures usually include television and radio (closed and open), audiovisual services (including film-making), measurement, and a very small group of behaviorists.

Unfortunately, the integration hasn't gone far enough. The fast-growing computer centers, which often include CAI projects, are not connected (see University of Illinois). More importantly, the library is still administered separately. As the library gets more involved with technology, this fragmentation will prove as anomalous as that between television and audiovisual. The new media structure often fails to have close links with the architectural and design people, with the result that new buildings are still going up without even the most obvious needs of educational technology allowed for (enough power points, lighting arrangement, etc.).

In the search for the best way of organizing media for a given problem it may be useful to look at education as a communications process and the educational institution as an information system. We are beginning to think about the modern library, for example, not as a pile of bricks and bindings but as information movement. The new information sciences have a big contribution to make to educational technology. Information and its handling are becoming the largest functions of a technological society. Thus we can ask the following kinds of questions in the design of media organization:

What information needs to be transmitted?

What and how is it stored?

What format should the information being transmitted take?

To what points/people should it be transmitted? At what speed?

What is best distribution device for transmission? How can 'noise' be reduced?

What type of access to information is required? At what speed?

These sorts of questions will help us solve educational communications problems at many levels of complexity. If this type of question has been asked in the Daly City, California, elementary school involved with the EBF/Bell and Howell $600,000 Discovery Project, then the first thing to enter the classroom would not have been a 16mm projector but acoustic carpeting.

Educational technology faces overwhelming problems of accessibility and these kinds of questions will improve the chances of finding solutions. The television producer has problems of access to visual material. What central libraries of film footage, slides, stills exist and how should they be expanded? How should nonprint materials be indexed? What types of access does the producer have to the library? Heaps of visual material wait to be used but are unknown, un-indexed, uncoordinated, or lost in the quicksands of copyright. Television and radio also face the problem of access to research data on audiovisual communication. Where is the data stored? How can it be made most accessible? How can research conclusions be rewritten so that directors understand them? These questions are being asked by ERIC, the Educational Resources Information Center at the Office of

Education. This is the kind of way that the science of learning can creep into the busy TV control room.

The audiovisual coordinator and the classroom teacher have problems of access to films, audiotapes, videotapes, slides. Poor accessibility radically lowers usage and interest. Libraries like the National Center for School and College Television, the National Center for Audio Tapes at Boulder, Colorado, and the National Medical Audiovisual Center at Atlanta are making an impact but much greater expansion and resources are needed. The McGraw-Hill NICEM project with the University of Southern California, which is cataloguing via computer all available educational media, is having troubles. Today's school administrator who has the task of purchasing educational hardware and software is being swamped by the quantity of firms and conflicting claims. Brochures, unscrupulous salesmen, "statistics," and gratuitous advice descend on him and he probably does not know a videotape recorder from a correlation coefficient. To help him, Educational Products Information Exchange in New York City is trying to do consumers' reports on educational media.

The most important asset that any media organization can have—whether it be a television station, an instructional resources center, or a state education department videotape library—is flexibility. Educational technology is changing faster than the media organizations. Media organizations should be busy diversifying and merging; instead too many sit still and say "Well, we are broadcasters, that's our job." WGBH is one of the few educational stations that has seen the writing on the wall and is busy in its Education Division investigating other aspects of telecommunications and educational media. The CBS EVR device may alter considerably traditional patterns of production/distribution. What is the best organization for production purposes may not be best for distribution.

There are many pressures which make media organizations inflexible and unwilling to diversify. One very strong pressure comes from the multitude of national associations which are set up to push their own particular medium. The dilemma facing NAEB is that they are talking about educational technology but their survival depends on local ground-based television and radio stations. The pull of the technology may be towards a grid system of regional media centers but the pull of the association is towards as many local stations as possible. The media hostilities, for example between television and audiovisual, are real barriers in the path of media equality and integration. The rechristening of DAVI is a step in the right direction. Media organizations that look integrated are often less so on close examination. The same mentalities are there but under different names.

A study of educational technology should devote much time to the study of the various types of media organization and come up with guidelines. What media organizations exist are needed to solve the problems of:

Production quality?

Storage and good retrieval/distribution?

Utilization?

Evaluation?

An interlocking system of local/regional/national centers needs developing which can swiftly upgrade the quality of production, distribution, and usage of "instructional television and radio . . . instructional materials such as videotapes, films, discs, computers, and other educational materials or devices."

A media organization, at university level, ought to contain as many of the following elements as the size and character of the institution warrant:

Television
Closed and open circuit

Radio

Audiovisual
Service and production aspects

Library

Computer center
CAI projects

Behavioral psychologists
To work in teams with TV, audiovisual, measurement, innovation strategists, in the manipulation of conditions of learning with the subject matter experts.

To develop programmed instruction in print, film, computer media.

To run research-and-development activities. Basic research should be going on besides applied work if only for prestige reasons vis-a-vis faculty.

Measurement team

Innovation strategists
To guide implementation of new projects. Innovation strategy has been neglected in the past.

Training unit
For technologists themselves
For faculty

Close links with budgeting office, involved with PPBS techniques

Close links to new building projects

Close links to department heads and faculty

Operations-research unit
Developing PPBS/systems analysis techniques

Special brief to keep media organization flexible and responsive to changing conditions

One of the key problems facing the media organization at university level is establishing relationships with the department heads who make the curricular decisions and the faculty who need time, encouragement, and assistance. This is a delicate problem. At Michigan State, the Educational Development Program reports directly to the provost and EDP's director has his office a few doors from the provost. When department heads come to the provost with an instructional problem, it can easily be passed to EDP for scrutiny. The Educational Communications Division at the University of Wisconsin reports to the head of Extension which is less favorable in terms of contact with the main university departments.

Another problem, related to this, is the degree of centralization. In a large university, decisions are made at various levels and at various distances from the center. A challenging task facing the educational technologist is how to balance enough decentralization to get faculty involvement and enough centralization to get the full benefits of technology (critical mass factor). At Ohio State University a mini-media organization has developed in the chemistry department because the chemists considered the central organization

(Telecommunications Center) too distant and too cumbersome. This problem of centralization/decentralization rears up in the discussion of optimal sizes for closed circuit systems, the relationship between local stations and national/regional networks and libraries. The pros and cons of centralization and decentralization have to be carefully weighed.

The question facing any media organization in its attempt to implement educational technology is: who should make what decision at which point in the process? The decision by the administration not to permit (for financial or other reasons) free time for teachers to preview films, work on objectives, develop strategies, *on a regular basis,* clearly affects the speed with which educational technology can be introduced. Educational technology is a technique by which the decision-making procedures of a whole system can be scrutinized and ordered. As with systems analysis in other fields "the objective is to *sharpen* intuition and judgment." [10]

A Personal Opinion

This paper has described the major direction which a study of educational technology should in my opinion take. A summary of these directions—in question form—will be found at the end. Before this summary I would like to append my own more personal feeling about the role of the new media—particularly radio and television. Educational technology is, I feel, the asking of the right questions. Here are some brief subjective answers to one or two of them.

Freedom

The most challenging function of educational technology is to liberate teacher and student. Technology, correctly and creatively applied, should enable the kinds of freedom in education which have often been dreamt of, but have only rarely found reality. Group-paced and group-prescribed instruction was a virtual necessity when the educational media available were restricted to live teacher and books. Individual differences had to be put to one side in any normal system with average teacher/student ratio.

But with the sudden blossoming of many different ways that students can interact with subject matter and with (not necessarily live) teachers, these individual differences can be taken seriously. The built-in monopolies of education are destroyed. The rigidity of what students learn, how they learn, when and at what pace, is no longer necessary. One teacher and textbook per thirty students are no longer the only solutions. New combinations of teachers, students, materials, space and time, can be dictated more by the existence of educational needs, and less by the absence of appropriate instrumentation. The live lecture as *the* medium of college undergraduate education can now be seriously questioned.

A new freedom in education is necessary if only because of the world beyond the classroom walls. The sort of society into which today's first-grader will step after high school is not *known.* Change is the only constant, and the educator can no longer be sure at all that he knows "what is good for the child." The sensitive use of technology in education will increase the alternatives, and will allow the student to find his own direction more easily. He can be surrounded by a richer store of experiences and realities. This store can be organized on modular lines so that he can combine the various units to his own specifications. (This same modular freedom must be given to the teacher so that she can have the choice of complete courses or single units according to need. Closed circuit TV has been obsessed with complete courses to the exclusion of providing individual units of vivid interest on the modular system.)

Educational technology—by analogy to the cafeteria studies—is able to place the student in the midst of a balanced diet of knowledge and exploration. Some of the units will be programmed behaviorally, others will remain much looser and less systematic. Thus self-direction, seldom achieved (I think actually inhibited) by traditional group methods, may become an attainable objective. This self-direction is indispensable in a world which has prospects of increased leisure and has demands now for nonstop learning through life.

Freedom has always been stated as a goal of education in a democratic society. But the only real training for freedom is the practice of it, rather than preaching about it. Technology makes this freedom more attainable. It liberates the individual from the group. Education is an intensely personal affair.

First-hand Knowledge

Many years ago, Whitehead wrote: ". . . we must rise above the exclusive association of learning with book-learning. First-hand knowledge is the ultimate basis of intellectual life. To a large extent book-learning conveys second-hand information, and as such can never rise to the importance of immediate practice. Our goal is to see the immediate events of our lives as instances of our general ideas. What the learned world tends to offer is one second-hand scrap of information illustrating ideas derived from another second-hand scrap of information. The second-handedness of the learned world is the secret of its mediocrity."[11]

Via educational technology, the student can encounter something nearer to first-hand knowledge than is customary. He no longer has to just read about the flora and fauna of Brazil, he can "see" it. The television can transport Brazil in two dimensions, the museum in three dimensions. Traditional education is one long intervention between the learner and the subject to be learned. Television has the power to bring the student face to face with reality as it unfolds. But more and more ITV series are canned and rented from libraries. Radio can go anywhere very fast and very economically and confront the student with the demonstrator himself, with the poor people's leaders at Resurrection City, with explorers in the Antarctic. Instead, school radio broadcasts some woman reading stories from a book about George Washington.

Knowledge and reality are too often needlessly filtered by textbooks and teachers so that by the time they reach the student they are predigested conclusions, neatly packaged, with complete multiple-choice tests, and thoroughly divorced from the "radically, untidy, ill-adjusted character" (also Whitehead) of reality. Schools television should dominate along with radio the teaching of current affairs in American schools—but they don't. Most of TV time is spent watching another teacher talking about something that is not shown.

If we had stopped to think more about the unique qualities of the medium, educational television and radio stations would behave less like canning factories. All schools programs are planned and committed a year in advance thus destroying the main benefit of the medium (over, say, film)—*spontaneity*. It is sad to think that those working in games theory and simulation are doing more to offer students an encounter with reality than live broadcasting. This is one more example where television and radio are being bypassed by other media. Education is the exploration by man of his environment. Educational technology has the exciting opportunity to help create that environment in and around the school, so that the student can explore it, manipulate it, and learn to accommodate himself to it. The newer media can ensure that this simulated environment is not too abstract.

Equality

Nearly all classrooms in America can have the luxury of hearing and/or seeing Sir Laurence Olivier play Othello. The cause of equality of educational opportunity can be furthered by educational technology. When the telecommunications network envisaged by EDUCOM is operational, the small college in the boondocks can have direct access to the greatest libraries in the country. At the moment, via the National Library of Medicine's MEDLARS system, doctors in Denver can get as much up-to-date bibliographic information on recent medical literature as doctors living near the central computer in Bethesda.

Why should the college student in Alabama not be able to see lectures by Commager at Amherst? This has been technically feasible for years. The dream of master teachers via TV—much talked of in the 50's—has never been realized. It has ended up with compromise candidates picked by the local establishment for local use. Great Plains is distributing college courses not by Gerald Holton at Harvard or Postlethwait at Purdue, but by faculty of Chicago City College. The promise is still there. Technology does not have to move people, it moves the effects of people. The limits placed on this movement are political, parochial, financial—not technological. Equality in education—by which I mean access to equally rich learning environments—is not possible in a country devoted to mass universal education without recourse to technology.

Relevance

The disadvantage of books and films is that schools (and students) have to use them for at least five years to get back the investment. But TV, radio, and the Xerox copier are in the front line of events. They can be the shock troops in the conquest of irrelevance in education. The challenge facing radio and TV is relating what is happening now to the classroom. Radio and television can make regular trips to the frontiers of science so that the high school physics student can identify with the bigger picture. The great quality of tape (audio and video) is that it can be erased and used again. It can thus make a dynamic—rather than static—curriculum. The xerox copier makes instant textbooks. Vietnam, civil rights, air pollution, famine in Asia are too often evaded in school. Technology can help to dynamite curriculum guides at regular intervals.

Creativity

Most of the latent creativity in students has to be expressed in writing essays, painting, making speeches. But the media of creativity outside the classroom are far broader. Educational technology should be moving towards the day when one student hands in an 8mm film on "Spring," another an essay, and a third a sound documentary. Screen education demands a place in school unless it is believed that television and film are still not as influential in modern society as the poem and short story.

The museum project at Berkeley, EPOCH, is a good example of the use of the new media to develop creativity. With the use of slides, discs, films, tapes, 3-D objects, whole environments are created around the student in a special circular chamber. It may be a scene from Bangkok, Thailand, or the four walls of a pharaoh's tomb, or a mix of Art Nouveau and modern psychedelic art.

Once the principle of media equality has been accepted, and the present restrictions have been listed on what constitutes art at school, a far higher level of creativity amongst all students will, I believe, be discovered. The creativity of the teachers themselves can be enormously stimulated by the multimedia lecture halls as at University of Wisconsin. Much of education is concerned with the different faces of perception, the different dimensions of reality. These dimensions cannot be squeezed into print, mathematical symbols, or the teacher's voice. The multi-sensory quality of a modern urban environment should not be stunted in the classrooms.

A Replicable System

Educational technology's ultimate goal should be the creation of systems of education that are replicable, and that are relevant to the needs of mass universal education. In the design of these systems, a majority of good teachers cannot be assumed: in Washington, D.C. during 1966-7, 45.1% of teachers were temporary.[12]

America's lasting contribution to the underdeveloped world will not be teacher-training colleges, but a science of education. Educational technology is the way we engineer and instrument that science. How do we get good education to those students not lucky enough to have good teachers? That is the question facing the educational technologist. By the year 2000 there will be 6 billion people living on this planet. Population growth since the 1950s has led to an *increase* in the aggregate number of adult illiterates living in the world.[13]

Summary

Educational philosophy
    What are the priorities of American education?

Science of learning and communication
    What are the trends in the way American education is organized?

    What scientific data can be brought to bear on the design of the educational environment and on the improvement of educational communications?

Educational technology
    How do we define it?

Educational media
    What are all the available media in education? *No discrimination.*

    What sort of data can be compiled, characterizing each of the above media?

Educational technology: a four-part process
    Objectives formulation: Who should select objectives?
                               Should there be objectives at all?
                               What input data should be collected to assist in formulation?
                               What constitutes "good" objectives?

    Identification of types of learning

    Manipulation of conditions of learning:
                               What are the constraints within which strategies must be devised to reach objectives?
                               Who should manipulate the conditions of learning?

    Measurement: Is measurement necessary?
                               What sorts of measurement?

Media organization
    How do we organize educational media to implement educational technology?

    How do we organize educational media to implement educational technology?

    How do we integrate media and curricular decisions?

    How centralized/decentralized should media organizations be?

    What media organizations exist/are needed to solve the problem of:

Production and quality?
Storage and good retrieval/distribution?
Utilization and evaluation?

REFERENCES

1. Quoted in *NAEB Journal,* Vol. 26, No. 3, May-June 1967, p. 27.

2. Mackenzie, R. F. *Escape from the Classroom.* Collins, London, 1965.

3. Travers, Robert M. W. *Research and Theory Related to Audiovisual Information Transmission.* HEW/ University of Utah, Revised ed., 1967.

4. Diebold, John in "The Nature of Automation" in Burke, John G. (ed.) *The New Technology and Human Values,* Wadsworth Publishing Company, 1966.

5. *Washington County Closed Circuit Television Report.* Hagerstown, Maryland, undated, p. 79.

6. Stearn, G. E. (ed.) *McLuhan Hot and Cool.* Dial Press, 1967, p. 296.

7. Hitch, Charles J. and Roland N. McKean. *The Economics of Defense in a Nuclear Age.* Harvard University Press, 1960, pp. 128-9.

8. Rodgers, Dr. William A. and Lawrence M. Gariglio. *Towards a Computer-Based Instruction System,* USOE, 1967, p. 26.

9. *One Week of Educational Television.* No. 4., April 17-23, 1966, Morse Communication Research Center at Brandeis University and National Center for School and College Television, 1966, p. 12.

10. Gene H. Fisher in David Novick's *Program Budgeting,* Rand Corporation, 1964.

11. Whitehead, A. N., *The Aims of Education and Other Essays,* 1959 ed., Macmillan, p. 79.

12. Passow, A. H., *Toward Creating a Model Urban School System: A Study of Washington, D.C. Public Schools,* Teacher's College, Columbia, 1967, p. 109.

13. Coombs, Philip H. *The World Educational Crisis—A Systems Analysis,* International Institute for Educational Planning, 1967, p. 13.

36.
Using an Experimental Laboratory for Identifying Classroom Multi-Media Problems and Requirements[*]

by
WILLIAM P. KENT[**]
WALT Le BARON
ROBERT M. PETERSON
System Development Corporation
Falls Church, Virginia

Summary of the Final Report

This study emerges from a conviction that new media have much of value to offer to education, but that there are problems in deciding where and how to use them, in what combinations, under what conditions, and for what purposes. A review of the multi-media field (including standard audio and visual devices, television applications, computer-assisted instruction, instructional data-transfer systems, and so on) indicates that current practices are generally rather ineffective and that research and development efforts have been limited in scope. New approaches are evidently required.

The feasibility and desirability of laboratory approaches to educational media were investigated by this project. Systems methods formed the background of the investigation, though the project was limited to conceptual exploration and to the analysis of past and present experience. No new laboratory was constructed for trial and evaluation, but expert opinions representing many disciplines and backgrounds were sought out, written accounts were reviewed, and innovative installations were visited.

An important conclusion of the study is that *"multi-media problems" neither exist nor can be solved in isolation from total educational systems,* including their political and social environments. A laboratory to address these problems should be concerned with a complete spectrum of activities, including research, system planning, design, operation, evaluation, and diffusion.

Six types of laboratories (or laboratory-like organizations) are distinguished as being able to deal in various ways with educational media. These are:

1. Planning and Policy Institutes (concerned with predicting future needs and with recommending goals and methods).

2. Basic Research Laboratories (concerned with discovering and verifying general principles).

[*]*Research performed pursuant to a contract with the Office of Education, U.S. Department of Health, Education and Welfare.*
Complete final report (ED-029-492) available from ERIC Document Reproduction Service.

[**]*William P. Kent is head of the Washington Staff of the Education Systems Department of the System Development Corporation.*

3. Component Development Laboratories (concerned with discovering, testing, perfecting, and demonstrating equipment, materials, and procedures in comparative isolation from their final intended environment).

4. Simulation Laboratories (intermediate between component laboratories and laboratory schools; activities take place in quasi-total environments in which as many factors as possible are either actually present or represented by more or less realistic simulations).

5. Laboratory Schools (concerned with discovering, testing, perfecting, and demonstrating equipment, materials, and procedures in actual educational situations: single classes, schools, or groups of schools).

6. Comprehensive Development Laboratories (concerned with continuously planning, supervising, evaluating, and supporting systematic educational improvements; aspects of the five preceding laboratory types are coherently combined).

Of these six types of laboratories, at least three already exist and function more or less effectively. These are basic research laboratories, component development laboratories, and laboratory schools. In addition, educational planning and policy activities are fairly widespread. The two educational laboratory types which do not yet clearly exist, and which promise needed assistance in solving multi-media problems, are simulation laboratories and comprehensive development laboratories.

Simulation laboratory approaches to educational problems have to date shown limited success in relation to costs. A semi-manual, computer-based laboratory utilizing time-sharing techniques is judged to have the greatest chance of improving simulation laboratory effectiveness, but its main contribution would be as a research vehicle. It would tend to bring appropriate models, data, and functional analyses into existence as both a condition and a result of its operation, but it could do little by itself toward reaching solutions to the major problems which lie in the areas of development and diffusion. It therefore does not represent a feasible approach to multi-media problems.

In the restricted sense of technical feasibility, a computer-based simulation laboratory for studying multi-media problems is indeed feasible. One could be constructed and operated on the basis of existing technology. A more important question, however, concerns the value or cost-effectiveness of such a laboratory. Taking this broader point of view—which can be referred to as "cost-effectiveness feasibility"—there are very serious doubts as to whether this type of laboratory should be recommended.

Current multi-media problems will not be solved merely by developing new techniques to facilitate investigation, in the sense of finding ways of doing traditional studies with greater finesse. Moreover, even going beyond a simple linear extension of current research methods and thus attaining a more comprehensive concept of research would still be far from enough. The enormous technical apparatus of a computer-based simulation laboratory is not what is needed in order to review, analyze, evaluate, and generate alternatives to current multi-media practices and the assumptions and institutions in which they are embedded. Obvious problems exist, and alternative solutions are already being proposed and—to a limited extent—tried out. But even an optimum simulation laboratory could do little by itself to define and implement solutions to multi-media problems. Additional basic research, it may be assumed, will always be required. But today there is no specific evidence that the great educational problems are awaiting further research results before they can be solved. The difficulties which seem critical today are those of putting into effect what we already know—of making educational goals explicit, and of caring enough to reconstruct educational practices and institutions so that they effectively reach these goals.

Problems of development and diffusion are currently of greater importance than those in the research area. It may even be a mistake to claim that research is of primary long-run importance, since (as has been repeatedly demonstrated in the past) research conducted in isolation from development and diffusion tends to be inconclusive, difficult to apply, and generally of doubtful value. For these reasons, the simulation laboratory approach to multi-media problems appears infeasible, in the sense that such a laboratory could do little by itself toward reaching major problem-solutions.

The *Comprehensive Development Laboratory* has as its distinguishing characteristic that it is concerned with integrated and continuous planning, supervising, evaluating, and supporting systematic educational improvements. As such, it combines in a coherent fashion aspects of each of the other five types of laboratories: planning and policy formulation, basic research, component development, simulation, and experimental schools.

No laboratory of this comprehensive sort as yet exists—at least in the full degree envisaged here. Educational Facilities Laboratories, established by the Ford Foundation "to help schools and colleges solve their physical problems by encouraging research, experimentation, and the dissemination of knowledge regarding educational facilities," is perhaps the closest approximation to the concept. EFL, however, does not emphasize systematic operations to the extent of ensuring fully integrated planning-development-evaluation activities.

Some of the Regional Educational Laboratories which have been established by special legislation also approximate to some degree the concept of a comprehensive development laboratory. None of these organizations, however, has undertaken to systematically attack the complete spectrum of problems related to the design, development, and implementation of major multi-media and/or telemedia innovations. There is reason to believe that the laboratories might reconsider their abilities to deal with such problems, but their primary contribution appears to lie in other areas. The kinds of problems envisioned for a comprehensive multi-media development laboratory will require a concentration of attention, and a freedom from pressures for short-term visible results, which do not presently tend to be characteristic of the Regional Laboratories.

The concept of the Comprehensive Development Laboratory emphasizes careful attention to phased system and sub-system planning, design, description, specification, production, installation and operation. Overall needs for "technical management and design control" and for "evaluation and evolution" are also specifically responded to. These phrases are brief reminders of vitally important system principles which have often been learned the hard way—by violating them or by ignoring them. Too many complex systems have been built and have failed (or have needed major reconstruction) because of insufficient attention to advanced planning (analyzing system goals, environmental constraints, and available resources), to specification of hardware-software-personnel functions and interfaces, to orientation and training, to testing sub-systems and the total system against stated goals, and to the need for evolving as new or unanticipated problems and opportunities arise.

The Comprehensive Development Laboratory includes research activities, at least in the sense of applied research, in connection with prototype developments which are usually advisable at various times during complex system development. Basic research is generally of a longer-range nature, and would not be attempted as an actual part of the process of developing a specific system. Experiments with parts, aspects, or simulations of a system under development are highly appropriate and necessary, however. They should be planned for and carefully managed, to insure genuine contribution to solving developmental problems. Applied research in a broader sense, including operations research and environmental analysis, is also pertinent.

Diffusion and dissemination are also essential functions of the comprehensive development laboratory, which must always be concerned with strategies and tactics for successfully sustaining operations in an increasingly wide environment.

Organization   Organizational structure should facilitate and reinforce laboratory tasks. A possible functional organization could be based on three fundamental types of activities—plans, operations, and evaluation. In addition, a "meta-development" activity is required in order to bring the laboratory into effective existence; various support activities are also necessary.

Planning, operations, and evaluation are all indispensable. It is important that no one of them be permitted to dominate the others, as often happens in organizations. At the same time, it is unwise to give operators the sole responsibility for planning or evaluating their own activities. Similar comments apply to the possible dangers of permitting either planning or evaluation to be undertaken for their own sake, without being thoroughly integrated into ongoing operations.

From another viewpoint, the organization of the Comprehensive Development Laboratory could distinguish those operations directly related to multi-media equipment from those which are more conceptual, reflective, or analytic in nature. In that case, a "research and development laboratory" could be distinguished from an "institute of advanced studies." This distinction, however, would be inappropriate for the laboratory here conceived, which emphasizes the integration rather than the separation of thought and action.

Facilities   The Comprehensive Development Laboratory will plan multi-media applications, directly or indirectly carry them out, and evaluate them as contributions to widespread improvements in education. At the outset, it is doubtful that such a program would require extensive physical facilities. Indeed, it would be safer to begin with the assumption that physical facilities other than office space are not needed, to emphasize that the success of the organization is to be judged by its impact on education, not by the magnitude or expense of its inventory and arrangements.

Without experimental facilities of its own, without a computer, and without a demonstration school to operate, such a laboratory can nevertheless be in a strong position to organize and direct a fruitful and influential program of activities to be carried out in a variety of schools and research centers. But of course the laboratory must be well-managed, imaginatively directed, and adequately funded. It must have a strong, capable staff, dedicated to its purposes and techniques, and intimately involved in all details of the activities it sponsors. It must have access in a variety of ways to on-going school programs for purposes of observation, trial, and evaluation of designs. All sponsored activities must be well-planned and clearly defined as integral parts of a coherent program.

It is possible that as the multi-media laboratory develops its programs, it will identify tasks which can most effectively be carried out directly by the laboratory's own staff. If so, it may acquire experimental facilities of its own. These, however, should be made to depend on later analysis and assessment, and should not be included in original planning. Such facilities would vary with particular programs of research, but might eventually include some or all of the following:

1. Menus of multi-media devices, equipment, and support facilities.

2. Resources for the development of experimental software and other programs for the multi-media devices.

3. Sufficient computer capability to permit the design of simulations, games, and other applications.

4. Facilities and equipment for "walk-through" simulations and related techniques.

In the pre-equipment stage of the laboratory (which may continue indefinitely), geographic location can be based on a comparatively limited set of factors, of convenience, including the availability of appropriate personnel, cooperative school systems and other educational organizations, and related research and development efforts. Proximity to a major center of air transportation would be of interest.

Personnel   The basic structure of the laboratory would evolve around a team organized for the systematic development of programs and tasks. Although various activities might require special staffing, the basic laboratory staff would include permanent expertise in the following areas:

1. Educational systems analysis, design, and development

2. Multi-media equipment design and operation

3. Multi-media materials development and production

4. Engineering and design of learning spaces

5. Learning theory, concept organization, and child psychology

6. Testing, evaluation, and psychometrics

7. Modeling, simulation, and gaming

8. Educational management, economics, and politics

9. Cost-effectiveness analysis

This group would constitute an interdisciplinary team who would find their common theme in the integration of their various specialties around major problems involving the design and implementation of multi-media systems. Each of these groups would analyze needs in its own area and would be free to recommend needed projects. Although skills devoted to major problems would change according to the problem situation, the essential task would remain the design, evaluation, and eventual implementation of complete educational systems optimally incorporating media.

Functions   A comprehensive multi-media development laboratory conceived along the lines indicated above would be engaged in a broad spectrum of functions. Its general mission would be to develop, test, and actively disseminate systematic cost-effective uses of telecommunications, media, and other technological innovations for educational purposes, in such a way as to begin and sustain changes of major significance throughout American education. In fulfillment of this mission the multi-media laboratory should devote its attention to:

1. Problems of system design and implementation

2. Measurement of alternatives

3. The development of implementation models

4. The development of improved information systems and feedback

5. The recording of replicable experiences

6. The assistance of interested groups in mounting and evaluating multi-media instructional programs

7. The dissemination and demonstration of worthwhile prototypes

Comments on aspects of these functions follow:

Operational Testing and Development   One of the most important functions required is developing and testing designs which embed instructional media and techniques in operational teaching-learning environments. This would permit the examination of technology utilization within a context of actual environments. It would be possible to identify those factors that complement, enhance, or hinder the effectiveness of the technology; and required modifications to media and other system components can be determined. By making the required modifications and engineering the total system as dictated by evaluated experience, the advantages and limitations of technology can be determined and the necessary conditions for its appropriate utilization specified. The objective would not be to perform comparative evaluations of the effectiveness of competing media, but to test and develop, by iterative cut-and-fit procedures, media and other components of the total instructional system. The end product would be demonstrably effective instructional media and techniques with documented specifications for their appropriate utilization in the school environment.

Empirical Research A laboratory, in a more conventional sense of the term, may be used to perform studies aimed at acquiring new knowledge through direct observation of the behavioral results of technology utilization in learning situations. It is useful in considering the specific focus of the laboratory to distinguish between experimental and exploratory studies. Experimentation and exploration are distinguished here on the basis of the extent to which the observation and data recording and analysis are guided by precise hypotheses and the degree to which rigid controls are exerted.

Experimental Studies. Some problems of educational technology may be amenable to rigorous experimentation, i.e., the formulation of testable hypotheses, the controlled manipulation of prescribed variables, and the measurement of concomitant variation in other variables. Such research requires formal theory to guide the formulation of hypotheses. Since it is doubtful that adequate theory exists for classroom learning in general or for educational media in particular, it will usually be necessary to resort to less formal techniques of empirical exploration.

Exploratory Studies. Even where understanding of a given problem is meager, that problem may profitably be represented in a laboratory or examined in the field for purposes of direct experience and exploratory observation. This approach is appropriate when there is inadequate theory to identify critical relationships and generate testable hypotheses. However, orderly search can make important contributions to the clarification of problems and to the stimulation of new insights and hunches that may lead the way to more formal experimentation or systematic trial.

Analytic Research A computer facility within a laboratory could contribute directly to analytic research, not only through straightforward computational support, but also through symbolic simulation. In order to deal simultaneously with a large number of intricately related variables, it may be possible to develop analytic models of those variables and their interrelationships which may then serve as the basis for computerized simulations. By this means it may be possible to approximate solutions to otherwise unsolvable problems through artificial sampling and other solution-by-analogy techniques. However, computer studies within a laboratory should themselves be carefully planned and evaluated. There have been far too many instances where computer operations have absorbed a disproportionate share of research resources, yielding results of little if any superiority to those derivable by less elaborate means.

Demonstration A laboratory can serve as an effective means of two-way communication between researchers and educational practitioners. It can provide the capability for live demonstration of the results and products of a technology research and development program, which in turn will provide direct experience to experts throughout the educational community as a basis for critically examining demonstrated results and posing new problems. This may well be the most effective means for promoting increased participation and expert criticism in educational research and development. This increased involvement may lead to improved user acceptance, and should accelerate the transition of technological advances to classroom application.

Integration   A laboratory should provide the opportunity to integrate the problems, results, and methods of other research and development activities. Where related problems or educational elements have been isolated for purposes of study and analysis, these problems and separate study results may be related and combined. There may also be advantages to be gained in integrating not only the content or subject matter of the research, but also the research methods themselves. For example, the use of classic experimental techniques with analytic simulation in some iterative combination may provide a power, scope, or efficiency not possessed by separate methods alone.

Techniques   An important aspect of the comprehensive development laboratory will be its conscious and explicit subordination of techniques to problems. For this reason, it will avoid commitment to a limited set of favored techniques. It should be prepared, on the other hand, to use any techniques which may be required and which are justifiable as probably yielding returns commensurate with their demands on the laboratory's resources in funds, people, and equipment.

Although *simulation techniques* do not appear promising enough to justify a laboratory devoted exclusively or primarily to their use, they should be considered as among the possible tools for a comprehensive development laboratory. Since the laboratory will have no predetermined commitment to simulation, balanced judgments should be possible on the value of simple or complex simulations in particular cases. The status of an issue may be such that simulation is not the right tool. Some problems are too vague for rigorous experimental treatment and require preliminary definition by means of field research or other research methods. Some problems are so highly specific, on the other hand, that simulation is too elaborate. Methods such as small-scale experimentation or graphic analysis should then be considered.

Similar comments apply to *digital computer techniques*. The computer has made possible vast new potentials for the understanding of educational behavior through its ability to deal with tremendous amounts of data at fantastic speeds. In fact, so great is the computer's potential for dealing with mass data, that its abilities have often overreached the current state of analytical sophistication.

Often, a computer's principal influence on a process or an investigation has been through the impetus it has given to careful analysis and evaluation. Since computers are expensive and precise, they tend to demand unusually painstaking formulations of issues and of results. It then frequently turns out that although clarification has been achieved and decisions have been improved, the computer in itself made no contribution, since its actual computations were either self-evidently true, or irrelevant, or derivable by other and simpler means. A multi-media laboratory should avoid wasting its resources on elaborate computation, when the actual requirement is for penetrating analysis.

In general, a developmental, problem-solving laboratory should be prepared to use and defend *less formal methods* than those which are usually associated with the idea of laboratory research. This will not be easy, since wide knowledge and considerable good sense will have to be substituted for methodological formulas. Traditional experimental methods will not often produce results having real impact on anything so complex as public education. In order to achieve the precision and control required by traditional methods, the phenomena of real interest are usually stripped out of the problem. The result is often a precise, unambiguous answer to a question that nobody has asked.

The following "informal" methods appear worthy of consideration:

Cut-and-Fit Methodology. This method requires establishment of behavioral objectives and a process of try, fail, try, succeed. The "success" may not be optimal and its causes are not always clear, but the process allows the elimination of the ineffective and some insight into the degree of change necessary within a situation. First trials should be small-scale and short-term, gradually building into more complete attempts.

Problem Analysis. A good research strategy for studying problems occurring in large, complex systems is initially to embed—really or symbolically—the system of interest in a noiseless environment, i.e., one which is completely deterministic. After having determined how the system behaves in this environment, disturbing elements can be added one at a time to determine their effect on the system's behavior. This procedure will not isolate all of the possible interaction effects or in general satisfy the requirements of ideal research design. But it is a systematic way to deal with very complex systems and does permit the addressing of problems that are unmanageable by traditional pure methods.

Informal Simulation. Informal simulations of some aspects of the educational situation are feasible and can contribute to educational improvement. Enough is known about student behavior so that its limits can be specified and the interesting points on a continuum can be identified. These and their assumed relationships to other educational factors can be incorporated in a model which can then be used in sensitivity studies. Such studies will not uncover new knowledge, but they can indicate where the potential pay-offs lie and guide subsequent empirical research and development.

Walk-through simulation is another promising technique for multi-media development. This consists of analyzing some complex process and then having a group of technicians "walk-through" or role-play the steps or events in the process. It can provide important insights and avoid mistakes prior to a full-blown field test. Walk-through simulations of this type are similar to new developments in micro-teaching, and offer great promise as relatively inexpensive, uncomplex research devices.

Delphi Techniques. The Delphi Method has as its purpose the utilization of expert opinion in situations which lack a theoretically convincing reason for selecting a particular action or a particular policy for action. It replaces direct debate by sequential individual interrogations interspersed with information and opinion feedback from earlier parts of a program. The methodology can have important consequences for educational research, especially as concerns the complex situations in which multi-media operate. A careful analysis of expert opinion across the many subject fields and specialties involved in the design and development of the learning situation could help to resolve both major and minor implementation problems.

Educational Planning Games. Great interest has been expressed recently in the use of games for educational purposes. One educational planning game uses four teams of educational experts, two of which represent groups of professional personnel, one represents community interests, and the fourth represents "inhibitors" or "reality screens." The first two teams develop a plan or strategy for attacking a significant educational problem and are then confronted by the countervailing forces represented by the other groups. The result, if the game runs long enough, is a compromise position which takes into account all of the factors pressing upon an issue. In this manner the participants recognize the forces acting in a situation and are able to develop a realistic solution.

Programs A great variety of activities would be appropriate for a comprehensive development laboratory with the structure and functions described above. However, it would *not* direct its energies primarily toward inventing or developing particular multi-media devices; producing software packages, instructional packages, or curriculum packages— except on a prototype basis; training personnel in large numbers; building or operating a school or institution for a long-range program of education; or carrying out controlled, experimental activities aimed at basic research or the creation of knowledge. Its programs of course might result in suggestions for any of the above activities, and in such cases recommendations would be made that they be supported by other agencies.

The laboratory's basic concerns would be with working out and demonstrating systematic sets of solutions to important educational problems. It would focus its efforts on particular tasks which could be formulated in terms of evaluatable goals, and which would give reasonable promise of contributing significantly to the advancement of education. The laboratory would intend to make a major difference in the conduct and results of education, not just a difference in theoretical understanding or in superficial appearance.

Difficulties Establishing a comprehensive development laboratory will not be easy. Many of the difficulties, though, will be more or less routine, in the sense that they could be expected in connection with any new laboratory or organization. These are such matters as securing adequate funding, acquiring an appropriate staff, and building up staff agreement on the significance of laboratory policies and methods.

Other difficulties which may be anticipated are present or potentially present whenever educational changes are tried out. Because of the fears which prospective changes always tend to create, the sensitivity of the field of education, and justifiable concern for the effects of research techniques and new developments on children, strong constraints may be placed on experimentation.

Special difficulties with a comprehensive development laboratory may be anticipated because educational situations, including those to which multi-media can make a contribution, rarely permit the explication of a clear-cut statement of aims and goals broad enough to account for the total educational experience, especially over a considerable period of time. While this complaint is often heard, and frequently countered by pointing to the development of "behavioral objectives" (or arguing that education is an art anyway), much remains unaccounted for in any deliberate educational experience. Frequently, any one experience will contain a number of incompatible goal systems operating within the same environment. This confusion of educational purposes makes output analysis difficult.

In addition, only limited information is available on the interrelations among significant elements in a total educational situation. There has been considerable research on parts of the problem, including the adaptation of mediated instruction, but there has been insufficient attention to the nature of the total situation and the effects of varying one or more elements.

Other special difficulties would be caused by the facts that many of the innovative techniques appropriate to the laboratory are in early stages of development, and that personnel who understand their uses and limitations are in very short supply.

The existence of these several types of difficulties, however, does not mean that a comprehensive development laboratory must be deferred until all difficulties cease to exist. On the contrary, it is implied by the laboratory's concept and methodology that among its functions will be clarification of educational goals, analysis of interactions among elements in total educational systems, improvement of its own techniques, and training of its own staff. All laboratories engage in shaping their own conceptual tools and in developing their own personnel. The comprehensive development laboratory is committed to iteration and evolution. Its participants will learn (through actual trials, through evaluation of successes and failures, and through progressive improvements) both how to think about and operate the laboratory itself, and how to improve education.

Feasibility   A comprehensive multi-media development laboratory of the sort described in this chapter is needed, is technically feasible, and would have an excellent probability of making significant contributions to education without excessive costs. "Multi-media problems" exist, and opportunities for fully effective educational uses of media are unlikely to be realized unless a much more comprehensive and systematic approach is taken than any that is being used today. There is no technical reason whatsoever to prevent a comprehensive multi-media laboratory from coming into existence and operating successfully. The difficulties would be those of inertia, institutional resistance, and a lack of support.

Financial support is the ultimate key to the feasibility of the comprehensive multi-media development laboratory. With adequate support, there is good probability that the laboratory would rather soon demonstrate its value and begin to establish the credibility of its methods. However, support should include sufficient guarantees of stability to ensure that there would be no undue pressure for quick results, and that well-qualified personnel would be attracted to participate in it. Annual costs can be roughly estimated at around $2,000,000.

An adequately funded laboratory of the sort described should be able to make major contributions to the development and diffusion of improved educational systems. In fact, if such a laboratory can not make significant contributions, then nothing else can, except perhaps through accidental or chance occurrences. The laboratory as defined would have a clear mission, effective methods, and resources and personnel capable of sustaining its efforts through the stages of discovering and designing what is needed, trying out and improving its designs until they can accomplish their goals, and catalyzing their widespread dissemination.

Implementation   There are several ways in which implementation of a comprehensive multi-media development laboratory could be carried out. For example, the laboratory could be established as an entirely new organization, or it could be based on some related existing organization which would be given a new direction and charter.

A "meta-development" activity is required in order to develop the laboratory itself, in distinction from the educational systems the laboratory will eventually be concerned with developing. In the process of developing a system, the system mission, functions, and configuration are established in what is often called the "Conceptual Phase." The present feasibility study is a contribution to that phase. Next should come the Definition Phase, in which desired accomplishments (objectives or "end items") are specified in greater degree; then the Acquisition Phase, in which the laboratory staff and organization are more fully specified, assembled, and evaluated as potentially contributing to desired accomplishments; and finally an ongoing Operations-and-Modification Phase, in which improvements are suggested, implemented, and evaluated on the basis of actual experience. In the Acquisition Phase, of course, considerable attention is paid to analyzing, identifying, and acquiring the resources necessary and justifiable for attaining objectives.

An *"adaptive" methodology* is implied by the foregoing remarks. That is, explicit designs and plans are constructed, but it is expected that they will need continual review and revision as experience is gained during their implementation. No one yet knows enough about educational technology to be able, merely by reviewing past experience, to write complete and ideal specifications for a comprehensive multi-media laboratory. What is needed (at two levels—both for developing the laboratory, and for the laboratory itself in developing multi-media educational systems) is a systematic program of planning, thought, tentative decision, trial, evaluation, and revision. Full-scale trials should usually be comparatively late, following after simulated, prototype, or small-scale trials. Adaptive methodology is required in order to increase chances of success in approaching situations which are not completely understood. Educational systems eminently represent such situations.

37.
Educational Research: Perspective, Prognosis and Proposal*

by DAVID R. KRATHWOHL
Dean, School of Education
Syracuse University

Do you feel like a pioneer? Do you think of the work that you are doing as venturing in relatively unknown territory? I suppose in some senses every researcher does, but the sense in which I mean it is in terms of the larger perspective of where we have come, where we are, and where we might consider going next.

Educational researchers tend to think of themselves as being in a very rapidly growing field, with deep roots in the past. We have been preceded by a host of distinguished researchers, so that we feel much closer to "having arrived" today. Yet I believe that education and educational research are today much more like they were in the past than they will be in the not very distant future.

In the longer time perspective, Judd and Thorndike, Buswell, Gray, Horn, Brownell, and other early empirical research workers were in reality only the advance scouts. Though I'm sure they never viewed themselves that way, they were our Lewis and Clark, Daniel Boone, and Father Marquette—men who advanced into relatively uncharted territory quite early and left their mark. You and I are the beginning of the mass of pioneers in covered wagons who will be the settlers to develop the territory. We are the ones to begin the hard work of research and development that are yet to come.

This picture of where we are and where we have been results from: (a) viewing past research efforts in the light of the funding patterns that supported them, (b) contrasting this with the tremendous changes that seem likely to occur in R and D in the future, and (c) the assumption that education will allocate a proportion of its resources to R and D, comparable to the average of 3% so allocated, according to NSF, by other segments of our economy. Education, by contrast, now spends considerably less than 1% of the operational education budget (it is estimated at 2/10ths of 1%) on educational research and development in all fields. It seems inevitable that as soon as we can show worthwhile returns from educational research there will follow a marked increase in its support. I am as critical as all of you of educational research, its quality and its problems, but I am equally confident that this day will come.

Is it too soon to look for such returns now? From the figures given of the USOE R and D funding, it is apparent that ¾ths of the major funds available for educational re-

*This paper was prepared for and presented at the annual convention of the American Educational Research Association, Los Angeles, California, February 6, 1969.

search and development have been allocated in just the past three years. According to Garvey and his associates,* it takes, on the average, at least four years from its start for a study to be completed and reported in secondary sources such as reviews. That's at least one year yet for the first batch of results to be ingested into the "packed-down" body of knowledge on which the development process and new research build.

Even though it may be early to see substantial results, the trend of the times is to "show and tell." The number of committees that have recently examined the educational scene, either as a prime focus or in passing as part of a larger review, makes an impressive list.

(a) A committee of the President's Science Advisory Committee, headed by Dr. Wertheimer of the Department of Chemistry of Harvard. (b) A committee of the National Academy of Education, chaired by Lee J. Cronbach and Pat Suppes, has examined educational research.[3] (c) A Special Commission on the Social Sciences, appointed by NSF and chaired by Orville G. Brim, Jr. (d) A parallel study by the National Academy of Sciences, with the assistance of the Social Science Research Council. (e) The Research and Policy Subcommittee of the Committee for Economic Development recently issued a statement, *Innovation in Education: New Directions for the American School,* with direct implications for R and D.[2]

Add to this Congress. Examples are the extensive hearings of the House Special Subcommittee on Education headed by Congresswoman Edith Green[6] and the Report of the House Committee on Government Operation, headed by Congressman Henry Ruess.[5]

We have been funded long enough that, even though it is still early, it has seemed appropriate to many to ask whether we have made the gains that we should have made and whether there are ways of better doing what we are doing.

The question of whether we have come far enough involves a value judgment and will be answered differently by researchers, legislators, superintendents, and teachers. Many of us see marked advances in the way we are now able to analyze teaching, in the use of new media, in the means for realistically individualizing instruction, in the wealth of instructional materials built with content and technical competence, in our knowledge of the effects of racial integration, in our better understanding of the use of programmed learning, in new ways of developing creativity, in increased sophistication in the use of the inquiry method, in the new process-oriented curricula, in simulation and gaming, and in our increasing understanding of the ways to apply the computer and the videotape recorder to facilitate learning. You can add more to this list from your own experience.

We are developing an enlarged capability. We have begun to attract researchers from other fields who also have an interest in education. We are creating centers and laboratories. We are developing relationships with school districts which permit experimentation. We have been increasing the physical plants, the staff and working relations needed to carry a project through. A substantial number of industrial learning combines have been attracted into the field. A number of smaller independent development companies are emerging. We have 20, soon to be reduced to 15, regional laboratories, and 9 Research and Development Centers at universities. The first fruits of the Title IV sponsored, doctoral research training programs are seeking positions this year, and a tremendous group they are. A substantial and increasing number of schools and colleges of education have a commitment to research and have developed organizational relations that permit them to draw on the resources of the rest of the university. Ours is the pioneering effort. We have not arrived, but we are on the way.

Though we may be proud of these and other individual successes, we need to take a very critical look at ourselves and, in particular, to take cognizance of some of the com-

---

A recent study by William Garvey and his associates[4] indicates that typically three years elapse before an educational research study is published in a journal, assuming it is accepted by the first journal to which it is submitted. (Rejection adds a year.) Since the heaviest funding was first available just three years ago, we would expect the results of that group of studies to be available this year. Further, according to Garvey's study, it takes another twenty months until such a publication is ingested into the reviews that suggest its significance as judged by fellow researchers.

mon criticisms of educational research and development. Others are carefully examining our field; we must do so too.

Educational research is often viewed as unrelated to practical purposes, too fragmentary and poorly related to an overall framework of education. Let us examine these charges in relation to a three-way formulation of the problems and then consider a proposal. First, we shall discuss the charge of irrelevancy as it relates to the extent to which researchers and practitioners have a sense of community, a relationship to which we shall refer as vertical integration. Second, we shall consider whether we have appropriate horizontal integration across the research community. Third, we shall examine the charge of fragmentation in the work itself. Finally, we shall consider a new way of organizing for the administration of educational research.

First of all, the charge of lack of relation to practical purposes, of relevancy, is a serious one. Universities are being challenged on all sides these days to be more relevant, and a mission-oriented field like education cannot ignore these demands.

Charges of irrelevance come mainly from consumers, potential or real. In the case of universities, it is largely the students, but in the case of educational research it is the superintendents, the supervisors and teachers. You can elaborate other examples from your own experience.

In these cases, one of the reasons for the charge is a lack of a sense of community among researcher, developer, state department personnel, superintendent, principal, teacher and (in these days especially), the student; a lack of feeling that they are on the same team, that they are working together toward common goals, and most important, that they need one another's help and support to make the system really move. We shall refer to this as vertical integration, for it is a sense of community that should go up and down through the levels of organization of the educational system.

The relation of the researcher and developer to their consumer, the schoolteacher and the school superintendent, while a very close one, in certain situations is not very obvious on the national scene. Further, the appearance of even greater distance was no doubt given by the AERA's move to leave the NEA—a move dictated by the ever-increasing militancy of the NEA as it seeks to compete with the Teachers' Union, and by AERA's own need to relate more closely to the scientific and academic research communities. But state department personnel, superintendent, principal, and teacher, all feel they have something to contribute to the researcher. Most often this is in terms of the definition of problems that would help to make research more relevant. Sometimes they have ideas for problem solution.

As one aspect of greater relevancy, vertical integration could make an important contribution in the setting of priorities on areas to be researched, in choosing those ideas which are to be carried through the expense of development.

A vertical sense of community seems also important, if one is concerned about creating a readiness for adoption and installation. If the consumer is in league with the researcher and is kept abreast of developments, he is much more likely to be ready to use the completed process or product.

This vertical liaison and sense of community should probably not be thought of as stopping with the superintendent and his administrative staff, nor with the teacher or student. In many instances those most eager for change, and most critical of change; most eager for the new ideas that will improve the quality of schools, and most suspicious of change; most ready to adopt the idea that will assist their boy or girl, and yet most resistant to change; are the ultimate providers of the funds both for research and for the implementation of its fruits at the local level—the parent-citizens. Vertical liaison should, therefore, extend deeply to these grass roots.

We have not seriously pursued ways of establishing this liaison. A number of options are open but it should be a sophisticated approach. We shall have more to say on this later, but the problem is more complex than merely making research reports available. The raw research idea in technical language will mean little to the schoolteacher and less to the parent. It must be stripped of its nonessentials and communicated in terms that suggest its usability and desirability. Perhaps it would be well for a variety of educational organizations to join together in the establishment of a journal which would present research and development in popularized form. There is no journal that does for education what *Scientific American* does for layman and scientist in providing a vertical sense of community. Perhaps we should establish a similar journal for educators.

Another important reason for establishing vertical liaison lies in the inevitable competition for resources. For convenience, the innovation continuum or sequence, that is the progress of an idea from discovery into use, may be thought of as proceeding through four stages: research, development, dissemination, and installation. Those operating the schools have so far little appreciated the potential of research and development and its funding has received little support from them. They have had their own severe problems of getting enough operating funds. Conversely, because the researchers have only recently been concerned with development, and still very little with dissemination and installation, they have not assisted in means to facilitate these phases. Vertical integration is likely to result in a joining of efforts to improve education through all stages of the innovation sequence. We need to understand each other's needs and programs so that we can pull together to increase the resources that we all need to carry our tasks forward.

In summary, we need to develop a kind of vertical integration which will heighten the researchers' sense of relevance, and which will make use of the practitioners' hard-earned sense of realities to assist in setting research and development priorities. Such a vertical sense of community will provide an appreciation and a readiness for the adoption of research ideas. It can help to provide a better understanding of how to cooperate to achieve greater resources for our tasks.

In addition to the need for vertical integration, there appears also to be a need for greater horizontal integration. We cannot yet really speak of a research community. For example, AERA has grown so fast that its members do not know each other well. There has been a seven-fold increase from 1200 members, when educational research received its first major funding, to 8350 members today.

There is evidence, whether for reasons of growth or for other reasons, that we lag behind other fields in this horizontal integration, this sense of being a community of researchers. Dr. William Garvey and his associates made studies of last year's AERA Convention paper reading sessions and compared these data with nine other associations of such diverse groups as heating, refrigeration and air conditioning engineers, sociologists, and aeronautics and astronautics. Educational research audiences have less foreknowledge about the presenter's previous work or what he is currently presenting than audiences in other associations. Comparable data from other organizations show two to five times as many listeners already have some knowledge of what they will hear. This may not be too surprising, but it is not a condition to be condoned.

Existing conditions are somewhat conducive to greater horizontal communication but, in addition, steps are being taken to facilitate it. The fact, for instance, that AERA provides a single convention, where educational research of all kinds is presented, is some boost in this direction. Making the AERA Convention program abstracts available before the Convention, as was done this year, should provide the opportunity for gaining pre-knowledge about the sessions. The establishment of interest groups in AERA provides the opportunity for horizontal integration through developing groups that cut across the lines of AERA divisions, established disciplines, universities, laboratories, R and D Centers, and public schools.

The *American Educational Research Journal,* like the Convention, provides for the complete spectrum of educational research. But the relatively small number of articles in each issue provides only a very thin coverage of an extremely wide spectrum of activities. In fact, another surprising and important finding of the Garvey study was that, whereas professionals in Astronautics and Aeronautics, an equally diverse field, had to scan only three journals on the average to recover 50% of the papers presented to their national convention, an educational researcher had to scan 18 journals, the largest of any of the nine fields studied. Sociology was also high with 13 journals. Among the remaining seven associations, the next highest level was only four journals for the geographers and the heating and air conditioning fields. The reason given is that the areas where the information is more easily recoverable have larger journals publishing more than one volume per year. Garvey recommends that educational research consider this method also as a means of increasing horizontal communication.

The horizontal scope of an educational research community needs also to extend beyond those now working on educational research, to include social scientists and also the biological scientists, especially those working on physiological processes related to learning.

There are some efforts under way to remedy this situation. For example, the USOE recently established a program with the National Academy of Science and the National Academy of Education to finance the efforts of researchers concerned with basic understandings of phenomena relating to education. Dr. Patrick Suppes is chairman of the guiding committee. Initially, it will funnel two million dollars into basic research relevant to education.

Unfortunately, this program has come at a time when the diversion of monies from a funding level inadequate for unsolicited research deprives those who are now working in educational research of badly needed funds. But, by the same token, because funds are universally tight, perhaps it will get us the attention of some scientists who might otherwise not look our way. Thus, although it means some of us must pull our own belts tighter, it is a program to support and encourage.

Similarly, AERA has made steady progress toward broadening its base to include disciplines which are oriented toward basic and conceptual research. It has, in this past two years, started two new divisions—one last year in History and Historiography and, this year, one in the Social Context of Education. By including the new divisions, AERA provides a membership home to social scientists in addition to psychologists. Because these divisions are represented in the Association Council, AERA provides room in the governing structure for *historians, sociologists, anthropologists, and economists.* This is a trend which should continue until AERA is multi-disciplinary and can count on its rolls individuals from all those basic disciplines having an important potential contribution to education.

In summary, one of our needed directions is to provide for a greater sense of community, both among those currently in the field and to bring in and integrate into the field those social and biological scientists not now working on problems of education but having important contributions to make to it.

Perhaps the most serious charge of fragmentation is that lodged against the research itself. This appearance of fragmentation seems to stem from two problems. The first of these is that the studies seem to be unrelated to each other in general and, in particular, unrelated to theory. The second problem is in part a consequence of the first and this is that the studies have not concentrated in any one area sufficiently to produce a sizable impact.

The first charge of lack of relation of the studies to theory is a reflection of a number of things—the emphasis on empiricism, the state of social science theory, to name two important ones. Empiricism is as old as educational research, but it received an important emphasis when nearly all the research which was given early support was empirical. In an attempt to develop a rigorous program that would stand public scrutiny, there was initially a very heavy emphasis on experimental research. But the problem was that, though carefully designed, these studies too often had either very little or a very circumscribed theoretical foundation.

As the field has matured, a heavier emphasis on integrating empirical and theoretical work has been apparent. But the social sciences themselves are not so rich in applicable theory that this front is able to proceed rapidly. One way of advancing theory building is to note that theory often grows out of observing the successful work of the skilled practitioner. The kind of horizontal and vertical integration discussed earlier may bring social scientist and practitioner together in a very important way, for often advanced theories only result as theory building catches up to practice. Progress has been and is being made in theory formulation, but we have yet to find the appropriate balance point between it and empiricism. The search for that balance should be our continued concern.

A second reason for the appearance of fragmentation of educational research is the very diversified front on which advances have been sought and the lack of any substantial massing of research to eradicate a given educational problem. If research were to continue on this basis, no doubt in time it would not appear so thinly spread. But if we continue as we have, we shall make slow progress toward this goal.

The reasons for this broad front attack are many. One of them is certainly the manner in which the USOE research and development program was organized, with a broad overall mandate to advance research in all areas. In addition, there has been the desire to support the best ideas in every area, so that a strong program would result.

It is easy in hindsight to see that perhaps it would have been better to follow the NSF model of concentrating in a few areas and doing these well. NSF has spent 120 million since 1954, in the areas of science curriculum improvement alone. Single courses received multi-million dollar support. When the USOE tried to go beyond the science areas with Project English and Project Social Studies, they established a large number of centers (for example, 16 in English) with a budget of about $50,000 a year for five years per center. The centers covered all grade levels, included a variety of approaches, and even included curricula intended to assist the culturally deprived. All these approaches are thoroughly defensible and desirable, but the possibility of bringing to successful fruition even a substantial portion of the 16, in English alone, would require substantial support. Bright and Gideonse[1] point out that full scale multi-media curriculum development can range in cost from two to six million per course. Thus, had the USOE concentrated only on curriculum improvement, it would have taken more than all of the funds put into educational research thus far to have covered course developments in the other subject matter areas. But there are so many fields needing assistance that we have funded projects over a wide variety of areas, from classroom climate to teacher training, school organization, pre-school learning, test development, and building design. In short, the whole range of school activity, while by no means uniformly covered, has felt some impact.

The pressures for concentration of funds in an area and the programming of research in that area have largely come from those less intimately involved with the research process itself. Various levels of the Executive Branch as well as Congress itself have suggested that some kind of focusing of effort is in order. The resistance to this thrust has come from many sides. In part it resulted from a desire to protect the necessary and traditional freedom of the researcher. There may have been a lack of certainty that a real breakthrough in any given area had occurred that warranted a massing of development funds. There was concern that, once the original broad mandate was factionalized into special groups, we would tend to distort what perspective there was on the overall scene. Finally, and perhaps most important, because no one really feels there are simple answers to the ills that plague the educational scene, programs might be devised too soon. To do so would be to treat the complex problems of education with too simple answers. We would then defeat the ultimate purposes toward which we are striving.

Nonetheless, the time may have come for a new evaluation. We need to mobilize our talent on a broader horizontal base, with greater communication among significant segments of that base. We need the vertical integration that will facilitate greater relevance in research and development and greater readiness to accept the fruits of that program. We need a greater integration of the research both proposed and completed. We need the massing of research and development at a level that will have impact on substantial education problems. We need a major breakthrough in support. Progress on all these fronts could result from a new constellation to administer the various steps of research development, dissemination and installation. If we are correct in reading the signs, progress more easily will come if we focus our efforts on problem oriented target areas.

A law appears to operate wherever there is competition for time, attention, talents and resources. This law is simply that a focused proposal, a clearly targeted effort, is more likely to win these resources than a broad-gauge or diffuse one. Why? For a number of reasons, the simplest one being that a targeted effort is more likely to succeed, and nothing succeeds like success.

Focused programs are not entirely absent from the educational scene. There are now, or have been, three examples in the U.S. Office of Education. One of these is the Bureau of the Handicapped. One can agree that this may be a special case, for aid to the helpless has obvious appeal to all those not so afflicted. But it is illustrative, for it is clear that this unit has continued to flourish and to move ahead its program, while, with the Vietnam War, the general research program fell on dark days. The Bureau of the Handicapped was pulled by legislative fiat out of the broad mandate research program, because there was concern that concentrated attention be given research in this area. To maintain this support, the Bureau has invited professionals, school groups, and interested lay associations, to hearings where the program administrative staff was exposed to the priorities and problems as seen by this group. More than any other research unit, it represents a priority oriented task force with a professional group ready to utilize its products and a group of parent and professional organizations interested and concerned that it does its work well, with adequate freedom and resources. Mark this model in your mind, for it parallels part of what I would like to propose!

There is a similar, but less pointed parallel in the educational technology and media program which at one time served as a focal point for the efforts of researchers, university and public school audiovisual coordinators, textbook publishers, educational film producers, and other industrial producers of instructional materials. Similarly, the vocational program has had both a limited target and vertical integration in its support group. These appear to be somewhat similar parallels to the National Heart Institute, the Cancer Institute, etc.

Where does all this lead us? Can we make suggestions for the organizations of research within the Federal government, the major current focal point of innovative effort?

I would propose that we urge the development of the National Institutes of Education. They would be separate from the Office of Education and, like the National Institutes of Health (NIH), a responsibility of the Department of Health, Education and Welfare. They would report to the Commissioner of Education in his responsibility as Assistant Secretary for Education of the Department. They would absorb the functions of the present Bureau of Research from the USOE.

The National Institutes of Education would consist of a central coordinating staff which would, like NIH, work with a series of institutes, each focused on a critical education problem. Each institute staff would develop the best possible research, development, dissemination, and installation program to solve the education problem for which it would be responsible. It would carry out the program largely by working with those in educational institutions, industries, and laboratories with appropriate capabilities. In-house research would be carried on only if there were clear advantages. Problems around which an institute would be constituted could be as broad as urban education, or as circumscribed as the program now carried on by the Bureau of the Handicapped.

What are the advantages of such a proposal? I have already alluded to several advantages in connection with the Committee on Economic Development proposal. One of those is, it could provide a kind of stability for planning and carrying through programs that the USOE, which changes both top personnel and orientation with each new administration, lacks. As a branch of the executive arm, the USOE is expected to emphasize those things which will further the President's policies. Second, through combining on its governing board all interested parties, it has the advantage of providing for both the horizontal and vertical sense of community that is now lacking. Third, there is greater likelihood that, as an off-the-executive-line agency which is one step removed from the pressures, it could resolve the priorities issue. Settling of this issue would be necessary to determine which institutes to first establish.

A fourth and obvious advantage is that it provides for a focusing in each institute which could markedly facilitate the development of both the horizontal and vertical integration that are needed. For instance, given a problem such as urban education, one could identify the socioiogists, psychologists, economists, political scientists, as well as educational researchers, with interests and ideas bearing on the problem. There would be a ready and concerned clientele in the schools that would benefit from such a focused effort; they, in turn, would be interested in helping to set priorities and advise on development. Further, there would be a variety of grass roots organizations to which the progrm could turn for suggestions and advice, and to whom progress could be reported. These groups would be concerned about the growth of effectiveness, the freedom to explore leads, and the provision of needed resources.

Hopefully, the Institutes, like NSF, would take responsibility for the nurture and growth of the manpower and physical resources necessary for research, development, dissemination, and installation, so that these could be developed and used in the wisest possible way for the improvement of education. This concern is at a very low level now in the USOE. There would need to be substantial analyses of the manpower needs of the stages of the innovation continuum and for the development and support of training programs as studies indicated. Similarly, studies of the adequacy of organizations and facilities would be required, which should result in corrective steps as necessary. New sources of competence, such as an increased use of industry, seem very likely.

Sixth, by removing these programs from the Office of Education, it would prevent the continually threatened break-up of the Bureau of Research. This organization, primarily concerned with educational research and development, has repeatedly been close to being absorbed into program support offices where the insatiable demand for resources is likely to defer the research that can be done tomorrow for the program that must be run today.

Seventh, it would of course make coordination with the programs of the Office of Education more difficult. But, as the Federal Interagency Committee is well aware, concern with the problems of education is spread throughout the government. It is possible that a less proprietary attitude could be built into the new Institutes so that greater cooperation among the Federal agencies would be possible. If the Institutes' boards, panels and committees are structured to provide the horizontal integration proposed, opportunities for greater cooperation could be built into this organization than now exist in any current agency.

Perhaps the major disadvantage of such a proposal is the difficulty of coordinating the program across the Institutes for the good of education as a whole. In the past, for instance, there were those who felt that the media program tail was wagging the education dog when the media program was in full swing. This is always a danger with a focused program.

Related to this is the concern that a "party line" might develop in a focused program, such as the National Cancer Institute has been accused of. Only research with certain orientations then receive support. For this and the previous problem, the best answer lies in the choice of staff with broad vision and the appropriate choice and use of panels and committees to maintain appropriate perspective.

A second major concern is that the establishment of such a set of Institutes would further divorce education from the social sciences on which much of its research program depends. Had last year's plan for a National Social Science Foundation developed, it might have been a good location for the Institutes. But the social scientists elected to cast their lot with the physical scientists in NSF, so this is no longer a viable alternative. Regardless of where educational research is located, it will now need to coordinate with the social science wing of NSF.

A final concern is the threat of Federal control of education which the in-house research capacity of such a unit poses. The control that a government could exercise over the educational system through in-house projects is potentially serious. However, there appear to be enough checks built into the government appropriation machinery that this is probably more a potential threat than a real one.

The proposed Institutes of Education would give a bold new thrust to Educational R and D as a factor on the Education Scene. They hold promise of solving certain problems that have resulted from the lines of development we have followed. They might permit us to maximize the contributions of research and development to education at new levels and in new ways. You may disagree and feel that the problems we face can be solved through the organizations we now have. If so, hopefully this discussion will have made you think differently about them and will have suggested new directions for present policies. I would seriously urge, however, careful consideration of the Institutes of Education proposal. Then, whichever stand you take, we can hope for real improvements in the field of education.

Epilogue

It is paradoxical that James Allen, one of the finest State Commissioners of Education in the country and a man whom, from personal knowledge, I have come to very greatly admire, should be appointed as Commissioner of the U.S. Office of Education just at a time that I am recommending major surgery to that office. There is no question that the Office has made progress under other fine Commissioners, like Frank Keppel and Harold Howe. I am absolutely positive it will under the new Commissioner. Perhaps under Jim Allen the research program might take a mighty leap forward. But, viewing the arguments pro and con and looking over the instability of policy that has historically adversely affected the growth of educational research, I would still argue the National Institutes proposal has considerable merit that would be demonstrated by its long-run performance record. I would, therefore, urge the serious consideration of this proposal.

REFERENCES

1. Bright, R. Louis and Hendrik D. Gideonse. "Research, Development and Dissemination Strategies in Improving Education." In Edgar L. Morphet and Charles O. Ryan (Eds.) *Planning and Effecting Needed Change in Education.* Denver, Colorado: Designing Education for the Future, an Eight State Project, 1362 Lincoln St.

2. Committee for Economic Development. *Innovations in Education: New Directions for the American Schools.* New York: The Committee, 1968.

3. Cronbach, Lee J. and Patrick Suppes (Eds.). *Disciplined Inquiry for Education.* A report of the Committee on Educational Research of the National Academy of Education, 1968.

4. Garvey, William D., Carnot Nelson and Nan Lin. "A Preliminary Description of Scientific Information Exchange in Educational Research." Baltimore, Maryland: The Center for Research in Scientific Communication, Johns Hopkins University, 1968, (mimeo).

5. House Committee on Government Operation. *The Use of Federal Research in Federal Domestic Programs.* Washington, D.C.: Supt. of Documents, U.S. Government Printing Office, 1967.

6. House Special Subcommittee on Education. *A Study of the U.S. Office of Education.* Washington, D.C.: Supt. of Documents, U.S. Government Printing Office, 1967.

38.
Educational Technology
In New York State

by NORMAN D. KURLAND
Director
Center on Innovation
in Education
N.Y. State Education Dept.

Theory, Practice, and the Future

I. Theory

In 1963 I wrote the following statement about educational technology:

> Instructional technology provides for the first time the potentiality for truly individualized conditions of *learning* for each student while affecting the efficiencies of *instruction* that can be achieved by mass education. With the new technology what is done well once can be multiplied a thousand-fold. The economies so realized can release resources to do for every child what once could be done only for a few. Thus education can become more effective even as it becomes more available. We can have *both* quantity and quality, though the latter will be much harder to achieve than the former.

That statement reflected reasonably well the hopes that many had at the time concerning the impact of technology on education. Needless to say, five years later we are a long way from realizing those glowing expectations. If we take New York State as a whole and take into account the time spent in school by all pupils, we would have to say that instructional technology plays a very small role. If all of the technology now being employed were to be eliminated instruction would continue with very little interruption. To be sure, teachers would have to fill in the hours taken up by films, television and recording, but not much of significant educational value would have been lost.

Instructional technology is largely supplementary to the two primary media of instruction: the textbook and the teacher. Eliminate either of these and the educational system would be transformed, eliminate all of technology and education would go on with hardly a missed lesson. In other words, instructional technology has not been made an integral part of the life of the classroom in the way it has become in life outside the classroom.

Why has this been the case?

In the first place, five years is a very brief time in which to see much change in a system as complex and structured as education. The rapidity with which technology has transformed *some* other areas of our lives has led us to expect similar transformations everywhere. We must note, however, that technology has worked best where *things* are to be changed and least well where people have to change. Thus we have produced magnificent automobiles and highways but have not been able to get people to use them safely.

One reason is the low investment in the equipment for instructional technology.

According to a recent publication of the Division of Educational Communications of the New York State Education Department, *Percentile Ranking of Educational Communications Programs,* the median expenditure for educational communications (including rentals, subscriptions and purchases of materials, equipment and services, but excluding personnel and major installations) is $2.38 per pupil or under $60 a year for a class of 25. The advanced standard adopted by the State calls for a per pupil expenditure of $31.00. No district in the State reaches this level nor the basic standard of $20.82. The closest are districts expending $12.50 per pupil.

The report notes that "only a small percentage of school districts meet the basic and advanced DAVI–N.Y. Standards"–the average percentages being 6.2 and 1.2 respectively.

For example, no school system can boast of a television receiver for every teacher (the advanced standard), although nearly every child comes from a home with at least one receiver. The median level in the State is one receiver to 27 teachers. Film and slide projectors, tape recorders, record players and overhead projectors are available in nearly every school building but seldom in sufficient quantity to encourage regular and sustained classroom use. There is evidence from a project in Buffalo, however, than when a school is provided with sufficient equipment and a large library of films, the use of instructional films goes up greatly.

The advanced and basic standards and State median for the above items are as follows:

ITEM	TEACHERS PER ITEM		
	ADVANCED	MEDIAN	BASIC
16mm Projector	5	10	11.7
Slide and Filmstrip Projectors	1	3	6.75
Overhead Projector	1	4	12
Audiotape Recorders (elementary level)	2	5	11
Record Players (elementary level)	1	1 (K-3) 1 per grade 4-6	

Clearly neither the teacher nor the taxpayer has yet seen sufficient value in classroom technological aids to demand or to grant them in great quantity. In the home the advantage of the automatic washer is easily perceived. Vast sums have been expended to entice the housewife into using it and in making it easy for her to do so. Nothing comparable has been done for the classroom. Washing machine manufacturers quickly learned to reduce operating noise levels so that the washing machine could be tolerated even in a crowded apartment. Controls were simplified so that any woman could operate them without difficulty. In the classroom, the movie projector still operates at an undesirable noise level and is sufficiently complicated to deter many a teacher from using it.

It is, of course, not alone the lack of equipment that explains the low rate of use of instructional technology. If there were the need and the demand, the equipment would be there. The fault lies more with the entire functioning of the educational system today. This can best be seen by considering what the role of technology could be.

The major contribution of technology to education should be help to achieve individualized instruction.

Under present instructional arrangements individualization can never be more than a dream. In most school situations, classes are not homogeneous or small enough or teachers able enough to adjust adequately to individual differences. Every learner is handicapped in some way–the fast, by being held down to the pace of the slower, with the attendant boredom, frustration, and loss of powers not sufficiently exercised; the slow, by never quite mastering a subject before being forced to move along to the next topic; and the average—but there is no one average in everything! With technology we can come closer to insuring that the fast learner moves ahead at a pace adjusted to his capacity and that the slow learns thoroughly each lesson before he is allowed to move ahead, thus eliminating the perpetual frustration which must be a major obstacle to his educational achievement.

Differences in maturation rates may also more successfully be accommodated. Slow maturers now may be handicapped permanently by being tagged in their early school years as "dumb" and by failing to master fundamentals before they are moved along to more advanced materials. The new instruction would adjust to changing capacity for learning throughout the learner's educational career and thus try to assure that each one would achieve to the maximum of his capacity. Moreover, once programs are developed for learners of different capacities, it should become possible to understand the obstacles to learning and to develop more effective strategies for helping learners at all levels to learn more and better. It is even conceivable that the difficulty of some slow learners may derive from an inherent incapacity for manipulation of verbal symbols. Machines permit the presentation of non-verbal stimuli-pictures, diagrams, or even things and thus may make educable individuals who now appear to be uneducable.

Another intriguing development is the provision of simulated experiences as a means of approximating the conditions under which knowledge is applied. Suggestive work is going on in adapting the technique of the game to education. A number of experimental games have been developed and are being tried out in school settings.

What of the role of the teacher in the new technology of education? It will certainly be greatly modified. Some teachers will be engaged primarily in the preparation of the instructional system in cooperation with other specialists. Such work will require a vast increase of understanding of both the learning process and the subject to be taught. Intelligence and imagination will be demanded as never before. When these qualities are present they will be available not just to the handful of students with whom even the best teachers now can work but to as many as the system cares to have them reach.

The primary role of the teacher will be to do what an automated system can never do—motivate, counsel, and lead students to those higher order functions which are the primary goals of education—to question, imagine, invent, appreciate and act. Instead of a purveyor of information, he will be the orchestrator of a rich array of resources—highly varied and diverse but brought by him into harmony with the needs of the individual student. Because he will be relieved of the burden of regular classes he will be able to devote more time to individual students and to his own studies.

When he meets students both he and they will be prepared together to move into intricate and challenging aspects of a subject. Although the number of such group meetings will be many fewer than today, there will be ample opportunity for contact between student and teacher and such contact will take place *only* when there is a real educational value to be realized, not because of the lack of more efficient means of communication. The teacher—and professor—will then have time for her own study *and* the more intimate, informal contacts which are the most rewarding parts of education. Under such conditions the teacher can be what, at her best, she always has been—a model, a stimulator, guide, planner, and fellow searcher after truth, meaning, and value. In this way we may yet preserve that vital personal relationship between student and teacher which is so gravely threatened by the depersonalization of our society.

A final benefit of the large-scale introduction of technology into teaching is that it will provide a basis both for raising teachers' salaries to professional levels and for differentiating among teachers of differing abilities. The obvious increased "productivity" and level of professional competence of the teacher who directs a learning "system" and participates in the creation of effective learning materials will justify a reward more nearly commensurate with the training and ability required for the task. The effectiveness, too, of teachers with lesser abilities, working in a team with able leaders and using well-designed materials, will be greatly enhanced.

Lest there be any illusions about technology increasing the teacher-student ratio, let me state that I do not see this as a likely long-run result. The effect of well-applied technology will be to improve instruction and alter the functions of teachers and their relations to pupils and each other. But the effect of improved instruction is almost always to put greater demands on the creative teacher. What we can hope for from the introduction of technology, then, is not a saving of manpower, but of "mindpower" and a level of education achievement more nearly up to the needs of our culture.

What then will the school of the future be like? We can, I think, envision a time of universal individualized education when every person will be educated and no two will be educated alike. Teachers deeply committed to the art of teaching and thoroughly versed in the science of learning will have at their disposal a full panoply of learning materials to which they will direct each individual student in accordance with his needs, abilities and interests.

There will be no lockstep and indeed no common schedule. Each student will proceed at his own pace through a curriculum uniquely adjusted to his needs. He will have, through many media, access to the best teaching and the best information on each subject along his way. Intrinsic motivation (the kind that successfully drives the child and that the schools largely kill) will largely replace extrinsic as the student early discovers the power of knowledge and the joy of learning, and has opportunity to grow in directions which attract him. He will move smoothly and early from directed, highly structured learning situations to self-directed, unprestructured activities where the learner plays an active role in learning.

Let me stress this latter point, since too little attention is paid to it in many current discussions of the new technology in education. Too often it is suggested that the impact of the new technology will be to make the student even more passive than he now is. This, of course, may happen, but it is *not* inevitable. A major thrust of much current work is to discover ways of stimulating and helping the student to become a self-motivating and self-directing, independent learner. Surely for a world of change, this is one of the most important outcomes that education can promote. This does not, of course, mean that the "new" student would work only in splendid isolation. To learn is to want to communicate, and contact with teachers, scholars and fellow students is an important source of stimulation and ideas. The sharing of ideas and insights would in part emerge as a spontaneous consequence of learning, in part be structured into the learning experiences where required for most effective learning. Fellow learners would come together with each other or with a teacher. Such encounters, while not occurring with the regularity of present classes, would be far richer experiences because of the level of readiness brought by the students.

Seminar and lecture rooms, laboratories, and other facilities would be located much as they are today wherever convenient. They would be used, however, on varied schedules in accordance with the needs of individuals and groups.

For example, a student who needs a laboratory for work in biology might sign up for (or rent) space for five weeks, another might need to consult an English teacher for two hours to work out some difficulty in his writing. One teacher might be available in his office for consultation on a regular schedule; another might schedule a series of lecture or seminar meetings every Thursday afternoon at two.

If one seeks a current model of this school of the future it is best seen in the public library. To the library each user comes with his own demands, and each is more or less successfully accommodated, though no two persons are served quite alike. There are almost no age or grade divisions—adult and child may work side by side and even at times use the same materials. Each proceeds at his own pace toward his own goals. Moreover, the library never presumes that it must supply all the users' needs for information. It does what it can do best and leaves to other agencies in the community portions of the task appropriate to them.

Now after this somewhat extended peering into the future, let me turn to a basic issue that must be confronted in considering the role of educational technology—the impact of the new technology of education on the individual. Will it transform him into a mere extension of the machine—mindful of the things needed to keep the social machine going; mindless about the things that make him human? Every technological development has been an extension of some human functioning. Whether man is mechanized or freed by them depends on how he uses them.

Here I note a peculiar thing in many of the discussions about the impact of technology in general and particularly about its impact in education. There is a tendency to assume that the conditions determining the character of the impact whether for good or ill are inherent either in the technology or the conditions of society and will work themselves out whatever anyone may do or say.

The counter view is that what we do can influence the outcome. The role of technology in education is now being invented. Its invention can be left largely to chance; it can be left to those businesses—the so-called "education industries"—which have a growing stake in the outcome and who will not be left out; or it can be done by educators working in consort with many other groups, especially those in the education industries. Together they can work out an understanding of what education in the future is to be. The result should not be pious manifestos about everyone's good intentions but institutional arrangements that can help insure that the new technology is infused with a fundamental orientation to human values.

II. *Practice*

A. Educational Television

The State's educational television network is the nation's largest system to connect independently owned and operated community television stations. It broadcasts on two channels simultaneously, giving each station a choice of three programs: two from the net, or a third of its own. The network is programmed entirely by the stations, but is administered and operated technically by the State University of New York. It was developed by the University and the Office of a General Services both working closely with the State Education Department and the stations. The broadcasts originate mainly from a Network Operations Center in Albany, although any station can originate programs for the other stations.

The network began its operation in October 1967. It links stations in Buffalo, Schenectady, Syracuse, Rochester, and New York. Binghamton and Watertown will be added soon. An eighth station in Nassau County will be developed later. The present five station network has a potential audience of 14.3 million people and serves more than 80% of the state's population.

A program committee of seven representatives (one for each station, plus two nonvoting members for the university and education department) selects all programming for the network. Each station retains the option to broadcast any program or not, or record it for a future broadcast. Besides its weekday daytime schedule, the network broadcasts University of the Air courses on Saturday, and programs from N.E.T. and the Eastern Educational Network each evening including weekends. Some live programming connecting several stations in town meeting style is also planned.

A major source of educational material is the stations themselves and the State Department of Education, through its Bureau of Mass Communications. One of the Bureau's most important jobs is to supply copies of tapes to the network and to the 177 school systems, reaching an estimated 1.6 million public school students. Duplication is supplied for the Ampex VR-660 and VR-7000 videotape recorders located in the schools. Most of these schools have received financial assistance for their recorders and closed circuit systems from a matching-funds program administered by the Bureau.

Tape copies (averaging 100 per week) are made from a library of more than 1500 programs, including many complete courses. The Bureau also makes available duplicates of some 8500 titles from its audio tape library on request and for the minimum cost of the audio tape raw stock. Duplicating of video tapes is done by replaying them on a quadruplex recorder, an Ampex VR-1200, or two Ampex VR-1100's for recording on nine helical scan VR-7000's and six VR-660's. Audio duplication uses an Ampex Model 3200 duplicator with two slave units. New York State's experience seems to indicate clearly that the availability of software in the form of usable content materials makes possible the systems approach to more learning opportunity.

New York's Operation Center in Albany uses the most modern transmission and studio equipment available. Videotape recording and playback is done on four high-band VR-2000 recorders, equipped for monochrome and color. In addition, four VR-660 and four VR-7000 helical scan recorders duplicate material for use by university campuses. For audio material, the network center has an Ampex PD-10 audio tape duplicator with three slave units. The two-channel color compatible microwave system connecting the stations allows origination from any station or from Albany.

At the university level, television will be playing an even larger role in the future. Ten of the four-year colleges, four university centers, and one two-year college are now planning extensive closed circuit television facilities. Presently, five of the colleges each have two Ampex VR-1200 recorders for local production, recording, and playback. A number of the colleges are also equipped with VR-660 and VR-7000 helical scan recorders.

B. Technology Demonstration Program

The New York State Education Department has initiated a Technology Demonstration Program. This program funded at $75,000 on a matching fund basis is designed to develop demonstration centers in instructional technology. The "mini-grants" between $1,000 and $10,000 go to programs which school districts wish to introduce into their instructional programs. A major criterion for awarding a grant is readiness to continue the program after the one year State grant ends. Having received a State grant a school district agrees to receive visitors, provide an annual report both written and audiovisual, and allow for State distribution rights for materials produced. Fifteen districts were funded in 1968-69. The projects ranged from dial-access systems to graphic communication centers. It is anticipated that this program will be a major step in assisting school districts in getting their technology program off the ground. The continuation of the program on the part of the school district after State support has been withdrawn and willingness to receive visitors and share information with the State and other school districts promises an impetus to instructional technology that has been lacking in the past.

There are a number of current activities in New York State which are described further in the Appendix. They are:

A. The use of educational data processing

B. The rural educational center in upstate New York

C. Computer-assisted instruction in New York City.

III. *Planning for the Future*

Recently the New York State Education Department sponsored a conference on the instructional uses of the computer. Reports were presented by some fourteen universities and school systems within the State describing the ways they were using computers to aid instruction. Uses ranged from full-scale CAI operations of the kind described above in New York City to simple rental of time-sharing terminals to allow students to explore the problem solving capabilities of the computer. In general, all of the programs are in an early exploratory stage in which there is plenty of enthusiasm for the potential of computers but little firm evidence that they can change the quality of instruction significantly.

The conclusions reached are equally applicable to the entire field of educational technology. The major conclusion was that a large, carefully coordinated research and development effort must be undertaken if the potential of the technology is to be realized.

The conference heard that no such systematic planning was now occurring at the Federal level; although reference was made to the possibility the Commission on Educational Technology might do something of this kind. If no national action is forthcoming, the conferees urged that the planning and coordination be undertaken by the State. The feeling was strongly expressed that unplanned, uncoordinated efforts must be avoided. Not only is this terribly wasteful, but a few unproductive or negative projects, particularly in a field where project costs run high, could kill all interest and support for years to come.

It was generally felt, therefore, that a major effort must be undertaken both to discover how to use computers effectively to improve education and to produce evidence of the relative value of the new technology in comparion with alternative approaches.

To do this it was recommended that the research and development effort in the field be much more carefully planned than it has been to date. Up to now there has been little systematic planning for development. Projects are undertaken with little or no relation to one another and the findings, if any, of one project are seldom used or followed up in others. To help prevent this situation it was felt that some agency in the Federal government or the State should work out a research and development plan to guide the funding of projects and to provide all concerned with a common reference.

One suggested planning approach was the following:

1. Identify all significant "alternative futures,"—that is, possible ways in which the technology may someday be utilized in education.

2. Obtain estimates of the probable dates when each "future" may become reality and judgments on the desirability of each possible future.

3. Determine the activities that must be undertaken to arrive at the most desired futures including how much effort is likely to be required, what the cost will be and in what sequence the activities should best be undertaken.

4. Assess the current status of research and development with respect to each activity and the agencies or individuals most competent to carry forward on next steps.

5. Estimate the costs of arriving at each desired future in specified time periods. This will provide an indication of the level of investment that will be required to arrive at a desired goal by any given date in the future.

6. For varied levels of expenditure during each of the next five years, determine what mixes of activities are possible and how much each "mix" will contribute to the movement toward desired futures. This will give a reasonable basis for determining how best to use limited funds.

7. On the basis of all of the preceding information, establish long and short range development goals and specify the sequence of activities that must be undertaken to achieve those goals.

8. In each funding period support projects that fit the development plan.

9. Assess progress annually and revise the plan as experience dictates.

These steps would be applicable not just to the development of computer applications but might even be more meaningful if done for the total area of automated or technological aids to instruction.

Some other conference conclusions that are relevant to the work of the Commission are the following:

1. The major problem in CAI development at the present is not equipment but the lack of adequate theories of instruction or readily applicable validated experience. Therefore, extensive research and careful development should be undertaken. Application of computers to instruction without such a foundation is not going to produce measurable results to support the advantage of computers over traditional methods.

2. The successful application of computers (or any other technology) to education requires total system redesign—another reason why careful planning and a large investment of money and time will be required.

3. The proper question is, not how can computers (or any other device) be used in education, but how can computers help improve the quality of education. One implication of this formulation is that computers should be utilized in ways that take maximum advantage of their unique capabilities, leaving to other devices and to people functions that they can perform better.

4. For the next few years Federal or State funds should not be used for direct "hands-on" experience for students or teachers. If schools or colleges wish to provide such experience with their own funds, encourage them to use relatively inexpensive available equipment such as computers being used for administrative purposes, time-sharing terminals, calculators, or very low cost simple computers.

5. Encourage development of both computer monitored instruction (CMI) where there is no direct student access to computers and computer assisted instruction (CAI) where there is interaction with the computer.

6. While some attention should be given to the application of computers to present curricular goals and methods of instruction, the main emphasis should be on the changing goals and methods that will be more appropriate for education in the computer age.

7. A major developmental objective should be increasing compatibility among computer systems so that instructional programming may be more readily exchanged among users.

8. Begin developing plans now for the utilization of computer systems that will in a few years make available very low cost services using languages and procedures that will require no specialized training. These plans should include familiarizing both laymen and professionals with the profound changes these developments will bring about.

9. One of the major obstacles to the development of CAI identified by many conferees is the high cost of telephone communication from computers to remote

terminals. These costs reduce the potential use of large systems and thus may make overall costs prohibitive. It was strongly urged that efforts be made to obtain changes in the FCC tariffs for live usage or that alternative arrangements, such as communication satallites, be quickly developed.

Educational Data Processing

The number of districts receiving data processing services, either from their own installations or from Boards of Cooperative Educational Services (BOCES), has increased from 100 to 342 during the period between September 1962 and September 1966. In addition, recent data has indicated that many more districts will soon join the growing ranks of educational data processing users.

Although the use of data processing equipment has become widespread throughout the State's elementary and secondary school community, there has been very little interaction between data processing installations.

This uncoordinated development of educational data systems, by both individual districts and BOCES, has resulted in a considerable amount of duplication of effort, since the record-keeping functions of the school districts are essentially similar. At the same time, it appears that the computer has become a status symbol to many school districts. In such cases, the computer has been procured more often as a means of raising the prestige of the district than as an aid to handling educational data.

Since the utilization of data processing equipment and techniques by the State's school districts and BOCES represents a sizable monetary investment (estimated at 6.5 million dollars for the 1967-68 school year), the State Educational Department could not ignore this trend towards uncoordinated expansion. In addition, the Department, realizing its obligation to provide technical guidance to the State's school districts, resolved to improve its expertness in this new field of educational data processing. Due to the above factors, the State Education Department decided to hire a consulting firm, experienced in educational data processing technology, to prepare recommendations for the development of a master plan for educational data processing within the State.

The consulting firm, System Development Corporation, proposed the system configuration described below. The recommendations have been adopted by the State and requests for bids to install the first phase of the system have gone out.

1. *Regional Centers*

    At the present time, twelve regional centers are considered adequate to meet the educational data processing needs of the State's elementary and secondary schools (excluding New York City). In addition to their normal regional center data processing activities, three of these twelve centers will have evaluation and training responsibilities. The regional centers will all provide the following data processing applications:

STUDENT SUBSYSTEM	Census
	Enrollment
	Attendance
	Grade reporting
	Permanent records
	Test scoring and analysis
	Student scheduling
PERSONNEL SUBSYSTEM	Payroll
	Personnel records
	Staff directories

	Retirement Professional qualifications
FINANCIAL *SUBSYSTEM*	Budget preparation Encumbrance accounting Accounts Payable Cost Accounting Purchasing
FACILITIES *SUBSYSTEM*	Inventory Control Construction requirements Maintenance Transportation Library and text book accounting Cafeteria accounting

Except for the three E/T centers, student scheduling will only be accomplished to the extent of preprocessing student requests and printing out the final schedule. The E/T centers will accomplish the actual class scheduling on their larger computers due to the internal storage requirements inherent in scheduling programs. It should also be noted that the applications listed as part of the above subsystems (packages) are not meant to be all inclusive and should be considered merely as representative of the kinds of applications that will be covered. The actual applications to be included in the system will be based upon user requirements.

2. *Evaluation and Training Centers*
   In addition to providing the class assignments in scheduling, the E/T centers will provide other services which require the use of a bigger computer, such as certain sophisticated statistical analyses which might be requested by a district.
   Besides accomplishing the activities stated above, the evaluation and training center will provide the following special functions and services:

   a. Design and evaluate new educational data processing applications.

   b. Evaluate new equipment and technological advancements in respect to the needs of the Statewide system.

   c. Train school and center personnel in educational data processing activities.

   d. Recommend changes to the Statewide educational data processing master plan.

   e. Provide field services to the regional centers.

3. *Center Roles in the Design of New Applications*

   a. *Roles of the Evaluation and Training Centers*
       Obviously, the Statewide educational data processing system cannot be a static system, but must react to changes in the needs of the districts, as well as to changes brought about by state and national data requirements. The availability of new types of equipment and processing techniques must also be considered for impact upon the system. In any case, the kinds of activities that will be discussed in this section are those concerned with new application design and checkout, and are not related to the basic system implementation.
       Due to the special skills and extra machine capability available at the E/T centers, these centers will have the major role in designing and testing new appli-

cations to be utilized in the Statewide system. It is anticipated that at least two of the staff at each of the E/T centers will be concentrating on improving the existing system packages and designing new applications. The NYSEDS Coordinator will need to closely supervise this new development activity, however, to prevent unwanted duplication of effort at the E/T centers. After improvements in old applications, or designs of new applications, are thoroughly checked out under operational conditions, the resultant program packages will be forwarded to the other regional centers for inclusion into the Statewide system.

b.   *Role of the Regional Centers*
The first task to be performed by the regional center system analysts and programmers will be to make minor revisions in the system packages, as required by "local conditions." Local conditions are those factors, at the district level, which make it necessary to accomplish certain *minor* revisions in programs in order to get the districts to join the system. These revisions must be minor, however, or the effectiveness of the Statewide system will be seriously degraded.

What will the system analysts and programmers do after the system is completely operational? This question has arisen repeatedly and will be answered herewith. In the presently envisioned system, it is expected that the regional center staff will be involved with the following developmental activities:

1)   *Implementing new applications designed and checked out at the E/T Centers.*

2)   *Designing new applications suggested by local needs.*
Creativity should be encouraged and utilized whenever it appears in the State. If regional center personnel get an idea for a new and useful application, they should be allowed to develop it. The number and kinds of new applications being developed at the regional level, however, will have to be carefully coordinated to prevent duplication of effort and wasted activity. It is suggested that such development activity be approved by the E/T center serving the area. Once the application is completed, it should also be evaluated by the area E/T center as to whether it should be included in the system package.

The Statewide coordinator should insure that there is no unwanted duplication in new application development across the State.

3)   *Developing special purpose one-time applications to meet local requirements.*
The kinds of programs anticipated here are special applications, requested by one or more districts in the region, which are considered feasible by the center staff. These activities may include special inventories, listings, analyses of student data, etc. It should be remembered, however, that the regional centers are primarily production facilities and their first duty is always to get the normal reports out on time. New development activity, therefore, can only be accomplished when time is available.

Rural Supplementary Educational Center/ A Case Study

An ESEA Title III funded project in the rural Catskill Mountain area of New York is a good illustration of the opportunities and problems associated with the introduction of instructional technology.

The project area in Delaware County consists of a number of small, relatively isolated school districts. Frank Cyr, a retired Teachers College professor long interested in the problems of rural education, conceived the idea of using television, telephone and other media to bring better education to these isolated communities. He won the support of local educators and community leaders, with an assist from a local philanthropist who offered to donate a building and land for the project.

The next step was a request for a Title III grant prepared for the first competition when the program was new and policy guidelines not established. The proposal immediately posed the first issue—cost. The request was for over $900,000 for a project to serve a relatively small number of pupils. It also included considerable funds for equipment, which many thought should not be the emphasis for Title III. However, the project was addressed to a problem that existed in every sparsely settled mountainous region of the State and Nation. If the project were to be successful it offered a solution to the need for equalizing educational opportunity for thousands of rural youth.

After much consultation between State and Federal officials, therefore, the project was funded by the U.S. Office of Education at a lower figure than requested but still higher than the State Education Department, it must be confessed, had wanted.

Then the problems started. The central feature of the project was to be the construction of a television antenna on the highest peak in the region to enable reception of ETV programs from four stations outside the region (Schenectady, Syracuse, Binghamton and New York) and the transmission of programs directly to the schools within range of the antenna. It turned out that an FCC license was required which, for a variety of reasons, was not routinely granted. It took nearly a year and a half of diligent effort by Dr. Cyr to get the license. It is doubtful if anyone with less experience and influence could have done this; and, without the license, the heart would have been taken out of the project.

The next set of problems arose from the fact that no one had experience with the design and construction of the kind of system called for. There were companies capable of installing the antenna, others ready to do the studio; other ready to lay the cable, but none that were immediately ready and experienced enough to take on the entire job. Finally a contractor was found; but lack of experience produced delays and problems that may well have discouraged a less determined group.

To provide the participating schools with services while the television system was being readied a telelearning network was established in cooperation with the local telephone company. Groups in several locations have "met" together and specialists and interesting individuals have been brought into the classrooms of the region.

Finally in the second half of the 1967-68 school year the television system began to work. A wide variety of programs off air and from tape are now being brought into the schools. Teachers are learning how to use this resource and the community is beginning to understand what it can do for its children.

This description of the program appeared in the Pilot Issue of INSIDE EDUCATION, published by the N.Y. State Education Department:

> An unusual program headquartered in Delaware County is helping to improve education in sparsely populated areas of New York State by stimulating educators to use all available means of communication to reach both students and the public.
>
> Known as the Rural Supplementary Educational Center (RSEC), the project was set up to provide facilities to expand and improve educational and cultural opportunities in the rural schools and communities of Greene, Delaware, Otsego, and Schoharie counties, according to project director Frank Cyr.
>
> The mountainous area served by the Center is located at the headwaters of the Delaware, Susquehanna, and Schoharie rivers and consists of 21 autonomous school districts in an area about 30 by 100 miles. The largest village in the district has a population of just over 1,200, and the total population of the area is approximately 56,000. The communities are small and scattered throughout the valleys of the area.

The major function of the RSEC, explains Cyr, is to assist schools and communities in the use of multi-communications for improving educational opportunities. This includes finding out what teachers want and continually seeking resources to meet these needs, and also providing assistance to teachers, pupils, and others in the use of new communications.

The RSEC was organized in January 1966 with the support of Title III of the Elementary and Secondary Education Act. It now has a professional staff of 12 and a para-professional staff of 19 employees, some on a part-time basis. This includes an aide at each school to assist local teachers in the use of services.

The small size of the Center's staff requires the performance of a wide variety of functions on a small scale by each staff member, Cyr points out. Therefore, personnel must each have more than one area of competency. The highly specialized departments, with highly specialized personnel, which are basic to large scale operations are not adapted to the rural situation, Cyr says, where the work load could not make full use of such personnel. "Here the local personnel must be competent in those skills which are required day by day, while highly specialized personnel are employed as needed for short periods and often by use of telephone conferences."

Provision of multi-communications is the primary purpose of RSEC. This gives each teacher an opportunity to choose the means of presenting ideas which best suit his purposes. He is not limited to any one means of instruction.

For example, the RSEC distributes books, microfilm, films, filmstrips, records, slides, transparencies, study kits, and other instructional materials to participating schools. At the request of teachers, these materials are circulated among the schools in a mobile van which makes twice-weekly visits to each school.

Exhibits of original paintings and sculpture with a total valuation of more than $70,000 have been circulated annually among the schools and to the public.

A unique Tele-Learning circuit among the participating schools has a central switchboard at the RSEC office and amplified transmitters and speakers in each school. A group of pupils or adults in their own schools can carry on a two-way discussion with similar groups in the other schools or with resource persons anywhere in this country or abroad where they can be reached by telephone.

In addition to a wide variety of resource people, pupils have carried on discussions with other pupils in four foreign countries. "The purpose of these calls is to motivate pupils and enrich the curriculum," says Cyr.

An educational television system operated by the Center is able to receive, record, and broadcast programs from four ETV stations. The system can also use prepared videotapes or films, or can produce programs indigenous to the rural area which it serves. By using videotape recorders and UHF translator towers on six mountaintops in the area, programs are carried into schools and homes directly and through seven small village CATV systems where these are available.

Each participating school is wired with coaxial cable and has equipment to monitor and record programs for use either directly off the air or for later use at the convenience of the teacher. The schools are also able to produce local videotapes of school and community activities.

Many of the district's high school students have been trained to operate the school's television equipment. "In this rural area," says Cyr, "where the chief means of earning a living is either in agriculture or in small, electrically powered industries, this practical training in television operation provides a skill not usually available to students."

Now comes the critical problem. Federal support, which will have amounted in all to about $1¼ million is about to terminate. The basic capital equipment has been acquired but the continuing operating costs are still high. The participating communities are not wealthy; school costs have been going up rapidly and, with active teacher negotiation just reaching the region, are certain to go up more next year.

While the project has thus far seemed to be successful it has not been in operation long enough either for the teachers and administrators to realize and use its full potential or for the taxpayers to be convinced of its worth. When faced with the need to cut back, people prefer to cut the new and not fully tried, even if it has great future potential, then to drop practices of long standing even if they are no longer contributing in proportion to their cost.

The local administrators are, therefore, convinced that the project cannot be continued unless support from Federal, State or other outside source is forthcoming. The participating districts have put up $60,000 currently to help support the telelearning network and they are ready to add to this amount next year, but not to the extent necessary to sustain the project. This comes at a time when Federal and State funds are also greatly restricted.

A further complication results from the fact that in New York State school aid is paid on a cost reimbursable basis. Expenditures made in one year are reimbursed at the district's aid ratio in the following year. Thus when a district adopts a new program it must pay the full costs the first year and is reimbursed the following year. Federal funds used to support a project are not reimbursable. In the present case, the participating districts would have to put up the whole cost in the first year of local support even though they will be reimbursed for as much as 90% the next year. This is a difficult burden. The State is exploring ways of overcoming this difficulty.

At the time of writing the fate of the project is uncertain. What is needed in this situation, and undoubtedly in the many others of similar nature, is a detailed cost-benefit analysis of the entire system. While the project budget appears large when presented as a single item ($180,000), it represents only 1.07% of the total operating budgets of the schools in the area.

If the local taxpayer could be shown what the costs and benefits are of other major segments of the educational system, it might be possible to show him activities that could be dropped with little loss in exchange for the benefits of the new program.

Alternatively, it may be possible to show that some things now being done could be done equally well or better with the aid of the new arrangements so that with little or no increase in outlay both new and old services could be supplied. Until such analysis is available one cannot blame the layman or the educator for preferring activities that time has proved to be "necessities" to activities that the system survived without until only a short time ago.

Still another alternative is to continue outside support long enough to demonstrate that the new services are as much "necessities" as the old. Given long enough to discover what technological aides can do for them, teachers and taxpayers will demand and pay for them.

New York City Computer-Assisted Instruction Project/ A Case Study

Another ESEA Title III project illustrates other problems in the introduction of instructional technology. A grant was made to the New York City Board of Education to enable it to contract with RCA for the introduction of a computer-assisted instruction system developed by Professor Patrick Suppes of Stanford University.

The project provided for the installation of some 200 terminals in about 15 different school buildings throughout the City, all linked by telephone line to a central computer. The instruction to be offered was drill and practice lessons in arithmetic and language arts in the elementary grades. About 6,000 pupils would be served, each spending about twenty minutes per day at the terminal.

Again initial costs were high in relation to the apparent immediate benefits and in comparison with other school costs. It was the potential represented by the project that led to its funding. The fiscal problems associated with assumption of local support may follow that described previously when Federal funds are terminated.

The additional problems illustrated by this project have to do with the introduction of change in a large school system.

There was first the task of working out a contract that satisfied all of the legal and fiscal requirements of the Board of Education and the City and was satisfactory to the U.S. Office of Education. This involved extended negotiation between RCA and the offices involved.

Then specific schools had to be identified in which the terminals would be placed. A number of local superintendents and building superintendents and building principals to whom the opportunity to participate was offered declined. Reasons given largely were that they had too many other problems to be bothered with this new idea. Finally, with assistance from the Superintendent of Schools, fifteen suitable sites were selected.

Next, the school building department had to be contended with. To install the terminals required some minor alterations and the installation of electrical and telephone outlets. To get approval for this work and its completion on time involved another series of confrontations with bureaucracy.

Still another set of offices had to be cajoled into expediting procedures when it came to finding space for the computer. School space never was found and this difficulty was only overcome when RCA agreed to lease commercial space itself.

The next series of problems involved the Telephone Company. It turned out that in the private sector, too, assurances of full support and cooperation from the top did not mean much at the operating levels. Equipment delivery and installation was slow. It was exceedingly difficult to get operating problems attended to. Furthermore, three different operating units were involved in the three boroughs in which the schools were located. It proved difficult to get them to work together to resolve problems arising from the need to connect their three systems.

Finally, the problems attendant on keeping the system operating continuously have proved formidable. When failure occurs, the problem may be at the terminal; it may be in buffer equipment in the schools; it may be in the telephone lines; it may be in the data-phone connection; it may be at the central installation or in the computer; it may be in the software; or, worst of all, it may be in some combination of all of these. All of these problems have occurred. When the system goes "down" pupils, teachers and project personnel are all frustrated. Fortunately the limits of this frustration have not yet been reached. It is hoped that the system is stabilized before the limits are reached and the school system decides to reject the idea.

It should be noted that all of the problems so far described have to do with the hardware side of the project. The instructional materials will undoubtedly present their own set of problems, but these will not become apparent until there has been more experience with a fully operating system.

This experience indicates the kind of practical problems that are going to have to be met if educational technology of any complexity is going to be introduced on any significant scale into American schools.

39.
Notes for a Humanist Critique Of Technological Innovation In Teaching

by LEO MARX
Prof. of English
and American Studies
Amherst College

1. Aims and Assumptions

My aim here is to suggest some reasons for the resistance to the use of technology in education. Why do many intelligent people express anxiety, timidity, skepticism, or outright opposition when confronted with plans for introducing new mechanical devices in the instructional process? What can the history of attitudes toward technological innovation teach us about the motives of such people? Is it possible to distinguish between resistance which has some basis in reality and resistance which stems from fantasy? And what about the feelings of the students themselves? Is it possible that their negative or ambivalent reactions, however inarticulate, have something in common with those of their more critical elders? Needless to say, I do not propose to offer comprehensive or final answers to these questions. But I believe that we can learn something useful from the past history of resistance to technology, and that it is possible for the intelligent proponents of instructional technology to dispel some of the anxiety and skepticism their plans invariably arouse.

But, first, let me be clear about my assumptions. In referring to educational technology, I follow James D. Finn's definition of three general areas of education in which technology can or is being applied: (1) general administration, (2) testing, and (3) instruction.[1] But, like Mr. Finn, I am chiefly concerned with the third area, and, more specifically, with the use of television and teaching machines in the classroom.

Let me also be explicit about my own bias. I write from the viewpoint of those humanists whose skepticism I will be describing. Proponents of technological innovation invariably insist that technology means much more than "machines" in the literal sense of the physical apparatus itself, but they consistently fail to credit those who are critical of the preferred uses of instructional technology with a capacity to grasp this obvious, common-sense idea. Thus Mr. Finn refers to the "curriculum people" who are unenthusiastic about audiovisual devices as "emotional Rousseauians"; he tends to think of his adversaries as simple-minded Luddites: ". . . reactions in some professional circles to the advent of television" he writes, "are similar to those factory workers of the 19th century who attempted to destroy the machines that were replacing their jobs."

It is possible, of course, that opposition of this primitive, mindless kind still exists, but it would be wiser and more useful for the advocates of educational technology to meet the arguments of their more sophisticated critics. In these notes, accordingly, I shall be adopting the viewpoint of those who have no hostility to the use of machines as such, and who in fact welcome the help of any labor-saving device whose use is consistent with the long-range aims of education as they define those aims. They understand that the problem is not located in the physical apparatus itself. Most writers who address themselves to the subject of technological innovation seem to agree—to the point of banality—that the essential problem is the subordination of mechanical means to humane ends. Much of the criticism of instructional technology comes down to the fear that even in the classroom men are in danger of becoming, to use Henry Thoreau's phrase, "the tools of their tools." Whether they mean it or not, the advocates of instructional technology all too often sound as if they were perfectly willing to allow the availability of certain mechanical devices to determine their goals. They would be in a far better position to avoid giving this impression if they knew a little more about the ideas and emotions which have surrounded the image of the machine in Western thought since the early nineteenth century.

2. The Critical Image of the Machine

Thomas Carlyle was the first writer, to my knowledge, to analyze the properties of the critical, post-romantic image of the machine as we now know it. In a seminal essay, "Signs of the Times," (1829) he announced that the new era was the "Mechanical Age," and that its leading symbol was the Machine. "It is the Age of Machinery," he said, "in every outward and inward sense of the word." He went on to describe three interrelated senses of the word—three ways in which the image of the machine serves as an effective synechdoche to express the essence of a new industrial style of life.

First of course he referred to the increasing presence of machines in the literal, physical sense. Mechanization at that time meant the rapidly spreading use of steam-powered engines of production, extraction and transportation. Their counterparts in this discussion are the computer, the television set and the teaching machine itself. But even in 1829 Carlyle recognized that the more complex problems accompanying the onset of the Age of Machinery could not be grasped by those who conceived of the new technology—the Machine—in this narrow sense.

Second, then, Carlyle recognized that the image of the machine would be used as the vehicle (or secondary subject) of a metaphor whose tenor (or primary subject) was the whole complex of institutional arrangements, modes of organizing human behavior, which accompanied industrialization. He had in mind the autonomous (or seemingly autonomous) market economy, the stock corporation, the neutral state, and a modern, capitalistic, relatively flexible, uncodified system of class and status—in short, all of the subordinate systems which, taken together, comprise what might be called the "social machine" or the "machine of society."

But notice that when we move from the first to the second of Carlyle's categories of meaning we are crossing the boundary between literal and figurative discourse. Whereas the first use of the image refers to the machine as a hard, physical object out there in space, the second does not. Of course an ambiguous border area also exists between the two. When proponents of instructional technology speak about the "automatic classroom," or contemplate the "automation" of education, or when student rebels refer to the university as a "factory," it is not easy to separate the literal and the figurative meanings of their words. I will return to the point. Right here it is only necessary to observe that this kind of language, whether used with a positive, negative or neutral purpose, is calculated to transfer certain attributes of the machine as object to modes of behavior. It transfers the qualities of efficiency, impersonality, organization inherent in actual machinery to institutions which are only "machines" in a figurative sense.

The third meaning that Carlyle attached to the image of the machine is by far the most subtle and prescient. He perceived that the new power-driven tools also could be said to provide a model for a new mode of consciousness—a mental equivalent, so to speak—of the technological apparatus that was becoming visible everywhere in England at the time.

So far as this new mode of thought derived from a body of express ideas, a systematic world view, it was traceable (according to Carlyle) to the British school of eighteenth century empirical philosophy—or scientific rationalism—associated with the theory of knowledge of John Locke and the celestial mechanics of Sir Isaac Newton. That this philosophical school was closely related, both in theory and practice, to the magnificent advances of applied science was obvious enough. The relationship was implicit in the popular name for the new school of thought—the mechanical philosophy. But Carlyle saw beyond the obvious connection. He recognized that the great success of scientific rationalism in advancing man's control over physical nature had encouraged claims for the universal validity of the modes of thinking essential to the scientific method: objectivity, impersonality, observation, logical rationality, quantification, etc. He was not criticizing the scientific method within its own domain, but rather he was commenting on the extent to which the values and assumptions inherent in that method had begun to manifest themselves in virtually *all* regions of thought and behavior, including those furthest removed from science and technology. In other words, the machine was a symbol for the age in the sense that it figured forth the dominant attributes of a new mental style, a structure of thought and feeling which embodied the essence of a new style of life—a culture, as we would say, in the 20th century anthropological sense—a culture which he would soon call (he may well have coined the term) "industrialism."

For our purposes the significant characteristic of this new life-style, as Carlyle and certain 19th century intellectuals defined it, was its well-nigh ideal suitability to the establishment of man's power over the external world. (That this power was in some measure, as we now know, illusory, is for the moment beside the point.) Like the machine itself, it was a set of mind perfectly designed, it seemed, to gain knowledge and control of physical nature, to produce material abundance, and achieve freedom from the tyranny of the natural environment—above all, freedom from scarcity. But Carlyle predicted that the chief defect of this undeniably potent system of value would prove to be a dangerous lopsidedness, or imbalance, in the quality of life—the culture of industrialism. All those concerns that originate within the psyche, which is to say, the private aspirations and feelings and moral judgments and ideals, the imaginings, intuitions and dreams, the spontaneous impulses of an erotic, mystical or even merely playful sort—in a word, the whole dimension of behavior we refer to as "subjective," would, in the new order, have to be rigorously disciplined and subordinated to the needs of the collective social economy.

In the emerging culture of the Machine Age, as Carlyle saw it, the very conception of the function of consciousness was to be essentially mechanical. It would encourage emphasis upon means or techniques rather than ends, and in all matters *except those entailing the control over external nature,* it would favor a conception of the function of mind that is essentially passive. The new culture therefore would undervalue the role of the private imagination, and on this point Carlyle's argument is in close accord with the criticism of industrial culture which has been mounted by most writers and artists of talent in the West since the late eighteenth century. Thus consciousness was to be conceived as primarily reflexive (anticipating modern behaviorism?) rather than shaping, leading or constitutive. The machine is an apt model for this mode of consciousness, in Carlyle's view, because the industrial culture, in its thrust toward perfecting the external arrangements of life, would find it necessary to discipline (as never before?), the spontaneous, unpredictable, unreliable energy that flows from individual psyches. A single part of an efficient machine has no meaning or purpose detached from the functioning of the whole. By the same token, the consciousness of the individual in the new society would be geared, through technical specialization—an increasingly refined mental division of labor—to the needs of the "social machine."

In this paper Carlyle's analysis of the symbol of the machine must serve as a representative example of recurrent, cardinal themes in the long-standing humanist critique of the culture of industrialism. Perhaps the heart of the argument is a concept of equilibrium in the psychic economy. The evident assumption is that something like a balance must be achieved, in a normal or healthy human situation, between satisfying man's external and internal needs. Industrial society, in this view, has placed an excessive emphasis upon man's attempt to "conquer" the external environment, repressing the needs of the inner self in the process, and thereby inviting what nowadays would be called, in post-Freudian language, an explosive "return of the repressed" in the form of various irrational, authoritarian social movements. Carlyle, to be sure, only dimly foresaw this last development, though a line of intellectual descent can be drawn from his concept of the hero to the superman of Nietzsche and the dictators of modern totalitarianism. (This dangerously authoritarian ideal of the charismatic political leader was conceived, of course, as a way of averting the predicted catastrophe of bourgeois culture.) In any case, Carlyle did suggest that the industrial culture would give rise to a new, secular kind of fatalism, grounded in the 19th century faith in Progress. Central here was the belief that once the physical arrangements of life had been perfected, once man's material needs had been satisfied (as they now seemed, for the first time in history, capable of being satisfied), the "rest"—as Carlyle put it—would take care of itself. Hence the machine was not only the literal instrument for controlling the environment and achieving this secular form of salvation, but it also would become a symbol of virtually religious trust and adoration.

So much, then for Carlyle's concept of the machine as fact and symbol. Elsewhere[2] I have tried to suggest why the image of the machine seems to have had an especially powerful impact upon the American consciousness. For one thing, the onset of the new industrial technology coincided with the founding of the Republic. The geographic, social, and economic environment of the United States was peculiarly hospitable to the development of machine power. At the same time, however, the fact that the movement from Europe to the unspoiled landscape of the New World was universally associated with the tradition of pastoral idealism, that is, a retreat from a complex society, overburdened by history, to a simpler world "closer to nature," gave many Americans, for whom Jefferson was a leading spokesman, a particularly strong aversion to industrialization. The result, which is much too complex to summarize in detail, was a peculiarly ambivalent attitude toward industrial progress. While America was committed, as no other Western society, to the most rapid possible rate of technological innovation, and while the American people actually directed their energies to increasing productivity, wealth and power, they continued to define their national purpose in the old way as the creation of a society in the image of a garden. The new society was to be the outcome of a movement, like the movement in the traditional version of pastoral, away from a complex social environment (associated with Europe and the penalties of European history), to a new kind of society conducive to the achievement of harmony, peace and economic sufficiency. America, in this view, was to be a nation conducive, in Jefferson's phrase, to "the pursuit of happiness" rather than the most rapid possible rate of increasing wealth and power. Thus industrialization brought to the surface of awareness a contradiction between action and belief, or social behavior and ideology. At first the contradiction was apparent only to the most percipient Americans—the most gifted artists, writers, statesmen—but since the middle of the 19th century it has become a commonplace of our cultural history. For all these reasons, then, in the American consciousness the image of the machine has been invested with particularly complex and ambivalent meanings.

3. Skepticism About the Use of Instructional Technology Arising from the Idea of the Machine as the Embodiment of Impersonal Organization

With Carlyle's analysis of the image of the machine in view, let me now return to the problem of current skepticism about (or resistance to) the introduction of new technological devices in the classroom. My purpose is to show the relevance of Carlyle's argument to our subject. But like Carlyle and most sophisticated humanist critics of modern technology, we shall assume that the first category of meaning—the image of the machine used to refer to the physical apparatus itself—is largely irrelevant to our concern. It is irrelevant because serious skepticism about the value of the new instructional technology seldom if ever is grounded in allegations about the physical characteristics of the devices. In this literal sense, in other words, a gadget like a television set is assumed to be neither "good" nor "bad" for teaching. This presumed "neutrality" of the machine can be argued on the basis of two quite distinct presuppositions about the impact of improved technology:

1. The value of a technological innovation generally depends upon the use to which it is put, not upon its physical attributes.

2. The consequences of all technological innovations are both good and bad. Furthermore, the good and the bad are inextricably related, and so they finally cancel each other out.

For our purposes there is no need to discuss the relative validity of these two propositions. The fact is that most skepticism about the use of technology in the classroom, to repeat, derives from the second and third categories of meaning that Carlyle attributed to the image of the machine.

First, then, let us consider the grounds for skepticism about the use of instructional technology which belongs to Carlyle's second category of meaning: the machine as a model for certain modes of organization. Here the introduction of new devices in the classroom would be understood as part of a program to achieve the kind of rationalization, impersonality or total organization that technological progress has entailed in, say, the production of automobiles or television sets. Thus, according to James Finn (in the article referred to above), the advance of instructional technology will result in an educational system that "is more highly organized and less random in nature . . ." When writers like Finn describe with approval "the trend toward a mass instructional technology . . . *governed by machines and systems* suitable for the purpose," [my emphasis] they seem to select a language calculated to associate innovation in education with industrial innovation. Apparently they feel that this vocabulary will elicit approval for their program. How else account for the repeated use of terms like "teaching machine" and "automatic classroom"? But is the "teaching machine" in fact a machine in any meaningful sense? In what sense can a classroom be called "automatic"? What the proponents of the new devices seem to ignore is the kind of anxiety and resistance this way of speaking about education is likely to arouse. Are they really in favor of techniques which would reduce both teacher and pupil to acting out a preconceived set of operations? No doubt they would say no. Yet their predilection for the new language of systems analysis makes one wonder. Here is another proponent of the new educational technology talking about the advantages of the systems approach for designing courses of study and lesson plans:

> You see a means-ends approach in any course outline or lesson plan. It goes like this: first, you state your objectives; second, you design or select appropriate activities; and finally, you evaluate in terms of the objectives. A modern systems approach uses this same means-ends organization, but it gives much greater attention to interim quality control of production at process points, with feedback loops to alter procedures according to the developing needs of the learner. In an unscientific use of means-ends, the teacher is left with the whole task of improvising the feedback loops, the quality control; but in the language of modern systems approach, these elements must be more apparent and more objective. The strategy is put together like this:

(I am omitting a graphic representation of the input-output systems approach.)

The purpose of objectives of the system is an output or terminal behavior, or product. This requires initial input. Based on analysis of behavioral possibilities, there is developed a sequence of operational steps with instructional inputs along the "production" line; the whole system maintains an appropriate balance with its feedback from interdependent controls along the line to maintain productivity at the stipulated quality level. That is technically the means-ends approach to instructional design.[3]

As the writer virtually admits, it is "the language of the modern systems approach" which chiefly engages him. Whether or not he is saying anything that could not be said more simply in ordinary English need not concern us. He evidently is infatuated with the metaphor which enables him to describe the learning process as a "production line" with "feedback," "quality control," and "productivity at the stipulated quality level." It is easy to forget, in reading this passage, that he is talking about the education of human beings, and that when he says that his system "gives much greater attention to interim quality control of production at process points," he refers to ways in which a teacher can check, in the course of presenting some subject or problem, to see whether the pupils understand. I quote the passage at length because it is an extreme example of a rhetorical tendency that runs through much of the literature favoring the introduction of instructional technology. It is a tendency to talk about people as if they were things, and to talk about education as if it were a system for producing commodities. This is all the more striking, in the case of a writer like Mr. Lange, whom I have just cited, because he notes that a "common pitfall in the means-ends or systems approach is when it loses perspective as to where that specific outcome of learning fits into the whole scheme of human living." Judging by his language, the systems approach fits into our whole economic scheme in that it takes as the model for education production for the market. But Mr. Lange ends up by invoking the conventional pieties about "developing technology for the enhancement of human values." "So the gist of my argument," he says in his final sentence, ignoring the fact that his words throughout have implied the opposite, "is that the history of human learning shows that it was technology that humanized man—technology can help man save himself, to make more of himself, always emerging into *a more human man.*" [His emphasis.]

Of course it may be said that so far I have been talking about the rhetoric used to advance the cause of instructional technology rather than what actually happens in a classroom when the new devices are put to use. That is true, and I do mean to keep the two kinds of argument distinct. At the same time, I would suggest that a writer's figurative language often provides a reliable clue to his root values and to implications which may be at variance with this overt statements. In any case, let us consider some of the ways in which the machine might in fact prove to be the model for what happens in the learning process.

One obvious consequence of the use of television or programmed learning is that both teachers and students will be expected to gear their behavior to a program originating outside the classroom. The advantages of this system are that the curriculum can be planned by experts, and that the teacher will be released from certain routine obligations in order to devote more time to the demands of individual students. Moreover, the procedures can be more or less standardized, hence they should be less subject to the idiosyncratic whims of second-rate teachers or to variations from one class (or one school) to another. The difficulty, as usual with the rationalization of "production," is the probable loss of spontaneity and individuality. Anyone who has watched a good teacher at work knows how much of his success can be attributed to minute-to-minute adaptation to the needs and moods of the students—to what can only be called continuous innovation. A good teacher of beginners in reading can take a shallow, mindless, unimaginative primer and invest it with life and pleasure. By the same token, the pupils are invited to innovate as the lesson proceeds, so that the primer itself merely provides the bare bones, the starting point for the rich, varied, unpredictable experience of reading. But if we are watching a lesson on a television screen, or working with a teaching machine, is there any possibility for this kind of imaginative, innovative, personalized learning? My point is that the analogy between the new methods replacing the fallibility of the individual teacher and the assembly line replacing the individual craftsman may not be "mere rhetoric." The danger, in short, is that the use of instructional technology, like the use of industrial technology, will rationalize the personal or innovative factor out of the productive process. Both teachers and students will come to think of themselves as essentially controlled parts ("cogs" is the word used by the student rebels at Berkeley and elsewhere) of a system that has been designed by anonymous, invisible experts.

One of Carlyle's points about the machine as a symbol for industrial culture is that it represents the tendency to synchronize all of the subordinate systems of society to the total organization—the "social machine." Given a society in which the chief motive for production is private profit, then, it is interesting to notice James Finn's remark about "the continuous, grinding, sweating struggle carried on by audiovisual specialists, dealers, manufacturers, and producers to introduce, one item at a time . . . [the various devices of instructional technology] into the educational system . . ." The point here is not that the campaign for instructional technology is a conspiracy of capitalists, but rather that it may in some degree derive from motives having nothing to do with the educational merits of the innovations. Not only does the new instructional method make possible standardized teaching, but it also encourages the production of standardized pedagogical "hardware." Here again there is a tendency for the means to determine the ends. Is there not a danger that once the new technology gets a firm hold on the educational Establishment, those subjects will be favored which are most conducive to the new machine teaching?[4] (In higher education nowadays we find that students often set out to discover research projects suitable for computer programming.) Then, too, the introduction of programmed teaching methods seems to entail, as in industrial technology, greater centralized control of education. Programming, says Mr. Finn, is "a matter of extreme organization . . . It is also a social problem. The heartland is programming. He who controls the programming heartland controls the educational system. Will it be a Foundation, a committee of scientists, textbook publishers and film producers, the NEA, the school superintendent, the board of education, the students, or the general public?" The fact that the question arises at all suggests the possible validity of the notion, insinuated by Carlyle's conception of the machine, that mechanization embodies a tendency toward super-organization and perhaps, for that matter, totalitarian institutions.

In sum, then, the concept of the machine as the embodiment of increasingly standardized, rationalized, impersonal organization has some bearing upon resistance to the introduction of instructional technology. We find that the advocates of the new teaching methods, whether they mean to do so or not, lend credence to this association between the actual teaching devices and the machine-like organization of the learning process. In part they do this because of their fondness for *the rhetoric* of mass-production technology and electronics, but in some part at least their substantive proposals would seem to entail a loss of spontaneity and individuality of the kind we associate with mechanization generally.

4. Skepticism About the Use of Instructional Technology Arising from the Idea of the Machine as the Embodiment of a Mode of Consciousness, A Structure of Thought and Feeling

Advocates of the new instructional technology seem to take for granted the desirability of the most rapid possible rate of technological development. Thus James Finn provides a chart in his article comparing the various stages of industrial technology with the equivalent development of instructional technology. Whereas industry had reached the stage of "Mass Production Technology" in 1800, he describes education in 1900 as "Still Pre-Industrial in Concept and Execution," and whereas industry entered the "Pre-Automation Period" in 1950, he says that education had reached only "Potential Mass Production Technology (Unrealized)" at that time. There are two basic assumptions here which are shared by many proponents of the new instructional methods. The first is that scientific and industrial development provides a model of what is desirable and necessary in education. Hence the fact that education lags behind industry obviously is to deplored. And the second is that the introduction of more sophisticated technological methods necessarily constitutes "progress," which is to say, a good thing. Thus Mr. Finn, discussing the use of television to create a "Continental Classroom," and the use of "new audiovisual teaching machines" developed by Hughes Aircraft, imagines that the two might become synchronized and standardized for the whole nation. "Think, for a moment," he exclaims, "about that one. It is now possible, not only to eliminate the teacher, but the school system." But then he introduces this modest afterthought:

> These may be considered extreme applications, but such applications, at least experimentally, are inevitable. . . . The point is that both the mass instruction systems and the technology of individual instruction—teaching machines—are getting terrific momentum. These technologies are going to hit education with a million-pound thrust.

Mr. Finn may well be correct in his analysis, but I feel that the passage conveys a curiously uncritical exhilaration at the thought of eliminating teachers and school systems, and especially at the thought that these developments, which will "hit" the system with a "million-pound thrust" [the power of an intercontinental ballistic missile, or is it an Apollo spacecraft?], "are inevitable." The tone, like the thought, comports with Carlyle's analysis of the dominant ethos of industrialism. The central symbol is the machine, and anything associated with the advance of technology may be expected to elicit a similarly uncritical, reverential and fatalistic attitude. The values being endorsed are efficiency, depersonalization, standardization, quantification, and—in a word—rationalization. There is an unspoken premise here to the effect that virtually anything technology is capable of doing is worth doing, and that technological innovation is the irresistible cutting edge of history.

But here again it may be said that I am taking the rhetoric at face value, and that while James Finn and his colleagues may talk this way at times, their real aims are to democratize and humanize education. Perhaps that is the case. On the other hand, it also is possible to imagine ways in which the use of the various new devices would in fact serve to make the learning process wholly "mechanical" in the pejorative sense.

It is illuminating to compare the use, with reference to the fundamental attitudes toward learning that they engender, of the television set (or teaching machine) as against the living teacher. One claim made for the new methods is their built-in correctness. Leaving aside the possibility that the programming might be based upon misguided principles, let us grant the point. We would prevent second or third-rate teachers from warping the minds of the young with error. A pupil working with a machine would learn to place total confidence in the knowledge meted out. At least it is difficult to imagine how the programmer would go about introducing error into the lesson plan. Yet is it certain that we want the child to learn this kind of respect for the infallibility of the abstract intelligence which manipulates the learning process? Every sensitive parent has learned that adult know-it-allness can be an impediment to learning. The child becomes easily discouraged by the grown-up world's seeming omniscience. One of the great advantages of the living teacher's relation with the child is that learning is a two-way process. A good teacher knows how to learn from the child, and to exemplify the ideal state of mind of a learner, that is, one who is prepared to learn, and—a most important function—one *who can admit error.* In the living teacher's classroom, moreover, there is the sense of impending revelation. Something unexpectedly illuminating may happen at any moment. The child may respond to a text in a fresh way and win the teacher's approval. But the child who faces a television set or a teaching machine is up against an essentially unresponsive, error-free, inexhaustible repository of knowledge. The situation is "closed" at one end, and it tends to make learning an accommodation to the inevitable.

A particularly threatening feature of the new standardized teaching methods, from the viewpoint of the teacher of language and literature, is the loss of individuality in the use of language itself. One of the great resources of language, as the new transformational linguistics has demonstrated, is its infinite variability. Yet the dream of the instructional technologists, it sometimes seems, is to have every third-grade child in the school system attending to the same program on TV (or built into the teaching machine) at the same time. Standardization is a dominant concern of the new methods. But in teaching children to write, a sophisticated teacher attempts to make them appreciate the resources of the language they already possess, with all of its local, ethnic and social particularity. Today we deplore the old-fashioned schoolmarm's effort to divest speech and writing of its colloquial coloring, and to give every child the imprint of genteel, standardized, "proper" English. Yet it may be that the new instructional technology constitutes an even more serious threat to a living, individualized language than the old schoolmarm herself.

Standardization, objectivity, rationality, quantification, impersonality—these would seem to be the values inherent in the new instructional technology. The method may be ideally suited to directing the child's attention outward to an allegedly established body of factual knowledge and ordered procedure. But, as Carlyle observed about the ethos of industrialism generally, the new methods would seem to be less useful in developing the child's control over those aspects of experience which originate within his own psyche. The whole world of imagination, feeling, moral judgment—in a word, the *subjective* aspect of experience —seems to be slighted by the theory of instructional technology. Whereas the method implicitly values man's capacity to perfect his relations with the external environment (the learning situation created by the teaching machine is in itself a model of adaptation to impersonal forces), it virtually ignores the problem of controlling and using the resources of the psyche.

5. Conclusions

I have discussed two general sources of resistance to, or skepticism about, the introduction of instructional technology. The first is the idea of the machine as the model of organization that accompanies the use of educational technology. The second is the idea of the machine as the embodiment of a mode of consciousness, a system of meaning and value, that would be disseminated along with the use of teaching machines. In both categories the rhetoric of the advocates of instructional technology lends credence to the fear that they do in fact accept and endorse these metaphoric extensions of the technological devices they would introduce. But the argument can stand apart from an analysis of rhetoric. There are good reasons for thinking that the use of instructional technology might carry with it support for mechanical modes of organization and for mechanistic styles of thinking. Yet at no point have I wished to imply that there is any necessary connection between the physical apparatus and these concomitant practices.

One final word. At the outset I suggested that it might be possible, on the basis of these observations, for intelligent proponents of instructional technology to dispel some of the anxiety and skepticism that their plans tend to arouse. But this statement is open to misinterpretation. It might be taken to mean that canny theorists of the new techniques, aware of the susceptibility of their program to such charges, should deliberately change their rhetoric in order to create an opposite impression. I suppose that it would be possible for them to divest their writing and thinking of the overtones which invite the charge of shallow technologism. Such a procedure, however, would be misguided and liable to exposure as a mere Public Relations tactic.

But there is another sense in which these observations might be useful in dispelling opposition to the use of instructional technology. What if the proponents of the new methods were to take the charge of mechanistic thinking seriously? Might they not reconsider the relationship between the techniques they favor and the fundamental aims of education? And might it not be possible to introduce safeguards against the use of techniques merely because they exist? Surely educators could encourage a greater awareness of the folly of using teaching devices chiefly because they share some attributes of machines. Might not the thinking and writing of educational theorists be informed by a sense of the very real danger, inherent in all technological "process," that the ends often come to be determined by the means?

Early in this paper I quoted the response of Henry Thoreau to an earlier surge of mechanization. "But lo!" he said, "men have become the tools of their tools!" Lest that insight be dismissed as the fear of a mere poet and dreamer, a hypersensitive man of ideas who was out of touch with practical realities, let me close by citing the words of a contemporary economist whose name often is cited with approval by proponents of educational technology. At the beginning of his most recent book, *The New Industrial State*, John Kenneth Galbraith asserts, somewhat less pungently than Thoreau, but to the same effect: "I am led to the conclusion, which I trust others will find persuasive, that we are becoming the servants in thought, as in action, of the machine we have created to serve us."

Let the admirers of teaching machines consider what it would mean if this gloomy observation ever should become pertinent to the technology of education.

REFERENCES

1. Finn, James. "Automation and Education: Technology and the Instructional Process." *A V Communication Review,* VIII, Winter, 1960, pp. 5-26.

2. *The Machine in the Garden, Technology and the Pastoral Ideal in America.* N.Y. 1964.

3. Lange, Phil C. "Technology, Learning and Education." *Audiovisual Instruction,* XIII, March, 1968, pp. 226-231.

4. A nice example may be found in Leslie J. Bishop's article on "Technology and the Possible Curriculum," *Audiovisual Instruction,* XIII, March, 1968, p.225. Bishop is explaining how curriculum planning might work into the new order: it would consist, the writer says, "Of individual and group experiences *as determined by analysis and by study of audio, video, or other methods of capturing evidence."* I emphasize the determination of the content by the study of the methods.

40.

Age Discrepancies
In the Understanding and Use
Of Modern Technology,
Especially the Mass Media.

or

How Parents and Teachers Fail to Tune
In on the Children's Media Environment. *

by MARGARET MEAD
Curator of Ethnology Emeritus
American Museum of Natural History

Education may be looked at in terms of *maintenance systems* in which children are simply taught what adults know—the system found in all primitive societies—*maintenance and change systems,* in which provision is made for teaching children what their own parents do not know but which some adults know—the system found in all societies with some provision for social mobility, or the absorption of immigrant groups—and *emergent systems* in which children have to learn what no adult has ever learned in the same way . . . the unique condition which we face in today's world.

It is useful to have a clear picture of the earliest system in order to highlight the contrasts. Among hunting and gathering people, there are simple forms of the division of labor, boys learn men's skills and girls women's, and the entire society reinforces the learning process. The same tools are used generation after generation, the physical environment is known in detail, adults have gone through the same experiences that each generation of children go through, and children, as they learn, reinforce the memories and the understanding of their parents and grandparents. In slightly more complex societies there may be specialists and children and young people, in addition to learning what all members of their tribe know and what all members of their age and sex are learning, who may learn special forms of hunting or fishing or magical charms. The emphasis is more upon learning, not upon teaching, although occasionally a genealogist or the last man to command some special knowledge may seek for an apprentice heir. Societies differ in the efficiency of these methods of transmission; sometimes secrets are only imparted at the near death of one who knows them; sometimes a young person never learns about a particular way of handling some event—such as marrying a widow—unless he finds himself confronted with the event. But in general such education, most of it completely informal, is remarkably efficient in transmitting the entire body of knowledge and learned behavior from one generation to another.

When we come to great civilizations, with division of labor, urban centers and rural peasantry, conquest of alien peoples, emigration and loss of skills, and immigration and

*This material is based in part on research done under an NIH research grant No. B-3303 to the American Museum of Natural History project: "The Factor of Allopsychic Orientation in Mental Health."

gains of skill or of a large number who need to be absorbed into the new society, we get the equivalent of schools of some sort. It is no longer possible to rely on transmission from parents and other adult members of the community, and there is a need for recruitment of new members of different groups, clerks, sailors, craftsmen, philosophers, from among the children of other groups, sometimes selectively. As knowledge spreads and new techniques are introduced into the society, like script, printing, systems of keeping accounts, navigation, and engineering, more and more people have to learn what was developed by a very few innovators. The requirement for learning the language of those who control a large state is one example of such a requirement, so as standard German, standard French and standard Italian became state languages, the people who had spoken dialects were required to learn to read and speak the standard language. The modern requirement of literacy that extends even to the most backward and isolated peoples is another example in which in one generation millions of people are required to learn a skill which was once confined to a very small number of adults and their children. Each such requirement introduces a generation gap but in the past the gap has been between many adults and their own children. Today the gap is between all adults and all children.

For we have entered into a new phase, which I am calling here *emergent,* in which change is so rapid that there is no time in which the first group of those who learn something new can teach their own children, who having learned something as children, can teach the same things as adults. Instead, the entire present generation of those who grew up before World War II, wherever they grew up, in New York or New Guinea, grew up in a world that was radically different from the world of today. Those born after the war have grown up in a world that is radically different from the pre-World War II world, and the links which used to bind the old and the new are missing. There are a few individuals who were reared in the extreme forefront of their own period, who understood, for example, thirty years ago what automation would mean, or that exploration of space was possible. But there are no adults alive today, in any country, born before World War II, who have had, or can ever have the kind of growing up experience of the post World War II generation. Those adults who do have a working comprehension of today's world are like people who have successfully mastered a second language as adults. But for none of them are the ideas and the technology a mother tongue. These adults' second language is the children's mother tongue, and because the changes are worldwide, all the children have a new mother tongue.

This new world condition, in which children in the arctic fastnesses of Alaska and the tropical fastnesses of south sea islands share through tape recorder, radio and satellites, can be characterized broadly in the following terms: Today's children have learned, often not explicitly, but implicitly, the way children and non-literate people nevertheless know the grammar of their mother tongue, that we now have the means to destroy the entire population of this planet and that it will require constant vigilance to keep from doing so; they know that the danger today is not that there will not be enough people to do the work or defend one's country, but instead that there is the danger of too many people who will choke the arteries of travel, exhaust the food supply, overwhelm today's institutions. They expect to hear about events as they happen and not after they happen, and therefore now relate to raw events rather than to history, as their literate predecessors did; they know that the adults who are their parents, and their teachers, do not seem to understand what is happening. Most of these adults still seem to think that nuclear war can be prevented for good by test bans, non-proliferation treaties, and the destruction of stock piles and that other countries but not their own should limit their populations, that television is a nuisance very much inferior to reading, that exploration of space is an expensive and stupid luxury, that the way our enemies make war is bad but that when we do the same thing it is good, that computers are some kind of mysterious monster—suitably signified by signs like the giant octopus painted on Brown University's new computer center. And if only there were some kind of political leadership (more conservative or more radical), more socialism in capitalist countries, and more freedom in communist countries, present day conditions which are thought of as being created by the mass media, or the Communists, or the Capitalist Imperialists, or the party in power or leader in power, would all be ironed out and the world would be something like it is imagined to have been before: everybody working, people who knew their place and did not have unreasonable aspirations, airports and highways that were not crowded, air without smog, unpolluted rivers, clean beaches, innocent amusements and no crime or drugs, no riots or questioning university students.

Stated differently, most adults still believe that most of the changes which are transforming the world are due to some sort of moral or political misguidedness which could be corrected by political coercion, moral suasion or individual conversion. The young people, often at a very inarticulate level, know that the world has changed radically and irreversibly, because of the new technologies which have made scientific warfare a continuing possibility. They know that we have now explored the whole planet, and have established the fact that all men, regardless of racial divisions are members of the same species, have put the whole world into immediate communication and simultaneous confrontation of major events, and have begun the process by which machines will substitute not only for human hands but for the more laborious and long time and detailed operations of the human brain. They know that computerization, automation, is not only here to stay but will proceed apace until the whole world has TV, that the protection of space and the inner space under the oceans will be as continuous a task as our present concern with borders and boundaries, and it will be cost, not time, that separates human beings on one planet from those on another.

These are some of the large scale differences in the views of the world between the pre-war and the post-war generations. But they effect everything that is taught and the reception that such teaching receives. Our history books are the carefully constructed and contrived versions of history which the peoples of a given period wish to convey to their children, worked over, pre-digested, highly selective. So are many of the mass media presentations, the big colossal spectacles, the great movie spectacles, the articles in *Life* and *Look*. These also are carefully edited to present particular points of view and a highly selective picture of reality. But just as a small town newspaper was once unable to distort the local news because everybody in town knew what had happened, children place the edited versions, the slow, ponderous, hopelessly out-of-date text books, some of which are as much as a generation out of date, and the more up-to-date, but also highly edited prepared versions of film and TV beside the reality of the raw news which is poured in from all over the world. The editing is done in ways which no longer make sense; the basic premises both about what children should know and do know, are all wrong. They are given arithmetic text books which assume that they should spend 8 years learning arithmetic, while they can glimpse on TV, new math, new physics, the computations that control a satellite, the way in which a computer predicts election results. They learn, from TV and from the ads which are seldom scrutinized for the same values as the textbooks and the propagandistic documents, just what is happening in the world, about the pill and IUD and organ transplantation and tissue propagation. They are learning about the possibility of test tube babies while the schools are still cautiously offering a few carefully sterile remarks about reproduction.

They know about the processes of manufacturing and have a new sense of what books mean. Very recently, all but the most highly educated people regarded books as something given. There was the Bible, the almanac which told the truth about each year, the dictionary, the calendar. They had no idea that books were a place to turn to for something new, something just known, and little sense of how books were produced. But today, children writing to God, write:

Dear God,
Could you write more stories. We have already read all the ones you have and begin again. Emily.

Dear God,
Church is alright but you could sure use better music. I hope this does not hurt your feelings. Can you write some new songs. Your friend, Barry.

Dear God,
Did you have as much trouble learning Hebrew as I do. Are there any easy ways to do it. I know you talk English too so, I am writing this in English. Respectfully, Jerome.

Dear God,
When you wrote the Bible you made up all the words and spelled them the way you like. That is great. Most of the time I do it like that but I am not doing so good. Ron.

Dear God.
Your book has a lot of zip to it. I like science fiction stories. You had very good ideas and I would like to know where you found them. Your reader, Jimmy.[1]

Children in nursery school, asked to draw pictures, draw rockets with the count down indicated even before they know their numbers in sequence, and put in "7, 5, 4, 2, 1." Children discussing space take up their position out on the moon looking out at the earth, while their parents are still positioned on the earth looking up at the moon, a moon still conceived as they conceived it in childhood and learned to recite:

> "*Oh moon have you done something wrong in heaven*
> *That God has hidden your face,*"

or when they were a little older,

> "*If you want to spoon, say please mister moon*
> *Be a good sport and turn off your light.*"

And it was only a few years ago in which, in a Bell Telephone Company special film about the earth's resources, the sun was represented with a grinning face, smiling down on earth men trying to do mathematical calculations. The film was called *Mister Sun!*

The pre-war generation grew up trained to "concentrate," to work in quiet libraries where people were punished for talking, to finish their lessons before they played records or turned on the radio. The post war generation has learned to read and study and think with several media going at once: TV showing a game with the sound turned off, the radio turned on to a radio commentator on the same game, a long playing record providing background music, as 9th graders, glued to the telephone, compare notes on the problems they are doing. Reading required concentration; the symbols on the page were such a fragmentary schematic part of the vast information that they conveyed, simple sentences invoked whole epochs of history, as "Rome fell," and "America was discovered." Children who learned primarily from books had to learn to concentrate on the whole evocative sequence that unrolled in orderly and linear fashion before them. Understandably, the better scholar one became, the less related one was likely to be to ongoing life. But today's children not only can deal in many media but find silence, especially silence in a group, something that is very hard to bear. Shut up for the first time in a strictly policed room to take a scholarship exam, they quail before the sounds of their own and their neighbor's rumbling stomachs, sounds that they have never heard before, in the noise-ridden world that they inhabit by choice. Educated adults still "watch" TV, organize themselves in comfortable chairs, and turn attentively towards the TV screen as if they were at a concert where coughing and sneezing were forbidden. Uneducated adults may sit glued to the screen. But today's children simply turn it on and keep an eye on it, as one might keep an eye on what is going on out in the street, while making up one's mind whether to go out and join one of a number of games. It's a window on the world—sometimes there is something very special, as a parade is a special variant of street life and one may fight for standing room, but in general it's part of life to which one can attend for hours at a time, or treat cavalierly as part of the scenery.

An instructive example of the failure of teachers to allow for the TV world has been the conclusions that were drawn about children from socially deprived backgrounds who were voted "unable to concentrate." But if the teacher to whose voice they do not listen is put on closed TV, they sit perfectly quietly, and listen soberly to remarks that are obviously addressed to them, as are the remarks of Captain Kangaroo.

> Dear God,
> If you do all these things you are pretty busy. Now here's my question. When is the best time I can talk to you? I know you are always listening but when will you be listening in Troy, New York? Sincerely yours, Allen.[2]

These children have often grown up in homes where it was not customary for adults to tell anything to children but only to give them orders to keep still or get moving. Where the teacher who expects attention can get no response, the trained expectation of something said directly to them which they want to hear, is available to start these small children listening and learning.

In one very instructive case, we have an instance of a little girl who learned to read from TV without anyone knowing she had. It took an agonizing year in first grade where she was pronounced mentally defective and three years in a special psychiatric residential institution to get her back into the mainstream of education. Yet this is only an extreme example of the way in which bright children who have learned not only content but process from the mass media, are crippled by the discrepancy between what they know and what their teachers and parents think they know.

At the 1968 Congress of the World Federation for Mental Health, Dr. Margaret Lowenfeld presented the case of a boy who was having great difficulty learning to read by standard methods, but who could already solve problems of many dimensions in his head, doing quickly what highly trained adults took three or four times as long to do.[3]

The school as it was invented in societies in Phase Two, the phase of Education for Maintenance and Slow Change, was conceived as a group situation in which the teacher could teach a large class, in unison, and the slow child was dragged along, the brighter child's learning ability modulated to the pace of the class, the multiple styles of learning of the different children in the group, combined in such a way that finally, all the children in the class learned to read and write and do a modest amount of figuring. The slow pace, the group recitation, the teacher's rebukes and encouragements to children with different sensory gifts, combined to provide an atmosphere almost as embracing as a primitive village where all the little boys learned to shoot bows and arrows or handle a harpoon. As long as change—in society and in methods of teaching was slow enough—this worked. All of the children who were not seriously mentally defective learned to read, and the bright child read ahead of the class and was not severely damaged.

But since the advent of many other media beside script, rapid, partly rationalized untested methods of education which change with great speed so that teachers teach in ways of which they have no previous learning knowledge, this system has broken down. Great numbers of children fail to learn to read, very bright children are severely damaged, children who come from backgrounds divergent from the assumed background for school children break down before they are given a chance to adjust. The method of class instruction in which the appeals to special abilities and the use of special sensory modalities were masked by a slow, well-tried approach no longer obtains. Moving with the group is only satisfactory when the teacher has moved in the same way and so transforms their difficulties and capabilities into something that can be mastered by another generation doing the same thing.

This seems to me to be a more satisfactory explanation of the lack of reading difficulties in Japan and Korea than the alternative suggestions that we have a much larger number of children with defects in vision, e.g., lack of binocular vision, and with learning defects due to new forms of malnutrition associated with synthetic diets of various sorts. A case can, however, be made, as Milton Tobias has shown in his studies of California children,[4] that maturational delay, temporary and correctable central nervous system difficulties, and ocular defects also play a considerable role. It must also be borne in mind that where our aim is to save even the most fragile infant, both new defects and new capabilities in individuals of types who in the past would never have survived infancy, may be expected to appear in our school population to challenge our educational technology.

In this connection it is worthwhile considering the kinds of educational ingenuity developed by Evelyn Ayrault,[5] herself a case of cerebral palsy, who has specialized in testing and teaching devices for severely handicapped children, and the recent efforts to compensate for the defects in the thalidomide babies, and the experiments with placing hearing aids on very young infants, so improving their use of their defective hearing that later they can dispense with the hearing aids.

The Russians have been exceedingly successful in teaching the deaf by combining the use of manual language, lip reading and typewriters, so that children enter the first year of school with well-developed, large vocabularies.

All of these devices for teaching the deaf, the blind, the crippled, those with birth injuries, and cerebral palsy, where a great deal of technical imagination has been expended because of the extremity of the need, should be re-examined to see how they can be adapted to solve the learning problems of less handicapped but severely one-sided children. Intensive listening through special earphones may strengthen a child whose hearing is dull and obtuse; intensive watching of specially constructed closed circuit TV may teach a child with tunnel vision to allow for his defect, or a child with very wide vision to narrow it and focus more centrally.

Furthermore, such technical devices can be organized to teach children how other people see the world. There have been instructive museum exhibits of a "dog's view of the world" and of the way in which monkeys or birds see the world. An essential for children who are going to grow up in a multi-media world is to realize where their own sight, hearing, and ability to use abstract symbols and respond to isolated stimuli or complicated patterns, stand in the spectrum of the human abilities manifested now by fellow pupils and later by friends, constituents, fellow workers, fellow team members, audiences, etc. Each step in which a child's consciousness of his special skills and special "blind spots" (using this term to cover defects in any aspect of perception) is developed, will be a step towards developing an effective citizen of the emerging world. Glasses in which children can experiment with near-sightedness and far-sightedness, binoculars, microscopes, and telescopes, should be part of the regular equipment for young children and not wait for the time when they are studying a laboratory science or beginning to take a serious interest in astronomy. The electronic microscope, and telescope, and surgical instrument for operations, are already part of their world as seen on TV. Children need a chance to try them out.[6]

Today's teachers will be increasingly called upon to teach in fields where they lack both childhood experience and contemporary knowledge and where many of the children in the class, who have been attending to the mass media, are more knowledgeable than they. Faced with this condition, we have several options. We can try to reeducate the teachers, to simulate the experience of learning as a child by a condensed experience of learning as an adult.

This process of placing today's adult teachers in the position of children who learn new things has been experimented with in various ways. Some brilliant young foreign students, when they go to a new country, spend considerable time associating with younger people so as to capture the steps by which their age mates reached their present position as college students or medical students. The field anthropologist does the same thing in learning a new language, simultaneously associating with young children, learning as the children learn, and using highly abstract linguistic techniques to approach the language analytically. One experiment in which teachers were gathered together for new learning, using films to give them a further understanding of the process, was carried out by Gertrude Hendrix at the University of Illinois Mathematical program in which teachers were taught themselves, saw children taught, and also were given films of the way in which young dogs learned in a few short weeks from experienced trainers. How much the original period of learning, as one learns a mother tongue, can be simulated by the use of a variety of film and sound tape learning devices, remains to be seen. But it is one device open to us. Experiments in the special classes in the Illinois project suggested, however, that it was easier to teach teachers who had taught but had never taught mathematics, how to teach the new mathematics than it was to teach mathematics teachers who had learned previous techniques. This suggests that unlearning specific skills may be a more serious barrier to learning new skills than earlier more generalized learning. Experience with trying to present new experiences in which there is no trace of old habits also suggests that in planning the reeducation of teachers less reliance can be placed on any situation where unlearning is required.[7]

The experiments in making instructional films for the teaching of mathematics, made at the University of Illinois project, are also illuminating. The construction of the films themselves, in which the same teacher taught two sections, a week apart, so that the film makers could learn which moments to concentrate on, was a magnificent innovation. But the cost of the films, although subsidized, has been prohibitive and has prevented adequate dissemination of both the method of teaching and the method of making teaching films.*

The librarian presents another model by which teachers themselves unfamiliar with the subject matter or point of view which they must now teach can nevertheless present it to their pupils in audiovisual forms. Librarians are taught to know about things and to guide those who want to use the library into realms with which they themselves are totally unfamiliar. Far from being ashamed of their specific ignorance they are proud of their capacity to deal with the unfamiliar. If suitable films and tapes are available and are constructed for the use of teachers who are themselves unfamiliar with the subject matter, packaged in a way which makes the teacher proud of exploration rather than ashamed of ignorance, this library model can be used very constructively. But any film or tape which assumes that the teacher has, may have, or should have, a kind of contemporary knowledge which she does not have, leads to antagonism towards the new material—and to the new media—and to a tendency to clamp down on pupils' discussion as too threatening. This undoubtedly is one of the reasons for the tremendous antagonism and faulty use of audiovisual materials. Those who have made the materials have wanted to provide a content which will compensate for what the teacher does not know, but they do not make any allowance for the way in which his or her lack of knowledge is presented to the teacher so as to prevent the feeling of humiliation which stems from the conception of a teacher as one who knows what the pupils do not know. Today the teacher must adjust to being a guide and counselor and fellow explorer into realms in which he not only does not know more than the pupils but often knows less.

The hostility to the use of audiovisual aids, and this extends to programmed learning, use of computers, and every sort of teaching aid which has a mechanical component, even such mundane instruments as typewriters and stopwatches, is also partly a function of the

*Teaching High School Mathematics First Course. 50 Films for Teachers of Elementary Algebra. *Produced by The University of Illinois, Committee on School Mathematics, with an Introduction to the UICSM Teacher Training Films by Gertrude Hendrix. Average purchase price for each film $170.00, total purchase price for 50 films $8400.00. Rental rate $6.00 each film for 3 school days, $12.00 for each film for 8 school days.*

different ways in which the two sexes deal with machines. Traditionally women have disliked and distrusted machinery while boys and men have in the majority of cases learned to enjoy it. All mechanical teaching aids are designed by men and implicitly set up to be used by men. Projectors are made too heavy for women to manage. Much of the equipment is unreliable and requires continuous monkeying with and adjustment. Visual aid departments have also been manned by men.

If the new technology is to be used constructively in the school, women who form and may be expected to continue to form the majority of our instructional personnel through high school at least, must be included in the planning. Machinery must be devised which can be used with a minimum of adjustment, and educational instructional materials adapted to the style of relatively foolproof equipment designed for feminine use—e.g., washing machines—instead of to the style of ingenious small boys who like making things that don't work, work. Women—their whole attention concentrated on the pupils in front of them—like things that do work, not things that have to be made to work. Not only is it necessary to take women into the designing stage for equipment and audiovisual content, because they will be constituting the majority of those who use it, but it is also essential to include children, at as early an age as possible. Only children know what children see and what children are learning on daily TV; only children know what automatically conveys the message—"This is an ad; don't watch. This is an ad, don't listen." The creators of the ads continually resort to new tricks of presentation, voice change, altered sequence, in an attempt to divert, amuse and cajole an adult audience who are resistant to any style they know. But meanwhile, the children are absorbing another set of messages at another level, and a beautifully conceived sound film may convey exactly the opposite meaning from that which was intended.

By the same token, instructional audiovisual or programmed materials must be constantly renewed. Children are keyed to the smallest clues, from a single shift of line in a comic strip, to a change in the introductory music in a film. If the message is to be fresh and learned, it must also be absolutely contemporary in every respect, *or* the datedness must be built in, so that teacher and pupils can laugh together at how strangely old hat the ideas of five years ago are, and how much new there will be to learn.

A further characteristic of the present emergent phase of change is that it is no longer easily demonstrable to children and to those who lack education that there is an absolute tie-in between the need to go through the same steps as their predecessors and the arrival at a position of adult competence. Here I think it is essential to bracket together the impatience of children and young people with the whole educational system, the demands of the poor and uneducated for a full share in all the benefits of an industrialized society, and the demands of the new countries for immediate industrialization and effective nationhood. They share the common characteristic of a failure to recognize that the repetition of steps which were once demanded of adults, the poor and the children of the poor, and the inhabitants of the economically backward areas of the world are, in any sense, relevant today. Parents, teachers, elders—all of those who in the past have commended the necessity and the rewards of appropriate effort to learn needed skills, and the appropriateness of smaller rewards to those who failed to learn—can no longer do so. Why, they ask, should anyone have to go through stages which are so obviously associated with obsolescent skills and ideas? So children fail to learn in school; college students drop out, rebel and demand relevance; the minorities and the uneducated demand immediate shares of our admittedly enormous productive ability; and nations barely born want airlines and atomic reactors. This has been discussed as a demand for "instant everything" by Hayakawa[8] and others. But I do not think this goes to the heart of the matter. The rationale of waiting, studying, learning, or accepting, as an adult, that owing to accident of birth, failure of purpose or lack of ability one must take a humbler place in the social system, has simply collapsed under the speed of change. Parents who attempt to explain are dismissed by children who saw a more comprehensible version on TV; teachers who attempt to teach from obsolescent text books are dismissed as out of date and irrelevant; and the barely literate poor demand the same standard of living as those who have waited and worked, often for several generations, always through childhood and adolescence. It is hard to see what kind of a workable world we can develop unless a new rationale is introduced which makes such orders of discrepancy comprehensible to children and to those whose present position is the product of previous lack of privilege.

The use of modern technology in education unless used more skillfully than at present simply deepens the generation gap. When a professor lectures on Plato and the student yawns, the student still knows that the professor knows more about Plato than he does. His only rebellious recourse is to say Plato is irrelevant to his interests and the needs of the contemporary world. But when the teacher shows astounding ignorance both of the content of the new media and the basic technology, then the student can really brush them aside, and, as in the case of the growing segment of youthful radicalism, say their elders are simply untrustworthy and incapable of managing the system in which they are still in control. It is essential that we recognize the inexperience—in the sense of not having grown up into it—of all adults in the contemporary world, and treat the whole of our present civilization, as understood by the young, as comparable to a second language. This must be learned, if we as adults are to continue to be able to use our mother tongue, and if the children are not to be as radically disinherited as the small survivors of Dachau and Belsen who had to be parents to each other. To make this possible, we have to institute new forms of learning together, in which adults are educated in ways of identifying and using the world as seen through the eyes of children and teenagers—as adults and youngsters work together on problems to which neither group knows the answer. Education has been built upon accumulated past knowledge and experience. It must now include articulate ignorance of the emerging future combined with a determination to master the skills necessary to shape the future for the well-being of mankind.

REFERENCES

1. Hample, Stuart, and E. Marshall, eds. *Children's Letters to God.* Essandess Special Editions. New York: Simon and Schuster, 1966.

2. *Op. cit.*

3. VII. International Congress on Mental Health, London, August 12-17, 1968, World Federation for Mental Health. Session No. 222 *Socio-cultural Problems.* Speakers: Dr. Margaret Mead and Dr. Margaret Lowenfeld: "Exploratory Procedures with Standardised Stimulus Objects: Their Use is Anthropology, Education and the Study of Individual Personality," Tuesday, August 13, 1968.

4. Tobias, Milton, and William B. Michael. "An Exploration into Child Ecology: Physiological and Maturational Indices as Predictors of Measures of Achievement, Aptitude and Adjustment." *Educational and Psychological Measurements,* 21, No. 4 (Winter, 1961), 967-974.

5. Ayrault, Evelyn W. *You Can Raise Your Handicapped Child.* New York: Putnam, 1964.

6. Mead, Margaret. The Factor of Allopsychic Orientation in Mental Health. NIH (National Institute of Health) grant M 3303 (C1) to American Museum of Natural History, 1960-1964.

7. Frank, Lawrence K. *School as Agent for Cultural Renewal.* Burton Lectures 1958. Cambridge: Harvard University Press, 1959.

8. Hayakawa, S. I. "Mass Media and Family Communication," in press *ETC.,* 1968.

41.
Technologies for Learning

by RICHARD A. MEISLER
Director of Freshman Programs
State Univ. of N.Y., College at Buffalo

Introduction

In the midst of a society pervaded by technology, the American educational community is in the process of assessing the ways in which it can use a variety of available technologies. If technology can help to improve the quality or efficiency of our educational programs, then American education, pressed by the large number of students involved in its great experiment in mass education, can sorely use that help. But the question of technology would be forced upon us even if we did not have the problems of many students and high costs. We do, after all, live in the most highly technological society in history. Our students have assimilated technology into their lives more fully and comfortably than any previous generation. It is therefore valid to wonder whether an educational system without radical *and* technological changes can effectively reach such a student population. I doubt that it can.

I would like to present an inventory of promising and as yet unassimilated educational technologies, and also to discuss some of the general issues and puzzles that appear to be important to a consideration of technology in education. But it is appropriate to begin with a few comments concerning the things that are to be included under the heading of "educational technology," "instructional technology" or, as I would prefer, "technologies for learning."

I wish to include techniques that are not "instructional" in a narrow sense. For example, a great deal is learned from participation in certain simulation games, but the games do not instruct in the simple ways in which certain types of lectures or educational films do. In other words "learning" in "technologies for learning" is to be construed broadly.

Nor do I wish to include only activities that involve mechanical or electronic devices. For I do wish to include programmed instruction, even when it is not presented in a machine format. And I also believe that sensitivity training and other types of group learning experiences are parts of the new technologies for learning. Programmed instruction and sensitivity training organized our energy and activities in new ways on the basis of knowledge of how we learn and grow. They are therefore as much a part of our educational technology as any projector.

An Inventory of Technologies for Learning

A. Audiovisual Media

1. Audiotape

2. Overhead transparencies

3. Slides

4. Motion Pictures

5. Intermedia configurations

6. Multimedia configurations

Tape recordings (and long-playing records), slides, films and overhead projections are widely used in the presentation of lectures and lessons. When they are well prepared and skillfully used they unquestionably improve instruction by conveying an expanded range of substantive materials through their images and sound. Even if these devices did not bring new subjects and phenomena into the classroom, they would be important for the interest and excitement they add to a teacher's efforts.

In their simple uses these media tend to be viewed as teachers' aids. This view can be limiting if the teacher feels that the media materials can never stand alone, that they must always be thoroughly assimilated into his own lesson. Some films and tapes are remarkably effective instructional tools as they stand, and the good teacher need feel no reluctance or guilt about letting these materials speak for themselves. Another way of stating this is that some teachers feel that unless all the activities in their classroom bear their personal stamp, then their students are being cheated. On the contrary, a teacher may best serve his students in some cases by making a film or tape available to them, and then getting out of the way.

We will use the term "intermedia configurations" to describe combinations of the common audiovisual media when they are used to present tightly programmed units of instruction. A tape and slide presentation may be used, for example, to illustrate the use of a laboratory technique or to give an analysis of a textual passage. Intermedia configurations are often used to guide students through a set of activities, not only to present a body of information. These presentations can be independent and self-sufficient units of instruction, which may be used by individual students or groups without an instructor's presence. Major advantages of intermedia configurations are that such units may be prepared to very high levels of quality in terms of visual images, oral presentation, and instructional logic. In some cases subject matters may be presented which would be difficult or impossible to exhibit without the media. These presentations may also be made randomly accessible to students, thus allowing them at the student's leisure. This characteristic becomes especially important if large numbers of intermedia presentations are available, for they may then be used in various combinations and for diverse purposes.

When they are well prepared, intermedia configurations may rival or surpass the instruction of an excellent teacher. But common audio-visual media may be employed in other less conventional ways, to exploit some of their creative and aesthetic potential, and to deal with subject matters in ways which employ less familiar instructional logics. I use the term "multi-media configurations" to refer to uses of the media whose internal structure is closer to that of an artistic event or happening than to that of an instructor's lesson.

Multi-media configurations tend to use a great deal of equipment, and to immerse participants in a complex media-created environment. The multi-media presentation may have a fairly linear and discursive message. But it may also be more complex; it may be a media message, to refer to McLuhan's pun. The involvement of each member of the audience may be quite different and unique.

On occasion students have chosen to prepare such multi-media presentations as part of their work in a course or simply out of enthusiasm for the new form. The results have been very impressive from several points of view. The preparation of a presentation turns out to be a fine means by which a student can demonstrate what he has learned in a course or seminar. It is a most effective and engaging way to share one's learning. And the process of preparing a multi-media presentation is invariably an intense learning experience, for it involves asking basic questions about the subject matter as the available materials are altered, arranged and ordered. As in the case with most of our technology for learning, these media seem to become most productive when the student rather than the teacher gains control and acts as the designer of the materials.

B. Programmed Instruction

1. Book format

2. Teaching machine format

3. Computer-assisted instruction

The strengths and weaknesses of programmed instruction are by now well known. The engagement of the student's active response, the careful articulation of the logic of a subject matter, and the opportunity for the student to work alone and at his own rate all contribute to making programmed instruction an effective learning technology. Many people have found programmed instruction to be boring and tedious. It remains to be seen whether the state of the art advances to a point at which most programmed instruction will be more pleasant and interesting.

There is little doubt that computer-assisted programmed instruction will overcome some of these limitations. Computerized systems for programmed instruction are coming progressively closer to the ideal of handling a large number of student-constructed responses, thus freeing programmed instruction from the fairly rigid and uninspiring format of the multiple-choice question. Computerized systems can handle much more complex branching and, in general, a more sophisticated range of instructional strategies than other programmed instruction formats. The computer can also respond to each student in the light of its record of the student's earlier performance. At present the computer is a medium for the communication of programmed instruction. At some point in the future it will become a unique and complex technology for learning in its own right. It is hard to speculate on the characteristics of that learning technology, but we do know that it will be capable of presenting highly individualized instruction, it will handle large and complex bodies of information, and it will offer a wide variety of approaches to learning.

C. Closed Circuit Television and Videotape Recording

Private television has been used for some time now in schools and universities. Closed circuit television and videotape have offered universities a solution to large enrollments in courses. One mode of use is to record an instructor's lecture at the beginning of the day and then to replay it several times in many classrooms. Sometimes a library of lectures or lessons is accumulated, and the tapes made available to groups or individuals.

Some large university systems broadcast their instructional programs. In all of these patterns the instructor usually behaves exactly as he would in the classroom in the absence of television cameras. This behavior is a tragic waste of resources. Television introduces the possibility of employing a wide range of visual materials and production techniques. Our students have grown up accustomed to learning and acquiring a great deal of information from television, and this medium is used commercially with great skill and sophistication. Our failure to abandon standard classroom modes of presentation in favor of those that are better suited to television results in the loss of a significant amount of learning and student involvement. The first step in private television's creative use will probably be to remove the teacher from the screen and to make him a member of a production team which will include writers, announcers, artists and media professionals. Private television offers the capability of reaching a large student population, but this potential must be pursued simultaneously with the development of televisions characteristic strengths and styles of presentation; otherwise we will be reaching a great many students with instruction of an obviously inferior quality. An excellent classroom lecture may well be mediocre when presented unaltered on television.

Private television offers a set of educational opportunities even more unusual than those represented by its potential as a creative medium for teacher-to-student instruction. Videotape recording permits individuals or groups to observe themselves in a wide variety of situations. An important situation, for example, is the normal class or seminar discussion, in which the dynamics of the group may be observed and analyzed. Significant phenomena and patterns of behavior, even those that ordinarily pass unnoticed, become quite obvious. They may be understood and dealt with when they are negative, and built upon and strengthened when they are positive. Many people remember the shock and surprise of first hearing their voices on tape. Videotape can offer a person or a group far more useful (and surprising) information. Groups that have an explicit introspective orientation, i.e. groups that are partially or wholly committed to examining and learning from their own operations, can find that a videotape facility is an elegant and powerful resource. Videotape recording offers the individual teacher an important opportunity to criticize and improve his own classroom work. Videotape is, in general, an important tool in many situations, ranging from those in which self-understanding is the goal, to those in which learning a specific skill (e.g. public speaking, interviewing, selling) is sought. On some college campuses there are also movements to explore the aesthetic potential of video-recording; this holds enormous promise for the enrichment of a community's cultural life.

D. Games and Simulations

This is a rapidly developing and very exciting field. The full range of subject matters that supports game or simulation is not yet clear, but I would judge it to be quite large. Various sorts of social systems, from a business corporation in an economic environment to an international organization in time of war, have been simulated in game formats. But games are not limited to subjects in the social realm; the properties of certain biological systems have been taught by games, as have parts of algebra and symbolic logic.

It may be helpful to mention, as examples, two of the many games I have tried with college-age groups. On several occasions we have used the Inter-Nation Simulation (INS), which may be the most widely used and one of the most complex games available in the social sciences. Players in INS work on teams, each teach representing a nation. Rules and responsibilities within each team are divided up among players, with special rules dealing with economics, diplomacy, military affairs, etc. The game consists of time periods during which players must make economic, military, and diplomatic decisions, the results of which are calculated and returned to the teams according to a fairly complex mathematical model of international relations and economics. Students finish the game with a greater under-standing of the principles of international relations, especially as postulated in the INS model, as well as with a greater appreciation of the emotional and interpersonal dimen-sions of the subject. INS, like many other games, elicits a tremendous amount of en-thusiasm and excitement.

Another example is a RAND Corporation simulation that I used in a non-disciplinary seminar on the future. Participants played the roles of national policy-makers allocating units of resource among development projects for different types of technology. In making resource-allocation decisions students had to try to predict the social results of each set of technological developments. In another part of the simulation, groups representing different segments of the population evaluated, from their perspectives, the predicted social conse-quences of specific technologies. Discussions became quite intense, as assumptions con-cerning the future, values, and the nature of technology were challenged.

It is interesting to note that the field of educational games and simulations is a spin-off of war-game techniques used by the military, of computer simulation techniques used by engineers and physical scientists, and of simulation approaches to social systems used in social scientific research. One natural result is that some simulations are computer based, thus involving some very complicated and sophisticated models of the subject matter. This is one of the most promising frontiers in the use of computers in education.

Most observers are extremely impressed by the enthusiasm and commitment elicited by many educational games. Although we have little hard data on the effectiveness of these games, we have some reasonable speculations. Simulations probably help participants to appreciate the functional meaning of theories and principles as they operate in concrete situations. Many teachers are reluctant to use simulations or games until all of the princi-ples of the subject matter have been mastered discursively. Such caution is probably un-warranted, and may deprive students of the opportunity to arrive at general principles through induction from concrete circumstances. Another interesting aspect of games is that the resultant learning is often social in nature, i.e. students learn together as they collaborate as team members. Participants develop a real interest in the competence and understanding of their colleagues. A result is that students teach each other in a natural and enjoyable situation. I have often interrupted, after an hour, an educational game being played by people who were initially strangers. Invariably I can point out that they are communicating about and helping each other deal with the subject matter on a level of comfort and good feeling that would usually take months of regular classroom association to achieve.

Many simulation games like INS involve students with a theoretical model of the sub-ject matter. One of the most important stages in the use of games is the examination, after the game is over, of the characteristics and limitations of the model. Participants may approach this examination by observations of what the rules of the game did or did not let them do, how realistic these rules are, and how realistically the consequences of one's moves are determined by the game's structure.

Some individuals or groups are able to get into the activities of altering old games or constructing new ones. Such ventures amount to attempts to create functioning and "play-able" theoretical models of a subject matter. It is hard to over-estimate the extent to which this involves the search for basic insights into the subject matter.

On a theoretical level we have good reason to believe that the urge to play in young (and old) organisms is an extremely adaptive learning process. Play has a natural attrac-tion for all of us, and its roots are intimately bound up with our need to learn in order to survive. Developments that allow us to return to and tap this part of our nature in the formal process of education have tremendous potential.

"Granting that childhood is playhood, how do we adults generally react to this fact?

We ignore it, we forget all about it—because play to us is a waste of time. Hence we erect a large city school with many rooms and expensive apparatus for teaching; but more often than not, all we offer to the play instinct is a small concrete space."

A. S. Neill
Summerhill

E. Mass Media

1. Broadcasting

   a. Television

   b. Radio

2. Long-playing records

3. Magazines and newspapers

"Educational" broadcasting, whether sponsored by a university school system, or educational network, has generally suffered from the failure to use the television or radio medium with imagination. As discussed earlier, there has been a stifling allegiance to traditional educational formats like lectures and panel discussions. The educational broadcasting networks have begun to move beyond these limitations, however, and they are achieving some very notable successes.

Whereas some schools and universities make good use of the available educational broadcasting offerings, educators largely ignore commercial broadcasting. Many of the criticism of the broadcasting "wasteland" are valid. Nevertheless, there is an important portion of television and radio programs that would enrich and be useful to almost any educational setting. Network news and special affairs programs are often excellent, and many programs do have significant artistic content. Also one role of education is surely the examination and criticism of popular culture in order to assist the student to probe and become aware of the cultural forces acting upon him. From this perspective it would be important to bring a wide sample of broadcasting matter into the educational environment, including programs which one would judge to be of low quality.

The availability and cost of both videotape and audiotape recorders make it possible for an educational institution to use commercial materials repeatedly and according to a convenient schedule. It is unfortunate that schools and colleges do not have continuing policies and facilities for making a wide range of radio and television programs routinely available to their teachers and students. How realistic is an educational system that insulates itself almost totally from the most vital and effective communications media of society? Similar comments apply to the printed mass media and long-playing records.

F. Sensitivity Training

We will use "sensitivity training" as a shorthand term to refer to a range of new or experimental techniques designed to help people to understand themselves and to relate to each other better. This field is remarkable for its enthusiastic adherents and also for its vehement critics. This is not the place for a review of the evidence on either side or for an attempt to make sense of the controversies surrounding sensitivity training. Let it suffice to point to a congruence between the professed aims of American education and the goals of sensitivity training.

"All of the arts, poetry, music, ritual, the visible arts, the theatre, must singly and together create the most comprehensive art of all, a humanized society and its masterpiece, free man."

Bernard Berenson

Many of our educational institutions reject a narrow definition of their mission. They are, they claim, interested in more than the development of the human intellect. They are concerned with the "whole man," with the liberation of creativivy, the training of moral sensibilities, the ability of an individual to understand himself and to relate to others in aproductive and satisfying fashion. Sensitivity training is intended to be responsive to many of these matters. It therefore seems reasonable that those segments of the educational community professing interest in these broader constructions of the aims of education should consider sensitivity training techniques as a possibly useful technology for learning, as a set of activities and structures that might be fully integrated into the fabric of their institutions and programs.

G. Electronic Communications

Amplified telephone and its auxiliary devices for transmitting written or visual information are quite promising. They have helped schools and colleges to overcome their physical isolation and their remoteness from the learning resources of people and events.

We may expect that the advance of communications technology, especially as satellites come into use, will continue and strengthen the trend towards overcoming the geographical isolation of learners.

H. Xerography

The advent of inexpensive means for reproducing images on paper offers a range of new opportunities for teachers and students. In addition to the ease with which original or existing printed material may be distributed, image and print reproduction may be used as a creative medium to stimulate learning or to exhibit its results. In a sense we have overcome the high costs and technical expertise associated with the publication of materials, for small and moderate numbers of people.

I. Independent Study Materials

There have been many projects in recent years involving the extensive use of independent study. Such projects have used a number of the techniques described above, such as independently available audiovisual units and programmed instruction. There have also been special study guides and independent study syllabi developed. The educational community has accumulated a significant body of experience with independent study. The following types of questions have been asked: To what extent should the student be responsible for the initial definition of the independent study project? What are the most effective manners for an instructor to intervene and support a project, and how frequently should this be done? What are the best ways to help a student explore the available human and other resources for his study? What processes are successful in the evaluation of an independent study project? To what extent should the definition of an independent study be open to alteration during its execution?

Many of these questions may have valid answers. It must also be recognized, however, that attempts to systematize independent study activities can be destructive. Independent intellectual work is risky. Attempts to diminish the risks too greatly or to control independent activities too aggressively can emasculate the whole enterprise.

J. Speed Reading and Effective Study Training

There seem to have been breakthroughs made in recent years in both these fields. We would be doing many of our students a great service if we could integrate such instruction into many or most of our educational institutions without attaching to them the stigma associated with "remedial" work.

K. Photography

Still and motion picture photography have become the favored forms of artistic expression of a sizable segment of our young people. (This is an instance of the natural way in which they make technology a part of their lives.) As an artistic medium photography provides the educational opportunities associated with other forms of art, opportunities for the development of the creative and perceptual faculties. But photography also turns out to have a great promise as a technology for learning, even in situations in which aesthetic goals are subordinate to the goals of learning specific subject matters.

Projects in the photographic media dealing with a wide range of subject matters can yield enormously powerful learning experiences. Let us take an example from the social sciences—a group of students (on almost any level) studying phenomena of poverty. A photographic project, in which students attempted to capture the visible signs and effects of poverty, the images of the culture of poverty, could have tremendous educational rewards. One would expect such activities to sensitize the student to the sociological and economic significance of what he sees. And the photographic media would allow students to share their perceptions and thus to help each other to deal with the subject matter. The range of subjects in which such projects could be valuable is large, including many areas in the arts and humanities as well as the sciences.

Principles and Questions

We have made some general remarks about technology, and we have formulated a list of contemporary technologies for learning. The remaining question is obvious: How, when, and in what configurations, are these technologies to be used? There is no simple answer, and the quest for an answer leads us to a consideration of some of the most difficult problems of educational philosophy and practice. Consider, for example, the questions raised by the range of possible relations between the technologies and the teacher.

Technologies for learning are often discussed as the means by which teachers are to be relieved of their petty and burdensome tasks, thus to be freed to attend to those parts of education which are truly central. The assumption is that the relationship of teacher to student is unalterably the major locus of education. Technology therefore may attend to the peripheral tasks, allowing for more time and energy to be devoted to the heart of the educational system, the interaction between teacher and student. This view of technology and of the educational process is widely held. It has also been used, consciously or unconsciously, to try to assure teachers that neither their importance nor their roles are to be changed by technological innovations.

But it is important to consider the possibility that the role of the teacher will change in its basis. The culture of young people is increasingly separate from the adult culture, and young people may well be learning more of what they learn from each other and the mass media rather than from their parents and teachers. A major effect of rapid societal change is the production of experiences which are common to younger generations but which are quite dissimilar from the experiences of older generations. These discontinuities, along with the availability of new communications technologies for learning, suggest that we might reconsider the familiar notion of the teacher's role in education.

To argue on a general level that the teacher must remain "central" to education or that he will be "displaced" does not make much sense. Before the real issues can be joined it is necessary to articulate the full range of a teacher's activities. Teachers have many roles. They convey information and help students to learn a great variety of skills. They approve of some things and disapprove of others, thus affecting students' value systems and personalities. Teachers give advice and counsel, and they serve as adult models for many types of intellectual and emotional behavior. Teachers create social environments of various types within which their students live. This list can, no doubt, be extended.

Cultural change in general and technology in particular are bound to affect the conglomerate role of the teacher. New elements, e.g. the preparation of materials for further development by media experts, may be added. Old elements may be deleted, e.g. the detailed evaluation of a student's performance may pass largely from the teacher to a testing specialist. Surely emphasis will be redistributed among the various parts of a teacher's functions, e.g. training for skills and conveying information may be deemphasized while attention to the problems of human relations may become more important.

We can be fairly sure that the meaning of teaching will change and that the change will be intimately connected with the manner in which technologies for learning are deployed. We cannot know, at present, exactly what those changes will be. One thing that we can hope, however, is that the changes will be produced in a context in which a full range of alternatives has been explored.

We need to identify or create a large number of educational institutions that will use technologies and teachers in different ways. Some institutions might implement systems in which teachers act out a radical change in emphasis among parts of their role, with technologies assuming some functions which traditionally have been served by teachers. Other schools might attempt a "symbiotic" approach between teacher and technologies in as many different functions as possible. There is a very large range of possible alternative configurations of human and non-human resources in the construction of learning environments. We are in a period in which there are many resources that have not been fully tested and whose promise is not completely understood. In such a situation we must encourage the deployment of our capabilities in many configurations and patterns, so that our eventual choices will be informed ones.

There are factors to consider other than the teacher's role, as we experiment with new patterns of technology. For example, it would be an elementary mistake to confuse the process of learning about technology with the process of learning by means of technology. Nevertheless, the two processes are not entirely distinct. The child who learns arithmetic through interaction with a computer has learned more than arithmetic. He has learned, at least implicitly, something about the nature and potentials of computers. (And if the medium really is the message, he may have changed in more subtle ways.) The nature of our society requires that we help our students relate to technology in a positive and liberating way, perceiving both the threats and the promises of the technological parts of their environment. The technologies for learning may be among the major ones with which the student is involved. As we experiment with different patterns of technology, therefore, we must remember that we are serving these broader educational goals.

If students are to be offered an environment that is both technological and educational, that environment should probably be quite responsive to the student's initiatives, and initiatives should be easy and acceptable. Many of the technologies for learning are found to be most effective in helping students deal with subject matters when the student himself takes over and becomes the designer of materials and activities. Our usual pattern of using technology, however, is to begin with applications that assume a passive student. The technology is a medium of communication from an instructor. This is also the assumption of the people who manage the machines; the closer the student's hand is to the machine, the more uncomfortable the manager is. When this pattern is overcome we find that the specific goals of subject matter learning can be pursued more effectively, as well as the more general goal of helping students to understand and deal with technologies. (It should be noted that the force towards technological patterns which are accessible to student initiative may be opposed, in some circumstances, by the need for teachers to use the technologies in professional and highly polished ways. Compromises in equipment and costs may be especially difficult when both of these desiderata are kept in mind.)

Before we conclude, let us mention two perennial questions in educational philosophy. These issues must be dealt with in almost any meaningful discussion of education, and a consideration of technologies for learning is no exception. As we consider and experiment with different configurations of learning resources, we must take a position, firstly, on the extent to which education is to be directed by the learner. The second question is related: What are the appropriate contemporary curricular and subject matter categories? These two issues are related, for a position in favor of traditional or disciplinary categories will usually imply methods which are strongly teacher directed; teachers (but not students), after all, are trained in and for the most part committed to those categories. If, on the other hand, one allows for unconventional curricular categories, learner-directed processes may make more sense.

The technologies can be used to create an educational environment in which the student's behavior is carefully controlled. They can also create an environment of great choice and student self-direction. Similarly we can use technologies in the service of standard subject matters or in programs involving other curricular categories. Our commitments in these matters will, to some extent, influence the technologies we use and the ways we use them. Programmed instruction may be neutral with respect to both these issues, and can be used in many ways. Network television, on the other hand, is not neutral with respect to curricular categories; it is not likely to support the traditional subject matter divisions, but it would support new ones. Sensitivity training, if it is an important part of an educational system, would be likely to reinforce student direction of learning but not commitment to our normal subject matter divisions. It would be possible to try to characterize all of the available technologies for learning in the light of these and other basic questions of educational philosophy.

The task that faces the educational community is the articulation, by experimentation and use, of the nature and possible uses of the available technologies. This must involve the construction of a wide range of educational environments, the deployment of human and technological resources in many configurations. And these attempts must be viewed from the perspective of all of the most basic questions that we can ask about education.

As we experiment with uses of technology, we must resist a simplistic view of the venture. Technologies are more than means to ends. They change our goals, for they change our very natures as organisms. I believe that educators can not refrain from extensive technological innovation. In doing so, however, they must sensitize themselves to the fact that the changes will ramify in profound and unpredicted ways.

42.
Instructional Technology
And the Purposes of Education*

by EMMANUEL G. MESTHENE
Director, Program on Technology
and Society
Harvard University

The Setting: Technological Society

The power, prevalence, and prominence of modern science and technology are serving to push to the fore certain characteristics of society that then begin to be seen as somehow fundamental to and definitive of society, i.e., as setting its basic structure and character and as differentiating it from other societies, past and present, in which science and technology are less prominent.

There are a number of fundamental traits that are thus gaining prominence as a result of the resources and emphasis that advanced societies such as ours put on the development and application of science and technology.

One such trait is *possibility*. The first-order effect of technology is to expand the menu of options or choices available to society by literally creating new possibilities or by altering the cost-benefit ratios of existing possibilities. For example, rockets for the first time offer us the option of going to the moon, and industrial technology lessens the cost of feeding, clothing, and sheltering the nation's population. This "freeing" of possibility or expanding of society's menu prepares the ground—opens the door, as the historian Lynn White has put it—to social change because institutional reorganization is usually required to take advantage of the new opportunities that technology offers as well as to guard against new problems that it also creates.

Another trait of a society in which science and technology are prominent is *institutional flux*. Institutions that were once separate and distinct tend increasingly to get mixed up and resemble each other. Government, industry, and universities, for example, once operated quite independently of each other, but are now becoming more interdependent and indistinguishable, as government regulates business, as business increasingly sells its products to government, and as both depend more and more on universities for knowledge and trained manpower.

A third trait is the *value change* consequent on technology. The alteration of the material conditions of experience by new technology affects the process of valuation and therefore creates a strong tendency for value change in society, just as new items or changed prices on a familiar menu can alter the order of one's culinary preferences. I have discussed

This paper is adapted from a talk delivered at a conference on computer-assisted instruction held at the University of Texas (Austin) in October 1968.

these three kinds of change in more detail elsewhere and will not pursue them further today.*

The Social Importance of Knowledge

I do want to stress a fourth characteristic of a technological society, more directly relevant to the purposes of this paper. This is the importance that society attaches to the generation and uses of knowledge. The term "knowledge" as I employ it in this connection is a quite general term that encompasses a number of elements. It includes first of all, of course, the actual content or body of knowledge that exists at any given time, as well as the methodology of knowing, the process of scientific inquiry. That is, it denotes what we know—what the natural and social sciences discover—and how we know. The term also encompasses the institutional forms of knowledge: knowledge organizations, such as universities, research organizations, R and D and planning divisions or departments in government and industry as well as the less formal but not less significant institutional forms that go with the professionalization of knowledge, such as professional associations or even less formal groupings such as what we call the scientific community.

Further, I also include in the term "knowledge" the various techniques, many of them of recent origin, that we associate with the uses of knowledge, such as techniques of information handling, of communication, of technology transfer, of linear programming, of systems analysis, and so forth. Finally, the term encompasses also the attitudes of commitment that go with the generation and use of knowledge: the receptiveness to knowledge, the ability to suspend judgment and act on probabilities, the willingness to commit resources to education and research, the readiness to act according to rational criteria, the confidence that knowledge can change the world, and the expectations, sometimes overdone, that this confidence inspires. In all of these senses, ours has been justly referred to as a "knowledge society." We are the greatest data-generating society in history and our decision-making in every sphere is more dependent on the availability and analysis of information than ever before.

Thus broadly construed, knowledge of course encompasses technology also. At the same time, I see technology as a condition without which knowledge probably would have very little social importance. That is, I would argue for the proposition that technological innovation is the cause of the social importance that accrues to knowledge. The enhancement of the social role of knowledge is in fact one of the foremost ways in which technology affects society.

Now, knowledge can be a rather heady thing, especially for intellectuals, of course, and even more so for public officials or for industrial managers who want to exploit knowledge —and intellectuals—for political purposes or for profit. That is where the danger is. There is a long and venerable tradition in the west that the scientific investigator is free—indeed, is duty bound—to advance knowledge in every area and as fast as possible, and to pursue the truth wherever it may lead. It has been a concomitant of that tradition that the *uses* of knowledge are not the scientist's or scholar's concern and that the intellectual, not only has no responsibility for what the practical man or the politician does with knowledge, but that, on the contrary, the knowledge enterprise would suffer if such concerns were allowed to influence it.

I propose that the prominent role of knowledge in our society has reversed this classic situation. The enterprise of knowledge is now likely to suffer, as is society in general, if scientific research is pursued without reference to its wider social ramifications. This is a difficult lesson to learn, because all of us have been brought up in the traditional scientific ethos. It is even more difficult to assent to, because the concern with social conse-

*For further discussion of these points, see E. G. Mesthene, "How Technology Will Shape the Future," Science, Vol. 161 (July 12, 1968) 135-143.

quence can be so easily turned into a distortion of the scientific enterprise for invidious purposes. This is what explains the reaction of the early nuclear scientists: while it was clear after the bomb that science could not be pursued independently of its political impli- cations, the scientists felt *they* had to assume the principal political responsibility because they were pure of heart. However naive the conclusion, the premise recognized a real danger.

What was true of nuclear physics and nuclear technology continues true of science and technology generally and of educational technology as well, therefore, although the simi- larities are less clear in educational technology because the situation is much more com- plex. The broader social implications of technical progress are so immediate and have such wide ramifications, that policies based exclusively on technological promise can be highly misleading. This danger is enhanced by the tendency of technical people to think that social issues are no different in kind from technical problems and that they are amenable to solution by some form of "technological fix."

Technology as the Answer to Everything

The undeniable promise of modern technology has given rise to a world view that sup- ports this facile attitude. This view holds that technology is an unalloyed blessing for man and society. Technology is seen as the motor of all progress, as holding the solution to all our social problems, as helping to liberate the individual from the clutches of a complex and highly organized society, as the source of permanent prosperity; in short, as the promise of utopia in our time. This technological optimism has its modern origins in the social philosophies of such 19th-century thinkers as Saint-Simon, Karl Marx, and Auguste Comte. It tends to be held by many scientists and engineers, by military leaders and aerospace industrialists, by people who believe that man is fully in command of his tools and his destiny, by the devotees of systems analysis, by those whom young people refer to as members of the Establishment with a capital E, and in general and quite widely, by many contemporary high priests of educational technology.

In 1966, Professor Anthony Oettinger of Harvard University wrote an article about the promise of educational technology that sounded a good deal like the world view I just described. It was called "A Vision of Technology and Education."* The vision included most of what we hear these days about how educational technology can be the salvation of American education, although Oettinger added a concluding section to his article called "The Cold Water." The vision described a nationwide, perhaps worldwide electronic in- formation network in which was stored all of man's knowledge in all branches of science, thus making it accessible to people anywhere and everywhere. Suitable terminals and computer consoles were located in schools, offices, and homes. Individual students could be connected instantly with the world's major libraries. They had at their fingertips audio- visual recordings of instruction and lectures on specialized topics prepared by the country's best teachers, as well as teaching programs designed in the light of individual differences of age and capacity.

Would such a vision, if realized, advance or distort the purposes of education? What would be its implications for a teacher's qualifications, training, and attitudes? What would happen to the teacher-student relationship, to the present balance between teaching subject matter and guiding or counseling students, and to the differential abilities of children? Would the problem of general as against vocational education persist? Might the transi- tion from school to work be facilitated, as former students continued to have access to the same information system with which they interacted during their years of formal training? Would such a system meet the growing need for life-long education in a world

*Oettinger, A. G., "A Vision of Technology and Education," Communications of the ACM, *July 1966.*

of widespread change? What would it imply for traditional relationships between school and family, school and community, school and government? What might happen, for example, to the baby-sitting function of the school or to local control of educational policy?

The Harvard Study

The Harvard University Program on Technology and Society organized a research group under Professor Oettinger's direction to explore those questions and to test the assumptions and implications of the vision. The group included an educational psychologist, a representative of the education industry, and a district superintendent of a large urban public school system. The group decided to concentrate on secondary education. It also decided to attend principally to a future ten years hence on the ground that such a time period is neither so long as to preclude reasonable prediction and extrapolation, nor so short that its conditions are already present and its shape determined. A longer glance beyond ten years was not excluded, but it was judged a potentially valuable exercise only if it could be based more solidly than on speculative prophecy.

Oettinger and his colleagues structured their approach by distinguishing between probable and possible developments in the next ten years. What will the average secondary school *probably* look like a decade hence? This estimate was arrived at mainly by extrapolation of trends now visible in such respects as numbers of students and teachers, birth rates, years of formal schooling, and growth of both gross national product and educational budgets. The estimate excluded the possibilities of a world as it might be if a third world war intervened in the next decade or of a nation as it might be if our goals changed so radically as, for example, to shift the totality of the defense budget to educational purposes.

What could the average secondary school *possibly* look like a decade hence? In contrast to an assessment of probability, an estimate of possibility inevitably involves a measure of speculation and normative judgment. It must take account, moreover, both of technological and of social possibility. There are potentialities even in present technology that are unrealized or poorly realized by reason both of technical ignorance and economic or political infeasibility. There are foreseeable additional potentialities in imminent technological developments whose exact nature will depend on the decisions about technology that we will be making in the next very few years. What may these technical potentialities portend for education if coupled with a school budget three to five times the present one in constant dollars, with greatly expanded educational research and development activities, with more effective policies, and with revised organizations, procedures, and attitudes in both the political and professional parts of the educational establishment?

The group's work began with a close look at conditions currently prevailing in secondary education, excluding the extremes both of the small number of avant-garde experimental schools and of the probably equally small number of schools in what might be labeled a "hopeless" category. This exclusion of avant-garde experimental schools is important, because it shows that the objectives of the study were broader than the technical prospects of educational technology. Given both the current state of that technology and especially the current organization of the school system, the group concluded that the average high school a decade hence is unlikely to be very different from that of the present time, in respect either to effective utilization of educational technology or to successful preparation of youth for the demands of a technological society.

Technological devices already introduced into schools in recent years have had only peripheral impact, partly because educational technology is as yet much more primitive than is generally appreciated, so that fragile, unreliable, and expensive devices often gather dust in a classroom corner after an initial wave of enthusiasm has subsided. Knowledge about how to apply the technology is even more primitive, in a number of respects. Teachers are often afraid that expensive equipment will be damaged and try to master the problem by defining a code of behavior toward machines that is reminiscent of the world of *1984*. Even when the machines work and classroom attitudes are attuned to their use, attempts to graft the new techniques to old curriculums have proved spectacularly unsuccessful and largely unrelieved as yet by imaginative technical and curriculum innovation tailored to the new demands and possibilities of education. As Charles Silberman pointed out somewhere, most teachers handle classes of four in exactly the same way that they handle classes of forty, and then wonder how true it can be that lower teacher-student ratios make for better teaching.

A major claim for educational technology is that it serves the individual needs of students better than the one teacher/thirty students organization of the traditional classroom. Oettinger argues, however, that an instructional program geared to allowing each student to proceed at his own pace implies a dispersion rate, even of an initially highly homogeneous group of students, so high as to create problems of administration, scheduling, and guidance that only computer techniques as yet undevised and modes of school organization as yet only vaguely imaginable could be expected to cope with them. It is unlikely that the next ten years will see improvements on these fronts sufficient to advance significantly the ideal of individualized instruction.

The primitive state of educational hardware and software, however, emerged as the lesser obstacle to the rapid and effective introduction of technology into the schools. The biggest barrier is institutional. The school system of this country may well be among the most resistant to innovation of all American social institutions, and the most successful in persisting in that posture. At one extreme, it has all the bureaucratic rigidity of a military service or government agency, with practically none of the countervailing centralized authority that ultimately makes the military and the government move. At the other extreme, the school system is characterized by most of the fragmentation and frustrations of small-scale organization—such as that of small business, for example—without its correlative freedom of response, initiative, and flexibility. In Oettinger's words, "the educational establishment in the United States seems ideally designed to resist change."

Oettinger and his colleagues thus began with a tendency to share the belief—prevalent in the Office of Education and in the "ed biz," and not infrequently fed by enthusiastic researchers—that the salvation of American education by a combination of computers and systems analysis lies just around the corner. They have since come to a more sober view.

They have found that a number of contemporary processes and devices do have promise, but they are badly in need of a hospitable soil. Progress is possible toward limited objectives in the direction of individualization, but as yet only under carefully controlled conditions. Neither educational technology nor the school establishment seems ready to consummate the revolution in learning that will bring individualized instruction to every child, systematic planning and uniform standards across 25,000 separate school districts, an answer to bad teachers and unmovable bureaucracies, and implementation of a national policy to educate every American to his full potential for a useful and satisfying life. Bridging the gap between limited success in the laboratory and useful impact in practice hinges first on understanding, then on removing institutional barriers to this transition, as well as on solving problems of scale-up, reliability, and economics that have scarcely been faced as yet. Current attempts to integrate technology with the educational enterprise are dominated by faddish orthodoxy and the artificial dissemination of innovations of unproved and often dubious merit. There is a serious danger, therefore, that the continuing adoption of change in form will serve to block change in substance. In short, human fallibility and political reality are still here to keep utopia at bay, and neither promises to yield to a technological fix.

From these findings, Oettinger has concluded that technology can bring substantial improvement to education only after we have learned much more about how learning occurs, how educational institutions work and change, how informal education agents—

TV, peer groups, apprenticeship training—interact with and affect formal schooling, how, even, to make existing technical devices work. We need also to look to the people involved. Dr. Strangelove's are not necessarily the best educators of the future. Mechanical teaching aids are unlikely to help teachers who are ill-prepared even for the the the jobs they are now doing; there is no such thing as teacher-proof technology. Moreover, industrial designers attuned to different markets often make the mistake of thinking that selling educational devices to educators is not much different from selling refrigerators to housewives.

Finally, Oettinger found that funding policies and R & D strategies must change if we want significant technological change in education. We must find institutional ways to support good ideas longer and encourage more risk-taking than either private or governmental programs now allow, and we must be able to follow through in depth with a small number of promising alternatives in genuine competition with each other. Buckshot research in education has no more to recommend it than shotgun marriage.

You can see from all this that Oettinger did not concern himself principally, or importantly, with technical evaluation of educational technology or with a critique of the various experimental projects now going on in California, Illinois, Florida, Pittsburgh, or elsewhere. The question he addressed was, rather, What are the probable social impacts of this technology and of such projects if and when they get out of the laboratory stage? What promise do they hold for educational reform, what are the obstacles in the way, what unwitting harm may they bring both to education and to the further pursuit of educational technology? What he found, basically, is that the social, political, economic, and ideological context in which development of educational technology is being carried out, promoted, applied, and exploited gives much less cause for optimism than the promise of the technology itself.

Educational technologists by and large do not understand this and are probably convinced that they do not need to understand it. Most of the papers I have heard and articles I have read by those at the forefront of research in instructional technology reveal a dedicated and enthusiastic pursuit of knowledge and technical improvement for their own sakes reminiscent of Galileo's valiant fight against the medieval church. Some writers argue that dollars constitute the only bottleneck to progress in educational technology which reminds me of the bigger-higher-farther-faster-at-any-cost philosophy that was abandoned a decade ago by even the most unsophisticated military services. This is the twentieth century, however, not the sixteenth, and what is good for educational technology is not necessarily good for education.

Some Pitfalls to Watch Out For

If those simple cautions are not borne constantly in mind by those concerned with applying instructional technology to the educational process, a number of dangers will threaten. One is the danger of force-feeding. Many researchers tend to eschew what they cannot deal with rigorously—i.e., how people learn, how they think, in what directions they need to be developed—and they concentrate instead on making mathematical models of only those parts of the educational process that are susceptible to such treatment. This attitude can be mistaken for scientific humility. It is more likely to lead to forcing scientific technique beyond its limits, which is no longer science, but scientism.

Another danger is that of premature exploitation. Industrialists who will sell an experimental drug as a tested cure are not unknown. Nor are public officials, anxious to move a logy establishment, who will advertise scientific possibility as operational readiness and wind up doing more harm than good by believing their own propaganda. Nor—I regret to say—is the technical man unknown who may be tempted to oversell his product to such overanxious buyers, only to let himself in for an awful letdown when the product fails to live up to the impossible, cure-all claims made for it. Scientific dedication may be unchanged since Galileo, but the equally traditional scientific caution tends often these days to be thrown to the winds.

A third danger lies in the seductiveness of rigor. The implicit claim of many researchers in the field of educational technology is a modest one: we are only trying to do better and faster what is now being done less well and slowly. But much of what we are doing now in education may be wrong, and if technology helps us to do it very efficiently, it may lead us beyond the point where we can detect and correct our errors.

This leads me to a final danger, which is the unconscious reinforcement of the values of efficiency and achievement that can result from technical improvement of present educational processes. There is more to education than the promotion of efficiency or the imparting of occupational skills. Education also has the functions of socializing individuals, of shaping their values, of preparing for citizenship, of conserving traditions, and of imparting some sense of awe before the wonders of the universe. To apply technology to the improvement only of the instrumental function of education may thus become an obstacle to a society that is trying to redress the balance of the heyday of achievement and economic productivity in favor of a greater pluralism in our values and our culture. And if that happens, educational technologists could find that they have contributed to technical richness at the cost of moral poverty.

Obviously, I am not saying that every researcher at the technical frontier of instructional technology must crank in such social-cultural considerations into his every technical calculation. He cannot do that and will only mislead if he tries. I am saying that the value of their inventions should not be judged by internal criteria only and that we should not conclude that they are good just because they work. The power of truth—of technology, science, knowledge—is very great these days. Those who seek after it, therefore, and those who are responsible for harnessing it to the welfare of society, have a duty to seek after all of truth, not just that part of it that can be comprehended by the two-valued logic of the computer.

43.
The Nature
Of Living Systems

by JAMES G. MILLER
Vice Pres. for
Academic Affairs
Cleveland State Univ.
and
V.P. and Principal
Scientist
EDUCOM

An Exposition of the Basic Concepts in General Systems Theory

General systems theory is a set of related definitions, assumptions, and propositions which deal with reality as an integrated hierarchy of organizations of matter and energy. General systems behavior theory is concerned with a special subset of all systems, the living ones.

Even more basic to this presentation than the concept of "system" are the concepts of "space," "time," "matter," "energy," and "information," because the living systems discussed here exist in space and are made of matter and energy organized by information.

1. Space and Time

In the most general mathematical sense, a *space* is a set of elements which conform to certain postulates. The *conceptual spaces* of mathematics may have any number of dimensions.

Physical space is the extension surrounding a point. Classically the three dimensional geometry of Euclid was considered to describe accurately all regions in physical space. The modern general theory of relativity has shown that physical space-time is more accurately described by a geometry of four dimensions, three of space and one of time.

This presentation of a general theory of living systems will employ two sorts of spaces in which they may exist, *physical* or *geographical space* and *conceptual* or *abstracted spaces*.

1.1 Physical or Geographical Space This will be considered as Euclidean space, which is adequate for the study of all aspects of living systems as we now know them. Among the characteristics and constraints of physical space are the following: (a) From point A to point B is the same distance as from point B to point A. (b) Matter or energy moving on a straight or curved path from point A to point B must pass through every intervening point on the path. This is true also of markers bearing information. (c) In such space there is a maximum speed of movement for matter, energy, and markers bearing information. (d) Objects in such space exert gravitational pull on each other. (e) Solid objects moving in such space cannot pass through one another. (f) Solid objects moving in such space are subject to friction when they contact another object.

The characteristics and constraints of physical space affect the action of all concrete systems, living and nonliving. The following are some examples: (a) On the average, people interact more with persons who live near to them in a housing project than with persons who live far away in the project. (b) The diameter of the fuel supply lines laid down behind General Patton's advancing American Third Army in World War II determined the amount of friction the lines exerted upon the fuel pumped through them, and therefore the rate at which fuel could flow through them to supply Patton's tanks. This was one physical constraint which limited the rate at which the army could advance, because they had to halt when they ran out of fuel. (c) Today information can flow worldwide almost instantly by telegraph, radio, and television. In the seventeenth century it took weeks for messages to cross an ocean. A government could not send messages so quickly to its ambassadors then as it can now because of the constraints on the rate of movement of the marker bearing the information. Consequently ambassadors of that century had much more freedom of decision than they do now.

Physical space is a common space, for the reason that it is the only space in which all concrete systems, living and nonliving, exist (though some may exist in other spaces simultaneously). Physical space is shared by all scientific observers, and all scientific data must be collected in it. This is equally true for natural science and behavioral science. Most people learn that physical space exists, which is not true of many spaces I shall mention in the next section. They can give the location of objects in it.

1.2 Conceptual or Abstracted Spaces   Scientific observers often view living systems as existing in spaces which they conceptualize or abstract from the phenomena with which they deal. Examples of such spaces are: (a) Peck order in birds or other animals. (b) Social class space (lower lower, upper lower, lower middle, upper middle, lower upper, and upper upper classes). (c) Social distance among ethnic or racial groups. (d) Political distance among political parties of the right and the left. (e) Sociometric space, e.g., the rating on a scale of leadership ability of each member of a group by every other member. (f) A space of time costs of various modes of transportation, e.g., travel taking longer on foot than by air, longer upstream than down.

These conceptual and abstracted spaces do not have the same characteristics and are not subject to the same constraints as physical space. Each has characteristics and constraints of its own. These spaces may be either conceived of by a human being or learned about from others. Interpreting the meaning of such spaces, observing relations, and measuring distances in them ordinarily require human observers. Consequently the biases of individual human beings color these observations.

Social and some biological scientists find conceptual or abstracted spaces useful because they recognize that physical space is not a major determinant of certain processes in the living systems they study. E.g., no matter where they enter the body, most of the iodine atoms in the body accumulate in the thyroid gland. The most frequent interpersonal relations occur among persons of like interests or like attitudes rather than among geographical neighbors. Families frequently come together for holidays no matter how far apart their members are. Allies like England and Australia are often more distant from each other in physical space than they are from their enemies.

It is desirable that scientists who make observations and measurements in any space other than physical space should attempt to indicate precisely what are the transformations from their space to physical space. Other spaces are definitely useful to science, but physical space is the only common space in which all concrete systems exist.

1.3 Time   This is the fundamental "fourth dimension" of the physical space-time continuum. *Time* is the particular instant at which a structure exists or a process occurs, or the measured or measurable period over which a structure endures or a process continues. For the study of all aspects of living systems as we know them, for the measurement of durations, speeds, rates, and accelerations, the usual absolute scales of time—seconds, minutes, days, years—are adequate. A concrete system can move in any direction on the spatial dimensions, but only forward—never backward—on the temporal dimension.

2. Matter and Energy

Matter is anything which has mass (*m*) and occupies physical space. Energy (*E*) is defined in physics as the ability to do work. The principle of the conservation of energy states that energy can be neither created nor destroyed in the universe, but it may be converted from one form to another, including the energy equivalent of rest-mass. Matter may have (a) *kinetic* energy, when it is moving and exerts a force on other matter; (b) *potential* energy, because of its position in a gravitational field; or (c) *rest-mass* energy, which is the energy that would be released if mass were converted into energy. Mass and energy are equivalent. One can be converted into the other in accordance with the relation that rest-mass energy is equal to the mass times the square of the velocity of light. Because of the known relationship between matter and energy, throughout this chapter the joint term *matter-energy* is used except where one or the other is specifically intended. Living systems require matter-energy, needing specific types of it, in adequate amounts. Heat, light, water, minerals, vitamins, foods, fuels, and raw materials of various kinds, for instance, may be required. Energy for the processes of living systems is derived from the breakdown of molecules (and, in a few recent cases, of atoms as well). Any change of state of matter-energy or its movement over space, from one point to another, is *action*. It is one form of process.

3. Information

Throughout this presentation *information* (*H*) will be used in the technical sense first suggested by Hartley in 1928, and later developed by Shannon in his mathematical theory of communication. It is not the same thing as meaning or quite the same as information as we usually understand it. *Meaning* is the significance of information to a system which processes it: it constitutes a change in that system's processes elicited by the information, often resulting from associations made to it on previous experience with it. *Information* is a simpler concept: the degrees of freedom that exist in a given situation to choose among signals, symbols, messages, or patterns to be transmitted. The total of all these possible categories (the alphabet) is called the *ensemble*. The amount of information is measured by the binary digit, or *bit* of information. It is the amount of information which relieves the uncertainty when the outcome of a situation with two equally likely alternatives is known. Legend says the American Revolution was begun by a signal to Paul Revere from Old North Church steeple. It could have been either one or two lights "one if by land or two if by sea." If the alternatives were equally probable, the signal conveyed only one bit of information, resolving the uncertainty in a binary choice. But it carried a vast amount of meaning, meaning which must be measured by other sorts of units than bits.

The term *marker* refers to those observable bundles, units, or changes of matter-energy whose patterning bears or conveys the informational symbols from the ensemble or repertoire. These might be the stones of Hammurabi's day which bore cuneiform writing, parchments, writing paper, Indians' smoke signals, a door key with notches, punched cards, paper or magnetic tape, a computer's magnetized ferrite core memory, an arrangement of nucleotides in a DNA molecule, the molecular structure of a hormone, pulses on a telegraph wire, or waves emanating from a radio station. The marker may be static, as in a book or in a computer's memory. Communication of any sort, however, requires that the marker move in space, from the transmitting system to the receiving system, and this movement follows the same physical laws as the movement of any other sort of matter-energy. The advance of communication technology over the years has been in the direction of decreasing the matter-energy costs of storing and transmitting the markers which bear information. The efficiency of information processing can be increased by lessening the mass of the markers, making them smaller so they can be stored more compactly and transmitted more rapidly and cheaply. Over the centuries engineering progress has altered the mode in markers from stones bearing cuneiform to magnetic tape bearing electrons, and clearly some limit is being approached.

In recent years systems theorists have been fascinated by the new ways to study and measure information flows, but matter-energy flows are equally important. Systems theory deals both with information theory and with energetics—such matters as the muscular movements of people, the flow of raw materials through societies, or the utilization of energy by brain cells.

It was noted above that the movement of matter-energy over space, *action,* is one form of process. Another form of process is information processing or *communication,* which is the change of information from one state to another or its movement from one point to another over space. Communications, while being processed, are often shifted from one matter-energy state to another, from one sort of marker to another. If the form or pattern of the signal remains relatively constant during these changes, the information is not lost. For instance, it is now possible to take a chest X ray, storing the information on photographic film; then a photo-scanner can pass over the film line by line, from top to bottom, converting the signals to pulses in an electrical current which represent bits; then those bits can be stored in the core memory of a computer; then those bits can be processed by the computer so that contrasts in the picture pattern can be systematically increased; then the resultant altered patterns can be printed out on a cathode ray tube and photographed. The pattern of the chest structures, the information, modified for easier interpretation, has remained largely invariant throughout all this processing from one sort of marker to another. Similar transformations go on in living systems.

One basic reason why communication is of fundamental importance is that informational patterns can be processed over space and the local matter-energy at the receiving point can be organized to conform to, or comply with, this information. As already stated, if the information is conveyed on a relatively small, light, and compact marker, little energy is required for this process. Thus it is a much more efficient way to accomplish the result than to move the entire amount of matter-energy, organized as desired, from the location of the transmitter to that of the receiver. This is the secret of success of the delivery of "flowers by telegraph." It takes much less time and human effort to send a telegram from one city to another requesting a florist in the latter place to deliver flowers locally, than it would to drive or fly with the flowers from the former city to the latter.

Shannon was concerned with mathematical statements describing the transmission of information in the form of signals or messages from a sender to a receiver over a channel such as a telephone wire or a radio band. These channels always contain a certain amount of noise. In order to convey a message, signals in channels must be patterned and must stand out recognizably above the background noise.

Matter-energy and information always flow together. Information is always borne on a marker. Conversely there is no regular movement in a system unless there is a difference in potential between two points, which is negative entropy or information. Which aspect of the transmission is most important depends upon how it is handled by the receiver. If the receiver responds primarily to the material or energic aspect, it is a matter-energy transmission; if the response is primarily to the information, it is an information transmission. For example, the banana eaten by a monkey is a non-random arrangement of specific molecules, and thus has its informational aspect, but its use to the monkey is chiefly to increase the energy available to him. So it is an energy transmission. The energic character of the signal light that tells him to depress the lever which will give him a banana is less important than the fact that the light is part of a nonrandom, patterned organization which conveys information to him. So it is an information transmission. Moreover, just as living systems must have specific forms of matter-energy, so they must have specific patterns of information. For example, some species of animals do not develop normally unless they have appropriate information inputs in infancy. Harlow showed, for instance, that monkeys cannot make proper social adjustment unless they interact with other monkeys during a period between the third and sixth months of their lives.

4. System

The term *system* has a number of meanings. There are systems of numbers and of equations, systems of value and of thought, systems of law, solar systems, organic systems, management systems, command and control systems, electronic systems, even the Union Pacific Railroad system. The meanings of "system" are often confused. The most general, however, is: A *system* is a set of interacting units with relationships among them. The word "set" implies that the units have some common properties, which is essential if they are to interact or have relationships. The state of each unit is constrained by, conditioned by, or dependent on the state of other units.

4.1 Conceptual System
4.1.1 Units. Units of a *conceptual system* are terms, such as words (commonly nouns, pronouns, and their modifiers), numbers, or other symbols, including those in computer simulations and programs.

4.1.2 Relationships. A *relationship* of a conceptual system is a set of pairs of units, each pair being ordered in a similar way. E.g., the set of all pairs consisting of a number and its cube is the cubing relationship. Relationships are expressed by words (commonly verbs and their modifiers), or by logical or mathematical symbols, including those in computer simulations and programs, which represent operations, e.g., inclusion, exclusion, identity, implication, equivalence, addition, subtraction, multiplication, or division. The language, symbols, or computer programs are all concepts and always exist in one or more concrete systems, living or nonliving, like a scientist, a textbook, or a computer.

4.2 Concrete system   A *concrete system* is a nonrandom accumulation of matter-energy, in a region in physical space-time, which is organized into interacting interrelated subsystems or components.
4.2.1 Units. The units (subsystems, components, parts, or members) of these systems are also concrete systems.

4.2.2 Relationships. Relationships in concrete systems are of various sorts, including spatial, temporal, spatiotemporal, and causal.

Both units and relationships in concrete systems are empirically determinable by some operation carried out by an observer. In theoretical verbal statements about concrete systems, nouns, pronouns, and their modifiers typically refer to concrete systems, subsystems, or components; verbs and their modifiers usually refer to the relationships among them. There are numerous examples, however, in which this usage is reversed and nouns refer to patterns of relationships or processes, such as "nerve impulse," "reflex," "action," "vote," or "annexation."

4.2.3 Open system. Most concrete systems have boundaries which are at least partially permeable, permitting sizeable magnitudes of at least certain sorts of matter-energy or information transmissions to cross them. Such a system is an *open system.* Such inputs can repair system components that break down and replace energy that is used up.

4.2.4 Closed system. A concrete system with impermeable boundaries through which no matter-energy or information transmissions of any sort can occur is a *closed system.* No actual concrete system is completely closed, so concrete systems are either relatively open or relatively closed. Whatever matter-energy happens to be within the system is all there is going to be. The energy gradually is used up and the matter gradually becomes disorganized. A body in a hermetically sealed casket, for instance, slowly crumbles and its component molecules become intermingled. Separate layers of liquid or gas in a container move toward random distribution. Gravity may prevent entirely random arrangement.

4.2.5 Nonliving system. Every concrete system which does not have the characteristics of a living system is a *nonliving system.*

4.2.6 Living systems. The *living systems* are a special subset of the set of all possible concrete systems, composed of the plants and the animals. They all have the following characteristics:

a. They are open systems.

b. They use inputs of foods or fuels to restore their own energy and repair breakdowns in their own organized structure.

c. They have more than a certain minimum degree of complexity.

d. They contain genetic material composed of deoxyribonucleic acid (DNA), presumably descended from some primordial DNA common to all life, or have a charter, or both. One or both of these is the template—the original "blueprint" or "program"—of their structure and process from the moment of their origin.

e. They are largely composed of protoplasm including proteins and other characteristic organic compounds.

f. They have a decider, the essential critical subsystem which controls the entire system, causing its subsystems and components to interact.

g. They also have certain other specific critical subsystems or they have symbiotic or parasitic relationships with other living or nonliving systems which carry out the processes of any such subsystem they lack.

h. Their subsystems are integrated together to form actively self-regulating, developing, reproducing unitary systems, with purposes and goals.

i. They can exist only in a certain environment. Any change in their environment of such variables as temperature, air pressure, hydration, oxygen content of the atmosphere, or intensity of radiation, outside a relatively narrow range which occurs on the surface of the earth, produces stresses to which they cannot adjust. Under such stresses they cannot survive.

4.3 Abstracted System

4.3.1 Units. The units of *abstracted systems* are relationships abstracted or selected by an observer in the light of his interests, theoretical viewpoint, or philosophical bias. Some relationships may be empirically determinable by some operation carried out by the observer, but others are not, being only his concepts.

4.3.2 Relationships. The relationships mentioned above are observed to inhere and interact in concrete, usually living, systems. In a sense, then, these concrete systems are the relationships of abstracted systems. The verbal usages of theoretical statements concerning abstracted systems are often the reverse of those concerning concrete systems: the nouns and their modifiers typically refer to relationships and the verbs and their modifiers (including predicates) to the concrete systems in which these relationships inhere and interact. These concrete systems are empirically determinable by some operation carried out by the observer. A theoretical statement oriented to concrete systems typically would say "Lincoln was President," but one oriented to abstracted systems, concentrating on relationships or roles, would very likely be phrased "The Presidency was occupied by Lincoln."

An abstracted system differs from an *abstraction,* which is a concept (like those that make up conceptual systems) representing a class of phenomena all of which are considered to have some similar "class characteristic." The members of such a class are not thought to interact or be interrelated, as are the relationships in an abstracted system.

Abstracted systems are much more common in social science theory than in natural science.

Parsons has attempted to develop general behavior theory using abstracted systems. To some a social system is something concrete in space-time, observable and presumably measurable by techniques like those of natural science. To Parsons the system is abstracted from this, being the set of relationships which are the form of organization. To him the important units are classes of input-output relationships of subsystems rather than the subsystems themselves.

4.4 Abstracted vs. Concrete Systems   One fundamental distinction between abstracted and concrete systems is that the boundaries of abstracted systems may at times be conceptually established at regions which cut through the units and relationships in the physical space occupied by concrete systems, but the boundaries of these latter systems are always set at regions which include within them all the units and internal relationships of each system.

A science of abstracted systems certainly is possible and under some conditions may be useful. When Euclid was developing geometry, with its practical applications to the arrangement of Egyptian real estate, it is probable that the solid lines in his figures were originally conceived to represent the borders of land areas or objects. Sometimes, as in Figure 1, he would use dotted "construction lines" to help conceptualize a geometric proof. The dotted line did not correspond to any actual border in space, Triangle ABD would be shown to be congruent to Triangle CBD, and therefore the angle BAD was equal to the angle BCD. After the proof was completed, the dotted line might well be erased, since it did not correspond to anything real and was useful only for the proof. Such construction lines, representing relationships among real lines, were used in the creation of early forms of abstracted systems.

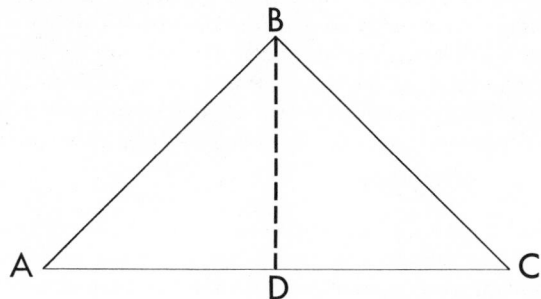

Figure 1.   A Euclidean Figure.

If the diverse fields of science are to be unified, it would help if all disciplines were oriented either to concrete or to abstracted systems. It is of paramount importance for scientists to distinguish clearly between them. To use both kinds of systems in theory leads to unnecessary problems. It would be best if one type of system or the other were generally used in all disciplines.

All three meanings of "system" are useful in science, but confusion results when they are not differentiated. A scientific endeavor may appropriately begin with a conceptual system and evaluate it by collecting data on a concrete or on an abstracted system, or it may equally well first collect the data and then determine what conceptual system it fits. Throughout this paper the single word "system," for brevity, will always mean "concrete system." The other sorts of systems will always be explicitly distinguished as either "conceptual system" or "abstracted system."

5. Structure

The *structure* of a system is the arrangement of its subsystems and components in three-dimensional space at a given moment of time. This always changes over time. It may remain relatively fixed for a long period or it may change from moment to moment, depending upon the characteristics of the process in the system. This process halted at any given moment, as when motion is frozen by a high-speed photograph, reveals the three-dimensional spatial arrangement of the system's components as of that instant.

6. Process

All change over time of matter-energy or information in a system is *process*. If the equation describing a process is the same no matter whether the temporal variable is positive or negative, it is a *reversible* process; otherwise it is *irreversible*. Process includes the on-going *function* of a system, reversible actions succeeding each other from moment to moment. Process also includes *history*, less readily reversed changes like mutations, birth, growth, development, aging, and death; changes which commonly follow trauma or disease; and the changes resulting from learning which are not later forgotten. Historical processes alter both the structure and the function of the system. The statement "less readily reversed" has been used instead of "irreversible" (although many such changes are in fact irreversible) because structural changes sometimes can be reversed; a component which has developed and functioned may atrophy and finally disappear with disuse; a functioning part may be chopped off a hydra and regrow. History, then, is more than the passage of time. It involves also accumulation in the system of residues or effects of past events (structural changes, memories, and learned habits). A living system carries its history with it in the form of altered structure, and consequently of altered function also. So there is a circular relation among the three primary aspects of systems—structure changes momentarily with functioning, but when such change is so great that it is essentially irreversible, a historical process has occurred, giving rise to a new structure.

7. Type

If a number of individual living systems are observed to have similar characteristics, they often are classed together as a *type*. Types are abstractions. Nature presents an apparently endless variety of living things which man, from his earliest days, has observed and classified—first, probably, on the basis of their threat to him, their susceptibility to capture, or their edibility, but eventually according to categories which are scientifically more useful. Classification by species is applied to organisms, plants or animals, or to free-living cells, because of their obvious relationships by reproduction. These systems are classified together by taxonomists on the basis of likeness of structure and process, genetic similarity and ability to interbreed, and local interaction, often including, in animals, ability to respond appropriately to each other's signs.

There are various types of systems at other levels of the hierarchy of living systems besides the cell and organism levels, each classed according to different structural and process taxonomic differentia. There are, for instance, primitive societies, agricultural societies, and industrial societies. There are epithelial cells, fibroblasts, red blood cells, and white blood cells, as well as free-living cells.

8. Level

The universe contains a hierarchy of systems, each higher *level* of system being composed of systems of lower levels. *Atoms* are composed of *particles; molecules,* of atoms; *crystals* and *organelles,* of molecules. About at the level of crystallizing *viruses,* like the tobacco mosaic virus, the subset of living systems begins. Viruses are necessarily parasitic on cells, so cells are the lowest level of living systems. *Cells* are composed of atoms, molecules, and multi-molecular organelles; *organs* are composed of cells aggregated into *tissues; organisms,* of organs; *groups* (e.g., herds, flocks, families, teams, tribes), of organisms; *organizations,* of groups (and sometimes single individual organisms); *societies,* of organizations, groups, and individuals; and *supranational systems,* of societies and organizations. Higher levels of systems may be of mixed composition, living and nonliving. They include *planets, solar systems, galaxies,* and so forth. It is beyond the scope of this paper to deal with the characteristics—whatever they may be—of systems below and above those levels which include the various forms of life, although others have done so. The subset of living systems includes cells, organs, organisms, groups, organizations, societies, and supranational systems.

It would be convenient for theorists if the hierarchical levels of living systems fitted neatly into each other like Chinese boxes. The facts are more complicated. No one can argue that there are exactly these seven levels, no more and no less. For example, one might conceivably separate tissue and organ into two separate levels. Or one might maintain that the organ is not a level, since no organ exists that can exist independent of other organs.

What are the criteria for distinguishing any one level from the others? They are derived from a long scientific tradition of empirical observation of the entire gamut of living systems. This extensive experience of the community of scientific observers has led to a consensus that there are certain fundamental forms of organization of living matter-energy. Indeed the classical division of subject-matter among the various disciplines of the life or behavioral sciences is implicitly or explicitly based upon this consensus.

It is important to follow one procedural rule in systems theory, in order to avoid confusion. Every discussion should begin with an identification of the level of reference, and the discourse should not change to another level without a specific statement that this is occurring. Systems at the indicated level are called systems. Those at the level above are *suprasystems,* and at the next higher level, *suprasuprasystems.* Below the level of reference are *subsystems,* and below them *subsubsystems.* For example, if one is studying a cell, its organelles are the subsystems, and the tissue or organ is its suprasystem, unless it is a free-living cell whose suprasystem includes other living systems with which it interacts.

8.1 Intersystem Generalization A fundamental procedure in science is to make generalizations from one system to another on the basis of some similarity between the systems, which the observer sees and which permits him to class them together. For example, since the nineteenth century, the field of "individual differences" has been expanded, following the tradition of scientists like Galton in anthropometry and Binet in psychometrics. In Figure 2, states of separate specific individual systems on a specific structural or process variable are represented by I_1 to I_n. For differences among such individuals to be observed and measured, of course, a variable common to the type, along which there are individual variations, must be recognized (T_1). Physiology depends heavily, for instance, upon the fact that individuals of the type (or species) of living organisms called cats are fundamentally alike, even though minor variations from one individual to the next are well recognized.

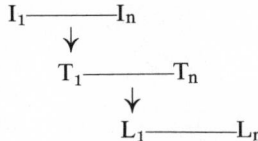

Figure 2.   Individual, Type, Level.

Scientists may also generalize from one type to another (T_1 to T_n). An example is cross-species generalization, which has been commonly accepted only since Darwin. It is the justification for the labors of the white rat in the cause of man's understanding of himself. Rats and cats, cats and chimpanzees, chimpanzees and human beings are similar in structure, as comparative anatomists know, and in function, as comparative physiologists and psychologists demonstrate.

The amount of variance among species is greater than among individuals within a species. If the learning behavior of cat Felix is compared with that of mouse Mickey, we would expect not only the sort of individual differences which are found between Mickey and Minnie Mouse, but also greater species differences. Cross-species generalizations are common, and many have good scientific acceptability, but in making them interindividual and interspecies differences must be kept in mind. The learning rate of men is not identical to that of white rats, and no man learns at exactly the same rate as any others.

The third type of scientific generalization indicated in Figure 2 is from one level to another. The basis for such generalization is the assumption that each of the levels of life, from cell to society, is composed of systems of the previous lower level. These cross-level generalizations will, ordinarily, have greater variance than the other sorts of generalizations, since they include variance among types and among individuals. But they can be made, and they can have great conceptual significance.

That there are important uniformities, which can be generalized about, across all levels of living systems is not surprising. All are composed of comparable carbon-hydrogen-nitrogen constituents, most importantly a score of amino acids organized into similar proteins, which are produced in nature only in living systems. All are equipped to live in a water-oxygen world rather than, for example, on the methane and ammonia planets so dear to science fiction. Also they are all adapted only to environments in which the physical variables, like temperature, hydration, pressure, and radiation, remain within relatively narrow ranges. Moreover, they all presumably have arisen from the same primordial genes or template, diversified by evolutionary change. Perhaps the most convincing argument for the plausibility of cross-level generalization derives from analysis of this evolutionary development of living systems. Although increasingly complex types of living systems have evolved at a given level, followed by higher levels with even greater complexity, certain basic necessities did not change. All these systems, if they were to survive in their environment, had, by some means or other, to carry out the same vital subsystem processes. While free-living cells, like protozoans, carry these out with relative simplicity, the corresponding processes are more complex in multicellular organisms like mammals, and even more complex at higher levels. The same processes are *"shredded out"* to multiple components in a more complex system, by the sort of *division of labor* which Parkinson has made famous as a law. This results in formal identities across levels of systems, more complex subsystems at higher levels carrying out the same fundamental processes as simpler subsystems at lower levels.

A formal identity among concrete systems is demonstrated by a procedure composed of three logically independent steps: (a) recognizing an aspect of two or more systems which has comparable status in those systems; (b) hypothesizing a quantitative identity between them; and (c) demonstrating that identity within a certain range of error by collecting data on a similar aspect of each of the two or more systems being compared. It may be possible to formulate some useful generalizations which apply to all living systems at all levels. A comparison of systems is complete only when statements of their formal identities are associated with specific statements of their interlevel, intertype, and interindividual disidentities. The confirmation of formal identities and disidentities is done by research.

What makes interindividual, intertype, or interlevel formal identities among systems important and of absorbing interest, is that—if they can be conclusively demonstrated— very different structures, which carry out similar processes, may well turn out to carry out acts so much alike that they can be quite precisely described by the same formal model. Conversely, it may perhaps be shown as a general principle that subsystems with comparable structures but quite different processes may have quantitative similarities as well.

8.2 Emergents   The more complex systems at higher levels manifest characteristics, more than the sum of the characteristics of the units, not observed at lower levels. These characteristics have been called "emergents." Significant aspects of living systems at higher levels will be neglected if they are described only in terms and dimensions used for their lower-level subsystems and components.

A clear-cut illustration of emergents can be found in a comparison of three electronic systems. One of these—wire connecting the poles of a battery—can only conduct electricity, which heats the wire. Add several tubes, condensers, resistors, and controls, and the new system can become a radio, capable of receiving sound messages. Add dozens of other components, including a picture tube and several more controls, and the system becomes a television set which can receive sound and a picture. And this is not just more of the same. The third system has emergent capabilities the first system did not have, emergent from its special design of much greater complexity. But there is nothing mystical about the colored merry-go-round and racing children on the TV screen—it is the output of a system which can be completely explained by a complicated set of differential equations such as electrical engineers write, including terms representing the characteristics of each of the set's components.

9. Echelon

This concept may seem superficially similar to the concept of level, but is distinctly different. Many complex living systems, at various levels, are organized into two or more *echelons* (in the military sense of a step in the "chain of command," not in the other military sense of arrangement of troops in rows in physical space). In living systems with echelons the components of the decider, the decision-making subsystem, are hierarchically arranged so that usually certain types of decisions are made by one component of that subsystem and others by another. Each is an *echelon.* All echelons are within the boundary of the decider subsystem. Ordinarily each echelon is made up of components of the same level as those which make up every other echelon in that system. Characteristically the decider component at one echelon gets information from a source or sources which process information primarily or exclusively to and from that echelon. It may be that at some levels of living systems—e.g., cells—there are no cases in which the decider is organized in echelon structure.

After a decision is made at one echelon on the basis of the information received, it is transmitted, often through a single subcomponent which may or may not be the same as the decider, but possibly through more than one subcomponent, upward to the next higher echelon, which goes through a similar process, and so on to the top echelon. Here a final decision is made and then command information is transmitted downward to lower echelons. Characteristically information is abstracted or made more general as it proceeds upward from echelon to echelon and it is made more specific or detailed as it proceeds downward. If a given component does not decide but only passes on information, it is not functioning as an echelon. In some cases of decentralized decision-making, certain types of decisions are made at lower echelons and not transmitted to higher echelons in any form, while information relevant to other types of decisions is transmitted upward. If there are multiple parallel deciders, without a hierarchy that has subordinate and superordinate deciders, there is not one system but multiple ones.

10. Suprasystem

10.1 Suprasystem and Environment The *suprasystem* of any living system is the next higher system in which it is a component or subsystem. For example, the suprasystem of a cell or tissue is the organ it is in; the suprasystem of an organism is the group it is in at the time. Presumably every system has a suprasystem except the "universe." The suprasystem is differentiated from the *environment*. The immediate environment is the suprasystem minus the system itself. The entire environment includes this plus the suprasuprasystem and the systems at all higher levels which contain it. In order to survive, the system must interact with and adjust to its environment, the other parts of the suprasystem. These processes alter both the system and its environment. Living systems adapt to their environment, and in return mold it. The result is that, after some period of interaction, each in some sense becomes a mirror of the other.

10.2 Territory The region of physical space occupied by a living system, and frequently protected by it from an invader, is its territory. Examples are a bowerbird's stage, a dog's yard, a family's property, a nation's land.

11. Subsystem and Component

In every system it is possible to identify one sort of unit, each of which carries out a distinct and separate process, and another sort of unit, each of which is a discrete, separate structure. The totality of all the structures in a system which carry out a particular process is a *subsystem*. A subsystem, thus, is identified by the process it carries out. It exists in one or more identifiable structural units of the system. These specific, local, distinguishable structural units are called *components* or *members* or *parts*. Reference has been made to these components in the definition of a concrete system as "a nonrandom accumulation of matter-energy, in a region in physical space-time, which is organized into interacting, interrelated subsystems or components." There is no one-to-one relationship between process and structure. One or more processes may be carried out by two or more components. Every system is a component, but not necessarily a subsystem of its suprasystem. Every component that has its own decider is a system at the next lower level, but many subsystems are not systems at the next lower level, being dispersed to several components.

The concept of subsystem process is related to the concept of *role* used in social science. Organization theory usually emphasizes the functional requirements of the system which the subsystem fulfills, rather than the specific characteristics of the component or components that make up the subsystem. The typical view is that an organization specifies clearly defined roles (or subsystem processes) and human beings "fill them." But it is a mistake not to recognize that characteristics of the component—in this case the person carrying out the role—also influence what occurs. A role is more than simple "social position," a position in some social space which is "occupied." It involves interaction, adjustments between the component and the system. It is a multiple concept, referring to the demands upon the component by the system, to the internal adjustment processes of the component, and to how the component functions in meeting the system's requirements. The adjustments it makes are frequently compromises between the requirements of the component and the requirements of the system.

The way living systems develop does not always result in a neat distribution of exactly one subsystem to each component. The natural arrangement would appear to be for a system to depend on one structure for one process. But there is not always such a one-to-one relationship. Sometimes the boundaries of a subsystem and a component exactly overlap, are congruent. Sometimes they are not congruent. There can be (a) a single subsystem in a single component; (b) multiple subsystems in a single component; (c) a single subsystem in multiple components; or (d) multiple subsystems in multiple components.

Systems differ markedly from level to level, type to type, and perhaps somewhat even from individual to individual, in their *patterns of allocation* of various subsystem processes to different structures. Such process may be (a) localized in a single component; (b) combined with others in a single component; (c) dispersed laterally to other components in the system; (d) dispersed upward to the suprasystem or above; (e) dispersed downward to subsubsystems or below; or (f) dispersed to other systems external to the hierarchy it is in. Which allocation pattern is employed is a fundamental aspect of any given system. For a specific subsystem function in a specific system one strategy results in more efficient process than another. One can be better than another in maximizing effectiveness and minimizing costs. Valuable studies can be made at each level on optimal patterns of allocation of processes to structures. In all probability there are general systems principles which are relevant to such matters. Possible examples are: *(a)* Structures which minimize the distance over which matter-energy must be transported or information transmitted are the most efficient. *(b)* If multiple components carry out a process, the process is more difficult to control and less efficient than if a single component does it. *(c)* If one or more components which carry out a process are outside the system, the process is more difficult to integrate than if they are all in the system. *(d)* Or if there are duplicate components capable of performing the same process, the system is less vulnerable to stress and therefore is more likely to survive longer, because if one component is inactivated, the other can carry out the process alone.

11.1 Critical Subsystem Certain processes are necessary for life and must be carried out by all living systems that survive or be performed from them by some other system. They are carried out by the following *critical subsystems* listed in Table 1.

Table 1. *The Critical Subsystems*

MATTER-ENERGY PROCESSING SUBSYSTEMS	SUBSYSTEMS WHICH PROCESS BOTH MATTER-ENERGY AND INFORMATION	INFORMATION PROCESSING SUBSYSTEMS
	Reproducer	
	Boundary	
Ingestor		Input Transducer
		Internal Transducer
Distributor		Channel and Net
Converter		Decoder
Producer		Associator
Matter-Energy Storage		Memory
		Decider
		Encoder
Extruder	}	Output Transducer
Motor		
Supporter		

The definitions of the critical subsystems are as follows:

11.1.1 Subsystems which process both matter-energy and information.

Reproducer, the subsystem which is capable of giving rise to other systems similar to the one it is in.

Boundary, the subsystem at the perimeter of a system that holds together the components which make up the system, protects them from environmental stresses, and excludes or permits entry to various sorts of matter-energy and information.

11.1.2 Matter-energy processing subsystems.

Ingestor, the subsystem which brings matter-energy across the system boundary from the environment.

Distributor, the subsystem which carries inputs from outside the system or outputs from its subsystems around the system to each component.

Converter, the subsystem which changes certain inputs to the system into forms more useful for the special processes of that particular system.

Producer, the subsystem which forms stable associations that endure for significant periods among matter-energy inputs to the system or outputs from its converter, the materials synthesized being for growth, damage repair, or replacement of components of the system, or for providing energy for moving or constituting the system's outputs of products or information markers to its suprasystem.

Matter-energy storage, the subsystem which retains in the system, for different periods of time, deposits of various sorts of matter-energy.

Extruder, the subsystem which transmits matter-energy out of the system in the forms of products and wastes.

Motor, the subsystem which moves the system or parts of it in relation to part or all of its environment or moves components of its environment in relation to each other.

Supporter, the subsystem which maintains the proper spatial relationships among components of the system, so that they can interact without weighing each other down or crowding each other.

11.1.3 Information processing subsystems.

Input transducer, the sensory subsystem which brings markers bearing information into the system, changing them to other matter-energy forms suitable for transmission within it.

Internal transducer, the sensory subsystem which receives, from all subsystems or components within the system, markers bearing information about significant alterations in those subsystems or components, changing them to other matter-energy forms of a sort which can be transmitted within it.

Channel and net, the subsystem composed of a single route in physical space, or multiple interconnected routes, by which markers bearing information are transmitted to all parts of the system.

Decoder, the subsystem which alters the code of information input to it through the input transducer or the internal transducer into a "private" code that can be used internally by the system.

Associator, the subsystem which carries out the first stage of the learning process, forming enduring associations among items of information in the system.

Memory, the subsystem which carries out the second stage of the learning process, storing various sorts of information in the system for different periods of time.

Decider, the executive subsystem which receives information inputs from all other subsystems and transmits to them information outputs that control the entire system.

Encoder, the subsystem which alters the code of information inputs to it from other information processing subsystems, from a "private" code used internally by the system into a "public" code which can be interpreted by other systems in its environment.

Output transducer, the subsystem which puts out markers bearing information from the system, changing markers within the system into other matter-energy forms which can be transmitted over channels in the system's environment.

Of these critical subsystems only the decider is essential, in the sense that a system cannot be dependent on another system for its deciding. A living system does not exist if the decider is dispersed upwardly, downwardly, or outwardly.

Since all living systems are genetically related, have similar constituents, live in closely comparable environments, and process matter-energy and information, it is not surprising that they should have comparable subsystems and relationships among them. All systems do not have all possible kinds of subsystems. They differ individually, among types, and across levels, as to which subsystems they have and the structures of those subsystems. But all living systems either have a complement of the critical subsystems carrying out the functions essential to life or are intimately associated with and effectively interacting with systems which carry out the missing life functions for them.

11.2 Inclusion Sometimes a part of the environment is surrounded by a system and totally included within its boundary. Any such thing not a part of the system's own living structure is an *inclusion.* Any living system at any level may include living or nonliving components. The amoeba, for example, ingests both inorganic and organic matter and may retain particles of iron or dye in its cytoplasm for many hours. A surgeon may replace an arteriosclerotic aorta with a plastic one and that patient may live comfortably with it for years. To the two-member group of one dog and one cat an important plant component is often added—one tree. An airline firm may have as an integral component a computerized mechanical system for making reservations which extends into all its offices. A nation includes many sorts of vegetables, minerals, buildings, and machines, as well as its land.

The inclusion is a component or subsystem of the system if it carries out or helps in carrying out a critical process of the system; otherwise it is part of the environment. Either way the system, to survive, must adjust to its characteristics. If it is harmless or inert it can often be left undisturbed. But if it is potentially harmful—like a pathogenic bacterium in a dog or a Greek in the giant gift horse within the gates of Troy—it must be rendered harmless or walled off or extruded from the system or killed. Because it moves with the system in a way the rest of the environment does not, it constitutes a special problem. Being inside the system it may be a more serious or more immediate stress than it would be outside the system's protective boundary. But also, the system that surrounds it can control its physical actions and all routes of access to it. For this reason international law has developed the concept of extraterritoriality to provide freedom of action to ambassadors and embassies, nations' inclusions within foreign countries.

11.3 Artifact An *artifact* is an inclusion in some system, made by animals or man. Spider webs, bird nests, beaver dams, houses, books, machines, music, paintings, and language are artifacts. They may or may not be *prostheses,* inventions which carry out some critical process essential to a living system. An artificial pacemaker for a human heart is an example of an artifact which can replace a pathological process with a healthy one. Insulin and thyroxine are replacement drugs which are human artifacts. Chemical, mechanical, or electronic artifacts have been constructed which carry out some functions of all levels of living systems.

Living systems create and live among their artifacts. Beginning presumably with the hut and the arrowhead, the pot and the vase, the plow and the wheel, mankind has constructed tools and devised machines. The Industrial Revolution of the nineteenth century, capped by the recent harnessing of atomic energy, represents the extension of man's matter-energy processing ability, his muscles. A new Industrial Revolution, of even greater potential, is just beginning in the twentieth century, with the development of information and logic-processing machines, adjuncts to man's brain. These artifacts are increasingly becoming prostheses, relied on to carry out critical subsystem processes. A chimpanzee may extend his reach with a stick; a man may extend his cognitive skills with a computer.

Today's prostheses include input transducers which sense the type of blood cells that pass before them and identify missiles that approach a nation's shores; photographic, mechanical, and electronic memories which can store masses of information over time; computers which can solve problems, carry out logical and mathematical calculations, make decisions, and control other machines; electric typewriters, high speed printers, cathode ray tubes, and photographic equipment which can output information. An analysis of many modern systems must take into account the novel problems which arise at man-machine interfaces.

Music is a special sort of human artifact, an information-processing artifact. So are the other arts and cognitive systems which people share. So in language. Whether it be a natural language or the machine language of some computer system, it is essential to information processing. Often stored only in human brains and expressed only by human lips, it can also be recorded on nonliving artifacts like stones, books, and magnetic tapes. It is not of itself a concrete system. It changes only when man changes it. As long as it is used it is in flux, because it must remain compatible with the ever-changing living systems that use it. But the change emanates from the users, and without their impact the language is inert. The artifactual language used in any information transmission in a system determines many essential aspects of that system's structure and process.

12. Transmissions in Concrete Systems

All process involves some sort of transmission among subsystems within a system, or among systems. There are *inputs* across the boundary into a system, *internal processes* within it, and *outputs* from it. Each of these sorts of transmissions may consist of either (a) some particular form of matter; (b) energy, in the form of light, radiant energy, heat, or chemical energy; or (c) some particular pattern of information.

13. Steady State

When opposing variables in a system are in balance, that system is in equilibrium with regard to them. The equilibrium may be static and unchanging or it may be maintained in the midst of dynamic change. Since living systems are open systems, with continually altering fluxes of matter-energy and information, many of their equilibria are dynamic and are often referred to as *flux equilibria* or *steady states.* These may be *unstable,* in which a slight disturbance elicits progressive change from the equilibrium state—like a ball standing on an inverted bowl; or *stable,* in which a slight disturbance is counteracted so as to restore the previous state—like a ball in a cup; or *neutral,* in which a slight disturbance makes a change, but without cumulative effects of any sort—like a ball on a flat surface with friction.

All living systems tend to maintain steady states (or homeostasis) of many variables, keeping an orderly balance among subsystems which process matter-energy or information. Not only are subsystems usually kept in equilibrium, but systems also ordinarily maintain steady states with their environments and suprasystems, which have outputs to the systems and inputs from them. This prevents variations in the environment from destroying systems. The variables of living systems are constantly fluctuating, however. A moderate change in one variable may produce greater or lesser alterations in other related ones. These alterations may or may not be reversible.

13.1 Stress, Strain, and Threat There is a *range of stability* for each of numerous variables in all living systems. It is that range within which the rate of correction of deviations is minimal or zero, and beyond which correction occurs. An input or output of either matter-energy or information, which by lack or excess of some characteristic, forces the variables beyond the range of stability, constitutes *stress* and produces a *strain* (or strains) within the system. Input lack and output excess both produce the same strain—diminished amounts in the system. Input excess and output lack both produce the opposite strain—increased amounts. Strains may or may not be capable of being reduced, depending upon their intensity and the resources of the system. The totality of the strains within a system resulting from its template program and from variations in the inputs from its environment can be referred to as its *values*. The relative urgency of reducing each of these specific strains represents its *hierarchy of values*.

Stress may be anticipated. Information that a stress is imminent constitutes a *threat* to the system. A threat can create a strain. Recognition of the meaning of the information of such a threat must be based on previously stored (usually learned) information about such situations. A pattern or input information is a threat when—like the odor of the hunter on the wind; a change in the acidity of fluids around a cell; a whirling cloud approaching the city—it is capable of eliciting processes which can counteract the stress it presages. Processes —actions or communications—occur in systems only when a stress or a threat has created a strain which pushes a variable beyond its range of stability. A system is a constantly changing cameo and its environment is a similarly changing bas-relief, and the two at all times fit each other. That is, outside stresses or threats are mirrored by inside strains. Matter-energy storage and memory also mirror the past environment, but with certain alterations.

13.1.1 Matter-energy stress. There are various ways for systems to be stressed. One class of stresses is the *matter-energy stresses,* including: (a) matter-energy input lack or underload—starvation or inadequate fuel input; (b) input of an excess or overload of matter-energy; and (c) restraint of the system, binding it physically. [This may be the equivalent of (a) or (b).]

13.1.2 Information stress. Also there are *information stresses,* including: (a) information input lack or underload, resulting from a dearth of information in the environment or from improper function of the external sense organs or input transducers; (b) injection of noise into the system, which has an effect of information cut-off, much like the previous stress; (c) information input excess or overload. Informational stresses may involve changes in the rate of information input or in its meaning.

13.2 Adjustment Processes   Those processes of subsystems which maintain steady states in systems, keeping variables within their ranges of stability despite stresses, are *adjustment processes.* In some systems a single variable may be influenced by multiple adjustment processes. As Ashby has pointed out, a living system's adjustment processes are so coupled that the system is ultrastable. This characteristic can be illustrated by the example of an army cot. It is made of wires, each of which would break under a 300-pound weight, yet it can easily support a sleeper of that weight. The weight is applied to certain wires, and as it becomes greater, first nearby links and then those farther and farther away, take up part of the load. Thus a heavy weight which would break any of the component wires alone can be sustained. In a living system, if one component cannot handle a stress, more and more others are recruited to help. Eventually the entire capacity of the system may be involved in coping with the situation.

13.2.1 Feedback. The term *feedback* means that there exist two channels, carrying information, such that Channel B loops back from the output to the input of Channel A and transmits some portion of the signals emitted by Channel A (see Figure 3.) These are telltales or monitors of the outputs of Channel A. The transmitter on Channel A is a device with two inputs, formally represented by a function with two independent variables, one the signal to be transmitted on Channel A and the other a previously transmitted signal fed back on Channel B. The new signal transmitted on Channel A is selected to decrease the strain resulting from any error or deviation in the feedback signal from a criterion or comparison reference signal indicating the state of the output of Channel A which the system seeks to maintain steady. This provides control of the output of Channel A on the basis of actual rather than expected performance.

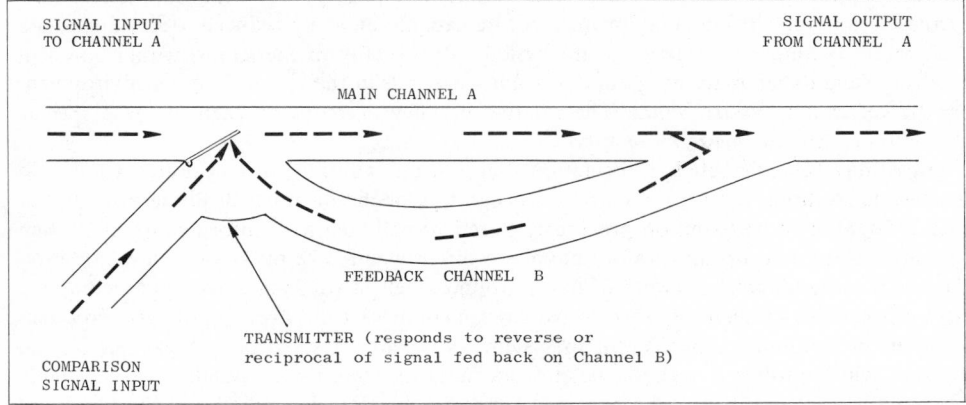

Figure 3.   Negative Feedback

When the signals are fed back over the feedback channel in such a manner that they increase the deviation of the output from a steady state, *positive feedback* exists. When the signals are reversed, so that they decrease the deviation of the output from a steady state, it is *negative feedback*. Positive feedback alters variables and destroys their steady states. Thus it can initiate system changes. Unless limited, it can alter variables enough to destroy systems. At every level of living systems numerous variables are kept in a steady state, within a range of stability, by negative feedback controls. When these fail, the structure and process of the system alter markedly—perhaps to the extent that the system does not survive. Feedback control always exhibits some oscillation and always has some lag. When the organism maintains its balance in space, this lag is caused by the slowness of transmissions in the nervous system, but is only of the order of hundredths of seconds. A social institution, like a corporation, may take hours to correct a breakdown in an assembly line, days or weeks to correct a bad management decision. In a society the lag can sometimes be so great that, in effect, it comes too late. General staffs often plan for the last war rather than the next. Governments receive rather slow official feedbacks from the society at periodic elections. They can, however, get faster feedbacks from the press, other mass media, picketers, or demonstrators. Public opinion surveys can accelerate the social feedback process. The speed and accuracy of feedback have much to do with the effectiveness of the adjustment processes they mobilize.

13.2.2 Power. In relation to energy processing, *power* is the rate at which work is performed, work being calculated as the product of a force and the distance through which it acts. The term also has another quite different meaning. In relation to information processing, *power* is control, the ability of one "master" system to influence in a specific direction the decision of a "slave" system at the same or another level, to elicit compliance from it. The system influenced may be the system itself—a man may be his own master; it may be some subsystem or component of it; it may be its suprasystem; or it may be some external system at any level. Characteristically, in hierarchies of living systems, each level has a certain autonomy and to a degree is controlled by levels above and below it. A mutual "working agreement" thus is essential.

13.2.3 Purpose and goal. By the information input of its charter or genetic input, or by changes in behavior brought about by rewards and punishments from its suprasystem, a system develops a preferential hierarchy of values that gives rise to decision rules which determine its preference for one internal steady state value rather than another. This is its *purpose.* It is the comparison value which it matches to information received by negative feedback in order to determine whether the variable is being maintained at the appropriate steady state value. In this sense it is normative. The system then takes one alternative action rather than another because it appears most likely to maintain the steady state. When disturbed, this state is restored by the system by successive approximations, in order to relieve the strain of the disparity recognized internally between the feedback signal and the comparison signal. Any system may have multiple purposes simultaneously.

A system may also have an external *goal,* such as reaching a target in space, or developing a relationship with any other system in the environment. Or it may have several goals at the same time. Just as there is no question that a rat in a maze is searching for the goal of food at its end or that the Greek people under Alexander the Great were seeking the goal of world conquest. As Ashby notes, natural selection permits only those systems to continue which have goals that enable them to survive in their particular environments. The external goal may change constantly, as when a hunter chases a moving fox or a man searches for a wife by dating one girl after another, while the internal purpose remains the same.

A system's hierarchy of values determines its purposes as well as its goals. It is not difficult to distinguish purposes from goals, as the terms have been used: an amoeba has the purpose of maintaining adequate energy levels and therefore it has the goal of ingesting a bacterium; a boy has the purpose of keeping his body temperature in the proper range and so he has the goal of finding and putting on his sweater; Switzerland had the purpose in 1938 of remaining uninvaded and autonomous and so she sought the goal of a military organization which could keep all combatants outside her borders or disarm them if they crossed them.

13.2.4 Costs and efficiency. All adjustment processes have their *costs,* in energy of non-living or living systems, in material resources, in information (including in social systems a special form of information often conveyed on a marker of metal or paper money), or in time required for an action. Any of these may be scarce. (Time is a scarcity for mortal living systems.) Any of these is valued if it is essential for reducing strains. The costs of adjustment processes differ from one to another and from time to time. They may be immediate or delayed, short-term or long-term.

How successfully systems accomplish their purposes can be determined if those purposes are known. A system's *efficiency,* then, can be determined as the ratio of the success of its performance to the costs involved. A system constantly makes economic decisions directed toward increasing its efficiency by improving performance and decreasing costs. Economic analyses of *cost-effectiveness* are in recent years frequently aided by *program budgeting.* This involves keeping accounts separately for each subsystem or component that carries out a distinct program. The matter-energy, information, money and time costs of the program are in such analyses compared with various measures of the efficiency of performance of the program. How efficiently a system adjusts to its environment is determined by what strategies it employs in selecting adjustment processes and whether they satisfactorily reduce strains without being too costly. This decision process can be analyzed by a mathematical approach to economic decisions, game theory. This general theory concerning the best strategies for weighing "plays" against "pay-offs," selecting actions which will increase profits while decreasing losses, increase rewards while decreasing punishments, improve adjustments of variables to appropriate steady state values, or attain goals while diminishing costs. Relevant information available to the decider can improve such decisions. Consequently such information is valuable. But there are costs to obtaining such information. Hurley has developed a mathematical theory on how to calculate the value of relevant information in such decisions. This depends on such considerations as whether it is tactical (about a specific act) or strategic (about a policy for action); whether it is reliable or unreliable, overtly or secretly obtained, accurate, distorted, or erroneous.

14. Conclusion

This analysis of living systems uses concepts of thermodynamics, information theory, cybernetics, and systems engineering, as well as the classical concepts appropriate to each level. The purpose is to produce a description of living structure and process in terms of input and output, flows through systems, steady states, and feedbacks, which will clarify and unify the facts of life. Future papers will indicate how these systems concepts can be applied to a particular class of living systems—educational systems. Particular attention will be devoted to the application of program budgeting and cost-efficiency analysis to educational planning and administration. Emphasis will also be placed on the potential of a particular class of artifacts—the new information processing technologies—for improving the quality and efficiency of educational programs and cutting their costs.

44.
The Living Systems Involved
In the Educational Process

by *JAMES G. MILLER*
Vice Pres. for Academic
Affairs
Cleveland St. Univ.
and
V.P. and Principal
Scientist
EDUCOM

How can the concepts of general systems theory be applied to increase understanding of the educational process? A number of levels of living systems are involved: At the organism level, there are several sorts of persons: the student, the parent, the teacher, the administrator, and other employees of educational institutions. At the group level: the class in the classroom, or the teacher and student in a tutorial session. At the organization level: in primary and secondary education, the school, and at a higher echelon, the school system; also in higher education, the college or university, and at a higher echelon, the statewide agency which coordinates higher education. At the society level: the national educational system, which has little centralized control in the United States but is much more centralized in the Soviet Union and elsewhere. Finally, at the supranational level: UNESCO, the Economic and Social Council of the United Nations, and other activities, are producing the first glimmerings of international coordination of education.

We shall now discuss in turn each of these levels of living systems involved in education, applying the concepts outlined in the previous paper.

The Persons in the Educational Process

The central person in all of education is the student. During the time he is in school the needs of his matter-energy processing subsystems must be provided for—milk and lunches for his ingestor; clothes and heat to warm all his subsystems; lavatories for his extruder; walks, hallways, and exercise facilities for his motor. There must be facilities for his information processing subsystems as well—lectures and artifacts such as books, television, computerized programmed instruction, and audiovisual aids for his input transducer; language teachers and language laboratories for his decoder and encoder; learning aids and tutorial assistants for his associator; academic advisers and counselors on personal problems for his decider; auditoriums and speech laboratories for his output transducer.

Students are of different types—male and female, all races, and many genetic strains. Their different physical, mental, and emotional characteristics mean that they have various needs which require individualized attention. Being human, students have highly complex nervous systems, decisions being made at several neural echelons, from the local adjustment processes of the spinal cord up to the subtlest creative processes of the cortex of the brain. As he matures each student must learn from his parents and teachers how to govern or control *(a)* his subsystems and components, his viscera and other organs (Freud used the term "id" to refer to such governance and the emotions related to it); *(b)* his entire system (Freud's "ego"); and *(c)* his system in relation to other persons in his suprasystem (Freud's "superego"). He must also learn how to use the common as well as the new and sophisticated artifacts which are becoming more and more important in our modern technological society. No education deals with the whole student unless it relates to his mental, emotional, physical, social, cultural, and technological adjustments.

Education is primarily an information processing activity of the student, involving many, and often repeated, information inputs to him and outputs from him as well as much internal processing in his nervous system. Thus he learns to use language, think, solve problems, make decisions, and adjust to the threats and stresses of life. Education involves learning many facts but it is more important for the student to discover where to find facts and how to make the adjustments required by a wide range of threats and stresses. One of the things that every educated person must learn, in one set of terms or another, is that adjustments are more adaptive if they are continually subjected to checks in order to discover whether they are optimally achieving their goals. This is accomplished by using negative feedbacks. A soprano checks her tones by playing back a tape recording she has just made. A student checks his progress by the monthly grades on his report card and, if he is motivated, works harder in those classes where he got the lowest grades. An athlete considers his previous year's batting average in deciding whether to try to make the baseball team again this year.

As they grow up students learn about power—how to influence others to do what they want of them. This is a fundamental part of life. A person usually exercises power to accomplish his own goals which are established in terms of his long-run purposes. All of this relates to the most intimate aspects of his personality, his motivations and his hierarchy of values. These are commonly learned more from informal and extracurricular personal interactions with parents, teachers, and fellow students than in the classroom. There is no indication that television or the computer or any other innovation of educational technology can in the foreseeable future substitute for this personal touch. Any educational system whose size or organizational arrangements can make such human contacts infrequent cannot accomplish one of its central missions. Anonymity is not the optimal climate for learning.

The individual student, somewhere in his education, must learn an economic approach to the planning of his life. He must learn to husband scarce resources—friends who can help him, his own time and money, and useful materials and services. He must learn that for every benefit there is a cost and that it is to his advantage to optimize the trade-offs of costs and benefits. This makes for efficiency of personal decision-making. Of course most human decisions are not calculated. Often their bases cannot be stated. But in actuality many personal decisions, especially major ones, involve cost-effectiveness evaluations. Education can develop a student's skills in making such evaluations.

Thus a student may be viewed as a living system, as can his parents, teachers, and the other individuals concerned in his education. Ordinarily all these are devoted to helping the student in his learning process. This is an altruistic goal which generally they all seek. But they are all human beings intent also on achieving their personal purposes. Otherwise there would not be teachers unions; otherwise some parents would be more willing than they are to help their children with their homework. Anyone who wishes to understand education or any other social process must recognize that every human being tends to optimize his own purposes and these cannot all be altruistic. Fortunately for students, many of them are.

The Class or Tutorial Session

The fundamental educational process is face-to-face—the simplest form being the tutorial relationship of one teacher or counselor and one pupil, Mark Hopkins on one end of a log and the student on the other. More typically there are one teacher and 20 to 30 students, a classroom. The classroom is made of walls, floors, and ceilings, material artifacts. In and out of the classroom matter must flow—students, teachers, school books, other supplies—and so must energy—heat and light. These flows change over time. But the most important flows in a classroom are information flows—the information in the books, on the television sets, and in the interactions between the students and the teacher. These information transmissions are integral to the fundamental learning process. They also are the means whereby the teacher maintains discipline and coordinates the students who are components in the concrete living system which is the class.

The spatial structure of the class importantly influences its processes. If students are arranged at desks facing the blackboard or television set, their interactions are different than if they are arranged in a circle or if they are arranged at laboratory benches. The classroom process varies also with the content of the information discussed and the teacher's approach to interpersonal reactions, which is often dictated by the teacher's philosophy of education.

Group learning situations differ in type: some are lecture sections, some discussions, some laboratories, some field trips, and some are extracurricular groups. The typical class is a face-to-face group and so it does not have echelons, but occasionally a large class organizes into echelons. The suprasystem of the class is an organization, the school, and its subsystem is the individual student or teacher.

Within the class there are many sorts of transmissions. Matter-energy such as laboratory equipment, experimental animals, or chemicals may be distributed to all the students. Information is processed when the teacher asks questions and the students respond, when the teacher writes problems on the blackboard and students solve them on their papers.

Also various sorts of steady states are maintained by the class. Ordinarily the teacher maintains the dominant control of these. With the help of the bell and the clock which signal the times for class periods, the teacher determines when the class begins and ends. The teacher usually divides the time available to the class more or less equally among the students, recognizing who is to speak, keeping the entire class in adjustment by quieting those students who speak out of turn.

Often the teacher varies the rate of information processing, sensitively reacting to signals in the students' expressions and comments which indicate how fast and well they are learning. A new topic is not taken up until most of the class have mastered the previous one.

Usually the teacher wields the primary power in the class, but often, as the students get older and enter the higher grades, this power is diminished. Sometimes students resolve conflicts among themselves, but often the teacher must step in as the decider in the group. The teacher is trained to understand the overall purposes of the course being taught and to set day-to-day and moment-to-moment goals to accomplish these purposes.

Of course there are significant costs in the functioning of any class. First there are the original capital fund costs of building the classroom. There are the operating fund costs of light, heat, supplies, and repairs. There are also the costs of recruiting, training, and equipping the teacher and of the information-processing media which bring information to the class. Besides the money spent there are also the costs in the human time which is consumed at the school. Since it is possible to evaluate at least roughly the effectiveness of a single hour in class or a single course, cost-effectiveness evaluations of a given class are possible.

What are the critical subsystems of the living system known as the class? The student who holds open the classroom door so others can enter is part of the ingestor. The teacher or child who distributes the graham crackers in kindergarten is part of the distributor. The laboratory assistant responsible for the stock of glassware and chemical reagents is part of matter-energy storage subsystem. The student who opens the window when the class gets too hot is part of the extruder.

The information processing subsystems are more central to the main purposes of any educational group. The child who comes in and reports on his experiences over the weekend in "Show and Tell" is a component of the input transducer. The girl who reports that the boy behind her is sticking her with a pencil is part of the internal transducer. The channel and net includes air through which the students talk as well as the examination papers they hand in to the teacher. Often the teacher alone is the decider, but at times some or all students may join with the teacher in this group process. The report from the teacher to the principal on how the class did that week is an output transducer function.

The School*

A school is generally a building or a set of buildings on some real estate, all together occupying physical space. This physical space is important because it limits expansion and restricts the size of auxiliary facilities such as football fields and playgrounds. Building a school alters arrangements in physical space, but it also changes the spaces of abstracted systems in which it is located. It becomes the locus of many community activities, such as the Parent-Teachers Association, which allow citizens to cooperate for the purpose of helping the school. It allows certain members of the community to exercise initiative and leadership and derive a variety of benefits from that kind of participation. It also becomes the center of a political unit for those persons who are concerned with financial and other support of that school. It affects real estate values in its immediate surroundings.

Time is a fundamental dimension in schools. In most of them a system of bells indicates the limits of class periods. The class programs and major activities are scheduled in terms of a school year calendar. One recent change in many schools has been flexible scheduling, based on the developments in individual classes. The availability of media, the use of CCTV and educational television (ETV) has added more flexibility to some aspects of school processes but more rigidity to others which are dependent on closed circuit TV or ETV broadcasts. The more individualized instruction, such as dial-access systems, that is available, the more flexible can the scheduling and operation of the school be.

In some systems-oriented planning studies students' time has been considered the major consideration, and lack of more student time was viewed as a constraint on all activities that occur in the school.

Schools have matter-energy relationships similar to many other organizations. As any school principal knows, planning about matter-energy structures and processes comes first whenever any new school is being constructed. The architect decides how to arrange the walls, floors, and roof on the lot and the contractor constructs the building from those plans. Fuel is brought in to provide heat and electricity to provide light. There are inputs of water, food, equipment and other supplies and outputs of garbage and sewage. Over time students come and students go.

Information transactions, however, are the main business of a school. In addition to the direct information interactions which occur between teacher and student, the administration and operation of the school as a whole require many types of information flows. Operational information is needed to coordinate and plan the educational process. Information is needed and collected for fiscal and administrative matters such as pupil attendance, which is a key factor in most school systems as a major portion of revenue depends on it. Payroll

This section and the next are contributed by Dr. Gustave Rath, Professor of Industrial Engineering and Management Sciences, The Technological Institute, Northwestern University, Evanston, Illinois.

information must be collected. Additional information is necessary for scheduling of students, teachers, and facilities.

A school is a system whose components are classes in classrooms, administrators in offices, workers in storage areas, cooks and waitresses in cafeterias, and maintenance personnel throughout.

Schools are open systems into which resources and people come and from which students graduate and the other people leave after a period of time. The processes which a school purposes to bring about are irreversible learning processes. A school is in some ways like a job shop in which a series of students are processed from station to station, from one learning experience to another. The experiences are similar but not identical. Nor is their order and timing identical for each student. The student's behavioral and cognitive changes are the key determiner of the timing. Skipping grades and ungraded schools attest to this viewpoint.

A school is usually part of a school system which is its suprasystem. Generally its components are class and other learning groups.

All the variables in a school are never in steady state. Adjustment processes reacting to negative feedbacks are continuously active. Feedbacks occur within the school in many channels between the principal, the teachers, and the students, as well as the parents and the citizens of the community. Many adjustment processes are required to keep the school operating under these many forces.

Power and conflict are critical problems in schools. In many of them today, power is chiefly wielded by the teachers. The principals are faced with the difficult position of being expected to resolve conflicts and bring about decisions to keep the system integrated which concern teachers over whom they have little control because of their tenure, teachers' unions, schoolwide curriculum decisions, and a suprasystem which makes the decisions allocating major resources. Often the principal feels that he is little more than the school's output transducer—a public relations man. Of course, in small schools, or independent ones, the principal or head master may be the key power figure. Conflicts also occur between outside and inside groups such as unions and faculties. Conflicts also occur inside schools between students and teachers. Interpersonal conflicts within the staff have always been with us.

The purposes and goals of a given school relate to the overall plan of its suprasystem, the school system. Individual schools are expected to apply their resources to maximize the educational objectives set forth by the school system. Typically these purposes and goals, of quite different sorts, may be divided into: (a) educational objectives, such as preparing a student for a vocational school, teaching vocational skills, preparing students for college; (b) social skills, such as good citizenship, developing good consumers and responsible citizens; (c) economic service objectives, such as keeping the students off the streets, baby-sitting for working mothers, and other such activities; and (d) community services, such as lighted schoolhouse programs, PTA's, educational programs in the evening, and the use of the physical plant by the community; also, the offering of recreation and entertainment for the community in the form of sports, and, in some cases, other things like movies or plays.

Costs of a school include use or expenditure of scarce resources such as materials—foods, equipment, supplies; energy—light, heat, fuel; information—books, audiovisual aids; budgeted funds; human time of all personnel in the school and many in the community. When these are measured and compared with measures of achievement of purposes and goals, cost-effectiveness evaluation of a given school is at least roughly possible. Effectiveness can be measured in terms of the number of students who graduate, the number who go to college, the number who drop out, how well students do in competitive examinations, how well they do in getting and holding jobs, crime rates among students and graduates, and other measures of undesired social conditions among them such as narcotics addiction, ill health, and unemployment.

The critical subsystems of a school may include guards who protect and maintain the boundary; the admissions office whose personnel register new students and so are components of the ingestor; workmen who cart equipment to various rooms in the school, parts of the distributor; the cooks in the cafeteria, components of the decomposer and the producer; bookstore clerk, part of the matter-energy storage subsystem; and the janitor, a component of the extruder. As to the information processing subsystems, the technician who operates the ETV controls is a unit of the input transducer; the teachers and students all participate in the channel and net; the librarian is part of the memory; the principal and teachers jointly constitute the decider, with the principal more in control in some cases and the teachers more in control in others; and the principal is a major component of the output transducer.

The School System

The matter and energy of a school system include all that of the schools which are its subsystems. In addition there are school bus transportation facilities, warehousing and shipping facilities, and other services which use the roads of the community which is the suprasystem of the school system. Time takes a new perspective as compared with the school's time units of hours, weeks, and the school year. A school system works in terms of many years. A bond issue and a consequent commitment to buy land and build on it is a multiple-year activity. Planning-programming-budgeting (PPB) for school systems always requires a multiple year plan.

Information processing is essential if personnel, facilities, and allocated resources are to be kept under control and coordinated. Resource allocation and control is a major function of a school system. Individual schools require resources and generate the information flows that lead to more revenues. The school board with its ability to propose bond issues, to help determine tax levies and schedule campaigns, gets involved in many political processes in the decider subsystem of the community, which is the school board's suprasystem. All this must be coordinated by information flows into and out of the system.

The structure of a school system is much more complex than that of a school. Some decisions are centralized and others are decentralized. In very large systems, many hierarchical levels occur. The processes involved are those of planning, control, training, logistics, acquisition of educational materials, and development of common services to serve all components of the system.

The suprasystem is the community and above that the state including the state school board of education, which is usually a very weak system compared to a school system.

There are matter-energy flows of supplies and equipment and of persons to some extent among components of school systems. Primarily, however, such systems are parasitic (or symbiotic) upon their suprasystem communities for such flows. Information flows, usually over the community channel and net subsystem, are much more fundamental. They provide feedbacks and control signals which maintain the adjustment processes that keep components of the system in steady states. Information on votes and bond issues, levies, the effect of the press, and public sentiments about the school system is processed. It is interesting to note that recently many school systems have shown great interest and concern in public relations activity and in developing instruments to measure how they are viewed by the public.

Power and conflict problems are much greater at the school system level than at the school level. Power not only involves power within the school system, but also the suprasystem of the community in which a school system is embedded—city government, citizens' groups, real estate interests, and political organizations, among others.

The purposes of a school system are ordinarily viewed over a longer time span than purposes of a school. A time horizon of five years is minimal because it is the least that covers all those children who are alive and living in the community but are not in the school system. A time horizon of seven years is minimal for such planning as the decision to buy buses, because seven years is the average life of school buses. In a kindergarten through eighth grade school system, a nine-year predictive span makes sense because that is the least that covers changes which will be implemented in the kindergarten and continue through into the eighth grade. Land buying commitments involve planning many years ahead, since bond issues and the public financing may take 20, 30, or 50 years to retire.

The purposes of the school system include the intention to give a high quality of education to all members of the community through programs which meet the individual needs of all, including special groups such as children with physical disabilities or learning disabilities, as well as an academic program for those who are going to college. This may be interpreted in specific goals like the operation of special education classes, an ETV station, or a junior college.

Cost-effectiveness evaluations are critical in school systems because a maximal possible level of expenditure exists at any given time, and the school system must achieve the optimal cost-benefit ratio for that level of resources. Thus, with a given budget, one tries to achieve the best possible programs. This is especially difficult as inflation, increasing salaries, and other pressures exert continuing financial pressures on the school system in spite of additional revenues. These forces may lead a school system to develop a PPB system. That makes it possible for alternatives to be presented for analysis to the school board in a way in which decisions can be made.

The critical subsystems of a school system include guards and community police that protect the boundary of its property. Warehouse personnel that receive shipments of equipment, components of its ingestor. Truckers who deliver such supplies to schools, parts of its distributor. Persons who build or manufacture supplies, part of its converter and producer. Warehouse laborers, parts of its matter-energy storage. And bus drivers, components of its motor. Closer to the school system's primary purposes are the subsystems that process information, including: The admistrators who bring back from national conventions reports on what other school systems are doing, components of the input transducer. Administrators who receive periodic reports from each school in the system, part of the internal transducer. Telephone operators, parts of the channel and net. Filing clerks, parts of the memory. The Board of Education and the superintendent, parts of the decider. And the president of the Board of Education, part of the output transducer.

The College

A college has as its territory the campus. Within its boundary are dotted clusters of matter which are its buildings. Into this campus enter many forms of living and nonliving matter —bricks and mortar, furniture, equipment, supplies, food, automobiles, bicycles. Also animals and human beings enter. And there are outputs of such things as well, many of them wastes. All these structural configurations and processes of input and output change over time. This change may be slow, for many colleges are traditional. They often endure a long time. Some European colleges are centuries old. Even in America, Harvard College has lasted more than three centuries and Yale for nearly three.

As at all other levels of educational systems, the types of processes which are most important and characteristic and which chiefly accomplish their goals are the information processes. Information flows into a college from all over the world—by scholarly journals, books, radio, television, the mails, but also by visiting scholars, students, and others who come there for varying lengths of time. There are many patterns of information communication and storage within the system. Interactions among students and faculty, learning by faculty and students, storage of memories in human beings and libraries, and publication of knowledge through books, broadcasts, and travel of professors and graduates to all parts of the world.

A college is a concrete living system with a structure usually clearly pictured in maps of the college. The process in that structure is often vigorous and always complex.

There are various types of colleges, classed by the content they study—e.g., general education, engineering, or law—by number of components, and by form of organization. The suprasystem of some colleges is a university. For independent colleges it is the community of which they are a part. The subsystems are departments, usually separated by academic disciplines, and other such components as student unions, fraternities, dormitories, and field stations.

The administration of the college, with the cooperation of many components, maintains a steady state relationship between the system and the suprasystem, through public releases, interrelations with the alumni, and citizens of the community. It also uses its power to maintain the appropriate adjustments between the students' demands for power and accomplishment, the faculty demands, and the demands of the other components in the total system. The administrators are a major aspect of the decider, which may often be dispersed to include others as well, and they make their decisions in the light of many feedbacks which they receive from all parts of the system and its environment. Often, and especially in recent years, they find themselves involved in the resolutions of interpersonal and intergroup conflicts.

Some colleges, like a Jesuit seminary or a school of agriculture and mining, are quite clear about their purposes. Others, particularly those concerned with general education and the humanities, are less certain. Nevertheless, they appear to set goals which lead toward certain purposes, vaguely or clearly outlined.

Any faculty member or administrator of a college who has ever made a budget knows that all the college's processes involve costs in matter-energy, information, and time of the human beings involved. Consequently it is possible to make cost-effectiveness evaluations of how well the system is achieving its long-range purposes and its short-range goals. The measurement of effectiveness of such a system is by no means easy because the organization's purposes and goals are subtle. Much though has been given to this problem of evaluation, however, and this effort has resulted in some progress.

It is not hard to identify the critical sybsystems of a college. The police who guard it are involved in its boundary subsystem. Those who bring in the necessary books, supplies, fuel, and food are parts of its ingestor, and the drivers of the delivery trucks and porters who take it to all parts of its campus are components of its distributor. In closets, pantries, and bookstores it has matter-energy storage. The cooks, heating engineers, and carpenters are components of its converter and producer. The drivers of the trucks that remove the wastes are parts of the extruder. In the information processing subsystems the Dean of Admissions and the mail clerks are parts of the input transducer. The Dean of Student Affairs does much of the internal transducing, learning how the students feel about various aspects of their college life. Both students and teachers are involved in learning and are components of the associator. The scholars and librarians are parts of the memory. The department chairmen, deans, and presidents help to make up the decider. The faculty who publish and go forth to lecture, as well as the alumni and the official spokesmen of the college, are components of the output transducer.

The University

Obviously a university is not fundamentally different from a college as a living system. It is usually larger, more variegated, more sophisticated. Because of their size and variety, as universities have grown from colleges they have developed more and more echelons.

Some colleges have only department chairmen and a president. But long ago deans intervened over department chairmen, and in the last 20 to 30 years provosts, vice chancellors, chancellors, and vice presidents have also flourished. Academic structures have become much more complex with components, subcomponents, and subsubcomponents—colleges, departments, and units of departments, as well as institutes, centers, and intercollege programs.

As the systems have grown in size and complexity decision processes have been decentralized and the systems have demonstrated less integration. The major programs or components usually represent content areas or disciplines—categories of information processed—instead of functions, which components almost always represent in large industrial or governmental organizations. Although the boundaries of university departments at first are often set by subtle academic logic, and so surround abstracted systems, eventually the different components so separated grow into semi-autonomous concrete systems—groups of people.

Management information systems are being used for the first time in recent years to evaluate the cost and effectiveness of these programs. The costs are easier to determine than the effectiveness, but to some extent arbitrary criteria have been set up, like the national ratings of the quality of graduate departments, the number of their publications, or the number of their graduates who pass professional examinations. These measures, though subject to criticism and clearly unsophisticated, are first steps toward effectiveness evaluation.

The critical subsystems of universities are similar to those of colleges. The main difference is that the decider subsystem is much more decentralized.

The Nation's Educational System

Countries vary greatly in the structures of their components responsible for education. Education in most other nations is much more centralized than in the United States. Since the United States is a union of states that were established by colonies which formerly considered themselves to be sovereign, the educational activities of the country are primarily controlled by state and local governments. The components of the elementary, secondary, and higher education of the nation have been described above. The national educational system is simply the sum total of these plus the administrators who determine policy for it, like the Office of Education, acting as interfaces between it and the total nation.

The national educational system of the United States has few operating units beyond those mentioned above, with the exception of the regional educational laboratories. Consequently the main emphasis in discussing this level of national educational system will concern how decisions are made in it. Day-to-day decisions in individual schools of course are made by its principal and teachers. Superintendents in schools and boards of education are probably the most autonomous decision-making units in elementary and secondary education, just as college and university administrators and boards of trustees are autonomous decision-making units in higher education. State superintendents of education, as we have said, have been relatively impotent so far, and until the last few years statewide controlling boards of higher education have not been powerful deciders, but the balance of power is rapidly changing from the colleges and universities to the administrators of statewide systems, including the governor and the legislature.

The United States Office of Education has been relatively impotent until this decade, but its decision-making power grew rapidly in the Kennedy and Johnson administrations. It is still much less influential in elementary and secondary education than the school systems, although the balance is changing. The fundamental influence in the Office of Education is through the funds it administers for building construction, educational subsidies, student loans, educational research, and educational technologies. As it gained this financial power the prestige of the national educational organization has increased dramatically. Through the networks of official communication channels and through professional conventions, local school boards and college boards of trustees are affected by national decision-makers. The granting processes of federal agencies and foundations have also become important aspects of the decision-making process. Now, for the first time, it begins to be possible to plan national resource centers which will provide the content for broadcasts by various media over national and international networks. When these begin to function, not only decision-making but also the educational process itself can be centralized nationally.

The International Educational System

Except for the interchange of publications among nations and for Fulbright, Guggenheim, and other visiting fellowships and scholarships, the educational systems of the world's nations have been almost entirely independent of each other and still are. With the establishment of the League of Nations and more recently of the United Nations—and particularly with UNESCO related to the United Nations—worldwide planning for education has begun. Someday there may be an international or supranational educational system, but we are far from it at present. Educators are communicating regularly by publications and international congresses. The educational leaders of nations know each other and intercommunicate. The first steps have been taken toward the development of international textbooks and television lectures, and the setting up by satellites of international networks interconnecting the national educational systems of the world. There will undoubtedly be rapid development of these technologies and consequently of the decision-making processes required to coordinate these. As of now, however, the international educational system is not a true system since there is no effective central decider. There are only vestiges which may sometime grow into a potent means for teaching the citizens of the world and hopefully aiding them in living together in harmony.

45.

A Ten-Year Program
For Developing, Evaluating
And Implementing
Instructional Technologies

by *JAMES G. MILLER*
Cleveland State Univ. and EDUCOM

Almost daily we hear of new instructional media, or novel, interesting, and versatile gadgets which can contribute to education. Their sophistication is rapidly increasing. The interest of educators is not in hardware and software for themselves alone, however fascinating they may be. Rather they are concerned as to whether these technologies can be used to achieve greater excellence of education from nursery school throughout life; to individualize that education and fit it to the needs of specific human beings; to share resources and scarce personnel in educational systems at all levels; and to cut costs in various scarce forms of matter-energy and information, including money for capital construction and operating funds, and the time of students, teachers, administrators, and staff members.

A national program to accomplish these purposes should be developed over the next decade by cooperative planning among schools, colleges, and universities, industrial organizations, and the government. Because they have the largest number of students, the *schools* should be the greatest users and constitute important proving grounds for the new media. The colleges and universities in their traditional research and development role should take the lead in the basic investigations underlying these new technologies, in their engineering development, and in trying them out in their own processes. Universities may also serve to protect the content information of the media from distortion by the profit motive or governmental control. The role of industry is to create hardware and software and operate communications systems. Government is likely to have four roles: (a) funding necessary basic and applied research and development; (b) subsidizing early operations, by such means as creating special rates for educational communications; (c) providing tax funds to support public education; and (d) regulating the technologies, as the Federal Communication Commission does of other sorts of communications, or as the Copyright Office does of uses of content materials.

Organizational Considerations

Five to ten major university centers for research and development on instructional technology scattered around the United States, each with long-term block grant institutional funding by the government in addition to other projects grants, would in all likelihood be the best basis for national initiative in this field. Multiple university centers are probably better than a single governmental institute comparable to one of the National Institutes of Health, for the following reasons: First of all, such institutes usually cannot pay salaries to compete the thorough development and field testing of specific techniques and content materials. Many workers in educational research have demonstrated in theory, or with relatively insignificant examples, that certain kinds of hardware and software can be useful in education. But careful development of instruments which have been systematically tested and are ready to use is rare. Complete segments of courses, full courses, and other sets of learning materials are urgently needed for instruction at all levels of elementary, secondary, higher, and continuing education. These should be carefully evaluated with groups in terms of their educational effectiveness and costs.

In addition a national program of federal government project grants for research and development activities should be established. Foundation and other private grants will undoubtedly supplement these.

Hardware Needs

Throughout the ten years of the program intensive research should be carried out to improve the hardware of present instructional media and to add to those now available. The initiative for such activities should come from educators and those involved in instructional research, rather than from engineers. The educators should determine the need and state the specifications. They can then turn to engineers on university faculties or to industrial engineers in order to produce the product as required. Each one must be carefully and well engineered and field tested with cost-effectiveness evaluation, in the same hard-headed way that a new airplane, automobile, or electric toaster is evaluated by industry.

Funds should be available, especially in the first five years of the ten-year period, for the development of a number of specific types of hardware like those listed below. The ones which prove out should be ready for industrial manufacture on a mass basis by the end of the fifth year.

Among the major types of instructional hardware which currently appear to be in need of development are the following;

1. *Computers especially designed for educational needs.* In recent years no computer has been constructed for educational uses primarily, except perhaps the Illiac IV, a pattern-recognition computer designed and built at the University of Illinois at Urbana, and the IBM 1500, industrially designed for computer-aided instruction. Educators should have a role in stating the specifications for computers needed for educational computer-aided on-line time-sharing systems.

2. *Inexpensive automated carrel to sell for less than $1000 when mass produced.* Such a carrel should include audio input, visual input on a screen which can show black and white and colored letters, figures, still graphic materials, and moving pictures; an electric typewriter which can be operated on-line to a computer; and a light pencil whose beam can be sensed by an on-line computer whenever it is pointed at any part of the screen.

3. *Portable microform reader.* Utilization of microform has been widely restricted because microform readers are large and bulky and because they rapidly tire the eyes of the user. As a result, libraries purchase expensive books rather than cheaper microform copies of the same materials which are available, because of user resistance to microform. This resistance could probably be significantly diminished if a portable microform reader were developed that could be carried in a small briefcase, perhaps

even pocket-size. This reader should be capable of enlarging to full size microcards with black letters on a white background, white letters on a black background, and colored materials, and with adequate illumination so that the user's eyes do not tire. It is possible to reduce ordinary book pages clearly 40- or 45-to-1, so that they fit on a single microcard. If such a reader were available, many books could be carried around in a single briefcase. Research and development are now underway on a small, portable microform reader.

4. *Automated carrel in briefcase.* An entire automated carrel in an attaché case is probably attainable within the next ten years if an effort to develop it is given priority and support. It could contain a television screen, light pencil, micro-optical information storage file, remote television camera and tripod, teletype keyboard, touchtone keyboard for communicating with the local storage or a remote computer, and telephone. It would be powered either from a power outlet or from a rechargeable, long-life battery. The user would set up the TV camera in its tripod to photograph himself. Then he could transmit his own image to a receiver anywhere on a network over phone-vision line outlets to which he would connect his briefcase. Over the same lines he could receive over a network from any location the image of someone he was talking to or data from a computer. What was not stored in the information file of the briefcase could be obtained over telephone or phone-vision lines of the network from a remote computer. In this way the user could get access to television lectures, documents, data, or computerized programmed instruction. The user could interact with a remote computer by light pencil, by telephone, teletype keyboard or touchtone keyboard.

5. *Optical print reader.* A machine is needed which can scan and rapidly read into digital storage entire books printed in ordinary type of many different fonts. Photo-readers exist at present which can read at the rate of a page a second, material typed in a number of fonts of typewriter type, but none yet can read, with adequate accuracy, many fonts of book type. Until such a machine exists, it will not be financially feasible to store massive amounts of textual material digitally in electronic memories which can then be searched for information that can be transmitted rapidly over electronic networks. If this development should occur, with mass memory storage hardware available now and soon to be improved, the operation of libraries could be greatly improved. For approximately the amount of federal money appropriated annually for libraries in the United States it would be possible to store the entire text of the Library of Congress, if the attendant complex legal copyright problems could be resolved. Thereafter schools, colleges, and universities could have access over networks almost on an instantaneous basis to the entire store of the Library of Congress. This would remedy the great shortage of information of this sort that exists in many parts of our country today and create a true nationwide democracy of access to such information.

6. *On-line electronic blackboard.* If in group discussion rooms and classrooms it were possible at will to retrieve printed and graphic materials in black and white and color and to magnify them up on large surfaces—on-line to a computer like electronic blackboards—many aspects of classroom teaching could be facilitated. Large displays something like this are presently in use in command-and-control rooms of American military installations, but they are probably far too expensive for educational use. A cheaper form is required for mass production.

7. *Home cartridge video-tape player and recorder.* Audio-tape cartridge players already are in wide use. It is reliably reported that in the near future, color television sets will be equipped to play and record video cartridges. This coming development can be of great value for home study by students in schools, colleges, and universities,

as well as by adults. Home television sets will become potential educational centers and can be used, therefore, both for recreational amusement and for education.

8. *Educational satellite.* Communications utilizing satellites are already in operation around the world. Satellites dedicated to educational communications are now feasible and are likely to be available by 1972. This broad-band facility will make possible transmission of all of the media that can be carried over networks, not only across the United States but around the world.

9. *Signal transmission by laser.* Laser beams are capable of very broad-band transmission. This means that very large amounts of information can be transmitted rapidly and inexpensively. This information could be both printed or graphic, still or moving, visual and/or moving, relating to all the electronic instruction media.

Other sorts of hardware will also undoubtedly be found desirable as educational research and development expand.

Software Needs

The experts agree that to create sophisticated and effective software is much more complex and difficult than to produce hardware. Many fundamental principles of software construction are understood, although improvements can constantly be made. The art of software development is young. There are basically two sorts of software: (a) systems software for operating the various types of computerized equipment in flexible ways which will be most useful for the educational process and (b) the programs of actual content material.

Throughout the ten years the phases of software development should be as follows: Basic research on software technology, including new methods of programming; creation of new programming languages; and work on basic linguistics in order to improve the ability of computers to translate text from one language to another or to search text and answer questions based on such searches.

In the first three years of the ten-year program, major content materials should be programmed in the different media for grade school, high school, and junior college curricula, and most popular college and university courses. By the end of three years, complete curricular materials in all these areas should be available, preferably from multiple courses and authors, to get different points of view. Between the third and fifth year of the ten-year program, such content materials should be expanded to most or all curricular fields. Thereafter there should be more and more varieties and duplications of these various forms of content material. It is essential that there be multiple versions of such materials and that any author who wishes should be encouraged to prepare educational materials to go on the network. Quality of the content can be best assured by such competition.

Efforts should be made through basic research and development to study man-machine symbiosis. We should allocate to machines rote teaching and other activities that can be best done by individualized instruction with machines. Human beings, teachers working in small groups and individually with students should carry out the functions which machines cannot do now and very likely never will be able to. The emphasis in production of educational materials for these new instructional technologies should be not on learning facts but on learning how to find and use facts; or developing wisdom and judgment and on discovering how to live a full and fruitful life.

Legal Activities

During the first two years of the ten-year period, legal task forces made up of educators, lawyers, engineers, librarians, computer experts, television broadcasters, and other special-ists should devote themselves to improving the present laws and regulations and spelling out ethical codes for the most effective operation of the instructional media. The Federal Communications Commission should establish rates and regulations that make possible the operation of all the media at local sites and also over networks. Furthermore, serious con-sideration should be given to special educational rates. One form of federal subsidy for education may be cutting the long distance communication rates for educational purposes below those for other purposes. In the development of new industries throughout Ameri-can history, such federal subsidy has been common. It is certainly appropriate to subsidize the newly developing educational industry, most or all of which is and always will be nonprofit and which, in addition, is utterly vital to the country.

Present copyright legislation must also be rewritten to take into account recent develop-ments in the new media and to provide appropriate reimbursement through royalties and licensing arrangements to authors and publishers while at the same time guaranteeing that all information useful to education will be freely made available. Copyright holders should not have the right to prevent their materials from being used on educational networks and other educational media. But they should have the right to receive appropriate reim-bursement for the use of their copyrighted materials.

Laws and regulations governing educational network operations should be established to deal with anti-trust considerations, potential negligence, censorship, and so forth. In addition, ethical codes and laws concerning privacy of information and procedures for guaranteeing it where appropriate should be worked out. This legal activity should be followed up intensively during the first two or three years of the ten-year period. At the end of three years, well worked-out codes of laws, regulations, procedures, and ethics for the use of educational technologies should be available.

Networks

In the first five years of the ten-year period pilot networks should be established, begin-ning perhaps with a single medium, like the Educational Information Network (EIN) dedi-cated to computers or like various educational television networks now in operation. These should be expanded to include all the instructional media which can be transmitted on networks, as planned for EDUNET.* Preferably operated by a university consortium and supported by the federal government, these pilot efforts should develop principles of operation, organizational structures and manning tables, rules for hardware and software compatibility, and methods of accounting and financing. Then they should obtain content materials and begin pilot operations. After evaluating their experiences, they should expand services which appear useful to all colleges and universities, schools, and other agencies in the society which can use them. By the end of the fifth year, these developments should be sufficiently advanced to begin to constitute significant factors in American education. Later they can be extended to other countries.

Evaluation

No educational process should be accepted for wide use without appropriate evaluation on a controlled basis in comparison with other possible ways to accomplish the same ends. Throughout the ten-year period there should be basic research on effectiveness measure-ment and cost-effectiveness evaluation procedures. Beginning with the second or third year of the ten-year period when significant amounts of software are becoming available,

*Cf. Brown, G. W., Miller, J. G., and Keenan, T. A. EDUNET. Report of the Summer Study on Information Net-works Conducted by the Interuniversity Communications Council (EDUCOM). New York: John Wiley, 1967.

these should be subjected to controlled evaluations of their costs and benefits or effectiveness. Comparative evaluations of competing materials should be made public by an agency sufficiently judicial not to be influenced by pressures from hardware or software development organizations, government, or any other source. This might be a quasi-judicial governmental agency, perhaps associated with a National Institute of Educational Technology, but perhaps independent.

Demonstration Centers

Because of the widespread resistances to change which have been mentioned above, few on-going educational systems are likely to make the radical changes in their structures and processes necessary to adapt themselves most effectively to the new technologies. Therefore it is recommended that, beginning with the third year of the ten-year program and extending through the eighth year (as soon as a reasonable mass of software content material is available for educational systems at any level), a number of federally supported demonstration centers be established. These centers would operate school, college or university programs using the instructional technologies as much as possible and comparing them with traditional forms of instruction. These centers would run the gamut from nursery school to continuing education, including special types of schools, as for the mentally retarded or for prisoners. The learning environment in them would include every automated aid but would by no means eliminate human teachers whose roles would be to deal with the motivations of the individual students, to adapt the materials to their specific interests and personalities, and to instruct in those matters which have not yet been automated.

Training in Educational Technology, Systems and Communications Science

There is a great shortage of persons concerned with the educational process who also have the background required to apply present knowledge in communication science and systems science to the use of the new instructional technologies. Therefore, colleges and universities should have bachelor's, master's, and doctor's programs in these fields. At the bachelor's level, educational technologists would be trained to be operators of the media. At the master's level supervisors would be trained with knowledge in depth of such matters as systems analysis, computer programming, computer-aided instruction course programming, and television script writing. Doctoral level training would be provided for those who are able to innovate and do research development in the new media and in systems and communication science. Those studying to teach in elementary, secondary, and higher education should be trained to use the media. In other professions, like medicine and engineering, it is universal practice for a student to get to understand the tools of his trade before he begins his professional life. It is strange that this is not generally true in education—particularly higher education. Educational administrators also should be trained in the media and in techniques for eliciting innovation from their teachers and professors, and for clearly indicating the administrations support for such innovation.

International Implications

Once the hardware and software has been developed and tested out in the United States, they can be mass produced at reduced costs for use throughout the world. Electronic instruments can be provided with their own power sources, if necessary, and taken anywhere in the world. They can be interconnected with the United States through international educational satellites and by other means. The content materials can be translated into other languages. If such materials are to be most usefully employed in foreign lands, developing as well as to established nations, they must in each place be articulated with the local scene. American provincialisms must be eliminated from them. Emphases should be changed to suit the language, culture, and traditions of each country. In addition, every effort should be made to render instruction and examination materials culture-fair, not biased for or against any given country. At the same time one would hope that large parts of the curriculum would be of general international interest. International education using these common materials could be a major force toward peace. In some countries adequate preparation for higher education is not available and, therefore, in such nations remedial education courses appropriate to the country would be essential.

It is unlikely that automated instruction would be entirely self-sufficient for providing a complete education anywhere. Human instructors almost always must be involved to deal with problems of the student's motivation to learn, to tailor instruction to the personality of the student, and—along with fellow students—to provide social facilitation to the learning process.

Funding

A rough suggestion about funding of a ten-year program by the federal government is indicated in Table 1. Of course, there would be other sources of funds in this country besides the federal government, including private foundations, school systems, colleges, universities, and industry. What is proposed here is a massive national effort over a decade, and the costs must be borne by many agencies. In addition, of course, international financing by foreign governments and international bodies, as well as the United States Government, are important if the entire world is to benefit from the instructional technologies.

Table 1.   Funds Needed for a Ten-Year Phased National Program for the
Development and Use of Instructional Technologies
(Amounts in thousands of dollars)

PURPOSE	1st Year	2nd Year	3rd Year	4th Year
Block grants to Research & Development Centers	2,500	5,000	7,500	10,000
National Institute of Educational Technology				
Intramural Program	500	1,000	1,500	2,000
Project Grant Program	2,500	4,000	5,000	6,000
Hardware Development	5,000	15,000	25,000	25,000
Software Development				
Basic research	1,000	2,000	3,000	4,000
Content material preparation	2,000	5,000	10,000	15,000
Subsidy to permit special rates for educational communications	1,000	2,000	3,000	5,000
Legal activities	100	200	200	150
Educational multimedium networks	500	1,000	3,000	5,000
Evaluation	5,000	1,000	1,000	1,000
Demonstration centers			6,000	12,000
Training	1,000	3,000	5,000	7,000
International programs	500	1,000	1,500	2,500
Totals	21,600	40,200	71,700	94,650

5th Year	6th Year	7th Year	8th Year	9th Year	10th Year
13,000	16,500	20,500	25,000	30,000	36,000
2,500	3,000	3,500	4,000	4,500	5,000
7,000	8,000	9,000	10,000	10,000	10,000
25,000	15,000	10,000	10,000	10,000	10,000
5,000	5,500	6,000	6,500	7,000	7,500
20,000	25,000	25,000	25,000	25,000	25,000
8,000	11,000	15,000	17,000	19,000	21,000
100	50	50	50	50	50
8,000	10,000	12,000	14,000	16,000	18,000
1,000	1,000	1,000	1,000	1,000	1,000
16,000	20,000	25,000	25,000	25,000	25,000
9,000	10,000	10,000	10,000	10,000	10,000
5,000	7,500	10,000	15,000	20,000	25,000
119,600	132,550	147,050	162,550	177,550	193,550

46.
Curriculum Change
And Technology

by NEIL POSTMAN
Prof., English Education
New York University
School of Education

As I see it, the major educational problem of the nuclear space age is that almost *all* formal schooling in America (for black and white, rural and urban, rich and poor) is more damaging to children than beneficial, and, in fact, reduces rather than increases their chances of future survival. The magnitude of this problem has been documented in recent years by Paul Goodman, Jerome Bruner, Nat Hentoff, Edgar Friedenberg, John Holt, Jules Henry, Marshal McLuhan, and George Leonard; before them, by Jean Piaget, Carl Rogers, Earl Kelley, Norbert Wiener, Ashley Montague, Aldous Huxley, and A. S. Neill; and before them, by W. H. Kilpatrick, Maria Montessori, John Dewey, A. N. Whitehead, et. al. In other words, the problem is not entirely new, but it grows more serious every day especially since so many people seem unaware of it (that is, act as if it doesn't exist).

The fundamental nature of the problem can be expressed in one word—change. All other "revolutions" we are undergoing are subordinate to the "change revolution." In order to sense the dimensions of this revolution, consider the situation of communications technology in the following way: Imagine a clock face with 60 minutes on it. Let the clock stand for the time men have had access to writing systems. The clock would thus represent something like 3,000 years, and each minute on the clock, fifty years. On this scale, there were no significant communication or technological changes until about nine minutes ago. At that time, the printing press came into use in Western culture. About three minutes ago, the telegraph, photograph, amd locomotive arrived. Two minutes ago: the telephone, rotary press, motion pictures, automobile, airplane, and radio. One minute ago, the talking picture. Television has appeared in the last ten seconds, the computer in the last five, and communication satellites in the last second. The laser beam appeared only a fraction of a second ago.

It would be possible to place almost any area of life on our clock face and get roughly the same measurements. For example, in medicine, you would have almost no significant changes until about one minute ago. Until a minute ago, as Jerome Frank has said, almost the whole history of medicine is the history of the placebo effect. Within the last thirty seconds, there have been more changes in medicine than is represented by all the rest of the time on our clock. This is what some people call the "knowledge explosion." It is happening in every field, and it's not going to stop.

The standard reply to comments about change is that change isn't new and that it is easy to exaggerate its meaning. To such replies, Norbert Wiener had a useful answer: the difference between a fatal and therapeutic dose of strychnine is "only a matter of degree." In other words, change isn't new; what is new is the *degree of change*. As the clock metaphor is intended to suggest, about 3 minutes ago, there developed a qualitative difference in the character of change. CHANGE CHANGED. The human situation is thus totally different from anything we have known before.

In the face of this situation, our schools have been almost totally paralyzed. A phrase sometimes used to describe paralysis induced by too much and too rapid change is "future shock," and our schools have got it bad. Among other fixations that prevent our schools from dealing with the change revolution is a venerable assumption that a major function of the schools is to transmit knowledge. This assumption is now not only irrelevant but actually harmful, and has been for at least 25 years. If you are over 20 years of age, the mathematics you were taught in school is "old"; the grammar you were taught is obsolete and in disrepute; the biology, completely out of date; the physics, a joke; and the history, open to serious question. The best that can be said of you, assuming that you remember what you were told and that you still rely upon it, is that you are a walking encyclopedia of out-dated information. Moreover, this is exactly what will become of the children who are presently in school. Most of the information now being transmitted to them will be out of date within ten years. The rate of information change is actually accelerating, and the process will not stop. We may have to face a situation soon whereby information change will occur so rapidly that knowledge transmitted before the Christmas holidays will be obsolete by summer vacation.

If you think I am exaggerating the problem, consider the case of what are called "subjects" in school. In elementary and secondary schools, even colleges, the subjects that are taught are roughly the same as those that were taught 50 years ago. And yet today (1969), there are at an absolute minimum 100 subjects that did not exist (at least in a developed form) 50 years ago, and which are arbitrarily excluded from school curricula. Why, for instance, is history taught? Why not archaeology, linguistic philosophy, psychology, anthropology? Why is geography taught? Why not demography, comparative linguistics, sociology, cybernetics, exo-biology? Why is English taught? Why not natural ecology, comparative symbology, futurology, semantics, cinematography, comparative theology, symbolic logic?

Even if the schools began to add such subjects and subtract others, the problem would not go away. The proliferation of new subjects and the rot of old ones is so persistent that a curriculum will always be out of date as long as the schools take as a major objective the transmission of a specific body of knowledge. Such an objective, however useful it may have been in the past, is now a formidable obstacle to any intelligent confrontation with the future. It creates the illusion of knowledge stability. It fixes people to ideas, constructs, and information whose life expectancy is far shorter than people's. This is extremely dangerous. "What you don't know can kill you," is an important slogan, but even more important is Josh Billings's line that the world is plagued not so much by what we don't know but what we know that ain't so.

Not only is the information which comprises a subject changing at an unprecedented rate, but the concept of a "subject" itself is shifting. A major characteristic of the knowledge explosion is the interconnectedness of knowledge. Biology and chemistry become bio-chemistry, which is joined to mathematics to become mathematical-bio-chemistry. Sociology and psychology make Social Psychology. Psychology, Linguistics, and Cybernetics make Psycho-cybernetic-linguistics. And so on. Knowledge is fluid and integrated but a "curriculum" is a rigid and segregated metaphor. Knowledge is changing and tentative but subjects are fixed and absolute. The schools are stuck on the horns of their own decrepid assumptions: their idea of what to do with a subject is old, and their idea of what to do with a student is old. Which leads to another set of assumptions presently preventing the schools from making a useful contribution to the well-being of their students: The schools have been and are presently committed to teaching certain skills—mostly the

3 R's. But changes in communications media, industrial technology, and in the structure of our political, social, and economic lives require new skills, new competencies, new patterns of behavior, none of which the schools, at present have much interest in. For example, reading and writing are still important skills, but not any more important than the listening, seeing, photographing, editing, speaking, recording skills demanded by television film, radio, tape recorders, LP records, etc. At present, the schools approach the teaching of communication skills as if the electric plug did not exist. The fetish about teaching children to read (e.g., *The New York Times* actually prints the reading scores of children throughout the city) is an excellent illustration of what is meant by future shock. Just at that point in communications history when reading has less importance than it has had for five hundred years, the schools have organized themselves for a full-scale attack on reading disabilities. In other words, the schools are just about 100 years late, and give no indication that they are even aware of it.

There is comparable future shock in the school's approach to intellectual competencies. At present, the only intellectual skill the schools genuinely value is memorizing and the student behavior most demanded is *answer-giving*. This, just at that point in technological history when electronic information storage and retrieval systems render human recollection behavior extraneous. Socrates feared that the written word would diminish the need to memorize. He was right. The computer diminishes the need further by a logarithm of about 10. The future does not require people who do badly what machines do well. And yet the typical classroom in America (in suburbia as well as the ghettos) is organized so that children will learn to playback a low definition version of what someone tells them. If you can remember 65% of what you were told, you pass. An exaggeration? Is there anyone reading this who knows of a school anywhere that provides sustained and systematic instruction in *question-asking?* I seriously doubt it. Schools are simply not designed to help children learn how to ask questions (the source of all knowledge) or, in fact, competently perform any intellectual operations (observing, inference-making, generalizing, verifying, etc.) that go beyond ventriloquizing (giving someone else's answers to someone else's questions). There are several reasons for this, not the least of which is that schools try very hard to train children to be obedient functionaries in a hierarchical economic system. A great deal has already been written on how children are grouped, graded, and otherwise "processed" in preparation for their tranquil entry into our economy. Public service television commercials which urge children to stay in school so that they might earn more money in the future give the whole game away. There is no other reason that would make sense to a child—given what he already knows about school. Nonetheless, it is somewhat grotesque that most school environments are so blatantly modeled after the working conditions of mass production industries: 5 day week, 7 hour day, 1 hour lunch, careful division of labor for both teachers and students, a high premium on conformity and a corresponding suspicion of originality (or any deviant behavior), and the administration's concern for product rather than process. Here, one needs only to add that of all the assumptions on which present school procedures are based, there is none more questionable than that which says that the future requires children who are responsive to authority, who are unable to ask their own questions, and who do not know how to find their own answers.

Which leads to still one more set of assumptions keeping schools from a satisfactory meeting with the future. I have already alluded to the obsolete conception of knowledge which guides the schools. To this, must now be added the fact that for most school people "self-knowledge" is considered neither reputable nor worthwhile. There are pitifully few curricula anywhere in the country which include any serious attempt to have students learn something about themselves. Inquiries in student self-awareness when they occur at all, occur as extracurricular enterprises. Attempts by students to inject their personal feelings into a lesson are uniformly considered intrusions. By "knowledge," our schools mean awareness of things outside one's skin. What is going on inside one's skin is not considered worthy of systematic or even haphazard study—to be referred to a guidance counselor or a friendly coach. Considering the fact that more Americans are hospitalized for mental illness than all other illnesses combined, that suicide is the second most common cause of death among adolescents, and that the most common cause of infant mortality in our country is parental beating, the exclusion of self-knowledge from the epistemology of the schools is intolerable.

The 21st century is only 31 years away and the schools are not as yet concerned to teach children how to think, how to master electronic media, how to deal with rapidly changing knowledge, how to produce knowledge, how to give direction to their own education, how to understand themselves.

I will not, therefore, discuss any procedures which use modern technology as a means of perpetuating the obsolete assumptions and structures of most school systems. Instead, I will describe a "school" program which will reflect my answers to the following questions: What should kids be doing in "school" today and in the years ahead? What should be the characteristics of such a "school"? What role can technology play in that environment?

The following quotations from *Walden* expresses compactly the major beliefs which generate the form of the program I will describe:

> Students should not play life, or study it merely, while the community supports them at this expensive game, but earnestly live it from beginning to end. How could youths better learn to live then by at once trying the experiment of living?

In other words, I am assuming (1) that learning takes place best not when conceived as a preparation for life but when it occurs in the context of actually living, (2) that each learner ultimately must organize his own learning in his own way, (3) that "problems" rather than "subjects" are a more realistic structure by which to organize learning experiences, (4) that students are capable of directly and authentically participating in the intellectual and social life of their community, (5) that they should do so, (6) that the community badly needs them, and (7) that in order to do so effectively, students need to have skillful access to all forms of communications technology. (This set of beliefs is sometimes referred to as the "judo" principle of education. Instead of trying to forestall, resist, or neutralize the natural curiosity, intelligence, energy, and idealism of youth, one *uses* it in a context which permits both them and their community to change.) Thus, the program I am talking about abandons the metaphor of "subjects" altogether; it reduces the reliance on classrooms and school buildings; it transforms the relevant problems of the community into the students' "curriculum," and (as you will see) puts "media literacy" at the center of the learning experience.

Let us assume that the students attending our "school" live in a fairly large city. We can be sure, then, that their community has serious problems with traffic control, crime and law enforcement, strikes, race relations, urban blight, drug addiction, garbage disposal, air pollution, medical care, etc. The students would be formed into teams, each team consisting of a teacher, a high school senior, perhaps a lay member of the community, and ten or a dozen students. Their task would be to select one of these problems for study, with a view toward designing authentic, practical solutions to it. They would do whatever they needed to do in order to learn about the problem (including previous attempts to solve it) and to communicate to others their own solutions. For example, imagine one team has selected the "crime" problem for study. Some students could spend two or three weeks at the police station serving in a capacity that would allow them to observe the problem from the perspective of the police. (Some might even go out on calls with police officers.) Others might report regularly to the criminal court, observing the problem from that vantage point. Students could spend many days on interviewing assignments: insurance men, police officers from other towns, ex-convicts, prison wardens, merchants, town officials, et al. Students could review the available literature (both non-fiction and fiction), correspond with prisoners, write to law enforcement officers in other countries. The classroom would be used, among other things, as a place of assembly when students need to assess their findings, and to plan and organize additional inquiries. It is important to stress here that the activities described above do not constitute "field trips." Most of the students' "school life" would be spent outside the school where the realities of the problems being studied are to be found. However, included in the process must be a serious attempt to offer solutions and to communicate these to the appropriate people. This might require meeting in school for the purpose of writing resolutions, letters, pamphlets, handbills, etc. Or the students might wish to publish a newsletter about the problem, or produce an audiotape for broadcasting on the local radio station (in which case some students might spend a week or two at the radio station), or prepare a photographic exhibit, or produce a film for presentation to the town council. The possibilities are almost inexhaustible. (More on this in a moment.)

Much of the teacher's work would involve making arrangements for the students' daily and weekly activities, e.g., arranging with the police, the court, the radio station, the newspaper, etc. for the most beneficial "internship" experience. The nature and locale of the students' activities would depend on the problem they are studying. A study of medical care problems would lead students to hospitals, doctors' offices, homes for the aged, welfare agencies, etc. A study of race relations might lead them to the Chamber of Commerce, the courts, the newspaper office, churches, etc.

In brief, the major idea is that the community itself will become a laboratory for the inquiries of students. The classroom, in this context, is only one of many resources that the students might choose to use. But the "community as laboratory" experience would by no means be the entire "school" program. If you will look again at the kinds of problems the students would try to solve, you will see that all of them are essentially problems in communication, or, as I prefer to call it, Media Ecology. The most succinct statement of what Media Ecology is can be found in *The Human Use of Human Beings* by Norbert Wiener. Although Wiener does not use the term anywhere in his book (or anyplace else), his fundamental thesis is "that society can only be understood through a study of the messages and the communication facilities which belong to it . . ." In other words, Media Ecology is the study of the transaction among people, their messages, and their message systems. More particularly, Media Ecology studies how media of communication affect human perception, feeling, understanding, and value; and how our interaction with media facilitates or impedes our chances of developing liveable communities. The word *ecology* implies the study of environments: their structure, content, and impact on people. An environment, is, after all, a complex message system which regulates ways of feeling and behaving. It structures what we can see and say and, therefore, do. Sometimes, as in the case of a church, courtroom, business office, or classroom, the specifications are more often implicit and informal, half-concealed by our assumption that what we are dealing with are machines and nothing more. Media Ecology tries to make these specifications explicit. It tries to find out what roles media force us to play, how media structure what we are seeing, why media make us feel and act as we do.

As Wiener would say, you cannot understand the "crime" problem, or the race problem, or the drug problem, etc. unless you have some understanding of the messages and the communication facilities of the society. And so, if there would be anything that could be characterized as a "subject" in the program I am describing it would be "Media Ecology." One way of studying Media Ecology is through the activities I have already suggested; that is, the students go out into the community, identify problems, try to understand the causes of the problems, try to offer solutions, and, most important, attempt to communicate their solutions to others. In short, the community as laboratory. But another and complementary way is to use the school as laboratory—in this case, a media laboratory. I am thinking here of a school which is designed as a media laboratory. Such a school does not need many "rooms." It is equipped instead with a wide aray of 20th and 21st century media. These would include, for example, computers, motion picture cameras and projectors, television equipment, tape recorders, stereophonic equipment, photo-offset equipment, radio transmission facilities, photographic equipment, etc.

Each student would be required to work toward the acquisition of "multi-media literacy." The intention is not to train technicians, but to have the student learn some of the important technical problems of several media, so that he may have some understanding of their creative capabilities and limitations. Indeed, if the medium is the message (or, if the medium is even *sometimes* the message), the students will need to know, in practical terms, something about the structure of various media. The best way to learn this is to *do,* to work with, to produce something in a medium. This is exactly what would happen when the students returned from their "community-lab" and entered their "media-lab." They would learn about media by using them in a real context in an attempt to communicate real solutions to real problems to real people. I have already referred to the newsletters, the radio broadcasts, the films, the pamphlets, the photographic exhibits, etc., that would serve as links between the students and their community. Plays, TV documentaries, and public service commercials are other possibilities.

Included in "media literacy" must be a consideration of the problems of interpersonal communication: its structure, its effects, its limitations, its creative possibilities. In other words, in personal terms, one's language as well as one's body and entire metamessage mechanism are media of utmost importance. The psychology of interpersonal communication can be studied by requiring each student to be involved in one or more T-Group experiences. The purpose of such an experience is two-fold: first, to offer the student an opportunity to learn about, modify, and extend his own repertoire of communication techniques (verbal and non-verbal), and second, to provide students with a laboratory for the study of interpersonal communication. I need not elaborate on how crucial such matters are if students are going to identify, offer solutions to, and otherwise relate to the problems of the people in their own community.

What I have described so far is entirely feasible for children between the ages of 8 and 16. (There wouldn't be much point in putting children in "grades," and there *would* be much point in "mixing" children; that is, having each team consist of children of varying ages.) What I wish to describe now may be viewed, to use a horrible phrase, as "culminating experiences" for the students. (The only thing to be said in favor of that phrase is that it is preferable to "terminal experiences.") In any case, I am talking about children between the ages of 16 and 18, who have had considerable experience in studying the problems, messages, and message facilities of their community. These young people would be involved (for at least two years) in what may be called media criticism. This means that they will produce, write, direct, edit, broadcast, telecast, etc. regular commentary about media of communication. The students will, in effect, monitor the media environment, addressing themselves to their community and possibly their own region of the country.

The students would produce a bi-weekly television program (taped in their own media-lab and aired on their local television station), a weekly radio program (taped in their own lab and aired on a local radio station), a weekly newsletter, possibly even a monthly magazine. Their object is to initiate and sustain a serious, informed dialogue with their community on the interaction between human beings and their communications technology. The departure point is media as environments (Media Ecology); that is, the effects of the structure and content of media on human perception, value, and understanding. Of paramount concern is the language environment itself—the uses and misuses of language, especially via the mass media. Here are some specific possibilities:

1. Review of the press, for which the students might take as their models the work of A. J. Liebling or Nat Hentoff. They would address themselves to such immediate and long-range questions as, How have newspapers dealt with important stories of the week? How do newspapers decide what is an "important" story? What are the

biases of different newspapers? What are their strengths? Who are the most reliable reporters? etc. An adjunct activity would be correspondence with individual news reporters and editorialists. Each student will correspond regularly with one news reporter, including radio and TV men, on the quality of his work during a specified period of time. (Before he died Albert Camus proposed that such a monitoring of the press be done. He would have been delighted to know that young students will assume this task.)

2. Criticism of print and electronic advertising, in which the agencies producing various advertisements will be regularly examined and evaluated, along with the aesthetic and social value of their work. (Good example: Currently, Phillips 66 is running a commercial which claims that some chemical which is put in their gasoline actually contributes toward reducing air pollution. This is not only untrue, but dangerously untrue. The students could form a special Science and Technology Committee whose function would be to check on suspicious claims made via the media by various advertisers.)

3. Criticism of radio and television programs, in which among other things, "ordinary" people (including students of all ages) are given the opportunity to express their opinions about network programming. One special feature might be the Weekly Murder Index, wherein an account is kept of the number and type of murders (and other brutalities) depicted weekly on network TV. Of a more positive nature, the criticism might attempt to make explicit the standards that might fairly be used to evaluate television and radio programs. (For this activity, it is almost certain that young people will be more perceptive than adults. Print-oriented adults—for example, most teachers —are largely inept in their attempts to evaluate electronically produced literature.)

4. Recording the Language Pollution Index, wherein students keep track of the important public utterances of the week, with a view toward calling attention to the best and especially the worst of (i.e., deceptive, illogical, oversimplified, vague, etc.) the use of language by public figures. With the increased outpouring of language through the mass media, it is essential that some check be made on the quality and direction of our semantic environment.

5. Description and analysis of the economic facts of the communications industry, by which the public is kept informed of the financial structure of various media of communication: Who owns the TV and radio stations in town? the newspaper? the movie theatres? What financial stakes do these men have in the development of the community? For example, in cable television, pay television, ETV? What is the role of unions in these media? etc.

Other subjects to be dealt with are:

Informing the public about relevant government hearings and legislation dealing with media and technology,

Informing the public of the substance of major professional conferences and meetings dealing with media and technology, and most important,

Informing the public about new technology and the effects they are likely to have on the structure of society. Here is an invaluable contribution since there is at present virtually no public dialogue on the proliferation of new technology nor of its possibilities for good or evil. Below are several questions (some requiring historical knowledge, others requiring highly speculative imaginations) that might be dealt with by the students:

What specific effects are television, film LP record, transistor radio, etc. having on youth? To what extent are such media-environments responsible for the "generation gap"? for student rebellion? for the search for "self" through drugs? What kinds of revolutions, if any, does electric circuitry provoke? Are books obsolete? If so, when will we find out? If not, what useful purposes will they serve? Why, indeed, can't Johnny read? Will he ever? Why should he? What are the long-range effects of the information explosion? Is it destroying hierarchies? organized religion? the industrial state? Who is programming the computers? What should computers be used for? What are they likely to use us for? Who should be forbidden to use them? What uses shall we make of bugging devices? of the television-telephone? What is technology doing to the concept of "privacy"? Will the electric car save our cities? At what cost? Are cities obsolete? Have big media "repealed" the Bill of Rights? Have they made politics an offshoot of show business? If so, what should we do about it? What new kinds of politics will we require? (To answer this last question, the student might convene a Constitutional Convention to which they would invite all interested parties from the community. Who knows? There might develop from this some highly practical guidelines for legislators to use in future attempts to modify our present Constitution.) What will our new literary forms be like? Of what use will "tradition" be? To what extent is technology remaking our language? etc., etc.

The purposes of the student's activities here are these:

1. The students will learn how to conduct responsible media criticism and will become, hopefully the nucleus of a cadre of media critics absolutely needed if our society is to deal rationally with present and future problems.

2. Our students will develop models of and standards for media criticism where presently very few exist.

3. The "school" would serve the community by becoming a major resource and focus for discussions of the impact of communications technology on society.

One more feature of our school program needs to be mentioned. Arrangements will have to be made for each of the students to serve as an "intern" (probably for a period of several weeks) to at least two different practitioners of the communication arts. The student will function as an "assistant" or in whatever capacity will offer the best opportunity for him to observe the inner workings of a medium of communication. The purpose here is to give the student a direct sense of what the media look like from the inside. Our students will "intern" with film directors, book publishers, newspaper and magazine editors, television, radio, and record producers, advertising executives, et al.

To conclude this memorandum, I want to acknowledge that, from one point of view, my proposals are irrelevant. If one is primarily interested in maintaining the present structure, function, and epistemology of the schools, then I have not answered the question put to me by the Commission. I am, of course, not interested in preserving any of it, and in fact believe that it is exceedingly dangerous to do so. Given that bias, I perceive the question put by the Commission in an entirely different context, and I sincerely hope the Commission will find my answers useful.

47.

The Technics and Techniques
Of Educational Technology

by WILBUR RIPPY
Instructor
Bank Street College
New York City

Technology is the rationale, the theory, the conceptual "surround" of both techniques and technics. Techniques are the ways we implement technology. Technics are the tools, machines, programs we use to implement technology.

The technology of mass education is presently unequal to the tasks imposed upon it. This primarily because it has absorbed the conservative, traditional postures of education. Onto this shaky technological structure created primarily to meet the needs, myths, values of an industrial age, we attempt to overlay "innovative" technics or techniques.

We see how fruitless a task this often is as we have watched innovations whether technic or technique: the new math, audiovisual materials, team teaching, individualized reading programs become absorbed, transformed, and modified in such substantial ways that we no longer recognize them as distinct entities. From this we deduce a simple fact. When an institution built on tradition, set in conserving its own structural integrity, encounters an innovative technique or technic it simply, easily, unhurriedly incorporates it and then transforms it into something other than what was intended. Still we live in a period of history in which technology itself effects changes in the society at large which in turn effect the schools. Thus the structure of schooling no longer holds together. This makes possible the consideration of technics, and techniques.

Both teachers, parents and students are undergoing transformations of a significant nature. It is not as if a new race is being created. It is more than a shift, a dislocation of energy, sensibilities, values has occurred. Curiously enough this seemed to have happened without our being fully aware of it. It is as though we were asleep and only now three months after the fact dimly begin to realise that impregnation has taken place.

And despite the apparent societal symptoms that indicate new winds are blowing some of us refuse to button our coats while others defying the elements rush out with umbrellas which we brandish about even as they are stripped bare by the winds.

We can only surmise what is happening. The following paper assumes:

There has been a shift in sensibilities particularly in the young. When this shift directly affects learning it is discussed within the paper.

There are technics and techniques which will serve and enhance the development of these sensibilities.

These technics and techniques center around materials, programs, presentations, which invite student participation on much broader levels than previously conceived and which redefine learning-teaching in such a way that self-corrective materials become focal to the educative process.

Participation redefines teacher-student relationships and redefines the nature of education. We begin by examining a specific technic and technique.

The Sullivan Programmed Reading Materials were used by the writer in an inter-age, non-graded, "free" school. Some of the findings which are useful in viewing any programmed material are as follows:

1. The materials were used by the children as a "cool media." By filling in responses, by exterpolating from the individual frames of the program, by using the workbook as a drawing board, they transformed it into a highly individualized, "idiosyncratic" material.

2. In most instances, reading skills were quickly advanced. Competency and increased skill emerged as a more important motivational factor *than did the content of the text*. Nothing succeeds like success. The assumption that content of the reader determines student's attitudes seems to be unfounded. Content relevance—in the early grades, soon disappears as motivational factor in advancing reading *unless skill is also advanced*. This is the rock upon which individualized reading programs flounder. Remediation at later grade levels requires both content and relevance and skill advancement. This is particularly so when neither have been present in previous reading programs. Hopefully, we will eventually be able to program *relevant content* which will advance skills economically in terms of time and energy of student and teacher. Pleasure will then act as reinforcement on two levels, content and advancement of skill.

3. Increased and pleasurable attainment of skills led the students to a creative use of language arts skills. The camera, spirit duplicator, tape recorder used simultaneously with the programmed materials resulted in maximum infusion of basic long-range goals of any relevant reading program, namely the effective, creative use of written and spoken word to record and communicate experience.

4. The programmed materials were not used in this situation as suggested by the author of the program in the teacher's manual. Less time was given to various drills and didactic lessons than suggested. Furthermore, it was found that some children moved back and forth from the Sullivan Materials to other reading programs available in the classroom, specifically the Stern materials, The Bank Street Reader, and the Merill series, or to individualized reading of literature or the creation of their own readers, cartoons, stories.

5. In some instances, the programmed materials did not seem to meet specific children's needs. Other instructional materials were used either side by side or separately from programmed materials. Programmed materials were thus only one part of the total reading program. It is interesting to note that research indicates children learn whether or not they write in the response assumed as integral part of the program.

6. Despite the acknowledged effectiveness of the Sullivan Materials, the teacher's sensibilities still respond to its content as vulgar. Vulgarity of kind is a quality most children enjoy. As disclaimer, it should be noted that most children seem moved into creating or reading literature with appreciable aesthetic merit.

7. There is no available research data known to the writer that helped him determine which child would make maximum use of programmed materials. Intuition, careful observation were helpful but inefficient.

Programmed texts and materials particularly in curriculum subjects other than reading, mathematics, science, social studies, rely on reading abilities that cannot be assumed at any particular grade level. Thus the use of programmed materials in these areas reinforce the erroneous notion that one cannot be a student, a learner, unless one is skilled in reading. We know from biography and autobiography of unusually talented inventive persons that this is a prejudice. Since programmed materials in various curriculum areas assume skills not yet attained by the intelligent, but non-reading student, they are ineffective as a method of individualizing instruction, for all but the student who has attained reasonable reading abilities.

This is a crucial area of instruction. For by creating programmed materials using ideograms, pictographs, or symbolic representations other than the written work, by programming with records and tape recorders the instructions of a program, learning and competency could be reinforced in specific curriculum areas. This would eventually affect the student's reading ability. No longer forced to define himself as an incompetent, simply because he had not as yet learned to read, he could regain confidence in his own potential.

Furthermore, he could enter the process of education in ways now foreclosed to him by the teacher's definition of the "good" student as one who reads by the ends of the first, second or third year. Schools might with the use of relevant programmed materials indeed become relevant.

Programmed materials are self-corrective materials. They engage the student. Interaction with the content or skill is essential. Still one only has to think of any subject that is distasteful to realize the limitations even when content is effectively conveyed by a program or teacher.

A self-corrective material need not be programmed. A piece of drawing paper determines limits by the extremities of its sides. It "self-corrects" the impulse of student to exceed the reasonable enclosure offered by it. Graffiti are self-corrective in the sense that they correct rigid correction of self-expression.

The Dienes Multi-Base Blocks, the Attribute Blocks, the Geo-board and the jigsaw puzzle all contain answers within the confines of rules as set by the proper use of the material.

The Cusinaire rods ask questions. Are a purple and yellow rod when placed end to end equivalent to a red and a white and yellow rod? Algorisms can be discovered as well as specific number facts.

The child's use of a self-corrective material depends to an extent on whether confidence, autonomy, curiosity have been sustained in his own character structure. The child can reinvent the wheel in the classroom in mathematical terms—but he is not obliged to do so with a flint stone hammer. With the use of specific technics such as the Cusinaire rods an economic time compaction is possible. As one child expressed it as he looked at the problem he has set and answered: "It used to be in the olden days that two add two equals four. Now one add one add two or two add one add one, or one add one add one add one or three add one or one add three equals four. Look I proved it!"

The pervasive use of such materials would free the teacher to do his essential task; namely to suggest the next problem when the child does not foresee the outcome of his activity and to help the individual student use the self-corrective material with maximal economy.

The deterrents to the widespread use of such materials are similar to those of any programmed materials:

Teachers are threatened by open-ended questions that do not follow the rigid sequence which they associate with proper teaching methods.

The teacher's fear that by freeing himself to become an individual teacher he will unleash a classroom of individual students which he will then no longer be able to control.

Authority is invested in the child and in materials as well as the teacher, thereby threatening status.

Notwithstanding the intrinsic propensities of programmed materials allowing each student to proceed at his own pace, Komoski has pointed out after the initial trial: "All too frequently in the end, the traditional class structure, its group logistics, and its time schedules win out over the new requirements of the new technology." [1]

Succinctly stated, teachers continue to reassert their role as master programmer.

Master programmers are generally identifiable by an absence of self-corrective programmed materials in the classroom. Master programmers program by maintaining complete control over the total curriculum. The shift in sensibilities, in proprieties, meets an obstruction of age and time.

Implicit in a self-corrective material as a functional part of the material is a built-in self-discipline. Self-discipline transfers discipline from the teacher as source of sensible behavior to the child's sense of what is proper. Propriety is demonstrated when we straighten an askew picture on a wall or when a child sharpens a blunted pencil. Or when we as teacher refrain from excessive verbiage. Or when a child remarks: "Why do you always ask about my painting? Don't you trust me? Why are you so greedy that you have to know everything?"

Common games which give pleasure have built-in disciplines. In "hide-and-seek" the rule is to remain silent for inordinate amounts of time. In schools there is a similar rule. In "hide-and-seek" the rule is functional, it advances the game. In schooling, the rule is non-functional; it advances the teacher's narrowly defined role of the "good" student. In the former game one has a good chance of being *"it."* In the latter game one has a good chance of becoming insensate. This to the extent that one succeeds in the game.

Techniques such as Viola Spolin's *Improvisation For The Theater* are exercises in self-discipline for the discipline is contained in the nature of the game problem. The "point of concentration" is whether the players effectively convey their chosen message to the audience by *showing* rather than telling. The game cannot continue without respect for the rule implicit in the game.

"The problem-solving techniques used in the workshop (game theater workshop) gives mutual objective focus to teacher and student. In its simplest terms it is *giving problems to solve problems.*" [2]

Game techniques are:

Multi-sensorial by virtue of games which use and expand the sense as the natural tools of objectifying the reality in which we are immersed.

Multi-disciplinarian by virtue of including games as communication, games that advance learning of self and other persons (role playing) games that define and elicit environments (social studies), games in which theories of maximal learning theory are made manifest, and finally by being the most effective method of teaching and learning dramatics.

The techniques suggested by Spolin have been furthered in relation to children and youth in the work of the Arena Theater, Washington, D.C. where game techniques have been used in public schools.

For the person unfamiliar with Improvisation Theater it is important to know that acting or dramatics as usually conceived has little to do with game theater. Memorizing scripts, increasing anxiety by placing persons on the stage separated from audience are the antithesis of game theater. Game theater is improvisation, a way of communicating between audience and participants and participants and audience. In game theater the audience is simultaneously participant.

Self-corrective materials, such as Game Theater, some programmed materials, art materials when not didactically imposed, all have four things in common. (1) They invite participation. (2) They allow and encourage the child to explore his own potential via the materials. (3) They are non-judgmental, non-argumentative. (4) Children enjoy them.

Both commercial and comics as media invite filling in. That this is not understood by educators indicates their own dependence on literality. Although television and comics are the most beloved educational experiences this culture offers to children they have limitations. Perhaps the greatest is that they are lonely activities. I will not here pursue the problems and potential of a genuine instructional television wherein the media is considered as an intrinsic part of the message, I do pause to point out that comic, commercial and television have reinforced filling in and participation as a style of learning for children in our culture today.

We need technics, techniques which invite participation, materials which invite specific responses and materials which invite open-ended responses. Workbooks in use in the primary grades invite participation—but they often foreclose it by linear sequential development of content which induces sleepiness. Reading-writing responsiveness can be advanced by use of blank spaces within the workbook for drawings, editorial comments by children (Ug! Wow! I liked this!) related or unrelated to the content of the workbook. More use should be made of the "balloon" and comic strip structure of the cartoon as indicated in the Greater Cleveland Reading Program, First Level (I.T.A.) materials. Whether the spectator arts of the industrial age are relevant to today's world is speculative. The immediate problem is that participatory arts have moved into the public domain. This movement is perhaps the most significant data allowing us to understand that a shift in sensibilities has occurred in the recent history of mankind.

Education would do well to join cause with the participatory arts in so far as they are expressions of rational human interaction response and communication.

Participatory arts have already made their inroads into schooling via specific technics. As Bruce Spalding, a ten year old participant in a film made by his peers put it: "I like acting. I like to *do* art. That's how I came into the films. It's not like art, but you can *make* art with movies." One of the films made by this group, Film No. 3, was about the filmmakers neighborhood. For reasons available to anyone who cares to think, the content did not follow concepts as set by social studies curriculum. The content followed the camera's eye. "The film showed streets, junk-strewn lots, cars, policemen (friendly) and rows of buildings. The sound had the youngsters telling about why they lived where they lived ('The kids aren't bad kids.' 'It's not a junkheap.') and discussion of how safe or dangerous it was to cross Webster Avenue."[3]

The difference between curriculum guides and the film are obvious. Curriculum guides tell us that "community helpers" clean the streets. The film showed junk-strewn streets. Curriculum guides tell us that our "friendly" policeman will help us across the street. The film tells us policemen are not always available when one needs them.

Thus film becomes a corrective device, correcting the banalization and the bowlderization of traditional curriculum content as designed by educators.

Indeed a highly educative exercise would be to have children film a neighborhood then compare the message of their film with the message of packaged audiovisual materials, or the message of books prepared for them by educators who have made certain assumptions about neighborhoods. A primary question might well be: Do generalizations serve the purpose of fantasy? A film verité done by students of some neighborhoods in New York City, including the junkies, pushers, prostitutes, pimps, the open sale of illegal goods, cops "cooping," and other such details familiar to the children who inhabit these neighborhoods but too frightening to the adults who presume to tell them about their neighborhood helpers could be helpful in establishing some reality.

A film on rats and cockroaches as a biological social reality entitled "Our Friendly Neighbors" would be informative and genuinely educative for those living outside these neighborhoods. For most impact this could be shown side by side with a film strip illustrating another favorite illusion of educators *Dick and Jane* as real people. A lively discussion analysis, evaluation would necessarily result from the presentation of such materials to students.

It is clear that participatory arts break down the rigid designation of the teacher and the taught. With engagement with participation the teacher may be either adult or child and either adult or child may be student. In other words a learning environment destructures rigid definitions of role in the participatory arts. Content is largely determined by what one knows through experience. A technique or technic such as filmmaking helps one explore the experience further, bring it to consciousness, and if desirable to communicate it effectively. Participants who filmed *The Jungle,* the 12th and Oxford Street Gang of North Philadelphia had no difficulty articulating their explanation about the content they had chosen: "We wanted to make it on the best thing we knew . . . and the best thing we knew was gang war." "We didn't want to make no Hollywood junk." "We didn't want to make that fantasy stuff."

While this has a refreshing ring of authenticity, we should know that gangs exist not only *in* fact but *as* facts which serve the illusions of the gang members, further that Hollywood's fantasies about gangs whether of the gangster, the cowboy, the soldier show us clearly where "it is at," namely power through physical violence as intrinsic to our culture. At the same time, cinema verité has the virtue of dispelling the illusion created in Hollywood that violence is aesthetic, i.e. that battlegrounds are "arranged" by decorators rather than bombs, that blood is similar to catsup, and that persons die while smiling bravely in the kleig lights or while puffing the last cigarette placed between their lips by their solemn companions.

Summed up, filmmaking in the hands of children and youngsters will increase knowledge only if it does nothing more than dispel illusions that prevent knowledge. We need not state it in such minimal terms. Filmmaking will: Increase the student's contact with reality. Engage him in a significant participatory art. Teach him a craft. Enhance his self confidence as he demonstrates his competence.

More critical is the definition of education *as* participation—for this is indeed what is being forced upon us.

Whereas mass media, movies, television, magazines-newspapers, direct themselves to an educated adult audience with the mentality of a ten to twelve year old, the participatory arts by unlocking symbolic representation, imagery, visual illiteracy and the processes of creative thinking provoke the sedentary, mentally enfeebled spectator to act rather than passively react.

The participatory arts are, we add, not addressed to the adult world of any age. Rock and roll, filmmaking, the underground press, the innovative theater subvert, even in the act of addressing themselves to the young. This forces a redefinition of who is important, who makes decisions, and finally elicits a reexamination of authority based on a dominant-submissive pattern determined by status *or* ability.

Before considering other technics and techniques that fulfill the requirements of participatory learning we might consider the imbalance between the rhetoric of educators regarding audiovisual materials and the practice of educators in the schools. Most reasonable intelligent educators will acknowledge that we learn with all our senses, that the eye focused on print and teacher, the ear listening to the voice of teacher is not necessarily the best use of the multi-sensorial learning organism with which we are endowed.

Most educators will then agree since learning is multi-sensorial we can use audiovisual materials to motivate and sustain flagging of teacher and student.

Most educators would agree that audio materials can be used to provide information, sustain interest, bolster motivation and relieve boredom.

The question given this rhetoric becomes why are audiovisual materials used primarily to give data which the reasonably effective teacher could give anyway and/or at least to furnish a momentary diversion from business as usual i.e., the inculcation of boredom.

The answer is not difficult to find. In fact educators do not believe no matter what they say that we learn through our senses. As one result of a misconception of their own misguided education they believe we learn from the *telling* that takes place when a student encounters a text book or a teacher. Believing this, but put upon by the educational theorists with fancy notions about multi-sensorial, multimedia, the teacher simply invests the machinery, the audiovisual materials with the properties he so assiduously cultivates out of the student's behavior. In other words he doesn't help the student to hear more, or see more, or move more, or taste, touch or feel more.

Instead a machine is moved into the classroom which will, by virtue of its "program," already decided what is to be seen, touched, smelled, felt, examined. Thus an unending series of trivia on any subject imaginable. Far from shaking up thinking and liberating the senses the student is besieged by a new form of idiocy which may momentarily titillate—after all any diversion is welcome in a sea of platitudinous irrelevancies—but will ultimately be incorporated as another bit of grain on the sandstone that erodes his spirits.

It follows that audiovisual materials are not generally used to revamp the way in which we see and hear. It is the thing furthest from an educator's mind that the students be helped to listen and see as well as hear and look, that audiovisual materials be used as media to increase rather than decrease visual and aural literacy.

That media could be used to educate the young in innovative patterns is imminently feasible but this would require substantial shifts in the traditional energy economy of the classroom.

Existing structures, by which we mean the energetic relationships which determine the form of the given organism or institution, accommodate and absorb, transform and modify, (1) technology as the theoretical extensions of man's mind, (2) technics as the tools which follow from those extensions, and (3) techniques as the procedural implementations of the technology.

The lesson would seem to be clear. If innovative technics, and techniques are to be practised in the school we must place these tools and skills directly in the hands of the students. Teachers must be trained not only in how to use audiovisual materials as how to insure that these materials are in fact used by the students. This might best be done by using older students as media specialists. Schools might train students in specific areas of curricula.

Specific programs available for immediate implementation in the school around high success-competency areas of communication are presently in operation. These need further rationale and implementation.

These can be discussed from the point of view of the technique required. The techniques suggested here are the camera, the tape recorder, and the spirit duplicator. All of the techniques have overlapping functions and for maximum reinforcement should be freely available to children in the primary grades. By freely available, I mean they should be used by children without, as well as with adult supervision. The projects assume that it is the children who photograph, record, print using specific technics as tools. A further assumption is that from work of this kind many different unique project dissimilar in kind but similar in intent and purpose will emerge within the context of a given classroom. The author has worked with these materials in a school setting and has found this approach extremely feasible.

These techniques are ways by which man can record and communicate. Used effectively, they become important tools of communication and recording. This is not to demean the written word. In fact, such techniques used effectively include the written word: the recording of a song, the duplication of a child's story, the photograph of a street sign. They reinforce communication which is the larger category under which we include: reading, writing, mapping, movie and still film, tape recorders, phonograph records, dance, music, and the applied and fine arts.

The tape recorder reinforces aural literacy. The camera and the spirit duplicator reinforce visual literacy. Visual illiteracy is an indigenous part of a culture overemphasizing print as *the* method of communication. The verbal and printed word assume absurd proportions only when man erects a myth of an assumed rationalism as defined by verbal sequence.

Visual illiteracy takes the form of our looking but not seeing. Aural illiteracy takes the form of hearing but not listening.

Visual illiteracy is reinforced by the ugliness of a man-made environment designed with machines rather than human beings in mind. Part of our not seeing is defensive. We have to protect ourselves against overwhelming ugliness and disorder. We reenact the legend of Perseus who when slaying Medusa looked into the mirrored surface of his shield in order not to be slain by her ugliness. We will learn to bear both the beauty and the ugliness around us by interposing a technique, the camera between ourselves and reality in order to gradually reestablish contact with reality.

Each technique mentioned above has a specific way of enclosing the field. This for simplification, we will call framing. Framing requires both cognitive and visual skills of a high order. To frame is to categorize, to select, to set priorities.

Miss Susan Wood working with children at the Henry Street Settlement in New York City, explored the following themes with rhetorically disadvantaged children: Dominant Color, Color Moods, Congruous and Incongruous Shapes, Dynamic and Static Lines, Macrocosm-Microcosm. The disciplines of attention, concentration, patterning, composition are implicit in the work. The photographs taken by the children are records of effective teaching and multi-disciplinary learning.

The camera records the environment with a detached lens. Its objectivity allows us to record subjective statement about reality. Subjective statements are none the less truthful for being personal and relevant. We do not have a commonly accepted vocabulary for such obvious phenomena as: sensations, body movements are the indispensable tools of the scientist. This because we elevate mind and degrade body. Puritanism continues to express itself in sensorial deprivation.

A program direction toward visual literacy and conceptual framing might include the following activities.

Register the most common objects as seen through the camera's eye: overflowing garbage piles, grafitti (as personal-social-folk media), oil slicks on streets after rain, geometrical man-made shapes, grids, bricks, cement blocks, building as cubes; windows, doors, pavement markings as rectangles, chewing gum stains on sidewalks, manholes, lamp posts, telephone poles as circles, globes, and columns; the parallel lines of railings, fences and building forms.

Map a neighborhood, assuming that a worm had a camera, then a dog, then a child, then an adult, then a bird. Map the people in the community with the cameral documentation, map the environment separately. Then place the two into correct juxtaposition.

Observe the camera asking different facts on different streets. Let the photographs ask the questions. Try to answer the questions by using the resources within and outside the school. Ask "old timers" or the corner candy store man why a building is vacant or what once occupied a now vacant space. Record the dialogue with the camera and the tape recorder. Record oneself recording.

Record objects. What do the identifiable "artifacts" tell us about a specific culture (community). Record broken wine bottles, refuse in the streets, a street cleaner at work. Send a letter to the sanitation department asking questions presented by the data.

As the data is collected, place it in easily retrievable categories. Let the categories shift as dictated by the data. Set up a cross reference system. Learn how to research with a camera and tape recorder. Prepare visual displays thereby learning how to communicate with economy, that is without being boring or redundant or imposing superficiality upon experience.

We will begin to see without the camera. The "ah, yes" recognition infiltrates consciousness when an idea, an object, a vision, a sound is placed within a meaningful conceptual structure. We induce the pleasure of learning by engaging in pleasurable learning.

There is no need to establish identity by placing mirrors in kindergartens or taking pictures of ourselves. Identity is established by engaging in significant work. Significant work is work which uses and increases skills in a demonstrable way.

The children create studies rather than study studies.

A program directed toward aural literacy might include the following activities.

Record with the tape recorder the sounds surrounding the photographs. At random select tape and photograph and determine whether they are congruous.

Listen for the sounds on the tape which one did not hear at the time of recording. The airplane overhead, the vague rumbling of the subway, the particular quality of voices, movements. Sounds of machines. Sounds of animals including people.

Use the tape recorder as media. "Bend" it to include a library of sounds: crunchy sounds, scary sounds, mechanical sounds. Overlay sounds by using several tape recorders simultaneously; one or two with prerecorded sounds.

Build a library of tapes. Record discussions. Record the sounds of animals in the zoo and cross reference the sounds with the photographs and the books, pamphlets, cards obtained at the zoo or through the library. Record the dialogue with keepers, zoologist, visitors. Record recorded information available at the zoo.

Record parts or all of manned space flights. Reenact these in informal dramatics using the tape as a script. Record imaginary adventures on distant planets. Check out fantasies by books in the classroom or obtained from the library about the planetary system in which we live.

"Frame" conversations and sounds by erasing, selecting, and categorizing.

Make the tape recorder available for recording the children's stories. Place these stories in the classroom library in tape and in written form.

The use of litmus paper to record acidity; the scarring of a tree by the insect who records its travel by reducing wood to another molecular structure; blueprint paper as a way of recording a three-dimensional structure two-dimensionally, can be examined as specific communication medias.

The technology of print can be explored via the potato print, silk screen, the hand press and the spirit duplicator.

A hand-operated, child-operated spirit duplicator is a functional component of a responsive educational environment. This because the duplicator duplicates, thereby affording communication on a wider scale. Given the choice of adding to the school library books in the often futile hope that they will inspire children or the buying of a machine with which the children can make their own books, one would do well to choose the latter. Books as used here, means anything from a folded paper with a picture inside to a collection of bound stories, dialogues, observations or studies.

In kindergarten, children should have the opportunity to place their drawings and speech (observations, dialogue, stories) on stencils.

The phases of learning to write may be described as follows:

Gross and subsequent fine motor movements. Signals.

Scribbling, drawings, paintings. Pictographs.

Symbolic representations of objects, including the alphabet. Ideographs.

Controlled use of the alphabet for form words, phrases, sentences. Alphabet.

Conscious selection of vocabulary, form and style to communicate feelings, ideas, experience. Literature.

All of these phases should be reinforced by recording and distribution of the recording via the spirit duplicator. We need to teach the importance of symbols as a way of communicating a message. From this, the recognition will emerge that the written word is a precise and economic method of communicating complex or simple ideas or feelings. Reading and writing then become intrinsically desirable from the child's point of view.

A primer typewriter should be available to children from kindergarten through third grade. The kindergarten-first grade child uses the typewriter to make calligraphic designs.

This brings awareness of graphics. The page will then be designed in terms of the spacial arrangement of the print. For reasons as yet unclear to the writer, the typewriter incites spacial exploration of the page when used freely by the five and six year old.

The children's language, whether story or dialogue, form the library. Communication through written spoken word when printed, assumes relevance by virtue of its spacial propensities. The printed word reinforces the child's self image as a constructing, competent person.

Science and the arts are not "objects" such as paintings, sculptures, magnets, batteries and bulbs. Science and arts are ways of looking and reacting with things clearly, relatedly, perceptively, sensitively until we know them subjectively in terms of how we feel about them and what they mean to us, and objectively in terms of what they are.

There is nothing mysterious about either science or art. Everyone who functions at all proceeds to make certain affective and/or rational decisions commensurate with scientific and artistic disciplines.

Specialization, the mystique of specialization allows us to believe that science and art are separate entities that belong only to genius.

The first step in freeing education from this mystique is to free the teachers to be truly objective and truly affective.

This is no small task, but then neither is teaching science and art under our present illusions. In fact the teaching of science and art have been in our culture a comprehensive failure. All they have managed to do is reinforce a separation of common man from the very forces intrinsic to his functional life, to make him think that art exists in a museum or a concert hall or resides in the body of an unkempt erratic person and that science exists in things such as computers, or rockets, or "electronics."

Science is a way of looking, examining, contacting things in such a way that we know them more completely than when we began to look at them. The Elementary Science Series work on similar premises. The difficulty again is that teachers think the science is inextricably bound in the subject i.e., mealworms, or balance, or bubbles.

Still to examine common objects is our only recourse. We need a science of common fixtures. Doorknobs, latches, switches, the valves on radiators, water and gas pipes done in plastic so we can see the action as it occurs. Models of things that show us how things work, that make simple yet mysterious things comprehensible.

We need simple explanations that follow upon constructive manipulative work with concrete, plaster of Paris, soap, wood, glues. Concrete for instance has changed the entire concept of enclosure by creating modular structures with blocks and sculptural structures with reinforcement. Concrete should be mixed, poured, reinforced, molded, shaped, textured by being formed in forms of cardboard or wood constructed or found within the classroom. Concretes with varying mixes of sand, cement and water should be tested for strength, for expansion, for durability.

The technology and techniques of glues have modified the work of the cabinet maker and carpenter. Plywood is a consequence of a durable bond. Glues should be tested, created, examined, questioned, used in the classroom. The technology and techniques of plastics should not wait for introduction into the classroom until industry has pre-empted the educational field.

Common objects and materials need examination and exploration. Phonographs can be taken apart, examined, explored, put back together. Motors of old phonographs taken out and used in the classroom for kinetic art shows. The tape recorder as technic de-structed and constructed within the classroom.

VITA (Volunteers for International Technical Assistance) has prepared handbooks (Village Technology Handbook) and catalogs (Village Technology Center Catalog) for making Technology available as a low cost locally developed means of village improvement. Schools are the under developed villages of our over developed cities.

To select a few of the many operable items from the catalog: solar water heater, sunlight projector, opaque projector, silk screen printing equipment, geletin duplicator, flashlight projection; wood lathe, grinding wheel, jigsaw—all powered by bicycle are exactly the kinds of things that when created in the classroom clarify the mystery of things by enhancing the everyday competency of students.

In the Handbook the use of raw materials, earth, sun, water for enclosure and power is clearly spelled out in specific technics.

Casein and fish glue, rubber cement can be made within the village (classroom).

The recipe for soap making would have been useful to the writer when he was teaching.

Parts of old machinery, television sets, war surplus, spare discards from electronic shops should be available in the classroom for examination and use as junk sculpture. Let the materials ask the questions. Let the questions be answered by exploration and resource personnel within and without the classroom.

Many parts of machines are beautiful, they should be seen as well as heard, examined, explored, not left to die a calendar death upon a shelf while we witness the spectacle as spectators.

The Technology, techniques, and technics of containers and enclosures should be carefully studied. Mumford points out that containers as carriers and storage may have been more important in man's development as technics than other more recognized tools.

Contemporary packaging, plastic "blisters," bags, styrofoam insulators, air in pneumatic houses, iron and bamboo "curtains" indicate the extensions of containers one might well consider. The concept that yolk and white are contained in a shell (egg) contained in a living organism (hen) contained in a factory (contempory "hen house') to be contained in plastic or cardboard which is contained in a store or home in refrigeration ultimately to be contained in breakfast food or cake and the human body are extensions of containers and worthy of consideration.

All the above could be implemented in some honest way in classrooms from first to twelfth grade. The structure of such learning would be the knowledge that we live in a "world," in a world made for man by man. This is to begin to know the man made world, to live in it as participant.

We will know our environment our total cosmic environment when we feel familiar with the things and the relationship of things within it.

Earth Works, a show of sculptured landscapes at the Dwan Gallery in New York City, Fall, 1968 indicates that art is moving out into the environment. We live on, over, and within environment—the earth whose earth works are easily framed by the window of a jet traveling at 20,000 feet and whose archetypal patterns and basic structure and design can be immediately apprehended by anyone who has carefully recorded in their memory bank the shapes, movements, and structure of micro-organisms with the aid of the microscope. The airplane as framing, aesthetic media has yet to be fully explored.

Consider some aspects of the classroom without walls, the world as a learning center. Since the average American moves rapidly in grand demographic shifts, transportation becomes as increasingly prevalant educational media. Education will necessarily take on the task of teaching the traveler to observe. What one sees is significant. Here I refer to land formations, population clusters, natural resources in so far as they are revealed in flight, on the road, on the sea, or from a car or train window.

Studies of distant cultures require transportation of the students to the site. Participating with a culture, we release education from pedantry.

Texts will be used as reinforcement of actual experience. Classes will be flown to Greenland for a week to study the effects of technology upon a preindustrial society. The Greenlanders will study the effects of an industrial society upon human propensities. Every class should take at least one hour airplane trip a year. This is an economic move which will teach, if reasonably planned and executed, more about geography, technology, transportation than all the books, films, time wasted in present studies. Trained observers travel with the class to insure minimal teacher interference with the learning process.

Industry must be called into service to implement this program.

Architecture is another way of indicating space enclosures. As a study, it can move quickly in the early primary grades to the actual problem of creating a humane environment within the classroom. Thus it becomes environmental art. Environmental art will be unlikely until we reach the level of sophistication attained by the Balinese centuries ago. They have no word for "culture," yet everything is beautiful—this because they simply do everything as well as they can.

Space variations in existing enclosures can be created by using flexible materials such as nylon stretch walls and flexible plastics. There would be no "decorations," only the work well done of the students, whether this takes two- or three-dimensional forms. Space can no longer be conceived of in modular horizontal-vertical terms, anymore than dancing can be conceived of as vertical movement on a horizontal plane. Exercise, such as transcribing the movements of a dancer into three-dimensional static or kinetic forms, will be common. Music will be defined as what happens when intense aural stimuli excites the total sensory apparatus of the student.

Techniques will be implicit in the use of materials. Crafts must be re-introduced not as a subject for those who are deficient in absorbing "knowledge," but for the intellectually and spiritually gifted whether they exhibit these gifts in verbal or non-verbal forms.

Already cooking as a comprehensive activity is rediscovered as a subject of highly charged yield in the primary-elevator classroom.

Participation rather than demonstration, "mixing and messing" with real material and tools resulting in edible foods is to place man's technological heritage in proper focus.

The grinding of grains, the mashing of potatoes, the grinding meat, the cutting of carrots are activities of consummate interest to the child in the primary grades. The exploration of common foods and common tools (knife, grinder, morter and pestle) allow focus on the ordinary wherein the commonplace becomes extraordinary.

Trips to ethnic neighborhoods to purchase specific items, difficult to locate, simple ingredients such as cocoa (mixes are more common on shelves) introduce the child to problems (synthetics) and solutions (transportation) of modern technology.

Recipe books duplicated and distributed suggests the written words efficacy in recording data for retrieval. The impermanance of materials, the dissolutions of sugar, salt in water, the effect of heat on corn (popcorn), on dough, the gel of gelatin, the change of cream into butter through movement, are matters of inherent interest to young children. To be able to control and predict for young children is more important and possible than to understand why these transformations occur. When life is considered important, it will center around the most common activities in order to insure their centrality: cooking, eating, dancing, sewing, weaving, furniture making of materials primarily other than wood. This will necessarily occur as we learn to care. The machine man is obsolete.

It is no longer possible to speak of environments without thinking simultaneously of ecologies. Ecology becomes redefined as the energetic affects of living and non-living things within a given space. The learning of ecology will be implicit in the creation of the learning environment, built in not as course but as process. As experience leads to definition, ecological considerations will become increasingly sophisticated, as the student becomes more conscious and articulate.

Ethnology as the study of animal behavior will include the behavior of man. Reunited with the animal kingdom, he then exercises his specific abilities not to "control" nature but to interact with it or any part of it for *mutual* benefit.

To reinforce ecological considerations, animal, vegetable, and mineral environments can be created within the classroom. No more caged-environments. Specifically designed environments for the specific animal housed within them can be created. Plants and plant life can be studied as a part of the interior-exterior landscaping implicit in environmental studies. These at the nursery-kindergarten through college levels. This indicates the return of the professional into the educational setting working with the children as authority by virtue of specific abilities and knowledge. There is nothing to keep us from immediately moving in these areas except inertia.

As Fuller would say, it is a matter of doing more with less. This does imply not additional monies but a genuine educational economy based on long-range rather than short-range goals within the classroom. "Subjects" will no longer be taught. That they were never learned has not yet been allowed to penetrate the structural defenses of teachers—or parents. This despite their own experience.

Consider the techniques and technics of social studies.

Through television with the instantaneous viewing of events, history has become the study of the present which necessarily includes the past and immediately becomes the past of the future which becomes the present.

As time and space compact through electronic media and the technics of movement— the jet, rocket, express train—"then and there" move into the living room. The living room becomes the jet rocket and express train or the air-conditioned car. We travel in a controlled environment in order to release the controls on habits which include ways of thinking and viewing the world. The points of reference to the past and future merge with the present. The past becomes important not as curio, not as episode that transpired long ago, but as event that has immediate transference, throwing light on the present. Thus one structural aspect of a discipline such as history is inculcated. Educator will reinforce and bring this inculcation to consciousness, thereby allowing the student a disciplined tool with which to examine his own socio-historical situation.

Commercial television is as yet the most effective multi-disciplinary media. It synthesizes experience, events, happenings, by showing anything, anyway, anytime it is significant. It operates outside sequence except as sequence is determined by contemporaneous relevance. In doing this, it escapes the limitations of instructional sequence as determined by the cognitive rigidities of educators.

The viewers' consciousness is expanded under the impact of local, national, global, cosmic events. The "there and then" is brought into the home in comprehensible visual metaphors and language.

The "here and now" curriculum can no longer focus on what we will know anyway given reasonable emotional conceptual development. Thus social studies as a series of concentric circles, moving from family to neighborhood, to city, to state, to nation, to globe and finally to cosmos, is obsolete to the extent that content of social studies fails to incorporate simultaneous absorption of data and to the extent that content does not advance the discipline inherent in social studies.

Since simultaniety brings confusion as well as richness, specific curriculum disciplines would do well to address themselves to this problem, particularly in relation to the elementary school child. To ignore the confusion and focus only on the smallest mediocrity of self-evident life around us is not likely to arouse enthusiasm in the student.

The "here and now" curriculum is no longer a *study* of ourselves engaging the contemporaneous. It is now an *engagement* in the present, from which certain higher, more effective forms of behavior emerge. Social studies for college students of the past ten years has been the engagement in the civil-rights, student protest, the sexual revolution, which through participation has lead to increased understanding. We need not agree with the conclusion reached by youth in order to acknowledge this has happened.

The news event which we view or read is one in which we are participants. "Teaching in the decentralized I.S. 201 Complex is like living in the eye of a hurricane. Every day you rush home to find out what happened to you in the papers."[4] "The convention (Republican, 1968) had demonstrated that no reporter could keep up any longer with the event unless checking in periodically with the tube . . ."[5] We see ourselves walking to work during a transportation strike. Generators provide current needed to present the black-out event to us when the electricity returns to the tube. We see ourselves making history—the Morrow family in La Grange, Georgia, see their son fall under artillery fire and the administration of aid by a medic during live coverage of the Vietnam war. The next day they receive a letter from the War Department saying their son has been injured.

We see ourselves making history not only in the present, but the history of the future—exploration of space, oceanographic explorations, cars jammed on the highway illustrating one aspect of urban crisis, dead fish in the water illustrating our pollution of natural resources. Single acts—being delayed on the thruway—are incorporated within a mass media vocabulary and awareness. Social studies becomes existential—the awareness of being and becoming.

This is illustrated in the lesson below. The poem by Langston Hughes is used as media for questions asked by the teacher, Charles S. Isaacs. The students are encouraged to ask their own questions. This possibility is implicit in the lesson plan.

Landlord, landlord
My roof has sprung a leak.
Don't you 'member I told you about it
Way last week?

Landlord, landlord
These steps is broken down.
When you come up yourself
It's a wonder you don't fall down.

Ten bucks you say I owe you?
Ten bucks you say is due?
Well, that ten bucks more'n I'll pay you
Till you fix this house up new.

What? You gonna get eviction orders?
You gonna cut off my heat?
You gonna take my furniture and
Throw it in the street?

Um-huh! You talking high and mighty.
Talk on—till you get through.
You ain't gonna be able to say a word
If I land my fist on you.

Police! Police!
Come and get this man!
He's trying to ruin the government
And overturn the land!

Copper's whistle!
Patrol bell!
Arrest.

Precinct station.
Iron cell
Headlines in press:

Man Threatens Landlord
Tenant Held; No Bail
Judge Gives Negro 30 Days
in County Jail

"Ballad of the Landlord"
by Langston Hughes

Questions:

1. Who is the man in the poem?

2. Why is he angry? Should he be?

3. What does he do to the landlord? Was he justified in doing so?

4. What happens to him? Does he deserve the penalty?

5. Would it happen if he were white? Why? Why not?

6. Does this poem remind you of things that happen here in Ocean Hill-Brownsville? What?

7. Why do you think Mr. Mayer has used this poem in our class?

—A social-studies lesson at J.H.S. 271[6]

To further the emerging consciousness of one's condition the teacher asks clarifying questions:—"Would it happen if he (the tenant) were white? Why? Why Not?" Teaching so conceived is to interject learning into the process of making history.

This means that educators will have to assume the specific job relevant to education at all times; introducing the child to a humane inter-active environment. Schools will necessarily address themselves to problems of human interaction, the arts and skills most enhanced by these interactions.

Social studies shifts to become primarily the specific group and/or individual interactions within the classroom as models; models of societal forms existing outside the classroom. Experimentation will be done with controlled and spontaneous groupings that take place in relation to archetypal social problems: conflict and resolution, autonomy and collectivity, power and authority. Through resource centers at home and in school, the child learns to ask increasingly relevant questions, to evaluate his questions and his answers. There is no need to teach what is obvious, i.e. mailmen are community helpers, transportation is a way of moving. The child can no longer be distracted from his essential task of defining and re-defining himself in relation to others nor can he any longer be placed in environments which use the most minimal potential of himself and his teachers.

It is impossible to sequester, divide, rigorously split the classroom into discrete areas of learning.

> "The very words 'elementary education' means starting with parts . . . They (educators) take the child and say 'Come here into our schoolhouse darling. We are really going to teach you something. Stop thinking about the universe. We are going to give you an A and a B and a C and you are going to learn how to put those simple little elements together. By-and-by we will make you so forgetful of the world around you and so sharply focussed by the blinders you put on now that you can become a great specialist.' This is how young life, the children, become damaged." [7]

Buckminster Fuller

Consider other statements taken somewhat at random from his paper: Comprehensivity is inherent while specialization was acquired.

We can no longer think in terms of single static entities—one thing, one situation, one problem—but only in terms of dynamic changing processes and a series of events that interact complexly.

In our day the bulk complexity and detail of our knowledge requires restructuring into assimilable wholes.

There is an enormous need in world society today to integrate since specialization itself is not normal, not inherent, not native to the individual.

Because Fuller is comprehensively aware of our needs I have quoted him here. But more the classroom itself must become comprehensive regarded as a total environment serving total learning needs.

Is the camera used so that the students may learn more about our technology of communication, more about a technic namely how to operate a camera and use it effectively, to reinforce visual literacy, to record an actual event which we may call dramatics or social studies or science (a photographic essay on the life, birth and death of guinea pigs in the classroom)? It will be used in all these ways and more. It will develop intrinsic conceptual, cognitive abilities *if* we place the camera in the hands of the students and with the light touch make available to him our knowledge of the camera's potential when placed in his hands.

Anyone who has examined children's drawings of urban riots, the assassinations and murder of leaders will be unable to say when content (social studies in this case), art (the media of color and paper), and sensibilities (the feelings of the children) can be separated into distinct entities or what such separation would serve.

Consider the exhibit of children's responses to the teacher's strike in New York City in the Fall of 1968. The exhibit mounted in the New York Shakespeare Festival's Public Theater included language arts:

> I think they should come back so we can learn.

> I don't need you. Don't even come back till next year I don't miss you.

> I think the teachers should come back and teach a little math. I love math. No homework. They shouldn't take advantage of children because they got no children.

> We need a new mayor. Teachers don't care. We have to have a good education.

> The white teachers are scare. . . . We love our own kinds. They don't want us, black children to get an education.

Are these simple concrete relevant statements about a significant social event in the lives of these children or are they simple emotive language arts?

Is the following statement posted as part of the exhibit play with words or a learning of acceptance of self through words, as the competent use of words creates self confidence?

> I dig me. Dig I me. Me I Dig. I me Dig. Dig Me I. Me Dig I. I feel good. Good feel I. Feel I good. I good feel. Good I Feel.

Participation, engagement, the use of language as technique, the use of the lobby as media on which to mount the message, all these and many more relevancies are included here.

Perhaps it is sentimental but considering the condition of the world we should consider Stephen Antonakos a 10 year old who has formed a Children's Organization for Peace when he says:

> "When you get older you're kind of spoiled. When you're young you can't do it because you're not allowed. Children could change America if their feelings got widespread.

> I think we could get people to realise what's been happening. Children just are not recognized as people. They are not allowed to take part in anything that's *happened* just because we're young." [8]

REFERENCES

1. Komoski, P. Kenneth. *Technology and the Classroom.* Educational Leadership Volume 25, No. 8, May, 1968.

2. Spolin, Viola. *Improvisation for the Theater.* Northwestern University Press, Evanston, Illinois.

3. *N.Y. Times.* December 18, 1968.

4. Manoff, Gregg. *Manhattan Tribune.* November 13, 1968.

5. Mailer, Norman. "Miami Beach and Chicago." *Harpers Magazine,* November, 1968.

6. Isaacs, Charles S. "A J.H.S.271 Teacher Tells It Like He Sees It." *The New York Times Magazine,* November 24, 1968.

7. Fuller, R. Buckminster. *Conversations on the Arts.* A Report of the Fine Arts, Project V, ESEA Commonwealth of Pennsylvania, Dept. of Public Instruction, p.11.

8. *N.Y. Times.* June 25, 1968.

48.

The Physical Science Versus The Behavioral Science Concept Of Instructional Technology

by *PAUL SAETTLER*
Prof. of Education
Dept. of Behavioral
Sciences
Sacramento State College

It will be useful here to make a distinction between the physical science (or prevailing conception of instructional technology) and the broader, behavioral science concept. The traditional and physical science concept of instructional technology dominates much of the thinking in both education and industry and defines instructional technology largely in terms of hardware—language laboratories, slide projectors, simulation devices, demonstration apparatus, videotape machines, computers, etc. The narrowness of the physical science concept is such that it tends to view instructional media as aids to instruction and to be preoccupied with the effects of devices and procedures rather than with learning and with the selection and organization of content for reflective problem solving. Closely related to this view, is the widely held presumption that a technology of machines or a collection of techniques is somehow equivalent to a science and technology of instruction. As a consequence, someone orders a number of overhead projectors and dumps them into classrooms where no one knows what to do with them; or a school installs a closed circuit television system or a language laboratory and then leaves the teachers without any guidance or technical assistance in their use.

So far as the purposes of education are concerned, the possibilities opened by modern instrumentation have not usually been understood by those using them for instruction, nor have there been more than a few systematic attempts to design a true technology of instruction. To date, it has to be said that the commercial market for educational hardware and software has expanded to a degree which is seriously out of proportion to their intrinsic instructional merit. The trouble is that a rather sophisticated technology of machines has been developed while a technology of instruction hardly exists. What has happened, as a result, is that much of the modern hardware at the educator's disposal is beyond his knowledge or training with regard to its implementation or function within the educational system in which he is working. Unfortunately, the recent introduction of "The Educational Technology Act of 1968" to Congress also largely reflects the physical science concept of instructional technology by its undue stress on hardware.

It is the writer's view that an applied behavioral science approach to the problems of learning and instruction is fundamental to instructional technology. The basic view of the behavioral science concept of instructional technology is that behavioral science theory and research, or other organized knowledge, should be applied in support of the practical art of instruction. Aside from the broad areas of the behavioral sciences (anthropology, psychology, sociology, etc.) and within them, the more specialized areas of learning, group processes, psycholinguistics, bionics, cybernetics, perception, psychometrics, cognition, organization theory and behavior, communication theory, etc., the behavioral science concept of instructional technology may include such related areas as engineering research and development (including human factors engineering) architectural psychology, logistics, game and decision theory, and operations research. The most important aspect of this concept of instructional technology concerns the application of scientific knowledge to provide a conceptual basis and methodology for the design, development, and evaluation of instruction and instructional products for the purpose of improving the related components of the educational process.

It should be clear from this description of the behavioral science concept of instructional technology that it would call for new organizational arrangements in education and the development of high-level specialists (e.g., systems programmers, computer technologists, learning bio-chemists, etc.) and generalists (instructional technologists) who could assume the task of instructional design in a research and development setting.

Toward a Technology of Systems Design

Many new technologies in other areas of society have important implications for education, but system theory and research is seen as offering a unifying focus for the application of new technologies in the design of instruction. In fact, the systems approach may constitute the core technology around which other relevant technologies may be clustered and integrated in application. Systems engineering—the invention, design, and integration of an entire assembly of equipment (as distinct from the invention and design of the components) geared to the accomplishment of a broad objective—is a concept which has been fundamental to practical engineering since the beginning of the industrial revolution. One of the most successful applications of the systems concept in the military sphere was the development of weapons systems. The systems concept has been applied in the development of man-machine systems in space research.

Modern systems technology is intimately linked with electronic technology, particularly computers, and with the development of such new branches of mathematics as game and decision theory and operations research. Also, there is the development of self-regulating machines whose fundamental principle is control (feedback) and communication (messages between machine and environment, and within the machine). This finds its principal expression in cybernetics principles which can be widely applied to educational problems.

It is important to point out that we agree with some recent outspoken critics of systems analysis who assert that the educational system is considerably more complex (for various social and political reasons among others) than other areas (e.g., military, space) in which this technique has already been successfully applied. We also view with suspicion the recent efforts of corporate coalitions to mould education into a system of cultural uniformity through their long-range plans to produce systems of standardized, prepackaged materials for mediated instruction. Whether instruction is mediated or provided by a live teacher may not be a significant factor in the educational process, but the excessive concern with specifying behavioral objectives tends to legitimatize those objectives built into the system by commercial producers because they can be easily described in schematic detail and quantitatively measured. Unfortunately, education rarely questions or examines the purposes of systems derived from commercial and military sources.

If teachers are to be bypassed by mediated instruction, for example, then it can be assumed that curricular decisions to be built into multi-media instructional systems will continue to move outside of education. This is not to condemn the concept of a systems approach, but merely to emphasize the importance of control of the production of educational materials and equipment. Consequently, one of the most important principles in the application of the systems approach to instruction is that product research and development must be under the direction and control of the educational establishment. Unless educational control exists over all the components of an instructional system, the testing of materials and procedures against goals and purposes embedded in the system cannot be accomplished.

The dependent role of instructional technology is nowhere better illustrated than in the development of the computer as a teaching tool. Since educators generally lack technical knowledge or understanding of the potential applications of the computer for the improvement of instruction, they are required to rely almost completely on computer manufacturers for the design of computer software. But if we see the computer as another instructional medium, we can see that education must begin to develop its own technical staffs skilled in computer technology in order to have the in-house expertise required to preserve a choice in selecting instructional strategies. However, the total design of instructional systems demands, primarily, competence in the behavioral sciences and in subject-matter, and it is unlikely that significant educational work can be accomplished with computers or in any other highly technical area without reference to these necessary competencies.

It is obvious that education is not ready to assume responsibility for the kinds of tasks suggested or implied in this memorandum. Unless or until some basic changes occur, the glowing expectations for instructional technology held by many may lead to progressive disillusionment and confusion.

A Proposal for Instructional Technology

Our proposal is designed primarily to implement a new research and development role for education. It is in no sense a fixed blueprint of an instructional technology of the future, but it does indicate in broad outline what could happen if education realized and utilized its potential resources, knowledge, and skills. Whether or not this plan, or details of it, are implemented, one thing is clear: The consequences of not planning well for the future will be that the control and direction of instructional technology will reside, by default, with the education industry whose primary function is not to improve education but to produce profitable products.

We shall elaborate our plan by focusing on three broad areas: (1) research and development, (2) development programs for instructional technologists, and (3) relationships between education, private enterprise, and government.

1. Research and Development

Instructional innovations depend inevitably on existing materials and equipment or on the development of new ones. For example, it is hardly to be expected that new ideas or curricula can be implemented without substantial reliance on textbooks, films, slides, videotapes, and a variety of other materials produced by private enterprise. Yet, we can hardly expect schools and teachers under our present system to develop the necessary skills to produce their own learning packages although there are direct and observable dependencies embedded in materials introduced into the classroom. It is obvious therefore that instructional technology is largely derived from and dependent on private industry. While there is nothing wrong with the idea of private industry serving education as producers of what education is not able to produce itself, it can be easily seen that the widespread use of instructional materials and equipment which educators had no hand in designing or testing means that it is the commercial producers rather than the educators who have much to do with determining the curriculum. Moreover, if the task of carrying out the necessary feasibility studies is left to industry, then the developmental process will be confined largely to those materials and devices for which there is an immediate and substantial market. Since it is frequently too expensive to change the configuration of an adopted or adapted product to accord with particular educational goals, the goals of education must and often do change to accommodate the product or system developed for different purposes. For example, the recent installation of a computer-assisted instruction system by the Philco-Ford Corporation in the Philadelphia public schools was a direct outgrowth of a research and development program done by Philco-Ford for the United States Government command and control system. It is, incidentally, a prevailing mythology that military and space research and development is necessarily relevant to a far more complex educational system.

On the other hand, it is distressing to note that, too frequently, educational research projects have been presided over by investigators whose personal or institutional prestige has guaranteed federal funding regardless of the intrinsic merit of their research concept or design. When the United States Office of Education funded the establishment of research and development centers and regional laboratories throughout the country a few years ago, there was considerable hope that such an instrumentality would produce a fundamental change in American education and that educational research would become a matter of national policy. Unfortunately, much of the work of the research and development centers and the regional laboratories, to date, has been disappointing due to failure to change the status quo or to consider viable alternatives to instructional procedures or the sacrosanct organization. The relationship of the research and development centers with schools, colleges, and universities has tended to be rather peripheral and meaningless. Their frequent refusal or inability to cope with a number of critical social, financial, political, and technological problems facing American education is nothing less than astounding. Further, their research and development approach has been fragmentary rather than comprehensive. No attempt, for example, has been made to deal with the total process of designing instructional systems in terms of curriculum development, content organization, media-message design, production of materials and devices, evaluation procedures, preparation of teachers and related specialists, and the relationships and arrangements required for linking all the components of an instructional system into a meaningful educational pattern.

In order to implement a different approach to research and development, we propose a revised and expanded regional research and development model which would focus on the present gap between knowledge production and knowledge application through the management of clusters of experimental schools within the region. Further, it is proposed that R&D Centers enter into contractual relations with school districts which would give the centers full administrative, legal, and financial responsibility and authority. It is further proposed that the contract contain an added proviso that public school personnel be involved in the research operations, planning, instrumentation, data-gathering and analysis, report preparation, and dissemination activities.

The purpose of our proposal is quite clear. It is to create a body of school personnel who see the value of the empirical-inductive mode of thinking and to develop a profession that turns to research to solve problems, not to justify what it is doing or happens to think is a good idea. Many administrators and teachers simply ignore good research either because it is laboratory research, or because it was not done in their district. An analysis of the Elementary and Secondary Act Title III projects seems to indicate that doing research in a school setting is not necessarily going to improve educational research nor will it automatically solve educational problems. If research is going to improve educational practice, the practitioners must be interested in and must be engaged in some phase of the process.

Our R&D Center model would provide leadership in creating teacher research teams to formulate proposals for research efforts. In this way the schools could be engaged in doing research on problems they want to solve. Experimental classrooms could be established where atypical instructional procedures would be the rule, extended observation and testing could take place, and where creative experimental treatments could be employed over a relatively long period of time. For example, one experimental theme might reflect the cognitive-field approach; another, the operant conditioning approach. Other experimental approaches might derive their themes from organizational patterns, values, individualization of instruction, creativity, etc. Thus the R&D Centers would provide an ideal experimental setting which the contracting schools themselves would be unable to offer. Selected educational administrators and classroom teachers could spend at least one year or longer working with the Center for purposes of observation and participation in educational research along with behavioral scientists. They would return later to their own schools to provide leadership in innovations which had been experimentally verified.

There is at present a serious gap between research and application that cannot be spanned either by the researcher or by the teacher, or even through the blending of efforts of these two. Since there is a growing conviction that more attention must be given to the developmental process if research knowledge is to be utilized, our model encompasses the establishment of educational products development centers and the spawning of a new breed of instructional technologist or educational designer.

We feel that the development function of the R&D Centers cannot be fully implemented until educational products are developed within the R&D Centers themselves. A major task under this function would involve the preparation of design specifications for educational products (materials, equipment, learning packages, systems, etc.), and the offering of contracts for the production, evaluation, and distribution of these products to private enterprise through competitive bidding. In other words, the relationship of R&D Centers and commercial manufacturers would be no different than that between industry and other sectors of society in terms of technological control. It is envisioned that such a relationship would ensure rigorous standards of evaluation and quality control as well as professional control over the whole process by which new curriculum ideas and instructional innovations are implemented.

Since the federal government has already made a beginning in converting research knowledge into instructional materials through the establishment of regional laboratories, it is suggested that some of these laboratories be transferred to the jurisdiction and control of the R&D Centers. Thus a total development process, from basic through applied investigation, to design and development, innovation or production, and evaluation, may be achieved in one place.

An important part of this model would be the development of a new instructional technologist who would combine skills that are urgently needed and that are not now taught. As will be seen in the following section, recommendation is made for the funding of developmental training programs for instructional technologists at those few, rather easily-identified institutions, long active in, or currently concerned with this problem. Therefore, it is further recommended that we develop and test prototypes of the R&D Centers we have described and locate them at those institutions that are providing leadership in the field of instructional technology. After these models have been tested in practice, we can begin to replicate them throughout the country.

2. Developmental Programs for Instructional Technologists

There has arisen considerable anxiety in some quarters concerning the adequacy of present curricula and environments for the nurture and cultivation of instructional technologists who can coordinate the developmental process. The programs that do exist at these few universities who are recognized leaders in this field have developed or are developing from programs which were essentially planned for the training of audiovisual specialists. It is now recognized by many that a new training program is called for which will develop a person competent in educational research, who can combine media and messages for effective learning, and coordinate and manage teams of specialists in diverse technologies in the design, development and evaluation of instructional systems. Without the development of a sufficient number of these new instructional technologists, education will not be able to undertake the kinds of instructional tasks envisioned in this memorandum nor will it gain technological control of its future development.

The training programs for instructional technologists clearly call for considerable variety and flexibility. There must be ample opportunity and encouragement to interact with the diversity of disciplines found in a college or university community. The model proposed here is designed to implement the behavioral science concept of instructional technology defined earlier in this memorandum. For example, the biochemist could contribute to the understanding of drugs and brain extracts to enhance learning; the neurologist to the functioning of internal neural systems (neural communications); the architectural psychologist to the relationship of space and form to effective learning environments; the human factors engineer to the study of living systems in transactions with their environments; the cognitive psychologist to an understanding of cognition and problem solving; the communication specialist to the use of media and message forms; the social psychologist to construction of models of small groups and interpersonal behavior; the computer specialist to methods for simulating entire instructional systems. In other words, there must be opportunity for interaction with a diversity of disciplines and technologies. In this sort of environment, students can pursue their interests while becoming involved in ongoing research projects. It should be emphasized strongly at this point that the training program should develop a perspective which would stress the importance of maintaining technological control on the design, development, and evaluation of educational products.

We have presented a general, long-range proposal for the training of instructional technologists in full recognition that at present such an ambitious program is handicapped both by a lack of adequate personnel and financial resources.

Therefore, as is suggested in the previous section, we propose that the federal government sponsor such developmental training programs for instructional technology, starting with those easily identified institutions which have already provided leadership in this area and those qualified institutions now actively initiating such programs. Since it is obvious that such programs would best succeed in an R&D Center context, the value of establishing new R&D Centers at institutions undertaking developmental training in instructional technology is evident. But the long-range goals seem clear: instructional technology must be transformed into an applied science. To do so, it will need a large number of developmental instructional technologists who value and use applied behavioral science and who can create the patterns and combinations of media and materials required to solve problems of learning and motivation.

3. Relationships Between Education, Private Industry, and Government

It is clear that if R&D Centers are to direct, to a great extent, the activities of persons working under contract in private industry, then new relationships will be required and new methods of evaluating and reporting on results will have to be developed. In any event, the present system of technological development and materials production must be changed to meet the growing needs of education. The extent to which industry and education can work together toward solutions to the problems of education will have a long-range effect on the quality of education.

It appears that any relationship between education and industry which does not provide for an interchange of personnel is not likely to be very productive. Not only is this type of arrangement advisable for mutual understanding of the constraints under which both education and industry operate, but it is essential for providing technical training to educational personnel and providing some direct contact for industry personnel with the problems of the classroom. In this connection, it is suggested that some type of leave of absence be instituted for educators to serve full time in industry and that industry personnel do likewise in education. Also, some joint appointment plan might be devised. One prototype of such a partnership between education and industry now exists in the joint undertaking of the University of Pittsburgh Learning Research and Development Center, the Pittsburgh Public Schools, and the General Learning Corporation to experiment in individualized learning for young children.

It is further proposed that private industry and foundations share with the federal government the cost of developing and evaluating educational products and instructional systems at R&D Centers. Although the federal government might in some cases make direct contracts with commercial manufacturers, this contracting function should remain, basically, with the R&D Centers. As is well known by now, all materials produced under contract with the federal government go immediately into public domain, and this involves a host of legal and ethical questions which may be solved more easily outside the realm of the federal government. In any event, some policy would have to be developed whereby schools, colleges, universities, and private industry could all share in the use of and profit from educational products in whose research and development they are involved.

49.

Technological Systems for Education Which Adapt Technology to People

by *ALEXANDER SCHURE*
President
N.Y. Institute of Technology

This paper envisions technology applied to education as being most effective when attuned to accountability of the various arrangements of the educational system. It hypothecates techniques which can identify and recommend the most effective implementations of techniques most responsive to the social and political exigencies that affect education. It suggests that occupational education can only be advanced substantially when the foundational base is made culturally responsive for minority groups and suggests additional support systems structured through technology to achieve a more responsive educational system. It also delineates an individualized system monitored by a computer to make present educational occupational programs more relevant in the higher education area. The paper concludes with the suggestion that technology may, in itself, be used to educate the decision-making segments of our society in the optimum method of employment of personnel so as to adjust our societal needs to these characteristics.

Technology applied to education must be broad based and go well beyond conventional interpretations of existing systems. Present day instructional technology must add to its hardware-software combinations exemplified by audiovisual, multi-media, computer-based, television, communications equipment and other resources. A new technology must emerge to include those total management and informational systems capable of relating the wide range of the social processes which encompass education. Within this technology, composites of machines, strategies and techniques may be abstracted for each individual human so as to yield the most effective combination pertinent to a given person and environment. All informational, managerial, predictive and decision yielding systems in themselves must become part of the technology.

This broader definition enables a new flexibility, adapting technology to people rather than forcing adaption of people to technology. It brings man a step closer to the zero reject concept in education. Realization of this philosophy would give to each person, at any time, an opportunity to reach his largest probable educational success level. Further, through an appropriate information and retrieval system there can be detected impediments to progress early enough to permit corrective action.

Technology with its predictive capability can provide guidance for additional assists or alternate paths. There would then be no failures—no rejects for any individual in a heterogeneous population—in fact for any useful member of an entire society.

One basis of success for technology, when properly applied to occupational and technical education, exists in its capacity to match (and coordinate) community needs to the regional resources required to alleviate these needs. As pedagogues, we tend to think the problems of developing and releasing talent can be solved by the school. Actually, the solution is essentially political and social. A free and open society which attempts to recognize the marvelous uniqueness and value of every individual must also have the wisdom to realize the school can do justice to its total constituencies only when its educational framework is truly integrated into other social formats. When we examine the persistent problems which impede the education of a wide spectrum of our children and youth, and relate the efforts of our school system to cope with them, it seems appropriate to indicate concepts of the educational framework in which better "solutions" than those now available may take place.

Education must prepare for a consistent performance in some socially valuable activity. This includes serving not only the intellectually gifted or the academically talented but those who must function capably in a range of prosaic occupations, in the graphic and performing arts, in the technical crafts, and in social leadership.

An educational format capable of satisfying the interacting logistical and economic demands of such an organized system are, or will be prime among the objectives of education.

If technology is to be used effectively, it must be attuned to the challenging and pressing problem of education for the culturally different. Success in contributing to a resolution of the myriad of problems within the social cultural context—how to deal adequately with students drawn from the urban slums or rural poverty areas; how to deal with minority groups; how to cope with the dropout; and how to harness increasing militancy of both students, teacher and local communities as they struggle for values important to them—will have the most profound effects upon the viability of the educational system.

It seems likely that much of our national energies in the future will, of sheer necessity, remain focused on the more persistent and recurring areas of concern that now make many of our public schools a battleground for varied and conflicting interests. There are no easy and quick solutions.

Present efforts are piecemeal and ineffective. Yet, unless an emergency status which recognizes the crises which now exist is perceived, it becomes questionable that there will take place that extent of reorganization of existing agencies, expenditures of Federal and State funds, and the development of necessary new patterns required to deal with present problems of the urban areas, their inner cores, and the people who constitute them.

Required are broad based focused programs which are feasible economically and operationally; are directed towards both majority and minority groups; point to long term and short term objectives, beginning with pre-schools and continuing into the adult years; and aim at stabilizing the inner city by providing means through which the requirements and desires of minority factions can in actuality be met. The needs of these constituencies go beyond welfare and employment. They include as a high priority the maintenance of dignity for the individual; his ability to exercise control over decisions that relate to his own life; and the means whereby he may develop his resources in directions that yield promise of substantial future returns to him. Solutions will be found in programs acknowledging the interactional relationship between majority and minority, directed towards the value and belief systems of whites as well as non-whites and other minorities. Technology, aptly and adequately applied, can provide the necessary tools.

The present educational systems are not without their strengths. They are least effective in responding to the needs of inner-city and minority cultures. If primary education with these groups is ineffective, whatever follows is remedial and patchwork. Hence, restructure of education at the earliest levels to be "culture responsive" is a necessity if there is to be subsequent success within the worlds of work and education.

To make a quantum leap forward in occupational education, education for the minority groups must be improved substantially. Involved in culture responsive systems are all the urgent problems common to, and complicating, urban, minority and migrant education. Pertinent factors include increases in the population, over-centralized control, non-white populations, little cross-class interaction, violence arising from extremist forces and the loss of tax base to the communities. Complicating the problems in minority education are the debilitating effects of insufficient primary and secondary education; the lack of motivation resulting from home problems; the lack of relevance to minority values; the shortage of competent counseling; and, the lack of financial support for professional education for the minority groups.

There is a futility to any single, uni-factorial direction. If there are solutions, they will be found in multi-factorial approaches. Current trends include the development of resources within particular regions and communities into new forms of urban educational institutions (one element within this structure is concerned with the training of leaders drawn from the inner city who will return to function within the inner city core); requiring all of the institutional segments concerned with occupational education to have closer relationships with industry; and, the stipulations that all elements projected for an emerging multi-factorial system must maintain a sufficiently well-organized research base to permit replication within chosen areas for those aspects of the model which are successful.

There are educational support systems which can be structured through the capacities of technology so as to achieve a more responsive educational system. One such system could well be a "redundant school system." The "redundant school system" term is used in the engineering sense, as an alternate or replacement when the primary system fails. Envisioned is a backup school system from pre-K—16, public or private, which has continuous, individualized education for maximum development of each student according to his abilities and vocational aspirations. Students can range from youngsters to grown adults.

The structure of education within the redundant system would be based on the most applicable technological techniques. These would certainly include administration of programming and referral through systems analysis. Special instructional materials would be utilized with grades or certification based upon units of behavioral increment. Progress in education would be gauged in terms of measurable output and made certifiable by achievement criteria. Quantitative measures of such improvement would be evolved and the systems structured to provide for educational patterns that assist in achievement of desirable goals, be they social or political.

Within formal schools, in community centers and industry, there would be access to the "back-up" or redundant school system. Attendance for remedial help could be encouraged. The facilities for, or access to, advanced work and vocational training would be provided as an alternative to the available back-up system within the formal school program. The ability to grant high school and advanced degrees through the back-up educational system, individualized programming, subject matter structured on continuums, with each step being known as a unit of behavioral increment, the enhancement of motivation through monetary rewards to families or to local community groups for a rise in level of performance to or beyond the normatively expected unit of behavioral increment and the involvement of community trained personnel could all be well within the purview of the back-up system.

The educational advantages of an individualized system include diversity, flexibility of feeder patterns, equalization of educational opportunities, academic multi-level opportunities and programming patterns which are innovating, flexible, and open. The learner then can be brought to understand the relevance of learning through its integration with the world of work, and of life itself. In a cooperative work-study milieu, payment for an appropriate unit of behavioral increment could yield appropriate motivations. The student's progress then becomes self-actualizing, dignified, and self-conceived. Individualized instruction provides a new climate where education has prestige and status for the student who is a non-performer in today's world.

The system must also be capable of beginning fundamental learning processes at an early age so that receptivity to educational stimuli can promote educational success at later times. The individualized instruction within such a system necessitates referrals between agencies within a given region, interaction between schools, community centers, industry, government training agencies and schools outside the back-up system. Such interaction must take place between project agencies, governmental, and the social agencies outside projects.

Within the system there must also be initiation of technical and paratechnical job training at any time for those who desire it so as to insure employment for the newly trained as well as the unskilled. The system must likewise initiate or provide access to a wide range of social services including social welfare and psychiatric services. Likewise, access to employment agencies is imperative. Again, modern technology can be utilized to insure immediate knowledge of available offerings to prospective employees for vocational counseling or job placement. Carefully formulated educational plans for our schools of the future must provide for diverse heterogeneous student inputs, with methodologies capable of matching the inventory and the potential of each individual they will service to his subsequent career environment. Such plans must also provide the means for transformations towards an interest goal, with a high probability of attainment. They must furnish the resources to develop human talent in an optimal way. Programs with these dimensions must be self-improving, therefore flexible.

Flexibility is the predominant trend, and attention to the individual the keynote of future efforts. Almost all the state plans now endorse this theme, and their goals for occupational education reiterate these ideas often as the means of achieving the central aim. Thus we find these points recurring in various state education department statements:

1. The structuring of an overall fundamental master plan that, once developed in consultation with all appropriate agencies, provides for the orderly development of occupational education in the region to be serviced.

2. The utilization of a variety of agencies and institutions tailored to provide programs and services to correct those educational deficiencies in people of different age groups, abilities, and educational status which could prevent such trainees from benefiting from instruction designed to lead to their employment.

3. A broadening of occupational educational programs to meet present and predictable employment and preemployment needs and skills.

4. Together with continuing vocational guidance and counseling at all levels, services are envisioned utilizing shared-service boards, the facilities of area schools, high schools, and public and private community colleges and technical institutes. Further, expansion of occupationally-related programs throughout the education system from elementary through post-secondary levels are ultimately foreseen.

5. The speeding up of the development of larger shared-service units to increase occupational education efficiencies.

6. The designing of special arrangements, including work-study or apprenticeship programs, where appropriate, or where special educational needs exist.

The concern for developing the maximum potentialities of each individual in the society has brought renewed interest in the development and structuring of new curriculum patterns, along with efforts directed at the improvement of existing courses of study. Add to these directions the availability of an information processing, retrieval, and communication technology ever increasing in sophistication, the broadening diverse role of the media in attaining instructional objectives, and the development of systems engineering and management techniques applicable to fundamental educational problems. All permit greater attention to the individual. Accomplishing such individualization is the task of properly utilized technology.

The need for successful individualized instruction runs like a common thread through the multiplicity and diversity of educational problems that challenge the American educator today. All the themes touched on—the "knowledge explosion," the problems of teacher training, the need for equality of educational opportunity, the population growth, the insufficiency of trained manpower for technological advance, the increase in our awareness of student differences in learning ability—all these stress the need for American education to develop a system of pedagogy that can identify and maximize individual student achievement regardless of level or category of learning ability. And with the recent incidence of failures of school budgets across the country, there is also the suggestion of a nationwide push for a more satisfactory investment—in terms of student attainment—of local tax dollars for schools.

The issue, of course, is more than one of mere facilities, curriculum or teacher proficiency. There is, and this is most important, the necessity of identifying a student's ability level, isolating what he *can* learn from what he *needs* to learn, and teaching him, on the basis of valid identification procedures, what he needs to know before he can proceed to more advanced levels of training. It becomes other than a question of teaching him to learn more in terms of speed and quantity; there is the need as well to determine what he needs to be fed if the student is to be expected to thrive on a properly balanced and nourishing educational diet.

What has become essential to provide is a self-improving educational system in which each student in a large heterogeneous population may receive the individualized instruction which would permit him to proceed along an educational path which, as far as he is concerned, is optimal. He also needs a system which would allow him to proceed towards these defined objectives with a high probability of attainment. The decision makers also require data that will permit them to manage the system with confidence.

No pedagogical or educational management process system has yet emerged as a validated total system that actually brings to fruition much more substantially than has heretofore been the case the possibilities for learning in this generation of students. One aspect of the problem is found in the inability to train or diagnose in or out of the classroom the various potential or specific causes for failure or under-achievement. The necessity of finding such a system—self-improving, individualizing, diagnostic and prescriptive—becomes more and more urgent.

Simultaneously, the invention of the computer has offered to education enormous possibilities for advancement. It has already been used for the automation of corollary information and data processing systems, but has only just begun to be explored for use in the educational process itself. The computer, in fact, offers tremendous possibilities for the management of the educational process, freeing the teacher from more routine tasks for more intensive kinds of consultation with students and individualizing instruction to a degree never before considered possible.

A substantial number of researchers have been investigating just such possibilities relating to the individualization of education for larger numbers of diversified students through a computer-based management system. This system does, via technology, what only very large numbers of staff and dollars could hope to do:

1. it discovers what the student should do to get an education;

2. it keeps track, by means of the computer's "memory" of the student's history and progress;

3. it assesses whether or not the student is being satisfactorily taught (i.e., whether or not his less than total success or failure is due to some weak quality in the course itself);

4. it provides the student and the teacher with validated information to enrich the rapidly-learning student or to intercede with appropriate correction for the slower-learning one.

The objectives of relevant ongoing programs aim to develop and refine an operant self-improving system which can provide individualized instruction to a heterogeneous population; to employ computer facilities and student guidance techniques for the purpose of helping a learner proceed along an effective path which is directed towards well defined objectives; to utilize computer capability to provide both the student as well as those responsible for his education rapid feedback concerning his academic progress and problems; to extend the material resources and media available to the learner which are relevant to his needs and appropriate to his level of attainment; to institute techniques for systematically evaluating the program so that it becomes inherently self-improving, and to achieve a viable articulation between elementary, vocational, high school, and lower college levels which offer a continuum for a diverse student population.

Although early systems for the computer-mediated management of the educational process are being tested, for practical purposes, in a specific curriculum context, the essential objectives of most of the research remain the development, refinement and evaluation of the system itself; the specific validated curricula that will emerge as well should be viewed as secondary to the main objective.

Essentially, such control will allow the administrator to devise and refine an educational system that eases the rigidity of the pre-determined instructional pace, loosens the ties of lock-step instruction, yields information relating to the success of instructional strategies and allows students to learn at a pace commensurate with their ability to grasp the contents of a course at any given time.

The two principal necessary phases are:

1. the "ordering" of the management system, and

2. the measurement of the efficiency of that "order" via the management system.

It is these elements that are now in development. In summary, the computer will be used by the schools:

1. for simulation of the interactions within comprehensive districts and/or the units which compose them;

2. for cost-effectiveness evaluation;

3. to serve as a diagnostic tool to facilitate the rapid evaluation of individual as well as group student performance;

4. for prescription of optimum mixtures of people, strategies, resources, media and materials appropriate to the different levels and degrees of learning that occur at any given time, thus individualizing the instructional program;

5. to institute much more rapidly, as a result of the computer-based profile-sensing, the most effective remediation measures (programmed instruction, audiovisual tapes, tutoring, supplementary reading assignments, special laboratory or class experiences, emphasizing the specific area of deficiency) thus avoiding the accumulation of confusion that often accompanies subsequent units of instruction;

6. for teacher and pupil guidance as appropriate;

7. to evolve networks, as easily used by lay personnel as by computer-oriented specialists, which can store, process, analyze and communicate relevant information to be used in all phases of educational endeavors.

Although management techniques and the approach of the systems analyst have become considerably more common in attempting to cope with the problems of the schools of today, there is still a long way to go before effective implemented systems are the rule rather than the exception. Adequate computer mediation schemes which form part of instructional management systems can make possible not only flexibility and individualization, but accountability of the elements within a system as well.

To test the concepts described previously, several models are being developed. One, Project ULTRA (at New York Institute of Technology) can serve as the type of prototype this author has in mind.

The following is a description of Project ULTRA, which is unique in several aspects. First, through a technologically-based system, education for large numbers of students is virtually individualized; special learning requirements, such as those of the disadvantaged student, can be successfully fulfilled here as a result. Secondly, ULTRA is not a purely academic concept. Its organization entails thorough cooperation with business and industry, as well as government.

Project ULTRA is based upon the utilization of a systems approach to education, the computer mediated analysis of the multi-faceted and sometimes problematic educational sphere. Such analysis should yield an orderly, integrated solution to occupational education capable of accommodating special situations, meshing individual requirements with societal demands. It is hoped that Project ULTRA will prove to be one cornerstone on which to rest continuous escalation through continuing educational cycles.

One of ULTRA's primary objectives is the construction of an organizational framework whereby every individual possesses a maximized opportunity of realizing the predicted match of his potential and occupational or school inventory with a high probability of success. No individual who desires to improve his education towards a career objective is rejected from ULTRA; however, an individual may be channeled towards a lesser occupational objective if his present abilities indicate a low probability of success for his initial choice. Alternate Skills Programs (ASP), Auxiliary Training Programs (ATP), College Preparatory Program (CPP), Institutional Off-Campus Programs (IOFF), Deficiency Correcting Phase-In Programs (PI), Industry-College Cooperative Associations Programs (CB), Differentially Paced, Self-Organizing Computer-Based Experimental Programs (X), and others are related to ULTRA's mainstream program through a computer-managed Information Center (IC). The Center constitutes that facet of ULTRA's central system which perpetually gathers data from all sources. It stores, analyzes, retrieves, and distributes information to appropriate locations (e.g., the Admissions Center (AC), the Diagnostic Examinations Center (DEC), etc.) where convergence of informational and decision-making processes fosters responses to activity areas and programs. The integrated operations of Project ULTRA necessitate the computer-oriented Information Center to handle the volume and processing of important data. Informational feedback from advanced stages of the program provide the source of improvement for the predictive functions of the Information Center, thus guaranteeing automatic self-correction. The flow chart (Figure I) is a schematic outline of the overall concept of ULTRA.

An additional purpose of Project ULTRA is to provide the opportunity for each student to achieve the educational success essential to his pursuance of a selected career objective. That objective is selected via a student's interests and abilities, which are diagnosed, discussed, predicted and interpreted by the combined skills of man-made examinations, computer-oriented methodologies, and man-machine interpretations. Of course, the human has final decision-making approval. In order to establish the qualifications for his chosen career, it is imperative that such requisites be precisely defined as part of ULTRA's initial process.

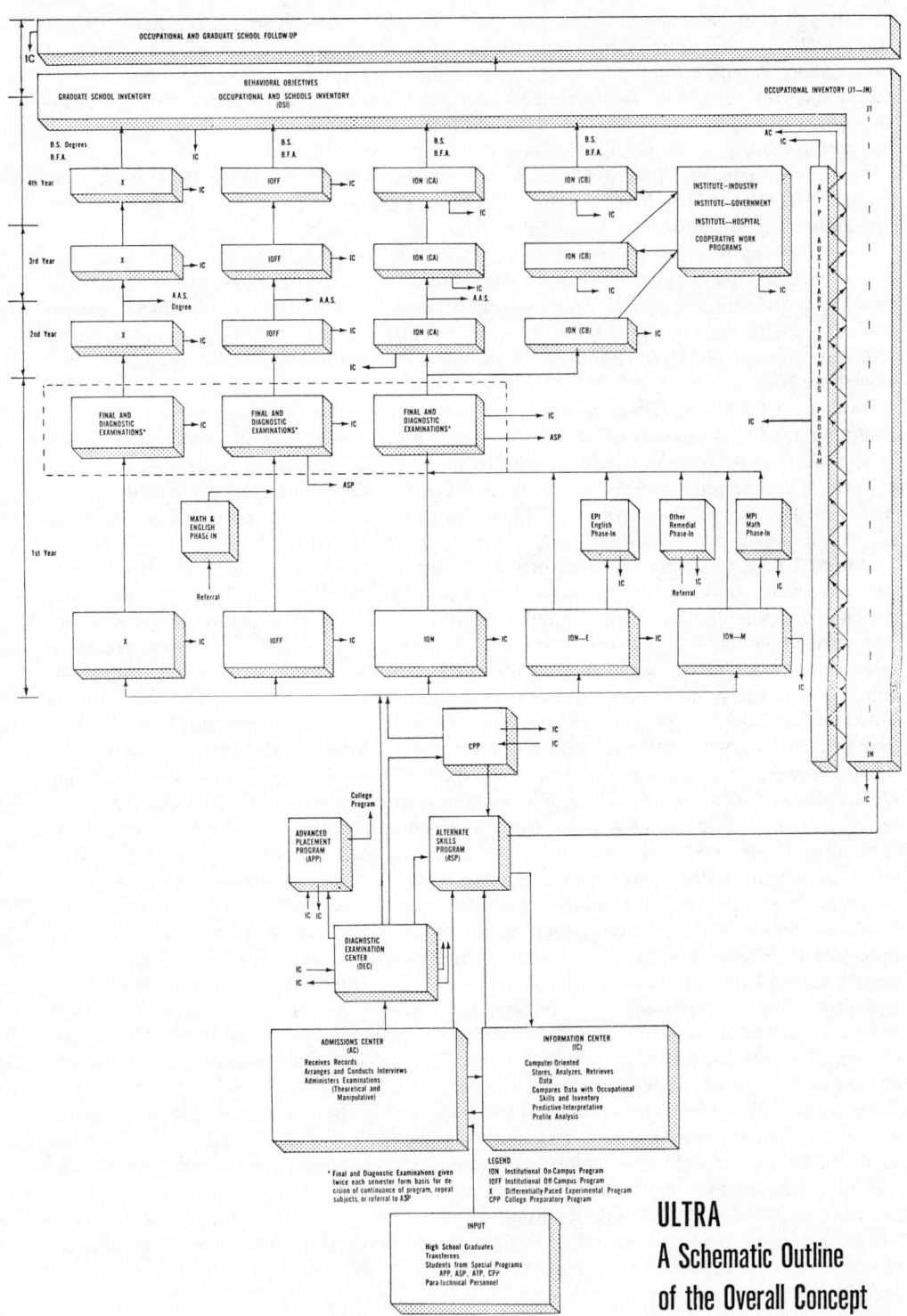

Figure I

The system invites high school graduates. These may be of recent origin, or have been in the occupational world for some length of time. The design also accepts as transferees, others who previously could not meet admissions standards for a college program, but who, on the basis of new training or experience, may have risen to acceptable standards. The Admissions Center receives student records and conducts interviews as an integral part of a pre-counseling service. College aptitude, plus manipulative and technical skills are tested through examinations administered by the Admissions Center.

The resulting data are fed into the Information Center, which compares them with the Occupational and Schools Inventory and issues a success probability prediction, which in turn is forwarded to the Admissions Center. This preliminary information also constitutes the initial basis of the applicant's profile. After the AC receives the comparative and analytic information from the IC, the next possible alternative is plotted.

If the success probability for the applicant in a specific college-level program is low, a match is made with an Occupational Classification (J..) of related interest and a high attainment probability. The student is referred to the Alternate Skills Program for training in related, career-oriented skills (J..).

The outcome of this training is not limited merely to the area of anticipated competence; the student can participate in the Auxiliary Training Program (ATP) which permits re-entry into the college admissions center upon certification of acceptable performance. Thus, the possibility of further educational advancement is always present.

Students who evidence college potential in the Admissions Center are processed through the Diagnostic Examinations Center, (DEC). In the DEC, achievement examinations are administered in reading, English and associated skills, and math and specialized subjects. Examination results are fed to the IC, where informational and predictive processes continue and predictive analytical results are returned to the DEC. At this time, one of the following decisions is made:

1. The applicant is ready for college education (with or without intensive deficiency phase-in programs in English and mathematics (EPI or MPI), or preparatory programs).

2. The applicant, not prepared for college education, is referred to the Alternate Skills Program (ASP).

3. The applicant already possesses college education or its equivalent, thereby qualifying him for Advanced Placement Examinations and subsequent phase-in to the College at an advanced level.

Those students found by the Diagnostic Examinations Center to be deficient in reading comprehension or any two specialized areas (e.g. English and math) but who nevertheless appear to have the aptitude and ability to attain rewards from college education will be directed to a College Preparatory Program (CPP). Here, intensive training in basic subject areas will be provided in order to raise the student to college-level performance. In keeping with the ULTRA philosophy, examination results will be fed into the Information Center, from which a returned analysis to the Diagnostic Examinations Center will in turn encourage one of the following recommendations:

1. Acceptance in the College Program

2. Direction to the Alternate Skills Program (ASP).

The Institutional On-Campus Program (ION) is the mainstream process which most closely resembles the traditional four-year baccalaureate programs. On-campus program (ION CB) is a work-study plan available to paratechnical personnel who may utilize this opportunity for continuing their college education.

Students diagnosed as weak in a particular subject area may pursue the normal course load, but in place of the conventional class, the student will enter an intensive training course in the area of his deficiency. Specialized instructional methods will be utilized here. Upon the successful completion of diagnostic examinations geared to the normal, functional course-work level, the student will be phased into a regular class.

Modern educational technology has facilitated the creation of off-campus degree-granting programs with emphasis on technical, industrial, distributive, business, and paratechnical areas. Academic excellence and social value can become an inherent part of this new design through the use of authoritarian agencies (such as the New York State Education Department and the Educational Testing Service Advanced Placement Programs). Students emanating from industry and chosen for advancement in the industrial framework can now earn either a degree or other appropriate certification. The gain serves as a protection against obsolescence and an inculcator of meaningful social status. Both are, of course, highly desired and urgently required. The generation of industrially related institutions is one of the primary objectives of IOFF.

One correlate of Project ULTRA has been the development of a self-organizing, computer-based educational system (X). In it, a computer makes diagnostic evaluations of the student's prior achievement, gives him required learning materials, gauges his progress and helps him to complete specified objectives. The computer then aids in the assessment of acquired knowledge as a measure of the student's ability to perform academically, and as a basis for beginning further instruction. The computer-designed profile of the student is based upon his knowledge, plus his abilities and personality characteristics.

This individual diagnosis allows a student to enter any learning situation at the point where he is most likely to perform optimally. Having discovered the precise limits of a student's knowledge in all subject matter areas, the computer selects his appropriate learning resources—the lectures he should attend, the texts for him to study, the films to see. These assessments, too, are geared to a student's interests and personality as well as his academic competence.

In this self-organizing method, the computer devises a mechanism for checking the learner's progress against a specific objective, whether it be the accumulation of course credits towards a degree, or the satisfaction of a need for continuing education, the modernization of professional backgrounds, or the mastery of technical skills. The student may leave the system without restriction of artificial time limitations, when his objectives have been satisfied.

Project ULTRA is founded on the assumption that technology is the key through which the door to a model educational system, generalizable on a mass basis, can be opened. ULTRA's prime objective is to extend the availability of college education to students who, under conventional educational systems, would find that goal unattainable; individualization of instruction insures their success.

The prognosis for movement towards full employment sources is good. There is still much new work to be done within the structure of our society to eliminate poverty, to revitalize and rebuild our urban centers, to strengthen our transportation systems, and to upgrade our health, medical and educational services. We can expect, over the long term, additional employment to be made available as the result of shorter work weeks, earlier retirements, later entry into the labor force and even the equivalent of sabbatical or educational leaves for members of the labor force.

These directions, however, will not come to pass in the immediately foreseeable future, and other methods must be found to achieve full employment. It may be necessary with all of the ramifications for education, both formal and informal and with the necessity of a much greater part of the total lifetime being devoted to the education process than has been the experience in the past, to use other approaches to break the unemployment concentration found in our minority groups and amongst the young and older members of our society.

One explanation for this concentration of unemployment in these groups has always been that, in our increasingly sophisticated society, there is less work for the unskilled to do. The role of the educator may, and indeed, must go beyond the viewpoint that the only cure for unemployment is education for those whose background is limited. Often, education for progressively higher levels of skill resulting in substantial achievement changes is a comparatively slow process. Vocational and technical educators may have to find a more corollary and pragmatic solution to the lack of education alone as a cause of unemployment, by educating the decision-making segments of our society against the concept that given the technology at any particular moment, there is the requirement that the totality of available labor forces must adjust to it. In lieu of this, our educators may determine (through technology information), in much more detailed measure than is now the case, the given characteristics of our labor force as they do indeed exist, and educate business and industry to adjust its technology to these characteristics. In time of crisis, such as a war, the latter philosophy often springs into predominance. An operation is required with a labor force that may not contain sufficiently educated or highly skilled people to mount the kind of technology envisioned by many as optimum. The existing labor force is found to contain different characteristics of skills or abilities and as a result, a varigated technology is needed and comes into being. Whenever there is an urgent and sufficient demand for particular products, industry finds the means to produce these products in a way which utilizes the labor forces available. Conventional usages of instructional technology are often the major methods by which the vocational or training task is accomplished.

Although education alone is not the sole key to the problem of unemployment, it will contain a majority of the elements necessary to the eventual solution of this problem. Education sharpens the skills, and through these skills, permits technological advancement of the society in direct proportion to the ratio of economic advancement in that society. Then too, education assists people in becoming adaptable to changing conditions. The loss of productivity is considerably less in societies characterized by higher educational attainment than it is in those of lower educational levels.

Augmenting its critical economic role, technology in the organized form of proper deployment of its mass media and resource centers distant from the formalized institution can free education and training from the shackles of its current on campus or in-school chains. It can open opportunities for a vast segment of population presently deprived of real and practical opportunity to upgrade themselves. It can coordinate the employment and educational potentials of government, business and industry.

The concept must be one of direction, not rejection. The value of a total system lies in its regenerative and improvement capacities. The more that enter such a system, the longer it is tried, the greater the data base—the more successful it will be. A realizable utopian dream? Many believe so.

50.
Systems Analysis In Education

by RICHARD E. SPEAGLE
Prof. of Finance
Drexel Inst. of Technology

Prologue

"System," thanks to wide military usage, has become a prestigious "in" term and is loosely dropped into ordinary conversation to lend it an aura of sophistication. At the opposite pole of usage, formal systems theory is an abstract topic with closely reasoned concepts emerging as an advanced field in higher mathematics.

This exposition is organized in four sections to:

(1) present a popular interpretation of the systems approach;

(2) use general systems theory to explain why the computer is a better learner (and reader) than "Johnny";

(3) obtain cues for needed remedial action in education through a cross-system comparison of the typical computer installation and school; and

(4) urge analytic systems studies as a continuing activity in the education field.

The reader-in-a-hurry may skip parts (2) and (3), trading off a gain in time against a loss in becoming more fully initiated into the workings of the systems approach.

1. A Popular Presentation of Systems

Despite their at times forbidding aspects, systems concepts are highly useful for the purpose at hand—rethinking and reorganizing the education function. At an intermediate level between theory and nonsense, a common sense version may be outlined with adequate precision out of which will grow a more formal definition later on.

In most minds the term "educational system" conjures up an image of school facilities; teachers, students, and administrators; course materials, and instructional techniques. Other "outside" elements admittedly are influential—to use jargon, the educational system is a "subsystem" of the larger social system—but many people choose to view such influences as marginal rather than central.

But are they? And who says so? Scientific tests (and future R&D) may challenge the conventional wisdom as to what is or is not crucial to a child's learning. To take a simple example, the ease with which a youngster absorbs his lessons may be deeply influenced by his food habits and by parental harmony at home. Moreover, temperature in the classroom, distance and mode of travel to school, and the degree of discipline enforced are other vital variables.

An organized, broad-gauged attack on the task of instruction—a "systems approach"—makes traditional boundaries and definitions crumble. If nutrition and family relationships prove important, a breakfast and a mental health program must enter the definition of a complete "school system," and similarly with other "extraneous" influences. The potential impact of and need for this type of systematic thinking to solve problems like that of the ghetto or the rural school is obvious.

General systems *analysis,* defined as the *application* of systems *theory* to the solution of problems, is a three-stage procedure which:

a. asks about the objectives of the job to be done;

b. searches for the most efficient way of doing it, and

c. evaluates performance.

Under a "systems approach," the analysis surveys the entire terrain without preconceived limitations, and examines all major premises. In tradition-bound education, as in many other fields, this is not being done, but now may be the time to start. In an important and broad sense, "instructional technology" means nothing more, nor indeed less, than a thoroughly rational approach to education.

The first stage of educational systems analysis, dealing with the question of objectives, was covered in an earlier chapter on R&D.

The second stage, the search for the best alternative means of instruction, blankets a series of techniques known collectively as operations research (OR). Generally, OR practitioners use such tools (largely mathematical) as linear programming, game theory, queuing theory, simulation, statistical decision techniques and cost-benefit analysis, to name only a few.

In school systems, OR finds its greatest use in the logistics area, including the configuration of computers and terminals that play such a large role in CAI. However, one of the OR techniques, cost-benefit analysis, is of more than routine interest because it probes deeply into the process designs of instruction whenever several alternatives, and media related thereto, compete for doing a given teaching job. This makes cost-benefit comparisons of sufficient importance to deserve a separate chapter.

The third stage of systems analysis, evaluation and control of instructional performance, is a follow-on to decisions about ways and means, and consists of two parts:

(1) the design of measures and measuring methods;

(2) the actual measurement procedure for feedback and control of activities.

A design for measuring "classroom" results must be built into each teaching experiment, and measures so validated subsequently become tools in finding optimal teaching techniques. The logical place to discuss this topic, therefore, is under cost-benefit analysis. The testing operation itself, once viable measures exist, is relatively routine and needs no separate elaboration in this study.

The much publicized planning-programming-budgeting (PPB) technique, increasingly used by government agencies, is an attempt to put public expenditures on a rational or performance basis through a systems approach. Broadly speaking, the initial "P" represents the first stage of systems analysis in a fiscal setting; the second "P" begins the second ways-and-means stage and the final "B"—budgeting—defines program details of organization and scheduling in terms of dollars required.

The third or evaluation stage of systems analysis is undertaken by administrative action, usually by internal audits and later by outside review. In the federal government, the latter step comes under the jurisdiction of the Bureau of the Budget and the General Accounting Office.

Other terminology for applying systems analysis to public expenditures includes "program" and "performance" budgeting. A trap to be avoided consists of adopting the outward form of program budgeting by calling everything that is now being done a "program," while blithely ignoring any substantive attention to systems thinking. In that case, the term "program" becomes simply an empty box tagged with a promising but deceptive label.

The Field of Systems Analysis in Education

The potential breadth and power of systems analysis applied to education is perhaps best illustrated by listing the major structural components which this approach brings under surveillance as it investigates the feasibility and promise of the new instructional media. The list is not exhaustive, but includes the following:

COMPONENTS	THEIR ROLE IN THE SYSTEM
1. Educational goals and objectives	Goals, the broader concept, identify reasons for the expenditure of scarce resources in education rather than, say, industrial production. Objectives define the task of instruction broken down into smaller steps.
2. Learning theory	Furnishes a body of scientific principles which explain learning behavior and orient instruction.
3. Teaching technology	Provides an efficient instrumentation of instructional activities through various media.
4. Educational testing	Measures learning performance in the broadest sense, and thereby helps in the evaluation of 1., 2., and 3.
5. Educational economics	Furnishes data for costing input and valuing educational output; helps to determine sources and uses of funds in education.
6. Teacher training	Produces qualified human resources for the educational enterprise.
7. Student population	Constitutes the "raw material" to which educational processes are applied.
8. School administration and faculty	Represent attitudes and vested interests that must be reckoned with in any change of existing school arrangements.
9. Education industry	Develops and sells teaching devices, school supplies, and educational facilities.
10. Organization of educational research	Helps determine the rate and quality and data output in 2.
11. National manpower needs	Define job opportunities for graduates and helped to direct educational objectives in 1.

12. Student home environment	Influences motivation to learning through living conditions and parental attitudes.
13. Educational politics	Recognizes the role of decision makers and their constituents in formulating educational policies, subject to 1., 5., and 8.
14. Educational strategy	Searches for a combination of above elements to achieve educational goals of 1. in the most effective manner.

It would be tempting to wade right in and begin outlining programs under each of these headings but that is not feasible, being the very kind of comprehensive (and costly) systems study that flows as an urgent recommendation from later sections of this chapter. For the moment, having arrived at this panoramic viewpoint, additional insights into the systems approach can only be gained at the cost of stepping up the rigor of the exposition, taking care to keep it as non-technical as possible.

2a. Computer and School Systems Compared

In its most general meaning, a *system* is a set of interrelated and interacting units having some properties in common. The *state* of each unit—the current condition of any characteristic that is subject to variation—depends in some sense on that of all the others.

Schools may be considered as *living* systems, a special category of *concrete* systems that exist in physical space and move forward in its time dimension. The fundamental binding agent of a school system, and the "glue" as it were of any system, is information (defined below) carried along on moving *markers* or "information-bearers" in a flow known as a communication process. Markers are physical entities or matter-energy, like a letter or electronic impulse, whose movement over space is defined as "action."

The principal function of the school system prototype is to produce and facilitate "learning," which is essentially the receipt, processing, storage and retrieval of information by a chosen clientele, the students. For this purpose the school system uses "specially patterned transmissions of information," a broad expression for "teaching" activities. These constitute an intermediate output of specialized system components, the teaching media.

Teaching output takes the form of *signals* and *messages,* the latter being simply a cluster of signals, which travel via audio waves, gestures, electric or other markers along a grid made up of channels which here may be acoustical, visual or metallic. While animate media, the instructors, are learning themselves when engaged in teaching, their learning is a byproduct and returned as input to the process of teaching students.

The foregoing description of a school may fruitfully be contrasted with that of a related but *mixed,* concrete system, the typical computer complex, inclusive here of hardware, software, programmers and technicians. Focusing on the non-living, equipment subsystem for the moment, it is similarly organized by information flows employing electronic markers that travel within wires or cables when sufficient energy is expended to get them moving along these channels.

The computer system, a man-made analog to the brain, has purposes fairly analogous to those of the school system, to produce and facilitate learning. The exception of course is that here the student is the bolted-down computer installation. Again, what programmers and technicians learn by operating the system is subordinated to the goal of teaching the computer to "learn" ever more efficiently. So far, some amazing learning results have been obtained.

At the next higher level in the systems hierarchy, computers and schools can be seen to belong to a "suprasystem," the education system, which involves additional and complex mutual relationships. These, however, lie outside the immediate concern of this discussion.

2b. Results of Intersystem Comparison

A comparison of the school and the computer points up some dramatic contrasts highly favorable to the latter. The computer system's development displays an impressive degree of perfection and performance. Ends and means of the system, properly matched in various input-output processes, are well and operationally defined. Messages are meticulously constructed from basic information units known as "bits," each bit defining a yes-no or binary possibility that corresponds electrically to the opening or closing of a switch or "gate."

Teaching in this context simply means programming a computer, that is, decomposing incoming messages into bits and then suitably decoding or translating this information into computer language for further processing. On the output or print-out side, incidentally, the process is reversed: computer language is encoded back into the popular idiom. Circuitry and memory units are scientifically designed under physical and information theory principles for the most efficient transmission and storage of impulses, i.e. data processing. The environment of the computer system, from space, heat and humidity requirements to materials specifications, is carefully controlled, having first been engineered with cost-benefit considerations in mind.

Not so in the school, where prevailing conditions border on the primitive:

1. System objectives are ill-defined, and so remain subject to vigorous debate.

2. Learning processes are virtually *terra incognita,* with no solid body of principles to guide scientific applications and techniques.

3. Poor communication means that what principles are discovered are by no means widely or fully applied.

4. The match between marker (medium) and message is a matter of guesswork.

5. Instructional messages are garbled, and rise with difficulty above distortion and random disturbances. On the other hand, information is frequently redundant.

6. The elaboration of more complex messages, like the course content or the curriculum in its entirety, lacks a well-organized rationale.

7. The influences of social conditions and of the academic environment on learning are largely ignored.

8. Roles and decision-making in the school are locked into a traditional power structure. Change is interpreted as a threat and strongly resisted.

9. Results of school activities are largely immeasurable; cost-benefit analysis is stymied.

In fairness to the school, the computer's inanimate state confers tremendous advantages on its human mentors through the precise control of variables in an artificial laboratory situation: the computer stays put while kids do not remain still even for a minute. However the computer must be taught everything that to a child comes naturally, and where the child may overlook or filter out a teacher's mistake the computer comes to a dead stop when it discovers even small programming errors.

A more deep-seated difference favoring the computer is in outlook. The typical computer facility is a no-nonsense, "straight-arrow" operation pointed at definite production goals. The school, on the other hand, still lacks a serious conception of educational processes as at least in part the equivalent of input-output relationships in a service industry. Instead, the typical school district behaves as if its chief purpose in life was to preserve a highly tenuous equilibrium between its political constituencies—administrators, teachers, students and parents.

System-Derived Directions for Education R&D

To discover some remedies for this discrepancy in progress between computer and school, it is necessary to take another step towards formality of statement. Following system-theoretical concepts, the organizing principle for this intersystem diagnosis is the notion of a "critical subsystem"—any process that is essential to a living system for survival.

To serve as an outline of this technique, Table A:

    a. lists these critical subsystems;

    b. describes their function; and

    c. identifies their location and comments on the performance in the typical school compared to a computer facility.

Fuller discussion and a derivation of possible recommendations for action follow immediately after the table which distinguishes three types of critical subsystems:

    1. processors of matter-energy (m-e), which deal with physical entities;

    2. processors of information, which deal with abstract entities; and

    3. processors handling both matter-energy and information.

Since both computers and schools produce services rather than engage in manufacturing (if computer manufacturing is excluded from the first system), the information processing subsystems turn out to be far more important than the matter-energy processing subsystems. The former of course have priority in the value hierarchy and thus determine the specifications of the subordinate "logistic" subsystems. It is teaching and learning which must primarily determine computer design or school layout rather than the other way around, even though engineering and architectural constraints influence what can be taught and learned in either case.

A rational system may be defined as one where the critical subsystems form an integrated whole, oriented to fulfill prime system purposes most efficiently. Failure to achieve such a rational organization, in schools, computer laboratories or whatever, may result in being stuck with a semirandom collection of semirelated processes, many irrelevant or even counterproductive to system goals.

The above cross-comparison of computers and schools pinpoints some crucial areas for action if the latter are ever to catch up. The school's "production subsystems" are not very productive, and other critical subsystems are plainly lacking in efficiency. The principal "hang up" of the school is its tragic ignorance about the very nature of its fundamental "production processes," learning and teaching. This severe and widening gap in "process information" has caused the instructional technology applied to humans to fall ever more behind the natural-science-based computer technology. The need of the hour is a massive, intense, and wide-ranging research effort in "learning sciences," covering at least the following:

FIELD	SUBJECT OF STUDY
1. Neurophysiology	Behavior of central nervous system.
2. Biochemistry	Chemical base of nervous processes.
3. Biophysics	Physical base of nervous processes.
4. Biomathematics	Mathematical modes of physiological processes.

NAME	SUBSYSTEM: FUNCTION	COMPUTER	PERFORMANCE BY: SCHOOL
I. Matter-Energy Processors			
Ingestor	Carry (m-e) from environment across system boundary.	Purchasing function performed on cost-effectiveness principles.	Fair efficiency of purchasing policies.
Distributor	Transfer (m-e) whether inputs from "outside" or "inside" products of system, among components of system.	Production functions performed on cost-effectiveness principles.	Housekeeping, administrative and support activities carried on largely in traditional fashion.
Converter	Change inputs into more useful forms as needed for special system processes.		
Producer	Combine both "outside" (m-e) inputs and outputs of converter into stable form to serve such system needs as growth, repair, or transportation of products and markers.		
Storage (m-e)	Retain "deposits" of (m-e) within system for length of time required.	Business-like inventory and warehousing policies.	Tolerable efficiency in inventories.
Extruder	Dispose of (m-e) in form of products or waste across system boundary.	Distribution of output in rational fashion; waste disposal a trivial problem.	Physical output and disposal problems are trivial.
Motor	Move system in part or as whole relative to environment, and rearrange parts of environment as needed.	No major problem in this area.	Transportation problems minor.
Supporter	Maintain proper distances among system components to prevent crowding.	Location of components determined by engineering principles and OR techniques.	Concept, location and layout of "school facilities" largely traditional.
II. Information Processors			
Input transducer	Sense and receive "outside" markers, such as punch cards, tape or other terminal inputs; process them for further transmission.	Standard part of equipment design.	Needed information fails to enter system, or when brought in, remains unused.
Internal transducer	Sense and receive "inside" markers informing about significant changes within system.	Highly sensitive and reliable process controls.	Difficulty in sensing "what's going on" at administrative, faculty, student and parent levels.

Table A (continued)

NAME	SUBSYSTEM: FUNCTION	COMPUTER	PERFORMANCE BY: SCHOOL
Channel and net	Serve as physical routing grid for marker "traffic" within system.	Close specification of transmission characteristics. Good interpersonal information flows.	At student level, characteristics of nervous system in handling information relatively unknown. Interpersonal communication channels often clogged.
Decoder	Receive outputs from transducer for "translation" into codes (languages) "understandable" to system.	Efficient translation of instructions and other messages into computer languages.	At student level, formation of sensory stimuli into neural codes imperfectly understood.
Associator	Form information items into enduring groups, as the first stage of the "learning process."	Art of organizing information input highly developed.	Theories of learning processes lacking; teaching techniques in ritual stage.
Memory	Store information in the system as the second "stage" of the learning process.	Strategies of marker storage for convenient "warehousing" and rapid retrieval well known; sophisticated disc and tape "memories."	At student level, processes and functions of "remembering" and "forgetting" imperfectly understood. Library management traditional but seeking more advanced concepts.
Decider	Play role of system executive by receiving and transmitting all information inputs and outputs for system-wide control.	Art of giving "instructions" well advanced. Modern decision-making in force.	For lack of educational theories, teachers don't know how to "teach" or students how to "learn" efficiently; at administrative level, primitive decision rules prevail.
Encoder	Translate information from "private" system languages into codes understandable to other systems in the environment.	(Reverse of decoding process.)	(Reverse of decoding process.)
Output transducer	Send markers across system boundaries, changing their (m-e) where necessary, for transmission over channels in environment.	Print, CRT and other types of output highly engineered.	Quantity and quality of output ("learning results") suffer from inadequate information input and storage; similar conditions exist for intermediate instructor outputs.

III. Processors of Matter-energy and Information

NAME	SUBSYSTEM: FUNCTION	COMPUTER	PERFORMANCE BY: SCHOOL
Reproducer	Give rise to similar systems in environment.	Capability inherent in technology.	Capability inherent in system.

5.	Bionics	Search for technological cues in plant and animal behavior.
6.	Psychology	Behavior of "normal" individuals.
7.	Psychiatry	Pathology of human behavior.
8.	Sociology	Behavior of social groups.
9.	Pedagogy	Application of teaching media.
10.	Philosophy of science	Educational objectives.
11.	Computer engineering	Design of computer complexes.
12.	Cybernetics	Simulation of self-organizing learning in computers.
13.	Systems theory	Cross-disciplinary organization of sciences.

Of course the thrust of investigation within these areas must be directed toward one question: how does the individual learn and how can that process be facilitated? Only with the aid of a comprehensive body of theory, gathered through the patient formulation of hypotheses, experimentation and accumulation of proofs, can one begin to specify the actual behavior and components of critical educational subsystems. That is the long-run path of system development in weaponry, in space vehicles and in communication complexes, and so it must be in instructional technology.

At this stage, it seems futile to ask the computer or ITV or any other medium, no matter how "advanced," to solve the school's crisis, by a simple add-on procedure so as to obtain a "modern" education system with all components working together in harness. Such complementarity is potential—it does not yet exist.

While the computer has proven itself as a great learner on its own ground, it cannot perform as a great teacher of humans, as envisaged by CAI and CMI, until its educational function is operationally defined. Without being told its precise role, the computer is a boob in the classroom. Small wonder that up to now no computers have been specifically designed for instructional purposes the way they have been for complex calculations, simulations, and volume routine operations in so many other fields.

4. The Need for Continued Systems Analysis

The study of generalized systems and the formulation of systems theory is not a finished task but is breaking new ground all the time. The previous section provides only a very small sample of the domain and the power of systems theory. Consequently systems analysis, the practical utilization of theory, is not a finished tool but is constantly being updated, strengthened and modified in many salient features.

A semantic confusion arises from a double meaning of the term systems analysis but this is easily clarified. In one sense, systems analysis is like a recipe for baking a cake: a specification of all the necessary ingredients, and their order and mode of combination. In a second sense, systems analysis may mean doing the actual baking by following the instructions in the recipe. How well the cake turns out depends largely on the skill of the cook.

Extending this analogy, systems analysis may mean either the art and activity of "writing new recipes," or the art and activity of "using known recipes to bake different kinds of cakes, pastry or other dishes." The point is that systems analysis is not any "one-shot" affair—something that is done once and finished—but a continuing type of endeavor on a theoretical and practical plane. Moreover, just as the author of recipes may work in a model kitchen while the cook is slaving over a hot stove, the theoretical systems analyst works out his "blue prints" in some "think tank" or research laboratory while the practitioner is out "in the sticks" surveying some school district.

The gastronomic explanation of the systems approach may be stretched to deal with more complicated concoctions, like a seven-layer cake. Here the recipe consists of three "sub-recipes," that of the cake, the filling and the frosting, which must be properly prepared and combined in the right proportions, the right order, and at the right time.

Systems analysis too deals with an often complicated hierarchy of subsystems which must be identified and separated, level by level, for special treatment and later combination. In education considered as a suprasystem, system analysis may focus at a low but basic level on the classroom situation; at a somewhat higher level on the local school district; at an intermediate level on a specialized subsystem like textbook publishing; or, at a level difficult to specify, on a complex, interpenetrating subsystem like national instructional television.

There are as many potential applications of systems analysis as there are systems at different levels. The difficulty of interpretation varies from relatively simple to highly intricate, as in the design of an effective missile defense.

For the moment, the application of systems analysis in education faces its biggest obstacle in the lack of knowledge of and R&D in learning processes, as mentioned before. Going back to the kitchen analogy, the situation resembles that where a recipe for bread calls for a certain amount of flour, and as it happens the cupboard is bare, the grocer is out of it, the miller has exhausted his supply, and the farmer is facing a crop failure. The outlook for genuine bread under those circumstances is extremely dim until the problem of flour supply can be straightened out.

There is no magic in a recipe as such, nor can there be in systems analysis, when some basic ingredients are missing. But knowing exactly *which* ingredients are lacking and *why* may lead to asking the right questions, and from there straight to action for prompt procurement. In that respect, theoretical systems analysis is able to put educational development on the right track, principally by organizing its R&D effort and by pointing it in the right direction. If the will and the funds are there, the job can be done.

51.
Major Problems
Facing Public Schools
In the Seventies*

by SIDNEY G. TICKTON, RONALD GROSS, and PAUL OSTERMAN
Exec. Vice Pres.   *Vice Pres.*   *Program Assoc.*
Editor-in-Chief

Academy for Educational Development

Introduction

The purpose of this paper is to describe the major problems facing American public schools in the coming decade, and to indicate alternative approaches toward solving these problems.

To hold a subject so wide in scope within reasonable limits, rigorous selection has been essential. Other observers might come up with a somewhat different set of problems, and, in some cases, different alternatives. Thus, for example, the church-state issue is not treated in this memorandum. However, most informed analysts of the school system would select the areas, which are taken up in the following pages, as presenting the most critical problems facing our schools today.

Goals

The Problem

The question of the essential role of the schools—what they should do and should not do—is increasingly important to everybody concerned about education, but particularly to those responsible for policy. The policy-makers today must be prepared, if necessary, to expand the role of the schools or be able to show why not.

Some people believe that systematic organized learning, with the emphasis on the academic and intellectual, is the special function of the schools. However, others—harking back to an earlier generation—believe that schools should play a positive role in building a new and better social order.

To the extent that this enlarged view of the schools' responsibility prevails, the task of the schools (as applied to the conditions of contemporary urban life) is made obviously so much the more difficult. However, for the schools to try to divorce themselves completely from community problems including matters of social and economic justice, could be an abrogation of essential community responsibility.

To raise such questions about the responsibilities of the public schools invites a debate

This paper is developed out of materials prepared for a number of Academy seminars and symposia.

on educational theory and philosophy. But as a practical matter, the schools have been increasingly extending their activities and scope. Even greater participation in community problems can be expected of the schools in the future.

Apparently, in fact, the prevailing belief that the schools' prime concern is "academic" has perforce made room for the recognition that schools *have* to offer programs in important areas—health, technology, citizenship, culture, recreation, and trade. This additional requirement is particularly acute where the home, the church, industry, and other institutions of society do not or cannot provide essential experience in these areas.

Related to this conflict is the question of the time-span of the school's program: should formal education begin very early in the child's life, prior to kindergarten or first grade, and should it continue, at public expense, beyond high school to embrace a year or two of junior college? The value of an earlier start is reinforced by recent findings in psychology, which indicate that early experiences condition a child's entire later development. Extension of schooling for an additional year or two grows out of the demands of an increasingly specialized labor market.

Today a good school system cannot ignore the influences—positive or negative—that home and community have on every child. It is bound to heed whether he comes to school well-fed or hungry; properly shod or barefooted; whether he walks to school or is bused; whether he comes from a cultivated household or a fatherless ghetto tenement.

In the big cities particularly, the aims of the public schools are woven into the aims and needs of the whole city.

Alternative Solutions

One approach to the problem of educational goals would be to maintain the traditional stress on academic and intellectual training, despite the momentous changes in social conditions nowadays. To do so, however, would necessarily ignore the individual needs of a large proportion of children for whom such goals, as commonly exemplified, have proven to be inadequate or inappropriate.

Going to the other extreme, the schools could try to spearhead the movement for overall social betterment—as vigorously advocated a generation ago by reformers like George Counts in his book, *Dare The Schools Create A New Social Order?* This approach would probably alienate most Americans, who seem to feel that, while the schools are necessarily concerned with the welfare of society as a whole and the child's development as a rounded human being, their role is *primarily* intellectual.

A middle position would be this: society's problems today are so critical that the schools must participate actively in the areas of greatest public need and, through such intervention, hasten redress of existing and potential inequities.

Those who support this middle position base their case not on theory but on sheer utility. The school is in a practical position to act where other institutions have failed or cannot act or don't exist. A good school *can* mitigate some of a child's family, social, economic handicaps. Gifted schoolteachers and administrators can take the home and community into their confidence, establish a dialogue, even try to change what is baleful. For some children, in the worst circumstances, they can if they will act quite literally in *loco parentis*.

The compromise position outlined need not rule out a commitment to the distinctively intellectual function of formal education, and this could serve to restrain the overextension and fragmentation of the school program. Perhaps the most searching examination of the goals for the American public school system was provided in 1963 by the Project on Instruction of the National Education Association. This distinguished group (whose work formed the basis for the NEA's present Center for the Study of Instruction) consulted extensively with experts and leading citizens throughout the nation, and concluded that schools should focus on intellectual competence as the distinctive goal of formal education.

It cited the definitive statement once made by the Educational Policies Commission:

> The purpose which runs through and strengthens all other educational purposes—
> the common thread of education—is the development of the ability to think. This
> is the central purpose to which the school must be oriented if it is to accomplish
> either its traditional tasks or those newly accentuated by recent changes in the
> world. To say that it is central is not to say that it is the sole purpose or in all
> circumstances the most important purpose, but that it must be a pervasive concern
> in the work of the school. Many agencies contribute to achieving educational
> objectives, but this particular objective will not be generally attained unless the
> school focuses on it. In this context, therefore, the development of every student's
> rational powers must be recognized as centrally important.[1]

The final report of this NEA group also recommended the development of specialized
vocational competence as a primary goal of schooling. Finally, it stressed the responsibility
of the school system in a democratic society for developing the potentiality of each child.

It is, perhaps, this stress on the importance of the *individual* that may best reconcile
diverse views of education's goals. Concern for the individual embraces his intellectual
development, his preparation for a chosen vocation or profession, the encouragement of
his artistic sensitivities and creativity, the nurture of his spirit, will, and sense of purpose.
But it is primarily through programs of organized systematic learning that the school can
exercise this concern.

Control

The Problem

Who runs the public schools? The superintendents? The principals? The boards of education? The teachers? The local governments? The mayors? Parents and students? Who? The
answer in a word is: "Everyone." The school systems of the United States, it would seem,
are everybody's business (and by that token sometimes, it appears, nobody's).

But however much citizens at large are, or could be, involved in the determination of
educational policy, it is the professional educators who must tend to the day-to-day running
of the schools. At this level of administrative control, the public schools throughout the
country face a problem familiar to businessmen: How can a large, necessarily bureaucratic,
and centralized organization preserve or encourage local initiative and creativity?

Decentralization of authority and responsibility are the order of the day in many corporations which want to offset the negative effects of bigness. But the present pattern of
school organization in most big cities tends to a higher degree of centralization. As a result,
many urban school principals and teachers feel insufficient freedom to plan programs for
particular school populations. This rigidity is, viewed from one angle, the bad by-product
of a good purpose: to further equality of opportunity among a city's schools through the
maintenance of common standards for both programs and services. But well-intentioned as
these procedures may be and as successful as they may have been in the past, they do not
meet the pressing problems of the present and the future.

Obviously the centralization of certain functions—for example, long-range planning,
purchasing, data processing, budgeting, building construction, and overall policy development—augments economy and efficiency. On the other hand, when decisions bearing directly
upon programs of instruction in particular schools and upon the relationships among principals, teachers, students, and parents are masterminded from a remote central office, the
school system takes on the character of a bureaucracy, and quality of performance and
satisfaction—of students, teachers, principals, parents—is apt to be diminished.

Alternative Solutions

It is no longer possible to ignore the question of school control. In city after city, parents and others have made it clear that they can and will disrupt the educational process unless and until they are made to feel a part of it.

One approach is to involve directly in the affairs of the public schools citizens who are neither board members nor teachers nor necessarily parents. A new kind of partnership is in the making. As Francis Keppel has said: "Education is too important to be left only to the educators."

Harold Howe II, who preceded Mr. Allen as U.S. Commissioner of Education, has cited some of the major considerations in bringing about a stronger school-community partnership:

> At a time when innovations and increased specialization make education more complex, nothing is more important to its healthy growth than simple and direct communication from the professionals who lead it to the laymen who are responsible for it. . . .

Another approach would go beyond improved communication. Today educators, in many cases pressed by minority groups in the large cities, are taking a new look at the possibilities for decentralization. (At the same time, in rural areas, the consolidation of inefficiently small school systems continues.) Even the U.S. Office of Education itself is in the midst of a program of decentralization through building up the capabilities of regional offices; state departments of education are being bolstered in the same way.

Ex-Commissioner Howe suggested the lines along which even more progress might be made:

> I propose that we take a step toward broader local control of education by increasing the number of school boards in the densely populated urban areas. It seems to be absurd that our large cities, with hundreds of thousands of school children, should limit the advantage of stimulation from interested laymen on a school board to a single group of 10 to 15 members. How can a dozen school board members give any sense of representation and participation to the many neighborhoods of a city differing vastly from each other in their economic and social make-up? It is worth exploring the notion, as New York City has, that perhaps our largest cities should have as many as a dozen school boards, each running a cluster of elementary and secondary schools, and each with a majority representation of citizens who live in the neighborhood. Such a system would bring a much greater sense of direct participation in the formulation of school policy. It would give district superintendents a much greater chance to advocate promising new ideas in education, and it would generate a most productive variety of experimentation.
>
> We must welcome and encourage a responsible interest in the schools by laymen who hold no official position except that of citizen. I know that superintendents frequently resent school-study groups made up of local busybodies or the occasional self-appointed saviours of either the school curriculum or the local tax rate. But these abuses should not blind us to the growing movement of reasonable citizen interest in education. Worthy organizations at the local, state, and national level express this interest, and we all stand to gain by it when it is well-planned and well-led.[2]

Still another approach is the one which the United States Chamber of Commerce's task force on economic growth and opportunity put forward in its report on education: competitive education. Under this arrangement the government would continue to finance the education of all children—but would offer, as an alternative to public education, financial support for private education up to the amount of the average expenditure per pupil in local public schools. The task force based this unusual suggestion on its conviction of the importance of sound education, coupled with a concern that the present institutional structure may not be the best or only way to achieve this end. The task force recognized that the suggestion raises constitutional questions, having to do with the participation of sectarian schools and with the use of the technique to permit racial discrimination.

Financing

The Problem

Spending money to get good schools is sound public policy: there is wide recognition of this fact. The reasoning can be entirely pragmatic. Research shows a high relationship between level of education achieved and personal income. Money spent on education is a good investment: it provides good rates of return to individuals, corporations, cities, states, and the nation as a whole. The economic progress of the nation, and the future of business and industry specifically, depends heavily on the provision of the best possible education for America's children.

Nonetheless American public education now faces serious financial problems. The system needs large additional funds every year—as it will for a considerable number of years to come—in order to fulfill its essential functions. But restrictions on educational financing, particularly in the large cities, has meant that important school needs have been neglected.

Heavy reliance on local taxes, together with legal limitations placed by state legislatures on the amount of school taxes cities could levy, has severely constrained the financing of many urban school systems, and faced them with serious deficits for years to come.

But more money for city schools, desperately as it is needed, would not be enough in itself. The very procedure of initiating, developing, and financing requisite educational change should be revised. In general, present procedures do not provide the basis on which to judge: (a) which programs to expand, (b) how much to expand them, (c) how the expansion of any particular program should be related to overall needs, and (d) how much money to allocate for the changes contemplated to achieve the results desired.

An improved procedure for financial planning is the "program budgeting" long used by business corporations and now being adopted by the Defense Department and other agencies of the federal government. Using this procedure, a school or school system determines *precisely* what ought to be done to improve educational programs, allocates the necessary money and people, and then does what has to be done to reach the specific objectives established. Evaluation of costs as related to educational gains is an important aspect of program budgeting.

Alternative Solutions

Where will the necessary increased funds come from? Since the great depression, property taxes—still the main source of school financing—have been declining relative to other sources of funds for public schools.

The levy of additional property taxes is one conceivable way to provide the additional money needed for education. However, property taxes based on assessments of real estate rarely reflect the true value of property, even after equalization techniques have been applied. More important, property values do not share proportionately in increased levels of income and production. And tax levies on property are subject to a wide variety of local resistances, including statutory and, in some cases, constitutional restrictions designed to prevent tax-rate increases. Organized opposition by taxpayer groups now appears to be augmented, in community after community, by a much broader opposition to increased levies for schools. In the years immediately ahead, therefore, property taxes can hardly be expected to provide the increased revenue needed to finance the improved education the times require.

An alternative solution is a combination of income taxes and sales taxes, since these would harness both state and federal taxing powers. Unlike the local property tax, these taxes reflect increased volume of income and production. They would meet greatly expanded expenditures for urban schools without hampering the economy, local or national.

A subordinate alternative would choose between state and federal taxes. In general, the basic principle of using statewide taxing power to equalize educational opportunities throughout the state has long been an established policy, and state equalization has undoubtedly encouraged educational improvement. Until now, however, only the federal government has recognized the special problems which high density and poverty bring to large city school systems; but federal funds, while growing in importance, are still not adequate to make a real dent in these problems. Therefore existing inequities in state equalization programs and what to do about them is a critical public policy issue.

There is no doubt that the people of the United States can pay for the kind of education and the quality of instruction that they want for their children. The problem is now, as it has always been, how to make available for public schools everywhere a relatively small— but at least adequate—percentage of the income and productivity of each city, metropolitan area, state, and of the nation as a whole.

Curriculum

The Problem

The schools are an agency of society, and society's needs and concerns at a given moment in history have always, within limits, legitimately shaped the curriculum. Today the American society is changing rapidly in many ways. These changes generate—perhaps more forcefully than ever before—this problem: What should the schools teach?

A brief look at some major social changes will help define the problem. In the first place, the fate of the United States is tied up as never before with the rest of the world. Are our boys and girls learning to understand the wide range of difference in human experience, belief, and culture among their contemporaries in other countries, and are we introducing children to these differences early enough in their school program?

Secondly, the United States is increasingly an urban and mobile society. Technological change climaxed by automation marks—and, at times, mars—our progress. Leisure time grows for most of our citizens. Minority groups are demanding the equal opportunities long promised but previously closed to them. Pressing problems—of racism, air and water pollution, crime, highway safety, misuse of natural resources—impinge more and more on the American way of life. Do the schools provide young people with enough knowledge and understanding of these problems so that they can relate them to their own well-being and to their responsibilities?

A third force affecting the school curriculum is the "knowledge explosion." The amount of new knowledge, together with the numbers of new jobs it produces, is so vast and multiplying so rapidly as to cause, in itself, an educational revolution. Schools have never been able to teach all that students should know, to be sure. The task has become so patently impossible that it places increased urgency on efforts to make formal education more selective in content, more centered on basic concepts.

Finally, the need to reach more and more students, vastly different in their capacities and interests, challenges the standard school curriculum. The challenge strikes education at many different points. Schools are having to develop curricula to meet the needs of teenagers who once might have left school, and at the same time to devise programs for pre-kindergarten children. The changing ethnic and socio-economic character of the school population, as a whole, has brought major new needs into sharp focus.

Alternative Solutions

Our society is changing very fast. One response is to keep the curriculum essentially the same, stressing the basic academic subjects and striving to make them more available and relevant for a wider range of students.

A second approach would be to broaden the curriculum constantly, striving to keep the various subjects up to date, and to meet the changing needs of different kinds of students. This is the add-it-on approach, constantly attempting to make room for more things in the curriculum—international study or African languages, new technical courses or more advanced mathematics offerings.

A third approach is to establish priorities among the elements of the curriculum. One criterion which has gained favor recently is: whatever will help students "learn how to learn"—using procedures and materials which help the student learn how to acquire the particular knowledge and achieve the understanding *he* needs largely on his own. With this approach, for example, schools would strive for greater student understanding of international affairs and of the dramatic changes and problems of American society, without introducing huge quantities of new material into the curriculum. Instead they would try to train students in the basic processes of discovery and analysis that specialists apply to problems in their fields.

Teachers and Teaching

The Problem

The most important—and expensive—single resource the school contributes to the quality of learning is the school's professional staff: instructional, supervisory, administrative, and special services (remedial instruction, guidance, psychological counseling, etc.). Virtually every school system in the country faces difficulties in finding enough qualified teachers. But the problem goes beyond mere numbers.

As the school population, particularly in the cities, becomes increasingly heterogeneous, schools will more and more need sensitive teachers who understand the nature of individual differences and who, by background and training, are prepared to deal with them effectively.

Teachers now and tomorrow must not only understand students better, but their subjects, too. Ten years from now, any body of knowledge mastered by a college graduate today will be largely obsolete. Yet ten years after college is just when a teacher is reaching the peak of performance and responsibility. Obviously, constant in-service training is a necessity.

Supervision of teaching raises other problems. The responsibility for instructional supervision in most American school systems rests primarily on the central-office personnel, on school principals, and, in secondary schools, on the department chairmen. This "standard" form has generally served the schools well.

There are, however, two major dangers in the standard approach:

1. The inherent possibility that the ends of supervision may come to be increasingly identified with systemwide uniformity and conformity; and

2. as well-organized supervision becomes increasingly "available" to both schools and teachers, teachers—particularly new, beginning teachers—may come to rely too heavily on supervisors for direction, make understandable efforts to satisfy what they perceive as the supervisor's wishes and suggestions, and be correspondingly less inventive and creative in their teaching.

Alternative Solutions

There is widespread agreement that we need more teachers, better trained teachers, teachers who are able and willing to keep their knowledge and techniques up-to-date, better conditions for teaching, and more effective supervision. How can these be obtained?

One approach is to merely continue the trends of recent years, gradually raising teachers' salaries to attract and hold more capable people, and strengthening pre-service and in-service programs wherever possible.

For example, schools could extend their efforts to recruit teachers whose familiarity with the social and behavioral sciences embraces more than a cursory and elementary knowledge of psychology, anthropology, economics, political science, and demography. A strong preparation in these fields, reinforced by clinical experience, assumes sharp relevance to the overall competence of teachers whose work will increasingly compel them to understand the day-to-day realities of life in city slums.

For teachers already at work in the schools, substantially better in-service training programs could accomplish much. Such programs need to give particular attention to:

a. direct and sustained efforts to improve and fortify the teachers' understanding of individual and group differences;

b. adapting instructional methods more relevant to both individual and group differences;

c. a better understanding of the existing social, economic, and cultural forces.

As to conditions of teaching and supervision, the constant pressure to reduce the size of classes and to provide additional help to the classroom teacher have certainly proved of some value. However, this approach has hardly brought about sufficient school improvement to meet present and future demands.

Some educators have suggested new ways to achieve better teaching. They suggest, for example, that while efforts to reduce the average size of classes be continued, schools should also consider other promising approaches to the matter of class size, some of which have has a limited "try-out" in enterprising school systems, but none of which has apparently been encouraged on a systemwide basis in many large school systems. Among these the following deserve special mention:

1. Team teaching, which provides flexibility in grouping and regrouping students into small, medium, and large groups, depending on the particular instructional purpose and method. Team teaching arrangements, typically, place responsibility with the teachers composing the team, and do not require any change in school-wide scheduling. The same flexibility in increasing numbers of secondary schools is being achieved through departmental responsibility for grouping and regrouping on a basis approaching "at once and at will."

2. Use of the new educational technology to facilitate instruction of large and small groups, and self-instruction as well. Television and the "self-teaching" machine are two examples.

3. Computerized scheduling which can, with careful planning and advance programming, achieve more flexible schedules with a minimum of irreconcilable conflicts.

4. More flexible treatment of time and the number of time periods into which the school day is divided.

5. Wider opportunities for independent learning under conditions which do not require the physical presence of a teacher.

6. The use of nonprofessionals to assist teachers and administrators. Their recruitment and training will be an important undertaking for the public schools. Key attributes for these aides are a liking for children and a willingness to work as a team member. Judicious recruiting of nonprofessionals could also encourage some of them to prepare for full-time careers in teaching.

As to the supervision of teaching, its major function should be to help the teacher to identify his unique strengths, to organize and improve them, and to teach at the top of his capacities. High-level supervision should be a stimulus to the teacher to be creative, to be self-critical, to improve. Imaginative supervision of this kind, many critics contend, is not apt to flourish in a highly centralized, bureaucratic setting. While in large school systems the central office obviously must assume overall responsibility, the fulcrum around which supervision is organized should be the individual school.

Facilities

The Problem

In the 20 years since building materials again became available for public construction after the close of World War II, the American people have built more classrooms, school libraries, gyms, athletic fields, auditoriums, lunchrooms, and other educational facilities than had been built in the entire previous history of the country.

Yet today, a generation after the start of the greatest school building boom ever, with some $50 billion of new construction already completed, the need for new schools and additional classrooms continues high. School authorities are constantly confronted with the need for additional educational space, better space, and remodeled space. Despite mammoth programs of planning, financing, site acquisition, designing, and construction, school facilities rarely keep up with the growth and change of population.

But sheer space is only part of the problem. The question is not only how much to build, but where and what. Most schools built today are built on the general model of the schools which school board members and school administrators once attended. Rarely is consideration given to the fact that the needs of the community and the requirements of effective instruction have changed or are changing rapidly. New ideas, ranging from educational parks to the use of carpeting, are not often considered. Flexible schools which permit teachers to break out of the egg-crate pattern of self-contained classrooms in order to experiment with team teaching, independent study, and other promising techniques are only occasionally designed. In short, educational problems, educational philosophy, and educational methods are changing faster than the design of educational facilities. The result: rigid walls that constrain education into old patterns and inhibit new ways to organize a school for maximum effective learning.

There is good reason, in many cases, for following this essentially conservative approach. Teachers are accustomed to traditional school design, and often resist innovation. Also, the problems and the costs involved in such construction are familiar. Undoubtedly, a very large proportion of the school construction in the Seventies will follow the traditional approach.

In addition to the problems of quantity and quality there is an additional problem which particularly afflicts the central core of the cities. Obsolete schoolhouses have for too long, in too many deteriorating neighborhoods been the very symbol of the surrounding decay, according to Harold Gores, president of the Educational Facilities Laboratories of the Ford Foundation. The school is almost never equipped to serve the community at large. Mr. Gores also says:

> Increasingly, society is asking that new schools be planned in such a way that they are integrated or, at the very least, so that segregation is substantially reduced. And the new schoolhouses must be equipped with, or designed to accommodate, facilities for the community services they inevitably will be asked to provide.

Alternative Solutions

One approach to problems raised by school facilities is to proceed cautiously, building schools when and as the need becomes critical, and designing them pretty much as we always have designed schools. This is the policy which is frequently followed, for a number of compelling reasons—because it seems more economical, because the community is suspicious of newfangled designs, because administrators and teachers want buildings like the ones they're used to.

A second approach is to speed up the process, by finding the money to build more schools faster, but still to plan, build, and place them in the conventional way. This approach meets the immediate problem, but is not apt to produce schools that encourage educational change or that help to alleviate the crisis in our cities.

A third alternative is to apply more money in new ways, planning and placing facilities so that schools can more easily adopt promising new procedures and can effectively assume their civic role.

To adopt this third approach, educational policy-makers need to know a great deal about school construction and design, plant modernization, space utilization, and building maintenance, as well as about the social dynamics of the community. To acquire such understanding and knowledge school systems, individually and in concert with other systems and with business organizations, should undertake a substantial research-and-development program.

Equality of Educational Opportunity

The Problem

Current public attention to equal educational opportunity might suggest that this is a new idea. It is, of course, nothing of the kind. Equal opportunity is the very basis—in theory, at any rate—of public education in the United States. But the country's present, long overdue concern with the civil rights of Negroes and other minorities has sharply accentuated the long struggle for equal educational opportunity.

The American public school was created to combat the social inequities of a system that provided education only for the rich or the very bright. The upsurge of concern with equality today is only the latest and most dramatic in a long series of confrontations going back 100 years or more between the public schools and pressing social or individual needs. Over the years America has constantly responded to demands for greater educational opportunity—including such developments as universal secondary education, education of the mentally and the physically handicapped, the advanced placement program, neighborhood schools, school-district consolidation, community colleges.

Thus public education has, over time, broadened its scope and procedures, and has tried to give each child the opportunity to become all he is capable of becoming. While educators and laymen agree that every child should have this opportunity, it is difficult to reach a consensus as to how equal educational opportunity may best be ensured. The difficulty is not surprising, perhaps: putting this ideal into practice hinges on many things we still don't know enough about and on which we often disagree—the conditions which foster equal educational opportunity keep changing.

What worked well enough for generations past, in school materials, school organization, teachers and techniques, will not necessarily work well for the latest arrivals in the seemingly never-ending parade of "disadvantaged" youngsters passing through our schools.

Alternative Solutions

One approach to this pressing and pervasive problem is to strengthen and increase "compensatory education" programs. The programs which have sprung up around the country in the last few years, strive to include the following elements: better staffing; more effective teaching; use of new materials, methods, and technology; provision of psycho-educational diagnosis and treatment; flexible grouping to fit different instructional purposes; extensions of the school; development of social support; wider and more stimulating out-of-school experiences; financial assistance; skilled guidance to opportunities in work or advanced education; remedial instruction in academic skills; procedures which seek to raise the expectations of teachers, students, and parents in order to overcome negative attitudes which impede learning; work with pre-school children in verbal skills, the arts, games, etc.

However, Dr. Edmund Gordon, who recently completed an exhaustive study of the nation's compensatory education programs, says: "Despite all our current efforts, tremendous gains are not being achieved. We are probably failing because we have not yet found the right answers."

If the compensatory-education approach falls short, what might work better? Some people argue that full integration is the only answer, but the demographic and housing concentrations in the larger cities makes this a long-range prospect at best. Of course, minimizing racial isolation, at least in school, is a basic aspect of compensatory education. Thus, a minimum program, which is properly directed at helping each individual child, arranges for students of different ethnic, social, and economic backgrounds to share significant and stimulating experiences.

Other, more enterprising strategies which have recently been tried with success include:

a. Capitalizing on a program of school modernization to facilitate, if only for a time, great increase in the contacts between students of different backgrounds from different parts of a city.

b. Open enrollment which leaves the choice of school to the individual (within limits of space and the ethnic makeup of the school population) but assures him of free transportation, sound assistance in locating an appropriate school, and the special compensatory guidance if he requires it.

c. Reorganizing the grades assigned to two or more schools to include a greater cross section of the community in each.

d. Concentrating most or all of the public school services on one site (or in large cities, on a number of strategically located sites) so that the children come from many different parts of the community from kindergarten age through high school. These concentrations are often called educational parks or school villages.

e. Developing a number of specialized schools (or specialized programs within comprehensive schools) which will, because of their excellence and uniqueness, attract students from all over the community.

f. Using school buses to move students to under-utilized schools which are more attractive physically, socially, and intellectually than those the students normally attend. This procedure has been used within cities and between them as well.

g. Drawing (and from time to time, redrawing) attendance boundaries in order that each neighborhood school may reflect something of the composition of the larger community.

h. Clustering a number of elementary-school districts, allowing students to attend any one of the schools in the enlarged district, and thus encouraging more diversified enrollment.

The results thus far of school experimentation along these lines suggest that no one arrangement or combination of arrangements is wholly satisfactory. The problem will continue to demand great ingenuity and creative endeavor.

Evaluation

The Problem

Public interest in education today is very strong. What happens in the schools and to the schools is important to everyone. Politicians, businessmen, PTA presidents, League of Women Voters study teams, civil rights leaders, members of school boards, schoolteachers, principals, parents, and many others are searching for an answer to the question: How good are our schools? How can they be improved?

This question is asked incessantly across the country by people concerned with the quality of public education. The answer they get usually begins: "It is impossible to measure the quality of education precisely because. . . ."[3]

Part of the difficulty is that the perceptions of those asking the question vary tremendously. Businessmen, politicians, and taxpayers generally would like to hear that everything is fine and that no tax increase will be necessary. Employers who hire school graduates have their views—often subjective—and are not about to change them no matter what a report might say on the subject. Parents in turn approach the problem with different perceptions and different blindspots.

The concern of educators with questions of educational quality is often discounted as the opening gambit in a campaign for more money. Many businessmen are prone to relate "quality in education" to "efficiency" in industry and business; they want "hard" evidence that spending more money for schools will produce correspondingly more efficient employees or lead to lower costs at a later time. Many Americans would be willing to spend more on schools if they could be sure money would produce quality.

Attempting to measure the quality of a school system is, and no doubt will continue to be, one of the most frustrating and least successful endeavors of educators, though some useful starts have been made.[4] Those who seek a simple answer are the most frustrated. The quality of education involves many intangibles which are difficult if not impossible to measure. It reflects, in sum, a delicate interplay between the child's home environment, the environment of the school, and the community itself. In some cases the home may reinforce, enrich, and otherwise strengthen the teaching and learning provided by the school, but the influence of the community may be negative or outright destructive. In other instances the influence of the home may be neutral; at worst, it may tear down or impede the efforts of the school.

Every public school system seeking to improve itself wants yardsticks by which to appraise its success. Actually, the extent to which a school system seeks evidence of its shortcoming (strengths are usually quite obvious), discusses them openly, and proceeds to do something to remedy them becomes one measure of quality. Given the importance of education to the individual and to society, plus its high cost, it is no longer enough to tell the public— children, parents, all interested citizens—that educational quality is too complicated to measure or to hide weaknesses under meaningless statistics or blame them on lack of money.

Alternative Solutions

Although the precise measurement of educational quality may be impossible, there now exist yardsticks by which to gauge a program or school or system. For example:

1. In a large city system, serving a multi-ethnic school population, is recognition given to the wide range of student capacities, talents, and needs? Does the system advance each child to his highest possible levels of achievement?

2. How well does the system draw on all available resources to meet the educational needs of each individual child? Does the system generally view these resources as limited to the school staff, the system-owned buildings, the school-owned equipment; or does it include the city, the county, the state, and for that matter, the nation as a whole? Large city schools tend to be particularly unimaginative in making maximum use of the myriad resources available—in the immediate neighborhood as well as far afield.

3. How successful is the system in releasing the creative abilities and innovative talents of administrators and staff? Does the system maintain a vigorous research program to find new ideas, and also encourage its personnel to do the same in their various assignments?

4. How well do the students do when they leave school, not just in their livelihoods but in their lives? Many people think this is the most important standard against which school quality should be judged.

5. Studies which follow the progress of individual students over the length of their school career and after are especially important in education. In fact, without such longitudinal studies of a carefully drawn sample of children, the impact of a school's program and procedures on each child can only be inferred from unrefined statistics.

6. Have appropriate steps been taken in recognition of the "knowledge explosion" and of the growing futility of trying to cram students with facts?

Innovation

The Problem

The educational problems facing America today cannot be solved, in the time and with the resources available, by merely attempting to duplicate conventional educational patterns. The nation's most imaginative educators recognize that putting more money into the old ways of doing things will no longer suffice. The world is changing too fast, the knowledge explosion, the urban crisis, and other pressing problems pose too great a challenge.

Quality and innovation are as closely bound together in education as they are in industry, but few people realize it. The major companies in the United States today spend between three and four percent of their income on research and development. It would be hard to exaggerate the benefits that could accrue if school systems and colleges spent three to four percent of *their* total budgets on planning new developments and improvements. A school system, however good its past and present reputation, which is not experimenting today with new ways of improving education is probably slated for decline. Today good education is largely synonymous with innovative education. Innovation means change.

The past ten years have accomplished much in extending the frontiers of education. The end is not in sight. The accomplishments fall into three major areas.

1. The Harnessing of Modern Technology to Education. The apparatus of schooling has been transformed. An industrialized society based on electronics, automation, and computers, for example, cannot afford to drag behind it an inefficient educational system still dependent on the blackboard and the slide projector.

2. The Radical Revision of Education's Pattern. The conventional ways of training, organizing and deploying teachers and students are coming under increasingly sharp scrutiny and reexamination. The standardized school, serving only a very limited neighborhood and composed of identical, self-enclosed classrooms, is becoming more flexible and functional educationally and geographically. Teaching is being tried in teams rather than solo, with each team member concentrating on his strongest technique or specialty. The system of grades has begun to disintegrate, with students permitted to progress at their individual rates in each subject. Teachers are beginning to assume a new look, too, through training programs which stress broad liberal education, meaningful practice teaching, sophisticated professional courses, and the use of technology.

3. The Development of New Ideas About How Students Acquire Knowledge and Understanding. With an increasing recognition of the great varieties of human ability unmeasurable by IQ tests, steps are being taken to exploit the student's intrinsic drive for learning.

In short, education in the United States has now entered on an intensive reexamination of some fundamental assumptions. Schools are looking hard at the old ideas—the fixed class size, the measurement of learning by the number of years spent in school, the self-contained school,—and often modifying them or replacing them by new principles. Especially in schooling for the disadvantaged, change—change in policy and practice—is the byword in most of our cities.

Still, the innovative approach which so permeates American business has not yet thoroughly pervaded education.

REFERENCES

1. *Schools for the Sixties.* National Education Association. New York: McGraw-Hill, 1963, p. 111.

2. Cited in *Quality Education in Milwaukee's Future: Recommendations to the Citizens Advisory Committee to Comprehensive Survey of Milwaukee Public Schools and the Milwaukee Board of School Directors.* New York, Academy for Educational Development, 1967, pp. 78-79.

3. The Chamber of Commerce's task force on economic growth and opportunity observed in its report on education that "There is little information to measure the quality of the public school 'output'—the student or graduate."

4. A recent publication of the National Education Association called *Profiles of Excellence* can be used by individuals or groups to review the activities of a school system or of individual schools.

52.

Implementing the Standards Established for School Media Programs

by LORAN C. TWYFORD, JR.
Chief, Bureau of Classroom
Communications
N.Y. State Education Dept.

Early in 1969, the American Library Association and the National Education Association published a booklet entitled, "Standards for School Media Programs."* The standards presented in this Publication had been prepared by a Joint Committee of the American Association of School Librarians and the Department of Audiovisual Instruction of the National Education Association in cooperation with an Advisory Board consisting of representatives from 28 professional and civic associations.

Although the American Association of School Librarians had revised their national standards in 1960 and the Department of Audiovisual Instruction had released standards in 1966, significant social changes, educational developments, and technological innovations had made it imperative to present new statements of standards. Adding impetus to the urgency for revision were the numerous requests from school administrators, audiovisual specialists, classroom teachers, curriculum specialists, school librarians, and other educators.

In describing the rationale for the standards, the booklet said:

> The two objectives that motivated the project are: (1) to bring standards in line with the needs and requirements of today's educational goals and (2) to coordinate standards for school library and audiovisual programs.

> The most important aim was, of course, to present standards for media programs that would best aid the schools in implementing their educational goals and instructional programs. The standards are designed for schools seeking to give young people education of good quality. Schools with innovative curricula and instructional techniques will need and want to go beyond the quantitative standards, but for schools which have not yet fully achieved their objectives, the standards can serve as a guide for charting goals to be reached in progressive steps over a planned period of time.

> National standards have many functions beyond the immediate ones of providing guidelines for media programs of good quality and establishing criteria for the media services, resources, and facilities essential in the educational process. They act as a stimulus to correct the serious deficiencies now existing in too many of our schools by (1) assisting in the establishment of media centers where no service is available, or (2) accelerating the improvement of media services in those

*Standards for School Media Programs, *American Library Association and National Education Association, 1969.*

schools where optimum programs are defeated because of lack of sufficient staff and resources or because of other substandard conditions.

The booklet then went on to say:

Although there is often a time lag between the appearance of national standards and their achievement on a wide scale, the standards are not visionary but firmly based on the very real educational needs of today.

The standards raised the question of what would be required to implement them and what it would cost. My calculations are that if the standards as established in the booklet are implemented at the "basic" level, the cost would be approximately $38 billion for schools, colleges, and universities, divided approximately as follows:

Public elementary and secondary schools	
Equipment	$ 8 billion
Materials	16 billion
Subtotal, equipment & materials	$24 billion
Professional staff	1 billion
Supporting staff	1 billion
Film rental and television	1 billion
Subtotal, public schools	$27 billion
Nonpublic schools	$ 4 billion
Higher education	7 billion
Total	$38 billion

Once this is attained the annual cost will amount to:

Professional staff	$ 1.4 billion
Supporting staff	1.4 billion
Film rentals and television	1.4 billion
Replacement of materials and equipment	6.8 billion
Annual cost	$11.0 billion

This amounts to 21 percent of the nation's budget for education.

Figures used in computing quantities in the standards were:

Pupils	45,100,000
Teachers	2,002,000
Schools	
Elementary	65,000
Secondary	27,500
Total	92,500
Teaching stations	
K-3	521,000
Elementary	1,042,000
Secondary	811,000
Total	1,853,000
Media centers	
Elementary	26,325
Secondary	20,000
Total	46,325
School districts	23,000

The cost estimates set forth above are based upon a detailed analysis of the various types of educational equipment and materials now used by public schools, and estimates of the quantity that would have to be obtained to meet the standards. The data and estimates assembled are in the tables that follow.

Table I lists the estimated number of items owned on July 1, 1969, and the number needed to meet the "basic" standard and the "advanced" standard.

Table II estimates the total cost for each item July 1, 1969 based on reasonable unit costs on that date.

The figures obviously are subject to a margin of error, but they are useful in indicating what the standards require as compared with the present situation.

Table I
Educational Technology in the Public Schools

ITEMS OF EQUIPMENT AND MATERIALS	NUMBER OF ITEMS ON HAND JULY 1, 1969	NUMBER OF ITEMS REQUIRED TO MEET STANDARDS	
		BASIC	ADVANCED
16mm projectors	251,000	555,900	1,158,125
Slide & filmstrip projectors	426,000	1,358,867	3,350,842
Record players	698,000	770,000	1,436,125
Tape recorders	320,000	694,650	1,667,450
Television receivers	187,000	1,630,000	1,676,325
Overhead projectors	453,500	1,945,650	2,038,300
Opaque projectors	91,600	74,000	216,650
Screens	919,000	1,853,000	1,853,000
8mm projectors	58,600	1,312,700	3,013,000
Radio	117,500	46,325	138,975
Central Distribution Systems	6,180	92,500	92,500
Darkened rooms	1,143,000	1,899,325	1,899,325
Slide or filmstrip viewers	163,000	2,289,754	7,491,487
Transparency makers	71,200	92,650	92,650
Microprojectors	6,180	92,650	138,975
Learning carrels	171,000	2,560,000	3,350,000
Electronic classrooms	26,650	399,000	522,000
Television studio control kits	5,330	80,000	104,500
Television cameras	16,000	240,000	314,000
Videotape recorders	16,000	124,000	372,000
Maps and globes	4,200,000	7,243,475	7,243,475
Earphones	576,000	4,940,000	15,200,000
Drymount presses	11,750	46,325	46,325
Reading devices	98,600	1,480,000	1,930,000
Rear screen projectors	22,200	334,000	436,000
16mm cameras	14,100	46,325	46,325
8mm cameras	7,200	46,325	46,325
35mm slide camers	27,200	46,325	46,325
TV Dist. systems	6,180	46,325	46,325
16mm films	1,315,000	69,000,000	69,000,000
Filmstrips	21,700,000	135,300,000	135,300,000
Tape recordings	2,020,000	203,000,000	203,000,000
8mm films	104,000	694,650	1,667,450
Disc recordings	7,200,000	67,600,000	67,600,000
2" × 2" slides	2,400,000	185,000,000	185,000,000
Overhead transparencies	5,230,000	185,000,000	185,000,000
Still & flat pictures	12,400,000	92,500,000	92,500,000
Reading programs	336,000	5,040,000	6,580,000

Note: *Increase amounts by 14 percent to include nonpublic schools and by 26 percent to include higher education. An increase of 15 percent each year is required to offset depreciation. Standards are those included in the booklet entitled* Standards for School Media Programs.

Table II
Cost of Meeting Standards for Educational Technology
July 1969

ITEMS OF EQUIPMENT AND MATERIALS	UNIT COST	TOTAL COST	
		TO ATTAIN BASIC STANDARDS	TO ATTAIN ADVANCED STANDARDS
16mm projectors	$ 600	$ 182,940,000	$ 544,275,000
Slide & filmstrip projectors	100	93,286,700	292,484,200
Record players	65	4,680,000	47,978,125
Tape recorders	110	41,217,000	148,219,500
Television receivers	130	223,294,500	193,612,250
Overhead projectors	180	268,587,000	285,804,000
Opaque projectors	320	0	40,016,000
Screens	60	56,040,000	56,040,000
8mm projectors	300	376,230,000	886,320,000
Radio	70	0	1,503,250
Central Distribution Systems	2,000	172,640,000	172,640,000
Darkened rooms	125	94,540,625	94,540,625
Slide or filmstrip viewers	40	85,070,160	293,139,480
Transparency makers	300	6,435,000	6,435,000
Microprojectors	150	12,970,500	19,919,250
Learning carrels	80	191,120,000	254,320,000
Electronic classrooms	8,000	2,978,800,000	3,962,800,000
Television studio control kits	5,000	1,866,750,000	2,206,000,000
Television cameras	2,000	448,000,000	596,000,000
Videotape recorders	2,500	270,000,000	890,000,000
Maps and globes	35	106,521,625	106,521,625
Earphones	30	130,920,000	438,720,000
Drymount presses	340	11,755,500	11,755,500
Reading devices	140	193,396,000	256,396,000
Rear screen projectors	700	218,260,000	289,660,000
16mm cameras	1,095	35,286,375	35,286,375
8mm cameras	250	9,781,250	9,781,250
35mm slide cameras	240	4,590,000	4,590,000
TV Dist. systems	3,600	144,522,000	144,522,000
16mm films	170	11,506,450,000	11,506,450,000
Filmstrips	7	795,200,000	795,200,000
Tape recordings	3	602,940,000	602,940,000
8mm films	20	11,813,000	31,269,000
Disc recordings	8	483,200,000	483,200,000
2" × 2" slides	.50	91,300,000	91,300,000
Overhead transparencies	1.50	269,655,000	269,655,000
Still & Flat pictures	5.50	446,050,000	446,050,000
Reading programs	450	2,116,800,000	2,809,800,000
Total Cost		$24,551,042,000	$30,025,143,410

Note: *Increase amounts by 14 percent to include nonpublic schools and by 26 percent to include higher education. An increase of 15 percent each year is required to offset depreciation. Standards are those included in the booklet entitled* Standards for School Media Programs.

Instructional Technology: Practical Considerations

a. IT and the Teaching Profession

53.
Training Personnel for Roles
In Instructional Technology

by DON DAVIES
Assoc. Commissioner
Bureau of Educational Personnel
Development
U.S. Office of Education

Education in the last third of the Twentieth Century is moving from the concept of mass instruction to the more pragmatic concept of individualized instruction. The proliferation of concern for team teaching, differentiated staffing, self-teaching curricular materials, programmed instruction, and countless other "innovations" are all attempts to reduce the pupil-teacher ratio while still permitting large numbers of students to participate more meaningfully in the learning process.

Not since the introduction of the chalkboard has the teacher in the classroom had a greater number of instructional tools than at the present time. And this is merely a prelude to the future. Hardware and software manufacturers are announcing almost daily that they have developed another new tool or process designed to be used in classroom situations.

However, schoolmen today are behaving toward technological equipment much the same as they have behaved toward other innovations. The tendency is to reject the "metallic beasts" as creatures with which they cannot live.

Partially this is due to unfortunate first experiences when some administrators were tempted to latch on to prematurely introduced equipment mislabeled "teaching machines" by their enthusiastic manufacturers. The promise of a new technology simply failed to live up to its billing when the "teaching machines" turned out to be little more than shiny boxes with disappointing innards.

In part the objection stems also from fear. Too many teachers and administrators see technology as a threat—an invader which could diabolically force them into a subservient role.

This fear and lack of understanding is perpetuated by the ways in which media are used in teacher preparation programs. All too often prospective educators are exposed to instructional technology used in the old sense of 'mass instruction.' So-called seminars are taught by absentee professors via closed circuit television, audiovisual media are scarcely used or used with little planning, study carrels with audio and visual inputs are used as a substitute for, rather than as a supplement to, classroom situations.

This type of exposure serves only to strengthen the feelings of frustration and distaste for instructional technology among educators-in-training. It does little to encourage prospective teachers and school administrators to play an integral part in the effective utilization of instructional media once they are in a position to do so.

Eventually technology and educational personnel will have to make peace with each other for a new education is emerging that calls for individualized programs in which students get facts and tutoring services from machines while a variety of specialized teachers and other personnel assume the more significant tasks of creating intellectual stimulus, of encouraging experimentation, of originating ideas, of analyzing and humanizing instruction.

The teacher should be looked upon as a consumer-utilizer and instructional technology as part of the toolkit of the professional educator. It is doubtful that programs designed to prepare educators include specific elements on the effective use of the chalkboard yet observation in classrooms where it is effectively used indicates that such preparation could, indeed, prove worthwhile.

The same statement could be applied to the entire range of hardware and software associated with instructional technology.

Two principles are clearly evident in the preparation of educators: first, that students learn a substantial amount through example; and second, that actually doing something ("hands-on" experience) is a better learning technique than talking about it or being told how to do it.

Applying these two principles to education in the utilization of instructional technology requires a concerted effort on the part of teacher-educators. Not an overwhelmingly different instructional task for the teacher-educator, merely a re-fashioning of the process used in the instructional program. It essentially means demonstrating the possible effectiveness of instructional media through its actual use in the process of training educators. It means prospective educators learning *via* instructional media . . . not about it.

"Hands-on" experience is quite similar to writing an essay. For the trainee to benefit fully from either they must master both the mechanical and the conceptual aspects. The student confronted with "hands-on" work in instructional media must develop an intimate knowledge of the capabilities and limitations of the hardware and then develop a careful plan for its use, involving many of the principles of good essay writing: developing the concept; researching the information; organizing the information for maximum meaning; developing creative and stimulating means of communicating the concept; and finally, packaging the whole topic artfully.

This process enables the student (regardless of the level of sophistication) to add the curriculum development phase to the consumer phase, rounding out the term 'consumer-utilizer' of instructional media.

Courses in audiovisual instruction are not the solution. Curricular programs in "Using the Overhead Projector" or "How to Prepare Computer-Graded Examinations" or "Transforming the Television From Mirror to Looking Glass" will not make effective consumer-utilizers out of prospective educators.

Student teachers who are continuously exposed to learning via the overhead projector (providing the learning materials and the techniques of the teacher-trainer are of high quality) can be made responsive to the creative use of the overhead projector as a classroom tool—vital to the visualization of difficult to visualize conceptual elements of the curriculum.

Good teaching via a variety of mass media can serve as an inspiration. Bad teaching can only lead to further estrangement.

One use of media which has received widespread favorable acceptance among institutions preparing educators is the 'micro-teaching' technique. Using a television camera and video tape recorder (often relatively inexpensive equipment), the educator-in-training is recorded in an actual teaching situation. Later, in the privacy of the instructors office, the tape is played back for the prospective teacher, thereby permitting him to see for himself how effective he appears to others. The flexibility of the video tape method, its ease of erasure and re-use, provide the opportunity to correct mistakes and bad habits before they become ingrained.

The teacher who has undergone pre-service training using this technique can readily appreciate its value. Instead of fearing the television camera, he learns to respect it. And, most important, he can translate the value of his experience into a tool for use within his own classroom if the equipment is available.

Imagine for a moment the cumulative effect which could be gained by exposing educators-in-training to a multitude of instructional media in "real" situations, relevant to what they will or could be doing in the classroom.

If there is a direct relationship between the way a teacher is taught and the way a teacher teaches, it is essential that teachers be taught in a manner consistent with desirable practices.

But assuming that instructional media is wisely used in the pre-service training of educators does not automatically mean that it will receive widespread acceptance and use within the education community.

Proper utilization of instructional media will come about only as part of a change in the way we use the people who staff our schools. The move toward the teaching team is part of this acceptance. There is less threat from instructional technology when thought of in terms of an external member of the teaching team, no different from the chalkboard or workbook.

Technology as a threat to the all-important traditional role of the teacher as the font of all wisdom is a concept that has already been eradicated. Teachers are, in most instances, not prepared to be experts in all disciplines. There is no relevance in perpetuating the myth of teacher omnipotence. It would be more realistic for the teacher to accept all the assistance possible to provide maximum opportunities for student learning.

The reason more teachers give for not using instructional media, the dehumanization factor, is also invalid. The fear of destroying the teacher-pupil relationship through the use of an impersonal medium such as programmed instruction, computer-assisted instruction, or televised instruction, is based upon a completely false premise.

In fact, the use of instructional media actually frees the teacher for more individualized instruction by providing a greater variety of instructional stimuli for the use of the teacher with large and small groups, or even with individuals. For example, the single-concept, loop films which can be manipulated by the student without teacher supervision permits the teacher to have several projects going simultaneously in the classroom, providing personal leadership inputs to individuals or small groups as required.

As students progress at their own pace, the teacher has greater opportunity for individual relationships with students. The teacher then assumes the role of diagnostician, continuously evaluating the instructional needs of the students on an individual basis and prescribing the stimuli which will fulfill those needs. The student has a wide variety of materials, all self-manipulative, with which to pursue this individually prescribed instructional program.

Another example of teacher-directed study utilizing instructional media is the production of multi-discipline instructional packages by student groups. Employing small groups of students, the teacher assigns a project to each group. Drawing upon the total resource potential of the school, such as films, overhead transparencies, slides, recordings, books, television tapes, etc., each group prepares to present its project to the remainder of the class. It might develop that one student does the actual instructional presentation while the other members of the group serve as technicians, program coordinators, or simply, monitors. Using several such groups in one class, the teacher can stretch his own preparation time while providing a highly motivated and stimulating series of multi-discipline discussions.

Concurrent with the adoption of new pre-service training utilizing instructional media, a major change must be made in the in-service preparation of teachers where instructional media may currently be in use or where future use is anticipated. This in-service training may prove to be more difficult than the pre-service programs already discussed.

Experienced teachers need exposure to successful uses in other schools, workshops demonstrating effective uses, and most important, the psychological preparation that the introduction of an instructional media program is not just one more handicap superimposed upon them by the administration. Teachers should play a major role in determining the use of instructional media and the in-service training should probably include heavy doses of actual preparation of materials (software) to be used with the hardware. By participating directly in the process of software development, they can be given greater awareness of the objectives of its use and the process by which it was developed, how it should be used, and how it can be evaluated.

Once teachers are involved in the developmental process they will be more likely to put the materials developed to maximum use. It would also follow that they will know how to use them properly since they had a hand in developing them.

Combination programs, involving both pre-service and in-service training components, are one means of infecting experienced teachers with the enthusiasm of prospective teachers. One such program involves both intensive and extensive training for the prospective teachers, coupled with an in-service program for the participating experienced teachers.

Prospective teachers, or teacher interns, are trained in the teacher education institution with the aid of instructional media. When they are brought into the classroom they continue to use the media with which they have been taught, reversing the procedure and using it as part of their classroom instructional technique. By demonstrating the effective use of instructional media in the classroom they can generate interest in the experienced teachers with whom they are working. These experienced teachers are then provided with in-service training to give them the necessary skills in media utilization.

Indifferent or negative reactions to instructional media often result from past experience with poorly planned or pedestrian media instruction. Learning can be characterized as an emotional experience with the best learning taking place where some emotional or dramatic stimuli are applied. A child may be told that to touch a hot stove is to be avoided since it could lead to personal discomfort. But true learning of this concept occurs when the dramatic personal reminder of the resultant pain confronts the child as he looks at the stove. This is not to suggest that we expose the children to danger as a means of impressing the consequence of that danger upon them.

It does suggest, however, that where dramatic approaches can be used as teaching devices they can serve to reinforce the learning situation. For example, one motion picture or television shot of a rocket blast-off can impress the student far more than all the verbal discussion of that process. And discussion of Newton's Laws of Motion cannot compensate for the simple demonstration of a moving pendulum hitting a standing one and the resultant transfer of motion.

Creativity, then, becomes an important element in the use of instructional technology. Creativity in the development of materials for the instructional system and creativity in their use.

School administrators, too, have a crucial role to play in the successful utilization of instructional technology.

First, administrators at all levels need sufficient background knowledge of the philosophy, capabilities, and limitations of instructional media to permit flexibility in evaluating how teachers use the various media. This requires intensive training in instructional technology for administrators, including the evaluation of programs using media. Such training should be part of both pre-service and in-service programs for administration personnel. Once again, good examples of the use of instructional technology as part of the formal education of prospective and practicing administrators can serve as a stimulus to better understanding of instructional media within their schools.

Next, it is incumbent upon administrators to create an atmosphere within their school systems wherein teachers are free to experiment with instructional technology, knowing that they will not be discredited when experiments fail. This, of course, is closely linked with the creative element. Experimentation by teachers should go beyond the perfection of teaching techniques using instructional media. They should extend to improvement of materials, development of new materials, evaluation of the impact of materials when used in different situations and in different ways. Administrators must become an integral part of the team in the entire process of instructional media utilization.

Finally, the administrator should exhibit a sensitivity to the reality that not every teacher operates effectively with instructional technology. Administrators should encourage teachers to use media, not force them. Where possible, administrators possessing the skills and abilities to present well coordinated, creative instructional technology programs should serve as demonstrators within their own systems.

Instructional technology is an exciting learning asset if properly used. As the space age progresses and by-products of the moon race become readily available for the use of educators there will be greater demands for teachers and administrators skilled in adapting and applying technology to the education process. Laser technology with its by-product, holography, cannot be ignored in the contemporary classroom. If the charge of irrelevancy is being levelled at educators today, think what charges will be made in the decades ahead if educators fail to keep abreast of technological change and its implicit potential for enhancing the learning process.

The drop-out of the Twenty-First Century may not be the student . . . it could be the educator who fails to avail himself of the benefits of the technological revolution.

54.

Educational Technology and The Teaching Profession

by LOIS V. EDINGER
Assoc. Prof. of Education
Univ. of North Carolina

While it may be true that there are members of the teaching profession whose first question (and real fear in some instances) may still be will educational technology replace the teacher, the vast majority have accepted the fact (or in some cases simply become resigned to it) that education must leave the era of "hand labor" and turn to machines to help increase the productivity of the human teacher. Statistics from population growth alone, both present and projected, are enough to convince one. Our elementary and secondary schools will have six million *more* children enrolled in 1970 than we had in 1960 according to present projections and college enrollments will have reached over seven million. Society cannot provide for the continuation of one teacher for a magical fixed number of pupils. One half of our population is now twenty-five years old and under; hence, the number of adults is too small to continue the present practice. One half of all college graduates would need to prepare to go into teaching to keep the present level, and this is neither likely to happen nor desirable, with the present needs for competent, skilled workers in many other fields and professions. That we must turn to the using of power tools in education to allow teachers to become more effective is a fact accepted by the teaching profession today, albeit with varying degrees of pleasure and readiness.

Although there are many aspects of this new technology one is tempted to explore, I shall address myself to the question posed by the commission and try to stay within the parameters suggested by it. What effect would the extensive use of instructional technology have on the teaching profession? By the teaching profession, I understand the question to mean not the process of using the technology in teaching per se; its advantages, and the like; but the changes or effects which may be predicted for teaching as a profession.

Extensive use of instructional technology will affect the profession in at least the following ways, I think.

1. It will facilitate and encourage the differentiation of staff.

2. It will increase the need for flexible organization of the school.

3. It will force the profession to reexamine teaching methodologies and look anew at learning theories and the most appropriate means of helping all children learn.

4. It will necessitate major changes in teacher education programs, both pre-service and in-service.

5. It will necessitate a reappraisal of certification requirements by State Departments of Instruction.

6. It will elicit a number of questions from the profession regarding the role of decision making of the teacher and the rights and responsibilities of the user (consumer) and the creator (producer) of materials for educational technology.

Facilitate and Encourage Differentiation of Staff

A major effect of the extensive use of educational technology will be to speed the movement toward differentiated staff. Only through the reorganization of staff and personnel can the new advances in teaching techniques and technology be effectively utilized. Much waste has resulted through efforts to superimpose new techniques on the old system. Innovations must be planned for, not prematurely introduced, and then they must be fully integrated into the system. The Research and Policy Committee of the Committee for Economic Development states in the first chapter of its book, *Innovation In Education: New Directions for the American School;* "If the schools are to make real progress in instruction, most of them must be jolted from their complacency by vigorous thrusts that will break through the old patterns and support experiment and innovation."[1] Increasing teacher productivity is a key to effectiveness in education. The introduction of team teaching and differentiated teaching functions should accompany effective utilization of instructional technology.

The National Commission on Teacher Education and Professional Standards, NEA, recently sponsored the Year of the Non-Conference to study the teacher and his staff. A number of papers, demonstration centers, and films were outgrowths of the year. "To add to the dialogue about school organization by suggesting some ways that teachers and technology can be brought together to create personalized educational programs" was the purpose given for a booklet sponsored jointly by TEPS and Center for the Study of Instruction.[2]

The Direct Instructional Team and Support Centers are proposed in this booklet. Let's stay with the idea of a team for a moment. Various groupings are possible for a team, but any grouping to emerge with extensive use of instructional technology would, I think, include technologists and paraprofessionals along with the instruction leader and assistant leader (Joyce), or professor and senior teacher (Allen). In any event, the profession must delineate roles and state responsibility, preparation needed, salary to be paid, etc., for the role performed. Teachers have been forced to be drill sergeants, clerks, traffic cops, nurses, substitute mothers and on and on for too long.

A breakdown of current practices shows the elementary teacher with 60.8% time for teaching, as opposed to 39.2% for miscellaneous tasks. The same study shows that the high school teacher spends 51.4% of his time for teaching, 29.0% for related out-of-class instructional activities and 19.6% for miscellaneous activities. Teachers are on record in this country with a request for time to teach. It is for this reason, if no other, I feel teachers will welcome the use of technology in education, for it will relieve them of much of the routine and drill activity they are now called on to perform. Educational technology has demonstrated that it can do routine jobs and some teaching tasks as well as, or better than, a teacher. Computers can carry out drill and repetitive jobs easily and often more effectively than a teacher. Skill subjects may well come under the programming of the computer. The computer is already being used in a number of school systems to relieve the teacher of tasks incidental to teaching such as roll taking, grading papers, taking inventory, keeping attendance reports of various sorts. Paraprofessional assistants may relieve the teacher of other related, non-teaching tasks. All of this is germane to the discussion of the differentiated staff and the effective use of technology. It must be made clear at this point that teachers will not welcome nor accept the use of technology if they are not clearly and definitely involved in decisions about its use. The teaching profession will be greatly concerned about this decision making role, and I shall have more to say about this later.

Whether we use the Joyce model[3], the Allen model or the Mort model[4] for differentiated staff is not the major question. The important thing is to define the roles performed by a teacher and establish differentiated staff based on these roles. Extensive use of instructional technology will force the issue, for the teacher will be using a means of communication dependent upon an extremely complex and expensive apparatus; one which is not under his exclusive control and one which requires special technical knowledge to operate and to program. We must of necessity then build our instructional teams including technologists and graphic arts personnel, programmers and mediated teacher as well as classroom teacher. The teacher who works directly with the students will be the diagnostician for the learning situation and will know what resources are available to meet the needs.

Flexible Organization

In discussing differentiated staff and team teaching, one moves, of necessity, into the organizational pattern of a school. Flexible organization for instruction is of major concern in the effective use of technology. There are two major organizational patterns in so far as organization for instruction is concerned. The name of John Goodlad is usually associated with reorganization of the elementary and junior high schools into an ungraded pattern, permitting the individual student to progress much more easily at his own rate. The profession, through its instructional leaders, has pointed out that the graded system is unrealistic in the sense of human variability. It might have been a technological solution to a chaotic problem in the nineteenth century, but it does not suffice today. Whether the ungraded elementary school is the answer for 1968 yet remains to be seen. The requirements in terms of materials, individualized instruction and the like are frightening when placed against what is now available.

The flexible system of organization applied to the secondary school is usually referred to as the Trump Plan after its originator, Lloyd Trump. Trump has attempted to break up the "egg crate", 30 students to a classroom situation in the high school and provide for large group instruction (40 percent) small seminar instruction (20 percent) and individualized instruction (40 percent). This concept, formally referred to as the Staff Utilization Plan, is based on the idea of team teaching. Various aspects of this plan have been tried all over the United States, and the idea seems to be moving into practice. Where teachers have had opportunity to use it, there has been general acceptance. It should be emphasized that the Trump Plan is also postulated on a much wider use of instructional technology than now exists in the traditional school particularly for large group and individualized instruction.

It is my observation that simply having various types of educational technology will not result in its being used for individualized study if this must all come after school hours. Through some such form of flexible organization as the Trump Plan, the students should be given time during the school day and easy access to materials in order to facilitate individualized study. I have seen this pattern in operation in several schools, and the remarkable thing to many people, teachers among them, is the constant and eager use being made by students of all the materials.

Organizational patterns, then, are directly related to and dependent upon instructional technology. The teaching profession will find itself moving more in these two directions, differentiated staff and flexible organization. For a look at how this might work, we may consider the model suggested by Dr. Joyce involving Direct Instructional Team and Support Centers which shows the close relationship between the teaching team and instructional technology.

In the Computer Center, the staff includes two teachers who are specialists in computer-assisted instruction, several paraprofessionals including computer programmers and personnel who are temporarily assigned to the center for various purposes. These people are specialists in the application of computer technology to problems of curriculum and instruction. They develop computer simulation, automate canned programmed instruction materials, adapt them for use in the local schools and work with other support centers to automate other procedures. One computer support center serves about twenty direct instruction teams.

The Self Instruction Center can serve five to six direct instruction teams. Contained in this center are programmed materials, self-instruction materials, either bought from commercial firms or made by specialists at the school. Such a center should have the capacity to develop materials on its own.

The Inquiry Center contains a wide assortment of materials such as slides, records, tape recording, listening and viewing stations. In this center there must be subject specialists who are responsible for seeing that materials are adequate in each subject as well as serving in other capacities with the team.

The Materials Creation Center calls for another group of specialists such as professional writers, artists and audiovisual specialists. By creating materials to meet needs in the school, the center frees the school from over-dependence on commercial firms and at the same time provides material uniquely suited in a given situation. It is far better from my point of view to have materials prepared by professional educators than to have the profession reduced to purchasing a product designed by industry just for marketing.

In like manner, specialists are needed for the Human Relations Center and the Guidance and Evaluation Center.[5] To be sure, this is an ambitious sort of model. Most of our schools will not have as elaborate structure as this right away, but modified patterns will be found in the majority of our schools in the next five to ten years, I believe.

Teaching Methodologies and the Learning Process

Coupled with the first two effects is a third which is that the teaching profession must accelerate its examination of the process by which learning takes place. To put it another way, we must be concerned with the psychological orientation of technological materials within the teaching-learning process. The profession must have some fairly firm ideas on this matter if the program in the machines and proposed texts are to be appropriate and valid.

Each new resource must be examined from the point of view of its usefulness in the learning situation. Will it contribute to learning for any child or any group of children? What are its special properties, its strengths, its limitations in the instructional context? Unless we examine each resource in this way, we may find we are simply doing better what we should never have been doing anyhow. We don't need glamorous ways to accomplish duel jobs which may have little learning value.

James Finn in dealing with this problem writes, "The current situation, however, within educational psychology is, to say the least, mixed. Very few theorists or practitioners would be willing to say that one given point of view has achieved all the answers. In the general practice of schoolkeeping today, an eclectic point of view as to theory coupled with a large portion of experience—passed-on-down constitutes the operational base." [6]

The majority of teachers are certainly familiar with Professor Bruner's point of view in the area of instructional technology today and of the influence this view had on the Zacharias group which began the national curriculum reform movement with the physics course of the Physical Science Study Committee. They are also aware of the current discussion of the difference between Bruner's and Skinner's points of view.

There are those in the profession who fear a conditioning of behavior such as Skinner's theory describes and others in the profession who are antitechnological, anti-any-machine. They see the machine as stifling creativity and learning. While they may not understand or completely accept the Skinner theory in totality, they, nonetheless, fear the overemphasis on machines. Serious questions have been raised about the extensive use of instructional technology—notably the computer. Mary Gardiner Jones writing in *AAUW Journal* lists a few of these fears which some people in the teaching profession have voiced. Students may depend too exclusively on the computer for validation of their identity and intelligence. The students may have their assumption reinforced that there is a right answer for every question. Students may be pushed into a purely reactive role, responding to stimulus but not initiating problems or questions. This reactive role would not produce creative, imaginative minds. Students may become "in essence mere extensions of the machine, informed about things which can be programmed and be computerized and mindless about the things which make man human." [7]

The fear that television or technology will replace the teacher has been put aside, I believe. If not, our earlier discussion of the specialized roles needed in the school of the present and future should help overcome any such fear. Indeed, we shall need additional personnel if anything, but of a different sort, and with different responsibilities and preparation. The teacher will not be replaced, but re-placed in the organizational pattern, perhaps.

In the man-machine era which we are now entering, technology can assist in routine drill aspects of teaching-learning, and free the teacher to do that which is intensely human; that which he is uniquely capable of doing—to question, imagine, invent, appreciate, act as guide, model or counselor. It may even be of some consolation to the student that a machine in a drill routine remains patient, encouraging and affirmative. At that point, it may be better not to have the humanness of the "real" teacher, whose human impatience may be an inhibiting factor in the learning environment.

Nowhere in my reading have I found any indication that the teacher will be replaced by any form of instructional technology, but there are strong indications that the teaching-learning process will be increasingly handled by a versatile teacher assisted by instructional technology of various forms.

In a speech delivered to the Mid-Cities Superintendents Conference, Dr. John Henry Martin makes a strong plea for providing for the use of all the senses in the structured environment. He states, "At present, we cannot predict differences in sensory styles from one child to the next. Consequently, curricular material has never been seen as needing to be prepared for those who are dominantly one sense minded as distinct from another. And if we could, there is reason to believe we shouldn't. This much we know: that whatever the dominance of one sense over the other, they are mutually supportive and in learning all are used. If the structured environment called curriculum or technology fails to make possible the conscious or unconscious exploitation of these separate pathways to the brain in the random fashion required by the range of human differences, then the curriculum and technology emasculate learning. We can and do learn through the eye alone. We can and do learn through our ears. But we learn better, and in some cases, we can only learn, if the learning environment, the technology, permits each of us to probe it with a sensory mix unique to himself." [8]

Dr. Wigren quotes Father John Culkin from a recent interview: "Kids are natural citizens of the electronic age. The new media are the liberal arts of that age. Kids learn more on the tube than they do in school." When asked what we should be doing about this, Father Culkin responded: "Educate the emotions. That's where the game is. Tune up the sensorium. Go after the kinetic, the tactile, the aural . . . Kids today are learners in a new way, products of the all-at-once environment. They feel out of it in a one-thing-at-a-time school environment. Introduce them to form, structure, gestalt. Guide them to be their own data processors, to operate through pattern recognition. Kids should be taught how camera angles lie, how cartoons are animated. Then they should makes films of their own. That's where it's at—an all media literacy, doing instead of consuming." [9]

Students should be encouraged to use the media to express their feelings; their ideas; to communicate. They don't always have to be consumers; they can become creators.

The teaching profession is cognizant of the need for options if a truly vigorous, personal, intellectually sound education is to be created. Teachers and pupils need a rich laboratory of books, audiovisual media, and other technological resources to create the basic types of learning situations to meet needs of students. Advancing technology and new understanding will make it possible for the teacher to prescribe for each child the learning materials and teaching strategies which closely match his achievements, ability and learning style.

Changes in Teacher Education

Effective employment of new instructional technology will demand new skills and more vigorous education of the teacher. Teachers should be taught to use the new technology and how to produce programs and materials. Not all teachers will desire to become skilled technicians, to be sure; but my experience with In-School Television convinced me that teachers used the media more readily and more effectively when they understood at least a little of what went into the production of the studio lesson. The same will no doubt be true for other forms of technology. No teacher training institution really prepares teachers for television or other mediated experiences. Most of the teachers learn on the job. Skill in the use of audiovisual or mediated materials is more desirable but not as common as production skills. When teachers move from users of materials to producers or creators of materials, they need the skills to help them create these materials. Another problem arises when teachers move from classroom to studios; for example, television teachers do not have the freedom to use copyrighted materials that classroom teachers have under fair use, and for this reason, they and other creators of materials need a broader understanding of the copyright law.

From this discussion, it is clear that teachers need new skills; they need to understand educational technology so they can use it creatively; they must understand the copyright law; they need to learn their rights and how to protect them; they need to learn their broader responsibilities as they use the technology. They must learn to evaluate technology as to its legitimate use in the learning process. Along with this must come basic changes in attitude and approaches for large numbers in the teaching profession. The extensive use of instructional technology then means changes in teacher education programs.

In education there is a tendency toward conservatism and resistance to change. There are obvious reasons for this, not the least of which is the fact that schools traditionally have reflected the dominant culture in society. Teacher education has played its part by preparing teachers to maintain the status quo in schools. Teachers are prepared for schools as they are at the present without much attention being given to what may be happening in a few years; hence, teachers begin looking for in-service courses almost as soon as they are in their first position.

Continuing education programs for teachers, or in-service programs, could be established on the basis of individualized instruction if we will use educational technology. If it works for students in the public schools, it should work for teachers. Not all needs could be met in this fashion, but refresher courses in skill subjects might be handled this way.

Because of the increased insterest in technology, there has come a concern for improving teacher education, for however sophisticated and useful the machine may become, it will always be an instrument employed by human educators. Teacher education therefore, must have curricula designed to include adequate instruction in values and use of both conventional and new educational media. Programs are needed to upgrade and update not only subject matter competence but capability in utilizing advanced teaching technology. Teachers need to know what technology to use, how to use it effectively, and how to evaluate its use in the learning environment. Some members of the profession will need to concentrate on programming for computers, machines of various sorts, or programmed textbooks. At the moment, industry is taking over the production of software; this was not the case in the writing of text books—a professional person was engaged to write. It is my belief that a professional person should be engaged, perhaps with technicians from industry, perhaps on his own, but more particularly in consultation with other teachers in preparing materials to be used in programmed courses. These materials should then be field tested under competent supervision. As we differentiate roles, teacher preparing institutions will need to reassess programs offered and plan for differing roles. All members of the instructional team may not need a full four years in college; some may need more. Preparation for various roles must be provided in schools of education and in technical schools where needed. Technologists and other specialists, perhaps some from industry, may make contributions to learning under the direction of competent qualified teachers.

Some efforts are being made to change teacher education programs to meet the growing utilization of instructional technology. In August, 1967, Multi-State Teacher Education Project issued a monograph entitled "Television and Related Media in Teacher Education." Dr. Harold E. Wigren in the introduction, made the following statement: "The widespread fusion of technology and education is rapidly becoming more the rule than the exception in our nation's schools and colleges. Innovative practices, which employ with considerable sophistication the use of television and other technologies are to be found in increasing numbers at all levels of education. These practices indicate the growing willingness—and determination—on the part of educational leaders to make creative application of technology in the solution of instructional problems." [10]

Since the experiments described deal primarily with the use of television, I shall not discuss them further here. This does, however, point up the growing concern of schools of education for the newer technology. Changes must come in teacher education programs if there is to be extensive use of technology; otherwise, teachers entering classrooms will not be able to make productive or effective use of instructional technology.

Certification Requirements

It should be obvious at this point that State Departments of Public Instruction and the certifying agencies of the state will need to reappraise the certification requirements and assignment of personnel. Whether this will mean new certificates with new programs, I know not. We will need to make provision for employing persons who are not licensed as teachers. At the moment, some states and school districts might have difficulty in getting the type personnel needed for extensive use of instructional technology. Schools will need a degree of flexibility which many do not now seem to have. It also appears to me that the profession will need a greater voice in the process of licensing teachers and in policy matters relating to organization and curriculum. Teachers will generally respond positively to innovations if they are involved from the outset and involved continuously. Since certification requirements vary from state to state, I shall not attempt a detailed discussion but suggest this as an area of concern.

Teacher Rights, Responsibilities and Decision Making

A final effect of the extensive use of instructional technology will be to raise questions from the profession concerning a teacher's rights—academic or legal—in this entire area and the role of teachers in decision making. One can safely say these rights are imperfectly understood at the present. The Division of Audio-Visual Services of the National Education Association as early as 1963 devised a policy statement concerning professional rights and responsibilities of television teachers. AAUP in its Autumn Issue (Sept. 1968) presented a statement on Educational Television, for its members' reactions. This statement contains many of the same principles contained in the policy statement of NEA.[11]

Little attention has been given to a faculty's authority in determining policies and procedures for the use of television or other media at either the public school or university level. Dr. Wigren puts this matter quite graphically in a recent address: "Admittedly, there exists in some quarters an uneasiness—and not without justification—that decision making with respect to the design and role of learning systems or packages will be gradually vested in a master educational engineer who is seemingly all-wise and omnipotent and who decides, in his great wisdom, what part (if any) the teacher will play in the system at any given time. Under this arrangement, the teacher becomes a monitor, or a cog in the system's wheel, with his own freedom of choice and initiative divested. When this happens, the teacher becomes "programmed" every bit as much as the computer! Fortunately, this need *not* be the shape of things to come!

"Properly conceived, a systems approach can—and *must*—provide ample opportunities for decision making on the part of both the teacher and learner to ensure that each develops to his full potential."[12] I believe that decision making will be one of the major concerns of teachers and is even now one of the items for negotiations in a number of school districts.

Since it is possible under the use of instructional technology for a teacher's demonstration and lecturers to be recorded and reused without the teacher's being present, a host of questions will be raised by the profession. Among these will certainly be the following: What will be the residual rights of teachers? Are there "residual" rights or only rights reserved in a contract? Who will own the television program, the packaged system, the programmed text material? Should the teacher have rights in regard to revision of the content? If so, what rights and to what degree? Should teachers have the right to withdraw a program if information becomes obsolete? Should the teacher have any control over the modification of his program by others? What controls, if so? Could some of these matters be handled through school or university policy in regard to salary adjustments, released time, etc., granted the teacher? Who owns supplementary materials that go to make up the packaged system? What sort of contractual arrangement should be made? Will problems of certification and accreditation arise at the public school level if non-certified persons are used to prepare materials or teach? What relationship should exist between local, state, regional and national agencies involved in production and dissemination of materials? What about local control of curriculum?

There will be other questions; these only suggest the range of questions likely to arise. These questions will need to be negotiated in every situation as they arise. The Division of Educational Technology (formerly DAVI of NEA) conducted a recent survey of practices on the professional rights and responsibilities of teachers in new media. Policies for television teachers were the chief concern from the survey, but it was the feeling of the investigators that policies for teachers in other media were based on much the same criteria. Key areas to be examined before an agreement is entered into were listed from the survey: salary, work load, program ownership, ownership of supplemental materials, revision of programs, terminating program use, reuse within the contracting institution, reuse within the contracting institution but for purposes other than originally intended, reuse outside the contracting institution, special use outside the contracting institution, contract reevaluation or renewal, liability.[13] For a more detailed understanding of some of the current contract practices, I would recommend a reading of the report.

There will be some difference in the approach from the public schools and from a college or university since public schools are turning more to the team approach which will be handled in one fashion, while at the university level, we still have primarily a solo performance by an individual professor. In any projections for expanded use of technology, the teaching profession will seek to find satisfactory answers to the questions raised here.

In an effort then to determine the effect which the extensive use of educational technology will have on the teaching profession, I have suggested and discussed six broad areas. All of these are related; some are interrelated. Any plan to promote extensive use of technology should be responsive to these effects.

The teaching profession finds itself caught between two realities; the need to increase teacher productivity through the use of instructional technology, and the need to maintain and enhance the teacher's uniquely human role in the teaching-learning process. To keep a proper balance between these two, will be a primary goal of the teaching profession as it seeks to meet its obligation to society to provide equal educational opportunity for all children and youth.

REFERENCES

1. Research and Policy Committee of the Committee for Economic Development. *Innovations in Education: New Directions for American Schools.* New York: Committee for Economic Development. July, 1968, p. 11.

2. Joyce, Bruce R. *The Teacher and His Staff, Man Media and Machines.* Washington, D.C. National Commission on Teacher Education and Professional Standards and Center for the Study of Instruction. 1967.

3. *Ibid.*

4. TEPS Year of the Non-Conference, *Occasional Papers:* Bernard H. McKenna, "School Staffing Patterns": (for the Mort Model.) Dwight W. Allen, "A Differentiated Staff: Putting Teaching Talent to Work." Washington, D.C., National Commission on Teacher Education and Professional Standards.

5. Joyce, *op. cit.* pp. 12-14.

6. Finn, James D. "The Emerging Technology of Education." *Instructional Process and Media Innovation,* Robert A. Weisgerber, Editor. Chicago: Rand McNally and Company, 1968, p. 306.

7. Jones, Mary Gardiner. "Computer-Assisted Education: A New Challenge in Social Responsibility." *AAUW Journal,* Vol. 62, No. 1 October, 1968, p. 4.

8. Martin, John Henry. "Making Technology Behave." An address delivered to the Mid-Cities Superintendents Conference, Pasadena, California, October 15, 1968.

9. Wigren, Harold E. "The Effects of Communication Media on the Educational Process." An address delivered at the International Conference on Communication Media in Education, Halifax, Nova Scotia, September 26-28, 1968.

10. Bosley, Howard E. and Harold E. Wigren, Editors. *Television and Related Media In Teacher Education.* Baltimore, Maryland: Multi-State Teacher Education Project, August 1967.

11. "Statement on Educational Television," *AAUP Bulletin.* Washington, D.C. American Association of University Professors. Vol. 54, No. 3, September, 1968.

12. Wigren, Harold E. "The Effects of Communication Media on the Educational Process." *op. cit.*

13. Mikes, Donald. "Contract Practices for TV Teachers." (Mimeographed) Washington, D.C., Division of Educational Technology, NEA. September, 1968.

55.
Teacher Training
In Instructional Technology

by *KEVIN RYAN*
Assoc. Prof. of Education
Graduate School of Education
University of Chicago

Eight years ago, in his book *The Schools,* Martin Mayer wrote:

> There are a million and a quarter classroom teachers, and by the normal curve
> of distribution, most of them are not especially talented. It was observed some
> years ago that most steel workers are not especially talented either—but they all
> turn out pretty good steel. The steel industry has developed technology that
> enables routine operatives to perform satisfactory work. The schools appear to be
> trapped in a technology that can be employed successfully only by good teachers.[1]

During the intervening years, the number of classroom teachers has grown to two million, but changes in their understanding and use of technology are not evident. It is the intention of this paper to deal with the question of how teachers and administrators can gain a more sophisticated understanding of instructional technology. Further, it will offer strategies and concrete suggestions to improve pre-service and in-service training, so that teachers and administrators acquire new competencies relating to instructional technology. This paper, however, is based on two assumptions. First, instructional technology of the more advanced type (television, data retrieval systems, audio- and video-tape recorders, film projectors) can be useful in the instruction of children. Even more, these newer means of instruction present the opportunity of a major improvement in the quality of education. Second, instructional technology of high caliber (both hardware and software) will not only be available, but also made easily accessible to teachers and administrators. At issue, in this paper, then, is not whether or not the more advanced types of educational technology are a good, or when and how they should be made available, but how teachers and administrators can make advanced instructional technology a routine and systematic part of what they are doing. It should be stressed, however, that training in the use of the new technologies should not proceed until material of high caliber is made easily available to teachers and administrators. To do otherwise would only deepen the cynicism and disappointment which school personnel already have for this subject.

A word or two should be said about the nature of the problem. Why is it that teachers and administrators do not use very sophisticated educational technology. For one thing, the use of technology is not part of the teacher image. When most of us think of teaching, we think of an individual using his mind and his voice box to present words to eardrums and, hopefully, the minds of others. This is the kind of teaching that most teachers have been exposed to from kindergarten on up. This is true, also, for their experience in teacher training. While most have had some formal instruction in audiovisual aids, and have become convinced that they can improve their teaching performance, this training rarely has strong transfer to the classroom. Most young teachers have experiences similar to the following: The newly certified teacher begins a professional career believing in many educational ideas, such as the value of using audiovisual aids, individualizing instruction and teaching non-authoritarian ways. However, the existential demands of teaching between five and seven hours a day take their toll. The teacher has little time for the careful planning for behavioral objectives, let alone for audiovisual materials which will help in the achievement of those objectives. All too often when the teacher discovers a film or record which does fit well into a lesson, he cannot get his hands on it at the right time. The system for obtaining films and records and other "content" can be quite cumbersome. Also, the maintenance of the hardware is a frequent source of disappointment and frustration. As a result of all these factors—the teacher image, professional training in education, the daily demands of teaching and the present systems for using technology—the level of educational technology in the schools is rather primitive.

The Necessary Understanding

Before any fundamental change in the behavior of teachers or administrators will be made, they must have a much more sophisticated understanding of educational technology. Understanding is not enough, but it is the first step. Since the term "understanding" is an abstraction, it is important that I specify in some detail the nature of this understanding.[2]

The Meaning of the Machine

In the education of teachers for the efficient and routine use of technology, the basic problem of instruction is the development of a concept of the machine itself above and beyond its educational function. Machines have certain generalized characteristics, and a broad appreciation of these generalized characteristics is prerequisite to any specific training in the use of the machine.

One of the basic criteria for the anthropological description of species *Homo Sapiens* has been the ability of man to use tools. Man, in his base wisdom, is a tool user, and to trace the history of tools is a reliable index to the development of cultural complexity.

The tool, though, is much more than it appears to be at first glance. Whether we speak of the most primitive hand axe or the most complex computer imaginable, they share common characteristics which define their nature, delineate a function, and instruct in usage. And, by the analysis of tool usage, one can generate an over-view of technology which helps to comprehend the problems of systematic thought.

First, a tool represents some way of basically standardizing behavior, although in varying degrees. Very simple tools such as the primitive hand axe modify behavior in general terms; the axe is little more than a crude extension of the closed fist, and the axe is generally used to perform those functions which the closed fist earlier performed. As the hand axe took on a sharp edge and a handle through technological development, so the behavior associated with the tool was modified and specialized. The "new" axe was meant to be swung, and this is a much more learned, specialized behavior as compared to the unspecific nature of the earlier hand axe.

But, compare the early hand axe to a tool as "complex" as the brace-and-bit-type drill. The appropriate behavior for the proper use of a brace and bit is much more highly sophisticated than behavior dictated by the axe, and this is a comparative demonstration of the degree to which a tool disciplines by complexity of operation. The lathe is much more complex than the brace and bit, and so on up the ladder of complex machines. So, the machine, any machine, has a certain behavior built into it as a discipline through its operating principles, and the major output of the machine process is *standardization.*

Standardization is a highly complex term, but simply considered, standardization is regularity or routine. The "randomness" of raw materials are fed into a machine, and they are reordered according to plan and design. Parts are rearranged and shaped; idealized configurations are sought and rendered through the inner processes of the machine, and in the end, machines transform nature's chance production into standardized reproduction. This means, of course, that the whole process of making can be rationalized according to plan—idealized wishes are transformed to purpose, purpose to machine processes, and processes to regularity of output, regular to a point of almost total predictability of ends.

So, in the last analysis, the machine is an expression of rational purpose, and technology is the logic underlying the structure of man's aspirations for transforming the material world of random shapes and functions into purposeful shapes and functions. Technology gives mute testimony to a rank order of problem solving, broad goals (transforming nature), direct purpose (definition of problem), specific objective (development of specialized operations), and concrete processes (the actual dynamics of reassembling the material from random to rational).

Comparing the hand axe to the computer reveals another point of similarity: both deal in a sense of abstraction. The abstraction is present the moment that a man-ape sees in his "monkey tool" a residual purpose which can influence events which have not yet happened. The reality of the present is converted into the abstraction of the future. The level of abstraction may be very low, but it does express a relationship between the immediate and the intended. The tool itself becomes purposeful rather than random. The computer, on the other hand, works almost totally in the abstract. Only to the extent that electrical pulses can be made to resemble something in reality does the computer touch the world of "things." But the "business" of the computer is the business of relationships of pure abstraction. In the realm of relationship, it never directly senses the pressure of a man's body calling it into action, nor does it ever experience directly the people for whom it makes so many decisions. Yet, though the computer's idiom is pure relationship and its language is the language of logic, it belongs to the same family as the hand axe. They represent extremes on the same continuum. Both use the same components, only in far different measure and at great distances in sophistication. Both represent discipline, but in different measure. Both represent decision making, but in different measure. Technology, then, means establishing the precise nature of conceived relationship.

Education and Technology: Use vs. Operation

The present relationship between public education and technology is incomplete, and the role of technology in education is poorly understood. The usual university course in educational technology requires one to learn how to operate a group of audiovisual devices. Threading a projector, operating a tape recorder, or making an overhead transparency of an outline, these are the breadth and depth of media instruction in the programs of teacher education. The subject matter used for illustrative purposes in these courses is generally banal, a mere means of demonstrating technique rather than teaching anything of a conceptualized nature, for the instructor assumes that the teacher will learn which ideas or skills they want to develop in the academic or methods courses.

But this assumption is probably false. Few academic departments use anything more complex than a record player or an occasional movie in their own instruction, and few, if any, offer any course within their own discipline on the structuring of content for media presentation. Many regard technology as a toy for teachers to use to entertain those too stupid to appreciate "the higher things." Few university instructors see technology as an instrumental aspect of the instructional process. Fewer still would accept the premise that to really know one's subject is to know how to use technology to teach it. The point is, today, only a few universities have considered the role of media and technology as being directly involved in the day to day matriculation of their student bodies.

A few imaginative teachers have been able to use the technology as it should be used, but for the most part, such things as closed circuit television, dial-access system, video- and even audio-tape recorders have had their real functions misappropriated. College teachers have looked upon media strictly as labor savers or as methods of exposing more students to the same presentation. The net result has been that lectures, which may be boring or unstimulating to begin with, have become even more stultifying and impersonal. The technology has been used to widen the gap between student and teacher. They have been used to impersonalize instruction without necessarily making learning one iota more rational, and this has been especially true in the university departments of English, History, and the Social Sciences.

That technology is so rejected in the social aspects of education is highly ironic, for the machines of teaching are fundamentally devices of *communication,* not simply reproducers of the written or spoken word. They will communicate at many different levels, and to truly *use* the machines rather than merely operate them, perhaps some guidelines can be established regarding the communicative functions of machines to better fit them into the instructional process.

The following are four functions of machines in classroom activity:

1. Machines can emphasize aspects of teaching: Certain parts of the instructional process are static. These can be conceived as the *givens,* the things to be remembered, or the boundaries of study. Generally they are rank ordered by some sense of logic, and one major premise may contain several minor premises and several examples. By using color coding, differentiated sizing, dimensional effects, and schemata, teachers can develop systems of presentation which materially aid the student in conceiving the *logic structure* of the discipline, possibly in several different ways.

2. Machines can portray dynamics: Certain aspects of the instructional process can be conceived as dynamic in nature. Under this aspect we would consider the operations of combination and synthesis or division and differentiation. The scope of these operations would range through the entire field of organized inquiry, from biological evolution to the character development of Holden Caulfield. Any process which changes shapes, properties or function in a predictable way can be graphically rendered in some way. Machines can slow down processes which escape the senses in their fleetness, or speed up those which grind with intolerable delay. Operations too small to notice can be enlarged and better comprehended. Things too large to comprehend can be reduced in size and scope. And technology offers us the wherewithal to accomplish it.

3. Machines portray emotions. Machines, especially media machines, offer us untold advantages in "humanizing" the sterile data. They enable teachers to reduce abstract conceptual generalization to human problems, complete with the emotional expressions which extreme tensions arouse. Pathos, sympathy, pity, humor, and fear are powerful, very powerful, learning devices, and yet, how many students have ever really been *moved* by the failures of Marcus Aurelius, the dilemma of Cicero, or the resignation of Tiberius Gracchus? The whole range of emotion is immediately accessible to the classroom, and most schools have the human resources to use them well with proper direction. Whether media

presentations use professional actors or student productions, media creates the common denominator for emotive comparison, and the power to move is the power to inspire.

4. Machines can involve people in activities: Machines offer us a chance to see and hear our favorite people, ourselves. They enable people to seriously analyze in retrospect their own role, and their role in relationship to others. And these machines will produce again and again a very finite series of actions so that each succeeding level of behavior is available for analysis. School behavior, socialized behavior, intellectual behavior, psychological behavior, all are there to be seen again and again. Technology, in the hands of the adroit, makes each lesson a triple lesson or even a quadruple lesson. However, the proper evaluation of actions requires more training than most of us possess.

Like all other machines, the machines of education enable us to rationalize our activity. Many teachers tend to fear machines. They visualize an automated classroom where cybernetics have replaced teachers and the educative process turns out conditioned automatons, responding on cue to the right stimulii and receiving the proper reward for appropriate actions. This would be the case if people were programmed instead of data. To make data rational, to make learning systematic is not to make it unhuman. Machinery simply makes us rationalize those behaviors which can be systematized. This frees the teacher for his real job, the job of humanizing the material and attacking the value problems of a generation in turmoil. Where reasoned activity is lacking and when there are no established criteria for judgment of appropriateness, then there is tyranny. The machines can help teachers do rationally those things which they should do reasonably, and to *use* the machine, rather than merely operate it, is to be aware of the reason for, and the rationale of, our teaching.

The crux of the problem is the understanding of the true nature of technology. Technology offers us a new perspective on the problem of the structure of learning, and the ability to utilize the technology will correlate highly to the teacher's ability to define purposeful activity, activity which is systematic, rational, and meaningful. The criteria for judging the purpose of classroom activity will be derived, of course, from two sources: the discipline structure of the subject area and the human needs of the learners. As these are molded into process descriptions and behavioral or performance criteria, so the specific purposes of the technology are defined at the activity level. "Program" becomes the logic and method of taking a learner from point X to point Y, and technology becomes the means of mapping the X-Y path.

To illustrate this point, one has but to look at the average football coach in either high school or college. While he does not possess any greater intellectual abilities than most of his colleagues possess, yet he is a master at the application of technology. The video taper, movie camera, and exerciser hold no mystery to him. He can tell you exactly where each fits into his instructional program, and he can demonstrate the proper use of each machine in terms of the purposeful activity. He knows what is appropriate for what machine; he would never order his players into the whirlpool bath prior to a scrimmage without a very special reason. He used the video-tape recorder for taping conditioning drills. As a matter of course, he systematically uses thousands of dollars worth of technological equipment without a second thought.

The football coach uses equipment well because he exactly understands the nature of his task. By understanding the nature of the discipline (the rules governing the game of football) and the needs of learner (in terms of physical abilities, understandings, and specific skills) he is able to use the functions of the machine to produce the desired affect in the skills, understandings, or physical abilities of his players. He sees the equipment as an embodiment of a logical program designed to bring about a given desired effect, and therefore, he uses it well. To develop this kind of functional ability among teachers of all subjects is the problem of teacher education, and it calls us back again and again to the problem of defining purposeful activity, and it forces us to consider the conditions and restraints which limit a full scale move by education into the age of technology.

Boundary Conditions for Change

Certain boundaries or limitations on the purposeful exploitation of technology now exist in the bureaucratic and value systems of education. Therefore, any recommendations or innovations must be derived from consideration of these boundaries. To solve the problem of technology and education, one must penetrate the wall of values and procedures which now insulate the present educational system from the forces of technological change which dominate progress in other spheres of institutional activity in the U.S.

These boundaries exist on two major levels. Level one consists of the value and procedural configurations which make up the teacher training institutions. Specifically, this problem subdivided into two major areas of activity—deans and administrators, and faculties of teacher training institutions. Level two is the general area of the public school itself, and this subdivides into three major boundary areas: (1) the administration and the support staff, (2) the faculty, and (3) the community. To bring about change in these levels, one must change the configurations of values and procedures within the areas.

In dealing with these levels, one can delineate the following boundaries or perimeters which now block the road of technological evolution in education:

A. Boundaries in Teacher Education

1. Deans and Department Heads, those who supervise and evaluate teacher trainers, put a low premium on technology in their own outlooks on teaching role. They themselves do not use it effectively, nor do they deem it important that their teachers use it effectively.

2. There are a lack of funds for use in implementing technology in teacher education. Expenditures for educational technology are a small fraction of expenditures on military technology, and until new sources of funding are found, it will be difficult for technology to become a routine aspect of classroom activity.

3. Professors and instructors, who train teachers, treat teaching like an art. Much of the content is vague, "how to do it," prescriptions. Too much of it is folklore, with the addition of a little behavioral science about the nature of the learner, and phenomenological experience.

4. Teacher educators are in a key position to affect what happens in the American classroom. They become models for their students of instructional technique. Frequently, however, the teacher educators give more attention to writing and research than teaching. In this, they are adhering to the ethos of the university. Since instructional technology has little place in university teaching (or so the ethos would dictate), teacher educators find no compelling reason to use it. Frequently, they are in the awkward position of urging their students to use media while never using it in their own teaching. Teacher educators have not defined the skills and performances that are expected of a teacher. The frequent result is that they teach no teaching skills. Performance criteria and objective norm levels would much enhance the use of technology in teacher training.

5. Funding, the problem of obtaining financial resources, is present at each level of

the problem. The problem of funds is an instructional problem as well as an administrative problem, and the needs are the same.

B. Boundaries in In-Service and Pre-Service Training of Teachers

  1. Like deans and department heads in teacher training institutions, administrators and supervisory personnel put little priority on exploitation of technology in their own presentation of problems and explanations of administrative decision making. They rely on words to convey ideas which could be better presented through media tools.

  2. They fail to put a high priority on media utilization in their evaluations of staff. Administrators do not generally base their evaluations and recommendations or their assignment of teaching personnel upon criteria of technological proficiency. No skills or basic proficiencies are defined which teachers may use as performance goals in evaluating their own teaching.

  3. Communities fail to appreciate the role of technology. Too often, if administrator attempts to develop a good media program in the school, the community tends to regard it as a "frill" or a luxury which increases tax load without improving the "product." Communities have to be educated to the fact that technology does better and faster many of those things which they expect schools to do. Learning can be interesting and still be learning.

  4. Teacher's professional autonomy is rising, and administrators may be unable to effect change in the traditional manner in the future. Teachers are now becoming more inclined to think of administrators as facilitators rather than decision makers and instruction leaders, so an administrator may be highly motivated toward technology, but lack the real power to actually change behavior patterns.

  5. Teachers vary tremendously in experience, competence and attitude. Training problems are different for new teachers as opposed to experienced teachers. New teachers may be lacking in security over the basic aspects of teaching (discipline, social relationship and image), while experienced teachers may be affected by too much security.

  6. Subject matters differ in adaptability to technology. Some subjects such as sciences, hygiene, drivers' training and business education lend themselves much more to technology than do highly expressive media such as arts, literature, and drama. Therefore, if there *were* an articulated evaluative program for teachers' ratings, a weighted scale would have to be devised for evaluation.

  7. Heavy demands are now made against teachers' time. Little time is appropriated in the teachers' day for improvement of instruction, and knowledge of subject matter demands so much extra preparation during vacations and holidays. Little time is left, nor is there much incentive professionally or momentarily for improved development of technological skills.

  8. Any program to substantially improve the use of technology by teachers must contend with the "loser image" which teachers presently have of technology. In the past, it has been over-sold. Improvements have been promised in the educational journals and popular press (e.g., programmed learning) which have never materialized. There are few teachers who have not been embarrassed by the projector which at the crucial moment breaks down. Therefore, what is done to improve the use of advanced technology by teachers should be based on a *reliable* future.

The Guidelines for Change

Although it is crucial that the teacher understands the role of technology and their relationship to instructional technology, understanding alone is not enough. Change is needed in the attitudes and behavioral repertoires of individual educators. Institutions, too, need to be restructured to accommodate innovations. In a chapter of the 1957 NSSE Yearbook, *In-Service Education,* Herbert Coffey and William Golden offered several principles from the psychology of change which may shed light on our problem. Although Coffey and Golden are referring specifically to change within institutions brought about through in-service training, many of these principles hold true for changing the faculties of pre-service teaching training institutions too.

> *First,* the individual is motivated to change when there is a disequilibrium between the tension systems of the individual and the surrounding social field. The dynamics of the process of change are seen in the attempts to restore equilibrium with the individual or to change the tensional quality of the surrounding social field.[3]

If teachers and administrators are to change their attitudes toward instructional technology and prepare to change their behavior, their normal equilibrium must be disturbed. Something must upset the balance and cause *tension* to develop. They must begin to feel dissatisfied with what they are currently doing. Next, they should see instructional technology as a means of alleviating the new tension.

> *Second,* in addition to needs growing out of physiological processes, many human needs are determined by the group to which one belongs or the status to which one aspires. Behavior which is characteristically human is most often in response to tensions arising in the field of social relationships.[4]

This principle reflects the human tendency to want to copy, or model ourselves after, those we like and admire. Also, it reflects the individual's tendency to seek to acquire the knowledge, skills, and behaviors of the social group to which he aspires. The prospective teacher feels tension until he has acquired the skills of the teacher. The admired faculty member becomes a model for his colleagues. While this principle can be a constructive force for change, it also explains the very conservative nature of teaching methodology.

> *Third,* the process of psychotherapeutic change comes about under conditions where the perceived needs of the patient are made the focus of attention, where the threats to one's perceptions are reduced, and where the relationship of therapist and patient are mutually collaborative. These are aspects of changed situations which can be generalized to any situation.[5]

This principle reminds us that those concerned with change must not overlook the needs of the individual. The individual, in this case, is the teacher or the administrator. Before he is to change, he must not only develop dissatisfaction with things as they are and develop a new level of aspiration for himself, but also he must see change as satisfying some of his needs. He must see that he is able to make the change, and that the goal is, indeed, attainable. The proposed change must be perceived as being helpful to him. The teacher or administrator must see that change is making him a more effective or happier individual. This factor is frequently overlooked. Often changes advocated that will make other people happy, but not those who are called upon to do the changing. This is particularly true of administrators who are in a position to see the need for change. They, then, insist or urge that their teachers change without particular regard to the affective consequences for their teachers.

> *Fourth,* individual behavior within a social system is determined by the role which is prescribed by that system. Roles contribute to the functioning of the system by creating within the individual highly internalized expectancies as to

how he should behave and how others will behave. Role behavior becomes highly fixed within the institution and is disrupted only under rather extreme conditions.[6]

Before any significant change in the behavior of administrators and teachers will be effected, their roles must be changed. This is the heart of the problem. At present, the role of the teacher requires a low level of competence in the manipulation of instructional technology. The expectancies of both the school professionals and the members of the larger community are few and vague. For real change in instructional behavior of school personnel to take place, a massive effort must be made to reshape, or perhaps recast the expectancies of teachers, so that new roles emerge which involve the informed and skilled use of instructional technology. The performance of these new roles must become the expectancy of school men and non-school men alike. Some of the means for this massive effort will be discussed later.

The school administrator is the individual who controls a major portion of the rewards and sanctions for his teachers. Change can be encouraged if the administrator uses his rewards and sanctions in the right way. Teachers must be encouraged to acquire the understanding of instructional technology and the related skills. Without the support and involvement of the administrator, whether he be dean of the school of education or principal of a small elementary school, a major portion of the incentive needed for change will be lacking.

> *Fifth,* the most significant barrier in institutional change is the resistance which persons express when such change seem threatened to roles in which they have developed considerably security. When the process of institutional change is facilitated by a number of conditions; a) when the leadership is democratic and the group members have freedom to participate in the decision-making process; b) When there have been norms established which make "social change" an expected aspect of institutional growth; c) When change can be brought about without jeopardizing the individual's membership in the group; d) When the group concerned is a strong sense of belongingness, when it is attractive to the members, and when it is concerned with satisfying member needs; e) When the group members actively participate in the leadership functions, help formulate the goals, plan the steps toward goal realization, and participate in the evaluation of these aspects of leadership; f) When the level of cohesion permits members of the group to express themselves freely and to test new roles by trying out new behavior attitudes without being threatened by "real consequences."[7]

The particular set of concepts clustered above refer especially to experienced teachers and teacher educators—the people who will be most threatened by a major role change. Since most will feel that they have already mastered the knowledge and skill of their profession, considerably skill and energy will be necessary to help them move into new areas. Beginning teachers in pre-service training, on the other hand, will not be as resistant to training. The problem is more complex for the experienced personnel because it means not only learning new skills and behaviors, but extinguishing old skills and behaviors. Also, for many experienced teachers, the change to a more sophisticated use of educational technology will mean drastically revising the way in which they conceptualize their role as teacher. The set of concepts above focuses particularly on the setting and dynamics of the training situation. Instead of having training thrust upon them, professionals should be given a choice. For a significant behavior change to occur among this group, the training must affect their minds and their *hearts.* Therefore, instead of directing professionals to undergo training, it should be presented as a valuable, attractive possibility. They must know that their efforts, however amateurish, to use instructional technology will be supported within their institution. As far as possible, they must have the security that their efforts to use advanced technology in the classroom will not separate them from valued peers. While every effort should be made to make the group training a rewarding social experience, there should be some opportunity for individual creativity of the part of the trainees. Frequently training experiences are highly standardized and allow for little human ingenuity or creativity. To get deep commitment and real involvement on the part of school personnel, there should be opportunities in this training for the expression of creative self.

> *Sixth,* any change within a given group must be supported by the organizational structure lest it become the storm center of ideological conflict within the institution. Therefore, communication must flow one hierarchical level to another. For a change must be sanctioned within the social structure. Resistance to change is to be expected at any level.[8]

Schools are complex social phenomena and are becoming more so all the time. If change is to take place in the school, many levels of the hierarchy need to be involved. Also, since change is disruptive by nature and threatening to many, it has great potential for generating conflict. It is important, therefore, that planning involves people from many levels within the hierarchy. Even if we are essentially talking about changing the behavior pattern of classroom teachers, it is essential that change has the support of, or at least no resistance from, the Board of Education, the PTA, the teacher union or professional organization, the administration, the administrative staff, supervisors, and more recently, student governments. Unilateral action is potentially disruptive in the interdependent life of the school.

Instrumentation

If administrators and teachers are to acquire the understanding and competencies necessary to use the more advanced instructional technology, the present system for initial and pre-service teacher training must be altered. The teacher training system can be altered at many different points. First, the complacency with the status quo must be disturbed and tension introduced. Second, a means for easing tension and acquiring a new level of equilibrium must become known. Third, the training, which actually brings about the new equilibrium, must be made available. Fourth, the new level of equilibrium must be recognized as legitimate and be rewarded. The concrete suggestions which follow are based on this four-step rationale.

The Introduction of Tension

1. Educators and those who support the schools and teacher training institutions (i.e., the public) must be convinced of the low state of instructional technology in the schools, and, also, what is possible. The mass media can play an important role here. Books, magazine articles, and, especially television, should be used to dramatize the disparity between what is and what could be. Hopefully, this exposition will not be an exposé. Administrators, teachers and teacher educators should not simply be of the targets of criticism. An honest, sympathetic picture of the state of instructional technology in the schools will probably do more good in the long run than an attack, which may arouse anger and guilt.

2. Educators can look to industry and industrial training as guidelines for expenditures on retraining. When an industry re-tools for a new process, they commit vast resources to the problem in anticipation of reward. The fruits of this commitment have been borne out enough times to convince them that it is good business to re-tool and retrain, even if it means very sizeable capital expenditure.

This lesson has been lost on education. To remedy this, teacher training institutions must get industry to present its approaches to problem solving through training and re-tooling to the public via the commercial media-television, periodicals, newspapers and radio. The cost of this to the public will be ultimately reduced if we can better fit the educational programs to the real needs of the learners. Riots, welfare programs and social service use more money than the cost of a first rate educational program, and industry has the image, the reputation, and the "know how" to sell this program to the public.

2. Exemplars of the sophisticated use of instructional technology should be made highly visible. While the NASA program and certain industrial training programs can provide startling examples of the advanced use of instructional technology, the heavy reliance on examples outside public education may just add to the "credibility gap." Prototypes within the public schools and teacher education need to be developed and publicized.

3. The professional organizations, like the American Association of Colleges of Teacher Education and the American Association of School Administrators, should be enlisted in a major effort to upgrade the use of instructional technology. The levers of influence and power within the profession should not be put on the defensive, but made part of the offense.

Directions for Reducing Tension

1. Educators must be made aware that sophisticated instructional technology is available for their schools and that training in the utilization of technology is also available. To accomplish both of these ends, new sources of funding will undoubtedly have to be discovered.

2. Boards of education and administrative officers within universities must be asked to support the training effort directed at teacher educators, administrators and teachers both in allocation of finances and time.

3. A film of extremely high quality on the use of instructional technology should be made. This film should be directed to the education community (teacher educators, boards of education, administrators and teachers). The film should not only deal with what is and what could be, but point the available means by which faculties can gain access to training. This film may show a lesson (or several lessons) presented in two different manners. The first approach may be a traditional lecture by a very good lecturer, and it would deal with a standard lesson which one may find being taught in almost any high school. The second approach would take the same content but it would use several types of media to dramatize the points and to map the processes put forward in the subject matter. The rationale for this presentation would be to show teachers and administrators that media will do better those things from which they already deem important. The film may conclude with a series of scenes from media centers, along with locations of these cities, where teachers may obtain help and assistance for their own projects.

Training Programs

1. Since industry will directly and indirectly benefit from the use of advanced technology in the schools, it should take on major responsibility for developing training programs. However, professional organizations should be consulted in the

design of these training programs. It is quite conceivable that special agencies for training which combine the best efforts of the industrial and education community need to be instituted.

2. Teacher trainers should be the primary target for training programs in instructional technology. Since they control the source of the profession, they could be the leaven for the profession. Therefore, teacher educators should receive intensive training and support in the use of the new media.

3. Since public school administrators still largely control the reward system, they are a most potent force for change in the schools. Therefore, they should not only receive intensive media training, but also their training should include methods of stimulating faculty in the use of media. If teachers are unable to procure the films, tapes, records, or other materials which they want at the times when they are most desired, this will tend to extinguish any motivation they have for using technology on the part of the teachers. As part of their training, they should receive instruction in systems of facilitating procurement of media by teachers.

4. There should be a variety of training programs designed to meet the needs of the different trainee groups. The skills and competencies needed by the Dean of the School of Education in this area are quite different from those needed by a third grade teacher.

5. Selection for training should not only be voluntary, but somewhat competitive. If an entire teacher education or public school faculty is pressed into training, there will be resistance. If only one or two from a faculty are trained, they could end up prophets without honor within their own schools. Therefore, a small group of administrators and teachers from an institution should be chosen for specialized training. Once the training makes a positive difference in their teaching, others will request training.

6. The training program itself should involve the most sophisticated use of instructional technology. The message and the medium should be mutually reinforcing.

7. The training program should allow for an immediate payoff for the trainee. Specifically, teachers and administrators should be able to identify and develop materials for their own use as soon as they return to their school.

8. Although a training program should be directed by behavioral objectives and clearly identified levels of performance, there should be opportunities for creativity on the part of the trainees. Trainees should not simply be on the receiving end.

9. Special time and special financial reimbursement should be made available for those who undergo training.

10. Training programs should have a follow-up in the schools so that skills and competencies are maintained.

A System of Rewards

1. Although the use of instructional technology must be intrinsically rewarding, the development of a high level of technology in the school will undoubtedly require the use of special rewards. Teachers and administrators who are innovative in the use of technology or who perform at special levels of competence, should be given special recognition in the form of national awards, money prizes, and public acknowledgments.

2. Eventually, the new competencies in skills required of teachers, administrators and teacher educators should become part of their normal and expected skills and competencies.

3. As part of the reward system, perhaps those who manufacture the media machines would sponsor an award or a series of awards to teachers and systems which successfully developed media programs. In order to prevent commercialism of the reward system, however, professional educational organizations should probably supervise and make final decisions on the recipients.

Conclusion

Of the major professional groups, there is probably none that is as *undertrained* as teachers. For this very reason, teachers and administrators will be responsive to relevant, superior training, especially if it helps them to perform their daily work with a greater competence and sense of achievement. It is quite conceivable that a quantum jump can be made in the use of technology if our on-the-cheap approach to the training of teachers is abandoned. In a sense, teacher educators, administrators and classroom teachers are so hungry for ways to improve their professional skills, that they could be captured by relevant and powerful training programs.

REFERENCES

1. Mayer, Martin. *The Schools*. Harper & Brothers, New York, 1961, p. 384.

2. I am indebted for the development of this concept and other contributions to this paper to William Guelcher. Mr. Guelcher is a Staff Associate in the Department of Education at The University of Chicago and a distinguished teacher with national recognition.

3. Coffey, Herbert, and William Golden. *In-Service Education*. 1957 NSSE Yearbook, p. 99.

4. *Ibid.*

5. *Ibid.*, p. 100.

6. *Ibid.*, p. 101.

7. *Ibid.*, pp. 101-2.

8. *Ibid.*, p. 102.

56.
Instructional Technology and The Teaching Profession

by *DAVID SELDEN* and *ROBERT D. BHAERMAN*
President   Director, Dept. of Research

Amer. Fed. of Teachers

Introduction

Most teachers tend to regard educational technological devices with deep suspicion. Teachers think of education as a more or less personal relationship between them and their students. Programmed materials, canned electronic "lessons", learner-operated machines, and even the older audiovisual aids tend to interfere with the generally parental interest teachers have in the success of their pupils. Hence, resistance to these devices among teachers is high.

A perhaps related reason why teachers are resistant to the new machines is that teaching has a built-in conservative factor. Other professions—medicine, architecture, and various kinds of engineering, for instance—tend to adopt new materials and procedures very soon after they have proved themselves in the laboratory. However, much of the knack of teaching is acquired through observation and imitation, giving heavy emphasis on tradition. Furthermore, it is difficult to establish hard truths about the value of an educational theory or an instructional technique. Thus it takes a long time for a new method to gain acceptance.

Teachers are not to be "blamed" for their slowness in adopting new methods. Many teachers carry on in a persistent aura of near-desperation. They are saddled with over-large classes, too many classroom hours a week, a curriculum whose relevance to the life of the student, currently or later on, must largely be taken for granted, and with students whose receptivity to schooling is at a marginal level. In desperate situations, most people cling to the safe and known. Under such circumstances, too, it is hardly surprising that new ideas emanate from supervisors and administrators, the administrative apparatus, rather than the grass roots. Thus new teaching devices have the double drawback of being untried and of being promoted by educational bosses who often lack credibility with teachers.

In assessing the likely effects which the use of instructional technology would have on the teaching profession, we hold that the organized profession is at a point in time where it still can determine the direction of this unresolved issue. Teachers are controlling more and more of their own destiny in matters effecting their economic security and working conditions. They also are securing a greater voice in educational policy, decision making, and goal determination. If teachers can clearly assess the problems and alternatives facing us, we will be able to determine the effects of instructional technology rather than assess the situation with analytical hindsight after the fact.

We have identified three major problem areas where distinct alternatives exist. The choices made will determine the future of the teaching profession for many years to come. These three areas are: (1) the question of educational objectives, (2) the question of educational standards, and (3) the question of the structure of the teaching profession. The first two will be examined briefly while the third, because of its major implications, will be explored in greater depth. However, beyond assessing what the potential effects of instructional technology will be, it also will be essential to explore ways to avoid or overcome their possible corrosive effects.

The Question of Educational Objectives

The first issue which teachers must face is not particularly difficult to identify nor is it especially a unique one. The problem of educational objectives—the clarification and priority of ends and means—is a recurring one. Yet, I cannot emphasize strongly enough my conviction that instructional media of whatever kind, new or old, offer only means to ends and never ends in themselves. Teachers have been presented with new "hardware," new tools, and new instruments. Nevertheless, it is the goals of education which should remain central and which should determine educational programs and methods, not the other way around.

Unfortunately, the use and evaluation of new instructional technology is to some extent inhibited by the distraction of promotional techniques which often seem more appropriate to Madison Avenue than to education and which imply a rationale which elevates them to the status of ends in themselves. This is not a new problem for it has arisen in the past with such "older" media as textbooks. It is imperative, therefore, that use of new technological approaches be based upon their contribution to the outcomes of education. The basic question is not how much use can be made of these devices, but how can the objectives of education be achieved most effectively.

While this paper certainly is not the place to become involved in an extensive discourse on philosophical objectives, several theoretical alternatives must be resolved by teachers if they are to avoid placing instructional means at a higher priority than educational ends. Teachers must have clearly in mind not only the most effective ways to utilize instructional tools at their disposal but, even more essential, they first should have resolved a number of elemental but extremely significant questions:

1. Is knowledge something that can be transmitted, as an object, from one human being to another *or* is knowledge the residue of one's unique and personal experiences?

2. Is the goal of teaching the mastery of factual information by means of demonstrations and recitations *or* is teaching a process of arousing personal response in the learner?

3. Is the learner conceived as a sensory receiver to be manipulated *or* is he an active and experiencing person?

4. Is the teacher conceived as a demonstrator and mental disciplinarian *or* is he provocator and instigator of activity—mental, emotional and social?

5. Is the educational process primarily one of absorption *or* one of self-discovery?

It is my belief that the alternative listed first in each of the five questions might *tend* to lead teachers toward an overemphasis on technology as an end in itself rather than as one of many methods for achieving educational goals. Conversely, I feel that the second proposition in each case would *tend* to focus technological devices in proper perspective as a means of achieving desired goals.

What Bhaerman means is that educational objectives should be determined by representatives of society and that educational methods should serve those ends. There is some danger that education may become McLuhan-ized.

Companies that invest millions of dollars in the development of new educational appliances are certainly doing so with an expectation of profit. Since many of these appliances not only determine teaching methods but actually *are* teaching methods, there is considerable danger that needs of society and the needs of the individual child may become secondary to the profit needs of the educational entrepreneur. And it isn't only big business that has this medium-message confusion. Individuals who earn their living advancing a certain point of view or a certain education theory also have a vested interested in process which could defeat goals. See Bhaerman's paragraphs below.

Teachers have a choice among two predominant philosophies: the philosophy which stresses the daily filling of twenty-five to thirty buckets in a classroom /or/ the philosophy which stresses the freeing of twenty-five to thirty human spirits. Their choice will determine to a large extent how well they use the new instructional devices or, conversely, whether they are used by them.

The Question of Educational Standards

A second problem closely related to the one above was raised recently and perhaps unknowingly by Congressman James H. Scheuer in a speech to the Council of Educational Facility Planners.[1] Congressman Scheuer pointed out that as a result of the Educational Television Facilities Act, the federal government was provided the seed money to establish state educational television networks. Scheuer remarked that the results have been *phenomenal* and that in September of this year the state of Kentucky turned on eight transmitters all at once. He also stated that virtually all southeastern states are building similar networks. Now this is significant—in a negative kind of way—when one realizes that Kentucky in 1967-68 ranked 45th among the states in the expenditure per pupil in average daily attendance. Not surprisingly, the other southeastern states ranked in significantly low positions on this same scale, e.g., Florida 30th; Georgia 38th; North Carolina 44th; South Carolina 48th, Alabama 49th; Mississippi 50th.[2]

In light of the relevant analysis of Dr. Martin Trow of the University of California at Berkeley, the implications of this should not escape us. Professor Trow[3] suggests that where educational standards are weak, the new technology will more likely be used only as a supplement for classroom instruction. Trow[4] quoted a significant item which appeared in the *National Observer* in the early 1960's when it was reported that on each day in South Carolina, courses in that state's history, algebra, French, physical science, geometry and electronics are fed in on television to nearly one-third of all the high school students in that state. Thus, what Congressman Scheuer said can be interpreted in another light. Rather than cause for joy, there is cause for alarm. In supporting a relatively untested educational approach, one which has not proven itself yet, the federal government may well be reinforcing the existence of relatively low standards of educational excellence.

Along this same line, educators must take a number of similar precautions in what seems to be overeagerness by some to shift to any new or different technological device, however unproven it may be.

Another way of looking at the problem of goals and methods is to take up some of the observations made by Callahan in his study "The Cult of Efficiency in Education" (University of Chicago Press, 1962). I cannot completely agree with Callahan's basic plea that the education of children has nothing to do with efficiency. The schools are not located on the big rock candy mountain. The cost factor cannot be omitted from any equation of educational productivity.

On a unit cost basis, the American public schools have been marvelously productive. They have achieved a low unit cost with a relatively high mass production by using low staffing ratios, low standards of teaching certification (cheap labor), and by not educating the roughly ⅓ of the students who are hardest to educate. When our society could absorb large numbers of unskilled workers, and when the fact that the uneducated third has an inversely correlated black racial characteristic was not morally offensive, our mass production educational system was adequate. This is no longer the case.

We could approach the problem of how to educate most of the "lost third" of the incoming population which our schools do not satisfactorily educate now by (a) using more teachers and better physical facilities; (b) new devices which increase the productivity of educational workers, or (c) by using a combination of increased staff, better technology, and better staff utilization.

One observation prompted by the above analysis is that individualized approaches to learning may be required for students in the "lost third." Diagnostic and remedial machines may be particularly helpful here. They almost invariably constitute new methods and they get away from adverse personal factors in the pupil-teacher relationship.

Thus, the new educational technology may provide a means for educating the lost third —but we should not delude ourselves by thinking that education is going to be cheaper as a result. Callahan was therefore right in one sense in decrying "The Cult of Efficiency" because no completely *cost-conscious* educational administrator would consider it worthwhile educating these individuals. Educating the lost third—with or without the new technology—is going to cost much more money per child than what it costs per child to educate the two-thirds who "make it."

The current level of education productivity must not only be maintained—it must be improved. Teachers must seek innovative ways to make the process and practice of education more fruitful. Not all teachers are unwilling to experiment with new instructional devices. And I believe that technology, if used as proper means to worthy ends, has the potential for increasing the productivity of our enterprise. However, productivity is being threatened in cases where teaching staffs are reduced, budgets decimated, and qualifications for entry to teaching lowered. Education must become more expansive with greater financial support for our schools, more qualified teachers for our classrooms and, perhaps in some cases, more "hardware," but only when such machines have been tested, certified and empirically validated in terms of being educationally productive.

In a word, standards in such areas as school staffing, class size, teachers' qualifications and instructional budgets must be maintained at levels where they are high and strengthened where they are low. As with educational objectives, high standards are a priority which must be paramount. When quality standards are established first, state-wide television networks will follow in due course as supplements to instruction. But let us not lose sight of quality standards and first priorities any more than we should confuse ends and means.

The Question of the Status and Structure of the Teaching Profession

The technological revolution in education involves forces working both to raise and to lower the status of teachers. And while it appears that lowering the status of teachers is more likely, this is an issue whose directions also can be determined by the organized teaching profession.

Professors Biddle (of the University of Missouri) and Rossi (of the University of Chicago) state the alternatives facing us in the following terms: Where teachers are in control of the new technology of instruction, teaching will assume more of the status of a profession and the teacher's activities will be governed more by their own determination than by orders from above; by contrast, where the new media supplant rather than come under the authority of the classroom teacher, the teacher will have less and less professional status.[5]

Biddle and Rossi project that the new media will provide a variety of new educational roles for both the teacher and supportive personnel. This, they foresee, will lead to increased specialization within the profession as we know it now and to the appearance of auxiliary positions in the school tables of organization. Some of these projected roles (planner, script writer, etc.) will be ancillary to the more basic job of instruction while others are likely to become separate jobs in and of themselves.

If that is all they lead to; that is, increased specialization and auxiliary positions subordinate to the more basic job of instruction, it would be one thing. The problem, however, goes far beyond this.

I welcome the appearance of auxiliary personnel. As a matter of fact, a major part of the American Federation of Teachers' program is geared to this. In the study, "A 10-year Plan to Save the Schools: Achieving Nationwide Educational Excellence," which Leon H. Keyserling recently prepared for the American Federation of Teachers,[6] the projection was made that non-teacher instructional staff positions will increase over the next ten year period from 188,000 to 1,523,000, including 1,100,000 para-professional or one for every two teachers. The implications of the concept of specialization are more complex, however, and provoke a more detailed discussion.

A number of educators, to whom I will refer momentarily, have written and spoken extensively on the effects of increased specialization. In fact, Dr. Carroll V. Newsom, now the Vice President for Education for R.C.A., speaking at the meeting of the Council of Educational Facility Planners,[7] even went so far as to say that the specialized use of faculty personnel *itself* is one of the new instructional technologies.

Professor Trow cogently observed a number of possibilities as a result of the increased specialization of the profession:

> The more centralized and extensive the planning of instruction through the new media, the more important will be the planning and administrative staff. These staff people already hold statuses (and earn salaries) higher than those of classroom teachers. The gap will be widened, and the administrative staff will come increasingly to include people directly involved in teaching (as television or "master teachers"), or in developing instructional materials (programmers). But in addition to the widening of status differentials, the rationalization of instruction will centralize power as well. The classroom teacher now has relatively narrow discretion in the shaping of the curriculum and the choice of materials. The new media, if governed from above, will further narrow the scope of his discretion. By thus further reducing the calls on him for other than routine skills and custodial functions, the new media will further lower the status of the nonelite teacher.[8]

Trow projects that the consequences of these innovations also are likely to affect the structure of the teaching profession, "replacing a unitary status by a hierarchy of profession and statuses".

Lindley Stiles and B. J. Chandler[9] make explicit the connection between instructional technology and the development of a hierarchy among teachers:

> Urban schools in the future will offer multiple opportunities for professional service, specialization, and advancement. Although it is to be expected that guild organizations will exert persistent pressures to prevent the professionalization of teaching services in city systems, it is highly probable that differentiations will be developed in the quality and utilization of teaching competence that will permit outstanding teachers to be rewarded for professional competence and contributions. Examples of such recognition of quality teaching are already available in television teachers, instructional team leaders, and specialist teachers in some school systems. In the future, it is likely that the uniform scale salaries that educational guilds defend so vigorously will apply only to the lowest echelon of teaching. Others who prove their professional competence will be able to advance within the function of teaching to higher assignments that carry greater professional responsibility and greater financial rewards.

Lastly, Professors Biddle and Rossi offer a number of similar speculations. They predict that as a result of the new technology and as more avenues of specialization appear,

1. the status of the teacher will rise;

2. the profession of teaching will appear to be less of a craft;

3. the teaching career will not be terminal but will provide many avenues for both horizontal and vertical mobility;

4. and the status of the "generalist", the traditional classroom teacher is likely to continue at a low level.[10]

Now this is surely a mixed bag of speculations. I believe the status of teachers has risen and will continue to rise mainly because of the success of teacher militancy as it is defined in the related concepts of collective bargaining and collective action. Collective bargaining is an orderly democratic process which permits representatives of teachers to negotiate as equals with representatives of their employers. On the other hand, it is only meaningful if teachers have the option of withholding their services in the event that it is impossible to reach agreement on ther terms of the written contract. Rossi and Biddle may have over-simplified the problem; it is difficult to hold to the idea that the status of the teacher will rise because of an increase in the avenues of specialization. The reverse is likely to be true, namely, the person we normally think of as a teacher may be submerged in a hierarchy of levels. (On this score, the first point made by Rossi and Biddle seems to contradict their last point. It is difficult to see how the status of the teacher will rise and the status of the "generalist," the traditional classroom teacher, is likely to continue at a low level.) How-ever, it is not difficult to see what the real problem is here, namely, the confusion about the issue of "What is a teacher?" The concept of a teacher needs to be clarified and stabilized. The problem, which I will deal with in the concluding pages, is how can these things be done.

That the profession of teaching, because of increased areas of specialization, will appear to be less of a "craft" appears to be splitting hairs. To polarize the teaching process into dichotomous elements always has seemed to me to be a moot question. Is teaching an art or a science? And now, is it a profession or craft? This kind of either/or thinking serves only to cloud the real issues. Lord knows it is difficult to define the teaching process and to reach limited consensus on a definition! (I suppose one could say that teaching is a "pro-fessional craft" or perhaps even a "crafty profession"!) The heart of the matter is not so much what you call it, but how you view it and, more importantly, how you treat it. That is to say, teaching will be less of a craft and less of a profession, not because of increased specialization, but less of both if we continue to treat it and support it in the substandard ways to which we have become accustomed.

Also, at the heart of the matter is the question of mobility, horizontal and vertical mobility. The latter form, particularly, adds a number of related problems which must be resolved: differentiated staff levels, ranking, and merit pay. That this problem is already at hand is seen in the position taken recently by the Massachusetts Advisory Council on Education which during the past year has been reviewing that state's program of teacher certification and preparation.[11] In the report of the Council a number of statements were made which I find quite shocking. First of all, a hierarchy is identified:

> Four levels of licenses are suggested: internship licenses for those in training; associate teacher licenses for beginning teachers; professional licenses for those who demonstrate ability to handle professional assignments independently of super-vision; and educational specialists for *high-level* teachers.

Then, the personnel policies of school districts, that is, collective bargaining contracts, are reconceived:

Policies such as employment qualifications, staffing assignments, salaries, promotion and tenure, should be related to the new differentiated uses of teaching talents. A key objective should be to provide opportunities for appropriate professional contributions, advancement, financial reward and professional prestige within the instructional team. School systems should move as rapidly as possible to adapt all personnel policies to the new differentiations of teaching that qualify teachers for higher levels of certification.

And lastly, vertical mobility is indeed undertaken:

Failure to maintain the level of performance for licensure could result in non-renewal, thus disqualification. In some instances, however, when the failure is inability to perform at an advanced professional level, such as professional or specialist, it may be decided to reduce the level of license to that of performance capabilities. Thus, a professional teacher who fails to maintain competence to perform independently might be licensed as an associate teacher and permitted to work under supervision.

TENURE	TENURE	NON-TENURE	NON-TENURE
ASSOCIATE TEACHER	STAFF TEACHER	SENIOR TEACHER	MASTER TEACHER
A.B. or Intern	B.A. Degree and State Credential	M.S. or Equivalent	Doctorate or Equivalent
100% Teaching	100% Teaching Responsibilities	3/5's Staff Teaching Responsibilities	2/5's Staff Teaching Responsibilities
1-10 Months	10 Months	10-11 Months	12 Months
ACADEMIC ASSISTANTS A.A. DEGREE OR EQUIVALENT			
EDUCATIONAL TECHNICIANS			
CLERKS			

Illustrated here is the Temple City, Calif., model of differentiated staffing. Temple City capitalizes on functions already existing in many schools, but formalizes them into a four-level teacher hierarchy: 1) The Associate Teacher, a novice, has a "learning schedule" and less demanding responsibilities; 2) The Staff Teacher has a full teaching load, aided by clerks, technicians and paraprofessionals; 3) The Senior Teacher, a "learning engineer" or methodological expert in a subject, discipline or skill area, teaches three-fourths of the time; and 4) The Master Teacher is a scholar-research specialist who teaches two-fifths of the time, but also has curriculum expertise, translating research theory to classroom possibilities.

From Florida Schools, *September-October, 1968*

Note: *The latest issue of "Education Recaps"[12] (October, 1968) reports that "teaching" salaries up to $25,000 appear to be a reality in the differentiated teaching staff plan adopted in Temple City. The plan began operating this fall with a single secondary level master teacher in social studies. In three years, the plan calls for the entire 4,500 student district to be on the schedule. At that time there will be six or seven master teachers, and one senior teacher for every eight or ten staff teachers. It is reported that master and senior teachers will be grouped around five disciplines. It is also significant that the editors of "Education Recaps" enclosed the word "teaching" in quotation marks.*

A number of significant educational issues are brought to the surface as a result of these three statements; for example, the evaluation of competencies, the obsolescence of teaching skills, and the renewal of certificates. And while they must be dealt with, the delimitations of time and space and the immediate topic before me force me to withhold discussion of these important issues until another time. The concept of differentiated staff, however, is directly relevant and must be assessed. There are a large variety of differentiated staff models which have been developed over the past few years. All are similar basically to the Temple City model found on page 395.

The scheme illustrated, tells us more clearly than anything most of us can say about the divisiveness which is gradually overtaking what was once considered a cooperative and egalitarian profession. Schemes such as this maintain and extend the disjunction which so often exists between teachers and administrators. I fear that it will not be long before it is impossible to distinguish between senior teachers, master teachers, and administrators, particularly since the various levels of teachers "teach" for varying periods of the calendar year. Such schemes are easy to develop on paper, which probably accounts for their increasing abundance. But it is another matter to carry them out, if one were prone to do so.

In the diagram above it is not at all clear who is responsible to whom, that is, are staff teachers or senior teachers or master teachers in the final analysis responsible for the key decisions needed in the educational life of each child? Or is accountability divided on a 2/5 and 3/5 basis too? The model assumes that "staff" teachers are something less than "learning engineers" (good lord!) and experts in subject matter and curriculum. It assumes that "master" teachers are superior in nearly everything and, hence, should be in charge. Such an assumption denies individual differences because most people are not superior in nearly everything! Surely there must be a workable and realistic alternative to this kind of divisive hierarchy arrangement. Such an alternative should be based upon a legitimate differentiation (if differentiation is the answer and I am not at all sure it is). Would not it make more sense to try to build a horizontal arrangement based upon differentiated assignments and tasks? While this has not been done to any wide extent, at least it would not tend toward divisiveness as does the hierarchical arrangement. In an alternative model teachers would be considered on the same level even though they may be performing individualized tasks. While the following diagram is only illustrative of one horizontal model, similar ones can be devised.

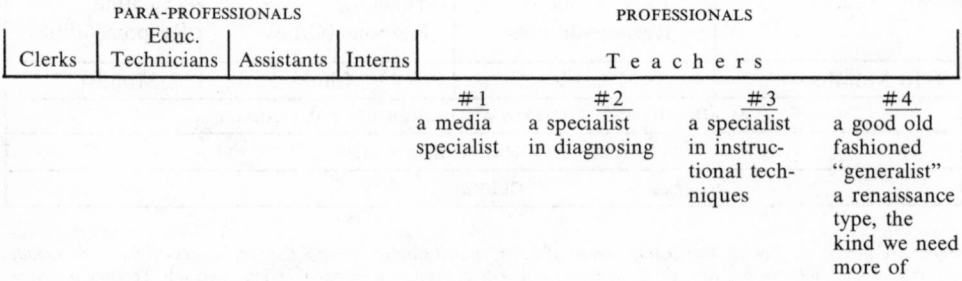

	PARA-PROFESSIONALS			PROFESSIONALS			
	Educ.						
Clerks	Technicians	Assistants	Interns	T e a c h e r s			
				#1	#2	#3	#4
				a media specialist	a specialist in diagnosing	a specialist in instructional techniques	a good old fashioned "generalist" a renaissance type, the kind we need more of

Bhaerman does a good job, I think, in pointing out the impact of new differentiated staff proposals on the status of teachers. A point that is not sufficiently stressed, however, is the fact that much of the new educational technology—that is the appliances—cannot be used in the traditional school organization. Diagnostic machines which can pinpoint why a fourth grade pupil hasn't yet learned to read cannot be used by the fourth grade teacher because they require large amounts of individualized attention, for instance. Programmed materials for older students, while useful for average and above average readers, cannot be used by below average readers without a great deal of help from a teacher or someone who is familiar with the materials being used. Thus, added staff will be necessary in spite of ingenious schemes to make small group instruction possible by accepting very large group instruction for part of the time, or by self-directed (teacherless) study. The added personnel required for use of the new technology will raise unit cost, unless varying pay grades for staff members are employed. This in turn, as Bhaerman points out, introduces the hierarchy concept.

At the present time almost universally throughout the United States, eighth grade students spend five classroom hours a week learning "American History." If, in a class of 30 pupils, six must be sent to a tutor, the cost of teaching that class American History is increased by the salary of the tutor plus the cost and maintenance of whatever technological appliances are used. Thus, a powerful force is generated toward paying the tutor considerably less than the eighth grade Social Studies teacher. At the other end of the scale will be a "specialist"—a quasi-administrator—who teaches less and is paid more than the Social Studies teacher. An even more ominous pressure will be generated to give the general teacher more pupils at a time to compensate for the costs of the specialists and the machines.

Finally a point that Bhaerman does not make enough of, I think, is that the use of differentiated staff requires a large increase in the amount of supervisory cost per teacher. A favorite remark of school principals when confronted by demands for faculty control is, "You cannot run a school by committee." While it might be a good idea to experiment with communal administration, I doubt that it is practical to teach eighth grade American History that way. Somebody must be in charge, like it or not, and I would make the further surmise that Parkinson's law will operate with tidal force to bring about bureaucratic proliferation, with the wind deadening effect.

To make a general rule, teachers will probably not be resistant to the new technology as such. To the extent that it can be shown that new educational appliances will make them more productive, teachers will actually welcome the added equipment. However, teacher resistance will increase as it becomes apparent that use of new technological devices require changes in staff structure, or are paid for with money which seems to come out of working conditions and teachers' pockets.

The length of time one teaches should be determined by contractual arrangement. However, the professional teachers should probably not teach 100% of the time since we should not ignore time needed for on-the-job training and for planning periods. Undoubtedly, some teachers should be specialists and some generalists. Nevertheless, all should be expert in their "subject, discipline or skill area." And, it seems to me, that with the aid of competent supervisors, teachers should be able to some degree to translate "theory to classroom possibilities." After all, it is the teacher who is in the classroom; hence, it is he who must translate theory into practice, not the scholar-research specialist who may be too far removed from the real concerns of a classroom. Just as the schools emphasize or claim to emphasize individual differences among students, the alternative should recognize individual differences in the faculty.

One final but significant point—the relationship of salary to the levels of teaching. It probably would be ideal if we had the omnipotent wisdom to be able to distinguish degrees of effectiveness among teachers—and pay accordingly. But the millennium is a long way off and the chances are we will not be around to see it. So we are left with a choice: to pay teachers according to the role they play (but who can judge priorities here?) or to pay teachers according to the level of their academic degree and years of experience (realizing the inequities that often exist here). Until we have found a workable and justifiable alternative, the salary schedule concept as we know it now is the only meaningful choice we have.

I trust the problem is now in clear focus: the duties of teachers need to be stabilized along lines similar to this horizontal continuum in order to differentiate him from his supervisors and from other adults who play important supportive roles. Even those teachers who train in areas of specialization need not be ranked at higher levels. Specialists are needed in this day and age, but so are generalists who can see more than one side of a problem. Who is to say which is the more significant role? Both should be remunerated according to their level of education and experience, not by their role performance. Remove even one brick from the base of a structure and it will collapse. Likewise, to a large degree, teaching is a cooperative and communal effort and so it should remain. Nothing must be injected to create divisiveness . . . not even new instructional technology. While we *can use* the new media, when proven that it effectively can meet our goals, let not the new media *use* us.

In short, we should attack the problem at the source: if the majority of teachers are not the most able or skillful, let us get to the root of the problem by identifying, recruiting and further developing the "raw material" into truly first class teachers who are able. Instead we concoct a hierarchy of levels and rewards, thus creating new and even more serious problems.

Conclusion

As I stated at the outset of this paper, I would deal not only with the potential corrosive effects of instructional technology on the teaching profession but also with ways in which I feel that the corrosive effects could be mitigated. I have attempted to suggest ways in which the concepts of the "teacher" could be stabilized. Let me conclude by offering two positive prerequisites which I feel will be necessary for this stabilization:

1. A reinforcement of our professional (or verbalized) attitude that teaching is a cooperative and fraternal effort, one which calls for centralizing the values of solidarity and unity among the teaching profession. While teachers may perform different roles, their unified force should be directed toward improving the status of children's learning and of the profession's well-being.

2. A demonstration of courage on the part of both teachers and administrators is necessary in order to encounter such schemes as the vertical hierarchy in the Massachusetts certification plan and the vertical differentiation in the Temple City plan.

Those two plans offered a thesis. We reject them and offer in its place a concrete plan of our own to complement the two attitudinal requirements stated above. Therefore, two specific programs are needed in order to stabilize the status and structure of the profession:

1. A teacher certification arrangement in which the state would require superior college-level preparation for certification, provide for expert supervision of beginning teachers for a period of at least three years, and then remove itself from further certification activity. In turn, local school systems would provide the stimulus, where needed, to encourage teachers to continue their education for improved competence. Presently, in many states teachers must secure additional college credit in order to continue the initial teaching certificate in force or to make it "permanent." This practice involves a type of coercion that does not lead to professional responsibility. The stamina and the dedication to complete three or four years of successful teaching, plus the optimum collegiate preparation necessary for regular initial certification, should be sufficient grounds for extending a certificate. Rather than the multi-levels of certification we offer the concept of certification as a dual-step process with continuing certification granted after a three or four year probationary period.

2. An in-service education arrangement in which specialization can be obtained by those who wish it and continued professional growth can be achieved by all. However, in-service approaches must not be more of the same old things. They must be meaningful and significant and, to a complete degree as possible, they must be personalized and individualized. It is trite to say that teachers must be continuously alert to the many new insights into educational theory, the learning process and, yes, instructional technology. Teachers obviously must never stop growing or they are dead. A way must be found to assure this growth. The question is not whether they do or whether they do not. It is: What is the fairest, most mature, and most professional way to insure professional growth. Obsolescence of skills can be overcome without the restrictions imposed by rigid certification levels and forced renewal. But the way will not be easy; nothing worthwhile ever is. Courage by teachers and administrators alike is needed.

Brave words! But how to make them a reality? One approach might be to encourage the development of jointly controlled teacher-administration research and development funds through more imaginative collective bargaining. As things now stand, R&D is carried on by colleges, grant farmers, and institutional research departments. Working teachers are not involved. Perhaps two or three percent of the operating budget of every school district could be set aside for research by teachers on a released time basis. Such research would have much more credibility and could command much more support from teachers than ideas which come "from the outside."

In dealing with the possible effects of instructional technology upon the teaching profession, it has been necessary to go beyond the initial elaboration and prediction of those effects. To reiterate, I believe the effects of technology are still being determined. The main alternative appears to be a choice between a hierarchical structure of the profession and a flexible, less rigid, and less divisive structure. I trust I have offered a workable guideline in order to achieve the latter goal.

REFERENCES

1. Scheuer, Congressman James H. "The Federal Interest in Education Technology." Speech to the annual meeting of the Council of Educational Facility Planners, Washington, D.C., October 10, 1968.

2. *Ranking of the States, 1968.* Research Report 1968-R 1. Washington: National Education Association, p. 55.

3. Trow, Martin. "The New Media in the Evolution of American Education" in Peter H. Rossi and Bruce J. Biddle, *The New Media and Education.* Chicago: Aldine Publication Co., p. 347.

4. *Ibid.*

5. *Ibid.,* p. 38.

6. Keyserling, Leon H. "A Ten-Year Plan to Save the Schools," *Changing Education,* Summer-Fall, 1968, p. 21.

7. Newsom, Carroll V. "Technology as it Affects Educational Planning." Speech to the annual meeting of the Council of Educational Facility Planners, Washington, D.C., October 10, 1968.

8. Trow, *op. cit.,* p. 348.

9. *Ibid.,* p. 338.

10. Biddle, Bruce J., and Peter H. Rossi, "Educational Media, Education and Society" in Rossi and Biddle, *The New Media and Education.* Chicago: Aldine Publication Company, p. 38.

11. Massachusetts Advisory Council on Education. *Teacher Certification and Preparation in Massachusetts.* Report Number 1. Boston: Massachusetts Advisory Council on Education, June, 1968. 132 pp.

12. "Education Recaps." Educational Testing Service. Princeton: New Jersey. Vol. 8, No. 1. October, 1968.

57.

How Teachers and Administrators Can Be Given a Better Indoctrination on the Potentialities And Uses of Instructional Technology

by A. W. VANDERMEER
Dean, College of
Education
Pennsylvania State Univ.

The question of how teachers and school administrators may be given a more solid and sophisticated indoctrination in the uses and possibilities of instructional technology presupposes that instructional technology can make a significant contribution to the achievement of the goals of the American system of education. Other papers in this series cite research and informed opinion which, in general, support this presupposition. The issue, of course, does not end here, for while there is little doubt that instructional technology is deservedly "here to stay" there are grave differences of opinion with respect to the dimensions of the contributions of this field. There are disagreements as to which educational goals it can help to achieve, and there are disagreements as to the extent to which instructional technology can make a quantitative difference in the achievement of these goals.

It is necessary to recognise that extreme positions exist in the spectrum of opinions regarding instructional technology. There is the minority view that to introduce any amount of technology into education is to dehumanize it. A major cliche on university campuses is that students are reduced to numbers to be manipulated by computers, and this attitude is clearly a part of student unrest in secondary schools. Instructional television, computer-assisted and other machine instruction, and even motion pictures are included as targets of this cliche. The existential primacy given to feeling as opposed to reason is easily extrapolated to justify an antagonism toward technology on the grounds that it is basically rational and scientist rather than affective and emotional. Then there are the devotees of the printed and spoken word who, since they cannot view nonverbal media as occupying any but a subordinate position on the hierarchy of intellectuality, resist technology on the grounds that it may divert the better minds from the necessarily arduous task of achieving a level of literacy that is commensurate with their aspirations and abilities. Even those who may agree with McLuhan that the linearity of verbal communication is at least somewhat anachronistic seem to emphasize the relevance of nonverbal media to the needs and desires for self-expression and self-fulfillment rather than to presentational and instructional applications.

On the other hand, there are the highly partisan advocates of instructional technology. James D. Finn, writing in "Planning for Effective Utilization of Technology in Education"[1] points out that extravagant claims have been made for the impact of technology on education for more than half a century, and documents this contention with a series of quotations beginning with Thomas Edison who is supposed to have stated for the New York *Dramatic*

Mirror's issue of July 13, 1913, "Books will soon be obsolete in the schools. Scholars will soon be instructed through the eye. It is possible to teach every branch of human knowledge with a motion picture. Our school system will be completely changed in ten years." More recently, E. B. Kurtz[2], writing of instructional television, stated ". . . this new instrumentality . . . bids fair to become the most potent agency for universal education ever conceived." Similarly extravagant claims could be cited for teaching machines and computer-assisted instruction.

A more analytical view of the potential of instructional technology assumes that it can make different levels of contributions to the achievement of different goals of education or that there are some kinds of learning to which instructional technology can be applied with salutary effects while there are others to which it has limited or zero applicability. For example, Harry Broudy[3] in a piece following that of Professor Finn's, writes "For this type of explicit instruction (imparting knowledge—either of facts or principles—for rote learning or for problem-solving) the traditional teacher is needed no more than covered wagons are needed for cross country transportation. If they *are* needed, it is for the type of teaching encounters that we noted in Socrates' teaching of virtue, or value education. This is the tacit, personalized phase of instruction. . . . The humanities, aesthetic education, molar problem solving, interdisciplinary explorations are a few of the areas in which encounter-teaching rather than didactic teaching is stressed. The human encounter, Buber's I-Thou relation, the imaginative sympathy entailed by such encounters—these will be the characteristics of their (the teacher's) styles. Such encounters cannot take place en masse."

Clearly, the whole strategy for giving teachers and school administrators a more solid and sophisticated indoctrination in the uses and possibilities of technology in education must aim at the reduction of the extreme points of view of the more radical partisans of and opponents of technology. The analytical approach suggested by Broudy seems to offer the greatest promise as a meeting ground for the reconciliation of the extremes.

One additional prefatory point must be made in advance of a consideration of specific tactics for the successful introduction of an indoctrination in technology into the pre-service and in-service education of teachers and administrators; namely, that we have to depend to an inordinate degree on what appears to be reasonable in judging the effectiveness of educational systems (and, indeed, of the teaching component of these systems) rather than on quantitative data. We have to recognize that there is little agreement as to valid criteria of teaching success or, by extension, the success of teacher education programs. Actually, the issue is in doubt as to whether we can hope to produce in the prospective or practicing teacher those behaviors that are required if he is to accept the worth of instructional technology and to use it effectively.

Dr. Donald M. Medley,[4] of the Educational Testing Service states "The direction and amount of change that should be produced in each teacher would tend to be unique to him, and few or no generalization can be made about what constitutes 'improvement' in teacher behavior—at least in our present state of ignorance.

"Perhaps the picture I have painted is too dark. Maybe there are not quite as many different types of teacher behavior all of which are equally effective, as I have imagined. But I am sure that this picture, pessimistic as it is, is closer to the truth than the simplistic model we have used in the past, the model which assumes that for any given definition of effectiveness there is one behavior pattern which is most effective for all teachers. Research has certainly not been able to identify any such pattern, and it has certainly tried."

Medley goes on to suggest the following characteristics of the model teacher education program which, he says, will provide the teacher with four things, " (1) an experimental attitude—a willingness to examine, evaluate, and modify his own teaching behavior throughout his career, (2) theoretical knowledge—familiarity with all that past experience and research has discovered which might be useful to him, (3) technical skill—control over the methods, techniques, and media of instruction (including his own behavior), so that he can implement the theoretical knowledge he possesses, (4) feedback techniques—ability to use objective methods for analyzing teacher behavior and assessing its outcomes so that he can learn from his experiences."

Clearly, if we follow Medley's anti-simplistic theses, we are compelled ourselves to apply technology to the process of education of teachers and administrators; we must think and plan in terms of behavioral objectives which can be attained through a variety of paths according to the characteristics of those being educated. We must consider, too, long- and short-range plans for the preparation of personnel for the teaching professions. In the short-range, attention is focused on producing an educator who is able to adapt to the current milieu while at the same time serving as an agent of change looking toward the schools of the future. In the long range, we must begin now to prepare personnel for an entirely new table of organization for the schools—one which will require professionals and support personnel that are now only dimly thought of. In the case of short-range plan it is opined that the responsibility of teacher education is to produce teachers and administrators who (1) know the uses and the *limits* of the uses of technology, (2) are able to exploit technology efficiently in the achievement of legitimate and agreed educational goals, and (3) take pride in applying technology effectively to those purposes for which it is appropriate, and (4) are secure and satisfied in assuming the roles that are appropriate when technology is thoroughly exploited.

With regard to the long-range plan it is assumed that the scope of teacher education must accommodate personnel other than teachers and administrators who will need to be prepared as a result of the application of technology to education as well as for the utilization of technology. For example, Broudy[5] envisions three types of personnel for schools distinct from the teacher: namely, (1) *instructional technicians* whose responsibility would be to assign pupils to instructional programs and to reassign them as the demands of individualized instruction dictate, (2) *instructional programmers* whose job it would be to write the programs that are fed into the system and (3) *instructional managers* whose responsibility would be to turn the instructional packages into schedules to be implemented by instructional technicians, and to exercise general supervision over all instruction. One can recognize the third of Broudy's non-teaching instructional personnel as closely similar to administrators, since, broadly speaking, it might be said that the function of school administrators is to make it possible for teachers (and other instructional personnel) to operate efficiently in the use of instructional technology.

In a complementary vein, Ward and Young[6] predict that "Technology will increasingly supplement but not replace the classroom teacher. So the present functions of the teacher will be performed more effectively as a result of the technological advances.

"A growing array of learning materials, media, and instructional strategies will be available. The teacher must be able to make rational decisions about their selection and sequencing.

"The teacher's role in the future is likely to feature: (1) a decreased emphasis upon information-giving; (2) increased attention to the development of higher order cognitive outcomes; (3) increased attention to the development of constructive affective outcomes; and (4) the integration of both cognitive and affective processes for the improvement of learner outcomes.

"Accelerating change, such as the information explosion and the rate of technological advances, demands a personal capacity on the part of teachers for thoughtful and systematic change.

"One of the major, relatively untapped resources in education is the self-instructional capacity of the learner. An increased function of the teacher role needs to be the provision of opportunities for students to learn how to learn.

"A realistic perception of one's self, and of one's interpersonal relationships, is crucial for highly effective teaching."

Several alternative models of teacher education programs can be envisioned to produce professionals who will have the competencies demanded by tomorrow's technologically-oriented educational system. What might be labeled the didactic model of teacher education presently is most commonly used. This model assumes that there is a body of content which can be mastered in more or less formal course work and then applied in classroom situations, first under supervision and later independently. It is necessary that the prospective teacher develop a high level of competency in (1) creating and/or selecting measures that describe relevant characteristics of children, (2) retrieving information about children, and (3) using information to diagnose and prescribe instructional procedures and strategies for the children. This clearly calls for a knowledge of a range of subject matter and of presentation modes as well as of characteristics of media; a thorough knowledge of a wide array and range of teaching and learning strategies; and the ability to relate both of the foregoing to such characteristics of learners such as maturity—motivation—sensory preferences—etc. While it must be readily conceded that not all of the content for this formal didactic instructional model for teacher education exists; it is clear that at least these three components will be represented:

1. Humanistic Studies   The teacher will need to understand a range of fundamental philosophical positions (perhaps realism, idealism, pragmatism, existentialism) and what characteristics of curriculum and method are consistent with each. What objectives are valid under the alternative philosophical positions?

2. Behavioral Sciences   Both sociology and psychology as well as, to a lesser extent political science and economics: The teacher will need to know the range of human developmental patterns, learning styles, motivations and value patterns, social structures and organization, etc. Also, of course, it is through the methods of the behavioral sciences that media and technological devices themselves are studied in terms of their own intrinsic characteristics and of the relationship between these characteristics and the characteristics of educational objectives.

3. Teaching Field or Discipline   A thorough knowledge of a wide range of content to be taught within the discipline of the teacher's competence. Under the present school organization, it is axiomatic that the teacher must have both breadth and depth of preparation in the subject or subjects that he will teach. This axiom is rooted in the assumption that the teacher's role is largely that of a dispenser of knowledge rather than as a manager[7] of a learning environment. While the latter is the only role that is consistent with the school of the future in the view of some people, the former is consistent with Broudy's dichotomy between explicit and tacit instruction and, of course, with his projected professional instructional manager. There is, however, no essential conflict here, although it will be necessary to modify drastically the technique whereby the content to be taught is mediated to the prospective teacher if he is to be fully equipped to use the new technology. Robert Glaser[8] describes as untenable the present assumption that "the way in which a discipline structures its knowledge provides the best structure for transmitting it to students." He goes on to observe that courses are too frequently organized in a way that satisfies the epistemological purposes of the body of knowledge involved, which organization is sometimes theoretical and logical and sometimes chronological and fortuitous. He favors rather than the exclusive attention to the requirements of the structure of the discipline at least equal attention to the requirements for transmitting the discipline to the student. Finally, he points out that a task for psychological research is to identify appropriate learning structures that can be incorporated into the epistemological structure of the knowledge in order to produce a more ideal learning process.

The prospective teacher must know his subject in three dimensions: (1) he must have more than a rudimentary grasp of its structure, its vocabulary, and its methods; (2) he must have sufficient breadth and depth of knowledge to be able to suggest viable alternative subject matter content that is appropriate for individual learners who differ from one another in such crucial variables as aptitude, maturity, motivation, and learning style; and (3) he must have a sufficient range of knowledge to work within the present range of curriculum offerings represented in the schools. As a general criterion, the prospective teacher should be able to read with understanding middle level journals in his discipline *and* in the literature of the teaching of his field. This latter includes the experimental literature on teaching and learning in his field, and the various curriculum proposals in his field.

To provide the beginning teacher with the kind of education described in the previous paragraph is a large order; one that is not likely to be filled by the present common array of discipline structured courses; rather it may be essential that at least a portion of the education of the prospective teacher in the content that he will be expected to teach should consciously and by design incorporate (1) a consideration of analysis of the knowledge into units that can provide building blocks by which the learner goes through an instructional sequence, and (2) the media and technology whereby these building blocks can be conveyed to the student. Such instruction would partake of a number of forms: (1) The college teacher would call attention to the way that he has organized subject for presentation, justifying this organization by consideration of alternative methods. (2) By the same token, *alternative* presentation modes would be considered incidentally with the presentation of subject matter. (3) The learner would be encouraged to introspectively and self-consciously examine the process whereby he himself is learning the subject matter and to verbalize for examination by his instructor and his peers the results of his self-examination.

The kind of "professionalization" of subject matter proposed in the preceding paragraph would not necessarily encompass the entire range of content learned in the course of the prospective teacher's education. More than likely it would be best placed *following* the mastery of the basic structure and vocabulary of the discipline and *prior to* a level of higher specialization within the discipline. Most of the latter would presumably occur at the post-baccalaureate level. "Professionalized subject matter" in the teaching field would, then, be the intermediate level of collegiate training, and would coincide with studies in the humanities and behavioral sciences as applied to education and as indicated in previous paragraphs. Correlation and coordination should, in this didactic model, occur at all levels between the behavioral sciences (including Education) and humanistic studies on the one hand, and studies of the teaching field disciplines on the other. While the teacher candidate is learning the structure of his teaching field he should also be learning the structure of, at least on the rudimentary level, philosophy, psychology and sociology. As he is learning the application of these disciplines to education he would be assisted in making connections across to the professionalized subject matter component of his education in his teaching field or fields.

In the model of teacher education described thus far emphasis has been given to shaping the environmental influences of the teacher education program in the interests of developing skills in the use of media and of creating a style of attacking the job of teaching in a way that is compatible with the fuller introduction of instructional technology into the school system. This is, perhaps, a verbose way of saying that the teacher education program should exploit the imitative potential of prospective teachers. One should, incidentally, reject vigorously the platitude that "teachers tend to teach as they have been taught." If this were true it would deny that teaching is a rational process.

The following points extend and make more explicit what has been implied in the didactic model of teacher education presented up to now; namely, that the program should exemplify the widest and best-reasoned use of instructional technology:

1. Obviously a wide variety of media should be used in the presentational aspects of teacher education, and these should be systematically evaluated by the

instructor and the students as an integral part of many if not most of the courses required of the teacher candidate.

2. A wide variety of media should be assigned as major sources for the prospective teacher. Instead of confining outside assignments to typical print material, the student should frequently be directed to recordings, filmstrips, films, tapes, and the like. Computers should be used for review, brush-up, and direct instruction by students. Assigned projects should require the prospective teacher to *use* a wide range of materials which, of course, presupposes a learning resources center that far exceeds in variety of resources, the conventional library. Instead of assigning reports to be submitted always as papers, students would be encouraged to report the results of their independent study in the form of film, tape, filmstrip, script, or the like.

3. Generous use of media in feed-back between instructor and student and vice versa should be characteristic of the teacher education program. A tape recorder could be used, for example, as a means whereby the instructor can communicate his criticisms of student performance (be it theme-writing or lesson presentation) to the teacher. Videotape and audio tape should be used for guided and independent self-analysis of performance in micro teaching and in internships.

4. A major activity of teacher education faculty should be research and development in instructional technology, and undergraduate as well as graduate students should be involved in these R&D processes. Such student involvement would, of course, pertain to individual projects of modest size as well as mission-oriented research and development. For example, John Pfeiffer[9] suggests an educational application of the Delphi method developed by Olaf Helmer and his colleagues in the early fifties at the Rand Corporation. The general idea of this method is to prepare successive rounds of questions designed to elicit progressively more carefully considered group opinions. Pfeiffer reports the results of a 1965 pilot experiment in which three groups of educators who had recently participated in various discussions of innovations filled out the Delphi questionnaire and produced a list of 93 proposed reforms, together with estimates of what the Federal Government would have to spend during a five-year period to carry out each reform independently. The result was a consensus regarding the allocation of funds among various proposals. It is easy to see how such a technique involving students and faculty members could produce insights and understandings in the realm of instructional technology.

What is, in essence, proposed in the foregoing paragraphs relative to teacher education in the wise use of instructional technology is the thorough immersion of the prospective teacher in a creative and self-conscious involvement in a system of education which, though it pertains to his own immediate goals, will bid fair to establish in him those professional techniques and ways of study and operation that typify the manner in which applied social scientists apply their professions. The focus is on active, thoughtful, self-analytical goal-related studies rather than on the plain acquisition of knowledge and skills. A fuller exposition of this concept has been presented by Mars[10] in a publication for the American Association of Colleges for Teacher Education.

Up to this point, no mention has been made of instructional technology as a subject to be studied directly. In the didactic model, formal study of this subject is definitely indicated. It is odd, is it not, that the curriculum of general education allocates so much time to the study of verbal language and so very little to the study of other forms of communication or even to the study of communication itself? It seems clear that it is essential that the teacher and the administrator have a high level of sophistication in communication. In the didactic model of teacher education this would come, presumably, as a result of a course taught well and within the environmental context previously described. The content of the course would include communication theory and models, analysis or existing channels and media, and practice in creating or producing as well as utilizing various media.

An alternative model of teacher education that is widely talked about but little used might be labeled as the functional model. Such a model is proposed by Bush.[11] In essence such a model proposes that at least the professional part of teacher education be geared to and grow out of the problems and observations encountered by teacher candidates in direct confrontation with students in public schools. The difference between didactic and functional models may be seen as largely one of tactics; agreement as to the skills, knowledges and attitudes sought would probably cover the major portion of the teacher education curriculum. In one study comparing these approaches, Torkelson[12] compared the effectiveness of a formal course in instructional materials with two approaches which integrated what was presumed to be the same objectives and content into practicum and methods in teaching. In general, his findings slightly favored the didactic approach; however, the functional approach was plagued with logistical problems and those who employed it had had the majority of their experience in more didactic approaches, so it would be wise to follow Torkelson's advice to avoid the temptation to generalize too far from his data.

Up to this point, pre-service training has been implicit in this discussion. Most of what has been written applies with equal force to in-service training. It is not to be expected that a pre-service education, however excellent, will last a lifetime. The pre-service preparation of the teacher must be followed by a continuing program of in-service education. It matters little whether these in-service activities are conducted by the universities, by school districts, by professional societies, or by a combination of these. The essential thing is that they be conducted and conducted well. Not only must education follow current graduates into the field, but also the existing instructional personnel presently manning the schools must not be neglected. In Pennsylvania, for example, the average number of years of service of elementary teachers in 1967-68 was nearly 15[13] while the average years of service of secondary teachers was nearly 12. It should not be inferred that these teachers had been completely innocent of in-service training during their years of service, but it should likewise not be assumed that their in-service training necessarily prepares them for the wisest and most fruitful participation in the applications of instructional technology.

What is true of teachers—that one can infer some need for in-service education from their average years of service—is even more dramatically true of administrators and supervisors. The average years of service of district superintendents was nearly 29 years. This was likewise true for supervising principals. Supervisors of elementary education and of secondary education averaged 23 and 26 years of service respectively, while county superintendents averaged a tremendous 35 years of service.

The content of in-service education in instructional technology does not differ much *in kind* from that suggested for in-service education; rather, it differs in level and in qualitative aspects. What the experienced teacher and administrator may lack in youthful energy and disposition toward change, he frequently makes up in insightful experience and dedication to quality education. Of particular importance, however, is the use of technology itself in bringing in-service education to the field. Modern extension work is pioneering the use of video- and audio-tapes, conference telephone hook-ups, and other exploitations of instructional technology. Such advanced applications of technology are, unfortunately, in the minority.

An excellent example of the use of technology in in-service education to instruct not only in teaching content but in the applicability of technology itself is reported by Riedesel.[14] Elementary school teachers in service in Williamsport, some 65 miles from the campus of the Pennsylvania State University were provided with access to CAI terminals in their home location. The response stations were connected with the computers at the University on a schedule which permitted the teacher to study a professionalized course in modern mathematics at her convenience. Not only did the teachers learn modern mathematics but they had a fascinating experience in the application of technology to teaching. A project whereby a similar course is taken to remote schools in Appalachia in movable van is under consideration by the Appalachian Regional Educational Laboratory.

Brickell has pointed out the crucial role that the school administrator plays in educational change. Clearly the skills brought to instruction by well-trained teachers can largely be frustrated in administrative situations where fruitful innovation is discouraged and where the means of instructional reform are not made available. The principle of managing the environment to support desired learning is applicable likewise to the education of administrators in-service and pre-service in the implications of instructional technology.

It goes without saying that a comprehensive study of the present and potential impact of technology on instruction and on school organization should be a part of the curriculum for the administrator. In addition to this obvious fact, however, experience should be given the prospective administrator in the use of the computer in various administrative tasks— scheduling, personnel records for pupils and teachers, accounting procedures, etc. By the same token, the applications of technology in educational planning should be taught to students of school administration in graduate programs and demonstrated to active administrators in the schools. If systems analysis concepts, procedures and tools are an important part of the administrators armamentum, he is very likely to behave in a sophisticated and supportive manner with regard to the application of technology in the instructional domain of the total school system.

It should be borne in mind that the school systems of the near future will require new types of administrative personnel. Graduate programs in educational administration should enhance the concept of differentiation of function by preparing administrative support personnel such as business managers, operation analysts, and instructional technologists.

One final element is required in connection with the indoctrination of teachers and administrators in the possibilities and use of instructional technology; namely, the preparation of professional education personnel themselves, that is, professors of education. By and large, the most neglected factor in Federal programs of support for education is that of the training of professors of education and their support personnel. A recent promising development is the Triple T program whereby the training of teacher trainers is to be subsidized through the U.S. Office of Education. Unfortunately, little emphasis is provided in the guidelines with respect to instructional technology. College professors, including professors of education are generally highly individualistic and highly verbal. Graduate schools of education need to turn their attention to the preparation of a new breed of instruction-oriented, technologically sophisticated professors of education. Research in media and instructional techniques should be central to the preparation of this group of professionals. Their model should not be the lecturer droning away at his podium but that of the manager of instruction who uses a wide range of media and techniques for the development of skills in his students, and that of the creative and scholarly researcher who exploits the discipleship concept of graduate education as he makes contributions to knowledge in the areas of instruction and technology.

REFERENCES

1. Finn, James D. *Planning for Effective Utilization of Technology in Education.* Designing Education for the Future: An Eight State Project, Denver, Colorado, August 1968, pp. 37-48.

2. Kurtz, E. B. *Pioneering in Educational Television.* Iowa City, State University of Iowa, 1959, pp. 70-72.

3. *Op.cit.,* p. 109. (See Ref. 1.).

4. Medley, Donald M. "The Research Context and the Goals of Teacher Education." Educational Testing Service, Princeton, N.J. Unpublished paper.

5. *Op.cit.,* pp. 108, 109. (See Ref. 1.).

6. *Ibid.,* p. 312. (See Ref. 1.)

7. Used here in a more general sense than of the specific professional person identified by Broudy, pp. 108-109.

8. Glaser, Robert. "Ten Untenable Assumptions of College Instruction." *Educational Record,* Spring 1968, p. 158.

9. Pfeiffer, John. *New Look at Education.* Odyssey Press, Poughkeepsie, N.Y., 1968, p. 152-156.

10. Mars, Walter J. *Professional Teacher Education.* AACTE, 1201 16th St. N.W., Washington, D.C., 1968.

11. Bush, Robert. *The Real World of the Beginning Teacher.* NCTEPS, 1201 16th St. N.W., Washington, D.C., pp. 12-14. It should be noted that this model could also serve as a semi-didactic model.

12. Torkelson, G. M. *An Experimental Study of Patterns for Improving the Preparation of Pre-Service Teachers in the Use of Audiovisual Materials and of Effects on Pupils.* Title VII Project #079, NDEA 1958. Grant #7-48-0720-034. College of Education, The Pennsylvania State University, University Park, Pa., March, 1965.

13. *The Calculator.* Vol. 10, No. 1. The Pennsylvania Department of Public Instruction, September, 1968.

14. Long, Samuel M., C. Alan Riedesel. *Use of Computer-Assisted Instruction for Mathematics In-Service Education of Elementary School Teachers.* Center for Cooperative Research with Schools, College of Education, Pennsylvania State University, University Park, Pennsylvania, October 31, 1967.

b. IT/Organizational And Administrative Changes

58.

Organizational and Administrative Changes Needed in Schools and Colleges in Order for New Techniques to Effectively Improve Instruction

by *ROBERT H. ANDERSON*
Prof. of Education
Harvard Univ. Graduate
School of Education

It may be useful at the outset to mention some of the ways that existing organizational patterns and administrative procedures tend to constrain and impede the processes of change. These patterns and procedures, most of which have their origins in the nineteenth century (or even earlier), were based on beliefs or conditions that no longer hold; yet they remain a strong force in the lives of most teachers and children and they serve to abet and encourage the essentially conservative posture of administrators, lawmakers, taxpayers, textbook publishers and equipment manufacturers, and others for whom the status quo proves to be more comfortable or more convenient than the seemingly more dangerous or expensive alternatives now being proposed.

In most states, prevailing statutes governing the existence and management of school districts and colleges, the ways that both capital and operating funds are raised and accounted for, the training and licensing of teachers and other educational workers, the powers of state agencies to influence or control local school district affairs, and the responsibilities of the schools were created in response to almost totally different needs than those we face today. In many cases, these often-obsolete provisions are built into the state constitution, and it is exceedingly difficult for them to be changed. In nearly all cases, their implementation over many decades has created a network of local "establishments" each of which is firmly entrenched within well-defined boundaries, jealous of its control over the various buildings, policies, and traditions that exist within those boundaries, and comfortably tolerant of the inequities, anachronisms, and even comic features of a nineteenth century schooling pattern in a nearly-21st century world.

It would be unfair to imply that the arrangement is totally ludicrous, or that sensible administrative and pedagogical practices are absent or even rare. Nonetheless, it is true that a wholesale revamping of school codes is desperately needed in most states, to make more satisfactory provision for school district organization, for fiscal support of the schools, and for the modernization of curriculum, staffing, and related policies.

Probably more serious than legal constraints, and the conservative posture of laymen who exercise leadership within the existing framework, are the constraints that educators tend to place upon themselves (and therefore upon community forces for change) as a result of tradition and experience. Some of the worst features of the schools as they are presently organized and administered are among the most familiar and popular practices within the profession. One finds disappointingly little genuine dissent, for example, among teachers with respect to continued use in the schools of (a) a September-June school calendar based upon an agrarian economy; (b) the self-contained classroom or depart-mentalized class with fixed pupil membership and an autonomous teacher; (c) the nomen-clature and policy trappings of graded structure; (d) competitive-comparative report cards; (e) 25-30 pupils as the predominant instructional group; (f) unilateral, didactic patterns of "teaching;" and (g) textbooks which determine the course content. It is uncommon to find teachers, individually or in groups (e.g., their professional associations), in the fore-front of local and state efforts to introduce Kindergarten and other pre-school offerings where they have not existed, or more elaborate guidance and health services, or curricu-lum revisions to include sex-education and other urgently-needed components, or even nonprofessional and paraprofessional support personnel as auxiliaries in the staff structure.

In some instances, the relative inertia of the profession with respect to needed reforms is explained by the weak power base from which teachers in many communities have customarily operated, and the lack of experience and sophistication they have had in legal and political affairs. For many, the job of teaching itself is so time-consuming and emotionally demanding that little energy seems to be left for an attack on basic problems. For most, however, it seems probable that the status quo is relatively inoffensive if not altogether acceptable, and thus the motive for revolution is actually absent.

Two of the major themes in the modest revolution that is underway in the United States today are (1) that schools must emphasize much more than the mere verbal mastery of subject matter, and (2) that packaging children in relatively homogeneous age-grade groups of 25-30 under the direction of an autonomous teacher is a generally unsatisfactory ar-rangement. Neither of these themes is easy for the typical teacher to accept and act upon, even though both have been much discussed in the literature for at least a decade.

In a recent A.S.C.D. yearbook, Rodney Clark and Walcott Beatty make this helpful observation:

> Most teachers now know that older notions of training the mind, mental disci-pline, and transfer of training were based on a kind of mythology. However, while these ideas were in command they generated methods of teaching and ideas about school organization which have been in practice so long that they now seem natu-ral and sensible. Thus the procedures linger on, long after their rationale has faded. Besides, many teachers have come to feel that it is not their province to try to understand learning, that whatever the mystery of the process, the teacher's job is to teach and the student's job is to learn.[1]

Though the rationale for many familiar teaching practices and organizational structures may have faded, loyalty to them remains remarkably strong. Old habits are not easily discarded, especially when even professors and school administrators provide reinforcement either to resist the new or to honor the old.

Conservatism has been a tendency of educators throughout the ages. Most societies have been suspicious of experiments with the education of their children; and there are many economic, social, and administrative factors that contribute to the sluggishness of educational change, including the high cost in time and resources of converting personnel, buildings and physical resources to the requirements of proposed new arrangements. For the educator, to propose and carry through significant reforms is often to work against heavy odds and to invite conflict with protectors of the status quo not only in the society itself but also in the educational profession.

The distinguished New Zealand educator, C. E. Beeby, has discussed the problem of educational conservatism, within a broader analysis of the quality of education in developing countries. Noting that many causes of conservatism are professional, he identifies five conditions which tend to restrain innovation in the schools. One is that the stated goals of education are not sufficiently clear, and teachers hesitate to leave the well-trodden path "because their goal is hidden in the mist."[2] Another is that reforms, to be effective, must be both understood and accepted by the teachers who are to apply them. Often, teachers with the responsibility for implementing a new idea either lack enthusiasm for it, or misinterpret it. A third problem is that the teacher is himself a product of the system in which he works, and there is a strong tendency for him to fall back on the familiar methods which may themselves be the object of the new reforms. Yet another problem is that teachers customarily work in isolation from their colleagues. Finally, Beeby notes that there is a wide variation in the effectiveness and the adaptability of the various teachers in any given school or school system. He comments:

> ". . . if teachers were not isolated, if they worked in hierarchic groups with common responsibilities, it would matter less that their range of ability is so great, that so many of them are vague as to the goals of their craft or fail to grasp the real significance of new methods proposed to them. Again, if teachers were not so deeply conditioned by their own experience as pupils, unsureness and doubt might lead more frequently to experiment with the new rather than regression to the old. This interlocking of factors produces a pattern of resistance to change that is probably unique."[2]

Experimentation with the new, or at least the creation and development of alternatives to the old, has been a relatively lively enterprise in American education since approximately 1955. The motivation for change has come primarily from outside the profession, stimulated in large measure by the enormous changes taking place within the society itself but also by the so-called "explosion of knowledge" and the growing capability of the mass media (notably, television) to inform, propagandize, and otherwise influence the thinking of John Q. Citizen and his children. Whatever the causes, however, there has been underway for some fifteen years what might well be called an educational reform movement of many dimensions. Terms like "revolution" have been used to describe this movement, although the slow pace of change and the relatively small impact of the reforms have led many observers to use less sanguine terms in describing what is happening.

The development and utilization of educational technology has been one of the most visible and exciting dimensions of the changing educational scene. Other categories of change include:

1. emergence of the school as an instrument and symbol of societal progress and change (and therefore, on occasion, a battleground in fields such as the civil rights movement)

2. increase in the age range for which the public, tax-supported schools take responsibility (to include pre-kindergarten, and junior college or adult-education)

3. effort to equalize educational opportunity, especially with respect to offsetting the disadvantages of poverty

4. updating and overhauling of the school curriculum

5. intensification of the commitment to meeting individual needs across the spectrum of human differences

6. development of clinically-oriented patterns of pre-service teacher education

7. new approaches to in-service development of professional staff

8. cooperation between school districts and universities (or other agencies) in research-and-development activities

9. collaboration among adjoining school districts in curriculum studies, research-and-development activities, or staff training programs

10. emergence of new professional staff patterns and roles

11. introduction of non-professionals and paraprofessionals in the personnel rosters of schools

12. decentralization of huge city systems, to permit closer ties with people of the local communities

13. consolidation of small, inefficient school districts to permit broader offerings and operational economies

14. experimentation with different patterns of school unit organization, such as the "middle school" serving youngsters in the age bracket 10-14

15. development of cooperative-teaching patterns as alternatives to the self-contained classroom

16. experimentation with new patterns of pupil-class scheduling

17. efforts to provide more flexible and adaptable school buildings and equipment

18. abandonment or modification of conventional graded structure

19. increased use of flexible and varied pupil-grouping and instructional arrangements

20. modification of conventional methods for evaluating, recording, and reporting pupil progress

21. deliberate mixing of pupils of different ages and abilities.

Probably other items could and should be included in this list, but the point has probably been made that educational change in America proceeds on many fronts and embraces many dimensions. What is perhaps less obvious, but important to appreciate, is that few if any of the twenty-two categories of change (including Technology) are incompatible with other categories. At least theoretically, it is possible for a given community or school to be actively involved in all of these types of change, the obvious exception being in items 12 and 13, where presumably only one could apply.

Specifically, we are here claiming that instructional technology can and probably should be linked in some way with each of the other dimensions of the changing educational scene. In some cases the linkages are more obvious than in others, but in no instance is there an actual clash (philosophically, or functionally) between the full development of technology and the type of other change that has been noted. The question is not, "Technology at the expense of what?" or vice versa, but rather it is "How can technology and (each of the other changes) best serve each other's interests?"

Such questions are easier to pose than to answer. From the vantage point of those whose interests and competencies lie not in the field of technology itself but rather in school organization and administration, certain arguments can be raised with respect to the kinds of problems that presently require solution and the types of structural mechanisms that seem most legitimate and promising in the present state of the art. Perhaps later, with these ideas in hand, the experts in technology can make the necessary connections.

Problems of American Schools

In the most recent (July, 1968) statement of its Research and Policy Committee, the Committee for Economic Development outlined certain problems of instruction in elementary and secondary schools.[3] Noting that research and technical invention are opening up new possibilities in instructional processes and methods, the report stresses "that there must be a basic change in the attitudes and approaches of large numbers in the teaching profession toward instructional organization, methods, and research."[3] It mentions four imperatives for the schools, including better organization for innovation and change, increasing emphasis on the dissemination and practical application of research, use of cost-benefit and cost-effectiveness analysis as a guide to resources allocation, and the establishment of a national commission to encourage research, innovation, and evaluation.

Significantly, the CED document is a fervent appeal to overcome educational conservatism and resistance to change, by means of such things as the reconstruction of school staffs, teaching patterns, and school organization; by the adoption of team teaching, differentiated teaching functions, and flexible salary scales; by the effective utilization of new educational technology (especially TV and audiovisual equipment); by improving teacher education and curriculum materials; by special emphasis on early schooling (especially for the culturally disadvantaged); and by elimination of the regimentation of students that results from conventional class units and the lock-step (graded) method of advancement.

> We believe that the combination of differentiated staffs, team teaching, and variable student grouping, together with the use of instructional television and other audiovisual media, has much promise for individualizing instruction.[3]

Elsewhere in the CED document it is indicated or implied that a heavy investment is necessary in compensatory education and in "Head Start" types of preschooling, in basic and applied research, in training teachers and administrators to judge the worth of new ideas and techniques, in strengthening state offices of education and the research-evaluation enterprise generally, and in the support of curriculum reform.

Setting aside the many implications of the CED report for federal, state, and local policies of educational finance, there are a number of recommendations and ideas in the document which deserve widespread support and implementation. Especially important is that the sprawling, disorganized, and generally ineffective network of educational research and development needs to be overhauled so that useful knowledge can be put more rapidly and more widely to work, and so that ineffectual ideas can be more quickly recognized and set aside. Whether it will prove possible to accomplish this overhaul without the intervention on unprecedented scale of the Federal Government or some other central agency, remains to be seen. One hopeful sign, noted recently by James Cass in a *Saturday Review* editorial[4], is that the Research and Development Centers established five years ago under the Cooperative Research Act may provide at least a nucleus group whose experience to date offers some hope.[5]

That *early education* deserves higher priority in the structure of American education is another CED conclusion warranting full endorsement. In the March, 1969, Vol. 50 issue of *Phi Delta Kappan,* this writer and some twenty other authors reported on the current state of scholarship about pre-primary children and the values of educational intervention at this crucial stage of human growth. Certainly one obvious conclusion is that public (and private) education, and the sources of financial support thereof, must be redefined so that educational opportunities will be guaranteed to every child in this pre-primary period (i.e., before the age of six).

As an aside, we might take note of an interesting observation by economist Charles Benson on the relationship between extending years of schooling and the national economic growth rate. In a passage dealing with the views of Edward F. Denison, whose studies suggested that the returns would be relatively small if a year of schooling is added at the end of the present cycle, Benson offers an intriguing idea: if the year is added at the beginning of school life, the opportunity cost would be smaller and the educational contribution to the economic growth rate might be twice as high.[6]

In the CED document, there is an unequivocal commitment to the idea of replacing self-contained classrooms with the collegial patterns for which the term "team teaching" is generally used. Although supporting argument is not provided, it seems reasonable to assume that the writers were impressed by several features of team teaching which are especially conducive to staff development, to avoidance of the "lock-step" in dealing with pupils, and to flexibility in the use of resources (both human and material). These features are adequately described in the literature of team teaching[7], but their special relevance to the problems identified by the CED and by the Commission on Instructional Technology may warrant further discussion here.

As Beeby (see above) noted and as most observers of American schools would now incline to agree, the long-cherished tradition of the self-contained classroom has been a great impediment to the professional growth of individual teachers and to the resolution of various other problems of the schools. It restricted the opportunities for teacher-to-teacher interaction (including the vital ingredients of "feedback" and constructive criticism), it slowed the development of specialization in teaching functions, it narrowed the range and the quality of pupil-to-pupil and pupil-to-teacher interactions within the school, it hampered the entire field of research-and-experimentation by offering only one physical-social setting within which questions of curriculum and instruction could be examined, and it encouraged the preservation of age-gradedness as the pattern of "vertical school organization." These conditions were found, by the way, in both secondary and elementary schools since the typical "departmentalized" teacher in junior or senior high school was no less self-contained than his counterpart in the elementary grades.

Team teaching, which has been in a stage of (distressingly) slow development in American schools for some twelve years or more, does not automatically insure that all the aforementioned problems or conditions will disappear, but it offers at least the strong possibility that they can be resolved. That the profession has accepted only gradually the arguments in support of teaming, and that most examples of team organization at the present time are only imperfectly developed, is admittedly discouraging. Yet, solid resistance to the idea of team teaching has virtually disappeared at the theoretical level and it would seem that the chief remaining obstacles to its full development are such problems as (1) how to reorient the veteran teachers and principals who were "raised" in the conventional tradition, (2) how to strengthen and modify pre-service training programs for future teachers and administrators, and (3) how to make more readily available to school people (and to interested citizens generally) the practical and philosophical insights that stem from the national enterprise of research-and-development (see above).

The "Theoretical Ideal" in School Organization

As we examine the literature and experience of school organization over the past decade or so, it becomes clear that the conventional arrangement of unit-age, graded, self-contained classes is inconsistent with the needs and the predispositions of children. In fact, the same may be said of youth and young adults at the college level. To be sure, there are times when people of the same age, and/or the same academic interests and history, are best grouped together. "Homogeneous" grouping is a legitimate practice under certain conditions and for a limited span of time, and among the options that should be available to each teacher (or group of teachers) is grouping on some criterion of homogeneity. However, it is equally important for a teacher to be able occasionally to combine children who are unlike each other in one or more important respects, including such variables as age, sex, interests, achievement history, speed of learning, learning style, and many other varieties of "academic personality." In the age-graded classroom of limited membership, fewer such combinations are possible than in a team which is multi-aged, multi-graded (or better still, nongraded), and large enough to require three or more teachers.

In a nutshell, then, we have defined the organization plan which is theoretically ideal. It calls for a group of adults, presumably with certain common interests but also varied talents, who will share the responsibility for teaching, at any given moment, a team of students who also have common interests but varied talents. Sometimes, all students in the team will participate in the same lesson, which is perhaps taught by just one of the teachers. At other times, every student will be working on his own, with or without the occasional guidance of one or more of the teachers. At other times, students may work together in groups of 3, 6, 10, 15, or whatever numbers are required. Hopefully, there will be frequent occasions when an older (or better informed) student will be teaching or tutoring other student(s), and depending on the size of the school there may be occasional student traffic to and from other teams (or even other schools).

The foregoing description is obviously too brief to include all the arrangements that are possible, but at least the general idea is clear. Now, then, let us carry the model to its logical conclusion. The basic idea is that each person in the organization should have maximum opportunity for interaction with other persons: some who are at a similar stage of development, some who have passed on to a more advanced stage, some who are at a less advanced stage; some who have similar needs and interests, some who have a different make-up. Presumably this argument can be extended to include interaction with materials of a wide variety, including the spaces within the building itself. The argument for a well-equipped Instructional Materials Center, with computer connections and other links to resources beyond the school itself, probably is at least implicit.

In a school so arranged and organized, the academic progress of each student would differ in significant ways, especially perhaps with respect to rate and quantity of learning but also with respect to the range and quality of topics explored, from that of every other student. It would be the responsibility of the staff, aided by technology, to keep track of each student's overall growth and to decide when and under what conditions that student should be allowed to move on to each new stage of learning. At intervals, perhaps every two years or so (but not necessarily in the month of June!) the student having reached a certain stage of development would be assigned to the team next up the line; and two or three times in the student's school lifetime he would be transferred to the next school unit.

Inasmuch as some younger students have very high academic potential and high motivation, it is possible that they could complete the work of the elementary school as defined in less than the typical number of years. Ordinarily, such students would then be allowed to proceed to middle-school work while remaining physically in the more child-like atmosphere of the elementary school. Later, when ready physically and socially to live in the middle school, they would be transferred to a higher unit. In some cases, especially where the child's physical and social growth is also relatively advanced, the very successful pupil would be transferred to the higher unit at a younger age. Pupils of high maturity and ability might, in fact, complete the entire K-12 program one or more years earlier than their age-mates; in such cases, the decision would be made either to permit the pupil to do college-level work while still in secondary school ("Advanced Placement"), or to enter him in a college at that point.

In the case of youngsters who mature and achieve at much slower rates, the reverse of the foregoing arrangements would occur: some additional time (e.g., a year or two) could be allowed in the lower unit, but social and physical maturity would be recognized as reason to transfer the pupils to the higher school unit (within which a less demanding program would be offered, as necessary).

None of this is novel, but it serves as a background for certain propositions that seem to deserve more earnest consideration. One, obviously, is that the several successive school units (pre-primary, elementary, middle school, secondary, college) should overlap each other to a considerable extent. Specifically, for example, the secondary school should offer courses (and other experiences) ranging in difficulty and sophistication all the way from "5th or 6th grade" level to upperclass college-level work. Teachers in the several adjoining school units should collaborate more with each other, and there should be more intellectual and physical traffic between the schools.

Another need is for far more elaborate record-keeping systems, whereby the chronological history (academic, physical, social and so forth) of each child's growth and performance during his school years is preserved and made available to the teachers, counselors, technicians, and others who work with him.

A third need is for a far more elaborate and comprehensive repertoire of testing and diagnostic devices, whereby the child's current status and needs can be determined and with the help of which the school program can both (1) avoid unnecessary and unfruitful repetition and redundancy (e.g., in exposure to "rules of grammar") and (2) insure that each unit of work will be properly chosen and well-timed in that child's experience.

A fourth need is for the school program, especially at the secondary level, to break away from the tyranny of 10-month courses and "carnegie units" or their administrative equivalents. Increasingly, it becomes evident that a subject such as Geometry I, if it is needed at all by given groups of pupils, can be mastered by some of them in a fraction of the time required by others. For the youngsters whose mathematical development in elementary school has been unusually complete, it is at least possible that the high school could (after diagnostic testing) "put him through" the usual Geometry I course in a matter of weeks, or even "excuse" him from the course altogether while making appropriate notation on the master record. The same could be done with all skills subjects, and the youngsters would thus be freed to pursue either more advanced skills, or substantive topics, or other worthwhile activities. Some of the work could be done independently, as in a tutorial course.

Much of the value in school experience, however, goes beyond the mere mastering of certain skills and bodies of knowledge. Increasingly, it now appears, technology shows promise of providing for these routine kinds of learning through the confrontations of individual pupils with machines and instruments; yet no one seems disposed to propose that schools as such may therefore be abandoned once machines and programs have been fully developed. On the contrary, the promise of the machine for educators is seen as the emancipation of teachers from the tasks that can be done mechanically, and the release of teacher energy for the pursuit of more important tasks. These will include a higher-level instructional role in the teaching of concepts and values; the analysis and shaping of attitudes; the search for truth and honesty in human relations; the therapeutic treatment of children's personal and conceptual problems; and even the savoring and enjoyment with children of certain joys and pleasures that stem from learning and living.

How might technology serve these loftier functions of the teacher in the school? For one thing, as mentioned earlier it may help the teacher to keep a more complete record of each child's developmental history, and to comb that record periodically for clues to the trends in his intellectual and other tastes, his ability to cope with and use powerful ideas, and his tendencies when confronted with certain types of problem-solving situations. For another, it may deliver to the teacher, more promptly than do professional libraries at present, instructional resources that promise to enliven and enrich the next "happening": a poem translated from the Russian, about this or that; a sound-movie interview with Robert Frost; pictures showing fish-eggs hatching; Franklin Roosevelt's voice on December 8, 1941; up-to-date information about the political struggle over the redwood forests.

At a more routine level, technology can be used within a school to help with the master-scheduling of people and resources. There is no reason why classes should meet every day at the same hour, or why teachers should not share the available space in the building in different ways from month to month or day to day. Even the idea of restricting "school" to the September-June cycle is obsolete, and with the help of computers it should be possible to enjoy far greater flexibility in the scheduling of space and activities over the entire 365-day year. Unless and until school administrators themselves show a greater interest in breaking away from the conventional and convenient patterns of utilizing time and space, however, it is unlikely that the full range of possibilities (with technological assistance) will be explored.

Vertical Adaptations

It would seem that the vertical structure of the entire American educational system is in need of rather drastic overhaul. Mentioned previously is that many children, especially those with superior academic talent can and should proceed rapidly through the "regular" school program so that by the time they are in high school they are already doing college-level work in some respects. It seems possible to claim that a substantial number of high-school students possess as much skill and knowledge (with some allowances for physical and social maturity) as did *college* graduates not so many years ago. Similarly, especially in the stronger colleges, the undergraduates pursue studies once offered at graduate level; and so on. Given these circumstances, it seems appropriate to ask such questions as

(1) *Why should not some high school students be given some of the freedom* (e.g., from daily-scheduled classes, from "Mickey Mouse" class assignments) *and responsibilities* (e.g., for one's own use of time, and for student-directed activities) *associated with college life?* Experience shows that this drastic a change from the prison-like control system in most high schools will require a great deal of planning and patience. Furthermore, the all-day *custodial* role of pre-collegiate schooling cannot be eliminated without creating numerous problems for families and communities. Nevertheless, a changeover in the direction of more flexible and appropriate arrangements is urgently needed; and in fact, the angry mood of many adolescents suggests that if schools do not take the initiative, some of these changes will be forced by the student rebellion.

(2 *Should not the academic route to the professions be radically shortened?* Especially since there is so much sheer waste and redundancy in the academic sequences that ordinarily precede medical, legal, pedagogical, scientific, and other professional studies, it would seem that young people could be spared a great deal of the dragged-out, expensive, and inefficient programs that pass for "pre-professional."

(3) *Could not equivalent economies be effected in the whole structure of collegiate and university education,* including programs for able students not pointing toward the professions? It may already be obsolete to view college as invariably a four-year sequence which ends at age twenty-two. Since the secondary schools now perform many of the functions left to the colleges a generation ago, the entire concept of "college" may be outmoded and it may be appropriate to view the lower unit of the university as a flexible, *transition school* in which enrollment may be for one to four (or more) years depending on the student's needs.

Other questions probably could be raised, but let us turn to the implications for the vertical school structure of the fact that *all* kinds of pupils (not only the university bound) have immediate and continuing educational needs that are not now being met. Lately a number of efforts have been underway to *redirect* the educational program, particularly in the secondary schools, so as better to meet the needs of young people for whom the usual academic program is unsuitable (or unpalatable). Efforts of this sort are of course expensive, and they require administrative and other changes for which only a fraction of America's educators are emotionally and intellectually prepared. However, unless schools can be made more relevant to youngsters of the sort who now do poorly or drop out, even more serious problems are likely to emerge.

It is becoming crucial in the United States to improve school programs with vocational implications. As the need for unskilled labor diminishes and, conversely, as the need for better-trained workers increases, the schools must offer more meaningful and efficient programs which equip young people with marketable skills. Among other things, technology has a great capability in helping to meet this need. Beyond the offerings in secondary schools, which themselves must include greater opportunity for work-oriented studies, there will be needed an expansion of two other types of post-secondary education: junior or community colleges (and technical schools), and adult education. These schools, within commuting range of the students served, can plan with local and regional industries and offer not only pre-occupational and work-study programs but also refresher training, advanced training, and adult re-training as needed. Since these schools will probably have difficulty in acquiring experienced staff, and since as new institutions they have greater freedom in establishing their own identity and style, it seems likely that they will offer particularly congenial settings within which the new technologies may be used.

Developing the Educational Professional

Adapting our sub-title from the Educational Professions Development Act, let us pursue for a moment one of the most important changes that must be made if educational workers are ever to achieve professional competency and status. In a nutshell, *the conditions of employment must be drastically revised in order that teachers, supervisors, administrators, and other certified personnel may have adequate opportunity on-the-job for continuing professional study and growth.*

In a time when (a) there is already an enormous gap between what should be happening in the schools and what actually is, (b) knowledge of all sorts (including what is to be taught, and how it may be best taught) is doubling every decade or so, (c) most teachers, even the recently trained, have only a fraction of the training and knowledge their job requires, and (d) schools are being asked to take on even greater obligations than before, it is simply outrageous that the schools continue to operate along lines laid down more than a century ago. The length and the nature of teachers' contracts, the work loads carried by teachers, the working calendar that is followed daily and annually, the nature of supervision and supportive help that is provided—all of these and related practices were developed in a time when far less was expected of the schools and the nation had only begun to understand the needs of its people and its economy. Granted that present-day schools are in many ways more elaborate and costly, it is nonetheless true that the typical teacher still receives virtually no time and support for activities other than those which keep the school in daily operation.

Given the rate and the range of new information and ideas that have some bearing on the teacher's work (what he teaches, or how he teaches), it seems reasonable to claim that the recent college graduate in his first year of teaching faces the need for being "re-educated" at least four or five times during his career. Within ten years, at least half of his own "education" will have become obsolete and most of what he knows will have been learned on the job. By the time he reaches his professional peak, perhaps only ten percent of his knowledge and expertise can be traced to his pre-service education. This being the case, it seems all the more urgent to insure that the quantity as well as the quality of his in-service educational opportunities will be significant.

In his address before the 1968 convention of the N.E.A. Department of Elementary School Principals, Harold Howe described the future role of the school as a training ground for teachers.[8] Pointing out that the principal is in effect the director of a teacher training institution, Howe noted that each school has the potential for developing and changing the skills of the various people (teachers, future teachers, aides) who work in it and stressed that team teaching offers an appropriate rubric within which people can learn from one another. That team organization does have this capability, by encouraging a far greater quantity and a more intense quality of interaction among teachers than self-contained patterns, makes it one of the most important ideas on the educational scene. However, the conversion from conventional structure to team structure is itself a complicated maneuver that requires much advance preparation and a great deal of developmental support at least in the early stages, so it would be reckless to assume that such a change can be made cheaply.

Ultimately, not only a collegial job arrangement but a basic change in the teacher's contractual obligations should be envisioned. Not all teachers need be shifted to more demanding roles, but at least a quarter of the teachers ought to be given greater responsibility and enjoy proportionately the privileges of professional-growth opportunity.

It may always be desirable to include on the roster a number of teachers with less training and/or commitment, whose work responsibilities will resemble those now commonly accepted by teachers on nine-month and ten-month contracts. Of the teachers who switch to year-round contracts and who express the desire to carry greater responsibility (e.g., as team leader or program specialist), perhaps not all will prove equal to the challenges of leadership. Some will, however; and in the school of the future we may hope to find many teachers on the job throughout the year, some of these in prestigious and significant roles. Furthermore, work with children would for most teachers occupy only about half to three-quarters of the actual time spent at school, the remainder of the time to be devoted to planning, research, staff seminars, materials preparation, and the like. Several months of each year would be devoted to professional activities and studies other than regular teaching, and the teachers would have much more contact with university professors, research-and-development workers, and others in frontier-pushing roles than has been possible for them in the past.

Probably there are practical administrative and financial problems in this proposal, but the general idea is that teachers no less than physicians and surgeons have need for study reflection, and basic professional renewal if they are to succeed and grow in service. Perhaps this is self-evident and needs no arguing in a document of this sort. What follows, then, is that technology can conceivably play an important role in the aforementioned activities. The media can be used to "reach" the teacher in service and put him in touch with new professional knowledge. Packages or kits, including not only written and audio-visual materials but also a variety of "games" and devices for individual and group study, can be provided as a part of the locally-sponsored effort in staff training. Teachers could watch and analyze video tapes of their own teaching and also of other teachers. And so on.

Also of crucial importance is intensification of efforts to re-define the total personnel structure of the schools, especially with respect to incorporating auxiliary personnel. Teacher aides, clerical aides, technicians, library assistants, and various other roles are appearing (though all too slowly) on the school scene, and with greater encouragement this trend could become one of the most important developments in the long history of education. One obvious benefit is that teachers when supported by auxiliaries can devote more of their time and energy to other-than-routine functions. Another is that it will be easier under such circumstances for teachers to engage in a lively in-service development program.

The emerging concept of auxiliary personnel in education has already created an impressive literature,[9] which has recently begun to focus on the important topic of training auxiliary personnel. Not only can technology play an important role in the training of such workers, but it seems increasingly necessary for these people to be familiar with technology as an aspect of their work.

One of the peculiarities of American education is the tradition of local autonomy and control. Just as the self-contained classroom has proved to be a limited and imperfect arrangement, so it may be said that the self-contained school and the self-contained school district are anomalous in a time of growing interdependence and collaboration. Among the most heartening trends in education today are those that involve the functional merging of adjoining schools, adjoining districts, university staffs, research agencies, and other groups (see nos. 8 and 9). Through such cooperation, schools and districts can afford to have services (e.g., computer scheduling), specialists (e.g., research directors, or psychiatric services), and pilot research programs that might otherwise be difficult to provide. Joint support of high quality in-service staff development programs is one of the most desirable types of cooperation.

Within and across districts, another desirable arrangement is "team administration," where the principals of several adjoining schools pool their resources (and specialize in functions) in much the same way that teachers team together for mutual benefit. Inasmuch as principals have at least as much need as teachers for working and sharing together, and since the team arrangement promises them the same opportunity for meaningful professional interchange, this is a trend that ought to be encouraged in every possible way by top administrations.

Admittedly, there is at this moment a great deal of discussion about the usefulness and the viability of the principalship as a major role in the educational structure. Some observers have noted that as teachers become more skilled and as teacher's associations obtain more authority for their members through contract negotiations, the principal may become a "fifth wheel" or supernumerary. Perhaps so. But one could also argue the opposite: that as the teaching staff becomes more and more involved in the limitless tasks of building better curricula and developing more sophisticated approaches to work with children, the local administrator becomes all the more important a person on the total scene. Given the right kinds of people in this role ("aye, there's the rub!"), schools can indeed become lively and productive places.

Unfortunately, the evidence stemming from studies of the effectiveness of principals is rather discouraging. Harking back to Beeby, it seems quite probable that the principal is often a voluntary prisoner of the conservative ideas and practices that were in vogue when he entered the teaching profession. Too, principals generally keep themselves busy with various functions of record-keeping, paper-shuffling, monitoring (e.g., cafeterias, bus operations and custodial functions), and supplies management that could and should be done by administrative assistants (serving several schools) or even by machines. Therefore principals often protest that they have insufficient time to visit classrooms, attend team meetings, work with teachers in program development, and keep posted on current educational developments.

Superintendents have many responsibilities, and especially in today's explosive social-political climate they are understandably preoccupied with such things as teacher militancy, community unrest, pursuit of financial support, and other urgent problems. Yet from the standpoint of their role as educational leaders, no responsibility is of greater importance than insuring that effective leadership is being provided "where the action is," in the individual school. Certainly the entire central-office superstructure is justified primarily as it facilitates and serves the work of individual schools, and the superintendent as top leader ought to have a particularly visible interest in the ways that he and his own staff either facilitate or hinder the active and progressive leadership of the building principals.

Although most superintendents might deny it, the fact seems to be that principals are more often rewarded for "holding the fort" and paying attention to administrative nitty-gritty than for venturesome efforts at program redefinition and vitalization. Rare is the situation where principals feel that approval will be expressed at the top if the audiovisual budget request goes up, or if teachers want certain walls removed, or if extra substitute teachers are needed so that a group can visit and study an exciting school in another city. Unusual is the situation where a principal can expect support if he wants to revise the reporting procedure, or adopt a more flexible school schedule, or ignore the regular course of study so that an experimental program may be introduced. Even more unusual, alas, is the situation in which a principal is under strong pressure from his superintendent to spend a great deal of time working in classrooms with teachers, and to report (in other than a mechanical way) on the efficacy of various supervisory techniques and procedures being employed.

It may seem strange that such situations are uncommon, but the simple fact is that supervision of instruction is given only lip-service in perhaps ninety percent of American schools. Unless and until the situation is reversed, it seems very unlikely that American teachers will make sufficiently rapid progress toward a true professional competency and status. In turn, new approaches to education *including* the extensive use of technology will gain in acceptance only very slowly.

Technology can, of course, be a useful tool in the reorientation and retraining of principals (as well as teachers), and also in the supervisory process. Doubtless other papers or documents available to the C.I.T. deal with specific ways and means; here we have merely described the problem and offered the (informed) opinion that the improvement game is likely to be won or lost at the level of local school leadership. Our suggestion, in summary, is that one of the most important changes that should be made in the schools, in order that technology may make an ultimate difference, is to invest new meaning to the term "principal teacher," forerunner of a term (principal) which lacks the lustre it deserves.

Finally, let us say a few words about the men at the top of American school systems. Already implicit in our argument is that superintendents should reorient themselves so that the principal-to-teacher relationship will assume fresh importance in the hierarchy of things. Another point we have stressed is that superintendents should themselves be enjoying some of the benefits of team work, through joint involvement in various studies and programs. A third, implicitly at least, is that the superintendent should think of himself somewhat as a college dean, in the sense that he heads a clinically-based graduate school in which hundreds of professionals are in various stages of training. Hopefully, in the same vein, he also feels like the director of a research-and-development center. That he is also in other roles, which very likely occupy the bulk of his time and energy, should never be allowed to divert his loyalties from those missions which have a staff-development focus.

School administration has become an extraordinarily demanding and difficult function, and the men and women who serve (particularly in the superintendency) are under pressures of the sort that perhaps only heads of government and of major industries may have felt in a previous generation. School districts are large and complex, with management problems as extensive as those in large corporate enterprise. The schools are caught in the middle of the current battles between progressives and conservatives, and they serve almost literally as the battle ground for some of the most painful and critical problems (e.g., the elimination of deprivation and poverty, the recognition of minority-group rights) with which the nation is beset. Of all the agencies that tax him and test his patience, only the school district is so easy for the taxpayer to attack and so responsive to his vote. Therefore it is rare to find schools staffed with a sufficient number and variety of specialists, for example in fiscal management or in school facilities planning, to insure that proper decisions are being made.

Typically, in fact, top-level school administration operates in an atmosphere of crisis. Decisions are made on the basis of insufficient or inappropriate evidence, and even so the superintendent is chronically faced with mountains of paper that ought to have been reduced to more digestible and manageable size through processing. All too little solid information is available to guide the superintendent and his staff, either in advance of decisions or after a decision has been made and results are subject to review.

The conclusion, then, is obvious. Educational administration, no less than other fields of administration, needs the technological and human resources that will enable its officers to function efficiently and knowledgeably. It needs especially to shed the habits-of-mind and the organizational structures that developed during a century of "local control," and to find new and better structures (e.g., metropolitan districts; consortiums) within which the necessary resources can be more readily provided and exploited. Clearly the new technologies can help such arrangements to come into being, and find proper place within them.

A Few "Loose Ends"

In a short paper it is impossible to deal in full detail with the many dimensions of this topic. However, a number of ideas that appear to be of some potential value are herewith included for the Commission's consideration.

1. Adoption of an innovation is fundamentally an individual decision, whether or not the individual adoption is part of a well-structured social system, according to Richard I. Evans.[10] Methods that have proved useful in *agriculture* in designing and diffusing solutions to problems may be useful in the field of education, according to Evans. Also of interest is his observation that standardized accounting procedures, which reward doing things the old way and fail to build in "seed money," tend to discourage innovation.

2. As a major dimension of the world in which they live, technology is a topic deserving of more attention in the curriculum experience of boys and girls. Children need guidance not only in learning how to *use* technology, but also in knowing how to evaluate its services and even how to protect human values against dehumanizing elements.

One good beginning, in providing information about technology in industry, is provided in *Teaching Children about Technology* by Mary-Margaret Scobey (Bloomington, Illinois: McKnight and McKnight, 1968).

3. A current project headed by Harvard professor Gerald Lesser, involving the use of home television as a medium of pre-primary instruction, is currently underway in New York City. It would seem possible that carefully-planned television programs *in conjunction with* various school-sponsored (or school-assisted) activities handled by parents and community persons (along the lines of Cub-Scout and Brownie "den meetings"), could very well serve to demonstrate the educational usefulness of the television medium.

4. Although "technology" in this study refers primarily to sophisticated equipment, it remains true that most teachers make little use of the simpler tools (e.g., tape recorders and movie projectors) that have long been available in the market. Sidney Eboch at Ohio State University has shown that when audio-visual materials are close at hand, and especially if clerical and professional assistance is available, teachers do make use of the materials. In most schools, however, neither the equipment nor the personnel are in adequate supply. NDEA and Title III have perhaps turned the tide by making new sources of funding available, and new interest is being shown by teachers. Is it possible that a

massive, one-shot capital-outlay effort, equivalent to the effort expended in financing a new school building, could be proposed in order to break the log-jam on audiovisual materials?

REFERENCES

1. Clark, R. A. & W. H. Beatty. "Learning and Evaluation." Chapter 3, page 49, in *Evaluation as Feedback and Guide,* 1967 Yearbook of the Association for Supervision and Curriculum Development, N.E.A.

2. Beeby, C. E. *The Quality of Education in Developing Countries.* Cambridge, Mass. Harvard University Press, 1966.

3. Committee for Economic Development. *Innovations in Education: New Directions for the American School.* July, 1968, p. 75.

4. Cass, James. "The Promise of R and D in Education." *Saturday Review,* January 18, 1969, p. 51.

5. See *Journal of Research and Development in Education.* University of Georgia, 1, Summer, 1968, for a full report on the nine centers.

6. Benson, Charles S. *The Economics of Education.* Second Edition. Boston: Houghton Mifflin Co., 1968, p. 50.

7. See especially (a) J. I. Shaplin and H. F. Olds, *Team Teaching* (Harper and Row, 1964): (b) R. H. Anderson, *Teaching in a World of Change,* chapter 5 (Harcourt Brace and World, 1966); and (c) *National Elementary Principal,* 44 (January, 1965, entire issue).

8. Howe, Harold, II. *Picking Up The Options.* Washington, D.C.: N.E.A., 1968. See Chapter 1.

9. See *An Annotated Bibliography on Auxiliary Personnel in Education.* Prepared by Bank Street College of Education for the U.S. Office of Education. January, 1969, p. 94.

10. Evans, Richard I. *Resistance to Innovation in Higher Education.* San Francisco: Jossey-Bass, Inc., 1967. p. 181.

59.

Implications of the New Technologies for School and College Organization And Administration

by T. H. BELL
Superintendent of
Public Instruction
State of Utah

I

Outline of a Proposed New Organizational Framework

A. The Need for New Organizational Patterns

New technologies available to effectively improve instruction are many and varied. They range from a simple audio tape to computers and television production studies. That teachers and college professors are not eagerly clamoring to utilize technology in the classrooms of America is a well known and broadly lamented fact. Critics of this circumstance often complain about the teacher and the professor for narrowness of perspective and rigidity of outlook. However, those responsible for the organizational circumstances, instructional staffing patterns and administrative procedures that actually inhibit the use of new technologies must assume much of the responsibility for the current state of non-utilization of new hardware and software in instruction in the public schools and colleges. The new technologies available to improve instruction have been superimposed upon an organizational structure and instructional staffing pattern designed for a teacher-textbook-classroom system of teaching.

What is needed is a new organizational structure designed to utilize a multi-media, man-machine system of instruction. This new organizational pattern must make it possible to individualize teaching. The school and college curricula must, in the years ahead, become more flexible and adaptive to the individual needs and abilities of students. Only through more extensive use of new technologies will this necessary individualization likely be possible.

One of the most significant problems in American higher education today is the depersonalization of instruction and the lack of student identity in the campus instructional machinery that tradition has geared to mass education practices. This problem is not much less acute in the large secondary schools of the urban and suburban areas of our country.

It should, therefore, be assumed that organizational patterns and administrative plans for implementing more extensive use of new technologies in instruction should focus upon meeting the problems of depersonalization and lack of self-identity in our large educational institutions. Technology must make it possible for teachers and professors to have more person-to-person dialogue with students. Technology should personalize and humanize the teaching and learning activities that take place on the college campus and in the public school.

It is the basic premise of this paper that new technologies will free teachers to teach by carrying out many necessary but routine instructional tasks. Simple demonstrations, the presentation of basic information, the carrying out of goal-directed practice and drill, test scoring, information storage and retrieval can all be done by machine.

It is technologically possible, for example, to have individualized instructional television available to college and public school students. No longer is broadcast television to classrooms necessary or desirable. It is economically feasible, through use of a low cost one-half inch video tape recorder, to provide televised lectures and demonstrations on an individualized basis. But teachers and professors cannot generate this capability (and many other potentially useful man-machine systems) until organizational patterns and administrative decisions are established to provide physical facilities, software, and time scheduling support.

The use of programmed learning, computer assistance to teachers and computer assisted instruction, dial access information systems, individualized 8 millimeter single concept film or tape loops, audio tape drill and practice units, and many other man-machine teaching possibilities cannot be effectively utilized until administrative leadership focuses resources upon organizing the potentialities of this vast array of technological capability. Ahead of invention of new technologies must come organizational provision to utilize what is currently available. The problem of bringing to fruition the full potential of the broad array of man-machine instructional capabilities must be facilitated by new organizational patterns and administrative arrangements before individual or departmental instructional personnel can even begin to hope for significant accomplishments.

B. Suggested General Provisions for a New Organizational Framework

We have had a piecemeal effort because educational administrators in command of the required resources have made only partial or piecemeal commitments. The lack of progress is not so much teacher indifference as it is myopia on the part of educational leadership. The orchestration of the strengths of individualized instructional television, computer assistance to instructional processes and practices, programmed learning units, dial access systems, 8mm single concept units, books and printed materials into a more completely harmonious systems approach to instruction will require the following:

1. Needed at the outset is administrative commitment on the part of the front office executive staffs comprised of large public school systems, colleges and universities. Administrative focusing of the resources available to large institutions will make the needed accomplishments in a multi-media, man-machine system of instruction possible.

2. A continuity of effort is needed over a period of years. If education is to develop software that will exploit the unique strengths of the instructional technologies available into a total system of instruction a continuous effort over a long period of time is essential.

3. We should alter physical plant facilities that have been designed—egg crate style—to teach groups of 30 students in traditional classroom organizational patterns. What is needed is *openness* of physical structure to adapt to varying types of grouping arrangements that fit unique learning patterns of individuals functioning in an individually prescribed curricula. (It is important to keep in mind that the traditional classroom was designed prior to the existence of most of the new technologies.)

4. We need to take administrative initiative in the organization of instructional media centers where software is stored and retrieved for use upon the prescription of certain learning activities made by teachers and professors. In addition to books and other printed materials, the IMC must stock vast numbers of ½ inch videotape programs, 8mm single concept loops, audio tapes, programmed learning units, computer software programs, models and charts. The IMC must have a similar functional relationship to the teacher or professor in educational practice that the pharmacy has to the physician in medical practice. Only through such provision will an individually prescribed curriculum be possible for thousands of students. The teacher cannot prescribe varied learning activities for students unless the media center is stocked with the software that will facilitate individualized learning in the new multi-media, man-machine instructional system. The professor must not be required to "cover a course" in a series of lectures. His role must not be focused upon the dissemination of information in the traditional lecture mode for much of this can effectively be done by machine. He must prescribe the software and permit his assistants and the students to dispense the information and observe the demonstrations. Machines must do most of the lecturing and information disseminating so that teachers may teach. This will be done to the extent that the professional is free to sponsor small group seminars where truly spontaneous teacher-student dialogue can occur. The media center must present the lectures by machine since this is a more appropriate role for a machine and a highly unproductive function for a professor.

The media center and the machine cannot engage in discussion, or debate. The machine cannot provide the supportive emotional climate necessary between a mature scholar and an eager, seeking young mind. When professors seek to perform as lecturing machines they cannot humanize and personalize learning for the student. So the machine should dispense information, provide drill and practice, present demonstrations, and repeat basic concepts. (The machine can repeat endlessly for the benefit of one person or a dozen. It can perform at 6:00 a.m. or at 11:00 p.m. It does not tire, nor lose patience.)

The machine cannot recognize a puzzled expression or respond to an uplifted hand. It cannot discuss the implications for life of certain ideas or issues as they relate to a specific person. It cannot motivate and inspire on an *individualized* basis. These most *crucial* and *highly necessary* instructional duties must be performed by the teacher/professor. The media center—with its software and machines—is the key to redeployment of teacher talent. The new organizational structure must focus software and machine resources to disseminate information, to demonstrate, and to tell so that the professional is free to teach.

5. We must alter the staffing patterns of instructional organizations such as single schools in a school system or departments on a college campus. More assistants to teachers, media technicians and computer terminal operators will be necessary in the multi-media, man-machine system of teaching. Teachers should be free from routine paper work that can be done at less cost and with more efficiency by others. The economic capability to provide these resources should come from the increased efficiency of individualized instruction that frees high cost professional time from many duties that can be performed by machine. The specific organizational frame-

work will vary with the unique role of the college or school. The structure, however, must be designed to utilize professionals only where professional insight and skill are required. Many instructional tasks can and should be carried out by assistants and aides working under the direction of professionals.

6. The organizational changes must establish an instructional management information system with computer storage and retrieval capability. Such a system must have evaluation and feed-back capability if it is to make the individualized, man-machine system dynamically self-improving.

In this essential instructional management information system two very complex bodies of information must inter-relate to the professors or teachers who function as the hub of the system: First, information about each student must be stored for instant retrieval in the computer. This information must be in a dynamically on-going stage of adjustment and adaptation as the learner progresses. The information system must inform both the student and the teacher of successes and failures, of subject matter mastery and of concepts and capabilities that are not yet attained and that need further attention. Simple computer terminals will make this vital information capability available to the professor or teacher when and where it is needed.

Secondly, the instructional management information system must give the teacher accurate, up-to-the-minute information on the availability of learning materials in the educational "pharmacy" (media center). These materials in the media center must match the immediate and ever changing needs of the learner. Information from tests that appraise the success of previous student exposure to certain learning experiences should also be available in the computerized instructional management information system. Such a system, if effective in the new multi-media, man-machine system, must keep a continuous inventory of what each student has yet to master in the curriculum. It must also present to the professional alternative possible learning experiences available in the media center as a next step in teaching.

This complex extension of the professional's memory is essential in a system that individually prescribes learning experiences for each student. Computers will play an increasingly prominent role in matching media and learner needs as the teacher observes student progress and prescribes new learning activities in the on-going *systems approach* to instruction in the schools and colleges of the future.

II

Organizational and Administrative Deficiencies in the Current Instructional System

American public education has devised an instructional system that is quite simple. It has been effective in meeting many of the educational needs of our people for a number of decades. Changes and modifications have been made but the basic framework for use of the teaching staff, physical facilities, and instructional materials has remained essentially the same.

The current instructional system is comprised of a physical plant containing classrooms with supporting laboratories, libraries, shops, and gymnasia. The design of the plant has been dictated by the function. The function has been governed by the basic instructional unit. The basic unit, in turn, has governed the system design.

The instructional unit is currently comprised of a teacher (with supporting personnel to be described later), a group of approximately thirty students, and a classroom of approximately 900 square feet (standard of 30 square feet per student) equipped with chalkboard, textbooks, and supplementary equipment and supplies.

This unit functions under the leadership of the teacher. The strengths and limitations of the teacher and the physical facilities and instructional supplies govern, to a great extent, the efficiency of each particular unit in the system. With these elements making up the basic unit, the quality of educational output varies from one classroom to another. It is limited to what the teacher can do as he works in his own somewhat isolated classroom.

The traditional instructional system places almost the entire responsibility for high quality, productive learning experiences upon the individual teacher. The teacher is in charge of (and almost totally responsible for) all of the essential factors that nurture learning for thirty students for an entire school year. Students, then, must rely upon the good fortune (and the good management) of the school district to provide unusual individual teaching capability. This unusual capability demands a wide variety of talents in: (1) understanding the school curriculum, (2) mastery of teaching methods, (3) using and adapting a multiplicity of complex instructional media to provide variety and differentiation to meet the varying and different needs of students, (4) diagnosing learning blocks and difficulties and adapting techniques to such needs, and (5) teaching and tutoring small groups on an individual basis while, at the same time, using the time of all members of the unit as productively as possible.

Thoughtful educational leaders have doubted that any teacher can meet *all* of the above demands to a reasonable level of efficiency. Even the acquisition of knowledge of the subject matter on a level applicable to all learners in the unit is a great challenge. To also efficiently provide all the other outcomes of education above and beyond simple knowledge acquisition is a near impossibility for one teacher.

Subject matter specialization has led to secondary school and college departmentalized teaching where each teacher teaches in his field of strength and meets from five to seven groups of thirty students each during a school day scheduled into time period segments of about 50 minutes each. The departmentalized system results in one teacher functioning in a classroom unit. The difference is that each teacher teaches a separate subject to from 140 to 200 students in a school day rather than teaching all subjects in the curriculum in one classroom to thirty students.

Departmentalized teaching is somewhat impersonal. With about 160 students being taught by each teacher in each school day it is difficult to learn of and adapt to the individual needs and varying problems of each learner. Also, the situation is still predicated upon the need for a "super" teacher who can be many things to each and every student.

The classroom unit system of teaching demands more than most teachers can produce. This is so in the departmentalized unit where class groups change every fifty minutes. It is also true in the self-contained classroom situation typical in the elementary school.

Because of these apparent demands for an unusually capable person in each unit in the system and because of the understandable limitations that many teachers have in measuring up to these demands, the classroom unit system of teaching has been supplemented with non-teaching professional personnel. These members of the school system's instructional team have been employed to provide support in plugging the more obvious gaps in the over-all efficiency in the system.

Specialists in educational diagnosis and counseling attempt to fill in for the "impersonalness" of departmentalized instruction of the masses. The school counselor keeps a record folder on each student for use of teachers. Test results and the complete educational history of each learner are kept in readiness for study and appraisal. Students are scheduled into the instructional system as a result of the expert knowledge the school counselor can bring to bear upon the study of individual needs. The counselor tries to see students as individuals and meet their needs as separate persons.

Remedial instruction is another example of supplemental effort to support the regular classroom unit system. The teaching of reading, for example, has met the needs of great numbers in past years. The exceptions stand out, however. We have non-reader dropouts. We have significant numbers of poor readers not equipped to move up the educational ladder. These are failures of our present system where too much has been demanded of the limited capabilities of teachers to meet the *individual* needs of *all* in a group teaching system in the basic classroom unit. We have sought to correct the mistakes and weaknesses of the basic system by establishing a sub-system of remedial teaching. (Some critics claim that schools have moved from teaching the three R's to six R's: Remedial Reading, Remedial 'Riting, and Remedial 'Rithmetic. This great need for remedial teachers is testimony for individualized rather than group teaching.)

School systems also have employed specialists to teach the subjects requiring special talents and insights. Music and art are subject area examples.

The supervisors, counselors, librarians, and subject area specialists all function in the present system. They have been added to supplement the efforts of teachers functioning in the *basic* classroom unit because of the inadequacies of the impersonal, group teaching system we have used for so many years. These nonteaching and supplementary teaching personnel are expensive. They have evolved as subsystems of the basic system out of necessity and concern for meeting the needs of all students.

As teachers deal with the frustrations of the demands of working in the basic classroom unit system, pressure emerges to modify the size of the unit. We are told that quality education will come when we reduce class size from thirty to fifteen. Teachers must also have time to study, plan, and prepare for teaching. It is a fact that many public school teachers suffer from suffocation of student numbers demanding attention every period of the school day. It is hard to be a careful, thoughtful teacher when the weight of numbers constantly frustrate creativity.

The organizational and administrative structure of most schools and colleges is geared to support group teaching in the classroom. Classroom teaching depends too heavily upon the capabilities of teachers working within separate classroom walls in isolation from colleagues and supporting services. Current organizational structure restricts all learning activities to the highly limited capacity of one person responsible for one instructional group. Not only the professional tasks but all functions that facilitate learning must be performed by a single teacher under the rigidities of the current system.

If professionals are to function on a level commensurate with the needs and demands of modern education they must have the necessary staff support. Professionals are currently forced to either perform many of the time consuming but perfunctory duties or they are forced to forego opportunities to utilize media and machines that will enrich the lives of students. Unfortunately, the current instructional organization and administrative supporting structure impedes rather than facilitates the use of multi-media technology to individualize learning activities that are varied in scope and comprehensive in curriculum content.

III

A Proposed Model for Providing Organizational Structure and Administrative Support for a Multi-Media, Man-Machine Teaching System

The new school, geared to optimum utilization of new technologies, must be organized with the media center as the heart of the institution. This center must exist to support the professionals and their assistants. The media center must be stocked with instructional systems packages that enrich and supplement printed subject matter content. The software developed for use in the machines must be well orchestrated with the texts and courses of study. A well-trained and coordinated instructional systems staff will make this level of sophistication possible in tomorrow's school.

The new school organization must provide for an open-space school where instructional teams work with students individually and in small groups and where flexibility and adaptability facilitate continuous learning progress. The instructional unit must be organized to adapt to the varied learning abilities of youth. The school must adapt to the learner rather than compelling the learner to adapt to the school. This can be accomplished when group teaching is replaced with individualized instruction.

On the next page is a proposed physical layout of a group of instructional suites wrapped around an instructional media center. Note the provisions for tutorial service, small group teacher-student dialogue, individualized study, and media utilization. (Note: This diagram was originally prepared by the writer in a position paper written for the Utah Instructional Systems Program. It subsequently was used by the Committee for Economic Development in its recent publication: "Innovation in Education: New Directions for the American School.")

The suggested new organizational structure would place many of the supporting staff in the media center. Teaching assistants, aides, and professionals will find a facility of this type more open and adaptive to individualized teaching supported by a multi-media, man-machine system.

The principal of this type school must be an instructional leader and the professionals under his direction must, in turn, direct the work of a supporting staff. It is suggested that the professional teacher-pupil ratio may be increased substantially to make it financially feasible to employ supporting staff. Such a change in administrative organization and instructional staffing will make it possible to utilize new technologies. It may also provide the potential for making professionals more productive, thereby making it possible to provide increased compensation for services.

To illustrate further possible staff structure and personnel dollar redeployment, let us consider a middle grade school designed to teach third, fourth, fifth, and sixth grade pupils. The basic unit for instruction will be comprised of 90 students housed in a large, open instructional area next to the media center. The new instructional system would include four instructional staff units (one for each grade or age level). It would also include an instructional media center staff.

Duties of members of instructional unit staff responsible for approximately ninety pupils:

    a. *Head Teacher*—Leader and director of the work of the unit . . . conducts meetings of the staff where planning is done—supervises all members of the

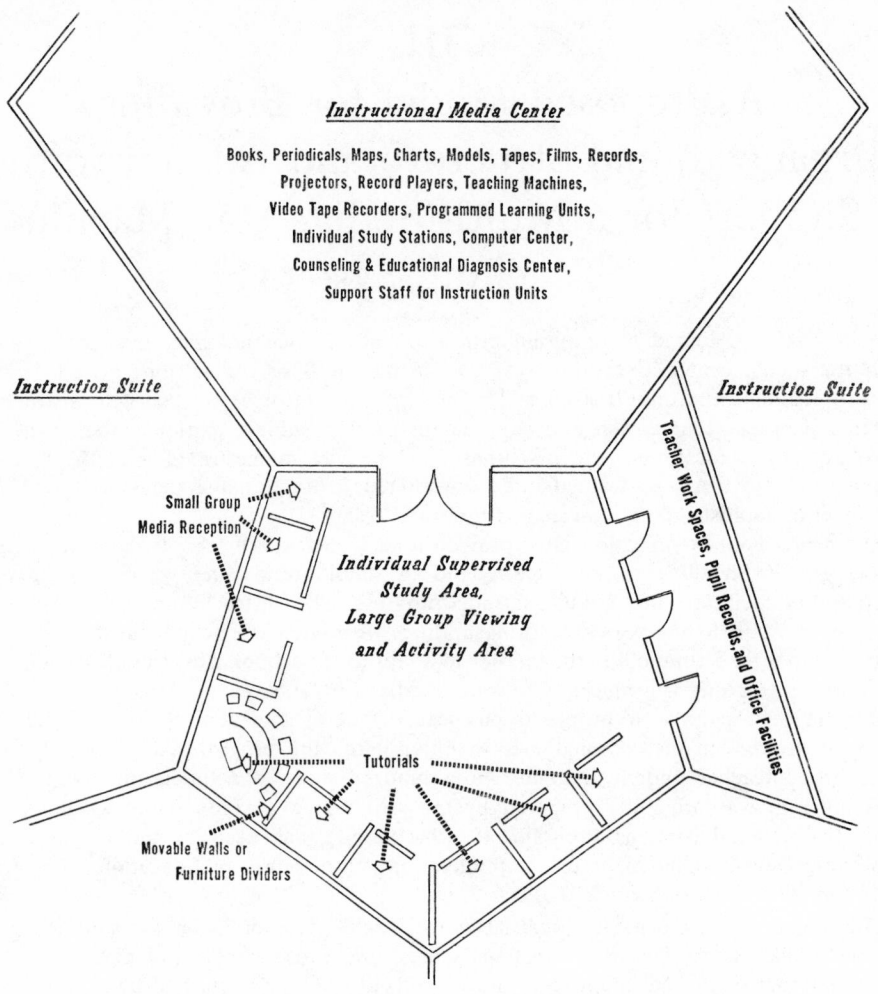

Possible Space Layout for Instructional System Facility
To Utilize Teaching Systems Packages,
Instructional Team Staff Pattern,
And Individualized Teaching Pattern

unit and coordinates their work—will require a very able person with organizational and leadership ability . . . salary should be high enough to attract ability and compensate for added responsibility.

b. *Experienced Teacher*—This person would provide professional teaching service to students under the direction of the master teacher. He would utilize the services of tutorial assistants and aides in individualizing instruction. This teacher would free himself of most routine work not requiring skills and insights of a professional level. Most learning would be in small tutorial groups of three to eight students and as individual students in self study or working with one adult staff member. The professional would prescribe many follow-up learning activities to be carried out by aides and pupils with extensive use of appropriate machine support.

c. *Tutorial Assistants or Intern Teachers*—These persons should be para-professionals with at least two years of college training. They should be interested in becoming teachers. The positions may, in fact, be filled with teacher interns or college students working toward a degree in education. The positions may be filled with four half time students or two full time paraprofessionals depending upon availability of candidates.

   These persons should provide a great amount of small group subject matter practice and drill activity to intermediate grade children working to master the rudiments of the basic tool subjects. They should, under the direction and assistance from the professional teachers, provide individual help to children.

d. *The Volunteer Aides*—Will serve on the staff out of motivation to contribute to their neighborhood school. Volunteer service to hospitals and neighborhood youth centers has resulted in a great deal of assistance to the public good. Many mothers endowed with a love for children and a desire to contribute to the cause of education of youth may be recruited to fill these posts. Personality characteristics that assure an attitude of service under the guidance of professionals will be important in recruiting these people. Some college background will be desirable, but intellectual ability to follow instructions and render teamwork assistance will be important.

   A modest compensation for expenses in being away from home and in traveling to and from school should be provided. The intent should be to reimburse for out-of-pocket daily costs and not to provide a salary.

   The volunteer aides should correct papers, prepare teaching materials, respond to on-the-spot needs of youngsters, supervise playgrounds, hallways, and school lunch, check on children to lend assistance during study time, pass out materials, and serve as a personal assistant to the professional teachers. The services of these persons should be a great value to the total unit, but this will be so only if their potential is fully utilized by the teachers. Training and orientation will be crucial. They will need to understand the limitations as well as the potential of their work.

   The school should honor and recognize publicly the persons who support education through volunteer service as aides to teachers. If this is properly done, reasonably capable talent can be recruited and a reservoir of applicants can be maintained. Orientation and training of volunteer aides will also be necessary if they are to function well in the system.

e. *Clerk-Pupil Progress Accountant*—This person will do clerical work for the unit. She will do the detailed accounting necessary in a system where individualized instruction encourages variable progress. She will also work with the person in charge of the computer input-output terminal located in the instructional materials center. The paper work of the unit will be computer assisted, and she will be the liaison person for the unit: updating progress data of individual students and retrieving from the computer system the information required by the professional staff.

The number of professional teachers is reduced substantially from those required in the traditional system. The professional teacher-pupil ratio is therefore increased from 27 to 1 to 45 or 50 to 1. However, the number of adult members of the staff will be increased to provide the supporting services from the instructional media center. Thus, the new staffing structure will provide more personnel, of varying levels of ability, to make it possible for new technologies to help to individualize the instruction for each one of the pupils in the unit. This will be accomplished through reliance on machines and assistants to convey information and do the lecturing and demonstrating.

The result should be the elimination of lectures and busy work for students in group teaching situations. Students should be more productively engaged in work responsibility for individualized learning most of the time. The effort should be to keep the learner active—not passive—during every hour of the school day. The responsibility for activity related to learning should shift from the teacher (under the traditional system) to the learner. He will be the one engaged in programmed learning units, in small group discussion, and in tutorial type activities. His exposure will be broadened with multi-media technology. His constant, active involvement in learning should emerge from a more varied program of individualized teaching and learning. (Note: This staffing pattern is now being utilized in four experimental schools under the Utah Instructional Systems Project.)

IV

Administrative Leadership to Facilitate Effective Use of Instructional Technology

Administrators and board members responsible for governance of our schools and colleges must initiate action to allocate resources leading to effective use of instructional systems technology. A sustained commitment (over a period of several years) of substantive resources of a large educational institution or school district (preferably working with a consortium of similarly committed units) will be needed to build the instructional system packages, establish media centers, train personnel, and gain actual broad-based field trials with refined corrective action based upon dependable feedback. (Utah, for example, has formed a consortium of school districts, universities, and the State Department of Education to develop its systems approach to instruction.)

The instructional level leadership will come when there is commitment on the level where the money is allocated and where other resources are deployed. This commitment apparently does not exist at the present time as evidenced by the piecemeal efforts that must be replaced by system-wide attention. Administrator-policy board recognition of the need to focus more on the invention of new instructional practice is the big logjam to attaining greatly enhanced learning opportunity for America's youth.

One of the puzzling things in academic life today is the lack of commitment and concern for the improvement of instructional practice on the part of the totality of what is known as the great American research and discovery enterprise. It is well known that our colleges and universities are in the forefront of a great drive to generate new knowledge and to develop programs that lead to application of such knowledge to solving our most urgent problems. It is also known that scientific and technological advances are outstripping progress in the social and behavioral sciences. If we are to improve the human condition in America education must become more effective.

More than ever before, we are justified in repeating historian H. G. Wells's famed statement that we are truly engaged in a race between education and catastrophe. That is why we have more at stake in the cause of educational research and innovation than we do in almost all the other research and development efforts combined.

It is hard to understand why colleges and universities concentrate such a great proportion of total research resources on biological and physical sciences and almost completely neglect the behavioral and social quests for discovery. Why shouldn't a great university focus some of its great research know-how upon how to improve its prime product: the human soul that marches across the graduation stage each June?

School district administrators and boards of education must spend more and worry more about the improvement of instruction. The invention of more effective teaching and learning practice is the most important research gap in our society. We need more experimental schools. We need more variation and less uniformity. We need more of our most creative minds pondering with intensity the opportunities that now exist to individualize teaching through a properly balanced and harmonized use of men and machines in the complex work of individually prescribing and executing curriculum and instruction programs for thousands of students.

Research and experimentation in the instructional process is the most productive field for new discovery that exists in America today. The biggest part of this task is to organize for the new potential and mount broad scale efforts where half measures and piecemeal attempts have been prevalent in the past.

V
Conclusion

These specific ideas and proposals are not offered as final solutions but as a means of communicating an approach to making organizational and administrative changes that will lead to more effective use of technology in instruction. Other promising alternatives will surely emerge out of more broadly based, system-wide commitments to change in instructional leadership, organization, and practice.

Reaching and converting the college president and school superintendent is a necessary prelude to gaining an understanding of the sleeping giant potential of current technology to revolutionize the teaching-learning process in our schools and colleges. This is the big challenge facing leaders in the U.S. Office of Education and State Departments of Education. There is not enough dialogue between the inventors and those with the power and position to implement. There has been too much isolated consideration of instructional TV, programmed learning, single concept film and tape loops, computer-assisted instruction, dial access information systems, films, audio tapes, etc. There has not been enough attention to the potential of building a systems approach to instruction through proper harmonization of the strengths and unique potential of all of these technologies. We need to set about this task with resources commensurate with the need. Top executive leadership on the state and local levels must first recognize the great promise of a multi-media, man-machine system of teaching.

Administrative commitment is lacking and must be attained.

SELECTED BIBLIOGRAPHY

Briggs, Leslie J., and others. *Instructional Media: A Procedure for the Design of Multi-Media Instruction, a Critical Review of Research, and Suggestions for Future Research,* Monograph No. 2. Pittsburgh, Pa.: American Institutes for Research, 1967. 176 pp.

Bushnell, Don D., and Dwight W. Allen, editors. *The Computer in American Education.* New York: John Wiley and Sons, 1967. 300 pp.

Campeau, Peggie L. "Selective Review of Literature on Audiovisual Media of Instruction." *Instructional Media: A Procedure for the Design of Multi-Media Instruction, a Critical Review of Research, and Suggestions for Future Research.* (Leslie J. Briggs and others.) Monograph No. 2, Pittsburgh, Pa: American Institutes for Research, 1967.

Carter, Launor F. "The Computer and Instructional Technology." *Current Issues in Higher Education: In Search of Leaders.* (Edited by G. Kerry Smith.) Washington, D.C.: Association for Higher Education, a department of the National Education Association, 1967. pp. 253-59.

Chu, Godwin C., and Wilbur Schramm. *Learning from Television: What Research Says.* U.S. Office of Education, Contract No. 2 EFC 708 94. Stanford, Calif.: Institute for Communication Research, 1967. 213 pp. (Draft)

Committee for Economic Development. "Innovation in Education: New Directions for the American School," (A Statement by the Research and Policy Committee), July, 1968.

Diamond, Robert M. "The Use of Multi-Media Instructional Materials Within the Seminar." (Abstract) AV Communication Review 12: 225; Summer 1965.

Edling, Jack V. *A Study of the Effectiveness of Audiovisual Teaching Materials When Prepared According to the Principles of Motivational Research.* U.S. Office of Education, NDEA Title VII Project No. 221. Monmouth: Teaching Research Division, Oregon State System of Higher Education, June 1963. 214 pp.

Edling, Jack V. "Media Technology and Learning Processes." *Man-Machine Systems in Education.* (Edited by John W. Loughary.) New York: Harper and Row, 1966.

Gilpin, John. "Design and Evaluation of Instructional Systems." AV Communication Review 10: 75-84; March-April 1962.

Goodlad, John I., John F. O'Toole, Jr., and Louise L. Tyler. *Computers and Information Systems in Education.* New York: Harcourt, Brace and World, 1966.

Guba, Egon G., and Clinton A. Snyder. "Instructional Television and the Classroom Teacher." AV Communication Review 13: 5-27; Spring 1965.

Joint Committee on Programmed Instruction and Teaching Machines. "Supplement II to Recommendations for Reporting the Effectiveness of Programmed Instruction Materials: Recommendations for Preparation of Technical Reports." AV Communication Review 14: 247-58; Summer 1966.

National Society for the Study of Education. *Programmed Instruction.* (Edited by Phil C. Lange.) Sixty-Sixth Yearbook, Part II. Chicago: University of Chicago Press, 1967. 334 pp.

Saettler, Paul. *A History of Instructional Technology.* New York: McGraw-Hill Book Co., 1968. 399 pp.

Smith, R. G. *The Design of Instructional Systems.* Technical Report No. 66-18. Alexandria, Va.: Human Resources Research Office, George Washington University (300 North Washington St.), November 1966. 85 pp.

60.

The Design of an Economically Viable Large-Scale Computer-Based Education System

by DONALD L. BITZER and DOMINIC SKAPERDAS
Director   *Asst. Director*
Computer-Based Education Research Laboratory
University of Illinois

The University of Illinois has been experimenting with a computer-based educational system (PLATO) for the past eight years. This system has evolved from a single terminal connected to the ILLIAC I (a medium speed, 1954 vintage computer) to a computer classroom of 20 graphic-pictorial terminals connected to a Control Data Corporation 1604 computer. Some of the areas in which studies have been conducted are electrical engineering, geometry, biology, nursing, library science, pharmacology, chemistry, algebra, math drill, computer programming, and foreign languages. This material has been presented by use of a variety of teaching strategies, ranging from drill and practice to student-directed inquiry. Based on these experiences and the data gathered over 70,000 student contact hours of credit teaching, this report describes the development of an economically viable teaching system. Some of our guidelines for developing the system's software and hardware are:

1. The computer should only be used when it is the best method of presentation. Less expensive methods such as programmed texts, films, slides, tape recorders, etc., should be used when appropriate.

2. The computer should be used as much as possible to simulate results in models constructed by the students rather than simply turning pages.

3. The system must be flexible and adaptable. It must be able to teach many subjects and present the lesson materials by a variety of teaching strategies. The system must change to meet the needs of the students and teachers, and not be limited to the off-the-shelf items presently available.

4. The method of integration into the educational system must be considered in the system design. For example, a school should be able to start with a single terminal for the incremental terminal cost instead of having to invest large sums of money for an entire system before the has determined if it wants or needs C.B.E.

5. The cost of computer-based education should be comparable with the cost of teaching at the elementary grade school level. Cost effectiveness should be determined by an hour to hour cost comparison (25¢-30¢ per terminal hour for use of the computer and terminal).

A present student terminal consists of a keyset and a television monitor as shown in Fig. 1. Information viewed on the television monitor is composed of a slide selected by the computer (random-access time less than 1 millionth of a second) and a superimposed image of graphs, diagrams, and/or alphanumeric characters drawn by the computer in a point-by-point fashion. The student uses the keyset for constructing answers, questions and for setting up simulated or real experiments as well as for controlling his progress through the lesson material. The computer responds to the student's requests within one tenth of a second.

The computer also controls other devices, such as movie projectors, lights, etc. The students at the terminals can interact with each other through the computer, thus permitting games to be played which require communication between the players.

In addition to keeping detailed records of the student's performance, the computer can provide individualized instruction, immediate feedback, and remedial training by the use of complex internal branching and the alteration of presentation or type of material based on the student's past performance. These unique features seem to make the computer an ideal instructional device for developing cognitive skills.

To encourage development of critical thinking skills, the author sets up the teaching strategy and presents the student with questions or problems so the student must think about what information he needs, about possible solutions to the problems or sources of information, interpret the data gathered, and test his solution. The computer immediately provides appropriate feedback to open-ended questions, thus reinforcing a correct approach, or in the case of an incorrect response, encouraging the student to a new approach.

The computational use of the computer appears in several ways. First, experiments can be simulated by the computer, immediately providing the student with results he uniquely requested. These same results might require hours or even days to calculate by hand. Second, a large amount of computation is involved in processing student responses. The more flexibility provided for the student to answer a question, the more feedback is needed to inform him of the correctness of his response. When only multiple-choice responses are required, the processing is relatively simple, but when the student is permitted to construct long alphanumeric and graphic responses the computer must analyze his answer to see if it is equivalent to a correct response, check for spelling and completeness of the answer, as well as inform him which part of an incorrect answer is unacceptable.

Whenever possible, algorithms are used to determine the correctness of the students' response. For example, when the student is asked to give a positive even integer, the student's answer is checked to see if it is positive and then it is divided by two and checked for a remainder. If there is no remainder, the answer is correct. The use of algorithms instead of comparing the answer against a long list of pre-stored answers not only makes the system more flexible but also saves memory space. In some cases this approach is almost a necessity. For instance, in teaching algebraic proofs, students can prove theorems in any manner as long as their statements follow logically from the available axioms and their previous statements. We have one example in which the author of the material was unable to prove a theorem in the twelve lines provided and, thus, was unable to supply even one pre-stored solution. Nonetheless, one student was able to complete the proof in the required twelve lines and was told by the computer he was correct.

To illustrate further how the computer interacts with the student we will describe some sequences taken from lessons in geometry, electrical engineering, and maternity nursing.

A user's computer language consisting of English directives was used to write a series of 15 lessons in informal geometry.* These lessons were to give 7th and 8th grade students an understanding of geometric concepts. A grid is provided on which the student draws and manipulates geometric figures. The computer is used to determine the correctness of the figure, independent of its size, location, and orientation on the grid. The student must select points of the grid to be used as the vertices of his figure. To do this, eight keys on

This project was supported by the U.S. Office of Education and by the National Science Foundation.

his keyset have been defined which move a bright spot around on the grid. (Figure 2 shows a diagram of these keys. The arrows on the keycaps indicate the direction in which the key jumps the bright spot on the grid.) Once a student has decided on a point, he communicates his selection to the computer by pressing the "MARK" key. He presses the "CLOSE" key to close the figure (connect the first point to the last point). To judge the figure the student presses "NEXT" and the computer either okays the figure or indicates the student's error.

In the following sequence,* the student is asked to draw quadrilaterals with a single line of symmetry. In Fig. 3a the student is instructed to draw a quadrilateral with one line of symmetry: the two possibilities are an isosceles trapezoid and a kite. He selects the points he wishes to use for his figure and marks them. Fig. 3b shows the partial construction of the trapezoid. When four points have been marked the student closes his figure and asks the computer to judge it. In Fig. 3c the completed figure is judged and the computer points out to the student that the symmetry line for an isosceles trapezoid does not go through the vertices.

The student then moves to the next page of the lesson and is asked to draw a quadrilateral with a single line of symmetry that does go through the vertices (Fig. 3d). The student, however, reconstructs the trapezoid. The computer, when judging the figure, recognizes the duplication and tells the student that he has drawn the same figure as he drew before (Fig. 3e). The student then draws a kite which has a single line of symmetry through vertices and the figure is judged "OK" (Fig. 3f).

For our second case we use a sequence taken from a circuit analysis course in electrical engineering (Fig. 4). The student has just analyzed a circuit containing a battery, a switch, an inductor, and a resistor, all connected in series. His task is to determine the value of the inductor and resistor that causes the current waveform to pass through the points marked on the graph after the switch is closed. He is instructed to make the resistor value small and notice the effect on the final value of the current. By manipulating these values, the student gains an intuitive feeling for the effects of the inductance and resistance, and he can proceed in an orderly way to determine their correct values.

The third example is taken from a maternity nursing lesson** where the student is presented with a question which asks her to name two cardiovascular compensations which occur as a result of the increased blood volume during pregnancy (Fig. 5).

The student, needing information to answer this question, presses the button on her keyset labeled "INVEST." She is then presented with a slide where she indicates that she wishes to investigate "Anatomic and Physiological Changes of Pregnancy."

After choosing her area of investigation, she is presented with a slide which requests further specification. Here the student indicates that she wishes information concerning changes which occur in the circulatory system during the third trimester of pregnancy. Having done this, she presses, the "Answer" button and the computer generated information tells her there is an "increase in blood volume, a 50 percent increase in cardiac work load, left ventricular hypertrophy, and vasodilation produced by an increase in progesterone." Deciding that increased work load is one compensation, she considers left ventricular hypertrophy, but needs to further clarify the word hypertrophy. By pressing the button labeled DICTIONARY, she is presented with a list of terms used in the lesson. The student types the word "hypertrophy" and the computer supplies the definition "increase in size of an organ or structure."

By pressing the button labeled "AHA," the student is returned to the question on which she was working. Here she types the answer "hypertrophy of the left ventricle" and the computer judges it "OK." However, the answer "the left ventricle" is judged NO, that is, correct but not complete. Next, the response "the left ventricle decreases in size" is entered.

*Figures 1. through 8. appear at the end of the article, after the bibliography.

**This project is supported by a PHS Training Grant, Division of Nursing, PHS, U.S. Dept. of Health, Education, and Welfare.

The computer responds "NO" and XX's out the word "decreases." Rewording the correct answer, the student types "the left ventricle enlarges" and the computer responds "OK." However, when the student presses the "CONTINUE" button to advance to the next page, the computer prints out "Duplicate Answer." Before the student can continue, she must change one of her responses to a correct answer which differs from the first.

Records of each student's request (his identity, the key pushed, and the time to the nearest sixtieth of a second is stored on magnetic tape. These data are processed by the same computer that is used for teaching. We have used these records for improving course content, designing better teaching strategies, as well as for planning new, economically viable computer-based education systems.

On the basis of CERL's experience with nearly PLATO systems, certain design philosophies for the proposed system have been formulated. First, each student terminal requires a keyset and a display, both connected to an inexpensive data transmission system which can also drive optional equipment such as random-access audio devices, reward mechanisms, movie films, lights, and so forth. Second, each student terminal must be capable of superimposing randomly-accessed color slide images on the computer-generated graphics. Third, the system should be controlled by a large-scale centrally-located computer rather than many small computers located at the classroom sites. This decision is based upon social and administrative factors as well as on system economics. Semi-conductor large-scale integration techniques may some day make the use of small computers as effective as large ones, but the added human expense of operating a computer center does not promise to scale as effectively. It is our opinion that the initial low cost of a single terminal will permit tightly-budgeted public schools systems to economically incorporate computer-based teaching into their programs. The number of terminals could be increased or decreased as the needs of the school system dictate. Fourth, the cost per student contact hour for the proposed system must be comparable with equivalent costs of traditional teaching methods.

Before discussing an economical system design from the technical viewpoint, it is necessary to consider the cost of producing lesson material. Reported costs have ranged over a factor of 10 for producing similar lesson material. The difference in author languages can account for this wide range. The author language must be just as natural for the teacher to use as the teaching strategy is expected to be natural for the student to use. However, in the long run, the cost of lesson material should constitute only a small fraction of the educational costs just as the textbooks and lesson materials represent only a small part of educational costs today.

Preparing a good CAI course is roughly equivalent in effort to writing a good textbook. Most good authors are quite willing to produce textbooks at a 10-15% royalty rate which yields to them approximately 80¢ per student. Most textbooks are used in courses which have at least 40 hours of classroom instruction. The cost of royalties, reproduction and distribution of lesson material total to $1.20 per student, and when used for 40 hours of instruction yields an eventual cost of approximately 3¢ per student hour of instruction. The reproduction and distribution of materials for computer-assisted instruction terminals promises to be very inexpensive (approximately 40¢ per student for visual and audio materials).

Statistical records of over 70 million requests of PLATO indicate that the average request rate per student depends upon the teaching strategy used, but the product of the average request rate and the average processing time is relatively constant. For example, when using a drill-type teaching strategy the average request rate per student is one request every 2 seconds and the average processing is 10 milliseconds. When using a tutorial or inquiry strategy, the average request rate per student is one request every 4 seconds but the processing time is 2 milliseconds. We will base our calculations on the 20 millisecond processing time which is equivalent to executing approximately 1000 instructions in the CDC 1604.

The request rate probability density function versus computer execution time is approximately an exponential curve; therefore, student requests requiring the least amount of computer time occur most frequently. For example, the simple and rapidly-processed task of storing a student's key-push in the computer and writing the character on his screen represents 70 percent of the requests. On the other hand, the lengthy process of judging a student's completed answer for correctness, completeness, spelling, etc., occurs only 7 percent of the time.

Several existing large-scale computers can perform about 4×10^6 instructions per second. Even if we double the number of instructions needed, providing 2000 per student request, it is seen that these large-scale computers require an average processing time of only 500 microseconds per request. Allowing a safety factor of two to insure excellent system response time, the system can accept an average of 1000 requests per second. This safety factor implies that the computer will be idle approximately 50 percent of the time. However, the computer time not utilized in processing the student requests can be effectively used for other purposes such as background batch processing. Since the average student request rate is ¼ of a request per second, the system can handle up to 4000 students simultaneously, allowing one millisecond to process a request.

Assume that the student input arrival time is Poisson distributed (a reasonable assumption for 4000 independent student stations), and that the request rate probability density function versus computer execution time is approximately exponential (PLATO statistical records substantiate this).

From queuing theory the expected waiting time E (w) that elapses before the computer (single channel) will accept a given student's request is given by

$$E(w) = \frac{p^2 + m^2 o_T^2}{2m(1-p)} \qquad (1)$$

where

m = request rate = 1,000 requests/sec.,
o_T = execution time standard deviation = 500×10^{-6} sec.,
$E(T)$ = execution time expected value = 500×10^{-6} sec.,
p = m E(T) = 0.5

These values yield an expected waiting time E (w) of 500 microseconds. The probability P(w) that a student's request will wait a time w or longer before being served by the computer is given by

$$P(w) = p \exp[-w(1-p)/E(T)] \qquad (2)$$

The probability that a student must wait for a 0.1 second or longer is negligible. Hence the probability of a student's request queue becoming long, or of the student experiencing a noticeable delay is very small.

Presently, each student needs to be assigned approximately 300 words of extended core memory to be treated individually. The maximum used in any teaching strategy has been 600 words per student. Let us allow on the average 500 words (fifty bit) for each student for a total of 2×10^6 words for 4000 student terminals. Our data shows that 20 percent of the computer instructions refer to these words of unique student storage. Therefore, the system must be capable of rapidly transferring data between the slower extended core storage and the high-speed core memory. Some existing computers are capable of transferring data at 10 words per second, requiring only 50 microseconds to transfer the data each way between the memory units. This transfer time is acceptable.

The peak data rate from the computer to each student station is limited to 1200 bits per second to permit data transmission over low-grade telephone circuits, a system feature made possible by the use of the plasma display panel discussed later. For 4000 stations the worst case data rate would be about 4.8 million bits per second, well within the present state of the art for buffering data out of a computer.

Summarizing the computer requirements, therefore, the central computer requires about 2 million words of extended core memory capable of highspeed transfer rates to the main computer memory, it must have an execution time of approximately 4 instructions per microsecond and be capable of transmitting data at a rate of 4.8 million bits per second. There should be a sufficiently large memory (64k to 12 Sk words) in the central processing unit for storing lessons (1k to 2k words per lesson) and for the various teaching strategies. Several existing computers meet these requirements.

The economic feasibility of the proposed teaching system is dependent upon the newly-invented plasma display panel (or equivalent device) now under development at the University of Illinois and other laboratories. This device combines the properties of memory, display and high brightness in a simple structure of potentially inexpensive fabrication. In contrast to the commonly-used cathode ray tube display, on which images must be continually regenerated, the plasma display retains its own images and responds directly to the digital signals from the computer. This feature will reduce considerably the cost of communication distribution lines. The plasma display is discussed in detail in the listed references. Briefly, it consists of a thin glass panel structure containing a rectangular array of small gas cells (about .015 inches density of about 40 cells per inch—see Fig. 6.) Any cell can be selectively ignited (gas discharge turned on or turned off by proper application of voltages to the orthogonal grid structures without influencing the state of the remaining cells). The plasma panel is transparent, allowing the superposition of optically projected images.

A schematic of a proposed student terminal using the plasma display is shown in Fig. 7. The display will be approximately 12 inches square and will contain 512 digitally addressable positions along each axis. A slide selector and projector will allow prestored (static) information to be projected on the rear of the glass panel display. This permits the stored information to be superimposed on the panel which contains the computer-generated (dynamic) information. The projector is digitally addressable, pneumatically driven, and contains a matrix of 256 images on an easily removeable four-inch square plate of film. The film plate is mounted on a Cartesian-coordinate slide mechanism and can be simultaneously translated along either of the two coordinate axes to bring a desired image over a projector lens. The positions along each coordinate axis are selected by a set of four pneumatic cylinders mounted in series. The stroke length of each cylinder is weighted 8,4,2,1, the length of the smallest being ¼ inch. Each slide selection requires less than three cubic inches of air at 8 psi. Based upon the prototype model now being tested, a low-cost image selector with approximately 0.2 second random-access time is anticipated.

Data arriving from the computer via a telephone line enters the terminal through an input register. As previously stated, data rates to the terminal will be held to 1200 bits per second. Assuming a word length of 20 bits, the terminal could receive data at 60 words per second, an important design feature when considering standard TV tariff for communicating. With proper data formats, data rates will be adequate for the applications envisaged. For example, packing three character codes per word will permit a writing rate of 180 characters per second, which is a much faster rate than that of a good reader. Using 18 bits to specify a random point on the 512×512 array, 60 random points per second can be plotted. If the $\times$ increment is assumed such as when drawing graphs, 120 graph points per second can be plotted. In addition, continuous curves requiring only 3 bits to specify the next point can be drawn at rates of 360 points per second. The keyset will provide the student with a means of communicating with the computer. The problem of converting the fast parallel output data from the computer into serial data for transmission to terminals at 1200 bits/sec. has been studied. This can be solved by the use of small size buffer computers performing the parallel-to-serial data conversion.

In the situation where a large number of students are located at considerable distances from the central computer, costs can be lowered drastically by use of a coaxial line instead of numerous phone lines. For example, the cost of a 4.5 MHz TV channel is approximately $35 per month per mile, whereas the rate for a 3kc telephone line is approximately $3.50 per month per mile. Each TV channel can handle at least 1500 terminals on a time-shared basis, each terminal receiving 1200 bits per second. Hence, for an increase in line cost of a factor of 10 over that of a single channel, an increase of a factor of 1500 in channel capacity can be obtained. In addition to a coaxial line transmitting 1500 channels at 1200 bits per second from the computer to the terminals, a data line for transmitting the student keyset information back to the main computer center is required. A data channel of 100,000 bits/second capacity, available from Bell Telephone can handle 1500 students, allowing 60 bits/second to each student. The costs for this line are approximately $15 per month per mile. Data to remote locations will be transmitted by a coaxial line to a central point; from this point local telephone lines rented on a subscriber's service basis would transmit the proper channel to each student terminal. A block diagram of a proposed distribution system to several remote points is shown in Fig. 8.

Over 200 cities, and on a more limited scale many schools, already use community antenna television systems or closed circuit TV. Because FM radio had already established itself prior to the spread of television, a frequency gap existed between channels 5 and 6 which is almost 8 channels wide. These existing channels can be used to communicate to over 12,000 home terminals.

The mainframe cost of a computer meeting the specified requirements is approximately 2.5 million dollars. The additional cost for two million words of memory and other input-output equipment is approximately 2 million dollars. An estimate for the system software, including some course development programming, is another 1.5 million dollars. The total of 6 million dollars amortized over the generally-accepted period of 5 years yields 1.2 million dollars per year.

Assuming that the 4000-terminal system will be in use 8 hours a day for 300 days a year, there are approximately 10 million student contact hours per year. The system cost, excluding the terminals, is thus 12¢ per student contact hour. In order for the equipment cost to be comparable to a conventional elementary school classroom cost of approximately 27¢ per student contact hour, the terminal costs must be limited to 15¢ per student contact hour, the terminal costs must be limited to 15¢ per student contact hour, or to a total cost of about 7.5 million dollars over a 5 year period. The cost for each of the 4,000 terminals, which included a digitally-addressed graphical display device and its driver, a keyset, and a slide selector must therefore be a maximum of approximately $1900. Present indications are that this cost can be met.

Table 1

SUMMARY OF COSTS

ITEM	TOTAL COST IN MILLIONS OF DOLLARS	COST/YEAR IN MILLIONS OF DOLLARS 5 YEARS AMORTIZATION	COST PER STUDENT CONTACT HOUR
Computer and extended memory	4.5	0.9	8¢
Software	1.5	0.3	4¢
4000 student terminals	7.5	1.5	15¢
Subtotal	13.5	2.7	27¢
Lesson material	-----	-----	3¢
Data distribution lines	-----	-----	4¢
TOTAL			34¢

Data distribution costs for a CBE center approximately 100 miles from the main computer are approximated as follows. The coaxial line rental is approximately $3500 per month, or $2.35 per terminal per month, based on 1500 terminals. The 100,000 bit/second wide-band data channel line is approximately $1500 per month, or $1.00 per terminal per month. Allowing $3.00 per terminal per month for a private telephone line from the coaxial terminals to each student erminal gives a total data distribution cost of $6.35 per terminal per month, or 4¢ per student contact hour if each terminal is used 160 hours per month. The author costs were discussed previously.

These costs, based on the above assumptions, are summarized in Chart I. The earning power of the computer for the remaining 16 hours each day and for the idle time between student requests, which would further reduce costs, has not been included.

Conclusion

Using newly-developed technological devices it is economically and technically feasible to develop large-scale computer-controlled teaching systems for handling 4000 teaching stations which are comparable with the cost of teaching in elementary schools. The teaching versatility of a large-scale computer is nearly limitless. Even while simultaneously teaching 4000 students, the computer can take advantage of the 50 percent idle time to perform data processing at half its normal speed. In addition, 16 hours per day of computer time is available for normal computer use. The approximate computer cost of 12¢ per student contact hour pays completely for the computer even though it utilizes only 1/6 of its computational capacity. The remaining 5/6 of its capacity is available at no cost.

BIBLIOGRAPHY

Avner, R. A. and Paul Tenczar. "The TUTOR Manual." CERL Report X-4, January, 1969.

Bitzer, D. L. and P. G. Braunfeld. "Description and Use of a Computer Controlled Teaching System." *Proceedings of the National Electronic Conference,* pp. 787-792, 1962.

Bitzer, D. L. and J. A. Easley, Jr. "PLATO III: A Computer-based System for Instruction and Research." *Proceedings of the 16th Internl. Congress of Applied Psy.,* Amsterdam, 1968.

Bitzer, D. L. and J. A. Easley, Jr. "PLATO: A Computer-Controlled Teaching System." *Computer Augmentation of Human Reasoning* (Washington: Spartan Books, Inc., ed. by Sass and Wilkinson) pp. 89-103, 1965.

Bitzer, D. L., W. Lichtenberger, and P. G. Braunfeld. "PLATO: An Automatic Teaching Device." *IRE Trans. on Education,* Vol. E-4, pp. 157-161, Dec. 1961.

Bitzer, D. L. and D. Skaperdas. "The Economics of a Large-Scale Computer-based Education System, PLATO IV." Paper presented to the Conference on Computer-based Instruction, Learning and Teaching Education, Texas, October, 1968.

Bitzer, D. L. and D. Skaperdas. *"PLATO IV: A Economically Viable Large Scale Computer-based Education System."* Presented at the National Electronics Conference, Dec., 1968.

Bitzer, D. L. and H. G. Slottow. "The Plasma Display Panel—A Digitally Addressable Display with Inherent Memory." *Proceedings—Fall Joint Computer Conference,* 1966, pp. 541-547.

Bitzer, D. L. and H. G. Slottow. *Principles and Applications of the Plasma Display Panel.* Proceedings of the O.A.R. Research Applications Conference. Office of Aerospace Research, Arlington, Va., March, 1968. (Also appears in the proceedings of the 1968 Micro-electronics Symposium I.E.E.E., St. Louis, 1968).

Bitzer, Maryann. "Teaching a Computer-based Nursing Course." Paper presented to the 21st Annual Meeting of the Conference of Catholic Schools of Nursing, June, 1968.

Goode, H. H. and R. E. Machol. *Control Systems Engineering.* McGraw-Hill Book Co., Inc. 1957, pp. 328-343.

Knight, K. E. "Changes in Computer Performance." *Datamation,* Sept., 1966, pp. 40-54.

Knight, K. E. "Evolving Computer Performance 1963-1967." *Datamation,* Jan., 1968, pp. 31-35.

Lyman, E. R. "A Descriptive List of PLATO Programs, 1960-1968." CERL Report X-2, May, 1968, Computer-based Education Research Laboratory, University of Illinois, Urbana, Illinois.

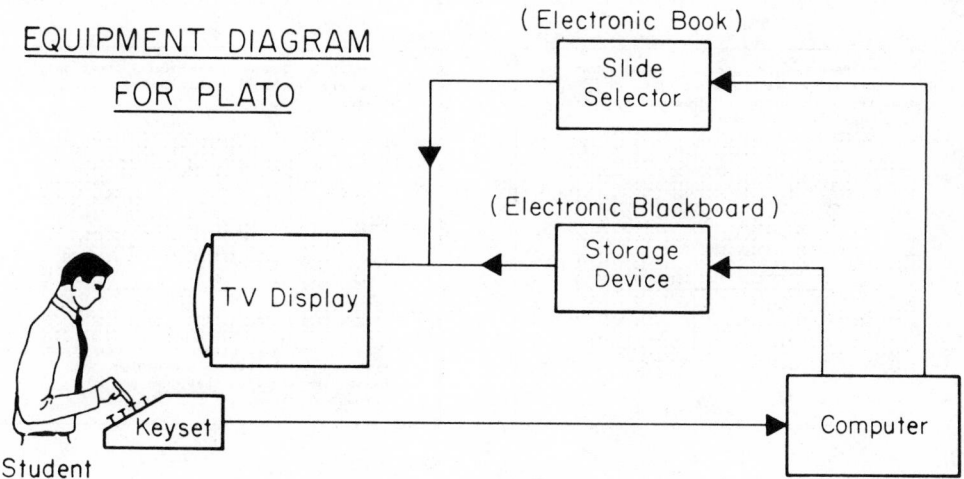

Figure 1. Equipment Diagram for PLATO

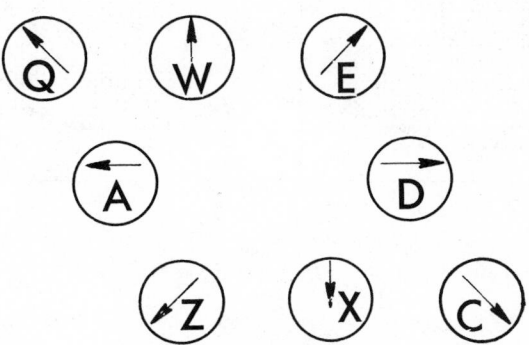

Figure 2

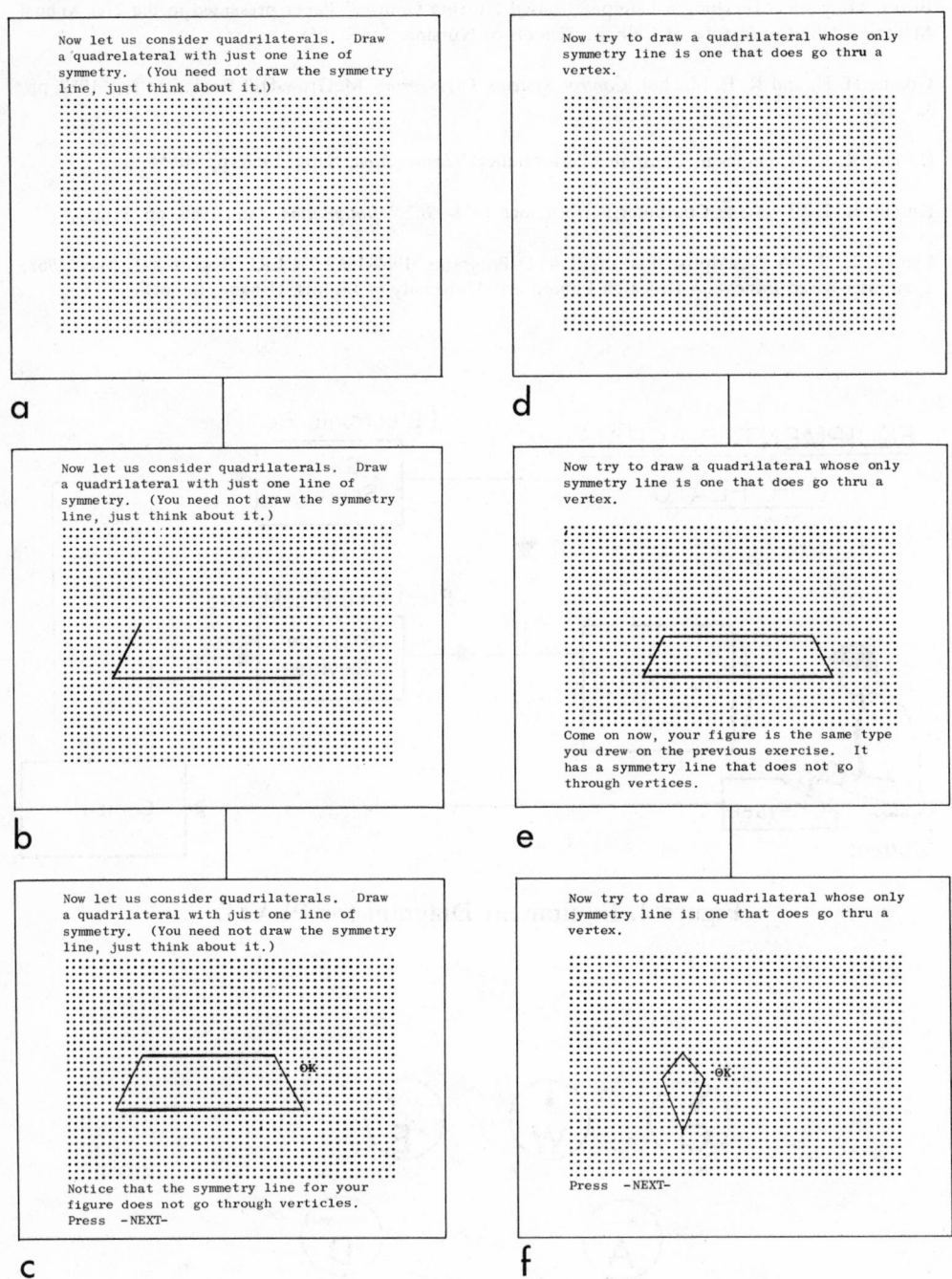

Figure 3

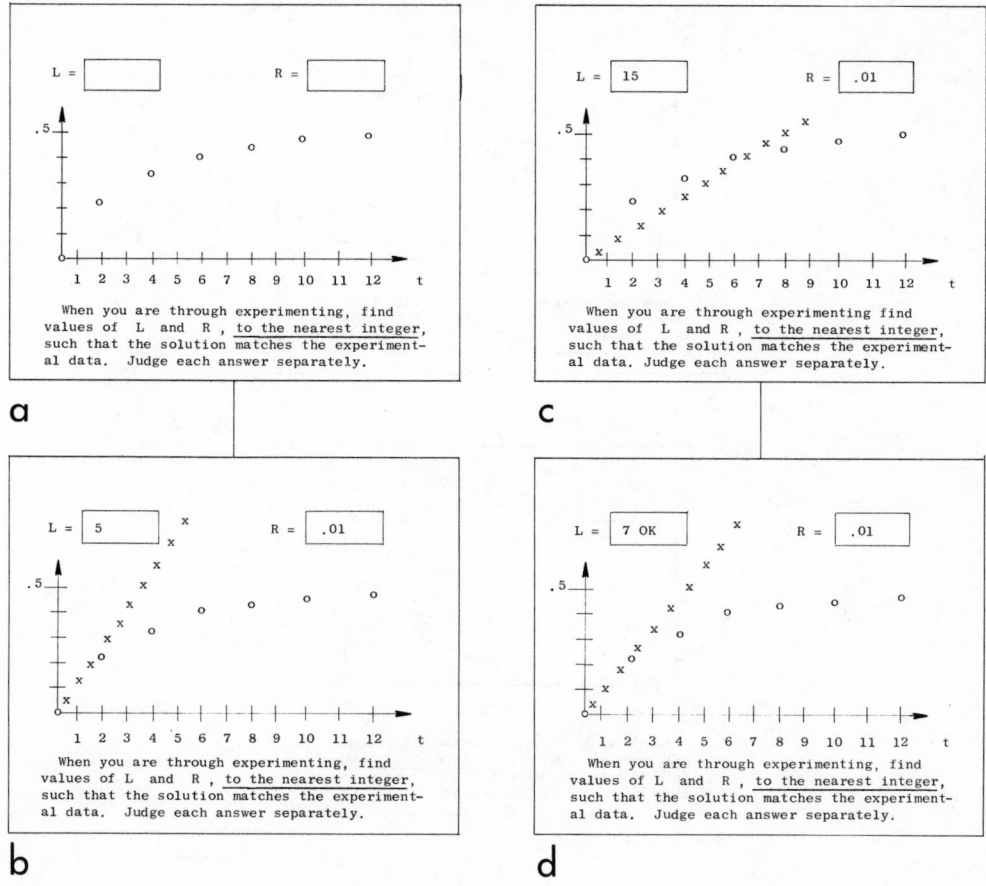

Figure 4

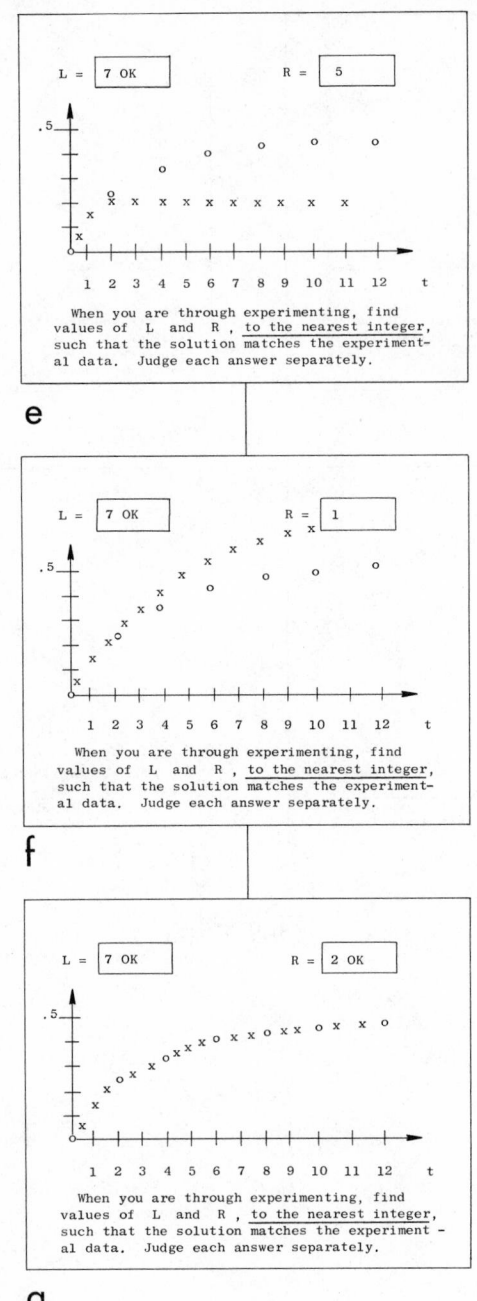

Figure 4 (Cont.)

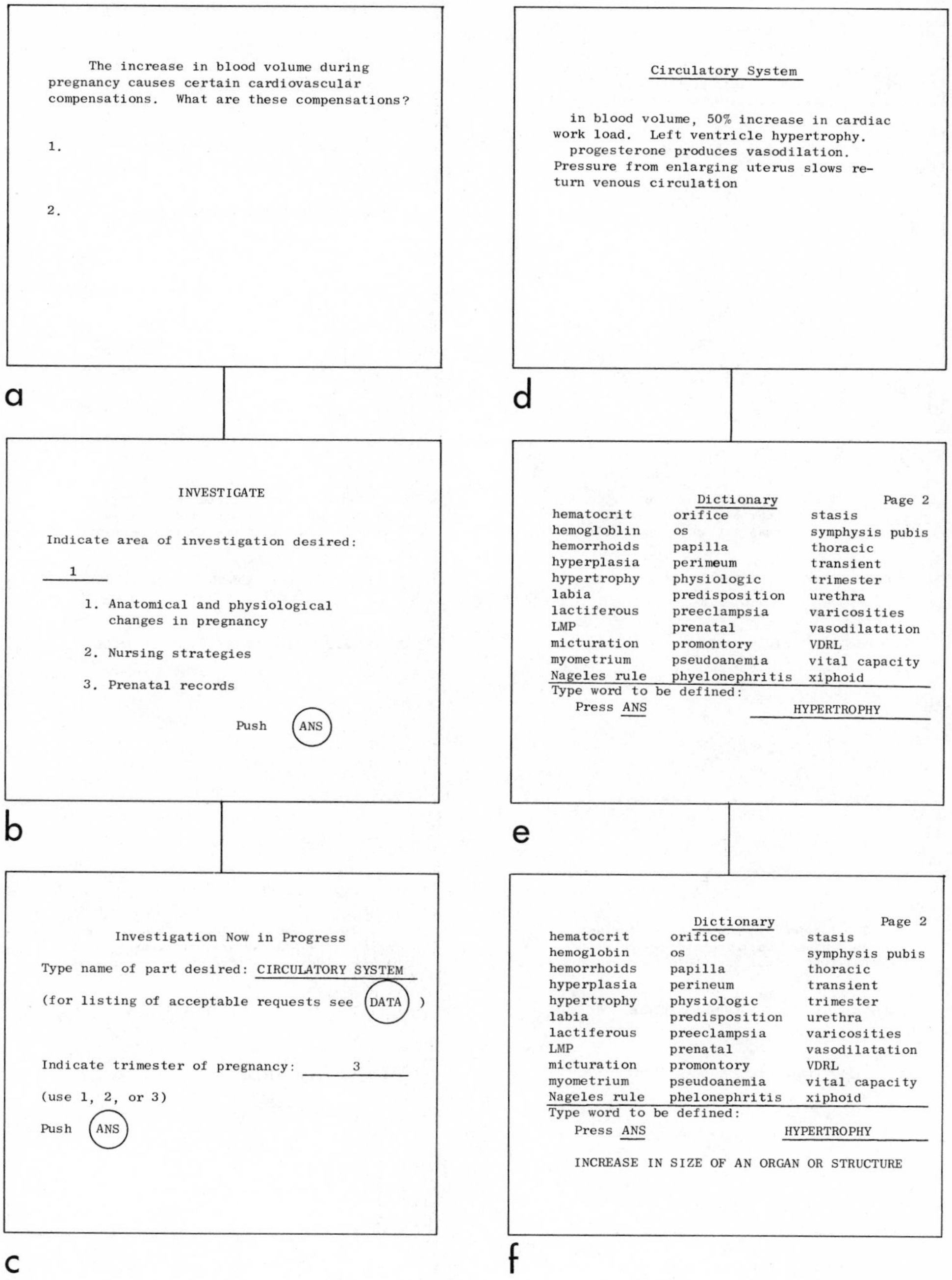

a

The increase in blood volume during
pregnancy causes certain cardiovascular
compensations.   What are these compensations?

1.

2.

b

INVESTIGATE

Indicate area of investigation desired:

  1

    1. Anatomical and physiological
       changes in pregnancy

    2. Nursing strategies

    3. Prenatal records

            Push (ANS)

c

Investigation Now in Progress

Type name of part desired: CIRCULATORY SYSTEM

(for listing of acceptable requests see (DATA))

Indicate trimester of pregnancy: _____ 3

(use 1, 2, or 3)

Push (ANS)

d

Circulatory System

  in blood volume, 50% increase in cardiac
work load.   Left ventricle hypertrophy.
  progesterone produces vasodilation.
Pressure from enlarging uterus slows return venous circulation

e

	Dictionary	Page 2
hematocrit	orifice	stasis
hemogloblin	os	symphysis pubis
hemorrhoids	papilla	thoracic
hyperplasia	perimeum	transient
hypertrophy	physiologic	trimester
labia	predisposition	urethra
lactiferous	preeclampsia	varicosities
LMP	prenatal	vasodilatation
micturation	promontory	VDRL
myometrium	pseudoanemia	vital capacity
Nageles rule	phyelonephritis	xiphoid

Type word to be defined:
  Press ANS   HYPERTROPHY

f

	Dictionary	Page 2
hematocrit	orifice	stasis
hemoglobin	os	symphysis pubis
hemorrhoids	papilla	thoracic
hyperplasia	perineum	transient
hypertrophy	physiologic	trimester
labia	predisposition	urethra
lactiferous	preeclampsia	varicosities
LMP	prenatal	vasodilatation
micturation	promontory	VDRL
myometrium	pseudoanemia	vital capacity
Nageles rule	phelonephritis	xiphoid

Type word to be defined:
  Press ANS   HYPERTROPHY

  INCREASE IN SIZE OF AN ORGAN OR STRUCTURE

Figure 5

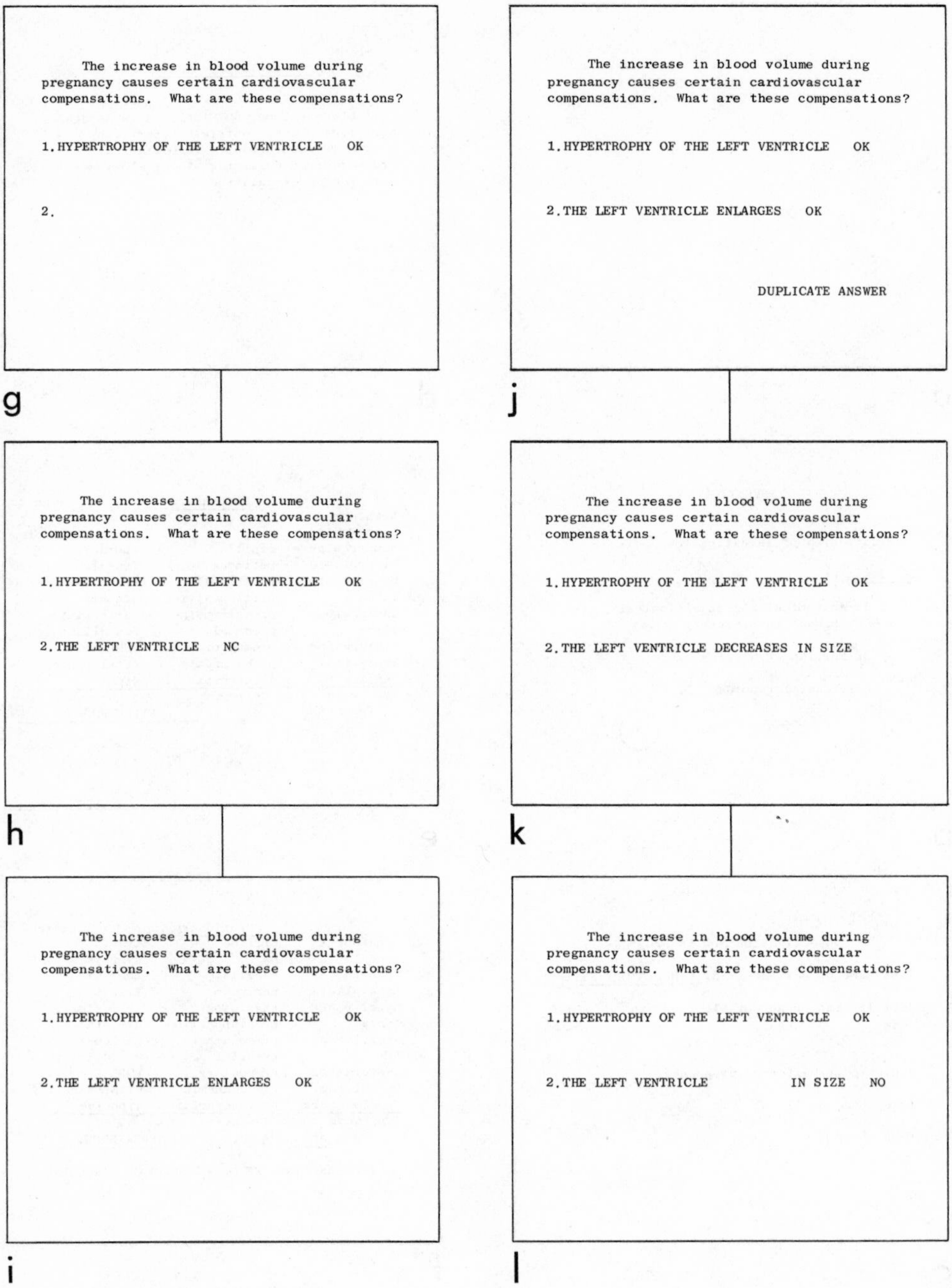

```
        The increase in blood volume during
pregnancy causes certain cardiovascular
compensations.  What are these compensations?


1.HYPERTROPHY OF THE LEFT VENTRICLE    OK


2.
```

g

```
        The increase in blood volume during
pregnancy causes certain cardiovascular
compensations.  What are these compensations?


1.HYPERTROPHY OF THE LEFT VENTRICLE    OK


2.THE LEFT VENTRICLE ENLARGES    OK



                              DUPLICATE ANSWER
```

j

```
        The increase in blood volume during
pregnancy causes certain cardiovascular
compensations.  What are these compensations?


1.HYPERTROPHY OF THE LEFT VENTRICLE    OK


2.THE LEFT VENTRICLE    NC
```

h

```
        The increase in blood volume during
pregnancy causes certain cardiovascular
compensations.  What are these compensations?


1.HYPERTROPHY OF THE LEFT VENTRICLE    OK


2.THE LEFT VENTRICLE DECREASES IN SIZE
```

k

```
        The increase in blood volume during
pregnancy causes certain cardiovascular
compensations.  What are these compensations?


1.HYPERTROPHY OF THE LEFT VENTRICLE    OK


2.THE LEFT VENTRICLE ENLARGES    OK
```

i

```
        The increase in blood volume during
pregnancy causes certain cardiovascular
compensations.  What are these compensations?


1.HYPERTROPHY OF THE LEFT VENTRICLE    OK


2.THE LEFT VENTRICLE          IN SIZE    NO
```

l

Figure 5 (Cont.)

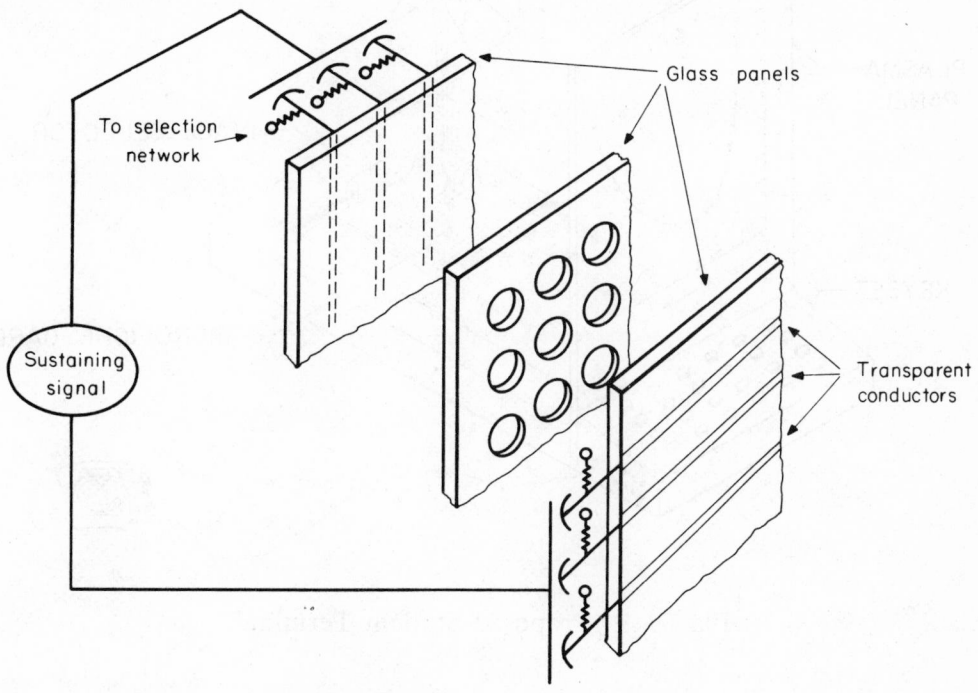

Glass panels

To selection network

Sustaining signal

Transparent conductors

Figure 6

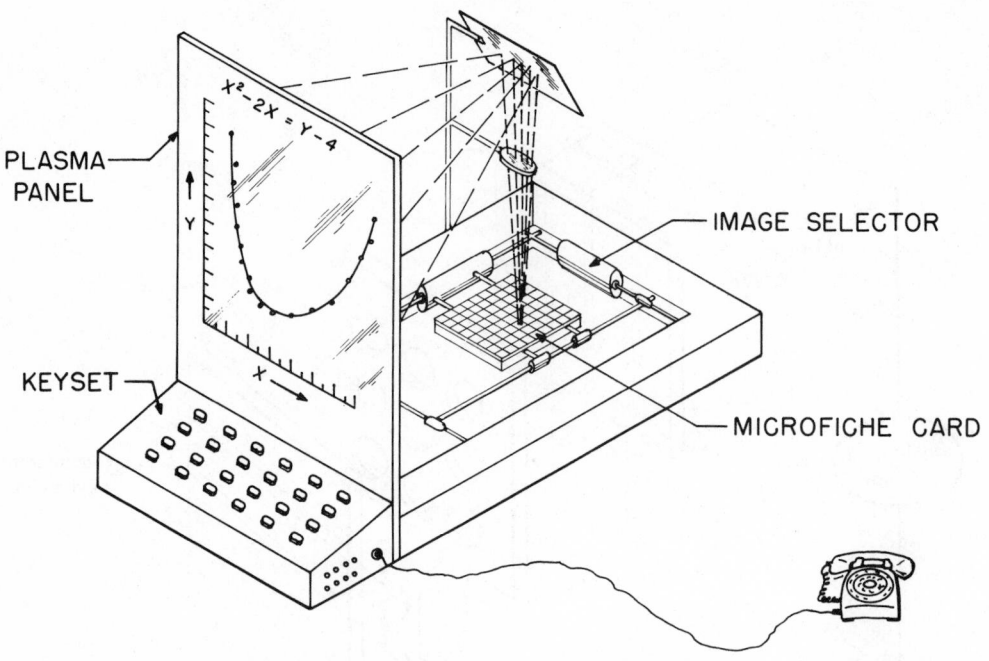

Fig. 7.   Proposed Student Terminal

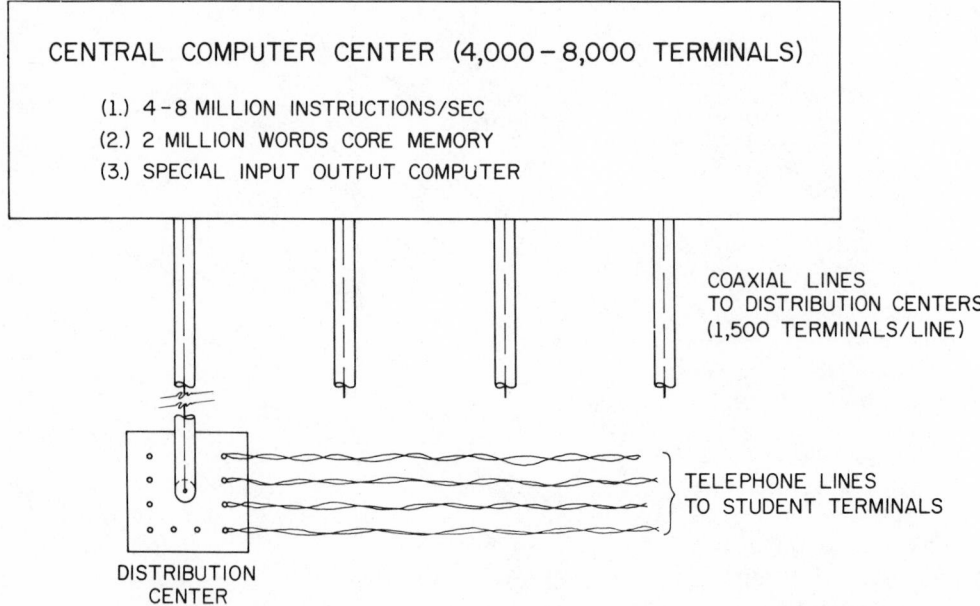

Fig. 8.   Block Diagram of Proposed Distribution System

61.

The New Technology: Its Implications for Organizational and Administrative Changes

by *JOHN O. BOLVIN*
Associate Director
Learning Research & Development Center
Univ. of Pittsburgh

One of the major weaknesses in the entire educational program today is the failure to recognize developments in technology and the implications these developments have upon the formal organization and structure of an educational institution. The present organization and administrative procedures employed in educational programs are not willing nor able to adjust to the instructional innovations that are currently coming onto the scene. Francis Chase in the *1966 NSSE Yearbook, The Changing American School,* states:[1]

> "Organizations and institutions, like individual organisms, tend to react to changes in their environments in ways which will perpetuate themselves. Sometimes the reactions appear to be unreasoned and largely defensive; sometimes they show evidence of calculation and planning. Sometimes the response is slothful; sometimes partial; sometimes prompt, but irrelevant; and sometimes characterized by foresight, orderly planning, and comprehensiveness. The more stable an organization or institution is and the more deeply it is entrenched in the larger society, the more difficult it may be for it to respond to changes in the environment. Hence, the so-called social lag—the piling up of challenges year after year without corresponding reactions on the part of social organizations and institutions until the cumulative effect becomes so great as to produce abrupt change in or even destruction of institutions—is always a real and present danger in education . . ."

The implications new technology has upon the organization and administration of educational institutions seem to indicate that major changes must take place if the new technology is to have a real effect upon instruction.

To get some insight into this problem, one only has to consider the possible effects that implementing programmed instruction into three or four subject areas would have upon the organization and administration of that entire school. If programmed materials do help students advance at varying rates, then the system presently employed of defining a course as a year's work would have little meaning. Promotion and advancement would be a continuous process, not something occuring at the end of the year. In turn, this continual progress would have an effect on the entire scheduling procedures. Additionally, the implementation of programmed instruction would change the role and function of the teacher. Rather than being able to prepare a full year's work before beginning the year, the teacher must be prepared to handle pupils at varying stages as they advance through the various content areas. A change in the teacher's role consequently changes the role of the administrator and supervisor, and so on it goes that just from the implementation of a single innovative program, one can see the changes necessary for the total school structure.

In considering the topic, what changes might be necessary in the organizational pattern and administrative procedures of schools and colleges for new technology to effectively improve instruction, one probably should start with what is meant by effectively improving instruction. One way of defining instruction would be the process of education in shaping a pupil's behavior toward achieving certain competencies. In this sense, instruction would contain two parts—the resources and the plan. Resources would include the teacher, learning materials, techniques of instruction available, the setting, and so forth. To plan effectively for instruction, several basic elements must be present. These are: 1) a definition of course objectives for the goals of instruction; 2) a knowledge of the student's entering behavior; 3) the resources, the techniques of instruction, and the instructional procedures that are available for assisting the student in moving from one goal to another; and 4) techniques of assessing student performance as to when he reaches the desired goals.

Bearing this in mind when considering the effective improvement of instruction, an additional factor enters the picture. When talking about effectiveness we are talking about effectiveness in terms of the pupil. This means that most instructional plans should be centered on the student and not a group of students. In view of the above, this is where the role of individualization comes into instruction. Since individualization is an important theme permeating education today, it is worthwhile to look at one model for individualization and the implications this model presents for school organization and administration.

The definition of individualization most commonly used is that the individualization of instruction requires the adaptation of the educational environment to individual differences. The working aims of a model for individualization are derived from this definition which include: (1) to provide for reliable assessible individual differences among learners, (2) to develop mastery of subject matter as the child moves through the curriculum, (3) to develop self-directed and self-initiated learners through instructional procedures that provide for self-selection and self-evaluation, and (4) to provide opportunities for the child to become actively involved in the learning process.

To meet these aims, the components of the model are as follows:

1. Well-defined, sequentially established, curricular objectives for each subject area.

2. Procedures and processes for diagnosing student readiness, needs, and accomplishments in terms of the objectives of the curriculum and the characteristics of the learner.

3. The necessary instructional materials for individualizing learning providing a variety of paths for attainment of mastery of any given objective. These instructional materials must be developed to permit self-direction, self-initiation, and self-evaluation on the part of the learner.

4. A system for providing individual lesson plans or prescriptions for each student prepared especially for him designating the learning tasks that the student is ready to undertake, suggested materials and techniques of instruction, and the standard of performance expected as an outcome.

5. Strategies for information feedback, either through the use of para-professionals or data processing equipment to provide the student and the teacher opportunities for continuous evaluation and assessment, and

6. The reorganization of the total school environment doing away with the arbitrary boundaries usually designated as grades but substituting organizational patterns to permit continuous progress. This reorganization typically provides opportunities for two or more staff members to work and plan together for

the same students, reallocation of duties and functions because of the involvement of para-professionals, and more freedom of movement on the part of the students.

To effectively improve instruction, certain assumptions are implied in this model. These are: (1) providing more effective self-study on the part of the learner; (2) planning the instruction of each student to maximize success in learning; (3) having available a variety of materials and resources related to various styles of learning; (4) the teacher must be provided with relevant information concerning the student's abilities, aptitudes, past achievements, success or lack of success on present assignments, and what materials and resource options are available at any given time, etc.; (5) the students can move through the curriculum at varying rates of speed; (6) the curriculum must be spelled out in detail prior to beginning instruction for any given child in order that the particular path for that child can be determined in light of future learning goals and past achievement; and (7) instruments for assessing student characteristics be available at all times for the teacher to select in order to determine the style of learning, past accomplishments, etc., on the part of the learner. In addition to these assumptions is the assumption that individualization of instruction cannot be done without the application of the new technology.

The implications these assumptions have for the administration and organizational procedures for the schools shall be examined in terms of the equipment and resources necessary in the schools, the time, the space available, personnel, and the community and family involvement.

1. Equipment and Resources   From the assumptions made concerning the improvement of instruction, one can readily determine that there is a need for instructional resources for self-study on the part of the learner. A great deal has been written about the pros and cons of certain self-study materials, and the qualities and quantities that must be available. Even though there are many unresolved questions regarding these materials such as what types of stimuli are needed, what pacing techniques are necessary, how immediacy reinforcement must be in terms of students' responses, what prompting and amount of practice are necessary for different students, and so forth, individualization cannot be accomplished without the availability of self-study materials.

The need for self-study materials implies that certain types of equipment and resources be readily available prior to beginning instruction. Since the equipment must be operable by students, it will vary depending on the age of the child, the learning outcomes desired, the type of material with which the child will be working, and the facilities available to house such equipment. One thing is certain, when individualizing instruction the teacher no longer has the opportunity to develop and create materials for students to work with prior to beginning the instructional process. Assorted materials must be available for reading, viewing, listening, writing, and for doing various activities under the supervision of the teacher. Facilities to house such materials should be spaced throughout the building in order that supervision and monitoring can be carried out by the teaching staff.

In addition to equipment and materials that assist in the learning process, it is also necessary to have equipment that provides the teacher with information relative to the student's past accomplishments and current progress. Computer equipment can store the relevant information and upon demand feed back to the teacher information which is needed to assist him in decision making when planning the student's learning experiences.

2. Time   The component of time and its effect upon the organization and administration of schools will have a profound effect with the application of new technology. Today, educational time at all levels reflects the many constraints group instruction imposes on the educational system. We generally think in terms of the school day beginning and ending at the same time for most students. We think in terms of "periods" when scheduling students to various activities. We think in terms of the "school year" or, at least large segments of time in the school year such as quarters, to begin groups of students in a particular learning activity. We think in terms of "courses," "C rnegie units," "credits," etc. based upon time in studying and learning. However, as we project to the time when learning is based on the needs and characteristics of an individual learner, the present constraints must be removed.

Present technological devices no longer make it necessary for groups of students to begin learning the same thing at the same time. Students can be introduced to new topics through films, videotapes, records, etc., and the amount of practice that a given student needs can be provided through paced learning with technological devices. When a particular child needs review, it can be provided for. Selected elements within a particular content area for which a given student can skip or pass over can be provided for through the new technology. All these factors tend to eliminate the need for the September opening and June closing of schools. If it is desirable for students to spend 200 days during the school year (which is very much open to question), there is no need for this time to be the same 200 days for all children. The "year around" school begins to take on a different concept. Students can spend their 200 days spread throughout the entire 365-day year. In a similar way, the time spent in studying different content areas should vary from individual to individual. The time that an individual spends in each of the content areas will vary for that individual. The use of technology will provide opportunities for the learner to remain with particular tasks depending upon his needs in that task and not the needs of the group. The differentiation between the regular school time and the after school time and the differentiation of tasks that are performed during these two times begin to take on different meaning. The type of instruction provided in the regular school time and the type of instruction provided in the after school time can be similar. The present model of correspondence courses may be closer to the model used for home study than the use of "home work" as presently viewed.

Time is also reflected in terms of personnel or staff of the school. When we think in terms of time for a professional staff, it is now possible to think about planning time during the school day not held by the constraint of group instruction. Time to teach takes on a different meaning, time for professional development becomes integrated with the regular school time, and so it goes. The component of time as we now consider it and the component of time with the new technology drastically changes the concept of school which, in turn, changes drastically the organization and administration practices of the educational institutions.

3. Space and Facilities The design of space and facilities must reflect the school's educational program. Since it is assumed that with the application of new technology the school's program will provide for more effective learning which, in essence, provides for more individualization in the planning and conducting of instruction for each student, space and facilities must be different than the building as we now know them. The equal-sized classrooms presently existing in most schools grew out of the position that teachers should have an equal load of students and students should be divided into groups according to age or ability with instruction generally being given to the entire group or, at best, two or three sub-groups. In place of the equal-sized classrooms, the facilities needed include: (1) Individual learning stations (both wet and dry-type carrels) spaced throughout the building yet housed in such a way that students' activities do not interfere with those of the other learners. (2) Student viewing rooms and small conference rooms must be provided for students to work with other students or for a teacher to work with small groups of students. (3) Science and math laboratories for individual and small-group activities must be provided. (4) The library as we now know it will become more of a learning resource center than it is presently. However, not all library catalogue materials will physically be found within the library. In essence, the library will permeate the entire school with individual learning carrels tied into an information retrieval system coordinated from the central library facility. Close to or as a part of the library should be student reading rooms. (5) Space must be provided for large- and small-group instruction. One change that technology will make in the utilization of space is the need for large-group instruction as presently being proposed by many educators. As you read the educational literature on buildings, the purpose of the large-group instruction area is to provide large-group instruction when possible in order to free teachers to work individually with students or to work with small groups of students. The application of technological devices will change the need for large groups from this point of view. Technology makes it unnecessary to have large groups of students together in order to free other teachers to meet with a small group. However, this does not rule out the need for some large-group instructional areas within the school facility. The purpose for which they are used and the amount of time they will be used will change. This means that the space needed for large groups must be flexible to get maximum use of space for maximum time. Changes necessary for students result in changes for teachers and other supportive staff. These facilities would include individual and team planning areas for teachers, a central information center accessible to all concerned, and administrative, health, food service, etc. as necessary.

4. Personnel and Staff The implications of new technology and the assumptions for improving instruction have been viewed in terms of equipment and resources, time, and space and facilities. Now let us look at the implications in terms of personnel and professional staff. Relative to personnel, the assumptions presented above imply changes in duties and responsibilities of various persons now assigned to the schools, as well as the addition of new types of assignments not found in most schools at the present time. Both of these factors will be considered when discussing the changes for personnel.

Since the core of the instructional program (in terms of staff assignments) begins with the teacher, any examination of the organization should begin here. Denmark[2] in an article, "The Teacher and His Staff," listed the following duties and responsibilities of teachers under the present conditions:

"Today's teachers are expected to . . .

1. Remain alert to significant developments in academic specialty and continue general education in order to avoid obsolescence of knowledge

2. Be a continuing student of the educative process and keep current with respect to innovations in teaching methods and materials

3. Plan with students and fellow workers

4. Work with curriculum committees

5. Experiment with different content, methods, and materials and keep systematic records of such studies

6. Read and evaluate student work

7. Confer with students and parents regarding pupil progress

8. Counsel and advise students on academic, vocational, and personal concerns

9. Maintain a cumulative file of significant data on each student

10. Develop reading lists, outlines, study guides, drill sheets, and visual materials

11. Prepare tests appropriate to the range of objectives established

12. Type and duplicate tests and other materials for classroom use

13. Arrange for field trips, outside speakers, and other programs relevant to the learning objectives of the class

14. Supervise homeroom, study hall, or luncheon

15. Supervise playground or recess periods

16. Advise student extracurricular groups, chaperon school functions

17. Keep attendance and academic records

18. Collect money for various drives and sell tickets for school events

19. Order and return films and other visual aids and operate equipment involved

20. Participate in professional-association and learned-society activities

21. Maintain an active interest in civic and community affairs and represent the school in the community

22. Orient and assist beginning teachers

23. Supervise student teachers and cooperate with area colleges in providing opportunities for observation and demonstration."

With the application of technology, certain roles of the teacher will change, some will be deleted, and other functions will be added. When applying new technology, teachers first of all will need an operationally sound theory of instruction to assist them in making the many decisions in planning for the student's educational development. The teacher's role in assessment, diagnosis, and planning will be the most important factors to be influenced by the new technology. The teacher will be required to make more and more meaningful decisions regarding exactly what it is that the given child is ready to do, what would be the best way for the child to accomplish the task, and when is it that the child should be changed to another mode of learning or moved on to another learning task.

The specificity of decision making required in self-instructional systems is not as crucial in the present teacher-centered situations. Under the present group-type learning situations, discrepancies and omissions in planning can be corrected as the teacher moves through the learning situation with the children.[3] However, when we begin to consider individual plans and self-instructional materials, independent learning, small-group instruction, the resources and plans must then be carefully thought out before instruction begins, must be carefully monitored throughout the instructional process, and carefully evaluated with the termination of the instructional plan. In order to have the time and resources necessary for proper decision making, certain organizational changes are necessary.

To provide flexibility and to adapt even now to some of these differences among individual students, the concept of team teaching has been employed. When considering the implications of improving instruction, one begins to reevaluate and reconsider the concept of team teaching. One change is a need for teams consisting of professional and paraprofessional personnel with differentiated task assignments. Many of the present team teaching programs provide some differentiation in the roles of team members. The teams are generally made-up of a team leader, some senior professional teachers, several intern teachers, teacher aides or technicians, and clerical aides. When considering the needs of individualized instruction, then the make-up of this team in terms of differentiated staff roles would follow very basically this same type of team operation.

The team leader, for instance, presently is considered to be an experienced, mature, master teacher of unusual talents. This person usually possesses a master's degree and is able to supervise other persons, is able to initiate change, has a firm knowledge of the learning process in the goals of education for the particular institution, and knows the community and students attending the particular school.

Depending on what level of education is being considered, the senior teachers on the team would either be subject specialists for a particular subject or generalists for several content areas as in the lower levels of education (the primary and intermediate grades for instance).

The intern on the team is generally a trainee who is involved in a teacher education training program and working under full-time supervision within the particular school.

However, unlike the present situation where a given teacher trainee is often assigned to a single teacher for supervision and training, the interns on a team are usually assigned to the team and operate with various teachers and professional personnel within the team structure.

The teacher assistants and technicians assigned to the team are usually mature adults who have had some training in working and supervising student activities. In many cases, these persons will make instructional decisions. However, the professional teaching staff has generally set limits within which these decisions must be made. These persons also relieve the teacher of much of the routine teaching duties such as supervising recess and lunch periods, supervising the arrival and departure of students to and from classes, supervising students involved in various activities independent or small group, supervising project and laboratory situations, helping the student to obtain materials, and general housekeeping-type duties.

The technician will assist the students in learning how to operate the various mechanical devices for himself, to keep the devices fundamental, to be aware of the placement of various devices, and to keep the entire team alerted to the introduction of new mechanical aids that will assist the teachers in assigning student activities.

On the other hand, clerical aides will relieve the teacher and the team of many non-teaching tasks such as typing, filing, recording, duplicating materials, assisting the child in obtaining materials, and the general clerical duties that are now either not employed or are done by the teaching staff as part of their regular assignments.

When examining the 23 teacher expectations given by Denemark, certain roles assigned to the teacher can now be removed and reassigned to members of the team. These deletions include: (1) Maintaining a cumulative file of significant data on each student. With the assistance of para-professionals and such technological changes as the computer, the teacher no longer maintains a cumulative file. This file is maintained for all teachers to use and the teacher simply calls up that information which is relevant for her or him at a given time. (2) Developing reading lists, outlines, study guides, skill drill sheets, and visual materials no longer becomes the responsibility of a single teacher. (3) With the utilization of retrieval systems, it is possible for a school or groups of schools to maintain an up-to-date file coded to various learning outcomes that would provide the team with reading lists, outlines, types of study guides available, and what kinds of visual materials are available for a given outcome. (4) The teacher no longer would be required to prepare tests for groups of students as done in most schools at the present time. These instruments would be prepared and stored for teacher utilization. To individualize instruction, this is not only desirable but necessary if we want to assess the student along various parameters as he moves through the learning process. (5) The typing and duplicating of tests and other materials for classroom use will no longer be a necessary role of the teacher. This task will be handled for all teachers by clerical assistants provided to the team. (6) The supervision of homeroom study halls, lunch room, playground, recess periods, etc. can all be assumed by para-professionals, thus freeing the teacher to have time to plan with fellow teachers and students, and to keep current with the trends in educational practices.

One must be careful, however, in generalizing the roles of various teams for different levels of education. For example, some aspects for teaching very small children will remain a human enterprise with technological devices being used sparingly and for very specific purposes. Implied here is that teams working with three- to eight-year old children would have a much smaller pupil-adult ratio than, say, teams working with 12 through 16- or 17-year olds. However, in teams working with all age groups, certain ideas can be generalized; e.g., when considering differentiated staff roles, we can also consider differentiated pay for the persons within these staff roles. The team leader would be a highly-paid professional person receiving a salary based upon a 12-month period and commensurate with administrative salaries of educational personnel today. Teachers on the team can be differentiated in terms of desire and request on the part of the teacher. There can be those teachers who wish to be professional personnel, working 12 months a year from eight in the morning until five, and receiving salaries commensurate with the time and additional effort they put into a job. At the same time, there can be other professional teachers on this team who, because of outside commitments (e.g., wives and mothers), would rather work for nine or 10 months per year and possibly prefer to work from four to six hours a day. Through their own choosing, these persons would receive somewhat less in terms of salary than would full-time teachers on the team. Needless to say, the salary structure for para-professionals would likewise be commensurate with their background, training, and responsibilities.

As the differentiated team concept is explored, it becomes obvious that the principal's role begins to change. In most schools, the principal is referred to as the school administrator responsible to some degree for supervision of teachers; other professionals and para-professionals; budgets; transportation; food services; public relations; physical plant design, utilization, and maintenance; teacher in-service education; identification and implementation of innovations; research; pupil scheduling; etc. With the development of instructional teams some of these duties are transferred from the principal to the team. These include supervision, pupil scheduling, in-service education, and many more. Many management functions now required of the principal can be assisted, simplified, and transferred to others by the implementation of technology. Thus, the role of the principal will become more limited permitting this position to be better defined and better staffed. The principal's role as educational leader and coordinator begins to emerge as the primary responsibilities of such a position.

Directly related to the changing role of the principal is the introduction of additional specialists into the organizational structure of the school. One of these specialists might be termed the "educational engineer." The major role of the educational engineer will be to assist the schools in bridging the gap between research and practice. One assumption that underlies the need for this sort of person is the inevitable increase of information and knowledge about learning and the learning process that will be available as we apply technology to the system. The education and training of persons for this position should include a strong background in the behavioral sciences with some emphasis in educational research. However, with such a background there is one word of caution that must be injected.

> "The successful educational engineer should probably have all of the training and instincts of the behavioral scientist. As such, he may often find guesswork and the inelegance of trial-and-error distasteful. He will be tempted to behave like a basic researcher, but this sort of behavior does not add directly to useful social invention. If the educational engineer is employed by a local school system, the economic sanction and social obligation which accompany his publicly-defined position will serve to bind him to a practical commitment."[4]

To be effective, the educational engineer would work with and through the principal with each team providing a resource that is currently missing in nearly all educational programs.

Other positions presently existing that will take on different functions or roles include: guidance staffs, curriculum coordinators, supervisors, and health service personnel. As the role of the teacher becomes more associated with instructional decision making and planning for individual students, the implications this has for involving guidance personnel as resource persons become obvious. It is evident that with the tremendous expansion of knowledge and information, individuals must begin to select alternatives for concentration. As educational institutions, schools must build into the system the opportunity for students to become actively involved in the decision-making process.

One role of the guidance staff should be to assist the student and teacher in formulating more meaningful long-range goals and, in turn, developing and implementing instructional programs that assist the student in reaching these goals. Closely related to this function is the necessity for relevant information concerning the student that is used in developing the instructional plans. Since instructional decisions are related to all characteristics of the learner, the guidance staff must be supported by specialists such as: psychologists, social-case workers, psychiatrists, medical and dental persons, and other specialists that presently serve the students but are often completely independent of the student's instructional experiences. It should be the role of the guidance staff to coordinate and translate information from these specialists to teachers and students.

When attempting to relate the present functions of curriculum coordinators and supervisory personnel to future demands of schools, several assumptions regarding curriculum building and decision making are implied. First of all, the present practice of curriculum building that supposedly goes on in most schools should be questioned. The research and development functions necessary before a new instructional program should be implemented requires both large amounts of funds and the involvement of many specialists that are not generally available to most school districts. An examination of the costs and professional input that are necessary in developing instructional programs such as the newer science and mathematics programs, should serve as examples of what is implied. However, the local school districts should be involved in this process by (1) assisting in the identification of needs for instructional programs, (2) assisting in the establishment of aims and purposes of these programs, and (3) assisting in field testing and the implementation of these programs into local schools. Thus, the role of instructional curriculum directors and supervisors relate to these functions in developing instructional programs.

The second set of assumptions effecting the role of curriculum coordinators and supervisory personnel are those related to decision making. In most educational institutions today it is assumed that "decisions are made at the top." This statement implies a hierarchy of decision making that is not applicable when considering potential changes in roles suggested to this point. The teachers plan with the students. The teacher plans with other teachers. The teacher plans with other professionals and para-professionals. The guidance staff assists the teacher and students in decision making. The curriculum directors plan with other agencies as well as with local staffs and community for goal setting. The principal works with and through the teams for management and educational improvement. All of these statements imply a complex organizational structure that is yet to be developed. However, this structure must be developed before we can efficiently improve instruction through the use of modern technology.

5. Community and Family Involvement   One of the major effects new technology should have upon the educational institution is the clarification of the roles of the community and family in the educational process. Up to the present time, the involvement of the community has been limited and often ignored for a variety of reasons. To make education more relevant for more people, it is now necessary to actively involve the community in: (1) examining and assisting in establishing the goals and purpose of education; (2) assisting in developing the educational needs related to vocations; (3) providing opportunities for learning experiences related to the individual student's goals; (4) providing information from all community agencies to a central source about individual students; (5) sharing in the instructional program by providing resources, facilities, and personnel to enrich the education environment; and (6) cooperatively working with educational institutions to provide for continuous educational developments of all people in keeping with the changes of supply and demand of the labor market. In general, what is implied is that educational decision making at all levels must involve the community and eventually the family.

The general effect new technology has already had and what it would have upon the family has been a major concern of many social scientists today. The decision as to the effects it could have should not be made by various institutions separately, but rather examined cooperatively. For example, should we provide public education for three- and four-year olds through "nursery schools" or could these same experiences be provided in homes through technological processes? Should much of the student's independent work be provided in the home rather than in the schools? Both of these questions imply that through the use of technology it is not always necessary to bring students to a central facility for all systematic learning experiences but it is possible to provide the same types of learning in the home. Assuming that the outcomes are the same or similar in both instances, it then becomes a question as to which is more desirable in terms of the family and other social institutions.

Summary

In essence, there are many organizational and instructional changes that must take place if the new technology is to effectively improve instruction. The limited view of the "school house" must be erased and in its place the concept of the community as the school must be substituted. The "hierarchy" of line and staff from chief school administrators, to assistants, to principals, to teachers, to students must be replaced with several interrelating organizational patterns that start with the student and feed back to the student. Finally, before technology can have an effect upon instruction, professional educators at all levels must be willing to forfeit certain traditional roles and practices by assuming new roles and assisting in the creation of new practices within the administrative organization.

REFERENCES

1. Chase, Francis. "School Change in Perspective." In Goodlad, John I. (Ed.), *The Changing American School, The Sixty-Fifth Yearbook of the National Society for the Study of Education.* University of Chicago Press, Chicago, 1966, pp. 271-306.

2. Denemark, George W. "The Teacher and His Staff." *NEA Journal.* December, 1966.

3. Loughary, John W. *Man-Machine Systems in Education.* Harper & Row, New York, 1966.

4. Anderson, Richard C. "The Role of Educational Engineer." *J. of Educational Sociology.* Vol. 34, *8,* April, 1961, pp. 337-388.

BIBLIOGRAPHY

Anderson, Richard C. "The Role of Educational Engineer." *J. of Edu. Sociology,* Vol. 34, *8,* April, 1961, pp. 337-388.

Bruner, Jerome S. "Education as Social Invention." *Saturday Review,* February 19, 1966.

Chase, Francis. "School Change in Perspective." In Goodlad, John I. (Ed.) *The Changing American School, The Sixty-fifth Yearbook of the National Society for the Study of Education.* Chicago: University of Chicago Press, 1966, pp. 271-306.

DeCecco, John P. (Ed.) *Educational Technology: Readings in Programmed Instruction.* New York: Holt, Rinehart and Winston, 1964.

Denemark, George W. "The Teacher and His Staff." *NEA Journal,* December, 1966.

Glaser, Robert. "Ten Untenable Assumptions of College Instruction." *Educational Record,* Spring 1968.

Goodlad, John I. "Cooperative Teaching in Educational Reform." *The National Elementary Principal,* Vol. XLIV, *3,* January, 1965.

Goodlad, John I. (Ed.) *The Changing American School, The Sixty-fifth Yearbook of the National Society for the Study of Education.* Chicago: University of Chicago Press, 1966.

Goodlad, John I. & Kenneth Rehage. "School Organization." *NEA Journal,* November, 1962.

Heathers, Glen. "Research on Implementing and Evaluating Cooperative Teaching." *The National Elementary Principal,* Vol. XLIV, *3,* January, 1965.

Hechinger, Fred M. *The Electronic Revolution in the Classroom: Promise or Threat? A Discussion.* Washington, D.C.: Council for Basic Education, March, 1968.

Loughary, John W. *Man-Machine Systems in Education.* New York: Harper & Row, 1966.

Martin, John Henry. *The Electronic Revolution in the Classroom: Promise or Threat? A Discussion.* Washington, D.C.: Council for Basic Education, March, 1968.

McMahon, Eleanor. "Principals' Views of Team Teaching." *The National Elementary Principal,* Vol. XLIV, *3,* January, 1965.

Miller, Richard I. (Ed.) *Perspectives on Educational Change.* New York: Appleton-Century-Crofts, 1967.

Mitchell, Donald P. "Housing Cooperative Teaching Programs." *The National Elementary Principal,* Vol. XLIV, *3,* January, 1965.

Shaplin, Judson T. "Cooperative Teaching: Definitions and Organizational Analysis." *The National Elementary Principal,* Vol. XLIV, *3,* January, 1965.

Shaplin, Judson T. & Henry F. Olds, Jr. (Eds.) *Team Teaching.* New York: Harper & Row, 1964.

Stevens, W. William Jr., & Irving Morrissett. "A System for Analyzing Social Science Curricula." *The EPIE Forum,* Vol. 1, *5,* January, 1968.

62.

Changes in Administrative Organization Aimed to Effect The Introduction of Appropriate Educational Technology

by *JOHN E. DIETRICH* and *F. CRAIG JOHNSON*
Asst. Provost   *Prof., Higher Education*
Michigan State Univ.   *Florida State Univ.*

Critical Background Assumptions

Considerable space will be devoted in this discourse to certain radical changes in university administration and organizational patterns prior to the introduction of appropriate educational technologies. Simultaneously, it must be said that:

> *Any change in college or university organization which is explicitly addressed to the implementation of educational technology will fail.*

The successful introduction of educational technology into any institution must be judged against existing operational patterns and specific problems facing that institution. Heads of at least two major university systems have given their view as to broad university goals and problems which form the background against which change should be judged.

> Paradoxical as it may seem, I am conviced that the tremendous and terrifying problems which now suddenly face higher education in America are the most fortunate developments to have occurred. They make it mandatory for us to examine, really examine, what we are doing, to assess our educational philosophy, to adopt new methods and adapt old ones, to find new resources in teachers, facilities, and financing, and generally to raise hob with the status quo. We shall have to solve these problems, or higher education will make a steadily decreasing contribution to the welfare of the nation, especially in the quality of its products.
>
> Samuel B. Gould, Chancellor
> State University of New York
> Fall, 1965

Can the large university retain its stability, its integrity, and its usefulness to society by continuing to carry on in the same way as before, doing more and more of the same things, or must it change?

It is my belief, and I hope it is yours, that it must change, that the pressures and strains are so intense and so persistent as to make innovation mandatory. We see old models, old attitudes, old methods, old values, being challenged and changed in society all around us. Can we expect the university, itself a social instrument, to escape unchallenged and unchanged? We cannot.

John A. Hannah, President
Michigan State University
Fall, 1966

The introduction and/or expansion of educational technologies cannot and should not be one of the central problems of the university. John Gardner in his "Agenda for Colleges and Universities" (1965) has reached to the heart of some truly central problems when he calls for the restoration of the status of teaching and learning, the reformation of the under-graduate curricula, and the improvement of institutional forward planning.

Any organizational or administrative change must be explicitly dedicated to solving problems of the magnitude Gardner describes—problems which no faculty member, regardless of his classical or traditional rigidity, can ignore. If educational technology is used to solve central university problems, it can and will take its rightful and prominent place. (A case in point—Michigan State University clearly employs more different technologies on a larger scale with general faculty and student acceptance than any other institution in America.)

Institutional Change Results from Stress

There is a truism abroad to the effect that "the only constant in our society is change." The truism is followed by a premise that "the speed of change is creating vast new stresses." While agreeing with the notion that change creates stress, there should be one added premise; namely, that "change is the direct result of stress," or expressed inversely "without stress there will be little or no change."

To illustrate—the key operational unit in a university is the department. If the department can arrange its curriculum in such a manner that each professor is given the opportunity to teach his specialty regardless of what the students may need to know, little will change. If the department has a limited number of undergraduate students providing the possibility of (by departmental definition) optimal section size and minimal advising loads, it will continue its old patterns. If the number of graduate students are balanced so as to accomplish the necessary "service" teaching and maintain modest-sized seminars and modest advising loads, little will change. If the faculty is free to give (by departmental definition) optimal time to research and publication, it will resist change. If the financial resources are available for new positions, more graduate assistants, adequate labor, supplies, services and equipment, few changes in the system will occur.

In all of these instances the department will respond to almost any challenge to its curriculum, undergraduate or graduate instruction, or research by maintaining that it is doing a superior job. Under these "ideal" conditions, the introduction of educational technology will be rejected by faculty because it "decreases the quality of instruction by reducing the personal interaction between the faculty member and the student."

Given these "ideal" conditions and the accompanying rejection of technology, one might conclude that the best procedure for introducing educational technology would be to create artificial stress on the system deliberately. However, there are enough stresses already present on the system, as argued by Gould and Hannah, so that such a move is neither desirable nor necessary. The more realistic process is to identify stress which is creating critical problems and then introduce educational technology to help solve the problems.

Stresses Relate to Curriculum and Instruction

The principal departmental balances suggested as ideal conditions were small section size, minimal advising loads, adequate faculty and staff, and sufficient support dollars.

Section size and advising loads are a function of student numbers in proportion to faculty. Public universities have been and will continue to be pressed by society to take more and more students. Rising enrollments, coupled with the radical shift from the private to the public institutions, have created increased stress on the system. Public universities and colleges are forced to respond to the premise that the opportunity for higher education must be provided for all Americans who can potentially profit from it.

Adequate faculty and staff is the function of both availability and resources. The ratio of Ph.D.s on our university and college faculties is, in general, decreasing while the demand is increasing. Simultaneously, the cost of trained faculty is running ahead of new resources, thus creating real stress on our institutions.

Sufficient resources for faculty, staff, labor, supplies, services, and equipment are a function of new dollars. At present, despite an influx of new dollars, the per capita student dollar is decreasing at a time when the worth of the dollar is diminishing. This phenomenon is bringing another stress on the system.

Finally, time for research or, for that matter, for the faculty member to teach what he wants, is a function of the number of students, adequate faculty and financial resources. As each of these ratios change in an undesirable direction, stresses on the system increase.

Institutional Stress Is Uneven

Thanks to the time-honored but dismal process of allocating university resources by historical "pie cutting," stresses are not comparable in all parts of the institution. Allocation of new dollars (departments are usually guaranteed those dollars they already have—i.e., the base) have generally not reflected shifts in need. As a result, those departments under the greatest stress appear to be making the quickest response to the challenge of change. On the other hand, those departments in which at least the student-faculty ratio is favorable appear to be the most resistant to change.

Despite the inequities created by tradition and the speed with which resources can be reallocated, most departments can demonstrate great need when present conditions are compared with traditional ratios or goals.

Since new financial and human resources cannot be provided in the desired measure, and present resources cannot or at least are not reallocated in tempo with academic change, most colleges and departments have deep and profound frustrations. It is to these concerns that administrative reorganization and educational technology can respond.

The Context of University Response

Prior to any administrative reorganization to bring about change involving educational technology, certain specific steps need to be taken. First, change procedures must be defined; second, a commitment to change must be negotiated and stated; and finally, a climate for change must be developed.

Problem Solving Procedures

A large majority of university studies resulting from stresses on the institution begin with an attempt to define institutional goals. While this may seem to be a highly desirable technique, it frequently proves to be fruitless. The goals of an institution are customarily stated in such bland terms as "to educate the individual to contribute to his society economically, socially, morally, and politically" or to the development of the "liberally educated thinking man." These general goals may read well in the front pages of college catalogs, but it is usually impossible to state them in specific action-oriented terms.

A much more fruitful procedure is to study emergent issues which result from stress. A series of mechanisms are available to identify problems and solve them.

Procedures for Identifying Problems

1. Faculty will consider seriously statements made by the president of an institution, such as those quoted earlier in this paper by Samuel B. Gould and John A. Hannah, particularly when they are followed by a series of clearly defined problems.

2. A prestiged ad hoc faculty committee can study broad institutional problems and make specific recommendations for modification. One example of this type of committee was the Select Committee established at the University of California, Berkeley, which brought more than 40 recommendations for major changes in the institution before the faculty and the administration. Another example is the Michigan State University Committee on the Future of the University, a prestiged faculty committee provided with released time for an analysis of the institution. Dozens of recommendations from this committee urged modification of the structures and procedures. A third example is the MSU Committee on Undergraduate Education which was, again, an *ad hoc* prestiged faculty committee which analyzed the problems of undergraduate education and made more than 70 recommendations for change. In each of these instances the committees were not a part of the normal administrative organization. In every case they had the advantage of being a select body of senior faculty commenting on critical problems. One brief quotation from the *Report of the Committee on Undergraduate Education* at Michigan State may indicate how a thrust toward implementation of educational technology was included.

   Faculty members, particularly those teaching large sections, should be encouraged to consult with personnel in Learning Service and in the Instructional Media Center concerning the possibility of using technical aids in their classroom instruction. Support for the development and use of such technical aids should be at a level sufficient to allow for a no-charge policy for departments using the service.

3. University position papers can be written. Such a position paper is exemplified in the Michigan State University Seven-Point Program which proposed seven academic concepts for use by all faculties in the evaluation, review and development of their programs. In this paper, one recommendation was directly oriented to the implementation of educational technology. This recommendation reads as follows:

   It is proposed to put to use discoveries already made concerning the learning process itself, and to stimulate further research, through the establishment of a Learning Resources Center (later named the Instructional Media Center) to include and encourage the use of closed circuit television, film, teaching machines, programmed studies, and other aids.

4. Prestiged outside consultants can be invited in to look at university problems. The University of Missouri, Columbia has used this procedure to advantage. This technique provides the opportunity to selected consultants who hold established points of view. For example, Professor C. Ray Carpenter of Pennsylvania State University has served this function for a number of different institutions.

The point of the preceding paragraphs is that procedures do exist for bringing about action-oriented recommendations for the solutions of major university problems which almost invariably include the need for further implementation of educational technology.

Developing the Commitment for Change

The process for identifying problems and recommending solutions implies a full commitment to the necessity of change. This commitment must be understood and supported by all sectors of the academic community. A clear-cut statement on the desirability of innovation including new technologies has been made by the Board of Trustees at Michigan State. The President, the Provost, and the deans have made public commitments to their position. Department chairmen have, in general, followed suit. Department faculties have been organized to examine their programs in the light of new developments in their disciplines. Even students have been encouraged to come forward with constructive proposals for the modification and improvement. In summary, all of the forces in the academic community have been encouraged to join in a common effort toward the solution of common problems.

Developing the Climate for Change

The university ad hoc committees, the university position papers, consultants, the stated commitment of administrators, faculty and students—all contribute toward developing a milieu in which change becomes possible.

Michigan State University has, in addition, made use of internal conferences dedicated to innovation. As early as 1963 a Learning Resources Conference, which brought in experts from all over the country, was held for the faculty. More than 60% of the faculty took time from their heavy daily responsibilities to attend one or more conference sessions. In 1966, under the sponsorship of the U.S. Office of Education, a National Conference to Stimulate Research and Development on Curricular and Instructional Innovations in Large Colleges and Universities was held on the campus, and the dissemination of its results helped create a climate conducive to change.

Assuming a problem-solving orientation, a broad university identification of problems, a commitment by all parties concerned, and a climate conducive to change, administrative organizational changes must be introduced which are geared to give immediate response in the implementation of change concepts as they evolve.

Administrative Reorganization
To Induce Change
And Facilitate the Introduction and
Development of Educational Technology

Administrative reorganization requires establishment of a central organization, coordination of university expertise, development of financial resources, and the establishment of adequate reward and communication systems.*

Reorganization of Central Administration

The central academic organization of the college or university should be reorganized to make the agent or agency for academic change an integral part of the administration.

Customarily the university academic administration may be characterized (to use an onerous military analogy) as a line organization which includes at its apex the provost or vice president for academic affairs, at its second echelon the deans of the various colleges, and as a third administrative echelon the chairmen of the various departments.

There is also a central administrative *staff* organization related to the vice president for academic affairs. The administrative agency concerned with change should be a part of this staff organization rather than the line organization.

One major inhibitor to the introduction of change has been the lack of such a staff organization. Customarily new dollars have been infused into the line organization with the result that there has been expansion and proliferation of present procedures rather than specific emphasis placed on review and modification of programs. A central staff agency can influence the allocation of resources to the line administration.

One of the principal difficulties encountered by most educational technology agencies, such as audiovisual or television centers, is that they have only departmental status and are frequently attached to a particular college, for example the College of Education. As a result, other departments and colleges tend to regard such agencies as mere appendages rather than as an integral and central part of the institutional development process. Central focus will avoid this difficulty.

Several other characteristics of the change agency should be considered. First, the name of the organization should be carefully selected to indicate to the academic community that its mission includes concern for improvement in curriculum, instruction and the use of resources. At both Berkeley and Michigan State, these agencies are called an Educational Development Program. At Florida State, the program is called the Division of Instructional Research and Service. In four other institutions, the University of Illinois–Urbana, Pennsylvania State University, State University of New York–Stony Brook, and the University of Illinois–Chicago Circle, the agency is called the Office of Instructional Resources or a variation thereof. In each case, the agency has been given a generic name which labels it as concerned with the common university good.

Second, the agency should be kept small. The appearance of empire building must be avoided. The agency must avoid proliferation or duplication of the activities of any other university group.

Third, the directorate of the agency should be given visibility. This can be accomplished by placing the director *ex officio* on major faculty committees and on the principal legislative councils of the institution.

Fourth, the directorate must have an overview of all university operations. Placement on major committees and councils will provide the opportunity to see and understand the problem from a faculty as well as an administrative point of view.

Finally, the purposes of the agency should be clearly stated and should be service or problem-solving oriented. Examples of such purposes are: (1) to identify major problems

For specific details of the Michigan State University Educational Development Program see John E. Dietrich and F. Craig Johnson, "A Catalytic Agent for Innovation in Higher Education," Educational Record, Summer 1967, pp. 206-213.

For a national survey and evaluation of key educational development programs in the U.S. see F. Craig Johnson, "An Evaluation of Educational Development Programs in Higher Education," Project Report No. 401, Michigan State University, March 1968.

in the curriculum and in the learning-teaching process, (2) to stimulate and conduct research which will suggest solutions to identified problems, (3) to undertake projects which give promise of improvement in instruction, (4) to provide service to all parts of the university community, (5) to facilitate implementation of approved solutions, (6) to identify and communicate progress in research, experimentation and implementation.

Organization and Coordination of Expertise

If the central agency for change is to have maximum effectiveness, the university must reorganize and coordinate all support services basic to implementing change.

A number of existing agencies can be brought together to provide a more concerted effort to improve the curriculum and instruction, and provide a broader definition to the term educational technology.

The technology of institutional research, applied human learning, media application and evaluation should be centralized and coordinated. The techniques of these groups can then be directed to the identified problems.

The Office of Institutional Research can make a prime contribution to the change movement by asking the pertinent questions, by collecting and reducing data, and by specifying problems. A Learning Service can help the faculty with the specification of behavioral objectives and the organization and development of contents. A Media Service, which should include expertise in film, graphics, closed circuit television, computer-assisted instruction, programmed learning, etc., can develop creative ways of reaching the defined objectives. An Evaluation Service, composed of testing and measurement experts, can help to evaluate experiments and improve testing, examination and certification procedures. Ideally, the libraries should be included within this framework since books are the most used learning resource and need to be coordinated with and treated like any other resource.

The purpose of this coordination is threefold. First, it will provide a centralized all-university service which can be controlled and supported to the equal benefit of all departments. Second, it will provide expert human resources which are necessary to the solution of instructional problems. It can be argued that today's professor is so concerned with keeping up with his subject matter that it becomes impossible for him to be an expert in learning, technology and evaluation. Finally, the coordination of these services will avoid duplication and competition.

If the various learning resource agencies report to different administrative offices, duplication and competition result. This can be demonstrated at almost any university in the authors' experience. In such instances, decisions relative to different technologies are not based on an analysis of the learning problem, but are frequently sold by avid devotees of particular brands of hardware. For example, if the campus has a film service and a closed circuit television service, these groups may complete. To make matters worse, in some institutions closed circuit television is free to the user while film production is charged to the user. In such a case, the user chooses closed circuit television because of its apparent economy, despite the fact that television and film are almost never equally appropriate to the solution of a learning problem. Coordination of learning resources permits a rational decision of the appropriate media application.

Administrative Allocation of New Financial Resources

Change in a university and implementation of educational technology depends heavily upon the allocation or reallocation of resources. The creation of an agency, such as an Educational Development Program, provides a powerful device for rechanneling new dollars.

As mentioned previously, line budgetary operations in all of the institutions with which these authors have had any contact are not based on a thorough and systematic evaluation of need, nor are they typically used to promote change. In an earlier portion of this paper we referred to historical "pie cutting" and pointed out the sluggishness of the dollar response to stress. A change agent can provide a critical review of present practices, and through forward planning the opportunity to bring strong pressures in the reallocation of resources.

At Michigan State University it can be clearly demonstrated that prior to the introduction of the change agent, new dollars were invariably used to produce more of the same. To be explicit, new dollars were placed where there were increased numbers of students, always within the framework of the same old instructional models and procedures and without much regard for evaluation of what was most effective (quality) and most efficient (cost). Few examples of radical change in instructional or curricular patterns could be demonstrated prior to the introduction of the change agent.

The new organization permitted taking new dollars off the top and assigning them to those groups who were willing to experiment with specific and real changes in instruction. In a sense Michigan State has followed the applied management science technology of industry. It has taken a significant percentage of its academic resources (one-half of one percent of its entire academic budget—small but a start) and used these resources to improve its principal product—instruction and student learning. Obviously, reallocation of these resources, while creating some (though remarkably minimal) dissatisfaction in the line operation, has stood as the greatest single example of institutional commitment to improved instruction.

External resources have an even greater impact. During the first three years of the Educational Development Program activity, the project was modestly supported on a matching basis by the Ford Foundation. Dollars coming from this source had the obvious advantage of permitting the institution to move sharply into the change process without appearing to withdraw support from the ongoing operation. Existence of outside dollars permitted MSU to phase in its own new dollars.

At the risk of being sued for heresy, we must maintain that the Federal Government, principally in the form of the U.S. Office of Education, has severely limited its impact on the change process by virtue of its granting procedures. Federal dollars are available for research, but not for development in any broad sense. Federal dollars are available for specific projects, but are not available to agencies which can, by virtue of being totally conversant with the instructional problems determine what kinds of projects can provide conspicuous results. Federal granting procedures frequently have unbelievable time delays which cool the enthusiasm of the faculty member or group interested in attacking immediate problems now. If there is one single recommendation which should be made above all others, it would be to change the direction of Federal support from research to development, and to change the granting procedure from project grants to catalytic agency grants.

The Association of American Colleges, in a recent statement, has urged that there be "federal institutional grants for instructional purposes." The principle is viable; the procedure proposed is doubtful. Their second guideline suggests:

> Support should be available to all eligible institutions of higher education for expenditure at their discretion within the generally accepted definition of instructional services and departmental research.*

Such grants are mandatory if we are to succeed in introducing instructional change and educational technology. By the same token, it must be argued that if the grants were to be made to institutions rather than to clearly defined change agents established within the institutions, the money almost certainly will go into line operation activities.

*For the complete statement see "Federal Institutional Grants for Instructional Purposes," A Statement by the Association of American Colleges, 1818 R Street, N.W., Washington, D.C., February 1968.

Finally, on the matter of dollars, it is important to recognize that small amounts of money applied at the right time and the right place can bring about remarkable change. The change dollars available at Michigan State have amounted to approximately $250,000 a year, yet these dollars have brought about more than 150 projects, of which almost 100 have been directly related to educational technology.

Administrative Development of Reward Systems

If an institution is truly interested in reshaping its curricular and instructional patterns, strong emphasis must be brought to bear upon the reward of those who take the initiative for the improvement. If an institution believes that it is essential to provide major emphasis upon improved instruction to balance the emphasis upon more and better research, it must introduce a clearly visible reward system. For example, at Michigan State administrative commitment has been given to the recognition of improved instruction. Modifications have been made in central administrative procedures as they relate to promotion, tenure and salary systems. Visibility and reward have been given to faculty members who have made significant contributions to instruction as well as those who made significant contributions in research. While the change agency makes no direct contribution to these modifications, its overview of the instructional process provides for ample opportunity to affect the reward system. For example, universities frequently offer distinguished faculty awards which usually go to senior research scientists. At Michigan State, there has recently been introduced an award system for both exciting young teachers and teaching assistants. These kinds of changes are shifting, albeit gradually, the attitude of the faculty to a balance between the two traditional functions of a university—teaching and research. Such a reward system is, of course, one more example of visible university-wide commitment.

Administrative Development of Communication Systems

Almost every university has a newsletter, a faculty highlights publication, or some kind of mechanism for pointing out current achievements. This is, however, not enough. Systematic communication of the change that is taking place, of the success and failure of instructional experiments, is necessary. Not only will such a system give visibility to the individual faculty, but far more important it helps to break down the disciplinary and departmental barriers to the change process. For example, at Michigan State we have found that successful multi-media laboratory techniques developed in Physiology have now been adopted in Soil Science, Nursing, Linguistics, Urban Planning, Biology, Engineering, etc. A careful internal communication system which pointed out the applicability of this technique in different disciplines was, in part, responsible for the crossing of the departmental and disciplinary barriers.

The overt communication system at Michigan State consists of two internal publications. One, EDP REPORT, which details the characteristics of various faculty projects. The second, EDP COMMENT, is a faculty forum in which new ideas and new techniques in learning, media and evaluation are discussed and frequently debated with argument and counterargument. EDP REPORT and EDP COMMENT are broadsided to the campus on a schedule of approximately one communication every three weeks.

In addition to the overt communication system, an intensive covert communication system exists. This is made possible by continuing liaison between the staff agency and the various line officers and through the device of *ex officio* positions on principal academic committees and councils with the faculty.

Ramifications of the Central Administrative Agencies in the Colleges and Departments

Since faculty innovators can be identified and the amount of change in various departments and colleges can be measured, the impact of the change agency reaches directly to the grass roots of the institution. At Michigan State, most of the relationships between the Educational Development Program and the faculty are extremely informal. They are brought about by the monitoring, evaluating and servicing of the operating projects. In addition, in several instances formal liaison has been established between the departments and the colleges and the agency by actually supporting, on a part-time basis, a liaison agent in the unit. Thus the faculty member becomes a focal point for change, readily available in the particular unit.

The Place of Educational Technology in the System of Change

This paper has concerned itself with the administrative process of bringing about change in an educational institution. It has attempted to place educational technology in its proper perspective. While it may not appear to have always been addressed directly to the subject of educational technology, almost every element of administrative reorganization is directly associated with the introduction of technology. As mentioned above, approximately ⅔ of all of the changes wrought at Michigan State have made significant use of technology. The place of technology has been assured because it has been introduced only in those instances where it fulfilled the three criteria of (1) appropriateness, (2) acceptance, and (3) cost.

By placing technology in its proper perspective as one, but only one, of the procedures to improve instruction, faculty disenchantment has largely vanished. In general, faculty has been convinced that the change agency and the Instructional Media Center believe in the improvement of instruction and will apply media only in those instances where it can solve instructional problems.

Having adhered with great care to the criterion of appropriateness, the university has been able to fulfill the second and extremely difficult criterion of acceptance. Faculty and student acceptance are genuine. Thorough evaluation of faculty and student attitudes have been rigidly coupled with each application of technology. The results of these evaluations clearly indicate that the technological applications have been successful and accepted.

Finally, new cost studies, while embryonic in form and somewhat crude in nature, relate the financial impact of technology upon the institution. While decisions concerning technology are not made on cost alone (they also include cost-quality, cost-trade off and cost-scope decisions),* cost analyses have supported the view that technology is not more expensive than other forms of quality instruction.

This paper has been devoted to the explication of an administrative reorganization model for institutional change. The model provides a major place for educational technology. The model is viable. Any institution which accepts the premise that a break with traditional instructional procedures is mandatory may profit from close examination of its characteristics.

*For details see F. Craig Johnson and John E. Dietrich, "Cost Analysis of Instructional Technology," A Paper Prepared For The Commission on Instructional Technology, October, 1968.

63.

Changes Required in Patterns Of School Organization, Management, Staffing, Facilities, and Finance for Technology to Effectively Improve Instruction

by *ROBERT M. FINLEY*
Superintendent
Glen Cove Public Schools
New York

Organization

We Now Have:

LAY PEOPLE	POLICY	TEACHERS	SUPERVISORS	ADMINISTRATORS
Aides	Board Members	Certified	Checkers	Principals
P.T.A.		By Elementary and Secondary	Evaluators	Superintendents
		By Degree		Directors

Should Go To:

COMMUNITY AIDS	DOERS	PLANNERS	TAPE CUTTERS
Citizen Committees	Teachers	Department Heads	Directors
Study Groups	Interns	Principals	Asst. Superintendents
	Lay Aides	Supervisors	Business Manager
	Para Professional		

POLICY SETTERS	POLICY DOER
Board Members	Superintendent of Schools

MECHANICAL AND TECHNICAL

A.V.	Public Relations
Art	Transportation
Clerical	Cafeteria
Electronics	Federal Programs
Supplies	

The accompanying diagram depicts the movement from the traditional to the modern approach to operating schools in a community.

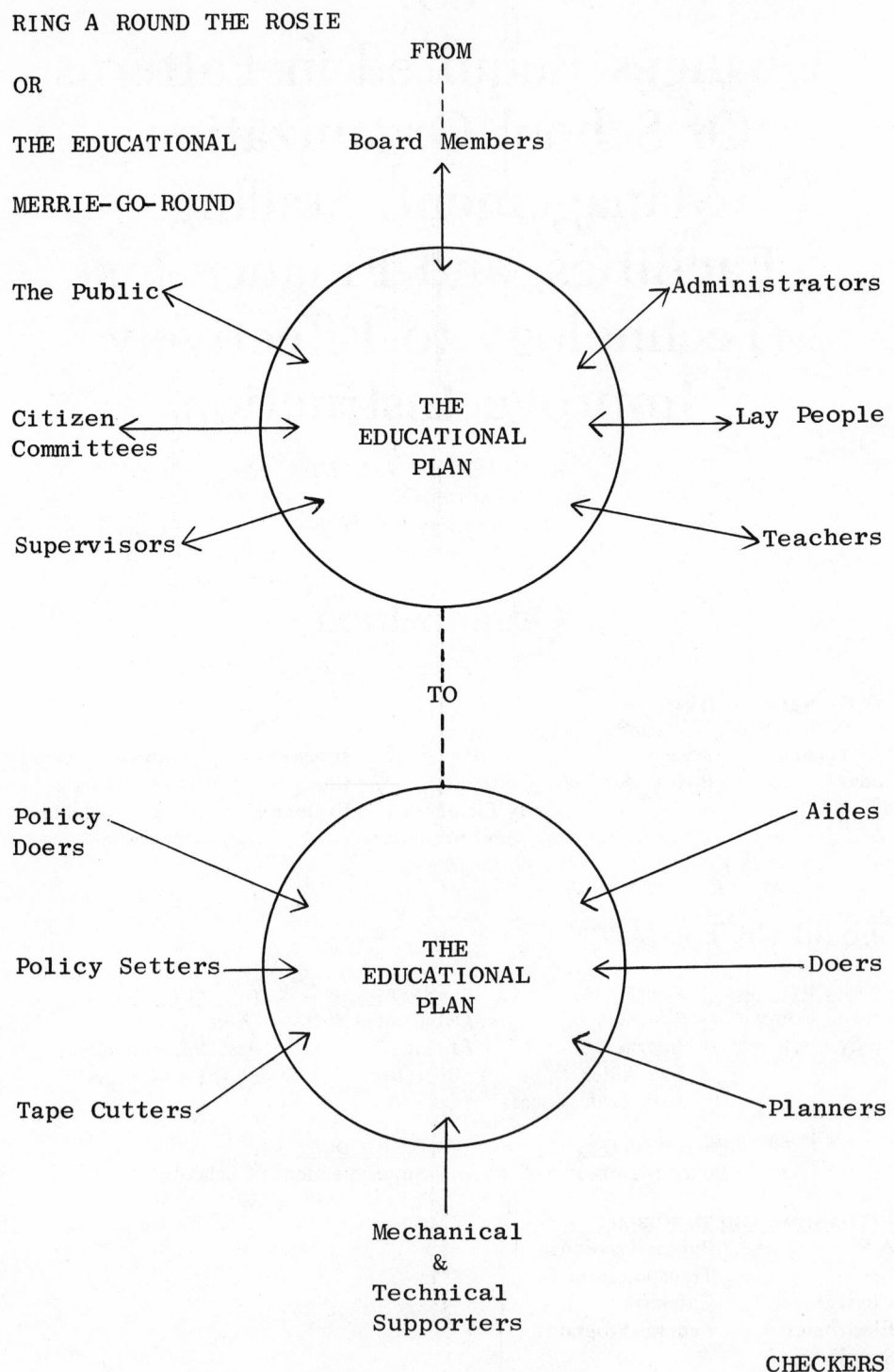

RING A ROUND THE ROSIE

OR

THE EDUCATIONAL

MERRIE-GO-ROUND

FROM

Board Members

The Public

Administrators

Citizen Committees

Lay People

Supervisors

Teachers

THE EDUCATIONAL PLAN

TO

Policy Doers

Aides

Policy Setters

Doers

THE EDUCATIONAL PLAN

Tape Cutters

Planners

Mechanical & Technical Supporters

CHECKERS (BITCHERS)

While most superintendents are not political in that the Superintendent does not run on a political ticket but in effect he is "elected" by the Board. He is also fired by the Board —in its ever-changing philosophy and desires.

The organization of schools is archaic—this is being challenged today by:

1. teacher militancy

2. Superintendent in middle

3. curriculum interest

Teachers are militant—and with good reason—because of the treatment of the past. In many ways, teachers deserved what they got—which wasn't much. In another way, the Boards of Education, acting like Industrial owners of the '20's, are getting their just returns. However, most of the blame for teacher militancy of today must be laid at the feet of the Superintendent. (I would have said "placed on the shoulders of the Superintendent," but usually in the past everything started and landed in education with the Superintendent's foot.)

The Superintendent has always seen himself in one of three positions:

1. Representative of the Board (Agent)

2. In the middle

3. Representing the teachers

Most Superintendents have allied themselves with the Board. This was natural since the Board hired and fired the Superintendent. Also the Superintendent usually carried out the policies of the Board. In the third place, the Superintendent's salary was determined by the Board. It was very natural for the Superintendent to be the lackey for the Board.

It has become quite popular lately for the Superintendent to be the "man in the middle"—since negotiations, that is. As a result of this stance, the Superintendent is nothing. He has taken the firm position of a man having his feet planted firmly in mid-air.

The third position of representing the teachers is a rare one—and one of the major reasons why we are now in such a mess. If the superintendent had represented the teachers for higher salaries and better working conditions and fought to provide teachers a chance to do the kind of job that they wanted to do—this present situation would not have occurred. Rational for this opinion is based on the fact that most superintendents were and are educators and that they should take stands when it comes to teachers—members of their own profession. Instead—lay members of the community, called Board members, ran the schools as though they understood what education was all about. It was a case of the sightless leading the seeing eye dogs. I'm afraid it is going to continue—at least until the lay Boards of Education change in makeup and the Superintendent returns to his role of Educational Leader.

Teacher training institutions are not preparing college students to enter into the world of teaching. Oh, yes, they are prepared for the 1940's, but certainly not for the 70's. The public schools have moved too quickly—and the colleges too gently.

The very graded organization from the kindergarten through the 12th grade is archaic and outdated. Although we have discussed and claimed to have "ungraded" or "nongraded" schools for 20 years—this has not happened. Schools are graded—although we know this to be educationally wrong—as an administrative convenience. Such an organizational pattern merely permits us to obtain prettier and more neat statistical tables. The question from the State Superintendent is—"How many children in the 2nd grade?" Answer —400. So what? Educationally, there is at least a four year educational span and any "second grade" teacher can attest to this. There is no such thing as a "second grade."

Such nomenclature merely provides information for census studies or reports to the country. It has nothing to do with education of children. Although it does produce beautiful, non-read statistical graphs and tables.

But how to break the line since we have been trying for 20 years and still have not ungraded? One suggestion would be the "Birthday Kindergarten." It is utterly ridiculous to stay a child's education for a year simply because he wasn't born before December 1st. Why not enter children when they reach their 5th birthday. Send them a Birthday card—and—as a gift—have them come to school. What a psychological gift. (School must be something wonderful.) As a result, children would be entering school each month—not all in September. This gradual entrance would permit us to pay more attention to small groups of children each month and therefore more reasonably plan his education. This would force an ungraded school—although I fear we would categorize the children then by months. Such as: John Jones—Primary—May 1; Sue Smith—Primary—March—3; etc.

Teachers' Negotiations

Teachers' negotiations will tend to bring about new trends in management and eventually in education. Teachers and their organizations are already demanding more voice in curriculum direction, evaluation, and actually the administration of the schools. I am not so certain they are wrong, considering the botch we are in. Since some teachers are practically receiving more money in 9½ months (per month) than many administrators, perhaps they should earn their keep in adding to the farce of school administration. It couldn't be much more of a mess with their help.

Teachers' negotiations can only lead to three logical conclusions—on the plus side.

1. A 12 month year of education

2. Merit salaries

3. Loss of tenure

If teachers thought these three outcomes would occur, I'm afraid negotiations might come to a screaming halt; but they haven't thought of these possibilities.

Why will this happen? Simple. At the present, teachers are dealing and bargaining with Board members. The public support is with the teacher—as well it should be. Teachers have been underpaid, etc., etc. However, Boards of Education are merely the controllers of funds—not the sources.

The source of the money is in the community. Since the community members are not yet aware of some of the salaries being paid for 9½ months, or 180 days, they have not reared their ugly tax heads. But this will come when the Boards can no longer come up with the demanded money—and the teachers refuse to teach. Then the news will become public that a new teacher, fresh out of college, will earn $8,000 and some teachers will get $16,000 to $20,000. When the man in the street compares this with his pay check—for 12 months—all hell will break loose.

Teachers have received support from the community because it feels sorry for them. This will disappear unless the teaching profession builds up a different image than is often depicted in The Chicago Tribune cartoon of the old maid schoolteacher on the opening day of school. The people will then demand that teachers work like other human beings—12 months or at least 11½. And then when the people discover that they really don't work 9½ months, but merely 180 days—watch the fireworks. Goodbye 2 weeks at Christmas, 1 week at Easter, all Holidays, etc. It should be an entertaining episode.

Then, also, people will question that all teachers should get the same increase merely because (1) years on the job and (2) what degree is tattooed on the forehead. This will probably lead to a form of merit salary. The good ones get more; the poor ones get less. It's the American way and it's bound to come.

It is interesting to note that in education today, teachers are asking to be paid extra for anything over and above their teaching: coaching, baton twirling, study hall, bus duty, chaperone, etc. . . . etc. . . . I am not saying this isn't right—nor wrong—but wouldn't it be interesting to see ā Board of Education grant an extra amount of money to a teacher for "a superior job of teaching?"

To have the audacity to predict that tenure will disappear in the future might be fool-hardy, but . . . the American public is a funny and often unpredictable lot. Someday, as less than average teachers (yes, we have some) keep getting better and better pay, some people of the community will demand that these teachers not be allowed to teach their children. I can't blame them. If we keep stating that education is so important, why then must we keep the incompetent? I don't want my children in the presence of a lousy teacher for a whole year. This must go—and the public will see that it does.

Yes, school organization is changing and it's about time. Changing in administration, Board relations and organization, teacher militancy, pupil grouping, and Federal, State and Community impact. The only phase of education that doesn't seem to be changing are taxes on real estate—and they really are—they're going up.

Management

When we think of management of education—particularly the public schools—we think of administration. Normally, as has been the pattern, the top of this management is the Superintendent. At least he was the top. Today changes are definitely taking place in this long cherished position. The forces causing these changes are terrific.

1. Boards of Education
2. Duties and Responsibilities
3. Lay and Citizens Groups—questionnaires
4. Politics
5. Public Relations
6. Changes in Education
7. Lack of Money
8. Paper work
9. Pressures
10. Federal programs
11. Transient teachers
12. War
13. Integration
14. Negotiations
15. Consultants

The trend is for the Superintendent, Principals, Department Heads, and Guidance personnel to form a management team and join the Board of Education and the taxpayer.

The militance of teachers has brought this about. Teachers want a piece of the action and a cut of the melon.

As has been the case for many years, the position of the Superintendent has been clear —as written—but not clear in actual practice. There is little or no doubt that the Board of Education legally has the responsibility for creating policy—and the Superintendent is blessed with the job of carrying out said policy. In brief, he has the administrative power —would that it were this simple. The problem arises in the understanding of what is policy and what is administration.

In almost any business of which I am aware, the administrative head is told what has to be done and then he is given his head to do it. If he doesn't succeed, a new man is appointed. The difference in business, however, is Evaluation. This has somehow eluded us in education. In business it is relatively easy to figure profit and loss. Not so in education. In business one can determine rather quickly if a salesman sells more or less of a product. Not so in education. In brief, business has objectives and goals that can easily be checked. Not so in education. How much did a child learn this year from this teacher? Only achievement tests tend to estimate—but we're not sure. Is this teacher (salesman) good or bad? Guess . . . Since we cannot absolutely be objective in evaluation in education, why do we keep trying. Why must we avoid subjective opinion. It is as good a criterion as any objective data that we have.

In the evaluation of the teacher we have merely added more money each year based on the number of years in the business plus the number of hours studying (more degrees). What a farce! And yet, we are deterred from using subjective opinion in determining good or bad since the association of teachers does not like or trust it. They would rather continue on the path of education for mediocrity. As someone has said—Education is the only business that when we find something is wrong or doesn't work, we continue to do it.

In some way the Superintendent must be protected from the whims of changing Board of Education members. In some way the chief administrative offices of the schools must be permitted to bring about better education without the Board of Education playing Mickey Mouse with his office. No business could long exist if it were run the way schools are. It would be bankrupt within a year. Board members must define their jobs. They must determine to stay out of education and let the Superintendent run the schools. Granted, the Board has many duties—but they are not administrative. I have found that most Board members are honest and hard working citizens. But they are too hard-working at something about which they know very little—modern education. It is true that each Board member went through school, and each is a well meaning and respected member of the community, but each member has to learn that "you can't please the community." There isn't such a thing as a community when you try to please it. There are many communities within the political boundary . . . and you can't please them all. Too many Board members want to be popular. That is not their job. Too many Board members want to "protect" the community. From what?—Higher taxes, Experimental programs in Education, Modernizing education, etc., etc. As a result of this motherly complex, we have protected the communities from excellent education.

Staffing and Facilities

For hundreds of years we have staffed schools according to the book. It hasn't worked but it has been administratively convenient. The package and the process has been very neat and convenient. It goes something like this:

STEP 1   Take the number of children in any "grade" and divide by 25 and this will tell you how many teachers you will need.
P.S. Sprinkle in a consultant or supervisor here and there.

STEP 2   Build one room 30×30 for each class. This will tell you how big the building will be—and above all the cost/square foot.

STEP 3   Build the building as cheaply as possible. The formula for this is repetition of the single unit (class) connected by hallways and stacked one upon another.

Now let us analyze the Formula.

1. What is the term "grade"? This seems to be the base for grouping children for learning. In some way this term "grade" is a magic way of putting children together because they are approximately the same age—Hogwash!
   The term "grade" is an artificial administrative convenience. It is used to inform the County or the State how many children we have in any one grade so that we can get money for each one. It has nothing to do with good education. This graded jargon begins with the kindergarten—and often the Nursery School—by setting down age criteria for entrance. For instance: To go to kindergarten, a child must be 5 years of age by December 1st. Now what does this mean? It merely suggests that a child is ready for formal education based on "how many years he has been on earth." What a base for education! By no means of the imagination could we possible assume that all 5 year olds are at the same degree of learning and readiness. As we enter children on the chronological basis, we merely instill and cement the outdated graded system. We have "talked" ungradedness and nongradedness for years—it hasn't happened and it won't as long as this entrance program continues.

2. Why the magic 25 to 1 ratio? Dr. Alvin Enrich tells me that the history of the 25-1 ratio dates back to the TALMUD before Christ. This obviously relates to the "handling" or "control" of a group of children by one person. Certainly it doesn't relate to the teaching of each of the 25. There is absolutely no evidence to show that 25 is the best size group for teaching. Rather than looking at the control or handling, why not look at what size group is best for teaching and learning. If this is done, we should then look at what we are teaching and what means of communication appears to do this best. For example:
   Investigation— 0-1—Independent Learning—Contract
                  1-1—Guided—Individualized
                  1-(6-8)—Discussion
                  1-(12-15)—Decision Making
               Large—One way communication
                    Stimulation
   If this is true, then we must take a look at staffing in order to bring this about. In interviewing teachers, we usually look for which "grade" the teacher wants to teach. We never ask:

   1. Do you work better with fast or slow children? mature or immature?

   2. Are you better working with large groups? small groups? individuals?

   3. Are you better at discussion? lecturing? or face to face?

   No, we ask what do you teach and they say 3rd grade. Rarely do we ask: What do you like to teach and what don't you like. No one can teach all areas in a superior fashion. I would want a teacher to say:

   1. I work best with small children

2. I work best with discussion groups

3. I like math best—hate English

I would have the teacher work in a team, teaching the sharper kids in discussion groups (6-8) in the field of mathematics. This would be her main responsibility. Not one grade, however. We must instill the idea that "if you don't like what you teach, don't teach." You won't fool the children. We administrators must create an atmosphere that will permit teachers and children to make mistakes. If mistakes are not made, then we are not trying anything.

Some people would surmise that we would not then teach the basics—not so. Basics or fundamentals should and must be taught to most children in the first 4 or 5 years of school. The next 3 years should be exploratory years followed by the directional years of the high school.

Somehow we must tear ourselves away from "preparing" kids for the Middle School, the High School, or for College. This philosophy is backwards. For too many years the curriculum has come from the top—that is, the University has said to the High School—you must teach thus and thus, the High School pass the word to the Junior High, saying such and such was necessary in order to succeed in "our" High School. Naturally, the Junior High School gave the word to the elementary schools. In other words, we are preparing the kids for the most conglomerate of grades, rather than having the High School change its curriculum to meet the needs of the incoming students. The order of the day has been "let's fit the kids into our schools" rather than fitting the school to the kids. It's easier but the day is coming. As a result of this stagnant thinking, we don't have "drop outs" today—we have "push outs."

Facilities

From the days of the Old Quincy School to the present, buildings for educational purposes have not really changed too much. In most of these monuments to mediocrity we still figure the superiority of each building by how many kids we can cram into the least amount of space; the square foot cost; etc. . . . etc. . . .

It is amazing that most businesses build a building and then proceed to advertise how expensive an edifice was. In education we are expected to brag about how cheap the building is into which we are to thrust and trust our most prized possessions—our children —and our school buildings look like it. They are cheap. Rarely do they do the job because the bonding power isn't enough to build the space that we really need. Rarely do we build until the present building is overly-packed with children and by the time the new one has survived the scars of cutting and skimping, it is almost filled.

Sometimes I think we should build 3 types of school buildings:

1. One that will automatically level itself at the stroke of midnight 25 years after being built.

2. The Bathtub School—that is one that you pull the stopper and the whole thing goes down the drain.

3. The building that can later be sold to business, etc. . . .

Using buildings, as we are today, that are 75 to 100 years old, is a disgrace to the community and its "pride" in education. Perhaps we should tear them all down, paint each brick gold, and attach a sprig of ivy to each and console each tax payer who attended "good old Main Street" by giving this mantel piece to each.

Buildings being erected today should be so built to protect the community in the future. Like most other businesses, education is changing, whether we like it or not. Schools of the future must be able to accept new ideas, new physical features, etc. Only if we build modular, clear space, fluid, organismic buildings can this be possible. Educators of the future must not be stuck with 20% of the building in halls; cracked asphalt, vinyl, or terrazo floors that have stood the test of time. Each building must be built for air conditioning since schools will be used year round. If the population continues as it has—and there seems no let up—perhaps we better build the roofs of these schools so that they may handle large helicopters. Certainly buses will not do the job in the future—if we want children there on time.

Much better thinking must be considered for the future in building schools. No longer can we merely build them as cheap as possible. Such building just doesn't pay—it never has. Few people realize that the cheapest part of education is the building—operation is where the money goes.

Finance

And finally, we come to the name of the game . . . money. In the past we have suffered under the delusion that we have "free public education." Nothing could be further from the truth. Free, merely means that we are free to go to school—but that's about it. Education is, and should be, costly. In fact, it is going to be more costly. If so, where will the money come from? In the past, local real estate taxes have paid the bill. Time is growing short for this method. The State and the Federal Governments are both moving in. Involved in this change is the fear of "loss of local control." There is little doubt that this is a vital concern; but the local community deserves to lose this control if the result of local control is the type of education resulting today. The local community with few exceptions has not done the job, mainly because the people of the community have not held education in high esteem. Therefore, they have not financially supported the venture. Witness low teacher salaries, dilapidated buildings and 20 year old textbooks. This can no longer be tolerated and, in fact, it won't be. But, can the local community face the increase—and do they want to? In 8 out of 10 cases, the answer is "NO." Therefore, enter State and Federal saviors. How it will be done is anybody's guess. But it will be done. It should be interesting.

With the foregoing as a preface:

What and where is the place of Practical Application of Technology in Public School Education?

Naturally, if you tend to agree with the above mentioned thoughts—without changes in structure, weight, organization, personnel, etc.—there can be no practical application of Technology. To be applicable and better education, certain things must change in order that technology enter the school and the classroom.

Curriculum
Finance
Personnel—(lay people)
Leadership
Control
Boards of Education
Viewpoint—Education to Business viewpoint
Evaluation—(profit motive)
Cost control

Cooperation—(public schools and colleges)
Maturation (we are in 20th century—helicopters, traffic, food, freedom)
Research
Break the mold—(Kindergarten, 12 months, merit, incentive)

How can instructional technology be best used in schools to meet the needs of each individual student for learning experiences truly relevant to their interest, concerns, and aspirations? A good question but a very complicated answer.

First, a little history that has to play a big part in any future use of technology in the schools. Technology is not new in the schools, contrary to much modern day thinking. In fact, what is new in the schools? I quote a modern statement uttered about 350 years before Christ by a man by the name of Plato:

> "Education and admonition commence in the first years of childhood, and last to the very end of life. Mother and nurse and father and tutors are vying with one another about the improvement of the child as soon as ever he is able to understand what is being said to him." (Dialogues of Plato, Protagoras)

I believe that we have been hearing the same words today. So . . . what of the latest utterances pertaining to technology in the schools? Is it true that big business has seen the light that education is big business and the great commercial groups of the country are pushing their products? This is true and yet how successful will this venture be if the fine products in the process of being turned out will not be turned on in the classroom? Do you remember when the first photograph entered the classroom? Neither do I, but I would venture to say that it was looked upon as being too expensive to buy the camera and the film, and what could the photo do that an art teacher couldn't. Yet today, almost every school has a camera—gathering dust when it could be used much better. Next recollection of course was the entrée of the victrola, better known as the phonograph. The same human cry went up then as we hear today. "The machine is fine but there aren't enough good records." Today, every elementary room is equipped with a phonograph, which of course is rarely used because of newer pieces of equipment—which are rarely used. As an aftermath of the War (which one I can't remember), the movie projector made its entrance into the school. Not the classroom, mind you, but the school . . . system. Gradually we have now a projector or two in each school, but the same human cry comes about. "If I can get someone to thread it and run it, fine . . . ; however, the films come late because we have to order them a year or two in advance, and when they come, we have already studied the subject or are not ready for the film." Very poor coordination. Teachers have never learned to use the projector and they are afraid of this little device. No wonder the colleges don't give a course that is mandatory in audiovisual aids, and these courses, if included in the colleges, are usually voluntary. How many States make this course mandatory? Very few. So the movie projector, as great as it may be, is not used correctly and the films are rarely previewed by the user. In brief, the movie today is sort of a breather for many "teachers" and the first showing of the film is as new to the teacher as it is to the children.

Remember the wire recorder? What a breakthrough. Then the tape? Also, remember we had one for each school district, also. Now we have one or two per school but usually few tapes. And again, find a teacher who could master the techniques of threading the device.

Enter the age of the slide and strip film projectors. Much hailed and greatly overused . . . and still the software was and is inadequate.

The language lab made its debut and everyone got on the band wagon. Most schools bought up the equipment as soon as Uncle Sam footed the bill. We felt that we needed language labs so badly that we rushed into the language lab with great gusto. Oh, of course, the public helped us so that we could begin teaching French in the first grade. Well, the lab was placed in the high school, and, of course, in a soundproof room, carrels, etc. . . . then we put ear muffs, ear phones on each child as if we needed them. After a few years, we have found the language lab to be a very expensive, seldom-used, educational toy. What next?

Now, we are playing with TV videotape recorders and waiting with baited breath for the computer. More of the same, no doubt.

The point that is being made is that no matter what the technological breakthrough that enters the school, there is always one deterrent to its success . . . the human being. The teacher, the principal, the parent. There is little doubt that technology is on its way; the problem will be—will we be ready for it . . . ever?

Now, we are caught in the middle. On the one hand large business firms are in the process of turning out technological advancements which, if used properly, could enhance our educational product. On the other hand, educators are screaming about individualized teaching and meeting the needs of the individual student, and yet the school people are ignorant about the use of this very advancement.

Technology in the schools will come. Some of it is with us in some schools now. More will follow. Several facets must be discussed if true use is to be made of this event.

1. What will come?

2. How should it be received?

3. What are the deterrents to success?

4. What are the advantages of further technology in the schools?

5. What are the steps toward providing a framework for successful introduction of technology to teachers in the schools?

What Will Come?

Without doubt the technological advancement within the schools will come with electronic devices. The main difference with these devices of the future will be that not too much software will be necessary, as in the past. By that, I mean that much of the input into the devices will come from the air or by wire. For instance, I believe that communication centers are needed in each school. I am not speaking of Learning centers nor Resource centers, but, instead, a center that would include the communications emanating from the outside world. If one stops to think of it, the school is the only institution or business that has little or no communication with the outside world. Unless a secretary has sneaked the radio on, there is no outside input of news. The school, which should be one of the first to know, is usually the last. Therefore, we are looking to the communications center which would include:

1. A large news map of the world. Much like the maps on TV during political elections. These maps should be complete with lights and flash news happenings as they occur for all to see. A newspaper could be printed for the people of the school as the news events happen.

2. A ticker tape to bring the news direct should be in operation. This could and should be a teletype machine with wire service.

3. A complete teletype bringing the world weather reports.

4. Radios which bring overseas foreign language programs.

5. TV tuned to constant news media.

6. Ear phones for listening to the broadcasts.

7. Either in the center or on the front of the building, a moving news ribbon, much like that in Times Square. This would keep the people up to date in the school and certainly broadcast the events of the school and community on the outside.

School Tie-Ups

In the future the schools should be tied together by either waves or wires for instant communications. This should be spread throughout the community for such events as closing schools, etc. . . . This is a real need.

TV

Although we have played with TV in the schools, we have not been sophisticated enough to really use this piece of equipment to the best results. Far better has this device been used in the home. The reason for this, of course, is that the home is not on a schedule, or can change its schedule, while the school tries to work the TV into its schedule. If the school schedule remains so tight, the TV cannot be worked into it. The schedule of the school must become flexible like the home if this piece of equipment is to be used. Of course, the videotape recorder is coming into its own, if we can train the teachers how to use it. We should look for TV tapes not only being used in the school but sent home to be attached to the TV set and played like a film on a projector.

Bus Education

A child spends much time on the bus these days . . . doing what? Why not take the idea from the commercial air lines and show educational TV or films on the bus. Even audio tapes would work.

Individualized Scheduling

One of the biggest booms to education would be the perfection of the computer that could schedule students individually, every day; not each year.

We must move to the individualized, smorgasbord curriculum and this can only be done with the aid of the computer. Granted this cannot be done yet, but if we can send three men around the moon, we certainly ought to be able to schedule a high school each day.

Summer Education

Electronics should endeavor to provide the students with summer education based on individualized cassettes, either film, audio, or TV. Very few teachers would be needed and the education would be set in action with the constant use of the very equipment that lays stagnant each summer.

How Should These New Devices Be Received?

Undoubtedly, the success of technology in the public schools in the future depends upon the acceptance and training of the personnel in the colleges and universities. We can train the personnel in the schools but this is temporary. This job should be done before the teacher comes to the school. This is our big problem today. The teacher comes fresh out of college without the least possible notion what team teaching, ungraded, etc, is. They must be taught in college, but the college prof must be first and this is a monumental task since most profs have all the answers now.

Once the teachers coming into the schools are taught, then constant in-service training throughout the calendar year must be brought about. Not just during the year, but also in the summer. This has to be done if we are to keep up with even later technological breakthroughs.

Reallocate Funds

Many people insist that money will not be available for this technological innovation. We must study the budget and reallocate some of the money that is not being spent well. Granted, that this means playing with about 20% of the budget, since the rest is in personnel. However, we may have to get along with fewer people in order to do the job.

It should be helped that the teachers will not fight this technological advancement, but they probably will since they will liken it to automation and possible loss of jobs. This should not be the threat since the teacher is indispensable. Some teachers, that is. The possible threat to the teacher will bring to their attention that only good teachers will be employed in the future.

More Men and Technicians

Since most women, and especially young girls, are deathly afraid of anything that moves mechanically, more men must be brought into the field of teaching. This should not be too difficult since the salaries are beginning to get competitive. Along with teachers of the male gender, we must begin hiring technicians instead of more teachers.

What Are the Deterrents to Success?

Cost: While I have talked of reallocating funds to meet the cost of these technological devices, the problem will be the original cost of each item until they become numerous enough to be cheap. The same happened to the video tape recorder and other devices. Somehow, some way must be found to make the objects reasonable for the schools. Some subsidizing might have to be used to do this such as the language lab.

Parent: Parent groups will naturally look askance at such innovations, as they have in the past with modern math, team teaching, etc. . . . Let anyone state that the little darling will not have the total attention of a mother hen for six hours a day and all hell will break loose. Together with these gripes will come the John Birch Society and the like, with the scream for return to the McGuffey reader, motherhood, and the flag . . . but not of the technological variety.

School Cooperation: Undoubtedly, at the start, no individual school will be able to do the job alone. They must cooperate and share. This will be a problem since each school likes to retain its individuality. Perhaps some of this individuality will have to be sacrificed in order to take advantage of the technological gains.

Buildings: Some of our antiquated buildings will need some going over in order to bring about conditions that will permit the use of technology. This will not be as important as the change in people, however.

Administrators and Boards: The real key to the implementation of newer thoughts and instruments of better education rests with the administrators and the Boards. The Superintendent is the real mover, and without his foresight and planning, we can be assured that the Boards will not move. Administrators must begin now to become educated as to the use and employment of these newer techniques. This is a must.

What Are the Further Advantages of Technology in the Schools?

Individualized Instruction: This has to come about. Something that we have been talking about for fifty or sixty years but haven't attained. Technology can bring this about.

More Kids, Fewer Teachers: With the cost of education going up, primarily because of teachers' salaries, something has to give. I believe that we will have to educate more children with fewer teachers because of the cost. Technology must be the answer.

Cover More in Less Time: Because of better planning and convenience in technology and not being so dependent on the teacher, we will and must cover more knowledge in less time.

Less Space: As we individualize and introduce technology, we will need less space in order to achieve more. All children will not have to be in classes nor come to school at the same time therefore saving the need to build more buildings and space.
   Year round, or extended schools, will evolve.

Standardized Minimums and Standards: Through technology better standards will evolve and comparisons will be more easily made. This could introduce a national minimum curriculum.

Immediate Testing and Evaluations in Less Time: Computerized testing and evaluation could be done in less time and more accurately, also bring about diagnostic testing.

What Are the Steps Toward Providing a Framework for Successful Introduction of Technology to Teachers in the Schools?

1. With Federal backing, set up about six pilot schools throughout the country where teachers can see the results.

2. Train the college and university teachers.

3. Have the business people educate the trainees.

4. Take time to have teachers understand the reasons before putting the technology into the schools.

5. Educate the parents before using technology.

6. Run pilot schools with the district before all schools.

7. Involve all schools.

Technology must come. It is inevitable as stated above. When and how soon is not the question. Why is the answer. We must now begin training and educating people why this must come. It is none too soon.

64.

Production Facilities Needed In a University to Satisfy Instructional Technology Requirements

by *CHARLES F. SCHULLER*
Director
Instructional Media Center
Michigan State University

From the vantage point of a large multi-university where over the past four years extensive, and highly effective efforts have been made to systematically design and carry through new undergraduate courses of instruction including production of required instructional materials, two conclusions are inescapable: The first is that higher education's needs for improved undergraduate programs and materials of instruction cannot be adequately met by institutions undertaking individually and independently to do the job. The second conclusion is that for an institution to attempt to do so independently can only result in waste of valuable time and human and financial resources which the nation can ill afford.

Coordinated Efforts Essential

The answer lies in coalitions of institutions, professional associations, regional production centers, and, perhaps, industries in which the combined efforts and expertise of all concerned can be coordinated and focused on common needs. It is generally recognized that technological hardware and circuitry are far advanced beyond the capacity of either education or industry to supply the essential programs without which technology has little meaning or consequence. For institutions, however prestigious, to attempt to solve all of their software production needs locally and in isolation is both self-defeating and abortive of higher education's present day resources and responsibilities.

Many problems stand in the way of the coordinated effort envisioned above. Not the least of these problems is the traditional separatism of institutions and the freedom of individual faculty member to deal with his particular disciplines as he sees fit. On the other hand, optimum instructional systems, by definition, are highly flexible and adaptable to local needs and the professor and student are built into the system. It must be the professors and their associates who make content determinations and who write the programs if programs are to be written. Furthermore, it is the departments and professors who, in the final analysis, both select the programs and the materials they will use and decide how they will use them. Finally, it would appear, that a relatively small proportion of the total course offerings of any institution is likely to be systematically programmed for some years to come. The above problems, do appear solvable.

Even if the proposed coordinated inter-institutional production system eventuates, there will still be a need on individual college and university campuses for production centers to accommodate a variety of local instructional needs. The balance of this paper is addressed to these centers, the facilities required, and to several factors which can significantly influence their effectiveness.

Factors Influencing Production Requirements

Nature of Faculty Use of Media

The nature and extent of production facilities required in an institution are dependent on the level and amout of media use being made by the faculty. Finn cites six levels of possible use ranging from a relatively simple "tool" level to a fairly sophisticated and complex "systems" level in which media become totally integrated and essential components of the system. (Finn, 1966) The more sophisticated the level of use, the more varied and extensive are production requirements.

Existing levels of faculty use are not, of course, the same for all faculty members at any given time nor can it be assumed that levels of sophistication and use will very long remain at the present level. Thus, while a production facility may be fairly modest in the beginning, it would be a mistake not to plan sufficient flexibility for subsequent development and expansion. This paper assumes a middle ground in which sufficient capacity is available for current needs plus reasonable possibilities for expansion.

Another assumption is that use will be made of commercial technical services whenever practicable. As an example, there is little point to an institution providing its own motion picture developing and printing facilities so long as these services are readily and quickly available commercially. Such services are purely technical and are performed on standard specifications. Further, these services are highly competitive and can normally be secured at substantially less cost than would be required for a university to provide its own.

Administrative and Organizational Influences

Other factors influencing the kinds and amounts of faculty use of technology and, consequently, the level of production capacity required are discussed in other papers prepared for the Commission. (e.g., Dietrich and Johnson, 1968) Some of these related factors are indicated here in order to assure a contextual base on which university production facilities may be considered.

1. *The institution has a climate in which innovation and instructional improvement are encouraged.*

The degree to which innovation and improved instruction are genuinely encouraged has a direct bearing on the amount and sophistication of production likely to be required for instructional purposes. Since production operations require substantial expenditures both initially and operationally, faculty and administrative commitment and support are necessary. This support should be based on a commitment, not to production per se but to the concept of instructional development and the needed changes and services necessary to bring it about.

On-going production costs may be fully subsidized by funds budgeted by the university to the production center as is normally the case with CCTV and computer operations in which operational costs are too high to be paid by production charges against academic department budgets. Ideally the same principle *should* apply to costs of production of instructional films, graphics, still photography and recorded materials. In practice, however, the latter costs are commonly charged, at least in part, to departments requesting them. In either case the costs are there and must be supported.

At this point, it might be observed that the only legitimate reason for producing teaching materials within an institution is to improve the effectiveness of teaching and learning. If such materials are determined as being needed (within a system of functional priorities) the fewer roadblocks put in the way of their procurement, the better. Cost is clearly a deterrent, particularly if charged against departmental budgets. Even worse, however, is a system in which some production services are ostensibly "free." This frequently may lead to media choices because they are "free" rather than because they are right for the job.

2. *Production facilities are part of a centrally coordinated organization of instructional services.*

A central organization of instructional services to assist academic departments in improving educational programs is another reflection of administrative commitment. These services include professional assistance in planning, development, and evaluation of new or revised instructional programs; the provision of learning resources including needed equipment, media systems, and materials of various types; and, the provision of the technical assistance required to make the technology and related materials readily and easily available to the faculty.

As a rule most, though not all, of the above services are provided through a media center having a library of instructional films, sound tapes, videotapes, and similar learning resources; a considerable variety of projection, recording and public address equipment and operator services; and production facilities for still and motion pictures, sound recordings, graphics, and closed circuit television. (Johnson and Swiger, 1968) Assistance with computer programming and programmed instruction are increasingly provided by such centers. Open circuit TV and radio services are normally separate operations not directly related to campus instruction.

The range and complexity of the above services obviously suggests immediately the importance of a central organization for the university as a whole, both to avoid costly duplication of facilities and to make possible the employment of professional staff members who are competent educators as well as experts in one or more aspects of educational technology. As technological systems develop on large campuses, there is justification for subcenters in individual colleges for additional faculty services including simple production services. All such units, however, should be coordinated so as to be mutually complementary, rather than duplicating, in the services provided.

3. *Provisions are made for stimulating faculty interest and competence in instructional uses of technology.*

Faculty members in colleges and universities have normally secured their advanced degrees with little, if any, preparation or prior experience in the art and practices of effective instruction. Further, promotions and salary increases are far more likely to be awarded on the basis of research and scholarly writing than for good teaching. Under these long-standing and traditional conditions in higher education, it is not surprising that high quality instruction has typically received little emphasis (or reward) in colleges and universities. For the same reasons, in most institutions, faculty acceptance of educational technology has tended to be slow and of limited effectiveness unless conditions were present to bring about a change in faculty attitudes.

One such favorable condition has been the presence on a number of campuses of media centers which provided campus-wide services of various types normally including one or more forms of production. Some of these centers have been staffed by educators of unusual competence both in teaching methods and media. These individuals have worked with faculties over a considerable period of years on resolving instructional problems in which media application could be helpful.* Unfortunately, the majority of colleges and universities have been without the benefits of enlightened and competent media services and are only now beginning to look seriously at the learning and instructional potential of educational technology.

Another major factor in instructional development in recent years has been the passage of educational legislation incorporating an emphasis on the new educational media and materials. While much of this legislation, beginning with the National Defense Education Act of 1958, was aimed at improvements in elementary and secondary schools, higher education institutions soon became involved in conducting Institute programs for improving elementary and secondary teaching in an increasing number of academic areas. Hundreds of directors of such Institutes in higher education institutions across the country have attended one or more of the Special Media Institutes.** There, in concentrated five day sessions, distinguished professors from 14 disciplines had their first opportunity [in most cases] to experience the potentialities of media in their own disciplines and to sample a variety of materials and techniques which could be used in the Institute programs they would subsequently conduct.

Title VI-A of the Higher Education Act has provided a good start on supplying much needed instructional equipment and materials (including production equipment) for higher institutions and Title III of that Act has provided substantial additional help for small developing institutions. It would also be difficult to overestimate the impact of Title VI-B of the Higher Education Act of 1965 under which over 90 institutes in Educational Media and Instructional Development have supplied new insights for approximately 4,000 college and university professors in a wide range of disciplines.

If we may assume that the conditions warranting media production facilities in a higher education institution can be met, it is necessary to consider requirements of the several kinds of production needed in a complete program. These types include closed circuit television, a computer system, film production, graphics production (including still photography), tape recording and playback distribution, and language laboratories.

Closed Circuit Television

The principal purpose of a Closed Circuit Television unit in a university is to help the faculty produce and to distribute effective instructional programs for substantial numbers of students. CCTV can also provide unique instructional benefits to either small or large groups of students through such capabilities as magnification, immediate playback, split screen, and other optical treatments.

*Among the institutions with centers having campus-wide orientation plus the staff and facilities to do significant work in instructional improvement are Michigan State University, Syracuse University, The University of Iowa, The University of Indiana, The University of Wisconsin, San Jose State College, The University of Nebraska, Wayne State University, and The University of Colorado. Representative smaller institutions with highly effective programs include Miami University at Oxford, Ohio, Kent University, The University of Massachusetts, and Stephens College. Centers such as these have been able over a considerable period of years to build a strong nucleus of faculty interest and acceptance not only of media use in instruction but, also, in varying degrees, of the principles of instructional development on a fairly sophisticated plane. In a real sense, they built part of the foundation on which recent forward thrusts in educational technology in higher education have been made.

**The Special Media Institute [SMI] program was conducted from 1965 to 1969 under the direction of the late Dr. James D. Finn of the University of Southern California at that institution and at Michigan State University, the Teaching-Research Division of the Oregon System of Higher Education, and at Syracuse University. The SMI program is now under the direction of Dr. Charles F. Schuller at Michigan State University.

Distribution Facility

A modern distribution facility for a university CCTV unit should include:

1. A transmission system (preferably in full color);

2. A minimum six-channel capacity;

3. Sufficient flexibility and staff to permit scheduling from early morning to late at night;

4. Coaxial cable connections to all principal classrooms, laboratories, and dormitories;

5. Capability for adaptation to individual carrel and random access systems when these become practicable.

Production Facility

A minimum production facility for support of a university CCTV service at the above level should consist of one studio, 40'x50', preferably equipped for color and staffed by key personnel with MA degrees. The Director, preferably a Ph.D. should have a good grasp of Instructional Development principles, at the higher education level, as well as of media applications generally. Depending upon the size of the CCTV operation, he should have one or more supervisory assistants in charge of operations including scheduling, production, engineering, videotaping and replay.

A system of the type described above, in color, would cost $500,000 to $750,000 in 1969 for space and equipment, $1,000 per classroom for reception, and $150,000 to $200,000 per year for staffing and operation. A black and white installation would cost approximately $240,000 less. (See Attachment on Cost Summary)

In addition to a central CCTV system, portable CCTV systems for departmental use in research and teaching activities are important adjuncts. The representative functions that can be served by portable TV systems include the following:

1. Mirror television: making it possible for the individual performer in such areas as speech, music, counseling, and teaching to see his own performance at an acceptable picture quality level.

2. Storage of visual patterns observed in real life such as animal behavior, child behavior in classrooms, public behavior, teaching behavior, and research equipment readings.

3. Training of students and faculty in televised communication such as courses in broadcasting, inquiry and expression, instructional media, communications theory, and others in which students communicate with each other by preparing televised reports. Equipment should be capable of flexibility and should include switching devices, talk-back lines, cameras with view-finders, etc., as well as editing capabilities in the recorder.

The cost level of the above three levels of sophistication will probably center around $1,000, $6,000, and $15,000, respectively.

Levels of Production Need

The volume and quality of local production and distribution requirements is determined by size of enrollment, extent of need, and availability of funds. It is neither necessary nor practical for every institution to undertake production of all of its own instructional programs as is still commonly attempted. A cooperative plan under which regional centers produce quality courses in basic areas of the undergraduate curriculum is as viable for CCTV as it is for broadcast television particularly with the wide range of use patterns employed in effective CCTV instruction.*

The smaller and less affluent institutions will likely be the first to break the classic mold of academic self-sufficiency in order to add new elements and quality to their curriculums. Others will follow, for no institution, as stated earlier, can effectively meet all of its instructional programming needs independently any more than it can produce all of its own text and reference materials. Effective use of limited available funds, time and faculty talents are even more persuasive reasons for avoiding wasteful duplication of instructional programming efforts. (Johnson and Dietrich, 1968)

This is not to say that any college or university can afford to be totally without CCTV production capacity. Very small institutions can probably meet most of their local needs with portable equipment. Somewhat larger institutions will require at least some distribution and studio facilities in order to realize many of the substantial instructional benefits available through CCTV. Institutions with large undergraduate enrollments stand, in addition, to pass up significant and cumulative cost benefits unless they get into the CCTV business.

Computer Instruction Facilities

The Rosser Report which indicated in 1966 that while like any new tool, the computer has been "over-promoted, abused, and misused" and that a great gap exists in the training needed by both faculty and students in computer use, nonetheless predicted a doubling of computer capacities on U.S. campuses by 1968. (Rosser, 1966) Subsequent reports in 1967 by the President's Science Advisory Committee (Pierce, 1967) and The American Council on Education (Caffrey and Mossman, 1967) supported both the need and the anticipated growth predicted in the earlier study. Consensus is that the computer is here to stay and its uses in higher education research, administration, and instruction may be expected to multiply in the years ahead. It is, accordingly, appropriate and necessary to deal with computers among the production facilities a university needs in order to satisfy its instructional technology requirements.

Since computers are expensive [compared to most instructional equipment] and are comparatively recent additions on the educational scene, it may be helpful to note certain considerations with respect to financing computer acquisitions and certain data on their current cost effectiveness in instruction.

Lease versus Purchase

The question of "lease versus purchase" has many facets. Typically, an institution may go the lease route when it is unsure of the extent and nature of the uses which will be made of the computer. Studies at Michigan State University (which has one of the larger installations among universities) indicates that its CDC 3600 purchased in 1963 would have cost an additional half-million dollars on a lease basis over a five-year period. A CDC 6500 now being acquired would cost from one-half to three-quarters of a million dollars more

---

*At Michigan State Univ. which has the largest CCTV system in the nation, use patterns range from single periods per week in a four hour course to total courses via TV. The faculty in all cases determines the nature and extent of use.

via lease at the end of five years depending upon the computer's resale value at that time. An additional factor is that although it is still common practice to depreciate computers over a five-year period, actual obsolescence is not that rapid; a more realistic depreciation period may be eight (8) or even ten (10) years. Thus, unless lease rates are adjusted accordingly, this situation reflects another consideration favoring purchase rather than lease.

Whether leased or purchased, however, large computers represent an expenditure well beyond the normal capability of most institutional budgets. There is a consensus among the various Study Commissions that substantial new sources of funds are necessary if the significant instructional potentials of computers in higher education are to be realized on American campuses. This conclusion also assumes the development of large central educational computing facilities located and equipped so as to be capable of serving a number of other smaller colleges and universities in a geographic area. The Pierce Report proposes interactive remote consoles in smaller institutions as the most practical and desirable means of providing necessary computer services: (Pierce, 1967)

> "One can visualize not only typewriterlike terminals in using areas, but also high-speeder readers and printers, graphical display devices, and small peripheral computers which store data and process it to some extent but call on the central computer for difficult processing and computation. Such terminals and problem-oriented languages and compilers open a whole vista of possibilities for university computation utilizing a central processor and time sharing."

Cost Effectiveness

Currently, computer technology has far greater application in research and administration than in instruction. Most analysts predict, however, that within the next decade or so a majority of college students will receive instruction on uses of the computer in their respective disciplines and that within two decades, the computer will be used extensively for individualized instruction in a variety of fields: (Rosove, 1968)

> "The Learning Resources Center may be comprised of various types of 'systems' by means of which the learners 'switch' themselves into sources of information. Such learning resources as teaching machines, computer-assisted instruction, computerized library information systems, closed circuit television systems, etc. will in 20 years be the basic tools of the learning facilitator (teacher)."

Computer-assisted instruction (CAI) is currently faced with costs which are excessive compared with other forms of instruction. An in-house study at Michigan State University comparing relative costs of CAI and SLATES (a scientifically designed system for individualized instruction in carrels) and CCTV showed CAI running about 8.5 times as expensive as a SLATE and as much as 26 times the cost of closed circuit television even when the assumptions (identical number of student stations) clearly penalized CCTV severely. Other studies show present computer costs—when divided by the total enrollment—to be comparable to annual library and freshman chemistry laboratory costs per student. (Pierce, 1967) It is evident that a combination of increasing demand and lower costs will be necessary before CAI can be integrated into the instructional program. The question actually becomes primarily one of how soon sufficient additional subsidies can be inserted into the higher education system and how rapidly computer costs can be reduced through competition and mass use.

Space Requirements

Space and facilities requirements vary widely in terms of the size and complexity of computer operations. A large installation such as that at Michigan State University requires approximately 2,000 sq. ft. of machine room space. A small installation would take about 500 sq. ft. of machine room space and a medium size installation approximately 1,500 sq. ft. Medium and large installations will take about one and a half times the machine room space for auxiliary equipment and five times the machine room space for offices, classrooms and storage. As in other types of media operations, storage is a critical and neglected factor.

Specialized Requirements

There are few specialized requirements, for computer equipment other than air-conditioning and acoustical control to contain the noise of equipment operation. Computer equipment requires controls to hold the temperature to 75 degrees and the humidity to 50%. (EEL, 1967) This is important not only to preserve the equipment but also [and more significantly] to preserve the magnetic tapes which tend to change their operational characteristics at extremely high or low temperatures. A highly efficient filtration system for dust removal is necessary in order to protect the reliability of magnetic reading and recording systems.

Computer equipment operates on normal 115 volt AC current. There is no problem here other than the number of circuits required which must be determined in terms of the equipment to be installed. For a typical load, EFL recommends provision of 20 KVA at 175 amps with protection against current surges of more than 5 to 10 percent. (EFL, 1967) Suffice it to say, it is simpler and less costly to supply a sufficient number of separate circuits and conduits when a building is being constructed than it is to install them later.

Another specialized requirement is the necessity for a 12″ to 15″ raised floor in the machine room to accommodate cables, air-conditioning ducts, and similar facilities.

Film Production Facilities

Universities rely on the motion picture medium to: (1) *record* visual motion and sound for purposes of observation, analysis, and documentary record in all areas of visible phenomena; (2) to *reproduce or play back* ("project") such recorded materials; and (3) to *select, organize and structure* ("edit") such recorded materials (i.e., shots, scenes) into films for instructional communication purposes. Essentially a motion picture facility *produces* required visual motion/sound programs (i.e., films).

Certain purely technical services—developing and printing—are unnecessary on a university campus since they are available commercially at reasonable cost and prohibitively expensive for an institution to provide for itself.

Shooting (Cinematography and Sound Recording)

The following representative camera equipment is recommended for the kinds of work normally expected of a good university film unit:

1. Studio camera systems for lip sync (e.g., blimped Mitchell, blimped Arriflex, Auricon 1200 self-blimped);

2. Field/location cameras (e.g., Eclair sync system w/Nagra recorder, Arriflex, Bolex, etc.);

3. Single-system sound cameras (e.g., Auricon 1200);

4. Middle-speed (to 500 frames per second) camera system (e.g., Millikan 16, Mitchell hi-speed 16);

5. High-speed (3000 fps on up) camera (e.g., Fastax-types);

6. Microcinematography systems (e.g., B.&H.);

7. Conventional animation system (e.g., Oxberry 16 or 35).

Along with the above cameras, certain accessory gear is necessary including tripods, dollies, and other equipment to anchor, stabilize, or allow various types of camera movement (such as shoulder harnesses, specialized camera mounts, hydraulic dollies, etc.). Basic lighting equipment includes conventional lights, fiber lights, standards, scrims, flags, cookies; cables and connectors and control panels; lenses, filters, shades, and masks. Recording accessories and units should include microphones, booms, pick-up systems, suppressors, equalizer and reverberator, various recording and playback units and other sound control components.

The precise items to be procured depend upon numerous local factors including the volume of filming anticipated, the nature of the subjects or events to be filmed, the availability of skilled personnel, and the standards of production sought.

A capable film unit should have the personnel and equipment to do thoroughly professional work for the purposes designated. Whether such work is, in fact, achieved is as much a function of the quality and creativity of the personnel as it is of the equipment.

Editing

Editing requires facilities to examine, view, evaluate, store, or archive film materials; to select, cut, edit, organize, splice, hold sync between image and sound, prepare prototype and master materials for laboratory use in mass printing or duplication, etc. Essential equipment is viewers, rewinds, splicers, editing tables and chairs, moviola-type sound/picture playback, projectors, sound readers, synchronizers, as well as storage cabinets, racks, bins, etc.

Sound Recording

The recording of sound is an integral part of the shooting step in film production requiring adequate recording instruments for either synchronized or post-narrated sound. Editing of sound recordings is subsumed in the editing facility. Sound mixing or the finalizing of tracks as prototypes may, depending on the volume and kinds of work to be done, be left to a commercial sound facility.

Floor Space

Small Studio	1,200 sq. ft.
Storage and Maintenance	400 sq. ft.
Editing	360 sq. ft.
Previewing	240 sq. ft.
Sound Control	240 sq. ft.
Animation	225 sq. ft.

Graphics Production Facilities

The purpose of a graphics unit in a university is to plan, design, and execute a variety of instructional visuals most of which require drawing or art work including such items as the following: chalkboard, flannelboard, and magnetic board presentations; charts, graphs, and diagrams; art work and reproduction for slides and transparencies; technical drawings, television art; and occasional displays. To perform these functions adequately, there must be a highly specialized staff incorporating the competencies of an industrial designer, a cartographer, an illustrator, a lettering artist, a photographer, and a construction specialist. There is also a need for a variety of graphic technicians and student helpers.

A graphics unit is normally made up of four sections: studio, reproduction, photography, and construction. To enable these sections to function efficiently, the following facilities and equipment are needed:

Studio   Design, lettering, illustration, and drafting work are performed in the studio. Each artist requires the following standard equipment plus certain specialized items:

1. drawing desk and stool;

2. taboret and drawing instruments;

3. lamp;

4. drafting tools;

5. drawing, inking and painting tools;

6. lettering guides.

In addition, each artist should have ready access to such items as an extra large drawing board, paper cutters, and electric pencil sharpeners. Further desirable items include enlarging devices such as the "Lucygraph," drymount presses, and a deep sink for washing pens and brushes.

Reproduction   The Reproduction Section needs the following pieces of equipment:

1. diazo reproducing machine for making varicolored overhead transparencies;

2. photocopy machine for making reflex type transparencies;

3. proofing press;

4. hot press for slide and film titles as well as television supers;

5. refrigerators to store diazo and film stock;

6. large assembly table;

7. drying racks;

8. laminator;

9. suitable storage cabinets.

Photography   Graphics photography is primarily copy work although the same personnel should be capable of most forms of still photography. Required equipment includes:

1. a good reflex 35mm camera;

2. lighted copy stand;

3. large format camera;

4. darkroom with separate light controls, temperature-controlled running water, and stainless steel sink;

5. developing tanks;

6. enlarger;

7. slide copier;

8. dryer or drying cabinet;

9. suitable storage facilities.

Construction   Representative graphics construction work for building study displays and exhibits requires both hand and power tools and a fire-safe paint booth plus work benches and extensive storage facilities. Needed equipment includes a good quality circular saw, band saw, jointer, drill press, sander, emery wheel, and paint spray equipment. Metal working equipment should also be provided if not available elsewhere on campus. Space requirements for graphics operations vary according to the number of personnel required. Each artist needs 64 sq. ft. to accommodate a drafting table and normal working instruments. Common assembly and specialized art equipment areas in the studio require approximately 240 sq. ft. The reproduction equipment listed above can be accommodated minimally in a 200 sq. ft. area. The photographic darkroom and adjacent copy work area should have 180-200 sq. ft. of fully enclosed space. The construction area must be in a separate room which is acoustically contained and adequately ventilated to exhaust paint fumes and dust. Approximately 400 sq. ft. are required for work, equipment and storage space in the woodworking shop.

Tape Recording and Duplication Production Facilities

The purpose of a tape recording and duplication facility in a university is to provide the technical support necessary to implement teaching through recorded lectures and various other audio materials. With escalating enrollments in universities across the nation, there is an increased use of instructional systems approach and self-instructional programs. Recorded information has become an integral part of these new approaches to learning.

To be of optimum use to university departments and faculty members, a tape recording and duplication production facility should be capable of providing the following services: Sound productions in monophonic and/or stereophonic audio-tape recording with narration, music, special effects (sound or electronic) and tape slide synchronization; turntables for playback of discs, re-recording of tapes, and mixing and equalizing of audio recordings; editing and splicing and duplication of audio-tapes, including high-speed duplication (60 ips) of standard reel to reel master tapes and high-speed duplication of cassette tapes from either reel to reel standard master or cassette tapes.

Maximum requirements for an efficient tape recording and duplication service are: two recording studios, a control room, and a tape duplicating room. Space and facilities needed for these studios and duplicating room are as follows:

Recording Studios   The recording studios should be completely soundproofed with acoustical isolation of floor, walls and ceiling. They should be air-conditioned with a diffused air exchange system to prevent noise of ventilation from being picked up by microphones. Our control room may serve both studios with the viewing windows on the studio walls (facing the control room) having double glass walls for soundproofing and located for easy visual contact between the recording engineer and the person(s) being recorded.

One studio should be large enough to accommodate at least two individuals (minimum of 100 sq. ft.) and the other should be larger for group recording. Microphone inputs should be installed under the window along the wall of the studio. Each studio should be equipped with: (1) monitor speakers for playback purposes, (2) a large time clock, (3) an intercom system with the control room, and (4) comfortable chairs and a table.

Control Room   The control room should also be soundproofed and air conditioned. A computer-type floor would facilitate equipment installation and maintenance plus accommodating necessary conduits and duct work. Adequate electrical power requires three 20 amp circuits with multiple outlets. Facilities should be available in the control room for rear screen projection of slides for viewing by a narrator in the studio to record tape-slide programs.

Tape Duplicating Room   It is recommended that there be a separate room for tape duplication adjacent to control room. The size of this room will be governed by the number and type of tape duplicating systems (standard reel to reel and cassettes) and tape storage cabinets used. Adequate electrical power and multiple outlets must be provided.

The following illustrative list of professional equipment is suggested on the basis of extensive trial and experience. Equipment having comparable performance standards may readily be substituted.

A. Studio Equipment

   1. Four Electrovoice microphones with stands

   2. Four Altec Monitor speakers

   3. Four Dyna 40 watt basic monophonic amplifiers

B. Control Room Equipment

   1. Two Magnecord master recorders with ½ track stereo erase, record, playback (optional ¼ track head available for playback)

   2. Two dual turntables for disc playback

   3. Two Dyna basic 40 watt monophonic amplifiers

   4. Two Altec monitor speakers

   5. One Altec filter

   6. One Altec equalizer

   7. Two Altec compressors

C. Duplicating Equipment

   1. One Ampex 3200D duplicating system with one master and two slaves

   2. One Infonics Cassette duplicator

Language Laboratories

Michigan State University has six (6) language laboratories with approximately 400 student stations for use in foreign language instruction and other subjects. Tapes are duplicated for the most part on the tape decks in the control rooms of the laboratories. Master tapes are prepared either in a sound studio such as that described above or in a small studio adjacent to one of the major laboratories. These tape decks, accordingly, are clipped together so as to perform typical duplicating functions. They are not duplicated at the speed or the quality which can be obtained with professional equipment but the quality obtained is adequate for the instructional purpose.

Summary

Strengthening instructional programs in higher education often requires the application of educational technology. Educational technology requires suitable instructional materials. Where materials of sufficient quality exist, they should be procured from commercial sources or from other institutions to avoid wasteful duplication; information and distribution systems are badly needed to facilitate such procurement. Where suitable materials do *not* exist, they must be produced. Most high quality production will probably occur within universities and colleges having systematic programs of instructional development plus adequate production facilities and professional staffs to operate them. The payoff on such systems will be more than sufficient to justify the administrative and faculty support necessary for their successful implementation.

Appendix A

SUMMARY OF TYPICAL COSTS FOR STUDIO PRODUCTION
FACILITIES FROM AN ENGINEERING FEASIBILITY STUDY
FOR THE MICHIGAN DEPT. OF EDUCATION
BY JANSLEY & BAILEY, 1968

Studio Production Equipment

A typical studio will be equipped with two professional live cameras, one film camera, film and slide projection equipment, audio, and auxiliary control equipment, test equipment, and a basic studio lighting package. Other technical supplies such as spare lamps, tubes, parts, shop tools, are not included since these are usually made a part of the operating expenses. A spare parts and equipment pool could be developed for a network system. This would offer the advantage of a stockpile sharing and avoidance of extensive duplication of technical supplies.

The following list contains recommended *minimum* technical equipment for use at a production studio. Development of program resources, exchange, and usage will require periodic additions and changes. Also, more complex production requirements and schedules can sharply increase these costs.

Summary
Capital Cost For Basic Television Studio

	MONOCHROME	COLOR
Building space—5,500 sq. ft. for one 50′ × 40′ studio, related work areas, electric service, and air conditioning. Estimated @ $30 per square foot:	$ 165,000	$ 165,000
Control room equipment—video	17,720	32,400
Control room equipment—audio	8,290	8,290
Film equipment	43,130	86,880
Video tape recorders	151,150	205,150
Studio cameras	51,300	177,500
Lighting equipment	8,620	8,620
Test equipment (partial)	3,090	3,090
Installation and test	15,000	15,000
Miscellaneous and contingent	15,000	15,000
One studio—total	$ 478,300	$ 716,930

BIBLIOGRAPHY

Caffrey, John and Charles J. Mosmann. *Computers on Campus.* American Council on Education, Washington, D.C., 1967.

Dietrich, John E. and F. Craig Johnson. "Changes in Administrative Organization Aimed to Effect the Introduction of Appropriate Educational Technology." Commission on Instructional Technology, October, 1968.

Finn, James D. "A Possible Model for Considering the Use of Media in Higher Education." National Special Media Institutes Bulletin, University of Southern California, Fall, 1966.

Johnson, Bettye and Denzil Swiger. "How Colleges Organize Media Services." College and University Business, Vol. 45, No. 5, November, 1968, pp. 78-80.

Johnson, F. Craig and John E. Dietrich. "Cost Analysis of Instructional Technology." Commission on Instructional Technology, 1968.

Pierce, John R., et al. *Computers in Higher Education.* Report of the President's Science Advisory Committee, The White House, Washington, D.C., February, 1967.

Rosove, Perry E. *An Analysis of Possible Future Roles of Educators as Derived from a Contextual Map.* System Development Corporation, Santa Monica, 1968.

Rosser, J. Barkley, et al. *Digital Computer Needs in Universities and Colleges.* National Academy of Sciences and National Research Council, Publication 1233, Washington, D.C., 1966.

Weinstock, Ruth, et al. "The Impact of Technology on the Library Building." Educational Facilities Laboratories. New York, July, 1967.

PART FOUR

c. IT and the Future Of the Book

65.

Instruments of Instruction: The Book Plus the New Media

by *LEE C. DEIGHTON*
Chairman of the Board
The Macmillan Company

After speech and writing, the most important human invention for transmitting knowledge is the book, and it may properly be regarded as the first instance of instructional technology. The book is not determined by its format or the materials of which it is composed. That is, it is not defined as consisting of paper, parchment, or vellum on which text and illustration have been imposed in ink or vegetable dye. The Chinese composed books from thin strips of bamboo on which characters were carved, the strips being tied together at one end.

The *idea* of the book, the novelty in the invention, is that it is a collection of thin uniformly-sized strips of material, bound together, which can be entered at any point with a relatively simple motion. The ancient scrolls were not books: the scroll had to be unrolled in a series of motions to the points of interest. Later refinements such as the index and table of contents, running heads, and sideheads improved access to the contents of the book.

The textbook as an instrument of instruction is a special kind of book, a modification of the basic invention. The textbook has the following characteristics:

1. It is a *presenter* of data

2. It is an *explicator* of relationships among the data. These relationships may be as to time order, cause and effect, likeness and difference, greater or lesser, etc., the basic cognitive structures through which man deals with experience.

3. It is an *illustrator,* providing charts, graphs, drawings, photographs to demonstrate data or relationships.

4. It is an *exerciser,* providing opportunities for use and practice of data and concepts through study questions, tests, exercises and the like. These are the means of interaction between reader and content.

The textbook as an instrument of instruction has certain unique values. It provides an orderly introduction to a discipline or subject matter. It provides ready means of continuous review, of comparison, of what Professor Bruner calls "retrogressive Integration." It permits contiguity of text and graphic illustration.

These considerable values and unique characteristics require consideration of the book as one element of instructional technology.

If this proposition is granted, it follows that instructional technology has not suddenly emerged in the second half of the 20th century. The first textbooks in American schools except for the *New England Primer* were imported from England. Following independence, it became clear to Noah Webster, Jedediah Morse, and others that textbooks of American origin were needed. Textbooks were followed by other technology. At a time when paper was expensive, Joseph Lancaster introduced slates for individual use. Later, blackboards were introduced, and in the interests of art education, the Milton Bradley Company designed and produced colored chalk. Wall maps and charts were developed. Following on the improvement of photography, the stereopticon was invented for group showings. The stereoscope, for individual use, provided the effect of three-dimensional views. Steel point pens replaced the quill, and eventually pencils and ball-point pens were made available when paper became cheap enough for classroom use. Paper itself for drawing, for exercises, for notebooks was in its time a new element in instructional technology.

There are four aspects of these early instructional instruments that are of special interest today: (1) They were characteristically either for individual use or for group use. Only the textbook could be used in both manners. (2) All of these instruments of instruction permitted in some degree an independence from the teacher's voice which had ruled the classroom for 2000 years. (3) None of these instruments except the textbook met with any substantial opposition. It is recorded that in the 16th century the faculty of the University of Salamanca protested against the printed book as likely to deprive them of a livelihood. The same view is held today by faculties in the colleges of some underdeveloped countries. (4) All of these instruments were adopted to the classroom, having been originally created for use in other contexts.

These four aspects of early technology have a bearing upon the introduction and use of newer forms of instructional technology in our time.

Instructional technology must be considered in the context of a significant non-technologic invention of the mid-20th century: *operations analysis.* While this analysis was not originally designed for educational purposes, the military have applied it to training and other forms of education with striking success, and it is beginning to find use in the non-military training programs of the federal government. Its usefulness in education is readily apparent. In simplest terms, operational analysis begins with a precise statement of specific objectives and permits a cost-effectiveness comparison of alternative methods of achieving these objectives.

In this framework, study of instructional technology begins with a statement of the objectives of instruction, affective as well as cognitive. The difficulty of defining objectives of instruction is well-known and well-documented elsewhere. The defining question seems to be: What do we want the learner to know, to believe, to feel, to be able to do as a result of a course of instruction?

Assuming that specific answers can be derived in terms of knowing, believing, doing, and so on, the next step in analysis is to consider the alternative means of achieving these objectives. It is at this point that a consideration of the newer means of instructional technology bogs down. Research has not clarified the unique values and capacities of tape recorders, film, television, radio, computers and other media. Until we know the difference between viewing a film and viewing television, we are not in a position to evaluate either.

Beyond this basic inquiry as to the unique values of the various media and devices, there is the question of how best to fit them into the classroom situation, and into the total set of conditions affecting learning what goals of instruction are most effectively sought in a group where everyone meets the same stimuli simultaneously? What goals of instruction are most effectively sought on an individual basis? Even more basically, can an entire course of instruction be presented effectively through a single medium? What happens when an entire course is presented by television, or can it be? What happens when an entire course is presented through programmed materials? Assuming that a combination of media is an effective method, which elements of a course of instruction should be assigned to which media? These are insistent and defining questions for which few answers are available. Without them, the choice of alternatives is a matter of guessing.

For the past 150 years the main concern of American education has been attendance. The major problems of our system today, including finance, arise from the success of the effort to get more students into the schools and colleges. A major effort is now required to discover what to do with the learners now in the schools. The preoccupation of psychologists with general learning theory in the first half of the century was not productive; psychologists are turning now with interesting results to particulars such as motivation, attention, arousal, anxiety, and to stages of intellectual growth. These are factors of individual learning, but as the Coleman Report dramatically demonstrated, they are not the only conditions of learning. The classroom is an interactive social system within the larger system of the school which is itself part of a community system governed by needs, values, and expectations of persons outside the school system. This is the total mix into which instruments of instructional technology must operate.

The basic questions to ask then are these: (1) What can the new instrumentation do? (2) What can it do in the total context of conditions of learning? (3) What can it do to make instruction more effective, less expensive, and more rewarding to learners and to teachers?

These questions can be made specific to the nature of the media. This paper began with a statement of the unique characteristics and values of the textbook as an instrument of instruction. A similar analysis is wanted for overhead projectors, simulators, computers, film, television and other instruments. The inquiry might begin with two considerations: (1) The textbook is a necessary but not a sufficient instrument of instruction. One cannot learn to speak a foreign language from a book, or to speak at all for that matter. One cannot learn manipulative skills from a book. A process can be described verbally, but it cannot be presented visually in a book. To place upon books the entire burden of instruction leads only to misuse and failure. (2) The newer instruments of instruction primarily present sight and sound. Learning games provide a different dimension as do computers and industrial machinery, but primarily television, radio, film, transparencies and similar media operate through more or less dramatically heightened light and sound. This factor determines their unique values but also limits their range of effectiveness since heightened light and sound may be distractive.

It is a basic assumption of this report that we do not yet know enough about the values and the effects of the newer instruments of instructional technology to make a persuasive case for them. We do know that they are in plentiful supply but not in wide use. We do know that their introduction to the classroom has been met with skepticism and resistance.

It would be easy to conclude that educators generally and teachers particularly oppose innovations. To anyone acquainted with the changes in our schools since 1900, this conclusion is inacceptable. It is time to consider the alternative: that the technology and its advocates are at fault. Perhaps the programmed materials really are boring. Perhaps the learner does not react well to the monochrome of an infinitely patient teacher.

Perhaps the films are not available at the appropriate moment; perhaps the content is irrelevant and poorly prepared. Perhaps the opportunities for interaction between learner and technology have not been sufficiently exploited.

The original motivation for introducing technologic instruments of instruction was a projected shortage of teachers: the machines would take the places of the missing teachers. The shortage has not occurred, but the image of technology as replacing the teacher has persisted. A different kind of motivation is required. In the military, the use of instructional technology to meet carefully defined objectives has substantially reduced the time required for instruction. In the military context, the saving of time and the consequent saving of money are of prime importance. In the schools, with the length of terms prescribed by law, time saving is irrelevant. A wholly different motivation is required, a motivation that would entail redefinition of objectives. It may well be that the failure of instructional technology in the schools and colleges results simply from overtooling, from the use of powertools in handcraft operations.

Crowell, Collier and Macmillan with which I am associated has produced tapes, films, filmstrips, phonograph records, overhead transparencies, and programmed materials—all of the materials of the newer technology except computer programs and machinery. This is the record of all the leading publishers of instructional materials. These materials have one common characteristic: they are conceived and designed as parts of a course of instruction with a textbook at its center.

There is one publishing trend that could make a substantial difference in the successful use of technology, particularly of computer-managed instruction. This is the trend to produce shorter units of printed materials bound separately rather than as a single large book. If adequate storage and transfer facilities are provided in the schools, teachers will be encouraged to use them for individual and small group instruction.

Summary

The extension of instructional technology will depend upon the following:

1. Identification of the peculiar values and limitations of media and devices including the textbook.

2. Identification of more specific goals of instruction in the manner of operations analysis.

3. A new motivation for use of technologic devices based upon the reality of what they can contribute and how they can be used.

Instructional technology is not a unique discovery of the mid-20th century. The aura with which they have been vested by enthusiasts tends to obscure their real values and real limitations. We have tried without success the strategy of dumping $350 million of materials into the schools through NDEA. Perhaps it is time to try a slower, more rational strategy.

66.

The Prospect for the "Book" As an Educational Medium

by FRANK G. JENNINGS
Director of College Relations
Teachers College, Columbia Univ.

It is no prophecy to say that the book will always be with us. It is simply a statement of low-grade physical fact, useful but trivial.

The book is not to be defended, but used. Its major technological virtue is its simplicity of construction and except in its gargantuan form, such as elephant folio, it is highly portable. It is important to make the distinction suggested by Albert Szent-Gyorgyi between books that hold information and books that use information; that is, between books that are repositories and books that are expositories. The former are used to relieve the mind from self-clutter, the latter to aid the mind in reaching beyond a current condition. The difference can also be expressed as between the position of the artisan and the artist. It is this distinction, however, which causes a great deal of trouble, and the book is hoarded and cherished as a treasure.

It *is* easy to learn to read. It is a low-grade skill that can be taught to all but the most severely brain-damaged. But to use reading too soon and to depend upon it too heavily in the processes of education is to blunt a good tool by inexpert use. Fifty years ago Alfred North Whitehead warned, "A merely well-informed man is the most useless bore on God's earth." Teachers and librarians know this truth in their marrow, and if they are uneasy before technology's open-handed advance, it is because they will not allow information to be mistaken for wisdom.

It is this impulse that impelled Gordon N. Ray, in his American Library Association address in New York in July, 1965 (as reported in PUBLISHERS WEEKLY, July 18th, 1965) to assert that the profession would be ill-advised to turn from the education of librarians to the manufacture of information retrievers and the training of servitors in "systems analysis." He complained about the long observed "lack of fellow feeling between librarians and faculty members, who ought to be united . . ." (as he said) "in the common world of learning." Mr. Ray told his audience in New York, "You should not only be librarians but bookmen. . . . Make it evident that your interest is in books themselves as well as procedures for making them available, that you are bookmen first, and administrators, technicians, and efficiency experts second."

Mr. Ray argued that "a compelling case can still be made for the book as the best source of information. Once one goes beyond the broad, elementary view of a subject, the opportunities which books afford for review and comparison, for immediate reference and prolonged attention to any step in the argument, and for all the other detailed operations that are a necessary part of close study, surely outweigh the advantages that electronic devices can offer." He also pointed out that in a world "conditioned to irrationality, books offer a way of staying human."

The librarians of ancient Alexandria must have said as much to the soldiers of Islam who put the torch to the recorded truth, wisdom and beauty of classical Greece. But— all such arguments are rather less than half right! The book is merely a lifeless artifact until someone knows enough about it to put it to some significant use, and it is the quality of that use that confers value on the book. Books do offer a way of staying human. So do tapes and records and films; so did the bards who sat by ancient campfires, thumping drums as they sang of gods and heroes. We stay human as we grow more humane, using language, recorded or remembered, to bring minded order out of the chaos of experience.

Book or tape or scroll or film; printed circuit or thermoplastic memory module: it's what we put into them that counts; it's the way we take out of them what others put into them that makes civilizations live and grow healthier and more fair. It is what we do with information that helps us to become wise and generous. It is the way we, the people of the book, exercise our vocation, serving all the muses, that will determine the quality of tomorrow's life.

That vocation needs constant celebration, no matter how imperfect its exercise. It is thrilling and terrifying to cite the titles of books that changed our minds or reshaped our worlds—there have been many of them. It is comforting to count off the authors, poets, philosophers, dreamers, knaves and fools who help us to tolerate what is inexact and arbitrary about existence. But individual titles, no matter how noble, how powerful, how filled with wisdom or terror, cannot adequately display the resources of the book. It is only as they are ordered and collected into libraries that their essential qualities can be comprehended and employed. Within libraries books become modules, integrated circuits, elements within a sentient network beside which any computer-based technology is merely an adjunct to our informed and educated intelligence. It is necessary, therefore, in dealing with the uses of the book, to consider libraries.

The library is more than a building, a staff, a collection of collections. It is more than methods and procedures, more than budgets and boards. But, what that more is defies language and rhetoric. Perhaps one can get near its meaning by way of metaphor.

In one sense, the library, writ large, is the mind of society. It is where all human experiences are recorded, assessed, translated, and treasured. It is the only effective repository of whatever is meant by the phrase "racial memory". Out of its resources, collective and individual thinking are tested, reinforced, and amplified. We read out the record; we assess the feedback; we use both as navigational aids on our mind voyages of intellectual and emotional discovery.

"Mind" is a slippery term that will not compute. Like "soul" and "psyche," it is more appropriate to the confessional or to the analyst's session. But only "mind" can handle— can tolerate—the irrational, the disorderly, the chaotic, the capricious, the tragic, and the generous in human affairs. Only a mind can "read out" the meaning in Pat Moynihan's observation on the death of President Kennedy: "You have to be an Irishman to know that sooner or later the world is going to break your heart."

Considered in this sense, the library as a particular building staffed with professionals and stocked with books, tapes, films . . . and clay tablets (the Philadelphia Free Library still circulates them!)—the library can and should determine the shape of its community and the quality of its life.

Librarians as well as teachers must know that theirs is a dangerous profession. Libraries, even more than schools, have in the past been attacked as seedbeds of social trouble, even sedition. One has but to read Richard Altick's marvelous book THE COMMON

ENGLISH READER to recall how some sections of the English public regarded the emergence of the free library.

In the mid-19th century even its supporters looked upon the free library mainly as a form of riot control, or at best a means by which to solve the problem of alcoholism among the masses. Free libraries would be, as one proponent put it, "temples erected by Literature for the votaries of Bacchus."

The opponents of the free library used stronger language. They condemned the institution as a kind of "socialists' continuation school," a place where the town loafer could amuse himself at public expense. Some of these 19th century bibliophobes sound like people who today are trying to cadge votes in California. Listen: "By providing public this and public that for the lower classes, you spoil and pauperize them. The best help is self-help. A man who drinks at the public pump, washes at a public bath, sots at a public house, and dreams away his days with a popular novel borrowed from a public library is not likely to be of much use to the State. . . . We are as a people getting far too much in the 'public line'." (Altick, 234-235)

We in the United States have a more generous tradition toward the care and nurture of the public library. But the War on Poverty and the associated struggle to build the Great Society have not enlisted the public library in any socially significant way. Some of us may be happy with this omission. Reflect upon it for a moment. We should be outraged.

Read in the September, 1966 issue of THE PROGRESSIVE magazine the article by Jim Fuerset and John S. Wiggins on "Libraries in Trouble", and know that others are reading that "In fourteen of our largest cities, combined, 20 per cent fewer books are now circulated by public libraries than were lent to borrowers thirty to thirty-five years ago. . . ."

Don't settle for cheap explanations about population shifts, the omnipresence of television, the incursions of the paperbacked book, and the changing shape of leisure. Ask why some library administrators "tend to be passive not only about attracting readers but toward local legislators and budget-makers". Ask why librarians are harder to come by today, why the profession does not appear to be an exciting option for our youth.

I am not competent to catalogue the ills of the public library, but as an unabashed bookman, I know what thrills me about the programs in Cleveland and in Pittsburgh and New York.

Take Cleveland as a case in point: The Cleveland library system is "reader-oriented". It constantly seeks to reach new people. It dispenses folders, and posters to churches, stores, social agencies, anywhere people come together. It considers itself not just a book dispenser but a community center focused upon learning, broadly conceived . . . and it does not worry too much about hurt books and scarred furniture. Cleveland's branch libraries are community culture centers . . . not merely places where genteel book review talks are given on rainy afternoons, but exciting and vital places where the voter registration drives are located, where issues of housing are not only discussed, but where plans for improvement are worked up—and possibly even implemented.

In the worst of the slums there is a branch that is not even called a library. It is known as the "Treasure House for Children". There the chief librarian, miracle of miracles, is the children's librarian. Everything about the place is there for the child. The furniture, the decoration, the reading materials—are all aimed at the child who is culturally deprived. Oh, yes, there are tunnels and other secret passages, there are—save the bookmark— amusement devices, game areas—everything designed (plotted is a better word) to seduce the children into the building and make them feel comfortable in the exciting surrounding where books are transformed into the reward at the end of the rainbow. And, yes, as I am sure you know, Cleveland leads all big cities in the number of books borrowed not only by children but by adults.

This is not to suggest that the uplifting of the poor should be the library's only concern. Yet ours is the first society in human history in which the poor are a helpless minority.

Therefore, one must measure the efficacy of our enterprises by our capacity to make a healthy difference in the lives of the least advantaged of our citizens. At the same time the library, functioning as the "mind of society", must be able to understand and act upon all of the reports of its social senses.

The world at large is undergoing great and fundamental changes. We use the word "explosion " to characterize many of them even when we really mean "crisis": the crisis in values, the rising tide of expectations, the population explosion, the cultural explosion. There is even an urban implosion and something that only the French can describe adequately as "l'explosion scholaire."

It is the sense of the horizon that thrills us; it is the explosions, the crises, the changes in our world that define our goals. And to achieve those goals we must gladly use whatever is at hand. The bound book is a marvelous instrument. It is sometimes even a work of art. There is exquisite pleasure in beautiful type assembled gracefully on a well-proportioned page of hand-laid paper. There is more than an antiquarian's joy in holding a volume of incunabula.

I have paid my homage to the book and I think that I can be at least as eloquent as Gordon Ray in the celebration. I love the feel of leather and the smell of old paper. I carry some book with me wherever I go. I have a personal working library of some four thousand volumes. I have a duly issued public library card and membership in two old private subscription libraries. I buy sixty books a year and read twice that number.

But . . . if someone produces an instrument the size of my thumb that will project any portion of the contents of an encyclopedia on any surface as I need it, I want the gadget. If there is a service available through the telephone company which will let me use my television screen as the read-out component for any archive anywhere in the country, I want that service. If books become micro-capsules the size of a dime which can be played through a projector-receiver which will allow me to add margin notes as I now do with a pencil, I want that too.

The shape of the book, which I treasure, is merely a function of the container that it is. The poets of Sumer may have resisted the innovation of the scroll, just as Politian resisted the plague of movable type. They all bowed to the new technology. It is the message that counts, and not the carrier. It is the idea that is important, and not merely the way you get it. It is a human mind communicating with other human minds past, present, and future that is the book-in-use.

One need not be oblique. We are talking about books and their technology; about tapes and computers, about thermo-plastics and micro-films, about instant read-out and print-out from nation-wide coordinated data banks and all the dreams of terror and hope that the word technology carries in its syllables.

There are many libraries, both public and private, where I can go with a slip of paper and order photo copies of however many pages of books and periodicals I need for whatever work I am about. There are others that will respond to a phone call and send me by messenger a micro-film of a dissertation or a scholarly paper of ancient vintage. Ten years ago I produced an anthology of short stories and had to destroy twenty books to paste up the pages for the printer. Today one typewritten order sheet will get me the same number of pages without hurting a single volume. This service permits my mind to work the scholarly lode and produce part of the next generation of books.

The library is the mind of society. Computer technology, cybernation, information theory, communication theory; all work to convert the metaphor into a definition. New equipment, new materials, new procedures will simplify some aspects of the library's task as they extend the range of its responsibilities.

So, let us consider the future. There will always be books, even as we have known them for five hundred years, but I am certain that there will come a time when some future librarian will display them as curiosities to be circulated, as clay tablets are today. There will be libraries and archives as identifiable as such, but different in ways we are already comfortable with, and filled with the great writers, the small songs, of the human record.

The foregoing discussion has laid heavy stress on the structure and function of the library, and this, I believe, is the most appropriate way to respond to the question posed. For it is when books are assembled into libraries, whether to serve an individual, a classroom, or a nation, that the efficacies of the book for its infinite purposes are most clearly displayed.

I must also repeat my comments about the book and technology. I am not concerned with the binding or the typography, although both may enchant me. I am not concerned with its manufacture, nor even with its physical shape. As I suggested before, given our ever-increasing technological sophistication, it is probable that books in some near future will bear less physical resemblance to papyri. The book of the future will probably be as different from present cloth or paper-bound volumes as the contemporary book differs from papyri or cuneiform tablets. What makes the book what it is will remain constant in every future age: the physical result of a mind or minds attempting with varying degrees of success to make contact with and inform other minds in future times. After all—this is one of the cardinal purposes of education, which is what every book, however made or used, is always employed towards.

67.

Educational Technology and The Future of the Book

by JOHN L. MARTINSON and DAVID C. MILLER

President	President
Communication Services	David C. Miller Assoc.
Corporation	San Francisco, Calif.
Washington D.C.	

Introduction

Mark Twain, a prodigious maker of books, might well have been speaking of the book form rather than of himself when he made his classic remark, "Early reports of my death have been greatly exaggerated." More recently, a 1967 position paper published by the Educational Facilities Laboratory observed:

> The book, which appears to have extraordinary survival power, has stood up thus far against the real and imagined threats of radio, film, and television. Witness its career since 1945, for example, when general television broadcasting began. The circulation of public library books in the United States has increased by more than 200 percent; and from 1960 through 1965, the numbers and titles of new books, and new editions of books produced in the United States, increased by more than 90 percent. *Publisher's Weekly* reports that the past two years were banner years for book sales, continuing an upward trend in annual overall book figures for more than a dozen years. In 1965, dollar volume ran to over 2 billion. In 1966, how to meet the bottlenecks in production and delivery caused by the demand became a major industry issue.

We do not propose to consider *whether* the book has a future, because we take that proposition to be self-evident. Rather, we wish to consider *what kind of future* may await the book form, especially in relation to education. First, however, we feel obliged to set forth some of the major premises which shape our speculations.

Anyone who speculates about the future applies a set of values, whether or not he is aware of doing so. Relevant values of which we are aware include:

1. The conviction that our society remains dedicated to the fulfillment of its citizens, both singly and collectively.

2. That human fulfillment requires personal freedom for its pursuit, freedom being defined as the right to make informed choices from a spectrum of real opportunities. The wider the spectrum of opportunities, the greater the freedom. Collectively, the free society is one in which there is an optimum distribution of options.

3. Freedom and fulfillment are possible in our technological society. Each new increment of technology provides us with another choice, another way to control

the environment and so another way to extend our freedom. In applying technology, whether to the book or to anything else, the challenge is to *realize* the potential. Such are the values we have in mind in considering the future of the book. But what do we mean by the terms "book" and "future."

With respect to "book," we intend the relatively narrow definition suggested by the following entry in the *Random House Dictionary of the English Language:*

> BOOK: a written or printed work of some length, as a treatise, novel, or other literary composition, especially on consecutive sheets of paper fastened or bound together in a volume.

The term "future" is more difficult to define, even arbitrarily. We hold that "future" can be meaningfully defined only with respect to the situation which requires the definition. At its nearest, the future "begins" immediately following the knife-edge instant of the present. At its furthest, the future extends to the "end of time", whatever that may mean. In the present context, we take "future" to refer to that period of time during which the recommendations of the Commission on Instructional Technology may reasonably be expected to have their major impact. Using common sense and some accepted conventions, we therefore use the following operating definition:

> FUTURE: For present purposes, that period of time beginning five years hence and extending to the turn of the century, that is, the period 1973-2001.

We feel obliged further to state our definition of "education," but defer that definition until later. Before proceeding, however, it is necessary to point out that what we offer are *speculations,* rather than predictions or forecasts.

Predictions are assertions concerning the simple occurrence of specific events at some time in the future, whether or not the time is specified. Forecasts, on the other hand, set forth probabilities for a specified schedule of specified events.

In the sense indicated above, the present paper is neither a prediction nor a forecast. It is rather something less, a set of *speculations* (hopefully informed) concerning general trends for the book during the future specified. We mean only to suggest where the book *may* be heading in future *if* present trends persist.

Keeping these definitions and limits in view, we begin our speculations by considering the general environment of communication within which the book as a form must compete.

The Future Supply and Demand for Messages

A basic trend in civilization for the foreseeable future is the apparent increase in scope and depth of complexity, interdependency and (consequently) interaction. Each individual and group is increasingly aware of links with more external parties in more dimensions. Our collective response to this situation is sustaining a rapid growth in all symbolic interaction, which promises to continue indefinitely. Thus we hear of the information explosion, and so forth. There is no evidence to suggest that this trend has spent itself, and a good deal of evidence indicates that the trend is increasing. It appears that in future all of us will feel the constantly increasing need to tell more and to learn more.

Another way to say the same thing is to say that the future demand for and supply of messages will increase at a rapid rate, the "message" being the package in which information is transferred. Every message must be contained in some medium or other, and the book is only one medium among many. In this sense, each medium must compete with all others for messages and the question becomes: How competitive will the book be in the future market for messages?

The best speculation, perhaps, is that the book can be expected to improve its *total volume* indefinitely but should be expected to enjoy a *decreasing share of the total message market.*

New media are appearing all the time—tape recorders, videotape recorders, polaroid cameras, etc.—and each medium captures that fraction of the message market to which it is best suited. As an example, daily stock market reports are not published in books and soon may no longer be published even in the daily newspaper.

Still, the total volume of messages to be sent seems likely to increase so rapidly that the absolute increase in book production will persist at a rapid rate of growth. The book, that is, will be produced in greater and greater quantities for as far ahead as can be foreseen, despite the fact that a decreasing fraction of all messages sent will be transmitted in books. We may look, however, for some significant shifts in the *kinds* of messages sent in books. To see why this is so, we must consider the declining period of the useful "half-life" of information.

The Declining Average Half-Life of Information

A widely quoted albeit shaky observation is that half of all that an engineer learns in college is obsolete five years after he graduates. That is to say, the average useful half-life of engineering knowledge is five years. While the exact rate is difficult to establish, it seems reasonably certain that many kinds of information become obsolescent much more rapidly than once was the case.

The Increasing Demand for Individualized Messages

Closely related with the declining average half-life of information is the rapidly increasing demand for individualized messages. Several apparent trends shed light on this relationship. The underlying explanation is that each of us finds his *need* to handle messages rising much more rapidly than his *capacity* to handle them.

First of all, there is the pervasive growth of interdependence, which simply means that each of us is concerned about more and more persons, things, places, and events.

Secondly, there is the fact that there is more to be known about everything. To choose a single example, a hundred years ago the sum of human archaeological knowledge might have been contained in a small library, while today a worldwide network of research libraries is unable to acquire and store new archaeological information as rapidly as it accumulates.

Thirdly, there is the declining average half-life of information already discussed. The state of affairs and the state of knowledge about affairs changes so rapidly that simply being aware of "what the facts are" requires a much greater effort than once was the case.

Taken together, these three forces—combined with the relative inability of the individual to process information more rapidly—are having an inevitable effect: Out of all that is known, each of us is more and more inclined to demand individualized messages. If our interest is in archaeology, we find less use than previously for a 500-page general survey printed five years ago. Instead, we search for a 100-page monograph published within the past year and dealing with all the latest details of some single aspect of interest. (In the 500-page survey, this one aspect may well have been dismissed with a summary paragraph written before the basic relevant discoveries were made.)

Implications for the Future of the Book

We have suggested the importance of the declining average half-life of information, and of the increasing demand for individualized messages. What are the implications of these trends for the future of the book? We see at least two important ones.

First of all, since books in their present form are designed for relatively long half-life messages, the traditional book will be displaced from many message markets. As an example, we foresee scientific and technical books diminishing in importance in those fields, simply because the state of knowledge changes so rapidly. Indeed, evidence of this trend can already be gathered in these fields. It is beyond the scope of this paper to make a field-by-field analysis in order to predict fields in which the book's importance may diminish, but such a survey could and should be made. On the other hand, new fields or types of information may emerge which exhibit a long average half-life; if so, the traditional book form will be highly competitive for such messages. Another study might well be conducted to examine the prospect for such new types of long half-life information.

Secondly, we foresee increasing competitive pressure on the book, causing it to evolve so as to become more suited to short half-life messages. As a means of identifying possible developments of this kind, we review below the basic stages of book production, namely: creation of the manuscript; pre-production processes; production; and distribution.

Creation of the Book Manuscript

Technological change is already affecting the process by which information is transferred from an author's mind to the manuscript page. Truman Capote's *In Cold Blood* or Oscar Lewis's sociological treatise *The Children of Sanchez* are certainly as much products of the tape-recorder as Don Marquis's *archy and mehitabel* or the poetry of e. e. cummings were products of the typewriter. Many new tools for creative expression are appearing: the tape recorder, the video recorder, and the computer, to name but three. We cannot now see clearly what impact these technological innovations will have on the creation of book manuscripts, but it seems likely that their combined impact will be substantial. Mark Twain, who invested (and lost) thousands of dollars in the effort to develop a typesetting device, is said to have been the first author to deliver a manuscript to a publisher in typewritten form. It is not unreasonable to expect that manuscripts will come to publishers increasingly in the form of decks of punched cards, reels of magnetic tape, or other machine-readable forms.

Book Production Processes

The future impact of technology can be foreseen more clearly with respect to the pre-production phases of book production. "Pre-production" refers to all those steps between the acceptance of the author's final manuscript and the time at which the book is ready for printing and binding. Here the current technological revolution in book production is clearly evident.

First, the traditional "hot type" processes face increasing competition by "cold type" methods based on typewriter-like machines combined with photolithographic printing processes. The extent to which these processes are controlled or monitored by electronic computers is also increasing. Technological changes in the steps preceding type setting have already been demonstrated to a considerable extent in another print medium, that of the daily newspaper. In prototype systems now under development a reporter "types" his story into a computer memory device and then rewrites it to his satisfaction while viewing it on a videotube display device. Copy and page make-up editors make their corrections and revisions in the same manner, and the result of these efforts is used to direct the output of a typesetting mechanism. Only when the finished page is ready for camera and plate-making does the data leave computer storage and assume its physically readable form.

This system has yet to be applied fully and seriously in the newspaper field, and the advent of similar systems for books lies even further in the future. If the previously identified trends persist, however, some such system will in time come into use, at least for special purpose publishing. The chief significance of these technological developments at the *editing* phase of the production cycle appears to be this: increasingly, the editor is relieved of the necessity of feeling that every page must stay on his desk until it is in *final* form. That is, the emerging technology makes it easier to think in terms of earlier and more frequent revisions to any printed work. The magnetic tape typewriter and other typewriter consoles using central electronic facilities on a time-sharing basis are good examples of such new tools for the editor. In the past editors working against production deadlines have been inhibited from making changes in camera-ready copy because a single change might necessitate re-typing an entire paragraph or page. The "playback" features of tape typewriters greatly relieve such inhibitions.

Beyond the editing phase of book production there are the composition and make-ready activities which precede actual printing and binding. The traditional "hot type" methods of doing page composition which require handling slugs of metal and locking them up in page format face considerable competition from "cold type" methods at this stage. An even more recent development, but already in widespread use, is *photo-typesetting* which cannot easily be characterized as "hot" or "cold" and is free of the "metal-on-metal" or the "metal-on-paper" requirements of all previous typesetting systems.* That is to say, "hot type" requires sufficient machine capability to actually cast characters in a linotype slug. "Cold type" allows the repeated use of a character cast in metal once it has been on the type bar of a set of typewriter keys. In use, of course, the metal of the typewriter forces ink or carbon out of a ribbon and onto paper to create a photographable image. In either case, however, engineering talent is required to design and build devices that assure that the machines will handle moving pieces of metal with speed and precision.

Photo-typesetting, on the other hand, requires that a *quantum of light* be cast on negatives or photo-sensitive papers. Instead of metal striking metal or paper, as in a linotype machine or typewriter, a bundle of light energy passes through a film or an etched glass matrix, and the image of a single character is cast on the receiving film or paper. Lenses and other optical systems for handling light waves now begin to replace machinery for handling pieces of metal. Instead of storing linotype matrices of different sizes in order to go from 10 point body type to 14 point headlines, the phototypesetter merely requires the adjustment of a lens in order to enlarge the image from 10 to 14 points. This is not to say that complicated machinery isn't required. Phototypesetting devices are certainly large, expensive, and complicated for the most part, but they operate with a speed and efficiency which is unimaginable by other composition methods. When these devices are directed by input from readily manipulable and erasable magnetic tapes (as in increasingly the case) it means that typesetting, like editing, can be thought of as a provisional rather than final process to a large extent.

Finally, it should be observed that the previous discussion has focused largely on systems of typesetting because we are largely concerned with the process of *reading*. Books, however, contain pictures as well as words. The implications of computer controlled photo-composition for graphic design have barely begun to be explored by artists and designers. Serious discussion of this subject is beyond the scope of this paper (not to mention the typing device on which it is being prepared), however, it seems clear that computer graphics and other techniques for preparing and printing illustrative material will influence the book form in the next generation at least as much as the processes already discussed.

Beyond typesetting and composition are the stages of make-ready, printing, collating, and binding. Here again, the trend away from fixed or finalized systems (requiring heavy

---

In passing, electrostatic printing should probably be mentioned since it too does not require the impact of an inked metal surface in contact with paper. Here we are not referring to office copying machines so much as the special techniques for imprinting on pieces of fruit, corrugated cardboard, and other irregular surfaces. These methods represent an important new tool in the development of information technology, but seem unlikely to affect BOOK production greatly in the foreseeable future.

capital investments) and toward easily prepared, easily discarded, (and therefore revisable) products seems clearly evident. In traditional letterpress operations a considerable quantity of heavy metal must be locked carefully into place before the presses can roll. Offset printing simplifies this process by using a light metal plate onto which an image from a negative has been "burned." These plates are made in minutes and can be positioned on the press relatively quickly. They are commonly discarded at the completion of the press run (the information is permanently stored on the negative) in contrast to the conserving and re-melting of lead in a letterpress operation.

The make-ready process is even further simplified with the increasing use of paper or other non-metal plates. Short-run offset printing is now frequently done without negatives and the burning of plates. In this case a camera is used which casts the image from original copy onto a special photo-sensitive paper. This paper is actually an offset plate since it is taken directly from the camera (no darkroom procedures are required) and placed on the press. Such plates can only be used for short runs and are thrown away after a single use, however, the ease with which they can be produced and placed on the press further simplifies the make-ready process and illustrates the overall trend toward easy revisability.

A related development which would seem to be a logical next step is the preparation of metal offset plates in the phototypesetting device itself. That is, instead of composing pages as negatives and then burning metal plates, processes may come into use whereby the phototypesetting device casts the image directly onto metal plates which are then positioned on the press. In any case, the quicker and cheaper the plate-making and positioning process becomes, the more the whole operation takes on the quality of a "throwaway" rather than a retained system. While books and other printed matter will inevitably lose the quality of "preciousness" as this happens, the same process will permit closer attention to the needs of smaller groups of information users.

Developments in the design of printing presses, collating equipment, and binding methods are too multifarious for detailed discussion here. One example from the printing field will be given, however, to illustrate the overall theme. Printing presses are either sheet-fed or web-fed depending on whether single sheets of paper are individually fed into the press or the paper enters the press continuously from a large roll and is later cut into pages after printing. In the past, the efficiencies of continuous feeding from a web or roll have been enjoyed almost exclusively by the owners of large (typically newspaper) printing establishments. These have usually represented sizeable capital investments in letterpress operations which could only be justified by the effort to serve mass audiences.

In the past decade, however, an increasing number of smaller, less expensive, web-fed offset presses have come into use. Quite recently, a web-fed offset press has been marketed which prints on 8½ × 11 inch pages. This might be viewed as a "super-mimeograph" operation or a "mini-newspaper" press. In any case, it illustrates a trend which permits production efficiencies formerly available to mass market suppliers to be utilized for much smaller markets or audiences. Whether the managers of information dissemination, and educators generally, will use the emerging technology for greater service to individual and personal needs remains to be seen. Such a question is probably a sociological and political matter more than an economic and technological matter. Many instructors with access to a Xerox machine and a good library can develop instructional materials for their classes on a par with those available from commercial publishers. But copyright problems aside, would such an instructor be likely to do so unless he gained as many professional "points" for such an effort as spending the same effort writing an expensive textbook that could be distributed nationally?

What is being developed in the interest of production efficiencies seems to have the following implications for education:

1. *A rising demand for more current and more highly individualized messages has already been suggested;*

2. *As such demands develop the use of computer or other machine based systems will be encouraged;*

3. *So long as information is held in easily erasable or manipulable form it can be readily and constantly updated;*

4. *These systems can be designed to provide personalized print-outs in response to individual needs.*

Should such methods for revising and producing books gain acceptance, books produced in this manner will be different from books produced by traditional means, but it will be reasonable to continue referring to them as *books*. The book as an object has a history which considerably antedates the invention of the printing press. The book survived the invention of the printing press in a new form; we see no reason to believe that the same won't be true in the post-computer age.

The idea of an "edition" as we know it may become irrelevant with the advent of quick print-outs from large magnetic storage systems. Other traditional aspects will change substantially as well, such as accepted notions of copyright, bibliographic citation methods, or even authorship itself (when numerous individuals contribute to the same repository of information). With changes in copyright practice or laws it seems likely that the system of royalty payments will also be modified. These represent social or institutional changes likely to come about as authors and publishers utilize and adjust to the emerging information technologies. These have not been our primary concerns in this discussion. Hopefully, they represent problems to be dealt with by others more competent to do so. Here we are primarily concerned with suggesting ways that the book is likely to be extended into other, less passive or fixed, formats. Within the traditional formats, however, some interesting changes can be expected.

Paper, for example, may be increasingly displaced as the favored material for carrying printed information. Paper has already been displaced in such specialized applications as children's books, moisture-proof cookbooks and laboratory manuals, etc. In the future, further displacement of paper by synthetic substitutes may be expected for two reasons. In the first place, as studies conducted or sponsored by Resources For The Future and others indicate, the demand for all wood products, including paper, will seriously over-tax the supplies likely to become available in the remainder of this century. With relatively long replacement times, it is easier to cut down forests faster than we can restore them. Secondly, the chemical industry (and especially the plastics industry) is producing more and more effective competitors for paper. Other considerations aside, economic considerations alone may one day dictate the displacement of paper by synthetics for book printing.

Other possible developments may accelerate this trend. Three dimensional images in books, for example, may be produced more readily on synthetics having special optical properties. Fluorescent inks are coming into use, and the prospect of self-illuminated pages for reading in subdued light is not unthinkable should it be desirable or necessary to do so. The utilization of synthetics in special print-outs seems even more likely than their use in conventional printing. To suggest the possible dimensions of such a system a hypothetical book reader of the future is described below. While any particular suggestion is more likely than not to be in error, the following may indicate something of what lies ahead.

Suppose that one fine day in the late 1980's John Smith wishes to have in book form the latest print-out of Richard Roe's *current novel*. Smith goes to his bookstore and consults a list which tells him that Roe's current novel in this month's version is 350 pages long. Smith then goes to the store clerk and purchases a 350 page "book blank" from the clerk. The book blank is a bound volume whose synthetic pages are in effect electronic "blackboards" upon which a magnetic signal can inscribe images which are readily readable and readily erasable. Smith tells the clerk which printout he wishes to purchase. The clerk slips Smith's book blank into an electronic receptable, dials the number of Roe's current novel and presses the Print button. In one ten-second pass the manuscript is copied from magnetic memory into Smith's book blank. The clerk hands Smith his book who retires to the shade of his favorite tree to examine what he has bought. In alternative versions of this fantasy there is no clerk, in fact there is no store, and Smith completes his book purchase transaction at home by telephone or desk-top console.

To repeat, it is highly unlikely that this particular version of the future, or any other specific version, is likely in detail or even principle. The example is suggestive, however, of the extent to which technological change may affect the future evolution of the book in certain directions. The really difficult questions, however, are those related to the problem of deciding what the implications of these developments are for educators in particular. This subject is dealt with in the following, and concluding, section.

Future of the Book in Education

So far, we have considered the future of books in general. In concluding this review, we turn to an examination of the future of the book *in education*. As a point of reference for the term, we refer to the following definition from the *Random House Dictionary:*

> EDUCATION: The act or process of imparting or acquiring general knowledge,
> developing the powers of reasoning and judgement, and generally
> of preparing oneself or others intellectually for mature life . . .
> The development of the special and general abilities of the mind
> (learning to know).

In this context, we identify three trends in education which can be expected to have a special relevance for the future of the book. They are:

1. The trend toward continuing education throughout one's active lifetime. This trend basically results from the average decreasing half-life of information cited previously.

2. The trend toward increasing individualization of formal instruction. This trend basically results from increasing interdependency and from the decreasing average half-life of information.

3. The trend in formal education toward aiding the student in "learning how to learn," that is to emphasize general principles and practice in the art of learning in contrast to specific field content.

The implications of these three trends for the future of the book in education are discussed in the following paragraphs.

We must distinguish at once between the future of the traditional book in education and the future of the book in new forms like those suggested above. We deal first with the traditional book form.

It seems certain that the book in its traditional form will continue to play a major role in formal education. Much of education, for instance, is properly devoted to conveying the best traditions cast up by the past. What Plato thought and wrote will be as significant in 1993 as it was in 1793; while there may be newer and better translations of Plato as well as commentaries more relevant than present ones to future times, Plato's works will certainly continue to be published in books. So it will be with endless numbers of classic pieces of literature. Furthermore, the number of copies of classics in print will certainly increase substantially.

In addition to classic works it seems likely that another kind of educational message will commonly be produced in traditional book form. These messages will have to do with basic principles and relationships, and especially with "learning how to learn." Today, despite much effort by social and behavioral scientists, we know very little about the different ways that human beings learn. But the state-of-the-art in learning theory suggests that we are poised on the brink of some important breakthroughs. If this proves to be the case, our future knowledge of how human beings learn will promptly be translated into new instructional packages. The average useful half-life of the information contained in these packages, as well as the number of persons for whom the messages will be intended will justify the production of conventional books in substantial quantities. While the state of knowledge about electronics may change rapidly, the basic principles of learning applicable to keeping up with changes in electronic knowledge will change much less rapidly. "How to Learn It" books in contrast to "What to Learn" books seem likely to play a central role in formal educational programs of the future.

On the other hand, many of today's standard education books will be transformed into computer stores. General and special purpose dictionaries, for instance, can be more effectively stored and accessed in computers than in printed volumes as soon as computers become widely accessible and commonly consulted. The same observation applies to books of mathematical tables, physical constants, routine formulas and equations, maps, etc. The rate at which such classes of information are transferred from books to computers is uncertain as is the sequence in which the changeover will occur. It seems highly probable, however, that many if not most of our reference books will in time be stored in computers for consultation when required.

Turning from conventional forms of the book to the newer forms suggested by computer print-outs, the trend toward individually prescribed instruction is especially relevant. Learning is, among other things, a matter of leaping from insight to insight. One acquires facts, retains them, manipulates them, and eventually makes deductions implied by combinations of facts and principles.

Today we know that there is an enormous variation among individuals with respect to the way facts and insights are acquired, the scope and sequence in which they are applied, and the methods by which learners test and verify what they think they have learned.

While we still know very little about the learning process, the complexity and variety of individual learning is beyond dispute. Master teachers are those who have an intuitive insight into these processes and stimulate and respond to each student according to his peculiar needs. As behavioral scientists learn more about the principles of learning, however, learning and teaching practices can be rationalized and reduced to proven systems. The advent of learning systems having acceptable degrees of reliability is probably closer than many now believe. As such systems come into use "book" and "teacher" will be integrated into machine aided learning systems.

Computer systems can teach extremely large "classes" of students, yet deal with each student individually. Such systems can keep thorough records about how each student learns best, what he already knows, what he is uncertain of, and what he does not know. Patient drill can be provided in any amount necessary. Test of knowledge can be integral and continuous. New information can be presented in optimum sequence and quantities. These are only a few among many factors suggesting that much educational experience now conveyed to learners in textbooks must eventually be presented in automated learning systems.

Despite much ballyhoo and propaganda by some behavioral scientists and hardware manufacturers, the day of feasible, widespread computer-based learning systems is not yet with us. At present, what we know about how humans learn is insufficient, as is our ability to express what we do know in the form of automated systems. Still, the state-of-the-art in learning theory and in educational technology is advancing rapidly. The simple fact of a continuing, drastic teacher shortage alone surely must hasten the diffusion of automated learning systems.

It is important to keep in mind, however, that the emergence of computer-based instruction is in part simply "an extension of the book by other means." Computers are not magic boxes which eliminate the need for creative thought and ordered activity by professionally trained educators. Titles may change, so that those we call "teachers" today may become "learning programmers" tomorrow. Today's "textbooks" may become tomorrow's "multi-media programs." But it is the *form* which changes, rather than the *principle*. Furthermore, it must never be forgotten that we are here discussing only one aspect of the book's future evolution. The book in traditional forms, as we have said, will remain with us indefinitely, in education and in general.

Finally, we consider the implications for the book in the observable trend toward continuing education throughout one's active lifetime. "Completing one's education" has ceased to be a meaningful phrase, if ever it was. Education is less and less thought of as "what happens to one in school between the ages of six and twenty-five." Educational institutions, like all others, are becoming less *place*-centered and more *person*-centered. There is much less talk of schools and teaching, and much more consideration of learning and learners. Education is coming to be seen as an integral aspect of everyday life for as long as one lives. Such a definition of education is not yet standard but society seems to be headed in that direction.

In this broader context it is difficult to consider the future of the book in *education*. It is for that reason that we have focused more on the future of the book generally. If it is more and more difficult to distinguish between living and learning, it is also more difficult to identify books which are *not* part of one's education. If education has a future (as we presume it must if civilization is to have one), then books have a future as well.

Summary and Conclusion

In this paper, we have *speculated* about the future of the traditional book form in education during the period 1973-2001 Specific predictions or forecasts have not been intended. Rather, we have tried to discern the general directions in which the book may evolve. We have suggested that the total demand for and supply of messages to be sent will continue to increase at a rapid rate. We speculate that the book in its traditional form will persist and increase in absolute volume, although it will constitute a diminishing fraction of all messages sent. We suggest that the declining average half-life of information and the increasing demand for individualized messages will displace the book from many message markets. The same forces are seen as causing the book to evolve in new forms more suited to future message-sending demands.

We indicate that technological change already has begun to affect the book at every stage of its existence, from the original expressive form to the final product in the reader's hands. We foresee that these changes will accelerate during the future specified, with change occurring especially in those phases of production between the final manuscript and the first reproduced copy.

We believe that the book in its traditional form has an important place in the world of the foreseeable future, although we foresee important changes, such as the replacement of paper by synthetic competitors. Turning to evolution of the new book in new forms, we see such possibilities as book blanks printed and reprinted instantly from computer storage upon demand.

With respect to the future of the book in education, we identify as especially important current trends toward lifelong learning, individually prescribed instruction, and advances in learning theory which will permit future educational curricula to emphasize "learning how to learn."

In this educational future, we see the book more or less in its traditional form conveying classics and traditions as at present, as well as new, relatively stable, "learning-how-to-learn" information. At the same time, "books" in the form of magnetically stored and computer manipulated programs bid fair to assume many of the drill and study tasks now prescribed in conventional books. We would emphasize that the evolution of books in this new direction is an evolution and need not be regarded as a "threat" to the book as we have known it. It is an *extension* of the book. We also see computer stores acquiring many of the reference works now stored in book form such as dictionaries, mathematical tables, etc.

68.

The Future Role
Of the Book
As an Instructional Tool

by *AUSTIN J. McCAFFREY*
Executive Director
American Educational Publishers Institute

In assessing the future role of the book as an instructional tool, it is necessary first to recognize that any predictions made in 1968 might well have to be revised several times by the end of the century. We live in an era in which what today is undreamed of is tomorrow's headlines, and next year's commonplace. This paper, then, will consider the prospect for the book within the framework of assumptions currently held as to future developments in educational technology and in society as a whole. For the purposes of the discussion "book" refers to educational books used in a formal program of instruction in elementary and secondary schools, colleges and universities. It includes teacher's manuals, workbooks, supplementary materials, paperbound books, children's books, reference materials such as encyclopedias, atlases and dictionaries used in the classroom and school library. We would also encompass those printed materials of instruction employed in certain adult instructional programs and in pre-school programs. Many educational books produced primarily for U.S. students are marketed throughout the world. Others are translated into the principal languages of the world as well as into local dialects.

Since Colonial days, educational books have been a staple and central item in the instructional process. The basic philosophy of the early schools was to teach the youngsters to read so they could study the Bible. In order to propagate the gospel and to perpetuate for posterity the principles of the Christian religion, the primitive Church established schools and instructed the pupils by asking questions, receiving answers, and offering explanations and corrections concerning the points of the new religious faith.

The hornbook was the first instrument used by the children when they entered school. This was a small, wooden, paddle-shaped implement. A sheet of paper, with the alphabet, numerals, the Lord's Prayer, and other reading matter was pasted on the blade and the whole was covered with sheets of transparent horn. Next came the Primer, the use of which can be traced back to the Middle Ages. The one most commonly used in the early American schools was *The New England Primer*. It has been estimated that three million copies were printed. The Primer contained a rhymed alphabet and an outline of Puritan theology.

The advent of the spelling book indicated the growing secularism of American education. Besides the alphabet and spelling exercises, it had a short catechism, prayers, psalms, writing copies and a list of "hard words alphabetically arranged and sensibly explained." Noah Webster prepared the most famous speller and most widely sold of American schoolbooks, *The American Spelling Book,* in 1783. The Spelling Book continued in use for more than a century.

Gradually as the country developed, more books became available to students, although until well into the 19th Century textbooks with different presentations of subject matter were occasionally used in the schools by students in the same class.

In general the earlier texts did not require much pupil activity except memorization and formal application of rules. The earliest rhetoric books required little writing; physics and chemistry texts did not require pupil experimentation until after 1875, and rarely did zoology texts imply laboratory work. Botany books asked for student activities earlier than was true in the other sciences. Usually it was suggested that the students gather and analyze plants and flowers and keep the samples in books.

Jedidiah Morse's *Geography Made Easy* and C. A. Goodrich's *History of the United States,* brought out in 1822 are examples of textbooks in new fields. Effort was made to make books more attractive and useful to children. Better paper, clearer type, more pictures, and more interesting reading material became the rule. Toward the middle of the 19th century graded readers began to appear. The McGuffey Readers are doubtless the most famous of these. Gradually the concept of graded textbooks was accepted.

With the increase in enrollment brought by the expansion of free public education, same courses of study, the improvement of teaching procedures, and the separation of pupils into rooms and grades, it became necessary to have uniform textbooks in each grade and in all schools under the same jurisdiction. Research studies inaugurated at the beginning of this century provided new knowledge about how children grow and the way they learn, enabling textbook publishers to build books specially designed for the needs of the students. Four major influences characterized the modern textbook: (1) child psychology, (2) the improvement of printing and binding, (3) research by authors and publishers, and (4) textbook publication as a specialized industry.

As the colleges and universities urged the need for teachers to know child psychology, methodology of teaching, individual differences and testing procedures, emphasis in textbooks shifted from subject matter to the learning process. More attention was given to color, illustrations, size of type and quality of paper.

The second half of the twentieth century has witnessed dramatic advances in educational publishing. Discoveries made during World War II in the various military training centers, together with Russian scientific achievements in the late fifties, spurred revisions in curriculum content and school organization.

The areas of mathematics, physical sciences and modern foreign languages were the first to receive the concentrated attention of scholars and scientists. For the first time, university personnel concerned themselves with pre-collegiate reform. Their expert knowledge of the subject areas was important in effecting a complete reorganization of curriculum content.

The early curriculum groups developed their materials primarily for use by college-oriented students. It was, after all, an attempt to rapidly upgrade our scientific and technical competence in order to compete on an equal basis in the world. These curriculum revisions have received widespread acceptance in the schools. Soon other subject area specialists began to examine their disciplines with regard to teaching and learning. English teaching is being subjected to close scrutiny as groups study various models of instruction. Some fifty studies were initiated in the social studies ranging from experimenting with presenting an individual discipline at a selected grade level to an integrated K-12 curriculum. The establishment of the Arts and Humanities Foundation has given impetus to curriculum studies in these areas.

Curriculum structure is also changing to take into account individual needs of students. Courses are being designed to accommodate varying rates of learning. Materials on non-Western civilizations are being included in social studies courses. English is being taught as a second language in the primary grades to students from non-English-speaking homes.

The contribution of minority groups to the development of the nation is receiving added coverage in American history courses.

The organization of the schools has also changed as educators recognize the need for individualizing instruction. The ungraded schools are one way of encouraging a student to proceed at his own pace through a particular course of instruction. Team teaching allows for enough flexibility so that students are exposed to large group lectures and can also obtain individual assistance. Pre-school programs such as Headstart are being introduced, particularly in the urban areas, as a result of research indicating that a child's early years are critical in establishing learning patterns.

Educational books, too, changed during this period. When the scholars reorganized the subject matter and approach to instruction, new books were needed. Since the basic approach to teaching used by the curriculum groups rejected rote learning, school books reflected this by emphasizing the discovery method, exposing the student to concepts and ideas rather than facts to be memorized. New theory called for more depth coverage of a subject, encouraging the student to explore and experience the many facets of the area. When a subject was introduced at a lower grade level, publishers had to develop appropriate materials. Interest in the needs of disadvantaged youth required books providing low skill achievement with high interest motivation; multi-level texts which allow students of varying ability in the same classroom to begin, each at his own proficiency level and to progress as fast and as far as his individual capabilities will allow. Publishers contracted with authors of non-Western countries to write books about their native lands. Both supplementary materials and core textbooks have increased their coverage of the minority groups and their contributions to the development and growth of America.

Introduction of technological aids into the classroom was responsible for the production of books to accompany educational television courses and books for programmed instruction. In many cases, publishers have developed systems of instructional materials which include both printed materials and audiovisual aids. Often publishers will work with motion picture companies to develop films or filmstrips to accompany the textbook. Others will arrange for slides or transparencies. In some cases it is a cooperative arrangement, in others the publisher produced his own materials. Elementary science books come with individualized equipment to conduct appropriate experiments. Foreign language texts might be accompanied by films, filmstrips, tapes and records to reinforce the child's audio and visual impressions. Workbooks, programmed books, special-purpose equipment for reading instruction, and planetarium instruments may all be part of a publisher's catalog.

Continuing research by the industry suggests changes in size, paper and type of illustrations. One company produced a history textbook in four individual volumes for easier student use. Another issues a weekly supplement to an economics text in order to keep data current.

Paperbound books are in widespread use in the schools, both as textbooks and as supplementary material, as well as in the school and classroom libraries.

In reviewing these developments in educational publishing, it is apparent that the textbook can no longer stand as the single instructional tool, the sole source of knowledge on a particular subject, that it once was. It does however remain the most effective way to sequentially present the ideas, concepts, facts, generalizations and abstractions relevant to the subject area. The textbook presents data; explains the relationships among the data; provides charts, graphs, drawings, photographs to demonstrate data or relationships; and provides opportunities for use and practice of data and concepts through study questions, tests and exercises. The textbook provides the means of interaction between reader and content; permits contiguity of text and graphic illustration. It is the one instrument which can be used in either group or individual instruction. The traditional format of the textbook may be modified and satellite materials introduced, but as Mark Van Doren has written: "It is hard to imagine this country without school books . . . From the first primer to the latest textbook in the rarest science . . . school books have maintained a central, controlling position in our common life."

In addition to changes in the products of publishers, methods of production have improved since the time when an individual author, usually a teacher, wrote the textbook, had it printed and marketed it himself in the surrounding area. Today, in the elementary and secondary area, it is virtually impossible to find a single textbook by a lone author. Instead, you will find large teams of authors, along with consultants, advisors, researchers, and academic and professional specialists who are engaged in conceiving and planning and developing educational materials. These large teams of specialists are together for a number of years to work on one particular series, with drafts classroom-tested and rewritten. Since the time involved in the development of text materials varies between three and eight years, an editor must be constantly alert to changes in the subject area which necessitate content changes in the materials in preparation. Publishers are involved in increased experimental development and research, usually carried on jointly with educational research centers and with institutions of higher education, often using existing classrooms as laboratories. Another change is the increased use of professional educators in developing materials that are for the in-service use of teachers, such as the teachers' guides and manuals. Publishers employ professional field consultants to be sure that teachers are familiar with how to use the new materials most effectively.

College textbook publishing is quite different from elhi publishing. The wide diversity among institutions of higher education and the independence of the college professor in determining what is to be taught and how it is to be taught is well established. College books are in large measure the work of the author. His manuscript, usually with some technical assistance from the editor, becomes the book. It may be widely adopted or used only in a few institutions. It may be the basic course of study or a reference work used in conjunction with other materials. Usually the number of copies published is small compared to the larger runs at the elementary and secondary school level. Nevertheless many of these books are distinguished works and contribute valuable knowledge to highly specialized subject matter disciplines or are used in research undertakings. Thousands of university scholars have been able to combine writing with their teaching and research. In this way, college publishing has provided an opportunity for ideas to be expressed, developed, and disseminated.

Book publishing is one of the fastest growing industries in the world. In many countries government expenditures for education are beginning to exceed those for the military. A desire to keep current, to develop new skills, and simply to acquire knowledge encourages people everywhere to read more books. The Annual Statistical Survey of the American Educational Publishers Institute reported in 1967 sales of 95,525,000 textbooks, both hard bound and paperbound, and 131,900,000 units of workbooks and objective tests for elementary grades. In high schools, total sales were 44,290,000 copies of both hard bound and paperbound textbooks and 21,170,000 units of workbooks and objective tests. Total number of units sold in college was 63,655,000 hard bound and paperbound and 5,970,000 workbooks.

The future role of the book will be influenced by many factors outside of the publishers scope. State laws affecting the adopting of textbooks are a direct determinant. In this country, twenty-three states adopt elementary textbooks at the state level and 18 states adopt secondary textbooks in the same manner. The procedures of selection and adoption vary, but generally the books are chosen by the State Board of Education or the State Textbook Commission. The number of books selected for each subject and grade ranges from one to six. These groups also determine the length of time the books will be used. The cycle may be four, five or six years, with a provision enabling the state to renew the contract for up to three years.

Teacher training in the coming years will have an influence on how the educational books will be used in the classroom. The teacher will remain the most important ingredient in the learning process. Interaction between instructor and student is essential, no matter what educational media is employed. The use which a teacher makes of the available instructional tools will determine the role of each.

The tradition of learning from books is a long and distinguished one. We have been served well by the educational books throughout the years. Our national interests and concerns are reflected in large measure in educational books. New discussions on science and technology are disseminated through books. Such tradition is not easily discarded. Just how firmly it will be adhered to in the future will affect the use of such educational books.

Educational publishers make no attempt to discount the value of technology to the instructional process. The contributions of audiovisual aids and electronic media are well proven. They have made learning more interesting, more challenging and more effective. The range of instructional tools available to schools is impressive: slides and filmstrips, transparencies, microfilm and microfiche, recordings and transcriptions, audio-tape, radio—open and closed circuit, instructional television, motion pictures, 8mm single concept films, programmed instruction, computer-assisted instruction, EVR units, and student carrels. Such a range of devices enables a child to learn, using all his senses, or just those to which his particular system responds best. The concept of systems of instruction was generated from the vast array of technological aids. Recognition that every child does not learn in the same manner has been reinforced by the ability to offer the pupil different ways of learning.

The educational publishing industry has reacted in several ways to the changing needs of the schools. In some cases, the move was to acquire additional capital. Since 1958 twenty educational publishers offered their stock for public sale. In the area of mergers and acquisitions, over 50 transactions have taken place in the past ten years and others are in process. In some cases, two publishing firms combined forces in order to serve a larger span of the market by uniting different levels of education, producing other instructional tools, or adding trade or textbooks. In other situations, the communications and electronic firms sought out publishing houses to help them produce materials for their new means of communications. Such concerns as Xerox, IBM, Raytheon, CBS, Litton Industries, ITT, Bell & Howell and RCA have acquired publishing firms. Others such as General Electric and Westinghouse developed their own educational divisions. Other educational publishers maintained their original structure and diversified from within. Publishers acquired instructional aids, to complement textbooks, which could be offered to schools as a unit. Contract agreements were drawn up whereby publishers would work with film companies to produce instructional kits.

Technology and the systems approach to learning will most likely be an integral part of the classroom of the future. The rapid expansion of knowledge available to man and the concentration of population into the already crowded urban areas has made such development both desirable and inevitable. Already the computer has made an outstanding contribution in identifying student needs and recording achievement data; in reinforcement; and in instituting flexible scheduling systems, grading papers and standardizing tests.

To what extent the newer technological media will comprise the instructional program of the future will be determined to a certain degree by developments within society. Schools are responsive to developments in the nation which are helping to shape change. Additional changes in the structure and organization of schools with the possibility of comprehensive educational parks in some areas and decentralized school systems in others; new developments in teaching methodology; emphasis on urban education as large numbers move into metropolitan areas, with minority groups becoming majorities in the schools will all affect how the school program is presented to the student.

In any case, it is to be expected that the educational book will maintain its central role in the instructional process. The educational book has certain unique characteristics which make it the most economical tool since it needs no equipment; most flexible in that it can be used in classroom, library and home. As an instructional instrument it is the most effective way to sequentially present the ideas, concepts, facts, generalizations and abstractions relevant to the subject area. The most creative minds in the country are employed to produce the materials as scholars and specialists in curriculum work together to develop a textbook for a particular subject. The book and the machine are being brought together in the corporate structure. They can live together in the schoolroom with both comfort and distinction. The responsibility of the teacher will be to select the tools most appropriate for an individual student. There seems little doubt that achieving the goal of individualized instruction will require computerized techniques. The need for lifelong learning in order to keep pace with developments is evidence that information storage and retrieval is necessary. The exact form will have to await the results of experiments now underway. It is possible that educational books may take different forms in some instances in order to provide the intellectual content for technological systems.

The prospect for educational publishing is one of continued cooperation with the educators and government officials, as well as others of the community concerned with education, in solving educational problems. As other industries enter the knowledge business, they too will join in these joint efforts. The resulting instructional instruments will include the educational book in its present form, but it may also be represented by various forms of input for the electronic media.

d. IT and the Education Of the Disadvantaged

69.

Technology and The Inner City School

by JAMES P. COMER
Asst. Prof., Child Study Center
and
Dir. of Pupil Personnel Services
Baldwin-King School Program
Yale University

Technological advancement and the resultant changes, as much as neglect and discrimination, are responsible for the crisis in education in inner city schools. It appears only proper then that the potential of technology be harnessed to facilitate the education of young people on which it is making new demands.

Prior to the past seventy years, most people did not receive a formal education and did not need one. Most could grow up and earn a living just as their parents and their parents' parents before them. But within the lifetime of today's senior citizens, America has moved from a horse and buggy age through the age of train and automobile to the jet and now super-jet age. In every field of human endeavor, there have been remarkable technological advancements and it is predicted that the changes from now until the year 2000 will be greater than those which have occurred since 1900.

Technology has changed or greatly modified life styles, politics, religion, recreation—indeed, every aspect of American life. Most critical, it has changed and will continue to change the way we earn a living. In general, physical labor is less necessary in all areas of work and employment today then ever before. There is every indication that the trend will continue. The better jobs today and in the future will require a relatively high degree of education and training. As a result, many Americans are faced with an unprecedented problem.

Since the late 19th century, there has been a general pattern of three generational occupational movements in many American families. Unskilled immigrants and other newcomers held jobs requiring no skill. Their children often acquired skilled labor jobs and in the next generation moved to professional occupations or jobs requiring a great deal of skill and training. Excluded minority groups, late-comers and isolated Americans did not move in this pattern very often. Now a disproportionate number in these groups are unskilled and the demand of the job market today dictates that those who want economic security must move from the unskilled labor class to the highly skilled and professional class in one generation—a task which is more difficult than is often assumed.

While there is some evidence that automated industry does not require the high degree of education and training often claimed, there is little indication that hiring practices will not continue to favor the better educated people. Thus it still holds that education is needed to insure economic security in spite of the actual level of education needed to do a particular job.

Public school education has always missed a disproportionate number of "special people." Immigrants, Spanish-speaking people, Southern rural blacks and whites, migrants to the city, Indians and other young people have failed to benefit from educational opportunities in disproportionate numbers over the years. In the past this was considered unfortunate but not a tragedy. There was work and other opportunities available for those who did not take to the academic program. Today the child who cannot learn is often destined to a future of economic insecurity.

There are serious social and psychological consequences for economically insecure people. A sense of personal adequacy for males is closely related to his capacity to provide food, clothing and shelter or basic necessities for his family. Being able to provide these necessities enables a man to give the social, economic and emotional security to his wife and/or the mother of his children who has a primary role in providing the love, limits, guidance and direction needed for adequate socialization and psychological development of their children. To the degree that the female parent does not receive support and security, she is less able to perform her vital role as wife and mother. When males are unable to meet these basic requirements, they often exploit their wives and children to meet their own psychological needs. Alcoholism, desertion and other methods of dealing with a sense of personal inadequacy all take their toll on family stability and adequate child development. Certainly similar problems occur at every economic level but a disproportionate number occur where economic uncertainty is more frequent and prolonged.

For many years now there has been a movement of the better educated, better employed people from central cities to the periphery and to suburbia. As a result, a disproportionate number of minority groups and other groups who have not had access to opportunities for occupational advancement remain in the central city; indeed they have become its principal occupants. It is often assumed that they will move to a higher occupational and security level as directly as previous groups. It must be remembered that previous groups often moved to a better occupational and economic position in large numbers, not because of marked educational gains, but because of union-gained benefits in a pre-automation age of industry. Today without critical attention to inner city education, such movement will not necessarily be the case.

Many youngsters in the inner city are intelligent, have received adequate nurturance, socialization and guidance and come to school prepared to learn. Their parents are enthusiastic about education, have high aspirations for the youngsters and are supportive of the educational process. Many youngsters show remarkable strength in spite of the difficulties they experience. In fact, independence, spontaneity and curiosity—where it is permitted —are observed among inner city youngsters perhaps more often or certainly as often as among youngsters anywhere.

On the other hand, a disproportionate number of inner city youngsters have been adversely affected by their pre-school social experience. Often desired experiences have been missed and numerous undesirable events and conditions have been experienced. Parents working more than one job, frequently changing residences within the city and between regions, insufficient supervision of play, crowded home with over-stimulation of all kinds, parents overwhelmed by their own problems being unable to respond adequately to the child's needs are but a few of the difficulties. Lonely, neglected, exploited, angry and abused children are probably found in disproportionate numbers in some inner city schools. Thus a disproportionate number of children showing developmental lags, skill deficits and other difficulties are found here.

In most classrooms, regardless of socio-economic level, some children will manifest impulse control difficulties, excessive dependency, inadequate curiosity, poor use of speech for communication and a variety of other problems. Where there are one or two children with such problems, teachers are able to develop special programs, give special attention within the classroom or supportive personnel are able to arrange for compensatory help outside of the classroom. In this way, the provocative and impulsive child eventually learns to get along with others. The dependent, restricted youngster gains support for independent thought and action permitting him or her to grow and mature psychologically and socially and so on. Children prepared, socially and psychologically, for learning do not lose out through classroom disruptions or excessive teacher attention given to children with special problems. But such adjustments are possible only where the number of youngsters requiring additional help is small enough, the teacher is trained to detect and deal with special problems and adequate support staff is available. Inner city schools often suffer on all three scores.

Many cities are losing taxable industry and business to suburbia or to the South and are trying desperately to attract new industry and redevelop business areas. Property owners have paid more than their share to provide for education services. The support of schools and other social service activities has been less than desired as a result. Thus for many years now inner city schools have been getting by with barely enough staff to maintain little more than custodial services in which education sometimes takes place—when exceptional children and teachers happen to meet. Complicating the problem, school systems short of funds or because of prejudice have often concentrated more and better personnel in schools attended by middle income, usually white youngsters. In one inner city school a paralyzed teacher unable to speak clearly was allowed to spend almost a year—to teach reading no less. In another, a frankly psychotic teacher frightened the youngsters. Teachers with personality problems are assigned to the "Siberia" of education—inner city schools—with frightening regularity. This, of course, is precisely the place they should not be. Many children with minimal deficits and difficulties in inner city could compensate if they had experienced, well-prepared teachers, administrators and support personnel in sufficient numbers.

Children unable to receive adequate help become more troublesome behavior problems, parents are unhappy, teachers are disappointed and some schools, even after an input of special programs, remain little more than places of custodial care. In such situations there is a high staff turnover, with all the instability this involves. Parents withdraw or are unwanted and can lend little support to education. Administrators are constantly involved in day to day emergencies and unable to give young teachers support in instructional areas or to develop school programs which would improve the spirit, morale and sense of purpose, order and stability which occur so regularly in middle income schools that it is taken for granted. Yet it is the inner city schools with a disproportionate number of children with certain motivational and developmental deficits which are more in need of creating such conditions.

The stage of program refinement which follows the stage of stability often cannot occur in many inner city schools. Careful analysis of reading skills and deficiencies of the individual child and special reading programs for individuals or groups with similar problems cannot take place. The achievement test is often treated as an object designed to embarrass the youngsters rather than a tool to be used to modify and adapt curriculum and teaching methods to better meet the needs of the children. Indeed, many if not most inner city schools have little time or personnel to develop in-service programs needed to focus in on the critical deficits and to design approaches necessary to meet these needs.

Recently very dedicated and bright teachers have been seeking inner city school assignments. But many are young and inexperienced and have limited understanding of the complexity of problems within the inner city school or the difficulty many families in the surrounding community experience. Too often there is a feeling that previous teachers and administrators have deliberately abused the children and there is a need to rescue them. Such teachers often clash with others who have "given up" or been overwhelmed by the system, and an atmosphere of chaos and controversy develops. Too often there is an investment in innovative techniques which do not allow teachers to look at the child as an individual, where he is in his development, and what is needed to compensate for deficits. Yet the involvement of such teachers is a hopeful sign. But if they are to be effective and to strengthen the inner city school, they should enter a system which has achieved a relatively high degree of stability and is prepared to assist them in becoming effective teachers in this setting. Without such support, they are likely to fail, leave or "give up" and remain, making adjustments which compromise their effectiveness.

To date, help for the inner city school has been an input of new ideas, people, programs, etc. without systematic attention to the critical aspects of basic school programs. Unlike the good football teams which, when showing signs of slipping, revert to fundamental patterns of blocking, tackling and passing, schools have gone for the razzle-dazzle plays. Cultural enrichment, ethnic relevance, new techniques, fancy new buildings and the like have been the response to the crisis in inner city education. The principal of one inner city school recently counted twelve new program inputs in his school within three years, all now abandoned, none carefully evaluated, with little apparent impact on the youngsters. Yet few things are more cherished in education than innovation.

One of the dangers of rapid innovation is apparent in the comment of a teacher involved in a special program. She said, "The children appeared bright enough but 'they' just didn't learn or certainly it wasn't reflected on their achievement tests." Some will acknowledge that the achievement tests are often "not valid" for inner city youngsters. But when a program innovation fails it is often suggested that it is either the fault of the youngsters or irrelevant measures of success or failure were used. Rarely does an innovator question the appropriateness of the innovation for the system into which it was introduced.

The twelve new programs mentioned were introduced into a school in which the administration rarely had a chance to respond to anything but behavioral emergencies. Continuity of program planning and development was hardly possible from day to day, not to even consider months and years. The coordination of special program work with the classroom teacher was not possible. Cultural enrichment when many of the children involved did not know how to attack or sound out a word was of questionable value. The participation of children in interesting, stimulating and exciting activities—different in kind than those they received at home but similar in impact—was fun but did little to help the youngsters learn to get along with each other and respect the rights of others. (These are necessary lessons to learn in order to go the long haul in education and life.) Often people participating in the program did not appreciate the important socializing function they needed to perform while working with children, some of whom would not receive guidance and direction along these lines at home or from other adults.

Instructional technology introduced into a school or system operating at a "survival level" can be another burden for administration and teaching personnel. Increasing the vocabulary of a child through instructional equipment will usually be of limited value in a chaotic system not capable of producing or sustaining a learning environment. Even in schools operating at a relatively stable level, available instructional equipment will not be used or fully exploited without sufficient preparation of teachers. In one Southern city, expensive television equipment has not gotten beyond the school warehouse because of staff unfamiliarity and lack of knowledge relative to the educational possibilities of the equipment. The use of such equipment was "somebody's good idea," an innovation, but that is as far as it got. Careful planning, preparation and integration of the equipment into a well thought out school program did not take place.

Obviously, improving the education of the inner city school is no quick and easy task. There is no magical person, technique or technical development which will bring the potential of the inner city youngster to fruition. Yet technology can facilitate the stabilization of a school or school system, improve staff effectiveness and facilitate the training aspect of the educational process when properly introduced and utilized in a school district or system. These are interlocking considerations and, like "old fashion" love and marriage, you can't have one without the other. The use of technological equipment for instructional purposes in the inner city school is much more likely to be of value after it has been adequately utilized to prepare teachers to work in the school setting and after it has been fully exploited to facilitate administrative functions.

Preparing the young teacher to work effectively in inner city schools could be an important and efficient use of instructional equipment. Like the young medical student the future teacher often does not see the future consumer of his services until very late in his training. It is true that both have little to offer prior to that time but they certainly have a lot to learn. Yet exposure to the classroom at an early stage of development is even more impractical on a large scale for future teachers than contact with patients is at an early stage of development for future doctors. But it is most important that the theory-practice gap be diminished. It is this gap which necessitates a "baptism by fire" which many young teachers do not survive. One way to do this would be through the use of closed circuit television observation of successful and unsuccessful teaching techniques. Other instructors observing with the students could help the students learn to observe as well as interpret the activities in the observed classroom.

One of the very important needs in teacher education is to help young students, 18-22 years of age, often struggling with their own negative feelings about authority, separate their own needs in this regard from those of their future charges—young children. Indeed a confusion between certain admirable social values and developmental needs of children is a huge pitfall for many teachers. "Freedom and justice for all" is a highly desirable state to achieve for mature people who have developed personal controls, a sense of responsibility and respect for the rights of others. To not set limits for a youngster doing what all normal youngsters do—test a given social setting for the range of permitted behavior—is to invite chaos. Chaos in the first few weeks of school often leads to pupil control of the classroom from which many teachers can never recover.

Permissiveness is not freedom. Children are free to explore and investigate, invest in ideas and activity when their social system is relatively stable and they are free—by virtue of a clear set of just and reasonable external expectations—from the effect of their own aggressive impulses and those of others around them. Yet young teachers often mistake a youngster moving from one object to another as a curious scholar in pursuit of more information about a fascinating idea. Dangerously impulsive youngsters are too often viewed as "beautifully spontaneous." Excessively hostile and self-destructive youngsters—hiding behind racial or class prejudice or a variety of other defensive tactics—are too often viewed as appropriately rebellious. When two black youngsters refused to attend the Social Issues class conducted by a white teacher because "only a black teacher could understand," the teacher agreed. She failed to consider the fact that the youngsters were not attending other classes and as it turned out, did not attend the Social Issues class conducted by a black teacher.

There is little reason that case studies—educational not clinical—could not be used to help future teachers understand the meaning and manifestations of child behavior. Methods and ways to deal with such problems could be demonstrated by master teachers and behavioral scientists through the use of film, film strips and television. This would be particularly helpful in areas where child behavior consultation is not available. The demonstration of the application of such techniques rather than simple theoretical discussions is critical in that the distortion and misapplication of behavioral theory can be more harmful than good. The complexity of a troublesome interaction can better be demonstrated through the observation of a real or simulated classroom situation than by a discussion of theory. Discussion could be around the concrete issues based on the actual observation.

A third major need in the preparation of young teachers is to help develop self-appraisal and appraisal of the effect of certain techniques. Education like other disciplines in which dynamic process variables—environment, relationships, etc.—cannot be easily controlled and measured suffers from "advocacy training." The latest and successful method being used in Ceylon which catches the eye of the visiting professor from the United States can become the "answer" for the needs of children in Harlem without critical evaluation. When the professor is popular, powerful and prolific in his publications, it is much more likely that "the method" will catch on and will be utilized without asking critical questions.

Every student should be trained to ask, "But will it work with some, all, or any of my students? Will it work in a given community? Is it what the parents want for their children? Is it what the children need to cope in their present and future environments?" A commitment to a given approach makes for teacher security but if it does not meet the needs of a given child at a given time, use of the approach is a disservice . . . indeed poor teaching. Master teachers and skilled educational diagnosticians—rarely available in isolated or low income areas—could help teachers learn to develop the skills to pick up learning problems and to test the effect and appropriateness of a given approach or technique. Such a development would permit teachers to become independent and flexible based on a pupil-centered guide rather than the rigidity of response fostered by dependence on "an expert and his notions." At a given time, with a given situation, a given school, a given child and community, there can only be one expert—the teacher on the scene. If that teacher is not an independent operator, capable of diagnosing the deficits and needs of a child or group of particular children and developing a program or technique to meet those needs, the children will pay the price. Through film, television, etc., it is possible to demonstrate the weakness of a method-centered rather than a pupil-centered approach. This is particularly important where schools of education are dominated by instructors belonging to a certain school of thought.

The individual school or school system can benefit from technological aids in many ways. Schools have now become exceedingly complex social systems. Children and adults are together. Teaching staff of varied backgrounds and experiences must interact with social service personnel and other helping professionals. Non-professional personnel—aides, community workers, custodians, clerical workers, often food service workers, etc.—are all supposed to work as a team with the professionals. Parents, volunteers, visiting teachers, helping teachers and others are in and out of the school. The potential for inter-actional difficulties to occur in this complex mix is high. When the mathematics specialist remains at odds with a classroom teacher, the children are cheated.

Someone must supervise the safety patrol program, student government, physical fitness, the special program in the creative arts, the language club, the choral club and the like. When sister service agencies need information on children and families, they send their questionnaires through the school. When the local university students want to do research, they call on the schools. The teacher aide program must be supervised and the good school maintains close relationships with parents and provides curriculum support for teachers. All of these programs must be coordinated through the principal. Yet the principal is often asked to collect the milk money, sign for bus rentals, lock the movie projector only in his office and fill out numerous reports.

The chewing gum company across town has a well-paid executive with a degree in business administration and a year of in-service training under supervision before he is given less responsibility than most school principals are asked to assume. Many school principals are ex-teachers with no background in administration. Many do not understand the importance of administration in facilitating education. Some wish to get away from the class-room and do not appreciate the importance of providing instructional support. Those who are competent and capable of providing administrative and instructional leadership are often overwhelmed by the sheer volume of demands. Only a small percentage of schools and school systems are utilizing the data processing equipment which facilitates the work of business and industry.

The presence of three new apartment buildings and a road project in an adjacent school district should not find a school unprepared for the 150 extra children it is forced to take. There is little reason that the 3rd grade teacher who works well with withdrawn children but poorly with impulsive children should have four children with impulse control prob-lems in her class while the 3rd grade teacher across the hall has no children with serious impulse control difficulties. Significant health and performance problems discovered in one grade should not be lost to the child's teacher the following year because of an avalanche of time-consuming record keeping. Achievement and learning diagnostic tests should not be meaningless ritual, with the results never being available to the teacher. Yet all of these conditions exist from time to time and at one time in some inner city schools. These conditions result in confusion, disruption, a lack of continuity, frustration and finally, in pupil underachievement.

Data processing equipment could facilitate planning of all kinds and at all levels within a school or school system. Profiles of a given community, school, staff and children could be maintained and utilized to develop all aspects of the school program. Cost analysis could be developed. Material selection could be related to student needs. Material acquisition would require less time. All of these actions would free the administrator from time-consuming detail and permit this time to be spent in support of classroom instruction.

There is well-founded belief that schools should be managed by people with classroom experience rather than professional administrators. Whether this is necessary or not is as open to debate as the question of whether the chief hospital administrator needs to be a physician. The likelihood is even greater in education that a former teacher will serve as principal. This being the case, "packaged" instruction in administration—particularly where formal training is difficult to come by—would be of help. Films, tape, etc. would be useful in this regard.

Every measure which facilitates smooth administrative procedure and reduces the time needed for it, permits more focus on the students. But most important there are direct uses of instructional technology which can be of value to children. Children learn through their various sensory modalities—sight, sound, touch, etc. Lecture largely utilizes only one modality and reading another. Children who learn best by hearing may not be stimulated by visual instruction and vice versa. Technological aides can easily combine one or all of the sensory modalities.

Several educators and social scientists have pointed up the fact that many inner city youngsters speak an English dialect. There is also some evidence that some do not hear all of the language of the teacher who is speaking with different voice inflections, intona-tions, phrasing, etc. Some "tune out" or remain confused. Yet it is important for the child to feel that the language of his home and neighborhood is not "wrong" or less good but different. Recorded instruction heard through individual head sets would permit children to hear the different language of the school under better conditions and without the risk of implying that the dialect was wrong.

A number of educators and social scientists have indicated that self-recording and play back has been of value in "opening up" abused and suspicious youngsters who are turning off the classroom fare. Such equipment enables the child to view himself as an agent of action; to hear his own voice and his own language as it is. One caution here is that classroom teachers who "open children up" and receive emotionally powerful responses should be trained to deal with the content. Otherwise the child becomes defensive again or feels tricked or violated.

Instructional technology probably has the most to offer inner city school programs in the area of basic skill development. The amount of drill time needed here can be sharply reduced. This is important where a disproportionate number of youngsters have skill deficits. On the other side of the spectrum, new technological aids offer children the opportunity to work out their own programs and proceed at their own rate of speed.

Educators have pointed up several major problems children from difficult backgrounds often present. Time-space orientation, synthesis of ordering of stimuli and/or focus on critical stimuli are some of the more important ones. Without these skills children may have trouble finding a point on a map, conceptualizing or understanding the point of a play or story, etc. Technological aids, particularly in the early grades, can be useful in developing these skills.

But education is more than learning skills necessary to get a job. Education should facilitate the total social, psychological and intellectual development of an individual. No machine or device is capable of doing this. Only a human agent able to stimulate curiosity, and a spirit of inquiry, evoke feeling and emotion, provide guides and help the youngster examine himself in relationship to people and things outside himself can be a total educator.

The cultural enrichment programs so widely used in inner city schools often fail to recognize the critical role of the teacher in making the experience relevant. A day at the theater may mean little to some youngsters unless it can be made relevant. Indeed the same is true of readers. *Dick and Jane* and their visits to grandmother's farm have been widely castigated as injurious to the self-image of the inner city child and as irrelevant and outside their experience bank. There is some truth in these claims—although probably more black children spend their summers "in the country" than middle-income blacks or whites. But many children, black and white, are able to get interested in ideas, conditions and things outside their own experience. Whether new experiences are relevant or not probably depends on whether the teacher has promoted a spirit of inquiry and is aware of the need and has the ability to help children integrate a new experience into their past experiences. One inner city teacher noted that his pupils "checked out" on a story about escalators because they had never seen them before. But when he asked them to imagine the stairs to the playground slide moving to the next floor, they checked back in with a great interest, evidenced by a flood of questions, after the explanation.

Even then it was not the teacher's diagnostic ability alone that saved the day. This was a teacher who had a positive relationship with his class. His relatedness, concern, interest—all demonstrated over time—were factors which helped the youngsters tune in. His pupils identified with him and accepted his interest—teaching and learning—as something worthwhile. This, of course, is of vital importance where parents have not transmitted this message.

The point here is that the machine cannot and should not replace the teacher. In fact, if the teacher does not embrace the machine, it can be tuned out. Technology obviously has a place in the inner city school; therefore, it should be introduced carefully, with much planning; and with demonstrations of its potential and limits.

Where regional or city-wide closed circuit television programs are utilized, another consideration must be made. Master teachers or specialists may be threatening to a classroom teacher or may be out of touch with classroom problems peculiar to a given school setting. Without contact and a chance for exchange and clarification, the helpers may be rejected. Seminars and visits between the experts and the classroom teacher could prevent the development of a barrier.

Most important, technological instruction should be planned in conjunction with parents and school staff where possible. The objectives and goals of a given school program should be taken into consideration. The most urgent and important areas of concern should be identified and given highest priority. To give equal emphasis to social studies and reading when 60% of the children are two years behind in reading is wasteful. Joint planning gives a local school staff an investment in a particular approach or technological aid. This will help teachers maintain enthusiasm and interest which is important in motivating pupils.

Finally, developers of instructional technology should think about the possibilities of helping teachers be more effective human beings. In all professions in which personal qualities are an integral part of the "tools of the profession," it is important that attempts be made to favorably modify troublesome characteristics. Psychotherapists, teachers, actors, social workers, etc. can motivate or fail to motivate their consumer, in part on the basis of personal style, relatedness capacity, etc. It has been argued that where such qualities are important, the best professionals are made in heaven and not in college. But this is an overstatement.

Many people simply have speech and voice problems which can be modified. Others simply fail to utilize their hands and body effectively. Some are unaware of their difficulty with closeness and physical contact—a very real problem with very young children. Some have trouble acquiring interest and attention. Often these problems are functions of deep-seated personal problems but do not come to a teacher's awareness. A young teacher "inch-ing" away from a child crowding her for closeness was surprised when an observer noted the reaction. She was able to correct her response in a very natural manner once she was aware of the problem. Technological equipment—tape recorders, television, etc.—could be used at the college level and in in-service training and evaluation programs in schools.

It can not be argued that instructional technology must wait until teacher education is adequate and administrative operations are functioning well. The point being stressed is the wide range of possibilities for technological aids in the school and their direct rela-tionship to pupil learning. The caution being stressed is that technology is not a cure-all, particularly when introduced into a mal-functioning social system. It can be—with adequate preparation—an important part of bringing quality education to inner city schools.

70.

Possible Uses of Technology for Educating Underprivileged Children

by WILLARD J. CONGREVE *
Superintendent
Newton, Iowa Community Schools

There should be little doubt that technology has definite possibilities in the educational process. Many affluent school districts have built new schools or renovated existing ones to specifically accommodate closed circuit TV, electronically controlled study carrels, fully automated lecture halls, rear screen projection, slides and film strips, tape and video tape recorders and playbacks, and storage centers of electronically trivial materials.

Unfortunately, similar examples are not being developed in ghetto schools. The old adage, "the rich get richer and the poor get poorer," seems to apply to the educational arena. Because of dependence on local financing, most schools serving the underprivileged have few funds to build technology into their programs. Such schools even suffer from a dearth of ordinary modern equipment (paper and pencils, fluorescent lighting, and up-to-date plumbing), as well as from a lack of technological aids. Where such aids do exist (many having been purchased from federal funds), few teachers have discovered their potential in the instructional program.

Nevertheless, each year, more and more single instances of the use of technology with impoverished children are reported. The Washington D.C. public schools, in conjunction with the Educational Development Center, achieved exciting results from placing simple science and mathematics technological equipment in the hands of poverty children. Major manufacturers of technological devices are offering to install their equipment into inner city schools at no expense if the teachers will try to create software which will work with underprivileged children.

Even in the affluent schools most of the efforts to use technology seem to be proceeding without the benefit of concurrent evaluation or research. Several reasons might be advanced for this situation. Schoolmen have never been evaluators. Living at a time of rapid technological development they seem to be pressed to install new equipment "to see how it works," before developing assessment procedures to determine comparative effectiveness. "Keeping up with the Joneses" is also operative. When one school district installs "the latest electronic gadget" its neighbors feel they must follow suit, or risk voter and patron conclusions that the schools are backward. Furthermore university scholars for the most part have not become interested in technology as a research topic.

**At the time the paper was written he was an associate professor at the University of Chicago and director of the Woodlawn Experimental Schools Project, Chicago Public Schools.*

The Media Is the Message

There is the chance, however, that even if extensive evaluation and research on technology existed it might be inconclusive. Technology as it is used in schools today is not an integral part of the program. Rather, it is an appendage to the "tried and true" (tired and predictable) methods in which the teacher is the dominant figure and the student is the homeostatic stimulus-reducing organism.[1] Few schools view technology as a media capable of transforming education.

In his several works on media, McLuhan emphasizes one thought: "The Media is the Message." [2] He demonstrates that each new medium which has wrought significant changes in the social scene has done so more because of the nature of the medium than because of the results made possible through the medium. The medium creates a psychology of being able to accomplish the same thing differently; it creates the new life.

In McLuhan's terms, the content required to break the language coding system, a content essential to learning how to read, is the same when learned through the media of Dick and Jane readers, Phonovisual charts, and a pleasant persistent teacher, as when learned through the medium of the "Talking Typewriter." The difference is not in the content learned. The difference is in things which engage the child, excite, interest and motivate him toward breaking the code. It is the medium which makes the difference, that which he manipulates and responds to either physically or mentally: the book, the chart, and the teacher, or the keyboard and the sound track. Just two weeks ago I was required to adjust from a technological situation of immediate access to a car to no car. My office is less than two miles from my home; my major contact points are less than one mile from my office. I am healthy and enjoy walking; yet I felt that I had been stripped naked. The time needed to move from place to place could not have been increased by more than ten minutes; yet I felt I was wasting hours. The problem came about not because the content of the new medium (walking) was different, namely getting there; rather it was the medium itself. It changed my entire psychic. When I again obtained an automobile, I felt released from bondage; I was able to live again.

The present use of technology for education is similar to how it would be for me if I never had free access to an automobile, but occasionally used a taxi or borrowed one for about thirty minutes a day. Under such conditions I would never have developed the auto-psychology which is now a part of me. Rather, the automobile would be an exciting, different, experience; but it would always be something quite a part from my real existence. Under such circumstances, if I were denied the use of the automobile, I would not be deeply affected. I submit that if the technology now being used in ghetto schools were withdrawn, there would be few if any frantic cries from the teachers or the children.

In the current school setting, the omnipresent teacher remains omnipresent when technology is introduced. Until technology can be tested with teachers who are programmed to allow technology to play its full media role, we can not know what technology can do nor we will find the new and proper role for the human element in the media package. Educational technology needs to be tested in a setting (perhaps microcosmic) where it can become the message. Such a setting would be as different from the present schools as is the "wheel era" from the drag-board era. An educational program designed to use all of the technological media now available might give ghetto children such an exciting experience that they would achieve absolutely unheard-of results.

Three Major Problems Confronting Inner City Children: Can Educational Technology Help?

I should like to posit three major educational problems confronting inner city underprivileged children and suggest how technology might be used to alleviate or solve these problems. These problems have no simple origins; they are a function of several conditions. The suggestions made for the use of educational technology, therefore, may not work in many cases. However, I believe they should be attempted.

My own personal research and observations of ghetto children suggest that poverty youth are confronted with three somewhat distinct, but interrelated problems. First, they arrive at school lacking the background necessary for developing the skills, knowledge and understandings which enable them to be productive members of society. Second, they possess a debilitating self-concept. Third, they sense little or no power over their personal destiny. Most educators feel that unless something can be done to alleviate these problems, little significant academic progress can be made.

The lack of skill and knowledge development may not be the result of a lack of experience in the child's early years of his existence. He has had experience; but not enough of the right kind of experience. Preschool experiences of most ghetto children are of high definition[3] requiring very little response input (other than emotional) from the person undergoing the experience. Because of many conditions in his life space, the poverty child spends many hours before the television set. He has witnessed many fights, tragedies, including death, and sensual excitement of one sort or another. But in each instance, the child is a passive recipient, and is satisfied with little intellectual response being required. The stimulus of the media is reduced largely through an emotional response.

Very few of the poverty child's preschool experiences have been of low definition, that is, of such a nature that in order for him to get something out of the experience he personally must put something into it. He has had few provocative conversations with his parents or peers; he has had little opportunity to interact with another person over the telephone; he has seldom been engaged changing a blank piece of paper into a picture, or of converting cardboard into shapes. Much of his early life has been one of semi-vegetation; responding to stimuli to reduce them, and then waiting for or perhaps even seeking, other non-provoking stimuli.

When the poverty child arrives at school, he is not prepared to respond to low definition or "cool" experiences. He knows little about interaction; about personally involving himself intellectually in an experience so as to get something out of it. Moreover, he is not equipped to carry on a dialogue in an experience, even if he felt moved to do so.

For the first few moments the child may think school is much like the movies or television. The actor is the teacher in the classroom. But this actor soon becomes a disappointment; it is not long before he requires the child to do things which the "hot" media to which he has been accustomed never demanded. The child's initial responses to teacher directions are, because of prior conditioning, often inadequate, inappropriate or negative. After a few attempts to engage the child the teacher concludes that the child is nonverbal and not print-oriented. This conclusion often becomes a tragic form of predestination.

It is quite apparent that the current situation in poverty schools needs special media to accomplish a reversal of this conclusion. Technology might be this media; teachers probably cannot. Initially, the media should be of high definition to be similar to the past experiences of the child. In addition, the media must demand some simple intellectual interaction and response. As the child works with the media it must require more responses and permit him to exercise more and more control. Eventually the child must discover that he is the major actor on the learning process; that learning really takes place when he becomes the hot media interacting with "cool" media.

The "talking typewriter" is one technological device which provides the child either a visual or oral stimulation to which the child must offer a response (typing). The machine persists without rancor or impatience until the child discovers and makes the appropriate response. Thus, the "hot" media engages the child but from the very beginning an intellectual response is required. This intellectual response does not eliminate the emotional response. However, the interaction with the media occurs in a private booth. Therefore the natural emotional reactions which accompany the child's intellectual response can be expressed unseen by his peers and his teacher. He can shout at the machine, pound on it with his fists, or do anything else he feels necessary to free himself from the emotional straight jacket of the "hot" media. Yet the machine quietly persists, saying "A", "A", A-white key" "A-white key" until the child gives the correct response.

The "talking typewriter," which the Responsive Environments Corporation claims is useful only for cracking the reading code, provides a media through which so-called nonverbal and not print-oriented children can be engaged immediately in verbal and print-oriented experiences. But as the language code is becoming understandable the media must be altered so to provide the child greater exposure to knowledge and skills. The workbook, the SRA reading kits and laboratories, films film strips and tapes of various kinds can be used. Each medium should stimulate the child and then require him to respond orally or in writing before he can go on. Eventually the child should join a seminar or small group discussion to further his ability to interact and respond. However, any media, be it the teacher or technology which does all of the talking or otherwise prohibits student response, could reverse or neutralize the progress which the initial machine experience may have attained.

Evidence now available suggests that technology can be useful for developing skills and knowledge. However, if technology is to be more effective than the teacher alone, it must begin with each student where he is and provide ever-increasing student response and control.

Such an arrangement requires a vast number of programs for the machine (software) and the programming of the teacher into the process to insure complementary rein-forcement. Such programs and programmed teachers are not common at present. In addition, the number and kinds of machines are still limited.

The impoverished child also faces the problem of a debilitating self-concept. This problem is highly related to skill and knowledge deficiency, but is sufficiently distinct to warrant identification and discussion. The child does not know who he is; he feels that he has little or nothing to offer to himself or to the world, that he is rejected or despised by those in authority, that his ability is limited, and that he cannot ever expect to achieve sufficient success and identification to make him feel that he is "just as good as the next guy".

Many preschool children feel quite good about themselves until they come to school and find that their response behaviors do not satisfy the needs of new conditions. When confronted with people and other environmental conditions which call for responses never before required of him, the child cries and wants to run away. Immediate success experiences are needed if the child with these new conditions is to avoid learning difficulties and subsequent emotional difficulties.

Early success can give the child an exhilarating experience, and technology can help the child achieve this success. Machines can be programmed so they do not proceed until the child discovers the correct answer. Therefore, each time the machine goes ahead the child has been successful. Other programs insure a high level of errorless experience.

Machines also provide immediate feedback in a private setting, allowing the child to make and correct his mistakes without being exposed to teacher or peer criticism. Computer-operated machines can "talk back" to the child informing him of his error in a quiet tone, never getting "its dander up". No matter how many times the child makes the same mistake, the machine will tell him so in the same controlled voice. It never gets angry; it never becomes disturbed because the child is "holding back the rest of the class".

Success also depends upon pacing. Bloom and his associates have demonstrated that 95 per cent of the population can learn almost everything society demands, if given enough time and the proper instruction to do so.[4] Properly programmed and integrated into the total learning setting the machine can provide the concentration of experiences and the necessary reteaching and review which the child needs to succeed. Having enjoyed success, the child is better prepared emotionally to interact with peers and teacher.

If the child is lacking in essential skill and knowledge development, and has a debilitating self-concept, he will undoubtedly feel little power over his future. But, even when skill and knowledge development and the self-concept seem satisfactory for his local community setting the ghetto child or young adult might for several reasons, look out at the world and decide that he is locked in.

A technology media might be quite helpful in amending this disappointing outlook of the poverty child. It could convince him that machines are simple that they need not be feared, and that he can make them his servants. In due course the child will set up and operate machines as well as learn from them. As he controls film and slide projectors, calculators, typewriters, and computers, he will gain confidence and enjoy experiences which could become the foundation for a technological career.

Carrying this idea further, I propose the word "career" be substituted for "vocational" and that the school become a career arts preparation center, or a career arts exploration center. Appropriate technology could be installed in the school to enable children to have a personal experience with several careers before they leave school. Beginning at about age ten, each child could be permitted to manipulate many pieces of equipment and machinery. Through phonovision connections with industry, hospitals, the courts and lawyers' offices, he could observe and carry on a dialogue with people working in almost any career activity.

It should be emphasized, however, that the media used in the career arts center must permit student interaction. The center should avoid the passive recipient process.

As children discover that they can do or have the potential for doing a number of career activities, they will begin to develop a sense of power over their own destinies. However, the school cannot solve the entire problem. If later on, the young adult is unable to enter a career solely because of hard-line prejudices against including certain people (blacks, appalachian whites, etc.) in the career line, then the experiences just suggested will result in greater disappointment and a deepened sense of despair. It may also lead to a greater tendency to revolt.

Responses to Specific Questions Posed by the Commission

I now turn to some of the specific questions posed by the commission. In attempting to provide answers I will be required to repeat some of what has been presented above. In evaluating these responses I hope the reader will keep in mind my one recurring thought: the potential of technology in education will not be realized until we embrace it completely into the teaching-learning process. We need to be able to say "Technology is the media, and the media is the message." Neither technology or the educator may be ready for that experiment. However, we should be willing to accept the assertion that technology has little value if it is used to do only what the teacher has been doing.

1. *How can instructional technology be used to improve the quality of teaching and learning in the ghetto schools, and schools in other poverty areas?*

The Talking Typewriter does help children break the language code and this improves their reading, writing and speech. The time on the machine is short and must be reinforced with work materials and attractive books related to the child's level of development.[5] The Craig Reader has been used with some success in grades four and above to improve comprehension and reading speed. It is now being equipped with an audio recording device to permit student interaction. This device should accommodate programs for assisting the young child to learn to read.

The adding machine and calculator are currently being tested in the upper elementary grades and in high school under the auspices of the Olivetti-Underwood Corporation. These machines help students gain an understanding of mathematical operations. They eliminate the hand number manipulations which often interfere with the student understanding what mathematics is all about. Just as the talking typewriter helps children gain a sense of the language code, the adding machine and calculator assist them in breaking the mathematics code.

As children gain confidence in interacting with media of high definition such as those just described, they should be exposed to media which require more responses from them both openly and to themselves. Such media are available in a variety of forms. Study carrels, electronically connected to a rich storehouse of films, filmstrips, tapes, slides, and other educational media, can bring materials to the student at the press of a button.[6] A few high schools in America are well along in developing such resource media facilities. The technology required is available. Two things stand in the way: money, and materials programmed in a form which machines can use.

The possibilities of such a resource retrieval center are almost limitless. For example, a child, who is going to pursue a general topic could enter the topic through a dial select system into the computer controlled resource center. He would immediately receive a list of subtopics. The child could then order these subtopics, enter them into the computer and obtain lists of books he might read, films he could view, and other materials to explore. He would organize his study sequence and then proceed to call forth the resources and pursue the inquiry.

The resource bank could also give the child the names of other students who have asked for similar information. Knowing this, he could arrange a discussion with some of them. The major topic could be a total class efforts; subtopics, the efforts of individual students. At various stages student groups could come together to discuss findings and raise new questions. The teacher would not be idle; he would react to children's findings and suggest other avenues for exploration. He might even spend time exploring an area with which he was unfamiliar.

2. *What kinds of instructional technology should be introduced into schools in ghettos and other poverty areas, and what kinds of financing arrangements are needed to put this technology to work with all possible speed?*

Some technology is in most ghetto schools. Movie projectors, films, filmstrip projectors and materials, slides, overhead projectors, and tapes recorders are now common place. Unfortunately, their availability does not guarantee proper use. A strong case could be made for placing these devices into storage until teachers create a setting in which they, the children, and this equipment become integrated educational media.

The technology most needed is that which demands student interaction. It should require children to touch it to make it work, and respond to it to make it proceed. It should ensure early success and, in that success, communicate to the child that he, not the machine, has been responsible for the accomplishment. As the new media eliminates the passive recipient or the oppressed respondent behavior, the child should begin to feel like a different human being. The most promising technology for inner city children presently available are the talking typewriter, the talking page, the typewriter, the Craig reader (when it is equipped with the audio-active recorder) the adding machine, the calculator, and other computer based devices.[7]

If the current fare of films, filmstrips and other media are to be used they should be so incorporated into instructional programs that student interaction with the media is part of the process. Unless this is done, these media should be used sparingly.

The new technology which allows for student interaction is quite expensive. Moreover, "software" for this equipment is scarce. Twenty "talking typewriters," with the limited programs available, lease on a five year contract basis for about $280,000 per year. The Craig readers, with audio-active attachments, if and when they become available, will cost much less. All other computer-assisted instruction devices are also quite expensive. The installation of calculators, adding machines, or electric typewriters would require a significant outlay of money. At present cost figures, the technology which seems to have the greatest potential for reaching ghetto children will increase per pupil expenditures about $500 per year. Furthermore, if the technology is to be effective, its installation must be accompanied by a thorough re-education of the teachers and will probably require significant changes in the existing structures. Adequate electrical outlets, lighting, heating, ventilating, air-conditioning, and humidity controls are not available in most ghetto schools.

The high costs and other impediments to installing new technology contribute to technological "tinkering." Rather than expect ghetto schools to adopt expensive media en mass, I propose that one or two experimental media schools be designed and set into operation. Financed like the U.S. space program and committed to the integration of machine, man, and program, such schools could be the first to incorporate new technology into education and could also serve as referents for existing schools as they build technological media into their program.

3. *Can technology significantly advance the learning of children who are non-verbal and not print-oriented? Can schools improve educational achievement by taking advantage of the average child's conditioning by TV and movies?*

First we should question whether nonverbal and not print-oriented children are inherently thus or are simply reflecting preschool conditioning. TV and movies can be viewed as preschool instructional aids or as preschool instructional deterrents. These high definition media which requires little or no intellectual response may contribute to nonverbal and non-print-oriented behavior. As such they should be viewed as things to wean the child away from, rather than as media to be used for the child's learning.

Recognizing both the principle that learning activities should begin where the child is, and the inherent danger in using movies or TV as a steady diet, computer-assisted technology which looks and acts much like a movie or TV, but which requires a response from the child is promising. This new technology can be programmed at the individual level, and will give the child the same instructions an infinite number of times without ever raising its voice. Through its use we may discover the extent to which so-called nonverbal or non-print oriented behavior is the result of prior conditioning.

4. *Can instructional technology help make learning relevant to the needs and lives of ghetto children and youth? What successful techniques, programs, and materials can be cited?*

Let us first ask, Does this question suggest that ghetto children have educational needs which differ greatly from those of other children? I suspect not. Ghetto children need and for the most part want to learn many of the same things other children need and want.

If the difference is in degree more than in kind, the problem of relevancy can be divided into two areas: deficiency and interests. With respect to deficiencies in skill and knowledge development and understanding, technology, properly programmed, can provide individualized experiences to children that are impossible when the learning occurs in a group setting with one teacher. With regards to interests, technology can take ghetto children on trips; it could give them experiences which more fortunate children enjoy at home or through visiting in their father's factory or office. Typewriters, office machines, lathes, punch presses, auto-driving stations, and even cockpits of airplanes could be elements in a career arts exploration center, giving every child experiences which would feed both his knowledge deficiencies as well as his interests.

Few if any successful techniques, programs and materials can be cited in ghetto schools. Most computer-assisted programs have been tested with advantaged children. They should work equally well with ghetto children if the software is written to suit the individual learning needs. The calculator, adding machine, typewriter, and other office machines are being used successfully with upper elementary and high school disadvantaged children.

Single concept films, slides, cassettes, or other new media which permit the child to be the passive recipient may not be useful. They could become technological busy-work to keep some children occupied while the teacher works with others. However, the greatest danger in looking to technology to help make learning relevant is that it will be seen as a relaxation activity rather than as an integral part of the learning program.

5. *How can technology improve the training for the ghettos, and—since the plight of ghetto schools is so desperate—can technology be applied immediately to upgrade the quality of instruction in ghetto schools through relevant and intensive in service training?*

Several technological devices can be used both in teacher education and in-service training. The video-tape recorder may have the greatest potential. It can record and playback micro-teaching segments of the trainee instructing a small group of children. Following an immediate critique, the trainee can repeat the activity until he perfects the technique being developed.

Videotape cameras can record an entire class period for later playback and criticism. If one camera can be focused on the teacher and another on the children the teacher can study how his actions affect the verbal and nonverbal behaviors of the children.

A simple tape recorder equipped with a sensitive microphone can pick up the entire events of a classroom from an inconspicuous location. Although the video is lacking the information can be used by a teacher to critique his instructional program.

The use of recording devices depends upon the teacher's willingness to expose his teaching behaviors to himself and to his critics. If seen as a positive and healthy activity, the teacher can identify behaviors which are dysfunctional to student learning and practice new techniques under watchful eyes.

A teacher who is reluctant can use the VTR or the tape recorder privately. As he gains courage, the teacher might ask a consultant to view or hear the tape with him. Once the teacher discovers how these in-service activities can improve his techniques, he may find himself selling the idea to others.

Closed circuit TV in the Chicago Public Schools has become a successful in-service training device for the classroom teachers. The participating schools are organized into a cluster and the classroom teachers located in the cluster schools work as a team with the TV master teacher to plan the TV lessons. They are also present in the classroom during the telecast.

Planning the lesson with the TV master teacher, observing their children's reaction to it, conducting a follow-up with the children, and then evaluating the lesson with the TV teacher, results in considerable professional growth among the classroom teachers. Whereas the learning results for the children in the closed TV clusters is still being assessed, there is little doubt on the part of the professionals that this intimate involvement in the curriculum-making process has had a positive and dynamic effect upon the classroom performance of many teachers.

6. *If, as the Koerner report suggests, the chief thing wrong with black America is white America, how can instructional technology be used to help change the attitudes of the white majority—e.g., white middle-class suburban children and children of ethnic groups who settled in the ghettos before the Negroes?*

I don't think it can. Certainly films, filmstrips, TV shorts, etc. will do little, if anything. Engagement with children and adults of differing races and nationalities in activities where all work together to achieve a common goal is about the only way attitudes can be changed. It might be possible to set up a technological learning center which would attract children and adults of many racial backgrounds. Here, all would use the technology and all would benefit from it. Interracial seminars could be organized in which all could contribute to the interchange. Such a technological center might help but only if personal engagement and equality of role are essential dimensions.

7. *How could technology be most effectively used to increase black children's pride in their own heritage?*

To increase black children's pride in their own heritage they must be confronted with valid information about how black heritage has contributed to their culture and to the world culture. To be effective, the information should be transmitted in such a manner that children have full opportunity to ask questions of the media, and to otherwise respond to it.

I should like to be more specific. In the past year, many teachers of black children have lined their classroom walls with pictures of black political leaders and contributors to history and culture. The mere presence of pictures has some impact on the child. But because they require no response from the child; they soon lose the significance they may have had when first seen. Pictures can be useful if they are discovered by the children in response to some question; hung for a purpose, and then removed when that purpose has been fulfilled. Pictures of persons who deserve continuous attention and respect, should be chosen by the class for definite reasons and then be hung for an indefinite period.

Much the same can be said of movies which depict the lives of famous black people, or which relate black music, poetry, or history. The movie experience should develop out of children's requests. Lengthy movies should be shown in short bits to allow children to raise questions, or otherwise respond. As the movie is being studied the children should discuss what they have seen, speculate on the importance of the work of the individual, and consider how society would have been different had the person not lived or the event not taken place.

Phonovision could connect children to black cultural events, and to black scholars, sportsmen, doctors, lawyers, business executives, and other contemporary black leaders. I suspect that if black children could talk directly with such individuals they would develop an increased understanding and pride in their heritage.

Closing Remarks

There are many inconclusive reports on the effectiveness of technology in education. Some reports depict technology as something which can enter the classroom and take over some of the functions of the teacher without making any substantial change in the present nature of the system. While there is evidence to support these conclusions, we must recognize that the presence of the technology does precipitate many problems. For a machine to truly individualize, a comprehensive diagnosis must be made for each student. Teachers are not programmed to make such diagnoses, and when such is indicated, they often pooh-pooh the request as being unnecessary and irrelevant.

The capabilities of technology to individualize and specialize at a high level also make clear that the programs created for the machine by the educator are not sufficiently personalized. Again the teacher is confronted with a perplexing problem which up to now he has pretty well ignored in his classroom.

Even though the machine has yet to be perfected to the point where it can engage the learner in a meaningful dialogue, it already requires some specialization or training on the part of its users and is already indicating the need for major changes in the instructional process. The educator, instead of pursuing the potential capabilities of this new media to transform the instructional process, limits the use of the machine to only things which the teacher has been doing.

The machine can be inflexible as well as flexible. It can be programmed to standardize or it can be programmed to individualize. Because the machine exposes the inadequacies of programs more readily than do teachers own up to the inadequacies of their programs, the machine can be quite an irritant.

Much must be done before we can hope to realize the full potential of technology. First, teachers must learn much more about media. They must see themselves as a form of media. They need to be helped to understand how other media can be integrated with their media; how their media can be enhanced by a technology which can transmit ideas and develop skills with a degree of effectiveness and efficiency not possible for the teacher.

When the teacher accepts the technological media for what it can do, his behavior can then be modified to emphasize its personalized significance. It is doubtful that technology will ever be able to listen to children as they describe their many concerns, to ask them questions, and on the basis of questions and responses assist them to find new ways to deal with their problems. It is doubtful that any machine can take on the cloak of fellow-explorer as a teacher can with a student. It is doubtful whether any machine can have the sensitivity to know when to tell a child what to do, and when to hold off and let the child find out for himself. I suspect that when technological media does come to full bloom, the teacher will discover that teacher functions are not diminished, rather they are transformed and raised to a higher state of professionalism.

There are many roles which technology can assume, but these roles will not be readily assigned by the teacher. In fact, if the teacher retains his present command of his classroom, it is doubtful that technology will ever get the chance to demonstrate its potential. However, let us hope that someone will soon create an experimental instructional program which integrates the teacher, the student and the machine. The result may be a completely new media, and this new media be an entirely new message for education.

REFERENCES

1. Getzels, Jacob W. "New Concept of The Learner: Some Implications for The Classroom." *Claremont Reading Conference,* Twenty-eighth Yearbook, ed. Malcolm P. Douglass, (Claremont, California: Claremont Graduate School Curriculum Laboratory, 1964).

2. McLuhan, Marshall. *Understanding Media: The Extensions of Man.* New York: Signet Book, 1964.

   McLuhan, Marshall and Quenten Fore. *War and Peace in the Global Village.* New York: Bantam Book. Inc, 1968.

   Stearn, Gerald Emanuel. *McLuhan, Hot and Cool.* New York: The Dial Press, Inc. 1967.

3. McLuhan describes two kinds of media—those which are "hot"—of high definition, and those which are "cool"—of low definition. High definition or "hot" media require little of the person in the way of response in order for the person to get the message. Low definition or "cool" media demand that the person interact intellectually in order for him to obtain the message. A movie is a "hot" medium; a telephone is a "cool" medium.

4. Bloom, Benjamin S. "Learning for Mastery." AERA Pamphlet, 1968.

5. Martin, Dr. John Henry. "Will They Ever Learn." London, J. D. Garrod, Ltd.

   Responsive Environments Corporation, Conference Report, February 8, 9, 10, 1968, *Responsive Environment Learning Center, "Feedback From The Field."* Englewood Cliffs, New Jersey.

6. Bergenfield New Jersey School System. "Utilizing AV Devices, Instruments and Equipment as Aids in Teaching Children and Informing Adults." *Educational Equipment and Material,* #2, 1968 Edition pg 17-21.

Brown, James W., and Kenneth Norberg. *Administering Educational Media.* New York, McGraw-Hill Book Co, 1965.

Bauer, Rudolf. "Industrial Arts and The Ghetto." *Culture and Education,* Volume 1, No. 4, pg. 3-5, Winter 1968.

7. Thatcher, David A. "Teacher VS Technicians: We Still Have A Choice." *Phi Delta Kappan* XLIX, No. 8, 435-438, April 1968.

Suppes, Patrick. "Computer Technology and The Future of Education." *Phi Delta Kappan* XLIX, No. 8, 420-423, April 1968.

Bundy, Robert F. "Computer-Assisted Instruction—Where Are We." *Phi Delta Kappan* XLIX, No. 8, 424-429, April 1968.

Barrett, Richard S. "The Computer Mentality." *Phi Delta Kappan* XLIX, No. 8, 430-434, April. 1968.

71.

Technology for Pre-Service And In-Service Training Of Teachers Of Ghetto Children

by ALONZO A. CRIM*
Superintendent
Compton (California) Union High School District

Urban educators have waited for years for technology to produce instant solutions to the problems they face in educating poor urban children. Technology has produced abundant amounts of new soft and hard educational materials. Much of these materials, however, can now be found collecting dust in school storerooms and teachers' closets. Technology has not yet found the elixir for the ailments of public school education in the cities.

Educators who are not mesmerized by the success of technology in the production of goods and in space anticipated the early failures of technology in education. They know that educating America's youth is a complicated task. It is at least as difficult today to successfully educate children from low-income urban areas to fully utilize their talents as to put an astronaut on the moon. As technicians come to realize this they will become more successful in their explorations in the field of education.

Technicians and business leaders who are now being enlisted by government to "save" public education will find that it differs vastly from the worlds of business and industry. The basic difference is that it is every American's right to receive an education. However, Americans differ markedly on what kind of education that they have a right to receive. There is far more agreement in business and industry on the kinds of products that they are to produce. Public schools are expected to produce diverse kinds of education on a rather miserly budget. Fifty-one million public school students are educated at an average annual cost of $550.[1] There is absence of flexibility in the public school budget for future planning or investing in promising technology. Schools are required to be more concerned with the here and now or the past.

Instruction by teachers remains the major method of educating students. There are certain teacher activities that machines can do now and no doubt machines will do more of them in years to come. However, machine costs are higher currently. Patrick Suppes estimates the cost computerized system for drill and practice to be $4.50 per pupil hour compared to less than $.60 per pupil hour cost for teachers.[2] Cost of computer time will probably diminish in time, but it will hardly be reduced in the near future to the level of present costs of educating a student.

Technicians who are now conducting experiments in applying technology to education

*At the time his paper was submitted to the Commission (November 1968) he was district superintendent of schools in Chicago.

have come to know the magnitude of problems that teachers face in developing adequate curricula for students. Suppes, in considering the problem, wrote:

> It is a straightforward matter to show that the number of problems of possible sequences of concepts and subject matter just in the elementary school is in excess of 10^{100}, which is larger than even generous estimates of the number of elementary particles in the universe.[3]

If it were only a matter of discovering the proper sequences of concepts and subject matter for ghetto schools, technology would in time be successful in identifying those things that teachers in ghetto schools should know. But it isn't that easy. Ghetto communities want much more from their schools and teachers.

People living in the ghetto feel that the public school should not only teach reading, writing and arithmetic, it should also be the springboard for social acceptance and employment. Thus, the public school has failed them even when it has been successful in teaching academic skills. For maximum utility, then, technology should be used in preparing teachers to eradicate this failure of long standing. It should not be used as it has in recent years to perpetuate unproductive programs. How effective have teacher in-service and pre-service programs been in preparing teachers for ghetto schools?

In-Service and Pre-Service Teacher Education

Teacher in-service education rests on the assumption that children's lives will not be changed very much unless the professional and personal lives of their teachers are made ever richer with fruitful experiences. To this point the National Commission on Teacher Education and Professional Standards has stated: "In-service growth is that growth which takes place after the teacher is on the job. It is a continuation of the professional development which was begun during the pre-service period of preparation. In-service education is a process inherent in any planned program designed to make the individual a more effective teacher. This type of education should be an integral part of any school program."[4]

School systems, however, do not agree on what constitutes professional growth. The Research Division of the National Education Association conducted a survey of activities accepted as fulfilling professional growth requirements in 1965. The results of that survey are shown in the following chart.[5]

The chart shows that the 307 school systems with 6,000 or more pupils enrolled generally accepted just three types of professional growth activities: college courses for credit, school system programs and travel. It should be noted that two of the three activities are teacher initiated, albeit found acceptable and probably encouraged by school systems through inducements of salary advancements on the salary schedule.

The apparent assurance of school systems that teachers will become more effective teachers because of increments of higher education is unfounded. Research data has not found a significant relationship between teachers effectiveness and the teacher's grades in university courses.[6] These findings hold true even in the teacher's major subjects.[7] These findings, however, could mean that the university courses are irrelevant and that teachers could be helped to become more effective teachers if they were enrolled in meaningful courses.

School systems' strong support of teachers taking university courses no doubt stems from the recent past when teachers had limited education. In 1890, relatively few teachers had received a high school education. It was 1910 before any state was to make a high school graduation the minimum requirement for all teacher licenses.[8] Through the years, teachers have received increased education. In 1966, the percent of teachers lacking the bachelor degree had declined from 22.2 percent in 1951 to 7.0 percent in 1966.[9]

The evidence concerning the value of the other two professional growth activities accepted by the 307 school systems is just as lacking as with university courses. There is

Activities Accepted as Fulfilling Professional Growth Requirements in 307 Reporting School Systems 1965-1966

PROFESSIONAL GROWTH ACTIVITY	STRATA BY ENROLLMENT			
	Total	25,000 or more	12,000-24,999	6,000-11,999
COLLEGE COURSES FOR CREDIT	100%	100%	100%	100%
Workshops or in-service training sponsored by school system	81.8	80.4	81.0	82.4
Travel	66.8	69.6	69.6	64.8
Non-credit courses or institutes not sponsored by school system	44.6	43.5	43.0	45.6
Research	34.9	45.7	34.2	32.4
Work on School Committees	32.9	37.0	32.9	31.9
Professional writings	29.0	39.1	22.8	29.1
Attendance at professional conferences or conventions	21.8	26.1	17.7	22.5
Supervision of student teacher	14.7	13.0	11.4	16.5
Holding office in professional association	13.7	15.2	10.1	14.8
Committee work in professional association	11.4	13.0	10.1	11.5
Community projects	9.4	17.4	7.6	8.2
Work experiences	3.9	8.7	3.8	2.7
Other	6.5	4.3	3.8	8.2
Number reporting	307	46	79	182

virtually no research literature on how teachers are improved through travel. There is an extensive literature of school systems in-service education programs, but the determination of the benefits of these programs is derived largely through the observations of the authors.[10] Definitive research on how teachers improve through participation in in-service education is limited, if at all available.

Knowledge is equally obscure in the identification of the individual needs of teachers despite the large number of studies done on this topic. J. W. Getzels and P. W. Jackson, in reviewing over 800 teachers' characteristics and personality studies in 1950, write, "Despite the critical importance of the problem and a half-century of prodigious effort, very little is known for certain about the nature and measurement of teacher personality, or about the relation between teacher personality and teacher effectiveness."[11] The lack of knowledge about how to improve the teaching of teachers of minority children has become critical in recent years. A new emphasis has been placed upon the pre-service as well as the in-service training of teachers of minority children since the 1954 Brown v. Board of Education of Topeka Supreme Court decision. It was with this decision that it was officially recognized that minority children received an unequal education. Teachers discovered during the 1950's and continuing until the present that old teaching methods would not provide equal education. Malcolm Provus summarized the problem as follows:

... that the slum child is a child of another world. Our laws do not bind him, our standard middle-class ambitions do not inspire him, our IQ's do not measure him and most of all our teachers do not reach him. Rules learned in college clearly don't work in the slum schools, but some teachers cling to them for no one has taught them otherwise.[12]

If Provus is right, what rules should colleges teach prospective teachers? And if such rules do indeed exist, can they be taught to teachers?

Much of the research on disadvantagement in the past ten years has been primarily focused on children. The rationale was that if the children's needs could be identified that teachers could fulfill these needs. More recently researchers have given greater attention to the qualities that teachers must have to be successful in teaching ghetto children. Ability to bridge social class differences that often exist between students and teachers is thought by some researchers to be of the utmost importance. Kenneth Clark claims that social class of the teacher is a major factor in the poor achievement of lower-class children.

> The clash of cultures in the classroom is essentially a class war, a socio-economic and racial warfare being waged on the battleground of our schools, with middle-class teachers provided with a powerful arsenal of half-truths, prejudices and rationalizations arrayed against hopelessly out-classed working class youngsters. This is an uneven balance, particularly since, like most battles, it comes under the guise of righteousness.[13]

A number of studies on the background of teachers have concluded that teachers are middle-class or have a middle-class orientation, although researchers differ on community origins of teachers.[14] Thus there is no sure way of testing Clark's beliefs until there are groups of teachers identified to have working-class orientations who can be compared to groups of teachers of comparable skills with middle-class orientations.

This debate of social class difference, however, has affected the education of teachers. Teacher education programs for school personnel to work with children of the ghetto are heavily oriented toward the sociological and anthropological aspects of slum children. The rationale being that these kinds of studies will give prospective teachers the new understandings of the cultures of ghetto children, thereby making them more effective. It is a basic premise that new understandings of the culture of the particular group of children are necessary if the teacher is to bridge the gap from the home culture of his students to the school culture and the culture of the larger society.

Because the teacher of ghetto children, typically, does not share a common cultural background with his students, and because he has middle-class values which his students have not acquired, it is assumed that he may have attitudes which form a barrier to his acceptance of his students, a barrier to which they may react negatively. Many programs, then, are designed to change attitudes of the teacher toward the children of the ghetto. These aspects of the programs are difficult to evaluate. William Kvaraceus in *Negro Self Concept* states:

> One significant finding, however, which we can be somewhat sure about, is the fact that education has relatively little impact on attitudes and behavior. Coleman's study of adolescent society, Jacob's study of college education, and the research reported by Sanford indicate that most students enter schools, whether it be high school or college, and leave it without any visible change except that they are four years older.[15]

If this is true, the standard approach to classroom instruction cannot achieve desired change in attitude because the standard approach tends to reinforce the student's self-concept. Kvaraceus concludes:

> Therefore we would propose a new approach. We would suggest that the utilization of the idea of deliberate effort to change the self-concept of students (in educational courses) will appreciably affect their total education as well as their personal experiences.[16]

A number of teacher-training institutions have made a "deliberate effort" to interest their students in seeking teacher careers in slum areas. Some of these programs are reviewed by Edmund W. Gordon and Doxey A. Wilkerson in a research project by the College Entrance Examination Board and the National Scholarship Service and Fund for Negro Students.[17] The salient features of these programs seem to be increased contact with slum children and their communities. Almost all programs seek volunteers; therefore, there is no measure of how students' attitudes were changed toward ghetto children by the college courses they have taken.

Bank Street College was funded by the Office of Economic Opportunity in 1965 to evaluate the teacher education programs for the disadvantaged at 122 colleges and universities. Seventy-seven institutions reported accomplishing this goal through courses—36 through student teacher experience in special service schools; 19 through field trips and school visitations in disadvantaged areas; 14 through special projects; 13 through workshops and conferences; 10 through tutorial programs; 6 through community services; 4 through special films and lectures; and 5 through other methods.

Reactions of the institution to how they evaluated the programs covered a wide range of responses from, "Most of our student teachers are placed in a middle-income community, but at times might be *subjected* to the kind of community you describe," to, "We believe all will be better teachers for understanding the teaching of children with vast differences in experiential background." A frequent assertion was that the new emphasis on teaching teachers to work with the disadvantaged had not raised the public image of this kind of teaching and not facilitated recruitment and placement of teachers in economically deprived areas.[18]

The responses from the 122 colleges and universities seem to confirm the previously drawn conclusion that college courses do not change the attitudes of prospective teachers toward ghetto children. The portents of this conclusion are: ghetto schools will continue to have difficulty in securing teachers; many of the teachers who are assigned to ghetto schools do not want to be there; the rate of teacher transfers from ghetto schools will likely continue to be high; and, teacher morale problems may be more frequent and of greater consequence in ghetto schools.

Technology can best help education immediately in the area of evaluation. Evaluation and evaluative instruments in education are almost nil.[19] Officials of the U.S. Office of Education have identified those common errors in evaluation procedures used by school districts applying for Title I funds:

1. Confusing ends with means.

2. Operating on assumptions that are not necessarily a reasonable basis for evaluation.

3. Equating correlation with causation.

Since evaluation is extremely limited in education, it cannot be done in a piecemeal manner. It must be comprehensive. We cannot continue in education in building expressways along old cow paths simply because cows and men have always gone these same ways. We must know why we teach certain subjects and what methods bring about the greatest results.

To establish such comprehensive and interrelated educational research and evaluation, Richard Miller recommends that the U.S. Congress establish a network of 50 experimental schools across the nation patterned after the well-known and highly successful agricultural stations.[20]

Miller suggests that these schools be established in all geographic areas and would specialize in various educational problem areas. All schools would be linked by telephone and closed circuit television. In essence, the schools would be a systems approach to the problems of education. Not only would it allow the type of interrelated research and development management systems that are essential next steps in our era of energetic innovation, but it would allow educational problems to be studied vertically over a 12- or 14-year period. Different patterns of teacher education could be examined and evaluated in such a program.

The problem of teacher education, however, cannot wait for such onslaught. We must determine what we can do well now. We should identify some of the good proposals that have been submitted to the U.S. Office of Education and experiment with them on a limited basis. Increasingly, researchers in disciplines other than education are being persuaded to lend their talents to the problems of education. This trend must be encouraged through adequate funding for basic research.

A system of incentives must be devised to induce teacher training institutions and school systems to try methods that have shown promise in experimental situations. Federal funding has given impetus for experimentation in recent years. Perhaps some funds should be diverted to encouraging the use of pilot programs.

Helpful Applications of Technology in Teacher Education

Technology has had a tremendous impact on Americans. In tandem with massive commercial advertising, technology has through regular improvement created a mystique of infallibility for the average person. It is often forgotten by Americans that technology builds upon present knowledge and practices. Its power comes from its ability to systematize what is known, divide the whole task into smaller units of work, and make the smaller units more efficient and productive.

In education, technology has had, thus far, little success. It has built on old practices which in many cases were not meeting today's demands of education. Education has been slow in changing. Greater efficiency brought about by technology in education will not necessarily result in greater quality. Thus, films, radios, recordings and television play little more than token roles in instruction.

If technology is to play a significant role in instruction, it will have to be applied with imagination to problems identified by the people who run the schools. Otherwise, the new devices that are developed will have little hope of widespread adoption by schools. The current crises in urban schools and college campuses are more related to who will run the schools than what is taught. What is taught is so similar in schools that who runs the schools does seem to be a major variable in the quality of schools.

To identify how technology can improve the training of teachers for the ghettos, then, it is necessary to identify problems that teachers have in teaching ghetto children. The problems discussed in this paper are not comprehensive but are acute problems that have been identified by many students of education.

Language Barriers

Students in the ghettos generally perform poorly in school. They have a high proportion of failure, of drop-outs, of reading and other learning disabilities, and of life-adjustment problems. They are especially characterized by deficiencies in reading and language, the two tools on which success in school depends.

Taba found that the schools often exacerbate the learning problems of lower-class children ". . . through the attitudes of the faculty and choice of curriculum. Deviation in cultural background naturally creates a discontinuity between the cognitive, perceptual, and emotional development of the child and the school curriculum and expectations."[21] This discrepancy is not merely a result of a deficit in academic skills. It is also a discrepancy in orientation to language as a medium of communication. For example, the difference among the linguistic style of habits of students and teachers can be an effective deterrent to communication and, therefore, to learning.

Perhaps computers can intervene and mediate the language barriers between teachers and students, similar to the computer procedures used in item analysis of tests? James Swanson reports a computer program in which teacher-made tests were scored, and test items analyzed. The IBM-1230 Computer used in the experiment scored 368,000 answer sheets in 27 days, did item analysis of each test, and further computer analysis was instituted for determination of new objectives.[22]

In the program described above it would seem that it would be possible to determine which concepts students fail to understand and cause students to continue to fail and teachers to despair. With the aid of the computer, lessons could be developed with words that can be understood by the students—the cultural gap between teachers and students can be reduced.

Sophie Bloom found that the students in a disadvantaged school in Chicago did not clearly understand 20 to 50 percent of the basic words used by their teachers.[23] National surveys of educational achievement directed by James Coleman (Coleman Report) found that there was a cumulative deficit in the academic achievement of minority students. At grade six the average Negro is approximately one-and-one-half years behind the average white. At grade twelve, he is approximately three-and-one-fourth years behind the average white.[24] It seems perfectly reasonable for the Negro student to achieve about 75 percent as much as the average white when he only understands about 50 to 80 percent of what his teacher says.

Cultural Gaps—Differences of Teachers and Students

To determine the words that teachers say that their students do not understand is not, in itself, sufficient to improve the educational achievement of children in depressed areas. Riessman points out that teachers must learn and understand the cultural characteristics of their students.[25] A promising tool to help new teachers to understand the students' environment and for in-service training teachers is simulation.

Bert Y. Kersh describes a classroom simulation experiment for the pre-service education of elementary teachers that could possibly be used as a model for a simulation program that could be particularized for ghetto schools.[26] Kersh's program is concerned with the teacher's ability to detect, diagnose, and resolve such teaching problems as confusion, inattention, distraction, and fatigue on the part of the learner. To carry out the simulated experience he uses films and written materials (cumulative records and community descriptions). There are 60 problem sequences on film with feedback to show probable consequences of teachers' actions. Testing and instruction requires ten hours and simulated experience requires from five to seven hours. Experiences can be practiced repeatedly.

With such a program, some teachers could be helped to understand their students and better anticipate their problems in learning the school's offerings. Furthermore, they could be shown how their own actions are sometimes damaging to the students. Perhaps, then, the teachers could take to heart John Holt's caveat, "We must try to free our teaching from ambiguity, confusion, and self-contradiction."[27]

Teacher Placement

Study of career patterns of teachers who begin their careers in lower-class schools by Howard Becker shows that teachers tend to transfer to schools which are attended by children of higher social class.[28] Becker gave as reasons for the pattern of teacher transfers their concern with pupil transgressions against deeply-felt moral standards, especially those of ". . . health and cleanliness, sex and aggression, ambition and work, and the relations of age groups."[29]

The training of teachers through simulated experiences could be extrapolated to new teacher placements. Currently, teacher personnel information in the public schools has not been maximally utilized for placement purposes.

It would be well worth experimentation to identify the most successful teachers in all schools, have them participate in the simulated experiences and record their responses to the questions asked them. If there are discernible patterns, new teachers who fit certain patterns in simulation experiences would receive teaching assignments accordingly. Follow-up studies of the performances of these teachers would attest to the viability of the experimental placement procedure.

Perhaps such a placement program would help to curtail the inordinately large number of teacher transfers from the ghetto schools. Also, the ghetto schools, when they do receive teachers, would receive teachers who have a good chance to succeed in those schools.

Conclusion

Technology has virtually revolutionized business and industry in recent years. Increasingly, technology is being applied to educational problems. Some people anticipate success similar to that enjoyed by business and industry. However, what they seem to ignore is that technology has been used in education for some while without producing any noticeable changes.

Technology has entered education in a big way. But to date, technology has done little other than produce streamlined versions of what has gone on in education for years—old books have been given new covers. The research on pre-service and in-service education of teachers of ghetto children has revealed little as to what kind of training is needed.

It is suggested in the paper that technology can best be applied in preparation of teachers for the ghetto by evaluating current practices in teacher training and through its use in applied and basic research. Technology, through this means, can bring to fruition changes in teacher preparation that are likely to work.

REFERENCES

1. Long, Luhan H. Editor. *The World Almanac.* New York: Newspapers Enterprise Association, 1968, p. 154.

2. Suppes, Patrick. "On Doing Computers to Individualize Instruction." Found in D. Bushnell and D. W. Allen (eds.) *The Computer in American Education: Issues and Applications.* Palo Alto, California: The Fund for the Advancement of Education, 1965, p. 5.

3. *Ibid.,* p. 17.

4. Moffitt, John Clifton. *In-Service Education for Teachers.* Washington, D.C.: The Center for Applied Research in Education, Inc., 1963, p. 26.

5. NEA Research Division, *Research Bulletin,* National Education Association, March 1967, Vol. 45 (1), p. 26.

6. Jones, Ronald D. "The Prediction of Teaching Efficiency from Objective Measures." *Journal of Experimental Education.* 1946, XV, pp. 85-89.

7. Fowler, H. Seymour. "Evaluation of an Institute for the Training of Elementary School Science Resource Teachers." *Journal of Educational Research,* May, 1960, Vol. 53 (9), pp. 358-59.

8. Elsbree, Willard S. *The American Teacher*. New York: The American Book Co., 1939, p. 350.

9. NEA Research Division, *Research Bulletin*. Washington, D.C.: National Education Association, October 1967, Volume 45, p. 3, p. 87.

10. *Ibid.*

11. Gage, N. L. Editor. *Handbook of Research on Teaching*. Chicago: Rand McNally and Co., 1963, pp. 715-805.

12. Provus, Malcolm, et al, *Staffing for Better Schools*. Washington, D.C.: U.S. Printing Office, 1967, p. 3.

13. Clark, Kenneth. *Dark Ghetto*. New York: Harper & Row, 1965, p. 129.

14. Gage, N. L. *op. cit.*

15. Kvaraceus, William. *Negro Self Concept*. New York: McGraw-Hill Book Co., 1965, p. 36.

16. *Ibid.*

17. Gordon, Edmund W. & Doxey A. Wilkerson. *Compensating Education for the Disadvantaged.* New York: College Entrance Board, 1966, p. 54, p. 59.

18. Klopf, Gordon J. and Garda W. Bowman. *Teacher in a Social Context.* New York: Mental Health Materials Center, Inc., 1967, pp. 186-195.

19. Fox, David J. "Issues in Evaluating Programs for Disadvantaged Children." *The Urban Review Center for Urban Education,* Dec., 1967, pp. 2, (3), 5.

20. Miller, Richard I. "Needed Experimental Schools That Really Experiment." *Phi Delta Kappan,* April, 1968, XLIX, 8, p. 417.

21. Taba, Hilda. *Teaching Strategies for the Culturally Disadvantaged.* Chicago: Rand & McNally, 1966, p. 9.

22. Swanson, James R. "Item Analysis," *Data Processing for Education.* January 1966, Vol. 5: 1.

23. Bloom, Sophie. "Improving the Education of Culturally Deprived Children: Applying Learning Theory to Classroom Instruction." in *Educating the Disadvantaged Learner.* Staten W. Webster (ed.), San Francisco, Calif.: Chandler Publishing Co., p. 487.

24. Coleman, James S. *et al, Equality of Educational Opportunity.* Washington: U.S. Printing Office, 1966, p. 273.

25. Riessman, Frank. *The Culturally Deprived Child.* New York: Harper and Row, 1962.

26. Kersh, Bert Y. *Classroom Simulation: A New Dimension in Teacher Education.* Monmouth, Oregon: Oregon State System of Higher Education, 1963.

27. Holt, John. *How Children Fail.* New York: Hill Publishing Co., 1965, p. 76.

28. Becker, Howard S. "Social-Class Variation in the Teacher-Pupil Relationship." *Journal of Educational Sociology,* 1952.

29. *Ibid.* p. 461.

72.

Developing Relevant Education Through Instructional Technology

by ALVA R. DITTRICK
Educational Consultant*

Rapid advances are being made with respect to educational technology and its application to instruction. Unquestionably, a decade from now the classroom and educational environments as we know them today will be drastically changed. We are at the threshold of reform in both the development and use of instructional technology. Single concept approaches, programmed materials and educational hardware emanating from responsive environment concepts are laying the groundwork for future changes in instructional strategies that cannot be fully envisioned at this time.

As an example of one of the efforts that are looking to the future in terms of instructional technology, the Research Council, since 1965, through the American Education Publishers Institute, has been working to accomplish the revision of instructional material in a manner that will bring greater relevancy to the inner city child. This past year a relationship has been established with Education Producers Council. Currently, seven of the great cities are involved in identifying needs and recommending to the producers of audiovisual materials the kinds of materials that will support efforts to improve effectiveness and quality of the teaching-learning process in the schools.

Firsthand experiences and observations indicate that the rate and extent of creation, development and application of educational technology will be dependent upon three factors: (1) availability of funds, (2) teacher preparation, and (3) development of new educational supportive systems.

The discussion that follows directs itself at a consideration of two general questions:

"Can instructional technology help to make learning relevant to the needs and lives of ghetto children?"

"What are some of the successful techniques, programs and materials?"

Instructional technology is defined for the purposes of this paper as those instructional procedures are products that are used to facilitate learning activities. Among these products are included radio, television, tapes, projectors, computers, programmed materials, the development of new learning strategies and instructional organization systems.

*At the time this paper was written Mr. Dittrick was executive vice president of The Research Council of the Great Cities Program for School Improvement, Chicago, Illinois.

Developments in instructional technology have been and presently are being sought, developed and tested by school systems throughout the country in an attempt to establish more meaningful contact with all children and especially children living in ghettos. Teaching aids of all varieties when used with advance planning and preparation of students have been recognized as a basic means for improving the output resulting from classroom instruction.

Over the course of the past thirty years, instructional technology has demonstrated value as a means of making conventional classroom instruction a more effective vehicle for learning. Experiences in both industrial and military training reinforce the observation that more effective instruction can take place when teaching procedures utilize a variety of means by which to develop skills, knowledge and understanding.

As a result of funds available through legislation such as NDEA and ESEA, central-city schools have increased their use of instructional equipment and materials. In several cities improvement of instruction is being sought through a saturation of technological devices in each classroom of selected inner city schools. The presence of additional materials coupled with in-service preparation of teachers is serving as a basis for making classroom instructional experiences more interesting and relevant for disadvantaged children.

The greatest use of technological aids as integral elements of daily educational operations has concentrated on the use of the following devices:

1. Projection equipment and the software in terms of films, transparencies, and slides have become a basic element of teacher training and classroom practice. Both enrichment experiences and presentation of specific instruction have been enhanced by the availability of audiovisual educational tools. The overhead projector is probably the most significant instrument introduced within recent years that holds promise of reshaping many conventional teaching-learning experiences.

2. Televised instruction has established itself as an important educational means, particularly as a device to strengthen teacher competencies in specialized areas such as science, music, and modern math. In these instances the general level of teacher preparation necessitates more specialized training. Television has enabled the presentation of instruction by a teacher who brings competence and appropriate facilities that make selected elements of education both meaningful and exciting. The availability of this resource is uniquely important in schools in which teacher turnover is high and fully trained teachers may not be available.

3. Language and reading instruction has been made more effective by altering conventional instructional strategies through the use of language laboratories, listening posts, language masters and systematically prepared reading materials. The opportunity to hear appropriate pronunciation is important to the development of language patterns of inner city children.

4. Library services have rapidly changed in both function and resources so that they support instructional activities as material centers. Films, charts, displays, models and other resources are available in each school. Resources are being expanded in most inner city schools so that teachers have supportive materials. Libraries have strenghthened their capability to facilitate classroom instruction and provide opportunities for individual study by adding study carrels, single concept films and audiovisual equipment designed for individual use.

In each of the above instances the ability of the teacher to select and integrate instructional tools into the learning process is the single critical variable in achieving successful learning. Instructional technology has served as a resource for the teacher to plan and implement successful learning activities. The preparation and introduction of students to receive and use technological media is in the hands of teachers. To the extent that teachers comprehend how to use technology, both in terms of preparation and follow up, any and all products of technology will be limited or enhanced.

When equipment is used as a diversion or ancillary aid to education, its effectiveness is limited notwithstanding whether students are in ghetto or advantaged educational settings.

At the present time, a direct assessment of the impact of instructional technology on making learning more relevant for ghetto children cannot be made adequately. Operational situations simply do not exist in which large scale coordinated use of instructional technology is being applied to classroom situations. Isolated success stories and promising practices related to the use of specific machines or programmed instructional materials can be identified. For the most part, they are singular instances without consistent application as a regular integral part of daily instructional activities. At this point in time, the application of instructional technology must be considered to be in a trial and error, exploratory period.

Teachers and administrators are becoming familiar with various technical aids to teaching. Equipment and materials are being introduced into classrooms as aids and additional resources with which to reinforce teacher oriented instructional styles. Within recent years, more and more instances can be found in which instructional experiences are being planned so that equipment, programmed materials and teacher-pupil activities are deliberately and systematically coordinated to achieve specific learning objectives. With availability of financial resources, systematic coordination between teacher-pupil activity interacting with machines and material is becoming more realizable.

A review of practices among the sixteen great cities school systems reveals considerable experimentation with programmed materials in reading, arithmetic, and language instruction. Television along with overhead movie and clip projectors have become standard operations as means for enriching and deepening instruction by going beyond verbally oriented student-teacher interactions. Scientifically developed manipulative materials and autotelic devices such as Talking Typewriters and Listening Posts have received enthusiastic reception by teachers. They add variety to classroom experiences, and at the same time, enable teachers to approach greater individualization of instructional activities. In the case of manipulative materials, abstract ideas can be made concrete, resulting in quicker and clearer comprehension of relationships such as with various geometric forms and arithmetic quantities.

Several examples are listed to provide an overview of the specific uses of instructional technology.

In the St. Louis School System emphasis is being placed on speech improvement in inner city schools through the use of tapes and tape recorders. Specially developed radio lessons are being broadcast over radio to strengthen classroom instruction in inner city schools.

The Baltimore School System has developed closed circuit television instruction in math for selected children in grades seven, eight and nine in schools with large concentrations of disadvantaged children. Longitudinal studies are being made to determine effectiveness of this technique over conventional approaches. A similar study is being conducted at the senior high level with experimental and control groups. Temac materials by Encyclopedia Britannica are being compared to conventional textbook approaches to mathematics instruction in an inner city school.

The Los Angeles Public School System has developed and is evaluating instructional programs designed to improve oral English of Mexican and Negro American children. Language masters, tapes, tape recorders and auto-tutors are being studied to determine their adequacy in improving oral English. Study Skill Centers have been organized at the secondary school level to enable teachers to obtain training and experience in effective use of equipment and instructional systems.

In San Diego electronic classrooms have been organized at the junior high level for the purpose of teaching foreign languages.

Closed circuit television is being used to transmit seventy-five systematically prepared tape lessons to facilitate teaching English as a second language.

The Cleveland Public Schools are studying the effects of programmed instructional materials on development of basic reading skills. Sullivan reading materials are being compared to other reading methodologies in an attempt to identify successful approaches with children in six inner city schools.

The New York Public Schools' "More Effective Schools Program" has made abundant quantities of equipment and instructional materials available to teachers. The effects of mechanical facilitators such as overhead projectors, film cartridges, film libraries and teaching machines are being studied.

The Philadelphia schools have developed a Language Arts Communication Media Program. Students are provided with opportunities to employ communication media as motion pictures, still photography, and tape recorders to extend their understanding and appreciation of literature and competence in spoken and written expression. Teachers are trained in techniques necessary to implement the program. Teachers and students work with various types of equipment. Much individualized instruction is required.

The San Francisco Unified School District and the Lockheed Missile and Space Company have developed a Language and Mathematics Learning Laboratory Program. The (EDP) Learning Laboratory is a partnership which combines the talents of the San Francisco Unified School District and Lockheed Missile and Space Company. The program utilizes a gaming-simulation approach to learning. Language and mathematics are supportive to an electronic data processing curriculum which, hopefully, will generate the motivation essential to success.

Various types of equipment are used including a keypunch, sorter, interpreter, etc. In addition, reliance is placed on a VTR System which includes a 7500 Videotape Recorder, a 326-22 Camera, a Telemation Switcher-fader Syno cart and supporting accessories. Complementing this multisensory approach are the standard classroom items such as photocopier, duplicator, tape recorder, etc.

Ninth grade students who were underachieving by three-or-more years in reading were selected to participate in a class schedule which locks in four periods daily.

The Boston School System has developed an Interdisciplinary Slide/Film Program. This material was created by ninth-grade students. The concept of The Hero was developed with an interdisciplinary context making use of a slide/tape presentation. Ancient history, English, and art are all involved.

Increasingly, observations of inner city classrooms reveal a greater use of instructional materials that have been developed in programmatic fashion with systematic consideration given to learning processes and human development patterns. Sullivan and Science Research Reading materials are cases in point.

Though many improvements have been made in the quality of educational experiences of ghetto children, evaluations at the present stage of development do not present consistent data related to effectiveness in terms of significant changes in behavior of children living in ghettoes. This situation is partially due to the ad hoc use of new equipment and materials rather than development and selection of materials designed to meet specific educational problems.

It is clear that in those instances in which an item of technology such as a teaching machine has been introduced into a classroom by itself without being part of a larger plan in which the machine is selected to attain specific objectives, the machine alone has little impact on the teaching-learning process. The successful use and implementation of technology in educational activities are dependent upon the existence of certain conditions.

   1. Equipment and materials must be selected for their unique ability to enable the attainment of predetermined instructional goals.

2. Skills of teachers must be sharpened through in-service training to be able to understand how equipment can be used to facilitate the solution of selected learning problems.

3. The software that accompanies equipment must have a direct relevance in terms of content, level of difficulty and time to enable its introduction into schools as they are now organized to accept change in educational strategies.

4. Materials and equipment must be available in sufficient quantities to enable teachers to inject their use into teaching-learning experiences at a time when it is most appropriate to a given learning activity.

5. Technological developments must operate within the realities of inner-city schools as they are with limitations in terms of space, resources and personnel. Consequently, their full effect may not be appreciated at this point in time.

To the extent that experience and daily involvement in the process of teaching ghetto children can be assumed to be a basis for valid, reliable judgment, several observations related to instructional technology and its possibilities for making learning more relevant, appears to be increasingly visible.

1. Instructional technology is helping teachers to establish *new educational contact* with ghetto children. Where traditional techniques have failed to develop a satisfactory level of achievement with children, new approaches, such as Listening Post Reading Activities, Language Masters, Talking Typewriters and other programs and equipment specifically designed to improve reading instruction, are providing a means to alter traditional classroom roles and environments. Consequently, children find themselves with new situations and new chances to receive and to respond to instruction. Though teacher control and responsibility has not been replaced, new associations between students and teachers are made possible by the integration of various instructional machines and programmed materials into learning activities. New responsibilities and expectations are being placed on the child. Materials and machines are creating environments that appear to be challenging children to respond in other ways than before.

In addition to altering the instructional environment, instructional technology is providing a new reward system that evokes individual, intrinsic motivation from within the child rather than from the teacher or peers. As an individual senses that he comprehends a relationship or idea, enthusiasm is generated for further learning.

Teachers assume new roles as organizers and facilitators of instruction rather than assuming the leading, star part. In those instances where the teacher has the know-how and competence to utilize materials and machines as reinforcing elements of a learning activity, relevance is an automatic occurrence. In those situations where the training or experiences of teachers have not succeeded in developing necessary skills, relevance of learning is a rare by-product for ghetto children.

2. Instructional technology appears to be facilitating *individualization of learning activities*. The increasing availability of instructional materials that have been developed systematically is providing teachers with means to hand-tailor instruction to individual needs. As a case in point, diagnostic tests are being used to obtain a more precise description of children's learning problems. As these specific problems are identified, appropriate learning activities and materials can be prescribed to enable ghetto children to master skills or acquire information related to a desired learning activity. Though software is still not available in sufficient quantity, it is clear that instruction related to specific topics or skills can be organized so that an individual child can proceed at his own speed. A case in point is represented by single concept film clips that can be used in carrels with film projectors or viewers.

Three-dimensional and manipulative materials suggest possibilities both as facilitators of general instruction before total class groups and as means for remediation with tutors or volunteers working with individuals and small groups.

The essential point, however, is that the development of instructional materials must be related to some elements from the ghetto child's background so that a basis for the acceptance of materials and identification with materials can be established. In too many instances, ghetto children reject learning activities because basic levels of familiarity are not easily established, thus creating obstacles to learning.

3. Instructional technology is in the early stages of affecting *instructional procedures and curricular organization*. Subject matter courses have always had a logical though not necessarily relevant bases on which they were organized. Chronological or topical organization has been common in skill areas such as mathematics. Progress has been made generally from less to more complicated relationships. The new and important change that instructional technology appears to be bringing about is that learning activities are more carefully preplanned. As in programmed texts materials of learning activities are organized in a step by step progression. The availability of such programs is affecting both curriculum development and instructional practices in classrooms in that teachers are becoming more aware of how to convey instruction with greater clarity, thus reducing chances of creating nonrelevant learning situations.

Instructional technology along with increased understanding of children and expansion of knowledge related to learning processes, have laid the ground work for a revitalization of the teaching-learning process.

Technological developments are altering the long established educational model which relied heavily upon books, chalk, blackboards and teachers. Particularly relevant to the education of ghetto children, is the fact that instructional technology is providing alternative educational strategies with which to work with children. The choice is no longer limited to the singular dimensions of books, work sheets, maps, charts and blackboards. Teachers and educational planners have never had such a large resource of instructional facilitators and vehicles with which the establish contact with children. Though computer-assisted instruction is still in its formative stages, the basic philosophy on which its development is proceeding indicates that it will have considerable impact on teaching methods. Specifically, more logically related organization of learning activities will be developed. This in itself should lead to greater understanding and relevance of learning.

4. Instructional technology is producing effects on *teacher preparation*. Micro-Teaching and video taping are two procedures that appear to be having a real impact on teacher preparation. Micro-teaching with its emphasis on systematic planning of segments of instruction helps teachers to develop learning activities with maximum clarity. Video taping enables teachers to see themselves under supervision of an expert. This procedure should result in more insight into teaching-learning relations.

The impact of instructional technology in terms of making available a variety of teaching aids is changing the role of teachers. They are more and more required to become diagnosticians, program developers, and managers of instructional activities. Training programs must be modified to include appropriate use of new instructional media. The availability of many technical devices calls not only for familiarity but also competence to integrate various mechanical aids into a learning activity to make it maximally meaningful for students. Teachers work with ghetto children must be assisted through in-service experiences to sharpen their skills in using mechanical aids.

The issue related to instructional technology as a means for making learning experiences more relevant to the needs and lives of ghetto children is much larger than a consideration of how, when, and where to use machines and materials efficiently. The availability of both the ordinary tools, such as projectors and also the more sophisticated systems such as computers, is rapidly raising basic questions that will lead inevitably to educational changes. A spirit is growing in recognition that an increasing need exists for systematic scientific approaches to educational designs at the classroom level. The effects of instructional technology are contributing toward a more systematic means toward educational development of children in ghettoes.

The introduction and successful use of instructional technology in inner city schools is dependent upon several factors that can act as constraints or facilitators.

1. Cost factors related to the development of software cannot be ignored. At the present time, the availability of appropriate instructional materials limits the use of equipment in inner city schools. New schools will have to be planned with provisions for electrical and space capability to facilitate closed circuit television and computer assisted instruction.

2. Teacher preparation is at the heart of the problem in terms of making instructional technology an operational reality.

   Pre-service and in-service experiences must be developed to enable teachers to see themselves in different roles within the teaching-learning process, the key element being know-how and skill in selecting appropriate products of educational technology to facilitate the resolution of specific learning problems and situations.

3. New educational support systems will have to be developed. Teachers will need the assistance of aides and para-professionals in order to integrate the use of instructional technologies into educational activities. Conventional classroom organization may not be appropriate as a setting for full use of new approaches to education.

   In effect this is resulting in a new orientation to the teaching process. It is resulting in a redefinition and alteration of the teachers role. Teachers are becoming planners and managers with time and resources to select and utilize the products of instructional technology to facilitate learning.

73.

Instructional Television and Other Forms of Educational Technology Serving Needs In Urban Areas

by *MARTHA A. GABLE*
Editor, The School Administrator
Amer. Assoc. of School Administrators
Washington, D.C.

It is a privilege to contribute a few thoughts to the compilation of the important study which is in progress as a result of Title III of the Public Broadcasting Act. The study no doubt will have enormous impact on the destiny of educational technology both nationally and internationally, and on the pattern and structure of the entire educational process. For any analysis of the uses of instructional devices, necessarily must be based on desired goals of education and methods of achieving them.

There is an insistent demand throughout the nation for change in education—new approaches, methods and motivation—to provide relevant and effective instruction for inner city children; to upgrade for all children the quality of education which will equip them to live productively, successfully and with sensitivity in the decades ahead. At the same time, there is a shortage of qualified teachers, which will become more acute as needed instructional services demand more specialized expertise; the volume of knowledge doubles every decade.

The dilemma is manifold: how can the educational process be improved *now* for pupils in traditionally planned schools with traditionally trained teachers; and how do we create flexible, open-ended education designed to progress from the present into the future, combining resources, present and to be developed, to meet widely diversified educational needs.

This is an awesome task, for which there can be but partial answers, but our children deserve the *best* answers at this point in time.

The report of the Commission is due at an opportune time when guidelines are desperately needed to chart a course through the maze of present complexities and proliferation. The problems of ITV are similar to those encountered in applications of other types of technology. For instance, millions of dollars worth of audiovisual equipment were provided to schools under the Elementary and Secondary Education Act, but hardly any of the money was spent to equip teachers, philosophically and practically, to use the devices well.

Another problem in the study of instructional technology is the existing scattered pattern of applications. ITV is used fairly widely—open circuit, closed circuit, 2500 MHz installations, at different locations; other schools have concentrated on the use of computers for rapid computations and for instruction—on a variety of computers; some use radio extensively; programmed instruction is used here and there. Several schools are conducting projects in a number of these applications, but they are completely separate. This has come about through a "bandwagon" approach to innovation. Decision-makers tend to concentrate on a technology in response to their own enthusiasms, and for which funds are available at a particular time. Many of these experiments can progress no further because the initial installation lacked the capability for expansion.

It is hoped that the Commission will emphasize (a) the importance to decision makers of planning future technological experimentation and/or installation with the capability for compatible meshing with other technologies, as may be desired later on; (b) the need for investment in software—human talents, insights and understanding, to develop the enormous potentialities; (c) the design of equipment which is simple to operate, or the provision of complementary technical staff for operation and maintenance.

The technical problems will be overcome. This statement is based on experience in TV as far back as 1941, when brilliant young men overcame monumental difficulties and took outrageous gambles to demonstrate TV to doubting educators.

The target is software.

Practitioners who have labored long in the pioneering efforts of radio and ITV earnestly hope, also, that the report of this distinguished Commission will emphasize the *positive*— what has been achieved, and possible future developments, to improve education. Those in a position of leadership, who must make decisions on sizeable investments in the form and substance of education, will look to the Commission for reliable guidance.

There have been reports of disappointing results of ITV—but there are reasons for the shortcomings which must be understood, if technology is to succeed in the educational process. For instance, the very excellent book written by the talented team of Mrs. Judith Murphy and Mr. Ronald Gross, "Learning by Television," gives a good description of the successes and inadequacies of ITV in our country. However, the greatest impact of the book for many readers occurs in the first three sentences:

> After more than a decade of intensive effort and expenditure of hundreds of millions of dollars, has television made a real impact on America's schools and colleges? Has it made a worthwhile contribution to education? The short answer to such a developing question would have to be 'no.'

If only the "no" had been followed by an elaboration of "why," the negative impression of the opening paragraphs could have become, instead, a *positive* impetus for understanding and correction. Much later in the book, on a page and a half, the authors get at the crux of the matter when they explain in effect that teachers were not prepared for the new device, and therefore misused or resisted it; and that ITV in most instances was a peripheral addition to the instructional pattern rather than an integral part of the whole. In other words, the message intended by the authors, as later demonstrated, is not "no" to ITV; it is directed rather to inept human use of a powerful potential.

Teachers say repeatedly: "No matter how excellent or efficient the equipment, if the content lacks substance, and the teachers on the receiving end are inept or resistant, ITV will not achieve its full potential."

The message seems to be clear: man's genius, skill and imagination, which envisioned and developed modern technological devices, must be applied also with the same commitment to the development of effective uses of those devices for man's improvement. Otherwise we are burdened with an expensive Frankenstein.

The following pages will present the views of a practitioner in the field of education, who has experimented with many types and applications of ITV in a large city school system, in cooperation with suburban districts. There will be an attempt to record some of these experiences, as a basis for recommendations which, hopefully, will be of some small help in the gigantic and significant task ahead.

This writer believes that ITV represents a powerful educational tool to motivate, to involve, and for the transmission of ideas and information. It also lends itself to a variety of combinations with other technology.

Program Patterns

Programs of Regional or National Application

It has been said that TV is a "window to the world," and this literally is becoming a fact. Probably one of the most important potentials of ITV is the bringing of outstanding personalities, material, demonstrations, performances, scenes from far and near, to enhance the learning process. One has only to visit a school and observe the absorption of children as they watch the hatching of chicks in an incubator, or the story of William Penn as the actual wampum belt, (borrowed under guard from a nearby museum), is presented to him by the Indians, or receive exciting science instruction from an astronaut, all via the TV screen, to realize the almost limitless possibilities.

Parents early recognized this value for their children; before Boards of Education were willing to invest in TV receivers, parents' associations in Philadelphia invested $500,000 in TV and radio sets for schools. At first, rich resources were readily available as performers and experts were intrigued by the new medium. However, as ITV expanded, non-commercial stations were established, federal and state funds became available, creators and performers considered ITV a possible business—a source of income and programming for ITV became vastly more expensive.

In order to capitalize on the potential of bringing the world to the educational process, and lessen costs, a pooling of resources began. Programs for general application are now being produced and distributed by such agencies as the Midwest Project on Airborn TV (MPATI), The Great Plains TV Library at Lincoln, Nebraska, National Instructional TV of Bloomington, Indiana, the Eastern Educational Network, and others. Fees for local consumers are pro-rated, and therefore are much less than initial production costs.

It would be helpful if efforts were coordinated to provide a greater variety of excellent programs on a regular basis, designed to meet recognized needs, which can be distributed, efficiently and quickly by micro-wave, cable or satellite, to the noncommercial stations, the 2500 MHz installations, and the closed circuit facilities. Such programs, on tape and film, would also be available as a part of computerized instruction, and possibly would become available through dial access when such systems are available.

Here are a few suggestions:

1. The finest talent available of various ethnic backgrounds to read the lines of classic and modern drama, to discuss modern literature in ways that are relevant to the pupils of today.

2. Short presentations dramatizing events in connection with the historic shrines and events in our country, in keeping with the needs of children in a multi-cultural society.

3. Series to demonstrate skills to prepare youth and young adults for employment. There is a tremendous opportunity in a number of fields to use TV instruction to shorten training time. The military services have demonstrated well this use of TV.

4. Short, single-concept presentations (three to ten minutes) on a wide variety of topics which may be used as a part of a lesson, for individualized instruction, or as part of a longer TV presentation; such as stop photography of cell division, a flower blooming, plant growth; presentations ending with "think" questions requiring applications of what has been learned. A TV teacher spent three hours with a micro projector, to record a hydra devouring a sea flea. This fascinating four

minute bit is now recorded for reuse for all ages in that city. It is the kind of material which should be made available through some regular procedure to tape libraries in all schools.

5. A series on American History made relevant to today's pupils, with inclusions of the contributions made by various ethnic groups. Pupils are demanding of their teachers "tell it like it is." A TV series which combines chronology with sociology-history as it involves and affects *people* could be a valuable addition to current availabilities.

6. Short, well-made "open end" situation programs of 5-10 minutes to stimulate discussion among teenagers on decision-making: on cheating, voting age, the draft, drugs, etc. Such discussions help teachers gain insights of pupil attitudes and needs, as pupils are turned on by situations with which they identify. A few such programs are now available on film.

7. Excellent programs by the nation's top teachers *for* teachers to keep them abreast of new knowledge and methods in such subjects as science, biology, mathematics, uses of new devices, such as ITV, radio, computerized instruction.

8. The linkage of three cities, and many schools, in such programs as "Cabinets in Crisis" should be expanded. Pupils in Boston, Philadelphia and Rochester and their teachers will long remember the excitement of participating in decision-making on the spot, as students representing three countries appeared on the screen, from studios in three cities. This type of "live" television, with maximum pupil involvement, demonstrates the value of state and regional station inter-connection.

The list of possibilities is long. Really good resources for such series are not within the budgets of any one community at this time.

This Commission, hopefully, will open the way to the establishment of production centers at strategic locations throughout the country which will be equipped with whatever is necessary to bring together leadership in education to pinpoint needs, and then produce programs designed to meet those needs. Probably a national office should coordinate the activities of these centers, so that they do not proceed independently of each other and thereby repeat the uneconomical duplication of effort which presently exists.

A linking of these centers by microwave cable, or by satellite, would permit rapid distribution of such programs through transmission and video recording exchange.

Also, it is hoped that ways will be found to secure the excellent programs produced by commercial TV. Purchase or rental fees are presently prohibitive. The excellent films on "Africa" produced by ABC, "The Nile," "Van Gogh," produced by NBC, are examples of riches which should be made available. The revised copyright law will no doubt curtail the reproduction of printed, filmed, televised material produced by both commercial and non-commercial stations. Perhaps an organization like ASCAP, which serves as a central clearance agency for music, should be established, through which reasonable arrangements may be made; to protect the rights of creative talent, and recognize the needs of pupils and teachers. At present, teachers are recording copyrighted material off the air. When the questionable legality of this was discussed, one teacher said: "I'll take my chances. I think the desperate needs of my kids will be accepted as a 'fair use' defense." Such interpretation is imperative without threat of litigation.

Local Programming

In addition to the types of programs cited, which have general applications, there is a large volume of programming which is produced locally, to meet a specific need. A few examples follow. "Delaware Valley, USA" was prepared for children in the Philadelphia area to help them appreciate geography, history, industry, government, and the cultural background of their environs. TV series to supplement local syllabi, in prescribed sequences, are offered in mathematics, science, arts, social studies, language, and music, at a variety of levels

An outstanding teacher with a rich variety of resources is able to prepare visual presentations which are not possible for the teacher in the school who has neither the time nor the resources for such preparation. Due to a serious shortage of experienced biology teachers at the senior high school level, an excellent TV course has been of particular value to both pupils and teachers, (in fact, one substitute teacher accredited only in general science stated that she learned enough from this TV course to pass the examination to become an accredited biology teacher.)

The sharing of talents of excellent teachers will become more necessary as needs of pupils for specialized expertise become more acute, and to help teachers keep abreast of new content and methodology.

During a period of unrest, black pupils confronted the school administration with a number of urgent requests, the most pressing of which was a course in Afro-American History. This request was deemed reasonable. Tension was high; swift action was necessary. TV provided the most rapid means to reach a large majority of high school pupils, since many classrooms are equipped with TV receivers. A committee of pupils, teachers, and community representatives, black and white, and a black commercial TV producer, planned and produced a short series. Announcements of the series in process were made immediately by TV. The programs were scheduled to be telecast 30 times per week on the open circuit UHF channel to permit some flexibility of viewing. The series was not all that was hoped for; but general reaction reflected satisfaction that steps had been taken quickly, a majority of high school pupils in the city had viewed the series, the results generally were productive and favorable. No other resource could have answered this local imperative need so quickly and so dramatically. A sense of involvement, so necessary to many of today's children, if their education is to be relevant, is possible with local production.

Teenage discussions on current local problems—dress, dating, the draft, "pot," school curriculum, student participation in the making of school policies, school facilities, are but a few of the current, burning topics which are arousing interest and participation of even the most apathetic pupils.

The teaching of foreign language to elementary pupils by TV has received much attention. Usually, there are few teachers with second language competence in the elementary schools—the TV teacher carries most of the responsibility, with a few directions for the teacher in the school. Excellent native French-speaking supervisors were employed to visit the schools to follow up the telecasts. A larger value, in this writer's opinion, is the combination of vocabulary and conversation with films of children in other lands—their country, dress, customs, art, family life—so that there is a cultural appreciation experience for the pupils. Several schools reported that pupils who received TV French for two years in elementary school were considerably more culturally oriented, and learned more rapidly when they entered regular language courses in secondary school.

TV Spanish received in elementary schools where there were both American and Puerto Rican children created a catalytic "mix"—the Spanish-speaking children helped the Americans with their Spanish, the Americans helped the Puerto Rican children with their English; both benefited. The foreign language experience provided a basis for needed rapport between the two groups. The principals of the schools capitalized on what they termed an unexpected "extra value" of ITV.

In response to a need to improve reading skills among children in deprived schools, a TV series was undertaken to motivate children to read for pleasure. A talented Negro

English teacher searched for stories relevant to junior high school pupils, and dramatized portions on TV, with attention to unusual words, locale, etc. The stories in booklets were distributed to the schools for follow-up after the telecasts. Requests for additional books—from children and their parents—increased not only from inner city schools, but from schools throughout the city.

In another experiment, a personable young Negro, an excellent teacher of American History, was trained for TV teaching. No particular announcement was made when he began. Negro principals reported that the word quickly spread that "a black TV teacher is teaching American History." There was a subtle change of attitude which greatly increased school audiences—and home audiences—for this series.

There are many exciting, creative possibilities, but software budgets are frugal. The old refrain.

Evaulation

There has been more general than specific evaluation of ITV. However, several outcomes are generally agreed upon:

1. Advance teacher preparation is imperative if ITV is to be accepted and well used. Teachers must understand the values and variety of applications of ITV, and their role in its effective use.

2. Administrative support, philosophically and financially, is another imperative if ITV curriculum planning and the entire teaching process are to be integrated. (An outstanding example of successful ITV is at Hagerstown, Maryland, where Dr. William Brish, the superintendent, involved his entire staff—administrators and teachers—in preplanning, for the production and use of ITV throughout the 43 schools linked by closed circuit TV cables.)

3. The funds appropriated for hardware must be matched for software—(a) personnel, materials, art work, film for program production, and (b) in-service teacher education, before and during the use of the new device, and (c) feedback and evaluative techniques.

4. The attitudes of teachers toward new devices influence the attitudes of pupils and their parents. Excellence or lack of it in TV presentations, however, are quickly recognized by pupils, teachers and parents; the audience attracted to ITV in the schools usually reflects the usefulness and quality of the respective programs.

5. The scheduling of pupil time to coincide with station programming is the greatest deterent to regular, general use of ITV, especially in compartmentalized secondary schools. The repetition of programs on the second open circuit UHF channel provided some flexibility, but the installation of video tape recorders and closed circuit systems in schools permitted recording of material off the air, and distribution of it to pupils and/or teachers as requested, which *tripled and quadrupled ITV use.*

6. Teachers agreed that the TV teacher, with excellent resources, and more time for preparation, could do a superior job of presentation. They said: "We have time now to better watch pupils' reactions, diagnose their learning problems, and concentrate on pupils' understandings and applications—the "think" part of learning. We never had enough time for this important part of teaching when we had to do what the TV teacher does better."

7. There is a need for a different kind of assessment of learning by ITV and other types of technology. After an ITV project teachers reported that pupils who were considered slow learners learned with surprising ease by the visual, verbal TV; they could draw the diagrams and explain the concepts well, but they could not read questions, nor write satisfactory test papers. Teachers expressed the need then for non-print-oriented testing which is a major consideration of today. It underscores the need to explore new testing as well as instructional procedures.

8. There is a tendency by adults not in the classroom to evaluate ITV by commercial standards of production—lighting, camera work, pace. The only *valid* evaluation must be based on what happens to the children for whom the programs were planned. A good teacher, with interesting demonstrations, a sense of pace and timing for *his specific audience* and a message of substance usually reaches the pupils. Lighting, sound and camera work of less than commercial standards do not get in the way of the children so long as they can see and hear comfortably.

9. Hundreds of housebound pupils benefitted from the variety of in-school programs, which permitted them to receive the same lessons as their classmates.

10. ITV is a particularly effective tool among the disadvantaged children, since they are familiar with TV at home, and the visual, verbal presentations by-pass reading and writing problems.

Organizational Patterns

Present day emphasis on individualization of instruction has caused some shortsighted labeling of ITV as a mass technique. ITV is as flexible as the ingenuity of the teacher in its application for desired goals.

Traditionally, ITV became another audiovisual aid in the classroom. However, as organizational patterns for teaching and learning became more varied, uses of ITV have been expanded.

Earphones are now available for TV receivers—one, or several pupils in the instructional materials center, or wherever, may use TV without disturbing others nearby. Individual pupils can view and follow the schedule of open circuit programming. Or, videotapes from a library in the school may be requested at any time, or as often as desired, by individual pupils, groups or by an entire class. The pupil who was absent may see the program he missed; the teacher may preview the tape before the pupils use it.

Team teaching has become an organizational device whereby teachers with particular competencies teach pupils in groups larger than the usual 30 at a time. One or two teachers assigned to such groups releases time of other teachers for more individual guidance, tutorial help, or other services for small groups. The expert TV teacher provides another specialized resource for the large group instruction. In an experiment sponsored by the Ford Foundation, 1957 to 1962, in 14 cities, the use of TV in large groups was studied. In Philadelphia, results revealed that the children in the TV groups learned significantly better in science, and social studies, and slightly better in language arts, than in traditional classes without TV instruction. The large group pattern of ITV, not more than 175 pupils, spread from nine schools to 50, voluntarily, as teachers and principals recognized the values of freed teacher time, and the partnership of skills enjoyed by pupils through the combination of the TV teacher and the team teacher. There were anticipated reservations about pupil discussions in large rooms housing groups equal to four or five classes. However, an alert Negro teacher, who sensed particular needs of his pupils, 98% black, motivated them to project their voices and to speak in sentences, and to express their thoughts with confidence before a group considerably larger than the traditional class of thirty. The lessons in history became also experiences in a "town meeting." This concomitant was recognized and utilized by all teachers in the project.

In several schools, where there was a serious shortage of experienced teachers, the large group TV instruction was used to teach not only pupils, but to help the teachers better understand both content and method. Several substitute teachers reported that they learned so well from the TV teachers that they passed the examination for regular certification.

This writer does not share the fear that large group TV instruction mechanizes, or dehumanizes, the teaching process, when it is used for specific purposes. The sharing of an outstanding expert with many, via TV, particularly where the development of appreciations, and the widening of cultural horizons are the goals, makes little difference whether the performance is viewed by one or hundreds if the viewers can see and hear comfortably. Helen Hayes reading excerpts from plays, or Marion Anderson singing or discussing folk music, can be enjoyed via TV in the school auditorium as well as in a theater. There is an eye to eye contact between the TV performer and viewer. Pupils repeatedly reported "I feel as though the TV teacher is talking only to me."

The Hardware of ITV

This section will focus on two aspects of hardware: a) for distribution of programs, b) the use of hardware itself in the learning process.

The open circuit non-commercial stations, and a few commercial stations, are the chief means of ITV distribution at the present time. However, in spite of extraordinary cooperation on the part of stations and schools, uses of open circuit ITV are limited by scheduling conflicts. The one or two channels available from local non-commercial stations cannot serve the variety of needs represented by metropolitan city and suburban school districts. Therefore, the 2500 MHz channels available are being rapidly requested in two, three and four channel groups to serve ITV needs of small school districts, and in larger areas to expand the services of open circuit channels. The FCC wisely has appointed area chairmen to coordinate the requests for channels, for maximum coverage.

In Philadelphia, in addition to channels 12 and 35, a feasibility study for a four-channel installation has been completed to serve all city schools, and which can eventually link city schools with suburban schools in four surrounding counties. The plan was also designed to link certain city schools with Temple University and others with the University of Pennsylvania. It includes channels for diocesan schools and other educational organizations. These channels will be available for repetition of programs produced in and recorded from the open circuit station studios, and a channel may be assigned full-time to the distribution of programs produced to answer special needs of children with language problems, with physical and mental handicaps, and to distribute films from the central library for preview by teachers and for other specialized services. It was envisioned that two suburban and two city schools will be linked, with two-way sound during TV transmission, so that inner city children and suburban children may produce programs for each other, and question each other as programs are received. *Where distance is too great for physical integration; TV will permit electronic integration.*

Computer distribution systems, for instruction and for information retrieval, also are well on their way into the technology complex. Programmed instruction represents another type of educational technology which has achieved rather uneven results. The school of the future will need these technologies in combination to meet diversified needs. Distribution systems must be designed to distribute a variety of software—video tape, films, slides, audio. The present isolation of each type of technology will present difficult meshing problems.

Another potential which has been almost untapped is the linkage of schools and homes in a district or neighborhood by CATV, for specific services. It is envisioned that CATV will become a valuable asset whereby health and sanitation programs, services to combat illiteracy, language and reading instruction geared to special needs of children in certain schools and of adults in certain neighborhoods, may be distributed without preempting large services of open circuit or 2500 MHz distribution.

Segments of neighborhoods (schools and/or homes) may be reached exclusive of others, by CATV. This lends itself to the concept of school district decentralization—wherein sub-districts may produce and use special programs.

This writer heartily agrees with the recommendations in the President's Task Force on Communications to greatly ease the restriction on the development of CATV services. However, owners of the CATV franchises should be reminded of their responsibility to make channels available for educational use, and decision-makers in education should at once move to develop the potential.

The channels of 2500 MHz and CATV also offer possibilities for distribution of video and audio material to computer-assisted instruction (CAI). For instance, CAI course in biology will probably need certain visual components. Rather than transfer visual material to computer language, which is time consuming and expensive, video tapes, films, slides, which now exist, or which will be produced, may be integrated electronically into the CAI course. For example, a pupil reaches a point in the CAI course when the computer dictates: "Dial number _____ for video tape on cell division," or the computer dictates: "Go to your instructional materials center after this lesson and view the film (or video tape) number _____."

As we envision the school of the future, *all* forms of technology—and some not yet developed—may be used, as children utilize films, tapes, video tapes, slides, audio tapes, records, micro-fiche in their rooms, in groups, as individuals, or in the instructional materials centers.

In addition, vast amounts of information will be stored in central or regional locations, so that the library will become alive with availabilities at the push of a button or turn of a switch. Distribution systems of ITV figure prominently in these service systems, since the channels are able to carry the variety of software mentioned previously to carrels, class-rooms, or auditoriums.

The teacher will become a manager of resources. Each pupil will progress at his own speed. Teacher time will be freed from much presentation-preparation to help individual pupils.

The Use of Hardware in the Instructional Process

Increasingly, "involvement" is stressed in education. Open circuit stations have not provided opportunity for extensive pupil involvement in program preparation, since the programs are distributed to the general citizenry as well as to the schools, and a professional standard of quality must be maintained. However, closed circuit installations, with videotape recorders, plus small vidicon cameras in individual schools have opened new paths for motivation and participation.

Another interesting feature of the closed circuit project is the employment of a local parent or other citizen interested in the schools, from the community, to operate the video tape recorder and the TV camera. It was realized that funds would not permit the employment of engineers or technical experts. On the other hand, reliance on a teacher or other school personnel, already in short supply, for this service would have been completely unrealistic. Therefore, one non-professional per school (34) was given intensive training, paid $100 per week, to coordinate the recording and distribution of open circuit ITV within a school, and to plan the operations of the TV camera and VTR to best serve that school.

The small TV camera in each school led to an exciting variety of pupil participation. Verbalization is one of the chief problems of the ghetto children. Following the example of commercial TV performers, children produced their own TV newscasts, which were distributed to TV sets in classrooms throughout the school. News, weather, sports and school announcements were presented by four pupils, with continuity by a master of ceremonies. The foursome changed each day; there was no reluctance to participate!

Pupils who had avoided reading and writing, became interested in their diction, in *reading* to search for news, in *writing* to prepare copy. Pupils in art classes prepared the titles to be used before and after the programs; they prepared 8mm film clips (which were televised from a screen in the studio, as there was no film chain) and selected their own background music. The entire production was pupil planned and produced. Teachers of English and Social Studies collaborated in encouraging this "communications" approach to learning. The newscasts were recorded. The performers subsequently studied themselves alone—from the tapes. This self-analysis technique, used with the natural motivation of TV, resulted in remarkable improvement in verbailization, and overcoming dialect problems.

Students also became proficient in operating the equipment. "Crews" were selected from volunteers. Pupils who were chronic trouble makers, truants and potential dropouts arrived promptly to set up lights, microphones, scenery, cameras, the tape, in preparation for TV recording and distribution. Several boys who intended to quit school are now graduated and enrolled in wireless technical courses to continue their work in some aspect of broadcasting.

The equipment was used also for self-analysis by pupils studying drama and dance, and in the reading of poetry and stories—often student created.

Self-analysis by teachers also has proved a valuable aid to improved instruction. Dr. Dwight Allen of Stanford University experimented with micro-teaching, whereby a teacher with four pupils concentrates on one technique (opening of a lesson, the use of gestures to sustain discussion, etc.) for five minutes on video-tape. The teacher studies the tape, and later reteaches the lesson with four different pupils, and views the second tape to evaluate progress. Teachers sometimes were reluctant to enter into this rather shattering experience, but after a few extroverted types took the plunge, the others decided to capitalize on the value. It was interesting to note the teachers' reactions: 'I use my hands too much'; 'I talk too much'; 'I say OK too often'; 'I distract by stomping about.'

Colleges of education are using this device to help student teachers study teaching techniques, and analyze themselves in action.

The TV camera also is being used in a ghetto high school to tape outstanding, successful Negroes in various careers who deliver forthright, hardnosed messages of encouragement, exhortation to work, and inspiration to black pupils. The response has been so favorable that these tapes are being duplicated for use in other schools.

In another high school, a returned drop-out addressed the entire student body, via TV, in classrooms (the auditorium accommodated only ⅓ of the enrollment) and recited the agonies of the dropout, and the wisdom of remaining in school. This talk, delivered in the language of the ghetto, had a profound effect on the pupils.

Realization of the values of closed circuit TV, with receivers and cameras in individual schools or small groups of schools, has just begun. Some of the uses are included here, to emphasize the importance of including it as a part of the hardware of ITV. If funds are provided only for open circuit TV hardware and programming, some of the exciting, productive aspects of ITV which are possible through local uses of closed circuit channels, 2500 MHz channels and CATV, will be lost. This will be a tragedy, and will frustrate many excellent teachers who see possibilities, but have been hamstrung by piecemeal, anemic budgeting.

Mr. Marcus Foster, a black principal* of a 4400 pupil high school, 99% black, where heroic

Mr. Foster is now associate superintendent in Philadelphia.

efforts are paying off to decrease the drop-out rate and place pupils into successful employment or continuing education, is a practical believer in the use of new approaches. His
school received a video-tape recorder, a TV camera, and a CCTV system under Title I of
USEA. He writes:

Teachers at North Philadelphia's Simon Gratz High School are committed to the
concept that their students want to learn. This is why they are quick to perceive
that the value of the textbook is limited with great numbers of them. It is not
that our disadvantaged students refuse to learn—most really want to. Rather, it is
that this segment of the student body learns *differently.* These young people are
not geared to the extensive reading assignments or to the Socratic question-answer
style of teaching. . . . They simply do not operate that way. It is not "their thing."
So we took a careful look at their learning style and turned to, among other
things, the Tube. (Our students watch as much as five hours a day, and they
like it. Often they talk about a program they watched, about a program that
aroused them, or amused them or intrigued them. The Tube is their friend, their
baby-sitter, their filler of silences. It occupies their minds.) And because that is
precisely what we sought to do, many of the staff at Gratz turned to TV.

Closed circuit television turned out to be an educational goldmine, for it allows
us to address ourselves to our students' cry for relevance, to their surging
interest in their identity as Black Americans, and it allows us to do even more.
It gives us a vehicle which capitalizes on how our kids like to learn and how
they learn most readily.

"Black Facts" seeks to replace the black threads in the tapestry of Western
Civilization. We can do what the blanched textbooks haven't done. We can
talk about the contributions of great Black Americans, Black Russians, Black
Africans. We can show those contributions graphically while we talk about them.
And we can bring notable Black and White Americans into our classrooms,
into fifty classrooms at once. "Color Us People" does just that. . . . We have
discovered that a student is far more likely to read about a person when he has
"a picture of him" to work with. He is far more likely to read about other men
and women like him, especially if he or his peers are able to converse with
the person. We have spoken of the milk and honey which the Black People have
produced. Now we can zoom in live on the cows and the bees. We can back
up our assertions. Further inquiry becomes tenable, student-initiated. It has
a basis.

The English Department found that students might be a bit more interested
in poetry if they heard an exciting interpretation (a reading and discussion of
it) from their fellow students. Especially if the reading is accompanied by
musical background played by their friends and if it is interspersed with sketches
or paintings done by still other of their fellow students. The Art Department
found that it could borrow a museum collection and display it before hundreds,
making closeups possible, having students provide explanation of impression-
istic canvasses or way-out sculpture or African masks. It became possible to
display the architecture of an entire civilization in fifteen minutes; it was no
longer necessary to plow through fifty pages of dull prose to get the message.

Aside from producing our own material, there is a large collection of films
and television programs which we have recorded from open circuit TV and
presented. We are presently seeking funds to get such series as "Of Black
America," a CBS masterpiece. Performances from professionally produced
theater groups and dance companies are available, too.

Filmmaking also represents a communications approach of "involvement:" 8mm
cameras were used by a social studies class to report a community need to transform
a small "dump" into a playlot. Films of the eyesore were recorded, plus visits to
community leaders, the cleaning up process, and the final victory. Audio tape narra-

tion and musical background made an interesting report by and for pupils. The writing, reading, speeches, discussions which this project motivated in a deprived school were amazing.

In an elementary school, pupils wrote their own stories, illustrated them with their own drawings, took still photos of the selected art work which were made into slides, recorded the story with music on audio tape to accompany the color illustrations. Creative writing, art, photography, and music were combined in this further illustration of appropriate combination of hardware and software. There are many such illustrations.

The Magnet Communications School Concept

In the new design for education, considerable attention focuses on non-reading, motivational approaches to learning, to overcome the handicaps of children who lack skills necessary for success in the traditional process. An experiment to use a communications approach to the entire curriculum is under way in Philadelphia. A school is being planned to house 300 pupils, divided into six "houses" within the building to lessen the sense of "largeness" to the pupils. The school will serve pupils from the community who seek a regular diploma, and will offer more intensive communications experiences for those who wish to enter communications careers. The latter pupils will come from all parts of the city and suburbs.

The following is an excerpt from an early report from the planning committee:

> A communications approach is understood to include radio, TV, journalism, filmmaking, drama, computerized instruction, language laboratories, speed reading machines, as tools which would motivate and enhance learning. It is envisioned, for instance, in discussing a story or play, the pupils will decide to produce excerpts on radio, in a TV sequence, or on film. There might be subcommittees, after the sequence is selected, for role playing, writing continuity, musical background (in cooperation with the pupils in the music courses), timing, placement of microphones, recording.

> Similarly, a social studies teacher and his pupils may prepare a historical event in history, for TV, or a series of newscasts, highlighting a significant event in the news; or the pupils may take a moving picture camera into the community and film conditions which they hope to change through presenting filmed reports to community groups. TV and filmmaking techniques will involve art work for titles, scenery design, musical backgrounds—in a wide variety of learning experiences related to a realistic situation which should challenge pupil creativity and energy.

> In addition to these types of presentations, small TV cameras and video tape recorders will be used for pupil self-analysis individually and in groups. This technique is presently providing to be valuable for both motivation and improvement.

> The communication approach does *not* mean less attention to subject content necessary for successful employment or college entrance. Rather, it should provide a variety of vehicles to make learning more relevant and challenging in all subjects, in addition to production skills in the communications media.

> It is considered as an additional dimension to learning which will stimulate pupils to greater achievement, as they broaden their backgrounds of skills and understandings.

> In addition, the instructional materials center will provide learning resources on slides, films, records, audio-tapes, video-tapes, books, through live storage or dial access.

There is a possibility that such a school will become a production center wherein programs on film, audio and video tape, produced by pupils, will be distributed over 2500 MHz channels when these are activated, or "dubbed" on 1″ tapes for individual school use, or, on occasion, produced for the open circuit public TV station for all schools and the community. Tapes may be physically transported to the various "head ends"; eventually a transmitter may be added to the school for micro-wave distribution to 250 MHz and open circuit transmitters.

A Few Estimated Software Costs—December 1968

Programming costs vary considerably in different parts of the country because of labor costs, overhead, teacher salaries, etc. However, the following represent average costs in one metropolitan area. Fees for the use of station facilities, including crew, lighting, rehearsal time, cameras, sound, projection, titles, music, basic furniture, are as follows:

Live Production, taped, and broadcast later	$1000/hour
Live Broadcast, not taped	700/hour
Live Broadcast, and taped for later re-use	800/hour
Taped Program from other sources	400/hour
Film	250/hour
The cost of tape, in addition to the above, prepared for use	300/hour

Therefore, a thirty-minute program, minus talent and materials, to be produced and recorded in advance of air time would require $500 for studio fees, and $150 for tape, a total of $650. The regular TV teacher is paid of an average of $100 per program, a guest expert may require $100 upward. Film prepared for the telecast costs about $300 per minute, with sound; $200 per minute, silent. Rental of commercial film is $1 to $1.50 per minute, although many film distributors insist that payment be made for the entire film. $10 to $25 is the usual fee, although only three to five minutes may be used. Artist charges average $25 to $50 for special work—it is more economical to employ a full-time artist for $100 to $200 per week. A good script writer asks $300 to $800 for a thirty minute program. A thirty minute local TV program on a metropolitan open circuit station ranges from "shoestring" costs of $900, to a desired *minimum* of $3000.

In-Service Education of Teachers

New content, new methods, are creating a sense of insecurity among teachers. It is imperative that experts on the frontiers of change reach the teachers of the nation quickly and effectively. TV series featuring the new math, modern science, new approaches to the teaching of reading, and analyses of effective uses of new technology for the children of the ghetto, by the most competent talent available, are but a few examples of the sharing of expertise. However, if distribution is confined to open circuit scheduling, the programs cannot be used by many teachers because of time conflicts. Here again, local recording within a school permits the development of a tape library for teachers which may be used at their convenience, and as often as desired.

Thousands of dollars now spent by large school systems to employ outstanding experts to conduct seminars for teachers, which reach possibly 20% of the staff any one year, might well be used toward the recording of excellent TV programs to reach *many* schools and school districts, and viewed with local discussion leaders, as desired, for *all* the teachers in a given school or sub-district. Or, these programs may be viewed by individual teachers at their convenience.

It is envisioned that the sources for in-service teacher education will include video-tapes, audio tapes, microfiche, as well as books—available in school or regional libraries, and eventually by dial access. However, important teacher education will not become a general, continuing experience for all teachers unless the time for self-improvement is *scheduled into the school day.* Plans to improve the instruction of children must include time and resources continually to upgrade instruction.

Software of ITV

Generally, there are two main categories of software: A) the talent, materials, substance which include the planning, packaging and presentation of strategic programming, and B) the people involved with the actual uses of ITV.

(A) If really significant ITV programs are to be produced regionally or locally, special-ists in content, psychology, and the *artistry* of teaching are needed to determine the what and how of programming. Here is where the budgetary consideration frequently becomes imbalanced—attention is paid to excellence in hardware, first, and what is left goes into software.

Therefore, it is hoped that the Commission recommendations will eliminate the unhealthy tug of war which operates too frequently between TV technical production personnel who understandably seek quality hardware, and the educator-producers who need expert, creative talent, films, art work, and other materials—for excitement and value in the message to be transmitted. Funds for ITV should be allocated to school districts, so that the development of software is under the direction of educators.

If such funds are allocated to other agencies, the educational decision-makers tend to be less directly involved, and ITV may remain peripheral to the total educational pattern.

(B) Orientation and preparation of teachers to use effectively material available through technology is the usually forgotten element in the total process. Or, it becomes an after thought, when the bulk of time and money have been allocated. Human beings are sus-picious of the unknown or of the misunderstood. Teachers sometimes view new devices as threats to their competence status, or as an eventual reduction of teacher positions, or as an expenditure of funds which will prevent higher salaries, or just plain nuisances which get in the way and take time.

Massive staff development programs are necessary to develop philosophical concepts and practical skills if there are to be acceptance, understanding and productive uses.

Therefore, it is suggested that the Commission include in the plans for procedures and funding, provisions for teacher and administrator workshops, demonstration centers, semi-nars, regionally and locally, which will bring together groups of teachers and adminis-trators to work with outstanding, knowledgeable leaders in educational technology, plus *teachers* who have worked successfully with various aspects of technology, who are able to instruct, persuade and inspire other teachers and educators. For example, seminar courses of two and three weeks, after-school seminars once a week for several weeks, Saturday morning sessions conducted by school districts, state departments of education in con-junction with universities and local ETV stations are among possible patterns. An experi-ment which featured TV teaching in large classes, was successful and accepted because the money was spent largely on teacher preparation, curriculum planning, and continuous teacher exchange of techniques. Resistance vanished as teachers acquired new skills and recognized values.

Funds allocated for ITV should include provision for staff development *each year.*

Pre-Service Training for Teachers

Staff development of teachers in service is a crucial need if there is to be productive change, and effective use of new devices. However, this may become an overwhelming task if all new teachers, fresh out of college, enter the profession with experience and background only in traditional education patterns. A *massive* attack on the problem *in the teacher colleges* is long overdue. Technology itself offers a potent facility to prepare future teachers for the use of educational technology. TV cameras and video-tape recordings are bringing to *some* student teachers the opportunity to observe a variety of excellent teachers with their classes in different schools. Schools located near teacher colleges may be wired with closed circuit TV, with a camera outlet in each room, the science laboratory, the auditorium, the instructional materials center which will permit student teachers to observe practically every activity in the school, without the disruption of the physical presence of strangers in the school. In addition, the student teachers may assist in the production of radio and TV programs for both pupils and teachers to meet differing needs of pupils from grades 1 to 6. Such student teachers will be well aware of ITV and radio, and have some notion of its uses when they begin their careers. Micro-teaching, study of ITV programs which exist, preparation of segments of ITV presentations, and the combination of these with radio, other audiovisual equipment, and computers, belong in the teacher education of 1969.

School Design

Educational changes literally are shaping the schools of tomorrow. The dilemma is to plan for maximum flexibility and function within reasonable budgetary limits, and which will avoid as much as possible the hazards of obsolescence. This is a large order, and requires the best brains available from education, technology, city planners, architects, and pupils.

Hopefully, the Commission will urge the provision of top-flight consultant service so that the school building design will accommodate to the maximum degree the new kinds of educational experience. Since buildings usually are planned to serve from 30 to 40 years, it will be vastly more economical to plan for and install the necessary spaces, conduits, etc., during construction, than undertake renovations later. TV studios, CCTV linkage, camera feeds, filmmaking laboratories, instructional materials centers, easily available to all parts of the school, carrels in strategic spots for dial access, computer-assisted instruction, are but a few considerations.

What Might Be

Envision then a school district with facilities to do the following:

1. By dialing or phoning a number, a desired video tape, film, audio tape may be projects for (a) a large group of pupils in a team teaching space, (b) a group of pupils in a part of a classroom, (c) individual pupils in classrooms, instructional materials centers, or other spaces which the modern educational center will contain. Such materials will be stored in a regional library, within the city, prepared by top flight groups of experts in designated production centers, or by groups of local teachers to meet local needs.

The receiving pupils, in a variety of locations, may raise questions by pushing a button, or dialing through a two-way sound system to a group of teachers with a variety of expertise, on duty at a center (in the city or metropolitan area) who will hear and answer questions, or guide pupils to further exploration.

2. Pupils in the instructional materials center in a school will use vastly expanded resources of printed materials, stored on microfiche.

3. Open circuit TV channels will distribute excellent programs, films, etc., which will be recorded and redistributed over multi-channel 2500 MHz installations as desired, and for recording and use in individual schools.

4. Programs from other countries will become available through satellite distribution. Two-way sound will permit pupils in the United States to talk with pupils in South America and Europe as the world becomes real and near in the educational process of its people.

5. Pupils and parents who need help with language (Puerto Ricans, Mexicans, foreign born), with citizenship orientation, health and sanitation, and enrichment of the home climate for learning will receive specially developed programs over CATV channels in their homes and schools. Parents and citizens will have a continuous flow of radio programs designed to meet a myriad of needs. (The poor listen to radio almost constantly, as home, and on the street.)

6. The communications approach to learning, through verbal visual pupil involvement in radio, TV, film, dramatic presentations, will be possible through the schools equipped for this purpose. Such approaches will combine music, art, literature, social studies, science—in fact, the disciplines necessary for successful, productive living. Such a school also will begin preparation of pupils for a variety of careers in communications.

7. Clusters of schools within the city and surrounding suburbs, will be joined by CCTV, with camera and sound inputs from each school, where pupils will share their skills, discussions and other productions (plays, art, crafts, foreign language activities, filmmaking) with pupils in the schools within the cluster. integration by technology—city and suburbs—may be a concomitant of this arrangement.

8. Pupils and teachers will use a facsimile system whereby a printout of material covered visually and verbally will be readily available, at school or at home, such as stories, plays, maps, pictures, etc.

9. Teachers will have available, through dial access, or other systems, outstanding experts in the various disciplines who present the best in content and methodology.

Recommendations

It is interesting to speculate on the future, and what further changes the genius of man will evolve. However, for purposes of this report, it seems more practical to suggest ways for better meeting the present needs of education, and indicate open-ended procedures which may anticipate both known and unknown potentialities of the future.

1. In order to lend strength and substance to existing applications and operations of educational technology and encourage additional study and development to meet present and future needs of education, it is recommended that a Central Agency be established and funded to undertake the following:

a. Subsidization of a "think" laboratory where research experts, psychologists, educators, will examine minutely the elements and processes of learning, the obstacles of learning, the overcoming of these obstacles, the organization of curriculum to meet pupil needs, the design of technology—single components and in combination—which will move the educational process forward with the necessary variety, flexibility and availability. Present uses of technology in education represent in large measure the fitting of educational uses into what is available. The developers of hardware, used successfully in business, have approached educators who experimented with what was designed mainly by manufacturers. Slowly but surely there is emerging a realization that *an analysis of needs in the educational process must determine the design of hardware*. One example of this trend exists at Oak Park, Illinois, where the educators planned improved teaching procedures, wrote specifications to achieve their goals, and then asked the manufacturers to produce the desired capabilities.

Billions of dollars have been invested in analyzing the problems of reaching the moon, controlling rainfall and then designing the means to solve them. Improvement of teaching and learning is also important, and deserves a subsidized research laboratory for intensive study.

Experiments and projects presently are fragmented. Some of the results have been excellent, but the dissemination of information, the combination of successful experiments for general benefit, are not coordinated—because there is no plan for coordination. Decision-makers are reluctant to expend the large sums necessary without some assurance of a return on the investment. The "think" laboratory also would determine what is better taught by other than technological means.

It is this writer's opinion that if the potential of educational technology is to be realized maximally, as that potential expands, applications must be based on the requirements of learning, some of which are yet unknown in our changing society.

Such a "think" laboratory might be subsidized in a university. Reports would be issued regularly; educators everywhere could use the results as a basis for meeting specific and general needs, regionally and locally. It would become a valuable, valid resource for a new plan of education, which would capitalize on what has been done, enlist the cooperation of innovators in various localities, and continue intensive research and experimentation. *Note:* President Nixon, in his campaign speeches, proposed the establishment of a National Educational Institute. Hopefully, it will be established, and undertake some of the functions herein described.

b. The subsidization of regional *production* centers to capture the best talent and resources in the country, in fact, in the world, on video tape, or on film, planned by the best brains available, supported by adequate funds, produced nationally or regionally, on a variety of subjects—exciting, up to date, relevant —to enrich the offerings in our schools through distribution to open circuit TV stations, closed circuit, CATV, 2500 MHz installations. Planning groups—government or foundation sponsored—including educators, behavioral scientists, psychologists, pupils to determine priorities of needs, in their respective regions, and to plan content and continuity, would provide both substance and prestige to the planning and production of programs. It is not enough for a few high-level individuals to "dream up" programs. These should be designed to meet expressed needs from the regions and subregions. The central agency will coordinate the programming to be produced and mesh distribution schedules to best serve the entire country, using interconnection and satellite distribution systems.

c. Subsidize regional or state *demonstration* centers, to prepare teachers for the use of educational technology, philosophically and practically. Centers may be established in schools which now use a combination of educational technology, and which may be expanded to meet model requirements where groups of teachers, administrators, parents and pupils from their respective subunits may be financed to observe, participate and receive instruction from experienced teachers and pupils for a week or more at a time. This could be an on-going activity, with workshops scheduled throughout the year. The plan may be so arranged that participants on their return to their respective subunits will transmit what has been learned to their faculties and communities at a local workshop, with the assistance of a series of TV programs, carefully produced, which will show and explain the uses of educational technology at the centers. Teacher and pupil reactions at the centers may be recorded and made available to the regional sub-units to support local workshops. Such a plan would result in a "fanning out" from the centers needed orientation and expertise, with the enthusiasm of teachers using technology, to develop a climate of understanding and receptivity among the consumers.

d. Take action in setting up reasonable arrangements to make available for ITV excellent films and tapes which have been or will be produced commercially. Present procedures to secure permission to use these excellent resources are too complex and time consuming for teachers who need given content *now;* most are priced far beyond present school budgets.

e. Assist teacher colleges with funding in the upgrading of their courses to permit students to observe, participate in, and study philosophically the uses of technology to meet pupil needs. Student teachers should have an opportunity to serve in schools using technology before graduation, if such experience is not possible on campus. The linking of colleges and local schools by TV cables for observation of classroom procedures, teaching techniques, pupil reactions by student teachers, and the preparation of ITV by future teachers, in cooperation with regular school teachers, children, and college staffs, and the use of CCTV for self-analysis, are important elements in the preparation of today's and tomorrow's teachers.

f. Establish and subsidize a committee of competent technical consultants, alert to the changing "state of the art," which will serve as a continually available resource for those who are contemplating sizeable expenditures. Obsolescence is a recognized fact of life in the technological arena. However, up to date information to keep decision-makers ahead of rather than behind new developments may reduce losses.

g. New curriculum and methodology already have had impact on school design. Throughout the country, exciting innovative schools are taking shape. School architects are pressing educators to project future needs. A new kind of resource is being sought—a technology expert who works with and for school districts to help educators translate educational needs into technological specifications.

It is recommended that the national agency activate sub-committees at the national or regional levels, including experts in school design and educational technology, to suggest school building specifications based on desired functions. Such sub-committees could evaluate school designs now in process, and formulate alternatives from new combinations of present technology or completely new technology to meet a variety of foreseeable needs as they arise.

This is not a plan to regiment school design, or crush local creativity. However, the costs involved, and the expertise required, to design functional schools for the future, prompts the suggestion to establish such a resource, in the interest of maximum value for the financial outlay. If school buildings as we now know them will become outmoded, the "think" laboratory of recommendation (a) should project such information.

h. It is suggested that the central agency use every persuasion to achieve standardization of hardware so that video tapes, computer materials, etc., may be used interchangeably among schools, and equipment may be used from a variety of manufacturers without encountering problems of compatibility.

2. It is important that those responsible for the funding of hardware recognize the importance of including CCTV for individual schools, and 2500 MHz installations, as integral elements in school ITV. The capability to record and redistribute ITV, audio, computer material as desired is imperative if there is to be maximum service. The TV station cannot provide scheduling with the necessary flexibility required by the hundreds of schools within range. The values inherent in the uses of video tape recorders, TV cameras, *by pupils* and teachers for creative expression and self-analysis are just becoming evident.

3. It is hoped that the Commission report will present a positive approach to the use of technology, citing successful examples of what has been, and exciting projections of what might be, to help pupils locate information, develop the ability to reason, act and react with sensitivity and intelligence in a dynamic society. It is suggested that parts of the report be prepared on video tape, and/or still slides with audio-tape narration, setting forth examples of uses of technology for the transmission of excellent content, and for pupil participation and self-analysis (there are hundreds of examples available) and displays of new school buildings designs, and suggest a plan of dissemination so that board of education members, administrators, legislators, parents, civic and government leaders will be strongly motivated to implement this report.

4. It has been indicated that funds for public broadcasting will be secured by and administered through the Public Broadcasting Corporation. The Carnegie Commission separated public broadcasting from instructional broadcasting; the Public Broadcasting Act also made separate provisions. Therefore it is recommended that instructional technology be administered through its own educational agency, to be created, or through an existing, representative educational agency such as the Joint Council on Educational Telecommunications (JCET), or the U.S. Office of Education.

5. Business and industry represent vast resources of expertise and financial support. It is recommended that cooperative arrangements be developed whereby closed circuit TV, CATV and other distribution systems, present demonstrations and other training to pupils in schools. The Department of Labor, the National Chamber of Commerce, may aid in bringing the large corporations together in such an enterprise.

The foregoing obviously is based on experience with instructional television. However, the problems encountered in the use of technological devices in education—the analysis of need, the design of hardware, and the preparation of software to meet those needs, philosophically and practically—are common to all. The focus of this paper has been on examples of productive uses of instructional television and some of the problems which must be overcome, (which are sizeable) possible combinations of instructional television with other technology to meet a variety of needs, and the inclusion of recommendations with implications for short and long range implementations. Somehow we must capitalize on the potential for excellence, for efficiency and for sensitivity so that the process of education will be exciting and satisfying for all.

Some of the wonders of today have been wrought by scientists, engineers and others who operate on the theory that nothing is impossible. Perhaps educators should take a page from their book—or more likely a printout from their computer. There must be a commitment of spirit, as well as of intellect, to the task before us.

74.

Racism and Attitude Change: The Role of Mass Media and Instructional Technology

by *ROBERT L. GREEN and RICHARD THOMAS**
Asst. Provost
Dir., Center for Urban
Affairs
Michigan State Univ.

The Report of the National Advisory Commission on Civil Disorders[1] (Kerner Report), concluded that centuries of white American racism were responsible for the conditions that led to open rebellions in the black communities of Newark and Detroit, during the summer of 1968. Racial discrimination in education, housing, and employment were listed as major factors that led to distrust, hopelessness, and finally to retaliation against a system that favored whites and abused blacks. But in addition to the indictment of those "un-American" practices directed at black Americans, the National Advisory Commission also cited the role that the mass media have played in urban disorders, and their indirect role in perpetuating white racism:

> Important segments of the media failed to report adequately on the causes and consequences of civil disorders and on the underlying problems of race relations. They have not communicated to the majority of their audience—which is white—a sense of the degradation, misery, and hopelessness of life in the ghetto.[2]

Specifically the mass media have failed to use their communicative skills to educate white Americans regarding the role that white-controlled institutions have played in planting the seeds of discontent in black communities throughout the nation. The Kerner Report states:

> What white Americans have never fully understood—but what the Negro can never forget—is that white society is deeply implicated in the ghetto. White institutions created it, white institutions maintain it, and white society condones it.[3]

If, as indicated by the Kerner Report, the major obstacle facing the black community in its efforts to become a viable force in American life is the negative practices directed at it by the white community, what role can mass media and instructional technology play in changing the undemocratic attitudes and behaviors of the white community?

The power of the mass media in shaping public opinion and directing action toward problems by governments and by citizens is well recognized. "Books, telephones, telegrams, newspapers, and more recently radio and television are man's formalized information processing and distribution institutions."[4] Political aspirants are well aware of the impor-

*Richard Thomas was a history major at Michigan State University at the time this paper was prepared.

tant role played by various forms of media in shaping the attitudes of the voting population. Indeed, President Nixon used a mass medium, namely television, most effectively during his second and successful effort to reach the White House. The image offered to the American public during Mr. Nixon's first presidential campaign was greatly modified through the use of television in 1968.

Mass media and its offspring, instructional technology, can be rightly viewed as very powerful forms of social control, and can be used to shape the attitudes and values of a given citizenry for constructive or destructive purposes. Adolph Hitler used mass media to convince millions of Germans that its Jewish residents were morally corrupt and inherently inferior and thus paved the way for the destruction of human life. Through the use of mass media, the United States assisted millions of Americans during the afer World War II in developing first hostile, then very positive attitudes toward the country of Japan, all within a span of ten years. Radio, movies, filmstrips and eventually television were used concomitantly in order to shape the views of Americans toward the Japanese. More recently, the medium of television was used very effectively during the early 1960's in order to portray white southerners (such as the police commissioner of Birmingham, Alabama, Bull Connor) as violent and brutal men who oppress black people. Yet this same technological tool several years later portrayed black people as rampaging citizens, lacking in inner control, who burned cities to the ground.

These examples might be multiplied many times to indicate the very important role that media can play in shaping the attitudes and values of people towards issues that vitally affect the direction this country might take regarding its political life. In fact, it might be said that the mass media have played a very important role in supporting the attitudes of Americans about a number of institutions—institutions such as education, the welfare system, employment, and the defense system (witness the manner in which the media, particularly radio and television, supported with little question the war in Vietnam).

In discussing the mass media and instructional technology, we should perhaps explore the power arrangements in American life since these are the arrangements which are usually supported by the media. Most societies are held together by very specific interacting belief systems. Such belief systems need not be objectively valid, as long as they perform functions deemed to be important by those who hold power positions within that given society. These belief systems are a very significant aspect of social cohesion. When a given belief system is threatened by forces within its society, the system reacts to that external threat. It may draw together or it may begin to disintegrate, precipitating chaos in other systems that interact with it.

American society has several belief systems that perform certain highly selective functions for the white majority. Racism is a very important belief system that appears to be functional for the white majority. Its tenets are rationales developed to perpetuate the *status quo* and explain away the oppressed circumstances of minority groups. We would need only to examine our political, legal, and social history to confirm the latter statement. American society has yet to deal effectively with the issue of eliminating racism as a major belief system operative throughout our culture. It may be argued that the belief system of racism is a major construct which weaves together other belief systems in our society, e.g., "Indians and Blacks are unemployed not because of racial discrimination, but because they are lazy."

The media have been used as a very effective set of technological tools to maintain and perpetuate the racist belief system. Minorities have been portrayed by the media with just those traits that the system allows them to possess. Thus, a kind of self-fulfilling prophecy is created and upheld.

At first, this was accomplished by newspapers—the printed word. Today, however, radio and television can do in an hour what print or word of mouth take years to do. Attitudes toward racism can be piped thousands of miles, hour after hour into the living room or shanty of any white American whether to reinforce his belief system regarding poor people, Indians or black people, or to counteract basic attitudes operative within that belief system.

In essence, television is a powerful medium of communications. It exposes us to a world which at times might be strange and frightening. It can bring into the most remote white rural living room the death moans of a black child dying of rat bites in Harlem. It can, for a moment, force a tear from a black nationalist viewing an unemployed white worker looking helplessly into the face of his starving young pregnant wife. It can move mountains of raw emotions to fever pitch, hatred, or even tender love. It could make us one family, if it would.

With the advent of radio, television, filmstrips, programmed learning materials, computers, and other communication tools into the area of formal instruction, the young field of instructional technology has developed rapidly. Some planners, recognizing the effectiveness of mass media, have suggested that the mass media become the educational institutions of our generation.[5] Thus, the order of business now is to determine how instructional technology with its great capacities might assist in developing democratic attitudes toward all people in American life.

Attitude development theorists argue that the attitudes of young children can be shaped more quickly than those of adults. If we are to assist large segments of the American public in developing democratic attitudes, then, our chances of success are much greater if we begin with young children. In addition, it has been found that the perceived prestige of the individual who conveys certain information significantly affects the amount of attitude change. "The higher the perceived prestige, trustworthiness, or expertness of the communicator, the greater the attitude change toward the position advocated in the message. Further, studies have indicated that attitude change is independent of the amount of factual information absorbed from the message."[6] So both the time at which information is conveyed and the prestige of the individual presenting this information are important factors in changing attitudes.

First, let's dwell on the age factor. Schramm provides data which indicate that "more than ⅓ of all children in television communities are watching the picture tube by the time they are three."[7] He further indicates that four out of five children view television by the time they come to school. "Almost all of them are regular television viewers before they begin to read the newspaper."[8]

How much time do children spend watching television? Schramm finds that small children tend to view television a little more than two hours each day. As children approach their early teens, their TV watching time exceeds three hours each day. "This means that from the child's third year of life until sometime near the end of high school, television comes near to filling nearly one-sixth of all the child's waking hours. It absorbs from one-half to three-fourths of all media time."[9] This suggests that TV is a very important mode of communication for preschool and early elementary school children.

Considering the amount of time spent in watching television, a unique opportunity exists for providing children with educational programs that are related to developing positive attitudes toward social justice. Cartoons are certainly powerful reinforcers for children and could be made enjoyable, funny, and at the same time carry a humanistic theme and/or some educational content. Yet, this has not been done on a wide scale. At present, many of the cartoons that are currently being watched have come under fire from citizens' groups around the country. Parents complain that the days of the Donald Duck cartoons have vanished. Modern cartoons are saturated with aggression and outright violence.

A promising innovation is the Children's Television Workshop; the main objective of this program is to provide preschool children with basic education and to develop healthy attitudes toward learning and toward their fellow men. Within the next year, 130 programs will be presented, directed mainly at poor children in the cities. Efforts are being made to make these Children's Workshop programs a series of creative, innovative presentations that will attain their goals.

The Children's Television Workshop, however, is only one small but important approach oriented toward positive attitudes through the use of instructional technology. Let us focus specifically on the general American population. There is much evidence to support the point of view that many white Americans still hold non-democratic attitudes toward minorities—e.g., the Kerner Report. The white community has historically held unhealthy attitudes toward black and other minorities, and minority groups have in turn developed unhealthy attitudes toward the white majority as a function of the mistreatment they have received. It must be asserted that attitude change will not come about unless conditions in our society are basically changed. Blacks will not change their attitudes about mistreatment in the area of employment until employers stop discriminating against black people who are trying to secure employment. However, even if rapid and basic changes could be brought about in American institutions today, attitudes developed as a function of historical facts may yet need changing. This change will not come about unless there is a major commitment by those who control media in America to deliberately present information that will assist in developing "Democratic Attitudes." Both the government and private industry, i.e., those who financially support mass media, can play a very important role in encouraging the communicators of information to take this approach. Whitney Young, in a recent speech to the National Association of Broadcasters, also reiterated this idea. He indicted the networks for rigidly preserving the *status quo* by their strict enforcement of regulations which permit only network personnel to plan programs for American audiences. It was stated earlier that when the government feels that its best interests lie in assisting *all* Americans to develop positive or negative attitudes toward other world powers, it does this through radio, television, films and newspapers readily and swiftly. This same kind of massive commitment must be made by the media in an effort to assist the white majority in developing positive attitudes toward black Americans.

In the past, the opposite has been true; witness Stepin Fetchit, Amos and Andy, and other caricatures of black people, where they have been portrayed as being not just ignorant, but also stupid or, at best, with what shrewdness they had, being directed to prolonging a lazy and shiftless way of life. Although blacks are not necessarily portrayed as Amos and Andy types in 1969, the mass media have not yet taken a strong enough approach to presenting blacks in a positive manner. There have been some first steps taken of late regarding the portrayal of black Americans, which are promising. Prominent entertainers such as Bill Cosby and Sammy Davis, Jr., have been presented in major shows watched by millions of Americans. Of late, such programs as "Black Journal," which focuses on the positive aspects of life in black America, has been piped into millions of white and black homes. And just recently, a major television show ("The Today Show") has presented the viewing public with a black newscaster. Portraying blacks in favorable roles such as this can lead to positive views of this major American minority, but much more can be done, particularly by the medium of television.

All over the country universities are starting black studies programs or installing in established departments certain black courses. From coast to coast, Harvard, Michigan State University, University of Illinois, and Stanford, black studies are being developed for the benefit of exposing the university community to the cultural life of black people, both domestically and internationally. Yet what is strongly lacking is a coordinating body that can make available to the non-university audience, e.g., high schools, adult education, religious groups, the benefits of this new body of knowledge.

Some universities can better afford black studies programs than others, and unless interested parties can afford to hop from school to school, they will obviously miss a lot. However, this can be remedied by a closed circuit TV network and a team of university and non-university coordinators, structuring a program where each university with a focus on a special area of black studies could televise that area.[10]

Many people, both black and white, in the non-university public are greatly interested in black studies. However, they have to wait until the national broadcasting companies decide to find room or sufficient monetary motives. Black people, in particular, of the non-university public are starving for all the black studies programs they can get. This need can be met again by setting up mobile television units in places which would be located in the black community (almost like the Christian Science reading rooms). The viewing audience could view these programs during the day when the universities broadcast them or later at night and on weekends. A coordinating body could help the universities to develop schedules that would benefit the work schedules of as many non-university viewers as possible.

Most schools, too, could be plugged into the national network and would be spared the expense of searching for and recruiting teachers for black studies programs. Instead, the history or social studies teacher could assist the program by leading the discussion groups in classes, after the viewing. The class would be exposed to the very best in black studies, from experts in special areas the nation over.

Such developments are presently being effected for industry and medicine. They are not futuristic ideas, by any means. Western Union is presently creating a nationwide utility which will gather, store process, retrieve, and then distribute information through connected computers. And the General Electric Company has already designed a system for the National Library of Medicine which not only locates articles of interest to students or individuals at dial-access terminals, but will also produce an offset film positive of it for printing.[11] Again, it only seems a matter of priorities in terms of the nation's needs; such systems can be established in areas of information distribution about attitudes, but the power structure will need to support them.

The public school system as well as colleges and universities throughout America have available to them a captive audience, an audience that can be presented with information that can lead to the development of very positive attitudes through the use of instructional technology. The Children's Television Workshop was used as an example of what can be done to assist preschool children in developing positive attitudes.

In reviewing the literature in the area of technology, most of the data indicates that instructional technology is used on limited basis in urban, predominately black schools, and is most widely used in very affluent suburban school districts throughout the country. Several reasons may account for this: (1) Suburban school communities can often afford the expensive costs of specific technologies, such as computers, 8mm loop projectors, and other forms of technology. (2) Urban teachers often complain that they are so heavily involved in matters related to upgrading the educational status of their children that they "do not have the time to experiment" with technology.

However, since instructional technology is so widely used in suburban schools, that population which may most negatively or positively effect poor communities can be easily reached. This is where educators have a positive impact on the developing attitudes of junior high school and high school students. Films related to human relations, filmstrips and 8mm films focusing on poverty and welfare conditions in America can be used to offset the attitude that people are poor because they are lazy. The interrelatedness of discrimination, lack of education, and poor health can be vividly portrayed through the use of film strips. Dial-A-Computer can be used to pump in statistics regarding the negative effects of poverty and discrimination in American life (many individuals will accept the data presented objectively in statistical form in contrast to the spoken word).

Another program could be in the area of a dialogue via closed circuit television between inner city black and suburban white students. Over a telephone-television system, black and white students could discuss various subjects which both would be studying simultaneously in their classrooms. After-school centers could be created to continue the dialogues, but in other areas of interest to the students. In the home economics department, black as well as white housewives could discuss preparation of certain meals via closed circuit television, and these discussions could then be televised to home economics classes at all levels of education. In these suburban school communities, due to their already wide use of educational technology, educators have an opportunity to develop programs that are specifically aimed at eliminating racist attitudes and to channel them into suburban classrooms throughout the country.

Ira J. Singer, in a recent article, indicates that instructional technology is used on a limited basis in urban school communities with large minority populations.[12] It is here that instructional technology can be used to good advantage to assist disadvantaged youth in making more rapid progress in efforts to overcome the effects of a past disadvantaging background and to improve attitudes toward work, government, and self. For example, computer-based dial access systems, film strips, movies, all can be used to inform minority youth of new opportunities that are recently available to them in America. Many minority youth, as a function of their own personal experiences and historical information, develop low levels of aspiration regarding their potential achievement in American life. Instructional technology can be specifically used to motivate youngsters to engage in tasks of an academic nature. Research findings indicate that students who participate in courses which use instructional media, such as programmed learning and classroom television, show a significantly more favorable attitude to the course than those taught through the typical lecture method.[13] It might be added that instructional technology could also be used to increase the actual learning ability of disadvantaged youth. The "Talking Typewriter," a computerized teaching machine using a number of media simultaneously, produced by the Responsive Environments Corporation, has shown remarkable success with disadvantaged students and illiterate adults.

In the area of community relations and attitude change, technology can also be very helpful. Dial-Access Information Retrieval Systems can quickly transmit information to any individual or group and can choose information which is tailor-made for a particular audience. Singer[14] points out that technology can be used to assist urban children and their parents in effectively utilizing community resources available to them. For example, "an expectant mother needs advice on prenatal care; an unemployed family head requires guidance for the receipt of welfare benefits; a police suspect seeks legal aid; a high school student needs information concerning availability of after-school employment—in short, information basic to life itself but generally unavailable in convenient form to the ghetto resident can be electronically dialed and transmitted in video and audio modes."

The dial-access system can also be used for teaching skills, when audio and video modes are combined. Such a system would be most useful in job training centers and school situations, in addition to preschool programs.

Another area for technological assistance would be community-police relations. The report of the National Advisory Commission on Civil Disorders offers a number of suggestions, one of which was: "Establish fair and effective mechanisms for the redress of grievances against the police and other municipal employes."[15] What kind of mechanisms? A centrally located information center could be established where black people in the community could check daily on the behavior of the police, i.e., their arresting patterns, patrols, etc. If it is suspected that someone is being harassed, responsible people could go to the center and not only report it, but demand that the officer question the suspect in front of a closed circuit television camera for later viewing. The community could then demand a viewing of any questionable procedures.

Ethnic groups could develop closer ties in their communities by setting up closed circuit television to inform people about daily events related to social justice. Community organizers could work with various segments of the community by channeling information pertaining to race relations to community residents from centrally based offices. Tutorial programs in race relations could be extended through television to millions of homes throughout America. All of these proposed approaches can positively affect and shape the development of democratic attitudes.

The task still confronting this nation is to use our communications technology in an effort to effectively eliminate racist attitudes in American life. However, there must be a major commitment to build a new ethic regarding fair treatment of the individual regardless of race, religion, or national origin. Mass media are controlled by moneyed people in our society. But the media and those who control them must be willing to run the risk of losing a bit of their profit for some period of time in order to engage in the business of facilitating positive attitudes toward such emotional issues as poverty and race. They must be willing to use subtle forms of attitude modifiers in order to infiltrate certain rigid belief systems.

Schools, churches and civic organizations would have to be organized to support the efforts of opinion-makers when such attempts toward attitude improvement are made. These community groups must watch and discuss their programs. Trained observers would have to be available to record or relay to policy-makers the positive or negative effects of new approaches.

Typically, a flurry of activity begins when a major disturbance, such as a riot, occurs in our society. We must not wait for riots and other forms of social disruption in order to begin to develop the kind of society in which all men can feel as though they are accepted. If we are to live out the democratic creed, this change should come about in an orderly democratic manner.

REFERENCES

1. *Report of the National Advisory Commission on Civil Disorders.* Bantam Books, New York, 1968, p. 10.

2. *Ibid.,* p. 20.

3. *Ibid.,* p. 2.

4. McIntyre, John P. "Mass Media—Alternative to Schooling?" *Educational Leadership.* 25, April 1968, p. 637.

5. *Ibid.,* p. 638.

6. Kumata, Hideya. "Attitude Change and Learning as a Function of Prestige of Instructor and Mode of Presentation." *The Impact of Educational Television.* Ed. by Wilbur Schramm, Univ. of Illinois Press, 1960, p. 157.

7. Schramm, Wilbur. "A Note on Children's Use of Television." *The Institute for Communication Research at Stanford Univ.* pp. 214-223.

8. *Ibid.*

9. *Ibid.*

10. Mr. Ron Lee, former Assistant Provost, Michigan State University, suggested that Fisk University could be the site of this national coordinating body, where a center computer system could be established on tapes; and flown out from the various special interested schools.

11. McIntyre. *Op cit.,* p. 640.

12. Singer, Ira J. "Media and the Ghetto School." *Audio-Visual Instruction.* October 1968, pp. 861-864.

13. Neidt, C. O., and D. D. Sjogren, "Changes in Student Attitudes during a Course in Relation to Instructional Media." *AV Communication Review,* 16, Fall 1968, pp. 268-279.

14. Singer. *Op cit.*

15. *Report of the National Advisory Commission on Civil Disorders: Summary of Report.* p. 17.

75.

The Reading Process
And Processed Reading

by SPENSER JAMESON
Lecturer & Professor
Urban Community Schools
Program
Teachers College
Columbia Univ.

and FRANCIS A. IANNI
Prof. & Director
Horace Mann-Lincoln
Institute
Teachers College
Columbia Univ.

In the past five years, industry has provided education with a variety of teaching machines and programs that purport to develop the basic reading skills of children attending schools in the ghetto. The excitement generated by the potential of instructional technology—particularly when joined with learning theory from the behavioral sciences—is widespread. One result of this interest has been an outlay of public and private funds of a magnitude without precedent in American education. Large numbers of youngsters attending schools in the inner city, however, are still not reading.

Education as a System

The reasons why urban man has been able to send rockets to the moon but unable to teach his children to read are associated with his failure to understand the nature of his urban life or to effectively apply technology to the teaching of reading for ghetto youngsters. In the first instance we have so far ignored the overwhelming evidence that learning is more than situational; it is in fact heavily conditioned by the culture within which it develops. If we rule out, for the moment, the many correlational studies of intelligence and family background or child rearing practices and personality, little systematic study appears to have been given to the child rearing antecedents of cognitive behavior and even less to the development of teaching strategies based upon such knowledge. And yet, if we consider learning as essentially an exploration of alternatives and one of the functions of teaching as the economizing of random activity in such choice, then teaching strategies must take into account the fact that the propensity to explore is heavily conditioned by the cultural context within which it takes place. That is to say, every culture produces predisposing factors which develop or inhibit the child's drive to explore and to consider alternatives. An adequate pedagogy then must understand these factors and develop an instructional system which builds upon or vitiates the predisposing factors.

The present mode of so-called diagnostic teaching illustrates the point. This teaching strategy, which places strong emphasis on individualized instruction, posits certain optimal conditions for instruction: (a) that the teacher operate within a system which identifies and exploits the antecedent experiences which predispose a child to learn; (b) that the information to be transmitted be carefully structured for optimal comprehension and presented in a properly programmed sequence; and (c) that the system comprehend the nature and placing of rewards and punishments. The cultural context is a critical, though largely overlooked, factor in the operation of this strategy. Obviously such elements as the degree of intellectual stimulation the child receives from his family, the value his society places upon learning, and the richness of his cultural environment will influence his predisposition to learn. But the structure of knowledge and the mode of presentation are equally dependent on cultural factors. We see, for example, the difference in instructional modes between our own and primitive societies: We teach the young by telling about an action—abstracting out of context; they instruct by showing the action itself. Finally the numerous examples of cultural differentiation of rewards and punishments are as obvious intraculturally from class to class as they are cross culturally.

Just as damaging, however, has been our failure to view educational technology as the product rather than the revolutionizing force of the learning process in urban areas. For all of our talk about a systems approach in education we continue to search for that single revolutionary device or technique which will make it possible to teach all children to read quickly, efficiently and painlessly. We scurry around trying to adapt this piece of industrial hardware or that academically developed strategy of instruction to urban education without ever actually looking at the systematic relations which make education work. Education has rarely been examined in this systematic fashion, particularly by educators. In fact, while there have been some studies on social climate in the schools, most research has concentrated on the learner as part of that system and, in recent years, on what is taught in that system. Little attention has been given to the total organizational structure of education viewed as a system and even less to an analysis of the structure as a device for administrative or management training. What is necessary here, and what this paper is intended to suggest, is that just such a theoretical framework must be employed if we are to understand and manage educational affairs as a system.

Each of the behavioral sciences has now adopted a systems approach which looks at behavior as part of a relational pattern of elements rather than as a series of discrete acts. Whether it is the structural analysis of kinship systems, a behavioral gestalt or a social system, the same intellectual methodology is applied. Elements in constant dynamic relationship cannot be fully understood in isolation from that interaction because constancy is an illusion when human behavior is properly seen as a series of interactions. Applied to education, the systems approach suggests an analysis of a total system of related organizations, behaviors and outcomes rather than the separate analyses of curriculum, administration and teaching. In part this new approach derives from the practical experience of educators who have seen the failure of piecemeal attempts to improve education and have come to appreciate the relational interdependence of the educational system. The very promising curriculum revolution of the 1950's and the 1960's was far less successful than it might have been because it had as its motive and its mode the improvement of education through the improvement of one component—and only one component of the system —the curriculum. There is now ample evidence that modifying the curriculum is a necessary but insufficient step in school improvement unless there are concomitant changes in the rest of the system.

In sum, these are the imperatives for a successful program of technological development in urban education: understanding the psycho-cultural system of the ghetto and developing both software and hardware out of an understanding of this system rather than imposing existing devices and techniques on it. Failure to adhere to these imperatives explains in most cases technology's inability to make any dramatic change in urban education. Nowhere is this more obvious than in the transformation of the reading process into processed reading.

The Challenge of "Bootleg" Education

Before exploring some of the ways instructional technology can be applied to the teaching of reading, it would be useful to look at a program that has been able to teach deprived youngsters how to read. Without books, programmed materials, teaching machines or even trained teachers, a group of youngsters in the East Harlem and Harlem communities of New York City were taught to read by men who themselves had failed in or dropped out of school—men who might be called "bootleg educators."

With just the teachings from the Koran and some written lessons that emphasized Afro-American history and the dignity and importance in being black, youngsters ranging in age from eleven to seventeen were motivated to learn to read 42 lessons. An alphabet and number system were incorporated into the program. The young people were given the alphabet, words beginning with every letter (e.g., "J is for Justice or Just ice") and, through a cross-referencing system to numbers which corresponded to the 26 letters, proper Islamic names beginning with each letter in the alphabet. In order to be admitted to a special peer group, a youngster memorized the words and names for each letter and number, and read and memorized the 42 lessons. When this was accomplished, the youngster obtained his Islamic name by using this coded system and joined the Five Percenters—one of the many splinter groups which came into being after the assassination of Malcolm X.

A byproduct of this initiation procedure was that many youngsters whom schools had labeled functional illiterates learned to read. When pupils in one classroom who had scored below 4.0 on the California Achievement Test viewed a filmstrip on civil rights, several were consistently able to identify and pronounce correctly words like "militant," "exploit" and "heritage." In a discussion which followed the film, they were able to articulate the views of black militant groups in an intelligent and forceful manner. Measured by the standardized test, these youngsters were not prone to learning. Yet they *were* learning in a bootleg fashion from the preachers of the street, many of whom use the miseries of the poor to further their own ends.

Has instructional technology with its machines and programmed systems met the challenge of the bootleg educators in teaching the inner city child how to read? If so, how? If not, why not?

When one teaching machine was placed in a school with youngsters from an inner city ghetto, the students were at first fascinated—fascinated with the fact that they had a machine that looked like a television set with all kinds of buttons they could push to make the picture move backwards and forwards. As the teachers and students began to use the program, however, not only did the content disinterest them, but the fascination of pushing all the buttons wore off. The content, a modified version of material developed in the 1940's, presented life in the country—cows, chickens, and the kinds of experiences which elicit neither recognition nor interest from inner city students.

Many companies are making an effort to focus software text and illustrations on the interests of the urban student. This is needed, but is it enough? When compared with the "teaching strategies" underlying the bootleg education described above, the effort represents merely an adaptation of traditional middle-class learning modes to an essentially different culture. Though frequently successful in the environment for which they were originally designed, these teaching materials and strategies, however modified, fail in the ghetto classroom.

The difficulty lies in the very process of materials development. Education companies are made up of people living in relatively affluent areas of the city or suburbs and working in midtown offices. They may make occasional visits to the ghetto and its schools or bring somebody from the ghetto into their office, pump him, and then design programs which, they assume, will meet the needs of the youngsters lacking in reading skills.

The bootleg educators, on the other hand, came from the same environment as their "students." They were from the ranks, often the same age as the young people they taught, and succeeded in gaining membership in the organization by learning the same 42 lessons they taught. A perpetual each-one-teach-one approach was used much along the lines of Laubach's adult literacy techniques. The curriculum designers and programmers, as well as teachers who live outside their students' neighborhood and know little about the life styles of the youngsters, will have difficulty matching the effectiveness of the person who is familiar with their needs and has their respect as one who understands their problems because he has himself risen above similar ones.

Companies can hire people from inner city ghettos to fill decision-making, writing and research positions by establishing criteria other than academic training. At present a few companies are considering the possibility of setting up independent black companies to produce software—with no strings attached. Like the development of more relevant content, these are effective and necessary trends, but again limited in comparison with the bootleg educator's approach. For even when companies embarking in new directions of instructional technology involve ghetto residents in materials development, they follow traditional publishing procedures which, to date, have failed to translate the learning methods at work in the street into marketable materials. The traditional procedures entail the design of software as a final product to be marketed in the classroom. Periodic revisions are sometimes scheduled, but contact between the classroom and the company is largely limited to an initial teacher-training session on how to operate the equipment and administer the materials. Occasionally materials are pretested in the classroom and modified to suit students' needs. But once again, the company *modifies* rather than *develops* materials for the inner city student.

These many problems concerned with developing effective reading materials for the inner city pupil are further complicated by the stark fact that the few programs and equipment which have evidenced some measure of success are too expensive for most schools to purchase. The result is that teachers are forced to use less expensive instructional aids which still utilize the traditional content that has failed to teach many inner city children how to read. Beyond this, large numbers of schools located in the inner city have anarchronistic facilities that are not readily adaptable to newer systems of instructional technology.

Meeting the Challenge: Community Learning Centers

Education companies can, however, break out of an approach which uses the classroom merely as a sales outlet for materials. They can tap the bootleg educator's techniques and involve poor readers in the reading process—rather than merely processing traditional reading materials through new equipment. And further, this can be done at a cost within the reach of school systems and community centers.

The large industrial combines that purport to turn out all kinds of educational materials can become active members in centers of learning, based on the inner city, where business and industry, local colleges and university schools of education, public school administrators and teachers, and parents, students, "drop-outs" and other residents of the community can meet together. In these community-based "Learning Centers," all members of the community—people living, studying, teaching or marketing—would have the opportunity to become involved in the solution of educational problems. They would learn from each other and learn together.

From the company's point of view, the value of a learning center, in terms of the quality of resulting products, new markets and profit margins, would depend to a great extent on how much each company brought to, and was willing to learn from, the centers. Nevertheless, some possible outcomes can be suggested:

1. Companies would begin to understand the needs and learning styles of inner city students and, on the basis of this understanding, develop software which was relevant to the observed needs of inner city students.

2. Companies would simulate the kind of individualized instruction offered by the Five Percenters by structuring relevant content into programmed materials and other self instructional aids which a student could use at his own pace.

3. Companies would design some software components as "core programs" for mass production and national marketing. The programs would teach basic skills at all levels and provide a model for supplementary materials which teachers and students could develop to suit their unique reading skills and motivational needs.

4. Companies would develop training designs for on-site workshops and training materials which would instruct teachers, community people and high school students on ways to develop the above components.

5. Companies would train and license individuals to perform technical services needed in the operation of technological instructional programs (e.g., coding machine instructions, taping audio scripts, developing slides, etc.).

6. Companies would provide students with "tools," such as tape recorders and still and motion picture cameras, to collect and create content material of interest to them, for use in their own reading instruction. This raw material would be adapted for software to be used in other urban schools by students with similar reading skill deficiencies and content needs.

Axiomatic to responsible leadership in the world of instructional technology is the idea that the teacher is not to be replaced but situated in a new position where his talent as a teacher and person may come to full fruition. It is nevertheless true that a major obstacle to the full execution of many programs lies in the resistance that many teachers put up to automated technology. One of the weaknesses of current reading programs is that teachers did not participate in the development of the materials—and consequently are not actively involved in administering them. Representatives of educational companies, participating at community-based learning centers as both learners and specialists, could help alleviate teachers' fears of automation by involving them in a variety of orientation and training programs.

In addition to involving teachers in the potential uses of instructional technology, companies participating in learning centers would work with educators on curriculum development, diagnostic testing in local schools and special educational projects in after-school centers, and adult training. The companies would have the opportunity not only to learn about needs and future markets but also to begin orienting school personnel to more innovative approaches in education. Through demonstration projects and teacher workshops conducted at learning centers, new methods in teaching reading could be introduced into the school system. From the initial stages, learning center programs would utilize and coordinate resources of the major segments of the community. For example, businessmen and educators together would adapt remedial and adult basic literacy skills to practical, job-related reading situations; specialists in instructional technology would work with university schools of education in developing techniques of teaching reading skills with various types of teaching machines and devices.

Each segment of the community would contribute in its area of specialty and at the same time learn from the others. Universities would provide testing and evaluation services as well as teacher training in subject areas. Business and industry would consult on management techniques, fund programs, and conduct special training and orientation to the world of work for young people. The public schools would make needs known, refer pupils and evaluate the effectiveness of new media.

Community parents and young people would define "relevant" approaches and collect raw content material. This latter contribution merits further clarification.

Materials by the Student for the Student

In much the same way that teachers often resist the idea that machines and self-contained materials can be effective teaching tools, experts in the development of educational devices and self-instructional materials sometimes resist the idea that teachers—and even students— can develop materials for themselves. Evidence attesting to the feasibility of this approach, however, is offered by the experience of the Community Resource Center of the Horace Mann-Lincoln Institute where during the past year elementary and high school students and high school drop-outs with poor reading skills have been developing their own reading improvement materials.

Small teams of students from our film workshop, using still and motion picture cameras, take pictures of people and things that interest them. These pictures serve as the starting point of a reading program. As the photographers look over their pictures, they describe and label them. Descriptions are written or recorded on tape, thus enabling nonliterate students to be immediately involved in the activity. Community residents working as tutors and teachers transcribe the materials for reading. Sequenced on film strips, pictures can also serve as short stories or episodes for discussion and/or reading.

Simple reading skills are developed as students identify elements of the picture or suggest titles for them. At a more advanced reading level, the pictures become the source for fiction and non-fiction reading materials. The student himself may interpret the pictures, thus determining the actual content of the materials. The teacher thus works from student-written materials which are immediately relevant to the students.

Specialists in educational technology could adapt such student-made products for use in teaching machines, audiovisual aids, or self-instructional programs. To carry this proposition one step further, older students could be hired by educational companies and trained to adapt the materials themselves.

These materials, combined with instructional equipment, could form a package that not only would help meet the need for meaningful reading instruction, but would also cope with the problem of the prohibitive cost of computer-based instruction and the complex set-ups for which our schools are currently unprepared. Computers in current use range in cost from $60,000 to over one million dollars including limited software. Compare this to the cost of our proposed package—$150 to $200 for a 35mm camera, a small portable tape recorder and an 8mm or 16mm movie camera—and meaningful contact developed by students to serve as the basis for a reading improvement program. This is clearly within the means of any school system. The package would be small, lightweight and portable and would embody the much needed versatility and flexibility.

The learning center would in effect represent the practical application of the systems approach to education. Through close proximity and day-to-day confrontation at the center, the various elements of the education system—community life, students, parents, teachers, administrators, instructional systems, media, and the corporate producers of materials— would be sensitized to their mutual existence and interrelationship. Once conscious of this interrelationship, they (and especially those concerned with improving instruction) could exploit it for the purpose of generating new methods and materials that would be effective and acceptable to the various parts of the system. Curriculum would emerge out of the needs of students; teachers and administrators would observe its effectiveness and learn to use it; companies would translate it into marketable materials with demonstrated effectiveness and acceptability.

In addition, the community-based center would help to redress an imbalance in the system. The psycho-social factors of the inner city, too often ignored or misunderstood by educational planners, would come into full play at the center. Through company cooperation with community parents, teachers and students and through the creation of raw material by young people themselves, community styles and needs would have their impact on final products, products that would build the reading process into effective processed reading.

76.

The Promises of Educational Technology In Ghetto Schools—Implementing The Coleman Report

by *HARRY A. JOHNSON*
Assoc. Dean
Virginia State College

Present day curricula in ghetto schools are not meeting the instructional needs of youth. It is not designed for them, not understood by them, useless to them and is the chief contributor to the problems of discipline and dropouts. The ghetto youth is academically and intellectually behind his suburban-majority counterpart; short of skills, verbal self-expressions, training and refinements, and all the other attributes which lend themselves to learning. He is, however, well aware of certain measures of self-protection, he has grown up and matured rapidly, formulated many mistrusts and survived the wear and tear of the ghetto and the fated hand of prejudice and discrimination when venturing from its confines. He sees the enemies; the police, the rent collector, the teacher, a drunken father, a grocery store boss—and they all dispute his passage. When he comes to school, if he comes to school, he comes with more of a complexity of burdens than any children anywhere in the world. He's concerned with being drafted for the Vietnam War, he's eighteen and plagued with an ignorance and fear of venereal diseases surrounding him, usually hungry or never quite full, dressed in clothes which he long ago learned to despise and he is already tired from the long walk to school from a tenement house where babies cried all through the long night, and equally frustrated parents fought either verbally or physically in an interminable conflict. He gets to school just on time, but most likely late to get the abuse of a battery of middle class rules and regulations from middle class school personnel with middle class values and an obsolete middle class curriculum planned around a scheduled set of time blocks that won't move an inch. At 9:00 a.m. he is greeted with a talking face, the same one he left yesterday, droaning on and on about dates, location and details of the Hundred Years War between France and England. And really, who gives a damn? Not even the teacher, who fifty-three times out of a hundred grew up in the same neighborhood, finished the local high school, and a city teachers college, all to come back to teach about a subject she knows little about and cares less about. Her meager, dull, uninspired "teaching" is all she can bring forth from an impoverished social, economic and academic past. So it goes on and on, cycle repeating itself, getting worse as the world around them moves into the age of technology and space. That is a part of the picture of a ghetto child and the school he goes to and the home he comes from. Wherein there are many exceptions to this picture, the mere fact that it exists at all should foster a disquieting and repugnant feeling to all Americans.

The survey known as the Coleman Report[1] sounds a ringing rebuke to the failure of contemporary American education to meet the needs of low status minority poor of this land. The survey represented a massive effort involving many quantitative measures. Complete sets of information were collected for more than 3,000 schools representing about 650,000 students in five grades of public school. More than 60,000 teachers, several thousand principals and several hundred superintendents in school districts also responded to this research. These data were analyzed in 1966 and the 737 page Coleman Report, *Equality of Educational Opportunity* was published by the U.S. Office of Education in the summer of 1966. Deep as it is in statistics, facts and fallacy, it is accurate enough to sound warnings of the presence of social and political dynamite ready to be ignited into the greatest social explosion since the French Revolution. Enough generalizations may be drawn from these massive statistics to get the message about the unequal opportunities in American education.

Some grave questions, however, should be raised about the Coleman Report. The report gives three sources as bases for pupil achievement: (1) family background; (2) characteristics of the school (teachers, curriculum, facilities, resources, etc.); and (3) attributes of peer groups. The report blatantly, through design or through ineptness, understates the importance of school resources in explaining variations in achievement. The instrument for measuring school resources is highly inadequate, especially in light of the potential of measuring resources and achievement. As a matter of fact, the only resources apparently measured in the report were those which could have been measured a half century ago, namely, the library and the presence of laboratory facilities. Consequently, absent were the modern tools of learning resources, of instructional technology, including instructional television, films and programmed materials, independent study materials and equipment, audio and video tapes, computer assisted instruction, and a wide variety of even the more traditional audiovisual materials for learning.

The Coleman Report research design, without a doubt, overestimated the importance of family background as well as underestimated the influence of school resources on student achievement. Henry Levin states that a particularly glaring example of the incomplete measurement of school characteristics is the absence of the measure of class size in the regression analysis.[2] Coleman reported that the pupil-teacher ratio in instruction: "showed a consistant lack of relation to achievement among all groups under all conditions."[3] Levin contends that the report obtained its pupil-teacher ratio by dividing the enrollment of the school by the number of teachers. Says Levin, "The survey's published data suggests that the teaching load per school varies from a low of about four to a high of six hours a day. This range of teaching loads implies a potential difference of as much as fifty percent in class sizes for schools with the same pupil-teacher ratio."[4] Thus, despite its sweeping assertion, the report could not possibly answer the question of how class size affects learning, in general or under particular conditions, since class size was never used in the analysis.

It should be pointed out also that the Coleman investigation was not successful in securing information from more than 40 percent of the sample schools. This alone has some validity for the acceptance of this report in its total. Other reactions to the accuracy and validity are of no mean interest. Noted Harvard statistician, Frederick Mostella, reports Mr. Levin, served as chairman of a task force which examined some of the statistical evidence underlying the Coleman findings. In viewing Coleman's technique of first "controlling" for student background before examining the role of school resources, Mostella's task force concluded that "the things used to control were so highly correlated with things being adjusted that school effects were largely removed."[5] Further: "In problems where we have such strong correlation between the background characteristics and where the situation is utterly confused, the adjustment can be misleading."[6] And, finally, "We believe therefore that conclusions drawn from this part of the analysis can be badly misleading."[7]

American education can indeed be grateful to Professor James S. Coleman, principal author, and his staff for the quantitative study *Equality of Educational Opportunity,* which points up to the American people the status of segregated urban education in America. Wherein the Coleman report points a bleak picture of the status equality of education in America, it is felt by many educators that the opportunity can exist for quality education.

The Systems Approach

The approach that is most likely to pay off big dividends in restructuring the curriculum and educational environment of ghetto schools is an instructional systems approach to learning with built-in technological resources. Many forces prohibit any other approach. Poorly trained teachers, outdated facilities, haphazard use of technology, ignorance on the part of administrators and teachers regarding use of mediated materials, absence of skills in constructing educational objectives and countless other reasons prohibit continuing in the manner in which we have gone. Over and over again we see in ghetto schools, language laboratories not operating, awaiting a repairman, several projectors and no film, or films and no light control for use. Few ghetto schools are equipped with the needed resources and facilities for independent study or small group work. Teachers tire of hunting down the custodian to release a motion picture projector that finally comes without the essential extension cord.

A Title XI NDEA Institute for school principals of ghetto schools recently was an eye-opener regarding the place of media in the teaching-learning process. Most of these educators had regarded media, if at all, as a shuffling back and forth of motion picture projectors to and from the library. All, and I repeat, all, were aghast at the present involvement of many schools already operating with systems approach to instruction, simple dial access facilities, electronically operated independent study carrels, team teaching, varying sized groups, teachers free to prepare materials for large group instruction, and a variety of other kinds of educational innovations. Heretofore, district level purchasing agents and administrators have been hoodwinked into buying scores of overhead projectors with no thought of securing materials, locally or commercially; or new reading machines for elementary schools which are designed and programmed for utilization in the junior high and high school. All of these problems and countless others demand a team approach to redesigning the curriculum, setting of behavioral objectives, restraining teachers, orientation of administrators, utilization of educational media experts, supplementary and supporting staff, all within an instructional systems approach to educating ghetto youth. This concept may surprise some educators because it implies that never before had there been systematic planning in educating children. Much like the term "programmed," "systems" has a new meaning in the realm of technological communications. Indeed, whatever system educators have used, never before have they included the many essential components of learners, teachers, schedules, facilities, media, different groupings, individualization, programming, stimuli, responses, technology, materials, curriculum planners, etc. Barry Morris describes a new use of media in a system this way:

> The newer media have led us to a new approach to instruction. This is a scientifically developed combination of instructors, materials, and technological media for providing optimum learning with a minimum of routine personal involvement by the teacher. The result is a carefully planned "system" consisting of subject matter, procedures, and media coordinated in a program unit design which is directed toward specific behavioral objectives. A variety of learning channels are combined in such a system. Decisions as to where and how to use teacher presentation, discussion, media presentation, programmed learning sequences, or other channels, will be made in terms of what and who is to be taught.[8]

A definition of "systems approach" by the Department of Audiovisual Instruction Commission on Technology sets forth in its official release of the following statement:

> An integrated programmed complex of instructional media, machinery, and personnel whose components are structured as a single unit with a schedule of time and sequential phasing. Its purpose is to insure that the components of the organic whole will be available with the proper characteristics at the proper time to contribute to the total system, and in doing to fulfill the goals which have been established.[9]

The information explosion, poorly prepared teachers, high turnover rate of teachers and learners in the ghetto schools, and the uniqueness of minority groups and their special needs all urgently cry for the ghetto teacher to change her role from principal presenter of the message to a more useful membership in a revised educational strategy. Technology is urgently needed in ghetto schools in an effort to ease the boredom of talking faces which add more to drop-out problems than perhaps any other single contributor. Under the present conditions, language laboratories, independent study carrels, television program sequences are used or not used at the discretion of an overworked and overwrought teacher, but within a systems approach they function in the educational process at the curriculum planning phase and in its execution. Technology should cease being used principally for enrichment learning, but should be an integral part of the process of educating. It becomes an integral component of the message.

To operate in a systems approach, media will take its rightful place in the teaching-learning process. The array of technology and media which would be plugged into a system includes the whole array of television and video, tape packages, 2 × 2 slides and filmstrips, motion pictures, realia, audio teaching tapes, telelectures, graphic materials, mock-ups simulations, and other more traditional audiovisual resources—all built into and claiming a portion of the whole, not in isolation, not at whim, but coupled with such other innovation as team teaching, new flexible facilities, and above all, a school-wide philosophy that believes in and encourages the permissiveness necessary to arrive at the objectives of such a dramatic and new venture.

To really be operational and testable, such a system will recognize first of all, not lastly, the essentials of stating goals and setting up specific behavioral objectives that are clear and unequivocally stated. Robert F. Mager coherently states it:

> When clearly defined goals are lacking, it is impossible to evaluate a course or program efficiently, and there is no sound basis for selecting appropriate materials, content, or instructional methods. After all, the machinist does not select a tool until he knows what operation he intends to perform. Neither does a composer orchestrate a score until he knows what effects he wishes to achieve. Similarly, a builder does not select his materials or specify a schedule for construction until he has his blueprints (objectives) before him. Too often, however, one hears teachers arguing the relative merits of textbooks or other aids of the classroom versus the laboratory, without ever specifying just what goal the aid or method is to assist in achieving. I cannot emphasize too strongly the point that an instructor will function in a fog of his own making until he knows just what he wants his students to be able to do at the end of the instruction.[10]

Far too many teachers in ghetto schools cannot do this. Teaching and testing at the present time in most schools is one long guessing game with students as to what they will be tested for and how to say it like the teacher wants it said. Clear, precise objectives stated and understood by teachers and learners at the outset in the systems approach will by and large eliminate the uncertainty on the part of the learners.

A Relevant Curriculum

By and large, ghetto children dislike or hate the school curriculum. Their greatest joy at school is often a denied opportunity to relate and react to each other. They have every right to this feeling. What they are required to do in the planned curriculum is irrelevant as to both content and method. Kenneth Clark puts it succinctly:

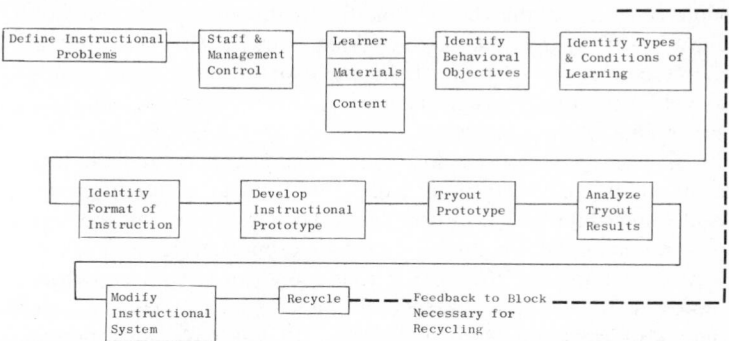

A Modified Systems Approach for Developing Instructional Systems for Ghetto Schools

What I believe I know about the nature of this crisis I think can be summarized in one sentence or, more accurately, one anguished explanation—namely, contemporary American education, urban public education, is a national disaster. A calamity. A catastrophic, inefficient situation. A social and political powder keg, awaiting just a capricious spark to set off a tremendous social explosion.

The chief victims of this calamity are clearly low-status minority-group children and other children from low-income families. The public educational system has broken down in terms of fulfilling the responsibility of preparing these children for a meaningful role in our society. . . . Specifically, these children, literally abandoned by our public schools, in terms of any meaningful definition of the term education, are suffering from a pattern of unsolved educational problems.[11]

Dr. Clark goes on to state further:

But the data that are available support without question the calamitous, catastrophic, criminally inefficient level of public education in deprived areas. These data support the fact that the retardation is cumulative; that the longer the children remain in school, the further behind they fall in the basic subjects when compared with more privileged children. Drop-outs are excessive, and analysis of the drop-outs leaves at least this observer to believe that these children are probably the more intelligent, in that they escape from a dehumanized and intolerable situation.[12]

In his address for the Educational Media Council on Television as an Educational Tool, Dr. Clark goes on to further state:

First, develop a parallel educational program on television. And, I'm suggesting, outside of the control of the present educational bureaucracy. A parallel educational program in basic skills of reading, arithmetic, communication—oral and written, etc.[13]

One may not agree with all of Dr. Clark's recommendations, but certainly must agree that ghetto schools and minority groups must shake off the shackles of the whole middle class aura that prevails from preschool to college. We have mimicked and aped and copied middle class values to such an extent that it has destroyed the very fabric of the educational system for minority groups. Let us look at Head Start programs and pre-school activities. These projects insist on modeling their programs on those of conventional middle class nursery schools. They contend that these children have the same needs and the same range of personalities as all children; therefore a child development center should have the same aims for their preschool experiences, etc. Middle class nursery schools operate on the theory that they can directly influence only the child's emotional and social development, not his mental growth. They assume that if they build up a shy child's confidence or redirect an angry one's aggression, a child's intellectual development will take care of itself. Therefore, they concentrate on getting along with others and other time-wasting objectives.

Slum children must make up for lost time from preschool and kindergarten through college. Teaching children to get along with others and to adjust to groups and develop appreciation of other children are outstanding objectives. However, they are not the most crucial to nursery school slum children. The poor cannot afford such luxuries. What they have not learned at home by the age of four, they must learn elsewhere and quickly. They must make up for lost time, unlearn old habits which is much harder than learning new ones, and also catch up with others who do not have such problems. Although Head Start centers are purely local operations, few of them have been innovative in their approach to teaching slum children. They have been based on the same principles as those for middle class children which does not emphasize intellectual development. Nearly all of these programs have failed to produce any great improvements in children's readiness for school. According to Dr. Samuel A. Kirk, an authority on retarded children, a given infant may grow up to have an IQ of 80 with a poor environment or 120 with a good environment. Only the outer limits of man's intelligence are fixed by heredity. But the older the child grows, the more difficult it is to produce a given amount of change in his intelligence. Therefore, since the most rapid growth of intelligence takes place before the age of four, efforts must be changed in these early years in working with children's intelligence. Some innovators of this point of view would send battalions of tutors into poor children's homes like visiting nurses and social workers to provide appropriate toys and to talk to babies to develop their intelligence. Others would set up the European type creche or children's day care centers on every crowded city block with educational programs that are geared to toddlers. Slum children of two to three years old would take part in specific learning sequences and would be taught to listen and repeat and to think and to respond. Perhaps, based on the famous Montessori techniques or educational methods, children will begin to develop their intellect in the slum area in these early years. The same type of a hard-nose approach to learning needs to be carried through the elementary and secondary levels and when economically deprived children and ghetto youth reach college age, they will either be skilled craftsmen or they will be ready for the academe of the college program.

Perhaps the most important reason for the multi-media or technological approach to instruction for the economically deprived lies in what Frank Riessman calls "style of learning." In planning strategies of learning for youngsters who have been disadvantaged, the fact that these patterns do exist should be a guiding factor. In individualizing instruction, each child's strengths and weaknesses should be diagnosed and treated through the most effective strategies available. Says Frank Riessman:

> One index of style relates to whether you learn things most easily through reading or through hearing, or whether you learn through doing things physically; whether you learn things slowly, or quickly; whether you learn things in a one track way or whether you are very flexible in your learning. The examples just cited are not to be seen as separate from one another. There can be combinations such as a visual-physical learner who learns in a slow, one track fashion.[14]

The tragic need for technological resources beyond those now offered to the slum teacher is reflected in the Coleman Report. "Fifty-three percent of the teachers have lived in the same locality most of their lives." [15] What this really means is that these teachers have grown up in the same slum neighborhood, finished the same ghetto schools and most likely have had college training in predominantly Negro colleges which are below the national ratings of institutions of higher education in almost everything. As an additional insult to ghetto youth the Coleman Report further states that only 46 out of 100 teachers in ghetto schools would not care to move if given the opportunity. Of these forty-six, it would be indeed interesting to know what percentage would prefer to stay because of their own insecurity and tragic shortcomings that would be glaring in a more demanding school district.

The answer then is technology. The ghetto teacher must be retrained to play a more important role in management of the learning environment and less of a role as presenter of information. The risk is too high to have it any other way. The systematic use of technology is going to prove even more upgrading in pupil achievement in ghetto schools than the predominantly white suburban schools. This assumption is indicated in the Coleman Report:

> The school of the minority pupil will increase his achievement more than will improving the school of the white child increase his. Similarly, the average minority pupil's achievement will suffer more in a school of low quality than will the average white pupils. In short, whites, and to a lesser extent, oriental Americans are less affected one way or the other by the quality of their schools than are minority pupils. [16]

What this is really saying is that our minority youth must look more to the school than other youth in preparing them totally for the society in which they are to enter. "The deficiency in achievement," states the Coleman Report in referring to minority groups, "is progressively greater for minority pupils at progressively higher grade levels." [17] Now let's look at some of the promises of technology in schools for minority groups which promise new directions toward achievement.

Dial Access and Information Retrieval Systems

Dial access and information retrieval systems would utilize materials designed for the ghetto youth. In a study of civics, he learns respect for police and how to get a job by learning something about taking examinations for police work, learning behind the scene responsibilities of police, hearing audio tapes by police and city officials regarding preparations for job requirements. Girls, in the privacy of a dial access system, learn about protection from pregnancies and venereal diseases and the dangers of abortions. Through multi-high school tie-ups dial access youngsters learn typing and shorthand skills, see examples of everyday economics for developing a perspective on consumer buying, see examples of the three branches of the federal government as explained on video tape by Ralph Bunche or Senator Edward Brooke.

Programmed Materials and Independent Learning

Programmed materials built into the system of a ghetto school will show infinite patience with the youngster who starts from behind as he attempts to grasp the concepts of the economy, the mortgage and interest rates on buying a car, carrying charges and real estate assessments. These, he can do at his own pace and at his own rate of speed. He builds his limited vocabulary with programmed materials; simple mathematical solutions, principles of combustion engines, and the process of how the local city government functions; all at his or her own rate and pace with no frustrating failures, no competition, no sarcasm from a teacher tired of repeating, no threats of failure. With programmed materials he has a wealth of properly programmed materials which paint for him a total picture in small sequences which he can handle, and the immediate feedback gives a sense of confidence and a sense of accomplishment.

Study carrels and independent learning through single concept 8mm film, record players, filmstrips, and color slides with earphones lend a person-to-person excitement. These properly programmed materials can follow through an inspiring teacher's introduction to general shop fundamentals of bricklaying, or carpentry, or typing, or music. The system employing carrels has in it as an integrated element the vast resources of 8mm single concept films for skill building in using saws and lathes, or 8mm sound films and music by outstanding Negro writers like Phil Medley or Undine Moore; Negro poetry recorded by Gwendolyn Brooks herself, or some materials by Diahann Carroll or Sidney Poitier, on the unglamorous side of the road to success, or an audio recording on "What It Is To Be A Man," humorously, but solidly delivered by Bill Cosby. Technology and the software yet to be produced will banish boredom, the talking face, and perhaps diminish the problem of dropouts.

Tape teaching, programming for flexible groupings, redeploying the teacher for more professional flexibility and personalized assistance, and programming learners into sequences utilizing audio tapes will prove to be one of the most profitable facets of educational technology. One of the serious problems in some ghetto schools is the high turnover rate by both teachers and students. A well-developed library of audio tapes can serve a variety of purposes. Each tape can be individualized instruction to the learner in a tutorial arrangement, and the tape is generally better planned and sequenced than most live lectures. Also, the learner can turn it on or off or replay as his needs demand. An additional feature is wiring a classroom or a laboratory to the tape recorder whereby youngsters are free to move about as instructions are given and to have both hands free for developing skills and participating in other activities. For example, in learning to use the library, there are such activities as dictionary usage, how to read a map, or how to set up electronically for furthering learning. The youngster puts on the tape (or an attendant may do so) and the tape patiently and slowly sequences the learning experience. This technique may be used in a language laboratory, science laboratory, or for instructions in the industrial education laboratory. Mr. Arthur Lalime, of Darien, Connecticut, has experimented with and found excellent results in tape teaching. He states:

> Taped lessons can be instructional and they can be fun. For example, stories may be recorded on tape and the students can "read to" via the tape playback and earphones. Students usually have a greater degree of comprehension through listening than when the student reads the selection silently. With book in hand, the student can read silently as the teacher on the tape recording reads the story. The earphone creates the sensation that the teacher is talking directly to the child. This type of tape lesson is also being used to help slow readers master the social studies and science material that may be too difficult to read without help. This is a "read with me" situation in which the teacher can make reference to new words, and explain illustrations. Once these taped materials are prepared by the teacher, they can be used at any time with one or many students.

> Prerecorded instruction makes possible the initial teaching of phonetic and word analysis skills as well as providing many opportunities for review of these phonetic skills as the need arises. Tape recorded lessons dealing with these specific skills are prepared in a planned sequence to insure continuity.

> Commercially prepared records can also be linked to the tape tables and earphones system. Many teachers believe that the earphones add a new dimension to listening. Teachers have indicated that recorded programs played to the entire

class were not effective, but when used with earphones the recorded programs were a "great success."[18]

Ghetto youngsters, out of necessity, through crowded experiences and the absence of privacy, have learned to become passive hearers, whereby they listen only when something affects them personally or they have an interest or need to listen. This need can be fulfilled through a special training for ghetto youngsters. Slum children can be taught to listen critically and they can be taught to paint their own creative pictures through listening, if the physical environment for listening has been properly established.

Learning by Television

Television can do more than any other educational media toward helping minority youngsters identify and develop a pride in race, origin and cultural heritage. By and large educational television has not begun to tap the potential it has for minority and slum children. Commercial television has recently made a start.

All three commercial networks and NET initiated special series defining, exploring, and explaining the plight of the black man in America. The most ambitious of these projects was the CBS entry, *Of Black America,* a seven part series purporting to deal in some cohesive fashion with the history, heritage and significance of the black American.

The advent of the portable classroom television recorder can assist teachers in building into learning experiences the resources of libraries of video tapes, made locally by students and teachers. The video tapes may be scheduled into small seminar group work and even independent work by students, or used with earphones in a variety of ways. If local talent is used for such programs it adds variety and identity for slow children.

The medium must use its fullest artistry and skill to produce educational and training programs just as it does to produce entertainment telecasting. A TV program must be kept totally in perspective. A television sequence showing a group of suburban, blue-eyed, fair-haired, happy kids in rural Wisconsin is one segment of our nation's great populus, just as a class of all black kids from an inner city school in Harlem. Therefore, educational television must, out of honesty and integrity, blend all segments to focus on the whole ball of wax when recording the nation's picture. This includes southerners, poor whites of Appalachia, the Mexican-Americans in the far West, the West Coast orientals, Indians throughout the country, Puerto Ricans in the East, the migrants, as well as Negroes and other minority groups. Each of these groups has contributed in its own way to the growth and development of America. Remiss TV will be if it fails to capture the greatness of our nation's melting pot and fails to foster in every citizen an appreciation for that diversity. Educational television must "tell it like it is."

Educational television can help to solve many of the pressing and vital problems of instruction from preschool education to adult education, and its content and format should be so designed. It has an even greater potential in schools where there are underpaid teachers, overcrowded classrooms, shortages of skilled and well-trained teachers, poor educational services, poor support, and dull unimaginative curricula. ETV can help boost the morale of teachers and even upgrade the level of respect for the teaching profession. It can succeed only as an integral member of the educational industry. School and community personnel, both, must be so integrated into the planning and production process as well as the utilization process, that program sequences and series are created from, and based upon evaluation and feedback from these consumers.

Educational television has a potential more than any other media for helping to equalize the quality of instruction. In reply to a question asked a teacher in a rural section of a southern state recently, "What important effect has educational television made upon you?" her reply was, "It has been the most thoroughly effective course in educational methodology I have had. My classroom teaching has improved from watching TV teachers. This includes everything from attitude towards children to skill-developing activities." This, and other concomitant potentials of educational television, should not be underestimated.

Television resources will give slow children an opportunity to deal with the vast, never ending information and knowledge explosion. Unlike his white middle class suburban brothers, the ghetto youth, in order to even survive in the mainstream competition, must play catch up!

Computer-Assisted Instruction

Computer-assisted instruction in the systems approach for minority youth can help catapult them into the mainstream of our society. Computers and their limitless promises seem to offer a portion of the solution. Ignorance on the part of educators as to the wide range of potentials of computers in education must be eliminated. Computer-assisted instruction and individualized instruction, coupled with other media and the teachers are ideal. A ghetto school with limited resources, poorly prepared teachers and a low level of achievement can turn to the computers because the computer can make decisions based on the assessments of student performance, matching resources to individual student needs. One such decision might be for the computer to present lesson materials directly to the student in a tutorial mode.

The computer is capable of serving a large group of learners simultaneously, dealing with the same problems. It therefore becomes a tool for problem solving, far more resourceful than a teacher in much shorter time. Before the student can make the computer solve his mathematical problem, he must analyze the problem and explicitly formulate its solution as a series of discrete, operationally defined steps corresponding to the computer's repertoire of operations. This type of high level experience quickly removes the bright slum child out of the restrictions and limitations of a mediocre ghetto teacher. Repeatedly, I refer to the poor quality of ghetto teachers. It must be remembered that just a few years ago, before any serious thought was given to racial ghetto education, few whites knew and most couldn't care less about the training of teachers for and the quality of teaching in ghetto schools. The products of these schools are mainly our ghetto teachers of today.

Let us explore briefly the RCA Instructional 70 System which has infinite potentials in upgrading the achievement of ghetto youth. The system is a multi-purpose computer-assisted instruction system designed to provide highly individualized daily instruction for up to 6000 students during classroom hours, and also to perform special after-hours instructional functions, a broad variety of educational services, and the administrative data-processing requirements of a large city school district, multi-campus university or other major educational activity.

The Instructional 70 System utilized an RCA Spectra 70/45 computer to drive up to 192 remotely-located student instructional terminals simultaneously, each terminal presenting curriculum materials continuously adjusted to the learning rate and capability of the individual student working at it. System response time at each terminal, all terminals operating simultaneously, is approximately half a second. Curriculum materials for use with the system are offered directly to system users by leading textbook publishers. Subject matter available includes elementary arithmetic, elementary language arts, and elementary science.

Simplicity is the keynote in operation; the System is designed to be used by professional educators, not computer specialists. Records are kept of each student's progress and reports are provided for the convenience of the teacher.

In an experiment at the BOCES[19] Demonstration Center in Westchester County, a New York project directed by Walter Goodman, efforts were made to try a computer system through the use of simulated techniques. The three economics games which were used in this project represent one kind of tactic in the broad strategy of simulation. Simulation, or the "simulated environment mode," is a methodological technique designed to provide individual students with substitutions for the significant features of a natural or conventional learning situation realized by the delivery of a teacher-made instructional program through the resources of a computer system.

This type of computer use has great potentials for ghetto youth, too. They could have invented simulation. They know all about it. They use it daily to survive. The computer has so much potential that the limit of its use is equaled only by the stretch of the imagination.

Instructional Resources Centers

Regional and district instructional resources centers may prove to be the most efficient hub around which the logistics of this paper could function. Educational programs utilized in the fullest potentials of educational technology must engage a partnership never before known involving teachers, supervisors, school boards, administrators, trainers of teachers, researchers, and the resources of the community, backed up by well-organized, well-staffed and well-equipped regional and district instructional materials centers. For too long, teachers and administrators have brought with them the unimaginative influences of the nation's teachers colleges where books and printed materials and the obsession with reading have been followed out of proportion as a need in ghetto schools. Some youngsters learn fast those essentials necessary for survival. It is a wonder they ever learn to read, considering the fares that are dished up to learn on. The regional IRC backing up every ghetto school will be far-reaching, for single schools will perhaps never afford the vast materials and equipment necessary. Such centers will include transparencies and masters, 16mm instructional films, 8mm films for independent study, audio tapes, video tapes, and kinescopes, production facilities with staff well qualified in producing local materials, flat pictures and filmstrips and color slides on meaningful subjects and minority identities. A functional distribution system will give each school what it needs.

Such a plan would be even more economical and operational in the Educational Park concept now being employed or planned for several urban areas. The Educational Park which is not entirely new in concept, collects enough students at one point to make better quality education economically possible. The more concentrated are the youth to be served and the more central are the physical facilities the greater the chances for really effective use of educational technology. Most of the proposals for the Educational Park are unique within themselves, but there are common elements which are critical because they stem from the same purposes. One is large size, with several thousand youth centered on one campus. A second and related aspect is location to serve its purpose. The Educational Park must be located so that it can draw from a variety of neighborhoods. And a third element is the effort toward excellence and variety in programming, instruction and facilities. It is within this third factor that a systems approach to instruction with educational media can make its greatest contribution. It is here that the instructional materials center comes into its fullest effectiveness, serving perhaps through underground cable or television requirements for the campus and through distribution by dial access means and other means fulfilling the requirements of systems tailor-made to the various aspects of the Park.

Research and Educational Technology

One might ask, what does research say about technology and learning? There are sufficient research results substantiating the need for the serious incorporation of technology into the teaching-learning process. Several publications are worthy of note here as listed by John Moldstad. Indiana University:

1.   Allen, William H., "Audiovisual Communications," *Encyclopedia of Educational Research,* pp. 115-137, edited by Chester W. Harris, The Macmillan Co., New York, 1960.

Reviews the research in audiovisual communication during the last decade under five major headings: (a) effectiveness of audiovisual materials, (b) audience-learner characteristics, (c) characteristics of the learning environment, (d) use of audiovisual materials, and (e) administration of audiovisual programs. Includes a 320 item bibliography of research studies.

2.   Chu, Godwin C. and Schramm, Wilbur, *Learning From Television: What the Research Says,* (U.S. Office of Education, Contract 2 EFC 70894), Institute for Communication Research, Stanford University, 1967.

Restricted to review of instructional television and includes the following six areas concerning the conditions of effective learning from television: (a) how much pupils learn from instructional television, (b) efficient use of the medium in a school system, (c) treatment, situation, and pupil variables, (d) attidues toward instructional television, (e) television in developing regions, and (f) learning from television compared with learning from other media.

3.   Finn, James D., and Allen, William H., Co-Chairmen, "Instructional Materials: Educational Media and Technology," *Review of Educational Research* 32: 115-221, April, 1962. (American Educational Research Association, 1201 Sixteenth Street, N.W. Washington, D.C.)

Reviews the research literature from 1956 to 1962 under the following headings: (a) theoretical formulations in audiovisual communications, (b) textbooks and other printed materials, (c) audiovisual materials, (d) learning from instructional television, (e) language laboratories, (f) self-teaching devices and programmed materials, and (g) administration of instructional materials.

4.   Godfrey, Eleanor P., *The State of Audiovisual Technology: 1961-1966* Monograph #3, Department of Audiovisual Instruction of the National Education Association, Washington, D.C., 1967, 217 pp.

Examines three surveys of national scope in audiovisual technology conducted during a six-year period from 1961-1966. Identifies the audiovisual resources available in the individual schools, describes the extent to which these resources are used by teachers in different grade levels and subject specialists, and considers factors that encourage or inhibit use.

5.   Kumata, Hideya, *An Inventory of Instructional Television Research,* Educational Television and Radio Center, Michigan State University of Ann Arbor, 1956, 115 pp.

Restricted to studies of the teaching of formal courses by television and includes (a) a review of research findings and (b) a collection of abstracts of pertinent articles. Intended as a guide to those interested in further study of the use of television in formal instruction situations.

6.   Lumsdaine, Arthur A., "Instruments and Media in Instruction," Handbook of Research on Teaching, American Educational Research Association, Rand McNally and Company, Chicago, 1963, pp. 583-682.

Part 1: Theoretical Orientations also include valuable background for the researcher.

1. Historic Exemplars of Teaching Method

2. Logic and Scientific Method in Research on Teaching

3. Paradigms for Research on Teaching

7. Reid, J. Christopher, and MacLennan, Donald W., *Research in Instructional Television and Film,* U.S. Department of Health, Education, and Welfare, Washington, D.C., 1967, 216 pp. (Superintendent of Documents, U.S. Government Printing Office Washington, D.C. 20402)

Presents a summarization of 333 research studies concerned with instructional films and instructional television in the period 1950 to 1964. The introductory review points out the direction in which the research has been going, the present status of the research, and some possible future directions.

8. Wendt, Paul R., *Audiovisual Instruction,* Department of Classroom Teachers of the National Education Association and the American Educational Research Association, Washington, D.C., 1964, 32 pp.

Discusses the nature of communication and the role of audiovisual materials in classroom instruction. Presents research material on audiovisual instruction which promises to be of most help to classroom teachers, identifies factors affecting the value of audiovisual instruction, and considers what audiovisual materials can and cannot do.

Summaries of the research papers presented at the annual Department of Audiovisual Instruction's national convention have been included in the following issues of *AV Instruction:*

Moldstad, John, "Summary of A-V Research, *AV Instruction,* September, 1964, pp. 492-497.

"Highlights of 1965 Research Reports," *AV Instruction,* June-July, 1965, pp. 528-531.

"1966 Research Reports Feature the Controlled Experiment," *AV Instruction,* June-July, 1966.

"1967 Research Studies Stress Stimulus Variables and Technology," *AV Instruction,* June-July, 1967, pp. 638-642.

Godwin C. Chu and Wilbur Schramm point up several encouraging and exciting research findings on the use of media, several of which are listed below. Each of these headings constitute an umbrella for a number of successful studies on the respective subjects. They are:

1. Given favorable conditions, pupils can learn from any instructional media that are now available.

2. Television and radio have certain advantages over films in flexibility and deliverability.

3. More complete control of film by the classroom teacher gives it a potential advantage over television.

4. There is some evidence to suggest that moving visual images will improve learning if the continuity of action is an essential part of the learning task.

5. Student response is effectively controlled by programmed methods, regardless of the instructional medium.[20]

Training Teachers for Imaginative Uses of Multi-Media

There is no longer any real doubt that children learn a great deal from technology, whether educational or not, so long as the experience seems relevant to them. It is the major task now of educators to provide the favorable conditions under which technology may be used.

The emotional content of meaning, such an essential ingredient in motivating our actions, is particularly difficult to get through to slum children through verbalizing and reading. The kind of training teachers colleges have afforded teachers is partly responsible for ignorance of these facts.

The training of teachers to work with slum children must get out of the doldrums of the conservative content of liberal arts courses and the abstract binds of professional education courses and into involvement with people.

Failure of teacher preparation to use the fast-growing resources of educational technology is reflected in a report on the results of a teacher-opinion poll published in the December 1963 issue of the *NEA Journal*. The NEA Research Division asked "a scientifically selected cross-section of the nation's one and a half million public school teachers" how their college preparation had fitted them for teaching. Every teacher education faculty concerned with change should have the results of that survey: over 60 percent of the teachers reported too little preparation in the use of audiovisual equipment and techniques; over 40 percent, too little teaching methods; and only 27 percent, too little in subject knowledge.

A well-designed teacher education curriculum will provide teachers with pre-service and in-service experience in many new techniques, whether in audiovisual courses or portions of methods courses is not important as long as it is related to the development of theory and practice.

A retraining of teachers in the imaginative uses of multi-media and the newer techniques is a prerequisite to understanding and solving the learning problems of children of the poor. But most important is attitude change. Old stereotypes and prejudices picked up from middle class American standards must be re-examined. Teachers must learn that, although poverty and racial discrimination may force many people to live in the slums, there can yet be found among them higher standards of conduct and family life, better manners, and higher life goals than are to be found in many middle class suburban families. This fact again points to the great diversity among ghetto youth and the need for individualized learning. Trainers of teachers must train them to develop the skills necessary for finding solutions to the many-faceted problems of the poor.

During the period of reflecting and researching for this paper, the writer went into several schools to observe and talk with teachers, children and administrators. Perhaps it is safe to generalize that many ghetto teachers are working against surprising odds. Class sizes from 38 to 40 and often 45 children seem the rule rather than exception. Outmoded architectural arrangements pour as many as fifteen hundred humans in one or two small corridors at once. There was evidence of little organization and administration of non-print materials, making mediated instruction almost impossible. The absence of a media specialist seems to be one of the most obvious personnel weaknesses in each school. Over-crowdedness in general is one of the most serious problems. Classes meet in cafeterias each hour of the day excluding the three shift services. The lack of opportunity for some privacy, small group instruction, individual study, team teaching facilities, instructional materials—all defy innovation.

On the other hand, to see three teachers, with a huge overhead screen and a public address system, working with over a hundred and fifty children in a cafeteria was wonderful. A typing teacher moving among her charges as the typing to music disc sent out a rhythmic beat and loud and clear instruction was great. A language laboratory or rather an electronic classroom built to the specifications and needs of the school, created by the industrial teacher, is a sight worthy to be seen. These and other efforts were bright spots in an otherwise intolerable climate.

In his article "Education: The Racial Gap," Christopher Jencks in reviewing the Coleman Report states:

> . . . pouring more money into Negro schools will probably accomplish little or nothing. While the Report does not prove that as yet untried improvements in school facilities and programs (e.g., computers) would have no significant effect on learning, it does provide a good deal of indirect evidence that this kind of innovation has made very little difference in the past.[21]

To accept any kind of research of this type without searching out every facet of the research is like using a slum child's I.Q. as the only instrument by which to judge his native ability and ultimate potential. Mr. Jencks writes about the Coleman Report as some Kentucky mountain folk talk about the Bible. What Mr. Jencks fails to apprehend and the Coleman Report misses completely is the likelihood of a combination of factors greatly increasing achievement in slum schools. These combinations would include newer building designs based on educational programs, smaller classes, more learner control of the learning environment, availability and utilization of a variety of educational technology coupled with innovations built into a systems approach to instruction.

The Coleman Report and Mr. Jencks review of it make a point of the lower test scores of teacher of Negro on verbal ability as well as the low verbal ability of Negro children. These unhappy facts are all the more reason to search for changes in the ghetto curriculum. Independent learning environment, variety of media and innovation will remove the teacher as the only presenter of information thus opening the learner's door to an increased verbal capacity.

Often, in our zeal and enthusiasm to encourage innovation and educational technology in ghetto schools, we risk misinterpretation of the increasing importance of the teacher. We pause here to stress the point that the classroom teacher is the essential factor in guiding instruction, in setting up objectives, managing the learning environment and assessing outcomes. The teacher needs all the help she can get, for nothing suggested in this paper has possibility for success without an effective teacher. It is therefore an urgent need to develop programs for retraining teachers and provide adequate funds for many new in-service experiences for these teachers. This means also an entirely new attitude by some administrators as to the importance of in-service training. These newly trained teachers might easily become the catalyst for change.

The promises of educational technology in ghetto schools are indeed limitless, with new programs recognizing the proper place of technology. Wherein psychology is providing us with much better understanding of the learning process, technology can begin to furnish the instructional tools that will enable educators to capitalize on these findings. The only successful use of technology demands a cooperative approach to curriculum development, a retraining of school personnel, and a plan of action whereby each teacher and learner knows the instructional objectives, the process of reaching them, and recognizes the need for constant evaluation. What this writer is talking about in this paper includes millions and millions of dollars from taxpayers. The Congress that appropriated less than two billion dollars for our poverty program but did not hesitate to vote twenty-seven billion dollars for the war in Vietnam, whose population, ironically, is about that of the American poor, must come to grips with the serious crisis in American education. The American people must understand that the urgency in America equals that of Vietnam and the appropriations necessary to save our cities, our poor, and even our civilization, is a small price to pay.

REFERENCES

1. Coleman, James S., and others. *Equality of Educational Opportunity.* Office of Education, U.S. Dept. of Health, Education, and Welfare, Washington, D.C., 1966.

2. Levin, Henry M. "What Difference Do Schools Make?" *Saturday Review,* January 20, 1968, p. 27.

3. Coleman. *Op. cit.*

4. Levin. *Op cit.*

5. *Ibid.*

6. *Ibid.*

7. *Ibid.*

8. Morris, Barry, Ed. "The Function of Media in the Public Schools." Prepared by a DAVI Task Force in 1962 as a position paper. *Audiovisual Instruction,* Vol. 8, No. 1, January 1963.

9. Ely, Donald P., Ed. (Prepared by the Commission) "Alphabetical Listing of Terminology." *Audiovisual Communication Review,* Vol. 11, No. 1, Supp. 6, January 1963.

10. Mager, Robert F. *Preparing Instructional Objectives.* Fearon Publishers, Inc., California, 1962, p. 3.

11. Clark, Kenneth B. "Unstructuring Education." *New Relationships in ITV.* Educational Media Council, Inc., Washington, D.C., 1967.

12. *Ibid.*

13. *Ibid.*

14. Riessman, Frank, "The Strategy of Style." *Education of the Disadvantaged,* ed. by A. Harry Passow, et.al. Holt, Rinehart and Winston, New York, 1967, p. 327.

15. Coleman. *Op. cit.*

16. *Ibid.*

17. *Ibid.*

18. Lalime, Arthur, W. "Tape Teaching." A report prepared for the Norwalk Board of Education, February 1967.

19. Wing, Richard L. "The Relation of Computer-Based Instruction and Other Media to Individualized Education." DAVI Conference, Atlantic City, N.J., April 4, 1967.

20. Chu, Godwin G., and Wilbur Schramm. *Learning from Television: What the Research Says.* National Association of Educational Broadcasters, Washington, D.C., 1967, pp. 84-95.

21. Jencks, Christopher. "Education: The Racial Gap." *The New Republic.* October 1, 1966.

77.

Educational Technology
And the Education
Of American Indian
Children

by *VINCENT KELLY**
Professor
District of Columbia
Teacher's College

Status of the Indian People

More than 600,000 persons belonging to over 300 different tribes in the United States are Indians.

For legislative purposes the term "Indian" also is applied to Eskimos and Aleuts; and any child who is at least one-quarter Indian and is living on or near a reservation is eligible to attend a federal school operated for Indian youth.

Most Indians live in rural areas; and the majority of these live in chronic poverty on fifty million acres of reservations, i.e., lands held in trust for the Indians by the Federal Government. Since these lands are generally not very fertile, many Indians—like the 115,000 Navajos on their thirteen million acre reservation live in relative isolation in order to seek out a feeble existence by farming the unyielding soil or by grazing sheep upon it.

The conditions under which the Indian people live are severe. As a result the death rate among infants is 50 percent higher than the national average and the Indian adult has six years less life to look forward to than his white fellow citizens. He is generally less prepared for life, having about two thirds the education of the average white American. Even today only 53 percent of Indians and Eskimos graduate from high school. As a result 50 percent of Indian people live on an annual income of less than $1500; 75 percent live on incomes under $3000.

The Bureau of Indian Affairs School System

About 151,000 Indian youth are of school age. Thirty-seven percent of these are served by the 244 schools which the Bureau of Indian Affairs (BIA) operates in seventeen states. These federal schools range from the one-teacher school that handles 12 students in an isolated Eskimo fishing village of less than 100, to the large boarding school at Brigham City, Utah, which has a student population of over 2200 students.

Obviously the educational levels among the 10 jurisdictional areas served by the Bureau of Indian Affairs are uneven. The geographic, economic, and socio-cultural needs and problems of each area vary greatly: in remote areas of Arizona and Alaska the native population

At the time his paper was submitted to the Commission (April 1969) he was Teacher Training Officer in the Division of Instructional Services, Bureau of Indian Affairs, Washington, D.C.

is almost totally dissociated from the mainstream of American culture and English is not spoken in the home. Ninety-five percent of the Navajo children who come to a BIA school at age six speak no English at all. Some do not even begin their education till much later.

In areas such as Oklahoma, most Indian parents have already adopted new cultural patterns, have "higher" ambitions for their children, and teach their children to speak English at home. Here the problems encountered in BIA schools appear similar to those of most schools dealing with the children of low-income families. However, many of the Indian children assigned to a BIA off-reservation boarding school have been assigned there because there were special problems in the home, because the child was unable to adjust in a public or private school, or because the child was a "social problem" in his home community.

Problems of Indians and Indian Education.

The purpose of Indian education, as of all education, is to improve the quality of life of the children and of their society. The needs and problems in the education of Indian youth are particularly challenging, if not, hopefully, insurmountable.

1. Poverty, ignorance, and isolation are the child's home environment.

2. The lack of adequate all-weather roads, rugged terrain, and severe weather conditions make travel over relatively short distances difficult and hazardous. Thus Indian children often must live away from home nine months each year to comply with the laws of compulsory education.

3. Whether due to feelings of inferiority, lack of management experience, or sheer indifference, Indian people have little control over the goals, the policies, or the practices of the schools attended by their children. Compared to 90 percent of the schools for the rest of the American population which are governed by a lay board of education, only 1 percent of the schools for Indian youth are directly influenced by local community leadership.

4. a. About two-thirds of the children entering first grade come from homes in which English is not spoken. The children must then enter the foreign environment of a kindergarten or first grade in which the teacher cannot speak their language. The child must learn to either "sink or swim" in the English language without much direct language instruction.

b. The interests, values, customs, and behavioral patterns of the children are quite "normal" for them, but they may appear "foreign" or "sub-standard" to the white, middle-class teacher who has little or no understanding of the child's home or community life. The curriculum, the methods, and the tests utilized in the classroom may not be appropriate to Indian children. The children, in turn, may not be motivated to achieve either in the direction or in the manner demanded by the teacher, the school, or by the system.

5. Many Indian children come from broken or disorganized homes. The father, mother, or both may have abandoned the child. Drunkenness may be a problem. Children from such homes frequently develop severe emotional or personality problems. An inadequate diet and lack of care may cause lifelong physical or mental damage. Furthermore, the child's experiences at home may have alienated him from the purposes and the activities of the school. Poor attendance accentuates learning problems among day-school children, and by the time they reach ninth grade many have already permanently dropped out of school.

6. The traditional culture of many Indian tribes is in a state of disorganization and

deterioration. Years of injustice, deprivation, and liquor have taken a heavy toll. Many of the important values and skills of Indian peoples in the past are no longer passed on to their children; hence, the children may have chaotic, inconsistent, and contradictory views of their cultural heritage.

The buffalo are long gone. The knowledge and skills of the hunter are no longer sufficient to provide for an Indian's needs or those of his family; since the weaponry of war has been improved by modern technology, the bravery and strength of the warrior find little outlet on the quiet reservation. Many Indians are trapped between two cultures: born too late to enjoy the power of a culture fully relevant to earlier history; too far away in terms of geographic and social distance to share the advantages of a modern technological civilization.

7. The medicine-man, the shaman, or the witch-doctor is still revered by many superstitious Indian people. At times, Indian children with serious injuries or illnesses are prevented from obtaining help from a medical doctor. The democratic right of freedom of religion makes the problem of eradicating superstitious practices extremely complicated.

8. Thus the Indian child desperately needs to form a self-image that will give him pride and self-assurance, both as a unique individual and as a member of the Indian race and culture. The high rate of suicide among Indian adolescents may well be due to a lack of self-esteem and a lack of hope for improvement in the future.

9. The dearth of industry or agriculture on the reservation makes it difficult to provide suitable educational experiences. What kind of vocational or commercial training will be of use to the child if he stays at home? Of what economic value is a high school or even a college education to the Eskimo who chooses to return to his frozen homeland? Certainly the fact that a returning high school graduate has to be closely watched so that he will not freeze to death while gathering firewood can only reinforce the conviction of many older Eskimos that formal education is a useless luxury.

Educational Technology and the Problems of Indian Education

The severe problems of Indian education will not lend themselves to easy solution by traditional methods. Certainly the amount of money needed in both federally operated and state supported schools is more than that required under normal conditions, yet historically the *per capita* expenditures for Indian education have been far below the national average.

Money is a necessary means, but it is not the whole solution. New, better methods, and techniques, media and materials have to be found and employed, and they must be used in a suitable organizational setting by dedicated human beings who are masters of their subjects and of the tools of their trade, and who understand the unique needs and problems of the youngsters in their care, of the society from which they come and of the society in which they will live in the future.

Technology refers to scientifically derived means of achieving a practical purpose. Educational technology refers to the sum total of means that are derived from scientifically established facts, laws, and principles, which are used to accomplish the needs and purposes of education. The physical "means" include media and materials; but ideas, methods, and techniques which guide human practice are also part of educational technology. Educators of Indian children should possess both technological knowledge and artistic skill in the exercise of their profession.

Let us see how technological means can serve to overcome the severe problems of Indian education enumerated above.

1. Various means of overcoming rural poverty and the effects of isolation have existed for some time. Since the middle 1950s technological developments have produced a veritable awakening for 115,000 Navajos on the reservation which spread through part of Arizona, New Mexico and Utah. All-weather roads have been and are being constructed; improved roads have aided the development of industry on the reservation. The improved possibilities for employment among Navajo adults have accordingly increased the demand for more and better education for Navajo youth. Furthermore, telephones, a radio station which broadcasts in the Navajo language, and television have vastly improved communication and increased awareness among the people.

2. Even more and better all-weather roads are needed not only as a prerequisite to further economic growth but also to provide educational opportunities within easy access of the home. Then, motorcycles, automobiles, trucks and buses are needed so that men and women can travel to work and children can travel to school each day.

Over the vast expanses of Alaskan wilderness "bushpilots" and commercial planes *airlift* over 2100 Eskimo children to and from boarding schools twice each year, enabling them to get the education that only a few years ago was unavailable to them. Similarly, it is now technologically feasible to utilize helicopters or other small aircraft in the vast expanses of the desert or in hazardous mountainous terrain. Thus the present practice of separating the child from his home and community by placing him in a boarding school for nine months each year could be eliminated or greatly decreased. When the war in Vietnam is finally concluded, surplus helicopters may become available, thus making such an innovative project financially as well as technologically possible.

3. Indian parents and community leaders must be actively encouraged to take part in school affairs. Adult education in methods of community development—such as those provided by Vista volunteers and the OEO Community Action Project have helped. The Bureau of Indian Affairs in its "Project Tribe" are developing the attitudes, knowledge and skills needed by Indian leaders so that they can participate in and eventually take over the direction of their schools. New methods of training such as sensitivity training, communication skills development, problem solving approaches and simulation techniques are being utilized.

4a. To reduce the problem of young children being thrust into a foreign environment with a "strange" teacher who does not know their language, the technique of utilizing a native teacher aide has been adopted in kindergarten and early elementary grades. Linguists and psycholinguists have shown that the child's native language can be utilized as a means of gradually introducing him to a second set of language habits. As yet no widespread attempt has been made, however, to teach Indian children to read and write in their native language before teaching these skills in English.

Nevertheless, a current project funded by BIA is Northern Arizona University's project to produce bilingual cultural readers in several Indian languages. Further contributions to the teaching of English-as-a-Second-Language have been made by Dr. Robert Wilson, who has demonstrated his linquistically based methods and materials to BIA teachers for the past several years in summer workshops. One of the Bureau's own English teachers, Mr. Vince D'Annunzio, has developed a three-volume set of English language materials based on a contrastive analysis of the English and Navajo languages.

b. An Indian teacher or teacher's aide can also serve as cultural mediator between the ways of the home-community environment and the ways of the school. Psychologists inform us that the child's personality develops through a succession of interrelated experiences. Sudden transitions may be traumatic and harmful to the child's mental and emotional growth. The sociological concepts of "life space," "social distance" and "anomie" lend further support to the wisdom of utilizing Teacher Aides. The Indian adult who has, at least partially, bridged the two cultures in his own life can serve as a temporary model for the child to do so. To further reduce the culture gap, Professor Roy Condy of the University of New Mexico has developed a social studies program specially adapted to the cultural background of Navajo children.

5. There is no technological substitute for human affection. Every child needs to be able to identify with and imitate adult models whom he can love and respect. Particularly Indian children in boarding schools or in border-town dormitories need to be in frequent, informal contact with both white and Indian adults. Pupil personnel workers, such as counselors, dormitory supervisors, social workers, and school nurses provide valuable professional services, but *somewhere* the ingredients of love, sympathy and warm human understanding must be added to their technological know-how.

Viable solutions to the problem of school drop-outs have been brought to light through recent research by social scientists. Charles Ray's *Alaskan Native Secondary School Dropouts,* published by the University of Alaska in 1962, contributed much needed information on the factors contributing to low educational attainment among Alaskan youth. A recent study by the University of Oregon presented data about American Indian students in 6 western states, which may soon lead to the solution of the high dropout problem in that area.

6. The sympathetic native teacher, teacher aide, dormitory supervisor, or dormitory aide can also help the child fuse together the conflicting, paradoxical elements of the dual society in which he finds himself. The child must be helped to form a unique, integrated personality and character from the diverse elements of his dual heritage. Unless the child can develop a healthy self-image he will be neither emotionally healthy nor socially effective.

The non-Indian teacher who has been taught some basic principles of sociology and cultural anthropology will also be better able to help the Indian child. Certainly an understanding of Indian history and of contemporary Indian culture can help the teacher overcome some basic prejudices and stereotypes that he might bring with him into his "foreign" school situation. As psychologists learn more about varying styles of learning and thinking, teachers might acquire greater patience and respect for students whom they had once deemed lazy, stupid or disinterested.

A special methodology for teaching Indian children has been elaborated by Dr. Henry Burger, of the Southwestern Cooperative Educational Laboratory. Entitled "Ethno-pedagogy," his manual on cultural sensitivity presents helpful techniques, derived from anthropological data and principles, for teaching across cultures by fitting together those ethnic patterns which are most compatible.

7. Principles of logical thinking and of science need to be taught effectively to children so that they can be freed from the intellectual and moral bonds of superstition. Good health practices and training in the disciplines of science and social science can be useful. It is most important that children learn to apply principles of good planning and problem solving to their personal lives. Students need to be involved in the process of scientific or logical thinking through new approaches such as "inquiry" and "role-playing." An artificial curriculum which presents "phoney" contrived problems for the child to solve by applying pat formulae or which presents an abstract, static model of government to be assimilated rather than participated in will be rejected, rightfully, by the child as irrelevant and meaningless.

The teacher who is aware of certain cultural barriers that might hinder the child's learning can help him overcome these obstacles. Some anthropologists assert that Eskimos tend to have great difficulty in dealing with abstractions, such as in mathematics. The stages of learning mathematics must be broken into smaller manageable steps for the child, who should also be given concrete experience in working with problems involving numbers and fractions.

8. It is certain that the study of Indian art, music, dancing, and history can have a beneficial effect in giving the Indian child pride in his native or traditional culture, and this, in turn, can help produce a better "self-image." Unfortunately, few non-Indian teachers know enough about the child's historical and cultural traditions to teach him anything positive about them.

There is much in the Indian culture that is beautiful, useful and worthy of being preserved in the lives of young American Indians.

At the same time all American youth, regardless of racial or ethnic background, require basic knowledge and skills of communication. They also need specialized knowledge and skills to be able to earn their livelihood in a sophisticated, technological economy, and broader cultural knowledge to be effective as citizens and as family members.

9. The question of *how* to teach an Indian child is not as imperative as *what* to teach him. The standardized curriculum may not be at all relevant to his needs or interests or to the desires of his parents. In a democratic society the question of goals and objectives of education must ultimately rest with the values and preferences of the community itself. Unfortunately, well-meaning, sophisticated non-Indian teachers and administrators frequently make these important value judgments *for* the Indian rather than *with* him.

There is great need for tests of achievement, talent and intelligence which are suited to Indian children. Levels of expectation for academic achievement based on national norms, which in turn are based on a standard curriculum are of doubtful validity and reliability in the case of the rural Indian child.

While the school staff has responsibility for educating the child, it is not the school's function to place a wedge between the child and his home or community in order to pry him loose from their influence. Is "upward mobility" synonymous with "whiteward mobility?" Non-Indian teachers and non-Indian administrators must avoid the error of giving the rural Indian child a second-rate replica of the education of the middle-class, white child of the big city. The psychology of individual differences demands, rather, that the school respond to the needs of *this* child by giving him the kinds of knowledge, skill, and experiences in the manner and at a rate at which the child can successfully assimilate them.

When lessons are adapted to the child's needs, they will be rewarding to him. When what the child learns in class is applicable at home and in the community, the parents will also reward and encourage his learning.

A coherent, continuous program of courses and experiences should be instituted by the school and the teacher which will gradually lead the child from his present level of interest and ability to new interests and new skills. No Indian child should have to leave school without an adequate preparation for a useful, profitable career. For a future in modern society, many more Indian boys and girls should be prepared and able to go to college and to graduate school. Educational technology can help to achieve this goal by providing greater opportunity for individualizing the curriculum.

Current Uses of Educational Technology in Indian Education

As was true in most rural schools throughout the United States, technological "hardware" was not used extensively before the late 1950s. Common media tools, such as motion pictures, slide projectors, overhead projectors and tape recorders were known and used on occasion, of course, but there was no concerted attempt to incorporate these devices into every classroom nor to train teachers to use them effectively.

One of the first coordinated attempts to utilize modern technological devices in Indian education was in the early 1950s. Young Navajos with little or no schooling were enrolled in a crash program designed to give them sufficient fluency in English and the manual skills to obtain employment. With language materials prepared by linguists, with the aid of such educational tools as tape-recorders, sound-scribers, and motion pictures, and in a well planned step-by-step teaching program, thousands of young Navajo adults became self-supporting, productive members of society.

Federal laws such as the National Defense Education Act, the Vocational Education Act, and the Elementary and Secondary Education Act have made funds available to the schools for the acquisition of specialized equipment. Tape recorders, soundscribers, and even language laboratories came into wide use in the teaching of English-as-a-second-language. Teaching machines and programmed instructional texts were provided to individualize instruction and to assist the slow learner. For teaching remedial and developmental reading, special devices such as tachistoscopes, shadow readers, and other timed reading machines were obtained in most larger schools, and virtually every classroom teacher had ready access to motion picture projectors, slide or filmstrip projectors, and overhead and opaque projectors.

The Bureau of Indian Affairs began including instructional materials centers in their new schools in the late 1950s. Standards for such "IMC's" were developed in the early 1960s and all new schools built by the Bureau have included a materials center, which distributes printed and non-printed materials to be used with a variety of instructional media.

The problems of teaching have not been completely solved by the new technology. In fact, the proper utilization of the learning centers and their equipment is a pressing need. One survey indicated that only about one out of every five IMC's is well utilized by the staff and the students. The major causes of this unsatisfactory situation are the following:

(1) the lack of professional preparation of the IMC director; (2) the lack of in-service training in the use of media and materials; (3) lack of procedures for evaluation; (4) poor production practices; and (5) inefficient scheduling.

In additon, two other factors interfere with the complete utilization of existing instructional materials centers: (1) lack of funds for adequately equipping the IMC and (2) a lack of orientation and training on the part of administrators in the new technology.

The "software" aspect of educational technology is still inadequate in quantity and in quality. A teaching machine without the programmed instructional materials for it is only an empty plastic box. Yet these materials are expensive. Traditionally trained librarians in charge of an Instructional Materials Center will seldom give priority on hard-to-come-by funds to such items. Even so, much of the commercially available material is merely a re-working of the old textbook. Programs based upon an extensive analysis of the subject matter and based upon valid psychological principles are needed. Unfortunately, discoveries such as those made by linquists and psychologists of learning have as yet made little impact on the textbooks, teaching materials or even on the teaching methods used in our schools.

In 1968 the BIA established an Instructional Service Center at Brigham City, Utah. One of its functions is to coordinate the purchase, distribution, and, when necessary, the maintenance of teaching media and materials. The ISC will help supply the needs of the schools' many Instruction Materials Centers across the country. When necessary, special materials, such as Super 8mm single-concept films and regular length 16mm color-sound films, are produced by the ISC's technicians and education specialists. The Center also sends out teams in mobile units to give on-site demonstrations or short-term workshops in the use of media and the preparation of materials.

One of the major functions of the Center is to implement training programs in Indian education. The Center has modern multi-media electronic classrooms for this purpose and can handle up to 500 students in a single summer workshop. Teaching materials can be programmed for sequential or simultaneous presentation and can be automatically operated by remote control. Training rooms also contain electronic devices for obtaining immediate feedback on students' understanding of the material presented, and for instantly evaluating responses and recording scores.

Among the most valuable contributions of technology to education is in the area of providing scientifically derived and tested methods for training human beings. While here certainly is much "art" in this complicated process, in recent years new concepts derived from the behavioral sciences have made great contributions. The "Systems Approach," "Behavioral Objectives," "Techniques of Objective Observation and Evaluation," such as the Flander's technique, "Micro-teaching," "Behavioral Management Techniques," "Communication Skills" and "Sensitivity Training" have all proven valuable to teachers, administrators, pupil personnel workers and Indian leaders concerned with the process of education. These new techniques are now being utilized in BIA's training programs for teachers, administrators, pupil personnel workers, auxiliary personnel or "aides," and for Indian leaders both at the Center and in workshops conducted for the Bureau of universities or private educational consultants.

Experimental Uses of Technology in BIA Schools

A few special uses of technology in Indian schools are "far ahead of the times." At Intermountain School in Brigham City, Utah, students are taught to play the piano electronically. Each student plays "silently" at his own electronic keyboard but can hear himself on a set of earphones. Meanwhile, the teacher can check each pianist's performance individually from a master control-panel.

At Chemawa Indian School in Oregon, ninth grade Indian students are using the modern math course developed by Professor Max Beberman at the University of Illinois. After being specially trained in a National Science Foundation summer institute in mathematics, the teacher now teaches congruence geometry and a function approach to fractions with a "stretching and shrinking machines." In this case, prior training enabled the teacher to master the new methods and devices provided by educational technology.

At Chemawa Indian School in Oregon lesson and classroom scheduling are planned with the use of a computer.

At Phoenix Indian School in Arizona, students with reading problems are being instructed with the latest materials devices: tachistoscopes, shadow readers, other types of timed reading devices, the SRA graded reading series, and other linguistically based materials.

The Phoenix school also uses dictaphones to teach writing. Students are encouraged to compose orally and then to transcribe what they have said on to paper. They also use these machines to listen to model compositions, and for playing back parts of the speech for further analysis.

While educational technology has made some definite advances in Indian education, there remain many more ordinary aspects of the child's educational environment that need improvement. For example, at one boarding school for Indian students thirty students were rejected from a driver training course because they did not have eyeglasses to correct their defective vision; at a vocational institute, students doing welding were not provided with safety goggles because they were "not covered in the budget." In some schools students are being trained for modern jobs on out-dated commercial and industrial equipment.

Unfortunately, some experimental programs that were promising at conception proved abortive. At an elementary school for Indian children in Isleta, New Mexico, a highly elaborate teaching system was set up under the direction of the Economic Systems Corporation. Daily tests were administered on the concepts they had been taught in each subject area. Students marked their responses for a multiple-choice test directly on IBM punch cards. The cards were processed by a computer which produced a print-out of the conceptual areas in which each child in the class was deficient and this information was given to each teacher before the beginning of school the next day. At the same time, several hundred preselected films had been catalogued according to the concepts they presented, and the computer searched out the films which corresponded to the areas in which most of the students appeared deficient. Another print-out was produced which showed the concepts contained in the film and indicated the channel and time at which the films could be seen the following day. The relevant films were transmitted by closed circuit TV throughout the school. Teachers could make the choice as to whether they wished their class to view a film, which film, and when. The elaborate program was discontinued the next year much to the relief of students and teachers. The term "concept" had not been properly defined, and many of the films which were shown to teach specific "concepts" actually were irrelevant to the teachers' purposes, or else the film took much too long to achieve what the teacher could do alone in a matter of minutes. Observers reported that toward the end of the school year most teachers left their TV receivers turned off all day long.

Some failures must be expected when innovative approaches are tried. By analyzing the faults and their causes, greater successes will be accomplished in the future. When one is aware of the difficult problems which have beset Indian peoples in the past few centuries, the accomplishments of the Indian people and of Indian education in the past decade or two appear astonishing. Even greater progress will be attained in the future if the American people and the government are willing not only to continue but to increase their support of projects to help improve the physical conditions of life on Indian reservations. Even more essential is the financial and morale support of programs for the development of the Indian's greatest resources—himself and his children—through education.

Although Educational Technology has helped, it can still play a greater role in improving educational opportunities for Indian children. If 50 percent of American high school graduates are considered capable of profiting from more advanced training in colleges, junior colleges, or technical institutes, why shouldn't we have the same goal and expectation for Indian children? And why shouldn't the necessary means to accomplish the goal be provided?

78.

Instructional Technology
For Black Children
In the Big City Ghettos

*by JONATHAN KOZOL**

The Commission has asked "what are the prospects and problems in using instructional technology to meet the needs of Negro children in the big-city ghettos?"

The first problem is posed by the wording of the above question. I think that the enterprise runs a risk of being very deeply compromised, if it is not rendered almost entirely archaic by the next few months of history, unless, before everything else, some thought is given to the assumptions which dictated the wording.

On the most trivial basis, there is the use of the word "Negro." Rhetorical or not, temporary or long-lasting, the will of a revolutionary minority, in my opinion, deserves to be respected. As a beginning, therefore, I think that Black Americans should be allowed their own adjective of self-description.

On a larger basis, it seems that the question assumes something bizarre, special, peculiar, perhaps unruly—certainly different—about "the educational needs of Negro children." This might well be a very useful working-assumption if by this it is meant that new and handsome materials will be available for children accustomed to all that has been old and ugly, technological devices of potential classroom-liberation will be available for children who have been eternally in bondage, and white-made, white-consulted, white-administered and white-profiting technology will be provided for kids whose parents have been almost totally excluded from the lucrative educational industry in which so many white people are involved: available with all the resentments, frenzies, frustrations and automatic areas of distrust and powerlessness which such a situation must entail.

Understood in this sense, the wording may be helpful. But if it means instead that the black inner city child is essentially less disciplined, essentially less curious, essentially less lively, potent, forthright, imaginative or patient in labors, then I think it is in error. I raise this point first because I believe it should be clearly understood that nothing carried out by a predominantly white organization, with ultimate executive authority belonging to white people and with quite enormous financial benefit accruing (even as a long-range consequence) to white-owned industry, is likely to be entirely pure of the racism inherent in our culture and, if we cannot be free of this racism and of all the assumptions it brings along in its train, we should at least clearly recognize its presence and the degree to which it cannot help but undermine the value of our judgments.

Jonathan Kozol is the author of Death at an Early Age.

Next, I would like to raise a question as to the impact of classroom technology upon the teacher's status and position. I think that it might have either very good or very bad results, depending on its nature and intent. There are, as I see it, beyond racism, two serious problems in the present role of the ghetto teacher. Either she is assertive, out-spoken, overbearing in a garrulous, dominating and manipulative manner which thrusts her own special and generally unhealthy values upon a class of children; or else, out of fear, timidity and professional training, she clams up, silences her opinions, lowers her hemline, wipes off her make-up and becomes a moral, social, sexual and emotional neuter. Briefly, there is either (a) too much domineering and manipulative personality or (b) no personality at all.

What is needed is a technology which will encourage the development of another human style within the classroom. A teacher who manipulates ruthlessly is simply given a better tool of mass hypnosis when she is allowed to sit behind an overhead projector. A teacher who has developed that special professional style of soul-less dehydration is simply dehydrated further when reading class is totally given over to a machine and when science and history lessons come from a television network. In other words, the two main dangers that I see are (a) technologies that heighten the manipulative mastery of classroom teachers, (b) technologies that will further thin out the already water-thin texture of many millions of our teachers.

The goals, therefore, should be as follows: technologies that heighten the individual autonomy of every child, technologies that seduce teachers into more open, affectionate and vulnerable postures in the classroom. By this word *(vulnerable)* I am thinking of a teacher who is placed, as the result of technological innovations, in a position of relative equality with the children in her classroom, where she is not permitted to hide behind either manipulative control or a neutral ruler-and-chalkboard personality, but must engage in open, equalized and often extremely painful interaction—ideological or otherwise—with a room of intellectually liberated children. This would require, clearly, a look not only at the nature of the technological changes that are introduced but also at the *content* conveyed by that technology. I will come back to this later. For now, I wanted only to point to the danger that better technologies, more clever ways of operating classrooms, might very well—if not carefully safeguarded—have the immediate result of allowing dull, watery and flavorless teachers to become still less tasty and less human than they are at present, while to the domineering and super-confident, manipulative schoolmarm they may simply provide more perfect and smoothly operating devices by which to increase a black child's assimilation of ignorant and arrogant assumptions.

This leads logically to the next point, which is the *content* question. What intellectual substance, what values and what attitudes are going to be purveyed by the new devices? What kind of school atmosphere are radical architectural innovations and space-changes going to create? What specific data, material and substance will be presented by all these televised, programmed, filmed, boxed, packaged and taped learning-systems which are soon going to be marketed?

It seems to me there is a dangerous assumption in this country that technological re-arrangements carry with them inevitably various forms of philosophical and intellectual maturity. I am afraid that the opposite has more often been the case. Ten years of brilliant and ceaseless scientific labor on the Manhattan Project enabled Americans to become even greater monsters, more morally bankrupt, than we were before. The development of the SRA reading-lab by IBM has enabled teachers to individualize a diet of racism and banality instead of presenting it to the entire class at once, as in the old days. New trickery for teaching children to read *quickly* raises a related problem. An EDL filmstrip method that has seen wide use in Boston recently did, probably, help to speed up reading-rates for children but by a method so wholly mechanical and dehumanized as to totally ignore the real basis for the children's reading difficulties. The real problem is that most books in our classrooms, both racist and otherwise, were not worth reading: they were poor

literature, boring, trivial and stupid. The EDL filmstrip sought to make up for this problem by a gadget which trained a child's eyes to move fast across a printed page. Perhaps
it worked, but it constituted an artificial detour around the actual problem. To my own
thinking, it was much like the hypothetical use of pharmacological means of sedation,
tranquilization and stimulation to guide, control, manipulate and ultimately enslave a
community of rebellious people. Or, for a simpler parallel, it was like a bad physician's
reliance on electroshock or pharmacology in place of genuine psychological processes of
discussion and confrontation. A cheap way out is a way that you generally pay for later on.

In this regard—of the relationship between the innovative technique and the content it
purveys—I am reminded of an additional problem: One of the largest and well-funded
laboratories of educational innovation is E.D.C. (Educational Development Corporation)
of Cambridge. In the course of some very expensive and long-lasting efforts, carried out in
various corners of the world, but almost entirely by white people, an effort was made to
develop a new social studies program—philosophically sophisticated and technologically
hip—which might then be mass-marketed for the entire nation. Working under the ultimate
authority of several well known scholars but, as it seems, with only the most indirect
supervision from them, the E.D.C. Elementary Social Studies team put together a package
entitled "MAN: A COURSE OF STUDY." While making a modest concession to the use
of the written word, the planners of this program sought to work around reading difficulties
as much as possible and did a great deal of work utilizing film and filmstrips, tapes and
tape recorders, as well as some ingenious games. Despite the best efforts of a large number
of intelligent people, employing as advisors and consultants a good many of the best experts in this area, the end-product fails seriously in a number of regards.

First, in seeking to translate modern ideas of anthropology into a subject-matter appropriate for study at the Fifth Grade level, the planners decided to select examples of animal
life and human society which would not be tinged with any kinds of nostalgia, fairy-tale
associations or subjective feelings on the part of children. As a consequence, the animals
chosen for study were the salmon, the herring gull and the baboon, none likely to awaken
very strong feelings of affection on the part of Fifth Grade children, and the human society chosen was the Netsilik Eskimo, an Eskimo group distinguished above all else by
its lack of interesting, affective and emotional qualities but, selected chiefly for its availability as a subject for filmmaking and for its technological ingenuity in dealing with a
difficult environment. E.D.C. has devised some extremely clever materials such as a series
of film-loops on the baboon and the Eskimo to be studied by children, on an individual
basis, with the use of film-loop viewers. Children, in both urban and suburban classrooms,
have been intrigued for a couple of days, usually by the mechanical device (it is, to most
children, as one can imagine, very much like a high-priced toy) but few children of my
acquaintance, white or black, have responded with any deep emotion to the actual material
which was presented on the film-loops. Nor, to be quite honest, to much of the other material prepared for them at so much expense and with the consultation of so many gifted
people. It is easy enough to see why they were not interested. In a year and a season
in which Martin Luther King was murdered, in which riots and riot control and bigotry and
backlash dominated headlines, in which Robert Kennedy was assassinated, Columbia University shaken with revolution and war still raging onward unabated in Vietnam, pupils
who had their eyes and ears open and who had access to their own minds and feelings,
could not take very seriously the problems of chopping a hole in the ice somewhere in
Greenland, or the mating habits of the herring gull and salmon.

All the technological cleverness and academic sophistication, heaped together, cannot
provide an adequate substitute for relevance, intensity and moral and emotional confrontation in the subject-matter. Yet there is grave danger, as the case of E.D.C. shows perfectly,
that an adult fascination with technological gimmickry and hardware, will blind educational
planners to the dehumanization of their subject matter. Children, so far as I can see,
reacted negatively to the material I have described not because it failed to hit head-on at

specific current issues like racism and assassination, but because, on a much broader level, it failed to invite the participation of emotional responses or to invoke ethical and moral judgments. Not Dr. King himself, not Senator Kennedy alone, but the whole territory of feeling and caring and the entire issue of fair-play and justice, weighed heavily on the minds of the children I observed: and it was this which was scrupulously avoided by the E.D.C. materials, no doubt to the enormous gratitude of thousands of teachers who were thereby spared the very painful and difficult task of coming to terms with troublesome matters like ethics and justice in the classroom.

"We are learning to be anthropologists. We are developing observation skills in social studies."

A superb reason: one of the most sophisticated rationalizations ever given to a classroom teacher. Now she does not have to think of herself as copping-out. She is simply behaving like an anthropologist: looking on at animal and human life with scientific restraint and without any unmanageable emotion. Thousands of miles from the schoolhouse, the frozen tundra and the icy salmon stream pass before the children's eyes in brilliant color. Then they turn off the machines, put on their coats and mittens, and—leaving school—they look around them once again at that actual world of guilt and pain in which they live and which their super-new social studies curriculum has so skillfully avoided.

The question arises as to how these mighty new curriculum projects are allowed to develop so fast and to consume so much money before their defects or possible misdirections are examined. I think it has something to do with the immense amount of money and effort which are likely to be put into such projects from their first beginnings. Once that initial investment is completed, those who have participated in the first stage feel compelled to defend and justify their labors. An excavation has been started and, since there is no easy way to fill it in without humiliation, the only solution is to keep right on and dig it deeper. There is also the fact that any program which involves a heavy use of new technology is likely to be highly profitable to a good many people, and it is here that various kinds of subtle propaganda enter the picture. The public relations carried out on behalf of the old history texts and basal readers are mawkish and innocent and childlike compared with the extremely skillful methods of propaganda increasingly available to those who launch the new curricula. The availability of prestige-names, the flattering of the teacher by associating her "in teamwork" with the names of neglected scholars—the "review committee" skillfully picked by a curriculum agency from among those who are already known to be its best admirers (and, occasionally, its consultants), these and similar factors seriously limit the degree to which either self-criticism or close-at-hand outside criticism is likely to be present in the process of developing these materials. The partnership of selected teachers and of academic planners with the manufacturers of educational technology involves both of the former in an elegant and profitable association which it is in the interest of neitner to question or to interrupt. Clearly, for this reason, a new factor of judgment and discernment must enter the picture at a very early stage, and this leads to the next point I would like to make.

The black communities, are, of course, going to have a very high stake in the nature of the new instructional devices and methodologies. All children will be affected to some extent, but those whose survival depends almost exclusively upon the degree of excellence available in a public classroom are obviously affected more than any others. A poor curriculum or a dehumanizing style of technology is going to be unfortunate for all children, but for those who cannot find jobs, buy homes, achieve dignity of even a marginal nature without the special passport handed to them by a high degree of quality in education—for them, such a technological failure will be murderous. In other words, the issues that we are discussing—while significant to all children—are going to be life-and-death issues to black children; and it is for this reason that their parents or representatives ought to be brought into the developmental process at the very earliest stages. Black parent groups, in short—or, for practical reasons, representatives of black parent-interests—should be contacted in the pre-planning period for all such enterprises, above all for those which are being abetted by the use of public funds, and such groups or such representatives should be invited to constitute advisory committees or parent review-boards with significant authority to veto unwanted projects. It is no good to tell a parent-body that options will be offered them later on, once the various curricula and machineries and architectural alternatives have been developed and completed. To offer Harlem or Roxbury the choice between IBM and Xerox is like offering them the choice between two brands of bread they did not bake, or two political candidates neither of which they had a voice in choosing. It is no choice at all. It is, indeed, *worse* than no choice, because it is the pretense of a choice, it is the semblance of respect and concern for a community's attitude when in truth neither respect nor concern are present. All you are doing, in such a case, is to seek the community's ratification of decisions and investments which have already been made and which in fact, by the time you ask for the community's opinion, are irreversible. At this point I have to return to the wording of the original question.

The wording asks about the "educational needs of Negro children in the big-city ghettos." I am going to take this question with as much seriousness as possible now and answer in the following manner: The first, last and most important "educational need of Negro children" is to believe that their own people have had some share in determining the nature of their education. This is a need which goes far beyond the token presence of one black member on a prestige commission, or of one or two or ten or twenty black consultants selected from among those who have already made their peace with white society and found comfortable niche within it. What is needed is the involvement of those people who have seldom, if ever, been consulted up to now because they did not appear to possess the degree of expertise required: when in fact it was they who possessed the only body of *authentic* expertise available anywhere in those areas of relevance and timeliness with which the various educational complexes purport to be concerned. For this reason I would suggest that all groups working in the area of instructional technology, above all when it is work supported by public funds and aimed at the inner city, be required by law or guideline to consult at the earliest stages with groups appointed from, and representative of, the major organized black parent-coalitions in a dozen or more of our largest cities. It would not, as many industrialists and experts frequently insist, be particularly difficult to select or locate such groups and individuals. I would be happy to suggest contacts in certain cities, and am in any case listing, at the end of this paper, the names and addresses of several articulate and sophisticated community leaders of the Boston ghetto to whom you might well turn for consultation.

Another point arises, I think, from the one I have just made. Black parents are not only properly resentful and suspicious of technologies—whether hardware or architecture or programmed teaching-systems—imposed from the outside without their consultations: they also are determined, once such innovations have made their way into the classroom, to be partners in *using* and *applying* them. In other words, community consultation in educational planning is only prefatory to community participation in the ultimate operation of the school. Despite the shrill and uneasy opposition of some of the militant teachers' unions, and despite the assumptions of certain educators that poor people, black or otherwise, have no real role or competence within a public classroom, the signs are up and the indications are quite clear that parent-control and parent-participation are going to be elemental ingredients of public education within the ghetto throughout the next few years. Parent-councils, parent-aids and, ultimately, parent-teachers are all part of the immediate future and ought to be taken into consideration during the earliest stages of planning new materials. Parents will be working beside teachers in the classroom: What kinds of space-arrangements will consequently prove to be most useful? Will it be helpful to have numerous small work-spaces surrounding central classrooms? Will there be electronic materials available requiring a degree of adult direction beyond the scope of very young children? If so, perhaps the operation of such machinery provides an obvious and useful "in" for neighborhood parents. One might, indeed, envision a public classroom in which as many as five or six separate members of a parent-council will work individually, exploiting new materials with children, while the teacher addresses herself to a general and unhurried, and, perhaps, at long last, a comfortable and happy type of classroom-supervision. Possibilities of this sort ought to be considered early in the game, for the nature of technological innovation will inevitably have to be affected by the degree of community-participation, and by the consequent adult-child ratio.

As the outside world is given access to a public classroom, so at the same time that classroom is going to be pushed out more and more into the world around it. The community will come in, and the school will go out. Classes increasingly will involve work and inquiry outside the actual building, and this will be not simply in the token fashion of a once-a-year field-trip to see the city and the Museum of Science, but in a continuing and perseverent effort to make the life of the classroom a viable continuum of the street and the nation and their urgencies. The age of a mortuary like I.S. 201—the aptly designated "windowless school of Harlem"—is clearly over, and the questions now will have to do with the degree to which architecture, technology and curriculum innovation can offer both symbolic encouragement and practical facilitation to the increasing humanization, opening-out and democratization of urban education. School-design and the nature of technology ought not only to provide for the possibility of parent-involvement and community-interaction within the process of the school-day, but they ought to pave the way for such developments by providing physical plants which will help to push a reluctant school administration in the right direction and which will make the participatory demands of community parents mechanically feasible from the viewpoint of the teachers. It is for this added reason, entirely apart from the argument of black self-determination, that parents' representatives ought to be brought into these technological planning projects at the earliest stages.

The early involvement of parent-groups, I suggest, may help to prevent the kind of expensive fiasco I have described above, in which a highly sophisticated, all-white and well-funded team of experts were able to dig themselves into so deep a hole with little or no opportunity for any serious self-criticism. Above all, I think that the participation of black parents will help to avoid that emphasis on "the skills of observation" as opposed to what we might call "the methodologies of change." Most curricula, after all, have for years been going after pretty much the same objectives as the E.D.C. unit I have mentioned, except that generally it was handled in a less subtle and more heavy-handed manner. Ultimately, the general objectives were quite similar: examine the landscape of life and learn to observe it with great accuracy, but do not imagine that there is a chance in the world that you can personally change it. "This is how little children live in China. This is what it is like to be a farmer in Nebraska. Eskimo hunters use these instruments. People in New York City go out for walks along this avenue . . ."

The tone and approach have almost been quite arbitrary, even in those cases where teachers have attempted to prove to themselves and to the class that they were being honest and realistic. "See it like it is and tell it like it is," says the hip young teacher who wants to convince her class that she's not square or frightened. But she does not generally add on the dangerous next step: "Now figure out the ways by which we can make things different." Instead, she avoids that uncomfortable area by assuring her children that "things are always gradually getting better." In this way, the sense of agency, of personal initiative, is quietly confiscated and the child is left with the deceptive impression that change, if it does come, will have little or nothing to do with his own efforts. This is a kind of confiscation which is unacceptable and brutally destructive to the minds of young black children. Children whose lives are painful, whose schools are dreadful, whose lot in life has, in many cases, been one of unending struggle for survival, cannot in conscience be asked to place high priority on the "skills of observation," unless the logical second step is made immediately apparent. A child cannot be asked to look quietly upon "the way things are" if that is a way which has been unhappy and devastating to his people. His need is not to learn to adapt to the world, but rather to learn ways to make the world adapt to him. This is where the word "revolutionary" is going to have to enter the minds of those who are planning new materials. But it cannot enter by means of academic reconsideration only: it must be positioned there by those who understand the need for significant change because they have already been participants in events and movements which were revolutionary in nature.

I might restate this somewhat in the following way: We live right now in an age which many people describe as revolutionary: Some, like President Kennedy and Dr. King, believed that a peaceful revolution might be possible. Others, including a number of black radicals and militants, have frequently said that violence is going to be the only way. Whichever the case, education which is going to be relevant to a revolutionary era is going to have to take the likelihood of revolutionary change into consideration. I see at least two ways—one positive, one negative—in which this fact might be affected by the development of educational technologies.

To take the negative first, there is the very great danger, alluded to earlier, that those who are working in this field will mistake an artificial and mechanical kinds of "revolution" for the real thing. The word, in recent years, has been used rather cheaply. Scientists talk about the "revolution in technology." Businessmen speak of a "revolution in administrative practices." It has come to the point where even the publishers of paperback books can call their industry a merchandising "revolution." In this way, a word which is essentially threatening to many people has been domesticated. But steel and stone and paper do not constitute the kind of change of which the world is thinking. It is only in the area of outlook and attitude, and of the nature of the relationship between a teacher and her children, that the use of the word "revolutionary" would become significant in education. And, without radical changes in these areas, all the technological gadgetry on earth will be quite meaningless. First, then, there is the preliminary danger that technological innovations, especially if they are quite clever and exciting, will blind us to the need for much deeper and more important changes: and may, indeed, even prevent us from recognizing this second issue as a separate problem.

But there is also a positive and encouraging way in which technological change may be able to affect this problem: Instructional devices, if developed with sophistication, may very well prove to be a seductive force in leading teachers and educators into areas of deeper transformation almost before they are aware of what they are permitting. This would depend greatly upon the intent and design of the new materials. A boxed reading kit, for example, which channels a pupil along through a carefully calculated rat-maze by means of an infallible yes-no or true-false self-checking system will, of course, compound only more deeply the sense of powerlessness and of helpless acquiescence which now afflict so many ghetto children. A reading-lab, on the other hand, which invited critical comment from a student, which provides not one channel but several alternative channels of movement forward, which asks few factual questions but confronts a pupil repeatedly with questions demanding personal choice and ethical and aesthetic decisions—this kind of innovation would be heading in the right direction. In technologies related to the teaching of social studies, the emphasis might well be on the presentation of *conflicting data* and of *contrasting viewpoints* which will not merely allow but compel a child to make significant judgments about important issues. A dangerous teaching-package is one which predicts, for the reader of the guide-book, a careful set of stages along which the children will progress toward a predetermined place of official wisdom:

"By the third week, children should recognize that our democratic process was not created fullblown by the Founding Fathers but has developed gradually, adding refinements and improvements under the stress of events and as the result of contributions made by many great Americans . . ."

"Lead children to understand why 'autumn stripped bare of her garment' is a beautiful and touching image. Lead them to understand that poetry is made up of many such beautiful images and that we call these images 'metaphors' . . ."

"Help children, by means of free discussion, to understand the major concepts which this film has illustrated. They should be led, by appropriate questions, to recognize that the baboon infant needs the use of his hands to hold on to his mother . . ."

The above, too close to materials in present use for easy ridicule, are examples of the wrong directions, and a dangerous technology is one which encourages teachers and school-systems in these tendencies. The ideal boxed packages, tapes or films for classroom usage, are those that will enable even very slow children to gain access to a profusion of views and materials which will place them in a position equal or superior to that of the class-room teacher: materials, for example, in the area of reading and social studies which are simply so profuse and richly multiplied that the teacher will have no time or opportunity to psyche out the entire area before the child gets there. I am thinking, for example, of a device, within the field of history, which might give pupils a private and direct and un-assisted access to an almost unlimited array of source materials. A teacher, rather than attempting desperately to plan and prepare every step and stage of progress, would be compelled instead to depend upon her pupils for the various kinds of information they are gathering, and children, for the first time in their school-experience might well have the sudden luxury of being able to tell their teacher something that she would genuinely want to know because she does not already know it. The satisfaction and the sense of confidence resultant from supplying a teacher with information she does not already possess might lead a pupil on to the point where he would also feel capable of questioning some of her opinions. It is at this point that a really satisfying democratization of the classroom might develop. Children might no longer feel compelled to read a poem or story, as always at present, to find out *why* it is good, but to determine *whether* it is good. Children might no longer feel compelled to accept with bland ingestion the preliminary sentences of the Declaration of Independence or the Constitution, but would be placed in a position where they could immediately contrast these words with passages of autobiography by men like Folk Douglass or James Baldwin or Nat Turner. The sheer possibilities for presenting an unprecedented multiplicity of source-materials, and the possibility for many dramatic new kinds of contrast and interposition are just two ways out of many in which technologi-cal innovation, if it is enlightened, can help to instill in young school children a sense of personal agency, private choice and individual decision, and to take away from the teacher that terrible semblance of omniscience to which so many children have been subjected and which, frankly, it is hard to believe that even the teachers themselves could very much enjoy.

With such a confiscation of intellectual domination from the teacher, and with the simul-taneous development in children of a sense of intelligent independence and defiance, of charting out at least a few of their own journeys instead of following always in the way their teacher went before them—in this manner, a classroom might become revolutionary in the very deepest and most creative fashion: by enabling those who are young to under-stand that they have information—or can obtain direct *access* to information—which is worth imparting to those who are their elders, and by enabling those who are poor and black and helpless to understand that they can draw into themselves the decisiveness and confidence to break out of their inward bondage. This cannot be conveyed by dictum: it must be learned by the way in which the classroom really operates.

This leads to the last point I'd like to make. Emphasis in these discussions is generally placed upon the root-word "teach," as in "teaching methods," "teaching styles" or "teach-ing machines." I think the active verb ought to be "learn." It is not just a game of words, but a real indication of the way we look at things. When we think of "teaching" we think inevitably of better and more dramatic devices for the teacher. If, however, we can think instead of the idea of "learning," then right away we are more likely to be wondering about devices which will enhance and facilitate the individual and active and aggressive pursuit of information from the direction of the child. Seen in this way, the ideal new technologies would be those that turned the classroom from a dinner-table presided over by a single fat lady dishing out one kind of nourishment from a single soup-bowl, into a smorgasbord set up on at least a dozen different tables, from which children were enabled to select nourishments of a thousand different kinds, some of which the teacher herself has never tasted. With this metaphor in mind, we might go on to imagine a situation in which one child begins to tell another what he's eating: in other words, when children exchange information and viewpoints with each other even before these viewpoints or pieces of information have been transmitted to the teacher. This image of a smorgasbord, I think, might well be in the minds of those who are involved with the development of instructional technologies. For it is easy enough to see with what inspiration a wise technology could make the idea of "self-service education" a reality.

There are two reasons why I wanted to end with this emphasis on "learning" as opposed to "teaching." First, I am convinced (as are many others), that people do not really "learn" things which are thrust upon them, even by the earnestness of excellent teachers. I just don't think that learning takes place like that. *Remembering* does. *Parroting back* and *repeating* probably do. *Thinking* doesn't. This point seems well enough established not to labor it; but the other point I want to make is less frequently made and one directly prompted by the question to which this paper is responding. This has to do with the issue of whether our present adult society, and in particular, our adult *white* society, does genuinely possess very much in the way of ethics of judgment or decision-making that ought to be passed on to children. We think of ourselves as those who transmit to the young an inheritance of culture which we have received from those who came before us. But it is possible, at this moment anyway, that a more appropriate image might be that of the narcotic addict who feels compelled to pass on his shame and his addiction to the boys out on the corner. We are disconcerted, I think, when our own children condemn our warlike policies. We are unsettled when they suggest that our own well-being might be founded on the misery of others. We are threatened deeply when they risk their own lives, without even consulting us, to redress a racial crime which we have always tolerated. Even the most generous and decent of teachers has a profound, if often totally unconscious, stake in preventing her pupils from discovering the tragic injustices to which she has anesthetized herself and which she has never felt it her responsibility to correct or influence.

Technology must therefore address itself above all to this problem and must help to emancipate a class of children from the chains which it is not humanly possible for most teachers to unlock. I think that I have suggested here a number of ways in which this might be attempted: by *individualizing* the use of new machineries, by a massive profusion of *conflicting and contradictory opinions and source-data*, by materials chosen with a specific view to *provocation* and to breaking down the whole idea that important questions generally have "right answers," by interpositions which will stimulate or demand moral decisions on the part of pupils, by devices which are more for the use of *kids* than that of teachers, and in all cases by the use of materials which take into consideration both *the future role* of the black community within the public classroom and *the future interaction* between that classroom and the revolutionary world outside. Finally, to return to the point where I began, it means going to the parents of the target-children at the earliest possible time, preferably right now, and certainly long before any irreversible decisions have been made. The sense of powerlessness is the number one psychological problem in the ghetto. It is not paranoid but an accurate picture of reality, and as educational technology develops there is every likelihood that that sense of powerlessness will be immensely heightened. It is within your power to help to prevent this possibility by means of foresight and specific action.

79.

Technology and
The Education
Of the Disadvantaged

by *JOHN HENRY MARTIN*
Former School
Superintendent
Mt. Vernon, N.Y.

Education for the disadvantaged, the children of the poor of our inner cities or Appalachia, the American Indian children, the children of the Spanish-speaking, has in the short space of the past five years moved from the remediation or correction of social and physical pathology to a recognition that education itself must be reformed. We agreed early that among the children of the poor, the high incidence rates of dental caries, eyesight problems, dietary deficiencies, physical defects, psychological disorders, as well as poor neighborhood conditions and inadequate family patterns of child rearing needed sharp additions of supplementary services. Each of these ills may be damaging to a child's capacity to learn; all require attention.

But we are now recognizing the unhappy truth that the remediation or correction of these pathologies is not enough to produce children who will then learn. It was comforting to those of us in education to believe that our educational failures were in effect environmentally produced; that our curricula and techniques worked well if a child was healthy and came from a stable home. If any mixture of deficits afflicted a child, then the removal of the difficulties were all that was needed to produce an eager and successful learner.

Head Start was conceived in these terms as a "total delivery system, broader than just education" to mobilize corrective medical, dental, social and educational components so that normal and regular schooling would be successful. We soon found that the spurts of measurable growth achieved during the Head Start period were not sustained or were erased subsequently in the kindergartens and the first grades. A clue to the reason can be determined from an examination of the educational programs of Head Start. For Head Start spawned a wide variety of classroom patterns ranging from baby-sitting, day care centers to replicas of middle class child development nursery schools. Basically, whether poorly or well operated, they shared in common a non-academic orientation with major emphasis for the most part being devoted to social and physical maturation exercises rather vague in practice and equally vague in the language used to describe them. The need for a rigorous reexamination of the central educational objectives with behavior goals and an equally disciplined description of the curricular options to fulfill these is now becoming clear. In other words, Head Start did accomplish much in the remediation of children's deficiencies in every area except that of education. But the central issue of the appropriateness of the educational program to the cognitive and language development of disadvantaged children was not met. Initially, the oversight in not designing an educational program specifically to meet the deficiencies of the disadvantaged youngster, was either not seen or was actually resisted as being unnecessary.

Coleman's study revealed that significant educational growth occurs where the social class mix in a school shows a clear numerical dominance of middle-class children over children with parents of low income. All other measurable educational reforms were of little or no consequence when measured against economic class. Neither class-size, nor dollars of expenditure nor remediation services, nor physical facilities, nor experience of teachers, made for significant differences in school achievement. Hidden in these findings is the startling interpretation that our schools can only teach children who come from homes which provide certain pre-requisites for learning. Looked at in these ways, the school curriculum and the teaching procedures seem to work when they work at all when the children of the middle-class white or black come to school with attitudes and behavioral dispositions in harmony with the schools patterns. For example, from infancy, the middle class child is raised in a home where parental approval is heavily weighted toward language development. "See the light." "Show Daddy." "Say, Da Da." "Say, Ma Ma." "Tell Grandpa." "Show Grandma how you can say airplane." Brightness in speech is the sure bestower of family awards. This frequently competitive exercise with siblings however physically damaging it may become, produces children well trained in seeking adult approval for verbal performance. Children spoken to, read to, and rewarded or denied approval, based upon parental estimates of language dexterity, enter school classrooms well prepared for a curriculum and teaching which maintains the same reward system and which presumes a language maturation able to cope with its materials and print media. But for large masses of our children, this family environment is only partially or not present, and our schools have as yet not designed a new pedagogy to fit these circumstances.

We are learning the tremendous importance of the first five years of life to the total intellectual growth of a human. Freud, 50 years ago, called attention to the decisiveness of these first five years of life to the emotional and personality development of every adult. We have recently awakened to the cumulative evidence indicating an almost equally controlling role for early childhood to much subsequent intellectual and cognitive power. Out of concern for family, or ignorance of early childhood's importance, education has until recently ignored these vital years.

We are also learning the consequences of the biological fact that by age four and a half; 50% of the total growth of the human brain is accomplished; that two-thirds of its growth is completed at age six. Bloom, at the University of Chicago, in an examination of over hundreds of studies of human growth and development, has concluded that the time for most effective intervention, or when the environment can have maximum consequences, is during the period when the organ or trait has its greatest rate of growth. Unhappily, the research shows that environmental neglect during this same early childhood period actually leads to a suppression of the growth of intelligence. Our antique assumptions about the genetic immutability of intelligence must now give way. We know that for millions of our children we have a system extraordinarily effective in reducing I.Q's by 20-30 points between infancy and adolescence. We can sometimes with great difficulty and expense bring it back. The evidence is now conclusive that with improved child rearing practices and the introduction of technology and other changes in education, we can enhance it.

Importance of Language Development

Some indications of what is needed came six years ago from the long-suppressed reports of Vygotsky in Russia. Vygotsky emphasized the central importance of language development in the growth of mental competence. Verbal symbols become the language of the brain. Enhance these at the appropriate growth periods in early childhood and intellectual fertility will occur. Similarly, studies now show that if this act is interfered with, if speech is repressed, cognitive growth is retarded. The phenomenon is world-wide and is most closely associated with poverty.

Israel has encountered language retardation with the children of oriental Jews. These households may be filled with the noise and the sounds of living, but not with the language of communication with infants. Children are told, not answered. In the inner cities of America, getting out of the way, shutting up, and avoiding physical punishment are early requirements for survival. It is a noisy world full of radios, television, loud voices, but with extremely limited language-building inter-relationships. Sub-verbal sounds, grunts, groans, commands, shouts, single-word sentences, are abusive not just to the sight of the child, not just to the personality of the child, but to that child's linguistic and hence cognitive and intellectual growth. This is what we mean when we speak of the educationally disadvantaged, as distinct from the physical and social pathologies in which they are immersed and until recently remained hidden.

Montessori, Italy's first woman physician, 60 years ago, between 1900 and 1910, developed Casa Bambini, children's houses in Rome, for the slum children of that city. The techniques she developed took institutionalized children, mental retardates and psychotically disordered, and made them capable of passing examinations in Italy's primary schools. Her principles, now being rediscovered and expanded, placed great emphasis upon re-evoking from children a sensory sensitivity to their surroundings. She found in the slums of Rome what Vygotsky found in Russia, Smilansky found in Israel, and Hunt and Deutsch in America: the children from nonverbal homes are dulled and depressed. She blindfolded them so that they could see through the feel of their fingers; she put the Roman alphabet on sandpaper so that they could feel the shape of sounds. She said that the act of learning is at its best when a child works his way through highly organized material, and that the thing to be learned should be structured so that the child can make his own discoveries. She developed, with a fertile brain, a host of these devices, some of which have become culturally obsolete, such as button-hook frames. Others continue in their simplicity to work effectively today.

Her program in the United States died before World War I, when Kilpatrick, high priest of Dewey's philosophy of education, pronounced her doctrine heretical.

In America we have suffered for 30 years with a distortion of a fractional truth called child development. Gesell, at Yale University, studying upper-middle class children from a suburban collegiate community, found normal behavior growing in ladder-rung precision. He and his followers announced what four-year-olds and five-year-olds and six-year-olds in theory could do. It followed that it was fruitless to teach earlier, since the stage of development of the youngster would not permit success. When he was ready he would learn. Readiness became an educational cliche that for all the gentleness of its intent served to prevent effective development of language growth and reading in our nursery and early childhood programs. Readiness was locked to the calendar and the clock, and we retarded all our children because at age five they weren't 'ready.' It would be grossly unfair to attribute all of these consequences to the Gesell School. Unfortunately, the widely supported application of these views was most damaging to the disadvantaged child.

With this brief background of some of the developments and some of the historical influences affecting the disadvantaged child today, we raise the question: 'What can be done?' May I point out that there is growing recognition that the billions we have spent in the past several years applying more of the time-honored solutions have resulted in little of consequence. We reduced class sizes, we added remedial, psychological and social services, we filled the cupboards of our schools with paraphernalia and gadgets patched on to a system that remained unchanged. In short, we have spent much and gotten little.

At this point we can either retreat to a negative view that black children, Indian children, children of the rural poor and children of Spanish speaking parents are doomed genetically to being inferior learners for whom no educational program will work or we can analyze what technology can do to change the content and style of education to match the needs of these children.

We believe that technology will make the difference. To do this:

1. A child to learn as an individual must be freed from the lock-step process within a group. Much learning is a private thing.

2. Technology ought to free the teacher from a concept of pedagogy which manipulates children.

3. That which is to be learned early through educational technology should be the languages of man's intellectual life: first and foremost, talking and reading and writing. Secondly, the languages of mathematics and music should be included. I am deliberately leaving to the side the role of the other arts as forms of expression and communication.

4. Educational technology must make it possible for the learner to correct himself. Rapid feedback of the consequences of his actions is important.

5. Instruments for learning, as I am defining them, produce in the learner a sense of competency. Learning with technology is largely tutorial in its appearance. However, the learner in a very private sense is doing it himself. We all can recall the sense of exuberance with which a child says, 'I do it myself.' and similarly all mothers know the muscular determination of the spoon-fed infant to grasp a spoon with strange vigor in the early months of life. The three-year-old's determination to put on his own clothing is a symptom of an internal compulsion that education has ignored. A child in a learning environment responsive to him can and does achieve the same self-learning.

6. Implicit in the above is a shift from efforts to motivate learning based upon peer and sibling rivalry and social competition exploited by the school to the learning energized by the self-growth and self-enhancement made possible by individualizing learning through technology. The disadvantaged child does not respond very well to the extrinsic reward and denial system of the schools typically withdrawing in either fright or hostility from these appeals. The act of learning produces an inner sense of well being. The power of this experience to generate additional learning is the central dynamic change technology can bring to the education of the disadvantaged.

Montessori, as every great teacher, has described the jumping up and down, the hand-clapping, the total exuberance that fills children when self-learning has occurred. Leonard, in the United States, has recently said that our goal in education should be the restoration of ecstasy to the human experience. Leonard realizes that this would put education in competition with other things. Technologically engendered learning bridges the artificial dichotomy between entertainment and education—the first sought the second imposed.

We have seen thus far that the need for change in education is great; that infancy is a new frontier of importance to the quality of society; that large numbers are now being reared or subsequently given a form of education that produces a literate and inquiring child or adult; that standard remedies are not working; and that a powerful educational technology can make a fundamental contribution to the relief of these problems.

If these are the ambitious, as well as vitally-needed goals, we now must ask how can educational technology reach them. It can do that if it isn't a gadget representing a fragment of the learning act. And it is a fragmented tool if it engages his senses only partially, if it excludes one or more of his sensory capabilities, and if it leaves him in a passive non-participating role. Consequently, technology to be effective in the basics of education must be multi-sensory in its capabilities.

A moment on the importance of multi-sensory media. Each of us attends to each experience with a unique mobilization of his senses. Some of us find it easier to see through our eyes while others see best by listening. Touch and grasp are of dominant importance to others. And labial learning is a common public display of our times.

At present we cannot predict differences in sensory styles from one child to the next. Consequently, curricular material for 'normal' children has never been seen as needing to be prepared for those who are dominantly one sense minded as distinct from another. And if we could, there is reason to believe we shouldn't. This much we know: that whatever the dominance of one sense over the other, they are mutually supportive and in learning all are used. If the structured environment called curriculum or technology fails to make possible the conscious or unconscious exploitation of these separate pathways to the brain in the random fashion required by the range of human differences, then the curriculum and technology emasculate learning. We can and do learn through the eye alone. We can and do learn through our ears. But we learn better, and in some cases we can only learn, if the learning environment, the technology, permits each of us to probe it with a sensory mix unique to himself.

The Learner's Active Role

A second major requirement of technology is that it be seen as a system whose behavior can be manipulated by the learner. The learner must do things. He must be involved. Passive sitting to 'look and listen' exercises bottoms more than brains. If this were not so our television-saturated society would not be confronted with immense problems in education. The learning setting, the specialized environment called technology and its curriculum, must respond to the initiatives of the learner. The learner's capacity to intrude is a high requirement of all good education. In technology it makes the difference between learning systems and gadgetry, however complex.

Learning is not a spectator sport. An aspect of this participatory learning is the requirement that the learner's dominant role permit his random exploration of the material. He must be free to go forward, to reverse himself, to repeat in his own style within the broad frame of the program design. Self-pacing is certainly a great virtue of teaching machines. But when speaking of self-pacing one must not assume that speed is the dominant difference among learners. This would ignore differences in human learning styles involving the senses as well as every child's needs for random exploration. This oversight stems in large part from a concept of programming largely linear in format. If material to be learned is structured in ladder rungs in step-by-step fashion, then speed of learning becomes the dominant observable variable.

From this concept of ten years ago we have come a long way. Programming capability has grown as technological sophistication has increased. Unfortunately, it is necessary to be critical of the continued narrowness of the conceptual design of both the instructional software and of the technological delivery system as they have circumscribed each other. If the program is linear, if the responses of the learner are limited to simple yes or no or multiple choice conventions, then the instrument may be a push-button machine and a weak version of what educational technology can and should be.

Excessive linearity, ladder-rung precision, however compensated for by periodic branchings, produces a rigidity foreign to the optimal behavior of a learner. The intake process from infancy through maturity filters the kaleidoscope of the environment. During the learning act the seeming irrationality of the learner's probes—who from moment to moment closes his eyes in order to hear, tunes out the sound of the teacher or the television announcer while seemingly continuing to attend to that learning situation—is a complex which technology and its programs must invite and not prevent.

When he is given control over these technologically structured pieces of the environment, he will pick and choose, more forward and backwards, call for repetitions in a random, personalized fashion. It requires an arrogance equal to that of the pagan gods to assume that a curriculum programmed in conventional style will do more than constrict most learners. As one of our associates has said, every human being has a learning print as unique as his finger print.

But if I left you with this picture of the functioning behavioral requirements of technology, I would seemingly have described anarchy. Structure enters this picture through an examination of the material, the subject, the skills, the concepts to be learned. Bruner, at Harvard, has made a major contribution to our thinking by pointing out that there is an internal integrity to human knowledge in many of its areas. Thus it is that to the teaching of reading we bring the findings of students of linguistics and language, to determine its internal structure, its phonetic base, and hence the concepts and skills needed to derive meaning from silent speech in print.

A second area that brings reason to the software instruction material programmed into the technology is our growing realization that words in print called textbooks are severely limited pedagogical instruments with and without teachers. An example is the way we have used art and graphics. Despite the ancient Chinese injunction about the value of a picture, art and graphics have been used as after-the-fact, patched-on affairs. We saw, thanks to the discipline imposed by the comprehensive instructional technology of the Talking Typewriter, and we are now seeing again in the Talking Page, that there is much in learning that can be graphically represented and that these graphics can and should carry a large portion of the content in harmony with and integral to the rest of the text. There is no reader who has not been irritated with a reference to an illustration several pages removed. An irritated adult is a child not taught.

The sound motion picture, 40 years old in entertainment and neglected educationally, showed us that the marriage of the human voice and other sounds with pictures and motion had a new efficacy in learning, despite its limitations due to its inability to permit the learner to get into the act. Now through a trilogy of graphics, text and sound, with as much pedagogical attention to each and then to their interrelationship, a whole new organization of curricular materials is made possible by a new educational technology.

Last, the responsiveness of the technology, this interaction with the material, the consistency of the environment's responses during the act of learning, all become vital to the learning efficiency.

A Sense of Discovery

We are rediscovering the importance of exploration leading to inductive reasoning called discovery. Hunt has called this the match, the spark that closes the gap between the known and the unknown. This is the discovery process in learning. Our old reliance on the deductive process, in which rules are given and applications mandated, is still too much with us and technology and its software should not prolong its excessive use.

How now do we examine the long and growing list of devices aimed at contributing to the relief of our major educational ills? We could catalogue overhead and filmstrip projectors, turn-tables and tape recorders, 16mm and Super 8mm projectors, television in broadcast and closed circuit, old-fashioned radio, light pencils and touch sensitive surfaces, new fashioned audiovisual instruments, dial access tapes and cassettes, the computer-based Talking Typewriter, computer assisted instruction and the Talking Page. We now need criteria based upon learning theory which will reveal for each of these their competitively established efficiency. Each of these will teach some things to some children. Some of them will teach uniquely well to some learners, under certain circumstances. Because they differ in total cost we must not assume they do not differ in effectiveness for particular kinds of learning. We have lived with a kind of hidden hypothesis that one of these would be better than all others for all purposes. This is not so. Each can induce learning but for some children and some situations, each of these devices has its own unique contributions. For example, a sound motion picture or television presentation of a dramatized situation is an extraordinarily effective means of having concepts understood and values learned by large groups. The same media has severe limitations in effectiveness and costs if used to teach technical skills and certain dexterities. Until we begin controlled research to delimit the behavioral parameters of kinds of technology most useful for certain learnings and for certain learners, we will continue our over generalized use of particular technologies. Systems analysis devoted to instrumentation in these terms holds great promise. We will then neither accept nor reject closed circuit television because it will or will not teach all subjects to all learners. In the meantime, in the areas of greatest educational need, where present methods continue to do poorly, we need technology that can respond affirmatively to these criteria:

1. Does it involve many senses?
2. Does it permit the learner to get into the curriculum?
3. Does it make possible the braided trilogy of sound, text, and pictures?
4. Does it bring freedom to the act of learning in the unique random style of each and every learner?

If it does, we have a learning system that can address itself to the present problems of the educationally disadvantaged. Partial instrumentation will fragment the effectiveness of the handicapped learner. Just at the school cannot parasitically exploit motivations and behaviors induced by middle-class child rearing modes to reach the children of the poor, technology addressed to these conditions must have an autonomy and multi-dexterity of behaviors that will induce learning in these children as they are. Such multi-dextrous instruments will empower a new generation of learners despite a social milieu which the schools cannot change and society must.

80.

Combining the Insights Of Linguistics and Educational Technology To Teaching Language In the Black Community

by CAROLYN NYGREN
Student
Univ. of Chicago

Linguistics and technology have been significant developments with many implications for education. The uses made of both fields, however, have too often been restricted to the externals, and these externals have been seen as capable of solving many of the problems of education. Language teaching has adopted the terminology of linguistics, but not its insights into language. Schools have adopted the products of technology, the equipment, but not the kind of thinking that made that equipment possible and makes it valuable in a classroom. Little has been done to use the insights and methods of either field to solve educational problems.

Linguistics has been hailed as the answer to all the problems of language teaching. Labeled as using "the linguistic method," a multitude of materials has been published and bought by school systems. It should be pointed out, however, that there is no such thing as "the linguistic method." Today's linguists adhere to one of several schools of thought. What they share is a belief in their research providing a model of language, but not necessarily a teaching model. The linguists most often cited in language teaching discussions are the structuralists and the transformationalists. Although it would be impossible to explain their theories here, a little background might be helpful.

Both schools of linguistics believe in the primacy of speech as language. Writing is merely a secondary form of communication. The structuralist looks at language as a set of habits involving speech patterns. He feels that the native speaker has internalized these patterns, and by using them their possible combinations, produces grammatical sentences. Foreign language teaching has taken this basic theory of language description and used it as a theory of language learning. Structural linguistics is the basis of the Audio Lingual method in which students first hear sentences using a particular pattern, then repeat the sentences. The goal of this method is to produce automatic responses on the part of the student.

Although the structural linguist might not be willing to guarantee the success of the approach, he would fully agree with the method most commonly used to arrive at the particular material stressed. The structure of both the target language and the mother tongue are analyzed, and areas where the patterns of one might interfere with the learning of the patterns of the other are marked. Analysis of a corpus of material also provides insight into the frequency of occurrence of various patterns. This ability to predict areas of difficulty and frequency of occurrence makes it easier for the teacher to find the most efficient ways to minimize the problems of learning and to determine proper emphasis for certain constructions.

The transformational school of linguistics is concerned with the rules necessary to account for grammatical sentences. It does not consider language as a set of habits but as the result of the innate competence of the mind. The purpose of research is not to specify the variety of patterns of the surface level of language, but to discover the underlying universal features of language. Writers of language materials, however, have adopted one external manifestation of transformational research. "The linguistic method" according to these writers is the attempt to relate one form of sentence to another. The active sentence is considered the basic form and the study is concerned with the formation of other sentence types from it. The question is, What are the rules that yield one form from another?

The major objection to the use of the linguistic theories, though, is not that they have not been proven to be relevant to language learning. They have not been proven irrelevant either. The objection is that usually only the terminology of the theory is adopted, while traditional approaches remain. While the teacher of traditional grammar taught sentence diagraming, the teacher of grammar based on structural linguistics may teach a skill called immediate constituent analysis which differs from diagraming only in appearance. Teachers using transformational grammar may teach the method of diagraming the steps in the generation of a sentence.

All too often the "new grammar," like the new math, is taught by a classroom teacher, who having no background in theory, expects the externals of the field to be the key to better learning for her students. This attitude is bad in any classroom, but it is disastrous in the black, where it provides yet another source of disillusionment and frustration for both student and teacher.

The result of this is that linguistics is deemed useless and is forgotten, and traditional grammars come back into the classroom. All of this happens without the teacher or student ever benefiting from the insights into language that linguistic research can offer.

Instructional technology has suffered a similar fate. Although the development of technology implies a more flexible approach to teaching, too many times the external manifestation, the machine, has been used without ever using the ideas of technology. Although the following statement is from a play satirizing the misuse of technology, it seems to represent the reasoning of many school systems.

> "We like to think of our items as magic wands and magic carpets, which in the hands of any teacher can change the world for the students, transporting them effortlessly to new knowledge."[1]

The products of technology are used as supplements to traditional teaching methods and often the success of a lesson is measured in terms of how many machines are used.

The misuses of instructional technology as well as the misuses of linguistics are nowhere so disastrous as in a classroom in a black school. Machines are not merely seen as supplements to teaching, but as replacements for teachers who have damaged their students. The machine is the answer.

> "It does not have preconceived notions about a student's lack of desire, or interest. It does not discriminate by color, weight, appearance, or attitude. It removes a certain amount of human contact which, for some ghetto students, is continually frustrating and abrasive. Mistakes are not penalized by scorn or sarcasm. Successes are marked by positive reinforcement of a 'correct' student response."[2]

Technology seems to provide an easy out, instead of attacking the real problem.

It is hard to imagine that the use of machines just for the sake of using machines will succeed. Instructional technology may be doomed to rejection along with linguistics, never having been given the chance to demonstrate its real value.

Instructional technology is not machines. It is the kind of thinking which the development of machines forces the planner to do. It assumes that behavior is the only measurable aspect of learning. It involves a careful identification of the specific content of curriculum and identification of the behaviors considered to represent the learning of the content. It then involves the devising of the means to effect the behavioral changes. The thinking behind the use of technology is far more important than the equipment.

Technology should be viewed as providing an opportunity to restructure the environment of the student to facilitate learning. No longer is the teacher the only source of the knowledge available to the members of the class. Technology provides the opportunity for the student to actively participate in his learning. This opportunity is especially important to the student in the ghetto school. The rigid environment of the classroom has been a contributing factor to his non-involvement.

Language teaching in predominantly black schools has been one of the greatest failures of the public school system. The effort until very recently has been really to erase all the "bad" language habits of the students and have them emerge as speakers of perfect standard dialect. The failure of most students to achieve this goal set by the school affects not just their achievement in language, but also affects their self confidence and expectations of achievement.

"Your speech is so sloppy." "You're just lazy when you don't add the "s" to that word." These are the comments made daily by the white language teacher in the ghetto school. She has labeled her students' language as incorrect English, and she sees her task as correcting every deviation from the standard dialect. She does not find her efforts very rewarding, and she begins to find the students as unacceptable as she finds their language. She feels they are not intellectually capable of learning, and her level of expectation for them is low. Since this attitude is often shared by most members of the faculty, little is expected of the students, and consequently little is achieved. The truism that performance equals expectation is never more devastatingly true than in a classroom in a black school.

Language instruction, then, is an important problem in black schools. Too often the solution for this problem has been that of the white curriculum planner or teacher. Recently these people have been adapting the Audio Lingual method to teaching standard English to black students. Unfortunately in many cases, foreign language materials have been used with very little modification. The importance of a careful contrastive analysis has been ignored. Staff members have seen the products of instructional technology as helpful tools for presenting the pattern drills. The first step to a more relevant solution to the problem should be the reexamination of the goals and methods of language teaching in the ghetto. This reexamination should employ the philosophy and insights from both linguistics and instructional technology.

I feel that the most profitable procedure would be to use the systems approach of Project ARISTOTLE as a framework for finding the best solution to the language problems in the ghetto schools. The findings of linguistics will be valuable in answering some of the questions posed. This framework would force the language curriculum planner to investigate previously unexplored goals, methods, and problems, both educational and non educational, in a search for an answer.

"As developed by Project ARISTOTLE, the systems approach to education consists of eight steps:

1. Need—the education/training problem;

2. Objectives—measurable learning goals;

3. Constraints—restrictions or limitations;

4. Alternatives—candidate solutions;

5. Selection—choice of the best alternative;

6. Implementation—pilot operation of the chosen solution;

7. Evaluation—measurement of results obtained against originally stated objectives; and

8. Modification—the change of the system to correct for the deficiencies noted."[3]

I feel that this approach would be invaluable to any school system in its search for a language program that would effectively serve its black students. Following this approach carefully will take a great deal of courage, for there is the chance that the solution arrived at as the best one may not be the one that fits into school officials' preconceived scheme. This approach will, however, provide a solution which will be most likely to yield results if implemented. I will include ARISTOTLE's procedures for arriving at the answers to the eight steps, and try to indicate the contributions linguistics might make in this procedure.

NEED

Definition: A statement of the real problem being faced by the society under consideration—that statement of a problem which initiates consideration of an education/training system as a potential solution.

Procedure: 1. Start with an expression of the generalized need.

2. Determine whether education/training constitutes at least a partial satisfaction of the need.

3. Determine in the light of the present state-of-the-art what type of manpower and what skills are needed.

4. Define more specifically and in greater depth the group of people and skill areas required to satisfy the need.

5. Verify the need and the delineation of the group concerned through the judgment of knowledgeable people in the real world involved.

This first step of determining need is the one which has usually been ignored by school officials. They felt that they knew the need. The need was to make black students speak "correct English." But is this the real need? A school system might dig a little deeper and decide that the real need is more communication between black and white people. The planners will have seen conversations between employer and prospective employee, between worker and worker, between agency and client, between teacher and child, result in misunderstanding, anger and disillusionment. Although the causes of this problem are many and complex, it might be assumed that the learning of standard dialect by the black students would partially satisfy this need. At any rate, some kind of education will have to be seen as necessary. The most significant part of this step is the necessity of verifying the need with members of the society affected. This is what has happened too seldom in the past. Research projects, government organizations, have studied the problems of the black community, found solution, and implemented them, all without consulting the people involved. The need here should be confirmed by the parents of the students and by the students themselves. What is most important is that this step be taken, and not ignored.

OBJECTIVES

Definition: The determination and specification of the terminal capability desired of students after having successfully completed a learning experience.

Procedure: 1. Define that portion of the need which can be satisfied by the education/training system.

2. Describe in measurable terms the observable act(s) which will be accepted as evidence of the learner having achieved the objective.

3. Describe the environmental conditions (stress, etc.) under which the desired end behavior must be demonstrated.

4. Define the minimum acceptable criteria for demonstrating terminal behavior objectives.

Linguistics can be helpful in determining the objectives of education. If the need is improved communication, then it is the job of the linguists to determine what behaviors will achieve this. The first problem would be to establish how much of the lack of communication has a linguistics basis, and how much has a psychological one. What elements of black dialect and standard dialect work against each other to produce confusion? Is the intonation of standard English such that the message it gives to the black dialect speaker cancels or at least affects a message the words are sending? Does the sound system of black dialect confuse the standard dialect speaker? Do the speakers of each dialect "block" the dialect of the other because of cultural differences, not linguistic? If the problem is linguistic, research would identify the specific areas that cause confusion and educational objectives would be established from them. Since standard dialect speakers are in the majority, it would be the burden of the black dialect speakers to become bi-dialectal. If the problem is cultural, another type of educational objective will have to be considered for both black and white students. Such research is very time consuming, and perhaps temporary objectives might have to be used.

CONSTRAINTS

Definition: Those real-world limiting conditions which must be satisfied by any acceptable system designed to attain the educational objectives.

Procedure: 1. Identify the applicable families (initial student behavior, facilities, financial, timing, staff limitations, administrative, political, etc.).

2. List specific constraints within each family and establish source of constraints.

3. Label the constraints by severity (physical law, short term but inviolate, financial or political, psychological or political, subject to change).

4. Rank constraints in order of effect upon the system design.

It is in this area that linguistics can say the most. Although it cannot speak to most of the families, it can give a great deal of information about initial student behavior. Previously constraints have been seen where they did not necessarily exist, and have not been seen where they did. Application of some of the findings of linguistic research shows where the constraints are.

Every language is a system. The most realistic approach is that of understanding that black dialect, even though it shares a close relationship to standard dialect, operates under its own grammatical, phonological, and paralinguistic systems. It cannot be considered a corrupt form of standard dialect exhibiting random errors. This kind of realization is necessary for the teacher who questions why her students can't seem to learn from her corrections.

They don't learn because they are faced with the same type of situation in learning standard dialect as they would be in learning French or German. It is not hard to understand, then, why corrections of random errors will fail to make a student fluent in standard dialect. A systematic attack on the problem, however, can only be made after exhaustive comparisons of standard English and the black dialects to determine what the areas of difference are. This is a necessary first step in determining methods and preparing materials for teaching the standard dialect.

For those not familiar with the idea, I shall include some of my work based on tapes of my students. One caution should be observed. My findings can only be considered valid for the particular people studied, until further research proves any of the patterns common to larger groups. It is to be expected that different systems may be operating in the language of speakers from other communities.

One of the most obvious differences between standard dialect and black dialect is in the use of "be" as an auxiliary and a copula.

In the use of "be" as the main verb, the non-finite form is used in all cases

They be about an hour and a half.

It be church.

As an auxiliary the same is true.

They be rushing and carrying on.

That's what the band be doing.

There is no grammatical difference between the auxiliary "be" in the present and in the future. Context determines the meaning. The next sentence was used to mean the future.

The local be stopping in Connecticut.

In past tense the same system operates.

They wasn't jobs that I like.

We was on the turnpike.

We was killing each other before we went over there.

Standard dialect has a choice between using the full form of the finite "be" plus the verb or using a contraction of the auxiliary. The usage of the two forms is determined by the social situation, usually with the former being used in formal situations.

He is drunk.   He's drunk.

He is drinking.   He's drinking.

Another reason for using the full form is for contrastive stress.

Black dialect maintains a distinction similar in form to the standard dialect, but not necessarily operating under the same system. The dialect has a distinction between the full form of the non finite "be" of the copula and the auxiliary, or no "be" form at all.

We on the same road.

They steamed up.

It be church. Well, I think it church.

They just saying it.

That's what the band be doing.

Standard dialect has a system of status using the word "do." The speaker can assert that a comment made by another person is not true.

You don't like that.

I *do* like that.

In this case contrastive stress is placed on the "do."

The emphatic statement is another indication of status.

I do like that coat.

The system is defective, however. It is impossible to use this emphatic "do" with any form of the verb "be"—as copula or auxiliary. The following sentences are impossible in standard dialect.

I do am right.

I do am hitting the ball.

These distinctions do occur in the black dialect studied.

I do be right.

I do be hitting the ball.

Other differences in the verbal systems are noticed. Standard dialect has a difference in form between present and past tenses. The dialect I studied does not maintain the distinction in regular verbs.

He walk to the store every day.

He walk to the store yesterday.

In this case the meaning of past is not carried by the grammatical system, but by the lexical.

Differences in the systems of what the grammarians call aspect were just hinted at in my data, but the implication is that further study in this area would be valuable. There is a distinct lack of agreement among grammarians about the meaning of aspect in English. Although languages such as Russian do have a distinct aspectual system, the use of the term for standard English dialect seems to be a case of trying to fit a language to a system, rather than a system to a language—something the science of linguistics is doing its best to eliminate. While standard dialect does not have a one to one relationship between form and meaning of the expanded tenses, indication are the black dialect does. It seems that black dialect expresses states and habitual action by the progressive tenses.

They be having drill practice every day when they be having their club meeting.

I be loving you.

It may be that simple tenses in black dialect have a meaning of completion, while the progressive tenses have a meaning of non-completion.

While standard dialect marks plurality in a noun no matter where else it has been marked, black dialect doesn't.

The U.S. government gave us a dollar and twenty five cent to eat off of.

We have had about two incident already.

We have soldiers that has went over there.

The last sentence above shows the marking of plurality in the noun if not marked elsewhere.

Some lexical items that are considered plural in standard dialect are not considered plural in black dialect, and vice versa.

Peoples come on the Center.

The staffs know this, but they don't get no act.

Are there any more discussion?

When contrasting systems it would be worthwhile to consider just how much of the standard dialect the students know. In some cases the forms of the standard dialect have been learned but not the situations in which they are appropriate. The instances of hyper-corrective forms should be included in the analysis of the two systems.

That's when Jimmy had told us they weren't doing the job.

. . . so I had signed up for it.

The two grammatical systems show several types of differences that must be distinguished. In the case of the same form representing both past and present in black dialect, but different forms in standard, we have the same concept represented by different forms in the two dialects. In the case of the contractions involved with non finite "be" in black dialect and finite "be" in standard, we seem to have different concepts but similar changes in form. In the case of the aspectual systems, black dialect may have an entirely different grammatical category.

The phonological systems offer equally important contrasts. Some black dialects may use a different inventory of sounds from standard dialect. In some cases the inventory may be the same but places where the sounds can occur are different. Standard dialect contains two inter-dental fricatives. The voiceless/ θ /occurs initially in "thin," medially in "method," and finally in "youth." The voiced/ δ /occurs initially in "this," medially in "Southern," and finally in "breathe." Black dialects often have those sounds either only in certain positions or they do not have them at all. For speakers without the inter-dentals in their speech, no distinction may be made between the inter-dentals and the labio-dentals/f/ and /v/. Occurrences of [θ] may be systematically pronounced [f], and those of [δ]

are pronounced [v]. Other speakers may make substitutions of other sounds in standard dialect or may use sounds not used in standard. Some speakers make different substitutions according to the position of the sounds.

Many speakers of black dialects do not have certain consonant clusters in their speech. While standard dialect maintains a difference between chest and chess, many black dialect speakers do not. Both words sound the same to these speakers. Black dialects are likely to have many more homonyms than standard dialect speakers do because of this. These homonyms must be identified.

Linguistic research has something to say in determining the psychological constraints, the removal of which might greatly affect the success of any program. For the teacher who accuses her students of using incorrect English, and of being intellectually inferior because of it, the knowledge that her students are speaking a legitimate language with a system of its own might be the first step in understanding her students. It might be worthwhile for the teachers to be put in the place of the students, and to try to learn to speak black dialect. Perhaps an understanding of the real problems of the students would be the beginning of an attitudinal change that might be constructive.

There are several insights of linguistics that might force teachers to reevaluate their students, and give the students a more positive estimate of their linguistic capabilities, for they have had their deficiencies drilled into them from their first moment in school.

All languages are equal. Even if a teacher grants the student the possession of a language, many assume that standard English is superior. They use the lack of inflection as an indication of the obvious inferiority of black dialect. The occurrence of many more homonyms in black dialect convinces them that the language is less precise than standard dialect. Study of the world's languages forces the linguist to dismiss all such examples as ridiculous. If inflection is considered decisive, then English would certainly be inferior when compared to some of the other languages of the world. We have only to go French or German to see this.

Teachers also tend to think that a person cannot reason in black dialect, and therefore we must teach standard dialect. Linguists have proven that every language is capable of saying anything it has the occasion to say. One language might express an idea grammatically while another expresses it lexically, but the idea can be expressed. Teachers must realize that if a person cannot reason, it is not the fault of his language, but of his background. Americans tend to be the most "linguacentric" people on earth. We know few foreign languages and expect that people from other countries will learn English. This attitude is the cause of much of the lack of understanding of the problems of the black student, who is essentially a person in a foreign country expected to speak the native tongue.

Another constraint is that of the black student's attitude toward language. Standard language has become for him the symbol of the world he has never been a part of. It is the language of the school, from which he has also been excluded. It is the white man's language. To use it is to sell out. The dialect which he shares with his friends is a mark of identity and strength in a threatening environment and a method of defying a society that has rejected him.

All of these constraints must be taken into consideration.

ALTERNATIVES

Definition: The generation of candidate systems which could achieve the objectives.

Procedure: 1. Gather data based on current and expected state-of-the-art with respect to potential means toward the specified end.

2. Solicit ideas from a wide spectrum of sources.

3. Keep written list of all suggested ideas—even if they appear to be impractical or to violate constraints.

4. Gather more data if the ideas are insufficient in quantity or scope.

Although the linguist would probably not want to commit himself about the validity of using one of the models of language for teaching, he can provide some suggestions not previously considered. A sample list might include the following as candidates: making the black dialect speakers literate in their own language before teaching the standard dialect, teaching linguistics, teach how language works using a discovery technique, don't teach standard dialect at all, teach standard culture to black students, black culture to white students, teach black dialect to standard dialect speakers.

SELECTION

Definition: The systematic evaluation of all alternatives in terms of objectives and constraints to select the one which is considered the most desirable.

Procedure: 1. Define the criteria which will be used to select the most promising system.

2. Establish a quantitative method for rating each alternative against the selection criteria.

3. Evaluate the relative importance of the selection criteria.

4. Utilize analytical methods (anything from logical thinking to mathematical models) to select the best alternatives.

5. Review the results of the analysis against mature judgment.

6. Make final selection of alternative(s) for testing.

Selection is in the hands of the school officials. Too many nonlinguistic factors are involved. The linguist can only insist that no matter what solution is chosen, it involves close linguistic research.

IMPLEMENTATION

Definition: The first adoption of the selected alternative to meet the specified objective.

Procedure: 1. Delineate the activity elements, schedule of events, and resource requirements.

2. Plan a program to evaluate the selected alternative(s) in utilizing a pilot program (as a test phase if possible, to minimize the risk).

3. Establish a controlled experiment.

4. Establish machinery to collect data (performance, financial, etc.) to use for evaluation.

5. Implement the program with conviction.

It is here where the external manifestations of instructional technology will be considered. The best means for implementing the selected plan must be devised.

EVALUATION

Definition: The determination of the conformance or discrepancy between all of the objectives initially specified and the performance that was actually obtained.

Procedure: 1. Reexamine the original statement of objectives and collect therefrom the specific measurable end capability statements.

2. Reexamine the original statement of objectives and collect therefrom the statements of the environment within which the capability must be demonstrated.

3. Develop as many reliable and valid tests as may be required to establish whether all the objectives are being met.

4. Incorporate in the tests diagnostic features that provide guides for corrective action.

5. Administer the tests to the experimental system.

6. Interpret the results of the tests both quantitatively and qualitatively.

7. At specified intervals, reexamine and evaluate the need and all elements of the system.

MODIFICATION

Definition: The process of modifying the designed learning system based on deficiencies in meeting the objectives as determined through evaluation.

Procedure: 1. Examine discrepancies between specified (objectives) and obtained (evaluation) system performance to determine probable cause for deficiencies.

2. Analyze the entire system to ascertain where the correction can best be made.

3. Develop a specific plan for correction.

4. Make the correction during the next system cycle.

5. Conduct a new evaluation and continue this cycle until the specified performance is attained.

Although the last two steps provide little opportunity for the contribution of the linguist, their importance to a program in language that involves black students cannot be over emphasized. For these last steps make implications as to where the responsibility for learning lies. Under this system the burden for failure falls on the teacher and planner. If learning was not accomplished the possibility exists that it was not the fault of the student. This is not the usual situation for the students in ghetto schools. Inferior intellectual ability is too often the reason given for student failure. If the systems approach to learning accomplishes nothing else, it removes the burden of failure in language studies from the student.

REFERENCES

1. Deterline, William A., "The Educational Technology Game." *Educational Technology.* September 15, 1968, pp. 4-10.

2. Singer, Ira J., "Media and the Ghetto School." *Audiovisual Instruction,* October 1968, pp. 860-864.

3. Lehmann, Henry, "The Systems Approach to Education." *Audiovisual Instruction.* February, 1968, pp. 144-148.

81.
Instructional Technology and The Disadvantaged Child

by *MEYER WEINBERG*
Coordinator
Innovations Center
Chicago City College

This paper inquires whether instructional technology has a special significance for educationally disadvantaged children. It is not concerned with those aspects of instructional technology which are equally important both for the advantaged and disadvantaged. Secondarily, the paper explores how educational technology can make school learning more relevant to the disadvantaged child.

The Technology of Anything

Any area of practical activity which is based on traditional techniques alone will resist change strongly. Practitioners whose only testing ground is experience will be suspicious of solutions that do not arise from daily experience. The suspicion may, in fact, be well-grounded. When daily routines are known to "work," even though the basis of that operability remains obscure, it is prudent to push no further. The medieval artisan who tanned leather without precise knowledge of the chemistry of the process was being rational when he rejected a new way of tanning. For, without scientific validation of the innovation—which was not possible, given the state of knowledge of chemistry—the contest was between the tried and tested and the untried.

Teaching proceeds in like manner. Age-old routines are perpetuated by practitioners who have—in Kelly Miller's phrase—the "knack without the knowledge."[1] Like the medieval tanner, the teacher must stick close to established ways. Middling success or failure is the common outcome. Neither extraordinary success nor failure can be expected or explained for either involves the "knowledge" that only a science of instruction could afford us. For better or worse, such a science eludes the theorist.

Technique takes on breath and color only as it enters the everyday world of practical activity. The path of its entry, however, is hemmed in by numerous constrictions of vested interest and social privilege. In a society of social class-allocated goods and services, innovations are weighed and measured for the differential advantages they bestow. Educational innovations, for example, are generally associated with schools serving middle and upper class children rather than those serving inner city, lower-class children.

Preoccupation with innovation often leads to an overemphasis upon technique. Frequently, this results in technologism, i.e., an unrealistic expectation of benefits from a simple change in what economists call the production function. This defective judgment results from an abstraction of technique from its social and cultural matrix. The innovation is viewed as an isolated tool or machine which, presumably, needs only be set in motion in order to produce immediate benefits. Those problems are sought that are amenable to the new process, while other problems remain unrecognized or ignored. The new technique may be politically useful as well, as social discontents are treated with mechanical devices. Thus, defective educational goals and methods in ghetto schools are expected by some to yield before the pressure of tools and techniques such as computers, opaque projectors, team teaching, and irregular time periods.

The contemporary innovation movement serves a similar function by directing attention to reform measures that operate within the school. So defined, the crisis in education is seen to consist principally of instructional problems. Accordingly, social-political issues are excluded by indirection. Non-material technology, especially when it consists of inventions such as decentralization or community control, becomes a near-irrelevancy.

The breakthrough-psychology is yet another defect of thinking about technology. This is the view of technological progress as the sudden appearance of apocalyptic devices and techniques which sweep before them whole series of practical problems. It is a form of magical thinking, fed by ignorance of technological history and based on a blend of blind faith and a diffuse desire for change. The breakthrough-psychology reflects the impatience of ignorance and oversimplification. The rise of slavery in the United States, for example, is glibly converted into a response to the cotton gin which is, in turn, explained as the fortuitous consequence of Eli Whitney's vacation trip to Georgia in 1793. Omitted are the long line of experiments in cotton ginning, the state and trends of the world demand for cotton, bases for slave economy other than cotton, the problems of discovering a variety of cotton that could be grown in dry, upland areas, and more.

In the field of education, the breakthrough-psychology can easily become a substitute for more fundamental thinking.

Disadvantagement, Dullness, and Technology

Lower-class persons are said to lack verbal ability, to be less "intellectual," and to excel in hand-work.

The psychological literature is filled with findings that disadvantaged children are more "motoric" than "conceptual," more adequate in physical activities than in sustained studying. This distinction is also said to characterize child-rearing practices of lower-class parents as contrasted with middle-class parents. In his influential 1962 book, *The Culturally Deprived Child,* Frank Riessman wrote about the "physical approach" of the disadvantaged child. He declared that teaching machines, standard mechanical devices, and other physical and visual techniques were "uniquely appropriate for culturally deprived children."

A year later, however, Riessman reported to a conference on urban education:

> . . . I had earlier advocated investigations of teaching machines and of program[ed] learning in work with low income youngsters. I did this on the grounds that the full approach was physicalistic in character, that there were clear-cut structural reinforcements, that it was a game-like technique, etc. I must tell you that my more recent informal experience in different parts of the country is that this "just ain't so." What happens when you try the techniques with these youngsters is that at first they say, "Oh, this is an interesting game"; "it's going to be fun"; "you get the answers right away." Later on they say: "I've been taken; this is just another reader," and a reading style is not the best style in

which to break through to the low income youngster. I report this to you as an impression independently gathered by a number of people around the country.[2]

Such are the vagaries of communication that Riessman's earlier discussion continues to be cited widely while his later one is all but ignored.

In Birmingham, England, Davis and Leith studied the use of programmed texts by children in two slum and two advantaged schools.[3] They found no significant differences between the performance scores of both groups. In one sense, the investigators held, the programmed learning was more effective in the former schools. They pointed to the fact that the slum children had been working at a level much below the advantaged children prior to the experiment. Davis and Leith observe: "Inspection of their workbooks indicated a level of work much inferior to their peers in the good environment. Further, children at both [slum] schools had suffered from the lack of continuity of untrained teachers, supply teachers, and the general lack of staff. Such base defects in previous training should have been reflected in poorer results."[4]

It is not possible to determine whether the lack of difference between slum and advantaged children was a lasting or a temporary phenomenon. Davis and Leith note that over a period of eight tests the slum students tended, especially in tests six and eight, to do more poorly than the advantaged students.[5]

Allison Davis has recently pointed out:

> About one-fourth of the more than 20 million slum children in this country under the age of fifteen have academic verbal superior to that of a third of the approximately 6 million upper-middle-class children under fifteen. . . . There actually are more able children, in gross numbers, in our slums than in our upper middle class.[6]

Nevertheless, the stereotype of dull, physicalistic intellects in the lower class is still widely accepted.[7]

If lower-class children were as dull as the stereotype prescribes, a question would still remain as to the special suitability of instructional technology in their schooling. In the absence of such correspondence, however, one must seek elsewhere for a convincing argument.

The Disadvantaged Child and Its Teacher

For the disadvantaged child, school has a very special significance. Much of that significance centers on the teacher. What does the research literature say on this subject?

Irwin Katz has emphasized that lower-class children, not having received a great deal of parental approbation for intellectual performance, "remain more dependent than middle-class children on social reinforcement when performing academic tasks."[8] Negro children, Katz continues:

> . . . are likely to be highly dependent on the immediate environment for the setting of standards and dispensing of rewards. . . . Teacher attitudes toward Negro children will be highly important for their classroom behavior.[9]

In the process of desegregation, the role of the teacher becomes crucial for the Negro child.[10]

Katz is concerned with *social* reinforcement, a concept that has little or nothing to do with the concept of reinforcement in conventional learning theory. He stresses the reinforcement of motivation that arises from interaction between student and student as well as student and teacher.

Geisel studied the self-concept of children in Nashville, Tennessee. He found a significant racial difference:

> The teacher for the white child is likely to be simply an instrumental agent of the school. For the Negro child she also represents a status position and a respected social role. . . . The Negro child who feels he is important in the eyes of the teacher is optimistic about the future and also thinks that education is very important. This pattern is much less pronounced for white youth.[11]

The significance of the school is strongly mediated through the teacher.

The Equal Educational Opportunity Survey (the "Coleman Report") attempted to account for academic achievement differences in terms of family background, quality of school, and attributes of the student body. Most important was the third factor; and it was especially significant for the most disadvantaged students. At the same time, the Survey reported:

> . . . Good teachers matter more for children from minority groups which have educationally deficient backgrounds. . . . For any groups whether minority or not, the effect of good teachers is greatest upon the children who suffer most educational disadvantage in their background, and . . . a given investment in upgrading teacher quality will have most effect on achievement in underprivileged areas.[12]

The Survey did not establish the empirical grounds of this connection. Unlike Katz and Geisel, for example, the Survey simply recorded the existence of such a connection.

One implication of the Katz and Geisel research is that the education of disadvantaged children proceeds best with a minimum of technological intervention between student and teacher. It seems to be the middle-class children—whose social need for the school is minimal—who can best "afford" technological interventions. The Coleman research is not inconsistent with such an interpretation.

Disadvantaged children bear the stigma of deprivation from an early age. In their school career, especially, is the lesson learned repeatedly. If we would help such children counterbalance the stigma, a deeply personal (and interpersonal) approach will need to be used. It is a fundamental defect of much contemporary educational technology that it stresses individual and isolated aspects of the learning process. One thinks, for example, of the single student using a tape installation in a private study carrel; or, a single student plodding his solitary way through a programmed textbook. A much more productive approach for disadvantaged students is to make classroom instruction almost exclusively a face-to-face transaction between student and teacher.

In England, Robson has discussed the problem of social isolation of the learner in programmed learning.[13] Such isolation, he reports, "is likely to favor those students who are less dependent on stimulation from group contact and on receiving encouragement from a human instructor."[14] In the light of Katz's theory, this would add an especially large disadvantage to the deprived child. As Robson puts it: "It is not inconceivable that one day a student will be as familiar with individual programmed instruction as with the now-conventional group instruction, but until that time comes we must remember that we are asking more of the student than that he become acquainted simply with our programs; we are also expecting him to adjust to what is to him an unfamiliar classroom environment."[15] Robson has experimented with combining programmed instruction with pairs of students in an effort to overcome, in part, the element of social isolation.

In still another way may educational technology be especially inappropriate for the disadvantaged. Many of the newer proposals assume, in Martin Deutsch's words, "that the child has reached a particular level in skills which underlie them."[16] Deutsch goes on to observe that such an assumption is unwarranted for the disadvantaged child, but not for the middle-class child. One characteristic of the "cognitive deficit" is its very irregularity. So irregular is it, in fact, that no standardized or mechanized strategy can be devised to counter it. Once more we are led to the need for an imaginative face-to-face encounter of student and teacher. The building of intrinsic motivation can hardly proceed otherwise than in a social-psychological framework between human actors. One could, of course, prescribe the educational task as one of mere response to extrinsic pressures of status and job preparation. Even this definition, however, would not obviate the task of creating or extending intrinsic motivation among the disadvantaged.

A claim frequently made on behalf of programmed learning is that it can release teachers for more individualized work with students. As we saw above, however, the disadvantaged student needs "individualized" teaching at all points of his classroom experience. It would, therefore, be robbing Peter to pay Paul for the disadvantaged student to suffer the burdens of instructional technology on the premise that individuation will come later.

Instructional technology is, apparently, one of the advantages that American society is willing to grant to the disadvantaged student. In more advantaged schools, to be sure, instructional technology plays a role, but a secondary one. Schools for the most advantaged children prefer to employ the most qualified teachers and to apportion their talents among modest-sized classes. Individuation is a constant password, if not always a working reality. Few reformers have prescribed automated classrooms for such schools.

On the other hand, it is the uncommon discussion of educational disadvantagement that fails to list instructional technology as a prime road to excellence. As we saw earlier, the research support for this argument is slight, at best. The contrary is more likely true. This suggests that the prescription is ideological. It complements the widespread myth of cultural deprivation. Both views regard the disadvantaged child as a helpless victim of cultural difference, so maimed by circumstance that he is beyond the possibility of becoming an autonomous, creative person. Consequently, he is allotted a meager share of the school's resources on the paternalistic argument that he could not profit from more. Regarded as a passive object of society's pressures, his passivity is to be strengthened by becoming an object of instructional technology rather than partner in a classroom transaction.

The ideological element in thinking about educational disadvantagement has been explored by a number of students in recent years. Although not well-known, the discussions deserve more attention than they have received.[17] It is but a short step to apply a similar analysis to the ideological element in thinking about educational technology.

A Socially Relevant Educational Technology

Educational technology can become more relevant to the education of disadvantaged youth. Such relevance hinges on a more meaningful classroom exploration of critical concepts. No single teaching technology has any special affinity to the topic. One can easily imagine an instructional role for programmed instruction, videotape, slide projectors, or motion pictures. The first task, rather, is to select that aspect or those aspects of the subject that will provide a short cut to relevance for disadvantaged youngsters. Here are two examples, described in summary fashion.

The Industrial Revolutions

These movements should be studied from the bottom up, so to speak. Large-scale economic changes produce social derangements. Thus, in England, Germany, or the United States, the first impact of industrialization was to create an impoverished class, which lost any traditional supports such as family and community. The growing instability of employment added to the low incomes that were aggravated by labor oversupply, produced unprecedented social instabilities. Factory production crowded unheard-of masses of people in small areas; housing and health problems multiplied. In the United States, a large part of the essential industrial work-force consisted of socially stigmatized Irish immigrants who were segregated in residences, employment, religion, and social life. All this, curiously enough, occurred in a general context of economic growth.

The pedagogic challenge lies in the ability of the educator to relate the life situation of the disadvantaged student to the broadly analogous circumstances of the earliest industrial work force. From this step, one can proceed to the technology of industrialism; next, logically, to the financial-economic structure of expanding industrialism; and then back again to an expanded view of the entire social structure undergoing change.

If we do this—or something like it—we will first have to dispose of all those educational films that present *the* Industrial Revolution simple-mindedly as a mere procession of machines and tools. And we shall need a great span of exciting materials which instructional technology has the capacity to produce. There can, however, be no excitement for disadvantaged or advantaged students in a hackneyed, dreary rehearsal of all the banalities of Arkwright and Watt—or was it Watt and *then* Arkwright?

The Negro in American History

The principal significance of the Negro in American history is the role he played in determining that history. Thus, his role must be delineated with reference to the role of white America as well as with the development of a Negro sub-culture. This involves an historical examination of racism in America—its foundations and functions in both its legal and customary forms; and of the political uses of racism. Essential is an examination of the institutions of Negro daily life, from their plantation beginnings to their contemporary urban forms.

It is peculiarly important to dwell on the intellectual expressions of Negro American life. The poetry, the historiography, the sociology, and the social commentary of black America can be presented as normal expressions of a people hard at work, thought, and life. We need to be ready to reevaluate old views by adopting, momentarily at least, new perspectives. How does immigration look to the only ethnic group that was ever forced to become immigrants to this country? How does the period of Jacksonian democracy appear to a people whose free contingent was deprived legally of one civil right after another during those years? How does a people view Lockean individualism after three centuries of being mere objects of commerce?

To approach these questions honestly and resourcefully is to be relevant to the great challenges of our day.

Instructional technology, then, has no special significance for educating disadvantaged children. Certain forms of it, in fact, have a built-in handicap for these children. Its greatest potential is to afford educators a further opportunity to apply new technical resources to enduring educational challenges.

REFERENCES

1. Miller, Kelly. *Radicals and Conservatives and Other Essays on the Negro in America.* Schocken, New York, 1968, p. 284.

2. Frank Riessman in *Guidance for Socially and Culturally Disadvantaged Children and Youth.* Yeshiva University, New York, 1963.

3. Davis, Terence N., and George O. W. Leith. "Some Determinants of Attitude and Achievement in a Programmed Learning Task." In Derick Unwin and John Leedham, Eds., *Aspects of Educational Technology,* Methuen, London, 1967, pp. 447-467.

4. Ibid., p. 453.

5. Ibid., p. 454.

6. Davis, Allison. "The Educability of the Children of the Poor." *The Unfinished Journey. Issues in American Education,* John Day, New York, 1968, pp. 69-70.

7. A straightforward rejection of the stereotype can be found in Joan I. Roberts in Roberts, Ed., *School Children in the Urban Slum.* Free Press, New York, 1967, p. 28.

8. Katz, Irwin. "Some Motivational Determinants of Racial Differences in Intellectual Achievement." *International Journal of Psychology,* 1966, MS p. 8.

9. Ibid., p. 13.

10. Katz, Irwin. *Desegregation or Integration in Public Schools? The Policy Implications of Research.* Unpublished paper prepared for the U.S. Commission on Civil Rights, November 1967, p. 18.

11. Geisel, Paul N. *IQ Performance, Educational and Occupational Aspirations of Youth in a Southern City: A Racial Comparison.* Unpublished Ph.D. dissertation in Sociology, Vanderbilt Univ., 1962, p. 211. (University Microfilm No. 63-1838).

12. Coleman, James S. and others. *Equality of Educational Opportunity.* Government Printing Office, Washington, D.C., 1966, p. 317.

13. Robson, G. A. "Group Integration Without Group Interference: A Method of Presenting Programmed Instruction." Unwin and Leeds, Eds., *Aspects of Educational Technology,* pp. 523-531.

14. Ibid., p. 524. A similar finding is reported in B. A. Doty and L. A. Doty, "Programmed Instructional Effectiveness in Relation to Certain Student Characteristics." *Journal of Educational Psychology, 55,* 6, pp. 334-338.

15. Ibid., p. 530.

16. Deutsch, Martin, and associates. *The Disadvantaged Child.* Basic Books, New York, 1967, p. 62.

17. See Norman L. Friedman, "Cultural Deprivation: A Commentary on the Sociology of Knowledge," *Journal of Educational Thought,* August, 1967; Edmund W. Gordon and Doxey A. Wilkerson, "A Critique of Compensatory Education," in *Compensatory Education for the Disadvantaged* (New York: College Entrance Examination Board, 1966); Bernard Mackler and Morsley G. Giddings, "Cultural Deprivation: A Study in Mythology," *Teachers College Record,* April, 1965; Diane Ravitch, "Programs, Placebos, and Panaceas," *Urban Review,* April 1968; and Murray and Rosalie Wax, Cultural Deprivation as an Educational Ideology, *"Journal of American Indian Education,* January 1964.

82.

Instructional Technology
For the Handicapped

by *FRANK B. WITHROW, JR.*   and *JOHN A. GOUGH**
Director
Div. of Educational Services
Bureau of Education for the Handicapped
U.S. Office of Education

Promises of the Use of Technology with the Handicapped

In response to the Commission on Instructional Technology's request for a position paper on the involvement of the Bureau of Education for the Handicapped with instructional technology, we have outlined our positions on (1) the promises of technology used with the handicapped, (2) specific applications through the Bureau of Education for the Handicapped's existing programs, (3) expansion of BEH's services, and (4) the legal authority for the development of media for use with the handicapped.

The handicapped child in the world today faces the same problem that all children face as they move into the adult world. That problem simply stated is, "How can I develop the skills and abilities that will enable me to participate in the benefits of modern society?" In the industrialized nations those skills are becoming more and more complex, consequently, the handicapped, the disadvantaged, and the poorly trained are at a point in history where they find their limited skills unusable and/or unsalable in the current market places. The pace of modern day education and the demands of our electronic society have very rapidly moved them further out of competition.

Instructional technology can, if used wisely, bridge part of the gap created by the increasing demands of our society for maximum development of individual skills. There are today an estimated 5,000,000 + handicapped children in the United States. Their needs vary with the type and degree of handicap. Some children need only short periods of special help each week or each day while others may require 24-hour intensive care. In 1968 we are providing educational services to only about 2 out of every 5 handicapped children. We have only 1 trained professional for every 3 professionals needed. Technology can provide help in eliminating these deficiencies.

The learning process for the severely handicapped child must be reduced to its most basic element. The learning strategies used are reality-based experiences that slowly evolve into symbolic experiences. Instructional technology can simulate reality, expand it, extend it, repeat it, and retrieve it in a systematic manner which can, in some instances, increase the learning experiences of the handicapped child through both group and individualized instruction.

The major promise of technology in education is that it may make basic changes in the

---

John A. Gough was chief of the Media Services and Captioned Films, Bureau of Education for the Handicapped, at the time this paper was prepared (November 1968).

relation of teacher to student, student to student, and student to his society. Up to the present the educational process has been too often characterized by teacher domination of pupils, pupils vying with each other for top wages known as grades and the student all too often learning the stuff of the curriculum only to forget it as soon as possible. Cheating, fierce competitiveness and anti-intellectualism are natural outgrowths of such a system. There can be little doubt that much of the turmoil permeating modern society has its roots in an antiquated, uncivilized educational system. How can educational technology change this system?

1. It can permit the *organization* of knowledge so that the teacher need no longer be the central figure in the learning situation. We are beginning to think in terms of learning methods rather than teaching methods. When learning is systematized so that it becomes more logical and available to the student through technology, then the role of the teacher can change to that of counselor and fellow-learner rather than taskmaster and paymaster.

2. Technology can *humanize* education. At present, education operates to great extent by the law of claw and fang. As technology takes over, each learner finds himself on a path of discovery that leads to the horizon and beyond rather than in a series of hotly contested foot races where few are winners. Thus the entire pattern of relations can change so that it represents the more humane aspects of our co-operative society.

3. Once education has broken out of the strictures of its current pattern and freed the learner to proceed at his own pace—motivated internally rather than by external forces—his outlook will change. He will come to regard learning as one of man's most significant pursuits, not merely a means to an end, but an end in itself. For, in this age of technology with its potentials for the reduction of labor needed to provide the daily necessities, learning will be the major challenge left to the mind and spirit of an intelligent being? With technology to extend the power of the brain to store and recover information, the dawn of learning and true education is only beginning.

Specific Applications—Media Services and Captioned Films

G. H. Rathe, Jr., in discussing the use of Computer-Assisted Instruction with deaf children states, "the primary advantage of CAI in teaching deaf children is that it does not discriminate between the deaf and the nondeaf." In effect the computer compensates for the handicapping condition and presents stimuli that are within the possibility of the handicapped child's response abilities based upon theoretical learning sequences.

If these promises are to be realized, it is important that the Federal Government's program of Media Services and Captioned Films for handicapped children must expand its services to include the following over the next 10 years:

1. To have an effective program of instructional technology, every classroom must be equipped with certain basic equipment. In the case of the deaf, the overhead projector, filmstrip projector, and screens were considered the minimal hardware of the initial phase completed at this time. More complex equipment must follow and the program must be expanded to other areas.

2. Hardware requires software. To make significant use of media equipment the class must have ready access to substantial amounts of significant resource materials. These are likely to be most effective if treated as a part of the total learning resources available in the school, hence library and audiovisual center become one

in the modern school. A study has already been made to set standards for such centers. These must be periodically updated and extensive developmental production must be undertaken to provide handicapped learners with the special materials which they need.

3. Innovations in use of technology in schools do not occur to any marked extent unless the administration is interested and understands the potentials. To create this kind of interest and understanding the Captioned Films program has held a series of annual symposiums on technology and the education of the deaf, inviting heads of schools to attend and participate. This orientation of top and middle management personnel of schools must go forward at an accelerated pace.

4. Teachers do not automatically adopt and use new methods when they are presented. Training is necessary. This is being accomplished through summer institutes, inservice demonstrations in schools and consultation provided through regional media centers. Expansion of these functions are important facets of a long range program.

5. Technological innovation does not consist merely of adopting what is already known but in discovering or developing new media—in short, research. In this particular program, applied research has been supported which has as its ultimate goal some direct application to the education of the deaf child. There has been an attempt to press for pragmatic answers to urgent problems within the limitations of a small budget. The primary aim was research and development that could be translated into classroom use. The next 10 years call for much more of this kind of activity as well as basic research.

Establishing the educational aspects of this program has required five years. It is evident, however, that changes are occurring. As new buildings are planned and constructed, provisions are being made for individual study carrels, closed circuit TV conduits and central learning resource centers directed by trained media specialists. Experimentation is going on in providing educational television for the deaf. In residential schools this is designed to serve both the classroom and living quarters so that the school day, in effect, is being extended. Teacher training centers are beginning to express interest in providing pre-service training in the use of new media and are asking for equipment to help make this possible. Teachers and students are beginning to develop their own innovative learning materials and are seeking ways to share these materials with others. These and many other new developments indicate that change is beginning to occur.

Expansion of Media Services to All Areas of the Handicapped

The long range goal for this service envisions that every classroom for handicapped children will have sufficient equipment with respect to hardware and software to deliver a maximum quality educational program to these children. At that time each classroom for handicapped children will have appropriate support systems to allow for individual prescribed instruction for all children.

1. A national media network for handicapped children will be established through the combining of the existing Regional Media Centers and Instructional Materials Centers for the handicapped.

2. Curriculum Development Centers must be established for the handicapped.

3. A systematic development of *Exemplary Mediated Teaching Environments* must be developed for each area of the handicapped capable of extensive and sophisticated evaluation of both process and content with respect to instructional technology.

4. Instructional Materials Centers must be developed at the building and system level for handicapped children.

5. Learning Resource Centers must be developed on a state and/or regional basis capable of developing individualized prescribed instruction. These centers would be capable of providing both computer-aided instruction and computer-monitored instruction to any classroom within their area.

In order to develop this system careful thought must be given to goals, process and materials, distribution, implementation and evaluation. There are a number of questions that may be raised by such a program. Who will set the goals? Will the process and materials dominate the curriculum or will curriculum dominate the development of process and materials? How and to whom will the materials be distributed? How will new and innovative programs be implemented on a large scale? What method of evaluation will be developed to assure efficiency of learning and cost-effectiveness? What will be the relation among Federal, State, and local educational agencies? What part will the education industries play in the development of such programs? Can educational industries develop total programs which school districts will purchase? Will these programs include content, the learning environment, and the personnel? How will the rights of the local education systems be maintained in such areas as the critical choice of curriculum? How will schools establish their own unique curriculum?

It is obvious that certain activities must be done at an overall level or the Federal level since large scale development and implementation of newer instructional technology will call for massive outlays of capital investments. For the same reasons some functions may be handled most effectively at the State level. Both of these systems can ultimately provide a wider choice at the local level for the building of curriculum items, therefore, widening the local participation in the development of curriculum for handicapped children.

It is our belief that the development of Captioned Films for the Deaf and the Instructional Materials Centers for other areas of the handicapped are providing a base for the Federal section of this program. The most urgent need of all areas of instructional technology, however, remains at the software level.

The major dissemination of didactic material going into the system will be through an electronic complex based upon regional, local, and national inputs. It will be computer-monitored and computer-based capable of a full range of auditory, visual, and tactile input to the child's interface with the learning process.

The completed system envisions local participation at the classroom and school level. Each school unit will have media and educational technologist knowledgeable in hardware and software. Sufficient additional equipment in terms of portable projectors, tape recorders, etc. that can be taken from the classroom to the home will supplement the electronic network. Specially tailored programs for the individual child's needs will be developed at the local level so that his formal learning experience can be expanded beyond the time and space limitations of the classroom.

The first level of involvement will be with the teacher and the learning process. A major shift in teacher-pupil relations will be required. Emphasis will be shifted from the "teaching process" to the "learning process." The professional educator will become a learning mentor capable of calling upon a wide variety of resources to assist the learner ranging from tutors to individual computer-monitored programs.

The second level of involvement will be support staff at the school unit level. Assistant teachers, librarians, media specialists, programmers, technicians, and technologists will be available to support the pupil and teacher through on-shelf materials and limited production of teaching aides and special units for specific children.

The basic individualized instruction systems will come from systemwide or third level data banks. This level will be located at either a large school system or a combination of small schools bound together into a satellite program for media development and transmission electronically of individualized learning sequences. This will be controlled, developed, and maintained at an intermediate level between the classroom and statewide system. It will have massive storage and retrieval capabilities.

The fourth level in the total network will be based at the State department of education. The prime activity of the State center is to provide information and collation of operational programs throughout its State. It will not maintain large data banks of individualized materials but will provide a storage and retrieval system for infrequently used and special resource materials.

The fifth level of the total network complex will be Instructional Materials Centers and Regional Media Centers which, by this time, will have evolved into research and development curriculum centers, capable of developing software, producing software, evaluating software, and disseminating it to the various substrata of the system.

Looking toward this future one sees the need for continuing massive support for acquisition of equipment, development and testing of materials, teacher training, stimulation of administrators and applied and basic research. As soon as possible, efforts must be made to reach into the preschool area and to provide training for parents that will enable them to become more effectively involved in the learning experiences of their children. Where children are handicapped or seriously disadvantaged, provision should be made for financial support to enable the parents to give more time to the handicapped child, especially at very early ages. In too many instances other family responsibilities of the parent deny the handicapped or disadvantaged child the attention that he should receive. To some extent television can help reach these parents, but, as with teachers, they will not necessarily adopt new ways just by being exposed. More intensive training is required. Through the use of new media this training can be vitalized and made widely available in ways that will be attractive and compelling.

Finally, adult education should be stimulated through media. Among the many possibilities of the involvement of new media in this area of education, motion picture production offers some of the most exciting possibilities. Although motion pictures are one of the most widely consumed art forms in America, few people are actively engaged in amateur production of films. That film study and film production at the grass roots level could do much to elevate the cultural level of the country seems obvious. To go back to our point of departure here is one sample of how use of technology can open a pathway of discovery not only for the youthful learner but for persons of all ages.

Administration and Authority

The immediate administrative structure and legal authority to provide the system outlined above is the Division of Educational Services and the Division of Research, Bureau of Education for the Handicapped. The legal authority is found in P.L. 85-905 as amended by P.L. 87-715, P.L. 89-258, P.L. 90-247, and P.L. 88-164. These laws authorizing Media Services and Captioned Films to expand its authority to educational development of media for all areas of the handicapped and authorize research in the development, production, and distribution of materials so that handicapped children may have a basic education equal to non-handicapped children.

The Regional Media Centers for the Deaf are funded through the Division of Educational Services, while the Instructional Materials Centers are funded through the Division of Research.

e. IT/Special Applications

83.
Instructional Technology
And Vocational Education

by *RUPERT N. EVANS, HENRY SREDL, BRIAN CARSS, and ROBERT W. WALKER**
College of Education
University of Illinois

General and Vocational Education—A Relationship

"World of work" has been a phrase heard in one form or another with increasing frequency since the early 1960s. The recommendations made by the late President Kennedy's Panel of Consultants on Vocational Education focused on preparation for the world of work and subsequently on the place of vocational education in the American public school structure: in a sense, the Panel's report marked the beginning of a period of respectability for educating the young and old for work. It is unfortunate, however, that it took a combination of a shortage of skilled manpower, growing unrest in the ghetto, and a clear challenge from a prestigious group such as the Panel to give vocational education respectability. Man has achieved his dominant role on this planet because of his ability, need and desire to work, and preparation for this work has been an integral part of his existence.

In a discussion embracing both vocational and general education, the problem of definitions is one that cannot be taken lightly. Vocational education has been defined in its broadest sense as "education preparatory to the entering of all occupations, both professional and non-professional, and thus encompassing the entire educational process."[1]

Most vocational educators would feel that this definition is both too broad and too narrow: too broad because vocational education as the term is commonly used does not include occupations for which a baccalaureate or higher degree is required for entrance; too narrow because it refers only to education for entering the occupation. Vocational education includes programs for employed workers. A commonly accepted definition is provided by the United States Department of Health, Education and Welfare in a 1960

Rupert N. Evans is Professor of Vocational and Technical Education, Bureau of Educational Research, College of Education, University of Illinois.

publication. Vocational education is education whose "controlling purpose . . . is to fit persons for useful employment." Vocational education "does not take the place of general . . . education: It supplements and enhances it for students who want training for a chosen occupation"[2] or a group of closely related occupations. Technical education is that part of vocational education which requires more extensive and intensive instruction, and usually is offered at the post-secondary school level.

This supplementary relationship between general and vocational education is the key to effective preparation for an increasingly complex world, a place which for most people is basically a world of work. Individuals have always prepared for a "place" in their world. Some prepared for occupations through formal schooling. Others prepared through apprenticeship programs, while still others prepared by imitation or by trial and error. Before the Industrial Revolution, the method used to prepare for the world of work was not extremely important: the technology used in industry was not rapidly changing, and time was not the factor in preparation for work that it is today.

As man found sources of energy to replace human and other animal power in industry, he was able to produce more products more efficiently. Since the Industrial Revolution, man's efficiency in industry has not only resulted in a different way of life but a different way of work and a different way of preparing for work. Technology demands more highly educated workers, and the availability of such workers permits a more sophisticated technology which demands still more highly educated workers. Both general and vocational education are required.

Most educators recognize that physicians who were once educated by apprenticeship must now complete a long program of general and vocational education. Similar changes in the occupational requirements for technicians and skilled workers are less extensive and more recent, so they are not perceived as clearly by the public. This leads to naive statements such as "industry prefers to train its own" being applied to all occupational education requiring less than the baccalaureate degree for entrance. Even in those highly specialized occupations where industry does not prefer to train its own, industry discriminates against certain groups (e.g. the less intelligent and the members of certain minority groups). This forces action by the public schools.

Two basic curricula should be offered in the community college (and in the secondary school until we arrive at a point in time when virtually all students have an opportunity to attend the community college). These two curricula, college preparatory and vocational, should each have substantial general education content. Approximately four times as many students should be enrolled in vocational curricula as in college preparatory. Even with considerable grouping by occupational families, probably 100-200 different vocational and technical programs need to be offered if students are to have the broad range of opportunities they need. This number is approximately the same as the number of different occupational specialties offered in a university for students who plan to enter the professions. Assuming approximately equal costs for development of software for vocational and for professional (including college preparatory) curricula, an enormous amount of money would be required. PSSC physics, a professional (not general education) course offered in many high schools, spent several million dollars on the development of instructional materials. Employment in physics and in the other professions needing the content of PSSC physics is small as compared with most of the occupational clusters taught in vocational education. Actually there is more general education in a vocational auto mechanics course than in a PSSC physics course.

General education is that part of the curriculum which prepares an individual to be a functioning member in his society. Since the American society is highly industrialized, general education must provide students with a basic understanding of the industrial aspect of that society. But if an educational system is to be complete, it cannot stop with informing individuals about their world in general: it must prepare each one for a functioning, contributing role in that world. Thus the educational system cannot be complete without the mating of general and vocational education.

While many educators and laymen agree to this relationship, the agreement has caused more conflict than harmony. Too much time has been spent attempting to identify the dividing point between general and vocational education, a point which in reality does not exist. Not enough time has been devoted to providing meaningful relationships between general education and vocational education. Whether a specific program is in fact general or vocational depends largely on the purposes and needs of the student. Vocational education is a means of building knowledges, skills, and attitudes toward the world of work, but it is also a method of developing certain individuals whose cognitive styles are not well suited to learning through verbal means. It is a means of social mobility for certain students. And, perhaps most important, it is a process which conveys to the student the relevance of certain parts of general education (and perhaps, by implication, the irrelevance of certain other parts).[3]

It is the contention of this paper that no amount of investment in instructional technology is worth anything, unless the curriculum material that is offered to the students is relevant. Relevance is a topic that is particularly timely. It asks whether the education that students receive during their school days and college days bears any relationship to the lives they will lead once they leave school.

The Use of Instructional Technology in Vocational Education from the 1940s to the Present

In public schools, and to an even greater extent in military schools and in training programs within industry, instructors of vocational education and the other practical arts have made far greater use of instructional technology than have teachers of most other subjects. Of this group, the driver education teacher probably uses instructional technology most extensively.

Undoubtedly the greatest use in vocational education has been that of simulated equipment. Whenever safety, cost, and space considerations permit, vocational education usually uses equipment, materials, and processes which are identical to those used in employment. However, much of the equipment used in each occupation is relatively unsuitable for instruction because its operating parts are concealed or because it is so sophisticated that the functions needed for instruction are obscured by refinements added for other purposes. All of these considerations have led to the use of simulated equipment. Unfortunately, little of this equipment is designed specifically for instruction. Rather, it is selected by instructors as being most useful from the array of equipment designed for other purposes, typically for laboratory testing or for low rates of production. Unfortunately, it is not always immediately clear whether a vocational shop uses older, simpler types of equipment because this equipment is more suitable for instruction or because no funds are available for replacement even though the equipment is obsolete for instructional purposes. It is certain, however, that criticisms of obsolescence of equipment are often unfounded. Indeed in home economics where manufacturers give new equipment to the school each year, the equipment is so complex and so atypical of lower class homes that it is quite unsuitable for instruction. In vocational machine shops a simple engine lathe is often used instead of a complex automatic lathe. The engine lathe has not changed significantly in 100 years, but the automatic lathe changes very frequently. Eninger found that the transition from instructional equipment to production equipment was accomplished in an amazingly short time—often in minutes.[4]

Other instructional devices which have been used heavily include models, mock-ups, cut-aways and the like to simplify instruction on complex equipment, materials, and processes. Most of these have been constructed individually by teachers, but a perusal of catalogs such as those prepared by Brodhead-Garrett of Cleveland, Ohio and the Vocational Agriculture Service of the University of Illinois, reveals a considerable range of instructional materials which are available for purchase or rent.

Sixteen millimeter films are available in large variety. But they, like the equipment, have too often been designed for some purpose other than instruction. Thirty-five millimeter slides are frequently made by teachers, especially in agriculture and home economics. Slides and filmstrips are also available in considerable variety from commercial sources. Commercial material prepared for the over-head projector is now becoming more widely available.

All of the visual media are dominated by software which is designed to sell commercial equipment, materials, and services, rather than to aid the instructor. Problems of timing the arrival of a rented or borrowed visual aid interfere with instruction. Too often it arrives after it is needed, but the teacher proceeds to show it anyway because it is there.

Visual aids are a perfectly natural tool for vocational education because such a high proportion of content can be introduced visually. The tape recorder, however, is little used in spite of the fact that much trouble-shooting is done by sound. Vocational teachers usually wait until a sound occurs accidentally, and then attempt to incorporate it into the instructional process.

Books have been relatively little used for two reasons: first, they, like visual materials, have often been produced for some reason other than instruction. Catalogs and handbooks have been common fare in specialized fields which have not had the high enrollment, and hence potentially high sales, of homemaking and agriculture.

Secondly, in many schools, students who enroll in vocational education have selected themselves out of the verbal learning style of the college preparatory curriculum. Their cognitive styles cope more readily with non-verbal learning. Since many of the vocational teachers have similar cognitive styles, books tend to be under-utilized. Books are used more frequently in technical education than in the lower levels of vocational education.

In spite of the fact that instructional technology has been used more extensively in vocational education than in most other school institutions, it has tended to be used piecemeal, rather than as part of an instructional system. One reason for this is the amount of teacher education provided to vocational instructors. Instructors in trade and industrial education in many states have a bare minimum of teacher education. A total of eight semester hours, accumulated after induction into teaching, is common. Teachers of adult, evening classes often have no teacher education.

Secondly, the tendency has been not to plan a curriculum, with supporting instructional technology, but rather to assemble bits and pieces of instrumental technology off the shelf, even if they were not suitable for instructional purposes.

The Needs of Vocational Education
for Instructional Technology

Professor Torsten Husen of Stockholm recently expressed "some thoughts concerning educational technology" in the *International Review of Education*.[5] While his thoughts reflected on education in general, they are especially applicable to that curriculum area responsible for introducing students to the world of work in an industrial society. Professor Husen mused that

> The practices that we observe in the educational plants of the industrially developed countries are still on the whole pre-industrial. This applies to 1) utilization of teaching personnel; 2) availability of teaching aids, . . . and 3) management and

administration. Teaching personnel of professional caliber are assigned to all sorts of school tasks, many of which could adequately be performed by janitors.[6]

Most of any teacher's time is devoted to the management of classwork and asking and answering questions. The vocational teacher contributes to learning because of his employment experience, but this contribution is often limited to demonstrations and critiques, and certainly demonstrations usually could be provided more meaningfully and with greater visibility and accuracy through audiovisual devices. Maryann Bitzer states the problem well:[7]

> Presently, the students are prepared for clinical experience by the traditional method of lecture, demonstration, and supervised practice. With this approach, the objectives of creative thinking and understanding may be attained, but are also often unconsciously prevented instead. One way this may be done is by demonstrating habitual actions to the inexperienced student. In these habitual actions, the intermediate steps which represent critical thinking are not shown to the student. The result is that the student learns the problem and the action, but not the process by which the action is developed from the problem.

The role of instructional technology in preparing individuals for the world of work appears clear. Instructional technology must provide the means to consider and account for individual human differences, as varied as they are, while preparing each person for a place in the working world; it must provide for differentiated staffing and CAI to handle the wide variety of tasks associated with education and to provide for the efficient utilization of both student and teacher time.

Instructional Technology—Three Contributions

Instructional technology can and must contribute to three aspects of education for the world of work. First, and perhaps most important, it must contribute to the motivation of students; it must help to create in each one the desire to become not only an active but a contributing member of this world. Second, instructional technology must assist in offering every individual the information and skill development needed to function in the world of work. Finally, instructional technology must contribute to the continuing education required of all working individuals.

    1. The contribution instructional technology can make in motivating students to learn about this world is an exciting one and should start at the earliest level of education. Anyone who has had the least contact with primary and pre-primary grade children has sensed the sheer enthusiasm, inquisitiveness, naivete, and fantasy so wonderfully common to this age group. Without the help of formal education these little people could be forming impressions of the world of work. Two generations ago, if you spoke to a child, or listened clandestinely to a group of youngsters at play, you would have learned some interesting things about the world of work. Children's play often revolves around the roles of respected adults with whom they have had recent contact. If their contact has not been with such people, their play revolves around the roles of story-book and television figures. With increasing specialization, increasing distance between home and work, and increasing security regulations by employers, the child gets fewer and fewer concepts of work from his parents and from his neighborhood.

    At this time in an individual's life, entertaining and enjoyable activities dominate his learning. Because of this, there is often little distinction between playing and learning; playing is fun and play which revolves around life-like situations is even more fun. Instructional technology at this beginning level of education could easily provide the means through which the education of the young can be expanded. To get an idea of where to start building such a system one needs only to take a slow walk through the toy department of any large department store. Successful toy manufacturers, individuals engaged in one of the most fiercely competitive businesses, have survived because they have been able to offer middle-class children technological hardware (toys) to satisfy and challenge the imagination. Toys which represent actual life situations including those pertaining to the world of work have gained an important place in the life of many (but unfortunately not of all) children.

Unfortunately, a change in the teaching-learning pattern occurs as a child progresses through the elementary grades. The individual's desire to learn, see and hear new things may not have changed but the process by which he obtains new information has changed. He becomes part of an audience held captive by an educational system which sets as its highest value, success in additional education, rather than success in living a full life. Learning about the world of work must be incorporated into the school. This learning lends intelligibility to much of the traditional school program. The imaginative application of instructional technology and the commitment of necessary monies are the only major barriers to a completely new, exciting and enjoyable learning about the world of work.

Instructional technology and its place in the motivation of students must not stop with the elementary grades. As a student matures, the sophistication of the instructional technology may also mature but the emphasis on motivation must remain. A working example of this point may be observed through a visit to one of the nationally advertised amusement parks (e.g., Disneyland, Six Flags Over Texas, etc.). A new pattern indirectly dealing with the world of work has emerged with the growth of these facilities. In effect, these parks are systems employing technological applications, many of which relate to instruction. While education is not the primary goal of these operations, the successful satisfaction of human needs allows learning to take place. In these parks both children and adults drive automobiles, "fly" airplanes, ride in and engineer trains, operate earth-moving vehicles and engage in many other activities common to the world of work. On a more sophisticated level, the world's fairs have provided similar educational experiences. It is perhaps at these fairs that the application of instructional technology to learning about the world of work is most evident. Learning about basic computer theory when one learns in a world's fair pavilion is, unfortunately, quite different from exposure to the same subject matter in the traditional classroom. The imaginative application of instructional technology at the fair makes the difference. Unfortunately, again the lower class child has relatively few opportunities to visit Disneyland and World's Fairs.

2. The second contribution instructional technology can make to the preparation of each student for the world of work focuses on the development of occupational goals of the student. Almost all counseling and guidance in public schools is concentrated in the high school and is devoted to educational planning. Usually this educational planning is designed for the college preparatory student. Students in the general and vocational curricula are used to balance out classes to achieve an economic student-staff ratio. Individual counseling is nearly an impossible task when so few counselors are well prepared and each counselor is responsible for 300 or so students. Computer-assisted counseling seems to offer real promise in providing individual counseling, and in providing information about the world of work. Most counselors have no knowledge or interest in work outside the professions.

The world of work involves more than fun and play and as the student becomes more mature, exposure to the world of work must become increasingly realistic. In the primary grades a general, comprehensive knowledge of the world of work is the goal. As the student advances, the terminal goal for each must include competencies which will allow him to take a working place in the world. However, since the world of work and the student are both changing, a student may and probably will have more than one terminal goal in relation to the world of work; each of these goals must allow him to function and contribute to this world of work whenever he decides to enter it formally.

It is in this phase of education that the use of instructional technology has received the greatest recognition to date. During the last five years much hardware has been developed to relieve the classroom teacher of routine, repetitive tasks. This hardware has the potential to enable students to study subject matter on an individual basis. Unfortunately, however, use of such hardware has generally been limited to those schools which have qualified for special Federal financial assistance. Even here, the necessary software is largely absent. The work of Ziel and his associates at the University of Alberta in Edmonton gives a hint of what could be accomplished. Programmed materials, single concept films, audio tapes, and slides are integrated in a system which introduces students to new equipment and processes in some ten stations within the practical arts laboratory. The educational effectiveness is very high.

The application of instructional technology at higher levels of learning can do more than relieve the teacher of mundane tasks. The hardware of instructional technology can be used as part of a total system which focuses on the individual. Total environments and specific problems can be simulated. While still foreign to public education, this application is not new to industry and the armed forces. Airlines have for many years looked to the aircraft simulator in preparing pilots. The space program involves nearly exact simulation as an integral part of its total educational program. Industry is increasingly using the computer to referee gaming situations which they hope will prepare decision-making executives for future roles. In addition to the use of the computer for educational and occupational counseling, it has marked potential for direct vocational instruction. At the University of Illinois, the work of Bitzer in using Plato for instruction in nursing gives a foretaste of what can be done. There is a remarkable gap between simulation for the very young through toys, and simulation for highly technical education. Obviously, little thought has been given to simulation for adolescents and for vocational education.

3. The third contribution instructional technology can make to learning about the world of work relates to continuing education. In a working world where change must be a part of life, continuing education must provide the means for individuals to maintain a proficient level of production. Continuing education must also provide the means for one to change his role in the world of work. This education must not be limited to a selected few whose needs and wants coincide with the needs and wants of traditional education. It should be an experience common to and sought by every individual. In this phase of learning, both motivation and realism are perhaps even more important than they are in the education of youth. Too often existing programs are extensions of the traditional classrooms which have provided an unsuccessful environment for previous learning. Instructional technology in continuing education can play a leading role in both motivation and learning. The exact nature and content of instruction will be determined by individual needs. Ideally, the content of continuing education should differ little from that of other school programs, but in practice, the individuals involved insist on instruction that is applicable immediately and are often unwilling to accept bland assurances of general education value.

The Role of Industry in Education

There are those who feel that the increased use of instructional technology will take direction for curricula or planning away from the educators and will give the curriculum director's role to the business world which will stand to profit from such developments. But educators have already surrendered their role of leadership in many instances and the surrender has not always been detrimental to the student. When children learn more about the molding of plastics from a kit which can be purchased for a few dollars in a toy store than they do in the school, more about anatomy through the construction of a toy plastic skeleton, more about the thrust of a solid fuel reaction engine through the electrical firing of a sixty-five cent solid fuel reaction engine, one cannot but wonder who is really providing the leadership in learning about the world of work. The business world is rapidly realizing that the inquisitive mind of a child makes learning a satisfaction, a relished experience, and that catering to this mind can be, in addition to other things, economically desirable. If businessmen can teach middle-class children and make money doing it, perhaps educators should take a look at some of the methods used here to see if they can be made available to *all* children.

Educating children is not the only activity of the business world. One four-year-old firm claims to provide among other things a "basic-education" for adults who have not learned the three R's in school. The price for this is $300 to $500 per person depending on how much monitoring of the instructional materials the firm must provide. One can question the validity of such education, which is based on individual student progress, the use of tapes, and so on, but in doing so he should know that 130 companies in thirty-nine states have already subscribed to the program in an attempt to supply themselves with people who can function in the world of work, and another two hundred companies are negotiating contracts; some of these firms include America's blue-chip corporations.

This paper cannot cover the extensive programs maintained by large corporations for the development of their employees or their role as a contracting agent for federally sponsored education. A good recent treatment of this subject has been published by the Departments of Labor and Commerce.[8]

The Role of the Vocational Teacher

Perhaps the key factor in successfully using instructional technology in preparing people for the world of work is the human factor, the teacher himself. Terminal education for the world of work on the secondary school level is presently taught by individuals who have had employment experience in the field which they are teaching. A large percentage of these teachers have learned their occupational skills through the traditional method of trial and error, on-the-job instruction. Today a man's qualification for a job in many occupations lies not in his native intelligence and his ability to learn from trial and error, but in his ability to pursue a training program for a specific period of time. An individual who established his occupational competence in the traditional way is not likely to abandon the system which worked for him and relegate much of his teaching responsibility, however routine and repetitious it may be, to a mechanized alternative. Hence, instructors who have acquired their occupational competence recently in employment where instructional technology has been used, are more likely to adopt instructional technology when they become vocational teachers.

The Two Major Issues

Many uncertainties are associated with the contributions of instructional technology to vocational education; many "how" questions are implied. The question of funding is certainly a basic one. But overriding these are two major issues: to what extent do we want as a nation, state, or local school system to prepare individuals for a functioning, contributing place in the world of work, and are we willing to adapt education to meet the needs of students who have different cognitive styles. Once these two questions are answered, much of the remainder falls into place. But to provide lip service to supporting change, to encourage teachers and curriculum people to revise existing materials, to feel that a new set of transparencies on a particular subject is marked progress, to feel that fancy teaching hardware is changing the learning situation and to hold isolated educational innovations as proof of this progress will not really change the human product, the graduate or dropout as we know him today.

As the world of work has increased in complexity, the cost of preparing for this world has increased. The final contribution instructional technology can make to the preparation of individuals for the world of work will be determined and limited only by the value we place on such preparation.

As we recognize that we are failing to provide an education attuned to the cognitive styles of many of our students, the complexity of educational planning will increase. The role of instructional technology in educational planning as well as in teaching is certain to increase. This is not to say that instructional technology has all of the answers. A practical and perhaps less expensive alternate to equipment purchase might be the provision of funds for transporting students to learn about the world of work, especially at the primary levels. In this sense, however, perhaps a bus may be viewed as a part of instructional technology.

Recommendations

1. There should be continued work on computer-assisted guidance and counseling systems, with heavy emphasis on preparation for the upgrading in, the world of work.

2. Teacher education programs should give greater emphasis to effective use of instructional technology. The need is greatest in adult education where teachers often have no preparation. Highly automated or self-instructing teaching devices would be very useful here.

3. Vocational education programs for technicians to assist in designing, developing, producing, operating, and maintaining instructional technology systems should be established. More extended educational programs for engineers may also be needed for this field of work.

4. The creative products of the toy industry, displays at museums, and fairs, and many other para-instructional efforts are relatively unavailable to low-income portions of society. This requires special efforts both in compensatory education to make up for their lack, and to incorporate the best of their products and services into the educational program.

5. Rapid changes in materials and methods used in the world of work cause rapid obsolescence of instructional materials in certain phases of vocational education. Similar rapid obsolescence occurs in some parts of general education. Such changes require a system for modifying instructional materials and for disseminating these revised materials.

6. Preparation of instructional materials by individual instructors is hopelessly inefficient. Instructors should have a variety of materials from which to choose, should have facilities for modifying materials, and a feedback system should be provided to enable producers of instructional materials to know of needed modifications and of modifications made by users.

7. The hardware needed for vocational education and for general education will

be almost identical, and the software will be more similar than is generally now thought. But the needs of vocational education will not be served by the common assumption of academicians that instruction which is designed for preparation for college will serve all students.

8. Vocational education should serve a large majority of students, and the amount of money required for instructional materials for this broadened vocational education will be at least as high as for college preparatory courses.

9. Experimental laboratories and classrooms specifically designed to make optimum use of educational technology should be developed for vocational education. Efforts of this type have in the past emphasized large lecture settings.

10. Much of the equipment in vocational education is selected for its simulation value. Yet most of the instruction assumes that the equipment is "real." Research and demonstration projects are needed on the effective use of simulators in vocational education.

REFERENCES

1. Personal letter from Bruce A. Campbell, Project Director, Industrial Test Development Section, Science Research Associates to Samuel M. Burt, Dec. 27, 1965, quoted by Samuel M. Burt in *Industry and Vocational-Technical Education,* McGraw-Hill Book Co., New York, 1967, p. viii.

2. United States Department of Health, Education and Welfare. *Public Vocational Education Programs.* United States Government Printing Office, 1960, p. 1.

3. For a further discussion of these points, see Mangum, Garth, *Reorienting Vocational Education* (Policy Paper in Human Responses and Industrial Relations #7, Institute of Labor and Industrial Relations, Ann Arbor, Mich.; Feldman, Marvin, *Making Education Relevant* (New York: Ford Foundation, 1966) Vocational Education: The Bridge Between Man and His Work (Publication 1 of the Advisory Council on Vocational Education, Center for Studies in Vocational and Technical Education, University of Wisconsin, Madison, Wis., 1968.

4. Eninger, Max. *Vocational Education, Process and Product.* American Institutes of Research, Pittsburgh, 1966.

5. Husen, Torsten. "Some Thoughts Concerning Educational Technology." *International Review of Education,* 13:1, 1967, pp. 6-13.

6. Ibid., p. 6.

7. Bitzer, Maryann. "Clinical Nursing Instruction Via the Plato Simulated Laboratory." *Nursing Research,* Vol. 15, No. 2, Spring, 1966.

8. Task Force on Occupational Training in Industry. "A Governmental Commitment to Occupational Training in Industry." 1968, Dept. of Labor, Washington, D.C.

84.
Museums, Media,
And Immediacy

by *RICHARD GROVE**
Staff Member
Arts in Education Program
JDR 3rd Fund

The primary, and characteristic, instructional medium employed by museums is the exhibition. It is very nearly peculiar to them, although trade fairs and international expositions sometimes use related communication means. In the sense in which it is being used here, an exhibition is a particular kind of learning environment: a planned, sequential, three dimensional, walk-through presentation employing a special set of elements.[1] These elements include space, light, color, sound, objects, works of art, words (in printed and recorded form), photographs, motion pictures, and occasionally touch and smell.[2] An expert exhibition designer casts the "message," effectively and economically, in terms which exploit the unique characteristics of the medium. You sense immediately that it could have been done in no other way.

Good exhibitions, of course, have always successfully spoken their own language. In recent times, however, museums, aware of the present-day theory and practice of programmed instruction and of general developments in the field of instructional technology, have undertaken increasingly sophisticated experiments in an effort to improve the educational effectiveness of exhibitions, to find out what works and what does not, and to make new knowledge and techniques available to the exhibition designer.[3] Two illustrative examples, still in progress at the time of this writing (October, 1968), are educational research projects funded by the Bureau of Research, U.S. Office of Education.[4] The first of these is going on at the Boston Childrens Museum and is entitled "Development of Validated Museum Exhibits." The project created an exhibition, designed modularly and readily alterable, which attempts to communicate a series of concepts (types of teeth and their functions) to young children. Results were directly observed and manipulative responses (the children work levers, push buttons, etc.) were recorded electronically. The researchers then tried to improve those components which were unsuccessful with considerable numbers of children so as to arrive finally at an exhibition pre-tested for educational effectiveness.

The second project is a joint undertaking by the University of Wisconsin-Milwaukee and the Milwaukee Public Museum. The principal investigator, C. G. Screven, describes the project's objectives as follows:

**At the time this paper was written (August 1968) Mr. Grove was Museum Education Specialist, Arts and Humanities Program, U.S. Office of Education.*

The research currently being conducted at the Milwaukee Public Museum is developing and testing experimental procedures for (a) obtaining continuing measurement of the pre-exhibit knowledge (entering knowledge) of the museum visitor, as well as his knowledge after seeing the museum display (exit knowledge), (b) securing the active involvement of the individual visitor with the concepts of the exhibits, (c) controlling the order in which a visitor attends to particular display elements, (d) adapting a fixed display to different age, educational and social backgrounds of visitors, and (e) selectively rewarding successful visitor performance . . .

Briefly, the chief goal is the design of a learning system which allows the visitor to interact with and be directed through the exhibit in such a way that learning occurs and the instructional objective of the exhibit is achieved. This system will eventually consist of three components: (1) the exhibit itself (including labels), (2) a device for presenting a set of programmed questions requiring the visitor to attend to specific aspects of the exhibit, and (3) a tape playback unit worn by the visitor containing conversational material which directs attention and emphasizes points.[5]

The present discussion is concerned with the more specifically didactic exhibition, whether in science, history or art museums. There are entirely valid uses of the exhibition which eschew this function, requiring the visitor to bring with him relevant informational and contextual data, or to seek them out elsewhere. In art museums, the latter view has a lengthy history and the extent to which the strictly educational function of the museum shall be stressed remains a live issue. "Art is an end," said Benjamin Ives Gilman in an article first published in 1904, "education a means to an end."

The office of an art museum is one which is warranted in itself; that of an educational museum is one whose fruits are its warrant.

Thus neither in scope nor in value is the purpose of an art museum a pedagogic one. An institution devoted to the preservation and exhibition of works of the fine arts is not an educational institution, either in essence or in its claims to consideration. While museums of science or of useful art are a part of our educational system, institutions auxiliary to our schools, our colleges and our universities, aiming at the diffusion of information about the sciences and arts to which they relate, museums of fine art are a part of our artistic life, serving the cause, not of any utility, pedagogic or other, but of art itself . . . The distinctive purpose of an art museum may be precisely defined as the aim to bring about that perfect contemplation of the works of art it preserves which is implied in their production and forms their consummation.[6]

"I follow Gilman," said Sherman E. Lee, director of the Cleveland Museum of Art, in a recent article.

The art museum has three major functions—preservation, exhibition, research and education. These are the assigned roles of the art museum in modern society. To this, except for a few fortunate institutions, is added the role of an indigent, marginal suitor for private or public funds. If the art museum is to be a force, whether an obvious or a subtle one, it must take a lesson from the art of war: the numerically inferior army does not disperse its limited powers, but by husbanding its resources and concentrating its blows makes its presence felt. And this presence is a visual one, not so much supported as confused by the simultaneous use of the sounds of Muzak or the words of Acoustiguide.[7]

Within this kind of theoretical structure, the experience of the art museum visitor is usually seen as taking place in a realm remote from language and information.

But by and large art museums today see themselves as having had thrust upon them an aggressive educational role, linked to the social and economic problems of the times. They must define their educational powers and somehow develop a formidable range of abilities. Without losing unity, they must see that scholarly work is not stinted, the essentially nonverbal nature of the visual arts is not betrayed, the connoisseur may confront works of art in something approaching "perfect contemplation," and the bewildered, turned-off, trapped ghetto child may be reached and helped.

Do museums of science, history, and art have special ways to contribute toward solutions of contemporary social and economic problems? To the extent that a museum takes this question seriously, it will be reexamining its function, the characteristics of its audience, and the relevance of traditional museum educational methods. And to that same degree it will be looking to current technological developments for assistance.

There are two other factors which help account for the fact that the museum world greeted the advent of the age of media with something less than passionate acceptance. The first of these is that the museum field is extremely weak in research and development. The second is a frame of mind. Museums are first and foremost places of the unique, the original object. All reproduction is counterfeit, translation into something inauthentic, a swindle for the unsuspecting. Museums, in this view, must hold to their essential purpose with renewed tenacity in a time when people are assailed, violated, saturated with the second-hand reality of the media, the air is full of language, and the impact of the object grows in power and consequence. "Electronic communication," says the Winterthur Museum's Craig Gilborn, "is, after all, every bit as artificial or vicarious as the printed word."

> Rather than liberate, it may yet further serve to restrict and banalize experience . . . Providing first-hand, exploratory experiences for the individual, not just in the classroom but in the larger world as well, is the only way, in the end, of reaching society itself.[8]

At the other theoretical extreme, a recently published brochure announces a proposed "Museum of the Media" in New York City which will be all media and no objects.[9] It will, the announcement sturdily claims, "inaugurate a sweeping change in the form of museums as we know them today."

> The primary function of the traditional museum has been to house and preserve collections of art objects. In this role, the museum has necessarily been confined to rich urban centers.
>
> The exhibits of the Museum of the Media, however, consist of audio tapes, movies, slides and programs. They can therefore . . . be easily and inexpensively duplicated.
>
> The Museum can thus readily make exhibits available to autonomous museums in small towns, suburban communities and ghetto areas which will thus be able for the first time to achieve a cultural parity with the central cities.[10]

Be all *that* as it may, the use of media to allow the museum to reach out beyond its walls is of interest here.

Museum-designed exhibitions themselves, of course, do not necessarily have to be housed in a museum. They may be designed to be packed up and reassembled in all kinds of buildings, including schools (although traveling educational exhibitions for schools are actually quite rare). An exhibition might travel with its own portable building. Or it might be moved from place to place by helicopter, in the manner of those lightweight structures designed by Buckminster Fuller. Or, in a more down to earth fashion (as it were), exhibitions may be designed to fit within boats and tractor-trailers. "In the end," said Stephen White, "the technological device of the first half century which is of most significance to the museum may turn out to be the ten-ton truck."[11] And, far from being hypothetical, museumobiles are on the roads on many parts of the country.

Another possibility, which has intrigued museums for many years, is the decentralization of the museum. Two notable experiments taking place today are the Smithsonian Institution's Anacostia Neighborhood Museum and the Brooklyn Children's Museum's Bedford Lincoln Neighborhood Museum.

With the qualifications stated earlier, museums in the United States have made considerable and often imaginative use of radio, sound recording, slide-tapes, film and television.

Museums of all types use film as an educational instrument and present it as an art form. (The Museum of Modern Art's film library is one of the most important in the world.) Of 2,752 institutions responding to a 1964 questionnaire, 644 reported that they program film showings.[12] Slide-tapes are frequently used as an introduction or adjunct to special exhibitions. Sound recording is widely employed. One familiar device has a funnel-like earpiece attached to flexible tubing. Pluck it from its resting place and it speaks to you. Electronic guide systems are commonplace,[13] usually supplying the visitor with either individually operated little tape recorder playback units, or portable radio receivers, similarly furnished with headphones, which pick up a continuous program emanating from a small broadcasting station. The latter equipment accounts for a curious museum phenomenon: blank-faced, hypnotized-looking people, sprouting antennae and shuffling from gallery to gallery in groups, heads swivelling in unison, rather like schools of fish.

A non-profit, national organization called the Museum Audiovisual Applications Group (MAVAG) meets yearly in connection with the annual meeting of the American Association of Museums. MAVAG publishes a bi-monthly newsletter devoted to "the exchange of information about audiovisual interpretation in museums, parks, zoos and similar non-classroom educational situations." Some of the questions posed by the editor of the *MAVAG Newsletter* in the July-August 1968 issue communicate a kind of indirect message:

> Do *you* need information? Are you having problems with actuating devices? Visitor reactions? Sound-label techniques? Pulse sensing devices? Recording techniques? Application concepts? Projection problems? Motion picture handling equipment? Automated exhibits? Communication and interest enhancement? Automated tours? Resychronization devices?[14]

Many audiovisual devices which are satisfactory in classroom use are ill-suited to continuous, daily museum use. Too, most museums cannot afford to have an audiovisual technician on the staff to attend to the machines.

The facilities and staff required for regular television programming limits it to larger museums. The Museum of Fine Arts in Boston has probably made as great a use of television as any other museum. The museum's Television Supervisor, Patricia Barnard, says that

> Twelve years ago the Boston Museum of Fine Arts decided to make a major commitment to television as an extension of its educational services. Since then we have produced some 1,000 programs—creative art courses for adults; programs for children; the popular IMAGES series, which weaves together photographs of works of art, background narrative, and music, with an end result similar to a motion picture film; and the unique weekly series, currently called MUSEUM OPEN HOUSE, which is produced in the Museum's galleries using our greatest treasures in the original. The Boston Museum was the first and is still the only major art museum completely wired for television.

This museum is one of the few to have attempted to create a characteristically museum use of television.

> We feel that formal art-history courses should be left to the universities. For our programs, aired in prime evening time, we hope to capture and hold a wider, more diverse audience. Television can help prepare the viewer for full appreciation of the actual work of art by stimulating his imagination; camera exploration of a painting, or of a photograph of architecture, can give the illusion of entering the scene and becoming one with it; skillful use of close-ups can give dramatic impact to significant detail; correlation of visual material, music, literature, and history can suggest the atmosphere of the period, culture, and circumstance out of which and for which the work was created.[15]

Museum-produced television programs by no means exhaust the possibilities. Other kinds of uses will undoubtedly be developed as museums explore the use of television in new varieties of multi-media exhibitions. The Metropolitan Museum of Art will open early next year an exhibition entitled "Harlem On My Mind." Thomas P. F. Hoving, the museum director, says

> It will be a multi-media show. In a penultimate gallery of that show there's going to be a closed circuit television set-up: one end in our gallery, the other at 125th Street and 7th Avenue, so that one will be able to have actual communication, conversation and confrontation—which I think is crucially necessary—with the people who live in that area of New York City.[16]

To the best of my knowledge, no one has yet used television and video tape in training teachers and docents, training museum workers (conservators might borrow from some of the television techniques developed for observing surgical operations), or to permit children to make their own taped museum programs for a school audience.

The computer has a great number of possible museum applications. More than one may turn out to have a revolutionary effect. Some uses have already been made; others are as yet only proposals.

The Institute for Computer Research in the Humanities at New York University has been assisting the Metropolitan Museum of Art in unlocking the coded significance of incised marks on Sevres procelain. As a by-product, the computer index was found to be a useful tool for detecting forgeries.

> Sevres has been tampered with and faked more than any other porcelain. Computerized variable indexes can reveal discrepancies with the normal pattern of agreement among the descriptors. Computer searches yielded a series of such discrepancies. It is known that hard paste Sevres procelain was not manufactured before 1768, yet earlier dates for some items were retrieved from the files. These specimens are being rechecked by the Museum.[17]

Other kinds of computer analysis are being done at the Metropolitan Museum of Art.

> "A cathode-ray attachment on a computer is helping us to classify Egyptian pottery," Virginia Burton, assistant curator in the Metropolitan's department of Egyptian art, reported.

> "We've taken the 12th-century Bury St. Edmunds Cross at The Cloisters—it is considered one of the greatest Romanesque ivories in the world—and are developing a computer program for it," William Wilkinson, the museum's registrar, noted. "We hope to come up with something that will enable the museum visitor to make inquiries to the computer and get significant information in depth from it."[18]

A pilot project at the Smithsonian Institution's Museum of Natural History is developing a computerized system of collection management.[19]

> In the Museum of Natural History, where Donald F. Squires is deputy director, there are 50 million specimens—17 million insects, 3 million mammals, birds and fishes, 12 million invertebrate marine animals, 13 million fossils, 3 million botanical specimens, and half a million rocks, minerals and meteorites, to call a part of the roll.

> "And we are adding new specimens at a rate of 1 million a year," Squires went on. "Even so, the problem is not in being able to find the specimens in the collections, but of making information about them immediately available for scientific study." . . .

> "The areas we selected for the pilot study are birds, marine crustacea and rocks," Squires explained. "We wanted to include a wide range of problems found both in the museum and the recording process."

> In time, a visiting scientist may come to the Smithsonian and, instead of groping for days, ask the computer questions such as:

"What insects occur in Colorado? Of these insects, give me a list of those found above an altitude of 8,000 feet. And give me a catalog number so I can go find them." [20]

It is apparent that if information about collections in one museum may be computerized, then information about the collections of several museums may be pooled. The way is then open for a national file: a research instrument and an educational resource of enormous depth and richness. A 1965-1967 study, supported by a National Science Foundation grant, was designed to "investigate the feasibility of inaugurating a nationwide inventory of ethnological specimens in museums and the subsequent creation of a file for that data." The project was limited to Oklahoma museums.

The objectives were to collect data on the time and cost factors in making an inventory, to devise inventory procedures which would provide information useful to scholars and which would insure consistency in the data to be entered into the file, and to experiment with various systems of rapid storage and retrieval . . .

One conclusion, not unexpectedly, was that use of the computer would be costly.

The volume of data projected for the inventory is large, and while at first glance a computer would seem to be the most feasible answer to the problem of manipulation of this data, the volume of data is not the only determining factor. Consideration should also be given to the complexity of data manipulation in the file during searches, the number of requests to be made over a given period of time, the speed with which retrieval of data is desired, the amount of new data to be added and old data to be deleted from the file, and the speed with which entires and deletions must be made. Our pilot study findings suggest that when all these factors are taken into consideration storage and retrieval procedures employing machinery less expensive than electronic computers may be feasible, at least until further developments are made in the computer field. [21]

However, a group of fifteen museums in New York City and the National Gallery of Art in Washington announced in December, 1967 that they have established a project called the Museum Computer Network with an office at the Museum of Modern Art. [22] Everett Ellin, former assistant director of the Solomon R. Guggenheim Museum, is the executive director.

This project will be a super-dossier on art, a vast continuous art book," says Ellin . . . "It will be an in-depth archive that goes beyond a listing and cross-indexing of titles, artists, descriptions, provenances and bibliographic references—even the images of the works will eventually be included in the data."

"All a teacher lecturing on Greek sculpture would have to do is to go to a console, dial a code number and have pictures and an arsenal of information about Greek sculpture available the instant it's needed." [23]

The Museum Computer Network plans to file data from northeastern museums and then proceed to set up a system of terminals in museums, libraries, and other educational institutions. Ties might be made with European museums. Ellin visualizes a new order of "museum without walls":

Ellin sees computers bringing art directly into the homes of the future. "With computerized programs we could call up what we wanted. Every man could become a curator and orchestrate his own exhibitions. The result would be a restoration of the personal eye." [24]

In April, 1968, the Metropolitan Museum of Art, with the aid of a grant from the IBM Corporation, sponsored "A Conference on Computers and Their Potential Applications in Museums." [25] The titles of the sections of this ground-breaking conference suggest the range of applications currently under way or being considered:

1. Documentary Applications

2. Stylistic Analysis by Computer

3. Visual Applications

4. Computerized Museum Networks

5. New Approaches in Museum Education

In a paper presented at the conference, Robert S. Lee, of the IBM Corporation, described a feasible but as yet imaginary "individualized museum environment."

> . . . with the computer, the entire museum visit as a total learning experience can be radically transformed.

> Let us consider, for example, a visit to the art museum of the future. The entrance hall, as is often the case today, might be devoted to setting the mood and orienting the visitor to the diverse possibilities open to him during his stay at the museum. On a high wall at the rear of the room, the visitor would see an everchanging kaleidoscope of projected pictures—these would be of paintings, sculpture and other art objects currently on exhibit throughout the museum. A closer examination of the hall would show that these changing pictures are generated as a result of various choices that visitors make at a number of individual exhibit stations placed throughout the hall. These are special stations where the incoming visitor can make inquiries and get a preview of what is on display in the museum galleries. He could, for example, touch a particular gallery on a map of the museum to call forth a series of slides and commentaries on what he might see there. He would also provide information on his background and his interests, and would give his personal reactions to pictures of various art objects . . .

> At the end of the inquiry session, on the basis of the profile developed on him, the visitor would get a personally tailored set of suggestions as to how he might most benefit from and enjoy his visit to the museum that day. In addition, the visitor would get an individually unique "key card" which he can use to start any of the interaction exhibits that augment the art objects on display in the specialized museum galleries. By means of this key card, the visitor's information profile would be available to all of the computerized exhibits throughout the museum. Each of these gallery exhibits will then be able to tailor its content and its style of presentation to suit the needs, wishes, background and even the personality of the individual visitor. Not only will the connoisseur be treated differently from the novice, but each connoisseur and each novice will be treated differently from each other one.

> By exploiting the adaptive capabilities of the computer, the museum of the future can become a place where every visitor, in a very real sense, creates his own learning environment.[26]

Quite evidently, the impact of the computer on the world of museums is going to be considerable.

An experimental laboratory, headed by museum professionals with the aid of a multidisciplinary staff, could, at this point in time, help greatly in developing new uses of technology in museums and in increasing the museum's educational flexibility, scope, and power.

Summary

The primary instructional medium employed by museums is the exhibition. It is a particular kind of learning environment with its own communicative characteristics. Some museums are presently conducting promising experiments in adapting programmed learning theory and practice to museum terms in an attempt to increase educational effectiveness.

Some museum professionals regard the instructional media with suspicion on the grounds that (1) aesthetic experience takes place during the direct confrontation of the visitor with the work of art and all else is intrusive and superfluous, and (2) museums are places of the unique, original object, hence all reproduction or translation is betrayal.

Museums reach out beyond their walls in ways which include traveling exhibitions, museumobiles, branch museums, radio and television. Film, slide-tape presentations, and sound recording are among the audiovisual methods used. Electronic guide systems are common.

Some museum applications of the computer have been made, including stylistic analysis and the experimental storage and retrieval of information about collections. A Museum Computer Network, involving sixteen museums, is in the planning stage. Computer uses in museum education promise new kinds of individualized guidance and instruction.

Research and development is needed to build upon these beginnings.

REFERENCES

1. For an earlier attempt to describe the nature of the exhibition in somewhat these same terms, see George Mills and Richard Grove, "The Exhibition as a Medium of Communication," *Clearing House for Western Museums,* n.s., nos. 5-6: 52-57, 1958.

2. The use of sound is not limited to recorded words. In an exhibition of sea birds at the Milwaukee Public Museum, the cries of these birds are heard. A great locomotive in the Smithsonian Institution's Museum of History and Technology is accompanied by an evocative recording of train sounds. In this same museum, there is an effective use of subtle, appropriate aromas in a nineteenth century candy shop exhibit.

3. For a historical survey, see Stephan F. Borhegyi and Irene Hanson, "Chronological Bibliography of Museum Visitor Surveys," in Eric Larrabee (ed.), *Museums and Education,* Smithsonian Institution Press, 1968.

4. Project No. 5-0245, Elizabeth Nicol and Michael Spock, Boston Children's Museum, Boston, Massachusetts, "The Development of Validated Museum Exhibits," and the project under C. G. Screven and Stephan F. Borhegyi, University of Wisconsin—Milwaukee, Milwaukee, Wisconsin, "The Application of Programmed Learning and Teaching Systems Procedures for Instruction in a Museum Environment."

5. Screven, C. G. "The Application of Programmed Learning and Teaching Systems Procedures for Instruction in a Museum Environment," in Stephan F. Borhegyi and Irene A. Hanson (eds.), *The Museum Visitor,* Publications in Musicology No. 3, Milwaukee Public Museum, 1968. A later report by the same author is "The Museum as a Responsive Learning Environment," *Museum News,* Vol. 47, No. 10, June 1969.

6. Gilman, Benjamin Ives. *Museum Ideals of Purpose and Method.* Museum of Fine Arts, Boston, Massachusetts, 1918, pp. 93-94.

7. Lee, Sherman E. "The Idea of an Art Museum." *Harper's,* September, 1968.

8. Gilborn, Craig. "Words and Machines: The Denial of Experience." *Museum News,* Vol. 47, No. 1, September, 1968.

9. The distinction between "realities" becomes blurred as technological media become art media, directly employed by the artist. One can imagine a future art museum entirely devoted to the work of such artists. The "art object" no longer exists.

A significant organization working in this field is Experiments in Art and Technology, Inc. (EAT), 9 East 16th Street, New York, N.Y. 10003.

10. "Museum of the Media," brochure, New York, 1968.

An article on the Museum of the Media is "Modules for the Millions," by Grace Glueck in the *New York Times,* June 22, 1969.

11. White, Stephen. "Implications of Technology for Museum Education." in Eric Larrabee (ed.), *Museums and Education,* Smithsonian Institution Press, 1968.

12. *A Statistical Survey of Museums in the United States and Canada,* American Association of Museums, 1965.

13. Some brand names are Lectour, Tour Disc, By Word, Sound Trek, and Acoustiguide.

14. *MAVAG Newsletter,* Vol. IX, No. 1, July-August, 1968. The editor of this mimeographed periodical is Katherine L. Nyce. The 1968-69 MAVAG chairman is Jon H. Larimore, National Geographic Society, Washington, D.C.

15. The two quotes are from Patricia Barnard, "Television Activities at the Museum of Fine Arts, Boston: 1955-1966," (mimeographed), November, 1966.

16. Hoving, Thomas P. F. "Branch Out!", *Museum News,* Vol. 47, No. 1, September, 1968.

17. "Sevres Porcelain Project—Hard Paste Index," *ICRH Newsletter* (Institute for Computer Research in the Humanities), New York University, Vol III, No. 5, n.d.

18. Esterow, Milton. "Metropolitan Museum is Studying Computer Uses." *New York Times,* January 12, 1968.

19. Project No. 7-1159, Bureau of Research, U.S. Office of Education, "An Information Storage and Retrieval System for Biological and Geological Data," Donald F. Squires, Smithsonian Institution, Washington, D.C.

20. Schaden, Herman. "Smithsonian Computer Spins Data Revolution." *The Evening Star,* Washington, D.C., February 6, 1968.

21. Ricciardelli, Alex F. "A Census of Ethnological Collections in U.S. Museums." *Museum News,* Vol. 46, No. 1, September, 1967.

22. Gilroy, Harry. "16 Museums to Study Computer Archive of Art." *New York Times,* December 9, 1967.

23. "The Electronic Museum," *Newsweek,* December 25, 1967, p. 42.

24. Same as 23, *Newsweek.*

25. *Computers and Their Potential Applications in Museums,* New York: The Metropolitan Museum of Art, 1968.

26. Lee, Robert S. "The Future of the Museum as a Learning Environment." in 25 (above), p. 383-384.

85.
Instructional Technology In the Armed Forces

by Lt. Colonel *HOWARD B. HITCHENS, JR.**
Exec. Director
Dept. of Audiovisual
Instruction
National Education Association

I. Technical Training

The vast amount of technical training in specific occupational skills within the armed forces is conducted to insure that adequate numbers of well-trained personnel are available to accomplish the tremendously complex job of defending the nation. Any view of armed forces training programs must be taken with that in mind—the armed forces conduct training as a means to assure the accomplishment of a specific mission.

The use of communications media in military technical training ranges from such rudimentary tools as the chalkboard to the very sophisticated computer. This report discusses the following broad areas:

    a. traditional audiovisual media

    b. television

    c. the techniques of programmed learning and instructional systems development

    d. the use of computers

The scope of the use of traditional audiovisual media (films, audio tapes, slides, transparencies, etc.) is difficult to depict. Since World War II the military services have depended greatly on such tools of communications for their training programs. As an example of the amount of effort and material that goes into training, Ft. Monmouth, New Jersey, produced more than 13,000 transparencies for the overhead projector for use in its training program in a recent academic year. In a recent year, Lackland Air Force Base produced more than 1,500 training devices of all kinds, and Keesler Air Force Base produced 4,000 graphics (flip-charts, posters, etc.). The inventory in each of the armed forces of such communication devices as overhead projectors, 35mm slide projectors, and the like, runs into the millions of dollars. These devices are used not only in the formal training conducted by Continental Army Command, Air Training Command, and the Naval Schools Command, but also in on-the-job and follow-up training on shipboard in the Navy and the various operational sites in the Army and Air Force.

A typical military classroom is equipped with at least one wall of chalkboard, a projector

---

At the time this report was written (January 1969) Lt. Col. Hitchens was professor of instructional communications at the United States Air Force Academy.

screen, and an overhead projector. Generally, equipment for the projection of 2 by 2 slides and 16mm motion pictures and a complete array of visual materials are available on request.

Each of the services has an instructor-development program, which includes formal preservice training for the military instructor. This training may be conducted at one central school facility (for example, the Academic Instructors' Course is required of each Air Force ROTC instructor) or an individual base-or-unit-level course. Without exception, training in the use of these conventional AV tools and materials is a required part of the course. Each of the services has a system of certifying the competence of the graduating instructor, usually by issuing him an AV equipment operator's license.

Television

Television is no longer a new medium of instruction within the military services. The Navy and the Army experimented with the use of television for various training purposes as early as 1949. The Army and Navy training establishment, or civilian institutions under contract with Department of Defense, pioneered research in the instructional uses of television. It would be nice to report that the television applications to training in the armed forces have been very carefully selected. Such is not the case.

The development of television has evolved in the same manner within the military services as it has within the civilian sector. Its introduction into training has occurred for reasons that range from seeking solutions to various training needs, to satisfying the felt needs of responsible individuals in the training process. For instance, the very large television distribution system which serves US Army's Continental Army Command (CONARC) was introduced to achieve standardization and more effective training methods in the technical training of Army enlisted men. There are presently 12 *regional* television production centers within CONARC which *annually* produce *1500* selected segments of courses on video tape for distribution to training programs at *26* CONARC posts. The largest distribution system consists of *30* channels used in training at Fort Gordon, Georgia. *Over 200,000 programs are transmitted annually on this closed circuit educational television system in direct support of USCONARC training.* An added benefit to Army training is derived from the CONARC TV System in the increased production of low-cost Army-wide training films (FY69—150 reels) using television techniques and transferred to 16mm kinescope film.

Currently the most exploited television capability is the providing of self-confrontation for students in instructor training. The small portable television record-and-playback units provide a very powerful means of allowing a person "to see himself as others see him."

The large television production systems have usually been established to provide experiences for the military classroom which could not be provided in any other way. For example, the bringing of a "real time" missile firing from Cape Kennedy into the classrooms at Redstone Arsenal, Alabama, was not possible before television. Since 1959 the television production facility at Redstone Arsenal has grown into one of the larger production centers in the Army. Similarly, the Air Force's Lowry Air Force Base introduced television into its technical training program in 1958, and it has since evolved into a large multi-faceted television production facility.

Part of the early evolution of television was to exploit its rapid recording capabilities—even before the advent of video tape. In the late 1950's the Army Pictorial Center developed a technique of making quick release films using kinescope facilities. This use of television capabilities continues to the present day, allowing rapid production of audiovisual programming through the television medium. In 1959, an entire course in Basic Electronics was produced on an experimental basis at Lowry Air Force Base. After demonstrating its effectiveness for technical training, the recorded materials were transferred from video tape to film and distributed to other Air Force technical training centers as films.

At present, the Army, Navy, and Air Force employ television extensively for training. Typical uses of television include:

1. Recording of dangerous or otherwise inaccessible phenomena for playback in the classroom.

2. The demonstration of manipulative tasks.

3. Introductory lectures on subjects ranging from technical to non-technical.

4. Enlargement or image magnification for demonstration purposes.

5. The aforementioned instructor training.

The administering of tests live through the television medium has been accomplished in several instances. Also, some use of the television medium has been made to lead students lock-step through programmed sequences.

One of the most unusual and innovative uses of television is the Navy's PLAT System (Pilot Landing Aid-Television). Television cameras and recorders on aircraft carriers monitor and record every aircraft landing. This enables the pilot and his supervisor to replay every detail of the landing—a superb tool for performance improvement.

In assessing each of the separate services' role in the use of this medium, it seems that the Army has consistently played a highly dominant role in the development of television for instruction. Most of the early research and experimentation that was accomplished was done either within the Army or under its auspices.

Programmed Learning

The programmed learning movement within the Armed Forces got its biggest boost within the Air Force, and not quite by accident. Soon after its inception in 1947, the Air Force exerted a significant effort in human factors research; it assembled a large number of highly skilled educational psychologists in dispersed research laboratories located at each of its training centers. Such people as Gagne, Lumsdaine, Crowder, Evans, Homme, and Glaser (all prominent behavioral psychologists today) worked in these laboratories. Much of their best thinking and many of their greatest contributions to the programmed learning movement came during their tenure in the Air Force. Unfortunately, these research and development laboratories were eliminated and the training research reduced in 1958.

In 1961 the Air Force's Air Training Command (ATC) introduced the concepts of programmed learning into its technical training programs. The use of these techniques involved systematic evaluation of the entire training process. As a part of this effort, ATC established Instructional System Development Teams at each of its technical training centers. These teams analyzed entire training segments and restructured courses in programmed form. This effort evolved into the Instructional Systems concept which all three armed services presently employ. Table I depicts the commonly agreed upon steps in systems analysis which the Army, Navy and Air Force use at this time.

Although the first course used for experimentation in each service's innovative surge was Basic Electronics, the courses in technical training which now employ programmed instruction run the gamut from Electrical Theory, Applied Aerodynamics, Mathematics, Physiology, Mechanical Principles through various specific procedural tasks and such mundane subjects as first-aid. In a few instances the programmed materials are used as the sole vehicle to accomplish the training. Virtually all of the programmed materials at this time are in textual form.

Table I
Instructional System Development Steps

1. Collect job data and analyze.
2. State training objectives.
3. Design: Content, Method, Media.
4. Construct course.
5. Field Test (Includes evaluation).
6. Implement.

The growth in the use of programmed instruction (PI) in the Air Force is depicted in Figure 1. Although a steady growth in its use is shown, PI has not been the panacea for training that the early enthusiasts predicted.

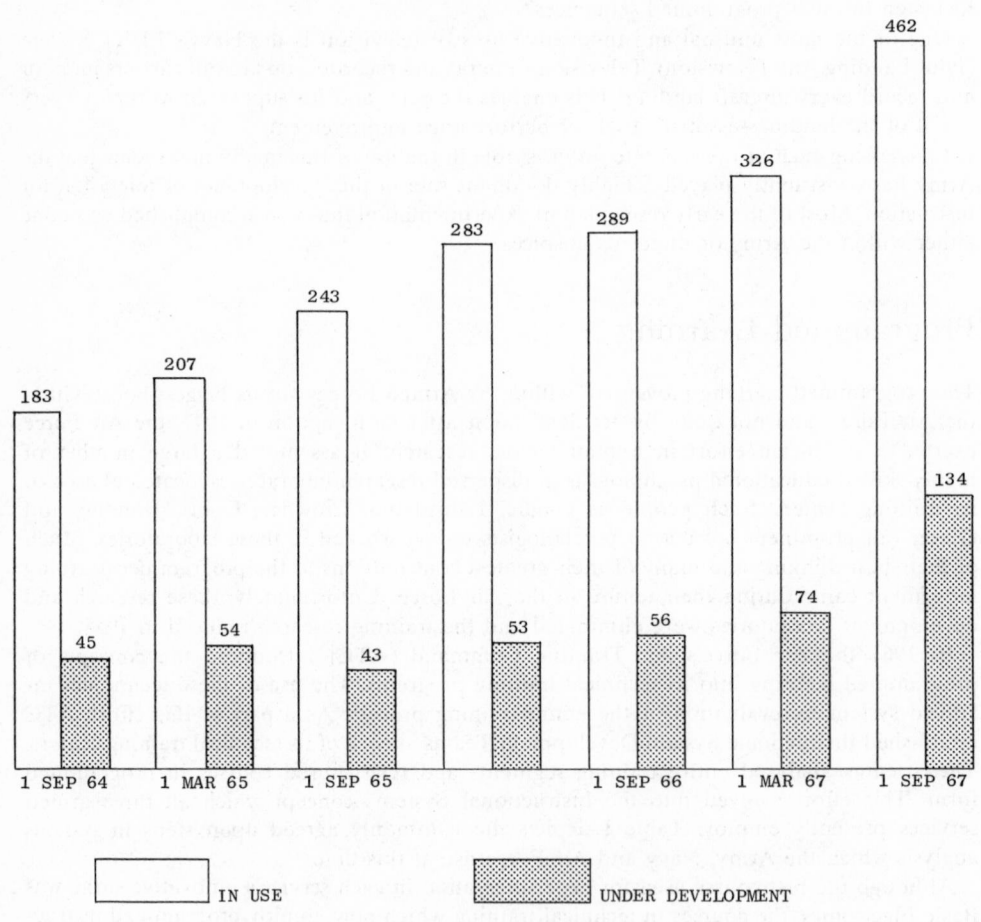

U.S. Air Force Programmed Instruction Summary
Figure I

One of the most effective applications of programmed learning has been in the school program of the Army Security Agency at Ft. Devens, Massachusetts. The systematic analysis that was made of jobs and tasks in the field resulted in significant changes in training and in the Military Occupational Specialties (MOS) descriptions. The training managers at Ft. Devens succeeded in changing the MOS descriptions based on their findings during the task analysis.

Currently the Department of the Army has initiated a five year program in all USCONARC schools and army training centers to redesign existing MOS producing courses, functional courses, career courses and Army Subject Schedules, based on techniques of systematic analysis.

The Memphis Navy Air Training Center has introduced programmed instruction rather extensively. Twenty-five courses use some programmed instruction materials. As of Fall, 1968, 411 PI booklets were in use; an additional 33 were completed and ready for use. Training managers at the Memphis Training Center have reduced training time by twenty-eight percent after introducing PI and have saved 235 man years in 1968 alone. Table II depicts some statistical data which was accumulated at Memphis. The costs shown seem to agree with those costs and savings which have been publicized by experimenters in civilian institutions and industrial training. In the Naval Schools Command, symbol learning has been programmed for electronic maintenance training, and, as a result, has moved out of the classroom to "homework."

Table II
Programmed Instruction Data
Naval Air Technical Training Command

Amount of programmed instruction time savings—43%
Amount of programmed instruction required to save one contact hour—2½ hours
Cost of producing one hour of P. I.—$278 (direct labor)
Cost of producing 2½ hours—2½ × $278 = $695
Airman 3rd class hourly pay rate = $1.36
Number of student outputs required to amortize 2½ hours P. I. in one year = $695 – $1.36 = 511
Quarterly rate of production, 60 programmers = 78 conventional hours
Programmer manhours per instructional hour—78

Similar developments in the use of programmed instruction have occurred within the Army. At Fort Rucker, Alabama, the United States Army Aviation School redesigned the entire Helicopter Instrument Flight Course by converting academic instruction to programmed format and adapting the technique of programmed, self-paced instruction to the flight and synthetic flight training. This redesign resulted in a significant reduction in course length. The Primary Helicopter School, Fort Wolters, Texas programmed the entire portion of the primary helicopter course. In both instances, programmed materials carry the entire instructional load. At Ft. Sam Houston's Medical Field Service School, approximately 300 contact hours contain some use of programmed instruction materials. In the Army's Signal School at Ft. Monmouth, New Jersey, 44 courses out of a total of 158 courses are using programmed instruction.

The San Diego Naval Training Center initiated a three week programmers course in order to develop programming talent within the Navy. By Fall 1968 ten programmers had been produced—and efforts in one school had resulted in twenty-four completed programs; eight more were in production; and seventy-five course hours had been replaced by the completed programmed instruction packages. The school in which this effort was couched was also rewriting all of its course objectives.

The best characterization of the effects of programmed instruction throughout the Armed Forces was stated by the educational advisor to the San Diego Service School Commandant, "PI has caused a 'cleansing' of the curriculum." He meant that the systematic analysis of training needs and procedures induced by programmed learning methods was very healthful. All of those personnel in Armed Forces Training contacted by the investigator were generally enthusiastic about the potential, if not demonstrated, effects of programmed instruction in making military training more productive. The general time saving of thirty percent is typical of military experience.

The most significant problem with the introduction of programmed instruction has been the fact that its use generally means the loss of the "lock-step" scheduling and control of students which is normal in military training. As a result, it is difficult for the personnel system to accommodate itself to irregular production of skilled graduates from training courses. As indicated above, the Ft. Devens experience of rewriting job descriptions (a combined effort by the trainers and personnel managers) demonstrated a beneficial procedure that can be useful throughout the Armed Forces.

Multi-Media Packages

One effect that can be attributed to the introduction of the systems analysis technique to military training programs has been a fresh look at the way in which conventional media are employed. Navy and Air Force headquarters staffs both indicated that the development of slide/tape instructional packages has made a significant contribution to their training programs. The skills involved in Navy pilot proficiency lend themselves to this technique. In fact, these sound slide packages, prepared by civilian contract firms, are extensively used in Naval aviation. Keesler AFB has also introduced a large number of slide tape/packages.

The EDEX (commercial name, from *ed*ucational *ex*cellence) Multi-Media Controlled System has been employed in driver training in both the Army and Air Force. The heart of the system, the programming console, permits the instructional programmer to carefully control the sequence of visual and auditory stimuli to which the students are exposed. The system is a "closed loop" in that student responder stations are integrated into it and determine the direction that the program moves in each instance. Again, the Armed Forces have used this system to satisfy a specific training need—driver education leading to the safe operation of motor vehicles. The Air Force plans to introduce this system with a packaged driver education course (all the necessary software in addition to the hardware) at most of its bases which have large personnel populations. Two years of feasibility studies have demonstrated that this system will, in fact, significantly reduce motor vehicle accidents.

In December 1968 the United States Army Infantry School, Fort Benning, completed a six months operational report on the effectiveness of the EDEX Instructional Systems. The recommendations contained in this report will be used as a basis for the possible extension of EDEX within the CONARC school system.

A similar evaluation is being conducted by the Air Force under the aegis of the Inspector General's office. Finally, the use of the device for training is being explored by other governmental agencies, such as the Internal Revenue Service, with Air Force assistance.

Uses of the Computer

As in the case of the Air Force's identification with the development of instructional systems and programmed learning, and the Army's identification with the development of television for instruction, the Navy seems to have the primary thrust for the development of computer uses for training in the Armed Forces. Most of the credit for this image goes to the major research and development projects being accomplished at the U.S. Naval Academy, but several other activities within the Navy are using computers within the general training context.

Computer *Managed* Instruction attempts to exploit the computer's ability to handle large amounts of data. A practical development of this mode is occurring at the Naval Air Technical Training Center, Memphis. Here the computer manages students' programs through carefully structured learning situations. Besides managing, the computer teaches the student in the tutorial mode and exposes him to individual audiovisual devices and programmed instruction booklets. The employment of this training concept has the potential for large, immediate payoff since this Center has a student population of 40,000 per year (14,000 at one time).

Although the Navy seems to have captured the leadership at the moment, all three services have been interested in the development of the computer within the context of the man-machine interface for years—specifically for training. Some activities within the Army and the Air Force have promise of great effectiveness. The tutorial mode is being used within the Army at Fort Monmouth, New Jersey. Basic Electronics training has been conducted on an experimental basis to determine cost effectiveness of CAI. The initial study resulted in no significant differences in student achievement, but did achieve a time saving of eleven percent. The researchers concluded that if a twenty percent saving of course time could be made, CAI would be cost effective.

The Army's Quartermaster School has under development the simulation of real life logistical situations on the computer. At Fort Benning, Georgia, the Army's Infantry School uses on line terminals with gaming information in order to teach strategy and tactics. A long-range Automatic Data Processing Systems (ADPS) Master Plan for the USCONARC schools system has been developed to satisfy its schools' academic and administrative mission. This plan is open ended to permit revision as necessary to insure that it stays in harmony with computer technology development in the school academic and administrative fields.

The Air Force is conducting a project aimed at exploiting the computer to teach the skills necessary to operate it. This project is associated with the massive buy of so-called Phase II Computers (Burroughs 3500s) for use throughout the Air Force. The development of software for this project is under contract to Systems Development Corporation.

An earlier project for the Air Defense Command was the development of a computer capability to handle the presentation of training sequences to train operators of the BUIC (Backup Interceptor Control) air defense system. This effort was accomplished by contract with Systems Development Corporation and was eminently successful. The Burroughs 3500 Operator Training Project is a refinement of this earlier effort.

The longest continuous project for the development of computer use in education is Project PLATO at the University of Illinois. This project has been funded repeatedly by all three services, and has provided a great deal of basic information concerning computers.

The most effective use of the computer to control student responses noted by this investigator was at the Army's security school. Here a dedicated CDC Computer is employed to present both Morse code information and typewriter keyboard displays to develop a simultaneous ability to the students to type Morse code responses. The classroom in which this training takes place is equipped to accommodate approximately thirty students at individual carrels. This project is in the advanced development stage and has processed more than 400 students quite successfully. The project manager cited the following advantages:

a. The computer based code trainer provides for individual differences in terms of quantity, quality, and rate.

b. The teacher can discriminate between typing errors and perceptual errors.

c. The cognitive perception rate of the student is stored and easily handled by the computer.

Simulation

One sphere of training activity in which the military is distinctly different from civilian education is in the use of simulation: providing a student training environment similar to the actual operations the student is learning will occur. An obvious example was the development of the Link Trainer to support pilot training during World War II; the Link Trainer, improved since World War II, is still with us. Many more sophisticated simulators have been developed and used since that time. Most expensive simulators are normally associated with weapon systems (aircraft, missiles, submarines, space vehicles) and are usually provided by the contractor at the time that the system is perfected and delivered. It is difficult to determine the exact number of simulators of all kinds that the Armed Forces presently employs. However, in Navy aviation training support alone there are presently some 215 major simulators in use and approximately 2,000 smaller portable simulators.

In the Navy, simulators are controlled and provided by the Navy Training Device Center. This is a centralized activity which has not only the logistical and distributive job, but also the research and development responsibility in support of Navy training. Incidentally, the Army Training establishment makes considerable use of the Navy Training Device Center's capabilities to manufacture and distribute various devices for Army training. The Air Force generally manages its major training simulators within the Air Training Command, and does not depend on the Navy Training Device Center.

One interesting attempt to simulate the operational environment is the "captive helicopter" used in Army aviation training at Ft. Rucker, Alabama. In this instance, a light helicopter was linked mechanically to a fixed ground control apparatus and was found to be a very useful way of accomplishing some flight maneuver training for Army aviation student helicopter pilots.

Simulators are used a great deal in the development of crew skills such as pilot and air crew, submarine crew, deck crew, tank crew and other performance skills in all three services. An entire ship has been reconstructed on land at Treasure Island for training in fire control procedures by the Naval Schools Command. Also a completely free floating ship's hull is used to train damage control technicians in emergency shoring of the ship's hull and structure during emergencies. In the latter case, a failure by the trainees results in a soaking as the hull takes on more water—a very practical simulator.

The discussion of simulators would not be complete without some mention of the use of the digital computer for this purpose. Some work is being accomplished in the area of mathematical representation of physical phenomena and allowing students to manipulate this data in a computer interface.

II. Pre-commissioning and Professional Training

Introduction

The Armed Forces conduct education and training solely to satisfy the need for effective manpower to support the nation's defense. Therefore, they consider education and training as a sub-system within the personnel structure. The Armed Services have formed similar organizations for satisfying their education and training needs: the Naval Schools Command, the Continental Army Command, and the Air Training Command. Although these training commands are thought to be the only centralized training functions in each service, that is, in fact, not true. The problem of interface between the education and training activity and its "customer" activity is very much in evidence in the Armed Forces. For example: the Air Force's Air Training Command (ATC) trains jet engine mechanics to a specific level of competence. To date, it is rare for the Strategic Air Command, Tactical Air Command, or Air Defense Command to employ the product of the technical schools of ATC without significant transitional or on-the-job training (OJT). Both the Army and Navy confront similar problems in their technical training; training is conducted at all levels or organization, in efforts that range from very informal to highly formal degree-granting schools.

Recipients of pre-commissioning, graduate, and professional training are generally officers, and the technical training student population is mostly enlisted personnel. While this distinction is not absolutely clear-cut, the investigator makes it in order to organize his observations. This monograph (first of three) describes the instructional technology in officer training of all kinds within the military services.

Pre-Commissioning Training

Within the Armed Forces the two largest facilities for development of Commissioned Officers are the Reserve Officer Training Corps programs of the Army, Navy, and Air Force, and the three Service Academies. (I am told the Army's Officer Candidate Schools produce more officers than West Point.) The service academies (Navy at Annapolis, Army at West Point, and Air Force in Colorado) are accredited undergraduate academic institutions. They are very similar to civilian colleges in their curriculum development and management; they are dissimilar in that their curricula tend to be more product oriented than the normal liberal arts college. All three institutions have developed the uses of traditional instructional technology in parallel with the growth of technology in American education. In fact, several technological innovations have originated within these service institutions. For example, the first use of the chalkboard in an American college was at West Point. At present, such traditional audiovisual media as the overhead projector, slide projector, motion picture, and language laboratory are thoroughly integrated into the instructional process in each of these institutions. Table III provides a comparison listing of the numbers of films and other conventional audiovisual equipment and materials presently in use at each of the academies.

Table III
AV Equipment And Materials At The Service Academies

	USNA	USMA	USAFA
16mm Films in Library	3310	940	2825
16mm Motion Picture Projectors	187	60	96
35mm Slide Projectors	79	81	126
35mm Slides in use	2000	26,169	13,280
Overhead Projectors	244	290	280
Film strips in Library	*	*	450
Film strip projectors	12	28	32
Audio Tape Recorders	106	75	130
Audio Tapes in Library	11,613	3,100	803
Video Tape Recorders	4	7	8
Video Tapes in Library	250	670	300
Opaque Projector	52	13	30
TV Receivers/Monitors	26	375	150
TV Large Screen Projectors	*	3	2

*Not available

All the services have accepted the overhead projector as a basic instructional device. This device, in particular, was invented several years ago by the Navy's Training Devices Center to serve the military instructors' need to face their students while presenting information. Since its initiation into military training, it has become almost as commonplace as the chalkboard. The academies reflect this same pattern of using the overhead projector in nearly every classroom. For instance, the Air Force Academy provides 280 overhead projectors to serve approximately 300 teaching stations.

The motion picture is used a great deal for instruction. From Table III, the extent of use can be generally gauged on the basis of numbers of film and projector holdings at each institution.

Similarly, 35mm slides and audio tapes are an integral part of the instructional process. The production of these photographic slides runs into the thousands each year. Audio tapes, while primarily consumed in support of the language laboratory, are used for such other purposes as recording of student and instructor presentations and providing recorded musical and dramatic selections in various classes.

The newer media—television, programmed learning, and computers—are each being used and/or experimented with in the academies. The Naval Academy is attempting to develop a breakthrough in the uses of the computer for learning. In a "Multi-Media" project which is funded in part by the U.S. Office of Education, a systematic structuring of the learning process has been undertaken. Under contractual arrangements, commercial firms are developing three complete undergraduate courses: Economics—Sterling Institute; Physics—New York Institute of Technology; Management Psychology—Westinghouse Learning Corporation.

Also at the Naval Academy, a tutorial mode experiment in computer assisted instruction (CAI) is under way. The courses being developed for CAI are Thermodynamics, Electrical Science, Modern Physics and Basic Russian. At the moment, one classroom with twelve fully equipped terminals is in use, with an additional classroom having eighteen terminals to be provided this academic year. Finally, at Annapolis, the use of the computer in the problem-solving mode is being exploited with seventeen teletype terminals to support eleven courses. Ten of these terminals are clustered in a classroom—the other seven are located conveniently for faculty and staff use in problem solving and course development.

The complexion of training in computer sciences at both West Point and the Air Force Academy is similar. Both institutions are concerned with the question, "What does a commissioned officer need to know about the computer sciences to serve his country successfully for the next 35 years?" West Point provides for both the learning of computer languages and the manipulation of electronics hardware in the curriculum. The Air Force Academy treats these two aspects of computer sciences, but with most emphasis on languages and less emphasis on student interaction with hardware.

The introduction of programmed learning into the curricula of the service academies has been slow. Generally, programmed learning has been used to satisfy remedial needs with the cadets and midshipmen, e.g. remedial programs in basic English, Mathematics, and Map Reading. The Air Force Academy mails both English and Mathematics programmed texts to entering students to complete before their arrival. It found this technique improved the verbal and mathematical skills of entering students who were weak in these areas. The Naval Academy and the Air Force Academy have programmed some out-of-class, or homework, activities in such subjects as Financial Management, Place Identification in Geography, Operations Research, Electronics of Weapons Systems, and Principles of Physics.

The use of television within the Academies has paralleled that of civilian institutions in the past ten years. All three institutions are still exploring the medium with the hope of some significant breakthroughs in its use. Few complete courses are being taught through the medium. Generally its ability to enlarge and reduce visual phenomena and provide everyone a front-row seat at demonstrations benefits most students. The Air Force Academy introduced the instructor-centered concept of TV program production (letting the teacher manipulate all of the audiovisual inputs into a television program by himself) in 1961. This innovation led to such devices as the Ampex Video Trainer, a self-contained, portable TV record and play-back unit. Television usage at the Naval Academy has undergone late development in the Naval Science Department and is only now beginning to enjoy wide-spread use.

The language laboratory is the only identifiable effort to give students access to informa-tion in a dial-access or remote-access mode. Even here students generally use the laboratory only under the direct control of a live instructor. The Departments rarely make the labora-tories available to the students outside scheduled classroom periods.

Some innovations in facility design are in process. The mobility of the Teletype terminal is being exploited to provide cadets with relatively flexible access to the computer programs at West Point. At the Naval Academy, the Multi-Media and CAI projects are evolving newly designed learning carrels. At the Air Force Academy, the need for more flexibility of scheduling caused the design of some intermediate-sized rooms (76 seats) when the new academic facilities were constructed. The architect dubbed these rooms "lectinars."

The issues and trends which seem prevalent at the service academies are the same ones occurring at civilian colleges and universities:

1. The individualization of instruction is recognized as desirable. However, tradi-tion mitigates against the breakdown of the very favorable student-instructor ratio (less than 20 to 1), which prevails at the academies. Because it is felt that control of the intellectual, social, and character development of these officer-leaders must remain in the hands of professional officer-teachers, the surrendering of the instructor's preroga-tives is difficult to accomplish. Obviously, increasing the use of machines and media seems at cross purposes with this human management of learning.

2. Standardization of instruction would seem to be enhanced by more use of the communication media. The issue at the academies is not standardization, but the proper balance between the employment of media and the human teacher to continue satisfying the requirements of the accrediting agencies. The academies must maintain a balance between becoming "trade schools" and keeping enough of a general educa-tion thrust to the curriculum to ensure that the degrees which they grant are recog-nized and have transfer value.

3. The keeping of the curriculum itself and its implementation as a dynamic process is very important. The rapid rate of technological change in weaponry and all the applied sciences does have a significant effect on the substance of these undergraduate curricula. This, coupled with the changing technology of instruction, tends to keep the programs of the academies dynamic.

4. The problems encountered in the employment of technology in the service academies, as in civilian institutions, are generally "people problems." Some hypotheti-cal questions, attributed to military professors as well as their civilian colleagues, illus-trate the problems: "Will the use of technology enhance my academic image?" "How will my colleagues in civilian education view me if my department has less instructors than theirs?" "Isn't this technology a dehumanizing influence on my students?"

The largest source of commissioned officers in all three services is the Reserve Officers Training Corps program. Detachments of active duty military personnel from the appropriate services conduct instruction in more than 400 undergraduate civilian institutions. Because this instructional program is embedded in a civilian institution, it generally tends to take on the methodological complexion of its host. Instructional technology is employed generally to ensure standardization of instruction and, hope-fully, learning across the several hundred detachments. The primary curricular tool is textual materials developed very carefully in each branch of the service through the course development and lesson planning process. Prescribing appropriate motion pictures and other training aids in each hour's lesson plan achieves some standardization. Generally, the logistical problems of supporting geographically separated and numerous detachments have inhibited the budgeting for and developing of newer media. There are exceptions. For instance, one of the initial courses developed and adapted for TV instruction at the Pennsylvania State University in the mid-50's was the basic ROTC Course. Again, the operation of ROTC instruction tends to imitate its host institution.

In general, however, the amount of instructional technology employed and the sophisticated level of use is far in excess of that employed in the typical civilian college. This is true not only at the ROTC detachments around the country, but particularly in the three academies.

Graduate and Professional Training

Degree Training

The Armed Forces conduct a number of high-level courses, often at the graduate level, primarily for their officers' professional development. These courses sometimes lead to graduate degrees and in more than half of the cases, although not aimed toward a degree, are essential for continued development of the officers. The military institutions primarily concerned with degree programs are the Naval Post Graduate School at Monterey, California, and the Air Force Institute of Technology (AFIT) at Wright-Patterson Air Force Base, Ohio, a sub-unit of the Air University. The Naval Post Graduate School is accredited to grant BS, MS and PhD Degrees. AFIT grants Masters and Doctoral degrees.

In addition both of these military institutions manage degree programs with several civilian colleges and universities around the country to assist in filling the need for officer education. In recent years, the total program of the Air Force, Navy, and Army (which does not have an "in-house" accredited graduate school) graduated approximately 2,000 students per year. The Naval Post Graduate School in 1967-1968 granted the following degrees: 252 BS Degrees, 323 MS Degrees, and 3 PhDs.

The Navy and Air Force resident graduate schools lean heavily on communication media to accomplish instruction. These media range from overhead transparencies through more sophisticated photographic products, programmed materials, television, and computers.

Characteristic of both resident programs is their use of television for such activities as instructor training (allowing the less experienced instructor to confront himself recorded on video tape) and distributing pre-recorded lectures by subject matter experts to students so that they may have the benefit of the best teachers the school has to offer.

The concept of use of television at the Naval Post Graduate School includes a considerable amount of decentralization of equipment. Facilities are provided for image enlargement in engineering and scientific classrooms, visual monitoring of hazardous experiments and getting at physical phenomena not readily seen otherwise.

Two distinctive developments at the Post Graduate School are (a) the use of video taped presentations of guest lecturers to precede a live telelecture and (b) the introduction of the "curricular officer" concept. The curricular officer concept arose from the fact that the Post Graduate School faculty, primarily civilian, faces the problem of keeping its training relevant, i.e., meeting the needs of Naval operations. To assure that the training is relevant and appropriate, a procedure of using officers who have been trained and have served in the professional skill within the Navy return for a tour at Monterey and translate the field's needs into the academic program.

Both institutions have rather exotic laboratory equipment. For instance, the Engineering Sciences curriculum of AFIT uses a working scale model of a 20 ft. wind tunnel, capable of producing velocities in excess of 300 miles per hour.

The Air Force Institute of Technology has a project under way to simulate the decision-making processes necessary in the Civil Engineering program within the Air Force. This ability to simulate such a complex process has only become possible with the advent of the large capacity digital computers presently available.

Non-Degree Training

Turning now to the non-degree professional training area, it can be seen in Table IV that professional military training takes place at seven possible levels. The approximate rank and years of service of the typical officer attending school at a given level is indicated in Table V. As an individual progresses through the seven levels of education he finds that the selectivity becomes more competitive and that fewer persons attend the higher level schools. For instance, less than fifty percent of the active duty officers in the Air Force graduate from the Squadron Officers School (level three); less than 700 officers attend the schools in levels six and seven out of approximately 700,000 officers in the military services.

Table IV
Professional Military Education Programs
Of the Armed Services

Level	Army	Navy	Marine Corps	Coast Guard	Air Force
1	(Commissioning Programs, i.e. academies, ROTC, OCS, and so on)				
2	Branch Schools (Orientation Course)	Surface Submarine and Flying Schools. Officer Special Schools	Basic School	Naval Schools	Pilot-Navigator, and Specialty-Training Programs of Air Training Command
3	Branch Schools (Career Course)	Naval Post Graduate School	Junior School	Naval Schools	Air University; Squadron Officer School
4*	Army Command and General Staff College	Command and Staff Course (Naval War College)	Senior School	Other Service Command and Staff Schools	Air University; Command and Staff College
5	Army War College	Naval Warfare Course (Naval War College)	Other Service War Colleges	Other Service War Colleges	Air University; Air War College
6	National War College; Industrial College of the Armed Forces	Same	Same	Same	Same
7	NATO Defense College	Same	Same	Same	Same

Between the fourth and fifth level specified numbers of officers attend the Armed Forces Staff College at Norfolk, Virginia.

Table V
Levels of Professional Military Education

Level Program	Equivalent Rank Average Officer	Approximate Years of Service
1. Commissioning programs	Cadet	0
2. Initial-training programs	Second Lieutenant	1
3. Career-training programs	Captain	5
4. Command and staff colleges	Major	12
5. Senior service colleges	Lieutenant Colonel	19
6. National and joint colleges	Colonel	22
7. Combined college (NATO)	Colonel	22

The methods of instruction in these professional schools range from highly individualized independent study (primarily in the preparation of reports and papers, language study, and reading improvement labs) to large lectures given live or over television. As indicated earlier, these schools use a great deal of traditional audiovisual media: slides and transparencies, motion pictures, and three dimensional models or mock-ups. Listed in Table VI is a summary of materials produced by the Audio-Visual Center at Maxwell Air Force Base for a recent year:

Table VI

2″ × 2″ slides	165,000
3¼″ × 4″ slides	15,000
16mm microfilm (frames)	567,000
35mm microfilm (frames)	600,000
Photostats	17,000
Transparencies (8″ × 10″)	2,500
Transparencies (7″ × 7″)	200
Charts, Posters, Graphics, Maps	22,400
Illustrations	1,500
TV special visuals	1,200
Displays	25
Magnetic Tapes	850 (hours)
Models and mock-ups	25
Tapes	1,000
Video tapes	100

Two formal courses conducted within the general realm of professional military training deserve special notice. The first of these is a one week indoctrination into the uses of television for communication which is conducted at Redstone Arsenal, Alabama, for middle-management officers of all the services. This course is highly mediated, using the technique of embedding the briefer in a carefully structured sequence of audiovisual events. In this technique the briefer works with television displays, live dramatic skits by other instructor personnel, and multi-media presentations on a wide screen. The course's purpose is to interest Commanders and military managers in the use of television for solving their problems; and it is quite successful if the enthusiasm of attendees is the measure of that success.

The other course intended to enhance the professional ability of instructors in the Air Force, is the Academic Instructor Course conducted at Air University, Maxwell Air Force Base, Alabama. The course is six weeks long, carefully organized, and emphasizes student performance; it develops an appreciation for the ability to use both the traditional audio-visual media and television for instruction. Though television has been used there for several years in instructor training, it is interesting to note that very little of the core instruction is accomplished through the television medium. In the context of this course, television is used as just another audiovisual tool to provide a self-confrontation and critiquing capability for the instructors in training.

Programmed instruction is in use in the professional programs, but generally only as textual material to be completed outside of formal classroom periods. Rarely, if at all, is a programmed text used to carry the main body of information to students in the classroom. Such programs as the Principles of Text Construction and Grading, as well as PERT techniques and other linguistic or procedural skills have been found amenable to programming. The use of programmed materials in officer training throughout the armed forces is much less than in the larger technical school system which deals with technical knowledge and motor skills.

III. Opinion, Trends, and Outlook for the Future

Trends

The public tends to view military training activities as extremely affluent and on the cutting edge of innovation and developmental activities, particularly with regard to technological applications to training. And it is true that the military services expend great quantities of money to insure that their personnel are adequately trained. This, perhaps more than any other fact, characterizes military training activities.

The most significant trend in military training seems to be the more careful specification of training. This is being accomplished systematically and, perhaps, grew out of the task analysis originally introduced in the programmed learning techniques. The Army labels this kind of activity "functional context training." This means that only those specific skills necessary to make the person capable of performing quite explicit tasks should be provided in the technical training schools. For instance, research within the Army's Human Resources Research Office (HumRRO) has demonstrated that a traditional basic electronics course is not necessary in the overall curriculum for an electrical maintenance technician. In fact, the Army Signal School has a carefully designed project under way to develop a Common Basic Electronics Training Course (COBET). Some work with the functional context notion at Redstone Arsenal is aiding this effort. Also, the Army has reduced the Missile Systems Maintenance Technician course from 19 weeks to 12 weeks through the course tightening which results from such analyses.

A second significant trend is to employ media in an even more systematic fashion in military training. Military trainers increasingly recognize the need for a strategy to use in managing the technological tools of communication. It is hoped that the major research effort of Army's HumRRO Project IMPACT will contribute more evidence to facilitate this trend.

The trend toward individualization of the learning process has been underway for some time in the military. Implementing that concept presents some difficulties. A classic example is assigning personnel to KP who complete a fourteen-week course in twelve weeks through the use of individually paced programmed instruction because "there's no other way to handle them." In spite of such difficulties the use of programmed learning has become nearly routine within the services—similar, for instance, to the use of a lesson plan.

Developments in both the general technology of weaponry and machinery of defense, and the technology of training will have an impact on the posture of military education and training in the future. An example of subtle technological change is the decreasing requirement for radiomen to know Morse Code—more sophisticated encoding hardware permits secure voice communication. As undersea exploration increases and America begins landing flight crews on the Moon and beyond, the defense posture must change. Just as the Mercury space flight project developed concentrated food which has become available in the supermarket, future space ventures will profoundly effect our military posture. Even though we sometimes believe that we engage in some human activities because our technology makes them possible, military technology must continue to improve. Military training will continue to depend upon the best empirical research results available and will remain in the forefront as a complete technology of instruction evolves.

Future

No discussion of media and technology is complete without some mention of future plans and applications. The future employment of traditional audiovisual media seems to be evolving within the systems development concept—approaches to training will become more systematized in the services.

Presently the Navy is developing both slide/tape instructional packages and 8mm cartridge films for follow-on skill training for use of personnel aboard ship. A skilled training specialist does not need to administer these packages. Complete "how to do it" packages for various jobs are being developed for circulation throughout the fleet in this form. The Air Force also has slide/tape packages under development for use in a "library" fashion on-the-job and has extended this technique to undergraduate pilot training for the day-to-day task of maintaining proficiency in certain skills.

Although television has become a readily accepted medium for military instruction, many of the training managers expressed some dissatisfaction with the way it has been employed. As an example of the kind of development taking place, the Navy is conducting a technical development project to reassess the role of TV in training. This project looks at television systematically as a medium for:

a. whole process learning (carrying the entire instructional message through the television medium)

b. supplementary learning

c. single concept learning

d. self-instruction

e. remedial instruction

f. presenting drill exercises

The Air Force applies portable television recording equipment to the problems of undergraduate pilot training, recording the cockpit environment and the pilot's perceptions outside the cockpit during various training maneuvers. Training personnel hope that using such recorded experiences in the ground classroom will facilitate the student's actual performance in the air. Television's ability to record visual images easily and play them back immediately excites the experimenters, and is being exploited more and more.

The greatest problem which deters trainers from using the computer more extensively is not the availability of hardware or money; it is instead the difficulty of accommodating the student to the machinery. Many of the researchers in all three services expressed the need for a more natural language for the computer user. A great deal of the research taking place in various civilian institutions with computer assisted instruction addresses itself to the development of more powerful and simpler computer languages. Additionally, the Armed Forces look at the computer not so much as a device for direct teaching as for a device to assist instructional decision makers and to make them more efficient. For example, the computer managed instruction project which is now underway at the Naval Air Technical Training Center has exactly that thrust. In this development project, the computer will only manipulate student data and help guide the student's sequence of learning activities; the student's primary learning activities will come through interface with various other more traditional audiovisual media (slides, audio tapes, films, etc.).

The major Army computer research project is the Human Resources Research Office Project IMPACT—a five-year advanced development project designed to produce three outcomes:

1. A prototype computer-administered instruction (CAI) system which the Army can put into operation;

2. Several CAI programs of instruction dealing with different kinds of subject-matter of critical importance to the Army; and

3. A decision model of the instructional process—a set of rules for deciding precisely which learning materials to present next to a particular student based on his personal characteristics, his previous "learning history," and scientifically established principles of learning and teaching.

The project, funded at 4.3 million dollars, is aimed at a very systematic evolutionary approach to organizing education and training within the Army.

Opinion

What is there in military education and training that the civilian education sector can use? Are lessons to be learned? Are specific techniques applicable?

It is "beyond the scope of " this paper to list specific techniques or methods which have been proven in the military and can be used by the rest of American education. However, some general principles can be cited and some useful observations can be made. It must be remembered that military education and training relates directly to the ability of the defense establishment to accomplish its mission. If the technician lacks the skill to maintain the computer, that electronic marvel will not perform.

For the above reason the Department of Defense expends great sums of money to insure that skilled personnel are available when needed.

On the other hand, the problems within military education and training are generally the same sort of problems that plague civilian education. An "establishment" comes into being, with all its conservatism and resistance to improvement which that sometimes odious term implies. On an individual basis, people themselves tend to become bureaucratic and resistant to change. Innovation, where it occurs, depends a great deal on the "climate" created by the leaders and managers of training. The military establishment knows its mission—it therefore can design the training process with a great deal more specificity than can civilian education. With this realization, the trend is clearly established toward even more systematic design to insure the desired training outcomes. Systems engineering is no longer applied just to the development of hardware or weapons systems. The techniques of systems engineering are being applied to the instructional process and much needed instructional design techniques are evolving. Military training activities are beginning to package segments of courses for the training consumer. Significantly, military trainers are reexamining the traditional audiovisual communication media with the hope of developing some *strategy* for their employment in the structional process.

Another factor which differentiates military from civilian education is that the provision of a complete spectrum of audiovisual support for the instructor has become traditional since World War II in the military services. Although the military instructor must operate certain pieces of audiovisual equipment, he has not produced the projectual materials, films, etc. that are used with this equipment. The fact that audiovisual support is traditional in military training has produced some very sophisticated training aids; working models, cut-aways, mock-ups, and other devices which aid the demonstration of concepts, processes, and procedures, are a normal part of the spectrum of support for the military instructor. This is clearly different from the support provided for the normal public school teacher (she often uses the janitor's talents).

Teacher training is clearly different in the Armed Forces. The instructor training courses conducted at all levels of training are organized around the rationale of "minimum theory, maximum performance," and these courses effectively develop skilled presenters of information, this, despite the fact that military instructors are generally "doers," not professional teachers.

The constant reexamination of the total training process has given rise to some significant changes in the training materials. Textual materials have been found wanting in many instances. Only recently, since the advent of Project 100,000, did the Navy realize that its basic Blue Jacket Manual was unreadable at the reading level of entering enlisted men. The manual has been rewritten. In like vein, the Air Force's dependance on "contractor provided" technical manuals as texts for maintenance training has come under scrutiny. Maintenance manuals are being restructured to make them more usable in training and in performing maintenance on the job.

The military services use the techniques of simulation a great deal in the teaching of psychomotor skills. Much of what we know about skill training has been contributed by them. Research findings of such activities as the Human Resources Research Office, Office of Naval Research, and the Air Force's Human Resources Laboratory do contribute to the steadily developing body of knowledge about learning processes. This information should be made more available to responsible researchers and educational practitioners in the entire country.

The people who are concerned with the introduction and management of instructional technology within the military services are generally quite enthusiastic about its potential and the realities of its use. This enthusiasm very often beclouds the real state of the art. As in civilian education, the enthusiasts are full of plans and programs that are not quite in being; however, the military education and training establishment taken in general is using instructional technology with the same degree of sophistication and naivete as the civilian sector.

To summarize, the most important aspects of the uses of technology for education and training within the armed services are:

a. There is a direct relationship of training outcomes to the accomplishment of the military mission which causes more careful specification of learning objectives and training procedures.

b. Considerably more deliberate design of the instructional process seems to be evident in the military than in civilian education.

c. Complete media support of the instructional process is traditional.

d. Competence in the use of hardware and other instructional materials is very much a part of the instructor training which takes place at all levels within the military training establishment.

e. The individualization of learning is being implemented in the military despite its inherent difficulties in the highly structured military training environment. Programmed learning packages which enable student paced completion are in rather extensive use. Most of the thrust here is to enable the person to learn while on the job, not in a school setting.

f. Simulation is used extensively to develop psychomotor skill learning. A great variety of simulators are employed, ranging from simple to very sophisticated electronic devices.

g. Military training managers continually expressed the need for more efficient information exchange between the civilian and military sectors, and between the researchers and the practitioners in the use of instructional technology.

Acknowledgements

This report is the result of selected visits to Armed Forces education and training activities and many conversations with personnel thus engaged in the military services. Obviously, all activities could not be visited and personal interactions could not be had with everyone; therefore, let me apologize in advance for those oversights or seeming lack of detail in this summary.

Many people assisted in the development of this study. I wish to acknowledge the specific help of the following: Major Ovid L. Bayless, Major Michael J. Grady, Jr., Mr. Harold Schulz, Mr. Thomas Dolan, and Mr. Thomas Gillespie. Many, many individuals lent their energies and time to this undertaking—though too numerous to name, I wish to express my sincere appreciation.

Particular acknowledgement is made of the help gleaned from the draft monograph on this same subject which was prepared seven years ago by Dr. Lee Campion of the New York State Division of Educational Communications and Dr. James Finn of the University of Southern California.

Finally, the assistance of the Office of Audiovisual Affairs under the Assistant Secretary of Defense for Administration is acknowledged. Colonel William Gallogly, Lt. Colonel Walter Halloran and Commander Paul Myatt were very helpful.

SELECTED BIBLIOGRAPHY

BOOKS

Crawford, Meredith P. *A Perspective on the Development of HumRRO*. Alexandria, Virginia: The George Washington University, Human Resources Research Office, August, 1967.

Shelburne, James C. and Kenneth J. Groves. *Education in the Armed Forces*. New York: The Center for Applied Research in Education, Inc., 1965.

Simons, William E. *Liberal Education in the Service Academies*. New York: Bureau of Publications, Teachers College, Columbia University, 1965.

PAMPHLETS AND REPORTS

Academic Resources and Technology Directory. West Point, New York: Office of the Dean, United States Military Academy.

American Institutes for Research. *Procedural Plan—Air University Learning Center*. Silver Spring, Maryland: American Institute for Research, September, 1968.

American Institutes for Research. *Training Plan—Air University Learning Center*. Silver Spring, Maryland: American Institutes for Research. October, 1968.

Caro, Paul W., Jr., Robert N. Isley and Oran B. Jolley. *The Captive Helicopter as a Training Device: Experimental Evaluation of a Concept*. Fort Rucker, Ala.: HumRRO Div. 6, Technical Report 68-9, June, 1968.

Computer Assisted Instruction Plan 1968. Randolph AFB, Texas: Air Training Command, ATC CAI Plan—68, 10 August 1968.

Curriculum for Data Systems Technician School: Class "C", AN/UYK-5 (V) Peripheral Maintenance. Washington, D.C.: Bureau of Naval Personnel, May, 1968.

The Development of Instructional Systems: Procedures Manual. Fort Devens, Mass.: U.S. Army Security Agency Training Center and School, 20 December 1967.

Evaluation of Controlled Self-Pacing Training Program of the ATC Standardized Electronic Principles Course. Randolph AFB, Texas: Air Training Command, Project Report N. 68-16, September, 1968.

Glossary of Terms and Abbreviations for Courses: 3AZR75100, Instructional Programmer. Lackland AFB, Texas: Air Training Command, June, 1968.

Group-Paced Presentation of Programmed Instruction. Randolph AFB, Texas: Air Training Command, Evaluation Project Report No. 65-2, August, 1965.

Guide to 3825th Support Group. Maxwell Air Force Base, Ala.: Air University, 1964.

Historical and Operational Data. Pamphlet, San Francisco, Calif: Treasure Island, Naval Schools Command, undated.

Human Factors Research in Support of Army Aviation. Symposium Presentations at 13th Annual Meeting of Southeastern Psychological Association. HumRRO, Professional Paper 27-67, June, 1967.

IBM Corporation. *A Feasibility Study of Computer Assisted Instruction in U.S. Army Basic Electronics Training.* Final Report Prepared for USCONARC at the U.S. Army Signal Center and School, Gaithersburg, Maryland: International Business Machines Corporation, February, 1968.

In-House Seminar on Computer Assisted Instruction. Report of the Department of Defense, Office of the Assistant Secretary of Defense (Manpower), 8 December 1967.

Information Concerning Programmed Instruction. Memphis, Tenn.: Chief of Naval Air Technical Training Instruction 1500.7E, Naval Air Station, 4 December 1967.

Instructional Programmer. Lackland AFB, Texas: Air Training Command, Plan of Instruction, Course No. 3AZR75100, June, 1968.

Instructor's Guide, Fort Sam Houston, Texas: Medical Field Service School, Brooke Army Medical Center, August, 1967.

Instructor's Manual. Monterey, California: Defense Language Institute, April, 1966.

Lovell, Dale F., Warren J. Anderson and Jackson A. Beaman. *A Study of the Effectiveness of the Track System in Basic Electricity/Electronics School at the Service School Command, San Diego.* San Diego, Calif.: U.S. Naval Training Center, October, 1968.

The Operational Framework for the Development and Implementation of the Basic Language Course of DLI, West Coast Branch. Monterey, Calif.: Defense Language Institute, 1963.

Parker, James F., Jr. and Judity E. Downs. *Selection of Training Media.* Wright-Patterson AFB, Ohio: Aeronautical Systems Division, Air Force Systems Command, ASD Technical Report 61-473, September, 1961.

Program of Instruction for Course 102-33 F20, Intercept Demultiplex Systems Repairman. Fort Devens, Mass.: U.S. Army Security Agency Training Center and School, March, 1968.

Project COBET Status Report. Prepared for USCONARC. Fort Monmouth, New Jersey: U.S. Army Signal Center and School, July, 1968.

Project IMPACT: Instructional Model Prototypes Attainable in Computerized Training. Technical Development Plan, The George Washington University, HumRRO, 2 December 1966.

Rigney, Joseph W. and Others. *Training Corrective Maintenance Performance on Electronic Equipment with CAI Terminals: I. A Feasibility Study.* (Project Designation NR 153-093, Contract Nonr-228(22). (Technical Report No. 51). Los Angeles, California, University of Southern California, Department of Psychology, December, 1966.

Rigney, Joseph W. and Others. *Requirements for a Computer-Aided Instruction System for the U.S. Naval Schools Command, Mare Island.* (PD NOOO 22-67-C-0181), (Technical Report No. 58). Los Angeles, California, University of Southern California, Department of Psychology, June, 1968.

Rigney, Joseph W. and Others. *Computer-Aided Technical Training Using Electronic Equipment On-Line with the CAI System.* (PD NR 153-093, NR154-251, Contracts Nonr-228(22), Nonr 46-26-16-360), (Technical Report No. 59). Los Angeles, California, University of Southern California, Department of Pyschology; Urbana, Illinois, Computer-Based Education Research Laboratory, June, 1968.

Training Device Developments. Orlando, Florida: Naval Training Device Center, NAVSO P-1300-41, April, 1968.

Training Digest, San Francisco Bay Area, San Francisco, Calif.: Treasure Island, Naval Schools Command, February, 1968.

Training Facility Standards. Aberdeen Proving Ground, Maryland: U.S. Army Ordnance Center and School, OSPAM3, January, 1964.

Utilization of HumRRO Research Products. CONARC Pamphlet 70-1. Fort Monroe, Va.: Hqtrs. U.S. Army Continental Army Command, 15 Feburary 1967.

ARTICLES AND PERIODICALS

Brown, Victor H. "Utilization of Instructional Television at BUPERS Supported Activities." *Naval Training Bulletin,* Summer, 1967, 1-5.

Caster, Paul. "Behind the Scenes in Army Film Making," *Army Digest,* Vol. XXII, No. 6 (June, 1967), 41-45.

Description of Project One Hundred Thousand. Department of Defense, Office of Assistant Secretary of Defense (Manpower and Reserve Affairs), periodic booklet, April, 1968.

Training Development Newsletter, Published periodically by Hqtrs., Air Training Command, Randolph Air Force Base, Texas.

UNPUBLISHED MATERIAL

Campion, Lee E. and James D. Finn. Unpublished monograph on instructional technology in the military services. (Typewritten) ca. 1962.

O'Connor, G. G., Major General. *Advances in Training.* Presentation to AUSA Meeting, Washington, D.C., 30 October 1968.

Report of the First USCONARC Training Innovations Conference. Fort Benning, Ga.: U.S. Army Infantry Center, 17-18 September 1968.

Shelburne, James C. Letter to Commission on Instructional Technology, 22 August 1968.

86.

Technology in Foreign Language Teaching

Prof., Modern Language Education
Purdue Univ.

"I don't advocate the use of machines . . . Give me a small class and plenty of resources. Let the lab be for 1984 and Big Brother . . . God preserve us from the machine!"

This defiant rejection is a school teacher's response to a questionnaire on the advisability of installing a language laboratory. Although its violence is not typical, such an attitude reveals a pervasive problem: the humanist's distrust of "machinery." Bookish by nature, training and experience, he tends to regard instructional equipment as a kind of profanation of the classroom.

On the college campus one finds the same attitude, especially toward motion pictures and computers. "The computer revolution is not an entirely bloodless one . . . In the Midwest a determined group of faculty members attempted to sabotage a newly installed computer system for recording grades by punching random holes in the cards." (*College Management,* February 1968, p. 33.) A wag has commented that the academic Luddites flaunt their innocence of electronic equipment—even television—"like a badge of honor or a warrant of electronic virginity."

The intransigent humanist is unmoved when reminded that his attitude and habits would be quite different if Gutenberg had invented magnetic tape rather than movable type. Yet this new battle of Ancients and Moderns is inevitably being decided, however slowly, by the sheer weight of numbers—too many students and too few teachers. Youth must be served, and moreover yesterday's youth are today's Assistant Professors.

Recent History

Although a Professor of Speech had installed a primitive language laboratory at Ohio State University some forty years ago, the very concept of audio-oral learning was soon discredited by the official "Coleman Report," which recommended a two-year sequence of study to attain a mere reading knowledge. This policy then produced a generation of deaf-and-dumb language majors—and teachers—whose failings made it necessary during World War II for the armed forces to train their own language specialists, notably in the Army Specialized Training Program. Contrary to popular legend, however, the ASTP made very little use of audiovisual materials and equipment, even prohibiting the spending of Army funds for the purchase of them. Although vigorously audio-oral, the so-called Army

Method relied on "human talking machines," otherwise known as native speakers. Too costly of money and time, this method was scarcely available to academic institutions, although a few universities, led by Cornell, gave it a good try.

It remained for Louisiana State University to install the first modern "language lab" in 1947, with a disc playback machine in each booth. Magnetic tape recorders were just becoming available, so after a few years they superseded disc equipment at LSU and other pioneering institutions such as Georgetown, Purdue, Michigan, Iowa and Wayne State. The language lab of today remains essentially unchanged from its prototype of fifteen years ago, save for improvements in ruggedness, convenience and—most important—quality of sound reproduction.

Because of the considerable cost (about $15,000 for 25 "positions"), such installations grew slowly in number, and almost solely in the large colleges and universities. Not until the NDEA of 1958, with its matching funds for the purchase of equipment, were the schools generally able to buy a language lab. The NDEA windfall was fated to be a mixed blessing.

With its flashing lights and chromium trim, the fancy new vehicle was impressive, even frightening to some teachers. To the public and not a few administrators, bemused by sensational articles in the Sunday supplement, it seemed a jet-propelled space craft to span the gap between languages and nations. But in truth it was only a group of booths for hearing and repeating the' words from the horse's mouth. And the horse—the familiar work-horse—was still the classroom teacher. Although nobody had ever dreamed of asking her to write the textbook, it was calmly and commonly assumed by administrators that she could devise and record the "program" for the language lab.

"The language lab as a teaching machine" was a perfectly sound concept of the programmer, but to the public and to many schoolmen it meant that the machine, as such, could teach. Not a few teachers actually feared for their jobs. Today it is common knowledge that the machine can only repeat the program fed into it, and that a good program requires almost infinite care and time to prepare, try out, and revise repeatedly. Looking back, we can summarize: the machine came first, the theory of programming followed, and the completion of expert, field-tested programs came several years later. Over a decade or more, the language lab used makeshift, homemade materials.

The results were sometimes disastrous. Lacking the facilities and techniques for successful recording, the high school teacher produced a sound track that was amateurish at best. More important, the content was often merely copied from the textbook, which was never intended for such use. When heard in the lab, the recorded "program" made the session a kind of amateur hour, tedious and repetitive. Sometimes the equipment itself failed, usually from misuse or neglect, sometimes because the teacher threw the wrong switch. When at length the boredom of pupils turned to vandalism the language lab became a disaster area which was locked up and abandoned. Such were the extreme misfortunes, not numerous but widely reported by word of mouth, as bad news always is. Of course there was good news too, from enlightened teachers in well organized school systems, but it came later, after the several years required for the preparation of superior materials. The good news was almost too late, and surely too little, for school teachers seldom have time to write for publication.

At the college level the results were less spectacular. With their superior resources, organization and technical expertise, the colleges could avoid major mistakes. Yet there were built-in handicaps: professors are usually not interested in the elementary course, for which the lab is used almost exclusively. Planning and programming were therefore delegated to junior instructors, although their primary concern was "publish or perish"; they did a job that was competent though uninspired, and they assigned graduate students to the supervision of lab sessions. Attendance by students was sometimes required and sometimes optional; in neither case was their oral performance likely to be monitored—that is, critically evaluated and corrected. Since self-criticism is impossible for most beginners, their performance was often an organized practice in repeating mistakes. In general, then, the lab sessions tended to become at best perfunctory, and at worst futile. Not surprisingly, the early enthusiasm for the language lab gradually waned. Early in the 1960s came relief in the form of expertly prepared courses which combined audio-lingual printed materials with tape-recorded equivalents followed by exercises based upon them. For the teacher there was a detailed how-to-do-it manual and sometimes also optional visual aids and "props." Gradually the book-and-tape combinations were widely adopted, but the optional materials less so. A few of the new courses included original color filmstrips or films, professionally excellent but seldom purchased. Although major publishers report that the film materials bring them little or no profit, school boards retort that the price is too high. Here is the old question of the chicken or the egg. What is certain is that the integrated films and filmstrips proved to be extremely motivating, while adding a new dimension to language learning.

Here for the first time was the systems approach applied to foreign language learning: *tape recordings* which provided native speakers as models; *printed equivalents* of the dialogues, followed by linguistic exercises; take-home *disc recordings* for every pupil's homework practice; *filmstrips* giving the visual imagery related to the dialogues; also, sometimes, movies which combined the audio and visual aspects of communication. Unfortunately, the very novelty—not to mention the cost—of this combination caused problems for everyone concerned.

Inevitably, most of the problems were passed down to the high school teacher, that work-horse of the profession, with her five daily classes. (The feminine form is used here because foreign language teachers, like their pupils, are usually females.) A major problem was how to conduct audio-lingually the classes of beginners who were, by definition, deaf and dumb in the foreign language. The only solution was for the teacher to be constantly lingual and for the pupils to remain eagerly audio in the intervals between their choral imitations. Repeated hour after hour (for most classes are composed of beginners), the teacher's performance was physically and nervously exhausting.

Presumably the tape recorder on the teacher's desk, if not the complete language lab, could spare the teacher's voice and energy. But in the early days of audio-lingual it was the self-same teacher who had to record the tapes, operate the lab and try to repair the equipment. With the advent of commercial tapes, discs and filmstrips the physical tasks were replaced by managerial busy-work: the cataloging and duplicating of tapes; the bookkeeping and inventory of take-home discs and recorders; the budgeting, ordering and accounting for supplies and repairs and—all too often—breakdowns or vandalism of the equipment.

Over the years these nagging miseries were usually overcome, but the experience was often discouraging if not traumatic. Especially in the early years, pupils were bored, parents disappointed, principals alarmed (by the costs and the vandalism), while some teachers longed for the good old days of "read aloud and then translate." No wonder that a few labs were abandoned! But the dedicated teachers and administrators fought their way through. When improved materials and equipment were combined with good teaching and administration, the results became evident in unprecedented audio-lingual skills. Although with great effort, the work-horse of the profession had successfully traveled the new road.

And then came the heartbreak: the driver disapproved! Always in the driver's seat but sometimes napping, the college professor awoke to find the schools moving in a new direction. Frequently he opposed it, for the new freshmen in his classes had not been taught to translate, they answered in the foreign language when he questioned them in English, they could not recite the rules of grammar, they had not read enough. Admittedly their speech was more fluent than accurate, more colloquial than literary. And no doubt those with mediocre training had acquired a mere smattering of the several skills. Altogether a very mixed bag. Perhaps inevitably, the sorting-out process relegated the audio-lingual students to the class of beginners, where they could start over, this time in the traditional method.

Such treatment was disillusioning to the students and maddening to their former teachers. "It is a pedagogical atrocity," wrote the late George Scherer, a distinguished professor of German and a pioneer in the audio-lingual revolution. His feeling was shared by other leaders, notably the officers of the MLA, who decided that, especially in the academic world, revolution can succeed only through education. The decision was followed by action.

The NDEA Institutes

Devised primarily by the Foreign Language Program of the MLA, the foreign language Titles of the NDEA (1958) included generous matching funds for the purchase of electro-mechanical equipment, and subsidies for special Institutes at which school teachers could improve their skills and knowledge, learn modern pedagogy and become proficient in using the new equipment, materials and techniques. Within a few years, millions of dollars were provided for thousands of language labs, while some 30,000 teachers were paid to attend the summer Institutes. This sudden largesse was almost overwhelming.

To appreciate the impact on the foreign language teacher, reflect that she had become a kind of academic outcast. Her share of the high school enrollment had dwindled, over a forty-year period, from a high point of 40 percent to an all-time low of 14 percent. There was also the long period of national isolationism which made everything "foreign" appear suspect; there was the war-time humiliation of foreign language "majors" and even teachers failing to qualify for special service; there was the general reduction or even elimination of foreign language requirements for college entrance or graduation. And then, after 40 years of famine, this neglected subject was proclaimed by Act of Congress to be essential to the national interest. Many millions were appropriated. To the lean and hungry teacher the NDEA was manna from heaven.

Divine guidance was lacking, however, and nothing less could have provided a wise over-all direction of this crash program, dependent on annual appropriations that were often late but must be spent at once or be "lost" (returned to the Treasury). Although the overworked staff in the USOE did its remarkable best, it could not possibly verify the details of hundreds of proposals, nor could it supervise the Institutes, whose annual number steadily increased to more than eighty. Aided by a special panel of advisers, the USOE at first awarded contracts by comparing the proposals and the reputations of the prospective Directors. Later, the reports of official inspectors could be consulted, but systematic inspection was possible only in the early years when the number of Institutes was small.

Sharing the elation of their colleagues in general, the inspectors tended at first to be more enthusiastic than critical; however it is likely that the first Institutes were indeed the best ones, for they were directed by outstanding men, and the morale of the participants was high. Even today we hear echoes of the indiscriminate praise broadcast in those early days when it all seemed too good to be true.

In fact it was only partially true, because of the many variables: the Institute might be as short as five or as long as nine summer weeks, housed in air-conditioned comfort or in monsoon misery, buoyed by a gung-ho spirit or rent by petty animosities. On balance the results were helpful but inadequate: a USOE officer stated publicly that the average FL teacher needed at least two or three summer Institutes, rather than a single exposure. Only a relatively few got two or three, and those few were usually teachers who were already proficient in the foreign language. At the lower end of the scale, the participants—full-time teachers of the language—needed instruction from a beginner's textbook.

According to the USOE *Manual for Participating Institutions,* the sponsoring institution should provide "a satisfactory language laboratory installation": the program should promote "mastery of new teaching methods and instructional materials," and facilities should include "language laboratory and other audiovisual aids."

Those specifications were met in varying degrees, depending mostly on the interests of the local director. In general there was considerably more emphasis on methods and materials than on equipment and how to use it. Although duly "provided," the laboratory was seldom a scheduled part of the program—not even for the children in the demonstration class. Commonly it was just "made available" for extracurricular use in one's spare time, of which there was little. Although some Institutes offered supervised practice in the use and servicing of the equipment, many simply provided a few lectures, perhaps by a representative of the audiovisual department.

Such tokenism was generous when compared with the treatment accorded to other types of equipment. (In fairness, however, it should be said that most of the integrated films and filmstrips are intended for the elementary school, and that there have been few Institutes for foreign language teachers at that level.) The 16mm projector was seldom used, and then only for the showing of imported feature films; the other projectors even less. One observer reported that in visits to a score of Institutes he found the overhead projector used only once. The use of such equipment, and likewise instructional television and radio, presumably was treated in the "methods course," based on the most popular "methods books." It is noteworthy that those books give scanty and skeptical treatment to all equipment except the (audio) tape recorder, which alone has been well received by the profession. Even this favored instrument was seldom used in the demonstration classes.

Because of their novelty and the large number of teachers involved, the influence of the Institutes has sometimes been exaggerated. What is certain is that they varied greatly. But one factor was constant: the site and the teaching staff represented higher education—specifically, language and literature (almost never school personnel or the Department of Teacher Education). When a university was the host the staff inevitably reflected the concerns of the graduate school.

The "participants," in turn, naturally wanted graduate credit, which would insure salary increases back home. In spite of the opposition of the USOE the local pressures were hard to resist; moreover the professors were not averse to recruiting candidates for advanced degrees.

Although there are good arguments on both sides, it seems clear that the requirements of the Graduate School (advanced courses in literature, primarily) tended to override the immediate practical needs of the school teachers. Certainly there was no graduate credit for practice in the use of the language lab and other equipment.

In general, then, the foreign language Institutes have done little to encourage the use of equipment and the learning materials devised for it. Although there have been exceptions, of course, and some exceptional professors even in routine Institutes, they only prove the rule. Undeniably the Institutes have done much pioneering, but—save for tape recordings—they have done it without benefit of educational technology.

After a few years of the Institutes the Presidents of the host universities and colleges received a form letter inquiring about the influence of the local Institute on the sponsoring department. Since Presidents lack the time and knowledge for composing answers to countless inquiries of all sorts, the letter was routinely forwarded to the department head, with a request for a draft reply. This bit of academic by-play may have served some local purposes, but it failed to elicit objective information.

After ten years of the Institutes such information has yet to be compiled and published. Probably it never will be, for usually the facts are known only by the teacher-candidates, rather than the faculty. This absurd situation results from the well-known antagonism between the Department of Education and the several academic departments. Although ostensibly and officially a partner in the preparation of teachers, the Department of Education is frequently ignored by the others.

"If you want to take Education courses you had better go and enroll over there. We

728/TO IMPROVE LEARNING/ Practical Considerations

don't communicate with those people." Such was the word spoken to a prospective gradu-ate student by an Ivy League department head. The graduate program of that modern language department is one of several which make no provision for school teachers; the M.A., if offered at all, is only a way station on the road to the Ph.D., which is still a research degree.

Alarmed by the whole situation, the MLA sponsored a special study and conference, directed by the late Archibald MacAllister of Princeton. A happy choice, for as Professor of Italian Literature and Director of the Language Laboratory, he was that rare com-bination—the true scholar-teacher. His preliminary questionnaire to the 52 Ph.D.-granting departments revealed that:

1. 51 employed inexperienced teaching assistants (who taught 80 percent of the lower-level courses);

2. 30 gave them no training in teaching;

3. most provided no effective supervision.

In his report of six years ago MacAllister anticipated the mood of today's students:

Dissatisfaction . . . with the cultivation of pure scholarship by and for individuals who for years must earn their living by lower-division teaching has grown more acute as the effects of our socio-economic revolution have made themselves felt on the nation's campuses . . .

The graduate schools should feel obligated to stop assuming that good teachers simply happen. The pressures have grown too great to permit such complacency to continue.

Yet MacAllister, although a vigorous exponent of instructional technology, was unable to persuade his conference colleagues even to mention the subject in their report. In a private letter he lamented that, in order to get agreement, the report had to be watered down, and that he had experienced opposition to the very mention of programmed in-struction, in a footnote.

It is significant that MacAllister's conference was composed of a score of distinguished professors of language and literature, with no representative of any other department or school. Although they devoted several pages to the undergraduate program for foreign language majors, they made no mention of practice teaching or professional courses. Their only approximation to such matters was a passing reference to Mr. Conant's "exhortations for better and longer language study" and "the improved teaching in the secondary schools that is beginning to flow from the language development activity of the NDEA."

Of those two references, the one to Mr. Conant is the more promising, but not for his specified exhortations. It is rather his advocacy of the "clinical professor" that is beginning to bear fruit. In a few enlightened universities one now finds a Professor of Foreign Lan-guage Teaching (or some such title). Usually he holds a joint appointment in Liberal Arts and Education, he is experienced in both school and college teaching, he gives the Special Methods course(s), supervises the practice teachers, and directs a doctoral program for prospective supervisors and professionals like himself. Lest he perish, he also publishes—usually articles concerned with research and development in his own special field.

His is an expanding field, concerned with methods and materials for use with the new media in varying combinations. Sometimes with the language lab director he may super-vise research (by graduate students) into such subjects as programmed instruction, the electronic classroom, dial-access to "mini-lessons," and even computer-based instruction, although the audio component—essential to language learning—is costly and therefore rarely found. With his teacher-candidates he uses the videotape recorder for observation of teaching in school classrooms; back on campus he uses it in the "mirror technique" or micro-teaching.

Although there are still relatively few such clinical professors, the prospect is encouraging; they bring Liberal Arts and Education together in much-needed cooperation; they use the computer, whose value is beginning to be appreciated even by some professors of literature; finally, the doctoral programs of the clinical professors now enroll more than one hundred students. Armed with their degrees and their specialized experience, the best of these bright but practical young people will themselves become clinical professors. As their tribe increases, so will the fortunes of modern foreign languages in our schools and colleges.

Conversely, the influence of the familiar NDEA Institutes seems certain to decline. Remedial and temporary by definition, they treated the symptoms rather than the endemic malady of poor teacher training. To a degree they were self-defeating, for some conservative language departments felt encouraged to "let the Institutes do it." There is no doubt that the influence of the Institutes on teacher education, even in the sponsoring institutions, has been far less than was hoped.

Now the initial fervor has passed and the number of FL Institutes has been halved. Of the remainder, a good many are concerned with the teaching of English as a new language or dialect for certain segments of our own society. Here is a bold new venture born of urgent needs. Concentrating solely on the hardcore problems of language learning, and unhampered by tradition or vested interests, it has the potential for making fundamental changes in the theory and practice of language teaching. With imaginative leadership and adequate funds for materials, equipment and personnel, it could make the conventional Institutes appear effete, by comparison.

Language and Culture

"The chief purpose in studying French should be to gain an understanding and appreciation of France." The writer of those words was not a contemporary anthropologist, but President Nicholas Murray Butler of Columbia University, in his annual report of 1918.

Shortly later our leading language departments began introducing courses in the foreign "civilization," meaning primarily the fine arts, literature and history, with considerable emphasis on literary history. Only since World War II have we known the anthropological concept of "culture with a small c." Popularized by the descriptive linguists, it has slowly infiltrated the ranks of the foreign language teachers, although firmly resisted by many. "The sum of man's learned and shared behavior, including his intellectual, social and artistic accomplishments" is a distasteful concept to some and a frightening one to others. Should—or can—such "culture" be taught in foreign language classes?

According to the descriptive linguists any language is an essential part of the culture it represents, and it can be understood only in the context of that culture.

For example, when a Frenchman hears himself greet you with *Bonjour!* his right hand automatically shoots forward and clasps yours. He does not shake your hand; he clasps it. Of such folkways is culture, the referent of language. The French intimate *tu* (or German *du*) arises not from rules but from human situations. Words are defined not by dictionaries but by their referents.

Generally accepted by the audiolingualists, this doctrine would ideally require that one learn the language abroad. Failing that, the obvious substitute is a specially prepared series of foreign-made films or television programs. Accordingly the last decade has brought us several "film and text" courses, the more ambitious ones spanning a three-year sequence.

Not to be confused with mere documentaries, these films are integrated with filmstrips, disc recordings, tape-recorded drills, textbook scripts and exercises, and sometimes "props" and "realia" (representative souvenir objects or pictures). Perhaps the most elaborate series is "En France (comme si vous y étiez)," filmed entirely on location by professional actors, and at astronomical cost. Lively, original, entertaining and pedagogically sound, this course has suffered disappointing sales although the films were widely broadcast by NBC. Much the same can be said of "Parlons Français," although it cost millions of dollars and was viewed year after year by millions of children in their classrooms. Less elaborate film courses, without benefit of television, have been moderately successful, thanks probably to the better sales organizations of the established book publishers involved. Of those consulted for this paper the most reassuring one reports that, although the sales of the audio materials are seven times greater than the audiovisual, the latter do make a reasonable profit over a five-year period, and their sales are increasing. But on the whole, the record is disappointing. Why?

Cost is doubtless a major problem, and the free TV showings served to emphasize the cost. But mental habits and attitudes are even more compelling. Most school boards and teachers think of language as book-learning. Even the MLA, after paying for an extensive series of films to accompany its *Modern Spanish,* neglected to advertise them, and the publisher never mentioned them. To this day they are generally unknown to teachers of Spanish.

The presentation of the foreign culture—indeed the modern concept of culture and its expression in language—these ideas simply have not yet reached the average teacher, or even the ambitious teachers who attended the Institutes. "Civilization" or "culture" was indeed a scheduled part of every Institute, but it consisted of a series of lectures and readings; apparently culture was something to be talked about or "learned" rather than experienced. And once back on the job, high school teachers don't have time even to talk about culture—they must "cover the book."

> Far too many students end their language study with the same naive assumptions they started with: that learning a new language is simply a matter of re-coding one's own, that languages are alike except for the words, that thoughts and ideas are universal and can be put into words by all languages in much the same way.
>
> John B. Carroll, quoted in
> *Foreign Language Teaching,* p. 74.

Television and FLES

A well-known cartoon shows a fat woman seated comfortably before the TV set while she watches a program of calisthenics. Reaching for another piece of candy, she comments, "I've been watching this program for a month, and I haven't lost a pound."

Unfortunately, learning a foreign language by TV is also sometimes considered to be a spectator sport. But the parallel is unfair, for the viewers—especially young children—do participate vocally and vigorously as they respond to the instructions of the TV teacher. It is certain that FLES by TV has succeeded very well in many school systems, but the success required much more than a TV set.

Ideally, FLES requires an expert teacher in the classroom every day. Since the expert FLES teacher is rare, she has entered most classrooms via TV, whose increasing popularity she has at once shared and promoted.

It is not generally realized that probably there are more students of modern foreign languages in the elementary schools than in the colleges and universities. A few years ago it was conservatively estimated that "Parlons Français" alone had a regular audience of at least two million children. And it seems certain that the overwhelming majority of FLES classes are taught at least partially by TV.

Peculiar to the TV screen is its special "magic"—the illusion of reality, of immediacy, of personal communication with the individual viewer. It is this strange fascination which makes children, despite their alleged short span of attention, sit spellbound for hours, to the annoyance of parents and teachers.

Peculiar to the child is his capacity to learn oral language—any language or several—to the amazement of parents when residing abroad with their children. But the child must be young, not adolescent. "Here the evidence is almost overwhelming. Practically every investigation of the matter, whether by linguists, psychologists, or neurologists, reinforces the conviction that young children have a unique capacity for language learning that can never be duplicated later in life." (J. Richard Reid in *Reports of Surveys* . . . Modern Language Association, New York [1962], p. 200.)

Unfortunately the MLA Statement of Policy (1961), omitting any reference to TV instruction, discourages all FLES teaching unless it is followed by a FL program continuing through grade 12. Clearly this position assumes that FLES is justified only if it leads to mastery of the language; if interrupted it is a waste of time. But to this view one may object that the cultural learnings for children may outweigh and even justify the linguistic learning. The by-products may be more important than the subject matter, as with other parts of the elementary curriculum.

It seems clear that intercultural understanding and tolerance, like language itself, can best be learned by the very young child before he encounters prejudices, and that therefore a sequence of a few years, if well taught, should be valuable.

Regardless of this academic controversy, and despite the many pitfalls of TV instruction, it is clear that a few FLES programs by TV are getting excellent results when supported by good follow-up practices in the classroom. By far the most widely used TV program is "Parlons Français," with 150 fifteen-minute films featuring Mme. Anne Slack. This three-year program is an example of instructional TV at its best, with these advantages:

1. Graded linguistic materials prepared by experts

2. Presentation by a gifted and winsome teacher

3. Sophisticated repetition and drill disguised by dramatics, puppetry, and songs and by identification with French children on the screen

4. Big-budget, professional production (at home and abroad)

5. Elaborate aids for local use: for the teacher, a detailed manual, practice discs, fifteen how-to-do-it films; for the children, practice discs and workbooks; for the school system, consultant services

6. A one-year trial program involving thousands of children after which the course was rewritten and the final filming was undertaken

The production of such an elaborate and costly program would be far beyond the financial and professional resources of any local school system. Like the automobile and other high-cost, high-quality products, it is feasible only with concentrated production and mass consumption. Nevertheless, scores—perhaps hundreds—of school districts have tried to produce their own TV instruction, usually with mediocre or even disastrous results. It is these local failures which have discredited TV instruction in the eyes of many educators. Having failed with their home-made "horseless carriage," they have given up on all such new-fangled contraptions.

The best TV programs are supplemented by disc or tape recordings, activity books for the children, perhaps even demonstration films for the teacher. The help of an itinerant specialist is highly desirable, for it provides personal guidance and encouragement for the classroom teacher who otherwise may well feel isolated and insecure in her strange new task. Even without such professional support the enthusiastic classroom teacher can provide successful follow-up activities to supplement the broadcasts. Well-documented research has demonstrated that this can be done and that the children not only make good progress in the foreign language but also do well in their other subjects simultaneously and later.

Even the average TV series provides at least a manual or guide for the classroom teacher. It may be an expert and detailed exposition of how to do it; more likely it is a mere synopsis of the broadcasts. In the latter case, the teacher is encouraged to think that the TV program provides almost total teaching. Nothing could be further from the truth, but such is unfortunately the assumption of many classroom teachers, parents and even principals.

At an international congress of ITV experts held in this country a few years ago it was decided to go and view an unrehearsed demonstration in a local primary school. A telephoned request to the principal was promptly granted, and the exact time and place were specified for the next day. Unfortunately, the principal neglected to notify the classroom teacher.

At the appointed time a bus load of international celebrities found the classroom and the children but no teacher, for she had gone out for a smoke. The TV set was turned on and so were the youngsters, but quite without reference to the program. The audio was drowned out by the shrill voices of thirty children who were playing various games and practically climbing the walls. It was indeed a demonstration.

Classroom TV sessions are usually less spectacular but not necessarily more productive of foreign language skills. Although the conscientious teacher can control the children, she cannot always control the local circumstances which may degrade the TV reception or otherwise minimize its impact.

"Many factors interact to produce an effective TV picture, and just one thing wrong— poor contrast, glare . . . the viewer's position, room lighting—can spoil the whole effect." (Alan S. Neal of IBM Advanced Systems Development Laboratory, in *A-V Instruction,* September 1968, p. 707.)

Accustomed to the good conditions of at-home viewing, classroom teachers do not realize the built-in handicaps of the average classroom, and they are unaware of such elementary requirements as the 30° maximum viewing angle. As for the pupils, even those with 20/20 vision can be partially blinded by "just one thing wrong."

Even more critical is the problem of hearing when the audio is in a foreign language. Audiovisual personnel and FL teachers are equally unaware of the fact that at least 8,000 cps are necessary to transmit the high-frequency sounds of speech. They do not realize that, thanks to "redundancy"—the clues provided by the oral context—the listener unconsciously "supplies" the mumbled or the high-frequency sounds which are not actually transmitted. The beginner in a foreign language course has no such resource, for he simply cannot imitate sounds that he does not hear. At school this general problem is commonly aggravated by one or more of the following factors: poor acoustics, since the average classroom is an echo chamber; the "little tin horn" in the usual TV receiver; excessive volume (the average teacher's response to any acoustical problem) and the resultant distortion; poor reception, so common in the big cities. Add to all this the competing sounds from the corridor or from outdoors, and in the classroom itself the shuffling of feet, the dropping of books and the teacher's commands to pay attention.

It is all so different from seeing and hearing in the quiet and privacy of the living room. In theory, school television can provide "the world at your fingertips," but in practice the little world of the classroom frequently intervenes.

Meanwhile the teacher may feel that the classroom is no longer hers. Here is perhaps the greatest problem of FLES by TV: the lack of any human organization or authority to provide leadership and guidance, and to which the teacher feels responsible. She is perhaps the only "foreign language teacher" in the school. Unable to speak the language and without the familiar resource of a book, she naturally feels insecure. Her colleagues and her principal can offer no help. The "little black box," as impersonal as the TV station itself, is concerned only with the program on the air. She feels, in the full sense of the term, helpless.

A few producers of TV or film series have undertaken to provide demonstration films or field consultants, and sometimes both. A major publisher reports to the author of this paper that the consultants represent a major cost in the marketing of the materials. Clearly it is a valuable service to the teachers, but a temporary one. On the other hand, the fifteen demonstration films for "Parlons Français" were seldom requested although available free, and were sometimes unused after being received. In large cities such films have sometimes been broadcast after school hours, but rarely watched. After-school meetings have been tried and abandoned because of poor attendance, unless it was made compulsory—seldom done, for obvious reasons. It seems clear that classroom teachers do not feel loyalty to a subject in which they are unskilled and for which they feel no local professional support.

It is a rare school system or organization which has moved to meet this problem. One such is the Minnesota Council for School Television, a cooperative society whose participating schools make a firm commitment to share the cost as well as the programs. Administrators and teachers hold membership in the Council and various committees. The headquarters office and staff provide leadership and specialized services such as counseling, testing and longitudinal studies of learning. The TV teacher provides weekly broadcasts for the classroom teachers, and he also visits classes and conducts local workshops. Such an arrangement suggests directions for other regions and states.

Recently some of the state education agencies have begun developing statewide TV networks and, with them, cooperative organizations with local representation. Here again the local TV teacher is no longer isolated and irresponsible. Such arrangements give promise for the future of instructional TV.

It is not suggested here that even in the best of circumstances television yields perfect results with young children. Their ability to mimic is probably greater with regard to melodic pattern or intonation than it is with pronunciation as such. Their imitative blunders in English are well known: "I pledge a legion . . ." and "Round John Virgin" and even "Harold be thy name." Supervision and correction are always necessary, but it does seem that very young children capture the new melodic patterns better than their elders, and retain them indefinitely. Likewise with peculiarities of syntax such as the final position of the verb in German. A similar capacity is the ability and willingness to imitate gestures and facial expressions as seen on the screen. Such advantages are unique to early childhood and it is unfortunate that high school teachers are unable to evaluate and give credit for them. Perhaps it is for this reason that some such teachers resent the "graduates" of FLES sequences. There are reports that some high schools have overtly or covertly opposed and destroyed FLES programs in their district.

As for films, it is often difficult to distinguish their use from that of TV. Obviously they are more conveniently available, they can be scheduled at any time, and repeated at will; also the film showing can be stopped whenever discussion or review seems desirable. Unfortunately the cost is high and sales are few. Those films which have sold best seem to be the ones which are so devised that the textbook and other materials depend upon them. This arrangement is not only strategic but logical, for language derives from life and not from books.

Supplementary films—those which are not integrated with any language course—are frequently of little value except for motivation. Unfortunately, a great many language teachers are unfamiliar with any other kind of "language films." Original and highly valuable, however, is the series of "filmed recitations" directed by Professor Howard Nostrand with a talented French actor on camera. Recreating the legendary figure of the French *diseur,* the actor performs (rather than recites) a considerable number of French poems embracing several varieties and appealing to various ages. Considerable field testing has revealed that even young children respond intuitively to the appeal of true poetry, even when they do not understand all the words. The children are given no explanation or analysis—simply the poem itself as interpreted by a sensitive and accomplished performer. There is no doubt that the audiovisual presentation is superior to sound alone, and the latter in turn to the printed page. Mr. Nostrand's initiative makes one long for greater resources of this sort. Much fiction and surely most poetic and dramatic art is best appreciated through sight and sound rather than through printed symbols.

Television and films are most used at the elementary level, less so in secondary school, and least of all in higher education. The rigidity of the high school schedule is a well-known obstacle, and tradition is another. On the 90-odd TV series screened at a recent evaluation conference conducted by National Instructional Television, only a handful were intended for the high school. Almost all were local productions intended to fit the local curriculum; most of them were poor. Far superior because of the greater funds available are the foreign-made series such as "En France" or the recent "Guten Tag" series, which promises to develop over the years. Such productions have technical excellence but they sometimes fail to understand the perspective of the American adolescent; also they try to aim at a wide range of ages; the shotgun technique has obvious weaknesses.

The most original and ambitious series for total instruction was doubtless Telescuola, intended to provide the junior high school curriculum to thousands of children in remote Italian villages which lacked teachers. Highly ambitious and yet successful, Telescuola has recently been drastically reduced in scope, apparently because teachers have now been found for those villages.

The college level has made very little use of language instruction by TV. Perhaps the earliest and surely one of the most successful was the French program begun in 1950 at Western Reserve University. Of the several TV programs conducted over the years by that institution, French was the only one whose enrollment justified a four-semester sequence. Full college credit was awarded, upon examination, to the TV students as they completed each semester. Many of them continued as resident students and at least one has gone on to the Ph.D. in French. All the Western Reserve TV programs were eventually discontinued because of difficulties not related to television.

Administrative problems have undoubtedly handicapped TV instruction at the college level and there have been other obstacles, notably tradition, inertia and academic freedom. Nevertheless there is slow but steady progress. Cooperative arrangements, state-wide or regional, have resulted in networks offering first-year and second-year courses primarily in Spanish but also in German and French. Broadcasts may be by open circuit, closed circuit or special micro-wave connections. The individual colleges are free to administer their own examinations for credit. It is currently estimated that more than 20,000 college students are studying Spanish by television. The FCC anticipates the establishment of some 40 state-wide ETV networks in the near future. Foreign languages will doubtless be included, and hopefully the lessons and the TV techniques will be superior to those of the past. What is urgently needed is a general service for consultation and long range planning to avoid the further duplication of courses, and especially the duplication of mistakes.

Conclusion

Although current research and experimentation in the foreign language field hold great promise for the future of instructional technology, it is teacher turnover which is most important and, in this case, encouraging. Probably no branch of our profession suffers a greater "generation gap" than the foreign language teachers, who for almost 40 years seemed to be the "vanishing Americans." Although today the greatest "gap" is found in the field of Latin, whose teachers now average more than 50 years of age, the same was doubtless true until a few years ago in the modern languages. But with the recent upsurge of enrollments there has been a rapid influx of eager young teachers, many of whom have attended the NDEA Institutes. Born and raised in the age of electronics, attuned to the spirit and needs of today's students, they will soon dominate their professional field, especially in the high schools. Like today's young parents, they are sympathetic to instructional technology, which has been well ahead of the profession.

Paradoxically, the field of Latin has produced the most lively and complete set of modern learning materials. Applying the principles of descriptive linguistics to audiovisual programming, Professor Waldo Sweet and his associates have also drawn upon the resources of the Hollywood "spectacular," combining commercial footage with scenes enacted by their own special cast using the original movie sets. The color films and filmstrips capture the grandeur that was Rome; the students can "see it now" while hearing it narrated in simple Latin. Then they hear and speak it in the language lab while doing their programmed exercises. Classwork reinforces and combines the several activities, providing mature guidance into the humanistic and enduring values of Roman culture.

Technology in the service of culture—such is the goal of the so-called "gadgeteers" in the foreign language field. They resent that term, and likewise the charge of being anti-literary, when in truth they are opposed only to the student's premature plunge into belles-lettres which causes fractured translation into his native words, with their native referents, and a cumulative distaste for the foreign literature and the culture it represents. This mis-fortune—all too frequent—is caused by teachers who, in the words of the late Professor W. R. Parker, want to eat their cake before they have it.

At stake here is a major issue of public education: who shall determine policy and goals. It is the thesis of Jencks and Riesman, authors of *The Academic Revolution,* that the graduate schools are by far the most important shapers of undergraduate education. It is Conant's thesis that the more distinguished the graduate faculty, the less they are concerned with teacher education, and "as for what goes on in the schools, they couldn't care less." Yet teacher education—at least four-fifths of it—is provided by the liberal arts faculty, much of it identical with the graduate faculty. Inevitably the elitist attitudes of these scholars are passed on to the teacher-candidates, who in turn teach as they have been taught.

Perhaps the new spirit of independence among students will make them question the assumptions and routines which have made foreign language a periperal subject, elected pri-marily to satisfy college entrance requirements. Our young teachers and teacher-candidates are becoming aware of the broader horizons and the deeper human understandings to be gained by an appreciation of a foreign language and culture. Thanks to the new tech-nology, rote-learning can be supplanted by simulated experience, and lockstep by individual inquiry. And thanks to the progressive policies of a new national society, the American Council on the Teaching of Foreign Languages, the young teacher will not lack enlightened leadership. Perhaps those leaders, by joining forces with the educational foundations and those vast new combines of electronics and publishing firms, will provide concerted plan-ning and action in place of the isolated nibblings of the past.

We can learn from abroad, too. Educational TV in Europe has long been superior to ours, and their highly developed use of slide sequences in "radiovision" is scarcely known in this country. Their radio alone, when used imaginatively, makes good the boast of "wide screen and full color." Pioneering work in linguistics, films and television continues in Europe while our own efforts disregard it.

In equipment, at least, we have almost infinite resources: the electronic classroom (off-spring of the language lab) should become *the* classroom of the future, while the lab itself ultimately evolves into computer carrels—descendents of the ill-fated "teaching machine." A long-term prospect, that, since the necessary audio component poses serious problems. Today it is available in very few installations, and even those are still experimental.

For the immediate future, the best prospect seems to be some form of Professor Samuel Postlethwait's audiovisual-tutorial system, of which the FLICS program at Ann Arbor seems to be a development: well-equipped carrels for the individual study of foreign art, music and social studies. The foreign language, like the wealth of equipment, is considered a medium of communication.

Such a fusion of form and content, of ends and means, points the way towards a sensible strategy of language learning *and use.* In order to develop and implement the strategy, there is urgent need of cooperative work by linguists, psychologists, media specialists, experts in speech, hearing and reading—and of course teachers and clinical professors. Only by such teamwork can we overcome the entrenched and absurd tradition of a little (rote) learning in order to pass entrance requirements.

In all this, it is certain that technology must play a major role, as it already does in out-of-school learning. The medium may or may not be the message, but as the twenty-first century approaches, the message is clear.

87.
Instructional Technology In Medical Education

by HILLIARD JASON
Prof. and Director
Office of Medical Education Research & Development
Michigan State Univ.

Introduction

The profession of medicine depends heavily on technology. Both practice and research have used and prompted new applications of technology for many years. Yet, instruction in medicine has not had a comparable orientation. Serious study and improvement of the instructional process in medicine has only recently begun. This attention is now leading to the implementation of approaches borrowed from other fields, as well as to explorations of new approaches specifically adapted to the particular needs of this profession.

These new developments, and the directions in which they will likely go, will be reviewed against the background of the recent history of medical education and its current major trends. This will involve an analysis of the central tasks of medical instruction and of the ways in which technology has made or can make its most important contributions.

Throughout this presentation the orientation will be exclusively toward technology as a factor in direct instruction, rather than a component of such administrative support functions as student record keeping, library management or budget handling.

Accommodation to the assigned space limitations required the setting of priorities, which have led to the selective exclusion of many issues. The highest priority and, therefore, most attention, has been given to those aspects of medical education which seem most in need of strengthening and to those forms of technology which are believed to hold the most promise as responses to these needs. It is emphasized that these priorities, emphases, and omissions are reflections of my own views and predispositions. While a wide variety of personal experiences as well as systematic studies of my own and others have contributed to this paper, the categories selected for attention, the conclusions drawn and the recommendations offered must be interpreted as a distillation of informed judgments and substantiated findings, not as exclusively the later.

The National Medical Audiovisual Center has compiled a bibliography of relevant references in this field, prior to October, 1966. We have developed a supplemental bibliography, bringing that one up to date. Both are attached as Appendices 2 and 3.

Background and Perspective

The Tasks of Medical Education

The applications of technology in medical education must be considered against the perspective of the instructional purposes which are to be achieved. Undergraduate medical education is charged with the rather staggering task of negotiating a virtual transformation in the young men and woman who are selected to become physicians. In some ways, this educational process is unlike any other. In addition to the huge and growing body of information and the large array of intellectual, manual and sensory skills which the students are to be helped to acquire, medical school faculties are increasingly seeing themselves responsible for helping students undergo some measure of personality modification. They are to enhance or develop the students' capacities for: establishing and sustaining high standards; making judgments and taking action in the face of considerable uncertainty; dedicating themselves to the notion that the welfare of others takes precedence over their own comfort and convenience; remaining productively engaged with experiences that tax the instincts and offend the senses; being supportive and empathetic while objective and clear-headed; putting aside a lifetime of becoming socially proper and discreet in relations with others, in favor of such activities as directly and comfortably asking virtual strangers for the most highly personal information; to mention only some of the highlights of this incredible educational challenge.

These and other goals must be fulfilled to an extent sufficient to grant each candidate privileges which are accorded no other group in society. In their professional roles they will no longer be bound by usual considerations of emotional or physical privacy, they will be entrusted with the judgments and tools of life and death, and they will be put in the position of having to give advice which can cause others to significantly modify their total life style.

The Characteristics of Medical Education

The pattern of the past century has been for almost exclusive attention to be given to the sub-task of helping students acquire the largest possible body of information, to the relative exclusion of attention to the many other sub-tasks noted above. These other sub-tasks are now coming to be increasingly recognized as in need of systematic instruction for optimal development.

Until relatively recently medical education in this country was a rather standardized process. With very little exception from school to school, the first two years consisted of lectures and laboratory exercises in the basic sciences of anatomy, biochemistry, microbiology, pathology, pharmacology and physiology. The next two years consisted of "clinical clerkships" in which the students rotated through full-time experiences on the clinical patient-care services of internal medicine, obstetrics-gynecology, pediatrics, psychiatry, and surgery with a possible special out-patient experience in addition. The most outstanding feature of this curriculum was its "lock-step" quality. The implicit assumptions of such a rigid system were that all medical students must learn in the same way, at the same rate, and that all M.D.'s must have an identical basic preparation.

The inflexibility of this system, coupled with its primary preoccupation with the acquisition of information led, predictably, to the employment of a narrow range of instructional methods and a limited use of instructional technology. The nearly exclusive application of technology in this traditional setting was: occasional slides to illustrate formal lectures, occasional 16mm sound movies shown to large audiences, microscopes and other laboratory equipment used according to proscribed, "cook-book" type assignments, and, using the broadest definition of aids to instruction, indigent patients, who served as subjects on which students could practice skills.

Current Medical Education

The above description is a necessary background for understanding the circumstances from which many medical schools are now emerging. While the characteristics described above remain more or less current at a significant number of schools, the majority of medical schools in the country are currently engaged in a serious reexamination and modification of their instructional program.

Within the past ten years an accelerating series of events has led to a significant alteration in the basic structure and orientation of the educational process in medicine. There are increasing efforts to introduce flexibility into the curriculum, through reducing the number and length of required experiences, adding elective options and free time, developing tutorial and advisory systems, and fashioning multiple-track rather than single-track pathways through the curriculum. Twelve medical schools have created offices of Research in Medical Education, in formal recognition of their efforts to study and improve their instructional programs, and nearly twenty other schools are now trying to identify suitably qualified individuals to develop similar units. In the largest national growth spurt ever, seventeen new medical schools are in the process of being developed as additions to the previously existing 86. Most of these new schools are capitalizing on the flexibility of their newness to test innovative instructional ideas. This country-wide spirit of change has brought many efforts at modification of instructional methods and introduction of new applications of technology.*

In this atmosphere of change, the growing variety of available technological aids to instruction is being adopted, even grasped at, with an eagerness that is both promising and worrisome. Of greatest concern is the propensity of many teachers to regard new *devices* as equivalent to new *ideas*. The act of accommodating old instructional notions to new packages, such as putting an old lecture on television or on a computer, can prove to be worse than no change at all. The glossy new packaging tends to deceive both the student and the teacher into believing that something new, and assumedly better, is happening. In actual fact, what has often happened is that considerable energy and money have been invested in creating a situation that is now even harder to change than was the conventional instruction it is mimicking.

There have already been repeated examples in medicine of live lectures, poorly delivered and stultifying in person, which became even more evidently so on the TV monitor. One can now find a small but growing number of computer-based instructional units which are, in actuality, electronic reincarnations of the pompous, arrogant professor whose instructional strategy is the demand of compliance from the student rather than the promotion of independent skills. Simply put: bad instruction isn't made good by inclusion in a new medium.

The basic issue is that the automatic response of many medical educators has been the accommodation of conventional instruction to available technology. The pressing need is for continuous study and modification of the instructional process itself, with adaptation of technology to the needs of that instruction.

The most recent data on changes in the use of technology in medicine were assembled as part of a survey on curricular innovations, conducted by a Steering Committee of the Association of American Medical Colleges, of which I was a member. These data are presented as Appendix 1.

The Uses of Instructional Technology

The conventional uses of technology have tended to reinforce the conventional approach to medical instruction: that is, the primary preoccupation has been with the transmission of information. One of the major changes now taking place in medical education is the growing awareness that in the domain of information-learning, acquisition is merely the first of three necessary steps. Simple *acquisition* of information at some point in time is of no value if the conditions have not been arranged for effective *retention* of that information and for its availability for *transfer* to a variety of different settings. A companion recognition is that retention and transfer are optimized by having the original acquisition occur in a setting that is maximally like the setting in which this knowledge will later be applied. For medicine, the implication is that much learning must occur in the context of clinical problems which require solution.

Other major changes taking place in medical education are the increased attention being given to the areas of highly complex intellectual skills, such as problem solving, and to the non-cognitive areas of learning, such as inter-personal relationship skills. Among the major requirements for effective learning in these areas are the provision of models of what it is the student is to become and opportunities actually to engage in the application of increasingly refined approximations of these models, in maximally real settings.

The foundation premises of the review that follows are framed in terms of the primary requirements of medical education. These are: (1) to identify the requisite knowledge, skills and attitudes of medicine, (2) to devise techniques and settings for the practice of these competencies, and (3) to provide frequent and reliable feedback to students on their success in acquiring these competencies.

The current major uses of technology can be seen as falling into four categories which derive from these requirements. They are the processes of: (1) transmitting information, (2) serving as role models, (3) assisting with the practice of specific skills, and (4) contributing to the provision of feedback. These four categories will be reviewed in terms of actual current applications, the directions in which these uses appear to be moving, and their potential for the decade ahead.

Purveying Information

The primary preoccupation of most instructors in most medical schools remains the transmission of information. The two primary vehicles for this transmission are still the spoken word and assigned readings in textbooks and journals. There has been a slow and steady increase in the use of projection slides, overhead transparencies, movies and, more recently, television for information transfer to large groups. An important but frequently unrecognized instructional aid for information transfer has become the ubiquitous duplicating machine. The distribution of lecture notes, diagrams, summaries and selected items from the published literature is becoming a more common practice. Nonetheless, the non-illustrated, non-supplemented lecture remains a very common instrument in American undergraduate medical education. The chalkboard is still its most common accompaniment, even in lecture halls where it is impossible for chalkboard writing to be seen by a large proportion of the audience.

Serving to offset the increasing use of aids in large group settings is the trend toward reduction of the proportion of instruction oriented toward large groups. The diminishing "core" of required learning in medical school and the growing recognition of individual differences in backgrounds and career plans have reduced the need for aids to knowledge transfer in large groups. While the balance is still some distance from being tilted toward the side of individualized instruction in medicine, there has been a growing interest in programmed texts, cartridge-contained self-view movies, projection slide-audiotape combinations, and more complex multi-media carrel arrangements. As in most other branches of education, the major problems delaying the growth of these approaches have been: lack of preparation of the teachers for the change in attitudes and skills required for new deployments of their own energies, as required for this different concept of instruction; the lack of administrative and financial support for the effort necessary to produce the materials to be used on an individualized basis; the absence of a systematic source of funding for the hardware necessary for these approaches; the failure of industry to take proper initiative in producing and distributing appropriate instructional materials; and the absence of any central agency or other systematic arrangement for sharing and distributing non-commercial materials among institutions.

Serving as Models

A very limited but potentially important use of technology has been the provision, on movie film or videotape, of expert examples of particular behaviors from which students might model their own behavior. This approach has been most frequently employed for presentations of skilled clinicians performing parts or all of a model physical examination of a patient. Less commonly, this approach has been used as part of the teaching of medical history taking. The most elegant application of this approach to date was directed by Dr. Allen J. Enelow (now of Michigan State University) while he was at the University of Southern California. He and his colleagues developed a series of ten videotapes which were programmed to give the viewer an opportunity to select among three options of possible physician behavior at multiple branching points in the course of the conduct of interviews of patients who presented particular paradigmatic problems. This imaginative technique appears to have maximized student engagement and growth and is coming into increasing use around the country.

All of these approaches to providing models for students are fundamentally different from the much shorter presentations of particular skills which are meant to be repeatedly viewed while the skill is actually being practiced by the student. In these cases, the presentations are providing "supervisory," more than "model," functions. They will be discussed below.

Facilitating the Practice of Skills

Two separate but related new approaches to the use of instructional technology hold great promise for improving the learning of complex skills in medicine. The first consists of short projection slide-audio tape, movie film or videotape sequences designed to serve as both models and reference checkpoints for individual students who are practicing particular technical skills. The instructional materials include the equipment, devices or synthetic models which the student practices manipulating, while referring to the visual demonstration, which serves as a "supervisor." A fair range of such units now exist, including instruction in such diverse skills as withdrawing blood from a vein, doing a spinal tap, scrubbing for surgery and plating out a bacterial culture.

The second application of technology in this category involves *simulation,* in which the technological device itself becomes the equipment with which the student interacts in the process of practicing the skills he is learning. There are three major categories of skills in medicine: manual, sensory and intellectual. Simulation techniques have begun to be developed for instruction in all three areas. They will each be reviewed.

One of the older instructional aids in medicine is the mannequin created to represent the female birth canal. Together with a doll the size of a newborn it provides the student with his first practice of the maneuvers necessary in delivering a child. At the other end of the continuum from this simple and straightforward simulation is the highly sophisticated application of modern technology known as "SIM 1." This life-size, life-like computer-controlled mannequin was developed under the direction of Drs. Stephen Abrahamson and J. D. Denson at the University of Southern California, with the collaboration of Aerojet General. It permits the practice and effective learning of many of the complex skills involved in the administration of anesthetics. SIM 1 breathes, has a heartbeat, pulse and blood pressure, and the pupils of his eyes dilate and constrict. All of these functions and many others respond appropriately to varying dosages of several different drugs, administered either by injection through a "vein" or by face mask through the "lungs." This is one of the most effective illustrations to date of the application of modern technology at a level of sophistication which matches in complexity some of the skills which must be learned in medicine. It seems clear that SIM 1 will be the forerunner of a large family of devices which will provide varying degrees of approximation of aspects of human functioning as a basis for the practice and mastery of the complex technical skills of medicine.

The most advanced approach to instruction in the area of sensory skills so far developed are the various "heart sound simulators," pioneered by Dr. Abe Ravin of Denver, Colorado. Using a variety of approaches, these simulators have in common the capacity to generate a virtually infinite variety of life-like heart sounds at controllable rates. Learning to distinguish a particular heart sound on a live patient may be nearly impossible, with that sound being buried amidst a variety of other natural sounds, while occurring at a rate of, say, 90 a minute. With the simulator, the particular sound can both be isolated for exclusive attention and can be slowed to the easily discernible rate of, say, 10 per minute. A gradual increase in the rate of repetition and the quantity of other sounds permits the systematic learning of the discriminatory skills which are required. It seems indisputable that analogous devices to assist in the learning of other complex sensory skills, such as interpreting breath sounds or eye findings, are needed and deserve to be developed.

In addition to instruction in manual and sensory skills, the acquisition and refinement of intellectual skills is now receiving increased attention. Technological reinforcement of this task is now made possible with the advent of the remote access time-shared computer. Probably the most generally required, and possibly the most poorly developed, intellectual skill in medicine is that of systematic *inquiry:* subsuming the skills of problem sensing, problem formulation, systematic information search and the formulation of judgments and plans for action. The characteristics of the computer make it possible to repetitively present the student with instances of sequential complexity which require the application of these component skills. These intellectual skills are less well understood than are technical and sensory skills such as drug administration or heart sound differentiation. As a consequence, we do not yet have the prototype application of effective instruction in the area of intellectual skills. Work is being done, however, in several centers which should lead to such a development in the near future. Potentially, the most powerful approach will involve the computer as a major instructional resource.

This review of newly appearing computer based and technological simulations has been all too brief. In my view, the instructional needs in medicine are of such complexity that simulation is likely to become the most important new educational development of the decade. To reemphasize the sources of this great potential, several of its major advantages will be mentioned:

1. The setting in which the knowledge and skills which are being learned will be applied can be maximally approximated.

2. The number of stimuli with which the student is confronted can be manipulated. This permits an avoidance of the sometimes overwhelming impact of having to deal with all the dimensions of the full, real situation and enables

a systematic acquisition of component skills, leading to their progressive amalgamation into a total set of skills.

3. The amount of "noise" in the system can be artificially reduced, permitting concentration upon the competencies being acquired. There can then be a gradual introduction of these distracting influences, up to the level actually found in reality.

4. The content of the material to which the student is being exposed can be made maximally relevant to his level of readiness and to his current pre-occupations. These usually derive from the other instructional activities with which he is then engaged. (A patient with a particularly relevant disease does not have to be searched for, he can be created.)

5. The student can repeatedly practice a skill as often as is appropriate for effective learning. (One cannot subject real patients to repeated procedures.)

6. The student is freed of the distracting risk of making a sick patient even sicker or an uncomfortable person even more uncomfortable. He can concentrate on the specific skill being acquired and can separately deal with whatever anxieties he might have about patients, under more appropriate circumstances.

7. The stimuli to which the student is responding are under precise control and therefore "standardized," so that the student's response can be accurately evaluated for purposes of "diagnosis" of his further instructional needs.

All of the above considerations regarding simulation have led to the recent development of an especially important innovation in instructional aids in medicine, although technology in its usual sense is not involved. This is the use of live people as simulators of specific medical conditions or of the general role of the patient. Doctor Howard Barrows of the University of Southern California pioneered this approach in training actresses to simulate the history and physical findings of particular neurological conditions, primarily to increase the reliability of student examinations. At Michigan State University, Drs. James B. Thomas, Norman Kagan and I have employed trained drama students and housewives as "patients" to help medical students begin to learn the skills and self-awareness necessary for the establishment of an effective and productive doctor-patient relationship. In combination with a feedback approach described below, this technique has led to rapid and lasting acquisition of some of the most complex competencies required in the field of medicine.

Providing Feedback

It can be safely asserted that learning occurs very inefficiently without effective feedback. In medicine, modern technology has very recently begun to make possible more sensitive and more complete readings on student behavior than had previously been provided. Potentially, it can carry this development forward dramatically.

The growing use of programmed texts, teaching machines and erasure or tab-test examinations has begun to contribute significantly to the quality and quantity of information students receive about their own learning progress. In addition to these increments in the area of knowledge acquisition, technology is now making possible the provision of comprehensive feedback in the previously largely neglected areas of intellectual skills and professional behavior.

In addition to its function as a large teaching machine, providing moment to moment feedback during the process of information and concept acquisition, the computer brings the exciting promise of providing feedback on the development of complex intellectual processes. A student who is engaged with a computer in the solution of medical problems can receive more than just item-by-item responses to his individual actions. The computer's capacity to retain a total record of all transactions in which it has engaged enables the student to be provided with the cognitive equivalent of a video tape of his thought processes. In fact, the computer print-out of the problem-solving process in which the student has participated is far more flexible than a video-tape. It is more like a map which can be scanned in its entirety and compared to other maps, for critical evaluation. Much like the golfer who makes startling progress through being confronted with a playback of a videotape of his own swing, the medical student who is learning intellectual skills, when provided with the feedback of a print-out, will certainly make unprecedented strides in areas that were previously barely touched by conventional medical education.

The memory and adaptability of the computer permits storing great ranges of evaluation materials and recording all its transactions with students, enabling the creation of an unusually comprehensive and elaborate evaluation system, both of student performance and instructional effectiveness. The singularly attractive possibility which emerges is that of *"computer-monitored"* instruction. In a way that has not been possible before, student progress can be assessed from day to day, rather than term to term, and instructional adjustments can be made, literally, as needed. This process can be seen as analogous to the continuous inventory which industries now use. It can, of course, be developed independently of whether or not the instructional program uses the computer as a teaching device. The extent to which this monitoring process might elevate our efficiency can, at present, only be imagined.

Television is now beginning to be applied to the provision of quite a different form of feedback, which is likely to have substantial impact in the next few years. Among the most complex of the skills to be learned in medical school are those of relating effectively to patients. The combined skills necessary to establish a productive, professional relationship have only recently begun to be carefully defined and explicitly taught. One of the central features of the doctor-patient relationship course using simulated patients at Michigan State University is the video taping of the medical students as they conduct this first series of interviews with patients. These interviews are witnessed, live, by instructors and other students and then immediately played back to the observing group and the interviewer. The playback can be stopped at any time for purposes of questioning and discussion. The feedback effect of being confronted with one's own behavior appears to be one of the most instructional factors of the many at work in this program.

Conclusions and Recommendations

As James Reston has pointed out, the ancient Chinese exhibited great wisdom in formulating two separate characters to convey alternative interpretations of the concept of "crisis." For them, crisis could mean either "danger" or "opportunity." Medicine in general, and medical education in particular, have been described as currently facing a severe crisis, in several forms.

There is mounting pressure for significantly more doctors to be produced. At the same time there is a strong push to create a new kind of physician who is more responsive to current social needs than were his predecessors and who is a far more effective continuing self-educator, among many other things. In addition, all this is to be accomplished in less time than medical education now takes.

These forces for a dramatic change in the character, effectiveness and efficiency of medical curricula come at a time when we do have an increased understanding of the educational process and when the number of potentially available technological aids to instruction have mushroomed. If the conditions could be arranged for us to take suitable advantage of the new resources available, the current crisis, which has all the earmarks of a dangerous situation, could be converted to a welcome, indeed exciting, opportunity.

It is asserted that the evidence is now in hand to indicate that instructional technology, appropriately applied, holds the promise of facilitating a distinctly more individualized, flexible and adaptable educational program. These characteristics, in turn, will significantly elevate the quality of medical instruction. The pressing need is for those changes which will encourage and enable the most appropriate exploitation of technology by the largest number of individuals. The key steps toward this goal are presented below. My major recommendations appear in italics.

More than anything, the effective use of technology requires careful planning. The instructor must have clearly defined his general goals, he must have ascertained the specific competencies his students are to acquire and the steps necessary to get them there, and he must have determined which instructional materials exist or need to be created for those purposes which can be best achieved with media. For understandable reasons, this type of advance planning is still rare in medical education. Medical faculty members bring with them an expertise in a medical discipline but no specific preparation for their role as instructors. The large majority tend to teach using the only model they know: the way they themselves were taught. Responding to the current ferment in medical education, as well as trying to exploit the potentials of technology, requires significant departures from that pattern. Medical faculty will need special help to learn how to plan instruction and use technology. *It is, therefore, strongly recommended that support be provided for programs that will systematically educate medical instructors in the applications of instructional technology.*

In addition to the educational program required to achieve a meaningful change in the teachers who are to deploy their own talents differently, there must be a change in the administrative format within which these teachers work. The medical schools will have to alter their reward system to provide suitable recognition for contributions to instructional programs at the level of detailed planning, instructional materials development and the fashioning of innovative techniques. *This transformation can be facilitated by modifying the basic support grants to medical schools to give high priority to innovative applications of instructional technology.*

It seems clear that the most promising instructional technology is both the most expensive and the least well developed at this time. The potential applications of multimedia carrels, television and computers can be imagined but have not yet been realized. *The need at this time is for government support of research and development projects and feasibility studies which design and test new ways to use technology.* It does not seem as justified, at this time, for support to be given to the implementation of programs using expensive technology unless they incorporate systematic experimental attempts to evaluate the differential effects of alternative approaches.

Despite the lack of systematic support and minimal institutional encouragement, many individual faculty members have begun to generate new instructional materials which are being used in their local setting. A major economy move as well as source of support and professional prestige for the developers of instructional materials would be the opportunity for regular dissemination of quality materials among other institutions. *It is recommended that the National Library of Medicine, through the National Medical Audiovisual Center, be invited to explore the possibility of serving as a central clearinghouse to facilitate and promote the distribution of quality materials throughout the country.*

An impediment to the effective application of instructional technology has been the failure of industry to respond to the educational needs of the consumer. The confusion created by the lack of standardization of equipment, especially in television; the efforts to foist onto unsuspecting educators equipment which was really designed for use in sales promotion and which is lacking in the flexibility needed for instruction; the relative absence of quality control of the programmed texts and other instructional materials being promoted; all indicate a need for some form of intervention. If we are to successfully profit from the potential contribution of American industry we must find ways to make it economically attractive for new avenues to be explored and for high standards to be maintained. To illustrate with a simple example: movie film will not have achieved its full instructional potential until it can be used like audio tape; that is, until it can have the flexibility in use which is made possible by fast forward and fast reverse controls in a simple cartridge mechanism. We would have had this breakthrough by now if suitable incentives had been available. *It is recommended that government support, guided by the best available educational thinking, be provided to encourage industrial innovations.*

This paper cannot be concluded without an examination of the frequently raised question: Can technology replace the live human teacher? B. F. Skinner could have been referring to all technology when he said, "Any teacher that can be replaced by a teaching machine . . . deserves to be!" Technology has indeed been demonstrated to do better than live teachers many of those things that teachers now spend time doing. The challenge we face was anticipated more than 50 years ago by E. L. Thorndike when he wrote, "A human being should not be wasted in doing what 40 sheets of paper or two phonographs can do. Just because personal teaching is precious and can do what apparatus cannot, it should be saved for its peculiar work." We have only barely begun to identify what is, in fact, the "peculiar work" of the live teacher. It clearly involves much more at the level of instructional planning, individual guidance, personal supervision and direct observational evaluation of students, and much less at the level of information dispensing than has conventionally pertained. Technology holds the remarkable promise of relieving the teacher of the burden of doing a variety of routine tasks which he can now carry out more effectively through the proxy of careful planning. He could then turn his attention to far more subtle and complex issues, including many for which his own abilities would be significantly bolstered by the proper use of technology. These changes could elevate the quality of medical instruction and medical learning to levels we have heretofor hardly dared imagined. This is not a hollow dream. The necessary educational expertise and technology are at hand to permit implementation of the studies necessary to convert this dream into a reality. Let us hope that the necessary support can be found so that this conversion process can be accelerated.

Appendix I

AAMC CURRICULUM QUESTIONNAIRE*
Section V. *TEACHING AIDS OR MATERIALS*

Question Posed:
Information is requested in the following table about selected teaching aids or materials used in your NEW CURRICULUM as compared to their use in the BASE CURRICULUM. Using the scale below, please assess the intensity of use of the aids or materials (listed vertically).

Summary of Responses Received:

TEACHING AIDS OR MATERIALS	USE IN NEW CURRICULUM				USE IN BASE CURRICULUM			
	EXTENSIVE	MODERATE	MINIMAL	NO	EXTENSIVE	MODERATE	MINIMAL	NO
Models & Mannequins	6	35	7	7	1	30	34	9
Programmed Instruction	7	22	35	20	0	5	30	40
Bibliographic Reference & Supplements	29	51	5	0	16	44	13	1
Projection Slides	52	28	5	0	42	28	4	0
Movie Films	14	52	17	0	9	38	25	2
Single Concept Films or TV Tapes	10	38	25	10	1	11	37	25
Live TV	9	37	20	17	1	9	27	38
Taped TV	11	34	22	17	2	12	23	39
Audio Tapes	6	25	38	11	1	5	40	26
Computers	10	16	35	21	1	4	30	41
Role Playing	2	10	33	30	0	1	24	47
Mechanical Simulators	1	3	29	40	0	0	16	55

Distributed to the 117 Canadian and U.S. Medical Schools, April, 1968. Data based on 103 returns received by June, 1968.

Appendix 2

A Bibliography of Significant Articles for the Medical Educator*
Prior to September 1966

OVERVIEW

Currie, D. J., and A. Smialowski. "Teaching and Audio-Visual Aids," *Journal of the Biological Photographic Association. 33,* 137.

Greenhill, L. P. "Communication Research and the Teaching-Learning Process," *Journal of Medical Education. 38,* 495-502.

Ham, T. H., and C. A. Miller. "The Need for Critical Review and Evaluation of Audiovisual Instructional Materials." *Journal of Medical Education, 40,* 792-5.

Harris, J. J. "Survey of Medical Communication Sources Available for Continuing Physician Education." *Journal of Medical Education, 41,* 737-55.

Markee, J. E., S. A. Agnello, and F. D. McFalls. "Medical Communications in Basic Science Teaching." *Journal of Medical Education, 38,* 226-38.

Orr, R. H. "The 'Newer' Media for Post-Graduate Education—Their Promises and Problems." *Journal of Medical Education, 37,* 137-44.

"Teaching with Audio-Visuals." *Lab World, 15,* 766-68.

AUDIO TAPE

Aitken, A. "Audio Methods in Continuing Medical Education," *Medical and Biological Illustration. 14,* 259-62.

Asher, H. "Teaching on Tape." *Medical and Biological Illustration, 12,* 253.

"C.M.A.'s Audio-Digest—A Decade of Progress," *California Medicine, 100,* 50-2.

Graves, J. "The Use of Tape in Medical Teaching." *Postgraduate Medical Journal, 41,* 208-12.

COMPUTER

"Electronics at the Bedside." *Medical World News, 7,* 52-63.

Feurzeig, W., P. Munter, and J. Swets. "Computer-Aided Teaching in Medical Diagnosis." *Journal of Medical Education, 39,* 746-54.

Harrington, J. J. "Computers and Health: Some Prospectives," *Harvard Public Health Alumni Bulletin, 23,* 14-23.

Swets, J. A., and W. Feurzeig. "Computer-Aided Instruction." *Science, 150,* 572-6.

FILM

Dryer, B. V., J. E. Markee, and D. S. Ruhe. "Selected Films for Medical Teaching. A Suggested Basic Motion Picture Library." *Journal of Medical Education, 40,* suppl., 1-76.

Prepared by the National Medical Audiovisual Center of the National Library of Medicine, USPHS, 1966.

Forsdale, L. "8mm Film: A New Tool for Research." *Papers and Proceedings,* Single Concept Teaching Film Conference, April 1-2, 1965, Public Health Service Audiovisual Facility, Atlanta, Georgia.

Humphreys, M. H., L. W. Nesmith, and S. L. Pohl. "Development of a Reviewing Procedure for Audiovisual Materials by Students of Medicine." *Journal of Medical Education, 40,* 742-52.

Leveridge, L. L. "Films for Medical Education." *Journal of Medical Education, 38,* 307-14.

McKim, J. W., T. C. West, and W. T. Stickley. "The 8mm Film as a Dynamic Instruction Medium in the Biomedical Education." *Journal of the Biological Photographic Association, 33,* 161-8.

McRae, R. K. "Eight MM. Filming By and For the Teaching Department." *Medical and Biological Illustration, 14,* 237-43.

Matthias, R. C. "Simplified Graphic Illustrations and Animation in Medical Film Production." *Journal of the Biological Photographic Association, 31,* 63-70.

West, T. C., and W. T. Stickley. "Reinforcement Experiment in Laboratory Pharmacology by Film: A Model for Cinematic Self-Instruction in Medical Education." *Journal of Medical Education, 40,* 990-2.

MISCELLANEOUS

Barabas, A. "Blackboard Drawing in Medical Teaching." *British Medical Journal, 5437,* 782-4.

Bowker, J. H., W. L. Kermond, and R. H. Jones. "Disease-Simulation Technics in Rehabilitation Teaching." *New England Journal of Medicine, 270,* 243-4.

Derbyshire, R. C. "On Science Fairs and Careers in Medicine." *Southwestern Medicine, 44,* 319-20.

Dobson, J. "The Training of a Surgeon." *Annals of the Royal College of Surgeons of England, 34,* 1-36.

Feder, R. J. "An Otologic Study Model." *Archives of Otolaryngology* (Chicago), *82,* 25-7.

Poppensiek, G. C. "Teaching to Impart an Understanding of Infectious Diseases." *Cornell Veterinarian, 53,* 575-619.

MULTI-MEDIA

"ASCP Steps Up Continuing Education Pace," *Lab World, 17,* 726.

Cole, C. R. "Teaching of Pathology in the Veterinary Medical Curriculum." *American Journal of Veterinary Research, 26,* suppl., 450-60.

Goodwin, A. H. "The Role of Medical Illustration and Photography in Medical Education." *New Physician, 12,* 449-51.

Heiser, J. J., and B. H. Traven. "Emergency Respiratory and Cardiac Resuscitation: Experiences with a Training Program in a Community Hospital." *Journal of the American Osteopathic Association, 63,* 945-50.

Huber, J. F. "The Multi-Media Approach to the Teaching of Anatomy." *Medical and Biological Illustration, 13,* 96-9.

Julian, L. M. "The Teaching of Anatomy in the Veterinary Curriculum." *American Journal of Veterinary Research, 26,* suppl., 401-13.

Kingrey, B. W. "Education in Large Animal Surgery and Obstetrics." *American Journal of Veterinary Research, 26,* suppl., 510-5.

Matzke, H. A., R. H. Geertsma, and C. F. Bridgman. "The Study of Anatomy: Current Perspectives at KUMC." *Journal of the Kansas Medical Society, 66,* 106-10.

Postlethwait, S. N. "Audio-Tutoring: A Practical Solution for Independent Study." *Medical and Biological Illustration, 15,* 183-7.

Sudman, E. " 'Phototheca Chururgica' and Audiovisual Series for Teaching General Surgery." *Medical and Biological Illustration, 15,* suppl., 72-3.

Taxay, E. P., W. Atkinson, and R. Jones, Jr. "A Bilingual Audio Visual Aid." *Journal of Medical Education, 38,* 80-1.

PROGRAMMED INSTRUCTION

Elder, S. T., G. R. Meckstroth, and C. M. Nice. "Comparison of a Linear Program in Radiation Protection with a Traditional Lecture Presentation." *Journal of Medical Education, 39,* 1078-82.

Geis, G. L., and M. C. Anderson. "Applying Principles of the Technique in Producing Materials." *Nursing Outlook, 11,* 662-5.

Geis, G. L., and M. C. Anderson. "Programmed Instruction in Nursing Education." *Nursing Outlook, 11,* 592-4.

Lysaught, J. P. "Self-Instructional Medical Programs: A Survey." *New Physician, 13,* 144-7.

Lysaught, J. P., and H. Jason. "Programmed Instruction in Medical Education: Report of the Rochester Conference." *Journal of Medical Education, 40,* 474-81.

Lysaught, J. P., C. D. Sherman, Jr., and C. M. Williams. "Programmed Learning. Potential Values for Medical Instruction." *Journal of the American Medical Association, 189,* 803-7.

Mathis, J. L., C. M. Pierce, and V. Pishkin. "An Experiment in Programmed Teaching of Psychiatry." *American Journal of Psychiatry, 122,* 937-40.

Miller, G. E., J. S. Allender, and A. V. Wolf. "Differential Achievement with Programmed Text, Teaching Machine, and Conventional Instruction in Physiology." *Journal of Medical Education, 40,* 817-31.

Nice, C. M., Jr. "Education and Training in Radiology." *Southern Medical Journal, 59,* 214-6.

Owen, S. G., R. Hall, and J. Anderson. "A Comparison of Programmed Instruction with Conventional Lectures in the Teaching of Electrocardiography to Final-Year Medical Students." *Journal of Medical Education, 40,* 1058-62.

Owen, S. G., R. Hall, and J. Anderson. "Programmed Learning in Medical Education. An Experimental Comparison of Programmed Instruction by Teaching Machine with Conventional Lecturing in the Teaching of Electrocardiography to Final Year Medical Students." *Postgraduate Medical Journal, 41,* 201-6.

Owen, S. G., R. Hall, and I. B. Waller. "Use of a Teaching Machine in Medical Education, Preliminary Experience with a Program in Electrocardiography." *Postgraduate Medical Journal, 40,* 59-65.

Polony, L. J. "Programmed Instruction and Automated Education for Hospital and Other Medical Personnel." *Hospital Progress,* February, 1965.

Weiss, R. J., and E. J. Green. "The Applicability of Programmed Instruction in a Medical School Curriculum." *Journal of Medical Education, 37,* 760-6.

Weiss, R. L., and D. W. Darby. "Continuing Education Outside the Dental School Setting." *Journal of the American Dental Association, 70,* 1488-96.

RADIO

Ebbert, A., Jr. "Two-Way Radio in Medical Education." *Journal of Medical Education, 38,* 319-28.

Woolsey, F. M., Jr., and W. T. Strauss. "Postgraduate Medical Education in Maine: A New Experiment Utilizing Two-Way Radio and Television." *Journal of the Maine Medical Association, 55,* 172-3.

TELEVISION

Agnello, S. A., J. E. Markee, and F. D. McFalls. "The Central Television Facility Duke University Medical Center." *Medical and Biological Illustration, 15,* 39-45.

Anderson, L. D. "Telecourse in Nursing." *American Journal of Nursing, 64,* 79-82.

Benschoter, R. A., M. T. Eaton, and P. Smith. "Use of Videotape to Provide Individual Instruction in Techniques of Psychotherapy." *Journal of Medical Education, 40,* 1159-61.

Berger, M. M., and D. M. Gallant. "The Use of Closed-Circuit Television in the Teaching of Group Psychotherapy." *Psychosomatics, 6,* 16-8.

"California Medical Television Network Helps Keep Hospital MD's Up to Date." *Medical Tribune, 7,* 22.

Cameron, C. S. "Five Schools Linked Together for TV Teaching." *Journal of Medical Education, 34,* 1077-81.

DiSanto, S. A. "New Techniques in Closed-Circuit Television for Dental Teaching." *Journal of the Society of Motion Picture and Television Engineers, 73,* 770-2.

Dryer, B. V. "A Nationwide Plan for Continuing Medical Education." *Journal of the American Medical Association, 189,* 35-9.

Engel, C. E. "Television in Medical Education." *Nature* (London), *200,* 725-8.

Groom, D. "The South Carolina Experiment in Medical Television." *Journal of Medical Education, 38,* 202-6.

Harris, J. J. "Television as an Educational Medium in Medicine: An Historical Purview." *Journal of Medical Education, 41,* 1-19.

Heiss, W. H. "Closed-Circuit Television in a Teaching Hospital." *Medical and Biological Illustration, 14,* 244-50.

Lennox, B., and F. C. Path. "The Glasgow Postgraduate Medical Television Series: Production Problems on the Medical Side." *Postgraduate Medical Journal, 41,* 220-2.

Lewis, A. A. "American Evaluations." *Postgraduate Medical Journal, 41,* 216-7.

McGuinness, A. C., "The New York Academy of Medicine TV-PG Efforts in a Metropolis." *Journal of Medical Education, 40,* 878-81.

McGuinness, A. C., H. Menzel, and C. Rogers. "Continuation of Medical Education by Open-Circuit Television: A Preliminary Report." *Journal of Medical Education, 39,* 735-45.

Markee, J. E., S. A. Agnello, and F. D. McFalls. "Examinations in Anatomy: Use of Video Tape Recordings." *Journal of Medical Education, 40,* 214-9.

Menzel, R., R. Maurice, and A. C. McGuinness. "Evaluation of the New York Academy of Medicine's Television Programs." *Journal of Medical Education, 41,* 826-43.

Michaux, M. H., M. J. Cohen, and A. A. Kurland. "Closed-Circuit Television in the Scientific Measurement of Psychopathology." *Medical and Biological Illustration, 13,* 49-57.

Moses, C., and R. Wolfe. "Grand Rounds via Television: An Experiment in Continuing Education." *Pennsylvania Medical Journal, 67,* 23-8.

Moses, C., and R. Wolfe. "The Pittsburgh Regional Medical Television Programme." *Medical and Biological Illustration, 15,* 247-52.

Pender, J. L. "Dietitian Teaches Patients via Closed-Circuit TV." *Hospital Topics, 44,* 46-7.

Ramey, J. W. "Television: Growing Pains of a New Teaching Medium." *Journal of Medical Education, 39,* 1107-13.

Rising, J. D., and W. D. Nelligan. "Practical Considerations in the Use of Television in Continuing Medical Education." *Journal of Medical Education, 38,* 75-9.

Robertson, G. J., H. F. Pyke, Jr., and E. M. Friedlander. "Boston Medical Reports. A Postgraduate Educational Television Series for Practicing Physicians in the State of Maine. A Preliminary Review and Report of Initial Evaluation." *Journal of the Maine Medical Association, 56,* 41-3.

Roy, A. D. "Scottish Television Experiment," *British Medical Journal, 5420,* 1321-3.

Ruhe, D. S., and K. C. Gentry. "Television in Medicine." *Journal of the Kansas Medical Society, 62,* 94-99.

Ruhe, D. S., S. Gundle, P. C. Laybourne, L. H. Forman, M. Jacobs, and M. T. Eaton. "Television in the Teaching of Psychiatry: Report of Four Years' Preliminary Development." *Journal of Medical Education, 35,* 916-27.

Samson, F. E., Jr., G. N. Loofbourrow, and D. S. Ruhe. "Utilizing Television for Laboratory Experiments in Physiology." *Journal of Medical Education, 39,* 780-4.

Schiff, S. B., and R. Reivich. "Use of Television as Aid to Psychotherapy Supervision." *Archives of General Psychiatry* (Chicago), *10,* 84-8.

Scott, G. B. "Demonstration of Histology by Closed-Circuit Television." *Medical and Biological Illustration, 14,* 251-4.

Seegal, D. "Videotaped Autobiographical Interviews. An Adjunct for Medical Education." *Journal of American Medical Association, 195,* 650-2.

Smith, G., and J. H. Wyllie. "Use of Closed-Circuit Television in Teaching Surgery to Medical Students." *British Medical Journal, 5453,* 99-101.

"Television in Higher Education: Ten Examples in the South." *Southern Regional Education Board,* January, 1966.

"Television for Hospitals—Network to go Nationwide with Medical and Nursing Programs." *Hospital Topics, 43,* 62-3.

Thomas, H. A. "Television as a Teaching Medium in Surgical Education." *Maryland Medical Journal, 14,* 49-53.

Trowbridge, M., Jr. "Boston Medical Reports." *Journal of Maine Medical Association, 55,* 83.

Trowbridge, M., Jr. "Boston Medical Reports." *Journal of Maine Medical Association, 55,* 174.

Appendix 3

BIBLIOGRAPHY OF INSTRUCTIONAL TECHNOLOGY
IN MEDICAL EDUCATION
September 1966-June 1968

OVERVIEW

Beckel, W. E. "The Teacher and the Taught." *The Canadian Medical Association Journal, 98:*1085-1089, 1968.

Jason, H. "Evaluation of Audiovisual Methods of Medical Teaching." *The Canadian Medical Association Journal, 98:*1146-1150, 1968.

———, "Self Instruction in Medical Education: Principles, Practices, Prospects." *British Journal of Medical Education, 2:*20-23, June, 1968.

Lysaught, J. P., Editor. *Programmed Instruction in Medical Education: Proceedings of the First Rochester Conference.* Rochester, The University of Rochester Clearinghouse, 1965.

———, *Self Instruction in Medical Education: Proceedings of the Second Rochester Conference.* Rochester, The University of Rochester Clearinghouse, 1967.

Lysaught, J. P. "Self-Instruction for the Health Professions: Trends and Problems." *Medical Times, 95:*1025-32, October, 1967.

Lysaught, J. P., Editor, *Individualized Instruction in Medical Education: Proceedings of the Third Rochester Conference.* Rochester, The University of Rochester Clearinghouse, 1968.

Lysaught, J. P. "Self-Instruction in Medical Education: Report of the 3rd Rochester Conference." *Journal of Medical Education, 43:*759-63, June, 1968.

Lysaught, J. P., Editor. Proceedings of the Fourth Rochester Conference on Self Instruction in Medical Education, (Forthcoming).

Manning, P. R., et al. "Research in Medical Education. Comparison of Four Teaching Techniques: Programmed Text, Textbook, Lecture-Demonstration, and Lecture-Workshop." *Journal of Medical Education, 43:*356-9, March, 1968.

Romano, M. T. "Audiovisual Education: Yesterday, Today and Tomorrow." *The Canadian Medical Association Journal, 98:*1127-1132, 1968.

Russell, W. O., and R. A. Kolvoord, Editors. *A Symposium: Implications of Developments and Trends in Educational Technology.* Chicago, American Society of Clinical Pathologists, 1966.

COMPUTERS

Abrahamson, S. "Evaluation of the Use of Computers in Medical Education." *Conference on the Use of Computers in Medical Education,* Oklahoma City, University of Oklahoma Medical Center, 1968.

Bowden, D. H. "Computer-Aided Instruction in Pathology." *Canadian Medical Association Journal, 97:*739-42, September, 1967.

Fonkalsrud, E. W., et al. "Computer Assisted Instruction in Undergraduate Surgical Education." *Surgery, 62:*141-7, July, 1967.

Harless, W. G. "The Development of a Computer-Assisted Instruction Program in a Medical Center Environment." *Journal of Medical Education, 42:*139-45, February, 1967.

Jason, H. "Computers in Undergraduate Medical Education," *Conference on the Use of Computers in Medical Education.* Oklahoma City, University of Oklahoma Medical Center, 1968.

Ovenstone, J. A. "Computer-Assisted Instruction in Undergraduate and Post-Graduate Medicine." *Medical Journal of Australia, 2:*487-91, September, 1966.

Shulman, L. S. "Inquiry, Computers and Medical Education," *Conference on the Use of Computers in Medical Education.* Oklahoma City, University of Oklahoma Medical Center, 1968.

Starkweather, J. A. "Computer-Assisted Learning in Medical Education." *Canadian Medical Association Journal, 97:*733-8, September, 1967.

INSTRUCTION

Balson, M. "Programmed Learning in Medical Illustration." *Medical Journal of Australia, 2:*176-8, July, 1967.

Hawkridge, D. G., et al. "Programmed Course in Biostatistics for Medical Students." *British Journal of Medical Education, 2:*36-40, March, 1968.

_____. "The Use of a Programmed Text During a Course in Genetics for Medical Students." *Journal of Medical Education, 42:*163-9, February, 1967.

Jason, H. "Programmed Instruction: New Bottle for Rediscovered Wine." *The Canadian Medical Association Journal, 92:*711-716, April, 1965.

McRae, R. K. "Illustrations in Programmed Learning: A New Linear Teaching Machine." *Medical and Biological Illustration, 16:*252-7, October, 1966.

Pishkin, V., et al. "Analysis of Attitudinal and Personality Variables in Relation to a Programmed Course in Psychiatry." *Journal of Clinical Psychology, 23:*53-6, January, 1967.

Stone, G. C. "Supplementary Use of Programmed Instruction in a Parasitology Course." *Journal of Medical Education, 41:*683-9, July, 1966.

Stretton, T. B., et al. "Programmed Instruction in Medical Education: Comparison of Teaching Machine and Programmed Textbook." *British Journal of Medical Education, 1:*165-8, June, 1967.

Weller, J. M., et al. "Programmed Instructional Material for a Medical School Laboratory Course." *Journal of Medical Education, 42:*697-705, July, 1967.

Wilds, P. L., et al. "Evaluation of a Programmed Text in Six Medical Schools." *Journal of Medical Education, 42:*219-24, March, 1967.

_____. "Programmed Instruction in Gynecologic Cancer at the Medical Student Level." *American Journal of Obstetrics and Gynecology, 100:*128-35, January, 1968.

MULTI-MEDIA SELF INSTRUCTION

Fiel, N. J. "A Preparation Laboratory for Advanced Mammalian Physiology." *Individualized Instruction in Medical Education: Proceedings of the Third Rochester Conference,* Lysaught, J. P., Editor, Rochester, The University of Rochester Clearinghouse, 1968.

Fiel, N. J., and P. Ways. "Multi-Media Self Instruction." Proceedings of the Fourth Rochester Conference on Self Instruction in Medical Education, (Forthcoming).

Garcia, E. N., et al. "A Multimedia Approach to Biochemistry Laboratory Instruction." *Individualized Instruction in Medical Education: Proceedings of the Third Rochester Conference,* Lysaught, J. P., Editor, Rochester, The University of Rochester Clearinghouse, 1967.

Garcia, E. N., and K. Ibsen. "Progress Report on a Program of Individualized Medical Instruction." *Self Instruction in Medical Education: Proceedings of the Second Rochester Conference,* Lysaught, J. P., Editor, Rochester, The University of Rochester Clearinghouse, 1967.

Harden, R. M. "Teaching Without Teachers: An Audiovisual Method of Self-Instruction." *Scottish Medical Journal, 13:*206-7, June, 1968.

Hood, J. H. "An Audio Visual Teaching Unit for Radiology." *British Journal of Radiology, 41:*150-1, February, 1968.

GENERAL AUDIOVISUAL AIDS

Broadbent, D. "Audio-Visual Techniques in Professional Medical Education." *Medical Journal of Australia, 2:*174-6, July, 1967.

Harden, R. M., et al. "An Audiovisual Technique for Medical Teaching." *Medical and Biological Illustration, 18:*29-32, January, 1968.

Hayden, J. Jr., et al. "An Initial Evaluation of Animated Serial Sections as an Instructional Method for Facilitating Three-Dimensional Awareness of Anatomic Regions." *Journal of Medical Education, 42:*447-52, May, 1967.

Jones, B. "Audio-Visual Aids in Medical Teaching." *Proceedings of the Royal Society of Medicine, 61:*89-94, January, 1968.

Manley-Cooper, N. C. "Projectors." *British Journal of Medical Education, 1:*221-223, June, 1967.

Russell, J. K. "Sound and Visual Teaching Aids in Obstetrics and Gynecology." *Medical and Biological Illustration, 16:*218-22, October, 1966.

Tuddenham, W. J. "The Use of Logical Flow Charts as an Aid in Teaching Roentgen Diagnosis." *American Journal of Roentgenology, Radium Therapy and Nuclear Medicine, 102:*797-803, April, 1968.

FILMS

Barrows, H. S. "Self-Instructional Film Cartridges in Medical Education." *The Canadian Medical Association Journal, 98:*1094-96, 1968.

Cree, R. P. "Use, Abuse and Misuse of Teaching Films." *The Canadian Medical Association Journal, 98:*1090-94, 1968.

Gueguen, Y. "Medical Film Production: Criteria, Problems and Potentialities." *The Canadian Medical Association Journal, 98:*1081-84, 1968.

Hirschowitz, B. I. "The Use of Motion Pictures in Teaching and Diagnosis." *Annals of the New York Academy of Sciences, 142:*455-60, March, 1967.

North, A. F. Jr. "Learning Clinical Skills through the Use of Self-Teaching Films." Journal of Medical Education, *42:*177-80, February, 1967.

TELEVISION

Bell, A. E., et al. "Scottish Television Medical Programs: A Preliminary Assessment." *Scottish Medical Journal, 11:*250-7, July, 1966.

Brayton, D. "Postgraduate Education in Medicine by Television," *Biomedical Sciences Instrumentation. 3:*81-8, 1967.

Brayton, D., R. R. Getz, and D. Sachs. "Encoded Broadcast and Video Recorders: Two Television Modalities Useful in Continuing Medical Education." *The Canadian Medical Association Journal, 98:*1133-36, 1968.

Green, J. H., and J. P. S. Thomson. "Use of Videotape Recording and Live Closed Circuit Television in Teaching Medical Students." *British Journal of Medical Education, 1:*135-43, March, 1967.

Groom, D. "Television in Post Graduate Education: Some Lessons from Five Years' Experience." *Journal of the American Medical Association, 198:*275-80, October, 1966.

———. "Experiences with Television Broadcasting: A Report." *The Canadian Medical Association Journal, 98:*1113-16, 1968.

Heinivaara, O. "Professional Television Facilities in a New University Hospital." *Medical and Biological Illustration, 18:*8-11, January, 1968.

Huber, J. F. "Intramural Closed-Circuit Television Teaching: Pre-Clinical Uses." *The Canadian Medical Association Journal, 98:*1106-09, 1968.

Hunter, A. T. "The Use of Broadcast Television in Continuing Medical Education." *Canadian Medical Association Journal, 98:*34-9, January, 1968.

Ide, T. R. "Educational Television: Problems, Resources and Utilization." *The Canadian Medical Association Journal, 98:*1140-42, 1968.

Judge, R. D. "Television in Clinical Medical Teaching," *The Canadian Medical Association Journal. 98:*1109-13, 1968.

Lennox, B., and F. C. Path. "The Glasgow Postgraduate Medical Television Series: Production Problems on the Medical Side." *Postgraduate Medical Journal, 41:*220-2, April, 1965.

Meighan, S. S., and A. Tresender. "Continuing Medical Education through Television." *Journal of the American Medical Association, 200:*762-6, May, 1967.

Meyer, T. C., et al. "Report on an Experiment in the Use of Tele-lectures for the Continuing Education of Physicians and Allied Health Personnel." *Journal of Medical Education, 43:*73-7, January, 1968.

Platzer, W. "The Epidiascope and Television in Medical Teaching." *Medical and Biological Illustration, 16:*243-5, October, 1966.

Ramey, J. W. "Teaching Medical Students by Videotape Simulation." *Journal of Medical Education, 43:*55-9, January, 1968.

Rechnitzer, P. A. "An Account of Variations '67, a Videotape Presentation." *The Canadian Medical Association Journal, 98:*1145-46, 1968.

Robertson, G. J. "Television in Continuing Education of the Physician." *Annals of the New York Academy of Sciences, 142:*487-92, March, 1967.

Robertson, G. J., and H. F. Pyke, Jr. "Television in Continuing Medical Education." *Medical and Biological Illustration, 18:*4-7, January, 1968.

Smart, C. R., et al. "Initial Experience with Encoded Two-Way Medical Television." *Journal of Medical Education, 41:*977-81, October, 1966.

Stone, D. C. "Educational Television Programming: Problems, Resources and Utilization." *The Canadian Medical Association Journal, 98:*1143-45, 1968.

Tampas, J. P., and A. B. Soule. "Experiences with Two-Way Television in a Teaching Hospital Complex." *Journal of the American Medical Association, 204:*1173-5, June, 1968.

Torkelson, L. O., and M. T. Romano. "Self-Confrontation by Videotape: A Remedical Measure in Teaching Diagnostic Evaluation." *Journal of the American Medical Association, 201:*773-5, September, 1967.

de G. Vaillancourt and M. Gill. "Continuing Medical Education by Television: A Canadian Experience." *The Canadian Medical Association Journal, 98:*1136-39, 1968.

Wagner, H. N., Jr. "Videotape in the Teaching of Medical History-Taking." *Journal of Medical Education, 42:*1055-8, November, 1967.

Waine, S. R. "Applications of Closed Circuit Television in Medical Education." *Medical Art, 16:*22-6, 1965.

Wilmer, H. A. "Television as Participant Recorder," *American Journal of Psychiatry, 124:*1157-63, March, 1968.

SIMULATION

Barrows, H. S. "Simulated Patients in Medical Teaching." *Canadian Medical Association Journal, 98:*674-6, April, 1968.

Dinnerstein, A. J., and M. Lowenthal. "Teaching Demonstrations of Simulated Disability." *Archives of Physical Medicine and Rehabilitation, 49:*167-9, March, 1968.

McCarthy, W. H., and J. S. Gonnella. "The Simulated Patient Management Problem: A Technique for Evaluating and Teaching Clinical Competence." *British Journal of Medical Education, 1:*348-52, December, 1967.

Ramey, J. W. "Teaching Medical Students by Videotape Simulation." *Journal of Medical Education, 43:*55-9, January, 1968.

MISCELLANEOUS

Adams, S. "Hospital Libraries as Learning Centers." *Bulletin of the Medical Library Association, 56:*175, April, 1968.

Barrows, H. S., et al. "Introduction of the Living Human Body in Freshman Gross Anatomy." *British Journal of Medical Education, 2:*33-5, March, 1968.

Dergen, S. S. "Use of Two Way Radio by a Volunteer Health Organization for Continuing Medical Education." *New York State Journal of Medicine, 66:*2694-7, October, 1966.

Doray, V. "Medical Illustration: Yesterday—Today—Tomorrow." *The Canadian Medical Association Journal, 98:*1097-1105, 1968.

Elkinton, J. R. "Self Assessment of Medical Knowledge." *Annals of Internal Medicine, 68:*247-9, January, 1968.

Geertsma, R. H. "A Student-Oriented Learning Center in the Biomedical Sciences. *Journal of Medical Education, 42:*681-6, July, 1967.

Johnson, P. C., et al. "Research in Medical Education. The Effect of Grades and Examinations on Self-Directed Learning." *Journal of Medical Education, 43:*360-6, March, 1968.

Netter, F. H. "The Role of Illustration in Medical Education and Medical Progress." *Journal of the Mt. Sinai Hospital,* New York, *34:*396-400, July-August, 1967.

Oakley, C. L. "Tape Recordings in Medical Education. The Pioneering Role Played by the California Medical Association's Audio-Digest Foundation." *California Medicine, 104:*534-7, June, 1966.

West, K. M. "Books as Clinical Tools. The Medical Center and Continuing Self-Education." *Journal of the Oklahoma State Medical Association, 59:*531, September, 1966.

88.

Instructional Media
In the Biomedical Fields

by *JAMES LIEBERMAN*
Asst. Surgeon General
Director, National Medical Audiovisual Center
Associate Director for Audiovisual and Telecommunications
National Library of Medicine

The traditional patterns for educating physicians and allied medical specialists face an unparalleled need for innovation in light of a teaching-learning crisis unmatched since the days of the 1910 Flexner Report.

Recommendations of a study recently completed under sponsorship of the Association of American Medical Colleges and supported by the Commonwealth Fund were accepted early in November by the Association.[1] These recommendations are designed to meet future needs rather than correct any grave deficiencies of the present in biomedical education and communication. They cover these major points:

"Medical schools must increase their output of physicians.

"Increased numbers of students should be admitted from geographic areas and from economic and ethnic groups that are inadequately represented today.

"The medical student's training must be individualized to fit varied rates of achievement, educational backgrounds, and career goals.

"Medical school curriculums should be developed by interdepartmental groups that include students.

"The medical schools must now assume a responsibility for education and research in the organization and delivery of new information as it is discovered."

In each of these areas, modern educational technology can make a decisive contribution. This includes not only the classroom instruction of embryo professionals but also the imperative dialogue between researcher and clinician; the continuing education of practicing biomedical personnel geared for the convenience of the practitioner; the ready accessibility of material from all over the world at any given time it is needed; and the essential improvement in the delivery of medical/health information to a public too often uninformed in matters vital to them.

The tools to which we now turn for help in these areas are not new in concept—their application, however, in biomedical fields is startlingly new.

More than 2,000 years ago in ancient China, the shadow show, forerunner of primitive audiovisuals, was attracting large crowds and educating newer generations in the folk lore of their antecedents. In the days of Rome's ascendency Athanasius Kircher used an oil lamp, reflector, and lens to amaze the court with a slide show that was more entertainment than educational. Some believe that the first experiment in visual education in America took place in 1703 during the Nouveaux Voyages when Louis-Armant explained the creation to an American Indian chief with the aid of an oil painting. It is more commonly known that one of the earliest experimental motion pictures demonstrated the sequences of a sneeze, enabling study of that particular physiological phenomenon. This may well have been the first use of an instructional medium in biomedical education.

Since that time, however, those in the biomedical field have been slow to explore and adopt new methods of teaching for undergraduate and graduate students and in the continuing education of practitioner and research.

Conservatism in this area is particularly difficult to understand since the World War II era proved conclusively that medical, and more specifically, paramedical personnel could be trained with speed and accuracy through the audiovisual media. The medical professions are still reaping the benefit of this wartime training which produced a cadre of personnel schooled in the health and allied sciences.

One of medicine's first attempts at electronic transmission of professional information over a large distance was made in 1947 when Philadelphia radiologist Dr. Jacob Gershon-Cohen and physicist A. G. Cooley sent the facsimile of a roentgenogram a distance of 25 miles by using ordinary telephone lines.[2]

Years later, Dr. Gershon-Cohen, while overseas, employed what he called "Telognosis"[3] on a patient whose chest films and EKG's were needed in Philadelphia for comparison with earlier patient records. Using the facsimile transmission facilities of the Associated Press for sending wirephotos, images of the films and EKG's were sent to Philadelphia within six hours and reports of the comparisons were transmitted back to Tel Aviv.

This innovation in medical care was one of the first in a series of dramatic experiments which resulted in the adaptation of twentieth century electronic technology to medical instruction and medical care.

Today, there is spread before the medical professions a collection of instructional media undreamed of by even the most farsighted at the time of the Flexner Report. Though maximum use is not yet made of these media, there has been in the last 10 years a significant increase in the profession's awareness of this technology and its potential. The hardware is well known. Its use in the field of biomedical education is less defined. This paper will mention each of the media known to be used in biomedical instruction from the most complex to the simplest and give examples of such use.

The Computer

A physician's judgement is no better than the information available to him.

Information should be organized efficiently; it should be reliable in order for conclusions to be drawn with assurance; it should be made available as rapidly as possible so that action taken will be closely related to need at the moment of decision. The importance of the computer in medicine is due in part to the fact that it can provide better information in all these ways. The importance of the computer to biomedical instruction is due to the same fact.

Dr. Emanuel M. Papper, professor of anesthesiology at Columbia University and author of two textbooks in that field, has become a pioneer in the use of computer instruction to improve medical teaching. At a meeting of the American Society of Anesthesiologists in 1967, Dr. Papper demonstrated an extensive training course in anesthesiology programmed into a computer 1,000 miles away.[4] Typing questions and answers on the computer console's keyboard, Dr. Papper showed how a programmed computer could ask questions, pick out mistakes, and give correct information to a student working with the program. Information fed into the anesthesiology instruction program was developed from course material supplied by educators at the University of Oklahoma and the University of California School of Medicine in Davis. Dr. Brandt, Director of Oklahoma's computing facility, believes that computer-assisted instruction can be particularly beneficial in anesthesiology, a specialty which most physicians realize is faced with a severe manpower shortage.

A computer processing system has been developed which permits transcontinental reading of electrocardiograms.[5] In a recent demonstration, electrocardiograms taken in France were transmitted via communications satellite to the Public Health Service computer in Washington, analyzed, and the results returned to France within seconds. Participating in the demonstration were delegates attending the First Congress on Medical Electronics and Biological Engineering in Tours, France, and scientists at the Medical Systems Development Laboratory in Washington.

The demonstration was performed to dramatize the capabilities of the computer processing system. Several programs employing this computer analysis are in operation in New England, and stations extend to the west coast.

In another instance recently, computers in Washington, D.C. and Houston were linked to an American soldier in a Tokyo hospital to provide "instant" diagnosis of his condition by medical research centers, thousands of miles away.

Information on the patient's condition was sped to the medical centers over a 50,000-mile communications link, via satellite and telephone company landlines . . . the demonstration underscored the growing application of communications in the solution of complex medical problems.[6]

A wide variety of material, stored and transmitted by computer, comprises a reservoir of teaching information which could be made available to teaching institutions throughout the world. A prerequisite to such a plan is an expanded national program, planned and designed to systematically catalog available material for widespread dissemination.

A novel computer teaching system was developed some years ago and applied to a problem in teaching medical diagnosis. Provided with thoughtfully designed case problems, the system should enable a medical student to augment significantly his experience and skill in diagnostic practice.

The computer program, called the "Socratic System," poses a problem to a student and engages him in "conversation" while he attempts to solve the problem.[7] Instruction takes place at the computer console. The "conversation" is accomplished through the use of an electric typewriter connected to and controlled by the computer.

Downstate Medical Center's fully computerized State University Hospital,[8] Brooklyn, New York, has been operating successfully with electronic data processing for nearly a year. The computing center at the $25 million hospital operates three on-line systems encompassing all phases of hospital administration.

Research on computer-assisted instruction is in progress in at least 20 institutions throughout the country—Stanford University, Harvard University, the University of Michigan, Ohio State University, Pennsylvania State University, and others.

Though computers and all other systems for scientific information transfer are potential tools for instruction, they can also be applied in myriad other ways for advancement of medical science—research, diagnosis, international communications, medical data storage and retrieval, etc.

Television

Educational television, now in its second decade, has begun to ignite the imagination of health professionals throughout the world. The speed of transmission, the facility with which space is traversed in seconds, and color capability have helped to spark a growing interest in television.

Today, there are more than 90 operational schools of medicine in the United States.[9] Approximately half of these are using television (mostly monochrome) in one or more departments. Of the schools using television, more are publicly than privately supported. Initial closed circuit television installations have most frequently been made in departments of physiology, pharmacology, surgery, anatomy, or psychiatry. Postgraduate education, departments of biochemistry, radiology, ob/gny, ophthalmology, and pathology were among the first to use the medium.

Currently, television installations in the medical schools range from the extremely simple, $2,500 single-camera chains to $300,000 installations that serve as many as 18 departments. In general, television has proved to be valuable in correlating clinical and preclinical teaching, and color has proved to be unnecessary for many applications. [However, some believe that color is vital in such areas as surgery, pathology, and anatomy, especially for fresh tissue and microscopic slides.] One of television's greatest potentials is its function as a delivery system for all audiovisual formats. Through television, motion pictures, slides, filmstrips, graphic material, previously recorded audio material, and all other media can be delivered as a comprehensive whole to the medical professions.

A recent development in television is the electronic video recording, or EVR, developed by the Columbia Broadcasting System.[10] It is a process designed to facilitate transfer to special film of material in a wide variety of formats. The playback device, designed to attach to a conventional television set, will permit an hour's worth of televised playback. One unit can play back through any number of linked receivers in auditoriums, classrooms, or other viewing areas of medical schools or institutions. It cannot be used for recording, and neither sound nor video can be erased during playback. Since equipment for making the special thin film recordings can be operated at high speed, with a 20 minute film being duplicated in 30 seconds, the cost of the cartridges should be much less than existing films; $7 has been mentioned, but whether this is laboratory cost or suggested sale price is not indicated.

Basic operation of the unit is like a long-playing record—the cartridge is dropped on a spindle in the playback unit. No threading, rewinding, or other handling is necessary. Normally, the film moves at a speed of 5 inches a second, but it can be stopped to examine a still frame at any point. The unit can be used for still pictures as well as motion pictures.

The possibilities of such a unit are limitless. In the classroom, the 8mm cartridge-loaded film concept would be expanded and accessibility improved. Regular length films could be screened either for the class on one or more television receivers, or individually, without requiring special equipment or room darkening. Students could consult film material, browsing through it to stop at particular sections or frames, as they now consult books. It is estimated that it will be 1969 before EVR will be available in the United States, but in the future the physician will be able to view at his leisure a televised lesson on digitalis as easily as he now listens to a Beethoven quartet on his hi-fi system.

In 1967, the National Medical Audiovisual Center, in cooperation with Emory University School of Medicine, Grady Memorial Hospital (Emory's teaching hospital), the Georgia Department of Public Health and its Mental Health Institute, and the Veterans Administration Hospital of Atlanta launched the first demonstration Community Medical Television System. This prototype utilizes the 2500 mHz bandwidth set aside by the FCC in 1963 for instructional purposes only; the system is a line-of-sight network with broadcast points at Grady Memorial Hospital and the National Medical Audiovisual Center. Since 1967, the network has expanded to include 15 public and private medical-health institutions, including the School of Nursing at Emory University. During 1968, CMTS transmitted a total of 896 hours which included 295 live air hours, 170 live and simultaneously taped air hours, 336 tape playback hours, and 95 identification and program promotion hours.

To illustrate the attraction of special programs for the practicing physicians, a course on "The Modern Treatment of Myocardial Infarction" had a registration of 225 physicians representing 27 states; a course on "Maternal and Fetal Physiology during Labor and

Delivery" (for the southeast region) brought in 315 physicians for the first day's symposium—a group of 40 Birmingham, Alabama physicians chartered a plane to attend.

Current member institutions of the network represent 25 per cent of the total number of general admission beds in the State of Georgia. The total potential audience of the CMTS member installations is estimated to be 12,000.

Similar systems are linking various components of individual medical-health teaching institutions, and some, such as the University of Nebraska System, are reaching out across larger geographic distances.

Meanwhile, such efforts as the Oregon Experiment[11] are available to take continuing education to the physicians via existing television resources. It has been found that many physicians do not participate in organized continuing medical education, either because they do not feel a need for it or because they lack the opportunity to influence the design of the educational courses offered. The Oregon Medical Association, in an attempt to solve both difficulties, has sponsored a series of television programs for the continuing education of its members. By delegating this responsibility to the State Medical Association, the entire membership theoretically becomes involved in attempting to design and organize an effective system of continuing medical education.

Working with the production staff of Oregon Educational Broadcasting, the association appointed a television committee of 17, each to be responsible for the development of one program. The TV network was made available at a cost of $200/hour of air time. Total cost for the entire 17-program series was $3,745. A major portion of the cost was defrayed by a grant received from the Network for Continuing Medical Education. Additional funds were contributed by the Oregon Medical Association and other groups.

Several factors influenced the patterns of television viewing. Although a primary objective of sponsorship by the medical association was to encourage active involvement of the members in planning their own continuing education, the organizational structure which developed permitted only very limited participation by the rank and file physician. Deficiencies were also recognized in the educational planning, chief among which was the failure to identify specific instructional objectives. Sound principles of education science and an organizational structure which encourages participation by the physician-learners are essential for the development of effective continuing medical education.

In another area of activity, "telediagnosis"[12] has proved itself with some impressive results, using a closed circuit television link between the patient treatment point (the first-aid room at an airport, for example) and the doctor's office in a major hospital. This method relies on the presence of a qualified nurse at the treatment point, but it allows a busy physician to diagnose and prescribe treatment—making "house calls" by television—without leaving the office. So far, the results have been encouraging, and the technique has won a high degree of patient acceptance.

With the advent of satellite-mediated communication systems, the fact of intercontinental information transfer is daily becoming a larger part of our lives. Special interest has been demonstrated in this technology by the Carnegie Corporation and The Ford and The Kellogg Foundations. Plans whereby excess revenues may provide a continuing subsidy have been discussed by some of these philanthropic bodies. Industry is developing an interest in educational media. Roche Laboratories has established a Network for Continuing Medical Education which is a cost-free video tape service for medical schools and hospitals with playback capability. At the moment, however, television is still a costly medium, and this fact should be taken into account by any medical educational facility contemplating its establishment. It is also still unfamiliar to many medical faculty members and sometimes causes resentment among faculties long accustomed to the simpler, less demanding lecture method. But television can and does bring to teaching the benefits of realism and versatility, permitting the instructor to move from patient to slide, and from slide to model or x-ray film, or chart, or film clip, or any other device able to teach man.

Motion Pictures

The nontheatrical motion picture and audiovisual field has become a billion-dollar industry. Expenditures for educational films increased dramatically in many areas. The fields of medicine and public health, however, made only modest advances, increasing only 9 per cent during the past year from $23 million to an estimated $25 million.[13] These figures paint a better picture than the 8 per cent drop in film production during the same period— from 400 to an estimated 370.

A major advance in the motion picture format for biomedical teaching is the 8mm film packaged in a plastic cartridge which can be shown on a TV sized table top projector in a lighted room. A study reported in the November issue of the *Journal of the Society of Motion Picture and Television Engineers*[14] revealed that there are currently 6,233 titles available in 8mm format as of September 1968. The largest number of these (1,645) is in the field of science.

Films are available on loan to the professions and professional institutions from a number of sources—the National Medical Audiovisual Center in Atlanta and selected agencies of the Federal Government; the American Medical Association; pharmaceutical houses and other commercial sources; Educational Film Libraries, and some university or medical school complexes.

In order to attain maximum benefit from the use of motion pictures in the medical fields, some compatibility of hardware and software is necessary. Similarly, there is need for a clearinghouse of information through which potential users will be steered in the direction of available materials. At present, the National Medical Audiovisual Center (NMAC) is serving this function under its mandate. NMAC, representing the Department of Health, Education, and Welfare—Public Health Service, is a member, with the Army, Navy, Air Force, Armed Forces Institute of Pathology, and the Veterans Administration, of the Federal Advisory Council on Medical Training Aids (FACMTA) and publishes each year the Film Reference Guide for Medicine and Allied Sciences, a catalog of audiovisuals listing all used by member agencies in educational programs for medical or paramedical personnel.

In addition to the Film Reference Guide, NMAC also produces the National Medical Audiovisual Center Catalog and selected listings of films on heart disease, cancer and stroke; mental retardation; mental health; dentistry, and other specialty areas. NMAC distributes some 1,000 individual audiovisual items, with more than 12,000 prints, available for free loan to medical/health personnel.

Historical medical films are also located at NMAC in the National Archives of Medical Motion Pictures and are available to professional faculty, students, or researchers for use in the study of biomedical subjects.

Research into new uses for the motion picture continues. At Loma Linda University in Loma Linda, California, and the University of California at Los Angeles, researchers are working on development of a method for improving 3-dimensional orientation in the visual presentation of anatomic material.[15] The method makes use of color motion picture film to show a sequence of stained serial sections of the anatomic area under consideration.

In film so prepared, the time factor makes possible development of a desirable illusion of depth. The film presents, at any one time, a 2-dimensional display of some particular plane of the area being studied. But as the film progresses, the plane of presentation changes so that the observer makes a visual excursion through the block of tissue. In the course of this excursion, his memory of what he has seen previously, coupled with what his eye sees at the minute, gives him a psychologically integrated concept of depth.

The teaching of 3-dimensional relationships in oral histology and embryology, particularly as these relationships relate to an understanding of differential growth, has long been a problem in medical and dental education. Moreover, such an understanding is vital for the skilled treatment of congenital malformations, such as cleft palate. Using color film showing animated serial sections improves the students' awareness of the 3-dimensionality of anatomic relationships and benefits not only education in the health fields, but also provides an additional tool for teaching the biological sciences in general.

Film is also contributing to the continuing education of the health professions. The Kansas State Department of Health, through its Division of Dental Health, has embarked on a program of continuing education for dentists by means of a Group Teaching System of Instruction called the Hu Mac Group Teaching System.[16] Programs for the system are developed at the Dental Health Center in San Francisco, with the intent of bringing postgraduate education to the dentist in his own community or region.

Equipment used in conjunction with the Hu Mac Group Teaching System of Instruction includes one motion picture projector, two slide projectors with zoom lens, a tape recorder, an accessories controller, and two large projection screens. The entire teaching system equipment is completely synchronized and controlled through inaudible high frequency sound signals on the tape of the tape recorder. After receiving information, participants are queried and may respond through a Port-a-Punch, stylus and IBM card. The question is then answered, and the reason for the correct answer provided. Participants may score themselves by using prepunched master cards.

Filmstrips and Slide Series[17]

Less expensive and less complex than the motion picture, is the still photographic image which for many years has been the front-line audiovisual in medical instruction. Most popularly, the still image is one photographed through a 35mm camera for preparation into a slide format for projection to medical students, physicians, and allied workers as part of a slide-lecture presentation. This form of teaching is currently enjoying a new spurt of interest, perhaps for the psychological reason that such a device provides comfortable transition from the pedagogic technique of lessons from humans to lessons from humans AND machines. 35mm slides are inexpensive, accessible, and easily stored.

The Instructional Media Center at Michigan State University is making a concerted effort to provide well constructed 35mm slides to faculty and students. In a questionnaire to medical students on the efficacy of using this medium to teach histology, these were the most common replies: it saved the physician's time; it stimulated group discussion; it was easier to understand the fine points and it was easier on the eyes (formerly more time was spent solely with the microscope).

It is important to note that the 35mm slide when combined with audio tape is an excellent teaching resource in which a tape recorder lecture is coupled with a strip of 35mm transparencies. This form of information transfer has barely been scratched by members of the medical community.

Radio and Audio Tapes

For 14 years, Dr. Frank M. Woolsey, Director for Continuing Education for the Medical School in Albany, New York, has used two-way radio to connect 70 hospitals in the New York, New England area in a network of biomedical education.[18] Using faculty from 28 different medical colleges in the New York area, Dr. Woolsey's network conducts professional conferences each day for physicians, nurses, dentists or other medical and paramedical personnel. Each conference is illustrated by 35mm slides pertinent to the subject under discussion. For the duration of the network's existence, more than 27,000 slides have been developed and used as a part of the radio curriculum. The FM broadcasting system covers a total of 100,000 square miles and offers staff officers, students, and practicing physicians a chance to question and discuss topics of immediate concern to them. Class D telephone lines are used to send information into offices, homes, or hospitals as it is needed. Dr.

Woolsey has estimated that it takes one-fifth more man-hour time for his faculty to prepare a two-way radio program than the time required to prepare a television program of the same length. Effectiveness of the system as a teaching tool is currently being measured, and results will be available soon.

In New Mexico, at health stations planned for remote areas of the southwestern part of the state, electronic sensors like those used in the space programs will tell a doctor miles away about a patient's heartbeat, respiration, blood pressure, and other life signs.

The physician (only 30 now serve the area) then will advise station personnel by two-way radio how to treat the patient. The stations will be manned by ancillary personnel appropriately trained to render emergency treatment.

Like radio, the audio tape, another effective and inexpensive teaching medium, is being used somewhat sporadically. Its great potential is not being realized due to the failure of teaching institutions to recognize its advantages.

The audio tape, a recognized valuable tool for teaching cardiology, has been used only infrequently in this field. Magnetic tape, cheap, durable, and compact, has been used to record human heart sounds in health and disease. A valuable collection of such heart sounds was made some years ago by Dr. W. Proctor Harvey at the Georgetown University Hospital in Washington, D.C. in conjunction with the Heart Disease Control Program of the Public Health Service. This economical and invaluable contribution to the study of auscultation should be available to any physician and student in the country for the asking.

In Wisconsin, the audio tape is used with the telephone to make brief recordings available to physicians for continuing education. As the system most commonly works, a number is dialed, and the physician is "tuned in" to an important message in the vital field of medicine. This service could be made available to students within the medical schools if learning resources centers were established at each medical complex to provide student, faculty, and practitioner with access to all of the media with a minimum of inconvenience.

National Efforts in Government

When the first Sputnik went into orbit from Russia in 1957, it launched not only an era of space exploration, but also an era of self-exploration among educators and scientists in the United States. Their findings resulted in greater attention to scientific and technical education and information exchange. In the beginning, the first of these was the major challenge—since then, the latter has demanded the most imagination and innovation. The first step toward National handling of new information was taken in 1957 with the creation by the White House of the post of Special Assistant to the President for Science and Technology. The Science Adviser to the President serves as chairman of the President's Science Advisory Committee (PSAC).

Recommendations of the first study of the President's Science Advisory Committee[19] resulted in creation of the Federal Council for Science and Technology, a confederation of agencies deeply involved in research and development activities—the Departments of Agriculture; Commerce; Defense; Health, Education, and Welfare; and Interior, as well as the Atomic Energy Commission; National Science Foundation; National Aeronautics and Space Administration, and the Office of Science and Technology.

The Science Adviser to the President is designated traditionally by the President to serve as Chairman of the Federal Council for Science and Technology.

The Council operates through standing committees, including the Committee on Scientific and Technical Information (COSATI), which is the 1964 successor to the Committee on Scientific Information (COSI), created two years earlier as a working group of the Federal Council for Science and Technology. COSATI's principal objective is to develop among the Federal agencies coordinated but decentralized scientific and technical information systems for scientists, engineers, and other technical professionals. It is concerned also with coordinating and cooperating with improved Federal and National systems for handling scientific and technical information. It reviews and makes recommendations on the adequacy and scope of present scientific and technical information programs. Its recommendations include standards, methodology, systems and management policies to improve the quality and vigor of these information activities.

Although these efforts are not educational by first priority, their concern with improvement and centralization of scientific and technical information makes them valuable assets to the improvement of material fed through instructional media into the biomedical fields.

Other important programs in the areas of science and technology are being conducted by government agencies in cooperation with industry.

After 1957, it was almost another 10 years before still further significant action was taken to close the gap between information discovery and transmission, especially in the medical sciences.

In 1965, the Medical Library Assistant Act[20] was introduced by Senator Lister Hill of Alabama and Representative Oren Harris of Arkansas. Under this Act, the National Library of Medicine (NLM) was empowered to make grants-in-aid for support of the Nation's medical libraries. Grants are authorized for the following:

1. Part of the cost of constructing medical libraries

2. Part of the cost of initial acquisition of medical library resources, including books and journals

3. Training of medical librarians and health science information specialists.

4. Research in medical librarianship

5. Financial support for biomedical scientific publications

In 1969 amendments were made to the Act which extended for three years the current program. Also in 1967, the Bureau of Health Professions Education and Manpower Training was established and placed under the aegis of the National Institutes of Health to concentrate on improved training of physicians, nurses, dentists, allied health personnel, research personnel and the further development of educational and research facilities.

Some 3 million people, including physicians, hospital administrators, dieticians, medical technologists, pharmacists, vocational rehabilitation counselors, veterinarians, dentists, nurses, health and radiology physicists, and biomedical engineers, among others, are served by the health science libraries of this Nation. Many of these libraries, in turn, are serviced by such modern technological systems as the NLM's computerized MEDLARS (Medical Literature Analysis and Retrieval System). NLM's current catalog is used by all medical libraries for acquisitions and is available from the Superintendent of Documents, Government Printing Office, in the future. The computer prints every two weeks a list of newly published books and journals.

There are several medical libraries in the United States that have put all of their holdings in a single computer in an effort to make resources more widely available. Library A then checks the computer to see what is available from Library B, etc., and borrows from that library instead of duplicating expensive holdings. The Harvard-Yale-Columbia Cataloging Project is one example of such a union catalog. The Medical Library Center of New York is a union catalog for some 10 separate libraries.

An important part of the Medical Library Assistance Act is the Regional Medical Library Grant Program, also administered by the NLM. Today, some six regional medical libraries are providing supportive services to other libraries in their regions as well as to individual users. Photoduplicated or facsimile copies of biomedical materials are provided also to qualified requesters for their permanent retention.

Also in 1965, President Johnson signed the Heart Disease, Cancer and Stroke Amendments to the Public Health Service Act, authorizing grants to help establish Regional Medical Programs to combat heart disease, cancer, stroke, and related diseases. The ultimate goal of the program is to help make the best in modern medical science readily available to all people who suffer from, or are threatened by, these major diseases.

To accomplish this purpose, the program drafted plans for the establishment of direct and continuous linkages between patient, his physician, his community hospital, and the Nation's centers of scientific and academic medicine. Today, it seeks to unite the health resources of the Nation, region by region, in close working relationships—to speed the transmission of scientific knowledge and new methods to the people whose lives depend upon them. By July of 1968, there were nine Regional Medical Programs in operation; as a result of the four newest ones added in 1969, by Nov. 1969 there were 44 operational programs. Geographically, the Regions have ranged in size from single metropolitan areas such as New York and Washington to multi-state areas such as the Intermountain Region (Utah and parts of Colorado, Idaho, Montana, Nevada, and Wyoming) and Washington-Alaska. They range in population from less than 1 million to over 18 million.

As a result of new and expanded NMAC programs in Audiovisual Systems Planning and Educational Studies and Development, medical/health institutions throughout the United States have become greatly more interested in the concept of learning resources centers on their own campuses. Evidence of this interest is shown in this list of institutions receiving consultation services from NMAC this year: The Ohio State University College of Veterinary Medicine; The Ohio State University College of Medicine; Schools of Medicine and of Public Health at the University of North Carolina; The University of Miami Medical Center, Coral Gables, Florida; The George Washington University School of Medicine; and the Mayo Clinic in Rochester, Minnesota.

Further Federal attention was given to communication in the Report of the National Advisory Commission on Health Manpower in November of 1967. The report of that Commission recommended that the Federal Government "markedly expand support specifically designated for research in the educational process for physicians and other health personnel." Medical educators have begun to experiment with new curricula in established schools as well as new ones. The general ferment that characterizes medical education today gives promise of significant change if support is forthcoming.

It was further recommended that schools of the health professions "study their positions in the continuum of education and develop and implement curricular revisions aimed at increasing intellectual stimulation and flexibility. Medical journals and standard reference texts do not perform adequately for the busy practitioner. New data processing techniques utilizing computers and adaptions of various teaching devices might greatly facilitate this task; they should be fully exploited as media for programs of continuing education." [21]

Among the most recent administrative steps in the direction of an improved National Program for biomedical communications was the joint resolution passed by Congress in August 1968 authorizing the establishment of the Lister Hill National Center for Biomedical Communications as a component of the National Library of Medicine. When operational, the Center will design, develop, implement, and manage a Biomedical Communications Network to accelerate the flow of new knowledge for application in medical practice; to improve delivery of health services, and to improve academic medical education.

The National Science Foundation, the National Academy of Sciences, and the National Research Council are adding further support to improved biomedical communication on a National level.

Each of these efforts, in its own way, makes a vital contribution to the motility of health information. There is little question that much is going on concerning instructional media in the biomedical fields. Nor is there question that much remains to be done. Most importantly—before the proliferation of technology and software gets out of hand, the fields of biomedical education and communication must sit down to plan together so that compatibility of effort, technology, technique and concept will be a commonplace. We desperately need to apply the administrative mechanisms, the existing hardware and software to the ultimate goal of improved patient care. For this reason, implementation of Title III of the Public Broadcasting Act is essential to the effort since it deals with broadcasting to the public, and education of the public in matters of its own health is in dire need of bolstering.

Only through the combination of improved professional education and improved public education will this Nation realize the full benefit of innovation in instructional media. This is equally true for biomedicine and for the other specialized areas of human endeavor with which society must deal successfully today.

Summary

Although information presented in this paper highlights a growing interest in modern instructional technology for the biomedical sciences, it should not be interpreted as total representation. Most of the Nation's schools of the health sciences still cling to tradition with a tenacity both remarkable and alarming. The Oregon Experiment was discontinued, and further study is underway to determine better ways to use television before the Continuing Education Project is resumed.

Although there are dramatic examples of the use of computers in isolated institutions, these devices are still too expensive and too demanding of programming talent to be in wide use throughout the biomedical fields. It would seem that the best application of the computer is illustrated by the examples which show several schools cooperating in the use of one computer to share the wealth of existing resources between campuses.

Television, too, is hindered in its growth as a biomedical teaching tool by the expense of equipment and by the lack of specially trained people who know how to get the most out of the medium for teaching medical/health subjects.

The primary requisite for making optimum use of modern technology in biomedical teaching is the preparation of a cadre of communications specialists who will know how to program the technology more effectively. With such a group of specialists working together, and some National compatibility of equipment and software, the potential for use of modern instructional technology in teaching biomedical subjects is limited only by our own imaginations.

And finally, new dimensions in biomedical communication must support the forward sweep of medical science by lessening the chances for obsolescence in health practice.

REFERENCES

1. Schmeck, Harold M., Jr. "Medical School Survey Urges Drastic Change in Study Goals." *New York Times,* November 5, 1968, p. 7.

2. Tompas, John P., M.D., and A. Bradley Soule, M.D. "Experience with Two-way Television in a Teaching Hospital Complex." *Journal of the American Medical Association,* Vol. 204, No. 13, June 24, 1968, pp. 83-84.

3. *Ibid.*

4. "Discourse with a Distant Computer." *Medical World News,* Vol. 8, No. 44, November 3, 1967, pp. 54-55.

5. "EKGs are sent by Satellite." *U.S. Medicine,* Vol. 3, No. 15, August 1, 1967, p. 1.

6. *Fortune Magazine,* LXXVIII, No. 7, December 1968, p. 35.

7. Feurzeig, Wallace, M.S., et. al. "Computer-Aided Teaching in Medical Diagnosis." *Journal of Medical Education,* Vol. 39, No. 8, August 1964, pp. 746-754.

8. Korn, Henry. "Successful Prescription for Hospital Management." *Data System News,* November, 1967.

9. *Journal of the American Medical Association.* Education Number, Vol. 206, No. 9, November 25, 1968.

10. "Broadcast EVR gets Rave Reviews." *Broadcasting,* Vol. 73, No. 23, December 4, 1967, pp. 38-39.

11. Meighan, S. Spence, M.B., Ch. B. FRCP, MRCP, and Anne Treseder, "Continuing Medical Education through Television—The Oregon Experiment." *Journal of the American Medical Association,* Vol. 200, No. 9, May 29, 1967, pp. 102-106.

12. "Computer Center on TV." *Broadcast Management/Engineering,* November 1968, pp. 34-35.

13. Hope, Thomas W. "Market Review: Nontheatrical Film and Audio-visual 1967." *Journal of the Society of Motion Picture and Television Engineers,* November 1968.

14. *Ibid.*

15. Hayden, Jess, Jr., D.M.D., Ph.D., T. R. Husek, Ph.D., and Ken Sirotnik, M.A. "An Initial Evaluation of Animated Serial Sections as an Instructional Method for Facilitating Three-Dimensional Awareness of Anatomic Regions." *Journal of Medical Education,* Vol. 42, No. 5, May 1967, pp. 447-452.

16. *Kansas Health Newsletter.* Vol. 34, No. 5, November 1966, p. 3.

17. Stinson, Al W., D.V.M., and Esther M. Smith, Ph.D. "Student Sets of Color Slides as an Aid in Teaching Microscopic Anatomy." *Journal of Medical Education,* Vol. 43, No. 1, January 1968, pp. 83-85.

18. Interview with Dr. Woolsey and Article in *Medical Tribune,* Vol. 9, No. 49, June 17, 1968, p. 8.

19. Barry, Lt. Commander Richard E., USN. Executive Secretary, Information Sciences Technology Panel, Committee on Scientific and Technical Information, Federal Council for Science and Technology, "Committee on Scientific and Technical Information Coordinates Inter-Agency Information Systems." *Navy Management Review,* April 1967, p. 3.

20. U.S. Congress. 1965. Medical Library Assistance Act of 1965, (Public Law 89-291).

21. Report of the National Advisory Commission on Health Manpower, 1967.

89.
Instructional Technology
And Continuing
Medical Education

GEORGE E. MILLER   and   *WILLIAM G. HARLESS*
Director, Office of   *Chief of*
Research in Medical   *Instructional Systems*
Education   *Section*
Univ. of Illinois   *Office of Research*
with the assistance of Hing-Kay Ho*

Introduction

The explosive growth of medical knowledge that has accompanied a rapidly expanding investment in biomedical research over the last quarter century, has produced mounting anxiety among medical educators that the medical practitioner's half-life of professional competence is steadily shortening. To sustain the currency of that competence medical schools and professional associations, as well as voluntary and public health agencies, have addressed increasing attention to programs of continuing education, but growing discouragement about the efficacy of conventional modes of instruction has stimulated a search of methods that will heighten the interest and attention of practitioners and achieve educational goals more effectively than past efforts have seemed to do. In this spirit they have turned to educational and communications technology.

The initial portion of this report will be descriptive in order to give some sense of the present and contemplated use of instructional technology in continuing medical education; the concluding segment will be devoted to issues which seem to have been overlooked in the headlong rush to get on with educational programming.

Tapes, Slides and Film

Since the major educational problem with which practitioners must deal is widely believed to be that of coping with a continuing flood of new information, most of the technical adaptations now employed attempt to provide more efficient means of delivering this information, or better methods for a harassed practitioner to retrieve from the vast store of knowledge which no man can any longer hope to master, or even to retain, the bits he needs, at the time and place he needs them. Printed words as they are recorded in books, journals, and more recently in succinct medical newspaper summary articles, are still the most widely used means of information dissemination. But many physicians prefer a summary lecture by an expert to the independent search which reading requires. Some years ago the California Medical Association attempted to provide such a mechanism by making available to its membership tape recordings of lectures delivered at professional meetings. The Audio Digest Foundation, which emerged from this effort, now produces weekly tapes

*Mrs. Hing-Kay Ho was an associate in the Instructional Systems Section at the time the paper was written.

in cartridge form which physicians may play while driving or shaving or engaging in other activities which do not require their full attention. This has proved sufficiently popular to lead the American Medical Association to announce a comparable service to begin in January 1969.

The Royal College of General Practitioners of Great Britain has adopted a similar plan selecting individuals who are both acknowledged subject matter experts and skilled in verbal communication to summarize a topic in a fashion that focuses upon the more general items that will be useful to a practitioner, avoiding the intricacies of a subject that may be especially appealing to an investigator. It has not always been possible to accomplish this goal, but their requirement of a preliminary script, a rehearsal, and thoughtful editing have made this a generally admirable collection.

The British have also added a visual element to the sound, using slides to illustrate points that require something more than words. By adhering to a rule of simplicity such that the tape will fit any standard recorder, and the 35mm slides any standard projector, they have made it possible for practitioners in all parts of the British Commonwealth to utilize the materials. At the present time the sound recording service loans approximately 1000 tapes each month.

In America the joining of sound and visuals has more often been automated than manual. The pharmaceutical industry which provides a large amount of continuing education, (commonly product rather than problem oriented) has supplied many detail men with portable solid state tape recorders and synchronized slide projectors that can be quickly assembled to deliver an illustrated lecture in a physician's office. This method is now being developed under other auspices to make brief and attractive summary presentations of current information available to physicians in places where they congregate, for example in the doctors lounge of a hospital. Utilizing a device that captures in a single cartridge both visual and sound, the Metropolitan Washington Regional Medical Program is preparing a series of illustrated lectures on the identification of ovarian malignancy to be placed in surgical dressing rooms for surgeons to view between operations.

Perhaps the most complex of the synchronized mechanisms is the "medical juke-box" developed in the Albany Regional Medical Program. An adaptation of a standard machine it will contrain 160 five minute LP recordings with synchronized visuals displayed from a self contained carousel projector. It will not only provide access to current summary information on a variety of topics, but also the means for a physician to record any unanswered questions. Periodic pickup of the question tape will lead to individual answers through the mails.

But audio tape has been used to do more than communicate information alone. The Royal College of General Practitioners has included in its collection an additional set of sounds whose recognition may facilitate medical diagnosis and treatment, for example the whoop (of whooping cough), the flight of ideas which characterize the schizophrenic state, the non-verbal communication of anxiety or depression which inflections and intonations convey, or the feelings about hospitalization and illness which patients rarely reveal directly to their physicians. The sounds heard through the stethoscope also lend themselves to recording. The American Heart Association has prepared an annotated collection of heart sounds on long playing records; another set is available on tape through the National Library of Medicine. Although simple to use, the sound fidelity has rarely satisfied cardiologists. The special heart sound recording device developed by Butterworth has minimized this problem, although at a very high cost. But all of these methods may soon be displaced by a new heart sound simulator that faithfully generates any kind of heart murmur, of any intensity and duration, in any part of the cardiac cycle, in the course of any cardiac rhythm.

Instructional films have long been available to those responsible for programs of continuing medical education but they have never achieved widespread popularity. There are probably many reasons, but two stand out: (1) most films seem to include more than most teachers want to show, and (2) the technical problems of making a projector work sometimes seem overwhelming. The development of small, portable, cartridge projectors has provided an escape from the second problem; the limited amount of film that a cartridge can hold has stimulated new production methods that deal with the first.

Single concept films are increasingly popular both for conveying summary information, and for demonstrating specific professional skills. The National Audiovisual Medical Center has been a major force in this development and now has an extensive catalogue of titles available on loan. The Washington-Alaska Regional Medical Program has utilized this method of reaching practitioners in remote areas. The University of Southern California is preparing a set of films for circulation to those in more urban settings; Wisconsin and Albany are planning the installations of projectors and film cartridges in community hospitals as information sources. It is clear that these devices will be easier to use than more conventional films. Whether they will produce the desired learning remains to be seen.

Radio and Telephone

Whatever the technical and content excellence of audio tapes, either with or without visual supplementation, when used as self-contained instructional devices they fail to incorporate what is generally regarded as an integral element of optimal instruction: direct teacher-learner interaction. The two way FM radio network established more than a decade ago at the Albany Medical College was designed to achieve this exchange in the course of bringing to physicians in their community hospitals the most recent information which a medical faculty could provide. The original network included six hospitals within a 50 mile radius of the College FM transmitter; with a new transmitter recently installed on New England's highest mountain, and with land line connection to other commercial FM transmitters in the region, the network now includes some seventy hospitals. The program format includes an initial 15-30 minute presentation by a panel of experts; the remainder of the broadcast hour is devoted to questions from audiences in participating hospitals. No more than fourteen hospitals are included in any single day so that staff in each institution may have an opportunity for active angagement. By repeating the program each weekday, all seventy are included in the course of a week. On each occasion the initial presentation is broadcast from tape; the interaction is live. In order to incorporate visual material, slides and printed handouts for use in the course of the broadcast are prepared in advance and circulated to the participating institutions. The Albany model has now been transplanted to other parts of the country and interlinkages between distant networks make it possible to utilize an even larger faculty resource than a single institution could provide.

The use of telephone lines for comparable two way teaching conferences has not been widely adopted, but the telephone has been used for other kinds of continuing medical education. One of the simplest is as a means of consultation on specific medical problems. While the telephone has long been employed for such communication between an individual physician and a personal consultant, only recently have several Regional Medical Programs attempted to facilitate this process by providing a cadre of experts on specific topics to whom access can be provided at any time.

A more imaginative development, most extensively used at the University of Wisconsin but being adopted in many other parts of the nation, is the provision of a library of 5-6 minute tape recorded summaries of current information on a variety of topics, to which any physician may have immediate access, twenty-four hours a day, by dialing the Department of Continuing Medical Education. The system is currently receiving nearly 20 calls/day from physicians, and another system has recently been established for nurses. Plans are now under way to expand the program to include tapes specifically designed to meet preceived information needs of other health professions.

Television

It is television, however, that appears to have aroused the greatest interest among those struggling to adapt contemporary communications technology to the needs of continuing medical education. A pharmaceutical firm was among the first to exploit the medium, through closed circuit transmission of surgical operations from a hospital amphitheatre to medical convention viewing rooms where throngs were captivated by the technical excellence, and the dramatic quality, of a live production. From such a beginning, designed to serve the objective of demonstrating to many what had previously been demonstrable to only a few, development of the medium has proceeded. But only in South Carolina, where a statewide network joining public schools was made available for medical use during scheduled evening hours, has the closed circuit method been widely employed for other than intramural programming. The cost of such systems has led to increasing utilization of commercial and educational channels, but a battle still rages over whether the instruction designed for physicians is suitable for public viewing. A variety of devices have been introduced to assure the privacy of such instruction: at UCLA the broadcast is scrambled so that it may be received only by sets with a decoding device; in Utah and Western Ontario the programs are announced only through personal mailing to the physician audience; in Oregon and Boston the broadcast occurs only after a ten minute break at the end of a regularly scheduled broadcast day. But neither in those instances where members of the general audience have inadvertently come upon medical programs, or in setting such as New York where programs were offered in prime time, has there been any public outcry about the nature or content of the programming.

While these productions have largely taken the form of one way communication, utilizing lecture and panel discussion and demonstration format (usually live but with increasing frequency from video tape), the opportunity for live exchange between experts and audience has been added in Pittsburgh and UCLA, using regular telephone channels for submission of questions during the broadcast period.

Since this medium has been regarded as one means of reaching large numbers of practitioners at a time and place more convenient for them than the usual course offering it is interesting to note that the number of viewers has varied from 4.8% of the potential audience in the broadcast area of WNYC-TV in New York, to 19% in the area of WUED-TV in Salt Lake City.

The high cost in money and man hours of originating carefully planned topic programs with the regularity that continuing education requires has produced several efforts to lessen this burden upon individual educational groups. A pharmaceutical firm, for example, has established a video tape network, supporting production of tapes by individual medical groups, and providing for their exchange through the U.S. postal network. An Association of Medical Television Broadcasters has worked out a similar exchange among members. In the former instance tapes are designed chiefly for local playback on portable tape recorders; in the latter, tapes are of broadcast quality. The UCLA group is now promoting a program of shared production as well as distribution resources, chiefly for the western Regional Medical Programs, but with an open invitation to others who might wish to join in such a cooperative venture. The National Biomedical Communication Network now under development by the National Library of Medicine will provide even wider production and distribution capability.

Although broadcast television may seem to have received the widest attention in continuing medical education, other dimensions of the medium are also being explored. For example the Community Television Network in Atlanta utilizes the 2500 Megahertz Band width for bidirectional sharing of educational efforts among a limited group of local institutions. Thus a medical grand rounds in one institution, a clinical pathology conference in another, a guest lecture in a third may serve all. Bidirectional closed circuits for medical consultation (such as that recently demonstrated between Logan Airport and the Massachusetts General Hospital) are also being explored as continuing education devices. And finally exploitation of the immediate feedback potential of portable video tape recording is increasingly recognized as a useful aid to physicians who are attempting to gain new professional skills or refine old ones.

Programmed Instruction

Medical educators were caught up in the tide of enthusiasm for programmed instruction and teaching machines which swept the entire educational community after Skinner's early publications. When a pharmaceutical firm reportedly received more than 50,000 requests for one of the linear programmed texts prepared under its sponsorship, there were many who voiced the hope that a solution had been found to the often frustrating problem of continuing medical education. As time has passed, enthusiasm has waned, for after an initial period of enchantment the linear programs become tiresome and even the more challenging branched forms rarely seem worth the effort required to flip back and forth through a scrambled book which can never be scanned, or used as a reference. And the machines which automated either linear or branched presentations seemed to offer no advantage, they merely required the learner to come to the machine rather than having instruction come to him.

Programmed materials are still being produced in limited quantities and for special purposes, but the initial hopes of medical educators have been replaced by more realistic views about the potential of such devices. It is probably fair to note a growing acceptance of the view that the learning principles underlying programmed instruction, should be incorporated in all forms of instruction rather than captured only in specific pieces of hardware or software.

Computers

Among educational technologies that have attracted the interest of medical educators computers are currently the object of most intensive study and development. Although the technology is changing rapidly, it now appears that the computer will be able to play at least three roles in the continuing education of physicians: 1) for retrieval of information; 2) as a consultant in the diagnostic process; and 3) as an instrument of instruction.

The *information retrieval* function is most vividly demonstrated in the National Library of Medicine MEDLARS system in which the world medical literature is periodically catalogued and stored. A bibliographic search can be instituted upon request, but the current rate of requests (approximately 5,000 per/year) represents less than 2% of the potential biomedical community of scientists and practitioners. This may reflect the simple fact that a single inquiry almost inevitably unleashes a flood of titles. For the scientist total retrieval may be essential; for the practitioner, however, a more selective output, or production of appropriate abstracts rather than titles alone, may be required. In order to provide more discriminating output, or to produce an automated abstract of original documents, a considerable advance in computer handling of natural language will be required. Steps in the direction of facilitating the abstracting function have been taken both at the University of Oklahoma, where the method utilized was a variation of cluster analysis, and at the University of Rochester, where techniques of factorial analysis were employed, but each represents a very small step toward untimate solution of the problem. The MEDLARS system is a superb beginning, and its extension to regional medical libraries has been useful to many scientists, but to be most successful as a mechanism for continuing education of practitioners it must probably become more selective and sophisticated in the kind of information it produces.

The consultative function is intended to provide practitioners with assistance in diagnosis or management of medical problems, or to provide some feedback about the nature or utility of their professional performance. At the University of Missouri, for example, the computer has been utilized to extract information patterns from a battery of laboratory tests to which each patient is subjected, in such a way that attention is focused upon elements that require further consideration, or which suggest with high probability a specific disease process. At the University of Utah a system that monitors a variety of physiological variables in the study of clinical cardiovascular problems has been particularly valuable in identifying congenital heart disease. At the Cleveland Metropolitan Hospital and the University of Wisconsin, computers have been utilized to systematize the acquisition and analysis of historical information taken from individual patients, or the management of problems identified in the course of investigation. Although the basic purpose in each instance has been to facilitate and standardize data gathering, the educational effect of such a device upon practitioner performance of these tasks in other settings may be very significant.

The consultative function has been served in a more general way by two other systems. In the Professional Activities Survey-Medical Audit Program (PAS-MAP), hospital records are systematically abstracted at the local level, entered in a central computer at Ann Arbor, and analyzed periodically in a fashion that produces extensive feedback to participating institutions on the extent to which the staff is fulfilling basic data gathering and clincial management practices according to acknowledged professional standards. It is unfortunatĕ that the vast collection of information which such monthly summary reports provide seems more often to end in an administrators file than in a staff meeting, but this does not deny its importance as a potential, if not widely realized, adjunct to continuing medical education. A similar system, focused upon a single disease problem, is the computerized cancer registry which has been most fully developed at the University of Utah. The storage of standardized information about every cancer patient in the state from the time of diagnosis to cure or death, provides a mechanism for assembling data on the diagnostic and therapeutic effectiveness of individual practitioners or hospital staffs, who may then compare their performance with some absolute standard or relate it to that of comparable groups. Either method provides a useful entry to further education at the point where education is most likely to be effective: identified and acknowledged deficiencies.

As an instrument of instruction, in continuing medical education, the computer is only now being explored as a tutorial device, and as a simulator. The University of Oklahoma Medical Center has focused attention upon the tutorial mode and has gained some experience in its use both in locally offered course work and in a national demonstration at an annual meeting of the American Medical Association. Physician acceptance of this unfamiliar tool was astonishingly positive, and preliminary studies revealed an encouraging level of learning associated with its use.

Simulations have been the focus of developmental work principally in two institutions. At the University of Southern California a life-like torso under computer control has been devised to respond in realistic fashion to administration of anesthetic agents, to the tracheal intubation that must often be carried out to assist respiration under anesthesia, and to develop the complications that may attend anesthesia (such as depressed respiration; vomiting, cardiac arrhythmias, for example) which must then be dealt with in the same manner that reality would require. At the University of Illinois a library of simulated clinical problems, now under development, will allow students at all levels to engage in independent problem solving, utilizing natural language to gather historical information from the computer, data about physical and laboratory findings, and to intervene with independently generated management procedures that may resolve the problem successfully, induce complications that must then be dealt with, or lead to loss of the patient to another physician—or the morgue. As instructional devices such simulations are exciting, and may under systematic study prove as effective as they now appear to be. But equally important may be their function in educational diagnosis—helping practitioners to identify personal deficiencies in clinical problem solving that may then be corrected using many instructional modes: Books, journals, films, courses or supervised experience. The automated system of simulated problem generation now under development will, if successful, allow almost limitless expansion of a problem library, and the establishment of a network such as that proposed by EDUCOM would provide wide access to such an instructional resource.

Exploitation of the computer as an instructional tool has only begun. Although an important start has been made there are still fundamental pedagogical problems to be explored, as well as technical problems (such a as natural language input and analysis), modeling techniques and system design to be resolved. The question of educational effectiveness of computers is yet to be confirmed, but assuming this is answered affirmatively there remains an issue that can be overlooked during the developmental stage but which cannot indefinitely be ignored—that of cost.

Questions and Issues

Although this account has been illustrative rather than comprehensive, it must convey a sense of the eagerness with which instructional technology is being embraced by medical educators. But the dearth of systematic study, documentation of worth, analysis of cost-benefit, or exploration of alternatives is in striking contrast to the rigorous scrutiny to which diagnostic or therapeutic innovations are subjected before being incorporated into the medical armanentarium. It is almost as though the spirit of inquiry had been replaced by a spirit of faith, when these educators moved from laboratory or consulting room into the classroom.

The process of continuing education, like the process of medical management, should begin with a diagnosis of need, be followed by prescription of a specific intervention to correct the diagnosed defect, and observed with sufficient care to determine whether the intervention had been effective. The preoccupation with technology that characterizes so much of continuing education is like shotgun therapy, random fire in the hope that a target will be hit.

Even granting that the greatest need in continuing medical education is to bring to practitioners the most recent advances in medical science (a view that will be challenged by many thoughtful persons who would aver that physicians are already drowning in the flood of information that reaches them) the real issue is not that of signal transmission, but of signal response. There seems little question that the technologies noted earlier have an immense, often incredible, capacity to transmit, but there may be real question about whether they are being used to transmit what is needed, or the extent to which they produce a desired response. Unfortunately very few of those responsible for continuing medical education appear to be trying to find out.

In reviewing the reports of technological innovations in continuing medical education one is led almost inevitably to the conclusion that in the minds of many writers the mere provision of an instructional method that reaches a substantial number of people who like what they receive is sufficient justification for its use. Virtually all reports of instructional innovation comment upon the number of listeners or viewers and their opinions about program worth, but almost none go beyond this superficial assessment of impact. Further in adopting such devices there appears to be widespread neglect of the principles of adult learning upon which there is general agreement among experts in the field, for example, the matter of active involvement in the learning rather than passive receipt of the learning which others have acquired, the facilitating effect of feedback, the emotional as well as the intellectual component of learning.

This is not to say that such elements cannot be incorporated in instructional technology —here and there they have been; but for the most part developers appear to behave as though the medium were indeed the message. And it may be—but not necessarily the desired one. The medical educator who is committed to television—or dial access or computers—will probably be no more successful than the physician who is committed to penicillin, whether the patient suffers from pneumonia, heart failure, or bunions.

In medicine there is clear need for further development of instructional technology that will involve all practitioners in active, self-directed and productive continuing education. But unless the developmental effort is accompanied by equally vigorous support of an educational research expertise among those who occupy leadership positions it may be found at the end of a decade that we have merely succeeded in creating more costly methods of doing the same old thing. For as one acute observer has put it, "We will never solve the problem (of information overload) by speed reading courses. What we need are courses that teach people to write things worth reading slowly."

And so it is with instructional technology where the need is for methods that produce a defined effect, not for tools that merely dazzle the beholder.

90.
Instructional Technology
In Vocational Training

Professor & Head of
Dept. of Educ. Research & Testing
College of Education, Florida State Univ.

Instructional technology may be defined in as many ways as there are definers though the expression seems most often to connote equipment, hardware, mechanical apparatus and, sometimes, programmed instruction. A more encompassing definition will be used for purposes of this paper. *Instructional technology* is the utilization of knowledge, research and invention in the facilitation of the human learning process. Much is implied in this general definition which needs to be made explicit. Learning is the more or less permanent modification of the learners behavior, which cannot be attributed solely to maturation. Learning will occur in school, though most learning will occur elsewhere. The basic conditions requisite to efficient human learning do not significantly differ from one environment to another. The principles governing behavior change in academic areas are much the same as in social or occupational settings. A consequence of this sameness is that it is pointless to discriminate between vocational and academic applications of instructional technology.

Clearly, what is happening in vocational and technical education today is the use of know-how and invention and is instructional technology of a sort. The blackboards, training aids, audiovisual equipment, etc., are tools however primitive and untested, upon which heavy reliance is placed by vocational teachers. Of more interest to us, is what might be called the *new* instructional technology—the technology which is not in widespread use. In the professional literature, educational, psychological, and engineering, one reads much of new techniques and tools for teaching and it is easy to erroneously assume that these are being employed in large numbers of schools. Such is not the case. The public schools are making far less use of the new products of instructional technology than private industry or the military. And in the public schools vocational education lags behind the academic programs in the utilization of technology.

What are these products of instructional technology? Which appear to be most promising for vocational-technical education? Why are they not being more widely used? Are they worth the effort of attempting to expand their use, and if so what steps might be taken to achieve this end?

Products of Instructional Technology

The products of instructional technology don't fall neatly into a systematic classification scheme. These products are sometimes things, sometimes a technique or strategy and in some instances barely more than a concept. They vary in the degree to which their "facilitation of the human learning process" has been empirically demonstrated. They also vary in the cost of their development and implementation and in the case with which they may be employed in an operational school environment. They also differ in where they may be used in the educational system. Some of the products impinge directly on the student in his learning experience; some relate more to changes in the roles of teachers and some to administrative procedures. Many of the products effect, and are affected by, several of the major independent variables in the educational environment, since these variables do not ordinarily operate independently. Perhaps the most important dimension on which these products vary is the thoroughness of their research and development. A description of some of the more important products of instructional technology follows.

1. Programmed Instruction

Programmed instruction has been on the educational scene for almost ten years and deserves to be treated first because almost certainly it has been an impetus for several of the other important developments in instructional technology. Behavioral objectification, individualized instruction, computer-assisted and computer-managed instruction are all specific by-products of PI. The most important contribution of PI, however, is a concept—the concept that instruction should be designed and presented in order to lead to intended outcomes; that if these outcomes are not attained the instruction, not the learner, is deficient; and that the instruction will be revised on the basis of learner feedback until it does yield predictable student learning. This concept is as useful to the classroom teacher as it is to the programmer (Morgan and Branson, 1964).

Linear programs of the early 60's tended to follow a fairly rigid format. The material to be taught was broken into small, sequenced steps with stimulus information presented to the learner with a response by the learner called for. He was then shown the right answer with which he could compare his own. These three elements—stimulus, response, and confirmation—were called a "frame." A program was constructed by writing series of frames which were intended to lead the learner, somewhat painlessly, to the attainment of the objectives. These frames were tried out on students and revised according to student error and learning. Traditional teaching and programmed instruction were compared, though many thought these to be specious comparisons. Generally, groups learning from well-constructed PI were at least as good as teacher-taught groups and often had higher average final test scores, a lower variability of student performance and less time to completion. Of course, not all programs of instruction did this well. Like learners, PI also had individual differences!

Early programmed instruction had several key features. It presented the instruction in small, logical steps. It required active participation from the learner. It provided immediate knowledge of results. It permitted the student to progress at his own rate, making relatively few errors. It was often devastatingly boring. As it happens the number of frames required to take the least apt student in a group to the objectives is considerably more than is required to take a good student to the same objectives. The printed page which was the medium for early programs was invariable in frame-size and number until Crowder developed the "branching" program and scrambled text. This technique allowed the students to receive varying information depending upon the answers they made.

The only teaching machine developed during this period which is worth mentioning was the "Autotutor" manufactured by U.S. Industries. It was designed to provide branched programmed instruction.

By 1968 PI had become more flexible in its format and is found in a variety of media. Oakland Community College in Michigan commissioned the development of a series of modular paperback programs of instruction in the vocational-technical area (Corrigan, 1965). These short programs of instruction, usually an hour or less of self-instruction, are components of their auto-instructional program and are published by American Book Company of New York City. There are also programmed slide-tape presentations being developed and marketed by General Programmed Teaching, of Palo Alto, California. James F. Wilkey of the Parks Job Corps Center, Pleasanton, California, has done important exploratory work in developing instructional television using principles of PI. The ITV sequence is developed to lead to specific performance objectives with the ITV sequence being revised as described earlier. Measures of learning gain for the job corpsmen suggests this approach may hold promise for instructional television programming.

It is difficult to estimate the number of students who will receive some portion of their instruction in 1968 by means of PI. Though a fairly large percentage of students experience some exposure to PI the dollars spent for PI are not a large fraction of the total amount spent for all educational materials—probably less than 5 percent. There are several possible reasons for this, one of which is cost. Pound for pound, PI costs the school much more than textbooks. Many programs of instruction are prepared to teach all or a large part of a course by self-instructional means. Students time-to-completion may vary from a few hours to several weeks and their finishing at different intervals is disruptive to a system geared to six, fifty minute periods. The design of shorter programs used as adjunctive or remedial at the option of the teacher will reduce the disruptive effect. The best justification for the use of PI is its validated teaching effectiveness to specific behavioral objectives. Yet, the publishers of PI rarely see fit to provide this information to the potential buyer. Demonstrated teaching effectiveness has never been a selection criterion for instructional materials so the publishers' behavior is understandable if not laudable. However, teachers and school administrators may one day demand this information from the producers of educational materials.

The variety of PI titles available from educational publishers is large but more limited in the vocational than in the academic areas. Size of identifiable consumer group is an essential factor in a publisher's decision to publish or not to publish. The vocational education materials market is small and fragmented and hasn't historically represented an incentive for the major publishers. Infusion of dollars through the Job Corps program, the Vocational Education Act of 1963 and the Manpower Development and Training Act have made this area more attractive for material developers.

Programmed instruction, as well as other instructional technology products, can add to the effectiveness and efficiency of vocational and technical training. This contribution can only be optimized in cost and effectiveness if certain other conditions in the training system are permitted to change.

2. Performance Objectives

The cornerstone of instructional technology is the proposition that the goals of education and training can be operationally defined in terms of learner performance. Defining training outcomes in terms of what a student is able to do at the end of the training is not new to the vocational educators nor the athletic coaches. The work of Bloom, Krathwohl, Masia and others in the development of taxonomies of educational objectives for the cognitive and affective domain has had much influence in educational thinking (Bloom, 1956; Krathwohl, 1965). A similar effort for the vocational area has been undertaken by McFann and his associates (McFann, 1968). These works, while conceptually interesting, have probably had less impact in the classroom than Robert Mager's, *Preparing Instructional Objectives* (Mager, 1961). Mager's inexpensive paperback book has permitted thousands of school teachers to attempt to state for themselves and their students the changes in student behavior which they hoped would result from the learning experiences they had arranged. Writing behavioral objectives is difficult and tedious, even in vocational education where the practitioners are not conditioned against thinking in terms of behavioral outcomes.

It must be recognized that the technology of performance objectification may be primitive compared to what it might be in a few years (Atkin, 1968). Likewise, it should be acknowledged by the antagonists of behavioral objectives that efforts in this area have received little federal or foundation research support. As underdeveloped as this tool is at present it still has a great utility. Even the most avid behaviorist would concede that not much is known about developing behavioral objectives in the affective domain (Deterline, 1968; Kapfer, 1968). Yet much learning time is spent in schools on the acquisition and retention of information, the development of skills, and the development of processes such as problem-solving. The fact that attitude development is also important in no way diminishes the significance of the others, and there is a growing body of experience in developing behavioral objectives for these latter areas.

Mager's experiment at Varians Inc., with new industrial trainees suggests furnishing the learner with explicit statements of what will be expected of him will, by itself, yield more effective training at lower costs than some formalized training programs. The Varians trainees were given the objectives along with information about materials or resource people who could help them in relation to specific objectives. From that point the trainees' activities were self-directed. They were not uniform in their entry level behavior and some needed to spend more time on certain objectives than did others. The results showed that the self-directed trainees reached the objectives better and in less time than their formally trained counterparts—and were happier in doing it. If one could generalize from this experience to the public school it might be concluded that we ought to give the students the objectives of the program, remain available to give help when asked by a student and otherwise keep out of the students' way.

Since behavior change is the effectiveness criterion against which instructional technology should be assessed more attention needs to be given to the development of this criterion (Altman, 1967). If we had objectives for all the subject areas, including vocational-technical, an analysis of the objectives would doubtless reveal a large number of needless and unintended overlaps across areas. It is likely that it would also reveal a number of important educational goals, thought to be served by the schools, which had fallen through the cracks found between disciplines. Bruce Tuckman of Rutgers University's Department of Vocational Education is attempting to develop a model for the analysis, evaluation and classification of behavioral objectives (Tuckman, 1968). His model, if successful, should permit the reorganization of objectives into coherent and learnable sequences independent of the disciplines from which the objectives were derived. Frank Lanham of Michigan University is heading a project which is attempting to catalog the behavioral objectives for the field of business education and office occupations. These projects are both part of a planned effort by the Bureau of Research of the U.S. Office of Education to develop performance objectives which can be useful to the classroom teacher, the school planner, the educational evaluator and the curriculum designer.

Some local efforts have experienced success in efforts to objectify their goals. One which is noteworthy because of its attempt to integrate occupational and academic objectives where appropriate, is taking place in the Quincy, Massachusetts Public Schools under the direction of Superintendent Robert Pruitt (Pruitt is now with USOE). Other attempts to merge vocational and academic for the mutual strengthening of both were made by the Office of Economic Opportunity's Job Corps Program and by the Richmond, California school system. This latter effort is presently being evaluated by the Stanford Research

Institute. The Quincy program is not far enough along to have evaluative data and the Job Corps effort, while probably the most extensive of the group, is not likely to be evaluated.

3. Computer Applications

The use of the high speed computer in education has been the most dramatic and publicized application of technology to instruction and, indeed, for many is the sum and substance of instructional technology. The computer seems to loom larger than life, deified by some and feared by many. These grey, blue or green boxes need to be placed in perspective by educators and be examined in terms of what they can do today and what that costs and what they are likely to be able to do in the next five to ten years and what that can be expected to cost. (A note of caution: One's personal prejudices can operate effectively in the face of empirical data; they are particularly potent in the absence of data.)

Perhaps the most extensive coordinate use of computers in attacking instructional problems in a school setting has been the effort in the Philadelphia Public School system directed by Sylvia Charp (Charp & Wye, 1968). Dr. Charp has used the computer with students in (a) simulation and games, (b) problem solving, (c) vocational training, and (d) computer-assisted instruction. She has used both Philco and IBM hardware. Computer-assisted instruction has been investigated by a group of researchers, the most significant of whom include Pat Suppes of Stanford, Harold Mitzel of Penn State, Don Bitzer of the University of Illinois and Duncan Hansen of Florida State University. It might be argued that Hansen's work is more legitimately computer-managed instruction in that the learner is routed off-line for some 90 percent of his instruction. The distinguishing characteristic of CAI is that the machine and the learner interact, with the machine performing an instructional role. This instruction may take the form of drill and practice as in the case of Suppes' work or the computer may perform as a tutor with characteristics of the branching program of instruction described earlier. While it is too early to draw anything but tentative conclusions about CAI, on the basis of results to date, one might make the following generalizations. CAI reduces time to completion of a learning task. While of interest to the psychologist as a dependent variable, reduced learning time is not a compelling sales point with schools, which in discharging their custodial function must still use up 100% of the students' fixed school time. Don Bitzer has retention data on students taught by CAI which suggests the forgetting curves of Ebbinghaus do not apply. His students showed little performance loss through time. Generally, the students learning by CAI have not been shown to be superior to students traditionally taught. The largest barrier to CAI's widespread use is its prohibitive costs which would be a factor even if its teaching power were unequivocally demonstrated. A study by Booz, Allen and Hamilton found that with commercially available equipment the cost of drill and practice by CAI would be in excess of $2.00 per hour per student. Drill and practice is probably the least expensive form of CAI. Tony Oettinger of Harvard University has taken a pessimistic stance in regard to CAI and speculates that it will be years, and maybe never, before schools can afford CAI.

Assuming that the teaching effectiveness of CAI is eventually shown there are some considerations that would surely alter the probability of its use in schools. First, even $2.00 per student hour of instruction is hopelessly non-competitive with most in-school instruction—but not all. Some vocational education and special and remedial education probably cost more and CAI could be efficiently employed in these areas. Second, technological developments could substantially reduce the cost of CAI. Don Bitzer and Dan Alpert have developed protypes of a plasma screen student terminal which could be served in large number (as many as 4000) by a central processing unit. Their projections of costs for a full system with five-year amortization of development costs would provide instruction at $0.25 per instructional hour. A third development which could effect the timing of CAI use is the rising personnel costs in the schools. Teacher militancy with its associated increases in teacher pay may accelerate the pace of adoption of instructional technology in general. A fourth development is the use of computer systems by schools to perform functions other than instruction where the bulk of costs are borne by these other functions (such as administrative data processing). It may be that the machine down time could be used for CAI at high per hour costs but be negligible in terms of the total system costs.

A more recent trend in instructional application of the computer is *computer-managed instruction*. There are several efforts presently ongoing, no one of which is far enough along to permit evaluation of this approach. Though the principals might not all agree that they are working on a CMI model the following projects may be so classified: Harry Silberman's work with the Southwest Regional Educational Laboratory and the Los Angeles Public Schools; Robert Glazer of the University of Pittsburgh working with the Oakleaf School in Pennsylvania; Donald Torr of Sterling Research Institute, Don Tosti of Westinghouse Learning Corporation and Alexander Schure of New York Institute of Technology all of whom are working with the U.S. Naval Academy. All of these projects are sponsored by the U.S. Office of Education. Another large project involving CMI is headed by John Flanagan under the sponsorship of the American Institute for Research and Westinghouse Learning Corporation (Flanagan, 1967). These studies differ in a variety of ways such as reliance on off-the-shelf materials as opposed to developing new instructional resources. They also address different academic levels and areas. Their similarities are greater than their differences, however. All are designing learning interventions based on carefully specified behavioral objectives and all are using the computer to mediate between the student, his individual performance on the objectives and the inventory of instructional resources related to the objectives.

In a sense, these projects are programming the instruction in modular pieces, using a variety of media with redundancy across the pieces. The computer, based upon earlier validation data, can select for a student a mosaic of learning experiences whose particular make-up is uniquely tailored to that student. The instructional power of this approach is yet to be demonstrated but will need to be very dramatic to justify the developmental costs which are estimated at around $30,000 per instructional hour (as contrasted with around $2,000 per hour for PI). Since the principle function of the computer in CMI is to prescribe and schedule, it could serve thousands of students daily and the operational costs of CMI should be less than traditional instruction.

Work by Leslie J. Briggs of Florida State University and David Markle of the American Institutes of Research suggests that the potential instructional power of this approach is great (Briggs, 1967). In the empirical development of an instructional system for a first aid course built for American Telephone and Telegraph Company, Markle was able to reduce the time to completion by 25%, increase the average final test score from 145 for the traditionally taught group to 270 for the experimental group (Markle, 1967). The standard deviation was reduced from 42 to 9 and the worst performer of the experimental group scored 44 more points than the best performer of the traditionally taught group. This study employed a mix of tailored media which underwent three revisions based on learner data. While this study is not conclusive, it does suggest that more effective instruction can be developed even without the computer.

The Naval Academy studies by Stirling Institute, Westinghouse, and New York Institute of Technology were designed to yield answers to some questions not dealt with in Markle's study (HRB-Singer Inc., 1968). How powerful can such a system be in terms of how much is learned in what period of time? Can we find principles governing media selection as opposed to blind trial-and-error? How much reckoning must be taken of what Jerome Bruner calls "learning style"? What roles can the computer effectively play in such a system? What is the minimum computer power required and what is the maximum that can be efficiently used? What are the most effective uses of human resources as contributors to the operating system? What different instructional approaches will need to be taken as course content varies from high-structure to low structure? What are the real development and operational costs of computer-managed, multi-media courses? What kinds of organizations can be expected to develop this type of curriculum? In a sense these studies should be guideposts for future curriculum development efforts, and their importance should not be underestimated.

One of the more promising immediate uses of the small computer in vocational-technical education is in simulating defects in a trouble-shooting exercise. A technique devised by H. R. C. Dale requires the student to make systematic tests using a schematic diagram in order to find the cause of improper equipment performance (Bryan, 1968). The difficulty of the simulated defect search can be increased as the learner gains sophistication. The computer permits many more diagnostic exercises in a given time than would be possible using real equipment. NASA and the AEC have made wide use of this technique and it is coming into use in electronic and TV training programs.

The U.S. Office of Education has sponsored in the past half-dozen years projects on computer applications in education costing several million dollars. Applications research include those previously described plus computer-based guidance systems, and flexible scheduling. Federal agencies such as the National Science Foundation, and the Department of Defense have also been sponsoring education related studies involving the computer. USOE, in an attempt to assess the state of development, formed an Ad Hoc study group to determine what had been accomplished and what were the most pressing priorities for future computer applications support. This study group collected information on the progress of the various on-going research projects, solicited the views of a number of computer technology experts both from within and outside the government.

The major conclusions drawn from this analysis were:

a. Of the several kinds of computer applications being researched, some should become operationally feasible before others.

b. With the existing hardware many of the more exotic applications (CAI, CMI and computer based guidance systems) would not become feasible for wide-spread school use unless significant reductions could be made in per student cost.

c. There are a number of non-exotic but useful functions which could be furnished to schools with the available technology.

d. Computer systems for schools should be developed to provide services currently available and be able to accommodate the expected newer functions at a future time with minimum disruption and systems modification.

e. The services provided by such a computer system probably should not increase the per student per year costs by more than 2%. In order to provide a range of services within this cost level it is reasonable to assume that a large central computer service with terminals extended to participating schools and school districts would be required.

As a consequence of this survey and analysis the Office of Education decided that one of its highest priorities would be to study the feasibility and desirability of supporting the establishment of such a computer center. In the planning phases this program has been called "A Computer Utility for Educational Systems" (CUES). In response to competitive bids, two contracts were awarded, one to International Business Machines and the other to General Learning Corporation to study this problem and to make recommendations for an approach. Questions that these two contractors were asked to address included: what are the services that are needed by schools today which can be offered with least delay, what numbers of students and numbers of schools in what geographic range would be required to meet the desired per student cost, what kind of equipment would be required at the computer center and what kinds of terminals would be appropriate in what numbers for providing these services, what computer programming would be required and what kinds of systems analysis would need to be done at the school and district level, what would be required in the way of non-computer software for supporting the services, what requirements would there be for staff-orientation and training?

While there were significant differences in the findings of the two investigators there were some remarkable similarities as well. In order to develop rapprochement between the two studies and refine the analysis a third contract was let to Computation Planning, Incorporated, under the direction of Mr. Herb Bright. These studies concluded that four services could be provided to a network of schools that would not require extensive research or development. These are administrative data processing, a basic course in computer technology, integrated problem solving and vocational training. Studies assumed that at a later time, computer managed instruction, computer guidance and career information systems and library services could be added. One or more of these services to be offered from the onset of the program are in operation in several schools in the nation at the present time. Only a few large school districts have all four of the services functionally operational.

The administrative data processing would include such functions within the school as student scheduling, classroom use, payroll and various other normal record-keeping functions.

The basic course in computer concepts would be offered for all students, probably at the ninth grade level, and would cover basic fundamentals of computer technology. It would be primarily designed to provide basic information about computers to the students but would also equip them with some rudimentary programming skills. This course would be regarded as part of the students' general education program.

The third use of the computer would be as problem solving device in appropriate courses within the existing curriculum. Problem solving exercises involving the use of the computer would be integrated into the physics, chemistry, mathematics, business education and other courses. The integrated use of the computer within these courses would be a standard part of the sequence of learning experiences for each student.

Vocational training application of the computers would be to prepare students as key punch operators and it should be possible for the students to actually punch the programs written by other students. Since all of the schools will have a remote card reader and printer and have a requirement for some form of production control, selected students can gain experience at an elementary level in that aspect of computer facility operation. Certain students in the vocational area should be equipped as beginning programmers.

The computer time required will not be equal for all three instructional applications. It is expected that students will have six to seven programs per year on the average, to be processed by the central processing unit. Problem solving and vocational training students will have a larger number of programs with smaller numbers of students involved. The course in computer concepts will have large numbers of students enrolled but limited use of computer time.

An early additional application anticipated, computer managed instruction has already been described.

The analysis compared time-sharing systems to multi-programming batch systems with a cost differential favoring batch processing of about two to one. A decision was made to design the system for multi-programming batch processing. Cost estimates for CUES on an operational basis range from twenty-two dollars to fifteen dollars per student per year, depending on the number of students to be served by the system and whether the system is leased or purchased. With 200,000 students in fifty to one-hundred schools within a seventy-five mile range, the cost of purchasing the central system and terminals with leased lines would be about fifteen dollars per student. This would be with five year amortization of purchase cost and would assume an average line length of thirty miles. These figures do not take into consideration any cost displacement or savings for administrative uses of the computer and the fifteen dollars per student should be accordingly reduced to arrive at the instructional expenditure for each student. The non-recurring expenditures for development and demonstration are not included in the operational cost and are expected to be approximately five million.

It is anticipated that the hardware required for the CUES System will consist of commercially available equipment, including a highpowered computer and related hardware at the central site and medium speed card readers and printers in the remote schools. Since the work load requirements cannot be estimated precisely at this time, it is not feasible to determine the exact central facility equipment requirements. The computer will be a high speed device with approximately one-half million characters or one-eighth million words of main (directly-addressable high speed) memory. Both high and low speeds secondary storage will be provided for input/output, library routines, and so forth. Four magnetic tape drives are to be provided in addition to one card read/punch and one high speed printer. The remote input/output station for the proposed system will include card readers capable of reading intermixed marked sensed and punched information at the rate of 200-250 forty column cards per minute. Printers will be used which combine medium speed (over one-hundred characters per second) and relatively low unit cost. Part of the administrative work load for which only limited input/output is required will be sent to and from the central facility via courier. The instructional functions of CUES will have first priority with most administrative jobs being processed after the end of the school day.

The next step is for a contractor and school district (or a group of districts) to be selected for the actual development of a CUES center. The advantages to educational planners and decision-makers should be several. Computers are expensive and unwise expenditures by schools can and have resulted in enormous waste of money. CUES should demonstrate what reasonable and desirable uses can be made of the computer in an operational school setting and what these services cost. School representatives will have a place to see for themselves the program in operation and will be able to talk to the actual school users of the system. Of significant value will be the detailed specifications of the required hardware systems, both central and remote, and the existing software—all of which can be borrowed or copied by other schools.

It can be anticipated that after CUES is developed and refined it can become a profitable enterprise. If this turns out to be correct, then it may be reasonable to assume that private enterprise, on its own initiative and with its own capital, working in cooperation with other school districts, will replicate the CUES model. It has been estimated that thirty strategically located centers, like that envisioned for CUES, would bring instructional computer services to almost 90% of the nation's school population.

4. Computer Based Guidance Systems

Another use of the computer is being made in the vocational guidance and career area. The kinds of information about career opportunities and training requirements for various careers that are available in most schools are not adequate for students. The student doesn't know enough about the jobs nor about himself to make wise career decisions and the result is that thousands of youngsters drift into jobs for which they are ill equipped in terms of training and aptitude. Many will shift several times in their occupational life—often to jobs which are no more suitable for them, virtually precluding a rewarding career pattern. David Tiedeman of Harvard University has been studying the career decision process of students for the past several years and has developed a career information system which permits machine storage of information about a large number or careers and for which there is actual employment opportunity in the region. His system permits the student to examine these career specifications and relate his own qualifications to specific jobs. Using the computer the student can simulate a series of decisions that are like those one would actually make in systematically analyzing a career progression. Tiedeman's project hasn't been underway long enough yet to determine whether a student's career pattern will be effected by these organized experiences and it will be several years before the real effects can be assessed. However, the approach appears to be logical and eminently sensible and on the basis of its face validity it will probably be utilized by other schools when its development is complete. John Flanagan is developing a similar program as a coordinate part of Project PLAN, which is likely to be operational before Tiedeman's program. Frank Minor of the IBM Corporation is also developing a career information and guidance system using the computer.

5. Individualized Instruction

Perhaps the most promising development in instructional technology at the present time is individualized instruction. It is promising because there is evidence that such approaches can be locally developed and operated without exotic equipment and without great additional operational expense. There are several programs of individualized instruction that are in operation and continuing development today. The two that have been underway the longest and are the best known are the Nova high school program in Broward County, Florida and the Oakleaf elementary school program in Pennsylvania. Both are being evaluated as development continues and in neither case is the evaluation data conclusive, nor yet exciting. Gary Foster of Florida State University has been in residence at Nova for the past four years collecting comparative data on the students in the program, and while his data analysis is not complete, the experimental students do not appear to be excelling the matched control students. The evaluation data on the Oakleaf project is being collected by Bob Glazer and his colleagues at the University of Pittsburgh and is equally tentative.

Two more recent projects are underway in the Duluth, Minnesota public schools and the Bloomfield Hills, Michigan public schools. Thorwald Esbensen of Florida State University (formerly Assistant Superintendent of Duluth) was the Project director of the Duluth program and Robert Boston, Assistant Superintendent directed the Bloomfield Hills effort. Both of these are too recent for any meaningful evaluation to have taken place. While there are differences between the four projects they are sufficiently similar for a description of one to suffice. In Bloomfield Hills, the entire curriculum for three schools has been individualized. The three schools, an elementary, a junior high and a high school, provide a kindergarten through 12th grade test environment. Teams of local faculty members in these three schools, working with central district office specialists and outside consultants, developed specific behavioral objectives for the entire curricular offering. There are terminal performance objectives, the sum of which make up a defined course of study, and interim performance objectives, a sequential group of which lead to a terminal objective. After developing the objectives the teachers analyzed the instructional materials available in the system and encoded portions of these materials against the objectives. For certain objectives, they judged no material to be suitable and developed their own instructional resources. Their next step was to develop instruments or techniques for determining whether or not a performance objective had been attained by a student at the specified level of proficiency. Finally, the products of these efforts was organized into a "student learning packet," which for a given block of instruction told the student what was expected of him in objective terms, what resources (including teachers) he might fruitfully employ in achieving these objectives, and, finally, how he was going to be evaluated on the objectives. The student could then proceed at his own rate, calling for assessment on any given objective whenever he felt he was ready. Indeed, many of the students were able to demonstrate proficiency on some of the terminal objectives at the beginning of the learning sequence, thus avoiding spending time on things they already knew.

A visit to any of these four programs, and talking to students and teachers, is a convincing experience even in the absence of evaluation data. While the youngsters are moving through the curriculum at variable rates, they are, as a group, tending to go faster than the traditional pace and some of the students are moving rapidly. A major problem which will have to be faced shortly in these individualized programs is what to do with the students who finish the present offering of the school before they reach graduation age.

What Needs To Be Done?

Much of the impact for instructional improvement by using instructional technology is lost because of the apparent inflexibility of the educational system and because the products of technology are usually employed in a piecemeal fashion, if at all. There are many critical variables in the educational system which affect student learning and these variables do not operate in isolation from one another. These include the instructional objectives, the role of teachers and administrators, the physical environment, the motivation and background of students, the administrative practices, the instructional processes and more. Research has been done on all these variables usually treating one independently of the others. Yet, maximizing the effect on student learning of any one of these is constrained if the educational researcher is not free to appropriately change the other variables. If all the major components in an educational program are to be optimally articulated, one might conclude that the smallest experimental unit for significant educational change is a whole school.

An application of systems approach to the re-design of the total educational program for a school is exemplified by a cooperative program presently underway called "Educational Systems for the Seventies." The U.S. Office of Education's Bureau of Research has joined with seventeen local high school districts located in fourteen states in designing and developing a new educational program at the high school level. These schools will serve as a flexible staging area where the interactive effects of the important components of the educational process can be tested and revised in terms of both contribution to student learning and cost benefits. The seventeen schools, currently participating in the planning of this program, will serve as test sites for its major components, and will later serve as demonstration schools for the operation of the total program.

The overall plan will identify all the activities that must be completed before the total new curriculum can be operational. These activities can be generally classified as either research, development, or demonstration. Because of the magnitude and complexity of the task, many diverse institutions and organizations will be involved in the effort. These will include universities, profit making and non-profit making organizations, and professional associations. The local schools will have primary responsibility for the definition and acceptance of the program as well as the try-out demonstration activities.

The specific tasks to be done range from the preparation of inservice training programs for staff to the analysis of design requirements for facilities. The plan anticipates that courses as we now know them, may be changed and that Carnegie Units as a measure of student progress may become inappropriate. Therefore, new accreditation and student certification practices may be necessary. The activity having the most pressing priority relates to the setting of the educational goals and operationally defining the performance objectives. The performance objectives define the output specifications for the system and must precede the design of the system. The ES '70 schools have already agreed upon their broad aims. Each graduate of this yet to be built program will receive a comprehensive education. He will have the requisite academic attainment for college entry and also for salable job skills. He will be equipped to cope with the socio-economic environment as an adult. These are ambitious goals and will require a powerful educational system if they are to be realized for all students. For these goals to become purposeful in a design of a new system they must be operatively defined in terms of behavioral outcomes.

An important reason for specifying the outcomes of educational systems is that it is necessary for longitudinal validation of the effectiveness of public education in preparing young people to cope with the social and economic environment when they leave school. Unless we know with what behavioral attainments a youngster enters the adult world, there is little basis for relating his later success, or lack of it, back to his school experience. Another reason for needing behavioral objectives relates to cost effectiveness of educational programs. The American taxpayer will inevitably grow weary of continuing to vote increased taxation for educational funds with no tangible evidence of the effect these funds have on the education of his children. With the performance objectives it should be possible to associate behavioral change with program cost. Student learning should certainly be the most if not the only basis upon which cost effective analyses are made in education.

Once these objectives are set, and agreed upon, all the other variables in the educational program need to be arranged in such a way as to optimize student attainment of the objectives. It should be possible to experimentally manipulate the other variables disregarding, where possible, the traditional constraints found in the educational system. This can be done by careful and systematic planning.

BIBLIOGRAPHY

Altman, James W. *A Behavioral View of Vocational-Technical Education.* (Prepared for the Commonwealth of Massachusetts Advisory Council on Education, Symposium on Vocational-Technical Education: Prospectus for Change), 1967.

Altman, J. W. *Research on General Vocational Capabilities (Skills and Knowledges).* Pittsburgh: American Institutes for Research, March, 1966.

American Institutes for Research. *Development and Evaluation of an Experimental Curriculum for the New Quincy (Mass.) Vocational-Technical School: Third Quarterly Technical Report.* Pittsburgh: American Institutes for Research, September, 1965.

Atkin, J. Myron. *Behavioral Objectives in Curriculum Design: A Cautionary Note.* Washington, D.C.: National Science Teachers Association, 1968.

Bitzer, D. L. *Some Pedagogical and Engineering Design Aspects of Computer-based Education.* University of Illinois, Computer-based Education Research Laboratory, (Position paper ASEE Symposium), 1968.

Bloom, B. S. (Ed.) *Taxonomy of Educational Objectives: The Classification of Educational Goals: Handbook I, Cognitive Domain.* New York: David McKay, 1956.

Briggs, L. J. *Sequencing of Instruction in Relation to Hierarchies of Competence.* Palo Alto, Calif.: American Institutes for Research, October, 1967.

Briggs, L. J., P. L. Campeau, R. M. Gagné, & M. A. May. *Instructional Media: A Procedure for the Design of Multi-Media Instruction, A Critical Review of Research, and Suggestions for Future Research.* Pittsburgh: American Institutes for Research, 1967.

Bryan, G. L. *Computers and Education.* (M.I.T. Symposium Series), May, 1968.

Bushnell, D. S., and R. M. Morgan. "A Systems Approach to Trade and Industrial Curriculum Development," *Guidelines for the Seventies 1967 Yearbook,* pp. 97-108, Trade and Industrial Division, American Vocational Association, American Technical Society, Chicago, Illinois.

Carter, C. M., and M. J. Walker. *Costs of Installing and Operating Instructional Television and Computer Assisted Instruction in Public Schools.* Booz, Allen & Hamilton, Inc., 1968.

Charp, S., and R. E. Wye. "Philadelphia Tries Computer-Assisted Instruction," *Educational Technology,* Vol. VIII, No. 9, May 15, 1968.

Corrigan, Robert E. *The Instructional Systems Approach to Tutorial Systems Development.* Anaheim, Calif.: Litton Instructional Materials, Inc., 1965.

Deterline, William A. "The Secrets We Keep From Students," *Educational Technology,* Vol. VIII, No. 3, (February 15, 1968), pp. 7-10.

Flanagan, John C. "Functional Education for the Seventies," *Phi Delta Kappan,* (September, 1967), pp. 27-33.

Gagné, R. M. *The Conditions of Learning.* New York: Holt, Rinehart, and Winston, 1965.

Gagné, R. M. "Educational Objectives and Human Performance," in J. D. Krumboltz (ed.), *Learning and the Educational Process.* Chicago: Rand McNally, 1965.

Glaser, R. (ed.) *Teaching Machines and Programmed Learning, II: Data and Directions.* Washington: National Education Association, 1965.

Kapfer, Philip G. "Behavioral Objectives in the Cognitive and Affective Domains," *Educational Technology,* Vol. VIII, No. 11, (June 15, 1968), pp. 11-13.

Krathwohl, David, (ed.) *Taxonomy of Educational Objectives: Handbook II, Affective Domain.* New York: David McKay Co., 1965.

McFann, Howard. *The Design and Evaluation of Vocational Technical Education Curricula Through Functional Job Analysis.* DHEW, USOE, Bureau of Research, Final Report, Project No. 6-1659.

Mager, R. F. *Preparing Objectives for Programmed Instruction.* San Francisco: Fearon Publishers, 1962.

Manion, R. C., R. M. Gagné, P. L. Quinn, W. M. Richardson, and R. M. Morgan. *Multimedia Course Development at the U.S. Naval Academy.* (Symposium presented at American Educational Research Association Annual Meeting, February, 1968, Chicago.)

Markle, D. G. *The Development of the Bell System First Aid and Personal Safety Course: An Exercise in the Application of Empirical Methods to Instructional System Design.* Palo Alto, Calif.: American Institutes for Research, April, 1967.

Morgan, R. M. "U.S.O.E. Launches Research, Designs CAI Centers," *Nation's Schools,* (October, 1968), pp. 65-67.

Morgan, R. M. and R. K. Branson. *Programmed Instruction—A Concept of Learning.* Los Altos, Calif.: General Programmed Teaching Corp., November, 1964.

Morgan, R. M. and D. S. Bushnell. "Designing and Organic Curriculum," *National Business Education Quarterly,* (Spring, 1967), pp. 5-14.

Morgan, R. M. and D. S. Bushnell. "How to Help Johnny Get—and Keep—a Job," *Air Force and Space Digest* (April, 1967), pp. 58-62.

Morgan, R. M. and D. S. Bushnell. "Vocational Training and Curriculum Design," *Educational Technology,* (June, 1967), pp. 1-8.

Morgan, R. M. and J. C. Morgan. "Systems Analysis for Educational Changes," *Trend,* (Spring, 1968), University of Massachusetts, CSSC, Amherst, Massachusetts.

Stansfield, David. "The Computer and Education," *Educational Technology,* Vol. VIII, No. 10 (May 30, 1968), pp. 3-8.

Tuckman, Bruce W. *Analysis, Classification and Integration of Educational Objectives.* (Paper presented at the meeting of the Educational Systems of the '70's network schools, San Mateo, Calif., May, 1968.)

Tuckman, Bruce W. *Structural Analysis as an Aid to Curriculum Development.* Rutger University, SCOPE Program, Incidental Report #1, July, 1968.

91.
Instructional Technology
In Dentistry

by DALE W. PODSHADLEY
Chief, Professional
Education Branch
Dental Health Center
U.S.
Public Health Service
San Francisco

Dental Education

The burgeoning population and ever-increasing individual demand for dental care has created a severe problem for dental education. In order to provide an adequate supply of dental manpower, new schools have been created and existing ones have expanded their enrollments. Between 1965 and 1975 the annual number of graduates will have increased 36 per cent, from 3,200 to 4,300.[1] Unfortunately, this dramatic and necessary increase in the student population has compounded an already critical problem—the shortage of qualified teachers.

Adding to the problem of teacher shortage has been an expansion of the dental curriculum. As a result of social change and increased social awareness on the part of the profession, many new courses are being added from disciplines previously only remotely concerned with dental education. Psychology, sociology, anthropology, and political science are but a few of these new curricular elements. At the same time, the knowledge explosion has added immeasurably and will continue to add to the content of traditional courses.

It is obvious that, with an increasing student-teacher ratio and increasing subject matter content, constant effort must be directed at facilitating the effectiveness and efficiency of both teaching and learning in the dental school environment. It is essential that the use of modern instructional technology be increased and effective educational innovations be applied rapidly.

In recent years, there has been a great deal of interest in the teaching-learning process. This interest has served as a catalyst in the development of new instructional strategies and instrumentation. These innovative developments attack a variety of deficiencies in the educational process. To alleviate the problem of personalizing and individualizing instruction, of combining the learning principles of immediate feedback, reinforcement, and active participation, programmed instruction, and recently, computer-assisted instruction have shown great promise. For the problem of teacher shortage and that of reaching a large number of students at one time, educational television provided a partial solution. To solve the problem of providing information when the student wants it, dial- and random-access capabilities for both audio and visual materials have been developed. To enrich learning experiences by involving more than one sense mode, simulation techniques were introduced and newer media and devices have been developed—these include cartridge-loaded and single- and multiple-concept films and filmstrips, 35mm slides with their easy-loading projectors, overhead transparency series with overlays for step-by-step presentations, and various other multi-media kits designed to help the students acquire important skills and knowledge.

Dental education has kept up with this growing technology. There is hardly any dental school that is not equipped with a fair variety of audiovisual equipment, and most dental teachers use some type of audiovisual aid in their teaching. This, of course, is to be expected since dentistry is visually-oriented. Clinical procedures, chairside demonstrations, examples and illustrations of anatomical structures, simplification of complex processes and magnification of minute objects lend themselves well to the use of audiovisual aids. There have been experimental and evaluative studies comparing the effectiveness of one medium with another or merely testing their feasibility, and in most of these studies, the results have indicated that audiovisual aids, when properly used, can make an invaluable contribution to learning. One such study was conducted at the University of Illinois College of Dentistry,[2] where the results of a study comparing the effectiveness of the lecture-demonstration with a synchronized tape-slide presentation in the teaching of dental technics showed the tape-slide group to be better performers. Another study, at Western Reserve University,[3] documented that dental students, when given the opportunity to pace themselves through the use of a manual and individual sets of colored slides, could save up to half the time traditionally provided for the learning of preclinical dentistry.

Even more important than research studies on the utilization of media is the preparation of the instructional materials themselves—the "software" in technological terminology. What is still needed, therefore, are more teaching materials, more efficient and organized ways of disseminating them, and a greater number of dental faculty trained to use them in an effective manner.

Single-Concept Films

Of the newer media, special mention should be made of the single-concept film. Dental education, with its emphasis on the teaching of specific procedural skills, has found this training aid to be of significant value. The simplicity of the projectors, the easy-to-load and protective cartridges, and the adequate film capacity to handle all but the most complex of dental procedures, have added a dimension to dental education that previously was unattainable. For example, a recent study at the University of Iowa[4] investigated the feasibility of condensing a two-semester course in operative dentistry into three weeks of intensive study. This project made use of single-and multiple-concept films on the conceptual and procedural aspects of certain clinical skills. The results clearly showed that procedures in clinical dentistry can be taught effectively in a shortened period of time. The films have since been placed in convenient locations for individual use by students for the recall of a particular procedure immediately prior to providing the service to a clinical patient.

Simulation

Dental educators have always been faced with the problem of providing adequate clinical experiences for future dentists. Although opportunities are provided for the students to experience a variety of situations during their clinical years, it is virtually impossible to expose them to many situations which they will ultimately encounter in their professional practice. It is true that there is no substitute for first-hand learning experiences, but since some problems do not occur at scheduled and at specified hours, the next best way to enrich the students' educational experience is to simulate life-like situations that are likely to occur in the dental office.

Simulation as a teaching method provides a unique learning experience whereby a situation may be repeated as often as desired, thus giving the student practice in discriminating cues that identify a particular problem. Since a group of students or a whole class can experience the same situation through simulation, a common frame of reference is established. In this way, the group can discuss a particular problem more realistically and evaluate the results more effectively. Many problems in dentistry, particularly those related to determining a diagnosis and a plan for treatment, are amenable to simulation.

In dental education, however, the potential of simulation as a teaching approach is just beginning to be realized. At the University of Oregon,[5] a series of filmed emergency episodes have been prepared that are of considerable value in teaching dental students to cope with emergency problems which may be encountered in private practice. This basic technique is also being used at the University of Alabama,[6] where community experiences are "acted out" on video tape to prepare students for their roles in society as community leaders in matters pertaining to oral health. And at the University of Michigan,[7] a series of short films designed for in-service teacher education is being developed. These films will simulate the most common teaching problems which occur in the laboratory or clinic and will illustrate good and poor solutions to these problems.

Even more realistic than filmed or video taped versions of actual situations are life-like, life-sized manikins, such as the computer-controlled SIM ONE, developed by the University of Southern California School of Medicine to improve the training of anesthesiologists.[8] It is planned that a similar manikin for the training of dental and dental auxiliary students will be developed by the Education Research Branch of the Division of Dental Health. This computerized head and neck manikin will simulate a variety of human characteristics and responses. For example, thermistors placed in pulp chambers will respond to excessive heat causing a pain response, salivation and circulation of blood will be provided, appropriate responses to correct and incorrect local anesthetic procedures will be included, and the maxillary and mandibular arches and contiguous tissues will be removable so that a variety of clinical problems can be presented to the student. Ideally, this manikin would simulate nearly every human response conceivable in dental practice, e.g., an allergic response to an anesthetic or a coronary occlusion.

Dial- and Random-Access Systems

A great deal of progress has been made in the area of information storage and retrieval during the past few years. With the tremendous amount of printed materials published and the rate at which new materials are being developed, the need to store and disseminate them effectively is of paramount importance. The availability of the microfiche provides a solution to the storage problem; the dissemination of materials, however, is still far from satisfactory.

This need has resulted in the development of the dial-access system. With this new technology, it is now possible for a learner to have immediate access to any prerecorded material he needs—audio and/or video—from any place and at any time by simply dialing a number or pushing a button. Even more promising than the dial system, where only one student at a time can be connected to the beginning of the program source, is the potential random-access retrieval system, where anyone who dials in to a program of his choice can be connected instantly to the start of the program.

Dial-access is already a reality in a number of schools throughout the country, but to date, the dental field has made only a modest beginning in the area of learning through prerecorded instruction. A significant amount of planning to introduce this system has been done by Loma Linda University School of Dentistry, but the system is not yet operational.

The concept of the retrieval system, especially if it is random-access and under computer control, has tremendous implications in the field of dental education. The immediate access to a library of prerecorded instructional materials when the learner needs them would provide the flexibility and individualized learning that is required if dental students are to progress in accordance with their individual capabilities. This element is of prime importance in the learning of psychomotor skills, where individuals differ widely in their conceptual and digital abilities. No longer will the student be forced into lock-step learning; no longer will he be held back or pushed ahead of his capabilities by other students in the class; no longer will he depend on the teacher or on the traditional library to dispense the information he needs at the moment. Since this dispensing of information can be done electronically, there will be more dialogue and communication between teacher and learner, and more time can be devoted to individual learning problems.

Television

An instrument that is capable of transmitting oral and visual information of any size to any group simultaneously is bound to have important implications for teaching and learning. For this reason, television has an important role to play in dental education. The capabilities of image magnification and image storage on videotape are particularly valuable.

Television was first used in dental education in the early 1950's at the University of Detroit School of Dentistry. Since then, a number of dental schools have made use of this medium of instruction. At the University of Texas, one of the pioneer dental schools to use television, basic science and clinical courses, as well as examinations, are televised into small laboratories and private operating rooms. Response mechanisms are provided to each student so that questions can be asked during the televised lectures and demonstrations. At the University of Kentucky, televised lessons are not only scheduled as part of a course, but they frequently are also immediately available for viewing by students who may have missed the lesson or who may feel the need for a review. The value of television in dental education has been documented by the University of Pennsylvania, as well as other schools of dentistry.[9]

At present, almost all the dental schools in the country have television installations or have access to television facilities. Research in television technology, however, continues. An example may be seen in the University of Texas Dental Branch where 3-D television to show perspective and dimension has been developed.[10] Another innovation is a prototype optical scanner for the inspection and display of intra-oral anatomy with remote television viewing, planned for development by the Forsyth Dental Center in Boston.

Unfortunately, one capability of television which would have immediate impact on the problem of the shortage of teachers is not yet being used to any appreciable extent in dental education. This capability is the sharing of great teachers through the use of videotape. The cause of this situation, however, is not entirely attributable to the lack of action on the part of dental educators; rather, a bigger reason probably is the lack of compatibility within the television systems.

With the continuing upsurge in technological innovations, however, it is conceivable that in the not too distant future, all classrooms and laboratories in each dental school in the United States will be equipped with television monitors linked to a computer, making it possible for a student to tune in a program or a course of his choice anywhere and at any time.

Programmed Instruction

Programmed instruction appeared on the educational scene only a few years ago, but it has already gained rapid acceptance in business, industry, and the military. This is so because training objectives in these fields are easily defined and the development of training programs are not bogged down by policy decisions. The acceptance of programmed instruction in educational institutions, however, has been relatively slow, and dental education has been no exception.

Perhaps the biggest single factor influencing the *applicability* of programmed instruction to dental education is the lack of agreement from one institution to the next regarding what is taught in a particular course. In other words, controversy over the subject matter itself over what ought to be covered or what should be emphasized blocks the widespread acceptance of material programmed by a single teacher or a group of teachers in one school. Individual teachers, therefore, are left with the task of preparing their own materials, or at least modifying what others have prepared to meet their particular needs. Unfortunately, because of the teacher shortage, few dental faculty members can affort the time and effort required to prepare their own materials or to modify those of others.

The use of programmed instruction in dentistry is still on a small and on an experimental scale. Programs developed to date are on dental materials, dental anatomy, gingivectomy, dental public health, operative dentistry, four-handed dentistry, oral cytology, oral pathology, endodontics, and a few others. However, the research that has been conducted regarding its feasibility and effectiveness has demonstrated the potential of this new approach to dental teaching.[11][12] This comes as no surprise since programmed instruction is an organized and systematic approach to teaching in the sense that it presents the information to be learned in small steps, requires active participation by the student, and provides immediate feedback and reinforcement. Here again, because it is a *self-instructional* method, its use would result in better utilization of students' time and would relieve the instructor of many routine classroom activities, thereby giving the teacher more time to devote to individual discussions with his students. From all indications, programmed instruction has a definite place in the field of dentistry. It is doubtful, however, that it will achieve this place until an easy way is found to introduce the teachers' objectives and knowledge into an automated system.

Use of Computers in Education

The latest technology that has appeared on the educational scene and the logical extension of simple programmed instruction is computer-assisted instruction (CAI). It incorporates many of the learning principles characteristic of programmed instruction but on a more sophisticated level. This system provides even more individualized instruction in the sense that course modification and revision can be made continuously by the author through the computer, in accordance with the student's individual responses. With CAI, therefore, there is an even closer interaction between author and student than in programmed instruction. Thus, while the hardware is an important part of the CAI system, it is still only a tool; what actually teaches is the computer program itself. Credit must be given to the author whose knowledge and application of important teaching-learning techniques are still prime requisites.

A few CAI programs in dental education are in the process of being developed. The Harvard Computing Center is planning to investigate the feasibility of CAI in the teaching of gross anatomy related to the oral cavity. This study will be concerned with improving the retention of anatomical information through the programmed display of perceptual aids to verbal learning through a CAI system.[13] In dental education itself, the Universities of Michigan and Iowa Schools of Dentistry probably have been the most active in planning for the future of CAI. Michigan has designed its new school with CAI in mind while Iowa recently developed a short course in a clinical subject for CAI.

Although CAI is a fairly new concept in education and therefore is still largely experimental, the computer itself is no longer a novelty. In business and industry, the use of computers in doing routine accounting procedures such as billing, filing, and payroll is commonplace. This usage of computer-based systems has now expanded into operations research, systems engineering, simulation models, and human factors analysis. Computer applications in educational institutions, although considerably slower than in business and industry, are gaining widespread attention and recognition. Most large universities and libraries in the country today are now relying on computers to do the usual administrative tasks of data acquisition and data processing.

Effective and efficient use of computers in an educational environment can be seen in simulating learning environments, automating and retrieving information, controlling variables for the study of learner-instruction interactions, integrating instructional media into the curriculum, and in decentralizing the educational system by bringing remote educational resources into the classroom, study carrel, library, and even into the home.[14]

The implications of computers in dental education and research are indeed far-reaching. The routine procedures of scheduling clinic time and chairs, determining patient load, keeping periodic records of individual progress, scoring and analyzing students' examinations, and a host of routine functions that will greatly increase the efficient use of time and facilities for the faculty and students are particularly amenable to computer applications. These functions, although only indirectly related to instructional technology, have a direct relationship to educational economy.

At the University of North Carolina, a computer project is now underway to test the feasibility of patient scheduling in accordance with the total patient care concept. In this project, the treatment needs of the patient are being matched with the level of ability of the student. Simultaneously, faculty-student ratios are being determined for specific clinics depending on anticipated problems.[15] Computers are being used by a number of schools, including the University of Maryland and the University of Southern California, to analyze quantitative and qualitative performance data on dental students. The University of Missouri at Kansas City has designed a dental examination and treatment chart to be used in conjunction with an IBM computer. New York University is presently investigating the use of various data processing methods for the collection and evaluation of students' work accomplishment and grades in the clinical departments.[16]

The real contribution of computers to education, however, probably will come about in the instructional process itself; it is not unreasonable to hope that in the near future, a few high-speed computers will be strategically located in various parts of the nation to serve all the dental schools as instructional centers. From these centers, programs written by subject matter authorities will radiate to the various dental schools where students can learn at their own convenience. And if the trend holds true for education as it has for business and industry, exciting possibilities are likely for systems analysis and computer simulation in the complex processes involved in and related to dental education and research.

Continuing Education of Dentists

There are about 100,000 practicing dentists in this nation today. The task of keeping them refreshed in the old and abreast of new developments in dentistry is formidable, since the "information explosion" in the dental field has increased geometrically in recent years. New skills, technics and procedures, new drugs, materials and treatments, and new applications of old procedures have all appeared, but they are of little value to the health of the nation until they are understood and fully utilized by the individual practicing dentist. Improved instructional technology is of immediate relevance.

The problems facing continuing dental education are both similar and different from those in undergraduate education. Much of the knowledge and many of the skills to be taught are alike; the problems of communication, particularly in relation to the level of the learner, are considerably different. Fundamentally, the difficulties center around the diversified needs of individual dentists, the geographic dispersion of dentists, limited teaching manpower, the lack of a broad curriculum in continuing education, and the lack of a coordinated system at local, state or national levels to plan, develop, implement and evaluate continuing education programs to reach the nation's dentists throughout their lifetime of practice.

Unlike the requirements for undergraduate education, the educational needs of the practicing dentist are highly personal and reflect his own characteristics and those of his practice. A determination of specific educational needs represents the base from which sound guidelines are drawn for administering programs, defining educational objectives and selecting topics, instructional materials, methods, and media. The best in instructional technology is of no value if it provides what the dentist neither wants nor needs. To solve this problem, during 1967-68, surveys have been conducted throughout six New England states, the South, Midwest and Western states in an effort to identify the dentists' needs and preferences in continuing education. In 1969, the Continuing Education Branch of the Division of Dental Health will publish these findings as a series of Profiles of Continuing Education.

Complicating the previous problem is the fact that nearly half of the nation's dentists are not located within reasonable distance of a dental school, the traditional setting for educating the dentist, primarily through providing short courses and post-graduate training in various topics. Even for those dentists who are able to avail themselves of these courses, several drawbacks are apparent. First, the dentist loses economically through the requirement to close his office during the period of training. Second, the public loses his services as a practicing dentist for the same period, a problem when a severe manpower shortage exists. It is obvious that both mass and individual methods must be found to bring continuing education to the dentists and still preserve high-quality instruction.

One answer to the geographic problem is a greater use of off-campus community settings for continuing education. There is ample opportunity in the community environment to present various courses, workshops, seminars and clinics in a highly personalized way. Subjects that do not demand intensive clinical instruction are especially suited to the community setting and a major portion of subject matter falls into this category. Even when material is presented which requires clinical application, the practitioner's office, the local hospital or the community clinic can serve as a substitute for the clinic facilities of the dental school. Mobile satellite centers also could bring continuing educational opportunities to the dentist in his own community.

Unfortunately, as has been mentioned previously, there is a critical shortage of teachers. The traditional role of the teacher, developing courses and presenting them to the students in a face-to-face relationship, is not possible. Fortunately, the use of live television, videotape, films, two-way radio, teaching machines, and other media has extended the teacher's time and talents. More effort must be devoted to course development, however, when a live teacher will not be available for the presentation. Clarity and the sequential organization of the teaching materials assume new importance when no one is present to answer the learners' questions.

The development of effective and efficient courses that can be considered self-contained almost always requires the use of a "team" approach. This team might consist of a dental specialist, an educator, an audiovisual specialist, a graphic artist, and a writer, each of whom assumes responsibility for certain elements in course development.

This team approach currently is being used by five dental schools, with the support of grant funds, in the development of course materials for off-campus presentation. The University of California, San Francisco, and Temple University are preparing self-instructional programs; Tufts University is presenting dental reports via open-circuit television and is activating mobile satellite teaching teams for demonstrations; the University of Iowa is preparing materials for evaluating teaching machines as well as developing "field" faculty among private practitioners; and the University of Pittsburgh is expanding existing regional centers for continuing dental education and establishing new centers, utilizing a wide variety of educational methods and media.

Although the methodology for course development in continuing education may be well-established, a major void still exists in that a curriculum has never been defined. Hopefully, this problem will be resolved soon. Under development are teachers' guides in the major areas of dentistry. These documents will define the "ideal" performance required by the student (as seen by dental educators) and will serve as a guide for teachers to develop appropriate course content and instructional methods and media. The guides also will have the potential of serving as self-evaluation tests which practitioners may use to determine their own continuing education needs. Eventually, this self-diagnosis of needs should be accomplished quickly and easily via computer.

At the present time, probably the biggest shortcoming in the continuing education of dentists is the lack of a coordinated system at the local, state, or national levels to plan, develop, implement and evaluate continuing education programs. The requirements of such a system are not simple. To provide educationally sound courses which are readily accessible and financially feasible, and which will meet individual and group needs without the physical presence of a teacher is a difficult but not hopeless task. The answer undoubtedly lies in improved instructional technology which emphasizes the systems approach. The eventual use of vast information storage and retrieval sources, computer control, and satellites for transmission may be the answer.

Dental Health Education of the Public

Dental disease has not received the attention from the public that it deserves. This is probably because of its universality and its non-threatening nature as a critical health problem. A wide discrepancy exists between the American public's knowledge about oral health and what it practices in meeting oral health needs. This situation is untenable since the individual can and must assume considerable responsibility if the oral tissues are to be maintained in a healthful condition.

To date, little has been done on a systematic basis to motivate the public to acquire good oral health practices. Although the professional associations and many commercial groups have prepared and distributed a broad array of informative pamphlets and audiovisual aids, few research studies have been conducted to evaluate the effectiveness of these materials in producing attitudinal and behavioral change. It is likely that dentifrice advertising has contributed more to the public awareness of the importance of dental health than any other medium.

Probably the most effective tool for motivation has been the patient education provided in the individual dental office. In the past, this function has been carried out largely by the dentist who, unfortunately, has not always had the training necessary to provide sound educational experiences for the patient. More recently, the role of patient education has been assumed to a large degree by the hygienist or assistant. Today, these efforts can be supplemented with a variety of educational materials, particularly programs on record-filmstrip devices. These devices and a variety of "canned" programs for individual use can contribute considerably through providing sound educational messages without a proportionate loss in productive dental manpower.

One of the most fundamental places for providing dental health education has been largely ignored. This place is the public school system. Whatever the reason, the lack of trained personnel, the lack of good teaching materials, or the lack of curricular time, little has been done to promote dental health in the schools on other than a sporadic and frequently unorganized basis. The public school system is also the place to begin educating socially disadvantaged children as to the importance of seeking dental treatment. Even when the economic blocks are removed, the socially disadvantaged are not prone to seek dental treatment; their values and life outlook militate against it.*

Perhaps one solution to this dilemma is through the use of educational television. With good sequential programming, many students could be reached throughout the primary and secondary years with proved motivational instruction. Audiovisual materials can be prepared which will produce fundamental changes in values among specific groups. This same approach might also be used to provide good dental health education to the public at large.

To summarize, there is not enough dental health manpower to perform the important function of educating the public. If the job is to be done at all, it can only be with the assistance of available educational technology.

REFERENCES

1. Hillenbrand, H. "The scope and urgency of the dental manpower problem." *J. Am. Coll. Dent.,* 35:113-122, 1968.

2. Barber, T. "Synchronized tape and slides as a method of teaching dental technics." *J. Dent. Educ.,* 28:43-53, March, 1964.

3. Vanek, H. G., M. K. Chen, and D. W. Podshadley. "Evaluation of a self-instructional method used in preclinical operative dentistry." *J. Dent. Educ.,* 31:34-43, March, 1967.

4. Darby, D. W., M. K. Chen and D. W. Podshadley. Experimental study of an intensive course in operative dentistry. *J. Dent. Educ.,* 29:419-425, Dec., 1965.

5. Jarabak, J. P. "Teaching dental emergencies through simulation techniques." Paper presented at the annual meeting, American Educational Research Assn., Chicago, Feb., 1966.

6. Ramirez, A., S. L. Miller, and W. J. Pelton. "Use of simulated experiences in teaching community dentistry." *J. Dent. Educ.,* 31:521-7, Dec., 1967.

7. Hansen, R. G. Personal communication. Oct., 1968.

8. Abrahamson, S. "A computer-based patient simulator for anesthesiologists." Univ. of So. Calif. School of Medicine, Los Angeles, July, 1967.

9. Romano, M. "Use of television in dentistry." J. Dent. Educ., 28:432-93, Dec., 1964.

10. Morrison, W. E. "3-D in medical-dental teaching." Paper presented at the DAVI annual meeting, NEA, Houston, March, 1968.

11. Podshadley, D. W. "Programmed instruction: highlights of its use in teaching public health." *Am. J. Pub. Health,* 55:887-91, June, 1965.

12. Podshadley, D. W., et al. "Learner attitudes as a variable in the use of programmed material." Paper accepted for publication in *J. Dent. Educ.,* 1968.

13. Stolurow, L. M. Personal communication. April, 1968.

14. Bushnell, D. D. "New applications of computer technology for the improvement of instruction and

A recent publication by the U.S. Department of Health, Education, and Welfare has this to say: "The diffuse fatalistic feeling of powerlessness which informs so strongly the relationships of the poor to the rest of society is embodied most pathetically in resignation to illness . . . For example, one finds very often the idea that total loss of teeth is ultimately inevitable . . . It is fairly common to learn that a person has had some or all of his teeth removed in preference to paying for their restoration to working condition."[17]

learning." In *The Computer in American Education—Issues and Applications,* Stanford School of Education Conference, Nov., 1965, 174-96.

15. Crandell, C. E. "The feasibility and merit of introducing the total patient care concept into the dental clinics through the use of linear programming techniques." Paper presented at the annual meeting of the International Assoc. for Dental Research, San Francisco, March, 1968.

16. American Association of Dental Schools. Report of research projects in dental education, 1965-66. Chicago, April, 1966.

17. *Low-income Life Styles.* U.S. DHEW, Welfare Administration Publication No. 14, Washington, D.C., 1966, VIII + 86 p., p. 59-60.

92.

Instructional Technology
In Service to
Vocational-Technical Education

by J. CHESTER SWANSON
Director of Project
Program for Research and Development
in Vocational-Technical Education
School of Education, U. of Cal. at Berkeley

Neither the term *Vocational-Technical Education* nor *Instructional Technology* has been standardized to the extent that it clearly defines a limit of action or a body of content which is uniformly accepted. The following definitions will be used in this discussion.

Vocational-Technical Education is an organized educational or training experience whose objective is to develop skills and provide knowledge related to a specific employment opportunity.[1]

This is a rather narrow definition in that it does not include many activities which support vocational education activities and in some instances are essential to its effective operation (e.g., industrial arts, basic education—the three "R's"—guidance, counseling, placement, etc.). Vocational education will be further delimited by not including education for professional occupations which normally require the baccalaureate or a higher degree.

This definition is broad in that it includes instructional and training activities in public and private schools—secondary, post-secondary and adult levels—and in business, industry, government and the Military. It includes work-experiences, apprenticeships, and internships as well as formal school programs. The terms "vocational" and "vocational-technical" will be used interchangeably. The hyphenated term is normally used to emphasize the fact that vocational education includes instruction which requires extensive knowledge and skills in mathematics and science.

Instructional Technology is defined as the use of any device of a technical nature in the learning-teaching process or in the ancillary activities which serve the student, the teacher or the administrative process of vocational-technical education,[2] (e.g., visual aids, auditory aids, computer scheduling, computer-assisted instruction, etc.).

This definition is more narrow than what might be developed from an etymological consideration of the Greek word from which "technology" is derived. This discussion shall consider only instructional processes related to machines, devices or instruments. The devices will be considered important only as they are related to the process of instruction.

Vocational-Technical Education is unique in its relation to *Instructional Technology* because much of vocational education is a process of teaching manipulative skills in the use and/or maintenance of technical devices. Thus much of vocational education is performed in an environment of technological equipment. This means that the vocational teacher is often very skillful in the production of technical equipment, in the knowledge of its operation and in the purpose of its use. The use of such devices by vocational teachers in the instructional process becomes very natural.

In any discussion of vocational education the great diversity and scope of its instructional programs must always be kept in mind. The following selected list of vocational programs in the high schools of California is given to illustrate this diversity.

Agricultural Production	Dental Technician
Accounting	Welding
Aviation Pilots	Computer Programming
Meat Cutters	Embalmers
Watch Repairmen	Electronic Technician
Food Service	Police and Fire Service
Locomotive Engineers	Printing
Nursing	Automotive Repair
Merchandising and Sales	Beauty Operators
Secretarial and Office	Commercial Artists

There are more than two thousand different courses in vocational education in the public schools of California. This diversity makes it relatively easy to find some program for which any specific instructional technology would be appropriate and is possibly in use. It also makes it quite difficult to make statements on, or imply general practice or applicability to, vocational education.

The Uses of Technology in Vocational Education

Technology in the instructional process of vocational education is quite old and has been extensively used. This statement might be illustrated by such examples as (1) the use of the record player to set a rhythm for the teaching of typewriting; (2) the use of "mock-ups" as operating models of mechanical and electrical equipment; and (3) the use of the film-slide and opaque projectors for presenting perspectives in mechanical and architectural drafting.

As more "software" became available—if this term can be used for projection-type equipment—with subject matter related to vocational practices, the use of the traditional and simpler audiovisual equipment increased at a rapid rate. During World War II many training films and filmslides were developed to assist in the instruction of skilled and semiskilled persons for war production and military training. A number of commercial firms greatly expanded their production of both audiovisual devices and the program materials for these devices during this period. After the war this production capacity and "know-how" was directed toward school and industrial use. Vocational teachers took advantage of these materials.

The "mock up" or display board showing in graphic form the parts and relationships of machinery, devices or operations developed into simulated devices which became working models for teaching purposes. Thus the flow of air in pneumatic devices, the flow of electrical currents in electrical circuits, and the motion of movable parts in machinery became observable in wall charts. This development of simulation devices became so sophisticated that a device for pilot training (the Link Trainer) was developed which significantly shortened the training period and improved the safety factors. The military developed many such devices in their extensive automation of instructional aids. Public schools, with few exceptions, do not have the financial capability to purchase, develop or operate such technical aides to instruction.

Moving-picture projection is used in many programs where training films are available—but relatively few are available. Television is used infrequently because few video tapes, films or live programs are available and because the listening-viewing audience is usually too small to justify the use of such expensive and limited facilities.

The military has used closed circuit television extensively as part of its basic training. It has had the financial ability and the number of students to justify its use.

The device which has grown in use most recently has been the continuous film loop projector. This is an inexpensive, small, simple to operate, sound (or silent) moving-picture projector which is threaded with a cassette of 8mm closed-loop film. One cassette provides several minutes of picture. These films can be produced locally. For many courses, any teacher could with reasonable financing develop a major part of his course material for individual instruction. The use of this type of equipment is increasing extensively.

Much of the audiovisual technical equipment has been considered in the past to be best used to reach large audiences. It now appears that the major use of technology may be to individualize instruction. The closed-loop film described above is a good example of such use. The video tape recorder with auxiliary equipment would do the same thing but at many times the cost and necessitating a trained operator. Various types of teaching machines have been suggested for use in individualizing instruction for vocational students. None of these machines is in general use. If materials were developed for these machines, some could be widely used and be within the cost limits. Magnetic card readers could also be used in such a manner.

Vocational instruction is being extended to reach more students. At the high school level many programs are being developed as basic courses for related groups of occupations. These developments may require the provision of courses for large numbers of students and thus make feasible the use of mass media devices. During the development of such conditions the technological problems are the same as for any instruction—the availability of the programmed material on film, tape, etc.

Technology as course content is a much more distinguishing feature of vocational-technical education than is instructional technology. Technology as course content may have more effect on vocational instruction than on any other instructional program. Instruction in electronic technician, computer programmer, electro-mechanical technician and medical technician are becoming quite extensive and are all courses resulting from extensive automation and mechanization of business, industry and household devices. The design, production, operation and maintenance of equipment for automated and mechanized processes require persons with more extensive skills and knowledge than has been traditionally demanded. Learning these skills often requires also more time and more maturity than secondary students possess. The result has been a rapid expansion of vocational-technical enrollments at the post-high school level.

Technology as course content does not present any unique problem for vocational education. It may require more expensive equipment than other programs and for some occupations it becomes impossible for the public schools to provide the necessary equipment. At times such instruction is provided as a "cooperative education" program where the skill training is provided by industry or business while the basic knowledge, related education and some of the field supervision are given by the school.

Technology in the management of instruction is probably the most important contribution of technology to vocational education. Technology is now being used in a number of institutions to assist in the scheduling for vocational instruction. The results of at least one research study[3] and the reports of institutions which have used computers for scheduling indicate that the use of such devices has proven very helpful but that their use for vocational instruction is not appreciably different from that for academic instruction. At the present time in most schools the number of classes and number of students do not make computer scheduling necessary except in relation to a large academic enrollment and the resulting complex class schedule.

Some schools are now using computers with auxiliary equipment to make certain types of information readily available. Such data retrieval systems are well known in business and industry and only the costs of installation, maintenance and operation prevent these systems from being much more widely used. Data retrieval systems could serve vocational instruction very effectively in the following ways:

1. Provide job description information with recent labor market data.

2. Provide evaluative information—placement data, enrollment trends, "follow-up" data on graduates.

3. Provide financial data—budget items, budget trends, unit costs, unit cost trends (maybe, in time, cost benefits).

These data would be available from the local, state and national levels and would be provided as appropriate to students, faculty, counselors and administrators.

Impediments to the Use of Technology in Vocational Education Instruction

The financial capability of vocational education is limited. Vocational instruction is in general more costly than academic instruction, due to greater equipment and supply needs and to smaller class size. These higher costs do not always prevail, since some non-vocational programs are very costly and some vocational classes are large and do not require expensive equipment. The competition for funds does prevent the operation of many vocational programs and also restricts major expenditures for existing programs. These factors greatly limit the extensive use of newer technological devices in the instructional program.

Federal funds have subsidized vocational instruction in public schools since 1917. Until 1963, however, no Federal funds could be used for equipment. In the first year in which Federal funds could be used to purchase equipment, some states spent the major part of these funds to replace, expand and update their vocational instruction equipment.

The President signed into law in October 1968 a new Federal law for vocational education. This law has the potential for providing almost $18 for every one dollar provided by the Federal government before 1963. Most of these funds must be matched on a 50/50 basis. There are severe problems in many public schools in the purchase of expensive equipment even on a basic subsidy of 50%. These additional Federal funds, however, will have a significant effect on the use of technological aids in instruction.

Certainly, a major impediment to the use of technology in vocational education programs is limited finances. The additional Federal funds will help. If school administration and instructional supervision were to increase its interest in such programs more money would be available. The focus on youth unemployment may create a growing concern for expanding vocational enrollment and developing more expertise in making this instruction effective. These factors would increase the use of instructional technology. The original cost, the operating costs and the maintenance costs are major factors in vocational instruction.

Walt Disney reported on one occasion that he organized the Disney Enterprises to produce educational films for schools. He said he had learned two facts in regard to educational films: (1) that schools did not have the funds to buy a significant number of films; (2) that if you didn't tell the public the films were educational, they would pay to see them as entertainment.

The physical environment is a factor in vocational education's use of technological devices. Often these devices require unique or quite exacting specifications for the acoustical and visual environment. If the technological devices are to be used to reach larger-size classes effectively, then larger rooms or more auditoriums are necessary. If these devices are to be used for individuals or for very small groups, then cubicle or alcove type spaces are needed, and usually these are not available. Some devices, particularly television, require unique electrical wiring, such as coaxial cable. If major computer equipment is used, air conditioning becomes necessary.

These problems related to the physical environment are in general no different for vocational than for academic instruction. However the noise level and the nature of shop buildings may make it more difficult and expensive to create optimum environmental conditions. Unless certain minimum conditions are available some technological types of instruction cannot be provided.

The logistics of technical devices often greatly impede their use, at times completely blocking their effectiveness. It seems unreasonable to say that technical devices cannot be available in the right place at the right time and in operational condition. Very few teachers have not had a projector and no film, film and no projector, or projector with burned-out bult create a very frustrating classroom situation.

The writer observed a condition in which 5,000 radios were given to the public schools in the Philippines with a powerful transmitting station. This equipment was to be used to improve the program of instruction in the Philippine schools. Since most schools in the Philippines did not have electricity these radios were battery radios, using automobile-type storage batteries. Most of them were never operational past the first two weeks because it was never practical to recharge the storage batteries. Technology solves this problem, not logistics—transistor radios with disposable batteries replaced the originals. This particular situation did not occur in the United States but such types of situations do impede technology, and administration for many reasons cannot always prevent them.

Teachers who experience such difficulties may soon cease to include such devices in their teaching plans. As technological aids become more sophisticated, the logistic type of problem becomes more significant. Computers cannot operate without a very special type of cord or tape. Operators are necessary since only rarely could a teacher program or operate the equipment. Related to the logistic type of problem are certain fears of the use of devices.

The human element in working with equipment becomes very important. Some very competent teachers have mechanical aptitudes that end shortly beyond the use of a ballpoint pen. Studies have shown that a large proportion of the language laboratories which have been installed are not used extensively and that the reason is the teachers' fear of the "gadgetry," or feeling of insecurity in its operation. Technical developments will solve some of these problems by making the operation automatic. Other situations will be solved by using equipment for which a trained operator must be available.

Another aspect of the human element in instructional technology is the psychological effect on the teacher. Some students of this phenomenon have asserted that the teacher, who has traditionally and historically had complete control of the teaching process, now feels that he is controlled by an automaton, a "thing," that tells him when to start teaching, where to do the teaching and what content to cover in any teaching period. The teacher then no longer is the *master* of the situation but more nearly the *slave* of a system. Such a situation would be an impediment to a teacher who either consciously or unconsciously reacted in this manner. This condition will not be considered in this paper.

Probably the most important human factor impeding the growth of instructional technology is lethargy. Any new process takes energy and time and creates uncertainties. It is much easier, much more secure, to continue in the methodology which the teacher has developed and used in the past. Good administration and supervision can overcome much of this apathy but it must be recognized in the planning stage.

The vocational teacher is as subject to the lethargy "virus" as the academic teacher. However, the vocational teacher in general has much more mechanical aptitude.

There may be many other human factors which impede such instruction now or may do so in the future. One condition has been discussed considerably in recent years. This is the problem of royalty rights. Some teachers have resented and resisted having their classroom practices and content reproduced on film or tape. It would appear, however, that the practice is relatively little different from publishing teacher-created materials. The problem will be readily solved as creative rights are protected by law and by accepted practice. This situation might be considered as a new type of problem resulting from technological developments.

Observations and Suggestions

Technological devices and processes should be used much more extensively to improve vocational-technical instruction. The following suggestions attempt to "spot-light" vital needs and programs which are within reasonable financial limitations.

Individualized instruction via the continuous loop moving-picture projector, the magnetic card reader, the tape recorder, the programmed teaching machine, is easily adapted to vocational instruction. The biggest problem in this instructional technology is the "software" or the content for these devices. Vocational instruction is so diversified and the number of students so small in most courses that it is impractical for commercial firms to produce such materials. The solution is for the Federal funds available to vocational education to subsidize the production of these continuous loop films, magnetic fact cards, audio tapes and programmed materials.

Commercial companies with Federal contracts could produce such materials. Or state and university curriculum centers could devise the content and process, and the commercial firms produce the final product.

The more popular high school vocational programs, with the larger number of students, should be produced first—courses such as basic electricity, the automobile (chassis, engine, body and automatic devices), typing, shorthand, merchandising, etc.

Studies should be made to enable the teacher in his own school to produce much of this material. The individual teacher using cassettes can now readily produce taped materials. Equipment is easily possible that the teacher could use to produce much of his own 8mm continuous loop film material.

Large group instruction can be made more effective and more efficient by the use of TV (video tapes), radio (audio tapes), and projection equipment. These devices, like those in use for individualized instruction, are not more widely used because of the lack of program materials—film, tapes, etc. They have not been produced extensively by commercial firms because of the cost and the relatively few students in any one subject matter area. The proper solution in this case is to segment the content material into modules and then produce the modules for which there is a large enough demand. Educational television stations should be forced to devote some of their day-time hours to ITV for schools. Some of this should be vocational. Larger school districts should operate their own TV stations with both live and taped programs. Such programs might be multi-class materials. For instance, certain lesson productions in electricity, gasoline engines, physics, chemistry etc. might be of value to vocational, general science, physics and probably other classes. The teacher in his follow-up would make the adaptation to the particular class. Scheduling between schools is a real difficulty but such mechanical problems can and will be solved when the program is vital enough.

The normal vocational teaching situation can be enriched and made more vital by technology. The materials for both individual instruction and large group instruction can assist in normal-sized class instruction. The additional assistance provided to individual students by such methods may make it possible for many students who formerly became failures to keep up with the class. This additional assistance might help considerably in striving for a "zero-reject" situation in student achievement.

The visual and auditory presentations and the material presented can do much to enrich and bring into the classroom that which clarifies and motivates the learning process. When it is practical to bring to the classroom the type of presentation that Walt Disney visualized, learning will more nearly be the ecstasy that is pictured in a recent magazine.[4]

Recently a situation was observed in which a typing teacher wore a "wireless" microphone in a classroom with 80 students. There were six microphones installed throughout the room. The teacher reported she could hear any pupil in the room and she could speak to the class from any position. She stated that she could serve the 80 students better than she formerly had served 35 students. This was the idea of a teacher with the assistance of a vocational electronics class. The potential for ingenuity in teaching by the use of technical devices is vast and the results might be phenomenal.

Ancillary services may use technology in the most significant ways to vocational instruction. Demonstrations are now rather common of the use of computers for information retrieval. It is easily possible at the present time to dial for vast amounts of information and obtain an auditory response, a projected visual response or a typewritten response. The costs are high for investment, operation and maintenance. However where large numbers of students and teachers are involved it may be practical to use these now. The costs certainly will decrease in the years ahead. A major use of such a device would be in vocational counseling where current data could be fed in at a state or large regional area and made available to students and teachers who normally could not have access to such information.

Computer-type devices should be used in the evaluation process. Some vocational tests—aptitude and achievement—are now available on programmed learning type programs. Many tests should be developed as a means of determining aptitudes before placement in training, and as achievement tests for termination of training or placement in employment. Some of these types of programs are now in use in state employment services.

The simplest, most common and oldest use of the computer is for data processing and tabulation. Very much more needs to be done in vocational education. The most recent national statistics for vocational education are 18 to 24 months old and errors and inconsistencies are easily detected. All state departments of education should record their operational data on tape or cards for rapid tabulation, analysis and print-outs. Many of the decisions required of administration would be much more easily and accurately made with more recent and complete data available.

State and Federal governments are demanding more complete and recent data for legislative actions. One type of data often requested is student "follow-up" data: What is the employment experience of vocational education students? Computers should be programmed to request such information at regular periods and record, tabulate and analyze the results. This activity should be performed by all large school districts and by the state for all other schools. There should be certain nationally accepted standards so that data from the various states would be compatible.

The demand and need for unit costs of vocational instruction are increasing each year. Such information has traditionally been impossible or impractical to secure. The procedure is now possible and practical. Some school districts are now pro-rating and programming all expenditures so that determining unit costs and program budgeting can be a routine practice.

Conclusions

The potential of our present technological devices is almost beyond our imagination. The actual use is insignificant by comparison with the potential, but yet is significant in amount and effectiveness. It is a temptation to boldly predict radical and immediate changes. Many have:

Mr. Edison said in 1913, "Books will soon become obsolete in the schools . . . It is possible to teach every branch of human knowledge with the motion picture. Our school system will be completely changed in ten years."[5]

Dr. George Zook, a U.S. Commissioner of Education, described the motion picture in 1940 as "the most revolutionary instrument introduced into education since the printing press."[6]

Dr. Thomas C. Pollock of New York University in 1957 said, "It now seems clear, however, that television offers the greatest opportunity for the advancement of education since the introduction of printing by movable type."[7]

A recent book (1967) states that "The impact of the computer on society, and hence on curriculum, has been compared to that of movable type and the printing press since Gutenberg."[8]

At least, all these prophets gave recognition to the printed page. It would seem however that many of the recent technological devices may have to "hang around" for about as long as the printing press in order that some of these prophesies be realized. It is to be hoped that means can be found to help vocational education reach the full potential of technological instruction much sooner and more effectively than has been true of other educational innovations. The following suggestions might be made toward such a goal:

1. Give visibility to the present achievements of technology in instruction—disseminate its success stories.

2. Encourage experimentation and pilot-type activities and their support services.

3. Make more funds available for these types of instructional activities.

4. Evaluate all such activities and obtain evidence as to any financial advantages or significant instructional effectiveness.

REFERENCES

1. This definition conforms with the definition of vocational education given in Public Law 90-576, Title I, Part A, Section 108, the most recent Federal legislation for vocational education.

2. This definition in general conforms with the description of instructional technology given by Robert Heinrich in "What is Instructional Technology?" *Audiovisual Instruction,* March 1968, pp. 220-222.

3. Allen, Dwight W. *Flexibility for Vocational Education through Computer Scheduling.* Research contract No. OE-2 CAD-570-94, U.S. Office of Education and Stanford University, 1966-68.

4. Leonard, George B. "Learning Can Be Ecstasy." *Look Magazine,* September 1965.

5. *Dramatic Mirror.* New York, July 13, 1913.

6. Hoban, Charles F., Jr. *Focus on Learning.* American Council on Education, p. 16.

7. From Stoddard, Alexander J. *Schools for Tomorrow: An Educator's Blueprint.* The Ford Foundation, p. 27.

8. Caffrey, John and Charles J. Mosmann. *Computers on Campus: A Report to the President on their Use and Management.* American Council on Education, p. 12.

PART FOUR

f. IT/Measurement And Evaluation

93.

Measurement and Evaluation In Educational Technology

by *JOHN B. CARROLL*
Senior Research Psychologist
Educational Testing Service
Princeton, New Jersey

Measurement and evaluation have long played, and will continue to play, a major role in the development of educational technology. This paper will first point out that educational measurement and evaluation is itself a technology: it will then proceed to describe how this technology has been applied, and can be even better applied than in the past, to the development and utilization of instructional procedures and materials, particularly those using newer technologies whereby the interaction between learner and content to be learned can be controlled and monitored more efficiently than in traditional classroom instruction.

Educational Measurement and Evaluation as a Technology

Educational measurement is a technology in the sense that it consists of a set of procedures and developed products founded on mathematical principles and scientific concepts.

At the base of this technology are the theories and formulations of mathematical statistics, which yield methods of collecting, summarizing, and interpreting both quantitative and qualitative data, particularly data that exhibit variation over populations or over samples of populations with respect to given characteristics. The research worker in educational measurement is required to be thoroughly familiar with such statistical techniques as multivariate correlational analysis, factor analysis, analysis of variance and covariance, tests of statistical significance, survey sampling methods, and the design of experiments.

Another discipline that is fundamental to educational measurement is psychology. Psychology provides educational measurement with basic information on the characteristics that differentiate individuals and on the processes of maturation and learning that are involved in changes in skill, knowledge, and performance. Indeed, a theory of individual differences (Anastasi, 1958) underlies all work in educational measurement and evaluation. This is so because educational measurement must take into account the status of the learner before he starts to learn a particular task or course content and also the processes of learning and motivation that come into play in behavioral changes.

A special discipline or field of inquiry that depends both on mathematical statistics and psychology is what has been called "test theory." Test theory is a theory of measurement as applied to the kinds of measurements that are used in psychology and education. As developed to a high degree of technical adequacy and sophistication by such writers as Lord and Novick (1968), it specifies methods whereby the reliability (accuracy of measurement in the sense of freedom from error) and validity (meaningfulness and predictive efficacy) of measuring procedures can be evaluated and/or improved.

Among the technological products that have been developed within the field of educational measurement are large numbers of standardized tests for measuring various aspects of intelligence, personality, vocational interests, social attitudes, and educational achievements (Buros, 1965). But almost of equal importance in educational evaluation are the instruments that can be, and are, constructed by teachers and research workers for the measurement of particular traits or achievements. To be sure, not all these measurement instruments have satisfactory reliability and validity for the purposes for which they are intended, but it remains true that a well developed theory of measurement is available for the design and evaluation of any particular measurement device or procedure.

Other technological products of educational measurement include standard experimental designs (Campbell & Stanley, 1963), computer programs, and special machines for scoring test answer sheets. The very extensive research literature can also be considered as a technological outcome of educational measurement and evaluation (Harris, 1960; Gage, 1963).

Definitions of Measurement and Evaluation

The ordinary meaning of measurement is fairly well understood. One measures some object or entity, with respect to a given characteristic or trait, by some operation that assigns that object a value on a scale. The scale may be purely nominal, consisting simply of an unordered series of categories, or it may be a quantitative scale in which successive values are at least ordered in magnitude. The units of some scales may have still other properties such as equality and additivity.

For example, one may classify or measure a person with respect to sex (where "male" and "female" represents two points on a nominal scale), scholastic rank in class (where the scale is merely ordinal), "intelligence" (where the units of the scale are approximately equal), or weight (where the units are not only equal but also additive).

Few educational measurements are based on scales with additive units, but many of them have scales whose units can be regarded as approximately equal; such scales are known as interval scales. The errors of measurement are frequently quite large, however, in comparison to those usually encountered in the physical sciences. Also, educational measurements are sometimes of questionable validity, in the sense that it is not certain exactly what is being measured. It is the task of technology in educational measurement to fashion measuring procedures that are as free from error and vagueness as possible.

Evaluation—the rendering of a value judgment—goes beyond measurement. It may utilize measurements as data entering into the judgmental process, but it depends more importantly upon the use of standards and criteria.

A simple kind of evaluation occurs when one interprets the result of an educational test. If one asks whether a given score is "average," "excellent," or "poor," with respect to a representative group of testtakers, the interpretation may be said to be *norm-referenced.* If one can interpret a score as reflecting a certain distinct range of behavior or a specific degree of mastery of subject-matter, we may say that the evaluation is *criterion-referenced.*

In a broader context, however, evaluation refers to the assessment of educational programs and their components with respect to the extent to which they achieve their stated goals and with respect to the cost (in time, money, effort, or incovenience) of achieving these goals. It considers the degree to which the program fosters or retards student progress, whether in subject-matter skills and knowledges or in the formation of desirable interests, attitudes, and personality traits. Evaluation may even extend to the assessment of the worthwhileness of the stated goals of a program, but such assessment must be made more with reference to a philosophy of education than with reference to technological criteria.

Evaluating Educational Programs and Their Components

Educational programs (or their components, such as curricula, textbooks, films, etc.) can be evaluated as final products, with a view to final acceptance or rejection. This is the traditional view of evaluation. Recently, however, it has come to be realized that an equally important kind of evaluation can be done in the course of developing a program, with a view to modifying and shaping it to yield best results. In the terminology introduced by Scriven (1967), the former type of evaluation is "summative" while the latter is "formative."

The work of evaluation, whether it is "formative" or "summative," begins with the attempt to state the objectives of the educational procedure or product being investigated, that is, to state in detail what kinds of changes in skill, knowledge, or performance are desired in learners. Further, it is important to include in the statement of objectives information on what kinds of learners these changes are desired in—their characteristics in terms of age, intellectual maturity, prior learning experiences, and (sometimes) personality.

The task of stating educational objectives is not as simple as it may seem. Sometimes the objectives of an educational procedure are couched in such global terms (e.g., "the attainment of skill in arithmetic," "ability in creative problem solving") that it is not immediately possible to develop an evaluative procedure. The designer of the educational procedure or product may have developed it without a clear and specific notion of his objectives, in which case it may be necessary to press him to make those objectives explicit before evaluation can begin. Frequently the effort to state objectives reveals a need to recast the educational procedure or product itself. Ideally, a statement of educational objectives includes specifications of detailed instructional content that the learner is expected to master, and specifications of the kinds of behaviors or performances that will, hopefully, certify the desired degree of mastery. When such statements are available, the process of translating them into evaluative instruments is facilitated, although it is never really easy.

Educational research workers find it useful, in formulating statements of educational goals, to make reference to a "taxonomy" of educational objectives such as that for the "cognitive domain" by Bloom (1956), or that for the "affective domain" by Krathwohl, et al. (1964). Bloom's taxonomy classifies objectives in the cognitive domain into the following broad categories: Knowledge, Comprehension, Application, Analysis, Synthesis, and Evaluation; each category contains a number of sub-categories. Bloom illustrates how these classifications can be represented by behaviors or performances that can be, within certain limits, incorporated into evaluative instruments.

It is usually helpful, also, to organize specifications of educational goals in the form of a two-way table in which the rows are labeled in terms of components of instructional content, and the columns represent kinds of behaviors (such as recognition, recall, problem solving, application to concrete situations) which will reveal mastery of that content. In filling out a table of this sort one is forced to decide upon the particular kinds of objectives for which one desires evaluation, and then to choose or select adequate samples of goal specifications upon which to base evaluation instruments. One also becomes aware of objectives that may be more than usually difficult to use as bases for evaluation, and that may, in consequence, be left out of account unless special pains are taken.

The Construction of Evaluative Instruments

There is both science and art in the construction of evaluative instruments, whether they be objective multiple-choice tests, essay examinations, rating scales, performance tests, standardized interviews, or systematic observations of behavior in natural situations. (In this paper we use the term *test* in a generic sense to denote a wide variety of measuring procedures, any of which may play a role in an evaluative program.) The scientific aspects involved are in the realm of such matters as item sampling, item analysis, the assembly of item composites into tests, and the assessment of the reliability and validity of the measuring instrument. A large part of test theory, in fact, concerns problems having to do with how best to assemble a composite of separate test items in order to yield a measurement instrument with desired characteristics of reliability and validity. But there are other aspects of test construction that require perceptive intelligence and creative imagination on the part of the test constructor—relatively rare qualities. In general, there is no way of constructing an evaluative instrument "by formula," even though certain aspects of test construction may be done by a computer. The construction of a test requires as much creative ability as the writing of, say, an essay—but a different kind of ability, one that involves insight not only into the subject matter (if it is a test of subject-matter mastery), but also into how that subject matter is perceived and learned (or can be misperceived and learned wrongly) by pupils. For example, in constructing multiple-choice questions the item-writer must not only be able to state clear questions but also be artful in proposing "distractors" (wrong alternative answers) that will be plausible to the student with limited knowledge and yet not attractive to the student with adequate knowledge. The work of the item-writer is to some extent controlled by the statistical results obtained with his items, as when statistical analysis discloses that an item does not adequately discriminate well between students possessing adequate knowledge and those who have only partial knowledge, or less. However, statistical analysis is no substitute for the perceptiveness and creative ability of the test constructor.

Certain types of educational objectives are easier to test than others. It is relatively easy to test for the presence of factual knowledge or elementary skills in such subjects as science and mathematics; it is more difficult to assess a pupil's creative writing ability, ability to speak a foreign language, "inventiveness" in mathematical problem solving, or grasp of major historical trends. Partly the difficulties are semantic—the objectives may be difficult to define in the first place; partly difficulties are practical and can be overcome only by unusual arrangements or efforts. Early examples of unusual yet ingenious and feasible procedures for measuring certain "difficult to measure" educational goals are to be found in the work of Hartshorne and May (1928), on the assessment of such character traits as honesty. Often, relatively simple evaluative devices can be found which measure certain objectives somewhat indirectly and yet validly. For example, certain kinds of objective tests of ability to discriminate good and poor writing have been found to be highly correlated with more elaborate tests of creative writing ability, and hence, for some purposes may be used as reasonable adequate substitutes for the latter.

It should be emphasized, in any case, that the development of satisfactory evaluative instruments often requires much effort, imagination, and technical sophistication. The evaluative instruments themselves must be evaluated. There is no guarantee, further, that in any particular instance a satisfactory evaluative instrument can be developed; some educational objectives seem to be essentially unmeasurable.

Evaluative instruments vary in the extent to which they are an integral part of the instructional process. The traditional practice has been to intersperse evaluative procedures in the course of instruction, e.g. a test at the end of every unit. Sometimes evaluations are completely external, as when a standardized test is given to a group of students under the auspices of an outside agency like the College Entrance Examination Board. At the other extreme, evaluation is built into the instructional process itself, as where a teacher uses a "Socratic" method to develop knowledge and insight in the pupils; similarly, "programmed instruction," whether purveyed by "programmed textbooks" or a computer console, characteristically proceeds by asking students questions covering the material presented, student progress often being contingent upon his successful response to these questions. In some types of programmed and/or computer-based instruction, the student may be "branched" to more advanced material if he is more successful than the average student, or he may be shifted to special remedial material if he has more than ordinary difficulty with the mainline program. This "branching" action of the program, if it is to be effective, depends upon the presence of appropriate diagnostic and evaluative features in the program itself. Thus, at least in situations where the prior planning and control of instructional procedures with built-in evaluative features is possible, the principles and findings of educational measurement can be usefully applied. (In fact, the problems posed by built-in evaluative procedures require special extensions of classical test theory.)

Enter Technology

In trying to propose a role for measurement and evaluation in "educational technology" I feel a need to state what I shall mean by this phrase. "Technology" is a relativistic term; it can pertain to any device or procedure which makes use of scientific knowledge. I have already indicated that educational measurement is itself a technology. Further, the very process of instruction can be regarded as a technology, to the extent that it is based on a theory of instruction. One kind of educational technology, for example, is "programmed instruction," which is based on a set of principles derived from psychological theory and which can be conducted with the simplest of materials or devices, e.g., the "programmed textbook." Yet it must be included in any definition of educational technology. One's ordinary associations with the phrase prompt one to think, however, of specialized machines or devices that are based on contemporary industrial technology and that are, or can be, used in educational settings for presenting, recording, or otherwise processing information of a visual or auditory character—devices such as the film projector, the television receiver, the tape recorder, and (above all) the modern computer. I say "above all" the modern computer because it can control an assemblage of other devices and can even supplant some of these other devices. We shall consider the role of measurement and evaluation in connection not only with programmed instruction but also with technological devices for presenting, recording, or otherwise processing information.

Three trends are seen in the development of educational technology:

(1) More efficient and flexible ways of presenting stimulus material (e.g., random access to a file of material to be presented visually), or of recording visual and auditory information.

(2) Increasing control and monitoring of the interaction between the student and the stimulus material (e.g., with a computer, capability whereby the student can respond to the stimulus with a light pen in such a way that the computer

senses and records the response and takes further action contingent upon this response).

(3) Increasing capability for complex processing of data from student responses.

Trend (1) has long been evident in the development of such devices as the phonograph, radio, film, and TV. Trends (2) and (3) have been more fully realized only with the advent of the computer.

Trend (1)—more efficient and flexible ways of presenting stimulus material—has aided educational measurement and evaluation in numerous ways. For example, the invention of the tape recorder made it more convenient to present auditory stimulus material in connection with certain kinds of tests. A number of school systems use their own radio or TV installations regularly to administer school-wide tests and examinations: such a procedure standardizes the conditions of test administration. Further, recording devices such as the videotape recorder have facilitated the storing of classroom observations and records of teacher performance for later evaluative analysis.

The Evaluation of Presentation Devices

As used in the conduct of instruction, technological stimulus presentation devices such as the phonograph, movie film, or TV are only as good as the material that is presented through them. Sometimes they have added advantages such as greater convenience, richer possibilities with respect to the variety of material presented, and greater interest and better attitudes on the part of the students, but these bonuses do not *automatically* accompany these technological devices. Student attitudes, for example, have been found to be partly dependent on the attitudes of their teachers towards the technological device, or upon the quality of the material presented. Devices that do nothing but present materials are likely to have certain limitations as instructional media: usually they do not allow self-pacing by the student or variations in the material presented to the various students in a class. It may be inconvenient for the student to take notes on the material, and the possibilities for immediate response and feedback are often quite small.

Most research studies attempting to evaluate the use of film or television have found "no significant differences" between the results of such use and those of more traditional methods of instruction (Allen, 1960; Reid and MacLennan, 1967; Lumsdaine, 1963). This is only a generalization, however, there are studies which have indicated ways in which films and TV presentations can be improved and used more effectively. Even the reshowing of a film can improve learning markedly. Further, even if there are no large differences between the use of films and TV and the use of more traditional methods, it will often be the case that the educator can confidently supplant traditional instruction by introducing newer media, with consequent economic benefits such as the conservation of teacher man-power.

In nearly all the research studies on the evaluation of newer media, educational measurement has played a large role in measuring the characteristics of pupils or classes at various points in the course of instruction—before instruction begins, during instruction, and at the end of instruction. Student achievements are measured by standardized or special-purpose tests, and their attitudes are assessed by various types of attitude scales constructed according to psychometric principles. Nevertheless, several criticisms can be made of these evaluative studies:

(1) The design of the studies often leaves much to be desired. (In one review of research [Stickell, 1963] it was claimed that of 250 comparisons between televised and face-to-face instruction, 217 were classified as "uninterpretable" because of poor research design.)

(2) The measures of student achievement are sometimes of poor psychometric quality, with low reliability and/or validity, insufficient attention being given to the construction of proper evaluative instruments. One of the most frequent errors is the failure to make certain that the achievement tests that are constructed cannot be passed by individuals who have *not* had the instruction being investigated. Otherwise, test items can frequently be passed by individuals on the basis of general intelligence or general information rather than on the basis of specific instruction.

(3) The studies are nearly always of the "summative" variety; very few attempt to find particular defects in the instructional material or its use and correct those defects by "formative" evaluation. One exception is the study of Gropper and Lumsdaine (1961) who used student responses (errors on test items) to make successive improvements in a kinescope—improvements that paid off in significantly better student performance. If more "formative" evaluation were done for materials presented by film or television, the advantages of such presentations would probably be much enhanced. Unfortunately, people seem to resist the idea of editing films and kinescopes, once they have been brought to production standards.

Measurement and Evaluation as Related to Programmed Instruction

Programmed instruction has three distinguishing characteristics: (1) It is based on a detailed analysis of educational objectives, the objectives being stated in "behavioral" terms; (2) the steps of the instruction ("frames") are carefully chosen, sequenced, and organized— usually they are relatively "small" steps where the student's attention is directed to only one or a very small number of newly-presented elements to be learned at a time; (3) the program is normally arranged so that the student receives immediate confirmation of correct responses. Most programs are intended to be given to students under self-pacing conditions. A special kind of "formative" evaluation is employed in the development of the better programs: programs are tried out on small samples of students to detect errors and are then successively revised until error rates are low. As noted earlier, testing materials are usually built directly into the program, both in the form of "prompted" teaching frames and in the form of "unprompted" frames in which the student has to demonstrate mastery without the presence of cues or other helps. Some programs also present, at the end, a final test of a fairly conventional character.

Because the object of programmed instruction is to produce complete or nearly complete mastery, it has sometimes been argued that conventional principles of item analysis do not apply to the testing materials built into programmed instruction or even to "summative" evaluation materials given after the student has completed a program. Conventional principles call for items that are passed by, say, 10% to 90% of the sample, whereas programmed instruction tests should be passed by 100% of the sample. This argument ignores the fact that even in the context of programmed instruction, test items must be reliable and valid indicators of something, namely mastery of the skills or knowledges which are hopefully taught by the program. Thus, they should discriminate between pupils who have learned through the program and pupils who have not had the program or its equivalent. The test represented by an unprompted frame should, indeed, be passed by 100% of pupils going through the program, but it should be passed by a significantly lower percentage of pupils who have not had the program or equivalent instruction. Holland (1965) has shown that many frames in poorly constructed programs do not really teach or test, because he finds that even when large portions of the material in the frame are deleted ("blacked out") the pupil can still give the desired response; his "black-out" technique, he claims, provides a measure of the degree to which the material is properly programmed. Holland's technique is thus a logical extension of traditional concepts of test construction, since he shows, in effect, that certain test frames in instructional programs do not discriminate between those who have mastered the material and those who have not.

In appraising "programmed instruction," that is, in applying "summative" evaluation to programs, workers in the field have tended to eschew attempts to compare the effectiveness of programmed instruction with that of other kinds of instruction. They are more concerned with demonstrating the effectiveness of this kind of instruction in terms of its own goals. They insist that properly prepared programs should be accompanied by detailed information as to (1) the kinds of learners for which the program has been designed and validated, and (2) the achievement attained by those learners (in terms of time to reach criterion performance, error rate, or performance on criterion tests). One definition of a "program" has it that it is "a vehicle which generates an essentially reproducible sequence of instructional events and accepts responsibility for efficiently accomplishing a specified change from a given range of initial competences or behavioral tendencies to a specified terminal range of competences or behavioral tendencies" (Lumsdaine, 1964, p. 385). The acceptance of this responsibility, on the part of a program writer, entails the responsibility to provide the necessary proof of effectiveness; that proof will often be supported by evidence from before-and-after tests and other observations of performance.

One can, of course, use standard experimental designs to compare the effectiveness of "programmed instruction" with other types of instruction, including traditional classroom instruction. In the relatively few comparisons of this type, programmed instruction has come off rather well (Schramm, 1964), often because it affords a more efficient approach to instruction in terms of time taken to learn and amount retained after a lapse of time. It remains true, of course, that there are both good and poor programs just as there are good and poor teachers. Therefore it is difficult to make any generalizations, and perhaps one should not attempt to make them, except to say that programmed instruction, like any other form of special instruction, merits careful consideration for regular use in schools. Although programmed instruction has not been the panacea that it was first thought to be, it seems to have attained a solid place in educational programs and may even increase in acceptance, as better programs are prepared. Its popularity in industrial and governmental training programs is a testimony to its usefulness.

Enter the Computer

In the above discussion of programmed instruction we might have mentioned the teaching machine, i.e., any device for presenting the materials of instruction and arranging for the correctness of student response to be confirmed or disconfirmed. In fact, simple teaching machines were developed as early as 1915 by Pressey, and Skinner's early work in programmed instruction, around 1954, included construction of several teaching machines. There has been some rather inconclusive research on whether use of teaching machines yields greater effectiveness than the use of printed materials like the programmed textbook. The machines used in this research were often somewhat unreliable, inconvenient, and too expensive. Further, most of them were relatively simple, being limited to systematic, sequential presentations with confirmations or disconfirmations of student response. Today, more reliable and complex teaching machines are available, but there has been little research to evaluate them.

The advent of the modern computer in educational settings, around the middle 1950's, brought a new realm of possibilities, including increased complexity by several orders of magnitude. The first computers, like the early teaching machines, were somewhat unreliable and expensive, but at this writing we are going into the fourth generation of computers—even more expensive than before, but fast and powerful enough, it would appear, to reduce the cost of the student instructional hour to a small figure, perhaps something like 25 cents (according to one recent estimate) even taking into account the costs of program development, author royalties, remote communication lines, etc. This figure is competitive with ordinary classroom instruction. After a period of frank skepticism, I have become convinced that the computer will play an increasing role in instruction at all educational levels, and therefore I feel justified in giving it special attention in this paper.

What gives the computer its special promise is that it makes possible, much more than noncomputerized "teaching machines," the development of the second and third technological trends mentioned above, namely, increased control and monitoring of the interaction of the student with the stimulus material, and increased capability for complex processing of data from student responses. With respect to the former trend, the computer can orchestrate a whole panoply of other devices (such as film display units, sound-track storage-and-display mechanisms, TV monitors, and special student response devices) along with the by now conventional teletype keyset. With respect to the latter trend, it may be noted the computer can not only store and analyze multitudinous data about student responses (speed of response, correctness, freely composed answers, etc), but it can also utilize complex logic in making well-nigh instantaneous decisions about those responses and what is next to be presented to the student.

The almost unlimited capabilities of the computer enable it to be used in a wide variety of educational settings, at all educational levels. It can even simulate, in a realistic way, a free dialogue between student and tutor, so long as the student is able to type his responses on a keyset. One of the obvious limitations of the computer (at least in terms of presently-available technology) is that it is largely limited to the exchange of alphanumerical information with the student, and to the presentation (not the reception and evaluation) of visual and auditory material. It cannot evaluate students' oral responses or motor performances unless those can be translated into the digital input required by the computer, and successfully evaluated by the computer logic.

There are numbers of ways in which the computer can be used in instruction; in "computer-assisted" instruction the student is "on-line" with the computer and stored in the computer configuration (Stolurow & Davis, 1965; Atkinson & Wilson, 1968); in "computer-managed" instruction, the computer helps the teacher to administer and guide the instructional process, but the student is not "on-line" with the computer (Brudner, 1968).

In computer-assisted instruction as it has developed to date, many of the principles developed in programmed instruction are applied: careful analysis of educational objectives, development of programs by tryout and revision, use of relatively small steps in the instructional presentation, use of immediate feedback to confirm the student's responses. What we have said about the application of educational measurement and evaluation to programmed instruction also applies, in large measure, to computer-assisted instruction. That is to say, the evaluative process is usually built into the program "software" that is operated by the computer, and the effectiveness of the system is judged in terms of the speed and efficiency with which students attain the stated instructional objectives.

As yet there are few studies comparing computer-assisted instruction with other forms of instruction. Experiences with computer-based instruction in reading, arithmetic, and Russian at Stanford University indicate that learning (as measured by standardized or special-purpose tests) is at least as efficient as under more traditional instruction. In the case of Russian, there were fewer drop-outs from the computer course than from the conventional classroom. It is likely that research of the "comparative effectiveness" type will yield the same kinds of conclusions as other kinds of comparative effectiveness studies— that in general there are "no significant differences" in attainment, and that attainment is a function, not of the machine itself but of the quality of the instruction, however conducted

—that is, the way in which the instructional content is put together, tried out, revised, and validated.

Lest the above paragraph give too pessimistic an impression, however, I hasten to say that I believe the computer will in time render an enormous service to education. It will make it possible to offer more different courses to more students, and to guarantee student attainment to an extent not previously thought possible. This will come about, at least in part, through the intelligent application of principles of educational measurement and evaluation. To be specific:

(1) Because of its capability for storing and analyzing student responses, the computer will facilitate the "item analysis" of instructional content and the tryout and revision of instructional programs. Already at the University of Illinois, it is standard procedure to print out daily error analyses for computer-course authors, who then try to revise their programs to reduce student error.

(2) The computer is an enormously convenient testing device. It can in the first place rather quickly diagnose the student's initial state of knowledge about a subject-matter, "branching" him either to easy or difficult material according to his needs. In the second place, it administers quantities of test materials in the course of an instructional program; the student is not allowed to progress through the program unless he demonstrates mastery at intermediate points. Three, it can easily administer most standardized tests, quickly producing not only the conventional raw score but also diagnostic information on particular types of difficulties, information on speed and correctness of response to particular items, plain-language interpretations of test scores, and the like. Use of consoles at remote locations might make possible the administration of standardized tests simultaneously over wide geographical areas—even computerized nationwide test administration (as of College Board tests) is not out of the question.

(3) The computer can accumulate and analyze data on large numbers of students —data on student characteristics, learning performance, backgrounds, etc. It would thus enormously facilitate the evaluation of different instructional programs and the tabulation of the results. Whether or not it is used in computer-based instruction, it could accumulate large amounts of readily-analyzable information on the total educational program that could be provided to educational researchers and administrators in easily comprehensible form. Already this sort of thing is done in the state of Iowa in the public education system.

(4) Specialized capabilities may be developed whereby computers can evaluate free responses of students as validly, and more efficiently, than they can be evaluated by teachers. Work is now going on at the University of Texas whereby students' answers to essay questions in science courses can be quite accurately scored by computer. Ellis Page, at the University of Connecticut, is working on programs to grade high-school students' English compositions by computer, to diagnose their difficulties, and provide remedial instruction (Page, 1966).

(5) The computer can also be used for various types of content analysis of instructional material. For example, work is now progressing on automating the process of measuring the "readability" of prose; readability (reading ease or comprehensibility) has been found to be an important variable in the effectiveness of textual materials. It may also be suggested (although this does not exactly fall within the purview of this paper) that computers may perhaps be programmed to generate instructional programs or at least certain components thereof.

Summary

Educational measurement and evaluation is itself a technology which is central to the operation and improvement of the educational process, because it enables the educator to know crucially important things about pupil characteristics and achievements. It also furnishes him with a valid basis for judging the worth and effectiveness of educational programs and innovations, and improving them in both gross and detailed features.

There is a long history of the application of this technology to the development and evaluation of various educational innovations such as film, television, and "programmed instruction." At present, the computer is seen to be the important educational tool of the future. As in the case of other educational tools, the computer will be valuable only to the extent permitted by the quality of the instructional materials and programs put into it. Much research and development, using the technology of measurement and evaluation along with other technologies, will be necessary to allow the computer and other educational media to reach maximal usefulness in education.

There is still a large gap between what is possible to accomplish through measurement and evaluation and what has actually been accomplished. This gap can be filled by training more research and development specialists, training teachers and administrators to utilize research and development results more effectively, and providing adequate funds for these training, research, and development activities.

BIBLIOGRAPHY

Allen, W. H. "Audiovisual communication." In Harris, C. W. (Ed.) *Encyclopedia of educational research (Third Edition)*. New York: Macmillan, 1960. Pp. 115-137.

Anastasi, Anne. *Differential psychology: individual and group differences in behavior*. New York: Macmillan, 1958.

Atkinson, R. C., and H. A. Wilson. "Computer-assisted instruction." *Science,* 1968, 162, 73-77.

Bloom, B. S. (Ed.) *Taxonomy of educational objectives. Handbook I: Cognitive Domain.* New York: Longmans, 1956.

Brudner, Harvey J. "Computer-managed instruction." *Science,* 1968, 162, 970-976.

Buros, O. K. (Ed.) *The sixth mental measurements yearbook.* Highland Park, New Jersey: Gryphon Press, 1965.

Campbell, Donald T., and J. C. Stanley. "Experimental and quasi-experimental designs for research on teaching." *In* Gage, N. L. (Ed.) *Handbook of research on teaching.* Chicago: Rand McNally, 1963. Pp. 171-246. [Also published as a separate by Rand McNally.]

Gage, N. L. (Ed.) *Handbook of research on teaching.* Chicago: Rand McNally, 1963.

Gropper, G. L., & A. A. Lumsdaine. *The use of student response to improve televised instruction: An overview.* Report No. 7 (Summary of six prior reports), Studies in televised instruction. Pittsburgh: American Institutes for Research, Rept. No. AIR-C13-61-FR-245 (VII), 1961.

Harris, C. W. (Ed.) *Encyclopedia of educational research. 3rd edition.* New York: Macmillan, 1960.

Hartshorne, H., and M. A. May. *Studies in deceit.* New York: Macmillan, 1928. 2 vols.

Holland, James G. "Research on programming variables." *In* Glaser, Robert (Ed.) *Teaching machines and programmed learning. II. Data and directions.* Washington, D.C.: Department of Audiovisual Instruction, National Education Association, 1965. Pp. 66-117.

Krathwohl, D. A. et al. *Taxonomy of educational objectives. Handbook 2: Affective domain.* New York: McKay, 1964.

Lord, F. M., and M. R. Novick. *Statistical theories of mental test scores.* Reading, Mass.: Addison-Wesley, 1968.

Lumsdaine, A. A. Instruments and media of instruction. *In* Gage, N. L. (Ed.) *Handbook of research on teaching.* Chicago: Rand McNally, 1963. Pp. 583-682.

Lumsdaine, A. A. "Educational technology, programmed learning, and instructional science." *In* Hilgard, E. R. (Ed.) *Theories of learning and instruction: Sixty-Third Yearbook. National Society for the Study of Education.* Chicago: Univ. Chicago Press, 1964. Pp. 371-401.

Lumsdaine, A. A. "Assessing the effectiveness of instructional programs." *In* Glaser, Robert (Ed.) *Teaching machines and programmed learning. II. Data and directions.* Washington, D.C.: Department of Audiovisual Instruction, National Education Association, 1965. Pp. 267-320.

Page, Ellis B. "The imminence of grading essays by computer." *Phi Delta Kappan,* 1966, 47(5), 238-243.

Reid, J. C., and D. W. MacLennan. *Research in instructional television and film: summaries of studies.* Washington, D.C.: U.S. Government Printing Office (Catalog FS 5.234:34041), 1967.

Schramm, W. *The research on programmed instruction: an annotated bibliography.* Washington, D.C.: U.S. Department of Health, Education, and Welfare, Office of Education, 1964. (Catalog No. FS 5.234:34034)

Scriven, M. "The methodology of evaluation." *In* Tyler, R. W., *et al. Perspectives of curriculum evaluation.* Chicago: Rand McNally, 1967. (AERA Monograph Series on Curriculum Evaluation, I.) Pp. 39-83.

Stickell, D. W. *A critical review of the methodology and results of research comparing televised and face-to-face instruction.* Doctoral dissertation. The Pennsylvania State University, June 1963.

Stolurow, L. M., and D. Davis. "Teaching machines and computer-based systems." *In* Glaser, Robert (Ed.) *Teaching machines and programmed learning. II. Data and directions.* Washington, D.C.: Department of Audiovisual Instruction, National Education Association, 1965. Pp. 162-212.

94.

Evaluation And Measurement Of Instructional Technology

by *FRANCIS KEPPEL* and *MICHAEL L. CORNOG*
Pres., Chrmn. of the Board   *Asst. to the Pres.*
General Learning Corp.   *General Learning*
Corp.

I. Introduction and Definitions.

The Commission's assignment was to comment on:

> What has been done or can be done about measuring the results of the use of various instructional technologies, and how can this be related to present educational "results?"

The importance of this question is matched only by the difficulty in answering it. It requires history and prophecy. Harold Howe II hinted at the promise instructional technology holds for education when he described the Commission on Instructional Technology's study:

> The new educational technology holds no more exciting prospect for American education than the possibility of providing—on a scale and to a standard far beyond our grasp—an educational system able to respond to the unique needs and abilities of the individual learner.

He also described the problems such a study was likely to uncover and in fact the difficulty of conducting such a study at all:

> One problem is: how do we do this economically, at a price both industry and educators can afford? Even more important: how do we design and develop this technology so that it meets the needs of both the individual student and the educational system as a whole?

An inquiry into "what has been done or can be done about measuring the results of various instructional technologies" requires some definitions first. In particular, it is necessary to establish what is to be meant in this paper by "instruction" and what is meant by "technology."

Instruction literally means "to build into." The *Encyclopedia of Educational Research* expands the literal meaning to a fuller definition: "to build into another knowledge, information, attitudes, skills, understandings, appreciations, behaviors." The *Encyclopedia* seeks to make a distinction between instruction and teaching, seeing instruction as a part of the larger whole of teaching. Teaching would include what is taught (curriculum), how it is taught (instruction), and how it is assessed (evaluation). We will follow this use of the word.

Technology proves harder to define. The strict derivation from the Greek *technologia* is the "systematic treatment of an art." It is one of those unusual words whose definition is broader in scope than its connotations. The common use of technology brings to mind a variety of things—trains, harvesters, oil refineries, cars, computers, and airplanes. The denotation of the word of the word technology directs us beyond all of its various manifestations to the process behind its manifestations.[1]

When the terms are combined to form "Instructional Technology," definition becomes more than doubly difficult. There is a common tendency to equate instruction with teaching, and all too often we fail to see beyond the things of technology to the systematic treatment of an art behind them. In this inquiry we shall strive to perform the two different operations required by our definition of instructional technology—focus at close range at the distinction between instruction and teaching and yet see beyond the confusing, compelling, and myriad manifestations of technology to the broader implications of its denotation.

One of the advantages gained from such an effort at double vision is a way of ordering those many things normally thought of when the term instructional technology is used. In a way, anything from a hornbook to the most elaborate computer is a manifestation of an instructional technology. They are unlike in many ways—weight, shape, size, cost, fashionableness. But the way in which they are most significantly unlike is the *process* by which each *builds into* the learner *knowledge, information, skills, understandings, appreciations* and *behaviors*. The first, the hornbook, regards the learner as a passive recipient of knowledge, skills, behavior, *etc.* The process behind the thing requires only that the learner be open and receptive. The computer, on the other hand, when used to assist instruction, requires reaction and response from the learner in the process of building into him the particular knowledge or skill or behavior that is the subject of the lesson. Teachers can and historically have operated in either mode or somewhere in between.

What we have then is two poles around which to cluster the various instructional technologies—one pole represents those instructional technologies that view the learner as a passive recipient in the learning process; the other regards the learner as an active participant. Of course such a division of the instructional technologies does not create two distinct parts. Halfway between the two poles can be found instructional technologies that can regard the learner as either passive or active, depending on their use in the larger context of teaching the learner. A computer can be used as little more than an electronic hornbook, a thing which holds information and displays it to the learner without requiring a response. In the larger context of teaching, correspondingly, a hornbook can be used by the teacher to evoke a response from a learner.

Obviously, such considerations raise the major contemporary educational issue which centers on the theories of B. F. Skinner and the behavioralists: how one measures the activity or passivity of a learner as he learns. Evidence of the importance of establishing definitions is the title of the first chapter in Skinner's latest book, *The Technology of Teaching*, "The etymology of teaching." He rightly identifies the metaphorical basis of much of the terminology used to describe the difference between an educated and an uneducated person. Dealing specifically with three concepts, growth, acquisition, and construction. he shows their limitations and urges that "any analysis of the interchange between organism and environment must . . . avoid metaphor."[2] His structure is well taken, though extraordinarily hard to follow. It is not easy to dispense with the rhetorical usefulness of metaphor. We can only make a start.

II. What Has Been Done About Measuring the Results of Various Instructional Technologies?

With this understanding of instructional technology in mind we must now consider how their "results" have been measured so far. Again it is helpful to make use of the *Encyclopedia of Educational Research's* division of teaching into three parts—curriculum, instruction, and evaluation. When we measure results we are making an evaluation of those results. Man has always made such evaluations. When one of our primitive forefathers turned his son loose with a bow and arrow against a bear or a rabbit he could readily evaluate how well his boy had learned. When we move from the prehistorical to the historical we encounter increasing ways of evaluating the results of instruction, including the results of instructional technologies. We have lost the appealing simplicity of the caveman's method of evaluation —his son either killed the bear or perhaps was killed in turn, either killed the rabbit or went hungry. While contemporary means of evaluation are certainly more sophisticated they can also be far less significant in terms of their impact on the ways of instruction.

The history of the scientific *evaluation* of the results of instructional technologies covers only a few decades. The first tests of instructional media, for instance, date back to the beginning of this century. Moreover, while a number of important studies were conducted from 1918 until 1940, World War II marks the beginning of the really intensive period of research.[3] For our purposes then, the most important period of research into the results of instructional technologies is from 1940 unitl the present.

The most concerted effort to date to bring some order to the process of evaluating instructional technologies is the Educational Resources Information Center's (ERIC) attempt to index recent studies. If we look through the ERIC Research Report Index from 1956 to 1965 we find at least 70 reports from that ten-year period on instructional technologies. The summaries of these reports give a rough picture of the successes and failures so far. We have made a simple categorization of this material. The reports that showed better results with a given technology than with the traditional approach were put in one group; those reports where technology fared worse than the traditional approach (which often involved some form of technology, too, but an older kind) were put in a second group; and those where there was "no significant difference," or where technology was "as effective" or "compared favorably" with traditional methods were put in the third category.

The results of such crude headcounting are revealing. In about one case in ten was a technology shown to be a poorer pedagogic tool than the existing methods, which may be small comfort to latter day Luddites. In one case in four the technological approach was definitely superior. The largest group was the third where "no significant difference" could be observed. Cost factors were not involved in these studies; the studies were pedagogical, not economic. There is no adequate evidence on cost-effectiveness of various technologies.

Doubters of the potential usefulness of instructional technologies often call into question the validity of both the second and third group's findings. The Hawthorne effect can always be cited. But the advocates of instructional technologies can respond that Hawthorne effect notwithstanding even those cases where there is "no significant difference" can be accounted successes. After all, they can argue, equalling the results of as complicated a phenomenon as a teacher is no easy task. All that remains is to be able to justify the costs of incorporating that technology into the educational system.

Common sense will suggest that teachers have probably had something to do with the technologies that have proved successful, and, for that matter, with those that failed. It has often been noted that an instructional machine, no matter how sophisticated, can not function well if the software it uses is poorly designed. It might also be noted that machine and software combined cannot succeed unless those that use them are convinced they work and should be used.

In such symbiotic relationships between teachers and machines it is probably now beyond our capacities to separate fully the influence of the teacher and the influence of the machine in the final product, the education of the child. To do so requires instruments of measurement that are more sensitive than those available to researchers today.

What has been done about measuring the results of the use of various instructional technologies is therefore of recent origin, and of a character which does not permit generalizations. The evidence is not clear as to whether instructional technology that regards the learner as an active participant is more effective than technology that assumes a more passive role on the learner's part, though the former on theoretical grounds seems to us the more promising path to follow. Since we lack any solid evidence of cost effectiveness of the various technologies, we can only conclude that a substantial research and development effort is essential before education should commit itself to any particular form of instructional technology.

Experience suggests that at least two areas deserve priority. The first is the need for large scale efforts extending over a number of years, and able to take into account the most important variables that affect learning results. Many studies up to now have been narrowly focused, and many others lend themselves to criticism on the grounds of the Hawthorne effect. Such a large scale effort is almost surely beyond the means of the education industry, and must therefore be mounted by government.

Second, as we have noted above, is the need for developing more sensitive measures and the skills required for their use. Education needs criteria to establish the kind or combination of techniques or technologies that will best solve a given educational problem. A rough consensus as to how to measure educational results has been reached so far by experimenters, but only a rough one. Achievement can be measured with reasonable accuracy, and attitude change also, though without the same measure of accuracy. It is at least possible to go beyond the simple-minded but eminently pragmatic approach that has been taken in schools which are unable to meet the educational needs and expectations of the students. If there are fewer absences and fewer broken windows following an innovation, it is tentatively assumed that the innovation at least brought about an improved attitude toward the school on the student's part. Logic suggests, if it does not dictate, such a conclusion. But it is scarcely a solid basis of evidence on which to plan educational policy.

In summary, a start has been made on measuring the results of various instructional technologies. The uncertain conclusions and the need for better measuring instruments urge caution upon those with responsibility for making policy decisions in education. Available evidence on "results" scarcely justifies huge operating expenditures now or widespread application of instructional technologies. But such evidence does justify further investment in research and development to measure more accurately the benefits of such technologies.

III. What Can Be Done About Measuring the Results of Instructional Technology?

In 1937, a study was made to predict what new technological developments were likely to occur in the next twenty years. The study failed to anticipate radar, jet propulsions, antibiotics, the computer, or atomic energy.[4] Even as it is we expect much of what we say here will prove incorrect and grossly unimaginative in a decade's time.

What we would like to do is alter the question. Rather than concentrate solely on what can be done we would like to consider what *can* and *ought* to be done. We sense, for instance, that techniques for evaluating present technologies are improving. We expect that such techniques will change in degree, not kind, in the years immediately ahead. The logic of using control groups, of testing achievement and attitude before and after the implementation of a new technology is hardly likely to be proven invalid in the future. The possibility of using bio-psychological instruments seems to be a considerable distance in the future. In the present, substantial investment needs to be put into refining present techniques.

Evaluative information on instructional technologies has been so far ineffectively used in educational planning and practice. The average teacher or administrator in this country is only dimly aware of the results of evaluation of instructional technologies. His information is more than likely hearsay. Language laboratories have been used in a neighboring school and the teachers who use them like them. Therefore language laboratories are adopted in surrounding schools. That teachers like them is not a bad criterion upon which to base adoption. However it does not necessarily mean that laboratories will improve the teaching of foreign languages significantly in those surrounding schools.

Hendrik Gideonse has considered the lack of coordination between what is going on in educational research and in educational practice in a recent article in *Science.*[5] He proposes a model to help visualize the three areas of activity he determines as central to innovation in educational practice. The first level represents "research knowledge" available or being discovered. Above it is the second plane, "development process," where knowledge from the research level is put into practicable forms. Above these two levels is the third, "operations-production," which seeks to direct the utilization of developed forms. Such a model is not radical in its conception. What is of interest is the concern Gideonse has for the interactions between the three levels, and how initiatives are carried through within and between levels.

> I have presented an output-oriented model of educational research and development. I have tried to show that the outputs of research, development, and operating educational institutions are quite different, that performers of each of the three types of functions have important contributions to make in identifying proposed initiatives in their own sphere as well as all the others, and that these conditions create special demands upon the administrator of research . . . The model suggests the importance of adequate dissemination and diffusion mechanisms among the different functions, the importance of the manner of performing the activities in each function in making transfer and feedback from one function to another possible. . . .[6]

We consider his approach basically sound. It has been used for years in science-oriented businesses. Our own corporation has for the past year and a half been involved with the University of Pittsburgh and the Pittsburgh Public Schools in a consortium that seeks to develop procedures, teaching strategies, and materials for early learning. Each partner in the consortium brings special abilities and resources to bear on the problems. Those concerned with research (in this case the Learning Research and Development Center of the University of Pittsburgh), those concerned with development (General Learning), and those concerned with operations (the public school administrators) operate within a framework that allows an interchange of information and initiative similar to that proposed by Gideonse.

Another development that might facilitate further measurements of the results of instructional technologies would be the creation of a group of educational agents who could pass from each of these areas to the next. Few such agents exist today—men who have had experience in education, industry, and government—and so far there has been little organized encouragement and support for their training. The Education Professions Development Act could be used to support such a program. Most important of all, of course, is the need for patient and long term support of research and development programs to evaluate the various technologies. Only a bare start has been made.

IV. How Can This Be Related to Present Educational Results?

Technology will continue to affect education as it will continue to affect all aspects of our lives. Anthony Oettinger is even more explicit about the dangers that can results from an unrealistic view of educational technology:

> Attempting to design an educational or any other social system with our contemporary scientific apparatus is rather like giving Lucretius an imperial grant to make the bomb starting with his atomic theory. Whether we are two thousand years or thirty years ahead of ourselves makes little difference, and we cannot predict with any degree of reliability how much time it will take for physical, biological, and social science to progress far enough.[7]

One step, however, is in the process of being realized. National Assessment's aims are impressive.[8] Its goal is to provide qualitative and quantitative information on what students are learning in our country. Designed not to be a ready tool for pedagogic inspector generals, it hopes to afford those interested in what our students know a broad picture according to age, geographical distribution, sex, economic class, and ethnic background.

Technology of course will play an important role in the sorting and analysis of the raw data that results from National Assessment. Once that data has become information, technology will be involved in a second way. As one of the many ways in which children are taught it may be possible, since some baselines will have been established, to draw some conclusions as to how effective some aspects of instructional technology have been. The teaching of reading might be an example. National Assessment gives promise also of providing a continuing stimulus for evaluation, a constant prodding of the educational community on its success with the education of the young.

National Assessment of course, will not dictate that a given technology will work in all cases. That kind of judgment would require more information than National Assessment can supply. There is no formula available into which educational expectations, subjects, and resources can be cranked, and the appropriate technology, teaching strategy, and curriculum materials earmarked for the educator. It is unlikely that such a formula will ever be available. Even if it were available it is not clear that it would be desirable. In practice in the next few years, available funds will be the determining factor.

The chances of rationalizing the decisions made by those responsible for educational policy and practice will be greatly increased by the results of the National Assessment program. The direct effect on measuring instructional technology will probably be relatively minor at the start. In the long run the identification of areas of greater need will guide the value system which in turn governs the social and economic justification of educational investments. Expensive technologies may be justified if the social need is considered to be sufficiently great.

Education clearly needs the setting of priorities to guide its search for innovations and its us of technologies. Simply to assume that technology is a good thing without regard to social or economic cost is, of course, nonsense. The establishment of baselines, of the sort which may result from the National Assessment program, on which to base the setting of these priorities, is probably the most important single step in relating instructional technology to present educational results. Without such data, public policy is operating in the dark. The Commission should strongly urge support of the program.

REFERENCES

1. Maurice Belanger gives an extended definition of educational technology in his reply to an article by Anthony G. Oettinger and Sema Marks, "Educational Technology: New Myths and Old Realities," in *The Harvard Educational Review,* 38, Fall 1968, p. 722.

2. Skinner, B. F. *The Technology of Teaching.* Appleton-Century-Crofts, New York, 1968, p. 4.

3. In the area of communications research the studies conducted by Carl I. Hovland and Samual A. Stouffer for the Army and the War Department during WWII and Robert K. Merton's Mass Persuasion became seminal works. See Paul Saettler, *A History of Instructional Technology,* McGraw-Hill, New York, 1968, p. 327.

4. Brown, Richard. "Part Six. A role for Higher Education in Post-Industrial Society." In *Ancillary Pilot Study for the Educational Policy Research Center Program,* Hudson Institute, Croton-on-Hudson, N.Y., June 28, 1968, p. 602.

5. Gideonse, Hendrik D. "Research, Development, and the Improvement of Education." *Science,* 169, November 1968, pp. 541-545.

6. Gideonse, *op. cit.,* p. 54.

7. Oettinger, Anthony G., and Sema Marks. "Educational Technology; New Myths and Old Realities." *The Harvard Educational Review,* 38, Fall 1968, p. 716.

8. See "How Much Are Students Learning? Plans for a National Assessment of Education." The Committee on Assessing the Progress of Education, November 1968.

95.

The Role of Measurement
And Evaluation
In Instructional Technology

by *RICHARD E. SPENCER*
Head, Measurement &
Research Division
Univ. of Illinois

There are, in existence, innumerable reviews of the research dealing with instructional technology (Lumsdaine, Torkelson, Allen and Finn). Included under the rubric of instructional technology are educational television, computer assisted instruction, programmed materials, teaching machines, simulation games, instructional films, filmstrips, slides and other materials, textbooks, etc. All such variables, as well as many more, since the introduction of the hornbook in the 16th century, have been researched, compared, evaluated, accepted, rejected, or ignored. Much of the research has been temporal or cyclical in nature; emphasis occurs on one topic or another as a specific piece of equipment is made available in the market place, or as federal funds reward certain types of innovation.

It is not the purpose of this paper to review specific research in the area. It is assumed that the reader can find such material elsewhere. Here, the purpose is to attempt to make an editorial comment on the field as a whole, to indicate some sources of assumptions, causes of the findings, the role of measurement and evaluation in the area, and a look to the future of educational technology.

If one looks at the research, one can easily estimate the popularity of various topics of concern. Discussions of the Big Three—Television, Computer-Assisted Instruction (CAI), and Programmed Instruction (PI)—compose a majority of the writings in the area. In general, one finds that the early research efforts in each area tend to be focused on the hardware; i.e., Can TV teach? Do teaching machines work? Later, concentration turns to theoretical developments, and more system or operational considerations. To a considerable extent, however, the hardware systems of instructional technology have been used in some operational settings with little regard for research findings.

All of the studies have some basic assumptions, but it should be apparent that there is a basic problem with instructional technology research and use which has been generally ignored. In the first place, the definition of instructional technology tends to emphasize hardware, generally to the exclusion of instructional content, or teaching strategies or methodologies. These items are variables which exist on ETV, or films, or are included in PI, textbook writing, or any other presentation of instruction. Publications seem to have been concentrated on the assumption that the hardware can do something unique, or operate independently of what someone puts into it. Such research normally results in an all too common finding in this area—no significant difference. The hardware (the media end of instructional technology) as used, results in learning to about the same level as a real, live instructor does.

As one progresses from concentration on the hardware to what is performed with the hardware (sequence of learning, audiovisual stimuli, reinforcement, overlearning, etc.) one finds small but statistically significant differences between experimental and control groups. Unfortunately such gains are usually temporary and disappear upon delayed recall evaluation. Thus, the general state of the art can be defined in either an optimistic or pessimistic way:

> Instructional technology can reach *just as well* as regular, conventional methods; or

> instructional technology can teach *no better* than regular, conventional methods.

Thus far, however, we have not defined "what" is taught, how something is taught, or what learning is considered to be. Secondly, we have not concerned ourselves with student "attitudes" toward the hardware style of teaching. Most of the effort in instructional technology has been put into one-shot programs, often developed for research use only, which rarely see the light of day in a continuous on-going instructional operation. Those that do develop into operational instructional programs show no better results (in achievement) than does regular instruction, and the students generally dislike it more. Reports of non-involvement, separation from the instructor, uninteresting materials, etc. are common for ETV; for CAI and Programmed Instruction the most common student response is that it is boring. What is the basis for these rather discouraging results? Is instructional technology doomed to play only a supportive role in American education? Why hasn't instructional technology fulfilled its potential?

Some of the assumptions underlying the use of instructional technology could stand critical inspection. There is a considerable "religiosity" associated with instructional technology—those that are in the field seem to believe that the potential is just lying there waiting to be tapped. With only a slight degree of effort, the technology will prove its worth. Faith is built into many research designs, but satisfaction occurs with no significant regularity. An evident assumption appears to be that the medium is in fact the message (McLuhan and Fiore). It is certainly true that one can study content, as a student, only according to what content is available. What university courses exist define for the student what he may study—he is, in part at least, led through an *a priori* system of content. ". . . the student's rate of learning is restricted to the teacher's rate of presenting; the amount to be learned by the student is limited by the amount the teacher presents; and the pattern of instruction by which the student is supposed to learn is determined by the pattern the teacher decides to use for the whole class." (Dial-Access, p. 5) Similarly he may only read from the reservoir of what has been written; he may see films only related to that which film makers consider worth filming. Practical applications of ETV, on college campuses at least, have resulted in the video taping of hours and hours of the head and shoulders of some professor performing precisely the way he does in class. If the media is the message, the message on this TV media is that education is a bore. This attitude has become so fixed in the minds of the students, perhaps because of the rather obvious comparison to commercial TV, that in order to obtain significant increments in learning with ETV, one has to exert considerable effort, and consider many different variables and factors in the learning situation.

A second apparent assumption is that one must concentrate on the INPUT to the instructional system rather than OUTPUT; i.e., the assumption is made that we know what the objectives of a course really are. The method by which an instructional segment becomes involved with instructional technology is to start with how it is done now—in the regular (i.e., conventional) classroom instructional setting. This methodology of approach may set the stage for the all too popular "no significant differences" that so often result. Instructional technology has been constrained by the already existing structural pattern. Knowledge, or content, has long since been carved up into segments, placed at levels, and defined by a rendition of the Sapir-Whorf hypothesis. As Sapir states (Sapir, p. 578):

"Language constitutes a sort of logic, a general frame of reference, and so molds the thought of its habitual users."

Such a theory may be applied to an educational system—one which has defined reality and the real world (see Jerome), divided it up into language arts, arithmetic, social studies, physical education, etc.; housed it in a certain manner, supplied the media (i.e., teacher and text), financed it, dated it (from September to June), timed it (8:30 to 3:15) to such an extent that the system becomes a reality as Benjamin so aptly points out in the Saber-toothed Curriculum. It is difficult to develop an independent developmental procedure, and a capability to stand aside and view the system, define its objectives and evaluate its outcomes without the constraint of the existing structure within which instructional technology has been operating. The organization and the institutionalization of education itself has formed the greatest barrier of the use of instructional technology. The research on instructional technology has consistently occurred *within* the system—affected and controlled by the systemization already in existence. This system controls what we may experiment upon, how we may experiment, and how we are to treat the results. The potential for significant differences may not exist; or those things upon which we determine significant differences aren't the important ones. The system itself may be the most important variable related to the future of instructional technology.

Those variables on which instructional technology research is conducted are largely based on those factors held dear by individual professors or teachers. An analysis of these variables can be conducted in two ways—(1) ask what educational objectives are, or (2) inspect the examinations used. The former approach yields descriptions of everything from "improving thinking" to "reducing the myoptic view of our culture." The latter indicates that most examinations contain a majority of factual, memory-type test items (essay or objective) toward which learning must be oriented.

The type of examination system used in an educational program represents to a considerable degree the ultimate objectives in that learning system. The examination, therefore, serves to direct, influence, and determine what is measured and evaluated—and thus the concentration by design, intent or accident, that the student will place on certain elements to the exclusion of others—regardless of stated educational objectives. The examinations state the objectives very concretely, and with more meaningfulness to the student, than does the instructor, course outline, or textbook. If the system is composed largely of factual material, that which will be learned will be factual, at the expense of attitudes, appreciations, or problem solving concepts and understandings. To the extent that the evaluative instruments represent a known goal, that which occurs in the classroom (regardless of media or technology) is that which the student will learn (Spencer). The student himself controls what he will pay attention to or learn; partly on the basis of his own interest and motivation, partly (but only slightly) on the degree to which the instructional program can develop interest, partly on the basis of his *a priori* attitudes toward the content of the instruction (he likes math but hates English), and on the basis of what he sees as the way he can maneuver through the system. Whether technology is used or not is irrelevant at this point—the overriding influence is the system. Any alteration in the system, such as moving from conventional instruction to some sort of instructional technology involves a relationship with an already existing institutionalization and reward system. If these later variables are related to instruction in such a manner that they reward convention more than newer procedures, the results of the newer procedures will tend to be depressed irrespective of content. This effect can operate on content, faculty participation, interest, and student response. An assumption underlying instructional technology experimentation exists which is relative to this area—that the system is adaptable to instructional technology, and that operations in this area will be welcome. Such an assumption has not been wholeheartedly validated.

As we have seen, examinations themselves may be classified as an instructional technology. CAI and Programmed Instruction have emphasized this variable in their operations, by attempting to supply immediate feedback of results to students as they work through an instructional sequence, in providing positive reinforcement (getting the test item correct), and in testing only that which has been presented. One major problem comparing instructional technology with conventional systems is the introduction of different examination variables into the picture. If one proceeds to "program" a course, and supply positive reinforcement and immediate feedback, one is varying a considerable number of factors other than the method of presentation (i.e. by computer, self-instructional programmed text, or T.V. film or whatever). One is also introducing a methodological difference (in the psychological sense); the *manner* in which the material is presented is different. One can find in the literature that changes in these methodological factors, within a conventional classroom system, can produce a significant difference. The media may have little to do with learning—what's on the media is the thing.

There has been considerable emphasis on statistical treatment of instructional technology research, primarily because many of the assumptions underlying the statistics used are not met by the research design (Lumsdaine, p. 593). A second problem is a determination of significance for what? What type of significance is one really after?

If we imagine ourselves setting up an educational enterprise from scratch, with no previous institution ever having been in existence, we see that we must get the naive (student) connected to the all-knowing (professor). When we accomplish this purpose we can note by tests of significance that the student/professor system results in more learning (especially if the professor makes the examinations) than does the lack of such a combination. Thus we conclude that *IF* what the student/professor system has developed is of *value* to the society, we recommend its continuance, elaboration, and extension. Some systematic education is better than random or no education. Now if we want to experiment with different types of educational systemization, we tend to prejudice our thinking in the direction of very slight changes (relatively), each *within* the student/professor system. Let's put the professor on T.V., or film, or radio; add a textbook, or program the instruction, or use a computer; self-pace or time-pace the student, put him into homogeneous groups of slow, average, or fast learners, etc. The amount of potential effect these variables can possibly have upon student learning is indeed small. The results validate this argument—but perhaps, our criteria have changed. The IF statements (if we can slip into computer language for a moment) have been changed. Now, we may want significance tests like IF we can do it cheaper, faster, to more people at once, with less effort, etc., the significance of the results is tested by a valid "no significant difference," i.e. we are successful if there are no differences. If however we are interested in the students learning more, we have other things to consider. Now we have stated a specific direction; we must define "more" of what, and our effort (time, money, personnel) is directly related to the extent of the "more" that we want. If we decide to do in half the time (one semester) what was done before (in two semesters), again no significant difference in criterion test scores is a significant difference—our real criterion is time, which (2×1) is significantly different. But this design assumes we merely want to do the same kind of job. This is another primary problem with our assumptions. We assume that we know what we need to get accomplished, and that the educators know how to (pedologically) get it done.

As McCleary states (in another context, but applicable here):

1. "The immediate applicability of research findings becomes a primary criterion in the identification of the problem, research design, and support."

2. "The field of investigation is limited prematurely and may exclude essential criteria and/or experimental variables."

3. "The factor of self-correction—control and verification of activities and conclusions—is suspect."

4. "The haste to state conclusions crystalizes thinking and precludes examination of assumptions."

5. "Projects are too ambitious for the personnel and resources, thus they contribute to loose speculation about observations made in different situations."

Lloyd E. McCleary

Educators are constantly arguing about what is a good teacher, and what is a "good" method of instruction. We are concerned about how to evaluate when a student has reached success or mastery. Our examination, evaluation, or grading system again gets in our way. Is an "A" given by a professor sufficient indication of mastery? Is one "A" equal to another "A" in another course or subject? In instructional technology research, one notices that criterion tests tend to be rather easy (as most classroom tests are). Most of the variance among students is determined by a spread of scores among the top 25% of the scale (between 75-100% items right). If we want to make comparisons, we obviously don't have much room to operate. A football team (on offense) doesn't often get a long run for a touchdown because most of the time they are very near the goal line and do not have very far to go.

An ideal test for comparing differences between treatment groups would be one which distributes the students around an optimum mean (midway between chance score and the maximum possible score). Thus, on an objective test with five alternatives per item, and 100 items, an optimum mean would be the maximum score (100) minus chance score (20) = 80. A range of 80 between 20 and 100 would put the optimum mean at 60. Most classroom tests have means higher than this; and thus, the room to show the differences is depressed artificially by the type of examination used. There is not enough range for the students to show the gains they may have made.

In programmed instruction, and CAI, the tendency is to devise tests which have a mean score no lower than 95% in order to retain the assumption of positive reinforcement. This theory is seriously open to question, both on theoretical and statistical grounds (if one wants to compare groups). Tests are approximations of criterion behaviors sought by an instructional program. One instructs or presents a specific type of content, to which students respond. In an open situation (i.e., instructive) as traditional classroom instruction is, learnings are permitted to vary two-dimensionally—in *amount* of material that is learned (horizontally on a sequence ladder); and in *kind* (vertically across sets of ladders). Learning includes a variety of types, including factual knowledge or vocabulary (a neat, sequential, additive type of learning), to appreciation (very imprecise). In a closed, structured siutation (P.I., C.A.I.) that which is taught is more prescribed and defined. There is less opportunity for horizontal movement. The two situations present very different instructional settings within which wide variation may occur. There is certainly a value to be gained by the use of instructional technology. It presents an opportunity to investigate and possibly change an instructional unit or program and it exposes the system to view. This in itself may yield changes which benefit the student, but the one who is changing is most probably the individual faculty member; thus, not only does he change his procedures for the TV or C.A.I. or P.I. course, he also goes back and changes the conventional course. This system has not been investigated, because of a hypothesis that arranging a course for TV, for example, is sufficient reason to yield significant differences.

The potential for instructional technology is far greater than its use to date. Although wildly expensive, for educational minds and pocketbooks, instructional technology could be used to produce extensive "significant differences." In the first place let us acknowledge that the forgetting curve for school learning is monumental—most factual learning is forgotten within a very short period of time and most school learning is factual. Instructional technology can be used quite effectively for providing a tachistoscopic-memory device that could almost guarantee set levels of memorization—even overlearning. One could flood the student's perception with mechanical systems which he could scarcely escape from (1984 is only 16 years away). Attitudes, understanding, problem solving, evaluation, concept formations tasks are more difficult—but again readily possible given the appropriate resources to accomplish the task. If one looks at instructional technology installations across the country, one is reminded of where data processing was first housed—in basements, garages, and converted steam rooms. Present instructional technology setups indicate that instructional technology has evidently not been accepted by society. As Coombs states:

> "Education's technology, by and large, has made surprisingly little progress beyond the handicraft stage, whereas remarkable strides have been made in the technology and productivity of many other sectors of human activity, such as medicine, transportation, mining, communications, and manufacturing." (p. 7)

Jackson agrees:

> "... there is reason to suspect that many of the bolder forecasts concerning technological change in education will not be fulfilled."

Coombs goes on to suggest four reasons which might contribute to this problem:

1. "First is *the sharp increase in popular aspirations for education,* which has laid seige to existing schools and universities."

2. "Second is *the acute scarcity of resources,* which has constrainted educational systems from responding more fully to new demands."

3. "Third is *the inherent inertia of educational systems,* which has caused them to respond too sluggishly in adopting their internal affairs to new external necessities, even when resources have not been the main obstacle to adaptation."

4. "Fourth is *the inertia of societies themselves*—the heavy weight of traditional attitudes. . . ."

Instructional technology offers the potential of communicating the necessary facts and information into the public domain, rather than keeping educational materials locked inside classroom walls. Confining ETV to closed circuit is an example of the degree to which financial restrictions and poor planning eliminate wide sources of education from public view. Perhaps the public is not interested; they certainly don't rush to watch NET, but the reason may be that the programs are:

1. highly "arty"—drama, dance, music (and cooking)

2. highly academic, and by this I mean dismally boring and uninteresting for the potential audience.

That the Beverly Hillbillies is more popular than NET should not cast blame on the populace, but on the programming of NET!

Given the necessary and adequate funding, with creative and imaginative producers and writers, ETV can be as interesting and communicative as commercial TV. ETV has gone underground—perhaps because the public would be horribly shocked at the state of teaching in American education. Why is there the attitude that we must not "entertain" our student audiences? Why are textbooks dull? There is simply no support, either financial or in the faculty reward system, for making an instructional program exciting and stimulating. There is no system to reward the innovator, and thus no particular reason to evaluate the results. Why evaluate if nothing different is going to occur? The academic institutions may be competent, but they may also be impotent.

There are certain other variables which demand consideration in regard to instructional technology, particularly in the area of specific evaluation procedures and research designs used. Objective testing has been considered the exemplification of empiricical research. Atkin (1963) for example indicated that innovation or creativity may develop beyond the capability of objective criteria to evaluate them. How then are the innovators with instructional technology to calculate their effects? The question resides, unfortunately, in the case of objective criteria, or subjective judgment, with *who* does the evaluation, and *how* the criteria are arrived at. Obviously, if one picks objective instruments which depress the capability for the measurement of creativity (whatever that is), it will not be discovered in the treatment or experimental design. Similarly, with subjective judgment as the method, one is dependent upon the capability of individuals to observe creativity. The criteria, however, remains constant in both cases—to develop a measuring instrument (be it observational, experiencial, objective, or performance) which will consistently (reliably) be sensitive to the behavior we are interested in developing. Secondly, it must also do the job the next time, or with different subjects, or different operators of the project.

The development of an instrument always is a less than perfect approximation of the behavior we might desire to measure—tests and people are sensitive and insensitive. Care must certainly be applied in order to prevent the instrument from concentrating, or over-structuring the intent of a project, or determining in advance the results one may potentially render. If only a single, objective instrument is used as the criterion measure, we are placing all our marbles in one bag. A multi-media evaluation model (using objective tests, observational records, performance criterion, etc.) would be more likely to discover changes in students than a single-media approach to evaluation.

The type of evaluation system employed also depends on what it is we are attempting to do. If the object of the design is to show that one system of instruction is better than another, evaluation design, and media may differ considerably from a project which is determining what is the best way to accomplish a specific objective, or an exploratory instructional system which needs feedback into the system as the instruction develops.

In the same vein, much of the research with instructional technology has been concerned with a "defensive" research design; i.e., ETV is as good, or is better than conventional instruction (considering learning as the only criterion). A more rational approach to instructional technology would seem to be in the direction of "How can instructional technology be used to improve instruction? When, at what age, in what areas, and with what types of learning? (See Carpenter, 1968)

It should be apparent from how instructional technology is used in education today that whole programs tend to be presented rather than single-variable stimuli; i.e., French I in 6th grade is presented as an entity, rather than, say, the concept of "carrying in two-digit addition." There has been little effort to discover where a particular media or technology would be of help. In general, this is primarily due to the fact that: (1) we don't know where certain procedures would help, and (2) we don't know where, in our conventional educational system, the most help is needed.

We do not normally include in our educational system a constant evaluation program to inform administration diagnostically where the good and poor points of the program are located. For example, can we answer questions like: (1) Is high school chemistry taught better than history? (2) Is long division learned to the same extent as multiplication? (3) Is the English they learn in high school enough?

The university level is particularly vulnerable to questions of this sort since there are few criteria for judgment. The graduate schools can make judgments about undergraduate education—but few undergraduates go to graduate school. Since, however, this relationship is one of the few which can lead to evaluations of undergraduate education, the lower level system tends, perhaps, to orient the program in the direction of graduate school—even when only a minority of students ever arrive there.

The college can evaluate high schools—but again not all high school students go to college. The high school can evaluate junior high and they, in turn, the elementary. In general this results in a system of constantly casting blame downward. Each in turn sets its own criteria for selection and promotion on the ever present evaluation lying one step higher. The evaluation system is one which merely exists—no one thought it out, planned it, or adopted it—it grew. Is it the proper one? If one were to determine the practical objectives of the use of instructional technology, one would have to conclude that the criteria are already built into the system—get more people into college or graduate school! This has lead, one could presume, to an over-intellectualization of instructional technology. From observation (if I may use Atkin's method of evaluation) one observes the primary resources going into college preparatory courses, material pre-determined by already existing course and curricular structure, required rather than elective courses, etc. Very little has been done with motivation, self-evaluation, vocational education, visual communication, inter-personal cooperation, selection and interest, reading cross-field educational designs, etc. We still operate in the structure developed a hundred years ago—the assumption must be that this is the way it ought to be done.

What instructional technology is used, how it is used, and on what is it applied ". . . is guided largely by force of personal conviction, and evaluation research is mainly of use in helping consumers decide where personal convictions to buy." (Bareiter, 1967, p. 192)

With the advent of instructional technology, some institutions have been altered in ways they had not foreseen. Film usage requires projectors, screens, and projectionists, as well as some delivery method for getting the supplies to where the students are. C.A.I. requires cables, a student station or more, a computer; TV requires a channel, a tower, a studio, etc., etc. To the extent that such mechanics are bought, or subscribed to, the students receive a different sort of instruction. The instructor may be a machine and not a person; it may be self-controlled rather than teacher structured, written not spoken, or presented by a stranger on a screen rather than a teacher within the womb of the classroom. It is obvious that the individual teacher, therefore, loses direct control of what is presented, how it is presented, and when it is presented. The teacher becomes more of a participant than a director of the learning. This may result in many problems and disturbances—from some teachers turning the TV set off, not ordering films, not fitting the material into the classroom sequence of things, etc. The author observed an elementary class receiving TV instruction in the New Math and was interested in how the teacher was going to handle the content after the presentation was completed. The teacher responded with considerable aplomb—"That's enough of that New Math stuff," she said. "Now let's get back to *OUR* Mathematics—open your arithmetic books to page 73; do exercises 1-10!"

There are several ways in which instructional technology can be used to improve education. Generally, the "replacement" system has been used, i.e. replace a course taught by conventional means with one taught on or by TV. This procedure merely accomplishes the same basic purpose with a little greater hostility from the students. Some procedures, notably the audiovisual people, use a "supportive" system—assist an ongoing program to do the job a little better (which is difficult to find validity for). Other methods do exist, but seem difficult for administrative, legal, or institutional means. These methods include concepts of repetition, time, difference, applied, review, availability.

For example, if something is repeated often enough, it is more probable that it will be learned. Why not repeat the presentation again, over a different media perhaps, with greater clarity for those who didn't get it the first time, or in abstract for those who want merely a summary and review? It can be presented by another person or system—programmed instruction *and* ETV, radio *or* film. It can be presented during supper hours, over open circuit TV, offered at night, dial-access, or on the telephone. One can flood the market place and hit the students with many ways of presentation, many times, at their convenience.

A large issue in this whole argument is one of criteria—what do we want the student to do after the instructional program that he couldn't do beforehand. Generally we keep this a secret—we don't very often meaningfully communicate to him exactly what is expected of him. Many students fail. Should we blame the student or ourselves? If there are methods which will improve the number who reach the criteria, shouldn't we try it? Many times failure occurs because the student doesn't know what he doesn't know. Procedures can be developed which could answer this problem, through the use of instructional technology. One example will be presented to indicate an application of instructional technology in areas in which very little now exists in order to acknowledge the fact that instructional technology possibly would obtain better and more usable results if the area of attack was a novel one rather than an already existing one.

If we may assume that most learning will be evaluated by an examination, or series of examinations, and we further assume that the items on these examinations represent the content of the course, and similarly the capability of the student to indicate the degree to which he has learned, then our objective becomes clear—i.e., to enable him to: (1) know the material well enough so that (2) he will be able to answer correctly the examination questions we will use to permit him to show us that he has learned the content (such questions may be objective, essay, performance, what have you).

The capability of the student to know what these test items are can certainly have an effect on his learning behavior. If the items are good ones and he knows what the items are (barring memorizing of the examination for the moment), his direction toward learning the correct answers to the items is the same as learning the content. That this is not always true should not alter the fact that if our assumptions are followed thus far, it should be true.

Given that he can obtain experience with these test items (takes a test, is graded, and learns his relative position in his class and the instructor's opinion of his efforts), the feedback will inform him of what he knows or doesn't know, or how much he does or doesn't know. Such information, if presented diagnostically, can offer him specific knowledge of his particular strengths and weaknesses, dependent on the feedback of which items he has missed and which ones he got right. Similarly, information could be communicated dependent upon his item results as to where he may find a discussion about the area that that item represented.

Usually there are few rather than many examinations given during an instructional program—the procedure takes away from instructional time, someone has to score them, etc. Instructional technology provides means whereby such problems need not exist. Optical Scanning equipment can read answer sheets, or student input stations can be used to record answers to objective questions, scored by computer, and fedback (by printout or video display) to indicate his evaluation. The student may desire many questions, or few, testing often or seldom; if the facilities are readily available, he may guide himself, or be directed to pursue a line of evaluation most necessary for him or the teacher.

Many instructors would find such a situation intolerable because students may see test questions before instruction related to them has been presented, may be able to memorize answers to test questions, or may be able to find right answers by answering incorrectly and being corrected. This should be considered improper only to the degree that test questions are limited in their number, for if thousands of questions are available representing all parts of the instructional program, these intolerablenesses become motivational and acknowledging variables to relate the student to the material. Knowledge of the test, type of test items, and self-analysis (anonymous) capabilities ought to improve learning. The only problem is in supplying items in sufficient quantity to form an ITEM BANK, which the student can sample for his purposes, and from which the teacher can sample for examination time.

The computer can store *ALL* multiplication, division, addition, and subtraction problems; can vary the numbers in word problems ad infinitum, can create questions on the basis of a test item model, can collect, file, and retrieve *ALL* questions ever used on tests. What is more, data on what students do with these questions can also be stored (how many, at what stage pass this item), and analysis information given to the student. The instructor can also obtain such data indicating where students are having problems. In the same manner a student can address the ITEM BANK with direction for what kind of test item he wishes to try:

> Give me some items on photosyntheses used in Biology 101.
> Give me two digit division problems.
> Give me French vocabulary review items Chapter I, II, and III.
>   Etc., Etc.

Depending upon the sophistication of the instructional technology, the items could be visually displayed, could include graphics, charts, pictures, and configurations, could be solved by writing, light pen, or response to a multiple-choice question. The test can become a learning tool, rather than a punishment or negative reinforcing device. The computer can be programmed to evaluate what a student asks for, how well he does, and on what he ought to be tested. Thus, a student who asks for a test item beyond the appropriate stage of the course can be automatically advised of this fact. If he gets the item incorrect, communication can occur to yield appropriate statements indicating he should, perhaps, try item 1489. If he gets an item correct he can be praised (within the limits of the programmer's skill in thinking of appropriate positive reinforcement phrases, like "good," "great," "wonderful," "very few students at your stage get this item right," or "Sorry—that's not the right answer; you didn't divide the last number by 2—would you like to try another problem of this type?", etc.).

Another aspect of instructional technology which is interesting to observe is the degree to which dullness has been supported so resolutely. No manifestation of Madison Avenue ever crops across the ETV screen or is included in programmed instruction or C.A.I. It is obvious from the life and death struggle on the commercial market and the glassy stares of many of the youth of America that commercial TV has something to offer; that commercial advertising—even for aspirin—does in fact work. Why haven't any of these procedures and systems been used in educational technology? Does commerce ask educational technologists for assistance in selling Volkswagens, or creating the Pepsi generation, or creating an image of a political candidate? The image of education suffers by comparison. We are in the business of selling knowledge, perhaps to a much greater extent than we realize—learning is not becoming an "in" thing. The establishment is getting criticized from right and left, and perhaps rightly so. Can we use as a viable criterion that we ought to be able to teach Geometry to the same extent that Crest can sell toothpaste? Or are we satisfied and content that what we are doing is good and right, and thus should rest on its own laurels?

We have discussed both evaluations of instructional technology and how to evaluate instructional technology. The picture is indeed less than adequate. What then can be recommended?

One of our major problems with the use of instructional technology is the educational system itself in terms of credit allocations, management, and administrative systems, methods of showing proficiency, and product control. A system does not exist which gives support (i.e. promotion, salary increase) to those interested in improving instruction. Administrative details and incapability to change structures the manner and mode which yields us indices of learning. The learning appears, sometimes, less important than how the individual attained it. In one instance we require 16 hours of a foreign language for a B.A. degree, and on the other hand, prevent a foreign student who is in our university studying in English from presenting either English or his native language as fulfillments for this requirement. We pass a student into the next level course if he obtains a "D" or better grade in the prerequisite but we refuse to grant proficiency credit to someone who already had a "D" knowledge in that course. The system leads to a considerable amount of "playing the game" rather than learning. Competitive systems are not permitted. The system in fact works antagonistically to innovation which includes instructional technology.

Recommendations:

1. Develop funding which will lead educational institutions to build appropriate reward systems for the improvement of instruction—careers in teaching, particularly at the college level, are prerequisites to improved instruction.

2. Supply means whereby politically separate educational institutions become interested and rewarded for producing instructional programs useful in more than one institution—duplication of effort is wasteful and costly; efficiency needs to become an educational criterion.

3. Provide year long grants-in-aid for faculty to pursue research toward the improvement of instruction; in order to improve, senior personnel need to be released for concentration on the teaching process.

4. Subsidize large scale educational TV networks and communal C.A.I. systems; to provide means whereby institutions can observe presentations from other institutions, or can use them cooperatively if they so desire.

5. Develop model building educational resources, whose function it is to produce an obviously better instructional program and provide such proven courses nationwide—what is lacking in the technology to date is the proof that it can offer something better.

6. Support, with emphatic funding, experimental innovations in instructional programming, which will not fail because of lack of personnel, writers, producers or directors, material or equipment.

7. Study and produce an alternative administrative system of the teacher role; to enable college departments to continue their graduate programs without relying on graduate teaching assistantships; to reduce the competitive jealousy developed between public school teachers and instructional technology.

8. Investigate the possibility of establishing a federal free-university which can develop and make available courses of study in direct competition, or support of already existing courses, possibly presented over national ETV.

9. Supply funding for the expansion of libraries to include programmed texts, C.A.I., and video taped or audio taped courses of study (remedial, advanced).

10. Develop systems to automate information retrieval for students, for single-concept film loops on long-division, to TV recordings of plays, presentations of specific points, recordings of lectures, synopses of presentations, etc.

11. Support innovative practices which deal with the management of education; i.e. credits, hours, requirements, grades, probation, required attendance, or the classroom concept.

12. Assist in the development of procedures which will serve to bring the student in closer contact with that which is required of him—such as larger scale proficiency and diagnostic testing, test item bank procedures, and self-analyses systems.

These recommendations are, of course, very general; but they are intended to point in the direction which will enable the *use* of technology to catch up with the engineering state of the art. The hardware development has far outstripped the software (programs, content, assimilation, structure). Most important, however, is the system itself—it is not, and unless some radical changes are made in the management/administrative structure of educational institutions, will not be able to advantageously incorporate instructional technology into the system to an extent which the potential demands.

BIBLIOGRAPHY

Allen, William H. and James D. Finer, Co-Chairmen. "Instructional Materials: Educational Media and Technology." *Review of Educational Research,* Vol. 32, No. 2, April 1962.

Atkin, J. M. "Some evaluation problems in a course content improvement project." *J. Res. Science Teaching,* 1963, 1, pp. 129-132.

Benjamin, Harold R. *Saber-toothed Curriculum.* New York: McGraw-Hill, 1939.

Bereiter, Carl. "Acceleration of Intellectual Development in Early Childhood." U.S. Department of Health, Education, and Welfare, Final Report, Project No. 2129, Contract No. OE4-10-008. University of Illinois, Champaign, Illinois, 1967.

Carpenter, C. R. "Planning for Colleges and Universities with Educational Technologies." Paper presented for the Illinois Conference on Higher Education, Monticello, Illinois, Nov. 2, 1967.

Coombs, Philip H. *The World Educational Crises: A Systems Analysis.* New York: Oxford University Press, 1968.

Dial-Access Information Retrieval Systems for Education. Newsletter, Special Issue #4, Vol. III, No. 3, May 1966. University of Wisconsin, Madison, Wisconsin.

Jackson, Philip W. *The Teacher and the Machine.* Pittsburgh: University of Pittsburgh Press, 1968

Jerome, Judson. "The System Really Isn't Working." *Life,* Nov. 1, 1968, pp. 67-70.

Lumsdaine, A. A. "Instruments and Media of Instruction." In N. L. Gage, (Ed.) *Handbook of Research on Teaching.* American Educational Research Association, Chicago: Rand McNally, 1963, pp. 583-682.

McCleary, Lloyd E. Status of Research on Education in Latin America. *Latin American Research Review,* Vol. III, No. 1, Fall 1967.

McLuhan, Marshall and Quentin Fiore. *The Medium is the Massage: An Inventory of Effects.* Bantam Books, 1967.

Sapir, E. "Conceptual Categories of Primitive Languages." *Science,* 74, 1931, p. 378.

Spencer, R. E. "The Improvement of College Level Student Achievement Through Changes in Classroom Examination Systems." U.S. Department of Health, Education, and Welfare, Contract #OEC-3-7-061147-0271.

Torkelson, Gerald M., Chairman. "Instructional Materials: Educational Media and Technology." *Review of Educational Research,* Vol. 38, No. 2, April 1968.

Whorf, B. L. *Four Articles on Metalinguistics.* Washington: Foreign Service Institute, 1950.

PART FIVE

Instructional Technology: Implications for Business and Industry

96.

Innovations in Industry
Likely to Affect
Instructional Technology During
The Next Ten Years

by HUGH BECKWITH
President
Beckwith Associates
Cleveland, Ohio

This report undertakes to examine technological developments likely to occur in the next ten years as a result of industrial innovation that can have a significant effect on instructional technology.

The content of this report is based primarily on assessment of the activities and plans of large companies currently involved in various phases of instructional technology; on extensive review of reports published on the subject; and on the knowledge and experience of this organization acquired in similar studies.

Every attempt has been made to make this report realistic. Yet it is only prudent at the outset to state several important caveats that should be applied to assessing its content.

1. The technological innovations described as likely to occur are not certain to occur. The pace of technological breakthrough and development is so rapid that progress can be a matter of leap frog advances rather than orderly progression from one point to another. The full benefits of a breakthrough often so far exceed the expectations of those who accomplished it that it has been necessary to coin words such as synergism and serendipity to describe the results.

2. While the companies from whom major innovations can reasonably be expected plan their activities well into the future, all plans are subject to change because of change in motivation, unexpected breakthroughs, new insights. There is also, of course, the possibility that significant innovations may come from sources other than those surveyed in this study.

3. The accomplishment of the technological developments described in this report does not necessarily assure that these developments will prove really useful as instructional technology. Nor would their usefulness necessarily mean that they would be widely used. Many developments in the past that seemed to hold high promise have not found widespread use in education. The reasons for this are rooted in such factors as economics, social attitudes, and human behavior.

This report is organized into five sections:

1. Broad Areas of Technological Advance

2. Examples of Specific New Products to be Expected

3. Innovation in Areas Indirectly Related to Instructional Technology

4. Basic Factors Required for Innovation to Occur in Education

5. Basic Problems in Accomplishing Innovation in Education

It is recognized that the scope of the work assigned to this organization could be encompassed in the first two sections listed above, and this is where major emphasis has been placed. However, consideration of technological advance alone without taking into account the implications of its application can result in distortion in its evaluation. Therefore, we have broadened the scope of our work to include Sections Three through Five.

Broad Areas of Technological Advance

This section examines the broad areas of industrial technological advance likely to occur in the next ten years.

It also introduces a theme which will recur throughout the report. Most people interested and involved in the developments that are to come share a common conviction. Almost anything of a technological area that it is desired to do can be done.

All of the developments which are treated in the following pages are part of the evidence that supports this belief. Further, as these developments are considered, it is possible to see the dependence of one development on another, and the relationship of one step forward to every other step.

Perhaps the single most important factor in the near and long term future of technology, including instructional technology, will be the computer.

More and more of our present activities will be computerized and new activities will grow out of the increased ability to computerize. The use of computers will proliferate to a point where a "computer utility industry" will evolve as basic to the country's economy as the power utility industry is today.

As this occurs, remote input and output devices tied to giant central computers, and in some cases individual computers, will become essential to the operation of businesses, schools, and, quite probably, homes. The skill to use these devices will become as essential and as commonplace as the skills required to use a telephone or drive a car are today.

Currently, the cost of using computers in many of the ways envisioned for the future is prohibitive. This is changing rapidly. The accelerating progress of the basic electronics technology used in computers is already making significant cost reductions possible. For example:

It has only been twenty years since the first practical application of transistors was made, only ten years since the first integrated circuits were developed and only about one year since large scale integration of circuits was accomplished. The results of these three developments have been remarkable. They have:

1. Decreased the cost of electronic circuits by 100 times or more

2. Decreased their size by a factor that may approach 10,000 times

3. Increased their reliability by a factor of 1,000 or more times

This kind of progress means that it will soon be feasible to use computers for any desirable purpose. Specifically, in education the possible uses for computers and the implications of their use seem to fall into three areas:

1. As data processing tools, for scheduling, grade reporting, billing, payroll handling, facilities utilization analysis, etc.

2. As a subject field to be included in the curriculum

3. As an instructional medium, probably in several variant forms such as computer assisted and computer administered instruction

In addition to these principal areas of anticipated use, computers are likely to be employed for such purposes as analysis of the use and effectiveness of instructional materials and of the techniques of preparing such materials.

The subject of computer-assisted instruction is treated specifically later in this report. From a broad technological standpoint two points should be made in summing up the potential for computers. First, they will play a major role in the most fundamental changes in technology for the rest of this country. Second, education will share in the change and will be changed by it.

Another broad technological innovation likely to affect instructional technology in the next decade is holography. This photographic technique, which may employ lasers, records wave fronts of light from an object. These are then used to reconstruct an image of the object in true three-dimensional form. This will make possible three-dimensional photographs, printed illustrations, projected slides, motion pictures, televised pictures, images at computer terminals, and microscopic slides. While the theoretical use of holography has been possible for some time, the employment of lasers is a recent development and represents a real breakthrough. "Scientific American" commenting on the development, states that a "holograph may prove as useful, for optical purposes, as the actual object itself . . . perhaps even more useful." Refinement of present capabilities in this area will greatly increase the effectiveness of all visual communication.

Lasers, which play a part in holography, will have a great effect on a wide range of human activities. The most important area may prove to be in the field of data transmission. Lasers utilize frequencies much broader than those used by current broadband communications. This will make it possible to transmit enormously increased amounts of information, perhaps as much as one million times more information, at far less cost.

Ultimately lasers may make it possible to transmit data, in such forms as three-dimensional television, facsimile, voice, etc., in quantities great enough to accommodate any reasonable demand.

When this ability to transmit data becomes a reality it will, of course, be necessary to greatly increase the capacity to manage what is transmited, to store and retrieve it easily in meaningful form. This demonstrates the interlocking nature of technological innovation, one breakthrough demanding another and making possible still another.

The use of computers will make management of data transmission and its storage and retrieval a great deal easier. So will another development . . . microforms.

Microforms have already moved into the second stage of their development, microfiche, and are moving to a third stage called ultra microfiche. Their effect on the capacity to store information is so great that it is difficult to comprehend. It is presently possible to store the contents of 20 average sized volumes on a 4″ × 6″ film strip. It has already been demonstrated that using lasers to reduce data signals, as many as 20,000 volumes can be stored in an area of 8″ × 10″.

Obviously the use of computers to catalogue and retrieve data, along with improved low cost data transmission systems and low cost printers and readers that are convenient to use, can revolutionize libraries in terms of what they can contain and how they can be used.

The next ten years are likely to see much more widespread and more sophisticated use of communications satellites for direct broadcasts to schools and homes. The previously described breakthroughs in the use of lasers, improvements in data transmission, storage and retrieval, will play a part in the increased use of communications satellites. This, along with improvements in computers, tape players, and film projectors, will greatly increase the potential for individualized instruction in audio and video forms, programmed and non-programmed.

It is the intent of this report to highlight the significant breakthroughs in technology likely to occur in the next decade. The developments discussed thus far have, therefore, been treated as just that, highlights, described in brief detail. Nevertheless, it is possible to see ample demonstration of the fundamental accuracy of the belief, widely held by those who are seeking technological breakthroughs, that *almost anything of a technological nature that it is desirable to do can be done.*

Hopeful as that statement may seem, there are thoughtful people who are disturbed by what it can mean. Such people fear that our ever-growing technological capabilities will so far outstrip our ability to manage what is accomplished that we may be confronted with chaos instead of progress.

The concern is not without basis, and the question is dealt with in somewhat more detail later in this report. It can be pointed out here, however, that there is already technology in existence, likely to be improved, that can help to deal with revolutionary change not as an avalanche but as a tide of progress.

For instance, the science of cybernation, the development of systems which can control, extend and correct themselves, is keeping pace with the other areas of technological progress. This is likely to make possible the creation of highly complex systems of much greater reliability, systems which will employ automation to develop one-of-a-kind variations. Such systems will, it is likely, be capable of empirical self-analysis and of self-adjustment to perform in the most appropriate and effective ways.

So far automation and cybernation have found their widest use in the manufacturing process. But there have already been significant breakthroughs in the use of these remarkable tools in the business management area. These developments may well find a place in the management of the educational process with a resultant improvement in the understanding and control of learning environment and activities.

The development of this capability will not, however, guard against the human frailty of doing things that are possible but not sensible.

There are many instances today where technology is misused, where its use interferes with rather than enhances the educational process, and where people could accomplish the objective better and at lower cost than machines do. Unless the intended use of technology is put to rigorous examination, the phenomenon of technological misuse is not likely to disappear.

There is yet another area of development which must be noted. Progress in the chemical, physical and biological sciences seems to have opened the door to the possibility of literally changing human beings, in the genetic and later stages of life, to provide increased capacity and motivation for learning. While this possibility raises highly complex moral, ethical and sociological questions, no one exploring the future can ignore the implications. Certainly any such improvement in the human capacity to learn, remember and apply knowledge, would have incalculable impact on education in the future.

Examples of Specific New Products to Be Expected

Almost all the hardware now in use in instructional technology will become more reliable, offer greater flexibility in application. Such hardware will be easier and more convenient to use and, in relationship to what it will be able to do, less expensive than is presently the case.

There will be new products on the scene and the usefulness of existing products will be extended to permit new uses as well as improvements in present applications. Here are some of the things that may be expected:

Rapid, high quality copying of printed material at low cost, perhaps as low as $.01 per page, in black and white and subsequently in color.

Large screen television display systems at acceptable costs.

Combination television receivers and motion picture projectors. Association or combination of video tape and film technologies to produce more flexible formats at lower costs.

Packaging of software in relation to hardware to produce more convenient, reliable, accessible use.

Long lasting, inexpensive (perhaps $20 or less) television receivers that can be optionally operated on battery power.

Inexpensive, easy to operate video tape players and recorders.

More rapid, lower cost copying of video tapes, and perhaps film, possibly with equipment which can logically be located at school sites rather than in central processing centers.

Small, battery operated, two-way telephones.

Light-weight, small, perhaps textbook size, microfilm and microfiche readers.

Use of microfiche technology to provide rapid random access, large capacity slide projection.

Television screens which will be able to receive an image and retain it as long as desired without the need to regenerate the signal. These screens will also make possible the display of overlays or other images.

Stand–alone devices which will be, optionally, computer interfacable and will present audio and video information which can be programmed to require and measure student response.

Much lower cost computer terminals. Substantial progress should be made in this field within five years.

The foregoing list relates primarily to items that are commonly called hardware. In addition to these developments and others which will undoubtedly come, it can be expected that greatly simplified methods for preparing various kinds of software will be developed.

Of all of these developments perhaps most important of all will be the creation of large quantities of instructional materials which will have precisely stated objectives and will include diagnostic preinstruction tests and criterion achievement tests.

These materials will be available in many of the forms listed above and others, including books. Many of these materials will involve the student in the learning process, require active response from him, permit him to progress at his own rate, and will allow him considerable control and direction of his learning activities.

When new instructional technology is considered, books frequently get little attention.

Yet these oldest of instructional tools are likely to share in the benefits of much of the technological progress cited above. More economical and rapid techniques for printing are in the offing which will make it possible to publish a greater variety of printed materials, and make it more economical to use color illustrations.

Innovation in Areas Indirectly Related To Instructional Technology

A number of factors are likely to affect the nature and extent of the changes in instructional technology in the next ten years. These factors include:

Changes or lack of change in other aspects of education.

Access to the educational environment . . . that is the location of the school, the ease or difficulty with which it can be reached, the ability to place some of the educational environment in the student's home.

The management and regulation of the educational process.

Among the innovations that seem most likely to affect instructional technology in indirect ways are these:

Educational Environment

More sophisticated architectural engineering, accomplished at least in part through utilization of computerized analysis, which will result in such things as stressed shells, pressurized skins, and geodesic domes.

Improved building materials which will affect building exteriors and interiors, providing such things as more efficient and economical lighting, temperature, and ventilation.

As a result of factors like those listed above, much lower cost buildings.

Much more economical and efficient methods, perhaps utilizing lasers, for making excavations that will make underground building far more feasible than it is today.

Physical Access to Education

Much more prevalent and convenient mass transit, perhaps including moving sidewalks.

New forms and uses of underground transportation.

New power sources for transportation from new forms of storage batteries, power cells, etc.

Another approach to access to education may entail the use of equipment which the student can take home to recreate part of the environment found in school.

Management and Regulation

The purpose of this brief section is not to debate the issue that if education were run like business, business would be out of education (or conversely that education would be out of business). It is demonstrable, however, that there are managerial techniques used in business whose use in education will be innovative and are likely to occur.

Two of the more obvious of these relate to procurement methods and to cost/effective measurement.

Equipment Procurement and Leasing

Currently, education buys most of its equipment. Obtaining funds for the purchase of new equipment, particularly equipment related to instructional technology, is difficult. Procurement is further complicated by educator's concerns that the equipment to be purchased may become obsolete before it has been used long enough to justify its cost.

In many instances both of these problems could be solved, or at least ameliorated, if equipment were leased instead of purchased. If acquisition of equipment were analyzed from the standpoint of use rather than ownership, the funding requirements could be quite different. They might, for instance, be related to operating funds rather than capital funds. Where there are concerns about obsolescence, renewal options could be built into leases which would allow schools to trade equipment in on newer models or to get rid of it.

Many variations of leasing are in common use in business today. Further effort on the part of education to develop leasing methods which best suit its needs would, in our judgment, meet with cooperation and flexibility from most companies which provide products for education.

With regard to instructional technology, leasing would seem likely to apply more to hardware than software. However, looked at from another standpoint, great improvement in the ability to duplicate many published materials will also tend to make it possible, and perhaps essential, to approach the acquisition of some kinds of software from the standpoint of paying for its use rather than for its purchase.

Analysis of Costs and Benefits

As pointed out in the July 1968 Committee for Economic Development Report: "Innovation in Education" and in other authoritative sources, greatly increased use of appropriate instructional technology requires more effective and specific analysis of the costs and benefits involved. This means analysis not only of new or proposed technology but also of current practice and costs.

One disillusioned instructional technologist has described the problem implied in the foregoing as follows: "The reason so little instructional technology is used in education today is that its visible faults always end up being compared with teachers' invisible virtues."

Methodology and technique for analyzing the cost/effectiveness and cost/benefit of alternative and new courses of action, including intangible factors, exist today and are frequently used in business to evaluate such things as research and development projects, marketing operations, etc.

Analysis of the management techniques developed by business, and application of those methods and techniques appropriate to education, will result in innovative improvements in education's decisions on whether, what, and how to use instructional technology.

It is not this report's intent to oversimplify the problems involved in making realistic cost/effective studies of instructional technology and of current educational practices, but it is the intent to:

1. Reinforce the point made earlier that enough products have already been developed to lend credence to the proposition that almost anything of a technical nature that is really desired from technology can be accomplished.

2. The means to evaluate current educational practices and instructional technology on cost/effective and cost/benefit bases largely exist and are currently applied in other fields.

3. Developing and applying the appropriate ways for education to evaluate what's old and what's new can be done right now. Doing this, in our judgment, holds greater promise, both in the short and long range, for introducing and expanding instructional technology in meaningful ways than almost any technological discovery or invention that can be envisioned.

Basic Factors Required for Innovation to Occur in Education

For innovation in education to occur in any significant way, particularly for new instructional technology to be adopted, there must first be a recognition of the need for change and a conviction that the proposed innovation meets the need on the basis of cost related to benefit.

For there to be useful innovation, the educational community must believe strongly that there is a definite need to do something new or to change something old. At the same time the general community which supports education must also recognize the need and be prepared to pay for the efforts to meet it. Unless there is a clear and definite recognition of need, the taxpayer will be reluctant to see money spent on innovation while the educator will be hesitant to encourage it because of the disruption that change usually brings.

Obtaining maximum value from instructional technology also requires coordination of all of the elements which are likely to affect and be affected by it. That is, faculty, administration, physical site, available software and hardware, must all be seen as a part of the total picture. Only by doing this can appropriate and realistic goals be identified, pursued and accomplished.

It is apparent at this stage of the report that a great deal of instructional technology, with the capacity or the potential to improve the educational process, already exists. Whether or not it will be employed to accomplish that improvement depends on the ability to recognize the need for innovation and to evaluate the worth of the various approaches to accomplishing it. In short, the real need for innovation may be in areas of how instructional technology is introduced, managed and measured.

Basic Problems in Accomplishing Innovation in Education

This final report section does not presume to reflect all the views or even the majority of the views and frustrations of people in industry who attempt to provide products for education. It is reasonable to believe that various people in industry who are knowledgeable about current educational practice would disagree with some of the statements that are about to be made. What this section of the report does attempt to do is state problems which many people believe exist. The solution of these is fundamental to making the use of instructional technology more meaningful in education.

Foremost among these problems, many people believe, is education's unwillingness or inability to accept and use instructional technology already available.

There are a great many reasons why some educators delay accepting new technological possibilities. Some of these reasons are rooted in common sense and others are completely invalid. Because they may wish to wait for the next product or service or improvement before acting, and because there is always a "next product" in the offing, some educators wait forever without acting . . . even when the value of an innovation has been demonstrated and its economic practicality is clear.

It is recognized that the NIH (Not Invented Here) syndrome is common in business, particularly among people engaged in trying to find new technological approaches. Some people contend, however, that there is a particularly virulent case of NIH in educational circles, causing automatic rejection of a new idea or, at the least, violent tampering with technology developed and proved in some other institution or setting.

There are, in some educational circles, doubts as to whether instructional technology means teacher extension or teacher extinction. Examination of the implications of valid instructional technology will, of course, show that it is not only not a threat to good teachers but is instead a way of enhancing the importance, effectiveness and satisfaction of their job. Nevertheless, if those who feel threatened by technology are not reassured, their fears can be as destructive to innovation as if they were well founded.

There is, of course, another side to this. Many new teaching approaches coming from technology have been presented as the means of cutting the costs of education; as the means to replace teachers. This has turned out to be nonsense. But if industry persists in offering products of technology as teacher replacers and not as teacher extenders, then teacher fear of technology will also persist.

In more specific ways, basic current problems of introducing instructional technology can be listed as follows.

There is fundamental need for agreement on learning objectives stated in performance terms, to make achievement of these objectives measurable, and to make possible comparison of new and current practices.

More effective means of testing, guiding, and measuring each student's progress are required.

Development of enough instructional material of high enough quality to permit individualized instruction is needed. The amount of media used by a student in an individualized learning program is many times greater than that required by a conventional program. This material can, and in due course will, be produced. However, until substantial use is made of material already available and proved effective, large quantities of additional material cannot be expected from publishers. Nor is it reasonable to assume that this need will be adequately filled by education itself.

A further aspect of this problem is the need to develop adequate copyright protection so that producers of instructional materials can be recompensed on their use rather than on the sale of material of which duplicate copies are then made.

The whole question of teacher training, pre-service and in-service, presents substantial problems in relation to instructional technology, particularly as it relates to individualized instruction.

Effective individualized programs depend in large measure on pre-testing of students, diagnosis of learning problems and accomplishment, prescription of appropriate instructional materials, and tutorial instruction. Teacher training programs currently do not emphasize these matters, and the requisite skills to deal with them are not acquired by future teachers in their training. This problem is, of course, complicated further for the new teacher who may also be asked to understand the use of such materials in conjunction with relatively complicated hardware.

The problem of in-service teacher training is similar, but because of the logistics of geographic dispersion and time even more difficult to solve. One course of action that appears likely to occur is much greater involvement in teacher training by producers of instructional materials. This may lead to the further development of private industry undertaking to market to education teacher training services related to instructional technology.

The viability of such an effort will depend not only on the quality and relevance of such services but as importantly on their acceptance and economics, as, in fact, will the participation of industry in all of the areas of instructional technology. Business must show a profit. It will pursue those markets where profit is possible.

One of the most basic problems is that of school organization and administration. Questions of certification, accreditation, allocation of funds between salaries and media, all pose limitations and restrictions even in areas where there is strong motivation to innovate.

Given the motivation to do so, it is probably possible to deal with and change these matters in due course, but many people wonder how this motivation in a sufficiently massive way will develop. As long as teachers are trained to perform in a conventional setting, and this setting is administered by former teachers who were also trained and are now ingrained in the conventional ways, it is difficult to see how education will ever be able to change itself. If not, the further question is raised whether change can or should be brought about by forces outside of education such as government and business. If the latter, a whole new set of troublesome problems is raised.

The direct involvement of government and business has, of course, occurred in some specialized educational efforts, the Job Corps, for instance. The successful aspects of this program might serve as a model for taking the effort further. However, problems such as how to apply elements of another program, like the Job Corps, to already existing schools appear to be particularly sticky.

A particular area of instructional technology which has received a large amount of attention is computer assisted instruction. In the minds of some people CAI has now run the full gamut from panacea to the opprobium formerly reserved only for teaching machines.

As the most sophisticated form of instructional technology now known, a brief examination of its past and present and some speculation about its future should shed light on the subject itself and on other aspects of instructional technology.

It was presumed by many early enthusiasts that CAI would take over most teaching on an individualized basis, not only in drill and practice and tutorial forms. but also in flexible dialogue modes that would allow the student not only to control his own progress rate but also to control the paths of progress in diverse and relevant ways. This has not occurred.

Some of the early enthusiasts have now not only backed away from this concept but have relegated the computer in education solely to administrative housekeeping tasks. Why has there been failure to achieve the early dreams and why the disillusionment?

There are a number of reasons. The development of programs which have instructional validity has turned out to be extraordinarily difficult. Communication between student and computer has been awkward. Costs have been prohibitive. With these problems and others, acceptance in education has been minimal. Is this the end of the road? We do not believe so. For instance, work being done on computer based education in the PLATO Project at the University of Illinois has these guidelines.

1. Normally the computer should only be used when it is the best method of presentation. Less expensive methods such as program texts, films, slides, tape recorders, etc., should be used when appropriate.

2. The computer should be used as much as possible to simulate results in models built by the students rather than simply turning pages.

3. The system must be flexible and adaptable. It must be able to teach many subjects and present the lesson material by a variety of teaching strategies. The system must change to meet the needs of the students and teachers, and not be limited to off-the-shelf items presently available.

4. The system design must consider its method of integration into the educational system. For example, a school should be able to start with a single terminal for the incremental terminal cost instead of having to invest large sums of money just to determine if they want or need computer-based education.

5. The cost of computer-based education should be comparable with the cost of teaching at the elementary grade school level. Cost effectiveness should be determined by an hour to hour cost comparison.

We believe that the work being done in Project PLATO holds promise that these guidelines can be met from a technical standpoint. Key among the guidelines, in our judgment, is the first one: "Normally the computer should only be used when it is the best method of presentation. Less expensive methods such as program texts, films, slides, tape recorders, etc., should be used when appropriate." Looked upon this way, we believe the computer, as a result of work being done in many other places as well as in Project PLATO, will find a highly significant place in the educational process. Its acceptance in education, however, will be affected by many other factors which have been referred to earlier in this report.

This report has suggested in a number of places that the key to the amount of instructional technology that will be used in education is the ability and motivation of education to accept it. Despite prime consideration given to this point, it seems appropriate to conclude this report with the further point that even given sufficient ability and motivation to employ appropriate instructional technology, adequate funds will be essential. New money and reallocation of funds currently expended in education for other purposes, must be made available for research in appropriate subject fields and for the introduction of new educational systems which utilize instructional technology. Such systems must hold the promise of doing the job better and/or at lower cost.

New methods, techniques, technology in all fields almost always cost more and fail to perform as well initially as the old, proven ways of doing things. It is only after new ways have been used long enough to be refined and long enough for people to get used to them that the promise that caused them to be tried is realized.

It is unreasonable to expect education to prove to be the exception to this rule.

97.

Should Educators Generate Specifications for The Purchase of Equipment?

by R. LOUIS BRIGHT
Special Asst. to the President
Baylor Univ.
Waco, Texas

I have heard many educators express their dissatisfaction with the current educational hardware that is being "foisted on the schools by manufacturers whose only interest is to make a fast buck." They state their belief that the only way to straighten things out is to have educators decide what they really need and issue functional specifications for the equipment they want to purchase. The purpose of this paper is to examine this premise in more detail.

There are two major problems relevant to the introduction and acceptance of new forms of educational hardware. The first is: Is it appropriate for the educational function intended? This question breaks down into two important sub-parts: Does it perform a useful educational function? and; Is the cost reasonable for that function?

This requires that one consider all of the costs associated with the utilization of that hardware including: The amortization of the purchase price and installation cost, taking into account any changes in the professional to student ratio, requirements for additional non-professional employees, maintenance costs, materials costs, and space costs.

As to whether or not it performs the educational function should most appropriately be answered on a cost effectiveness basis in which one compares the education effectiveness of the system using this hardware with that of other possible alternative costing the same amount. In other words, could one perform that educational function as well or better by hiring additional people, using other types of equipment, or by some other technique for the same dollars?

The second major question relevant to the introduction of new hardware is the "Chicken and Egg Problem." No one will buy a piece of equipment unless there is a large library of course material to go with it, and no one will invest in the development of special software until the machine is in wide use.

Unfortunately, these two questions are not independent; they are inexorably related by the fact that the cost of a piece of equipment depends upon the size of the production run, both because of the direct economy of high production and because the engineering development costs must be distributed across that production run.

Thus, the probability of obtaining a favorable answer to the first question (cost effectiveness) depends critically upon the solution to the second.

I think that the most productive way of analyzing the efficacy of "educator developed specifications" is to see if they would ameliorate either of these problems.

The major consequence of these problems in the past has been to give us a line of educational equipment almost all of which was basically designed to serve some other purpose. I think the reasons for this are twofold. One, closely related to the question of this paper, is due to the fact that in many cases educators become familiar with and intrigued by the possibilities of equipment used for other purposes, for example, television and audio tape recorders. Television was clearly developed primarily for the home entertainment field, tape recorders were initially developed for military purposes and then put into production form for home entertainment. Having seen these devices in the home, many educators had the imagination to see applications for them in education and either used them without modification or asked suppliers if they would supply units altered in some relatively minor way. The other reason, of course, is related to the "Chicken and the Egg Problem" in that by simply making slight modifications on equipment whose development cost had been written off in other market areas, manufactures could introduce equipment at a much lower cost than if they had begun from scratch.

The results are, however, that very little of this equipment really makes much sense if one asks the first question: Is it appropriate; does it perform the function well; and does it do it at a cost which makes it competitive with the alternative ways of achieving the same function? The common error here is that in very few cases do people consider the total cost. For instance, with conventional audio-visual equipment (primarily modifications of motion picture cameras and projectors that were designed for the home entertainment field), most people pay attention only to the initial cost. They do not compute the tremendous cost of inventory, the cost of acquainting teachers with these materials, the professional time spent in previewing materials, or the maintenance costs, all of which are certainly real operating costs in any educational system.

One example of equipment that was specifically designed for educational use is the overhead projector, and I believe that a comprehensive analysis would show that its instructional cost effectiveness does compete very successfully with the alternative of a blackboard, particularly where teachers make extensive use of industrially prepared transparancies.

In writing specifications for hardware, it is only natural for educators to fall into the trap of only specifying those things that they have seen in use, thereby perpetuating this use of equipment designed for something else. Few educators are really familiar with the physical science research and development programs which are continually extending the techniques that could conceivably be brought to bear on the solution of educational problems. Few educators are even familiar with the educational research which tries to define optimum conditions for learning. Again the tendency is to simply perpetuate present teaching techniques or minor alterations of them. Most educators have not had the experience necessary to estimate high volume production costs of equipment, nor are they sensitive to the fact that small differences in the design and specifications can make major differences in development and production costs.

Once can give several examples from the rapidly developing art of computer aided instruction; e.g., it was early evident that an interface in which one simply had a pictorial and printed display and a key board by which the student could respond, was not adequate, particularly with very young children. It was necessary to have some type of non-alphanumeric manipulative input for the student. One very attractive solution is to use a light pen (using a technology developed for the military).

It is technically possible for a student to draw figures, letters, lines and so on upon a cathode-ray tube and have the computer receive and analyze this information. Unless one digs more deeply, it is not apparent that the ability to draw a line with a light pen costs about $600.00 in initial cost per student station and requires a much greater computer capacity than a $60.00 alternative in which the student uses the light pen to point to a fixed position on the screen and the computer detects where he is pointing. There is a very real question as to whether the ability to draw a line is worth ten times as much as the ability to point. Careful consideration of this situation seems to indicate that in almost all educational situations, the ability to point is an extremely useful function, but the additional ability to draw a line is seldom worth the cost.

Let me give a specific example of the use of alternative approaches. One of the reasons some educators were so enthusiastic about writing with a light pen was so that children could draw letters and have the computer check them for correctness. Although this is theoretically possible, it is both very difficult to define the tests that a computer must make to decide whether a letter is "correct" and still more complicated to have it indicate what was wrong, and, as has been pointed out, it is expensive to provide this writing capability. Actually the educational objective is not really to have a computer judge whether the letter is correct or not, but rather to have the child decide whether it is correct or not. In other words, it is necessary for the child to discriminate between a wiggle that society considers to be an acceptable "A" and a somewhat similar wiggle that society will not generally accept. This discrimination can be elegantly taught by displaying sets of related wiggles on the screen and asking the student to *point* to the best "A." Experiments have been conducted that show that this latter (and much cheaper) technique is much more effective in teaching children how to make letters than the former.

I again want to emphasize that I do not think that it would be obvious to most educators that these two, apparently only slightly different functions, (writing and pointing) would have more than an order of magnitude difference in cost. Still other examples from the same field can be given. For example, it is desirable to have a large number of pictorial displays available at random in a very short access time from a large store of pictures. Careful analysis seems to indicate that the cost of providing even quite a detailed black and white line drawings at a given access time from a given size store, will be an order of magnitude cheaper than providing grey tone drawings and perhaps still another magnitude cheaper than color continuous tone pictures. The educational problem must be faced as to what kind of educational situation is a colored grey tone or picture significantly more functional than a line drawing. If one were to look at the beautiful line drawings in a medical anatomy text, it is apparent that this question is a real one. No one, to my knowledge, has yet worked on this problem of comparing the cost effectiveness of computer-produced line drawings on a cathode-ray tube with that of color slides on a computer-controlled projector, where again total cost, including initial cost, maintenance, library and so on, are considered. Even in the more traditional audiovisual fields there are many questions that the educator has generally chosen to ignore. For example, the total cost of an audiovisual system is dominated by the inventory cost and not by the initial cost of the equipment. If one looks at this, one finds, of course, that the inventory cost of motion, either whether provided by video tape or motion pictures, is at least an order of magnitude, and probably two orders of magnitude, more expensive than storing an equivalent amount of course material on slides, film strips or other still picture techniques. Is this difference in one or two orders of magnitude in cost really reflected in a difference in educational effectiveness? In some cases such as the study of the life of primitive tribes in Africa or in viewing a Shakespearean drama, I am sure that motion is very desirable. However, what few experiments have been done indicate that in very few traditional subject areas does motion appear to have any significant advantage. In fact, in many cases it appears to be distracting. Certainly the costs of the preparation of the materials are also significantly different. In many cases, if the amount of money spent on a motion picture production had been spent on a careful analysis of the educational objectives and the production of a series of well prepared slides, the student learning would have been improved.

In summary, I don't think that the solution to the first problem, cost effectiveness, is likely to be solved by educator developed specifications. Rather it is very necessary that there be a constant interplay between people familiar with educational problems, educational research, hardware technologies and production and development costs so that it will be possible to make intelligent trade-offs among various alternative approaches.

The second part of the analysis is to decide whether educator developed specifications assist in the "Chicken and the Egg Problem." I think an interesting example can be given here: Last year one of the foundations felt that there was a real need for a low cost projector having certain characteristics and estimated there would likely be a market for about 10,000 such units. They approached a major audiovisual company and asked them if they could make a projector that would sell at a specified cost. The answer was, "At that number of units, yes, we can. Will you guarantee to reimburse us for the unrecovered development costs if our market does not reach your estimate within a two year interval?" The answer that the foundation was forced to give was, "No, it could not guarantee the development costs." The company did not produce the equipment.

As we look in more detail at educator developed specifications, it is immediately apparent that they are likely to fall into two distinct categories. One is where the educator wishes to conduct research on learning and wants a particular type of environment or presentation. The second is where the educator is planning to purchase the equipment for regular operation use in a school. The economic constraints on these two are clearly very different. For example, many researchers are able to specify the type of experimental functions they would like to have. With our present technologies, the hardware supplier can supply almost any conceivable type of function or environment if the customer is willing and able to pay for it. In many research projects, the researcher is amply endowed by Federal or foundation funds and orders it, and the hardware companies produce it. In some such cases it is not the large volume manufacturer that would respond, but in nearly all such cases you would find at least a few speciality houses that would be willing to design and build the equipment.

For the other type of requirement, the operational requirement, the size of the order is seldom large enough to justify the expenditure of any significant amount of development funds by the supplier. Or, putting it in another way, the development costs amortized over the number of units requested would result in a higher unit cost than the customer could justify. The only way in which educator specifications seem to assist in the "Chicken and the Egg Problem" is in the case where the customer is large enough to control a sufficient number of units to really justify the investment of significant development dollars. This could conceivably occur if some of the major states purchased hardware for all of the school systems within that state in a single order.

I believe another serious situation would result if this was a common practice. If each of the major states came up with its own set of specifications and suppliers responded to these, it is unlikely that there would be any standardization between the states. Equipment and materials developed in one state would not be interchangeable with that used in another, nor is it likely that there would be more than one supplier competing for second round orders. The problem becomes even more serious if one is concerned about driving the cost down to levels which can be attained by really mass production, i.e., if one is concerned about actual unit production costs as contrasted to simply the distribution of developmental costs. Here the number of units involved must be extremely large in order to realize the economies which are possible through automatic production. Another important factor in the overall situation involves the maintenance of competition. In the long run, a hardware system is likely to be much lower in cost if there are several manufacturers supplying the same type of function. This is closely related to the establishment of standards so that tapes, films, and other types of software programs developed for one manufacturer's machine will run on that of another without modification.

This emphasizes that there are dangers inherent in not specifying what you need. There is at the present time very little incentive for manufacturers to standardize their products. In fact, the major suppliers intentionally try to avoid standardization so that there will be less likelihood of their encountering competition on second round orders. I believe that the only way this problem can be solved and the resulting economies achieved is for the educational community to issue specifications in the following sense: Educational users should be represented on all appropriate industrial standardization committees and should agree to specify that all equipments they order must be in compliance with the standardization recommendations of those committees unless there is some urgent educational reason for deviating.

That route also has its dangers in that it tends to standardize on existing techniques and, hence, discourages the introduction of new and different types of hardware. In order to really solve the "Chicken and the Egg Problem," I believe that it is essential that the Federal government or major states provide development support directly to manufacturers of both equipment and software in order to encourage these companies to develop and introduce new products without the necessity of having a guaranteed market against which they can write off their development costs. This is certainly not a new concept. It has been applied to the construction of railroads, the subsidization of air mail, the research and development of sea water desalination and pollution control, to say nothing of defense or space. If this technique has been successful in bringing new products to these other areas of social need, why should not the same technique be applied to education? Many people react negatively to this concept in that they feel that it would give the company, who has received the development funds, an unfair competition. This may be the case for a short time; but if there is a requirement that the developments be licensed to other companies at a reasonable fee, and if all companies have an equal chance to apply for such development funds, it seems to me that there has been a competitive situation established.

In order to obtain the social benefits resulting from the educational utilization of the latest technologies, such support programs should not be limited to competitive bids against specific specifications but should also provide companies that have invested much of their own funds on research the opportunity to present attractive ideas in the hope of getting sole source support. This is not discrimination or favoritism if all companies have this same opportunity.

The fundamental question should not be whether it gives a company a momentary advantage but rather whether it is advantageous to society that such a product be developed and made available. Certainly, particular railroad companies were given competitive advantages in certain areas as were particular air lines, but the fundamental question was asked, "Is it of benefit to the society to have these geographical regions accessible?" The benefits to society are obvious.

I believe that another consequence of providing development support will be similar to that existing in other technical areas. If companies knew that there were major governmental development funds available to support imaginative and unsolicited programs relating to education, they would very quickly within their own houses assemble very impressive teams of educators, psychologists and hardware specialists that could continuously interact in the evaluation of various techniques, so as to supply an answer to the first question, "Is the function appropriate?" This would be particularly true if the reviewing agencies in deciding which proposals to support made their selection primarily on the basis of "does the investigation proposed likely lead to an attractive cost effectiveness solution?"

98.
Major Areas of Emphasis
For Instructional Engineering

by RUSSELL W. BURRIS
Executive Officer
Center for Research in
Human Learning
Univ. of Minnesota

A major concomitant of introducing technology into teaching and learning situations has been the exposure of many difficult and sometimes painful questions about the processes of learning and the practices of teaching. This paper attempts to identify and label several areas from which these questions seem to arise. These areas represent the writer's views and interpretations and to the degree that they are personal and subject to bias they may be faulted; they are based, however, on several years of experience working with faculty and students in many units of the University of Minnesota on instructional design and development projects, with other colleges and universities as a consultant for the development of teaching and learning resources and with several regional and national groups and agencies concerned with developing instructional systems and resources. It needs to be stressed, however, that these problem areas are interrelated and are in fact sub-areas of the general problem of instructional engineering.

Objectives, Criteria and Evaluation

Many references in current literature clearly indicate an expected use of technology to improve teaching and learning; optimal design, however, is at this juncture indefinable because of the lact of well-formulated objectives, adequate criteria and appropriate and powerful evaluation techniques.

It is rapidly becoming possible to do anything for or with students that one wants to do. Further, it is possible to keep a complete record of every move of the instructor and student through the course of doing so. But such power suddenly exposes our inadequacies. It has not been enough to tell an educator that his instruction should have objectives, that the content and structure of a course should be determined with reference to the objectives and that the course should be evaluated in the light of achievement of the objectives. Most of this guidance has been metaphorical. There has been little clear meaning to the "structure of a course" and the actual evaluation of objectives has been only weakly appropriate. The relations of objectives to particular steps taken in the pursuit of a course have always been problematical.

The writer feels that research efforts must be directed toward establishing a firm theoretical basis for use of instructional technology rather than the mere putting together of instructional components with old teaching-learning models. Two major questions must guide these research efforts. The first is: What is it that the student knows when one is willing to say that the student has mastered a given learning task at some appropriate level? This is the basic problem of describing what it is to "understand" a subject matter, "know" a language, to be able to "do" a skill, etc. The second question is inexorably intertwined with the first: How can one assess what it is that the student knows? If one can describe the subject matter effectively, the next step is specifying the status of the student with respect to that description. Such measurement needs to be doubly diagnostic for the purposes of systematically developing instructional technology. It must describe the learner's state of knowledge and it must specify his advancements in such detail that it can be used to evaluate the success of procedures, programs, experiences and the like which have been manipulated to achieve changes in his states.

In summary this research effort must be directed in three major problem areas: (1) the development of adequate characterizations of the subject matter in particular domains of knowledge; (2) the devising of techniques for describing and evaluating the state of knowledge of a learner vis-a-vis a subject matter; (3) the development of models of the learning process that permit an optimal sequencing of events in instruction.

Characteristics of Individual Learners

Some current data seem to suggest that certain learning strategies may be appropriate for one learner and not for another. Several questions arise from present interpretations of these data. Many questionable practices occur in education as a result of limited understanding of the implications of individual differences for instructional practice. Our current understanding of individual differences does not permit answers to the following questions: (1) Are there different preferred learning strategies among individual learners? (2) Is there evidence of a relationship between such preferences and individual capacities? (3) Are these differences a result of "set" or of deeper aspects of individual behavior structure? (4) How do these individual behavior differences relate across the different kinds or categories of learning? (5) Can a learner's preferred strategy be changed to another strategy without losing, and perhaps gaining learning effectiveness and efficiency?

Instructional Components and Instructional Design

The major issues in this area have to do with the research and developmental efforts required to identify the critical characteristics of specific teaching-learning situations. It is not enough merely to specify a sequence of components in a teaching-learning situation. It is necessary that the components, i.e., the procedures, practices, experiences, be understood as the environments in which learning occurs. As the processes of learning are better understood there is a need to study the critical variables in lectures, discussions, laboratories, tutorials, text and reference reading, etc. as they relate to learning.

This writer has studied current instructional practice at the undergraduate level, and the data show that approximately 80 percent of instructional design at that level can be accounted for by lecture, instructor-led discussion and textbook assignments. This suggests that the components used in instructional design are based upon traditional models. However, to imply that enough is known about the critical features of each component so that selection of appropriate components for particular kinds of learning and for particular kinds of learners would be false, if not dangerous, at this time. What is needed is a heavily supported research program across the basic to applied (or field) spectrum which identifies the critical features of the learning environment as they relate to characteristics of individual learners.

Clearly, more flexible approaches to the design of learning and teaching situations are needed if the often stated goals of developing individual intellectual initiative and of aiding the student to develop skills for continuing intellectual pursuits after graduation are to be realized. Learning experiences are probably desirable in independent study, group (including student-led) study, tutorial, seminar, as well as lecture, discussion and laboratory environments. Continual effort must be directed toward the selection of the components in instructional designs appropriate to both the content to be learned and the manner in which it should be learned.

In summary, the major problems in the design of instruction cannot be solved in ignorance of the processes of learning, and the critical aspects of instructional components must be related to what the learner is to learn.

The Use of Devices

The evaluation of devices in instructional situations can be done only after a better understanding is reached of the structure and processes of learning and the critical characteristics of the components used in designing teaching-learning situations. Optimal uses of information resources, new techniques and equipment in the learning and teaching programs require aid and support beyond that which can be expected from specialists associated with the library, television, audiovisual and computer fields. Students and faculty are faced with complexities as they approach the new and developing technologies beyond those which specialists in particular areas can help solve. These complexities have to do with questions of why and how the resources can be best used to meet instructional objectives and learning expectations. The responsibilities associated with using devices as media for the instructional components also include evaluations of learning and teaching. Magnifying the exposure of a lecturer to a greater number of students, using a programmed instruction unit in the course of instruction, and simulating a problem for the student to solve at a computer terminal can be evaluated only in terms of the effectiveness these components have in the total instructional design.

The Support of Instructional Research and Development

Data gathered by this writer indicate that more than half the faculty in higher education feel that adequate support for instructional improvement is not available. Further, about the same number of faculty state that no one is really interested in evaluating the quality of instruction. These two observations give some hint about the difficult problem of providing support for instructional research and development. This writer's interpretation of the current support programs is that many features are lacking for achieving success.

Instructional improvement must be a higher order goal within the educational institutions *and* within the disciplines. This must be the case in order to enlist the support of the most respected members of the various disciplines who are also the most respected faculty members of the major institutions. However, this goal is next to meaningless unless the criteria of improvement are meaningful and shared and unless the methods and outcomes of evaluation are seriously developed and applied by all those in significant positions within the institutions and disciplines.

This writer believes that only large scale efforts are apt to be successful in applying instructional technology for instructional improvement. A model which comes to mind is the Co-operative Research Programs in agriculture. The present basic and field research and development problems in education have similarities to such problems in agriculture at the beginning of this century. The need for major programs based and coordinated at large universities and the need for the participation of many scientific research specialists and technologists seem obvious. Further, the research and developmental efforts at universities must have formal ties to the field applications.

Privacy

A major part of developing instructional systems is use of data banks in which the response data of an individual's educational history are stored, from preschool through college and possibly beyond. While there is evidence for the value of this information in the design of instruction for the individual, the fact that this information exists in machine memory has rather serious implications.

Copyright and Publication

If the major publishing houses and other newly formed industries related to instruction are serious about their future roles as suppliers and distributors of instructional materials, they must take an active part with educators and government in solving problems having to do with copyright, rights of authors and developers, use of microforms and computers, and instructional system packages. There is evidence that many decisions being made in some of the businesses ignore current state of the art positions and developmental trends that are fairly obvious.

99.

The Quality
Of Instructional Materials

by C. R. CARPENTER
Research Prof. of Psychology and Anthropology
Penn. State Univ.
Univ. of Georgia

Introduction

This is the final report of a study done for the U.S. Office of Education, Bureau of Research, preparatory for the Commission on Instructional Technology as authorized by Title III of the Public Broadcast Act of 1967. The Commission was appointed in the spring of 1968 and began its formal work during the early summer of that year. Extensive staff work was done for the Commission by the Academy for Educational Development, including the collecting and making available to the Commission members of over two hundred documents. Support of Commission and staff work was provided by the U.S. Office of Education.

On July 24, 1969, the report of the Commission on Instructional Technology was submitted by its Chairman, Dean Sterling McMurrin, to James E. Allen, Jr., Assistant Secretary for Education, Department of Health, Education, and Welfare; and Commissioner of Education.

The Public Broadcasting Act of 1967 had three titles: one which extended provisions for television and radio broadcast facilities; one which authorized the Corporation for Public Broadcasting, as recommended by The Carnegie Report; and one which authorized a Commission on Instructional Technology to conduct studies on a large number of different media ranging from teaching machines through advanced printing technologies and computers to research laboratories and production centers to satellite distribution systems.

General knowledge from the results of a special Study Group on research needs* of the U.S. Office of Education and the extensive reports and recommendations of the Advisory Committee for Media which was mandated by the National Defense Education Act of 1958, Title VII, served as the basis for predictions that the Commission on Instructional Technology would urgently need background information on all aspects of problems of the production and effective use of instructional materials. The latter, throughout its ten-year life, with its successions of alert membership, called attention repeatedly to needs for more instructional programs of high quality to match equipment development and procurement. It was not necessary to await the work of the commission, therefore, to know that a crucial area of its deliberations and recommendations would be that of high quality

The members were C. R. Carpenter, John Carroll, Robert Gagne, Eric Gardner, Arthur Lumsdane, Mark A. May, and Wilbur Schramm.

new instructional programs to be provided for the large and growing media distribution systems of the nation. More importantly, perhaps, the commission would confront the problems of relating high quality programs to critical social and educational needs. If the commission should define more clearly and broadly than had been done in the past the role of the federal government in the area of production and distribution of programs for instructional media, what would it need to know and say on the problem of quality of instructional materials?

Recognizing problems that the commission would need to deal with, the U.S. Office of Education, Bureau of Research, contracted for the study and preparation of reports in a half dozen or more areas. One among these was that of the high quality of instructional materials. What is it? How do you get quality? What are conditions, factors, and contingencies which affect quality? What research results relate to the building of high quality in instructional materials? Are the technical and operant qualities of instructional materials inherent in them or are they merely attributes of media programs? Are there conditions other than these inherent characteristics which limit or accentuate quality? How is the cost of increments of quality determined?

These were a few of the questions discussed by Andrew Molnar, project coordinator, with C. R. Carpenter, the prospective project director in arriving at agreements basic to a contract with The Pennsylvania State University to study the problem of quality. A proposal was prepared, processed, and accepted for a year's study entitled: *Conditions, Requirements, and Variables Affecting the Quality of Complex Learning Mediated by Instructional Materials.*

The Problem

The problem of attaining high quality in instructional programs has been extensively explored theoretically, and by research and development efforts sponsored by federal agencies and foundations. The greatest effort has been made by the U.S. Office of Education, Bureau of Research, which has conducted research and dissemination efforts for ten years, 1958-68. The definition and delineation of factors, conditions, and determinants of quality and/or effectiveness have largely eluded the grasp alike of investigators and practical educators. The disturbing and ubiquitous findings of "no statistically significant differences" have arisen by the hundreds to smite those who have striven by neatly controlled research and analytical procedures to bring the variables and contingencies of quality into ordered conceptual and operational frames.

Two intersecting trends have arisen again and again relative to the quality problem. Research and development work involving the use of "new" media in education, instruction, and training is one trend that began importantly during World War II and was accelerated by the National Defense Education Act of 1958. The other interacting trend was extensive and persisting attempts to apply "learning principles" to instructional situations by means of the media (including print, audio and video) and complex media systems including computer regulators of learning behavior.

Two subordinate developments contributed to an increasing interest in the awareness of the problem of quality. *First,* there were many efforts made, about 400 for television alone, to answer the question of what medium and patterns of use of media are more effective, practical, and economical. Here emerged the effectiveness, productivity cost/benefit ratios kinds of thinking about instruction and media. *Second,* "programmed instruction and teaching machines" swept into the educational bivouacs disturbing their structure while at the same time contributing to the art of writing specifications for instructional materials and the formulation of criteria for learned performances.

Orienting Concepts

The questions that were of deep concern to the project director were these: What orienting concepts, approaches, methods, procedures, and techniques could possibly make *new* contributions to thinking about and research on the quality problem? What could be gained that has not already resulted from great effort and sustained research and development work for twenty years to improve quality of media programs? What conventional and unconventional methods might be used to collect useful information and to draw conclusions for the prospective Commission on Instructional Technology which would affect the recommendations it would make to the President and the Secretary of Health, Education, and Welfare? How could a broad and useful perspective be developed based on the results of previous research and development that, with the impetus given by the commission, could make a significant practical difference in the effectiveness and extent of use of media in the educational systems of the nation?

Studies of developments in the fields of education, learning, communication technologies, and related theories suggested that the following orienting concepts may be useful:

1. Concepts using the "systems approach" of instructional technology.

2. Concepts involving functional and operational approaches which specify precisely what operations shall be carried out by what instruments or people to achieve stated learning objectives.

3. Concepts of multi-media and multi-mode patterns or configurations which, when organized, operate together as interlocking instrument-human systems.

4. Concepts of fields of forces (as contrasted with single variables) in which the parts interact algebraically (with plus and minus effects) to produce learning.

5. Concepts of sequential operations in which prior operations determine, limit, facilitate, and interfere with subsequent events.

6. Concepts of *feedback loops* or nets of a more general cybernetic system.

7. Concepts of design specifications with criteria for judging behavioral changes that can be detected or observed and thus known to result.

A simplified conception of the task was that of working within a modified systems concept to select and use methods, procedures, and techniques which would define the factors, conditions, and contingencies that have negative and positive effects on any one or all of the steps and operations included in the procurement and/or production, distribution, and use of instructional materials. Accordingly, it was expected that application of appropriate procedures would make it possible to define in more detail than has been done heretofore the necessary and enhancing conditions as well as the barriers and barricades which have deterministic relations to effectiveness or high quality of instructional programs.

It was believed that a number of research and development practices in the past have led to blind alleys and statistically nonsignificant difference findings. In a sense, these were the misconceptions and erroneous expectations:

1. That any limited sets of single variables, e.g., color, music, first person commentary, direct address, would make significant differences in complex learning.

2. That transfer occurs widely from one to another and different sets of stimulus conditions, or from one set of responses to others, and from a learning situation to other and different situations of application.

3. That exposure to stimulus materials or programs of instruction will directly and certainly result in the expected learning with different learners.

4. That behavioral changes characterized by adaptation and learning are affected by limited ranges of cognitive and emotional experiences, for example, that learning in one "course" is separate from other courses, and that learning occurs separately from the storms and stresses of personal adjustments.

5. That learning can occur on a significant level without active participation, involvement, and appropriate kinds of responses and practices.

6. That elaborate, complex, and dramatic stimulus conditions (which are often very expensive to produce) will be more effective generally than simple, clean, and strong patterns of stimulus conditions.

7. That learning can occur without being targeted to clearly specified learners' characteristics and without having well known objectives and that learning can occur without feedback of information to the learner about degrees to which he approximates in his learning the specified or ideal response objectives.

These orienting concepts and critical viewpoints began to point generally to the methods which might be used feasibly in the conduct of the project for the commission dealing with factors contingent to high quality of instructional materials and programs.

Methods and Procedures

The problem of instructional quality, the consideration of alternative approaches, and orienting concepts and viewpoints all indicated that somewhat different methods and procedures from the traditional should be used for the conduct of this study of quality. Clearly time and funding limitations precluded the making of a research and development approach, nor was this expected. However, the anticipated needs of the commission were that the result of theoretical research and development investigations and studies in brief form were urgently required. Therefore, a first and very conventional procedure was indicated: namely, the collection, abstraction, and production (on McBee edge-punched cards) of abstracts of the literature pertinent to the problem of instructional quality. The developing ERIC Media Center at Stanford University was not yet in a position to be of great assistance to the commission. Furthermore, the media literature is so scattered and varied, characterized by limited and special publications, that it is extremely difficult to survey the published information in an orderly manner. It was planned to send copies of the abstracts to the Academy for Educational Development which was responsible for the staff work for the commission, to the U.S. Office of Education and to the ERIC Media Center. It was not proposed once again to make a review of the literature.

It was decided that the main procedure would be to confront directly selected people having informed, mature, and experienced judgments with the problems of defining the conditions, requirements, and variables affecting the quality of complex learning mediated by instructional materials.*

Nine places were selected in the eastern part of the United States where it would be practical to organize small groups of professional educator-media professionals for intensive discussions about instructional materials and especially on the quality problem. Men and women were invited who were well known in their professions, and who had research and

---

*In early plans, emphasis was put on television programming for instructional purposes. However, as the project evolved and conceptualizations deepened and broadened, the study came to include a very wide spectrum of instructional materials including both "new" electronic media and print. This viewpoint was communicated to the Commission.

extensive practical experience. The invited seminar members were persons who were recognized for their interests and competencies in research, development, and the application of instructional media to varied problems of education, the sciences, engineering, and the arts. Since a large number of such persons were at Penn State and since this university had the contract for the study, four seminars were scheduled there. Similar harvest seminars of information and authoritative judgments involved participants from five other universities. Three seminars were scheduled in places conveniently located for specialists and authorities from other educational organizations and from the military services. A total of about 100 people who could make substantive contributions to the thinking on the central questions of how to achieve high instructional quality of materials that are produced for and used in schools, colleges, universities, continuing education, and professional training programs was selected and invited to attend the seminars.

In the beginning the harvest seminars were exploratory and yielded information on how best the other seminars could be conducted. These first sessions were a seminar at Indiana University and one with faculty from both the University of Notre Dame and Purdue University. It became evident that due to the high level of deliberations, the broad perspective involved, and in general the complexity of the judgments and decisions that were required, an outline or framework was necessary for guiding the discussions. Consequently, the project director designed the attached chart (p. 872) for the primary purpose of having a general guide for subsequent seminar discussions. Actually, this chart has become a format or outline for the whole project, and it has served many other purposes including a framework for presenting conclusions of the study.

In order to have focused discussions, attention was sometimes directed to particular media like instructional films, television, or computers as they might be brought to bear on problems of teaching and learning in a course of instruction, or in a more limited or more general area of the curriculum. However, the perspective was always broad and references were made to all media and to a wide spectrum of their uses.

The settings of the harvest seminars and the procedures used were selected and designed to yield unrestrained and imaginative thinking about the quality problem. The seminar members were encouraged to bring their best focused judgments to bear on the problem: *quality factors in instructional materials.* Freedom of thinking and conceptual explorations were encouraged while severely critical reactions, typical of academics, were discouraged.

The harvest seminar settings were arranged to be out of the mainstream of activities and away from distractions. Sufficient time was provided for reorientation and disengagement of seminar members from their regular work, and for becoming personally involved in the issues of what high quality instruction means and how it can be attained in a very broad spectrum of educational efforts in this nation.

Orientation of the discussions, that is, the setting of the problem, was most important. Discussion group leaders usually challenged the members from the beginning to define and understand the quality problem and to formulate expectations of results from the extended and intensive discussions. Participants were challenged to make substantive, significant, and realistic recommendations for the proposed Commission on Instructional Technology. These recommendations centered on what needs to be done throughout this country to produce and make available instructional programs of the highest quality and effectiveness.

In the beginning of a seminar each member was told that near the end of the discussions he would be asked to make for the record one, two, or three of the most important statements that he could make on the general question, "how best to improve the quality of instructional materials for use in a wide range of available technologies at specified levels of education."

In some of the seminars simulation and role playing techniques were used. Members were instructed to assume realistic decision-making roles in areas of responsibility for which they believed themselves most competent. This was done in some instances by asking the question: "Suppose that you were responsible for drafting the recommendations to the

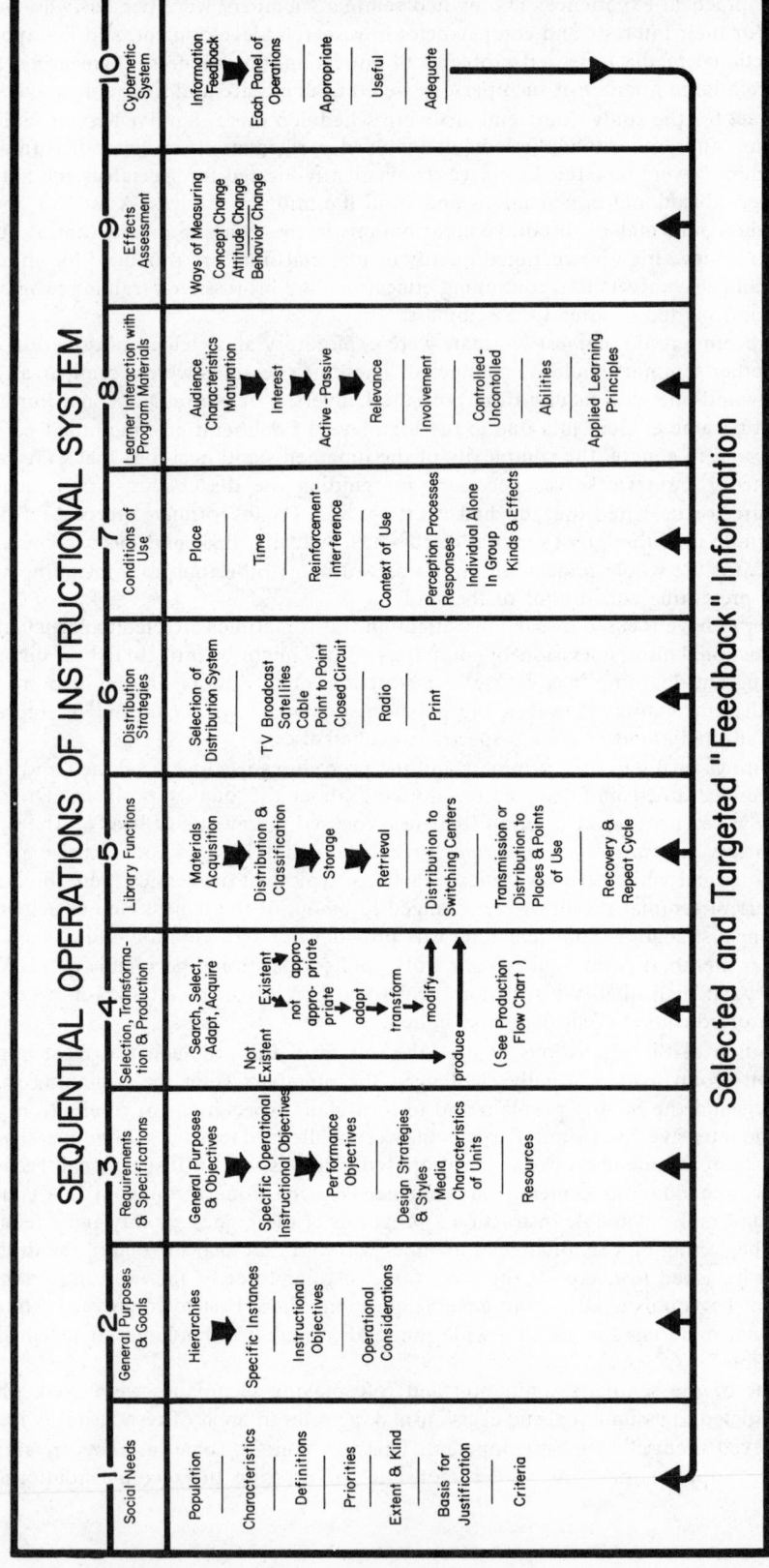

SEQUENTIAL OPERATIONS OF INSTRUCTIONAL SYSTEM

Selected and Targeted "Feedback" Information

1 Social Needs

Population

Characteristics

Definitions

Priorities

Extent & Kind

Basis for Justification

Criteria

2 General Purposes & Goals

Hierarchies

Specific Instances

Instructional Objectives

Operational Considerations

3 Requirements & Specifications

General Purposes & Objectives

Specific Operational Instructional Objectives

Performance Objectives

Design Strategies & Styles

Media

Characteristics of Units

Resources

4 Selection, Transformation & Production

Search, Select, Adapt, Acquire

Existent — appropriate / not appropriate

adapt

transform

modify

Not Existent — produce

(See Production Flow Chart)

5 Library Functions

Materials Acquisition

Distribution & Classification

Storage

Retrieval

Distribution to Switching Centers

Transmission or Distribution to Places & Points of Use

Recovery & Repeat Cycle

6 Distribution Strategies

Selection of Distribution System

TV Broadcast Satellites Cable Point to Point Closed Circuit

Radio

Print

7 Conditions of Use

Place

Time

Reinforcement-Interference

Context of Use

Perception Processes Responses

Individual Alone In Group

Kinds & Effects

8 Learner Interaction with Program Materials

Audience Characteristics Maturation

Interest

Active - Passive

Relevance

Involvement

Controlled-Uncontolled

Abilities

Applied Learning Principles

9 Effects Assessment

Ways of Measuring Concept Change Attitude Change Behavior Change

10 Cybernetic System

Information Feedback

Each Panel of Operations

Appropriate

Useful

Adequate

President of the United States for the commission on how adequate instructional programs for the media are to be produced on the highest possible levels of quality and effectiveness, what would be the content and form of your recommendations?" Or, again, "What are the most important requirements and conditions for producing instructional programs of the highest quality in your field of teaching?"

Early in almost all harvest seminars, the issue arose of how quality was to be defined. In order to expedite discussions, it was decided to define quality for all seminars after the first as being synonymous with effectiveness, and therefore, the full instigation, stimulation, and assurance of the production of the intended specified changes in the behavior of the defined population of learners.

There were two subordinate ideas: *first,* quality or effectiveness is a continuum of degrees of quantity that invite measurements and not an absolute quality or quantity, and *second,* the intended or proposed changes in behavior must be specified and clearly expressed so that the instructional objectives can be known by all those responsible for the management and regulation of the teaching and learning operations, including learners themselves.

The harvest seminar deliberations and discussions were recorded on audio-tape, analyzed, and written up in reports. Both the audio recording and the typed abstract of discussions became the main products and primary data base for this study.

Report Results   The early harvest seminars yielded two other results: *First,* it became clear that intelligent, experienced professionals who are interested in the useful and practical consequences of instructional methodology and in the contextual validation of the results of instruction cannot deal with the problem of quality when limited to inherent characteristics or attributes of instructional materials alone. These educational media professionals believe that integral sequences of events and broader contexts must be controlled and managed if high quality is to be achieved. Related to this viewpoint is the contemporary reluctancies to evaluate a single or even a few "independent" variables, or to make comparative effectiveness studies except for practical management purposes. This is clearly due to a growing realization that a large number of factors, conditions, and contingencies, including residues of the life history of the learner and the life history of units or programs of instructional materials, affects the changes of behavior known as learning. *Second,* there are large macroscopic educational management problems, priorities, finances, methodologies, production, procurement, distribution, use, and evaluations that must be solved satisfactorily before the fine microscopic research problems and their solutions can be dealt with effectively or indeed can have any significant practical effects on learning. Often the macroscopic override the microscopic factors. Not only during the early harvest seminars, but also during the entire series of twelve seminars involving a total of 117 hours of deliberation, a limited number of references were made and there was a lack of emphasis on the finding of controlled research and its relation to the quality of instructional materials for learning. The harvest seminar reports, without serious content editing, were included in a principal report entitled *Quality Factors in Instructional Materials.*[1]

Special Studies   The basic harvest seminars, the literature searches, and contemporary practices suggested special studies, two of which were speedily undertaken, subject to the limitations of time, funds, and staff assistance. First, it became abundantly clear that the prescriptions and formulas that are offered for the production, testing, revision, and retesting cycles in the preparation of instructional materials cannot be done practically except in centers which have the necessary characteristics. Therefore, more practical and short-cut procedures will continue to be required. Once again it was emphasized, also, that forms for guiding informed human judgments in assessing instructional units, lessons, and programs will continue to be needed and will serve useful purposes. Therefore, continuing a process begun fifteen years ago, yet another attempt was made to revise and make useful a measurement form, *Practical Procedure for Assessing Instructional Film and Television Programs.*[2] This judgmental form was tested by program professionals who used it to judge television programs and films nominated as being superior. The intent of this effort was to improve the evaluation form and the practical procedures for its use.

A second problem for study early emerged. It has been evident for several years from studies sponsored by the U.S. Office of Education that it is necessary to have a national complement of instructional material production centers or laboratories. These are required especially for production of nonprint materials. In some respects the research and development centers and regional education laboratories sponsored under Title IV of the Elementary and Secondary Education Act of 1965 served as models for developing, creating, producing, and testing instructional and experimental materials. These agencies are not expected to specialize in production. It was expected, therefore, that the Commission on Instructional Technology would need to consider whether or not to recommend federal support commensurate with the needs for a national complement of production and testing centers. Consequently, a special study was made of the places and facilities known to be producing instructional programs of high quality for the electronic media. A special report was written, Educational and Instructional Television Facilities Evaluation: Preliminary Practical Procedures.[3] The objective of the study was to begin to develop planning and evaluating procedure on the basis of direct observations of existent facilities and from inquiries made of all National Education Television (NET) stations. Television was accepted as a multi-media originating-distribution system and viewed as a good example of the kinds of demands that may be made in the future on new and advanced instructional material production centers.

A fourth substantive document was prepared. As was previously reported, members of the harvest seminars were invited and expected to present clear, succinct statements on their proposals of how to solve the quality of instructional materials. These statements, some of which were made orally, were edited and produced under the title of *Quality Factors in Instructional Materials: Significant Statements by Authorities.*[4]

The *Quality Factors in Instructional Materials* and *Significant Statements by Authorities* are the two main substantive reports. Those on program assessments and on facilities are expected to contribute to methodology. Whereas the assessment report will be found useful by teachers, producers of instructional materials, investigators, and users of the instructional media, the report on instructional television facilities will be the most useful to those who put into effect the recommendations of the Commission on Instructional Technology which have relevance to national complements of production centers.

In an attempt to engage the attention of the commission members, an audio tape recording was made especially for them. It presented a selected number of oral statements by authorities who commented on critical aspects as they saw them, of the quality problem of instructional materials. This tape was presented to the commission during its first meeting in Washington and a reference copy was deposited with the U.S. Office of Education.

A third kind of report has been presented. Earlier it was stated that the project on the quality problem would be recorded and reported in multi-media form. One hundred and seventeen hours of sound recordings were made of harvest seminar discussions. Typed transformations and records were made of all these tapes. Furthermore, in an attempt to produce a report that may be seen and heard by a larger than usual audience, working with WPSX-TV of The Pennsylvania State University, a ninety-minute summary report of the project was produced on videotape. The general and special titles were *Conversations on Educational Technology; C. R. Carpenter.* Marlowe Froke was the moderator. A separate sound tape of the commentary was made and put into circulation through the Audiotape Library, Audiovisual Services, The Pennsylvania State University.

The Investigator-Commissioner

In April 1968, the project director was invited to be one of nine members of the Commission on Instructional Technology. He was later made a member of the Executive Committee. Therefore, before the extended study for that commission was completed, its director was put into an extraordinarily favorable position for directly transmitting to the commission the general and special reports in printed, video tape and audio tape forms, but perhaps more importantly he was given the opportunity to communicate information and the effects of the study directly to the commission. Conditions of instructional technology, critical needs, and mature judgments based on evidence could be communicated verbally to the commission with appropriate timing and cogent arguments. Rarely has an investigator had a better opportunity to directly and speedily affect plans and policy proposals. It is believed that as a consequence this study had unusual effects on the work of the commission and the kinds of recommendations proposed to the President and the Secretary of Health, Education, and Welfare.

The staff work for the commission was done under contract with the Academy for Educational Development, Washington, D.C. As a commissioner, it became possible for the project director, partially as a result of this study, to give special assistance to the Academy in selecting staff members who represented the media professions, suggesting subjects and possible authors for contributed and commissioned resource papers, providing early and special bibliographies for commissioners, and recommending a special purpose Academy Information Center on the very large field of instructional technology. In addition, assistance was given about places and facilities which should be studied and observed by commissioners and staff members, and in arranging for instant seminars on urgent problems, modeled somewhat after the harvest seminars of the present study.

Transition

Therefore, it is clear that both the selection of the quality problem for the study, as it developed, and the selection of Penn State for conducting the study were fortunate. The results of the project had direct channels to the Commission on Instructional Technology. Some of the conclusions surely have corresponded with some of the recommendations of the commission.

Two additional observations complete the preparation for describing generally the results of this germinal study on conditions, factors, and contingencies of quality in instructional materials.

First, for ten years, much of the work in media of the U.S. Office of Education has been done under the headings of research and dissemination. However, most of the classes of activities designated as research have been development and application. Most of the dissemination activities sought to promote involvement of significant people and to influence them by instruction, information, and interactions to accept and to use instructional media.

The harvest seminars became, in the judgment of many participant-observers, extraordinarily effective as a method for communicating and exchanging information and for influencing the actively committed participants themselves. A basic condition to these effects was the selection of professionally competent and strongly interested men and women to compose the seminars. They were, also, personally involved in important live issues of the effectiveness of teaching and learning, and were interested in having for their work teaching materials of high quality. The groups were small, under twelve in number, and rather intense interactions occurred among seminar members. There was no escape for the timid into anonymity. Furthermore, each individual had final specific assignments for which the first part of the seminar could be preparation. This period could be used for scanning of experiences and knowledge, for selecting of a few most important points, and for formulating statements and recommendations. Each participant had a serious job of public, professional performance in the making of his personal statements before his colleagues and for the audio recording as well as for later publication. Finally, participants, by having role assignments, reacted with realism and the belief that their language may have consequences in terms of public policies.

The harvest seminars were also germinal seminars. They gave active responsible people from the same or neighboring universities and educational agencies the chances they continuously need, but rarely have, to think deeply and exchange judgments about fundamental issues of neglected subjects of teaching and learning, and about the quality of learning materials, resources, and technologies in terms of their effects on students.

The seminars were germinal in a second sense. They provided the somewhat unusual experience for most people to act as if, and with hope, that they could influence future legislation and federal support programs on matters of great importance, the improvement of the quality of instructional materials, of teaching and learning, and hence, the effectiveness and relevance of the educational system to the life of the nation.

Subject Headings and Key Terms
A Finding Procedure
for
Abstracts of Seminar Discussions
on
Quality Factors in Instructional Materials

The condensed substantive content yielded by the harvest seminars does not permit effective summarization. Therefore, the vast range of concepts and expressions necessitates a finding procedure. The following subject headings give also abbreviations of the reference seminar like *PSI* meaning Pennsylvania State University, Seminar I, and page number where the concept occurs.

Studies of the problems of the taxonomy of the media literature have led to the conclusion that work is urgently needed to compile key terms. The harvest seminars have yielded, by means of a deductive procedure, an extensive list of terms that may be used in discussions of instructional media and those factors related to the quality and effectiveness of instructional materials.

The subject headings are organized under the general panel headings of the chart entitled "Sequential Operations for Instructional System." * The selection and organization of key terms was done by Ruth J. Carpenter.

ABBREVIATIONS

Ind   Indiana University

ND   Notre Dame—Purdue Universities

*See chart on page 872.

Ill   University of Illinois

PSI   Pennsylvania State University—Seminar I

PSII   Pennsylvania State University—Seminar II

PSIII   Pennsylvania State University—Seminar III

PSIV   Pennsylvania State University—Seminar IV

Wash   Washington, D.C., National Association of Educational Broadcasters.

Atlanta   Atlanta, Georgia, Southern Regional Education Board

BR   Boca Raton, Florida Atlantic University

UGA   University of Georgia, Center of Continuing Education

QR   Quail Roost, North Carolina

Subject Headings and Key Terms
Quality Factors in Instructional Materials

1. SOCIAL NEEDS: (Ind 1, ND 1, PSI 1, PSII 1, Wash 1, Atl 1, BR 1, Ga 1, QR 1)
    1.1   National Goals (Ind 1)
    1.2.   University Role (PSII 1)
            1.2.1.   Administrative Decision Making (PSII 1)
    1.3.   Definitions (PSII 1)
            1.3.1.   Quality (PSII 1)
    1.4.   Priorities (ND 1)
    1.5.   Criteria (ND 1, Wash 1)
    1.6.   Extent and Kind (PSI 1, PSII 2, Atl 2, QR 1, ND 1)
            1.6.1.   Vocational Education (PSII 2, Atl 2, QR 1, ND 1)
            1.6.2.   Adult Education (PSI 2, Atl 2)
            1.6.3.   Education of the Disadvantaged (PSI 1, QR 1)
    1.7.   Federal Legislation (PSII 2, BR 1, QR 1)
    1.8.   *Basis for Justification*
    1.9.   *Population* (BR 1, Ga 1, PSI 1)
    1.10.   *Characteristics* (Wash 1, Ga 1)
            1.10.1. Specific Uses (Wash 1)
    1.11.   Logistical Support of Instructional Systems (Atl 1)

2. GENERAL PURPOSES AND GOALS (Ind 1, ND 2, PSI 2, PSII 3, Wash 2, PSIII 1, Atl 5, PSIV 1, Ga 2, QR 1)
    2.1   Instructional Objectives (Ind 1, ND 2, PSI 2, PSII 3, Wash 2, Atl 5, PSIV 1, Ga 2, QR 1)
            2.1.1.   Information Transfer or Proficiency Development (ND 2, QR 2)
            2.1.2.   Motivation of Students (ND 2, PSI 2, PSIV 1)
            2.1.3.   Counseling (ND 2)
            2.1.4.   Peer Group Reinforcement (ND 2, PSI 3)
            2.1.5.   Continuing Education (ND 2)
            2.1.6.   Research in Educational Methods (ND 2, PSIV 1, QR 2)

Results

What in general resulted from the study of factors, conditions, and contingencies affecting complex human learning?

First, to understand and to be able to produce instructional materials of high quality and effectiveness in a very wide range of kinds, those materials for a unit, a course, or a curriculum must have favorable conditions and factors operating over a very wide spectrum of resources, decisions, actions, interactions, and people-thing contingencies. Stated differently, to understand the *quality factors* of instructional materials requires the use of a systematic analysis of all significant and relevant conditions which operate during the life history, and over the full context of the conception, design, procurement, distribution, use, and evaluation of the materials. The discussions, after the first three *harvest seminars,* ranged over ten broad sets of factors or conditions. These headings symbolized generally the sets of factors and conditions that are believed to relate significantly to quality.

The following lists give some of the general subject headings that represent many but not all of the factors and conditions that are judged to be contingencies to *quality,* when *quality* is defined to mean the learning associated with defined and observable or detectable behavioral changes.

Sequential Operations of an Instructional System

1. Social Needs.

2. General Purposes and Goals.

3. Requirements and Specifications.

4. Selection, Transformation, and/or Production.

5. Library Functions.

6. Distribution Strategies.

7. Conditions of Use.

8. Learner Interactions with Materials.

9. Assessment and Measurement.

10. The Cybernetic Sub-system.

The Ideal Context

Within this complex operational system of elements and conditions which determines the effectiveness and efficiency of instructional materials, there are networks of interactions at all steps leading from the completion of the performance specifications and patterning of designs to effects assessments. Included are the sub-cycles of events that characterize procurement or production and testing. The library and distributive functions are equally interactive. Learning theory applications occur in the preparation phases and in the conditions or situations of use of the learning materials. Measurement and assessment procedures provide for the cybernetic network of effects which ideally are reported to the learners and which influence all interactions within the Sequential Operations System.

Themes   There were several major themes that developed, recurred, and were emphasized over and over again during the 117 hours of the deliberative discussion:

1. The "systems approach" and strategies were generally approved and used as a frame of reference for conceptualizing contingencies to quality of instructional materials.

2. There was agreement that the results of controlled and quantitative research on learning processes are most valuable guides, but they require translation, transformation, interpretation, and synthesis before useful application can be made for regulating learning.

3. Educators, teachers, and students must master the technologies of instructional media and avoid permitting the media to manage them.

4. For most complex instruction, several *modes* of communication will need to be used, preferably in optimized patterns, and herein lie three acute problems: (a) What are the interactional effects among two or more communication modes, e.g., sight and hearing and tactile modes? (b) What are the modes that are the most effective for defined kinds of learning tasks and for different learner characteristics? (c) How can estimates be made of the trade-off values in selecting and communicating theoretical concepts?

5. There was an agreement on a theme that was frequently reinforced, namely, that facilities acquisition and equipment developments had greatly out-distanced instruc-

tional program production and services for all media except print. Furthermore, the model of procurement used by publishers of instruction content and its organization and validation, seems not to be an effective model for the nonprint electronic media.

Systematic Approaches and Methods   The systems approach in education is being widely recommended and accepted on theoretical levels. The Systems Development Corporation, the Human Resources Research Organization, the American Institute for Research and many companies like IBM and RCA have developed and are promoting the concept of systems of instruction.

Generally, there has been oversimplification of the concept to the point where heterogenious assemblies of media have been described as systems. More correctly, a system includes all of those components, elements, factors, operations, and conditions which are significantly related to the results and objectives of a defined educational effort. The people parts of a system are often the most important determinants of the system's level of performance.

Thornton and Brown, in their excellent book, *New Media and College and University Teaching* (published by the Department of Audiovisual Instruction, NEA, in collaboration with the American Association for Higher Education) defines an instructional system as follows.[5]

> The materials, equipment, and other interrelated elements (including human components) of an assemblage that operates in an organized manner in handling the appropriate encoding of instructional messages and the distribution, use, and refinement of information. To be effective such a system must be sensitive to various stimuli and include elements for appropriate response, feedback, and adjustments. (p. 119)

Major Faults   With an understanding of the complexity of interacting factors in ordered interactional systems that affect the quality of media programs, it becomes clear that we are now in a position to diagnose faults, weaknesses, barriers, and barricades, in the instructional media programs, and thus we are in a position to correct them. What are *some* major faults in instructional media programs of schools, colleges and universities?

1. Failure to meet the difficult requirements of completing and perfecting the design phase for the sequential operations, and in particular, the failure to write performance specifications which are then compared with learning results or the changes in the behavior and performances of students.

2. Failure of not properly and accurately estimating and providing the essential resources of time, human competencies, funds, facilities, and materials that are essential for producing, testing, and effectively using media units and programs. The attitudes of educational poverty and unrealistically low expectancies associated with poor management result in attempts to do too much with too little. These conditions have dominated and deteriorated vast numbers of media programs and have made them ineffective even though acceptable locally where produced. "The wine is bitter but it is our wine."

3. Failure to provide adequate physical bases for work, including buildings, equipment, and facilities. Especially the lack of trained technical and professional people who have advanced skills in educational media production.

4. Failure to solve the *non*print library problems. Lack of access or difficult and delayed access to nonprint materials for use are major barriers to incorporating effectively media materials in instructional programs both in their preparation and production stages and in using them.

5. Failure in the area of inappropriate or ineffective conditions of use. Good distribution systems from media resource centers or from other sources are rare. Display systems in classrooms could be greatly improved. As a consequence, there is faulting of potentials for student interactions as well as restricted utility which increases costs per unit of instruction. Institutional independence and autonomy, the lack of broad cooperation, and the resulting limited utility, even of the few good materials, constitute a major fault in the application of contemporary media systems. In this connection, the use of distributive media and procedures could be a corrective step, and extensive interconnections as proposed by EDUCOM would be highly desirable national developments.

6. Failure to overcome *passivity* of the learner, involving the lack of response arrangements and records of the performances of students in mediated learning systems. Related is the frequent failure to provide for learners *knowledge of results* of their efforts to learn, and suitable reinforcement at the proper time and in the most effective form. The reactive and responsive media including those that are computer regulated are beginning to correct this fault.

Two Positive Suggestions　There are two considered and much debated proposals which, when applied, will reduce the resistance to the acceptance of media programs and greatly increase their instructional effectiveness. These proposals are aimed at levels of instruction from junior high school through higher, continuing, and professional education.

First, interactions of students with media productions and presentations should be directly with the information, the content, the stimulus materials. This kind of interaction can reduce many interference factors, including those related to activities of teachers, and can provide focus of attention in the perceptual fields for learners and clarity of meaning for the student. The potential for both individual and group learner interactions should be exploited. The focus proposed is on the essential primary information and not on a human mediator or teacher. Therefore, another favorable condition is accomplished: the avoidance of the introduction of a surrogate teacher into the learning situation because such surrogates may meet resistance from the person directly responsible for instruction and for the students in situations of use. Finally, if the materials can be kept cohesive, short, and flexible so that the new and adaptive patterns and sequences can be arranged by teachers and learners, levels of acceptance and use may be increased greatly as a consequence of involvement factors.

The second positive proposal is a radical reorientation in many current practices of producing and using instructional materials. It is that carefully produced and empirically tested instructional units should deal with the very core of units of courses for learning. The units of the course should be carried in the proper form by the required media and have included the basic essential conditions and regulators of that unit of learning. The units should have instructional completeness of treatment and be tested against what is required for a high level of learning. Instruction that is media based should not be complemental or supplemental to what a teacher does, but rather the other way around, the teacher should adapt, apply, explicate, and extend the mediated core materials.

Problems, Questions and Recommendations*

The discussions of the *harvest seminars* have led to the formulation of the following recommendations which have been made available to the Commission on Instructional Technology.

The important contribution of Lane E. Carpenter to the work of abstracting and formulating this statement is acknowledged.

Social Needs

1. There is an ubiquitous need for "on-the-job" training and information programs for working teachers. Radio and television local, regional, and national network programs could be used as a means of reaching and informing millions of teachers throughout the country.

    What proposals of the commission could create the "will" to do this and provide effective programs for the unlimited task of teacher training and development?

2. Assuming that solutions to social needs and conditions require accelerated rates of change, by the application of modern communication technology to education, it would be a possible means of achieving appropriately these degrees and rates of social change.

Goals and Purposes

3. National goals for education require continuous study; therefore, a national commission may be desirable to study continuously national goals and how they may be achieved including the uses of technology.

4. Periodic reformulations should be made in statements of national goals and policies reflecting current social needs and trends of social change. How are these adaptive reformulations to be accomplished?

5. Application of systems analysis to school and college work requires evaluations in terms of learning as an edn product or outcome; therefore, the consideration being given to requiring *minimum standards* of learning on a national basis is supportive of the recommendations for using the system analysis approaches to education and technology for getting the job done.

Planning and Legislation

6. Planning, designing, and administering educational enterprises require knowledge of the potentials and uses of instructional technologies by the *responsible and principal planners and administrators of education.* The appropriate employment of instructional technology cannot be included in educational planning by peripheral technologists who do not participate in central and important planning operations.

7. Informed opinion holds that the future will bring great increases in the speeds and capacities of *computer centers* which can be used on a cooperative basis by many different institutions. One problem is to develop effective educational uses of this great and growing computer capacity: (1) for regional and national administrative data, (2) for direct instruction, (3) for storing research and development data on a wide range of defined problems, and (4) for training uses and operation of computers.

8. What proposals could be the basis for creating *search* and *scanning procedures* for excellent existing instructional materials and for producing new programs of instruction and providing new supplemental units?

9. Policies are needed which would broaden and extend the many narrow and limited research and development projects conducted with federal funds, and also, to encourage creative inventiveness in the development and production of instructional materials.

10. The use of satellites requires many decisions in the near future which educators are not prepared to make. What should be done to ensure timely and valid decisions of the *educational and instructional* uses of satellites distribution systems?

11. Procedures are needed for vigilant and continuous definitions and redefinition of the *problems* of educational-instructional technology, and for designing and proposing solutions. What agency can be proposed which will serve these functions?

12. The commission should recommend whatever needs to be done at the national level to teach educators to write *clear and intelligible specifications* for apparatus, equipment, programs to meet instructional needs.

13. How can educators and industrial people of like interest make arrangements to work together from the statements of educational needs and problems through all steps to design equipment, facilities, and program development which will meet the needs and help solve the acute problems of instruction?

14. There is an urgent need for authoritatively based descriptions of the scale of *priorities of needs and instructional functions, and descriptions of the characteristics of the peoples to be served by specified media and media configurations wherever they live.*

15. Learning theories are needed for planning educational developments; therefore, a task force of distinguished scholars and psychologists should be appointed and supported continuously to work for sustained periods on the formulation of *valid and useful guiding theories* related to the practical management of learning processes. A part of the responsibility of the Learning Theory Task Force would be to derive a system of *theories of teaching* and another system of *theories of media applications, use and educational orientation of those who use media,* especially the producers of instructional programs.

16. Planning should be done which estimates *accurately* the practical requirements and alternatives of adequate means, including the uses of instructional technology for reaching important educational goals, and thus, assist moving education out of an accepted and prevailing culture of poverty.

17. The systems approach, including multi-media design features, suggests that a number of federal agencies and organizations now serving special media could be consolidated, coordinated, and related to more general educational functions and purposes.

18. What can be proposed to foster the creative production of varied and effective programs of instruction which serve principal functions of teaching and provide the essential conditions for learning? For example: Interactance? Responsiveness? Feedback? Personalization? Individualization? Responsible effort? Congruence of scope with complexity? Developing learner autonomy?

19. Rarely have the new broadcast media been used for testing and assessing *learning progress,* yet excellent models of possibilities exist for using these media for different kinds of testing and evaluations. What proposals can be made to foster development of the uses of measurement, testing, and assessment with appropriate media technologies?

20. What procedures and precautions are necessary to prevent mismangement in the purchasing of equipment, its lack of use, and its misuse?

21. A large and growing amount of computer time is available which could be used through telephone interconnections for research development, training, and direct instruction. What is required to encourage the use of *available* and *increasing* amount of computer time and capacity?

Organizations, Agencies, and Institutions

22. A system of *national production centers* for instructional materials should be planned and financed both with capital and operating funds. This should be a *production* network and not a broadcasting network. The system will need coordinating on the state, regional, and national levels. What should the commission recommend?

23. In case instructional production centers or laboratories are recommended, the question may arise of how the centers may be characterized. The following statements begin this characterization.

    a. They should be funded on a permanent basis.

    b. Centers would use teams of experts in content, productions, evaluation, and other essential functions.

    c. Centers should be free operating agencies without overlays of too much federal and state administrative control.

    d. All production must be tested under conditions of actual use.

    e. Centers must be responsive to the educational "marketplace."

    f. Centers must be staffed by highly trained specialists who speak a common language.

    g. The centers must be very well equipped.

24. Generally, throughout the country, the tendency is for schools, colleges, and universities to try to build their own *independent* and *complete* production facilities. A considerable body of opinion would have this supplemented by cooperative efforts, shared facilities, and shared uses of products.

25. The established research and development centers and regional education laboratories should be urged to provide and focus on efforts of using technologies as development forces, both in formal and informal instruction.

26. Institutions which train teachers at all levels should conduct media familiarization and indoctrination programs, and they should be provided with the best materials, new equipment, and financial support for this instruction.

27. Universities are important "change agents" and, therefore, should be given special means and responsibilities for appropriately introducing instructional technology into education at all levels of the educational system.

28. There is need for new extra-educational agencies or changes in old agencies, along with a corps of trained professional people to use *effectively* existing and emerging educational-instructional technologies for solving national problems and meeting social needs. What new agencies can the commission describe on the federal level?

29. There should be established working *instructional laboratories* as places where a full range of new equipment and apparatus is being used successfully for carrying out the essential sets of functions of teaching and for providing favorable conditions for learning. Such laboratories should have the most modern and proved types of equipment, and therefore, they should be magnificent showcases of the recent developments for industry. The laboratories should have frequent replacement of new equipment so that the latest models would be always on display.

30. What can be recommended for reorganizations of educational institutions that will prepare the way for the justifiable acceptance and use of instructional technology?

31. Support is needed for a wide range of *experimental explorations in* searching for new and effective kinds of programs for instructional technology. The pattern of proposed effort would be more like that of the "experimental theater" than like analytical experiments dealing with controlled variables.

Public Relations, Information, and Dissemination

32. The general public, and many special publics, urgently need new and valid information about schools and colleges and related technologies. Therefore, it is advisable to recommend the use of an extended base of the broadcast media to describe, demonstrate, and inform the public about instructional technologies and their effective uses in education.

33. Educational efforts should be made to convince educators of the validity and efficaciousness of *"representative"* (symbolic) communications compared with real three-dimensional objects. By using media, models of good teaching may be made more informative than actual "in-person" demonstrations. Also, some chemistry, biology, and physics demonstrations can be made more informative than some kinds of regular laboratory exercises.

34. Programs are needed to describe vividly and to explicate *social issues* and *educational efforts* as a means of informing the public about education. How can the public and legislators be informed about the availability, potentials, and valid uses of instructional technology?

35. The public is probably confused about, or does not make discriminations between, *instructional* and *public* television and radio, and between these and *educational* television and radio. Therefore, the commission must clarify these distinctions as a basis for making recommendations.

36. To be convincing, there needs to be some clear, evident, and dramatic cases of successful applications of instructional technologies, and the setting for such demonstrations could be the "inner" or the "central" city or impoverished rural areas.

37. What proposals can be made to implement the multi-media systems approach when currents of opinion runs so strongly for working with separate media? Instructional television, for example, is itself a multi-medium. Consideration from the system's point of view must be given to all channels and modes of television as well as to relevant events *before* and *after* instruction by television. How can these complex ideas be made clear to the public and to teachers at all levels of education?

38. What proposals can be made for providing information about plans and productions of programs for the media which will serve as a basis for reducing the amount of duplication throughout the nation of productions of instructional units, courses, and curriculum.

Professional and Educational Development and Training

39. Attention should be given to the rewards and incentives and to changes in values that

attract college and university professors of superior talent to the demanding work of producing instructional programs.

40. Means and programs must be proposed for meeting the acute shortages of professional people who are especially qualified to work in the media field and especially for producing and testing instructional programs.

41. There needs to be a clear definition of the *roles of teachers* and the *roles of "technology"* and their interactions, as well as interactions with different levels of learning, subject matter, and learning audiences.

42. How can the fear be reduced of the threat of mediated instruction to the statuses of teachers? What compromises in the interest of gaining acceptance can be made *at the various levels* of the educational system?

43. Process histories should be made and shared of research and development projects, especially of those dealing with the production of instructional materials, so that both what was done rightly and what was done wrongly can be known and reviewed.

44. Programs of graduate training are needed which emphasize the development of *science educators* in order to produce more *scientists*. The same need for professional development exists in other fields.

45. Professional development in *curriculum design* should require advanced professional training in communications *using media* for subject specialists, media professionals, and those people who organize curriculum.

46. The training of professional media producers required interdisciplinary development in three areas: content, learning theory, and message design, now therefore, how is this interdisciplinary training to be provided by universities that are so tightly organized along departmental lines.

PUBLISHED REPORTS

Carpenter, C. R., and Ruth J. Carpenter. *Abstracts of Seminar Discussions on Quality Factors in Instructional Materials.* The Pennsylvania State University, University Park, Pennsylvania 16802. U.S. Office of Education. Project Number OEC-1-7-071142-4372. ERIC Media Center, Stanford University, California. 1968.

Carpenter, C. R., and Susan S. Reilly. *Quality Factors in Instructional Materials.* The Pennsylvania State University, University Park, Pennsylvania 16802. U.S. Office of Education. Project Number OEC-1-7-071142-4372. ERIC Media Center, Stanford University, California. 1968.

Carpenter, C. R. and Marlowe Froke. *Description of a Practical Procedure for Assessing Instructional Film and Television Programs.* The Pennsylvania State University, University Park, Pennsylvania 16802. U.S. Office of Education. Project Number OEC-1-7-071142-4372. ERIC Media Center, Stanford University, California. 1968.

Carpenter, C. R. and Lane E. Carpenter. *Educational and Instructional Facilities Evaluation: Preliminary Practical Procedures.* The Pennsylvania State University, University Park, Pennsyvlania 16802. U.S. Office of Education. Project Number OEC-1-7-071142-4372. ERIC Media Center, Stanford University, California. 1968.

Carpenter, C. R. *Selected Bibliography of Summarizing and Capstone Reports No. 1.* For the Commission on Instructional Technology and Academy for Educational Development. The Pennsylvania State University, University Park, Pennsylvania 16802. U.S. Office of Education. Project Number OEC-1-7-071142-4372. ERIC Media Center, Stanford University, California 1968.

Carpenter, Lane E. *Statements made by Harvest Seminar Participants on the Quality Factor Problems—Audio Tape.* Library—Audiovisual Services, The Pennsylvania State University, University Park, Pennsylvania 16802. U.S. Office of Education. Project Number OEC-1-7-071142-4372. ERIC Media Center, Stanford University, California. 1968.

Froke, Marlowe. *Conversations on Instructional Technology: C. R. Carpenter.* A 90 minute Video Tape. The Pennsylvania State University, University Park, Pennsylvania. 16802 (WPSX) 1968.

REFERENCES

1. Carpenter, C. R., and Ruth J. Carpenter. *Abstracts of Seminar Discussions on Quality Factors in Instructional Materials.* The Pennsylvania State University, University Park, Pa. 16802. U.S. Office of Education, Project Number OEC-1-7-071142-4372. ERIC Media Center, Stanford University, California, 1968.

2. Carpenter, C. R., and Marlowe Froke. *Description of a Practical Procedure for Assessing Instructional Film and Television Programs.* The Penn. State Univ., Univ. Park, Pa. 16802. U.S. Off. of Educ., Project No. OEC-1-071142-4372. 1968.

3. Carpenter, C. R., and Lane E. Carpenter. *Educational and Instructional Facilities Evaluation: Preliminary Practical Procedures.* Penn. State Univ., Univ. Park, Pa. 16802. U.S. Off. of Educ., Contract #OEC-1-7-071142-4372. ERIC Media Center, Stanford Univ., Calif. 1968.

4. Carpenter, C. R., and Susan S. Reilly. *Quality Factors in Instructional Materials: Significant Statements by Authorities.* Other information same as Ref. 3.

5. Thornton, James W., and James W. Brown. *New Media and College Teaching.* Publication-Sales Section, National Education Association, 1201 Sixteenth St., N.W., Washington, D.C. 20036, 1968, pp. 185.

100.
Some Problems
Of Technological Innovation

by *THOMAS P. HUGHES*
Prof., Hist. of Tech.
Institute of Technology
Southern Methodist
University

The purpose of this essay is to raise questions about the process of innovation; hopefully, questions that might be asked by those interested in technological innovation in the field of education. The questions, if some are the right ones, should focus attention upon problems arising when technological innovation in education is considered and sought. If anticipated, the problems can perhaps then be met with considered decisions rather than hastily improvised responses so often the case with technological change.

Questions about technological innovation in education will be ones that can be raised about technological innovation in general. The assumption is that from the history of technological innovation in many fields a general concept of the innovation process can be formulated and that questions based on the general model will be relevant to the particular case of education. Admittedly the question may appear unsophisticated to the expert in the field of education but the author hopes that the expert will find the point-of-view fresh and accept the lack of sophistication as a challenge leading to further refinement and definition.

The author has formulated his concept of the innovation process from study of the history of technology in the nineteenth and twentieth centuries, both here and abroad. He has concentrated almost two decades of study upon invention, development, and innovation in the United States, Germany, and Great Britain. Focus has been upon the lives of inventors, engineers, and entrepreneurs working in electricity, chemistry, and guidance and control. Certainly for the purposes here, concentration in information technology would strengthen the author's credentials, but it is also relevant to observe that his concern has been with complex technology involving many things, diverse organizational structures, various processes, multitudes of people, and very large sums of money—factors not unknown in education.

Before proceeding some definitions seem desirable because analysis of the process of innovation has not yet become so familiar as to preclude semantic difficulties. The word invention, for example, is variously used. In this essay invention refers to both the inventor's intellectual conception of a thing or a process and to the simple physical model that manifests the conception. The invention is the inventor's response to a problem delimited by circumstances within which the invention should function. Because the invention is primarily intellectual activity and the inventor is not able to anticipate and comprehend all the variables, the circumstances envisaged and the idea of the invention are usually simplifications.

Development follows invention. Development is the designing of models of the invention that will function effectively in more complex environments than that originally conceived of by the inventor. The more complex environments range from mathematically simulated ones to scale laboratory reproductions and field tests. The process of development usually reveals inadequacies and opportunities not thought of earlier; sometimes these lead to sub-inventions that improve the total invention. Invention has so captured the popular mind that the ingenuity and engineering ability demanded by development is not fully appreciated. If technological innovation in education is desired, provisions should be made for thorough development.

Innovation comes when the developed invention is introduced into the actual environments or circumstances in which it must function effectively. Often these actual environments differ in detail from those anticipated during the development process. Therefore, it is important to note, innovation also reveals inadequacies and opportunities, and the responsible enterprises and entrepreneurs continue development and even sub-invention after innovation. In education, the classroom is one example of an "actual environment"; the social environment is a more encompassing one.

Though the term innovation is useful in describing the introduction of the developed invention into the actual environment, the term is also used to designate the entire process from invention to use. The term innovation is used in this paper in both the limited and the broader sense, the author trusting that the context assures clarity. Usually the expression "innovation process" is used to designate the encompassing process. The individual or enterprise presiding over the encompassing process of innovation is called the entrepreneur while those who develop inventions are termed engineers. "Inventor" still serves well to identify the conceptualizer and first creator although the term has unfortunately fallen into disuse, having been replaced by the vague term researcher. Technological innovation in education will involve inventors, engineers, and entrepreneurs.

Too often in the past innovation has been discussed without introducing the idea of a system. This omission has not simplified the discussion but limited and sometimes distorted it. If one insists upon thinking of an invention only as a component rather than a system then consideration of many of the major inventions of the past and future is precluded. Thomas Edison should be remembered for a system of incandescent lighting involving a generator, a distribution network, and an incandescent bulb—this is the systematic way in which he consciously conceived his invention. The creators of Ford's River Rouge plant conceived of a system of integrated units for producing automobiles from raw materials, and their conception can with reason be called an invention. It seems likely that technological innovation in education has and will also involve the invention of complex systems; thus it seems advisable to introduce and use the term in this discussion.

The essence of a system is the interdependence of its components. Most of the components are variables dependent upon other components in the system. A component in the system, however, may be independent of the influence of the other components dependent upon it; in short, an independent variable as far as the system is concerned. This independent variable is dependent, however, upon forces in the external environment if the system is an open one. If the system is closed, then this independent variable grows or changes according to some internal logic. A system has usually been created to fulfill a purpose or to solve a problem, and the purpose or problem is the organizing principle of the system. In the case of educational technology, the system output—the independent variable—may be information or methodology provided the student. The system would then seem to be an organization of teachers, machines, and processes systematized to provide the information or methodology. Though superficially the student appears to be the environment, defining the needs and posing the problems to be responded to by the innovative process, further consideration suggests that the students may be dependent upon a larger system, perhaps society, with their needs defined by the larger system. Therefore, innovation may be a response to the needs and opportunities of the larger system (society), or to a subsystem (the students), or both.

Finally in the matter of definitions, the author will refer to "those presiding over or stimulating" technological innovation. This reference is to governmental agencies, private foundations, congressional committees, and other organizations that wish to act as catalytic agents, initiating or accelerating the innovative process but not participating directly in it. These catalytic agents should be distinguished from the entrepreneur who manages and participates in the invention, development, and innovation.

The terms having been defined, attention can now be turned to the first question that might be asked by those interested in innovation in education—will the innovation be the introduction of a new system or the improvement of an existing system? Whether the innovation is a new system or an improvement influences the character of the invention-development-innovation process and the options of those stimulating or presiding over innovation. To explore this question, the case of Thomas Edison introducing a new system will be presented; subsequently, an example of improvement will be described and analyzed.

About 1878 Thomas Edison, already famed for his inventions in the field of telegraphic devices, decided to invent a system of electric lighting that could take the market for interior lighting then supplied by gaslight. There was of course the possibility for an inventor to improve the existing gaslight system and this was subsequently done with the incandescent mantle. Edison, however, experienced in electricity—but not in gas lighting—decided to try a new system.

His decision was not as bold as it might first appear. Edison, the electrician, knew from the technical literature and the patents here and abroad of the many electrical generators on the market, knew as well of the success of pioneers in the field of electric-arc lighting, and also of the efforts of others to invent an incandescent bulb. The state of the art and his self-confidence convinced him that the probability of his successfully inventing and developing the new system was high. He also took into account the material and human resources he could draw upon because of his fame and his growing wealth.

Before allocating these resources for the project he analyzed the need, or market. He and his helpers decided that New York's Wall Street district was a suitable environment for innovation. Many factors entered into his decision including the need for light in tall closely-packed buildings cut off from daylight; the high population density which minimized the length of distribution lines; the wealth of the potential customers; and the publicity that could be obtained in circles able to finance lighting systems elsewhere. In his analysis and decision Edison was fulfilling a cardinal requirement of successful invention, development, and innovation—establishing the existence of a need and defining the problem arising from that need. Successful innovators like Edison are not men ahead of their time and out of place like the garret inventors of legend are presumed to have been.

Having accepted a practical problem, Edison set to work his invention and development staff at his Menlo Park laboratory. The team possessed competence in electrical and chemical invention, machine tools and machine design, glass blowing, and even in higher mathematics. As the leader of the invention and development team, Edison decided what the major subsystems and components of his lighting system would be and then assigned the associated problems to the most competent members of the team. Because he was inventing and developing a new system, not improving an old one, he thought about the major components in relationship to one another, and he and his team developed them simultaneously. Out of the thinking and the experiments came his decision to strive for an economically competitive and technologically feasible high-resistance incandescent bulb, a low-voltage direct-current generator, and a system of parallel distribution. There is no need to describe these here, but it is important to stress that the characteristics of one component determined characteristics of another. Furthermore the laboratory and test models of each were tested in conjunction with the others to optimize the system. These are some of the realities of systems invention and development.

Though Edison worked in the last century, his development techniques were ones still viable in technological innovation today. To avoid costly errors in full-scale or production models he tested or experimented with mathematical models, physical simulations, and pilot plants. As the models and the environments became increasingly complicated, or more like the actual ones in which the system was to be used, inadequacies and opportunities were discovered and responded to. Even after a station on Pearl Street was supplying customers with light, post-innovational development continued. Subsequent Edison stations embodied the improvements. There seems reason to anticipate that the innovation process in education technology will involve a similar approach.

Edison's innovation was not financed by the gaslight companies. Those with vested interest or fixed capital in the prevailing system of lighting did not preside over or manage the innovation of a competing system. On the other hand, the gaslight industry might have financed an Edison innovation that would have improved the gas lighting system. Fortunately for Edison he had won such fame as an inventor that he could interest Wall Street financiers in backing him against vested interests. The problem of a would-be entrepreneur finding financial support for a new system of technology that would displace the prevailing way of doing things in the educational field might prove an even greater challenge than that faced by Edison.

Nor did Edison turn to existing enterprises to manufacture and market his system. He and his co-workers established new companies to manufacture the generators, the light bulbs, the insulated distribution lines, and the other necessary components. An Edison company was also established to operate the Pearl Street Station. Eventually these manufacturing companies piled profits on top of those earned by licensing the system, but the fact that Edison as entrepreneur carried the entire project through from conception to marketing suggests the tremendous drive, resources, and persistence demanded in this outstanding example of systems innovation. Many of the major systems inventors have had to nurse, cultivate, and launch their inventions (Fulton, Morse, Westinghouse, McCormick, and Ford are a few of the inventor-entrepreneurs that come immediately to mind). Edison and others innovating systems have had to create institutions for each stage: invention and development (research and development laboratories); and innovation (manufacturing and marketing organizations).

Many examples of innovations to improve existing systems can also be drawn from the history of technology. The case of Elmer Sperry improving ocean transportation should be sufficient to establish a contrast with Edison's systems innovation. To describe Sperry's improvement of a system, it is first necessary to think of a ship as a system of transportation functioning in an ocean environment. If the ship is viewed in this perspective then it is seen to consist of, among other things, a hull, a propulsion system, and guidance and control components. (The latter include a compass, a helmsman, a helm, a steering engine, and a rudder.) In the decades before World War I the ship system had evolved from a wooden sailing ship to an iron-hulled steamship.

The inventors and engineers who contributed to the evolution of the ship did not follow a preconceived systematic plan as did Edison and his staff with their electric-lighting system. Instead, innovations followed upon recognition of inadequacies or opportunities revealed by unbalances or reverse salients in the evolving system. In the case of the ship, for example, the introduction of the iron hull established an inadequacy of the magnetic compass; it became a reverse salient in an expanding front. The problem arose because the steel hull shielded the magnetic compass from the earth's magnetic lines of force and the iron hull took on magnetic characteristics of its own which confused the compass.

The sea captains might have been content to accept the errors of the compass and steer somewhat off-course if competition among the world's navies on the eve of World War I had not stimulated efforts to perfect the technology of naval warfare, especially gunnery. The inadequacies of the magnetic compass stood starkly and ominously revealed when it could not provide a precise reference line for the long-range guns. An improved compass, a ship system component that superficially seemed of minor importance, would increase the overall efficiency of the innovating navy. Only with an improved compass could the advantages implicit in the higher quality gun powders, the better steel gun barrels, and improved methods of controlling and directing the turrets be realized.

The stimulus of competition with similar systems played a leading role in compass innovation. After learning in the first decade of this century of the success the German fleet was having with a gyrocompass, the American Navy encouraged an American inventor familiar with gyroscopes to invent and develop a compass that would be an improvement upon the German. The account of how Elmer Sperry created his gyrocompass for the Navy is an interesting case of directed invention and development, but here it is important to stress that the Navy, with a vested interest in the naval-warfare system, presided over the improvement of the system. The Navy not only provided the ships for testing the Sperry gyrocompass, but held out the promise of contracts when the compass was proven. These contracts subsequently provided Sperry the funds to enlarge his manufacturing facilities and to carry on post-innovational development.

The subsequent history of the gyrocompass throws more light on the process of improvement of existing systems. Introduction of the more accurate compass created imbalances, or revealed inadequacies, elsewhere in the system. It was discovered that the newly acquired precision was often lost in communicating the information from the compass to the gun crews or gunnery control. To rectify this reverse salient an electrical communications system involving repeater compasses and information display devices was invented and developed by Sperry, now deeply involved in the system and aware of its inadequacies and opportunities. All of this was on the eve of World War I; immediately after the war Sperry took advantage of the opportunity offered by the improvements in the compass and communications of the ship to invent and develop automatic steering. The system was continuing to expand as improvements introduced new imbalances and, in this case, opportunities.

The Edison and Sperry cases raise the large question whether those interested in technological innovation in education wish to preside over the innovation of new systems, or improvements of the existing ones. Before the catalytic agencies can meaningfully answer this question they must define the educational systems that might be replaced or improved upon. Edison defined his electric system by its output to the environment (the placing of light in a dark interior environment); the Navy did also (the placing of destructive shells precisely in an enemy environment). Defining Sperry's gyrocompass from the position of the naval officers responsible for the efficiency of the ship, it was an improvement in the system. From the point-of-view of a magnetic-compass manufacturer the gyrocompass was a new compass system dependent upon the gyroscope and the earth's rotation rather than upon the magnetic needle and the earth's magnetism. From the perspective of an architect, Edison's incandescent light was an improvement in a building while the gaslight interests saw the Edison light as a new system. To define the system, despite the difficulty, is necessary, however, in order to organize thought and action. It will also help anticipate the attitudes of those persons in positions to encourage or discourage innovation.

After the system has been defined and after the question of replacement or improvement has been considered, other related questions, suggested by history, follow. Is the innovation to be planned and managed as was the case with Edison, or is it expected to occur by the free action of laws perhaps analogous to those found by Adam Smith? If a system is to be replaced, can those with interests vested in it be expected to plan it or accept it? If one is to be improved, how will the inadequacies or opportunities be revealed if the system is not in close competition with other systems? If the system is to be replaced will those planning it be able to coordinate the invention and development of the numerous components; if the system is to be improved how will those responsible anticipate the imbalances and the new opportunities? These are only a few questions which may be applicable to the educational situation; history and thought can raise countless more.

Assuming that the existing educational system will be replaced, or at least improved upon, by technology, then a troublesome and infrequently recognized problem may arise. Will the technological innovation take on a momentum opposing further innovation? The character of technological momentum and its effect can be illustrated by reference to the Edison and the Sperry histories. In the Edison case his system involved generators, transmission lines, lights and so on; in the case of Sperry the compass required extremely complex components. Both the lighting system and the gyrocompass required expensive manufacturing facilities. Not only were these expensive, but the facilities used in invention and development were also costly. The compass and the lighting system represented considerable investment of capital and were durable. This long term investment in a particular way of doing things built up a technological momentum. The men and instructions responsible for the momentum then made decisions and took actions maintaining it.

Consider, for example, the technological momentum of the Edison system and its effect upon subsequent innovation. Edison, his companies, his financial backers, and the central stations that were his customers all had vested interests in the particular characteristics of his system. The manufacturing plants were tooled to make the many components that fit into his system, and the central stations were built to use them. Threatened by the introduction of other systems with different characteristics, the Edison people and companies, especially Edison, himself, put up a determined resistance known as "the battle of the systems." In order to make it appear unsafe, the Edison interests even went so far as to successfully promote the use of the competing high-voltage alternating-current Westinghouse system for electrocution in the New York State Prison.

In the last century technological momentum has increased because of mass production. The increase has resulted from heavy investment in labor-saving devices—machines and processes—which are durable and demand full utilization to repay investment. These machines and processes have under the mass-production system usually been highly specialized, all of which makes innovation and the change in product economically unattractive. The remarkable similarity of the incandescent bulb today to Edison's, for example, results in part from technological momentum. To change the voltage, the screw base, and the overall dimensions after these have been embodied in the production and use system would involve not only a large expenditure but also considerable inconvenience to consumers. Because education involves a mass market, the tendency to mass production and heightened technological momentum seems likely.

Technological momentum as a factor retarding innovation has more complexities than can be explored here. Emphasis has been on the economics of fixed, specialized, capital, but other forces contributing to technological momentum can be indicated. Once a way of producing, or doing, has been established by machines and processes, for example, the people who have learned how to work with, or manage, the technology are reluctant to abandon it for new systems. Elmer Sperry found, for example, that while naval officers under the pressure of competition from other navies adopted the gyrocompass, the merchant-marine officers and men were extremely reluctant to do so. Not subject to the same intense competitive pressure, they resisted changes in the customary way of doing things. The new compass brought many operational and maintenance problems strange to the crew. It seems reasonable to assume, however, that humans in technological systems are more resourceful and flexible than machines.

The resistance offered by technological momentum to innovation has been stressed here in order to suggest that this momentum will develop as a result of technological innovation in the educational system unless steps are taken to counter the tendency. The educational system is one subject to mass production because of the large number of students involved. Therefore the danger exists that if new educational technology involving machines is introduced, the drift will be toward mass production in order to lower costs. This raises the question whether those interested in technological innovation in education should consider going against the American trend by avoiding standardization, limiting heavy investment in durable and highly-specialized machines, and accepting the higher costs of small-scale production of non-standardized technology.

It might be argued that customary ways of doing things have usually raised barriers to innovation whether or not machines have been involved. There is truth in this, but the investment in durable and specialized technology contributes most to technological momentum. Instead of equating technological innovation with machines and utensils as did inventors and engineers in Edison's and Sperry's day, those interested in innovation in education today might consider the invention and development of systems in which man is placed as a major component. This might introduce in the system resourcefulness and flexibility that would reduce the build-up of technological momentum, and encourage subsequent innovation.

To overcome technological momentum, if it exists, and to generally direct and carry through invention, development, and innovation entrepreneurial force and an entrepreneur are needed. Attention will now be turned to this important aspect of the innovative process. These terms have customarily been used by business and economic historians in connection with businessmen and institutions, but in this discussion focus will be upon the inventor and engineer who functions as an entrepreneur.

The inventor-entrepreneur is the individual who leads and directs invention, development, and innovation of technology. His prime commitment is to invention, but he follows through with development and innovation because of his determination to see his invention used. Both Edison and Sperry insisted that their work was more sweat than inspiration. The invention was the inspiration; the development and innovation the years of sweat. Sperry often attributed his success to persistence and courage, characteristics associated with the entrepreneur. As a young man he learned by failure in innovation that to his genius as an inventor had to be added the knowledge and experience of the development engineer, and the abilities of a fund raiser, business organizer, and salesman. Edison, as noted above, also had these capabilities in large measure. In order to promote innovation in educational technology the entrepreneurial types must be identified, attracted, and supported.

The entrepreneurial function can be institutionalized. Outstanding examples have been the research and development laboratories established by inventor-entrepreneurs to amplify their potential. Edison's laboratory at Menlo Park, New Jersey, and his larger laboratory at Orange, New Jersey, were both objectifications of his own inventive, engineering, and innovative inspiration and sweat. Sperry's gyroscope company, founded in 1910, gave him a staff and facilities for exploitation of the gyroscope field by the introduction of new applications. The Sperry Gyroscope Company remained primarily an invention and development company even after it began manufacturing its innovations. Edison's, Sperry's and many other inventor's institutionalization of their powers by the creation of laboratories and research and development firms should suggest the fallaciousness of the assumption that an inventor or inventor-entrepreneur is always a "lone" inventor. Those interested in innovation in the educational field should look for the inventive-entrepreneurial essence whether embodied in an institution or a person.

The difference between an independent inventor-entrepreneur and one who is dependent needs to be stressed for the two tend toward different kinds of innovation. The independent inventor-entrepreneur, whether an individual or an institution, is not a part of a larger organizational structure upon which he depends for a definition and as assignment of problems. The dependent is easily recognized as the employee or the research and development laboratory of an industrial corporation or government agency. The larger organization of which the dependent inventor-entrepreneur is a part has a vested interest in existing systems, and through its other departments, especially sales and service in the case of an industrial corporation, is aware of the needs and opportunities of the system in which it is heavily invested.

The characteristics of the two general types of inventor-entrepreneurs and of the innovation which is likely to come from each of them can be suggested by a brief exploration of the histories of Edison and Sperry and related laboratories. For a few years Edison acted as inventor-entrepreneur for the Edison companies that were forerunners of General Electric, but he then asserted his independence by establishing and maintaining his own laboratory; G.E. then founded the General Electric Laboratory in 1900. For a time Sperry's gyroscope company was used "by the Navy Department . . . as nothing short of a 'brain mill' and experimental laboratory," but Sperry's research and development company became more independent after World War I when the Navy established its own research and development facility, the Naval Research Laboratory. The most significant aspect of these events from the point of view of those interested in technological innovation is that Edison and Sperry eventually chose the independent course while General Electric and the Navy established dependent research and development facilities.

To explain why Sperry and Edison preferred to choose their own problems and do undirected research would demand an exploration of the psychology of the inventor; to explain the needs of General Electric and the Navy is less difficult. Both wanted a dependent research facility to improve upon the existing systems in which they had deeply vested interests. An outstanding example of directed invention and development at the General Electric Research Laboratory was the introduction of improvements in incandescent bulbs. By the end of the nineteenth century the carbon-filament lamp, the core of the Edison and then General Electric system, had reached its limits. In Europe several scientists introduced new lamps using metallic oxide, osmium, tantalum, and tungsten filaments. All of these filaments were commercially developed and when introduced in America challenged the dominance of General Electric and its carbon filament. When it became obvious to General Electric that it had to innovate to retain its place, the company had its laboratory focus upon the improvement of incandescent lighting, especially filaments. Dr. Willis R. Whitney, the first director of the laboratory, introduced in 1904 the greatest improvement made in the carbon lamp since the early 1880's; then in 1911 the laboratory completed the development of the ductile tungsten filament, a major technological innovation and a commercial triumph. This is not the place, however, to explore the remarkable successes of the industrial research laboratory. The intent is to argue that thinking historically and logically one would expect the dependent research and development facility to stress systems improvements.

One reason the dependent facility is effective in inventing and developing improvements in existing systems is that the sales and service department, in close contact with the market in which the system functions, keep the research and development laboratory informed of system inadequacies or opportunities. In the case of Elmer Sperry and his company, he personally conducted the company sales effort because the customers were few and large, and because he knew the highly complex product. As a result of his full exposure to the Navy system, when he and his company were closely tied to it, he frequently saw and acted upon the opportunities for systems improvement. According to one story, he realized the need for an improvement in the communications system of the battleship when one turret captain misunderstanding an order almost sank the ship on which Sperry was observing rather than the target vessel. Sperry soon had a visual display incorporating compass readings, gun positions, and gun-control orders.

The independent inventor-entrepreneurs have a less obvious and direct way of identifying need. The question arises how those interested in promoting innovation would contact and motivate the independent inventor-entrepreneurs. In the cases of both Sperry and Edison, publicity, the state of the art, and the availability of capital were prime factors. When Edison decided to invent and develop his electric-light system considerable publicity was being accorded the new electric arc-light systems in Europe and America. These systems were publicized in the popular press and fully described in the technical. Critics of the systems pointed out that the arc light was not suited to confined spaces. The state of electrical technology and science as described in the technical journals and patents indicated to Edison a favorable state of the art. Furthermore, the temper of the times was such that the successful Edison could interest Wall Street in investing in invention. In the case of Sperry, the naval armaments race during the decade before World War I publicized the needs of the Navy, and increased funds made possible modest appropriations supporting invention and development. In short, the independent inventor-entrepreneur does not have a related institution to probe the environment or market for needs and opportunities, but must depend upon generally available information and that publicized at professional meetings, in trade journals, and in scientific periodicals. Sperry seldom missed a professional meeting in his area of interest and he regularly surveyed the literature. Edison's library, preserved at his Orange, New Jersey laboratory, shows his professional interest in the literature. The intention here is to suggest that those interested in technological innovation in education should widely publicize the needs and opportunities in the field. It should be made known if research and development funds are accessible. Furthermore, it seems wise to encourage critics of the existing educational system to publicize their views in sources read by inventors and engineers, especially if technological solutions are indicated.

History has been analyzed in this essay to raise questions that, in the judgment of the author, should be explored by those interested in technological innovation in education. In conclusion, a sequence of logical propositions, precipitated by the questions, are offered as stimulus to further and more refined reasoning by those best informed about the educational system. In the first place, the assumption is made that technological innovation in the field of education will be induced rather than passively awaited. Then it becomes critical whether the innovation will be induced by those who are a part of the present educational system or by those outside it. If the innovation is presided over by those within the system it is probable that technology will be used to improve upon the existing system; if by those from outside then it is more likely that the existing system, or systems, will be replaced through technology by new systems (for example, information will no longer be provided by a teacher using technological "aids," but the technology organized by a "teacher" will directly provide the information). If the innovation is to be presided over by those in the existing system, then they would be advised to establish dependent research and development facilities. These facilities, informed of the needs and opportunities of the existing system by those in it, could invent and develop technology in response. Competition with other educational systems, perhaps involving public versus private or one national system against another, is likely to stimulate identification of system needs. If on the other hand invention and development is to come from those outside the system, and the innovation of new systems is favored, then invention and development will probably come from independent inventive-entrepreneurs stimulated by publicity given to the inadequacies of the present system and by knowledge that research and development funds are accessible.

101.

Toward the Development Of Effective Instructional Technology for American Education

by P. KENNETH KOMOSKI
Director
Educational Products
Information Exchange
Institute (EPIE)
New York

Development During a Decade of Change

About a decade ago, when a number of forces in our society had successfully begun militating for changes in American elementary and secondary education, I had two experiences which I now offer as "anecdotal background data" for the discussion at hand.

The first of these experiences occurred during a visit to the office of an educational publisher in early 1958 before Sputnik and the passage of the National Defense Education Act. We were speaking of one of that publisher's most successful mathematics textbooks at the time, and I was told of the difficulty in editing the text some years earlier because the original manuscript had been written entirely on large sheets of brown wrapping paper by an impecunious but talented retired teacher. Just why the publisher had risked his investment of time, money, and an editor's eyesight on that particular teacher I do not recall, but it was perfectly clear that those investments had paid off. The textbook that resulted from the manuscript had clearly met the test of the educational marketplace; it had sold many thousands of copies and had been used to teach hundreds of thousands of students. The cost of turning that manuscript into a textbook, including printing and marketing, may have been as much as but probably not more than $75,000. For this sum (a portion of which had been the investment of a retired teacher's "Free time" in the hope of royalties), the publisher had got a product he was able to mass-produce for potentially every mathematics student in the country.

The second experience came about a year later at a conference where I met a number of people newly associated with the first federally funded curriculum development project. The project was being organized to produce a course in high school physics and, like subsequent federally funded curriculum projects, it had enlisted the services of dozens of scientists and science educators, who organized and designed the course, and who were to be assisted by scores of teachers, writing and field-testing the materials with high school students prior to commercial large-scale distribution. The cost of developing these materials (books, films, laboratory equipment, etc.), all designed for a market containing only a small segment of the country's high school population, has been estimated by a reliable source at about $7-million.*

These two cases from the annals of instructional materials development have not been cited to raise the question of whether the materials for a physics course, produced at a cost some ten thousand times more than the cost of materials for a mathematics course, are ten thousand times as instructionally effective. Whatever the answer to this question, given certain economic, political, technological, and educational trends that have developed during the last decade, the question in that form is irrelevant. The questions that *are* relevant are: "How do we develop instructional materials, equipment, and systems that are *demonstrably effective* in the sense that they do what they have been designed to do with specific types of individual learners?" and "What are the chances that instructional technology of this quality will be produced in any quantity during the decade ahead?"

While we are attempting to come to grips with these critically important questions, we will also be forced to look rather closely at the growing interdependency of education and industry in this country,[1] it is important first to examine three trends that have shaped the development and present condition of instructional technology during the last ten years. These are: one: a trend away from the "intuition-honed-by-experience-and-shaped-by-an-editor" school of development toward the "multi-disciplined-team-working-to-achieve-specific-learning-objectives-through-field-testing" school of development (i.e., a major step in the evolution of a rationally based instructional technology); two: a trend away from the standard textbook toward the development of more complex multi-mediated, expensive materials, equipment, and systems; and three: a trend away from a master curriculum for all students in a mass-instruction program toward multi-mediated, multi-level programs intended to facilitate individualized learning. As we shall see, the question of whether today's emergent instructional technology may effectively meet today's changing educational needs depends on a number of factors related to these trends. Some of these factors seem to point to an affirmative answer and suggest specific and successful responses to these needs; others seem to prohibit the possibility of fulfilling these needs for some time to come.

The Present Pattern of Developing Instructional Technology

As a result of the events of the last decade, the instructional materials being developed today are seldom, if ever, created by retired teachers armed with teaching experience, perseverance, brown wrapping paper, and a good editor. On the other hand, most of today's materials are not yet being developed by the large complex multi-disciplined teams of scholars, teachers, writers, producers, editors, technicians, cameramen, artists, psychologists, instructional technologists, and field researchers working together to produce materials designed to achieve specific learning objectives with individual learners.

The prevalent pattern of developing instructional materials today usually does involve a team, but a modest one made up of one or more subject matter specialists and a few writers and editorial people organized and funded by an educational publisher. The team usually works together over a period of years and is often titularly headed by an educator with a national reputation. In reality, the team is more apt to be directed by an editor of the publishing company financing the project, and the actual creation of the materials may be done by one or more junior editors. Most often, the team does *not* include field researchers whose job it is to force the team from intuition toward empiricism (if not sci-

Some of this expense must be attributed to the "start-up" costs of the whole curriculum reform movement, which may be legitimately allocated to this first large-scale project.

ence) by providing the creators of the materials with systematic feedback, collected from learners, on the instructional effectiveness of the materials as they are being developed.

The cost of having such a team develop sufficient materials for a year of instruction, without systematic formative evaluations in the field, may run as much as, but usually not more than, two hundred thousand dollars. Thus, the costs for today's common pattern of development are greater than similar costs were ten years ago, but they do not approach the costs associated with the method of materials development represented by the large federally funded curriculum projects described earlier. Of course, those federally funded teams continue to produce materials and those materials are marketed by commercial producers. However, only a handful of the many commercial producers who do not have access to materials so designed have been willing or able to invest the large sums of developmental capital needed for the empirical shaping of instructional materials by "inhouse" teams. In their defense, it should be noted that in some cases the cost of such evaluations can be so great in relation to the cost of developing the materials themselves and to the size of the potential market for these particular materials as to lie well beyond the funds of all but the largest educational producers. This cost of pre-marketing formative evaluations is clearly an inhibiting (and in some cases a prohibiting) factor in the large-scale development of effective instructional materials, systems, and services that will demonstrably meet the needs of learners.

When it comes to the prevalent pattern of developing instructional equipment or "hardware," the overriding fact is that with very few exceptions such equipment is not developed specifically for the purpose of instruction. Most so-called "educational hardware," i.e., projectors, recorders, television systems, etc. have been created for the general consumer market. The cost of creating hardware systems for the specific purpose of making instruction more effective has never seemed economically justified to equipment producers. (The largest producer of such "hardware" did only 20% of his business in the education market in 1968.) In one sense, one may argue that this makes it possible for education to acquire equipment it might not otherwise have access to, but this dependence on "what is available" has made it impossible to discover how effective technology developed specifically for educational purposes might be. One exception to this general pattern of "hardware" development during the last decade has been the teaching machine, but it, more than any other "hardware," has suffered not only from chaotic incompatibility, and from a dearth of effective "software," but from premature commercialization that took the form of blatant claims of universal effectiveness generalized from a handful of well-developed teaching machine programs. The only piece of "hardware" that has been primarily developed for educational use and has worked well is the overhead projector.

All of this adds up to a present pattern of development that may be described as an almost random groping toward the development of effective artifacts of instructional technology. But perhaps this is all anyone has a right to expect after ten years of zealous effervescence and sporadic efforts. The questions to be answered during the next ten years are "How can this technology be used to produce effective and desirable educational results?" and "How can we best know what specific technological artifacts ought to be developed?" The answer to the latter question does not lie, as is so often suggested, in having educators, or for that matter anyone, arbitrate what sorts of products the education industry ought to set out to produce. Such an approach, at best a futile exercise, at worst could develop into an effort by educators (who tend to think that "improving the use of instructional technology" means using more of the products they have been using) to build an educational Maginot Line of 16mm projectors and record players as their answer to the challenge of the future.

Whether a decade from now we are to end up safe and sorry or equipped with new and effective tools of instruction depends to a very great extent on how the changing education industry continues to change and how much value is placed on the task of developing effective instructional technology—not just by that industry, but by the Congress,

State legislatures, local school boards, and individual taxpayers. At the present time, the prognosis for the next decade seems far from good. In an effort to understand why, let's look at the changing education industry and the "education market" it serves.

Present Business Strategies and the Present Pattern of Federal Funding

The present strategy of most (not all, but most) companies in the education industry is to give the educator what he wants to use at the price the educational market will bear. This has been a sound successful business strategy for many years and, in the view of many, there is no reason to believe that it could not remain so for many years to come. There is some question, however, as to how sound and successful an educational strategy it might be. The reason this question may be validly raised is, as we have already mentioned, that when the working educator, with little time left over from "running the shop," thinks about what his needs are, he tends to think in terms of products that are familiar and already available, rather than of those that are unfamiliar or those that "ought" to be available. Thus, for the most part, industry cannot learn what it needs to know from the educator directly. In a technologically dynamic society in which he has not been particularly active, the educator has few answers as to what instructional technology ought to be developed to meet changing educational needs.

From the business standpoint, therefore, the safe thing may be to continue to produce the traditional sorts of mass-instruction materials, thereby satisfying the educational purchaser, but not, unfortunately, the educational consumer, who is the individual learner. He, the student, is increasingly frustrated by these traditional educational materials; he has been told all his life that he is to be given every opportunity to develop as an individual, and that he will be allowed to make his own choices as to what products he uses in developing his individuality. And he has had his individual choice in so many other areas—from "variety packs" of cereal in the morning to any one of the stations on his very own transistor radio at night. But the education industry is still far from making technology as responsive to the individual as other industries have managed to make it, for instance, in the areas such as mass communications and food processing. And, even if educators and industry could discover and agree upon what products ought to be made and marketed to meet the needs of individual learners, products designed to meet those needs will not necessarily be forthcoming, because of what might be called the confounding economics of the new instructional technology. Some economic peculiarities arise from the traditional economic and social facts of American education life, with which hitherto noneducational corporations are often totally unacquainted. Others are functions of more substantive educational factors.

One extremely important economic fact is that, despite the frequently cited bit of information that the educational sector of our economy expends some 50 billion dollars annually and is expanding, the actual market for products and services traditionally purchased for educational purposes is only a very small percentage of this figure. Close to two-thirds of the total monies expended each year on public education are spent for the professional salaries of public employees engaged in teaching or in managing the country's largest locally controlled public service. Another large percentage of these monies goes toward maintenance, repair (one large city system is reported to have spent over $1,000,000 repairing broken windows last year), and construction of buildings. Other large amounts are spent on amortization, transportation, and an array of general administrative expenses. As a result, and much to their chagrin, many new corporations in the education industry have discovered that the portion of the total education market for which they are competing with other companies is worth perhaps two or three billion dollars rather than 50 billion. The question is whether a two or three billion dollar market is large enough to justify the competitive efforts of a Xerox, a Litton, both an RCA *and* CBS, a Westinghouse *and* a General Electric, a Time-Life *and* a McGraw-Hill, a Sylvania *and* a Raytheon. The answer to this question at present would seem to be "no"—Xerox, RCA and Raytheon have recently cut back drastically within their education divisions and other companies maintain a "wait and see" attitude. To make the answer "yes" will clearly require the opening up of markets for new types of educational products and services. It is also quite clear that this "market development" cannot be accomplished by the industry alone, not only because of the economics of the situation but because nothing has been done to spell out what is needed. Even after ten years of federal funding, which has increased the local school systems' purchasing power by a really large factor, the market has not changed materially. The increased funds have been used, as might be expected from what has been said earlier, to further increasing use of existing technologies for traditional instructional purposes.

Therefore, federal support has not (except in the case of some of the large-scale curriculum projects and of programmed instruction) led to the development of new technologies or individualized applications of existing technologies. Seldom, if ever, has federal money been given directly to the education industry for the purpose of developing entirely new products and services (a phenomenon which occurs frequently in such "public service" sectors of the economy as transportation, communication, aero-space, national defense, and even agriculture). When federal dollars do support developmental activities, it is usually through the indirect mechanism of a joint project with a federally-supported, university-based research and development center or a regional laboratory, often conducted at the risk of strained industry-university relationships, and some questions about the university professor as entrepreneur. And even this indirect funding raises fears on the part of some local educators that the federal sponsorship will result in undue influence on local decision-making because the donors will eventually establish specifications (in this case, curriculum objectives) of the sort that are established by the Department of Defense when it contracts with industry to develop a new weapons system.

Some of the new corporate conglomerates, experienced in providing goods and services to the military, might welcome the specification of "good clear curriculum objectives" by any agency whether federal, state, or local. These military-system-builders-turned-educational-suppliers are learning that in the "software" field it is very hard to pin educators down. They are also learning that most of the companies now selling "hardware" to education are marketing products (projectors, tape-recorders, television equipment, etc.) which were developed for sale in the general consumer market—and perhaps modified slightly for sale to school systems. These established hardware producers (over 90% of whose business may be in markets other than education) will resist any requirement to change their products to conform to purely educational specifications.

But given what some believe will be a period of federal cutbacks in support of instructional technology, many of the large systems producers are, as mentioned earlier, cutting back and moving toward marketing more traditional types of instructional materials, developed by and sold through well-established (and recently acquired) subsidiaries experienced in making and selling traditional educational products to a traditional educational market. As Edward Katzenbach put it before he vacated the presidency of the Raytheon Education Company: "The money is not in the new stuff, it is in the old stuff." From a "hard-nosed" business standpoint, continuing to sell the "old stuff" may be the best possible solution to industry's present frustration with the peculiarities of the education market. Thus, for the time being, there could be no discernible division within the industry—only intensified competition among the "old pros" selling traditional mass-instructional products dressed up with new packaging and sporting new labels which carry symbols of the prestigious corporations that are now standing behind the old familiar names. Those who rationalize the desirability of such a situation point out that, "We have never really made use of all the things already available for use in education," adding that, "Most schools do not have enough readily available films and other media including books," and capping their arguments with, "There are school systems where students don't even have their own textbooks for each of the courses they are taking." For such people the better distribution through more massive marketing of existing mass-instructional products seems to be the best and only economical solution to the problems of both the education industry and the educational system it serves. The only problems not apt to be solved by this possible turn of events would be those of the "ultimate consumer"—the individual learner.

The Immediate Outlook and the Conditions Necessary for the Future Growth of Effective Instructional Technology

If this is indeed the turn that events take in the future, what will the effect be on the three trends we identified at the outset? (the trend toward more complex and more expensive patterns of development and the building of innovative multi-media instructional systems; the trend toward the development of rationally-based instructional technology, and the trend toward the use of the new instructional technology to individualize instruction). In returning to look again at these trends after an examination of some of the economic and political factors that surround the changing education industry and which contribute to the peculiar nature of the educational market, we cannot be encouraged. While the trend toward more expensive materials will undoubtedly continue, this increased cost is apt to be paid for more or less traditional products sold to a market supplemented by federal funds that must be spent in a given year. The trends toward the development of a rationally-based technology of instruction and toward individualized instructional systems are apt to be talked about a great deal, but probably few materials will appear which have been systematically developed and thoroughly evaluated to the point where they will be demonstrably effective within an individualized instructional program. Those so developed will undoubtedly be too few to make a significant impact. What then of the continued growth of these trends toward the improvement of American education? Such growth depends on three things—one: our society's willingness to pay the full cost of adapting educational curricula for individualizing instruction; two: the ability of the developers of new instructional artifacts to make materials, equipment, and systems that are continually adaptable to the changing needs of individual learners; and three: the willingness of professional educators to use and shape these technological artifacts by responsible, on-going evaluation of their performance in a range of instructional settings.

Were these three things to occur on a reasonable scale, we might indeed expect to see great strides in instruction at all levels of education. The fact that none of the three is likely to occur to anything like the degree needed to cause significant increase in the development of effective instructional technology during the next decade indicates rather clearly that certain conditions necessary to that growth are not present.

Those conditions are not as simple as a lack of acceptance of new approaches to instruction on the part of educators. Contrary to the opinion of these who would place all blame on the immobility of the educational establishment, there are enough educators willing to introduce effective new instructional technology to bring along their colleagues during the next decade. What is lacking is understanding of how to do what needs to be done to develop a really effective new instructional technology.

Practically all present attempts to create effective instructional materials, equipment, and systems suffer from an incomplete cycle of development. The truth of the matter is that although developers of instructional technology have learned a good deal about the nature of the full developmental cycle they have not learned all they need to know, and, because of inertia and the exigencies of the educational marketplace, they have not applied what they have learned. Many people, both in the education industry and in the schools, seem to feel that the first problem is what products to make. That will always be a problem, but the problem which industry, the schools and the government should address first is how to make products that are effective. Educators and school board members have listened to a decade of excited claims and testimonials about new technology with no clearly evident increase in effectiveness of instruction. In time these purchasers will begin to demand a guarantee of a product's effectiveness. They may question why a nation which can put a man on the moon cannot plan for effective individualized instruction. They may even demand the recall of entirely ineffective systems, which can have as high a potential for danger—though of a different sort—as a defective carburetion system in an automobile.

While such a situation is conceivable, it is not likely to occur immediately because, as the educational market is now constituted, the increased cost of transforming products that are educationally attractive into products that are also educationally effective would have to be passed on to the consumer. At present, the consumer is in no position to absorb these costs. Given a choice between a product which costs "x" dollars and may or may not be effective, and one that costs "x+" dollars and will probably have to be reworked by the producer and adapted to by the school system to be made effective, most educators will select the less expensive product. Of course, were the school system guaranteed that the product would be immediately effective, they might very well be willing to pay the higher price, but given the nature of instructional technology, it is not very likely that such guarantees will be forthcoming. Therefore, despite the fact that there are likely to be more and more demands for effective instructional technology during the next decade, it is questionable whether the conditions or climate necessary for the development of instructionally effective technology will be present. Yet "effectiveness" is technology's most essential attribute; i.e., technology is man's process of organizing his mental and material resources to do what wants doing effectively. In the process, efficiency and economy may also be achieved, but they are valued "side effects" which may or may not occur. For too long, technology has been applied to education in the hope of achieving efficiency and economy—hardly, if ever, has it been viewed as that element within education that has to do with achieving educational effectiveness. Since that day a decade ago, when the decision was made that the United States would put men on the moon, the central concern and only acceptable criterion of success has been to get them there and back effectively. Once we accomplish that, we will then begin to concern ourselves more with how we can get people there more efficiently and economically. (Had the recent Apollo 8 Mission been done more economically or efficiently, but less effectively, it would not have been any more impressive, and could have been tragic.)

The fact is that the same sort of commitment to effectiveness simply does not exist within our society when it comes to instruction. Were it to exist during the next decade and were the commitment to be backed up a billion dollars of federal support*, there is little question that we would be able to boast of having created the world's first universally effective instructional technology. In time, it might even become "efficient" and "economical."

---

*This is approximately the amount spent in a decade on our space program. Much of the money has been granted directly to industry by NASA.

How Progress Toward More Effective Instructional Technology Might Be Made

All this implies, and I think correctly, that whatever small progress we do make toward a more effective instructional technology during the next decade will depend on the ability of school boards, educational producers, federal funding agencies, and the citizenry in general to tolerate what may be construed as inefficient and uneconomical practices in the effort to produce instructional systems that work. This tolerance must take a number of different forms. For the companies in the education industry willing to show such tolerance, it will mean a willingness to forego immediate profits and "hang in there" for the long pull (something many companies have talked about but which few are doing). It will also mean a willingness to develop a demonstrably effective product (perhaps just one to begin with that is effective with only one type of learner). In addition, it will require a willingness to keep in touch with the users of the product (both students and teachers) to be sure that it is working as effectively as possible, and to revise and redesign faulty elements. (This implies the ongoing training of teachers in the use of the product in some instances.) Finally, (and this will be the toughest one of all) it will mean the willingness to forego the ingrained prejudice that those instructional products are best that sell best, whether effective or not. In an "unnatural" market where companies supply "educational consultants" to write requests for federal funds with which to purchase what is available, the "natural" evaluation of products by the marketplace cannot be relied upon.

Of course, few education companies can at present afford to gamble on the corporate strategies implicit in the foregoing four points. However, it seems likely that more of them would be willing to carry out these strategies if federal funding were directly available to them to develop effective new products. What this implies for federal funding is a greater willingness to provide substantial incentives to companies ready to take on a sustained (perhaps ten-year) commitment to the building of effective instructional systems. Under the present style of federal funding, such a relationship to the commercial sector is not likely, but when one considers that for the past ten years the federal practice of supplying funds for buying traditional technology has not only been sustaining but supplying an increasingly rich diet for those within the commercial sector content to market traditional instructional technology, the changes proposed here seem justified.

Now there are those who may argue that the large amounts of federal support that have been made available for the development of computer-assisted instruction (CAI) during the last few years is proof that this type of federal support is already available to industry. This type of support is not what is being described here. The support for CAI did not include commitments from and to companies in the education industry to support the sustained development of that technology over a number of years along with a program of ongoing evaluation in terms of its effectiveness on learners. While federal support of CAI has been large, it has also been largely unsystematic with the hope of efficiency and economy taking precedence over the concern for effectiveness. Furthermore, because it has been support specifically for CAI, it has put the Office of Education in the position of seeming to favor CAI over other aspects of instructional technology. A different pattern of funding would be necessary were federal funding agencies to help sustain the development of the effective use of technology in education during the next decade.

It would be presumptuous to say precisely how this should be done, but it is clear that in general the federal government should be willing to make a significant amount of money available through whatever channels there are (a Commission on Research, Innovation and Evaluation in Education of the sort recommended in the recent report of the Committee for Economic Development might be an excellent mechanism) to any company willing to undertake the development of a specific instructional system or artifact to the point at which it is regularly achieving a designated set of objectives in a significant number of school systems that have voluntarily elected to use the system at local expense. Proposals might be granted support on the basis of formula containing such factors as: "innovativeness," "the educational need being responded to," "the amount of investment the company is willing to make relative to the estimated cost of development and the size of the company," "the number of pilot school systems which have committed in advance to use the product until it is proven effective or discarded," "the ultimate contribution the product might make to the growth of instructional technology." Special recognition of some kind might be given to those companies whose products were eventually proved effective in a wide range of schools. A product's effectiveness would be judged on the basis of the effect the materials were having on learners and on the willingness of a significant majority of the pilot schools to adopt the product at local expense once it had been developed. Ideally, any company having an adequate number of pilot schools might be given one such grant on request.

It may of course be argued that such a program would constitute an intrusion upon the working of the "natural education market." But that market has been "unnatural" ever since the National Defense Education Act went into effect, when schools were given money to purchase either "more of the same" or a variety of new products of uncertain effectiveness. The companies that have benefited from this pattern of federal support to local purchasers may feel that there is nothing unnatural about the pattern at all, but the fact of the matter is that, as has been shown, this nourishment has tended to put fat rather than muscle on the growing field of instructional technology. Furthermore, this pattern has tended to produce sales and profits for companies with established market visability while less well-established companies with more effective products have difficulty competing in a market where effectiveness is not rewarded by adequate support or recognition. By means of the plan suggested above, all companies, large and small, established or new, independent or part of a conglomerate, would have an equal chance to acquire proportionate developmental subsidies. That is, the formula would allow a smaller company undertaking a million-dollar product development project to acquire a subsidy of, say, $750,000 while a company that was four times as large might be able to acquire only $250,000 for a project of the same size. This aspect of the plan would greatly lessen the possibility that the education industry will coagulate into a few large producers living on federal subsidies.

There is also a need for this kind of sustained commitment on the part of the schools as well as government and industry. Too often during the last decade educators have rushed to use a promising product of the education industry only to abandon it at the first sign of difficulty, or on occasion, because federal funds were available for an even more promising "innovation" in the same area. However, it seems likely that there are enough school systems willing to commit themselves to the voluntary and sustained use of a particular artifact or system of instructional technology until such time as both they and the producer of the product agree that it is providing effective instruction—or should be abandoned. At the point of judging it to be effective, presumably the school system would be willing to adopt the product for broad and continued use at its own expense.

As indicated earlier, a company would have to enlist a number of such volunteer pilot school systems in order to qualify for a product development subsidy or grant. If, at the end of a number of years of sustained development, the majority of these volunteer systems decided to purchase out of local funds the materials, equipment and (presumably) services required for continued use of the product, it might reasonably be concluded that the product had been proved effective, at least, for the types of student using it in those volunteer schools. Given this specific concrete evidence in the form of a commitment on the part of the pilot school systems, it is likely that other school systems would feel they could move with confidence to adopt the materials.

A second thing that the educational community could do (and in a sense is beginning to do on a modest scale[2]) is to sustain a self-supporting cooperative exchange of information about the effectiveness of specific products of instructional technology. When fully developed, this exchange will give all cooperating school systems and companies ready access to impartial, accurate, and up-to-date information on the performance of specific products and services being marketed by the education industry. Such data would be used to prepare "product performance profiles" describing a product's ongoing record of use with specific types of learners in schools across the country. These data would be collected from teachers, students, and supervisors, and made available through an independent, non-governmental, non-industry "professionals' cooperative." Decision-making based on such dependable information could go a long way toward guaranteeing an effective "corrective feedback" to the education industry—a feedback based on continuous product evaluations by teachers and their students.[3]

Were significant commitments to be made by industry, the federal government, and the schools, real progress toward effective instructional technology might be made in the decade ahead. At present, only partial components of this inter-dependent system exist.[4] That is to say, there are a few companies that seem committed to a sustained effort to develop their products through to the point of effectiveness. Likewise, there are schools (more than many people suspect) willing to work in a sustained way with such companies. In addition, a significant effort is being made to build a cooperative exchange of professional information on product effectiveness. However, there is no available mechanism for sustained government support for those companies and those schools willing to do whatever it takes in time, talent, and effort to develop effective instructional technology. Until such financial support is broadly available, we cannot look forward to real progress in the development of this emergent technology.

Epilog

As we have seen, the education industry is no longer what it once was—a specialized off-shoot of the publishing business. At this point in our history, it has the potential of becoming a unique, extremely large, and profoundly important industrial and social phenomenon in American society. The great electronic boom of the fifties and sixties has made possible heretofore undreamed-of instructional techniques, as well as changing radically the environment in which the learner exists.

Thus, the continuing increase in the size of the American educational enterprise since World War II and the dynamic nature of the American economy and its growing dependence on educated manpower, have inevitably made technologically-oriented corporations aware of the direct pragmatic value of education not only to their own well-being through trained manpower, but as a newly developing market for educational products and services. The emergence of what has been called "the learning society" is a major reason why corporations have felt they would not only do well by actively entering the education market, buy why many have talked about doing "good" as well.

Whether they can manage to do either is, at this point, far from certain. The position of this "position paper" is that the answer to this important question is not entirely under the control of this new industry nor should it be, nor more than it is, or should be, under the control of the federal government, or, for that matter, the educational establishment. Nor is this a question to be answered in a general sense, definitely and once and for all. Rather it will have to be dealt with over and over again in terms of specific products that will have to be shaped and reshaped by educational producers, practitioners, purchasers and, hopefully, by the ultimate educational consumers—individual learners. The suggestions made in this paper, if carried out, could increase the number of times this question is answered in the affirmative during the next decade.

REFERENCES

1. Komoski, P. K. "The Second Industrial-Instructional Revolution—The Growing Interdependency of Industry and Education." 14th Annual Educational Media Leadership Conference, University of Iowa, 1968.

2. See Stake, Robert. "Designing for the Future: a Eight-State Project." *Planning for Effective Utilization of Technology in Education,* 1968, pp. 302-307.

3. See also, Komoski, K. P. "The EPIE Institute, Improving Educational Technology through the Exchange of Product Information." Proceedings of Project Aristotle Symposium, 1968.

4. See Komoski, K. P. "The Second Industrial-Instructional Revolution." Keynote—14th Annual Educational Media Conference, University of Iowa, 1968.

102.

Instructional Technology:
The Capabilities of Industry
To Help Solve
Educational Problems

by *ROBERT W. LOCKE*   and   *DAVID ENGLER*
Exec. Vice Pres.   *Gen. Manager*
McGraw-Hill Book Co.   *Instructional Systems Division*
McGraw-Hill

We are pleased to offer this statement of our view of instructional technology, and by way of introduction should state the frame of reference in which it is written. First of all, our concerns are those of a business firm, and we therefore have something to say about the capabilities of industry to help solve the problems of education. Second, McGraw-Hill being among the more diversified of the education companies with respect to the media of instruction, we believe that we are relatively objective as to the efficacy of different kinds of instructional products, whether hardware, software, or combinations of the two. Third, we have become increasingly concerned about the preoccupation with educational *products* instead of educational *processes*. Finally, we have some strong convictions about the proper role of private enterprise in the public concern for education.

There are three sections in this statement. The first argues for a clear definition of instructional or educational technology. The second considers the disappointing state of R&D work in education. And the third argues the case for greater involvement of the businesses associated with education, suggesting some modified relationships that we believe would serve the public interest.

The Need for Definition

We strongly urge the Commission to help clear up the confusion about what constitutes instructional or educational technology. (We use the terms interchangeably in this paper.) Most people involved in education, including the great majority of the teachers and administrators who will have to decide what changes to make in their teaching strategies, have only the vaguest notion of what educational technology is; and most make the serious but common error of defining it primarily in terms of hardware. This has greatly confused the issue because it has focused too much attention on the relatively superficial issue of what products are worth buying, and too little on the highly significant work being done through the *process* of instructional technology to produce teaching strategies that are relevant to the learning abilities of individual students.

The members of the Commission will, of course, be familiar with the various definitions of educational technology as a process, and perhaps should develop a new one in terms that can easily be understood by teachers and by intelligent citizens who are concerned about the schools. We suggest something along the following lines: Instructional technology is the process of applying the findings of behavioral science to the problems of instruction. This process manifests itself through the analysis of the relationship between subject matter content and student behavior both before and after instruction.

The importance of definition, it seems to us, is simply that educators will run the serious danger of making poor decisions about instructional strategy and of wasting their limited resources unless they have a clear understanding of the principles that underlie the alternatives that will increasingly be open to them. Their decisions are too often based on the characteristics of hardware and software and too little on what their objectives are and how these can be best achieved. They are putting the cart before the horse.

We might cite a few cases to support this concern:

1. The programmed instruction movement has been seriously misunderstood by most observers, with the result that great misjudgments have been made about it. For some people the movement was an effort to use machines to teach—and indeed for a period in the early 1960's many viewed programmed instruction primarily in terms of teaching machines.

   When the machines turned out to have relatively little value, these same observers dismissed the entire movement as having little value. Others with a more sophisticated conception of programmed instruction realized that the machine was much less important than the program and were neither surprised nor discouraged when the machines failed. They came closer to seeing the process involved and therefore made more intelligent decisions. But very few people focused on the much more significant point that programmed instruction was one of the first attempts to develop a strategy of instruction based on the findings of behavioral psychology. Had the development of programmed instruction been seen by most educators in this light, rather than in terms of physical products like teaching machines and programmed books, it is quite probable that there would be now have been much more progress in the use of the technique in schools.

2. Enormous amounts of money have been spent on instructional television without (as yet) any really satisfactory judgments about its value. Most of the analysis of ITV has been in terms of teacher-student ratios, the relative costs of capital equipment and teachers' salaries, and the simple-minded assumption that a medium that has such proven capacity for entertainment (leaving aside questions of value) must have a great capacity for facilitating learning.

   Very little of the analysis of ITV has been in terms of how well it can be adapted to an instructional strategy that takes into account the differences in learning style and rate. Again, the focus has been on the medium and not on the process of learning.

3. Perhaps most serious, the narrow view of technology as hardware, coupled with the serious doubts that many educators have about hardware, makes it that much more difficult to gain support for the promising work being done by behavioral technologists, who are beginning to apply the processes of technology to the development of improved instructional strategies. The work being done by people like Glaser at the Pittsburgh Learning Research & Development Center and by Flanagan at the American Institutes for Research is more promising than the work being done in, for example, computer-assisted drill and practice, but gets much less attention in the press and is less well understood by educators. This may be all right, but not if doubts about the ability of the schools to afford CAI make it more difficult to get support for the more basic work being done to individualize instruc-

tion. (For a good example of how a preoccupation with hardware and a failure to understand the process of educational technology can lead to pessimistic conclusions about the concerns of this Commission, see the article entitled "The Myths of Educational Technology" by Dr. Anthony Oettinger that appeared in the May 18 issue of *The Saturday Review.)*

Since part of the Commission's charge is to advise the Office of Education, the Congress, and the people of the United States about how technology is likely to improve instruction, we consider it critically important for the Commission to develop and state its conclusions within the framework of a broad definition of instructional technology: that is, one that views it as a process.

The Shortcomings of Research and Development

It goes almost without saying that the U.S. educational system needs a better mechanism for research and development than it now has, and the Commission could make a major contribution by proposing some new approaches. There is too little research, too much of it is of low quality, too little is relevant to the most serious problems of education; and in general, there is too little direct relationship between research and implementation.

Furthermore, there is great confusion about what constitutes research, development, or implementation.

The following is an incomplete list of the shortcomings of educational R&D:

1. The amount of basic research is very small. By "basic" we mean research in learning theory, of the sort identified with Piaget, Bloom, Bruner or Gagne. Compared with basic research in the physical sciences, for instance, it is far too limited.

2. By and large, the best basic research has not been done in the colleges of education, which one would consider to be the logical source of educational research, but in the departments of psychology in universities—thus creating a communications barrier of some consequence. Happily, this condition has been somewhat alleviated in recent years as it has become respectable for other researchers to associate with their colleagues in the colleges of education.

3. Applied research, too, has been neglected. Much more of it is needed, and more of it should take place on a broader scale. What modest efforts have been made in recent years have tended to be fragmented into small projects. More experimentation on a scale comparable to, for example, the Oakleaf Project should be a prime objective.

4. The so-called education business has done too little R&D work. It has done a great deal of experimental product development, often as a means of implementing research, but even this work could be done on a more rigorous basis. The education business has an R&D capacity that needs to be stimulated, both through the incentive of direct contracts and through the insistence of schools that products be properly evaluated. (More on this later.)

Since one of the great promises of instructional technology is its potential to help individualize instruction, the Commission should encourage broadened research and development in several critical problem areas. Experimental projects over the last few years have deepened our understanding of both the techniques and problems of individualized instruction.

From our vantage point, which is the design and development of instructional materials, we see a growing need for stronger theoretical bases, as well as applied techniques for dealing with the major factors of the instructional situation.

The three major factors with which the instructional designer must deal are:

1. The nature of the subject matter content;

2. The nature of the learner;

3. The nature of the learning environment.

The work done by Bloom and his colleagues on the taxonomy of educational objectives, and particularly the work done by Gagne on the analysis of learning tasks, have provided instructional designers with useful tools for analyzing subject matter.

What is needed now is a taxonomy of instructional strategy and media related to these taxonomies of learning tasks. Such a tool would help educators deal more rationally with the learning environment. It would, however, require the generation of substantial empirical data to serve as a base for the development of useful techniques.

We also need to improve our techniques of diagnosing individual learners. Our long-standing emphasis on standardized norm-referenced measures of ability and achievement are not adequate for the kind of individualized instruction now emerging in our schools. We need to strengthen our skills in diagnosing student behavior before instruction in terms of both mastery of prerequisite skills and prior mastery of stated instructional objectives.

Beyond this, we need instruments that will begin to help us diagnose differences in learning style so that we can effectively use the taxonomies of learning tasks, strategies and media in relation to the variations in the way different individuals learn different things.

Finally, there is a great need for broad experimentation with the techniques of cost-effectiveness or cost-benefit analysis in education. This will be increasingly true as we continue to individualize instruction and develop alternate instructional routes to accommodate differences in the way individuals learn. The useful application of these techniques to decision-making about instruction will provide educators with a badly needed tool for rational analysis of instructional problems.

It seems to us that these improvements in the technology of instruction will come about only with a broadened and deepened research and development effort. The Commission would make a major contribution by stimulating a high level of research and development in these problem areas.

The Role of Industry

Now for some special pleading. We hope that the Commission will consider the contributions that industry can make to education through applications of instructional technology. Despite the highly generalized assumption that industry has capabilities that can be used effectively in education, there has yet to be developed an acceptable rationale for its greater involvement, and this has inhibited both industry and education. The two key questions are (a) how to use industry for educational R&D work, and (b) how to maintain quality control of educational products and services. Implicit in both is the protection of the public interest.

R&D Work by Industry

It is reasonable enough to assume that the so-called education industry has the capacity to do worthwhile R&D work in areas connected with teaching and learning. However, it should be noted that the industry itself is highly diversified and that capabilities found in one firm may be quite different from those found in another; likewise there is a wide range of activities that make up the continuum from basic research in education to the development of practical applications. (It would be helpful to have a competent and thorough study of what capabilities exist in what kinds of organization.) Nevertheless, a few generalizations can be made about the capacity of industry to do R&D work, and they will suffice to make some other points.

First, industry has very little capacity to do basic research, and we feel that this function should be left primarily (although not exclusively) to the universities and other research-oriented organizations. Basic research in education is mainly research in learning theory, and we have already suggested that there should be more of it.

On the other hand, there is considerable capacity in industry to do applied research; for example, in the area of instructional media as it relates to differences in individual learners and in subject matter content, as noted earlier in this paper.

Third, industry clearly has the capacity to apply research findings to experimental product development. In fact, the chief contribution of industry to the improvement of teaching and learning comes through its ability to translate the findings of research and creative experiments into products and services that have wide application in education.

Fourth, industry has some capacity for developmental work in new techniques that may be useful in education, such as cost-benefit analysis and systems analysis.

Fifth, industry has begun to develop the capacity to do evaluation studies, an activity that is heavily dependent on research techniques, and about which we will have more to say.

Finally, industry generally has the capacity to supply management for research efforts.

As noted earlier, the education industry is highly diverse, and different companies are likely to have quite different capabilities for educational R&D work. The fact remains, however, is that these capabilities do exist, and it is important that they be used to the best advantage of education.

There is not present mechanism through which the R&D capabilities of industry and the needs of education can be matched. The natural inclination of industry is to put its money where there appears to be the greatest market potential, but this is not always an area in great need of development. Essentially, the allocation of business resources is made according to the goals of the individual business firm which may or may not at a given moment be consistent with the goals of education. In this respect, the education industry behaves much like the consumer goods industry, making investment decisions based on analyses of market trends, buying practices, competitive moves, and internal capabilities. However, the educational market differs greatly from the consumer market, in that it is public rather than private, and that it helps to accomplish societal goals. That is, education as a market for goods and services exists only because the public has created it, and has chosen to leave the production of goods and services to the private sector of the economy. Although schools are increasingly specific about what types of products they want to buy, they have only indirect control (through their buying decisions) over the characteristics of the products offered to them, and in common with other economic activities virtually none over the R&D decisions made by their producers.

This arrangement is not inherently bad, but we should recognize that it is not likely to result in an optimum match between the needs of education and the R&D capabilities of industry. In fact, it is almost certain to result in a time lag between the recognition of an educational need and the allocation of industrial R&D resources to the fulfillment of that need.

It seems to us that the interests of education would be better served—and the interests of the education business protected—if there were some mechanism for enlisting the R&D resources of industry in greater accordance with the needs of education. On the one hand, a strong case can be made for the maintenance of a strong and independent private industry devoted to the development and sale of goods and services for education; but on the other hand, perhaps the educational community should have more say in the priorities of the business firms.

To make the matter more difficult, education itself is less than unified in its determination of objectives and goals. Because of the highly decentralized nature of education—looking at it from a national standpoint—there are few effective means of agreeing on priorities. To be sure, there is fairly general agreement on the broad, critical needs, such as the improve- ment of urban education, the integration of the schools, and so on; but general agreement on areas that have become critical is very different from the development of discrete goals that have the potential to make significant improvements in education. It is difficult to build an R&D program around such a generalized goal as improving urban education, just as it would be difficult to build R&D programs in the defense area around a generalized goal like preventing World War III.

We need, therefore, a means of analyzing the needs of education on a systematic and national basis; and then of influencing the allocation of R&D sources according to these needs, whether the resources are in education itself, in non-profit research organizations, or in industry. Further, whatever mechanism is developed for this purpose, it needs to be structured in such a way that the independence of local or state educational units is not jeopardized.

This last, it seems to us, makes it difficult for the Office of Education to be the main arbiter of educational priorities. Even if the Office could be staffed in such a way that it clearly had the competence to do the job, it seems neither likely nor proper to us that the Congress should place this responsibility solely in the hands of a powerful agency of the federal government; and there is clearly a reluctance among state and local educational officials to see much more authority given to the Office.

Therefore, we believe that some new mechanism needs to be created, and we are im- pressed by the recommendations made in the recent CED report, *Innovation in Education,* that there be created a national Commission on Research, Innovation, and Evaluation in Education, supported by but not controlled by the federal government. If an agency were created for the purpose of influencing and contributing to the R&D work done in education, if it were adequately financed and received its support from both the federal government and the private foundations, and if it were governed by a prestigious board of directors chosen on a basis that assured its independence, then we believe this agency could do much to help match the educational R&D resources of the country of our long-term educational needs.

Returning to the matter of R&D in the education business, such an agency could also be the vehicle through which R&D contracts could be made with private industry, since such arrangements would be consistent with an analysis of what resources are applicable to what problems, and because they would avoid the difficulties of direct contracts between federal agencies and private industry in the area of education. (The sensitivity of Congress and the various federal agencies to the matter of R&D contracts with industry strikes us as highly naive as to the intentions of the business community, but we see no sign that it is likely to change.)

Dissemination by Industry

The power of the education industry to disseminate new applications of R&D work in education is very great, and in fact remains the chief means by which new techniques for teaching and learning reach the teachers and students. Properly used, this dissemination or marketing capability can make important contributions to education. The problem is to influence it without controlling it. Again, we see a need for a new mechanism, to which the proposed Commission on Research, Innovation, and Evaluation could make an important contribution.

Schools, colleges, and other educational institutions are entirely free to buy whatever teaching and learning systems they consider best suited to their particular needs (subject only to the limitations of local economics and occasional forms of local censorship), and any attempt by a national agency to influence or control these local buying decision would clearly be a violation of our policy of state and local responsibility for public education. Therefore, it may be more effective to influence the sellers than the buyers, and we suggest that this can be done through the development of standards for both the development and representation of educational products.

The need for standards was not so great when the choice of teaching and learning materials was limited largely to textbooks. All teachers have used textbooks as students and taught from them as teachers, and have a generally adequate frame of reference with which to make wise selections. However, the development of newer and less conventional forms of teaching and learning materials and systems presents teachers and schools with the problem of making choices without adequate frames of reference. Teachers who know what to look for in textbooks find it difficult to evaluate programmed materials, and even more difficult to decide whether or not equipment-based learning systems are appropriate to the needs of their students. Thus, the development of the new instructional technology carries with it the growing need to help educators make wise purchasing decisions.

We feel that the best solution to this problem is for the producers of educational materials and systems to develop standards for the evaluation of their products, and for educational institutions to insist on being given the data derived from field testing. Ideally, each new instructional program should be designed around a carefully developed set of behavioral objectives—that is, what learning it should facilitate for what kinds of students, and under what conditions—and then tested in actual classrooms during its formative stages in order to measure its effectiveness and to determine how it can be improved. Then the detailed statement of behavioral objectives and the field-testing data should be written up in a technical manual. The manual would help potential users determine how closely the objectives of the program match those of the school and students for which it is being considered, and the data would provide reasonable evidence as to its effectiveness under specified conditions. Technical information of this type is commonly provided by the publishers of standardized educational tests, and there is no reason why it cannot be supplied by producers of instructional systems. Some, in fact, are beginning to do so, and it is the firm intention of McGraw-Hill to publish evaluative data for new programs with increasing consistency.

This approach to evaluation would help the producers to maintain quality control and the schools to make intelligent buying decisions. Further, because it would be a form of self-policing, it would leave both educational companies and schools with a maximum of independence. It would avoid the pitfalls of using some central agency to monitor either the production of instructional systems or the purchasing decisions made in education.

However, it is unlikely that this ideal state of things will be reached in the near future. The cost of evaluation is sufficiently high that education companies may be slow to undertake it on the scale suggested here, and the technical problems of evaluation are probably beyond the present competence of all but the most sophisticated producers of instructional systems. Therefore, it would be highly beneficial if some combination of both pressure and assistance could be applied to the problem, and we see this as another highly useful function of the sort of agency proposed by the CED.

Such an organization could perform two services in the area of evaluation that would greatly help its progress without seriously limiting the freedom of action of either the education companies or the schools and colleges. The first would be to undertake studies of the process of evaluation itself, in order to provide the producers with some technical assistance that they badly need. The second would be to show schools and colleges how to interpret evaluative data, and more important, how to determine their own instructional objectives with enough sophistication to create a framework within which to consider the new instructional systems being offered to them. Both services would apply indirect pressure on the companies and schools to get on with the job, and at the same time would help them do it.

Conclusion

Several different and largely unrelated developments in education have combined to create an unusually good climate for change. Much the most important of these developments is that behavioral psychologists are beginning to understand the different ways in which people learn. Of less but still great importance are (a) that developments in the media of instruction (from films to computers) have created new options for the individualization of instruction, (b) that the public increasingly recognizes the key role played by education in the achievement of social, economic, and technological goals (from getting a man to the moon to solving the problems of the cities), (c) that we are willing to use the broad taxing power of the federal government to help finance change in education, and d) that the education business has acquired new capabilities. Instructional technology is one of the chief means by which change will take place, and as a process has great potential to bring about change in a much more systematic way than has generally been possible in the past. From the standpoint of national policy, therefore, it would seem to us highly advisable to foster a climate in which the maximum resources will be allocated to the improvement of education by all of the segments of society that can make a significant contribution, including the various parts of education itself, the major government units at the federal, state and local levels, the non-profit R&D organizations, and the business community associated with education. The greatest single need is for competent research in the design of instruction, and effective means of implementing research findings in the classroom.

Research in the design of instruction and its implementation in the classroom, however, must be done in the delicate political climate that pervades education. While virtually all of public elementary and secondary education and much of public higher education is controlled at the state and local level, it makes little sense for R&D work in instructional design to be done for purely local purposes. This makes educational R&D more difficult to administer than, for instance, defense R&D, and considerably more sensitive politically. And yet, unless the present R&D effort in education is both expanded considerably beyond its present levels and also coordinated in at least some informal way, there is a real danger that the opportunity to improve education will be dissipated.

More than anything else, we urge the Commission on Instructional Technology to examine the issue of how to research in instructional design can be furthered, and how research findings can best be implemented in a highly decentralized educational system. Speaking for our own interests, we believe that the education companies are capable of playing a major role in both the design of instructional through R&D work (more D than R), and in the implementation of instructional innovation through dissemination to the schools. We recognize, of course, that our business is the private sector of a public enterprise and that greater involvement will mean more subordination to public control. The problem will be to devise relationships between the public and private interests in education that provide the greatest natural incentive to work for the public good.

103.

The Multimedia Age

by *JOHN W. MEANEY*
Prof., Communication Arts
Asst. to V.P., Academic Affairs
Univ. of Notre Dame

It is urgently necessary for the United States to arrive at policy guidelines on the question of who should be encouraged to do the media software job of production. The basic reason for this urgency is the fact that the lead times in hardware and in software production are very different, favoring hardware consistently. More than that, the hardware engineers have been at work for a long time already and are even now practically in a position of saying, "Here is your multimedia system. What do you have to put into it?" If the software people are going to stumble around for years they may, in the process, discredit the entire potential of instructional media.

Moreover, the kinds of software that we refer to here are rather different from what we have known up to now, far more complicated. We have come to the end of the single medium era, the time when educators were willing to concentrate their bets on a favorite runner in the media derby, some on audio tapes, some on film, some on television, some on time-shared computers. Now it is becoming clear that these are all winners, in their special ways. The best combination of winnings may be to have audio tapes where the auditory sense and economy are primary factors, films where the high definition color picture is the chief requirement, television where you need live pictures or erasable recordings, computers for student feedback and drill, etc. In other words, the multimedia age is upon us. The goals of instruction will be increasingly well defined, and the media as the most efficient and thoroughly field tested means toward different portions of these goals will tend to take their logical places. Much of the teacher's transfer-of-information function will be shifted to these media tools, and the role of the teacher will in consequence, reach an even higher professional level, prescribing and supervising the mix of media for the individual student after getting to know him personally, after diagnosing his learning problems. The textbook in this age will expand into a whole spectrum of related learning devices, including but not limited to print, audio, graphics, slides, film, video tape and computer programs. This implies a wholly new kind of publication industry geared for electronic delivery in which basically similar pulses will produce either voice, picture, or print.[1] It also implies a new kind of library system in which digital storage with automatic retrieval and low-cost reproduction may lead to very limited original sales but a very extensive system of reproduction royalties. Clearly, all of this also implies a revision of the copyright act that will not inhibit such technological breakthroughs.

In addition to the diversity of media involved in these new developments there will probably also be required a great deal of redundancy or overlap among the software materials produced for such media. This arises from the fact that one student may have a greater facility for visual learning, another for auditory learning, and another for the inter-active processes available with computers. If the teacher is to vary the mix of media in order to meet the needs of the individual student without changing the basic goals of the course he will have to have this flexibility of choice.

But specifically how many sets of the new and expanded software materials for a given field and grade level should a teacher have available for this choice? Teachers in most fields have long been accustomed to having five or six nationally distributed textbooks offered them, texts that have probably been accounting, all together, for as much as eighty percent of the market sales. But if the multimedia packages of production are going to be many times more expensive than the old, single-text investment—as is certainly the case—how many competing series may we expect to have?

That we definitely want some multiplicity of choice in the new age we may take as one of our initial policy assumptions. Our commercial television system affords us three networks. The public television network that we are building after the pattern of the Carnegie Commission's report projects at least two national production centers. We have a long tradition of hostility to monopoly, especially in press and information fields. We may also take it, then, as an absolute requirement that our instructional system will continue to offer teachers a multiplicity of choice. Failing that, we would doubtless prefer, as a nation, to continue with the system that we have now.

The next policy requirement of the new system would probably be a degree of compatibility and standardization that will permit a flexible flow of materials between the media themselves and between the sources of production and distribution. This is a necessary correlate of our first requirement of multiplicity—whatever multiplicity we can afford must not be further whittled away by practical incompatibilities in hardware systems. We cannot, as a nation, afford in the instructional field the kind of fiasco that we have struggled through in the long-playing record field, for instance, where the battle between the big hole and the little hole led only to a waste of our industrial resources and the considerable inconvenience and deprivation of the consuming public. If greatly strengthened government standard-setting procedures are what we require now to head off such a development in instructional media, such procedures cannot begin too soon. We see already the wallowing of the industry in the standards morass of the helical scan video tape recorders. The industry clearly needs to be saved from itself and from the fragmentation that seems to be resulting also, in part, from its fears or experiences of our antitrust authorities.

A third policy requirement of the multimedia system of instruction must be its creativity. It must be, in its results, qualitatively better than what we have now—or else we do not wish to make the change. To be better, it must be humanized and humanizing. It must not only aim at but it must demonstrably attain a better human development in the learner, and it will be most likely to offer such a result through a redeployment of teachers as the humanistic exemplars in the teaching-learning community of the future. It must give to these teachers some creative opportunity to help with the construction of the media environment that will meet the needs of the individual student.

Where are we likely to find the kind and amount of media software production implied by such assumptions? It seems clear that the electronics-publishing mergers have been taking place with a view toward just such a task. This view seems to agree, also, with that of a recent report by the Committee for Economic Development which says that:

> "The joint efforts of subject matter scholars, education experts, and technicians are essential to the effective upgrading and updating of instructional material and methods in all fields. Publishers and other producers of instructional materials and manufacturers of educational equipment should assume a larger responsibility in this enterprise." [2]

There seems to be a kind of logic involved here: if you want to go from the textbook into multimedia materials start with the textbook company and add electronic capabilities. And yet, now that we are five or six years into this development and can see relatively few multimedia materials being marketed it may be time to reassess the situation.

Xerox seems to have touched off the wave of mergers in 1962 when it bought out University Microfilms and then went on later to acquire Basic Systems, Inc., the American Educational Publications series from Wesleyan University Press, and Ginn and Company. Xerox president McColough was quoted as saying, "Publish or perish is a phrase sometimes heard in universities. In industry, it will become 'educate or erode.' "[3] Last August Xerox's education division seemed to be showing some signs of erosion—eighty of its personnel were eliminated in a consolidation move.

RCA bought Random House with its L. W. Singer textbook division in 1966, but this year president Bernstein of Random House said: "Large businesses are still working very hard to find ways of improving education. But they are finding it a very difficult task."[4]

IBM bought Science Research Associates in 1964 with a view toward developments in computer-assisted instruction, but practical achievements have not as yet been extensive.

In 1965 General Electric Company and Time, Inc. joined to form the General Learning Corporation. Now, this year, Time, Inc. has gone on to buy Little, Brown & Co., the Boston book firm. Since Time's textbook firm of Silver Burdett had gone into the General Learning merger the Little, Brown acquisition appears to represent some corporate second thoughts.

Raytheon has bought the textbook firm of D. C. Heath & Co., and the most visible result has been a $400,000 contract to supply educational materials for Gondishapour University in Ahwaz, Iran. This may be some evidence that the international market, with all of its complications, is still an easier one in which to move instructional materials than is the domestic market.

Crowell-Collier now includes, besides Colliers Encyclopedia, the Macmillan publishing house, Brentano's book stores, the LaSalle Extension University, the Berlitz schools, a magazine entitled *Grade Teacher,* and an Institute of Continuing Education.[5] This array suggests a commitment to be found among other mergers, as well, a commitment even broader than formal education, and it may also give evidence of a pattern of specialization in some of the mergers.

CBS in 1967 bought Holt, Rinehart and Winston, and the CBS Board Chairman, William S. Paley, said: "The acquisition of Holt will give CBS a prime spot in the knowledge industry which is largely based on corporate partnerships that wed electronics and the printed work so as to participate in the U.S.'s education explosion."[6] But the potential seems even broader than electronics and the printed work in a corporation that also owns Columbia Records, four musical instrument companies, two educational film companies, a "Creative Playthings" company, and the New York Yankees. It is clearly too early to anticipate the kinds of production that might result from this amalgam.

In early 1966 Litton Industries bought American Book Company which had been publishing elementary, high school, and college textbooks, as well as educational discs. Even before that, Litton had been involved in instructional activities via management contracts for Job Corps centers.

The Ford-Philco merger of 1966 also seems to have multimedia implications from the fact that Philco has two Job Corps contracts to run trade schools in Oregon and Kentucky.[7]

There are many other mergers on the fringes of the multimedia age, including the old educational film companies which have been expanding to fit the pattern: Encyclopaedia Britannica Films has become part of Encyclopedia Britannica Educational Company, and McGraw-Hill has bought Spitz Laboratories which makes packaged planetariums. Former president Maurice Mitchell of the Britannica organization expressed their intentions thus: ". . . we will publish no textbook, make no film or tape, prepare no set of programmed learning materials that is not designed to be used as part of an integrated system."[8]

However, by September of 1968 all of the electronic-publishing merger corporations were moving so slowly and with so many organizational and other difficulties as to prompt the observation: ". . . while no one was saying flatly that the industry-in-education boom had fizzled, there was general agreement that the early glitter has all but disappeared. Products born of the industry-education marriages are few and far between; most companies are simply selling what their acquired subsidiaries always sold. . . ."[9]

Part of the difficulty in which the new corporations find themselves may arise out of the nature of the educational market: fragmented, conservative, resistant to change. Part of the difficulty may arise from the lead time required to plan and produce such a complicated and broad spectrum of materials. Part of the difficulty may arise from hesitations of corporations under antitrust scrutiny to allow their subsidiaries to work very closely together. At least some of the delay must be traced, however, to a reexamination of the size of the market. As Frank Keppel, Chairman of the Board of General Learning Corporation, explains it:[10] the vast education market of fifty to sixty billion dollars per year turns out to be very largely committed to teaching salaries and buildings. The only part actually available for investment in instructional materials may be about one billion dollars per year. Now if you assume an average industrial investment of 5% of gross sales in new research and development it becomes apparent that something in the order of $50,000,000 per year would be indicated. Private industry is simply not prepared to make a yearly investment of that size for research and development in the educational field, particularly when our national education legislation over the last six to ten years has clearly indicated an understanding by Congress that the funding of basic research in education is the responsibility of the federal government. Now under a Republican administration and virtually the same Democratic Congress it remains to be seen how this understanding can be translated into action.

It may be that a federal tax credit arrangement can be devised to stimulate the research and development of multimedia materials. Such a course of action would not be out of step with our general industrial requirements and recent experience. As Lawrence Lessing writes: "The propulsive force of this new age will be that chemical-electric-electronic-aerospace complex which now contains the country's technological elite, and which is phenomenally growing and intermixing into one giant, highly competitive innovative industry. The major companies in this complex, such as Litton, Lockheed, GE, DuPont, and RCA are all involved in one degree or another in the new developments coming up. . . ."[11]

C. R. Carpenter has recently called for a federal program on the assumption "that the strategy of publishers is not going to work satisfactorily for producing the combinations of electronic, printed, and other visual material which should characterize the patterns of modern instructional materials."[12] He feels that we must have legislation by Congress to begin the development of a network of educational and instructional materials production centers in which educational institutions and private industry will be brought into effective patterns of cooperation.

Certainly there is adequate precedent since the Elementary and Secondary Education Act of 1965 for federal contracts with private industry in the area of education. However, such a program must necessarily be open to participation by nonprofit agencies, as well, and there may be several kinds of these which will have important interests here.

When we visualize commercial textbook firms expanding into instructional materials production we may very well ask ourselves the question: "What of the university presses?" Are they likely to have an interest in being included? And, if so, why have they not had a major share of the textbook publishing in this country when so many of the authors work on their own campuses?

One answer seems to be that our university presses have largely relinquished the textbook field by deliberate choice out of their conception of themselves as nonprofit enterprises. In some cases they have, in fact, developed successful series of texts, only to transfer them to commercial houses when they became profitable, as at the University of Chicago where:

> "The writing and publishing of improved textbooks was a legitimate, indeed necessary, activity of a University in the opinion of President Harper, who was himself one of the editors of the Press's first venture in this area: the Constructive Bible Series for religious education. This textbook series began in 1900 and had grown to thirty-five titles by 1939, when it was transferred to commercial publication by Harper and Brothers."

> "Experimentation with teaching methods in the mathematics department of the University High School led to a series of high-school textbooks in mathematics which the Press published for thirty years before handing them over in 1937 to Laidlaw Brothers. And a series of foreign-language textbooks for high schools and colleges, in French, German, Spanish, Italian, and Latin, developed by experimental work in the classrooms of the University, was successfully established by the Press in the years 1925 to 1934. Then a joint publishing arrangement was made with D. C. Heath and Company by which they became the well-known Heath-Chicago Language Series."[13]

The university presses have not always been entirely consistent or rigid in the purity of their nonprofit motives, however; for at times they have accepted as part of their subsidy the profits made by their printing plant operations:

> ". . . at the University of Toronto Press, the surplus from the press' printing plant helps offset an overall loss on scholarly publishing. . . . Princeton University Press is similarly able to operate without a general annual grant from the university, in part because of the printing plant that was given to the press along with its buildings, early in the century."[14]

It is difficult to see, on principle, why the profits from a successful textbook line could not be used as well as profits from the printing plant to offset losses on other scholarly publications. The continuing financial frustrations of university press directors may suggest that this step will, in fact, be a logical one for such presses to take in the future. Chester Kerr, director of Yale University Press, has expressed the frustration this way: "We publish the smallest editions at the greatest cost, and on these we place the highest prices, and then we try to market them to people who can least afford them. This is madness."[15]

Another kind of nonprofit institution that could conceivably make a bid for some of the software production in the multimedia age is the regional educational laboratory. Jerrold Zacharias "recalls that one of the main reasons for the establishment of regional labs, in which he played an important role, was to insure a variety of up-to-date and imaginative courses and materials."[16]

James Koerner's judgment is that the labs are not now fulfilling their original purpose:

> "Unhappily, however, the regional labs, as they are now working out, show little awareness of the intentions of Zacharias, Singer, Keppel, Gardner, and others who promoted them. It is both instructive and disheartening to compare the rather grand vision that such people originally had of the regionals with the kind of agencies they are turning out to be. Gardner once spoke of these labs as 'combining the resources of MIT, IBM, and the New York State Board of Regents.' Francis Keppel spoke of them in an equally ambitious way at Congressional hearings before the passage of the 1965 Education Act."[17]

As one critic summarized the situation for Koerner, the labs "are nothing but schools of education with lots of money and no students." This capture of the new institutions by the Establishment is not likely to endure very long after such criticism comes to the attention of Congress which will be facing the problem of continuation funds and balancing such needs against those of other programs. Meanwhile, if there should be a federal tax incentive program for stimulation of innovative multimedia materials production we might well see a number of the labs being approached by industries interested in forming new consortia with clearly objective research components.

Finally, a federal program to stimulate multimedia materials production would be very likely to arouse great interest in some of the public television production centers around the country. After all, many of these centers are doing a relatively large volume of very low budget instructional materials production now. The typical daytime programs offered by the public television stations are enrichment-type lessons for the elementary and secondary schools—with the costs of acquiring or producing and broadcasting these programs being borne by the participating school systems. Many of these lesson series involve printed teacher manuals for the utilizing teachers, and some of them even involve printed student manuals. Other media than television and print are not as yet generally involved, but the approach to the multimedia spectrum might conceivably begin as logically from the television base as from the textbook base.

It is a fact that these school television productions are expected ultimately to shift to closed circuit and 2500 mgH facilities. Robert B. Hudson, Senior Vice President of NET, has recently predicted this,[18] as has Richard H. Bell of Ampex.[19]

Nevertheless, the production and recording for these series may very well continue on in many of the public television production centers where they occur now. In fact, this would be very much in keeping with the goal of the Carnegie Commission's report seeking to build up the production capabilities of the public television centers to first rate levels. The more that fragmentation of production can be prevented, the more that high volume and high-budgeted production can be concentrated the stronger these production centers will be. In fact, the more challenging instructional production that can be contracted for by·public television centers the more likely we are to see erased eventually that sad disparity between the documentary and artistic finesse of broadcast public television at its best and the production penury and neglect that is apparent in the instructional program that merely records a teacher in front of a blackboard. Instructional television has been of such poor quality that many public television authorities will be happy to see it leave their air and go to closed circuit.

There is no essential reason why the instructional television productions of the future should not be as excellent as the public television offerings—and perhaps the two could be practically interchangeable in many areas. But this cannot happen until reasonable production budgets are made available to instructional people and until the productions are concentrated in adequately equipped and staffed centers. This, in turn, would presuppose a considerably lessened volume of production commitment at local levels. As long as television represents for the schools only an intercom system with pictures there is nothing but casual mediocrity to be expected. The vast duplication in every field that has amounted to a national frittering away of our production resources has long been noted by foreigners as a great illogic. And yet, our efforts at spontaneous pooling of resources at state and regional levels have generally not been successful. We seem to be institutionally as well as temperamentally unprepared for this.

The entry of public television stations into this field has recently been called for specifically by James L. Loper, Station Manager of KCET, the public television station in Los Angeles. His advice to his fellow managers is that:

> "The marketing of ETV software is not to be entered into lightly or without considerable research but the rewards both in contribution to education and operating revenues, could be great."[20]

There are a number of other nonprofit agencies on the horizon but none with important production capabilities. The instructional materials libraries, for example, operated by the Eastern Educational Network, the Great Plains Instructional Television Library, and National Instructional Television of Bloomington, Indiana are basically distribution agencies, although the latter contracts for some production improvements and modifications in the series that it accepts. Such agencies could enter into consortium proposals along with public television production centers, thus supplying the national distribution potential that the public television centers would normally lack in such closed circuit work.

The recent passage of the "Networks for Knowledge" act also opens up the possibility that regional instructional materials centers under the aegis of leading universities might come into being. In some cases these might happen to coincide with important public television centers, thus lending another source of strength through coalescence. Such regional materials centers would be half-way houses between the local instructional materials centers currently existing in many schools and colleges and the national instructional materials distribution that will surely come about eventually by means of distribution satellites. The regional centers would be in a position of recording and holding satellite materials for local center scheduling much in the way that participating institutions in a cable or microwave system now use the helical-scan recorders to hold the closed circuit network offerings to meet local scheduling requirements.

A federal program to stimulate production and distribution of innovative multimedia software should, of course, be open to all existing agencies having an interest in this development, plus others not yet born. There is already some evidence of the kinds of industry-education consortia that might be expected to result. For instance, the General Learning Corporation has entered a consortium arrangement with the Pittsburgh Public Schools and with the regional educational laboratory at the University of Pittsburgh to develop and test primary educational materials for a comprehensive curriculum starting at age three and including an individualized instruction potential. RCA also has a cooperative project with Stanford's Institute for Mathematical Studies in the Social Sciences and Brentwood School of East Palo Alto, California, to explore computer-assisted instruction in reading and math applications for one hundred first grade students. Such are the kinds of consortia beginning to appear even now on a small scale with miscellaneous support from foundations, National Science Foundation, and the U.S. Office of Education.

Given a coherent program to stimulate just such developments we might find, in one case, a university press joining with a commercial film company to make a proposal. In another case an electronics-publishing corporation might work with a regional public television production center, each supplying its complementary parts of the package. Or, again, a regional educational laboratory with direct interest only in the research function could serve as prime contractor for a materials series that might involve subcontracts with other agencies for both production and distribution functions. Competitive bidding for several series of materials in each principal field and grade level would insure an adequate degree of multiplicity, compatibility and creativity, while at the same time permitting the new types of production centers and consortia to shake down and evolve on an empirical basis without detailed federal government blueprinting in advance.

The long hesitations and difficulties of private industries in getting into motion in the field of instructional materials production, in spite of their evident interest in doing so, suggest that this is an area of such high risk as well as national need that it justifies stimulation at the federal level. Under the policies of the new national administration it would appear that the most acceptable means of achieving this would be a program looking toward capitalization by private industry—even in consortia arrangements with nonprofit institutions—based on tax incentives. Such a program would constitute major support and go far toward guaranteeing the success of Mr. Nixon's proposed "National Institute for the Educational Future to serve as a clearinghouse for ideas in elementary and secondary education and explore the revolutionary possibilities that modern science and technology are making available to education." [21]

REFERENCES

1. Weiss, E. B. "The Communications Revolution and How it Will Affect All Business and All Marketing." *Advertising Age,* November 21, 1966, p. 106.

2. Committee for Economic Development. *Innovation in Education: New Directions for the American School.* A Statement on National Policy by the Research and Policy Committee, July 1968, pp. 36-37.

3. *Newsweek.* September 30, 1968, p. 82.

4. *Ibid.,* p. 83.

5. *Business Week.* May 14, 1966, p. 124.

6. *Time.* March 10, 1967, p. 85.

7. Siekman, Philip. "Henry Ford and his Electronic Can of Worms." *Fortune,* February 1966, p. 119.

8. *Newsweek.* January 24, 1966, p. 76.

9. *Newsweek.* September 30, 1968.

10. Keppel, Frank. Unpublished address to A National Conference on Trends in Education. University of Notre Dame campus, October 26, 1968.

11. Lessing, Lawrence. "Where the Industries of the Seventies Will Come From." *Fortune,* January 1967, pp. 97-98.

12. Carpenter, C. R. "A Critique of Educational Technology." *Audio Visual Communication Review,* V. 16, No. 1, Spring 1968, p. 23.

13. The University of Chicago Press. *Catalogue of Books and Journals.* Chicago, 1967, pp. xxi-xxii.

14. Hawes, Gene R. *To Advance Knowledge.* American University Press Services, Inc., New York, 1967, p. 83.

15. *Ibid.,* p. 5.

16. Koerner, James E. "EDC: General Motors of Curriculum Reform." *Saturday Review,* August 19, 1967, p. 58.

17. *Ibid.,* p. 58.

18. Hudson, Robert B. "The Future of Educational Television." Unpublished talk at the *Toward Century 21* symposium, Stanford University, April 4, 1968.

19. Bell, Richard H. "The Challenge of ITV." *Educational/Instructional Broadcasting,* Vol. 1, No. 1, February/March 1968, p. 17.

20. Loper, James L. "Who Should Market ETV Software?" *Educational Broadcasting Review,* Vol. 2, No. 5, October 1968, p. 37.

21. Nixon, Richard M., quoted in *American Council on Education, Higher Education and National Affairs,* Vol. XVII, No. 38, November 1, 1968, p. 3.

104.

Technology and Education: Who Controls?

by THEODORE R. SIZER
Dean
Graduate School of Education
Harvard University

DAVID L. KIRP
Asst. Prof. of Education
Exec. Dir. of Center for Law and Education
Harvard University

The new educational technology* is not an end in itself, worthy of encouragement for its own sake; it is a means of effectively carrying out educational ends independently fixed by those whose central concern is the education of children. In the context of "control" of education, this suggests that the best hedge on the possibility of supplier-dominated education is not the technologists' self-checking process, but rather the creation of a new force, an independent "consumers' union" for education which would test and evaluate all materials. In the context of the training of teachers, the understanding and intelligent use of technology as a means, rather than an end in itself, can best be maintained by including exposure to the new technology as part of substantive courses, so that the technology will serve the objectives of instruction, providing new ways of reaching those objectives.

Policy questions about the relationships between education and the new technology are essentially questions about control. The technology itself is neither monster nor miracle worker, but merely an aid (like blackboards and books). Used properly, that tool can assist teachers and school systems to accomplish what they deem should be done; used improperly, the tool can become an end in itself, subverting the legitimate aims of education.

Presently, the suppliers of educational goods and services exert a large and perhaps unhealthy influence on that market. The recent entrance of industrial giants into that market, viewed in light of their conduct thus far, raises the unhappy spectre of an educational oligopoly, dominated by companies interested primarily in short-range profits, not longer-range, research-supported contributions to education. While the diffuseness of the public education "system" provides some safeguards against takeover by the technocrats, the capacity of public education to evaluate new materials, and thus to have a voice in the creation of those materials, remains limited. This paper recommends the utilization of state and regional evaluation centers, and it strongly urges the creation and public support of a non-profit, independent consumers' union for education, which would shift control back to the educators.

In training teachers in the new technology, technological competency, the capacity to

*"New technology" refers to recently developed equipment designed to facilitate some aspect of learning (and teaching); it includes programmed materials, television, motion pictures, computer-aided instruction, information retrieval systems, etc.

understand the relationship of technology to all aspects of learning, and now mere mechanical know-how should be stressed. Existing "audiovisual aids" courses, which consider the technology apart from the curriculum courses and child development courses, fail to meet this need, and for other reasons are likely to be distrusted by teachers and school systems. New approaches to teacher training (both in-service and pre-service) which undertake to relate the technology to learning process are needed.

The Conventional Wisdoms

The conventional wisdom is of two minds concerning the impact of technology on education. To some (including, but not limited to, those engaged in developing technological applications) technology is a miracle worker, capable of remaking education in its own benign image:

> One can predict that in a few more years millions of school children will have access to what Philip of Macedon's son, Alexander, enjoyed as a royal prerogative: the personal services of a tutor as well-informed and responsive as Aristotle.[1]

The variety of available technology is cited as proof of its value:

> Recent technological aids to individualization include magnetic tapes, microfilms, and teaching machines. Programmed instruction offers a rich new supply of materials designed for independent study. Computer based instruction, now in early phases of development, will allow highly individualized learning. Dial-selection systems offer another valuable approach to independent study. Newly developed facilities—carrels, seminar rooms, and learning resources centers—contribute valuable settings for the conduct of individualized instruction. Computer-based record systems are being developed that will offer vastly improved means of analyzing, storing, and retrieving information about individual students. Computers are also being used to accomplish individualized scheduling in high schools . . .[2]

To those who adopt this position, the sources of resistance (generally, teachers) represent traditionalism at its most dangerous.[3] The technologists attempt to reckon with these sentiments by reassuring the teacher that:

> . . . these devices are surely [his] liberator . . . their capacity to learn is nearly infinite, and they never forget. Also, they never get tired, they never lose patience, and they never look askance and embarrass the somewhat slower student.[4]

The teacher, however, reads the description and is far from reassured; the machine appears to be ever so much less fragile than he or she is. For this continued unwillingness to seize the technological day, the teacher is scolded, accused of fearing change.

> [Administrators and faculty] are comfortable in the existing framework and prefer the status quo. The effective use of media raises curriculum and evaluation questions that are not only difficult to answer, but the responses also shatter major assumptions. . . .[5]

To others, the technological invasion of education is to be resisted, not because of fear of loss of jobs or unwillingness to alter seemingly fixed patterns of instruction, but out of concern for the survival of human values. They shudder when they learn of an "individualized" learning that leaves no room for happenstance, but rather guides a student from one predetermined point to another, as programmed instruction materials typically do. James Ridgeway, doing research for a piece on the "Computer-Tutor," reported on his dialogue with a history-programmed computer:

The computer asked, "A legend connects Betsy Ross to George Washington; according to the story what did Betsy Ross do?"

"I do not know."

"Try again, making your answer an affirmative statement."

"Betsy Ross made flags."

"Whose flag? Which flag?"

"She made U.S. flags."

"The U.S. flag did not exist as such until after 1870. This legend refers to an earlier period. Whose flag? Which flag?"

"She made American flags."

Then the computer began to give hints:

"She made — — American flag. Try again."

"She made the first American flag."

"Right, she made the first American flag." [6]

Nor are educators mollified by the clever computer that learns the name of its tutee, and greets him with "hello, Johnny," rather than with the less personal "hello, X." They are concerned with the subtle effects of a child's dependence on a machine for answers, and for the formulation of questions, on his ability to cope with individuals and communities.

At its most simplistic, this position represents intellectual Ludditism: destroy the machines. Yet in its most responsible form the position does pose crucial problems of personal identity, and of control, that need to be faced up to in coming to terms with the technology. The educator's concern about control has, at its best, a moral basis. This concern is ideological, not necessarily measured in changing school structures or changing market patterns. The educator typically regards himself as charged with the task of conveying ideas, principles, values that are essentially human and democratic; indeed, he may well view education as concerned principally with the transmission of these values, rather than with the speedy and efficient conveyance of a fixed body of knowledge.

> We like to believe [that in the "human-based school"] children and youth are inducted into their culture; individual potentialities are identified and developed; individuals take on a sense of identity and ultimately transcend themselves; and the young are inculcated in those values that make for the ideal adult.[7]

Frequently, the technocrat appears a threat to this set of values, one who by running schools more effectively (however measured) than the educator has in the past will seduce those who ultimately fix the educational priorities into viewing education as understandable from a systems-analytic viewpoint.[8]

Much of this concern derives from the demands that the technologists make on those whom they ostensibly serve. They call for regularized procedures, for formulae that can be reduced to punch card codification. While such procedures are feasible—and indeed may be necessary—for the business inspired by a profit-motive, they are less appropriate when the end sought is something as nebulous as learning or growth. Yet the educator must be able to assert these latter goals if education is to permit freedom as well as formalism, serendipity as well as scientific method.

I. A. Richards has reminded us that we "are products of the assistance we can accept . . . potential victims of those who, for whatever motives, would like to run things for us." [9] That victimization needs guarding against, especially as it relates to controls over educational goals. To the educator, technology should be regarded as means and not end. To let the technology define educational objectives—whether these be in training teachers, in evaluating materials, or in whatever educational endeavor—is to do a disservice both to the technology and to education. Carried far enough, it converts the school system into blank-check-writer, acquiescing in the gospel of gadgetry; it converts the teacher into tinkerer, one who starts up the equipment, and then waits for mechanical mishaps. The awesomeness of the technology demands a reassertion of human values, and human control. "The greatest intellectual challenge of our time is not how to design machines that behave more like humans, but rather, how to protect humans from being treated more and more like machines." [10]

The Education Market

The increased use of technology in education is seen by some educators as a move towards the "takeover" of education by "outsiders," the developers and suppliers of educational goods who are supposed to serve the educational system. The educators fear that technologists will occupy an ever-increasing role in influencing and making decisions about the educational enterprise. Such a concern about power, and about numbers (who will be doing what in education) upsets many. Writing in *The New Republic,* James Ridgeway describes in apocalyptic terms the ambitions of the ardent computerists:

> They want to design a school system, provide it with innovative materials and equipment, and then test the finished product—in this case, the student as he comes out of one system and goes into another. The long-range thrust is toward making the computer into an effective teaching machine. If this can be done, *the present school structure will radically change. It is conceivable that the school as we now know it will go out of existence altogether.*[11]

The school today, of course, is profoundly influenced by those "outsiders" whom the educators fear. That they appear unaware of this influence is traceable to two factors: they don't see the textbook salesmen as "outsiders" and they are not as conscious as they might be of the influence of existing teaching materials on the school's program and on the children's capacity to learn. While it is difficult to ascribe effect in any scientific sense, it is reasonable to argue that the textbook and the workbook are the *principal* influence on the shape of the school program today. All too many teachers are ill-prepared to teach the subjects assigned them and thus are obliged to rely on the text as a crutch. Most teachers are overworked (those who deny it should spend six unbroken hours responsible for thirty-five lively ten year olds) and have to fall back on materials, often workbooks, to keep the children "busy." Most school syllabi are so vague as to be useless; the assigned texts determine in critical substantive ways what is taught. The "education business" has, in sum, a major influence on school practice today. To say that the new technologically-based industries are the first to threaten educators' autonomy is to avoid the obvious but usually overlooked facts of the situation.

Seen in this light, the recent entrance of new, large manufacturers—large enough to package broad scale, multi-media programs—into an already supplier-dominated market arouses real concern. In the mid-1960's, companies such as International Business Machines, Xerox, Radio Corporation of America, General Electric, Raytheon, and Sylvania (industrial giants all) acquired smaller educational materials outfits. At each of these occasions, there was talk of two sorts: of the debt that American industry owed to education, and of the vast untapped potential of the educational technology market.

These industrial giants do have the capacity to undertake the research and pre-marketing evaluation necessary to produce decent materials. As one writer, describing the trend two years ago declared:

> The companies now coming into the market have resources—of manpower and talent as well as of capital—far greater than the education market has seen before.

They have, in addition, a commitment to innovation and an experience in management that is also new to the field.[12]

They also have the capacity—the sales and promotional and fiscal resources—to overwhelm the market with textbooks and technological gadgetry which provide more slickness than substance. The record of these companies over the past several years is discouraging: thus far, many have stressed short-term profitability rather than long-range planning. Many companies have been unwilling to make substantial investments for basic research, preferring the surer and more immediate gains that come with almost-instant marketing of new products. While companies argue that the market structure makes industrial influence of a new and happy kind difficult to achieve, these companies have not moved to begin providing shopping lists of curricular materials of differing kinds—related texts and films and tapes, and the exposure of teachers to those materials—which would encourage thoughtful planning and selecting by the teacher in a subject area, but have instead produced a text *or* a film *or* a tape, to be plugged in at some arbitrary point in the progress of a course.[13]

The education market is assuredly big: school expenditures for the 1966-67 school year were estimated at 48.8 billion dollars, making education the second biggest national market (just behind defense).[14] Yet American public education is not really a single functioning "system" at all. There exist more than twenty thousand school districts, each of which operates almost wholly independently. On specific matters of school policy, control resides at various levels within the school districts. One organization, which sought to illustrate the advantages of the computer in performing administrative tasks in a school system, found that it should appeal directly to school superintendents; the P.S.S.C. course planners concluded that the physics teacher would have to be wooed as an individual, that no superintendent's directive could persuade him even to buy the P.S.S.C. materials, let alone to use them. This dispersion of power, and consequent difficulty of acquiring a position of control, is likely to increase. The political winds favor structural school decentralization, which will yield even more school districts to contend with, and, more radically, increasing community power in schools, which will require that the technologist seeking to market his products convince parents as well as educators that the item is worth trying out.

For other reasons, education seems peculiarly inhospitable to takeover by the industrial technocrats. There are difficulties of measurement, and of comparison of competing products. "Effectiveness" in education is not readily defined; alternative approaches are not really trying to accomplish the same end. And even if one way of doing something could be shown to be demonstrably "better," this doesn't guarantee its adoption. In this sense, analogies to other supplier-consumer markets, and the ways companies come to dominate those markets, may mislead. In the typical market situation, the person buying the good is the one for whom increased efficiency will make a difference by making the good more obviously useful to him. Thus, appeals to the consumer can be couched in terms of enlightened self-interest. In education, however, the ultimate "consumer" is really the students; it is he who most directly benefits or suffers from the quality of goods and services that the school system buys. But this "consumer" has little or no influence on those who do the "buying," the professional educators and, to a lesser degree, the parents. The decisions by these surrogates for students are based in part on the students' needs, as these are perceived, but they are also based on political needs including the felt need to maintain a tradition of cautious action and, most critically, on financial realities.[15] These other factors may argue against using the very equipment that would most benefit the students, and the schools. At the worst, the "consumers' interest" is not in the hands of the true consumers at all, but in the hands of surrogates who fail to understand or give serious weight to the students' needs.

Centralization of some functions would doubtless be useful. Individual teachers, or individual schools, or even individual school districts—the groups that presently make most of the *ad hoc* evaluations of new materials—have neither the time nor resources to do that job effectively. Two innovations would be of particular value: (1) increased reliance by schools and school districts on state departments of education, and on regional school district associations, for testing and evaluating educational materials; (2) the creation of a consumers' union for education which would provide the forum for an independent evaluation of educational materials. Neither innovation would culminate in state-approved lists of, say, "social studies texts and films deemed appropriate for the sixth grade;" both would provide independent, detailed evaluation and comment on new materials. The schools' dependence on the suppliers for "evaluation" would be lessened and schools and teachers could exercise legitimate control in making more careful and intelligent choices about materials.

This latter entity—a consumers' union for education—is of especial importance and could represent an important new force in the political mix that "controls." The union could give evidence, often necessarily initial and incomplete evidence, but the best that there is at any rate, and such evidence would inform those making decisions about materials. The practice of asserting the "success" of a program or text because some "Nobel Laureate endorses it" would give way to assertions based on real data (data which that same Nobel Laureate has, presumably, been taught to respect in his own discipline). Such a consumers' union for education could not be supported in any way by industry; it would most likely have to be an independent non-profit corporation funded by the government, foundations, and co-operating school systems.[16]

In sum, technology—or the materials' "business"—should be the servant of humane goals set for children by their parents, educators, and the community at large. This will only be possible if there is an effort to establish non-partisan assessments of materials. A "consumers' union" is an essential element in proper control.

The Training of Teachers

Linus: This "new math" is too much for me.

Lucy: You'll get on to it . . . It just takes time. . . .

Linus: Not me . . . I'll never get on to it!

Linus: How can you do "new math" with an "old math" mind?

"On Adaptability," from *Linus on Life*

Technologists, amazed that teachers have not accepted machines that promise to reduce error, increase efficiency, hasten learning, and generally make education a rational process, complain of the paucity of training programs designed to acquaint teachers with the wonders of the new technology. Indeed, such programs are few: only a limited number of universities, U.C.L.A., Catholic University, and the University of Pittsburgh among them, have extensive course offerings in the field; many schools of education do not offer any exposure to the technology.

Even at those schools which offer some instruction in what is commonly called "audiovisual aids," that instruction is unsatisfactory. It is generally lumped into a single course taught at the end of the curriculum. Machines of increasingly byzantine complexity are wheeled into the classroom, and they are demonstrated; this is supposed to enable the teacher to operate a film projector without constantly splicing the film, or a tape recorder without erasing the day's lesson.

These "audiovisual aids" courses accomplish several ends, not all of them intended. By having teachers operate actual equipment, they may reduce the teacher's fear of the machine; to that extent they are useful. However, such courses may limit a teacher's notion of suitable equipment, by stressing the presently available.

More significantly, the timing (and, indeed, the very existence) of separate audiovisual courses affords the teacher a notion of what the audiovisual is for: it is for show, for gimmickry, a device to be used to recapture flagging attention. Unlike books and black-boards (which are, after all, only other kinds of "aids"), audiovisual equipment is talked about as if it constituted a separate subject. It has nothing to do with science, or social studies, or language; applications of the technology are not explored in the curriculum classes. It has nothing to do with different learning processes; the technology is not discussed in child development classes. It has, in short, nothing to do with anything else; it occupies a marginal role in the teaching of teachers, mirroring what will be its marginal role in the teaching of children.

In learning about technology, the teacher needs to know more than how to turn on and off a battery of machines; he needs to acquire technological competence. While it is unlikely, and perhaps unnecessary, that he will fully understand the mechanics of the available tools (for that, trained specialists might well be more appropriate), his training should enable him to develop some sense of how technology bears on what he thinks he is doing as a teacher. With such a sense, he could determine what he needed in order to present material more effectively, what a machine might do that would be helpful. Armed with that under-standing, he could intelligently negotiate for the sort of equipment that would suit his needs.

The central point, however, is that the training of the teacher must start with the objec-tives of instruction and with the means to reach those objectives. Novice teachers should be shown alternative teaching strategies, and in this context learn about the "technologies." The aids—whether as simple as blackboards or as complex as computers—follow from and depend on the objectives; they are part of the pedagogy related to the material being taught. That material and the objectives it addresses govern the choice and employment of the technologies, not vice versa.

The foregoing is obvious, but usually ignored. In industry, for example, there is evidence of more research and development in "hardware" rather than "software," on complete technological programs rather than resources to expand and support flexible and varied curricula. While it is often asserted that "technology follows the ends of education," there is little evidence that this is presently a governing factor. How much interest has the edu-cation industry, particularly the new technologically-based companies, shown in the ends underlying education? One cannot assume that there are givens, simply to be accepted and acted upon by industry. Technology shapes ends, in that it may make available new means: ends previously unreachable may now be within grasp.

Industry and education need closer ties, a recognition of the fact that materials follow objectives, and that constant interaction between teachers and material developers is there-fore essential. Furthermore, teachers must be trained to see the importance of this inter-action and to partake in it.

The need for technological competence compels teachers, and schools of education, to face up to many questions: questions involving the processes of learning, and how any situation relates to those processes. About such matters much research also needs to be done, for precious little is understood. One can talk about "ordered procedures generated by and re-flecting human intelligence," [17] but the specifics of what those procedures might be, and how that intelligence is to be defined and measured, remain elusive. Faced with this lack of information about how learning happens, the teacher is not readily persuaded that the technician's stress on speed, efficiency, accuracy, and clear directions should prevail over the need—presently unsatisfied by the technology—to develop the student's confidence in his ability to determine goals.[18] As a study of "New Media Research in Teacher Educa-tion" concluded:

> Studying media in combination will improve our knowledge but will constitute only one step toward the most central and complex issue in the use of new media in teacher education: what can each device and combination of devices do best for different kinds of students, under different educational conditions, with respect

to different educational objectives, and when used by different teachers? Obviously, no single medium or combination of media will accomplish the full job of training the teacher. No single criterion or set of criteria for successful teaching is likely to emerge, and no single best pattern for the training of all teachers is likely to be identified. In the same way, no single best pattern in the use of new media is likely to emerge as most effective under all instructional conditions.[19]

In-service training programs, as presently conceived, do not appear to offer substantial hope of awakening classroom teachers to the potential of the technology. Except when such programs are being offered for small numbers of teachers by a professional staff well versed in the uses and limitations of technology, their value has been marginal.[20] Companies have traditionally offered day or weekend-long programs to promote their own products, but this hardly equips the teacher to deal intelligently, and independently, with the technology. For this reason, public schools have not provided substantial financial support to such programs.

> In-service teacher training is the slum of American education . . . Public school systems have not been willing to make a significant financial commitment to in-service training and staff development activities . . . Colleges and universities have found offering courses for school teachers and administrators lucrative but have not allocated major financial or academic resources to the activity.[21]

Even when in-service training is available, it is more frequently viewed by the teacher as a way of satisfying state education requirements (and of making more money) than as an opportunity to become a better teacher.

> Teachers typically have seen in-service training as 'something somebody else does for us.' The policies and ground rules have been set by certification officials, school boards, school and college administrators. Typically teachers have docilely accepted both policies and offerings and have seldom even questioned the system.[22]

Schools may be reluctant to subsidize teacher training in educational technology for another reason. The schoolteacher trained in the new technology immediately becomes attractive to the many industries that use and develop similar equipment; these companies can offer salaries and working conditions to the technologically-trained teacher that public schools presently cannot match, and thus are able to lure him away from teaching. This tendency of the technologically competent to leave teaching has dissuaded many administrators from sending teachers to training courses that promise technological literacy.

One way of combatting this reluctance would be to give financial encouragement to school systems, enabling them to include on their staffs professionals who could develop programs which utilized the new technology, suggest equipment to classroom teachers, help evaluate new materials, etc. The availability of such positions might keep many of the technologically competent in the teaching profession, as well as provide school systems with personnel that understood the equipment that was available.[23]

Conclusion

Any discussion of the policy implications inherent in the development of new technology for education raises questions of competing social values, questions of control. Properly understood, the technology can serve both as a way of accomplishing more successfully the independently-fixed goals of education, and as a way of broadening those goals by providing the capacity to accomplish the heretofore unaccomplishable. The advent of the new technology, and the training of teachers to technological competence, should be viewed in this light. This necessitates rethinking what learning is about, and how any technology, be it blackboard or computer, affects learning; reconsidering the structure of education, including the need for an independent force, a "consumers' union" to help in confronting and evaluating potentially revolutionary changes, of which the new technology is but one example.

REFERENCES

1. Suppes, P. "The Uses of Computers in Education." *Scientific American,* September 1966, pp. 218-219.

2. Heathers, G. "Individualized Instruction." U.S. Congress, Senate Committee on Labor and Public Welfare, Subcommittee on Education. *Notes and Working Papers Concerning the Administration of Programs Authorized Under Title III of Public Law 89-10. The Elementary and Secondary Education Act of 1965 as Amended by Public Law 89-750.* Government Printing Off., Washington, D.C., April 1967, Ch. 7, Sec. B., pp. 177-178.

3. In his thoughtful essay, *The Teacher and the Machine,* (Pittsburgh: The Univ. of Pittsburgh Press, 1967), Philip Jackson cites studies of teachers' opposition to technological aids.

4. "Technology in Education." National School Public Relations Association, Washington, D.C., 1967, p. 5.

5. "Expert Answers to Urgent Questions." *College Management,* October 1968, pp. 17-18.

6. "Computer-Tutor." *The New Republic,* June 4, 1966, p. 20.

7. Goodlad, J. "The Future of Learning and Teaching." *AV Communication Review,* XVI, Spring 1968, p. 6.

8. This moral concern arises whenever technology may have an impact on policy: ". . . the people who occupy leadership positions in management can hire technologists. But often they are not able to transfer to them the fabric of their values. It is becoming difficult to continue the apprenticeship of wisdom that normally flows between the man who manages and the technologist. The manager may feel that his outdated technical training is inadequate and this fear may be communicated in the transmission of his values as manager to those next in line. It is essential that the non-scientist stop worrying about the gap between the two cultures and admit that there is a management of science." De Carlo, "Perspectives in Technology," in E. Ginzberg (ed.) *Technology and Social Change* (New York: Columbia University, 1964), p. 41. See also Raymond Callahan, *Education and the Cult of Efficiency,* (Chicago: University of Chicago Press, 1962) for a study of the effect of Taylor's "efficiency" movement in the early 20th century.

9. Bushnell, D., and D. Allen, Eds. *The Computer in American Education.* Wiley, New York, 1967, intro. xviii.

10. Jackson, P. *The Teacher and the Machine.* p. 66. Professors Ellis and Tiedeman have considered similar matters in discussing computerized guidance systems: "Because machines and human beings are different media, to expect one to act like the other is more like expecting a poet to literally paint a portrait with words. We must let the machine stay a machine, but recognize that the activity of counselling by human beings is a means to an end, this end being some desired condition in which the client will eventually find himself. Our interest thus centers on the possibilities of a machine achieving this same end even though it does so in a manner clearly different from human beings." "Can A Machine Counsel?" (Unpublished paper, 1968.)

11. Ridgeway, J. "Computer-Tutor." p. 19. (Emphasis added.)

12. Silberman, C. "Technology is Knocking at the Schoolhouse Door." *Fortune,* August 1966, pp. 120-121.

13. The structure and market power of the suppliers of educational materials has been inadequately studied. No one has seriously considered, for example, whether "the market" about which primary concern should be voiced is the "textbook market," the "science textbook market," "the biology textbook market," or some very different entity. The recent record described in the text suggests the need for careful study by economists, lawyers, and educators of the present state of the educational materials market, of recent trends in that market, and of particular aspects of that market where concentration appears particularly acute.

14. "Technology in Education." National School Public Relations Association, Washington, D.C., 1967.

15. McCusker and Sorenson describe the economic characteristics of education as "(1) a high degree of labor intensity; (2) a low degree of specialization of labor; and (3) a low level of research and development activity." In the analysis of possible effects of new media it is anticipated that little change will occur during the next decade. They predict that education will "remain massive in size, diversive in form, complex in function, pervasive in effort, and conservative in nature." "The Economics of Education," in P. Rossi & B. Biddle (eds.), *The New Media and Education: Their Impact on Society,* Aldine Pub. Co., Chicago, 1966.

16. The "union contemplated here is similar in some ways to Educational Products Information Exchange (E.P.I.E.), a New York-based organization which publishes a monthly report providing specifications for the materials in a particular subject area. The proposed union would also provide critical evaluation of the materials, and would offer teachers and school districts individualized assistance, based on their own assessment of needs.

    Reference to this idea has been made in the recent report, *Innovation in Education,* pub. by the Committee for Economic Development, New York, 1968, which proposes "the creation of a Commission on Research, Innovation and Evaluation in Education" p. 70.

17. Ellis, discussion of *"Educational Technology: New Myths and Old Realities,"* Harvard Educational Review, XXXVIII, Fall, 1968, (forthcoming).

18. Oettinger and Marks discuss the computer-programmers' claims regarding "individualized instruction" extensively in Chapter 4 of their forthcoming book, *Run, Computer, Run.*

19. Lesser and Schueler, "New Media Research in Teacher Education," *A V Communications Review,* XIV, Fall 1966, p. 352.

20. This has generally been the history of training programs designed to explain new curricular materials, like P.S.S.C. physics, to teachers. The caliber of training has declined as the number of those being trained increased. For much curricular material, no teacher training at all is provided.

21. Davies, "Teacher Education." U.S. Congress, Sen. Comm. on Labor and Public Welfare, Subcomm. on Educ. *Notes and Working Papers Concerning the Administration of Programs Authorized Under Title III of Public Law 89-10, The Elementary and Secondary Education Act of 1965 as Amended by Public Law 89-750.* Gov. Pr. Off., Washington, D.C., April 1967, Ch. 15, Sec. B, p. 295.

22. *Ibid.,* p. 297.

23. How such "media specialists" are to be trained poses another and very much open question. See V. Gerlach, "The Professional Education of the Media Specialist." *A V Communication Review* XIV, Summer 1966, p. 185.

105.
The Media Manufacturer
And the Educator

by *ROBERT G. SMITH, JR.*
Dir. for Program Development
Human Resources Research Org.
Alexandria, Virginia

The Problem

This paper has been prepared for the Commission on Instructional Technology, to discuss the following questions:

> How can the educational community best specify its needs in order for industry to respond with the most appropriate equipment, programs, etc.? How can the educational community and industry establish a closer working relationship and better mutual understanding so that industry can more closely meet education's technological requirements?

These questions raise a number of answers, which deal with matters which are not easy to resolve. The origins of potential solutions must be sought in the ecology of education, the systems approach to instruction, and the process of social change.

The Ecology of Education

Political Factors

The most common form of political control of education is the local school district, governed by a school board. The school board, in turn, is influenced by the local power structure in the major decisions made about the schools. This influence has been described by Kimbrough (1965). The major decisions are made by the influential persons in the community in informal meetings completely outside formal governmental procedures. The influential people generally develop through shared informal interaction a frame of reference upon which these decisions are based.

Actions of the local school boards are in turn constrained by state laws which deal with such matters as certification of teachers, attendance and curriculum. School books are often selected on the state level, or at least a limited choice selected, from which the teacher may choose.

In recent years, the federal government has made a variety of attempts to encourage innovations in the schools. However, because federal funds have been used as a kind of "bribe" to encourage school desegregation, there are strong pressures to simply pass on the federal funds to the states without any federal control at all. If this happens, the push toward innovation will be gone.

Traditionally, the classroom teacher has exercised little decision making power. The educational specialists and supervisors have been able to exert some influence in making decisions. However, the major decisions concerning the schools are still likely to be made by persons who are not educators.

The schools have been under severe attack on one ground or another for about ten years. The launching of Sputnik by the USSR in 1957 set off a major criticism of the schools for failing to develop scientists and engineers. College professors have been critical of the way their subjects have been taught in the schools, and have involved themselves in the preparation of school courses. More recently, the schools have been criticized for their failures to teach children in the inner city. Student unrest, starting in the colleges and universities, has begun to reach the high schools.

The effect of all this criticism has been to make educators and teachers less tolerant of even modest proposals for change. School administrators have objected to the modest proposals for a national assessment of education. Teachers are becoming unionized, and turning to the strike as a means of securing their demands.

The implications for those who wish to develop and sell equipment to the schools are clear. There are many groups which may have influence on the decision to buy. They must all be reached.

The Educator and His General Characteristics

As Biddle and Rossi (1967) have pointed out, education is labor-intensive—that is, relatively little equipment is involved in the educational process. The capital investment in the public schools in the main consists of the real estate on which the school stands, the buildings, and the furniture.

The industrial revolution, then, has not yet come to education. The teaching process most commonly means the students and one (or sometimes more, in the case of team teaching) teacher in a room. At the primary level, especially, there is little differentiation of functions. The teachers are viewed as nearly interchangeable units, so that a given teacher may be assigned to teach in a different grade each year.

In an insightful article on why so little change occurs in education as a result of educational research, Travers (1962) has described some general characteristics of educators. Sieber (1968) describes related matters.

The first point to be noted is that educators represent a highly selected subculture. A rigorous self-screening takes place because of the requirements of teacher certification and the courses needed to obtain a certificate. The selection process is still more stringent for the principals and superintendents. They generally must have both a teaching certificate and experience as a classroom teacher.

Travers points out that while educators tend to be above average in intelligence, they tend not to include many of those who are very high in intelligence. They are generally not very innovative or scientific; rather they prefer the day-to-day routine of teaching or administration, and are conservative in outlook.

The human aspects of the relationship between students and teachers tend to be highly valued by educators; as a result they tend to resist the idea of replacing any human function with equipment or other media. One form this resistance takes is a tendency to label innovations as just another "aid" to the teacher—even if the innovation could (and perhaps should, for maximum advantage) radically change teacher functions.

Even those who are convinced of the need for radical reform in our schools, make statements about "nothing ever replacing the teacher." In addition, every time any piece of equipment comes into the schools, or is even suggested, the question of "what about human warmth?" is raised. This suggests an ideal which forgets that there are also such qualities as human indifference, anger, sarcasm, and laziness.

While the teacher or principal may have little direct decision-making power over the major matters, they can certainly affect equipment usage, and thereby purchases. The legendary "closets full of unused audiovisual equipment" which are supposed to exist in the schools, certainly do not promote the sales of new equipment.

Further, one can hardly blame the teacher for neglecting to use equipment which he has not been taught to use with ease; which is awkward and clumsy to move around; which is difficult to check out of the supply room; and for which there are no new and up-to-date tapes, films, or slides.

The Role of Media in a Systems Approach to Education

The Concept of an Instructional System

The present author (Smith, 1966) has described the concept of an instructional system as an integrated set of media, methods, people, and equipment, performing efficiently the functions required to accomplish one or more objectives.

This concept implies that:

1. There are clearly defined goals for the system. For instruction, these goals are objectives which describe the behavior we wish to produce in the student.

2. There are functions that are to be carried out by the media, methods, people and equipment. The particular way these functions are to be carried out, and by which means, is a matter to be decided on a cost-effectiveness basis. Thus the system concept is neutral as to whether a particular function requires people or equipment. It only asks that the least expensive way that accomplishes the objective be selected.

3. The various elements that make up the system are properly integrated to carry out the objectives of the system.

An Example of a Non-System

In order to try to illustrate the nature of an educational system, let me describe a non-system. This is the true story of how my daughter learned to hate French through educational television.

The City of Hampton, Virginia was proud of the fact that they used educational television. Stories on the use of television in the schools regularly appeared in the newspapers extolling the features of television for education. Three times a week, for a half-hour period, a course in French was broadcast. For three years, during the fourth, fifth and sixth grades, under three different teachers, here is what happened to my daughter. Three times a week, the teacher quieted the pupils, and turned on the television set. The broadcast was all in French. When the program was over, the teacher turned off the set and moved on to other subjects.

The children thus learned that French was a dull subject that no one could understand.

When I talked to the teachers, they admitted that they didn't like the situation, but none of them knew any French and they could not support the broadcasts with explanations or practice exercises. But they did know if the principal came by and looked in their door window, they had better have the television set on.

When I talked to the principal, he told me that he knew of the problem, and had complained to the administration. He felt that special training should have been provided the teachers, or at least a traveling French teacher to help his teachers. But he did know that if the language supervisor happened to come by, those television sets had better be turned on.

When this situation is analyzed from the system standpoint, the objectives were not clearly established, all the functions needed to accomplish them were not effective, and there was no coordination among the components which should have been carrying out the functions.

System Objectives

Objectives are the purposes of an instructional system. They are an explicit statement of the performances expected of the student at the end of his instruction. As described by Mager (1962), in order to be sufficiently specific the objective should specify (a) a statement of the performance, expressed in action words; (b) a statement of the conditions under which the performance will be observed or measured; and (c) a standard of accuracy and/or time.

Ammerman and Melching (1965) point out that objectives are organized into a hierarchical structure:

1. *General objectives* describe an entire course or a major part of a course.

2. *Terminal objectives* represent meaningful units of job or life behavior subsumed in the general objective.

3. *Enabling objectives* represent knowledges or skills that must be mastered if the student is to attain the terminal objectives.

The present author (Smith, 1964) has described the processes involved in deriving training objectives for specific jobs. The basis for training objectives is a detailed description of the job. The problem of deriving educational objectives is more difficult, and the basic questions are much broader. Which parts of education are similar to job training? Should we base educational objectives on preparation of the individual to fit into society, or should we try to develop each individual to his greatest potential? To what extent should the individual student develop his own objectives? Are each of these rationales appropriate to different aspects of education?

These broad and fundamental questions are as yet unresolved. In order to proceed with the design of an instructional system, it is possible, although not desirable, to by-pass them. What is essential for system design is that objectives be specified in terms of Mager's criteria—that is, performance, conditions, and standards—and then organized in accordance with the suggestions of Ammerman and Melching on defining general, terminal, and enabling objectives.

Objectives specified in these terms provide a guide to the selection of media, methods and other equipment, and to how the instructional staff and students should perform.

Instructional System Functions

Smith (1966) has identified several functions which must be performed in an instructional system.

The Practice of Performance   This function is concerned with the practice of a terminal objective or an enabling objective which requires performance. The most important requirements are simulation of the cues and responses involved in the objective, coupled with a way of providing the student with knowledge of the results of his practice.

The Practice of Knowledge   This function deals with the practice of enabling objectives representing knowledge. The means for practicing knowledge include workbooks, programmed texts, and classroom communicators, such as the EDEX system. As with the practice of performance, knowledge of results should be provided.

The Presentation of Knowledge   Here the concern is with one-way presentation of knowledge or information to the student. Research results suggest that the message is more important than the medium, although the characteristics of the medium may limit the kinds of messages which may be sent.

The Management of Students   In this function are included all the things that are necessary to keep the student profitably occupied in the functions described above. Included here are ways of dealing with individual differences between students, and ways of motivating students to learn.

Quality Control   The function of quality control requires four general processes (Smith, 1965). The first is the development of tests to measure the attainment of objectives. The tests are then administered to the students. The results are fed back to the system managers. Finally, action is taken to improve those parts of the system which are not accomplishing the objectives.

The Role of Technology in an Instructional System

In an instructional system, the various functions are carried out by a variety of components. The system concept is neutral on the point as to whether these components should be human or not. The decision on the means for executing system functions is made on a basis of relative cost and effectiveness.

A particular element of the educational technology, such as a tape recorder, will perform one or more of the functions required to accomplish an objective. Whether a specific element is suitable will depend both on the objective and the function being carried out.

If a school has adopted the system concept, it will be relatively easy to specify the requirements for equipment and programs. They will perform the required functions to accomplish specific objectives.

Educational Innovation

It was noted earlier that education is a labor-intensive enterprise. The introduction of any item of equipment into such a situation represents a fairly major innovation. Thus it is important to consider the problems of innovation in education.

A review of the recent literature on innovations and their spread, made by McClelland (1968) in a study of the process of effecting change, has shown that the principal emphasis in the literature falls on the difficulties of innovating.

The diffusion of innovations has been described by Rogers (1968) as being affected by four key elements: the *innovation, communicated* to members of a *social system,* who adopt it over a *time* period.

Considering the characteristics of an innovation, Rogers describes the following as being the features that appear to affect the rate of adoption:

1. Relative advantage—the extent to which an innovation is visibly better than what it supersedes.

2. Compatibility—the extent to which an innovation is consistent with the present values and previous experience of the potential adopter.

3. Divisibility—the extent to which an innovation may be tried out on a limited or partial basis. Divisibility favors adoption.

4. Complexity—the characteristic of an innovation which involves difficulty on the part of people to understand or use it. More complex innovations either will spread slowly or must be integrated with a carefully planned program of training.

5. Communicability—the extent to which the results of the adoption of rejection of the new idea or item are visible to others. This characteristic explains why material things diffuse more rapidly than concepts.

The Human Resources Research Organization and its staff have had extensive experience in assisting the Army to use training innovations based on research. We have learned a number of lessons about factors that increase the likelihood of successful implementation of research results:

1. Only rarely do research innovations become adopted on the basis of a formal written report. Instead, the results of the research (provided that the innovation is superior to existing practice) must be clearly communicated to every decision-making level.

2. Adoption is aided by the involvement of military personnel in the research and their later endorsement of the value of the innovation.

3. It is worthwhile to do a great deal of work to engineer the innovation so that it can fit relatively easily into the existing training structure.

4. For some innovations, it has been necessary to conduct training programs and prepare guidance documents for Army personnel who are to use the new technique.

A point which should not be overlooked is that the Army generally is interested in using the results of training research and development as a means of obtaining not only improved training, but a return on its investment in research.

We will return to these points when specific suggestions are made for improving the likelihood of innovation in education.

Institutionalized Innovation

The American way of organizing education involves thousands of relatively independent school districts. Many districts are not sufficiently large to have a long-range planning staff whose function it is to systematically seek for innovations and to make sure that they are institutionalized in an orderly way. However, it is not inconceivable that the larger districts, or confederations of smaller districts, could develop such staffs.

The only institutions, to my knowledge, which have developed such a planning staff are the Armed Forces. The general characteristics of this process will be described below.

Projection of the Future

In the Armed Forces, planning is developed which covers a series of time periods, ranging up to about twenty years into the future. For each of these time periods there is a projection of the characteristics of the future which are of importance to national defense. The most important point for the topic of this paper is that each of these plans is periodically revised to bring new developments into their proper perspective, and the new plan for the farthest year is developed. Thus there is a series of plans and projections of the future, each regularly modified and refined.

Plans for New Weapons and Organizations

Along with projections of future conditions, there are projections of new organizations and new weapons that will be required to deal with the problems of the future. This process of outlining new organizations and weapons in turn becomes more detailed and specific as time goes on.

Another part of the planning process is the development of technological forecasts which not only predict the state of technology of the future, but also represent goals toward which the scientists and engineers can work to make the predictions come true.

Bringing the Innovations into Being

As technological developments make new weapons and organizations feasible, plans are developed for bringing the innovations into being and phasing out the obsolete.

New weapons are designed as complete systems. Not only are the hardware components integrated, but also requirements for real estate, power, and other aspects of the system—especially for personnel. The equipment is designed for human use, although there may be trade-offs in which the human engineer loses out to the hardware engineer. The new jobs required are identified, as are the numbers of men who will be needed in each type of job. Training plans are developed to bring the people and the hardware together at the same time.

As equipment becomes available from the manufacturers, it undergoes various tests, including tests of the complete system including personnel, before it is finally adopted.

Another aspect of the process is the development of doctrine—the policy and procedures for the use of the new equipment and organizations. It provides the system commanders and managers with guidelines on how to use the new equipment effectively.

As with any complex human endeavor, there are problems aplenty in bringing a complex combination of men and machines to completion. Coordination and decision problems abound, because many different agencies are involved, as well as different kinds of specialists. It is no accident that many of the new management techniques, such as PERT, cost-effectiveness, and program budgeting, have been developed by the armed forces in order to deal with these problems. The concept of the system itself received new impetus from the work of the military in developing new weapon systems.

Despite the problems, the services are far ahead of other groups in having mechanisms for the orderly introduction of innovations.

A Planning System for Education

It seems appropriate for education to begin to develop a planning system which could bring innovations into use on a planned, regular basis, and thus provide a means of self-renewal. This system should encompass the following features:

a. Forecasts for varying time periods of the major trends in our society which have implications for education.

b. Technological forecasts in all the fields which may have implications for education, as well as regular monitoring of actual developments. These fields might include:

(1) Behavioral Science

(2) Communication

(3) Operations Research

(4) Architecture and City Planning

(5) Information Science

(6) Data Processing

c. Explicit formulation of requirements for new systems and supporting organizations.

d. Introduction of these systems and maintenance, until it is time to introduce a new one.

At stage c. above, requirements for industry will be developed.

Suggestions for Solving the Problem

In the preceding material, background has been developed for posing some suggested answers to the problem of how to create better cooperation between the educator and industry. We have seen that educators are homogeneous members of a labor-intensive enterprise, so that nearly any introduction of hardware means a significant innovation. The systems approach has been reviewed, and the process of change has been discussed.

Now we are in a position to make a number of suggestions, both for the short-range and for the long-range, for both educators and industry.

Short-Range Suggestions

For Educators

1. Work toward specifying the objectives of instruction in terms of specific performances to be developed in students. With such objectives it will be possible for both

educators and industry to see how specific media and programs can be of assistance in meeting the objectives.

2. Provide industry with feedback on how various pieces of hardware and software work—or don't work. If an item is too cumbersome to use, and winds up in the store-room, say so.

3. Maintain surveillance of new developments and be willing to make and support appropriate innovations.

For Industry

1. Keep in mind that the education establishment, representing a labor-intensive enterprise, doesn't really feel it needs you. Its members will probably view you with suspicion, as being concerned more with profits than with service. Further, you represent change, and change can be uncomfortable. Therefore, it is up to industry to take the initiative with regard to contacts with educators. Join educational organizations, attend meetings, and learn the characteristics of the educator.

2. Develop the kinds of innovations that have a high likelihood of spreading. These should be:

   a. *Of high relative advantage.* Learn enough about education so that you can learn what the problems are as viewed by educators. Then develop items that will have a clear relative advantage in solving those problems.

   b. *Divisible.* For the short-run it is desirable to develop items that can be put to use on a trial basis in part of a school. In this way, others can hear about the new item.

   c. *Yielding highly visible results.* The effects of the item in solving an educational problem should be highly visible. Thus industry will have to do much more in the way of sponsoring evaluative trials of the item so that clear data on its capabilities can be developed.

   d. *Simple to use.* The item should be "human-engineered" to make it easy to use. Instructions should be tested for clarity. If training is required, training plans and programs should be developed. Provide suggestions for the optimal use of the item.

3. *Identify the innovators.* Despite the general conservatism and resistance to change of educators, there are persons who are willing to innovate. These persons should be identified, for they may be willing to give your products a first trial, from which others may learn and decide to adopt. Some organizations within the galaxy of educational societies are likely to contain more than their share of potential innovators. These are the associations concerned with audiovisual devices, data processing, broadcasting and programmed instruction.

4. Learn how important educational decisions are made. In most communities the power to make the most important decisions does not lie with the educators. The amount of funds, the degree of innovation, or the curriculum may be guided more by persons in political or economic power than by educators. These people should be studied and influenced toward innovation and change.

Long-Range Suggestions

For Educators

1. Work toward the admission into your ranks of people with a diversity of backgrounds, so as to encourage new and different views of the educational process. Work toward the changes in teacher and supervisory certification legislation which will make this possible.

2. Work for a system of long-range educational planning that will permit orderly trial and introduction of innovations.

3. Work toward acceptance of the system concept, with clear definition of objectives and specific functions to carry out those objectives

For Industry

1. Work toward reducing the forces making for homogeniety among educators. Lobby to change certification requirements.

2. Work toward the acceptance of the view that equipment can perform many educational functions as well as, or better than human beings. Your problem is to make education less labor-intensive. Your techniques may include lobbying, advertising, and other forms of persuasion. The concept of the systems approach to education contains the important ideas toward which you should be working.

3. Work toward a system of long-range planning that will lead to planned innovation. Each of these innovations should open sizable markets to you.

4. Educate those in power to change their views toward the amount and scope of educational innovation and the need for equipment and programs.

5. Sponsor demonstration systems. In order to show what could be done by really innovative approaches, industry associations could build complete instructional systems. With the potential of present day technology which is not being used, such systems could be strong stimuli toward change, if given adequate publicity.

BIBLIOGRAPHY

Ammerman, H. L. and William H. Melching. *The Derivation, Analysis, and Classification of Instructional Objectives.* Human Resources Research Office, Technical Report 66-4, May 1966.

Biddle, B. J. and P. H. Rossi. "Educational Media, Education, and Society." In B. J. Biddle and P. H. Rossi, *The New Media and Education,* Garden City, N.Y. Doubleday Anchor Books, 1967.

Kimbrough, R. B. "Community Power Structure and Curriculum Change." In Leeper, R. (Ed.), *Strategy for Curriculum Change.* Washington, D.C.: Association for Supervision and Curriculum Development, 1965.

Mager, R. F. "Preparing Instructional Objectives." Palo Alto: Fearon Publishers, 1962.

McClelland, W. A. "Process of Effecting Change." Presidential Address, Division of Military Psychology, American Psychological Association Convention, 1968. Professional Paper 32-68, October 1968.

Rogers, E. M. "The Communication of Innovations in a Complex Institution." *Educational Record,* 1968, Vol. 49 (1), pp. 67-77.

Sieber, S. D. "Organizational Influences on Innovative Roles." In *Knowledge Production and Utilization in Educational Administration.* Columbus, Ohio: University Council for Educational Administration, and University of Oregon: Center for the Advanced Study of Educational Administration, 1968.

Smith, R. G., Jr. *The Design of Instructional Systems.* Human Resources Research Office, Technical Report 66-18, Nov. 1966.

Smith, R. G., Jr. *Controlling the Quality of Training.* Human Resources Research Office, Technical Report 65-6, June 1965.

Smith, R. G., Jr. *The Development of Training Objectives.* Human Resources Research Office, Research Bulletin 11, June 1964.

Travers, R. M. W. "A Study of the Relationship of Psychological Research to Educational Practice." In R. Glaser (Ed.), *Training Research and Education,* Pittsburgh, Pa: University of Pittsburgh Press, 1962.

Instructional Technology: Economic Evaluations

106.

Cost Study of Educational Media Systems and Their Equipment Components*

by GENERAL LEARNING CORPORATION

Introduction: Volumes I and II

The purpose of this study was to investigate the cost of instructional media systems. The first objective was to provide the educator with a set of guidelines for realistically estimating the total cost of such systems. To gain this objective it was necessary first to identify and investigate a set of commonly used or proposed media systems and to develop a methodology for determining total system costs.

The data collected and analyzed during the study achieved the second objective or providing a data base for use by researchers in further studies relating to the selection, implementation, and operation of instructional media systems. A final objective of the study was to present recommendations which can result in cost savings when media systems are used. The recommendations are in the areas of media utilization, application of new technology, and educational system organization.

Selection of a Media System—An Overview

Estimating the costs of purchasing, installing, implementing, and operating a media system is not an isolated activity. Rather, it is part of the broader overall process of media system selection. The major steps in media system selection appear graphically in Figure 1.

The selection process begins with an examination of the educational setting in which the chosen media system is to function. Most educators agree that this setting consists mainly of an administrative component and an instructional component. Each component contains limiting factors which shape the specific data used in later stages of the selection process, namely specification of appropriate sensory stimuli, design of alternative media systems, cost estimation of the alternative systems and, ultimately, selection of the appropriate system.

Final selection of a media system is followed by the customary procedures of contract specification, review of bids, and award of a contract for equipment and installation. Two

*This study was conducted by General Learning Corporation for the Bureau of Research, U.S. Office of Education, under contract number OEC-1-7-079006-5139, May 1968. Inasmuch as space limitations prevented the reprinting of the entire three-volume report, only a brief summary is provided in this paper.

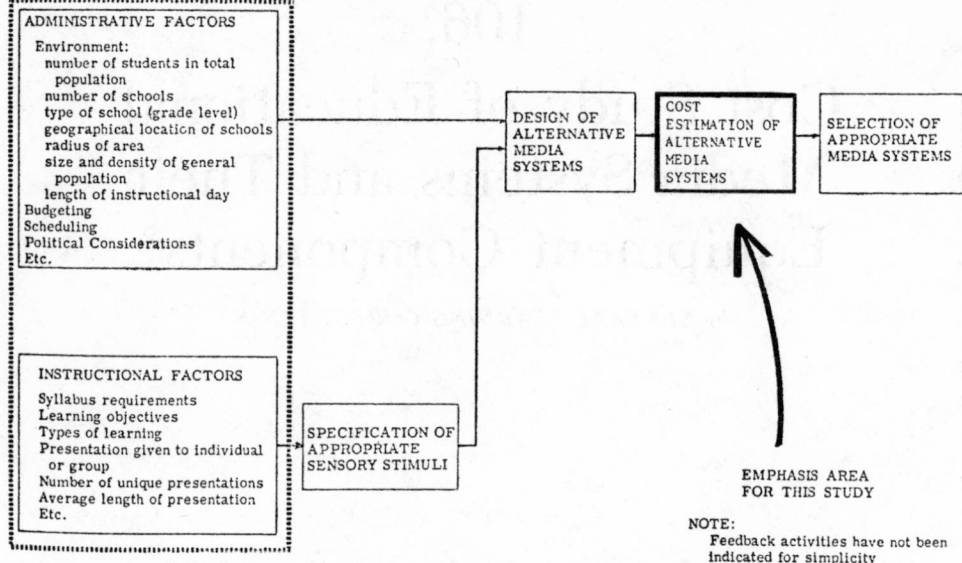

Figure 1. Selection of a Media System—An Overview

other "post selection" activities are essential at this point—implementation (training and operation) and evaluation. Logically, planning for these activities should be completed well before this time.

Figure 2 illustrates the sequence of general steps taken to determine the system's configuration. Blocks 3, 4, and 5 develop the costs in each of the three divisions into which the system has been separated. Block 6 sums up all costs prior to the selection decision that is made in Block 7. Actually, decisions are made throughout the entire process and some systems may be rejected or modified well before Block 7 is reached.

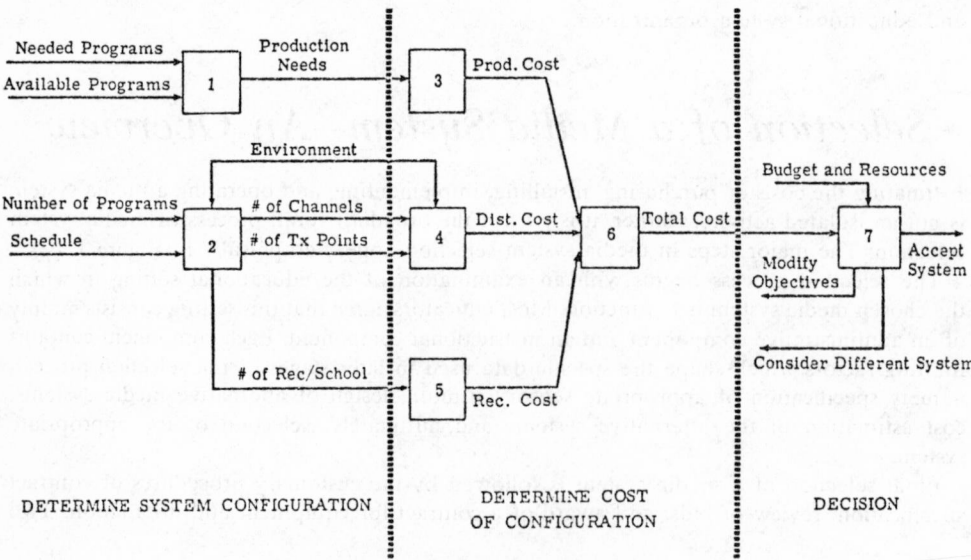

Figure 2. Cost Determinations

Methodology

The method of the study involves the specification of a task and an environment. The task describes "what the system is doing" and the environment describes "over what area and for how many people it is doing it." A valid comparison of media systems can be made only when a single real environment and the actual educational task are specified in detail for each case under study. To attempt this type of approach would mean the illustration of hundreds of cases consisting of different systems and their variations applied to many educational tasks over many different environments. This monumental effort would still involve some generalizations and assumptions and would only produce a larger group of system costs which might result in more confusion than clarification. Therefore, we chose a general expression for the task and a small number of generalized environments to construct a framework for media costs.

Environments Defined

Local District Model   The smallest environment is the school district which may vary in size from a few hundred to over a million students. The size chosen for this study was 15,000 elementary and secondary students in an area of approximately 80 square miles. Although the majority of school districts in the United States are much smaller, those with 3,000 or 4,000 students will not have the distribution problems which become extremely important in larger systems. Also, some of the media systems are too expensive (even in their smallest configuration) to be supported by a small district.

The school district used as the model consists of 14 elementary schools and four secondary schools. The school district is irregular in shape, but all the schools are within a circle whose radius is six miles.

City Model   The city covers an area of 70 square miles and has a total population of about 800,000 with approximately 11,500 people per square mile. The shape of the city is roughly rectangular and the entire area can be encompassed by a six mile radius circle. There are 150,000 students in 136 elementary and 46 secondary schools.

Metropolitan Area Model   The population of the metropolitan area is approximately two million. Its perimeter has an irregular shape and surrounds an area of approximately 1500 square miles. Because of its irregular shape, a circle with a 30 mile radius (2800 sq. mi.) is necessary to completely cover this area.

The metropolitan area, which contains a number of school districts, has 546 elementary and 183 secondary schools with a total of 600,000 students.

State Model   The state has a population of about 4.5 million people. It does not contain a metropolitan area as large nor as populous as described above, though about 60 percent of the population is urban. It has an area of about 40,000 square miles and a population density of about 110 per square mile. Approximately one million students are distributed among 920 elementary and 310 secondary schools.

Regional Model   The region is approximately a 10 to 1 extrapolation of the state, but a smaller population density is used to bring this figure closer to the national average. The region has an area of 550,000 square miles and a population of about 42 million. There are 10 million students in 9200 elementary and 3100 secondary schools.

Educational Task Defined

The task assumed in the report is: To provide each student with material via some medium during an average of 10% of his actual instructional time. In reality, no subject is taught entirely by the use of a media system. Some subjects may not use the media system at all. More than 10% of some subject may be presented by a media system. This task is general in nature so that it may be applied to any system.

A difficulty with respect to this study is not that the task is general in nature, but that it is not defined in units that have a relationship to system design. To bridge this gap, an exercise is offered in the report to illustrate the method used for this study to convert the general 10% task into an annual requirement for hours of unique program material for each of the defined environments.

Cost Structure

The stated task, to provide each student with material via some medium during an average of 10% of his total instructional time, offers a common source of data for the design of each media system. The definition of environments provides a method of examining systems as they are affected by an alteration in the size of the environment.

Classification by Function Analysis for cost estimation can be further aided by classification of the elements of each media system as they relate to production, distribution, and reception.

Production Production costs are those incurred in the inception, creation, development, and preparation of the instructional content. The acquisition of media programs and its related costs, such as selection and order handling, are also classified as production costs.

Distribution Distribution costs are those incurred in changing or copying the material from its original form, if necessary, and sending it to a point at which it will be reconverted to a usable form for the student.

Reception Reception costs are those incurred in changing the form and presenting the distributed material so that it is useful to the student. Examples are antennas, TV sets, film projectors, screens, headphones, and carrels.

Classification as Capital or Operating Costs Production, distribution, and reception costs can be classified as either capital (initial) costs or operating (annual) costs. Costs classified as capital costs include all purchases of goods and services that have a useful value of longer than a year or that are not incurred every year. The following items are considered as capital costs.

1. Initial planning

2. Initial training

3. Facilities

4. Initial equipment and programs

Costs classified as operating costs include all purchases of goods and services that have a useful value of less than a year or that are incurred every year. The following items are considered as operating costs.

1. Operation of equipment

2. Maintenance of equipment and facilities

3. Training

4. Administration

5. Related materials

6. Current programming

7. Research, Testing and Evaluation, for Program Updating

Equivalent Annual Cost   To simplify cost comparisons, the capital costs can be amortized over the life of the investment and added with interest to the average annual operating cost to form an equivalent annual cost. The result is a uniform yearly figure which includes amortization and interest. These costs can be examined for each environment to determine cost trends as they relate to student population, area serviced, etc. To calculate the equivalent annual cost, first a capital recovery factor (c.r.f.) is obtained from standard financial tables for a particular interest rate and life of the purchase. For example, the c.r.f. for five years and 1% interest is a little over 20%. The capital cost is multiplied by the c.r.f. and the product is added to the annual operating cost to obtain the equivalent annual cost.

Cost Structure Model

A cost structure can be established which encompasses the capital and operating costs for production, distribution, and reception for each system in each environment. This cost structure is illustrated in Figure 3.

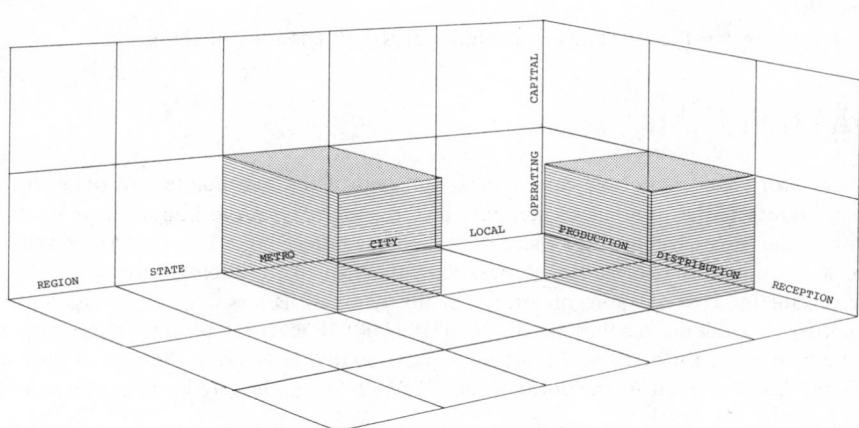

Figure 3. Cost Structure Model

Cube "A" illustrates an area of costs which is associated with the operating expenses during the production (acquisition) of educational material to be used by a media system in a metropolitan school environment. Cube "B" is symbolic of operating costs for distributing instructional materials within a local school district.

Sources and Use of Cost Data

The collection of cost data pertaining to an element of a media system usually resulted in a range of costs, not a precise value.

To estimate total costs for the systems investigated, a single value for each item was selected from the range of costs collected.

The actual dollar cost per system may not be directly applicable to a specific educator's unique problem, but it can indicate general cost trends. The value of this cost structure lies in the generality of its approach. The variables of a real situation can be applied to the structure to provide more realistic comparisons for an actual situation. The cost structure might be looked upon as a tool which can be applied along with measures of "media effectiveness" to solve "real world" problems.

Cost Estimates

Costs were estimated for each of the media systems investigated using the basic model discussed in the previous section. (The detailed cost data are presented in the original study, available from the ERIC Document Reproduction Service.)

Graphical illustrations were prepared from the cost data. There are two major sets of graphs presented and discussed in the full report. Each graph in the first set presents the production, distribution, and reception costs for one instructional media system. A second set presents graphical comparisons of the costs of media systems. Production, distribution, reception, and total costs are shown individually.

Comparison of Costs

The full report presents graphs illustrating the equivalent annual cost per student of the production, distribution, reception, and total cost categories for all media for each environment.

The following are the summary statements of the discussions of the graphs.

Production Costs

Production for visual materials can be accomplished at the reasonable cost of several dollars per student if the number of students in the system is in the hundreds of thousands. Moreover, the price structure for the materials must reflect large volume. At present, television production cost is considerably less than the cost of producing films.

The production cost of audio materials for the 10% task is less than $1 per student when the number of students reaches the level of 100,000. If teachers produce their own tapes or if the somewhat limited number of tapes now available is used, the cost is only a few dollars per student even at the local level. Each of the audio methods is inexpensive to program at the city level.

Distribution Costs

Television and radio are both available for the city and/or metropolitan areas at less than $1 per student for distribution. In the local school district, the distribution cost of the language laboratory and radio system is considerably less than any other system, about $2 per student per year. The radio system is a high-powered service which can serve homes as well as schools 18 hours per day. Film or classroom dial access distribution can be accomplished for $3 to $6 per student per year depending upon the size of the area. The VTR in the school is not an efficient method under the assumptions presented in the model. Among the television systems, for distribution cost alone, the ITFS system is cheapest for the local and city areas. For the larger areas, only a change in FCC rules to permit higher power will allow ITFS to be competitive with UHF or airborne for the state and region.

Reception Costs

Television reception cost—including $2.50 for teacher training—is about $6 per student per year. The reception cost for closed circuit or VTR network is slightly more than for the other television systems. Film reception cost is somewhat more. The reception cost for radio is about $2 except for the local area where it is about $3 per student per year. The reception cost for the language laboratory is slightly more than for radio. The classroom dial access cost for reception is very low, about 50¢ for the city or the metropolitan area.

Total Cost

Audio instructional materials can be supplied by radio for as low as $2 to $3 per student per year. Visual materials costs are about $10 per student per year when they are delivered by television in the city or metropolitan areas. Several new methods are available for coverage of wider areas at about the same or slightly lower cost. Smaller school districts must cooperate with one another or pay considerably more.

Effect of Number of Channels and Task Size on Cost Per Student

The cost figures presented in the discussion of television and radio have been costs for a four-channel service. The four channels accommodate the defined task of 10% of student time with a considerable margin for repeated broadcasts and expansion. There is, of course, the possibility of changing the task and/or changing the number of channels. An estimate of the cost of doing this is illustrated in the full report.

Cost-Saving Considerations

One objective of this study was to investigate ways in which costs in instructional media systems could be reduced. This section serves two purposes. The first is to present an overview of how cost savings may be achieved, the second to present suggestions which may lead to possible cost savings through organizational changes in the educational systems.

Three areas can be identified where changes are necessary if cost savings are to be achieved:

1. The utilization of media systems,

2. The technology of media systems, and

3. The organization of educational systems.

Production Cost Savings from Increased Utilization

Significant savings will result if a production effort can serve a larger number of students. However, if materials are to be accepted for widespread use, the quality of content and presentation must be improved by making more effective use of learning theory, techniques to motivate students, and studies of the curriculum needs of the schools. Preparation of materials in this manner would result in an increase in overall production cost but, through wider utilization, would also result in a decrease in production cost per student.

Savings in quality production are predicated on the assumption that the need for materials is relatively uniform in widely scattered school districts and that reliable, convenient distribution and reception systems would be available to transmit these materials. The existing widespread adoption of the same textbook would seem to indicate that these assumptions are reasonable. However, some coordinating mechanism is needed to guide the production and distribution of materials for the newer media. The cooperation of school districts is an essential ingredient in the development of such a mechanism.

Distribution Cost Savings from Increased Utilization

The distribution cost per student can be reduced if

1. More students can be served from a central facility, or

2. Mass reproduction methods can be found for making inexpensive copies of original materials.

The service of a media system can be increased through the use of network television techniques—higher transmission antennae, increased transmission power, and the electronic relay of materials between school districts. Satellite and airborne television systems are also well suited to covering vast areas containing large numbers of students. More intensive use of such methods can reduce per student cost considerably, but only if materials and schedules are appropriately tailored to the educational needs of participating schools. To accomplish this, transmission centers must have multiple channels available, and schedules and materials must be coordinated with the schools.

The critical factor in lowering the cost of reproducing original materials is the anticipated volume of distribution. Unless the volume is large enough, the development effort required to find inexpensive methods of duplicating films and video tapes would not be worthwhile. Present copying techniques are based on high quality broadcast standards and low volume. Although high speed reproduction of video tapes is potentially possible, the necessary techniques have not been developed. The price of a film print is many times the cost of making the print because of the low recovery rate of production and marketing costs. Assurance of a high-volume market for copies of video materials or federal financing of the needed research would encourage low cost reproduction methods of copying video educational materials.

Reception Cost Savings from Increased Utilization

Savings in reception costs can be effected through

1. Increased student utilization of some portions of the reception system, and

2. Lower costs of components through the adoption of mass production methods.

Portions of the reception system would cost less per student if more student hours were devoted to the media. The central reception and distribution segments in the television reception systems are examples of areas where greater utilization would lower per student cost. However, since most of the reception cost is for the television set and teacher training, more students in the schools would not necessarily lower costs per student. The students would still need a television set and a trained teacher.

The discussion above shows that an increased number of students using a media system tends to lower per student costs. Also, there is another increase in the utilization of the media which would tend to affect cost favorably, i.e., the increased use of the system by the same students. Although the actual cost per student would rise as the system is expanded, the cost does not increase as rapidly as service is increased. Therefore, if total educational costs are considered, more intensive use of media systems may be desirable since the change in the cost of providing additional units of instruction is quite small. This would be one step toward the achievement of optimum "cost effectiveness." The operation of media, the monitoring of learning experiences, and other similar responsibilities could be assigned to paraprofessionals. This work, currently performed by the teacher, could be effectively accomplished by persons without the professional qualifications required of members of the teaching staff. Hence, a "cost saving" may result when a school system is organized along these lines.

The discussion of wider utilization of media systems indicated the cost savings are possible when the system is used by larger numbers of students. For example, a dramatic decrease in annual cost per student for the production of television material occurs as the number of students increases from 15 thousand to 10 million. The per pupil cost of the distribution portion of the media system is also favorably affected as the number of students increases in the area served by the system.

Wider utilization may reduce cost, but it may also present organizational problems. For example, if 11 states were to be served by the same instructional satellite system, the educational programs of those states would have to be coordinated.

If production costs are to be shared, the material must be acceptable to all of the participants. Therefore, the user schools must be involved in the design, development, testing and evaluation, and revision of materials. The financial arrangements to support the production of materials must be agreed upon. All of the above considerations would affect the present organization of the user schools.

Regulatory Implications

Electronic Systems

Some of the multichannel instructional television systems proposed in this study are not explicitly covered by the present regulations or policies of the FCC. Specifically, the higher-powered ITFS specified for the state and region, the four-channel UHF system, the UHF airborne system, and the use of satellites for direct transmission on the 2500 MHz frequencies are all somewhat outside established practice. These departures were made for two reasons, cost and regulatory tardiness.

Film System

Some cost efficiencies in a 16mm media system could be realized with a favorable outcome of the current copyright legislation. Unfortunately, Congress is trying to develop a piece of universal legislation that will satisfy both the author and the publisher of all art forms for all communication media, both commercial and educational.

Sixteen millimeter film programs could become less espensive if the following steps were taken:

1. Redraft the current copyright bill to better serve the needs of educators and commercial producers.

2. Create a national cataloging service so that schools can locate short film segments that best fit their needs.

3. Permit films that were produced with federal funds to be sold at less than commercial prices.

4. Permit curriculum groups to market or distribute newly developed materials.

Abstract of Volume III

A general model is developed in this volume of the report which allows the graphic portrayal of economic factors pertinent to the use of computer-assisted instruction; i.e., how costs are incurred and how they react to changes in instructional methods.

Specific guidelines are directed to the sponsor, the contractor, and the user in order to broaden their understanding of this new field and to facilitate communication among them.

A discussion of the present educational technology industry, its problems, and public policy measures which provide feasible alternatives for the timely development and potential expansion of computer-assisted instruction into public education concludes this volume of the report.

107.

Cost Analysis
Of Instructional Technology

by F. CRAIG JOHNSON   and   JOHN E. DIETRICH
Prof. & Research Assoc.   Assistant Provost
Div. of Instructional Research   Michigan State Univ.
and Service
Florida State Univ.

At present, cost data on educational technology is almost nonexistent. The lack of these data severely impedes the academic decision-making process. Regardless of costing procedures used (several are suggested below), ways must be found to place costs of educational technology in perspective. Present inadequate cost data are frequently so subjective that they are nothing more than pious hopes. The time is here to come to grips with the reality of cost analysis in the academic decision-making process.

Cost benefit analysis is typically used to help make a choice among alternatives when confronted with several products or plans which yield similar results. Seldom in higher education is this the case. Similar results are rarely found or even stated as desirable objectives. Rather than facing alternate paths, fiscal planning is a process of justifying past action with little concern for uniform results. Based on the decade of experience with cost analysis at Michigan State University in the Office of Institutional Research and special studies done by Professor Gardner M. Jones of the Department of Accounting and Financial Administration, we have come to several realizations which bear directly on cost analysis of instructional technology. (Jones, 1965.)

Problems of Cost Analysis

Costs Are Seldom Linear

When we plot quarter-by-quarter expenses relative to a course against enrollments, we find some expenses directly proportional, some scattered, and others independent of enrollment. Other expenses are fixed over narrow ranges of volume but variable over wide ranges of volume.

Cost Records Are Not Adequate

Because costs are not linear, we find we need, for planning purposes, to make studies of individual expense categories separately. We do not, nor do other universities, maintain historical records of expense categories in sufficient detail over long enough periods to construct meaningful expense output relationships.

Not All Relevant Costs Appear in the Accounts

The notion of "opportunity costs" is important in considering how resources are used. If a faculty member's time is used for research, the opportunity for him to teach is lost. The loss of his time for one purpose is valued by the lost opportunity to use his time in another way.

Data on Teaching Loads Are Unreliable

We collect data on teaching, research, service, and administration time spent by faculty. The methods for distributing the time are as varied as the definitions of a "full load." In most cases, the department chairman or his secretary fills out the forms for the faculty. Sir Josiah Stamp's famous story serves as an appropriate caution here. (Stamp, 1929.)

> The individual source of the statistics may easily be the weakest link. Harold Cox tells the story of his life as a young man in India. He quoted some statistics to a Judge, an Englishman, and a very good fellow. His friend said, 'Cox, when you are a bit older, you will not quote Indian statistics with that assurance. The Government is very keen on amassing statistics—they collect them, add them, raise them to the nth power, take the cube root and prepare wonderful diagrams. But what you must never forget is that every one of those figures comes in the first instance from the *chowty dar* (village watchman) who just puts down what he damn pleases.'

Gardner Jones (Jones, 1965), after many years of trying to make cost analyses of instructional technology at Michigan State, concludes:

> Evaluation of instructional costs in a large modern university is a baffling exercise in splitting joint costs and measuring intangible, invisible joint products, in a type of establishment where established accounting procedures and employee personalities are not geared to cost accounting.

Uses of Cost Analysis in Decision-Making

These serious limitations in the cost analysis technique do not diminish in any way the need for cost data even at the highest levels of decision making in our Federal Government. On June 2, 1965, for example, in hearings before the Education Subcommittee of the United States Senate Committee of Labor and Public Welfare, cost data on instructional technology were presented in support of Senate Bill S. 600. Those testifying for Michigan State were impressed and concerned by the Senators' eager acceptance of cost data. (Schuller, 1965.) State legislators and university trustees often feel more comfortable with cost data than with the less familiar problems of the esoteric research and teaching topics faculty often discuss. Within the universities, the availability of adequate cost data for instruction and particularly educational technology is of paramount importance in making academic administrative decisions.

Michigan State University has made some attempts to collect adequate cost data and to use it as a base for making cost decisions. In our experience, several issues arise as we try to make quality, trade-off, or scope decisions based on cost data.

Cost Decisions

Unless there are radical differences in cost, academic administrators seldom make decisions on cost alone. Obviously, the cheapest instructional model (for example the correspondence course) is not the prime criterion for acceptability.

If CCTV, for example, were radically more expensive, a clear-cut cost decision could be made to eliminate it. On the other hand, if CCTV costs indicated extreme savings while gaining general quality acceptance, a cost decision could be made to expand its use. Usually, however, these academic decisions involve additional factors.

Cost-Quality Decisions

The costs of CCTV seem to be reasonably similar to traditional modes of instruction unless the number of students involved in each course exceeds 500. If a pure cost decision were made, CCTV might be eliminated for all courses whose enrollments numbered less than 500. The cost-quality problem is not so simple. Some of the most significant uses of television may well be the highest cost uses; e.g., magnification of surgical procedures or the introduction of materials not otherwise available in the ordinary classroom. Decisions now become more subject to cost-quality decisions as to what method at what cost will produce the "best" educational result.

To cite an additional example, initial cost figures for multi-media laboratories, if they include the cost of material preparation, are clearly more expensive than traditional instruction unless very large numbers of students are affected. A pure cost decision would reduce or eliminate multi-media laboratories. However, in the case of the SLATE laboratories (Structured Learning And Training Environment) at Michigan State University, there appears to be some increase in learning and a vast improvement in student attitude (11% of the students approve of the traditional laboratories; 93% approve of the SLATE laboratories). In this instance a cost-quality decision has led to the further expansion of the multi-media laboratories. (Davis, 1968.)

Cost-Quality-Trade-Off Decisions

If the administrator assumes reasonably comparable costs and reasonably comparable learning and attitudinal responses, how then can a decision be made? Frequently, these decisions are reached in terms of trade-offs. For example, specialized problems of time, movement and space at Michigan State demand the continuation of closed circuit television. Without a CCTV network, Michigan State would have less adequate use of student stations, less adequate use of afternoon and evening class hours, more long distance student movement about the campus, higher student density on the central campus, more repetition of lectures by senior faculty, and in addition would have to build additional auditoria. These factors then must be traded off against any differential in costs. However, without knowing the comparative costs of CCTV, a trade-off decision becomes almost impossible.

Cost-Trade-Off-Scope Decisions

There is fear and insecurity on university campuses about the possibility that the "machines" may take over higher education. There is some basic logic to this fear. Indeed, in some large beginning courses or small departments that rely heavily on lecture presentations, it would be possible, for example, for CCTV to replace the entire faculty. Thus, the university administrator is faced with cost-trade-off-scope decisions.

Again using CCTV as an example, there is a point at which a given "originations facility" reaches capacity. Any further expansion implies the complete duplication of the entire system of both machines and crews. Despite the fact that CCTV may have proved its economy and quality, the academic decision is now one of trade-off and scope.

At Michigan State we "believe" (a subjective judgment) that students should be given as many different kinds of instructional situations as is feasible. For example, it may be decided to limit CCTV to its present capacity regardless of cost factors, even though other instructional models may be more expensive. A trade-off is chosen to "protect" the students' education.

The application of this principle may well affect all kinds of educational technology. Despite the fact that comparative cost no longer is a consideration, no rational, though subjective, decision can be made without realistic cost figures as a base point. The following sections present the several attempts Michigan State University has made to establish some base points for instructional technology.

Cost Analysis of Instructional Technology

There are three ways to analyze instructional technology costs using student credit hours as the measure of productivity. The first assigns costs from academic budget funds, the second from direct instructional salary costs and the third from direct and indirect costs.

SCH/Academic Budget Expenditures

The simplest way to measure cost of instructional technology is to divide the cost of the technology by the number of students taught and get a cost-per-student enrollment figure. (If it cost $100 to produce a slide-tape segment and 500 students used it during the year, the cost per student is $.20.)

Certain technology cannot be treated in this simple manner. Television, for example, might be used more than once by each student during the term. Some universities compute use of television by adding up enrollments in all courses in which TV is used at least once and then dividing by the annual cost of operating the system. (If courses enrolling 20,000 students use TV during the year and the system costs $60,000 to operate and amortize, the cost per student is $3.00 per student.) A refinement of this transforms student enrollments into SCH's, and assuming a three credit average, the cost is $1.00 per SCH. This technique obviously gives television undue credit, and the cost figures are unrealistic.

A more realistic way of counting instruction using technology is to add up only the time per week a student is actually interacting with the medium. One formula which can be used in to calculate technology SCH:

$$TSCH = \frac{credits}{class\ hours\ per\ week} \times T\ hours \times Enrollments$$

where

T = Technology

SCH = Student Credit Hours

Example: CCTV is used in a three credit course with five class hours per week. Two of the five class hours are on TV and there are 60 students in the course.

By substitution:

TSCH $= 3/5 \times 2 \times 60$

$\qquad = .60 \times 120$

$\qquad = 72$

This formula can be applied to courses which only use media occasionally during the term by substituting *term* class hours for *weekly* class hours.

TSCH $= \dfrac{\text{credits}}{\text{class hours per term}} \times \text{T hours} \times \text{Enrollment}$

Example: Films are shown four times during a ten week five credit course that meets five times per week and enrolls 1,000 students.

By substitution:

TSCH $= 5/50 \times 4 \times 1,000$

$\qquad = .10 \times 4,000$

$\qquad = 400$

SCH/Direct Instructional Salary Costs

A second way to arrive at a cost estimate is to use direct instructional salary cost data applied to courses in which technology is used. In order to understand this technique, several basic definitions need to be presented.

1. Student Credit Hour Production (SCH)   The number of students enrolled in each section multiplied by the number of credits assigned each section. Total production figures are based on a fiscal year which includes all four terms. (Each course section taught from summer term through spring term comprises the annual SCH production for the fiscal year. A three credit course enrolling 5,000 students during a given fiscal year would have an annual SCH production of 15,000.)

2. Direct Instructional Salary Costs (DISC)   General fund salary dollars for academic staff (graduate student through full professor) who taught at least one student during the fiscal year and held an appointment in an instructional department or research unit. (If an associate professor with an annual salary of $12,000 per year was paid half time from Federal funds, his direct instructional salary would be $6,000 per year.)

3. Section Credits of Teaching (SCT)   The credit-hour teaching load of an individual instructor, determined by summing credit values of classes or sections he taught. (If he taught four 3 credit sections of introductory work, three 3 credit courses for majors and one 3 credit seminar, his total section credits of teaching would be 24 for the year.)

4. Direct Instructional Salary Cost Per Course   Instructor's salary assigned to sections in proportion to the credits in the sections he taught. (If an associate professor taught 24 credits during the academic year at a direct salary cost of $12,000, then each credit he taught would be assigned $500. If he taught four 3 credit sections in the introductory courses, $6,000 would be assigned to that course.)

5. Difference Between SCH Production and DISC Expenditures   For each course the percent of the university SCH production for one year compared with the SCH production of another year and the same comparison for DISC expenditures of each course. (If a course produced .10% of the SCH with a .10% of the DISC in 1963-64, and in 1966-67 increased its SCH production to .22%, it should expect to increase its DISC to 22%. If, however, the DISC decreased to .02% in 1966-67, there would be a difference of .20%.)

When this difference is computed in terms of an approximately twenty million dollar 1966-67 DISC budget, the total difference is $40,400. The arithmetic follows:

Difference Between SCH Production and DISC Expenditure for A Sample Introductory Course 1963-64 and 1966-67

	UNIVERSITY TOTAL		INTRODUCTORY COURSE			
			% OF UNIVERSITY		ACTUAL	
	1963-64	1966-67	1963-64	1966-67	1963-64	1966-67
SCH Production	1,040,000	1,400,000	.10%	.22%	1,040	3,080
DISC Expenditure	$12,600,000	$20,200,000	.10%	.02%	$12,600	$ 4,040
Expected DISC*				.22%		$44,440
Difference				-.20%		-$40,400

Based on SCH Growth and University DISC Budget

  This technique makes it possible to compare the productivity of a given course over time. It is also possible to compare the difference between SCH production and DISC expenditures with cost of instructional technology. It is possible to do this for any course regardless of which technology was involved. For example, the unit cost savings of courses which use television and other courses which do not use television can be compared. One medium can be compared with another. General statements to those responsible for allocation of university resources can be made about the impact of media upon institutional resources.

SCH/Direct and Indirect Costs

While the two techniques described above provide a cost estimate related to student credit hour production, not all indirect and overhead costs have been assigned. An attempt to assign these costs was made by Dr. Gardner M. Jones in two separate studies of a CCTV operation. (Jones, 1965 and 1968.) He established several basic cost categories:

1. Instructional Staffing Costs of instructional personnel or an instructional substitute therefore in the form of the instructional personnel cost portions of taped programs. Instructional personnel include all those in the classroom, or performing on TV, but do not include student engineers or studio staff or tape room staff.

2. Room Costs Room occupancy, including building maintenance, viewing set maintenance and repair, depreciation on classroom buildings and equipment and viewing sets, and channel charges. In the case of several courses, it also includes talkback equipment (telephones and related connections, wiring, etc.)

3. CCTV Operating Costs This includes the costs of studio operation in the case of live telecast, and tape room operation for replays. If taping is done during live telecast, such taping is considered to be for the purpose of subsequent telecast by replay, and no part of the live telecast production cost is assigned to taping.

  Administration and overhead for studio and tape room are included, and are assigned arbitrarily to the two functions of studio operations and tape room operations. For both studio and tape room, repair, maintenance, and depreciation on equipment (i.e., amortization of original cost) are recognized as necessary operating costs.

  CCTV operating costs are recognized on an hours-of-operation basis. Thus, a production using xxx hours of studio time will be charged with related costs at $y.yy per hour. Tape room costs are attached similarly to replays on a time basis: so many $ per hour of replay time for a tape for a course.

Total costs of studio operation are divided by the practical studio operating capacity per year, of 2,000 hours, to arrive at an average hourly operating cost. This is the rate at which studio costs (exclusive of crew costs) are applied to programs using studio time. Total costs of tape room operation are divided by an annual tape operating capacity, 14,000 hours (7 units @ 2,000 hours each.)

The specific costs of a studio crew as required for a particular program are identified and applied on an hourly basis to the program. Some programs require differently constituted crews, thus, there is no "standard" studio crew. Crew costs, then, are not included in the "average per hour studio costs" described above.

Each of the three basic categories of cost is constructed from the "best" information available about it, and is broken down to some basic unit. Each cost is then applied to each course for each term according to the most closely identifiable related usage factor.

Any of these techniques can provide an estimate of cost-over-time of instructional technology. The difference in cost accounting and the implications of each is presented in the following section.

Three Cost Analysis Methods Applied to the Same CCTV Operation

To illustrate how several cost analysis methods can be applied to a single use of instructional technology, the three year operation of CCTV at Michigan State University was selected. This TV system is large and complex. It produces about 75,000 TV SCH per year covering 10% of the undergraduate instruction of the university. As many as seven video tape playbacks and two studios are active during peak hours with an average of four program sources feeding the system from 8:00 a.m. to 10:00 p.m. five days a week.

SCH/Academic Budget Expenditures.

The first analysis, found in Table I, presents enrollments, student credit hours and television student credit hours during a three year period.

TABLE I
Basic Data For a CCTV Operation
1964-65 to 1966-67

	ENROLLMENTS	TOTAL SCH	TV-SCH	ACADEMIC BUDGET EXPENDITURES
1964-65	31,324	93,972	26,026	$228,083
1965-66	53,250	159,750	56,440	$267,426
1966-67	62,263	186,786	73,372	$303,072

Ratios of costs based on academic budget expenditures are found in Table II.

TABLE II
Cost Ratios For a CCTV Operation
1964-65 to 1966-67

	COST PER ENROLLMENT	COST PER SCH	COST PER TV-SCH
1964-65	$7.28	$2.43	$8.67
1965-66	$5.02	$1.67	$4.74
1966-67	$4.87	$1.62	$4.13

Cost ratios are computed for each of these measures. Any measure of the TV system indicates increased production without a corresponding increase in general fund expenditures. The more accurate TV-SCH is most often used at Michigan State; however, in some reports, a SCH ratio is necessary to compare costs with other data used by the university. When given the choice between reporting enrollment or student credit hour data, the enrollment figures turn out to be a better approximation of the more accurate TV-SCH figures.

SCH/Direct Instructional Salary Costs

The second analysis is found in Table III which shows the amount the CCTV system is helping to "save" instructional costs, based on the assumption that if a course produces 1% of the university SCH it should have 1% of the university direct instructional salary costs and that an increase in SCH production will yield an increase in instructional costs. Earlier in this paper it was noted that perhaps a major contribution of instructional technology is this saving in instructional costs.

TABLE III
Difference Between SCH Production and DISC Expenditures for a Sample of Ten Courses* that Did Not Use TV 1963-64 but Used TV for a Major Part of the Instruction Between 1964-65 and 1966-67

	UNIVERSITY TOTAL		10 CCTV COURSES			
			% of University			Actual
	1963-64	1966-67	1963-64	1966-67	1963-64	1966-67
SCH Production	1,040,000	1,400,000	5.7%	8.4%	59,652	117,174
DISC Expenditures	$12,600,000	$20,200,000	5.2%	3.0%	$293,177	$606,690
Expected DISC				4.9%		$989,800
				-1.9%		-$383,110

*Enrollment in these 10 courses represented 63% of the total SCH produced on CCTV 1966-67.

Total General Fund Expenditures For All CCTV Operations 1966-67 $303,072

The sample includes all courses which did not use CCTV prior to the three year period but became major uses during the period. The cost comparison is between the cost of instruction prior to going on TV and the cost of instruction during the third year with equated SCH production. This analysis indicates that the growing system described in Table I is saving more in instructional costs per year than it costs in general funds to operate the system. These ten courses account for the majority of the SCH production of the entire system. An analysis could be made for the remaining courses; however, the many minor uses would require attaching so many qualifications to the analysis that its meaning would be severely limited.

Both the analyses deal only with university general fund expenditures for closed circuit television operation and direct instructional salary. They do not deal with the more complex issue of indirect and overhead cost.

SCH/Direct and Indirect Costs

The data presented in Table IV assigns both direct instructional costs and indirect costs of TV production and room occupancy to a course in accounting. A detailed breakdown of the TV production costs assigned is found in Table V.

TABLE IV
Detailed Cost Analysis of a Basic Course in Accounting

Accounting 201:

	Fall '66	Winter '67	Spring '67
Instructional Staffing	$ 7,050	$ 8,900	$ 6,800
Room Costs	730	694	456
CCTV Operations	3,859	3,859	3,859
Total Costs	$11,639	$13,543	$11,114
Sections	14	13	8
Enrollment	656	526	354
Costs per Enrollment	$17.74	$25.61	$31.66
Cost per Credit Hour	$ 3.55	$ 5.13	$ 6.40

Accounting 202:

	Fall '66	Winter '67	Spring '67
Instructional Staffing	$ 5,500	$ 7,950	$ 6,850
Room Costs	403	595	697
CCTV Operations	3,859	3,859	3,859
Total Costs	$ 9,762	$12,404	$11,406
Sections	7	11	11
Enrollment	311	461	412
Costs per Enrollment	$31.39	$26.91	$27.70
Cost per Credit Hour	$ 6.28	$ 5.38	$ 5.54

TABLE V
Detailed Cost Analysis of TV Production

Cost Per Broadcast Hour
Production Personnel:

Cameramen	2 men for	1¼ hrs.	@ $2.96	$7.40
Director	1	1¼	@ 3.88	3.88
Audio	1	1	@ 1.45	1.45
Video	1	1	@ 3.54	3.54

Repairs, average cost per hour of broadcast	8.50
Depreciation on equipment	10.63
Depreciation—studio	4.17
Administrative and office expense	27.64
Total Cost per hour	67.18
Hours telecast per quarter	50
	$3,359.00
Rental of talkback facility	500.00
Total	$3,859.00

The analysis made by Gardner Jones covers only one course. Here, in addition to instructional costs and CCTV operation costs, room costs are added and CCTV detailed on a broadcast hour base. It is interesting to note that the average cost/SCH using this technique is $4.71 and that the university carries the cost at $5.17 without the additional TV costs. Further, using the method illustrated in Table II it can be demonstrated that this course "saves" $36,491 per year in direct instructional salary costs.

A final kind of analysis is possible using the more detailed procedures of Table VI to compare the TV costs with the cost of teaching accounting without TV, based on equivalent enrollment data and the course model necessary if TV were not available. The assumptions for each term of the course are:

Assumptions: Students have two lectures a week, two recitations, all 75 minutes long.

Fall: Three lecture sections; two by full professor, one by assistant professor, who also has two recitation sections. Remaining sections staffed by graduate assistant @ $2,700 annual rate.

Winter: Same as for Fall.

Spring: Two lectures by full professor; all recitations by graduate assistants.

TABLE VI
TV and Non-TV Costs For a Basic Accounting Course

AFA 201 Summary:						
	Fall '66		Winter '67		Spring '67	
	TV	Non-TV	TV	Non-TV	TV	Non-TV
Total Costs	$11,639	15,554	13,453	15,088	11,114	9,848
Per Enrollment	$ 17.74	23.71	25.61	28.68	31.66	27.51
Per Credit Hour	$ 3.55	4.74	5.13	5.74	6.33	5.50
Enrollment		656		526		354
Lecture Sections	1	3	1	3	1	2
Ave. Lecture Size		219		175		177
Rec. Sections	14	14	13	13	8	8
Ave. Rec. Size		47		41		44
AFA 202 Summary:						
Total Costs	$ 9,762	9,382	12,404	11,246	11,406	11,246
Per Enrollment	$ 31.39	30.16	26.91	24.39	27.70	27.44
Per Credit Hour	$ 6.28	6.03	5.38	4.88	5.54	5.49
Enrollment		311		461		412
Lecture Sections	1	2	1	2	1	2
Ave. Lecture Size		155		230		206
Rec. Sections	7	7	11	11	11	11
Ave. Rec. Size		44		42		37

As can be seen, TV costs are higher when enrollments are under 500 and TV costs lower when enrollments are over 500, suggesting a break-even point of 500. If, however, prerecorded taped lectures are used over and over for several terms, TV costs will be substantially less than non-TV even though enrollments fall well below 500.

In a music course, for example, 4 sections met fall term three times each week with two sections staffed by a full professor and two staffed by an assistant professor. When TV replaced these faculty for winter and spring terms, the TV cost showed considerable savings.

TABEL VII
TV and Non-TV Costs for a Music Course

Music 272 Summary:

	Fall '66		Winter '67		Spring '67	
	TV	Non-TV	TV	Non-TV	TV	Non-TV
Total Course Costs	$3,578	6,596	3,470	6,596	3,473	6,596
Per Enrollment	$36.88	68.00	24.10	45.80	18.90	35.84
Per Credit Hour	$12.29	32.69	8.03	15.27	6.29	11.98
Enrollment	97		144		184	
Rec. Section	5	4	4	4	4	4
Ave. Section Size	24		36		46	

Each of these analyses has its own contribution to make in gaining an understanding of cost analysis of instructional technology. Hopefully, in the years ahead, these techniques can be improved so that better decisions on the uses of instructional technology can be made.

BIBLIOGRAPHY

Davis, Robert H. "SLATE Your Students for Structured Self-Tutoring." *College and University Business,* Vol. 44, (April 1968), pp. 78-83.

Jones, Gardner M. *A Procedural and Cost Analysis Study of Media in Instructional Systems Development.* U.S. Office of Education Contract No. OE-3-16-030, Part B, September 1, 1965.

Jones, Gardner M. *CCTV Cost Study Report.* Michigan State University, 1968, (Mimeographed).

Schuller, Charles F. *The Economics of Instructional Media in Higher Education.* Michigan State University, June, 1965, (Mimeographed).

Stamp, Sir Josiah. *Some Economic Factors in Modern Life.* London: P. S. King, 1929.

108.

On the Economic Analysis Of Educational Technology[*]

by *HERBERT J. KIESLING*
Assoc. Prof. of Economics
Indiana University

Introduction

Economic historians have long held that one of the most important causes of all social change is technological change. On the heels of three decades of accelerated advance in the field of educational technology, and in the face of much more to come, American education finds itself in the midst of a searching self-appraisal concerning its traditional teaching methods.

While quick change is exciting, it is also hard for those functioning in its midst to adequately analyze it. This paper represents an attempt to build an analytical framework which would allow a semblance of orderly empirical investigation, using the professional expertise of the political economist. It is the appraisal of an "outsider," as the author has had little direct experience in audiovisual technology before embarking on this study. Hopefully the drawbacks coming from the author's lack of technical expertise in some of the concerns of the paper will be counter-balanced by the advantages of a fresh and objective viewpoint.

This essay will explore methods of assessing the actual and potential efficiency of alternative instructional strategies, including strategies which depend heavily upon mechanical and electronic instructional aids. It will compare the problem of evaluating educational outcomes with that of evaluating government outputs in general. The strengths and weaknesses of the systems analysis approach will be discussed. Finally, an extended example will be given which is meant to illustrate the analytical procedure suggested in the paper and at the same time give the reader some insights into the place of audiovisual materials in the contemporary education scene.

Education is itself a public product of course, and the professional economist whose specialty is Public Finance is not unacquainted with problems such as that posed above. It should be instructive to discuss some of the special problems which the economist has in analyzing the efficiency of government services because these problems are directly relevant to the task of this paper. Our understanding will be aided if we start by discussing the task the economist faces in the private sector.

Consider for a moment how one would set about finding the most efficient method (the

[*]*Dr. Kiesling acknowledges the help of the following people in the preparation of this paper: Laurence Brown, Polly Carpenter, Edwin Cohen, David Garloff, Eleanor Godfrey, Dean Jamison, Steve Johnson, John Moldstad, Edward Pfister, Roderick Rhea, Edgar Richardson, and Mendel Sherman.*

method with lowest average cost in terms of total resources used per unit of output) of rolled sheet steel. Finding the *most* efficient method presupposes we know all the possible alternative production methods and that we then compare the per unit cost of each method. There is nothing in this procedure which is impossible. Engineers can provide us with alternative technologies for producing steel sheets and if we impute a cost to each we have the answer.

The political economist who would find the most efficient method of providing a public service is not so fortunate however. This is because public sector outputs, *by their very nature**, are to some extent intangible and therefore cannot be quantified into meaningful output units such as tons of sheet steel. To appreciate this one merely needs to ponder the problem of measuring the units of "national security" or "law and order." But without a meaningful measure of output it is impossible to evaluate the efficiency of government programs.

Faced with this situation the economist has two choices. First, he can give up. If he does not wish to do that, he must compromise somehow and accept the fact that his analysis will not be as precise as that of his counterpart in the private sector. The concept of "systems analysis" which seems quite stylish just now in the audiovisual literature is one method he has for compromising. The principle of sub-optimization is another. Each of these concepts is discussed in turn.

Systems Analysis and Public Outputs

After a rather concentrated reading of some of the audiovisual literature, I am surprised at the amount of attention that the concept of systems analysis has been receiving and am somewhat sympathetic toward Professor Oettinger's position that systems analysis is currently being oversubscribed. On the other hand, Oettinger's reaction to this also seems extreme.

Systems analysis is little more and little less than another name for economic analysis. Considering again the steel mill discussed above, the rolling mill constitutes a "system," or indeed, the entire steel company might comprise a system. Our inquiry into the most efficient production method was systems analysis pure and simple. As Kershaw and McKean put it.

> . . . systems analysis is the comparison of alternative means of carrying out some function, when those means are rather complicated and comprise a number of interrelated elements. Such analysis could often be called "economic analysis," since the aim is to find the best use of one's resources, but the word "systems" is useful in calling attention to the complex nature of the alternatives being compared.[1]

Kershaw and McKean go on to explain the rudiments of systems analysis very succinctly:

> The purpose of comparing one system with another is to show which is better. Or, more frequently, since quantitative analysis can rarely embrace *all* considerations, the purpose is to compare systems in a way that is relevant to a choice between them and helps one to decide which is better. Only one of the systems compared will ordinarily be an existing one, for the object is to "try out" innovations and new proposals in the comparisons—to compare a system as it exists with what it might be after one or more proposed changes are introduced. Indeed one of the main products of making such comparisons is the devising of new and better variants— the designing of new systems. . . . It is characteristic of analytically interesting

---

**The private property system owes its fundamental justification to the desirability of having those who benefit society reap a corresponding return and those who impose costs should pay a corresponding price. When goods can easily be priced to individual recipients, the market system accomplishes this task well. But when benefits or costs of activities cannot be priced to individuals, i.e., when many of the costs or benefits are intangible in nature, it then becomes necessary for collective intervention.*

systems that there are many, many ways of varying the inputs. In education, for instance, not only can there be different pupil-teacher ratios, but different salary schedules and levels, different teacher training, building configurations, uses of television, degrees of emphasis on athletics, and so on almost to infinity.[2]

The most important criterion for meaningful systems analysis (economic analysis) is that there exist a meaningful measure of output. It is on this that all else depends. As we saw, analyzing a steel mill is not trick because we know precisely what a ton of rolled sheet steel with a certain chemical composition is. On the other hand, a systems analysis of the entire United States defense establishment is impossible since no one has the slimmest notion of what one unit of national security is. The problem of educational outputs is somewhat more manageable, however, and it may be possible to analyze a school or school district as one system, using achievement scores in basic subjects as the output measure as Kershaw and McKean suggest. Several economists have done work along these lines, including the author. After spending several years with this type of analysis, I am not sure that using achievement performance for a complete school or school district is not overaggregating. If it is not, however, the systems analysis approach for evaluating alternative instructional strategies would be simple if only achievement score performance is accepted as a meaningful measure. The researcher merely needs to experiment to see which instructional strategy yields the best results within the budget constraint of the school district.

The Concept of Sub-optimization

Let us return to the problem of analyzing public outputs whose benefits are mostly intangible. Defense is always the obvious example although it is easily possible to argue that there are too many dimensions in the public education product to be able to analyze them with one set of test scores. The compromise which the economist must make in this case is that he has to find a lower level of production such that a useful measure of output becomes available. This technique is called "sub-optimizing," and it is a very important one for the analysis of public outputs. Thus, while it is impossible to measure units of national security, it is possible to measure the number of days it would take to deliver a fully equipped paratroop division to some spot in the world. In education, examples of sub-optimization outputs might include science achievement in grades 4, 5, and 6 of pupils who come from middle-class socio-economic homes. Another output might be the same achievement for pupils from disadvantaged socio-economic backgrounds; another the amount of French vocabulary taught in high school, etc. In my judgment it is often true that these different outputs should be treated separately.

How would systems analysis be applied in a framework of sub-optimization? Again, what we have is merely economic analysis of an exactly specified "activity." But to illustrate, let us take an example from education. The output chosen is reading skill of grade school children from disadvantaged homes as measured by the Iowa Test of Basic Skills. A number of instructional strategies are chosen to accomplish the goal. Careful accounting procedures are instituted such that the amount and cost of all resources going into teaching reading to these children is known (program budgeting). An overall long-range plan is made for spending resources on this program (planning). Each technique or "activity" is carefully evaluated and the strategy is selected which optimizes pupil performance within the constraint of the funds available for the task. Finally, if there are any costs or benefits of an intangible nature which, while important, do not show up in terms of money cost or in terms of the output measure chosen, these are carefully "noted in the margin" such that the proper decision maker is conscious of them when he makes his decisions.

An important drawback to the sub-optimization approach is the fact that some decision-maker must in the final analysis decide the relative importance of increasing the outputs of the various "sub-systems." But this is often no more of a problem with sub-optimization than it is with higher level systems analysis. Thus, even though we can relate all school inputs to achievement performance, some decision-maker must still compare the value to society of achievement performance with additional police protection or the installation of sidewalks. It is only when all outputs can be quantified in *dollar* terms that an overall comparison is possible. When this is done (somewhat imperfectly) in the public sector it is termed "cost-benefit analysis." Cost-benefit analysis would only be possible for the education sector if all increases in achievement performance and other performance could be related to dollar rewards to society. While economists have done some crude studies of this kind, they are not important for our purposes here.

Let us summarize this discussion by listing the steps which need to be taken for a meaningful systems analysis in the school.

1. Define Meaningful and Concrete Objectives   It must be kept in mind that it will not be possible to include every nuance of educational output in such a set of objectives. This is more true the more aggregated the level of analysis is. However, it must be kept in mind that some intangible objectives may be automatically satisfied at the same time as major quantifiable objectives are satisfied.

2. An Output Measure Which Is at Least Semi-cardinal Must Be Found for Each Objective   A cardinal measure is one that has intervals which have interpretable units of width such as number of test questions answered correctly, etc. An example where such units do not obtain is when one program is thought to be "better than" another.

3. Accounting Techniques Must Be Instituted Where the Inputs Are Costed Carefully According to Each Objective

4. Ingenuity Must Be Exercised in Constructing Meaningful Alternative Ways in Which the Objective May Be Reached

5. Each Method for Realizing the Objective Is Tested and the Experimental Results Analyzed   The cost of each alternative is carefully computed and this is also analyzed. Even if it is impossible to test differences in effectiveness, the cost analysis would still be quite valuable to the decision-maker.

6. The Relative Benefits from Each Approach Are Compared to the Costs of Their Inputs and a Cost Effectiveness Summary of the System Made

In the opinion of the author, this is the framework in which a proper analysis in education can proceed. It is an approach very similar to that given by Briggs and others in their study of instructional media which is published by the American Institute for Research (8). An extended example of its working is given in the next part of this paper.

Some Suggestions for Implementation of the Analysis

There are a few more points about this approach which are germane to our discussion. First, it should seem obvious to the reader that the approach would require careful experimental control, as well as much patience and hard work. Because of this need for high quality control, I would suggest that research funds be channeled into a few extremely high quality experimental situations as opposed to a great many lower quality experiments. I would envision, for example, somewhere in the neighborhood of four to six experimental schools (or school districts) in the *entire country* wherein continuous research is conducted concerning the effectiveness of alternative instructional strategies with respect to the teaching of pupils from varying types of socio-economic backgrounds and with vary-ing levels of ability.

The use of a few experimental schools instead of widespread experimenting would ac-complish two other desirable results. First, it would be anticipated that if techniques become widespread which use objective test scores as the measure of performance, there becomes the danger that school teachers and administrations will begin to explicitly "teach for the tests," with the probable consequence that other, less tangible, but not unimportant, edu-cational goals would be neglected. This would not occur if there were only a few experi-mental schools. Secondly, this scheme would control the effects of "experiment enthusiasm," the factor which makes much published research suspect concerning educational experi-ments which have been conducted in the past. In the experimental school, participating personnel would come to accept varying instructional strategies as a matter of course. Finally, experimental schools should be similar to "typical" American schools in as many respects as possible.

Sub-optimization and School Organization

With the expanded possibility for using mechanical and electronic instructional devices, and adopting a systems approach by program, it appears to me that a fundamental change in the organizational structure in most American schools would create an institutional framework wherein there is a natural tendency for the most efficient instructional strate-gies to be adopted for each task. Briefly stated, the idea would be to have an independent decision-maker with his own budget responsible for each lower-level educational objective in the school district. There can be no doubt that the new instructional devices are caus-ing change to move in this direction. Consider the following observation concerning the use of a grammar program in Manhasset:

> The introduction of *English 2600* led the teachers to question previously un-examined assumptions about teaching, to consider prerequisites to the study of the subject, to examine the value of teaching certain material, and to analyze the needs of students. At the same time they found themselves organizing for instruction in new ways, using large group teaching of a rather unusual kind, individual confer-ences once or twice a week for each child, a lay reader who also held student con-ferences, a class in remedial grammar, and a system of grouping homogeneously by accuracy and speed in English grammar.
>
> The teachers also found themselves using a substantial portion of their two free periods each week for joint planning and evaluation of their program. The team, at first under the leadership of the teacher who had started the program, devel-oped an associate relationship involving joint planning, teaching and evaluating of the program. When the need arose, one teacher could take over any one of the eighth-grade groups, and pupils could be transferred from group to group whenever necessary. Yet no formal team-teaching structure was developed, and unlike teachers in many schools experimenting formally with team teaching, the teachers believe that their work load has not really increased. Rather, the work of planning has been transferred from home to school, and work time at school has become more con-centrated.[3]

As I see it, this organization will be one in which the department chairman becomes a responsible decision-maker as he is in many universities.* One department, for example, might be "History" in a small high school or "Eleventh and Twelfth Grade History" in a large school. The chairman has his own budget and participates along with the principal in hiring decisions for persons in his department. He is a master teacher and has a good

This is not to say that university departments are themselves efficient. The reason, again, is that the chairman is responsible for too many sub-functions. But that is another story.

knowledge of the strengths and weaknesses of the various audiovisual media. He has a hand in the planning of the curriculum and in daily lesson plans such that he can step in on short notice and perform *any teaching task* in his department without loss of continuity. He is free to substitute audiovisual media for teacher time and vice-versa at will as long as he stays within his budget and satisfies his superiors that the instruction is effective.

There will be ongoing evaluation of the educational "product" of his department both by the chairman and by the office of the assistant principal for evaluation. Finally, each school has an audiovisual media center which supports the department chairman's requests for equipment use and which coordinates the demands of the various departments.

A Detailed Analysis: Instructional Strategies for Elementary Education

Not the least of the virtues of looking at public services in the manner outlined above is that it provides a convenient framework for thinking about the problem in systematic fashion. As a way both of illustrating the technique and at the same time examining the potential of alternative instructional approaches in elementary education, this part of the paper will deal with the costs and outcomes of alternative instructional strategies for the teaching of science, reading, and arithmetic to elementary school pupils. Time did not permit the author to be as exhaustive as he should have in the treatment of the literature and many of the numbers in the analysis are not obtained in scientific enough fashion for them to be trusted. This is especially true on the effectiveness side. Cost investigations were somewhat more thorough.

There are four basic steps to the analysis. First, a specific output measure needs to be isolated. This is relatively easy at the elementary level since performance in basic subjects form a large percentage of elementary education. In the example here we have used reading, science, and arithmetic studies, with "science" being interpreted quite broadly in one instance (learning how to dial the telephone).

The second step is to carefully isolate *in detailed form* a number of major strategies for teaching this information of which the traditional reliance of a single teacher in a classroom is one. The purpose of the strategies would be different according to the aims of the individual researcher. If the evaluation is to be one of the experiments that have already been performed—such as that in this paper—then the researcher need pay attention only to strategies that have been used and perhaps also, for instructive purposes, some extrapolation of strategies close to those already performed. The drawback to this approach of course is the fact that many of the studies in literature are not strictly comparable. As Briggs points out:

> Many experiments were designed to compare the overall effects of one medium with another, or with a combination of media, over an entire course. While such experiments are of value for the practical purpose of choosing among existing packages of instruction on particular topics, they do not represent a basis for designing an analytic procedure for planning new instructional courses. When a lengthy course or sequence, representing several kinds of learning, is prepared in two different media and the results analyzed, the most frequent result is a failure to demonstrate a significant difference. One reason for such a finding could be that each of the media compared was more effective for some elements of instruction and less effective for other elements, so that the differences in effectiveness among media were canceled out in the overall analysis.

Briggs goes on to succinctly state an even more frustrating problem:

> Another problem in employing the classroom literature for the present purposes

was the failure to describe the content of instruction in sufficient detail that the type of learning involved could be identified. When it is suspected that the materials used in an experiment did involve several types of learning, it would be necessary, for the present purpose, to be able to identify specific criterion test items which correspond to the separate types of learning presented during the experiment. Almost no investigators report data which make this kind of analysis possible.[4]

Despite these problems, the approach can have a great deal of value and is probably the best one for putting existing empirical work into a meaningfully ordered analytical framework.

The second approach is to design and conduct experiments according to the various proposed strategies. This of course requires the professional expertise of the trained educational psychologist who keeps in mind the relative theoretical effectiveness of different instructional techniques for teaching different tasks—perhaps using the Gagné 8-fold classification of subject matter or concepts of the like.

Based upon the 21 experiments outlined in Chart 1, my own knowledge of educational practice, and some imagination, I have constructed a set of twelve possible teaching strategies for basic elementary-school subjects. Each strategy is different in some major respect from all the others. Depending upon the patience and resources of the researcher, a great many more strategies could be isolated although in most cases the additional effort would not be worth the candle. Thus, the major inputs varied in the twelve strategies are seven: Administrators, para-professional personnel, secretaries, TV instruction, teachers, films, and programmed learning, this last to include computer-assisted instruction. An analysis where more detail is introduced would include such things as filmstrips, overhead projectors, etc., as variables, not to mention strategies which utilize school buildings 12 months per year. In this paper it is assumed that the use of such devices is usually *in addition to* the resource inputs of the twelve major strategies and, moreover, that the incidence of their use is relatively stabile between strategies, and therefore, they are not considered in the analysis. This does not imply they are unimportant.

Each of the strategies is now discussed in more detail. There are two major variations with respect to administration—traditional and with departmental organization. The first six are traditional; the last six departmental.

Strategy 1. Traditional Single Teacher Instruction This is the strategy which has proved durable over many decades. Some audiovisual aids are used but the teacher carries the main burden of all the instruction and course organization. There is little supervision of curriculum detail by higher administrators and therefore, there are only about three to six principals and supervisors for every forty teachers. No TV is used; nor is there programmed learning of any type, although some films are used. Our strategy assumes three principals and supervisors per 1000 pupils (a figure based on a New York study by the author), no para-professional people, two secretaries for each principal and supervisor, a full-time teacher, no TV, no programmed instruction, and two 15-minute films shown per week.

Strategy 2. Traditional Single Teacher with Additional Use of Televised Instruction This strategy is essentially the same as Strategy 1 except that the teacher depends on audiovisual aids more heavily and it is therefore somewhat more expensive. The teacher uses some combination of five 60-minute, ten 30-minute, or twenty 15-minute televised periods per week.

Strategy 3. Traditional Single Teacher with One Period (60 Minutes) Per Day of Instructional Television in Large Classes of 150 Pupils This strategy is identical to the previous one except for the fact that the children attend the ITV lectures in large groups. The assumption made is that one teacher gives the lecture while another monitors the large lecture section. Since we assume one teacher per 25 pupils otherwise, this strategy releases four teachers during the TV instructional period.

Strategy 4. Traditional Single Teacher with Programmed Instruction This strategy is the same as Strategy 1 except that it adds 300 minutes of programmed instruction per week. There are two variants: Variant A uses computer-assisted instruction for drill and practice programs while Variant B uses teaching machines. These same two variants are used whenever there is programmed instruction.

Strategy 5. Traditional Single Teacher with Programmed Instruction with Pupils in Large Groups This strategy is identical to Strategy 4 except that pupils receive programmed instruction and view films in groups of 100. During programmed instruction one teacher answers questions and another either answers questions or assigns work to the pupils who finish the program.

Strategy 6. Traditional Single Teacher Except That Films Are Shown to the Pupils 60 Minutes Per Day in Groups of 150 It is assumed that only one teacher is present during the time the film is shown thus releasing five teachers for one hour. The sixth teacher could of course easily be replaced by a para-professional person at some savings.

Departmental Organization Strategies

Above was discussed the author's ideas of the departmental organization structure which would be required if there is to be efficient substitution back and forth between audio-visual materials and face-to-face teacher instruction. The chief difference is that more administrators, secretaries, and para-professional personnel would be used than are used in most schools presently. In most small elementary schools as they now operate little change in organization would be necessary. For a school with an enrollment of 500, say, required would be two additional assistant principals to head up phases of the curriculum. This represents perhaps a tripling of administrative personnel and the assumption used for the departmental organization strategies is that three times as many principals, supervisors, and secretaries would be required as are presently required. It is to be noticed that department heads have been classified as administrators and used full time for administrative tasks despite the fact that all of them would do some teaching.

Strategy 7. Departmental Organization with Pupils Instructed 1/5 by TV and 1/5 by Motion Pictures in Groups of 100 With this strategy a teacher is never used in the classroom to monitor TV and film instruction. This is done by para-professional people.

Strategy 8. Departmental Organization: Same as Strategy 7 with Programmed Instruction Substituted for Films Unlike for films and TV, the assumption is that a teacher will always be present during programmed instruction.

Strategy 9. Departmental Organization: Heavy Dependence upon TV Instruction with Some Film Instruction In this strategy, TV and film presentations are made in individual classrooms with teachers present in class 15 minutes out of the hour for discussion.

Strategy 10. Departmental Organization: Strategy 9 Except That the Pupils Are Instructed in Groups of 150 This is the most inexpensive of the twelve strategies.

Strategy 11. Departmental Organization: Half-time Single-Teacher Instruction and Half-time TV Instruction to Groups of 100 Pupils

Strategy 12. Departmental Organization: Heavy Use of ITV, Films, and Programmed Instruction, Groups of 100 Pupils; Single Teacher Otherwise This is the most "capital-rich" strategy presented. Despite this, the average pupil sees a classroom teacher during 42% of his total instruction time.

Costs

Having constructed a meaningful set of alternative instructional strategies, the next step is to estimate the costs of each on a per pupil basis. This in turn requires estimates for the per-pupil costs for the relevant inputs. This was straightforward for the four labor inputs used, since it is relatively easy to assign salary levels which are approximately correct. The salary levels assumed for a 36-week school year are as follows:

Principals and Supervisors	$10,000
Teachers	$ 8,000
Secretaries	$ 4,000
Para-professional Personnel	$ 4,000

The costs of the three "capital" inputs are much more difficult to obtain, however. The next three sections include detailed discussions of per-pupil costs for closed circuit TV, films, and programmed instruction (computer or teaching machine). As the reader will see, the estimates obtained are merely approximate, although I feel they are reasonable interpolations of what I have found in the available literature on costs. The two most important single sources used were the detailed study by the General Learning Corporation (GLC) (18) for all the major audiovisual media and the Booz-Allen-Hamilton estimates of the cost of instructional television and computer-assisted instruction which were prepared for the Committee on Economic Development (11). Cost estimates on computer technology also appear in Oettinger's coming book, and in work by Jamison and Suppes. I have also spoken at length with a number of people in the excellent audiovisual department at Indiana University (especially concerning film and teaching machine costs) and also at the National Center for School and College Television. Finally, I have found the discussions of costs of instructional television in Hagerstown, Maryland (6) most valuable. Throughout I adhere to the convention of making estimates in terms of ten percent blocks of instructional time. Unless otherwise stated, a school district of 20,000 pupils is assumed.

Cost Estimates for Closed Circuit Television

Three basic sources were used for CCTV cost estimation—Hagerstown, General Learning Corporation, and Booz-Allen-Hamilton.

The GLC estimate for ITV costs for 10% instructional time in a 15,000 pupil school district is approximately $33.00 per pupil per year. This includes some "in-house" production costs of "minimal Quality" (teacher lecture—some visual training aids). With greater reliance upon a national programming source the cost would be a few dollars less. The GLC estimate for a city with 150,000 pupils is only $11.00 per pupil per year.

Cost estimates in the Booz-Allen-Hamilton study vary greatly depending upon the software utilized. For a school district with 100,000 pupils B-A-H estimates ITV (for 1/6 time) would cost $800,000 for $50.00 per hour software and $3,200,000 for the exclusive use of the most sophisticated software produced in house. Their cost estimate for various combinations of software is $2,400,000. Few school districts would employ highly expensive software and many would undoubtedly concentrate upon the same type of software as that used in Hagerstown, which is relatively inexpensive. Thus, I have selected a compromise figure of $1,600,000, which is half-way between the two lower figures. This comes to $16.00 per pupil per year for 16.7% time or $9.60 per pupil per year for 10% time for 100,000 pupils.

The Hagerstown estimates are the only ones here coming from direct experience. I averaged required TV usage for grades 3-6 in Hagerstown which comes to 13% of instructional time. There are some optional TV courses also and, adding two percentage points for that, we have a 15% elementary school program of ITV. For this 15%, Hagerstown spends about $300,000 in operating costs. They claim buildings for the TV cost about $225,000 although this seems low. With debt service and a forty-year write-off this comes to about $11,000 per year. I assume $20,000. Dividing $320,000 by 20,000 yields the very low cost of $16 per pupil per year for 15% of total instructional time. There is no provision for rented program material in this although Hagerstown does in fact produce most of their own programs, using their own teachers with large TV viewing audiences.

To summarize the foregoing, we have the following estimates for 10% time by size:

			SIZE	
STUDY	15,000	20,000	10,000	150,000
General Learning Corporation	$33.77			$10.81
Booz-Allen-Hamilton			$9.60	
Hagerstown		$10.67		

The GLC and B-A-H figures seem reasonably consistent while that for Hagerstown seems low. If the Hagerstown figure is reasonably close, the GLC figure is undoubtedly too high.

What cost figures to use for a school district of 20,000? It is difficult to reconcile the different size, but let us assume that the *relative* cost differences by size are correct as given by GLC. Using that relationship, the figures reduce to the following for a district with 20,000 pupils, 10% time.

Hagerstown	$10.67
GLC	32.92
B-A-H	16.36

The arithmetic mean of these three estimates is $20.00, which is the figure I will use in this paper.

But this is merely for the first 10%. How much would additional blocks of 10% time cost? There is little in the literature to serve as a guide on this point. Certainly there must be some economies of scale in closed circuit television. General Learning Corporation at one point estimates that the cost per pupil of closed circuit TV going from 10% to 20% for a metropolitan area goes from $10.00 to about $13.00, or approximately 30%. Using this information, my guesstimate is that cost would increase 50% for each additional 10% and therefore, the figure assumed here is additional 10% blocks of closed TV instruction cost $10.00 per pupil per year. Further, and having nothing to go on (except some economic theory perhaps) I would think that after some point it becomes relatively expensive to provide TV again. Thus, I assume that after the percentage of instruction becomes 40%, the cost per hour per pupil again becomes $20.00.

Cost Estimates for Films

General Learning Corporation estimates that in a local school district (15,000 pupils) per pupil annual cost for using films 10% of the time would be $51.71, with $36.59 going for production (including acquisition of rented materials), $6.13 for distribution, and $8.99 for reception. The GLC estimates for acquisition costs seem high however. Rental fees at the Indiana University Audiovisual Center for five days' use are approximately $4.00, $9.00, and $13.00 for 20-, 60-, and 90-minute films respectively for black and white, double this for color. Assuming half usage of 20-minute and half of 60-minute films, half in color and half in black and white, and also assuming the films are shown to two groups of fifty students each week, total rental fees per student per year comes to $14.58 per pupil per year. Further savings could be realized by using more long films (which are becoming increasingly available) or by using a larger room for each showing. It is not reasonable to assume school district production in most instances of film material, although there is no reason why film production costs could not be almost as low as TV program production costs in Hagerstown, for example. Therefore I have adopted the figure of $15.00 per pupil per year for production and acquisition costs. Using the GLC estimate of approximately another $15.00 for distribution and reception costs, this yields a figure of $30.00 per pupil per year for 10% instructional time which is the figure I use.

8mm Film

While 8mm film is not specifically considered in this paper, a note should be added concerning this interesting new media. Perfect for individual and small group instruction, it costs only $10.00 for the purchase of a four-minute cassette and $55.00 for an 11-minute cassette. Small rear-screen projectors cost from $100 (silent) to $350.00. While the resolution is not quite as good as for 16mm, the 8mm film can also be shown to larger groups with projectors which cost about $400. The technology of 8mm films seems most adaptable to classroom teaching, with the possibility of the teacher stopping the film at any point to show one frame, going over material a second time, etc.

Cost Estimates for Computer-Assisted Instruction and Branched Programmed Learning Using Teaching Machines

There does not seem to be much agreement concerning the costs of computer assisted instruction. Part of the reason is that some writers look at present technology and others think in terms of what will be possible in the future. Also, there is some disagreement over what the computer would be asked to do. If it were a full-scale tutorial program, it would be much more expensive than a simple drill device.

Booz-Allen-Hamilton arrive at the conclusion that CAI cost per student for 1/6 of a day per year in a school district of 10,000 for drill and practice would be $340,000, while in a district with 100,000 pupils it would be $272.00. Oettinger, in his forthcoming book, presents figures which are fairly much in line with these estimates. On the other hand, Oettinger cites studies which state that equipment costs (not including software) would be 2% of a school's budget (Bright) and $50.00 per year per student (RCA). The 2% figure would run only $10.00, an unbelievably low figure. Oettinger cites another study which projects Philadelphia expenditure for CAI at 10% of their total budget, or about $50-$60 per pupil per year. Also, Suppes, in an unpublished comment on Oettinger's book claims that we "could aim at" $30.00 per student for a drill and practice program. Dean Jamison, finally, estimates a yearly equipment cost of $90.00 per student for an IBM 1500 computer with 32 terminals. Jamison also discusses a modified CAI system which does not have continuous access to computers, uses audio and other shortcuts, which would cost a total of only $45.00 per year.

The Booz-Allen-Hamilton estimate for production cost is $200.00 per year while Jamison's for the IBM 1500 computer is $90.00. Using Jamison's figure for production and leaving everything else unchanged, for a 10,000-pupil district this comes to $230.00 per pupil per year and for a 100,000-pupil district, $162.00 per pupil per year. This is for 1/6 time however. For 10% time and for a 20,000-pupil district, this figure comes to $133.50. On the other hand, the original B-A-H figures of $340.00 and $272.00 convert into a figure of $200.00 per pupil per year for 10% time.

The General Learning Corporation, while discussing computer assisted instruction in some detail, at the same time feels that it is premature to make cost effectiveness analysis simply because it is so difficult to measure effectiveness. They do give some trade-off figures, however, which help establish costs. Investment per student with top utilization rates is given at about $2,000, a figure which undoubtedly is well in excess of $200.00 per pupil per year, although this is undoubtedly for more than 10% pupil time.

Finally, Patrick Suppes gives a detailed breakdown of a system which has 1,000 terminals with 40 students using each terminal which only costs $30.00 per student per year. With some misgivings (because of Suppes' figures) I have adopted the figure of $200.00 per pupil per year for CAI for 10% time. It is probably too early in the game to make a decent estimate for this technology however.

There is probably no reason to assume that further 10% blocks of instructional time would be less expensive and therefore, I assume each additional 10% instructional time also costs $200.00.

Other Programmed Technology

Computer-Assisted Instruction in its simpler applications is basically programmed instruction. Thus, there are other less expensive programmed instruction technologies which are available. One of these is outlined by Dean Jamison, and is a branching program which uses a minimum of computer time. The student follows the course (at his own level) with earphones and a workbook. Jamison estimates that costs of this scheme would vary between 15¢ and 25¢ per console per hour. Using 20¢, this comes to 60¢ per week, or about $22.00 per student per year for 10% time.

Finally, there is the alternative of using teaching machines. Some types of machines make it possible to use a fairly sophisticated branching program similar to the simpler tasks that can be performed by computers. One machine which can accomplish this is the Auto-tutor, which sells for about $1,250 and lasts almost indefinitely. Software costs $110.00 per program and a student uses perhaps one program per week on the average. With a 25-year amortization and a $5.00-per-year maintenance cost, yearly cost of hardware is $10.00, and if six pupils per day use the machine, this is $1.67 per pupil per year. The cost to be imputed to this technology is closely related to the useful life of the software, however. Many writers assume that programs become obsolete after three years, although this seems extreme for such things as grammar, arithmetic drill, etc., as are often used for this type of program. More realistic figures might be seven or even ten years. The seven-year figure is used here. Per pupil software cost per week is therefore $110/7 \times 6 = \$2.62$ for 16.7%, or $1.57 for 10% time times 36 weeks. This is $52.52. Adding the $1.67 cost of hardware gives a figure of approximately $60 which is somewhat higher than that of Jamison's scheme. Since the Auto-tutor method is presently in use, I have adopted the $60 figure for branched program instruction using teaching machines. With mass-produced software this cost could go down significantly, however.

Relative Costs of Media

It is now easy to compare the relative costs of trading off one media for another which is a chief advantage of structuring the analysis in this way. The relevant information for doing this is as follows:

	COST PER PUPIL PER YEAR					
	PERCENT OF INSTRUCTIONAL TIME					
	FIRST	SECOND	THIRD	FOURTH	FIFTH	SIXTH
INSTRUCTIONAL INPUT	*10%*	*10%*	*10%*	*10%*	*10%*	*10%*
Teachers	$ 32	$ 32	$ 32	$ 32	$ 32	$ 32
Para-professionals	16	16	16	16	16	16
Television	20	10	10	10	20	20
Films	30	30	30	30	30	30
Computer Assisted Instruction	200	200	200	200	200	200
Teaching Machines	60	60	60	60	60	60

It should be remembered that in order to replace a teacher it is necessary to spend some funds upon para-professional personnel. But if one para-professional (teacher-aide) can monitor a classroom of 100 pupils while a one-hour film is being shown, this allows the administration to free four teachers for that hour, assuming as we do that it is necessary for there to be one classroom teacher for every 25 pupils. Thus, in this example, the cost would be that of the media plus of the equivalent of one fourth of a para-professional (since one such individual is monitoring four regular classes) while the savings would of course be the salaries of the four teachers for that hour, assuming they are being efficiently utilized elsewhere.

From the figures just given, it is obvious that computer-assisted instruction is by far the most costly of these technologies. Even teaching machines, of the Auto-Tutor type, with branching programs, are relatively expensive when judged alongside the other technologies. Of all the media, closed circuit TV is the least expensive. The reason TV is less expensive than films can be found in the copyright laws which forbid films to be shown through the TV facilities of an entire school or school district.

Cost Analysis of Alternative Instructional Strategies

Cost per pupil per year for each strategy is given at the bottom of Table 1. As the reader can see, the most economical strategies are those in which it is possible to take advantage of using groups of pupils which are at least 100 pupils in size. Thus, of the traditional single teacher strategies, the two most economical ones, numbers 3 and 6, both use groups of 150 pupils for media presentation. It is noteworthy that the traditional single teacher strategy is much more expensive than the two best strategies. Of course, when it is necessary to maintain a relatively full time teacher plus using audiovisual devices, the cost becomes greater, as with strategies 2 and 4. This is particularly true with computer assisted instruction.

As discussed above, when teachers are replaced and large classes are used for media presentation it is necessary to introduce more administrative planning using a departmental organization. Despite increased administration costs, the departmental scheme seems to yield economies, with all except strategy 9 being at least as inexpensive (using Teaching machines instead of programmed learning) as any single teacher scheme. The most inexpensive scheme of all, strategy 10, utilizes classes of 150 pupils for viewing films and television, with teachers providing 15 minute discussion periods after each film or TV presentation.

Effectiveness

Up to this point only the costs of alternative strategies have been considered. Nothing has yet been said about the effectiveness of each.

Chart 1 gives in summary form the effectiveness of 21 studies which are relevant to the teaching of grade school basic subjects and which represent, at second hand, reasonable approximations to at least some of the strategies given in Table 1. They are meant to illustrate in crude fashion a preliminary attempt at evaluation.

Most of the studies mentioned in Chart 1 are closest to our strategy 2, which merely adds television instruction to single teacher instruction. Counting the two racial groups in Study number 11, there were 12 of these experiments, of which three showed the TV treatment as significantly better, one inferior, and the others showing no difference. From these studies it would be difficult to conclude that strategy 2 is much better than strategy 1.

Five of the studies could be (with some awkwardness perhaps) construed as fitting into strategy 3 which uses large TV classes. Of these, four are significantly better, one shows no difference, and one is insignificantly worse. One of these experiments is the experience of Hagerstown, Maryland, which had positive results over a great many replications. There is a suggestion at least, therefore, that strategy 3 is more effective than strategies 1 and 2, as well as less expensive.

Strategy 4 employs single teacher relationships but with the addition of drill-and-practice type programs provided either through the medium of teaching machines or computer assisted instruction. There are three teaching-machine-programmed-learning studies listed in Chart 1 and one experiment using CAI. In two of the three teaching-machine-programmed-learning studies high ability pupils did significantly better than control groups and the third reports simply that good students had time left over to do other things. For average ability children two of the studies showed no difference while the third (Manhasset) showed experimental groups doing significantly better although there was some question raised about the testing procedure. One study reported specifically on low ability children and found poorer performance although not statistically significant. Many programmed learning studies complain that low ability pupils often fail to finish and therefore lose interest.

We have listed only one study for strategy 4A (or 5A), i.e., the one that uses computer assisted instruction. In that study, of which I have only a preliminary fragment, Suppes reports by class and therefore does not differentiate by ability level. In two experiments Suppes finds no difference in one and significantly better performance for the programmed learners in the other.

To summarize with respect to programmed learning, if I were a department head with the responsibility of dealing with higher ability children, I would look into programmed learning for rote skills very carefully. Otherwise the results do not as yet seem to warrant the additional expenditures required. There is no doubt that this technology will have a definite role in future instructional strategies.*

There is only one study which more or less fits strategy 6, which uses films one hour a day or so, shown to large groups. That study, by Slattery (36), also does not use as large classes as called for by strategy 6 and filmstrips were used besides motion pictures for the teaching of fifth grade social studies. Slattery found both filmstrips and motion pictures improved performance with best performance coming with heavy use of filmstrips.

Since the departmental organization structure assumed in the last six strategies in Chart 1 does not correspond to many real-world school situations there are not many experiments which fit those six strategies, although most of these strategies have their single-teacher-organizational-structure counterparts. Thus, strategies 7 and 11 are similar to strategies 2 and 3 for example.

Roughly speaking, the Milwaukee experiments in elementary science (number 15 on

---

The investigator cannot read into the literature on programmed learning very far without noticing the fact that it is an instructional technology which has very different impacts upon pupils with differing levels of ability. More specifically, the chief attraction of programmed learning technology is the speed in which it can teach some rote skill subjects such as grammar and arithmetic to high ability pupils. The technique should not properly be compared to the progress of all pupils therefore, but with pupils with high, average, and low ability levels, somehow defined. This is another example of the benefits to be gained from sub-optimizing the analysis to the point where the program and pupil population is homogeneous.

Chart 1) look as if they could easily fit into strategies 10 and 11. Of the 12 strategies, number 12 relies the most on mechanical instructional aids. There have probably been no experiments where A-V materials are used this heavily. Of the experiments listed in Chart 1, number 19 is perhaps the only one which came close to using this technology.

General Summary of Results

On the evaluation side of this analysis, there seems to be a great deal of evidence that many of these strategies are of equal effectiveness, at least insofar as average ability-level pupils are concerned. If I had to hazard a judgment, I would say that mixed-media schemes which use 10 to 20% instructional TV seemed to provide the best results. It seems most clear, also, that face-to-face teacher instruction, preferably in small classes, is the one input necessary to make all the other ones "go."

If we can believe the many findings in the literature of "no difference," then the task of comparing efficiency is simple; we merely need to compare the costs of each strategy. Thus, of the strategies using traditional organization, numbers 3 and 6 are best, while strategy 10 is far the most inexpensive overall. Of the strategies which use traditional single teacher organization, it is important to notice that the most inexpensive are those which utilize large groups of pupils for audiovisual media presentation. My final overall impression, considering both cost and effectiveness, is that the most efficient general teaching strategies for average ability elementary schoolers would be some combination of strategies 3 and 6.

If the outcomes are significantly different for the various strategies, however, and as the number of relevant strategies becomes larger, more sophisticated analysis is needed. This is available in the form of linear programming analysis and it would not be difficult for economists with a knowledge of managerial economies to set the problem up and solve it in a linear programming framework. Until more precise evaluation of alternative strategies is possible this will not be necessary, however. It will be enough for the administration to choose the strategy which yields the best pupil performance subject to the limitations of his budget.

Postscript: The Future of "Capital" in Education

While not germane to the discussion in the main body of this paper, I should like to venture some observations concerning the future of mechanical and electronic instructional techniques based upon some simple economic theory. Professor Baumol has capably demonstrated the plight of the labor intensive industry in a capital-rich economy both in his book written with Bowen (5), and more rigorously in a paper published in the *American Economic Review* (4). Briefly put, sectors which cannot increase their productivity by deepening of capital are at a serious long-run disadvantage relative to those sectors which increase productivity through improved capital equipment. The reason for this can be understood best from a consideration of the following chain of circumstances. Technological progress occurs in some sectors of the economy, for example, in steel production, automobile production, coal mining, etc. Such progress allows higher profits and for some reason or other—let us say it is because of union activity—wages rise to keep pace with the rise in productivity. With small exception this has happened throughout much of the past two centuries. Wages in these sectors are higher but *because of the increased productivity*, prices of the products do not go up—over time they may even decline. But since each national economy is a single labor market, wages do not go up in half of the economy without their being bid up in the other half as well. Over time wages tend to seek one level (and degree of unionization seems to have no effect on this) just as water tends to seek one level. Now, with wages having gone up in sectors where it is not possible to deepen capital and so raise productivity per worker (such as most government service, live symphony orchestra music, and barber services) the only resource for these sectors is to raise prices. There is no theoretical end to this process—if it continues long enough, prices in the labor intensive sectors will become infinitely high! With higher prices in these sectors, consumers substitute their purchases and buy more and more products where productivity has kept pace and less and less where it has not.

Until the 1960's, American Public Education, with a traditional resistance to change, has remained a highly labor-intensive sector with the result that prices of educational services have been rising rapidly. But the more prices increase, and the more the prices of the labor inputs—mostly teacher salaries—increase, the more economic pressure there is to substitute capital for labor. Thus, we should expect to see a much greater use of capital in American Education in the next fifty years.

This situation in the American Education Industry today (on all levels) is not unlike the situation in the American coal industry thirty years ago. It appeared at the time that American coal was being priced out of the world market and that any more increases in the wages of miners would kill the industry altogether. But John L. Lewis, an adamant man, led the union to seek and get much higher wages anyway. And what happened? Faced with higher wage costs, mine owners strained to introduce labor saving equipment, which they did so successfully that today American coal has a competitive *edge* in world coal markets. Part of the reason for this is that the high paid miners are themselves happier and more efficient than otherwise!

With teacher salaries having gone up a great deal in the past several years, I feel that American Public Education in the 1970's will be in the same position as American coal in the 1940's. Let us hope that the end of the story is equally happy. If it is, much will have been gained, for American Public Education will have high quality teachers using sophisticated instructional materials.

CHART 1
A Representative Sample of Experimental Findings: Audiovisual Techniques

AUTHOR	GENERAL DESCRIPTION	NATURE OF EXPERIMENT	CONTROL	EFFECTIVENESS (EXPERIMENTAL VERSUS CONTROL)	SCHEME MORE-OR-LESS SIMILAR TO STRATEGIES IN TABLE 1
Almstead and Graf (1)	Reading instruction, Grades 4 and 6, using talk back-equipped TV	Full reading instruction by TV where student could "talk-back" to TV teacher. Para-professionals as monitors possible	Face to Face Instruction (FF)	Grade 4: +3.6 Months Grade 6: +2.8 months Iowa Test Basic Skills	2, 3, 7
Amirian (3)	TV Instruction, Science Informa-tion, Grade 5	In science, 30 half-hour classes on TV during academic year	FF	No difference	2
Carner (9)	TV instruction, fifth and sixth grade reading	Total time and half time instruction of reading by TV	FF	*All TV:* Superior students: significantly poorer. Average students: no difference. Below average students: significantly better. *Part Time TV:* no difference	2
Curry (13)	TV instruction, seventh grade mathematics and sixth grade science	Mathematics: 20 minute periods plus face to face instruction. Science: 30 minute TV periods plus face to face instruction	FF	Above average students: no difference. Average and below-average students: poorer	2

AUTHOR	GENERAL DESCRIPTION	NATURE OF EXPERIMENT	CONTROL	EFFECTIVENESS (EXPERIMENTAL VERSUS CONTROL)	SCHEME MORE-OR-LESS SIMILAR TO STRATEGIES IN TABLE 1
Curry (12)	TV instruction, fifth grade science	20 minute TV lessons every other day 10 minute teacher discussion. Also: TV instruction with high pupil involvement versus TV instruction with low pupil involvement	FF TV instruction with low pupil involvement	No significant difference	2, 11
Dietmeier (15)	TV instruction, fifth grade science	90 classes total. In 24, TV instruction with teachers trained in TV. In 24, TV instruction with teachers not trained in TV. In 24, TV instruction with teachers not trained in science or TV	18 classes FF	No significant difference in any group	2
Enders (16)	TV instruction, sixth grade science	1. Twenty 15 minute TV programs during a 20 week period 2. Twelve 15 minute TV programs during a 20 week period	FF	The TV group were significantly better; the 12 lesson group did best	2, 3, 7
Gordon (19)	Speech Sound Instruction, TV, third grade	Two 15 minute instructional TV periods per week with 3 face to face periods	FF	No significant difference	2
Hall (21)	Various standard subjects taught to elementary pupils	Large group TV instruction, some whole periods and some partial periods	FF	Face to face instruction slightly better; not statistically significant	2, 3, 7
Himmler (23)	TV instruction, fifth grade reading and arithmetic	Reading: 25 minutes of ITV and then 25 minutes of face to face instruction, 20 classes Arithmetic: 25 minutes of ITV and then 15 minutes of face to face instruction, 20 classes	FF 19 classes	No significant differences; instructional variety found most effective	2
Johnson (25)	TV instruction, fifth and sixth grade science	Large and small TV classes	FF	White students: TV significantly better Negro students: No significant difference Students in large TV classes did as well as in small classes	2, 3, 7, 10
Anderson (28)	Learning to use the telephone, grade 5	1. Film Strips 2. Motion Picture Film with manual 3. Film Strips, Motion Picture Films, manual	FF	Multimedia instruction most effective. Face to face instruction only least effective	6 (except groups are small)
Romano (34)	Use of films and slides for teaching of sciences, grades, 5, 6, 7	Experimental groups used films and slides	No films and slides	Experimental groups better than control in all tests	6 (except) groups are small)
Slattery (36)	Fifth grade social studies instruction	Use of filmstrips and sound motion pictures	FF	Both filmstrips and sound movies improved performance; filmstrip presentation was the most effective	6
Suchy and Baumann (37)	Elementary science	First year: Instructional TV in large classes. Full period TV lessons Second year: Same as first year except 30 minute TV lessons	FF	TV significantly better	3, 7, 10,11

AUTHOR	GENERAL DESCRIPTION	NATURE OF EXPERIMENT	CONTROL	EFFECTIVENESS (EXPERIMENTAL VERSUS CONTROL)	SCHEME MORE-OR-LESS SIMILAR TO STRATEGIES IN TABLE 1
Herbert and Foshay (22)	Programmed Intruction: English 2600 Program, Grades 7 and 8	First year: grammar taught with program in three 30 minute sessions per week and at no other time Second year: Programmed grammar sessions for four classes at once in large room. When a pupil finished, he went to another room where he was assigned themes to write	FF as before, as part of the 90 minute social studies period	Significantly better except for low ability pupils perhaps. During second year average score +6.0 months compared to prior years	4B, 5B
Schramm (35)	Programmed Intruction: grammar written in house, grade 10	Program used to teach grammar	FF	Above average students: significantly better Other students: no difference	4B
Thelen and Ginter (39)	Programmed Instruction: fourth grade multiplication	Programmed instruction given in three 40 minute periods per week during the tenth through twentieth weeks of the term	FF	No significant difference except good students had time left to do other things	4B
Sadetsky (41)	Multi-media usage for instruction: filmstrips, slides, projectors, teacher aides	Individual learning for pupils in carrels	FF	Faster learning, not statistically significant	none 12 ?
Suppes (38)	Programmed Instruction, Computer Assisted, Drill and Practice, Mathematics	Ten minute daily drills as a supplement to the regular teaching program, two experimental schools and two control	FF	Statistically significant better learning in one experimental school and no difference in the other	4A, 5A
Hagerstown Schools (6)	Closed Circuit televised instruction, lectures by teachers. Music, art, mathematics, science, French	About 12% of total instruction in grades 3, 4, 5, 6 given over TV, mostly full hour periods	prior experience (FF)	Statistically significant and in most instances large increases in achievement performance in arithmetic, science, reading	3, 6, 10, 11

TABLE 1
Twelve Instructional Strategies, Seven School Inputs

Strategy	Input 1 TEACHERS	2 PARA-PROFESSIONAL PERSONNEL	3 CLOSED CIRCUIT TELEVISION	4 FILMS	5 A. COMPUTER ASSISTED INSTRUCTION B. PROGRAMMED INSTRUCTION WITH BRANCHING	6 PRINCIPALS AND SUPERVISORS	7 SECRETARIAL	
			% of Total Instructional Time					
1. Traditional Single Teacher	100			3.3 (two 30 minute films per wk)		1	1	$367
2. Traditional S-T with one period per Instructional TV	100		16.7 (five 60 minute or ten 30 minute sessions per wk)	3.3 (as in Strategy 1)		1	1	$394
3. Traditional S-T with one period per day ITV where pupils in large classes of 150 pupils	88.9 (one teacher gives lecture; one teacher monitors the large lecture session)		2.8 (as in Strategy 2 and divided by 6 $\left[\frac{150}{25}=6\right]$)	0.6 (as in Strategy 1 and divided by 6)		1	1	$330
4. Traditional S-T Branched Programmed Learning with CAI or Teaching Machines	100			3.3 (as in Strategy 1)	16.7 (five 60 minute or ten 30 minute sessions per week)	1	1	A. $701 B. $467
5. Traditional S-T with CAI or Teaching Machines where pupils are in large groups of 100 pupils while taking Programmed Learning	91.7 (during Programmed Learning sessions one teacher answers questions and another teacher answers questions or assigns work to pupils who have finished the program)			0.9 (as in Strategy 1 and divided by 4)	4.2 (as in Strategy 4 and divided by 4)	1	1	A. $343 B. $337
6. Traditional S-T with one period per day of films shown to groups of 150 pupils	86.2 (only one teacher present when film shown)			2.8 (five 60 minute or ten 30 minute or fifteen 20 minute films or some combination & divided by 6)		1	1	$322
7. Departmental Organization: 40% reliance on TV and Films shown in groups of 100 pupils	60	10 (one monitor for each TV or film session for 100 pupils)	5 (20% divided by 4)	5 (20% divided by 4)		3	3	$307

Strategy	1 TEACHERS	2 PARA-PROFESSIONAL PERSONNEL	3 CLOSED CIRCUIT TELEVISION	4 FILMS	5 A. COMPUTER ASSISTED INSTRUCTION B. PROGRAMMED INSTRUCTION WITH BRANCHING	6 PRINCIPALS AND SUPERVISORS	7 SECRETARIAL	COST PER PUPIL PER YEAR
8. Departmental Organization: 20% ITV and 20% CAI or Programmed Instruction. TV and Programmed Instruction in groups of 100 pupils	67.5 (for TV, one teacher lectures; for Programmed Learning, one teacher answer questions and one teacher answers questions or assigns work to pupils who have finished the program)	5 (as in Strategy 7)	5 (as in Strategy 7)		5 (20% divided by 4)	3	3	A. $400 B. $338
9. Departmental Organization: very high dependence on Film and TV: Teacher Discussion 15 minutes per class	25	76.7	66.7	10 (six 30 minute Films per wk)		3	3	$410
10. As with Strategy 9 except Film and TV shown to classes of 150; Teacher discussion in classes of 25	25	12.8 (76.7 divided by 6)	11.2 (66.7 divided by 6)	1.7 (10 divided by 6)		3	3	$202
11. Departmental Organization: 50% Instructional TV to classes of 100; single teacher otherwise	50	12.5	12.5			3	3	$277
12. Departmental Organization: heavy use of ITV, Film, and Programmed Instruction, Groups of 100 pupils; single teacher otherwise	41.8 (one teacher teaches the TV and two teachers are present for Programmed Instrction)	13.3	8.3 (33% divided by 4)	5.0 (20% divided by 4)	8.3 (33% divided by 4)	3	3	A. $428 B. $312

REFERENCES

1. Kershaw, J. A., and R. N. McKean, *Systems Analysis and Education*. The RAND Corp., RM-2473-FF, Santa Monica, California, 1959, p. 1.

   This important work, to my astonishment, has been completely overlooked in discussions of systems analysis I have seen in the educational literature, including one complete book on the subject by Pfeiffer.

2. *Ibid.,* pp. 1-2, 2-3.

3. Herbert, John and Arthur W. Foshay. "Programmed Instruction in the Manhasset Junior High School." *Four Case Studies of Programmed Instruction,* Fund for the Advancement of Education, New York, n.d., 24, (22).

4. Briggs, Leslie J. *Instructional Media: A Procedure for the Design of Multi-media Instruction, A Critical Review of Research, and Suggestions for Future Research.* American Institutes of Research, Pittsburgh, Pa. 1967, p. 24.

   This excellent discussion is the best I have been able to find on the analysis of multi-media instruction and is the one that incorporated the best understanding of the approach outlined here.

   Briggs' remarks illustrate a great problem that exists in the educational literature which has to do with the shameful quality of the reporting of educational experiments.

   A very tangible virtue of the procedure outlined herein is that it would impel investigators to report findings in a more scientific manner.

109.
Cost Effectiveness Evaluation Of Instructional Technology: The Problems

by HENRY M. LEVIN
Assoc. Prof. of Education
Stanford University

Introduction

Over the last two decades our society has experienced a revolution in decision-making processes. Where government and business once chose strategies on the basis of very meager information and intuition, modern decision-making relies upon the use of abundant sources of data, sophisticated analytical techniques, and high speed digital computers. Since most enterprises operate with a limited budget, they wish to make decisions that maximize output for any given cost or, conversely, minimize the costs for any given outcome. Such goals have stimulated the development of a set of tools for determining the probable costs and benefits of alternative management strategies. These methods are classified broadly under the term of cost-effectiveness techniques since they are designed to aid in choosing those approaches which yield the best outcome for any given cost.[1]

Concurrent with the recent revolution in management science and its particular branch of cost-effectiveness analysis has been the proliferation of new instructional technologies for the schools. Some of the best known of these techniques are: computer-assisted instruction; individually programmed instruction; the responsive environment or "talking typewriter;" educational games; and that relatively old example of the new technology, educational television.

At the same time our society has become increasingly frustrated by the failure of the schools to teach or motivate large numbers of disadvantaged youngsters. Complicating this failure has been the fact that spending additional money for so-called compensatory education has not improved to any significant degree these educational outcomes. Indeed, it appears that where there has existed a basic failure among traditional educational approaches, the simple expedients of spending more money on reduced class size and additional remedial services are inadequate for resurrection. So, increasingly in the post-Sputnik era the bankruptcy of the schools has led to many demands and proposals for substantial changes in the instructional process.

Given these three coinciding developments, one might expect a significant interaction among them. That is, we might expect to find the new instructional technologies being evaluated for their relative efficiencies in producing educational outcomes; the ones showing the greatest effectiveness relative to their costs would replace the allegedly less efficient traditional schooling processes. Paradoxically, this interaction has not taken place. The typical school continues to carry out its tasks in the same manner as it has always done. In fact, no reliable information on the relative costs and benefits of the new instructional technologies (or even the old ones) has become available. Schools and school districts have no objective data with which they can make determinations based upon the relationships between costs and performances of alternative instructional strategies.

Given this dearth of data, the schools have been very slow to adopt new techniques, and this conservatism has strong justification. There simply is no available knowledge that schools can draw upon to determine whether the new instructional approaches will be more effective, once costs are taken into account, than are traditional instructional approaches.

The purpose of this paper is to explain this paradox by outlining the problems that arise in applying cost-effectiveness evaluations to instructional technologies. It will be shown that most of the requirements for sound cost-effectiveness analysis cannot be satisfied given our present knowledge of the educational process.

Requirements for Cost-Effectiveness Evaluation

Like other productive enterprises, schools can be said to have three general properties which taken together define a "production process." First, there are educational objectives which can be defined as the *output* of the process; second, there are students, teachers, administrators, buildings, and other materials and personnel which provide *inputs* into the educational process; and third, there exist techniques of combining the inputs in various combinations to produce the aforementioned educational objectives.

Before we can compare the benefits and costs of different educational alternatives, we must possess some reasonably reliable data on the relationships among inputs, processes, and educational outcomes. That is, the task of cost-effectiveness analysis requires knowledge of the physical relations between inputs and outputs. Unfortunately, this information does not exist, even in a rudimentary form.

The inability to carry out cost-effectiveness analyses without these data can best be illustrated by presenting an example of how cost-benefit analysis has been applied to an area where it has yielded successful results, the evaluation of water-resource projects.[2]

Assume that we have a limited budget which must be allocated to that set of projects which will maximize benefits. Before the cost-effectiveness analyst sharpens his pencil he is given data on each of the proposed projects. Thus, he would be given information on such inputs as the amount of dredging required, the size of and specifications of the dam that will be built, and so on. He is also given a set of probable outcomes for each project; the degree of flood control, dimensions of the body of water that will be created by construction of the dam, hydroelectric output, and so on.

Given this information the cost-effectiveness analyst can estimate the value of social benefits that derive from reduced flood damage; new sources of water for irrigation, industrial, and drinking purposes; production of hydroelectric power, recreational potentialities and other outcomes. He can compare these with the initial and operating costs for the project and any indirect costs. Having taken account of the benefits and costs of all projects, he can select that combination of projects which will maximize the returns to society for any given cost. What is important to note in this example is that the physical relationships between inputs and outcomes are given to the analysts by hydrologists, civil engineers, and other water resource experts. It is these basic data which are required before the economist, statistician, or operations researcher can estimate the resultant costs and benefits. Why is it that comparable information on the schools is not readily available?

Outputs

The prime difficulty in evaluating outcomes of schooling derives from the multidimensional aspect of education as well as severe inadequacies in our abilities to measure even single dimensions of output. Anyone who seeks to list educational objectives is faced with a bewildering array of goals that are claimed for the schools.[3] While some of the goals are straightforward, others appear to be vague, and almost all of them defy measurement. Certainly the schools are expected to provide students with adequate knowledge of and literacy in language skills, mathematics, sciences, and social studies. Then there are the more esoteric objectives of inculcating a set of common values, civic pride, patriotism, appreciation of culture and aesthetics, and so on. It is often stressed that the schools are also responsible for preparing students to properly assume adult roles in our society. In actuality, the words describing these objectives tend to lull one into thinking that the objectives can be easily defined. Unfortunately, experience has shown that the specific goals which are masked by these descriptions are neither readily evident nor are they measurable.

Accordingly, the outputs which have usually been chosen for an analysis of school effectiveness have been standardized achievement scores, dropout rates, expected lifetime earnings, and rates of college attendance among high school graduates.[4] To the degree that these measures mirror to a great extent the ostensible successes or failures of individuals in middle class society, they are certainly important criteria. Nevertheless they may merely reflect that part of student behavior which is measurable in some gross sense. Unfortunately, like the visible portion of the iceberg, the greater part of educational output may be hidden from view.

Yet, one salient feature of educational output must be emphasized strongly. No matter which type of outcome one wishes to measure, the goals of the schooling process must be viewed as those of changing the potentialities, proficiencies, and attitudes of the students who enter that process. That is, schools are expected to change people in socially desirable ways (and one might also wish that the reverse were true). Students enter the schooling process as a relatively raw material, and the schools as well as concomitant family, community, and other influences transform these students into what might be characterized as "more-nearly finished" products. Thus the output of the school must be conceived of as the *value-added* to its student input—the difference between the value of the student output and student input.

In this sense the absolute levels of high school dropouts, college attendance, or achievement scores should not be used as measures of school output. Rather, the effectiveness of a school along these dimensions must be gauged by its success in *decreasing* dropout rates, *increasing* educational motivation, and *increasing* achievement among a given set of students. In particular, students of lower socio-economic status generally enter the schools less well prepared and with less educational support from their families than their middle-class counterparts. Even if the same amount of change were to take place among both groups of students, the disadvantaged students would show lower proficiencies at the end of the educational process. Therefore, it is the "value-added" in performance, attitudes, and other behavioral dimensions that must be related to schooling inputs. Unfortunately, many commentators appraise the performance of schools on the value of the student outputs alone, without taking account of differences in the proficiencies of incoming students.

Simply taking account of the social class of students in looking at differences in achievement levels—as some researchers have done—does not solve this problem.[5] Indeed, outputs must be directly measured as changes or growth along the pre-specified cognitive and affective dimensions. One way of doing this given the ordinal nature of test and attitudinal instruments is to measure the relative differences on a normalized scale at two points in time. That is, a school might have students who score at the 38th percentile on a standardized test of reading comprehension at grade 4, and at the 51st percentile in reading comprehension at grade 6 (using national norms for similarly constituted student samples at each grade level). The relative position of other schools might deteriorate. This approach represents a crude approximation of relative value-added, though it tells us nothing about absolute gains and is subject to all kinds of testing aberrations.[6]

One value-added measure that seems useful is the increase in productivity and lifetime income attributable to additional years of schooling. Even after adjusting for differences in students' abilities and opportunities it appears that additional schooling yields substantially higher earnings to the average individual.[7] Yet, we have no information which would relate changes in the *quality* of schooling and the implementation of particular instructional techniques to changes in productivity and life-time earnings. One possible approach is that of relating instructional techniques to changes in standardized achievement scores and subsequently relating differences in standardized achievement scores to differences in earnings (after accounting for such intervening factors as the returns to higher levels of schooling).[8] Much work needs to be *done* in the area of specifying and measuring outputs.

Production of Schooling

Assume that we could measure educational output satisfactorily. The next goal would be to find out how these outputs are produced; satisfying this objective we could specify inputs; and finally we could assess costs and benefits. Unfortunately, even given a specified outcome, we do not know how it is produced. That is, the complexity of the world in which education takes place has thus far prevented us from inferring specific and reasonably predictable relations between educational strategies and educational results.

Indeed the basic lack of specific knowledge on how learning or attitude formation takes place represents the greatest obstacle to cost-effectiveness analysis. In the case of water resource projects we know that by building a dam, some fairly predictable outcomes will ensue. In the case of education we have the problem that even if we arbitrarily select and measure both outputs and inputs, there are enormous difficulties in ascertaining how changes in any specified set of inputs will change outputs. The interactions among inputs and outcomes are so complex, and psychological processes are so little understood, that even sophisticated statistical techniques, the best available data, and the most advanced computers have not been able to reveal answers *in this area* where we lack basic theory.[9]

Thus, not knowing how schooling is produced we probably know even less about the specification and measurement of educational inputs than we know about outputs. It is true that we can measure per pupil expenditures, pupil-teacher ratios, physical facilities, and so on. Yet, if we have learned anything about the learning process it is that we must measure inputs in relation to their interactions with students. By this standard, it is the quality of the prime inputs that we must be concerned with as much as their quantities.

In the present schooling process, teachers represent about 70 percent of the current budget, so we must be especially concerned with the teacher input. The standard measures of teacher input tell us little about the quality of interaction between student and teacher. The traditional measures have been class size, the teacher's degree level, and teaching experience. These measures have been used because of their visibility. Yet, little evidence is available that shows any relationship between such measures and school effectiveness.

Even fairly substantial reductions in average class size do not seem to have improved the quality of teacher-student interactions.[10] Moreover, such factors as the degree level and experience of teachers vary so much in quality among teachers that they, too, have rarely shown any relation to school effectiveness.

Recent evidence suggests that those teacher traits which have not been readily visible such as attitudes and verbal facility show stronger associations with student achievement than do any *of the former measures*.[11] Moreover, experimentation is just beginning to denote those particular teachers' attitudes, that seem to affect the *performances* of students.[12] Yet, our state of knowledge is still too sparse to be able to accurately specify and measure those teacher attributes which are most highly related to educational outcomes.

Further, non-teacher inputs seem to be measured in very naive ways. For example, the presence of certain facilities or the age of a building is considered to be a reasonable measure of physical schooling facilities. This approach ignores the relevance of physical inputs by measuring them in such a way that student-facility interactions are ignored. For example, the presence of science laboratories tells us little about the quality or quantity of science instruction. Most high schools contain science laboratories as a standard part of their institutional design. Yet these laboratories vary in their equipment, their extent of use, and the degree to which they are integrated into the science program. In many schools science laboratories exist but are rarely used because teachers with science training are in short supply due to existing salary policies.[13] Yet a recent survey by the U.S. Office of Education used the presence of science laboratories as one of the two facilities measures that might affect verbal achievement.[14]

Likewise, the existence of educational television or some other form of instructional technology must be analyzed as an input in the way that it interacts with students and faculty. Simply specifying that some schools used closed circuit television and others did not tell us little about the schooling process. That is, the existence of a physical facility tells us little about the extent or quality of its use.

In short, just as outputs are highly speculative and poorly measured, we have very little available information on inputs into the schooling process or the learning process. Attention has been devoted to measuring quantities of visible inputs with little attention devoted to their qualities; and emphasis has been focused on the presence of certain visible features of schools rather than asking the more basic question of what constitutes the schooling process.

But the job of the cost-effectiveness analyst is that of evaluating the costs and benefits of different strategies. Information on inputs, processes, and resultant outcomes are the necessary prerequisites with which he must work, and the delicate job of translating this morass of information into a set of alternatives that can be readily compared by the decision maker is his science. If his information requirements are not satisfied, he cannot satisfactorily execute his task.

Some Confusion

Yet, so-called cost-effectiveness analysis is taking place in education with far too much claimed for it at this stage. One such effort has stated that it can translate expenditures on Title I programs into all kinds of educational outcomes including increases in lifetime earnings.[15] While no mechanism is shown for accomplishing this formidable task, the non-technical reader is seduced by flow diagrams, mock computer printouts, algebra, calculus, and a discussion of properties of statistical functions. Unfortunately, none of these solve the difficult problem for which the report claims it has the framework for solution.

Another report on cost-effectiveness analysis estimates actual benefit cost ratios without knowing the true costs of programs, what the programs consist of and their effects on student outcomes. That is, it never examines the ingredients of the programs; it merely assumes a casual link between changes in aid-to-the-disadvantaged and any improvement in their performance level over a period of time.[16]

Yet, I am optimistic enough to believe that many of these problems will be substantially overcome, and cost-effectiveness analysis will soon yield benefits greater than its own costs. Recent evidence, for example, has suggested that recruiting and retaining teachers with *higher verbal facility* is five to ten times as effective per dollar of teacher expenditure in raising achievement scores of students as the strategy of obtaining and retaining teachers with more experience.[17]

But before meaningful progress can be made we must be honest about the current state of the art as applied to education. Anthony Oettinger has stated this point succinctly:

"The systems analyst . . . owes it to the ideal of professional integrity to tell his client the truth as he sees it, not as the client would like to hear it. He may or may not have a useful prescription. Polio has been conquered, a mumps vaccine has just come out, but the common cold and cancer are still with us."[18]

The point is that we must recognize the formidable height of the barriers placed in the path of cost-effectiveness analyses in education rather than pretending that our hurdling ability is sufficient over any course. It is only by recognizing the magnitude of the hurdles that we will be able to surmount them rather than stumbling into them headlong.

REFERENCES

1. An overview can be found in Thomas A. Goldman, Ed., *Cost Effectiveness Analysis: New Approaches in Decision-Making,* Frederick A. Praeger, Inc., New York, 1967.

2. Cost-benefit analysis has been used by the Corps of Army Engineers for more than 30 years. For a discussion of techniques used to evaluate water-resource projects, see John V. Krutilla and Otto Eckstein, *Multiple Purpose River Development,* Johns Hopkins Press, 1958.

3. See, for example, Benjamin S. Bloom (ed.), *Taxonomy of Education Objectives Handbook I: The Cognitive Domain,* David McKay Co., New York, 1956.

4. For a discussion of outputs see Jesse Burkhead, et. al., *Input and Output in Large-City High Schools,* Syracuse University Press, 1967, Chaps. I-II. For some original work which discusses the effect of compensatory education programs on the alleviation of poverty within a cost-benefit framework, see Thomas I. Ribich, *Education and Poverty,* Brookings Institution, Wash. D.C., 1968. And for a cost-benefit analysis of dropout prevention see Burton Weisbrod, "Preventing High School Drop-outs," in *Measuring Benefits of Government Investments,* Robert Dorfman, ed., Brookings Institution, Wash. D.C., 1965, pp. 117-167.

5. See the discussion on this point in Samuel S. Bowles, "Toward an Educational Production Function," a paper presented at the Conference on Research in Income and Wealth, Univ. of Wisconsin, November 15, 1968, pp. 23-27.

6. Burkhead used a variant of this technique in the work previously cited. Unfortunately, problems with his data, statistical approach and specification of inputs prevented him from deriving useful results. See *Input and Output in Large-City High Schools,* pp. 53-56, 71-73, and 83-84. An example of the problems inherent in using test scores as measures of output is the fact that the test scores will improve simply by taking tests more frequently. That is, students can develop test-taking abilities that will improve scores. Holding other things constant, schools with extensive testing programs would show larger relative gains than those with more modest programs.

7. Becker, Gary S. *Human Capital.* Columbia Univ. Press, New York, 1964.

8. This technique might be used in a crude form with the recently available follow-up and earlier set of data collected by Project Talent.

9. For an example of the controversy on the validity of evidence derived in one of the largest studies on the determinants of scholastic achievement see, James S. Coleman, *Equality of Educational Opportunity,* Cha;. III; Samuel S. Bowles and Henry M. Levin, "The Determinants of Scholastic Achievement," *The Journal of Human Resources,* Winter 1968, pp. 3-24. See also the communication by Coleman in the *Journal of Human Resources,* Spring 1968, and those by Marshall Smith; Glen Cain and Harold Watts; and Bowles and Levin in the *Journal of Human Resources,* Summer 1968.

10. For strong evidence on this point in the light of drastic reductions in class size and student/teacher ratios see David J. Fox, "Expansion of the More Effective School Program," Evaluation of NYC Title I Educational Projects 1966-67, Center for Urban Education, NY, 1967, pp. 32-44.

11. See for example the evidence in Henry M. Levin, *Recruiting Teachers for Large-City Schools*, Brookings Institution, Wash. D.C., forthcoming. See also, Samuel Bowles, op. cit.

12. See, for example, Robert Rosenthal and Lenore Jacobson, *Pygmalion in the Classroom*, Holt, Rinehart & Winston, New York, 1968. Also see Ned A. Flanders, *Teacher Influence, Pupil Attitudes and Achievement*, U.S. Dept. of HEW, Off. of Education Cooperative Research Monograph No. 12, Gov. Pr. Off., Wash. D.C., 1965.

13. See my *Recruiting Teachers for Large-City Schools*.

14. Coleman, James S., et. al. *Equality of Educational Opportunity*. U.S. Dept. of HEW, Wash., D.C., 1966. On the basis of science laboratories and library books alone, the Report concluded that school facilities show little or no relation to achievement. See p. 316.

15. See Abt Assoc., Inc., "Design for an Elementary and Secondary Education Cost-Effectiveness Model," Report on the Mathematical Design Phase, Contract OEC 1-6-001681-1681, U.S. Off. of Educ., February 1967.

16. See Robert Spiegelman, et. al., "A Benefit/Cost Model to Evaluate Educational Programs," Stanford Research Institute, January 1968.

17. See Henry M. Levin, "Cost-Effectiveness Analysis and Educational Policy—Profusion, Confusion, Promise," a paper presented to the 34th National meeting of the Operations Research Society of America, Philadelphia, November 8, 1968.

18. "The Myths of Educational Technology," *Saturday Review*, May 18, 1968, p. 91.

110.

Deciding Whether and How to Use Educational Technology In the Light of Cost-Effectiveness Evaluation

by JAMES G. MILLER
Vice Pres. for
Academic Affairs
Cleveland State Univ.
2nd V.P. & Principal Scientist
EDUCOM

What do we mean by "educational technology"? Sometimes this phrase may refer to any form of learning situation planfully established by an educational system, including a tutorial session, a group conference, a school class, or a large university lecture, as well as a wide range man-made artifacts. Its more common usage includes all artifacts that aid in the learning process—books or journals, printed programmed instruction, computerized programmed instruction, on-line computer aids to learning and scholarship, closed circuit lectures on a public address system, educational radio, dial-access audio tape recordings, instructional television—both broadcast and closed circuit live, as well as tape recorded broadcast, closed circuit, and dial-access; facsimile transmission of documents by electronic circuits; various automated sorts of information storage and retrieval of written and graphic materials; as well as the many standard audiovisual aids such as wall charts, physical models, transparencies, slides, movies, and displays. The communication channels and nets which make possible widespread use of these technologies also should be included in any consideration of educational technology—word-of-mouth transmission in human interaction situations, transmission by courier, by the mails, or by telegraph, teletype, telephone, or television lines, microwave, laser, national, or international communications satellite.

Comparative Evaluation of the Media

We must evaluate, in terms of their comparative benefits, effectiveness, and costs, all these technologies, which have flourished so suddenly in recent years, as available artifacts that can serve as prostheses aiding the learning process.* It is incumbent upon us, with this new-found wealth of resources, not to continue traditional methods of education unless such evaluations of their cost-effectiveness trade-offs demonstrate them to be the most useful and desirable. We must ask what each methodology can contribute to improve education, or cut its costs, or both. Under what circumstances should one technology be employed rather than another? How does each serve to accomplish the long-range purposes or short-range goals of the system? Which contributes most to the individual organism in the educational

*Cf. Miller, J. G. The Nature of Living Systems, pages 36-37.

system, to the group in the classroom, to the school or university as an organization, to the society's educational system or to an international educational system?

These instructional technologies should be viewed only as adjuncts to human beings, rather than as substitutes for them. Over the centuries that man has used scrolls and books he has become accustomed to the idea that the book is an aid to the teacher or the professor, usually not a replacement. Apprehension about automation—replacement of the worker by the machine—which exists in many trades and professions today, appears to prevent a general understanding that all the other educational technologies should be used as books are. They are aids to the human beings involved in the educational process. Television or computerized programmed instruction, for instance, should be viewed as means to save the time of students and teachers, freeing the latter for the subtle and vital teaching functions which only human beings can carry out, at least at present. The new technologies may be able to assist in some rote learning functions, or provide more accurate and complete memory, or transmit information more rapidly and to more people than human beings can. This should relieve a load from the educators so that they can then devote themselves to smaller groups of students or individuals, dealing with such matters as those students' motivation to learn; problem-solving—using principles the students have learned in relation to real tasks in their own lives; students' manual dexterities; their attitudes and feelings about what they learn; ethical, moral, and religious issues; philosophical interpretations of the meaning of the knowledge; and other such concerns in which machines will quite possibly never replace human beings. Certainly such gifted machines are nowhere on the horizon now.

Any educational innovation ideally should be employed, at first, in a situation which permits comparative, controlled, and hopefully continuing cost-effectiveness evaluations. Such evaluation should take into account various sorts of costs: in scarce forms of matter-energy including land, buildings, and hardware; in forms of information, including books, documents, programmed instruction, and other learning materials which are in short supply; in short-range and long-range expenditures of funds available for either capital construction or operations; and in the time of students, teachers, faculty, administrators, and service personnel.* The costs of other related and essential activities must also be calculated, including research on the learning process, procedures for evaluating new technologies, and instruction of teachers and other personnel on how to use the technologies. The fact that several quite different sorts of costs are involved complicates any cost-effectiveness comparison of educational procedures.

Even more difficult is the problem of evaluating educational effectiveness. A number of criteria of educational effectiveness have been suggested by the Subcommittee on Efficiency and Innovation in Education of the Committee for Economic Development:[1]

> "Can the proposed technique be effectively employed in the cultivation of an open, inquiring mind? Or does it tend to produce conformity, dogmatism, and regimentation of thought?
>
> "Is it capable of communicating and facilitating an understanding of complex concepts? Or is its usefulness limited to the management and manipulation of simple ideas?
>
> "Is it capable of cultivating sensitive insight, originality, analytical facility, and creative intellectual skills?
>
> "Can it be employed to induce and deepen artistic and moral sensitivity and appreciation?
>
> "Do the benefits gained justify the costs incurred? Is the initial cost affordable?"

Evaluation of educational benefits or effectiveness is unsophisticated and superficial unless it takes into account considerations like those above. But educational psychology and the other

*See Miller, J. G. The Nature of Living Systems, Op. cit., 45; also Miller, J. G. and Rath, G. J. Op cit., 21-24.

behavioral sciences have supplied us with few effective, reliable, and valid instruments to measure such subtle aspects of human behavior, personality, and social interactions. We are, therefore, in danger of neglecting important variables in the educational systems we are evaluating because we do not have adequate ways to measure them.

Resistance to Change in Educational Methods

Any new instructional technology also should be evaluated in the light of a realistic appraisal of the sociological facts about man's resistance to change. Almost every important innovation in education, or any other field for that matter, has been resisted by people who are entirely satisfied with the current state of things or who have entrenched interest in maintaining the present state because they would lose certain benefits, comforts, or sources of support if changed occurred. When the horseless carriage appeared, the voices in the street cried "Get a horse." When the Wright brothers first flew their plane, the voices proclaimed, "If God had meant man to fly he would have provided him with wings." The modern version of the last complaint is, "If God had meant us to fly without propellors, he would have designed planes with jets."

Comparable attitudes toward new educational inventions have been demonstrated by teachers, professors, and administrators in recent years. Nevitt Sanford has asked:[2]

"How can colleges or universities—essentially conservative institutions—be induced to change? We consider faculty members, note that they have interest vested in things as they are, and suspect that they do not wish to change. We note, too, that the activities of individual teachers are interwoven with those of the institution as a whole and, hence, that even if a teacher wished to change nothing much would happen unless the institution itself was prepared to change. And as for the institution's changing, we are forced to recognize that our colleges and universities are embedded in the larger society, and that they rarely change according to their own plans but only in response to broad social forces.

"Gloom begins to envelop the class, and notes of cynicism are heard. Students who have been planning to go into higher education with the thought that they might help to improve it begin thinking instead of how they might adapt themselves to the existing systems. Some members of the class point out, hopefully, that innovations *do* occur in our institutions of higher learning, that today in fact innovation is very much in the air. But others are quick to respond that innovations in established institutions are usually quite superficial, that for important improvements in undergraduate education we have to look to new or rapidly growing institutions, and that even here it is too early to tell whether new models are going to be sustained."

A detailed analysis has been made by Evans of how professors in one university, "Metro University," reacted to an effort to introduce one particular form of innovative educational technology, instructional television.[3] The very real facts of life concerning such faculty resistance are demonstrated. Anyone who does not consider this social phenomenon in his attempts to employ and evaluate educational technology is neglecting a major factor. Strategies for introducing innovations must include plans for countering opposition to them.

The Central Social Issues About Education

Pressing social considerations demand that our concern for instructional technology be more than perfunctory. The rising costs per student of education and the increasing demand for it by all the people face the society with costs that are causing taxpayer revolts. The dollars required for the traditional modes of elementary, secondary, and higher education make it reasonable to ask whether there is a limit to what the society can afford to pay for it. The quality of much present instruction is devastatingly low by any standards. Many educational systems are not putting out educated students. Or if some education occurs, it is limited, parochial, superficial, and far worse than the best that can be produced. Inequalities of access to education throughout the population are directly related to social class, race, sex, and age differences. In one state—Ohio—out of 100 students who enter grade school, only 14 complete college and fewer than that go on to graduate education. Yet a much higher percentage of the population could profit from advanced education. Furthermore, continuing education in adulthood is much less extensive than it might be. Yet, despite its great costs and its many problems, education is almost universally recognized as a necessity, the primary fashioner of a society's future. Many of today's overwhelmingly difficult national and international problems, it appears, can only be met by more and better education. This fact gives it its high priority among all of man's activities.

The Strengths, Weaknesses, and Costs of Various Instructional Technologies

Table 1 lists the major media of educational technology available today, together with a brief description of the strengths, weaknesses, and costs of each.

The terms which describe the media in the table make clear what they are, with perhaps one or two exceptions. "On-line computer aids to learning and scholarship" refers to such technologies as Project MAC at MIT. An individual user of Project MAC can get access, by a remote terminal on-line to a large time-sharing computer to a wide range of programs that can help him solve mathematical, scientific, and engineering problems, routines for displaying the results of such problem solutions, tests of students' content knowledge in different fields, psychological and behavioral tests, and references or abstracts of articles relevant to many academic tasks. All of these materials are almost instantaneously available for the user to interact with in a "conversational" mode that requires little or no understanding of mathematics or computer programming. The final medium in Table 1, "Other standard audiovisual aids," actually represents several different items such as wall charts, physical models of crystals or parts of the body or machines or houses or mountains, microscope slide projectors, ordinary slide projectors, overhead projectors, moving picture projectors, and so forth. A number of other variants and combinations might be listed, but this table is sufficient to give a panoramic view of the alternative media available to educational systems today.

Many educators are scarcely aware that there are as many alternative forms of educational technology, or at least they have not had direct personal experience with them. One reason for this is that the number of media has risen dramatically because of technological developments in the last decade or two. When the educators were themselves in school or college they were not yet available.

These technologies are fundamentally products of the Second Industrial Revolution—the information-processing revolution—which burgeoned about 20 years ago, although it began in the last century with the telegraph, the telephone, and radio. The First Industrial Revolution flourished around 1800, being characterized by such major developments as the invention of the cotton gin, the steam boat, the steam engine, the electric motor, electric lights, the automobile, and the airplane. And it continues vigorously up until today with the developments in missiles, space travel, and atomic energy. Of course, the earliest such inventions occurred far back in history or prehistory, with the domestication of animals and the construction of dams and wheeled vehicles. This first revolution produced artifacts which operate as prostheses to living systems at various levels to carry out matterenergy subsystem processes. These machines can carry out these processes faster or more efficiently or with less cost in *human* energy (although there may be more over-all expenditure of energy) than human beings can themselves.

Now, with the appearance of the computer, with its rapid increase in capacity and sophistication, with the perfection of new communications technologies, and with the general increase in efficiency and speed and compactness of the machinery which processes information, the second revolution is well underway. We see in operation prostheses to aid living systems in the activities of the entire range of their information-processing sub-systems. These include input transducers—microphones, sonar, radar—which can receive signals that cannot be detected by any unaided living system; channels and nets which can transmit information at the speed of light and for great distances; computer aids to learn-ing, to memory, to management decision-making; and output transducers like slide pro-jectors, public address systems, radio, and television that can transmit messages rapidly, accurately, over greater distances, and to more people than can any living system.

Any educational system that is conscientiously intent upon raising the quality and lower-ing the costs of its functions would do well to undertake cost-benefit or cost-effectiveness analyses, studying the trade-offs among these alternative technologies, attempting to de-termine which will provide the greatest excellence under what circumstances, and which will be cheapest.

Any such analysis will reveal that it is not enough simply to add these technologies to procedures already in use. This will increase costs and will, in all probability, not permit optimal use of the new methods. Rather both structure and process of the system must usually be altered, often quite fundamentally. People must change their ways. Budgets must be adjusted.

A brief inspection of Table 1 indicates a number of things about the various instructional media available today. First of all, it is apparent that there are a good many of them, the number varying according to how they are classified, but one does not need to extend one's self to list seventeen, as in this table. The first two listed involve only living systems and do not require any artifacts as protheses. For this reason they are separated by a dou-ble line from the other media below them. These are the traditional media which have been used for generations, and the choice between them has classically faced educators—whether to use large class lectures or small discussion groups (including individual tutorial sessions).

If one looks across the columns on the chart, it is apparent that no one of the media has exactly the same characteristics as any of the others. This fact makes evaluation of their costs and benefits or effectiveness in different situations essential.

A large body of research on learning, in general psychology and educational psychology, gives us some idea of what constitutes an optimal learning environment. One cannot say that this knowledge is yet definitive, and it clearly differs from individual to individual since each one's genetic characteristics and past experiences result in differences in be-havior, personality, and temperament. Nevertheless, one can say with some confidence that aids to learning are most useful if the student can (a) carry them around, for then they are available whenever needed; (b) use them individually rather than having to coordinate his activities with class groups or other students; (c) use the aids anywhere, both at school or college and at home; (d) determine in terms of his own needs and sched-ule when to use the materials; (e) control the rate of flow of information inputs and out-puts in the learning process, and repeat inputs at will if they are not understood; (f) inter-act actively with the aids, since active learning is generally recognized as being better than passive; (g) be able to have outputs from him influence the next input coming to him. This "branching" arrangement assures that, if he knows one fact in the progression of the learning process, he is not given special training on it but goes on to the next one and so forth until he comes to a fact which he does not know or a problem which he cannot solve properly, after which he is given special training on that, his time being used for practice only on those facts or problems which he does not understand; (h) receive inputs in more than one sensory modality, since multiple sensory modalities represent multiple channels of input which reinforce each other. Learning aids are more useful if they can be

INSTRUCTIONAL MEDIUM	Can user carry it around?	Can user use it individually at school or college?	Can user use it individually at home?	Can user determine when it is to be used?
1. Class lecture	No	No	No	No
2. Small discussion group	No	No	No	No
3. Books and journals	Yes	Yes	Yes	Yes, unless another user has it
4. Printed programmed instruction	Yes	Yes	Yes	Yes
5. Computerized programmed instruction	No	Yes	Rarely	Yet, unless number of terminals is limited
6. On-line computer aids to learning & scholarship	No	Yes	Rarely	Yes, unless number of terminals is limited
7. Closed circuit lectures on public address system	No	No	No	No
8. Educational radio	No	Yes	Yes	No
9. Dial-access audio tape recordings	No	Yes	Rarely	Yes
10. Broadcast live instructional TV	No	Yes	Sometimes	No
11. Closed circuit live instructional TV	No	Yes	No	No
12. Broadcast tape-recorded instructional TV	No	Yes	Sometimes	No
13. Closed circuit tape recorded instructional TV	No	Yes	No	No
14. Dial-access instructional TV	No	Yes	No	Yes, unless number of terminals is limited
15. Facsimile transmission of documents by electronic circuits	Terminals can be portable & attached to any telephone	Yes	Possibly	Yes, during hrs. sender is able to transmit to user
16. Automated storage & retrieval of written & graphic materials	No	Yes	Rarely	Yes
17. Other standard audiovisual aids	Usually	Yes	Often	Yes

Table 1. Characteristics and Costs of Various Instructional Media

Can user control rate of information flow & repeat if not understood?	Can user interact actively with input?	Is individualized "branching" possible?	Senses used	Can signals be sent on electronic network?	Costs (in dollars per user hour)
Rarely	No	No	Vision & Audition	No	0.15-3
Sometimes	Yes	Rarely	Vision & Audition	No	0.50-15
Yes	No	No	Vision	No	0.05-10
Yes	No	Yes	Vision	No	0.05-10
Yes	Yes	Yes	Vision & Audition	Yes	2-25
Yes	Yes	Yes	Vision	Yes	5-100
No	No	No	Audition	Yes	0.02-2
No	No	No	Audition	Yes	0.01-1
In some systems	Rarely	No	Audition	Yes	0.01-2
No	No*	No	Vision & Audition	Yes	0.02-10
No	No*	No	Vision & Audition	Yes	0.03-3
No*	No*	No	Vision & Audition	Yes	0.01-5
No*	No*	No	Vision & Audition	Yes	0.03-2
Sometimes	Rarely	No	Vision & Audition	Yes	0.50-5
No	No	No	Vision	Yes	2-15
Yes	Sometimes	Yes	Vision	Yes	2-100
Yes	Sometimes	Rarely	Vision & Audition	No	0.05-8

Table 1. (continued)

*See pg. 1015

transmitted over electronic networks so that they can reach the student at any place he happens to be, coming rapidly and accurately from any other geographical location. It is also desirable for their costs to be minimal in dollars per user hour, as well as in the time they consume of the student or instructor involved.

None of the media listed in Table 1 is optimal in all these ways. Some are better than others, and some are more appropriate than others for certain situations or when certain amounts of funds are available to the educational system. These differences among the media make careful analysis of the trade-offs among them mandatory.

For instance, the first column shows that only a few of the media at present are truly portable. The user can carry around with him only books, journals, printed programmed instruction, a number of the standard audiovisual aids such as wall charts, slide and moving picture projectors, and—under certain circumstances, near telephone outlets only—terminals for facsimile transmission of documents. None of the other media, in their present form, are truly portable so far as the average student is concerned. Technical advances may make some of them much more portable in the near future.

The second column in Table 1 shows that students working alone at school or college can profit from most of the media, the exceptions being the class lecture, the small discussion group, and closed circuit lectures on public address systems. Students can use few of the media at home except books and journals, printed programmed instruction, educational radio, and some others under certain circumstances. Technical improvements in a number of these could render them readily available for home study.

A major constraint upon several of the media, as the fourth column indicates, is that the student must fit his schedule and convenience to that of a group, which limits the most effective use of his time. This is true of class lectures; small discussion groups; closed circuit lectures on public address systems; educational radio; and broadcast or closed circuit, line or tape-recorded instructional television. Indeed, it is probable that any form of radio or television which requires large numbers of students to use the medium simultaneously regiments them undesirably. This may be a major reason why instructional radio and television have not been more effective. The custom of herding students into classes at certain hours is so ingrained in the American educational system that it is hard to break. Many teachers forget or actually do not believe that the optimal learning situation for most students is probably one in which they set their own schedules and study independently.

If the individual student can control the rate of information flows during learning, he is not likely to fall behind in understanding the content or be bored waiting for new concepts to come to him. Many of the media, as the fifth column of Table 1 shows, give the student this sort of control, but some do not. Students rarely exert any influence on the rate of progress of class lectures, which is one of the primary reasons why lectures are far from perfect learning situations. Sometimes students can exert such influence in small discussion groups. If the group is very large, however, some of the students are likely to be too passive or too shy to request a change when the rate of information flow is not optimal for them. Tradition dictates that the experienced, senior person—the teacher—determines information flow rates. Closed circuit lectures on public address systems, educational radio, television broadcasts, and closed circuit tape-recorded instructional television all have these shortcomings as well. So does facsimile transmission of documents by electronic circuits.

Most of the media do not permit the user to interact actively with the input. This is one of the great advantages of the small discussion group and a major point in favor of computerized programmed instruction and of on-line computer aids to learning and scholarship. Under some circumstances, dial-access audio tape recordings make such interaction possible. For instance, a language laboratory tape may present a student with a word or sentence in a foreign language and give him an opportunity to repeat the word or sentence, which is then tape-recorded and later listened to by a teacher who corrects his pronunciation. Similar procedures are possible with dial-access instructional television. Under some circumstances a student or professor can interact with automated data banks for information storage and with some of the standard audiovisual aids. Table 1 shows a number of asterisks in the columns concerned with user control of rate of information flow and user interaction with information input. These asterisks refer to recent technological developments which may in the future be applied to education. A number of these novel forms of television and related technologies which may be of educational value have been described by Licklider, including specialized transmissions to individual users which he calls "narrow casting" and techniques which permit the receiver to respond actively to television transmissions as well as employ television channels to use a variety of other instructional media.[4]

A major potential of programmed instruction and on-line use of computers is individualized instruction. With them a student does not need to rehearse a second time material he already knows. Instead he uses the time for further practice on what he does not know. This can enable the student to save time, or at least allocate it better, in the learning process. Lectures and broadcasts do not usually have such a potential, although on occasion very small discussion groups or individual tutorial sessions do. The programming technique whereby each student is given practice only on what he does not know is called "branching." Such branching is less personalized, flexible and sophisticated in the best printed programmed instruction than in the best computerized programmed instruction and on-line computer aids to learning and scholarship. Various automated storage and retrieval technologies also permit a close tailoring of the process to the needs of the individual user.

As the eighth column of Table 1 indicates, the fact-to-face human situation in classes and small discussion groups has the great advantage of using both vision and audition, as well as some of the other sensory modalities on occasion. Books, journals, printed programmed instruction, on-line computer aids to learning and scholarship, closed circuit lectures on public address systems, educational radio, dial-access audio tape-recordings, facsimile transmission of documents by electronic circuits, automated storage and retrieval of written and graphic materials, and some standard audiovisual aids do not use both sensory modalities. Other standard audiovisual aids do, such as sound moving pictures. So do all the different forms of television. This is one reason why television is probably superior in conveying a sense of intimate and direct human relationships to books, computer terminals, radio, and other solely auditory presentations.

If educational materials can be transmitted over electronic channels and networks, they can, in principle, be initiated at any geographical point and be used at any other point. This facilitates diffusion of knowledge and makes possible democracy of access to educational information. The face-to-face relationships of class lectures and small discussion groups do not have this potential, nor do books, journals, printed programmed instruction, or the standard audiovisual aids. As the next-to-last column of Table 1 shows, all the other media do, since they are electronic. In the last few years educators have, thus, been presented with a challenge: How can the new network media be most profitably and creatively used in future educational activities?

Now we come to the question of costs. The last column of Table 1 lists only dollar costs in various sorts of matter-energy and information, although, of course, costs in student, teacher, administrative, and other staff time are also important. The dollar estimates include both operating funds and an appropriate portion of capital construction funds. For all of the media there is a wide range in costs, because it is extraordinarily difficult to make even rough cost estimates with our present knowledge of the media. This is an important area for future research and investigation. Many variables influence the dollar cost per user hour of these different media. Among these are: the number of students using the medium at a given location and at a given time; the ratio between the number of students and the number of instructors; the amount of hardware employed in the particular system under study; the number of hours the hardware is used on the average by each student; the original costs of the hardware (which over the years recently have been rapidly decreasing); whether the hardware is bought in large quantities; and whether the software needs to be written for the local system or has already been prepared for another system.

All the costs listed in the last column of Table 1, because of the fluctuation of these many factors, have a range such that the highest cost is one to four magnitudes larger than the lowest. A few general observations can be made: (a) Large class lectures are less expensive than small discussion groups. (b) Even though none of the electronic media have all the advantages of direct human contact, some of them appear to be, at least potentially, as cheap or cheaper than traditional methods of teaching by direct human contact. (c) Books, journals, and other printed materials are, in general, cheaper than most of the electronic technologies, though this is not necessarily true. (d) Electronic technologies involving both vision and audition are somewhat more expensive than those that involve audition alone. (e) Those media which involve on-line access to computers are, in general, significantly more expensive than the other media, at least at their present stage of development.

The Effectiveness and Costs
of Instructional Television

Though in most educational systems the use of instructional television is desultory and its potential is not realized, there are some exceptions. Among these are Chicago's Television College, broadcasting entire junior college course sequences, a closed circuit television system which centers in Hagerstown, Maryland, and the extensive televised on-campus courses provided by Pennsylvania State University at State College, Pennsylvania. As Murphy and Gross note, good instructional television can create a powerful learning environment:[5]

"If TV has one quality that is peculiar to the medium, it is its *immediacy*—its ability to transmit experience instantaneously. 'Creative TV,' says Patricia Swenson, supervisor of radio-TV for the schools of Portland, Oregon, 'is vivid, human, informal, warm, compelling. There can be, strange as it may seem, an astonishingly intimate relationship between TV teacher and child.' The Portland schools have been proceeding slowly in their use of television, aiming at quality rather than quantity, but the unpretentious series Dr. Swenson produced, *Let's Explore Science,* has gained disciples all around the country. Throughout the series, the writer-tele-teacher, Peter Taylor, uses the camera to sweep youngsters along as colleagues in his inquiries into such things as the pendulum, simple balances, rolling balls, and household liquids. The programs evoke rather than overwhelm the child's curiosity about the everyday world.

"Another good example of ITV's breaking out of the old molds is the series of brief, weekly programs called *Roundabout,* produced by the Washington, D.C., ETV station, WETA. Inspired by the Head Start idea, and produced by Dr. Rose Mukerji of Brooklyn College, these programs—probably the first of their kind—are designed, with imagination and skill, to appeal to preschoolers living in urban slums. Now being broadcast for the second time in the Washington area, the taped series has been made available for national distribution and is currently being shown in New York City. Most of the fifty-two programs, which are set in familiar neighborhood backgrounds, make use of Negro children and a young Negro male who is neither teacher nor actor but rather an older brother. They deal with a splendid variety of simple but eye-opening topics; barbers and bus drivers, art (the use of clay and paint), hinges, jobs, families, the ways of turtles. The most controversial program, called *Living or Dead?* inspects a dead parakeet, compares a live goldfish with a dead one, and relates the concept of life and death to human beings, in a very matter-of-fact way.

"Less ambitious, but also direct and lively, is a news program that is put on every morning by children in a Larchmont, New York, elementary school, and that goes by closed circuit to every classroom. Children from the fourth, fifth, and sixth grades—with four teachers as advisors—write, edit, cast, and produce the show, which includes news, weather, editorials.

"Closely allied with immediacy is intimacy—the fact that TV can bring one face to face with the action in a peculiarly close relationship. For example, the televised scientific demonstration makes it possible for a great many students to see with clarity on the screen what only a handful could see with their own eyes. As an experienced surgeon performs an intricate operation in an amphitheater before hundreds of students, each of them has an over-the-shoulder view, thanks to television. An extension of this idea is postgraduate education by TV. UCLA's series for doctors, for instance, is broadcast weekly forty weeks out of the year from Los Angeles's new ETV station, KCET (scrambled, to spare the squeamish layman), and goes to eighty-one hospitals and an estimated audience of 3,000 to 4,000 doctors. An incidental footnote which raises more questions than it answers about the medium's peculiarities: KCET finds that doctors experience the same immediacy with taped programs as with those that are live. Films, no; tapes, yes."

What is the validity of television as an instructional tool? The answer is that it works, as Chu and Schramm said in 1967 after a careful analysis of the evidence:[6]

"We have recently reviewed, up to 1966, 207 published studies in which television teaching has been compared with conventional teaching. Of the 421 separate comparisons made in these studies, 308 showed no significant differences, 63 showed television instruction to be superior, and 50 found conventional instruction better.

"Therefore, all these summaries show that in the great majority of comparative studies, there is no significant difference between learning from television and learning from conventional teaching; and that where there is a significant difference, it is a bit more likely to be in favor of television than of conventional instruction."

A study on the costs of some of the new educational technologies carried out for the Committee for Economic Development by Booz, Allen, and Hamilton, Inc. recognized that there are many cost variables in costs in the production of instructional materials and their dissemination. They recognized also that widespread use of the media would result in reorganization of the processes going on in the systems that used them, which hopefully would upgrade the quality of the instruction.

Making certain assumptions about the nature of an educational system that uses television, they calculated that the hardware costs for a 24-classroom school would be about $30,000 and that the costs for supplying a school system of 100,000 with one hour of television programming a day for each student would range from $800,000 to $4,600,000 a year. This would be between 4 and 24 cents per user hour. At this rate the annual cost for television in our national elementary and secondary school population would range from $265 million to $1.5 billion. There would be certain savings in scale if program materials were prepared jointly and if there were control administration of a massive national program of instructional television. Public school expenditures for the United States in the 1967-68 school year were estimated at $30 billion, including operating expenses and capital expenditures. Therefore, the study concluded that a television bill ranging up to $1.5 billion could be accommodated, and it would certainly bring about some offsetting savings.

The Effectiveness and Costs
of Computer-Aided Instruction

In a survey questionnaire sent to 2503 superintendents of school systems in 1968, which elicited 746 replies, the respondents rated promising educational innovations in the following order: first, individualized instruction; second, vocational and technical training; third, in-service training; and fourth, instructional television. Computer-assisted instruction was much less popular, being second or third from the end. There is no question that the use of instructional television is better understood and more appreciated by education today than is computer-aided instruction.

Nevertheless, computer-aided instruction has real strengths, as pointed out by Mary Gardiner Jones, a commissioner of the Federal Trade Commission:[7]

> "The introduction into our educational system of the computer and of the wide variety of associated electronic and mechanical teaching devices, together with entirely new programmed instructional material, presents us for the first time with unique opportunities to deal effectively with many of our educational problems. Use of programmed instructional materials will enable schools to offer a type of individualized instruction geared to the backgrounds and experience of each student. The student can proceed at his own pace and through the branching ability of the computer, the teaching materials can be tailored to the particular difficulty being encountered by individual students. To a certain extent, the student's manipulation of his own computer console can compel him to participate more directly in the educational process and presumably will not enable him to day-dream undetected through entire classes. [Also, as he learns he can create a complete computer record of how far and how fast he went in the process. This record can be substituted for examinations.]

> "At the same time, computers and other mechanical teaching devices can consistently exercise a degree of patience, encouragement and affirmative support for the struggling learners which no teacher has either the time or the saintliness to display at every moment of the day and on every day of the week. [As long as universities have 20-to-1 ratios of full-time-equivalent students to faculty, no faculty member will ever be able to give as much undivided attention to the 20 full-time equivalent students for whom he is responsible as a computer potentially can.]

> "With respect to the sheer acquisition of information and the basic technique of learning, these devices can take over much of the routine drill aspects of teaching and thus free the teacher for those aspects of education which he or she is uniquely capable of doing, namely, to question, to imagine, to invent, to appreciate, to act as a model, a guide, a counselor and fellow-searcher after truth, after values and after meaning and understanding."

Writing on the basis of several years' experience in computer-assisted instruction, Atkinson has reported results from the first year of an experiment using computerized programmed instruction to teach reading to first grade students.[8] He and his associates compared an experimental group with a matched control group. Each group was made up of about 50 first grade students from "culturally disadvantaged" homes, with I.Q.'s averaging 89. The experimental group received their instruction by computer-aided instruction and the control group by traditional classroom teaching. The fastest student taking computer-aided instruction completed over 4,000 more "central" problems during his whole course of study than the slowest student. This indicates how individualized computer-aided instruction can be. Both groups were tested with conventional instruments before the project began and again near the end of the school year. The two groups were not significantly different at the beginning of the year, but at the end the group receiving computer-aided instruction was significantly better on all of the following posttests: California Achievement Test, Vocabulary Subtest and Total Score; Hartley Reading Test, Form Class Subtest, Vocabulary Subtest, Phonetic Discrimination Subtest, Nonsense Word Pronunciation test, Word Pronunciation Test, Nonsense Word Recognition Test, and Word Recognition Test. There was no significant difference between the two groups on the California Achievement Test Comprehension Subtest. These findings as a whole constitute an impressive indication of the potential effectiveness of computer-aided instruction.

There is no clear agreement about the present or probable future costs of computerized programmed instruction.

Atkinson and his colleague, Suppes, at Stanford University have developed computerized materials for learning language skills for grades 4, 5, and 6. They calculate that in a school with 100 terminals which maintained an active program for at least two years, the total cost of using these materials would be about $1.80 per user hour, including all expenses such as terminal rental and royalties. To develop 200 40-minute instructional units cost them about $60,000, or $300 a unit.[9]

Preparation of such instructional units, according to Bacon at the San Jose laboratories of IBM, costs between $500 and $3,000 per student hour, varying greatly with the media, amount of branching, and types of materials.[10] The following uses of computer-aided instruction he believes are within practical cost ranges today: (a) For the early grades, simple drills coupled with diagnostic tests showing weaknesses, in such fields as arithmetic and reading. (b) Either before college or earlier, remedial mathematics, grammar, and other subjects. (c) In advanced professional fields, medical diagnosis, business games, computer-aided design, technical simulation, simulation of organizations, and logistic problems.

A study by Kopstein and Seidel compared the costs of traditional classroom instruction with computer-aided instruction in public elementary and secondary schools, higher education, and military technical training.[11] They calculated that in elementary and secondary education, costs of traditional instruction will average about 38 cents per student hour in 1971 and rise to 42 cents by 1974-75. For higher education the cost is higher, rising from between 37 and 46 cents per student hour in 1949-50 to between 82 cents and $1.02 per student hour in 1963-64, the last date for reliable data. In military and technical training they believe that $1.80 may be about the average cost per student hour. Making a certain number of assumptions, they calculated that the total costs of computer-aided instruction at present amount to $3.73 per student hour and concluded that unless this medium can be shown to be at least ten times more effective than traditionally administered instruction, a replacement does not now seem to be justified. They believe, however, that with further developments which seem likely to occur in the field of computer-assisted instruction, a forecast of costs of 11 cents per student hour for computer-assisted instruction seemed probable in a few years.

According to Zinn, costs for computer-aided instruction are reported by various workers as ranging between $2 and $15 per user hour, although one project claims it has achieved a cost of only 27 cents per user hour at consoles which include a keyboard, graphic display, and image projector.[12]

The Booz, Allen, and Hamilton group which studied instructional television concluded that the costs of computer-assisted instruction are relatively much higher. They calculated that for a 100,000 student school system the annual rental cost for present hardware needed for one student hour a day of drill-and-practice computer-aided instruction would be $20 million; $6 million would be required for other services; and about $765,000 would be consumed annually for software, making a total of about $27 million for a 100,000 student system, or about $1.35 per user hour. If the more complex tutorial mode of operating computer-aided instruction were employed, they calculated that one hour of software would cost about $30,000 to produce. (This cost is much higher than the cost of some such software now being produced.) For one hour of such instruction daily in a school system of 100,000, the annual software cost would, therefore, be about $5 million, hardware rental about $50 million, and other services about $17 million, for a total of about $72 million, or about $3.70 per user hour. It seemed to this group that at an annual cost in this range the large-scale use of computer-assisted instruction is at present too expensive when possible benefits are considered, but they believed that probably such costs will come down in the not-too-distant future and recommended research to decrease them.

Examples of Introduction of New Technologies into Various Levels of Educational Systems

When instructional technologies are introduced into educational systems, one or more prostheses are made available to aid the human beings in the system. This may or may not relieve them of processes they are carrying out or reorganize those processes. It is desirable insofar as possible to introduce these technologies into the system only after cost-effectiveness analyses are made and reviewed. Sometimes these can be quite precise and quantitative, particularly if management information systems exist in the educational system which provide data relevant to these decisions. Under other circumstances, only a rough calculation of costs and benefits or effectiveness is possible, either because the relevant data are not available or because so many variables are involved that it is not feasible to measure them or to collect information about them. Below is a series of fictional examples of how such an approach might be taken to decisions on whether to use new instructional media in educational systems at various levels:

1. A School

An elementary school which has a large number of underprivileged children concludes that it may be desirable to use carrels in its first grade classrooms. Its purposes in using such carrels include: (a) To socialize children to the learning environment of the school by giving them periods when they are isolated from most extraneous information inputs and can carry out independent learning experiences. (b) To prepare the children for independent study in automated carrels which the school expects to introduce within two years at grades 3 and above.

Carrels are booths which constitute an interface between the student and some artifact from which he can receive information inputs. They can be classified into two general types: general space carrels, an enclosure with a door by which the student may isolate himself from the environment for periods of self-initiated study; and multimedium carrels, which include in the booth a typewriter on-line to a computer terminal, a source of auditory inputs, a screen capable of showing letters or figures, graphic material, or television pictures, and a light pencil with which the student can respond to inputs by pointing to any part of the screen, which signals the computer where he is pointing.

Inside the general space carrel the student could use a book, a television set, a projector showing slides or movies on a little screen, or a record player with headset. In terms of effectiveness in learning how to carry out tasks in multimedium carrels, such a carrel would probably be best for the first grade, even though the student could not yet type, although they might push a few keys to send a limited repertoire of signals to the computer. They easily could look at the screen, use the light pencil, and listen to the auditory inputs. On the other hand, both the general space carrel and the multimedium carrel would accustom the student to a period of independent activity each day separated from the other students and inputs from them. In this latter learning experience they would probably be equally effective, and in the first grade this type of effectiveness would probably be more important than the other. The difference in cost of the two sorts of carrels is great. In calculating the costs of the carrels, the following considerations must be included: The purchase cost of each carrel and the rate at which it must be depreciated. The number of carrels for each classroom of 30 students; this might be either five carrels (each student spending one hour out of the six hours in the school day in a carrel) or ten carrels (which would permit each student to spend two hours a day.) Maintenance costs of the carrels. Costs of supplies and equipment used in the carrels. Maintenance of equipment used in the carrels. Payment for extra time of teacher aides for using the carrels and supervising students in them. Even with extra equipment in the general space carrel, the average cost per student hour in each carrel if there are five carrels per room would be 25 cents in the general space carrel but at least $1.25 per hour in the multi-medium carrel. In a school that has 300 first grade students the difference in cost would be $7,500 a year for the general space carrels versus $37,500 a year for the multimedium carrels. The cost of the latter would be far too great for the benefits obtained, so the former must almost certainly be chosen. This is particularly true since adding these carrels would relieve no teacher time. It would simply improve the quality of education of the underprivileged children who had not been used to solitary activity before coming to school. By the time the pupils got to third grade, the amount of individualized instruction that could be obtained from a multi-medium carrel and the saving in teacher time might well be enough to justify the relatively high expenditure for such carrels.

2. A School System

This particular school system has already installed a closed circuit television system connecting all of its high schools. It now is trying to decide whether or not to buy video tape-recording equipment. The purposes and benefits which it expects such equipment to achieve are as follows: (a) To be able to develop special instructional programs that can be re-used at various times of the day or week for different sections of the same class as well as in subsequent years. (b) To be able to use in the training of teachers video recordings of student-teachers operating in classes and of experienced teachers operating in classes. (c) To be able to produce for commercial television special public service programs about the school system. (d) To increase the student-teacher ratio in some courses by having classes given by video tape lectures rather than by live teachers.

Among the alternative procedures to be considered are live teaching in traditional classrooms and moving pictures.

The costs of this proposed innovation include the money expended to buy the new equipment; teacher time used in learning to use the new medium and in taping materials; as well as lowered morale of those in the teaching staff who oppose the new procedure.

An analysis of cost-effectiveness ratios relevant to the decision to introduce the tape recorder is shown in Table 2.*

For the video tape-recording system, we assume that the probability (P_i) of it being accepted is about 50-50 (.5). This is determined by the school system management that makes the decisions whether to purchase the equipment, usually based primarily on attitudes of the teachers. Compared to movies or live teaching, its utility (U_i) may be rated relatively high (10) because of its convenience to the teachers. Its cost will be $10,000 and so C_i is 10,000. This is the cost-effectiveness measure for the teacher and we will add to it a cost-

*This presentation is based on the mathematical approach to the setting of priorities outlined in the following paper: Miller, J. G. & Rath, G. J. Planning-Programming-Budgeting and Cost-Effectiveness Analysis in Educational Systems. March, 1969.

effectiveness measure to the students based on the same formula, as follows: To the students it is not especially helpful and there is no great joy in seeing black and white television (2). The price is $4,000 for the year, which is the cost of the machine plus some technician time to operate it. It is an identical cost for teachers and students because it is the same equipment for both of them. The live performance on the television has a probability of being effective which is much higher (.9). The cost of $10,000 is the same in both cases, and high, because the medium requires having one or more live persons available. It is highly acceptable to teachers because they do less work than if they prepare television tapes (50). The students like to participate in a live professional teaching performance, so their rating is 10.

FACULTY $\qquad$ STUDENTS

$$E = \sum \frac{P_i \times U_i}{C_i} \qquad E_i = \frac{P_{fac,i} \times U_{fac,i}}{C_i} + \frac{P_{stu+i} \times U_{stu+i}}{C_i}$$

$$E_{vtr} = \frac{.5 \times 10}{4,000} + \frac{.5 \times 2}{4,000} = 15:10,000$$

$$E_{live} = \frac{.9 \times 50}{10,000} + \frac{.9 \times 10}{10,000} = 13.5:10,000$$

$$E_{film} = \frac{.1 \times 5}{2,000} + \frac{.1 \times 20}{2,000} = 12.5:10,000$$

E_{vtr} = effectiveness of video tape recorder

E_{live} = effectiveness of live teaching in traditional classrooms

E_{film} = effectiveness of moving pictures

Table 2.
Cost-Effectiveness Evaluation About Use of Tape Recorder

The moving picture has the lowest probability of success (.1) because it is difficult to find films that will do the job. On the other hand, films, when they are available, are cheap ($2,000). For the teachers the film has a low utility because they have to choose the film, load the projector, and show the picture. The students prefer films over black and white television because they like the color and the high quality of production; there is generally much better entertainment value in films than in homemade television broadcasts (20). Finally, looking at the cost-effectiveness ratios the decision is to invest in the videotape recorder.

Obviously the alternatives are close enough that other factors might decide. If a grant were offered to create a film library, so that the operating budget did not need to support it, that would swing the decision to moving pictures. On the other hand, if some of the best teachers enjoyed live teaching so much that they would leave if taped television or moving pictures were used, the wisest decision might be to raise the teachers' salaries and forget the video tape recorder.*

3. A College

At a state supported urban college a new president, much more aware of the implications

*The last two sections were adapted from materials provided by G. J. Rath, Professor of Industrial Engineering and Management Sciences, The Technological Institute, Northwestern University.

for higher education of the urban crisis than his predecessor had been, determined to increase the percentage of the students living in urban central city slum areas from 2 to 20 percent over a three year period. Then the admissions staff began to interview the high school graduates from such areas. They found that their preparatory education was seriously lacking, so that they needed individualized remedial education. There was no subsidy available for such remedial education, however, so the college was under stringent financial necessity to carry out this individualized training as inexpensively as possible. They discovered that computer-aided remedial instruction programs in mathematical skills and language utilization were available without cost, so they made an effort to determine whether computer-aided instruction was the most feasible way to give this remedial education. Alternative plans were to hire individual tutors, to lighten the ordinary teaching load of volunteer faculty members so that they can tutor, or to pay junior and senior students to give this remedial education to incoming freshmen.

The college's purposes in instituting this new program were as follows: (a) To increase the probability that urban slum students in need of remedial education, would be able to complete their freshman year and continue into the sophomore year and work toward a bachelor's degree. (b) To improve the basic mathematical and linguistic skills of these students. (c) To raise the freshmen grades of these students.

Once it was determined that the computer-aided instruction programs of remedial education could be obtained free of charge from another university, the costs were calculated of giving each student in need of remedial training three hours a day of instruction in computer-aided instruction. This involved obtaining an IBM 1500 Computer with 30 terminals. The cost with this configuration for 30 students was $22 an hour. On the other hand, if the configuration was enlarged to 120 terminals and used in four 3-hour shifts each day, the cost was reduced to $8.82 per student hour. Furthermore, pretests indicated that the learning rate of students with this form of individualized instruction was about 20 percent faster than with human tutors. At the end of the first year it was found that the course grades of students taught with computer-aided instruction were significantly better than those taught by traditional tutoring methods.

With student tutors paid at the rate of $1,000 a year, each of whom tutored three students ten hours a week, the cost was $1.80 a student hour, including administrative costs. With volunteer faculty who received reduced loads (the loads in half of the departments having to be made up by teaching assistants that were hired especially for the purpose), the costs were $2.88 per student hour. It was unclear from any evidence whether the students learned better with the student tutors or with the faculty tutors.

The administration finally made the decision that the advantages of computer-aided instruction were great enough to justify its extra cost even though it represented a severe drain on the total college budget. This decision was made after it was learned that 300 students in need of remedial training would be in the freshman class in the next year. Unless this number could have been recruited, the computer-assisted instruction costs would have been exorbitant. One loss to the college was that there was not so much employment for junior and senior students who needed jobs as tutors. On the other hand, an advantage to the college was that the faculty were not taken away from their regular teaching activities, which represented its major strength.

4. A University

A private university over a period of 15 years had grown from 4,000 to 15,000 students. Most of the buildings used by the College of Arts and Sciences had been designed before this period of rapid growth. They had been built an average of 44 years before. A few large classrooms in the buildings could accommodate a maximum of 80 students but most of them could accommodate no more than 40 students. Small classes had been universal at the university until ten years before. It now became clear to the administration that if tuition were to be kept low enough that most of their applicants could afford it, they would need to raise the student-faculty ratio and have larger classes. Two alternatives were considered: (a) To build a new building including two classrooms capable of holding up to 500 students each, at a total cost of $2,500,000, and (b) To install closed circuit television in all the buildings of the College of Arts and Sciences.

The goals which the college's president wished to accomplish were: (a) To increase the student-faculty ratio from 20 to 1 to 28 to 1, in order to keep tuitions within range. (b) To maintain or improve the quality of instruction as reflected by students' performance on various tests. (c) To minimize expenditures for capital construction and equipment.

The cost of the new building had been set at $2,500,000. Of this $1 million was available in cash and the rest could be obtained from long-term loans. The building could be depreciated over at least 50 years. Maintenance costs for the building would be $9,000 a year. With interest charges included, the cost per year for the building would be $88,000.

A closed circuit television system for all the buildings in the College of Arts and Sciences would have the following costs: Laying of television cables between all the buildings, $83,000; interconnecting all rooms with television cables and installing black-and-white television monitors in each room, $680,000; television studio, tape banks, and tape recorders, $128,000. Total $891,000. This cost could reasonably be depreciated over at least a 20-year period, so the cost per year would be $45,000.

Research on live as compared to televised instruction suggests that students like televised instruction less but that it is not less effective. Use of televised instruction would make possible an average student-faculty ratio of 35 to 1, so that if the college were to achieve an overall 28 to 1 ratio, one quarter of the faculty time could be devoted to small group discussions and individual conferences as a result of savings by using closed circuit television. This would also be true if large classrooms were used.

For a time it appeared that the nature of gifts and grants available meant that the administration could obtain capital funds but not equipment funds. Finally an agreement was reached, however, whereby the money could be used for either purpose. The management decision was then made to install the closed circuit television. At the same time that this decision was made, the hiring rate of all departments in the college was slowed down over a four-year period so that gradually over that time the college would increase from its former 20-to-1 to the desired 28-to-1 student-faculty ratio. Costs were cut significantly and there was no clear indication that the effectiveness of education suffered. It might even have been improved. At the very least, tuition rates were kept down in an inflationary period.

5. A State System of Higher Education

Over the decade between 1955 and 1965 the number of state-supported colleges and universities in one state had increased from 5 to 13, and the number of students had more than doubled. The state budget for higher education had gone up from $125,000,000 a year to $280,000,000 a year. The percentage of the total statewide higher education budget devoted to libraries had crept up from 3 percent in 1955 to 5½ percent, and in three of the new universities it was up to 7 percent. Despite this four of the campuses in the state had libraries of less than 250,000 books and only one had a collection of more than 1,500,000 volumes. There was a very unequal distribution of books among the various campuses of the state. This inequity would continue for many years, if it could ever be corrected, even though the percentage of funds going to libraries rose to an unacceptable level.

Consideration was given to continuing previous policies, gradually increasing the percentage of the statewide higher education budget devoted to libraries up to 8 percent. But this policy would mean that for the next decade 8 of the 13 campuses in the state were predestined to have collections inadequate for extensive graduate work. An alternative was to establish a single statewide computerized union catalog and a network for facsimile transmission of documents from one campus to another.

The purposes of the state Board of Regents were as follows: (a) To equalize access to scholarly information on all campuses of the state. (b) To make available to every campus a library of the highest quality capable of supporting both undergraduate and graduate education. (c) To spend no more than 6 percent of the total higher education budget in any one year for libraries and library services.

It was expected that the statewide budget for higher education would increase an average $20,000,000 a year for the next 10 years so that this 6 percent of the budget that was spent for libraries, over the next ten years the library services budget for the state system would average $22,800,000 a year.

This amount of money would purchase and catalog 2,280,000 books a year by traditional methods at an average cost of $10 a book. These purchases divided around the 13 campuses would mean that at the end of a decade the average campus would still have only slightly more than 500,000 books and journals.

An alternate plan was to store certain classes of books in each library based on a joint acquisition policy. Each campus would have a core collection of 100,000 volumes of standard works and an additional 50,000 volumes of microfilmed journals and books. Calculations indicated that such a core collection would meet 83 percent of the demand on the typical campus. In addition each campus would keep the other books and journals it already had but transmit facsimiles of them statewide on demand. It was calculated that, with these procedures, on the average 7 percent of the demand would not be met locally. Since 7 percent of the demand represented an average of 183,000 volumes a year, efforts were made to calculate how much it would cost to transmit copies of these documents over a facsimile network. Two percent could be saved because 3 of the 13 universities were close enough to each other so that a courier could be used to carry books or journals from one to another. Including administrative costs for this system it was found the average transmission costs for a book would be $13, including an average royalty of $1 per book paid by agreement to the publisher. This included long-line rental charges and local terminal charges of $12,000 a year per campus. On the average a volume could be available by long distance xerography in an hour and a half from any place in the state. The total of 175,340 (183,000—2 percent of 183,000 or 7,660) volumes requested times $13 per book would cost $2,279,420 annually to transmit. This plus the cost of the local collections added up to $21,400,220 annually. This total program meant that statewide availability to a library totalling nearly 4,000,000 volumes could be provided within 10 years, and although browsing of these volumes was not immediately possible, access to every volume could be obtained within an hour and a half anywhere in the state, except those where delivery was by courier, which took a maximum of four hours. The state thus could have a very large and diversified collection, since no more than one copy of any volume needed to be purchased. When there was a demand for a second copy a facsimile could be made. This alternative library plan was accepted by the state since it was clearly more efficient than the first and no more expensive.

The fact that browsing was not at first possible could spur scientists in the state, in cooperation with others throughout the world, to carry out research on basic linguistics so that ultimately digital storage on computer memories of the complete text of books might be possible, making feasible computerized searching of the contents of the texts over networks.

6. A National Educational System

Promising alternatives to our country's traditional methods of education should be reviewed at the national level. If there is no democracy of access to information in any state, it is obvious that this is even more true nationwide. If it is desirable to share library resources by a network throughout a state, it is obviously even more desirable and profitable to share the resources of book libraries and stores of many other media nationwide. This sharing of resources, if properly arranged, can raise the quality of educational information services and cut their costs. It therefore seems desirable and feasible to establish national networks for knowledge, or educational networks, as described in the book EDUNET.[13] A consortium of universities throughout the country working together can share the resources of all the electronic media listed in Table 1.

The costs and effectiveness of such a national multimedium network are hard to evaluate. Many variables must be considered. The amounts of time and money required to put such a system in operation are very large, but its potential benefits are probably even greater. If a serious effort is to be made to establish such a network, undoubtedly cost-effectiveness analyses must be carried out. All we can do here is to state the obvious need for serious consideration of this multimedium adjunct to university education. For optimal services such networks probably should be interdisciplinary; include all useful information-processing media; provide similar services to all parts of the country; provide on-demand access of all sorts of information to the user; and be operated as a nonprofit system with appropriate collaboration between colleges, universities, and schools as well as other nonprofit institutions in education, industry, and the government.

7. International Education

From an engineer's point of view there is no reason why what can be done for education by the use of the new technologies on a national basis cannot be done internationally. When other countries become involved, however, the problems of organization and technical cooperation become vast, just as the possible benefits become tremendous. Educational satellites and new laser transmission systems are under study which may enable us to transmit information in very large quantities at rapid rates throughout the world. This can be done either over electronic networks, or by shipping electronic or other forms of memory through the mails, by ship, or by plane. For example, computer-aided instruction terminals with programs stored on magnetic tapes in cassettes and with self-contained power systems could be sent to any part of the world. If they were mass produced they could be reasonably inexpensive. Problems of translation and embedding of such an educational system in the local culture would be serious, but could be solved. This is perhaps the only way that some of the developing nations which have few adequately trained teachers to educate the younger generation could afford to take a big leap forward to catch up with the twentieth century as it is known in the more developed lands. At the very least an intensive review of the role of the new media in international education is indicated.

REFERENCES

1. Research and Policy Committee, Committee for Economic Development. *Innovation in education: A new direction for the American school.* New York: Committee for Economic Development, July, 1968, p. 45.

2. Sanford, N. Foreword in R. I. Evans. *Resistance to change in higher education.* San Francisco: Jossey-Bass, 1968, pp. xiii-xiv.

3. Evans, R. I. *Ibid.*

4. Licklider, J. C. R. "Televistas: looking ahead through side windows." In Killian, J. R., Jr., Chairman, Carnegie Commission on Educational Television. *Public television: a program for action.* New York: Bantam Books, 1967, pp. 201-225.

5. Murphy, J. and R. Gross. "The unfulfilled promise of ITV." *Saturday Review,* Nov. 18, 1966, 50, 89, 103.

6. Chu, G. C. and W. Schramm. *Learning from television: what the research says.* Stanford: Stanford University, Institute for Communication Research, 1967, p. 10.

7. Jones, M. G. "Computer-assisted education: a new challenge in social responsibility." *American Association of University Women,* October, 1968, 62, 3.

8. Atkinson, R. C. "Computerized instruction and the learning process." *American Psychologist,* 1968, pp. 23, 225-239.

9. Atkinson, R. C. Personal communication, March, 1969.

10. Bacon, G. Personal communication, March, 1969.

11. Kopstein, F. F. and Seidel, R. J. "Computer-administered instruction versus traditionally administered instruction: economics." *AV Communication Review,* 1968, 16, pp. 147-175.

12. Zinn, K. L. Instructional uses of interactive computer systems. *Datamation,* 1968, 19, pp. 23-24.

13. Brown, G. W., J. G. Miller, and T. A. Keenan. *EDUNET. Report of the Summer Study on Information Networks Conducted by the Inter-university Communications Council (EDUCOM).* New York: Wiley, 1967.

111.
Planning-Programming-Budgeting
And Cost-Effectiveness Analysis
In Educational Systems

by *JAMES G. MILLER*   *and*   *GUSTAVE J. RATH*
Vice Pres. for Academic   *Professor*
Affairs   *Industrial Engineering*
Cleveland State Univ.   *and Management*
and   *Sciences*
Vice Pres. and   *The Technological Institute*
Principal Scientist   *Northwestern University*
EDUCOM

Excellence in education is determined by diverse, subtle, and interwoven factors, ranging from the morale of the institution's instructors through the familiarity of the faculty with current scholarly achievements to the warmth of food served in the cafeteria. These factors always are influenced by economic realities. With a given level of resources available, the task of school, college, or university administrators is to select the policies, people, facilities, and equipment that will give the students the "best and biggest education per buck." From this basic but limited view, education is essentially an economic choice in which educational effectiveness must be related to resources in short supply in order to attain specified purposes and achieve certain goals that help to attain them.

The History of Programming-Planning-Budgeting

Pioneer work in analyzing large and complex systems with interacting technical, social, and political variables from an economic standpoint was done by Charles J. Hitch and his associates. He was once head of the Economic Division, the RAND Corporation, later was Assistant Secretary of Defense (Controller), and is now president of the University of California. The concepts of program budgeting (also called programming-planning-budgeting or PPB) which he advanced are now used by the United States Department of Defense and by contractors doing work for that department. These concepts also are relevant to problems which arise in educational decision-making. The following quotation from Hitch states his basic assumptions: ". . . being truly economical does not mean scrimping—reducing expenditures no matter how important the things to be sought. Nor does it mean implementing some status doctrine regardless of cost. Rather economics is concerned with allocating resources—choosing doctrines and techniques so as to get the most out of available resources. To economize in this sense may imply spending less on some things and more on others. But always economics or economizing means trying to make the most efficient use of the resources available in all activities in any circumstance."[1]

In the military, as in educational and many other governmental institutions, classical forms of budgeting are usually not carried out in a way most conducive for the planning of future programs. Tradition, state statutes, and other considerations cause most educational budgets to be broken down into such categories as academic personnel, nonacademic personnel, fringe benefits, equipment, supplies, travel, capital construction, and so forth. And it may be necessary to continue to use budget categories that are acceptable to state auditing, accounting, and budgeting officials as well as the relevant legislative bodies. But educational institutions may well conclude that they will benefit from using PPB in addition, as was done in the Department of Defense at Hitch's instigation. It said that the chief officials of his department ". . . were convinced that the financial management systems must also provide the data needed by top defense management to make the really crucial decisions, particularly on the major forces and weapons systems needed to carry on the principal missions of the defense establishment. And we were well aware that the financial management system, as it had evolved over the years, could not directly produce the required data in the form desired. It was clear that a new function, which we shall call programming, would have to be incorporated in the financial management systems. . . .

"But the existing budget structures serve some very useful purposes. It is organized, essentially, in terms of resource categories: (1) Military Personnel; (2) Operation and Maintenance; (3) Procurement; (4) Research, Development, Tests and Evaluation; and (5) Military Construction. . . .

·This division of the budget by broad input or resource categories provides needed flexibility for the adjustments in the program that are invariably required in the course of the budget year." But it was not the ideal form for program planning. Therefore a new form of planning, programming, and budgeting was developed.

Identifying and Categorizing Programs

Continuing to refer to the application of these methods to the Department of Defense, Hitch states that the problem ". . . was to sort out all of the myriad programs and activities of the defense establishment and regroup them into meaningful program elements, i.e., integrated combinations of men, equipment, and installations whose effectiveness could be related to our national security objectives. These are the basic building blocks as well as the decision-making levels of the programming process. As I noted earlier, the B-52 bomber force, together with all of the supplies, weapons, and manpower needed to make it militarily effective is one such program element. Other examples are Attack Carriers, F-4 Fighter Wings, the Manned Orbiting Laboratory development project, and Recruit Training. Wherever possible program elements are measured in physical terms such as numbers of aircraft per wing, numbers of operational missiles on launchers, numbers of active ships, and so forth as well as in financial terms, thus including both 'inputs' and 'outputs'—costs and benefits. Of course, such program elements as research projects can only be measured in terms of inputs."[2]

Sometimes in the military a program is a component. Rarely it is a subsystem. Often it is an abstracted system. It may be the development and operation of a concrete system like a missile, a battleship, or a national air attack warning system. At other times it is an abstracted system such as the total Navy personnel procurement activities, all recruit training, or the intelligence-gathering functions.

What Hitch noted about defense programs is equally true about educational programs: "We recognized from the beginning that the defense program is extremely dynamic and that changes would be required at various times during the year. Accordingly, we established a formal program change control system."[3]

And he also noted that: "To facilitate the conversion of program costs to the budget and vice versa, we also had to break down the costs of each program element by the various budget appropriation accounts in which it is financed. Operating costs typically are financed in the 'Military Personnel' and 'Operation and Maintenance' appropriations and, where operating spares are involved, in the 'Procurement' accounts as well. Initial investment costs typically are financed in the 'Procurement' and 'Military Construction' appropriations.

". . . The entire program is subject to continual change and is, therefore, updated every other month. Whenever a change is made in the cost of a program element in the current fiscal year, it must also be reflected in the budget for the same year and vice versa. Considering the vast quantities of data involved in the planning-programming-budgeting system, the only practical solution was to transfer the entire operation to a computer system. This we have now accomplished.

"The next task was to relate the program elements to the major missions of the Defense Department. The objective here was to assemble related groups or program elements that, for decision purposes, should be considered together either because they supported one another or because they were close substitutes. The unifying principle underlying each major program is a common mission or set of purposes for the elements involved. We now have nine major programs:

1. Strategic Retaliatory Forces

2. Continental Defense Forces

3. General Purpose Forces

4. Airlift and Sealift

5. Reserve and Guard

6. Research and Development

7. General Support

8. Retired Pay

9. Military Assistance." [4]

Also Hitch observed that there was ". . . need for military-economic studies which compare alternative ways of accomplishing national security objectives and which try to determine the way that contributes the most for a given cost or achieves a given objective for the least cost. The extensive and comprehensive use of these 'cost-effectiveness' studies or systems analyses was the second major innovation introduced into the decision-making process of the Defense Department." [5]

"Virtually every attempt we have made to explain the inexorable logic of relating cost to military effectiveness seems to shatter itself on the argument—'Nothing but the best will do for our boys.' And the 'best' usually refers to some particular characteristic of physical performance, such as speed, altitude, or firepower, or even unit cost!

"Implicit in this challenge is the deeply rooted feeling that national defense is far too important a matter to be inhibited by cost. If one weapon system performs better than another, then we should buy the higher performance system, regardless of cost; the country can afford it. Indeed, the people who hold this view feel that it is somehow sinful, or at least unpatriotic, to try to relate performance or military effectiveness to costs; that considerations of military effectiveness and cost are antithetical." [6]

It would not be hard to find educators, in some of the nation's best country day schools, in the high schools of some of our wealthiest suburbs, in Ivy League colleges, and in a few of the most privileged state universities, who hold the same view about education. But realistically we can no longer hope to finance such a policy anywhere. Modern education is inherently too complex and the demand for primary, secondary, and higher education is too widespread in the society. Too great a proportion of the gross national product would go to education, leaving unmet other competing demands for other socially worthy purposes as, e.g., housing, highways, urban renewal, health, mental health, and welfare. We must look for educational innovations which will maximize quality and minimize costs, and we must have an accurate idea of the productivity and expenses of any educational program we undertake. The first major use of PPB, as we have indicated, was in the Department of Defense beginning in 1961. Since that time it has been designated as the official method for all budgeting in the federal government, the State of California, and other political jurisdictions. While the inertia of such huge governmental budgeting apparatuses has not yet wholly yielded to PPB, it appears to be just over the horizon for much if not all of public sector fiscal management, including that of educational institutions.

The Fundamental Principles of PPB

PPB, according to Jungherr, is ". . . aimed at helping management make better decisions on the allocation of resources among alternative ways to attain government objectives. Its essence is the development and presentation of relevant information as to the full implications—the costs and benefits—of the major alternative courses of action." [7] The chief steps in its use are as follows:

1. Identify the main purposes and goals of the educational institution.

2. Identify programs which are directed to achieving these purposes and goals, and alternative programs which might do so.

3. Identify all processes or activities, regardless of where in the system they are or would be located, which contribute to these programs.

4. Consider the likely development of these programs in future years.

5. Calculate all related costs.

6. Select among possible alternative programs in terms of their costs and benefits.

To implement PPB budgeting, the executives who carry out the decision-making begin by agreeing on the ultimate purposes of their organization. If purposes are wrongly selected or described, the analysis will go wrong. For example, if it is assumed that the only purpose of a physical education program is to build strong bodies and the development of individual initiative is neglected, the allocation of resources is not likely to be optimal. Then the deciders must state operationally what goals must be attained to achieve the purposes they have selected. In other words, "to provide a college education to qualified students" is certainly a purpose of any university, but it is not an operational statement of a goal. The questions "What is a college education?", "What does it mean to provide a college education?", "Who are qualified students?", and so forth, are not explicitly resolved. An example of an operational statement of a goal might be "This university intends to provide the faculty and the supporting staff and facilities necessary to enroll at least 95 percent of all applicants who have the admission requirements and who wish to be trained as engineers in a curriculum as prescribed in our catalog, and at least possible cost."

After defining a set of operational goals, the decider or deciders or the staff propose possible programs which would carry the organization toward the achievement of its goals. If a goal is teaching engineers as suggested above, then various alternative engineering curricula would be proposed as possible programs. This can be the most creative and innovative stage of PPB development. New uses of instructional technologies can be proposed. The PPB procedure does not ignore the reality of how hard it is to change traditional modes of operation. Rather, it attempts to choose the "best" program. PPB forces all present and potential alternatives into competition. The result of this is both the "best" program or programs, according to the criteria established by the goals, and the costs of not pursuing the "best" alternative become recognized. This procedure does not insure that the "best" procedure will be implemented, but it does give the decider new and additional information. Often, new and unique alternatives are conceived and found feasible; a different combination of existing programs proves to be more desirable; or, at the very least, the costs of following and not following the current mode of operation are explicitly identified.

In education a program may be a concrete system like an Institute of Urban Studies in a university or an abstracted system like a preschool training program or a program for improving reading of children in the elementary grades.

Once a set of programs which are capable of achieving the desired institutional goals are chosen, the budgeting phase begins. A program budget may include both a set of indicators of the activities involved (e.g., the number of students, the number of faculty and staff, the amount of physical space, etc.) and the fiscal reflection of these physical activities (e.g., faculty salaries, support costs, research costs, administrative costs, etc.). All costs directly associated with an activity are listed under that activity. Those costs which are indirectly attributable to several activities should be allocated appropriately among them. In the case in which a cost cannot be assigned at all, a supporting or secondary program (in essence a dummy program) is sometimes included—an abstracted subsystem or component. All these indicators and costs are then extrapolated for a number of years into the future—say, three, five, or ten—to gain a systems-wide perspective of dynamic change over time.

The implementation of a PPB system is often a difficult and arduous task requiring a large data base. Since the information gathered by a traditional accounting system is usually oriented toward a traditional fiduciary-type budgeting system, an early prerequisite of a meaningful and operational program budget is an extensive and properly designed management information system. With it a simulation model of the educational organization can be constructed and consulted when institutional decisions are made. The field of simulation is new and can become much more sophisticated than it is today. Even though most simulations are still quite primitive, and they are used in only a few educational organizations, a well constructed simulation model provides significant advantages to academic administrators. It would be an extremely time-consuming and laborious task to calculate by hand all the essential variables in an adequate PPB array. But once the output routine of the simulation model is programmed, an analyst can feed data from the management information system data banks into it and produce a program budget display in a few minutes of running time on a computer. Planners and administrators are enabled to consider a large number of alternative program proposals or proposed changes to existing programs with relatively little effort.[8]

"In order to choose one alternative over another one we must have a 'test' or criterion. The central problem in many economic choices is selecting an appropriate economic criterion. In industrial situations the criterion may usually be taken as profit optimization. In educational situations, however, the positive values (objectives) and the negative values (resources used up) seldom have a common measure. In addition, there may be multiple objectives which even among themselves have neither common units of measurement nor comparable costs. In most educational analyses we have to be satisfied with some approximation of the ideal criterion.

"To sum up, the educational planning activities must be placed in the context of economic choice. This does not mean that analytic aids or computing machines must be used for every problem. What it does mean is that economic choice is a way of looking at educational problems."[9]

Let us now look in more detail at the technique of PPB as applied to a series of different types of educational systems—all of them at the organization level or above.

Determination of the System's Purposes and Goals

Precise descriptions of what the system is, what its environment is, and what its suprasystems and subsystems are, are prerequisites in any systems analysis. One must then determine the major dimensions or variables by which the system can be described and how they can be measured. Then one can proceed to discovering its purposes and goals.

For an educational system these can be established in two chief ways. The suprasystem may specify what they shall be, or they may be evolved internally by the system itself— though never, of course, without interactions with its suprasystem.

What purposes can a university have—to take one type of educational institution as an example? One class of purposes may be to meet demands of the community and society of which it is a part, its suprasystem. A university graduates educated ladies and gentlemen. Or perhaps it produces married, socialized ladies and gentlemen, which is a different thing. Perhaps it graduates useful citizens, or contributing workers. Perhaps it produces leaders, who, instead of conforming to the society, irritate it and its establishment. Maybe the purpose of the university is to achieve a proper conformity-innovation ratio between the university and the society, and perhaps universities are, therefore, always out-of-phase with society. The hope of somehow getting the university to conform to its environment may be mistaken, because any organization that leads, by definition, cannot so conform. Perhaps the main purpose of a university is to produce ideas. Perhaps the university meets the special demands of the trustees or regents, the alumni, the parents, the government, or the church.

The university may strive to meet internal goals. These may be intellectual—to improve the accuracy, speed, or completeness of its information flow; to maximize the cost-effectiveness ratio of its information flows or matter and energy flows; to speed the rate of learning of the average student, the best student, or the minimal student; to increase the generality of students' learning or the depth of their specialization; to increase the number of scholarships or amount of research; or to raise the amount of faculty time devoted to teaching. Or the internal goals may be social—to increase the time students spend with people in the university who are known personally to them, or the number of student-faculty contacts, or the number of student-student contacts. Perhaps a goal of the university is to improve the careers and increase the convenience of the faculty, and this goal should not be discarded out of hand, since the institution that neglects it entirely cannot keep its faculty.

Obviously these goals conflict in many ways. Any one of them can be maximized or minimized, and each of them has its costs. Until purposes and goals are made specific, performance criteria cannot be rationally established, and decisions as to allocation of personnel, effort, and time will be largely arbitrary. Any institution's goals, of course, must constantly be reevaluated.

Three major techniques may be employed to discover and measure an educational institution's purposes or goals. These are: First, interviewing persons in the system, including leaders and followers, to find what they believe the system goals are. Second, observing how people actually behave in the system, so that one may infer what their goals seem to be. Third, studying documents, both private and public. Each method permits some quantification, enabling one to count the number of persons supporting various views of their organization's purposes and goals.

Classifying and Operationalizing the
System's Purposes and Goals

The goals of an institution may be classified into those of the trustees or the school board, those of the administration, those of the teachers or faculty, those of the students, and those of the parents and other citizens of the community. But the executives usually make the final decisions, and their views therefore become the primary determiners of action.

Some goals may relate to the objective excellence of education or the breadth of the population educated or the effectiveness of the research carried on. Some of the goals are much more personal, such as achieving prestige, enjoyment, or satisfaction at being in an advanced educational system, or at having a special degree of communication among the students. Whatever it is, to operationalize a goal there must be at least one precise measure of how nearly it is achieved. There exist proximal measures of achievement of goals and distal measures of accomplishment of purposes. Cost-benefit analysis uses distal or ultimate measures. These are generally difficult to define and to operationalize. An educational system strives for development of citizens, scientists, and other contributors to society. Measures of such accomplishment are distal or ultimate criteria. Cost-effectiveness analysis in educational systems, on the other hand, is in terms of proximal goals like the number of students accepted, the number of students graduated, or the number of papers written by the faculty. They are much easier to measure but far from ultimate.

Techniques for Deciding on Priorities Among Programs

Priority determination in an educational system is the process of deciding which set of programs should be implemented and in what order. Analytical and cost-effectiveness techniques suggest the best alternatives to an administrator, committee, or board. They should always make the final decision. Even though a majority of the time one might accept the analytical decision, the final human evaluation can avoid some gross errors.

Six techniques used for establishing priorities among programs are:

1. *Analogy.* In a recent study carried out for a technical school, the problem was posed of how to evaluate, within a very short time, different possible physical plant designs. A quick review showed that the main inputs into the school were students who paid their own tuition at the rate of a good private university and engineers who were recruited from industry to do the teaching. Both these groups had to be attracted to keep the school operating. The outputs were students trained and ready to work in industrial settings. This suggested that the physical plant should look like a modern engineering laboratory—for the students come because they feel that it will prepare them for the work they desire. It should not seem like more nonvocationally oriented education. If engineers are to transfer from engineering to teaching, they must feel that the new environment will be as acceptable as the environment they are leaving. The future employer must believe that the school's training will transfer to his business. If he sees in the school a plant like that in which the student will work, he will be more assured that the training will transfer. This analogy can serve as a basis for evaluating plant design alternatives. Should this school have air conditioning? The answer is "yes." Modern engineering laboratories have air conditioning. Should the faculty be given individual offices? The answer is "no," because engineers typically do not require individual offices. Engineers do not punch time clocks, so the faculty should not be required to punch time clocks either.

2. *Checklist.* A checklist for rating a program is constructed on the assumption that

all its items are weighted equally and that one can determine priorities or make choices among alternate programs by seeing how each program scores on the check-list. Individual judges or panels of judges rating independently, may use checklists. The latter procedure of pooling judgments of individuals scoring independently may improve the rating process.

3. *Weighted techniques.* Weighted techniques involve the assigning of weights to items on a checklist. This may be done by multiple correlation techniques, regression analysis, or negotiation among judges or decision-makers.

4. *Cost-effectiveness or cost-benefit ratios.* This is a mathematical approach to the setting of priorities among programs which has been popular in the aerospace industry. Priority is given to the program with the highest cost-effectiveness ratio (E) calculated as follows:

$$E = \sum_i^n \frac{(P_i \times U_i)}{C_i},$$

where P = probability of the i item occurring
U = utility of the i item if it occurs
C = cost of the i item
i = 1,2,3 . . . N Number of alternatives or components.

5. *Mathematical models.* Many mathematical models exist that may be used to evaluate alternatives if problems can be mathematically formulated, mathematical condi-tions are met, and the solution can be computed. These models come from opera-tions research.

6. *Simulation.* Simulation techniques, especially those which use digital computers, can compare the relative effectiveness of various educational systems. Special com-puter languages such as Simscript and GPSS aid the programmer in efficiently carry-ing out his simulations.

Measures of Benefits or Effectiveness

If cost-benefit or cost-effectiveness analysis is to be used in studying educational systems, the first step is to produce satisfactory measures of benefits or effectiveness. These include:

A. *Measures of population saturation.* The contributions of any educational system increase as the percentage of its students that it influences increases. To measure such influence one starts with a description of the input population and some index of their levels of achievement. The range of types in the population is also an important variable because an effective educational process should influence as many types as possible. Knowing the percentage of the student population which can be trained by any technique is important. If 30 percent of the students in a course have a certain level of achievement on the first day and at the end of the course 90 percent have reached that level, the class appears to be effective. On the other hand, if a course starts with 85 percent of the students at a given level of achievement and ends with 90 percent at that level, one questions its value.

B. *Measures of achievement.* These include standardized measures which allow one to compare an individual's or a group's degree of achievement to that of a normative population, as well as measures by which one compares the achievements of an in-dividual or group at time "a" and at time "b." Both of these are important in edu-cational evaluation. Among such achievement measures are:

1. *Cognitive tests.* These evaluate thinking processes in many fields, such as mathematics.

2. *Affective tests.* These measures of emotional adjustment include projective techniques, situational tests, and other procedures.

3. *Social tests.* These include attitude scales, observations of behavior in new situations, and sociometric measures. They measure the relationships among persons, for example, whom students select as partners in play

4. *Value internalization measures.* Values are difficult to measure partly because they are hard to describe. Attitude studies, interviews, and situational measures are used. Some such tests measure the degree to which a student accepts cultural norms—attitudes toward cheating, for example.

5. *Physical measures.* Physical condition and achievement are easy to measure, by physical examinations and by tests of muscular strength and skill, athletic ability, and manual dexterity.

C. *Measures of social benefits.* Education influences the productivity of groups, organizations, and societies as well as individuals. Such measures as company productivity or gross national product or productivity per worker hour can be interpreted (with great caution) as indices of social benefits from education.

D. *Critique of these measures.* Anything as subtle and many-faceted as educational effectiveness is most difficult to measure with any validity. All single or joint measures so far proposed are primitive, and only partially valid. Furthermore, there are many pitfalls in the field of measurement. On the one hand, one is tempted to accept the newest measures because of their convenience and availability. On the other hand, one may develop, at much effort, a measure for a special purpose and then become committed to it because of effort devoted to its development. Some tests have low reliability. Others are not valid. For some there are no norms. The cognitive and physical variables are relatively easy to measure and noncontroversial. On the other hand, some measures are hard to standardize, like most exams which teachers give. Yet they are helpful because they are often precisely directed toward the objectives of the education. A total evaluation of the benefits of an educational experience should take this whole range of variables into consideration. An example of this is Project Talent, which in 1960 tested 440,000 American high school students with aptitude, achievement, and information tests. It is important in measuring educational effectiveness to pay attention to accepted considerations of test development and psychometrics—the reliability and validity of the measures used, and the overall dimensionality of the domain of effectiveness, as determined by factor analytic or related methods.

Measure of Costs

In cost-benefits or cost-effectiveness studies it is essential to measure not only benefits and effectiveness but also costs. Such measurement deals with several sorts of costs.

A. *Matter-energy, information, and time.*

Money is a particular form of information which circulates throughout the society and is widely accepted as the common denominator of all costs. Therefore it may be used to measure many aspects of an educational system, but there are other key resources in a community where expenditure involves cost. These include materials for buildings, gas, and electricity, and in another valuable commodity which cannot be, in many cases, completely translated into money. There are scarce human resources, valuable no matter how much money exists. The number of Ph.D.'s in the United States, for instance, is in short supply and is not going to change radically for years. Their time is a national shortage. Expenditure of anything which is scarce—matter, energy, information, or time—is a cost. In cost analysis indirect informational effects, such as on prestige or political power, must also be considered.

B. *Human effort.*

1. *Student time and effort.* Student time expenditure is a major consideration in resource allocation in an educational system. Students are available only a limited number of hours a week and this time must be used optimally. Measurement of students' time has usually been done in units of scheduled hours. Cost of student activity may be viewed in other ways. Older students, especially in agricultural regions and other communities where the students contribute significantly to local income, can have their class time measured in terms of their hourly earning power. Another approach is to analyze the alternative costs to society of student time in an educational institution as opposed to time in the army or time when they are unemployed and require, consequently, additional police, judicial, and correctional facilities.

2. *Teacher and faculty time and effort.* In recent years, effort reporting of faculty has been a key issue in many schools, colleges, and universities. The issue of measurement of work has been the subject of many controversies ever since the introduction of industrial engineering. The same basic units of time may be used to describe teachers as students, that is the working hour, or module in the case of the schools which can operate on a modular basis. Effort reporting has been done by using sheets in which one fills out how one spent his time, by sampling and observation, by the prescriptions of curriculum committees and supervisory personnel, or by estimates by supervisors. Direct observation is the best measure and the most difficult to arrange. There are also unobtrusive possible measures such as the use of substitutes, the number of recess periods, the amount of audio-visual aids used, or the number of trips to the library. Such indices sample teacher behavior and suggest how teachers expend their efforts.

3. *Administrative or technician time and effort.* The technical problems of measuring administrative or technician problems are similar to that of teachers and faculty, but there are not as many professional or status problems involved. Office or technical personnel, except in the top echelons, can be required to keep time records and in many cases they punch a time clock.

C. *Monetary costs.*

1. *Short run.* Capital expense cash flows have to be controlled but usually the long-term availability of capital is known and can be planned for. Accounting for short-term costs is also well understood and in general straightforward. Most of the commitments in an educational institution involve salaries. These are committed generally through a contract and so vary little within any year. The most difficult problems in short-run cost accounting concern the allocation of overheads.

2. *Long run.* (a) *Capital.* Long-term capital costs involve three issues. The first is the time value of money, which is a standard investment question. The second is depreciation. The third is the problem of raising the necessary money by levies, bonds, or private gifts. Certain forms of long-term financing may be economical from a short-run cost viewpoint but have a direct effect on the ability to borrow more money at a later date, which may make their use inadvisable. (b) *Operating*

activities on a long-run basis. Operating activities in the long range must consider service, inflation, and consequent increased personnel, equipment, and supply costs.

Cost-Effectiveness Measures

Having measured both costs and benefits or effectiveness, one proceeds to compare educational programs in terms of their cost-benefit or cost-effectiveness ratios. We have already discussed these ratios, along with the mathematical models and simulation procedures which can aid in the process of selecting among alternative educational programs. An example of how the costs and the effectiveness of achieving a particular goal—in this case instruction tailored to individuals—must be weighed against each other is given in the following quotation from a report of the Committee for Economic Development:

"Individualized instruction, geared to the individual's interests, abilities, and learning rate, is one of the cherished goals of American education. . . . Yet the schools are making very slow headway in this direction through present means, principally through efforts to reduce the pupil-teacher ratio. Over the past decade, while the nation has increased its annual expenditures for its public schooling from about three percent to nearly four percent of the gross national product, there has been a reduction of only three pupils in the average class size of elementary schools. To achieve any fundamental reduction in average class size, while maintaining the traditional instructional practices, would . . . put a serious drain on the trained manpower of the country and raise the costs of staffing the schools to unacceptable levels.

"More important, we question whether the pupil-teacher ratio provides an adequate basis for determining educational policy. We believe that the key to achieving effectiveness in education lies in increasing the productivity of the individual teacher, and that the means are now available through . . . the reorganization of instruction, the redesign of curricula, improved and new audiovisual methods, and the improvement of teacher education.

"What will these and other innovations cost in relation to the benefits they secure? Fortunately, new ways of measuring, testing, and assessing effectiveness and efficiency in education are being developed. Techniques of cost-effectiveness analysis and systems analysis, when used in the broadest sense, can now be employed in assessing the efficiency of school management. Moreover, research in the methods of measuring intellectual growth and attitudinal changes promises to increase the capability to evaluate a school's educational effectiveness. Although there are numerous imponderables in education that cannot be quantified or measured, we believe that these techniques will assist the schools in setting priorities and designing programs. . . .

"Any spending proposal, such as raising the starting salaries of teachers, could be assessed against the other possibilities for spending the same amount of money—e.g., determining what this sum would purchase if spent on such programs as the retraining of teachers. It would remain a matter of judgment whether the benefits of spending the money on retraining teachers would outweigh the benefits of improved recruitment. The choice among such alternatives would involve many factors, as for instance the policies and bargaining power of teachers' organizations. But however difficult the cost-benefit analysis when such factors are included, it should always be in the picture.

"Program accounting encourages school authorities to make useful comparisons of this kind. Perhaps most importantly, program accounting encourages the forecasting of the cost of new programs over a period of years. Grievous mistakes have been made in failing to take account of the cost in future years of programs that were superficially attractive but proved eventually to be bad educational investments.

"Program accounting will be particularly valuable in comparing the benefits that may accrue from other forms of resource allocation lying outside the scope of this statement. We have in mind the possibility, now being explored in various parts of the country, of gaining efficiency in the use of school facilities through their use after hours for adult education or other programs, or through the lengthening of the present school year, a legacy of the nation's agrarian past. . . . Program accounting will assist decision-making by providing comparisons that take into account the various costs involved in such proposals as against alternative costs accruing, for example, for plant expansion to provide for new pupils." [10]

Computerized Management Information Systems and PPB

As we have indicated above, the management of any educational system needs extensive and up-to-date information before the decisions which are inherent in PPB can be made. This, in most organizations of any size, today requires a computerized management information system.

A. *How to build and operate one.* A computerized management information system should be the product of a systems analysis which determines whether such an aid to decision-making is needed and what type is required. Automation is not a panacea. It has a place in many organizations. Bad automation is worse than a poor manually run system. People are usually able to adjust and correct human errors. A computerized system is not so adaptive.

The development of an automated management information system follows decisions made in systems analysis. One must specify what types of data to process, who will receive the information outputs, what information flow rates will be involved, what the costs will be, how confidentiality of information will be maintained, and other requirements.

B. *Establishing a data gathering system.* It is necessary to specify how many reports will be needed, when they will be required, who is going to contribute data, how many data will have to be stored for what length of time, and many other such details. A detailed plan for the flow of information must be worked out, and the forms used to input data, the handling procedures, and the timing must be adapted so that they will be appropriate for data processing. A computer system must be selected. Adequate documentation must be prepared to describe all the procedures. Personnel must be trained in the input behavior necessary to develop the system. Then the operation begins.

Once it is operating, field tests and upgrading of the management information system will continue, and it will be gradually extended to deal with other aspects of the organization.

C. *How to use PPB based on Management Information Systems in educational systems.* Though individual students, at the organism level of living systems, plan, program, and budget, their problems are not so complex that PPB is useful. The same is true of the classroom, at the group level, the next higher level of complexity. At the next higher level, the organization, and above, complexity is so great that PPB is potentially of great value. A school, providing secondary education to students in a given region, if it is relatively large, can profitably employ PPB. So can the next higher echelon, serving a whole town or city, a school system. A college, providing higher education, can, and so can a more complex university. At a higher echelon a state system of higher education can employ PPB. At any higher level—society or supratational system—it is in this modern age almost essential to efficient operation.

1. *A school.* A single school may be so small that it does not realistically justify a computerized management information system to implement PPB. A school of a thousand or more students, on the other hand, might make good use of it. In a school, the principle information needed involves a student data bank containing information about students, a comparable teacher data bank, a data bank about the curriculum and related materials, a data bank about rooms and other space in the school, and one about budget and other administrative matters. Programs would also need to be written to manipulate and interrelate the data from these different sources and to enable a computer to print out such reports and charts as: Time schedules for each student; time schedules for each teacher and administrator; time schedules for each room in the school; lists of students for which each teacher is responsible in each class; budgets; accounts; schedules for use of various sorts of reports on short-range and long-range costs in money and student, teacher, and administrator time of all sorts of energy, information, and services used in the school; reports of grades; scores of achievement, personality, and intelligence; cost-effectiveness comparisons, employing various measures of cost and improvement in grades or scores on various tests as measures of effectiveness. The principal can compare various courses or programs against criteria of how well they accomplished the purposes of the school as viewed by teachers, principal, superintendent, or school board. Other alternative programs can be considered and decisions made, on all the available updated evidence, whether to initiate them in future years, or maintain or expand current programs.

Suppose that a principal were considering whether the physical education program of his school was meeting its fundamental purposes and immediate goals or whether it should be altered in some way. He might proceed to restate the purposes and goals as follows:

Purpose A: To develop physical skills and fitness to the extent of each pupil's ability. *Specific Goal A;* To achieve a mean score for our students in the top 25 percent on the physical fitness screening test of New York State.

Purpose B: To provide wide experience in sports to students, both as player and as leader. *Specific Goal B:* Each of our students to develop skill in three team and five individual sports or activities.

Purpose C: To develop the leadership attributes of courage, self-control, sportsmanship, aggressiveness, poise, and perseverance. *Specific Goal C:* Each student to advance, from the beginning of the school year to the end, 10 points on a leadership rating scale filled out by his fellow students.

Purpose D: To provide outlets for physical activity. *Specific Goal D:* Each student to take exercise a minimum of one half hour a day outside of school hours.

The principal might then list the major feasible alternative programs for achieving the purposes and goals of the physical education program. In this case they might be the following:

1. Continue the existing program, using resources at the current rate.

2. Continue the existing program and increase the rate at which resources are used.

3. Continue the existing program and increase the rate at which resources are used 20 percent.

4. Reduce rate of expenditure of resources for athletic contests with other schools 50 percent and allocate resources saved by this to other activities.

5. Reduce class activities 50 percent and allocate resources saved by this to intramural activities.

6. Eliminate intramural activities and athletic contests with other schools and increase the resources allocated to class activities by the amount saved by these reductions.

7. Eliminate intramural activities and athletic contest with other schools and allot the resources saved to corrective activities and activities for the physically underdeveloped.

The principal might then calculate the costs and potential benefits of each alternative program and on the basis of this evidence select one. In future years he would determine the actual costs and effectiveness—how well the specific goals were met —in deciding about whether to stick with the alternative selected or to switch to another program.[11]

2. *A school system.* The management information system for an entire school system would store many more data than one for a single school—enough more, in a large system, to justify use of a fairly large third generation computer in a timesharing mode with remote terminals at each school and in the control office to transmit and receive data and interact with the computer. The data banks for the school system would contain much the same information as for a single school, but collected and constantly updated for all schools and programs in a uniform way. In addition the school system would have data banks on characteristics of the community, demographic trends, political factors, and sources of grant funds, as well as more complex and sophisticated programs used to analyze the data for PPB and other purposes.

Such a system can prepare a budget by computer annually or more frequently, for the superintendent and school board. The budgetary data can be broken down not only in the traditional chart of accounts but according to programs, indicating for a program category like spelling or reading how much is spent in each school and in the whole school system. Each program can have associated with its cost measures its effectiveness evaluation measures. Each program can include a breakdown of funds and time allocated to it by any categories desired. Also comparisons can be made with previous years.

The automated system can also be used by the superintendent and his staff for planning purposes. Systems analyses can be carried out when new programs, new personnel, new materials, or changes of existing plans are proposed. Thus the proposer has available data to help analyze and defend why the alternate program he suggests will be an improvement in cost or effectiveness over the *status quo.* Furthermore, planning may be carried out for the next budget cycle at such key times as when contracts for teachers are negotiated for the following year. Analyses may be made at any time, by grade level, by school, by vendor, or by many other breakdowns. Accounting questions may be asked and aswered at frequent intervals —such as whether each responsible group is staying within its budget. If not, the management information system can assist the superintendent in deciding how funds can be reallocated to meet existing needs for the rest of the year. The system can provide for daily attendance reporting, and for scheduling of such resources as substitute teachers, substitute drivers, and extra equipment. The locating of children or teachers in emergencies is another important function for it. It can also maintain updated student, teacher, and employee health records and facilitate control of petty cash, and small funds.

An illustrative example of how PPB using such an automated management system can be carried out in a school system may be found in an analysis of a school bussing program. First, criteria are set up to indicate how well the program's goals must be fulfilled. For instance, suppose the goal is to bus all students who live more than two miles from school. The criteria will define such needs as maximum allowable travel time for students, acceptable range of arrival times, and other factors.

The superintendent or school board that must make the decisions might have alternative bussing programs evaluated within the framework of available resources and necessary constraints. Resources include such things as school budgets, personnel, existing facilities, future income, supportive attitudes of the school board, and so on. Constraints include the legal, federal, state, and local situation, the attitudes prevalent in the school system, any negative mood of the school board, the demands of teacher unions, and other factors.

The output of this PPB analysis, as in all others, would be a set of alternatives, each with benefits listed and costs shown. The alternatives are evaluated, ranked and presented to the decision-maker who can then select a preferred set.

PPB requires multiyear planning. In a K-8 school system, several time spans can be considered for planning. Traditionally, organizations talk about 5 to 20 years when they talk about long-range planning. One can look at the existing population of preschool children who will be entering the school system, which suggests looking five years ahead. Or one can consider how long it takes for any decision started at the kindergarten level to ripple through the whole system. This suggests a nine-year planning span.

One possible set of programs for a K-8 school system appears below:

I. Administration

II. Instruction
   a. Social Studies
   b. Mathematics
   c. English
   d. Science
   e. Foreign Language
   f. Arts and Crafts
   g. Physical Education
   h. Special Education, etc.

III. Teaching Aids
   a. Audiovisual Aids
   b. ETV
   c. Miscellaneous, etc.

IV. Research and Development
   a. Administration
   b. Instruction
   c. Teaching Aids
   d. Supporting Activities

V. Supporting Activities
   a. Library

      b. Lunchroom
      c. Building Operation
      d. Maintenance
      e. Transportation

   VI. Miscellaneous

When constructing a program, it is important to accumulate under it all relevant activities. Major activities involve using facilities and other supports to achieve given goals. Some programs may continue through the life of the long-range plan, such as teaching English; others may be short-lived, like an experimental program designed to study speech disorders in order to recommend a plan for the entire school system.

Each program has outputs. Some programs will have neat goals that can be easily evaluated, while others will have objectives that are very difficult to evaluate or must be evaluated subjectively. It is not necessary, however, to wait until one has a certain quantitative set of objectives before starting the programming.

PPB must cover all costs and all parts of a school system. It does not make sense to have a program budget only for the English program or only for the building program while leaving out maintenance or any other costs. All costs and all parts of the educational system must be covered.[12]

3. *A college.* An organization of the complexity and size of the average junior college or private college can profit significantly from a management information system, access to which is preferably available on-line by multiple remote terminals from which inputs to the system can be made, in order to update it, and outputs obtained to give information to various departments of the college and to aid them in their matter-energy and information processing activities.

The primary components of such an information system are data banks for academic administration (concerning students, alumni, and faculty—part of the personnel data bank), for financial administration (concerning personnel, accounting, investments, materials, plant and equipment), for institutional research, planning, and development. The interrelationships among these data banks, according to one plan, are indicated in the following figure:

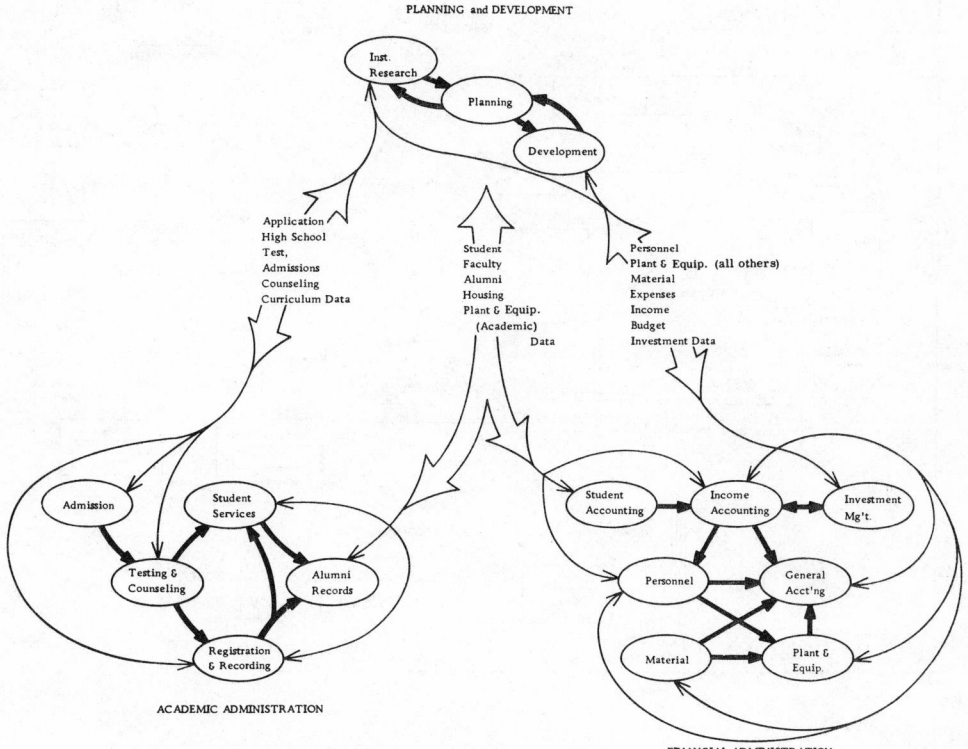

Data Interrelationships

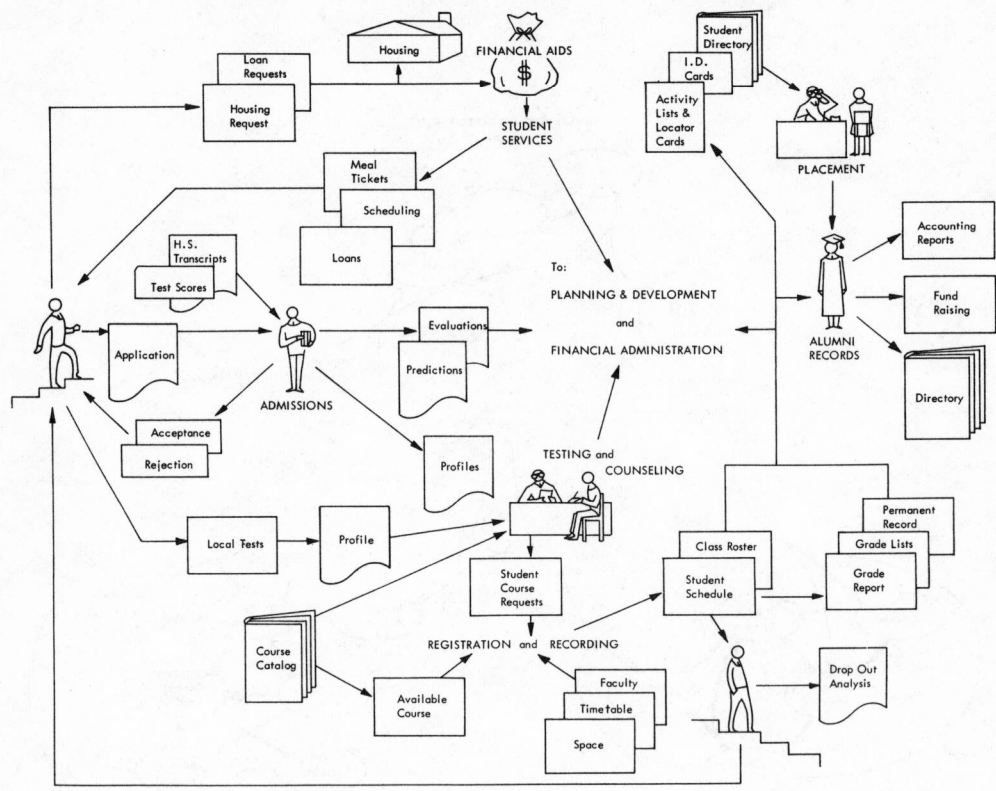

Academic Administration Data Bank

There are many parts with different arrays of data in a part of the overall system above, the data bank for academic administration, which stores information for the academic units of the college. They are shown in the figure above.

In this data bank is a master file of information about each student. Its collection begins when he applies for admission and continues until he graduates and even afterward when he is an alumnus. Information is included from the Admissions Office, from Testing and Counseling, from the Registrar's Office, from the faculty members who taught each student, from various offices which provide student services, and from the Alumni Office. Personnel data on the faculty and academic staff are also in this file. So are data on the effectiveness of faculty members, performance, such as how many students they teach, how much they publish—rough measures relevant to PPB cost effectiveness computations. The parts of the data bank for financial administration are shown in the following figure.

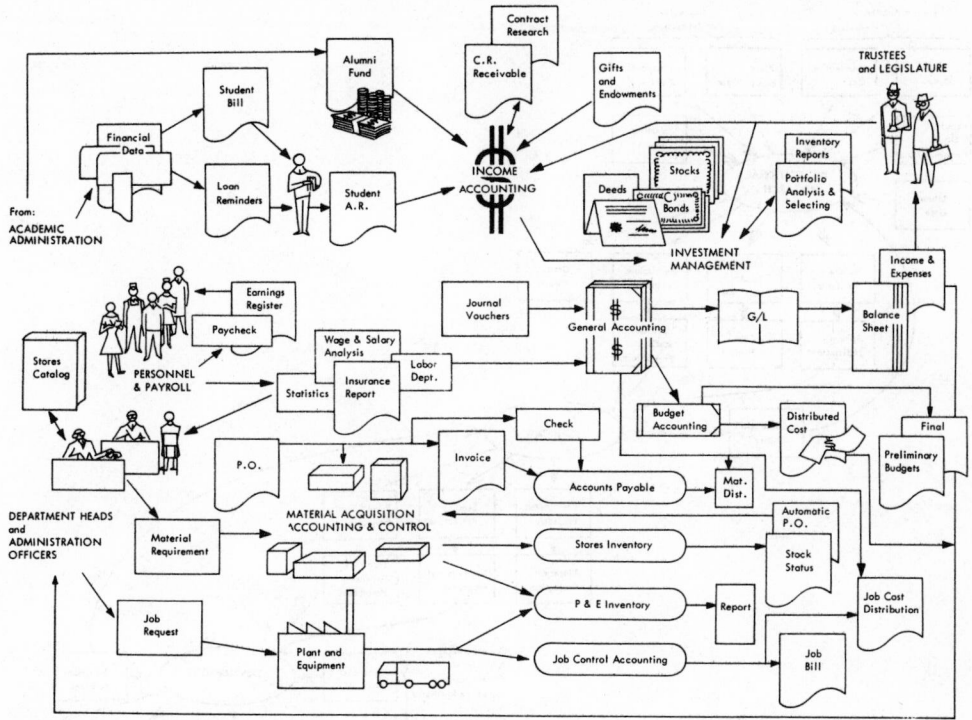

Financial Administration Data Bank

In the financial administration data bank are components for student billing and accounting, including student loans, scholarships, fees, and tuition. Then there are the many sorts of information required for personnel files for academic and non-academic personnel and payroll management. There are data on purchasing and inventorying of materials, for budgeting and accounting, and for investment management. Various measures of costs can be obtained from this data bank—some of the essential data for PPB.

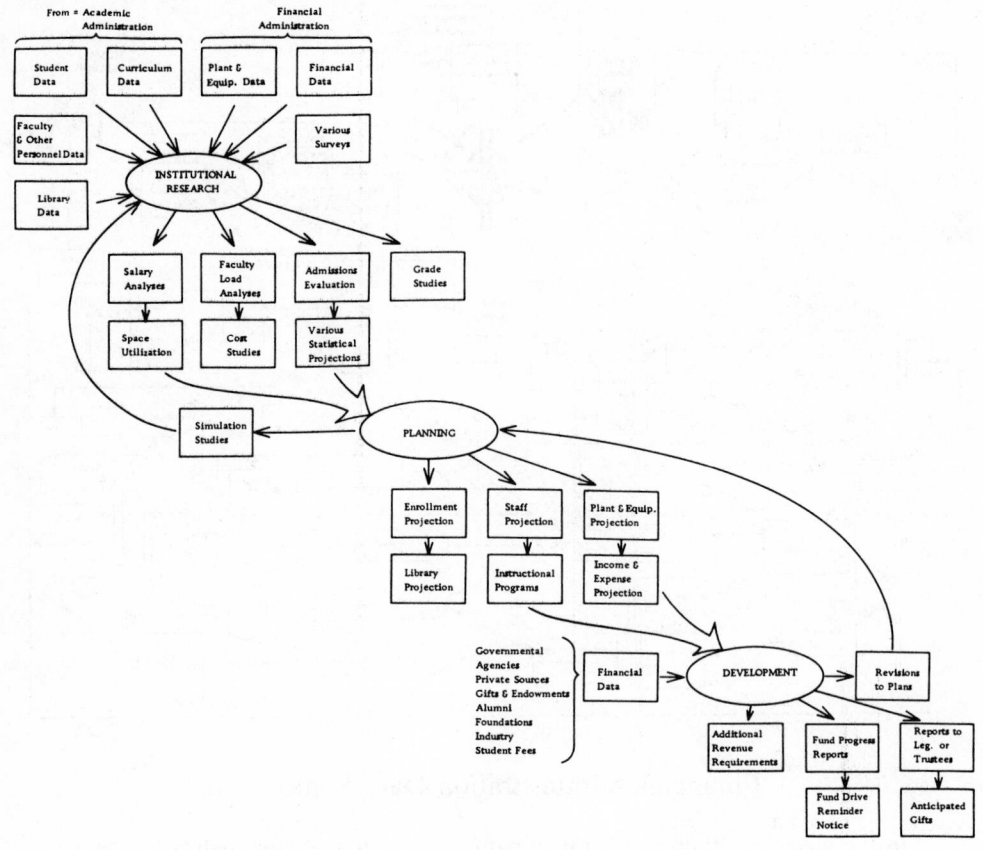

Institutional Research, Planning, and Development Data Bank

The data banks for institutional research, planning, and development are pictured in the figure above.

These data banks contain much of the information relevant to PPB. A good deal of it is calculated by computer from the other data banks previously mentioned. Faculty loads, from student and faculty records; faculty costs, from faculty and budget records—both are measures of costs for cost-effectiveness computations. Examples of charts of such cost measures appear in the next figure.

8

COLLEGE UNIVERSITY

INSTITUTIONAL RESEARCH OFFICE

FACULTY LOAD DISTRIBUTION

2/10/64 DATE

DEPT	INSTRUCTOR NAME	INSTRUCTOR NO	THIS DEPT % FTE	% TEACH	% RSCH	% WRITE	% DEPT SERV.	% OTHER STUD. CONT.	% FIELD SERVICE	% OTHER
10100	GRAVES, GLADYS	003461278	75	48	21	10	5	14	1	1
10700	BARK, SHERMAN	001286934	100	27	59	4	0	6	0	4
10700	CAN, CHARLES	098361249	100	31	19	37	2	1	8	2
10700	MOX, JOHN	081274311	85	68	0	20	5	6	0	1
10701	CURTIS, HELEN	043216858	100	51	16	18	4	6	4	1
10701	LEWIS, JEAN	001231244	50	10	6	12	2	15	5	0

COLLEGE UNIVERSITY

INSTITUTIONAL RESEARCH OFFICE

FACULTY COST DISTRIBUTION

COLLEGE LIBERAL ARTS

2/10 64 DATE

DEPT	INSTR NO	% APPMT	% IN DEPT SALARY	TEACH		RESEARCH		WRITE		DPT. SERV		OTHER STUD. CONT.		FIELD SERVICE		OTHER	
				%	AMOUNT	%	AMOUNT	%	AMOUNT	%	AMOUNT	%	AMOUNT	%	AMOUNT	%	AMOUNT
10068	003416875	100	8200.00	40	3280.00	10	820.00	10	820.00	2	164.00	0	0	20	1640.00	8	656.00
10068	086121145	100	9600.00	60	5760.00	8	768.00	20	1980.00	4	384.00	2	198.00	2	198.00	4	384.00
10068	089743582	75	7000.00	20	1400.00	60	4200.00	6	420.00	2	140.00	10	700.00	2	140.00	2	140.00
10075	004317682	100	10,200.00	35	3570.00	18	1836.00	16	1632.00	10	1020.00	10	1020.00	3	306.00	8	816.00

Faculty Load and Faculty Cost Distributions

Institutional research commonly investigates the comparative costs and effectivenesses by various measures of different programs in the college computer models and simulation techniques enable institutional researchers to investigate possible alternative programs quantitatively and to extrapolate program development into future years. They can put their findings before administrators as a basis for planning, setting up of development program goals, and other fundamental management decisions for the college.[13]

4. *A university.* Colleges are complicated institutions. Universities may be an order of magnitude or so more complex. The huge multiversities like the University of California and the State University of New York, each with well over 100,000 students, are so vast that they are almost out of management control. In such large organizations there are many degrees of freedom for program experimentation. Consequently sophisticated management methods properly applied, can result in important improvements in quality of educational functions and major savings in expenditures of money and time.

How a computerized management information system can be used for PPB in a large multicampus university can be illustrated by the following example. Fundamentally data banks are set up like those suggested above for a college. The task of establishing the data banks and keeping inputs to them current is, of course, much greater. University programs can be categorized as in the figures on the following pages.

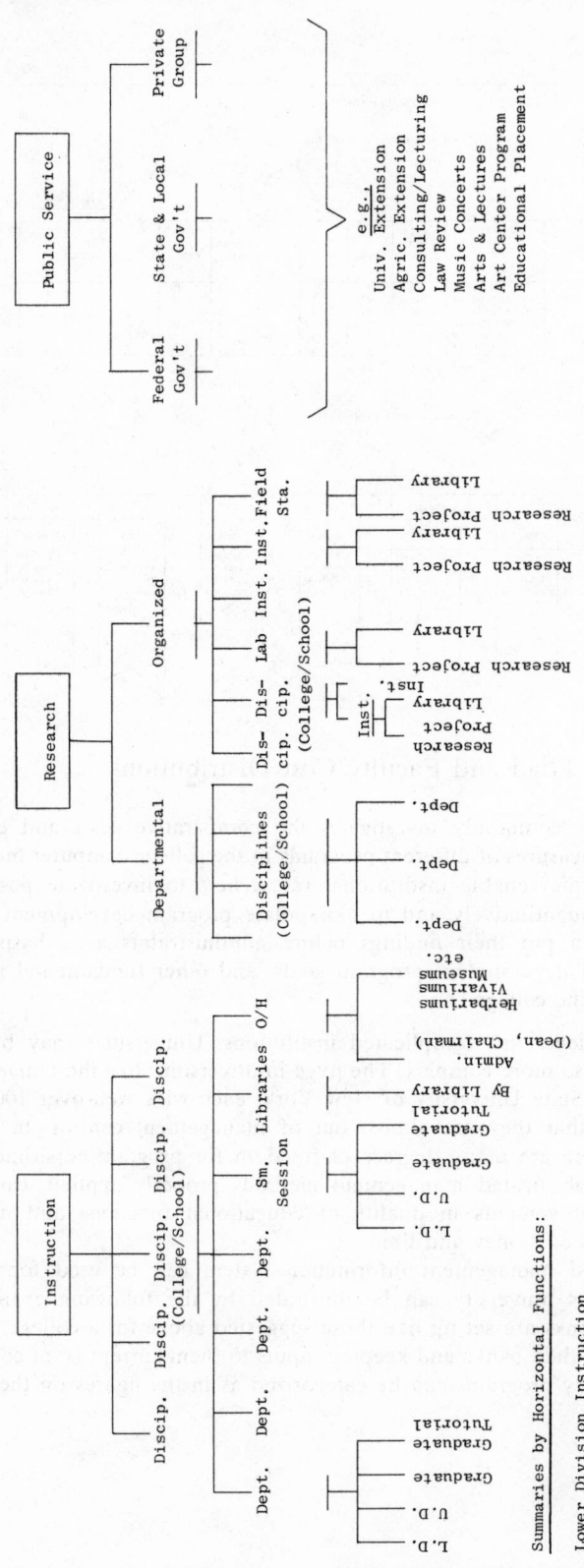

Primary Programs

Supporting Programs

LIBRARIES	GENERAL ADMINISTRATION	GENERAL STUDENT SERVICES
Special Collections	Chancellor's Office	Dean of Students
Government Publications	Architects & Engineers	Student Health Service
Periodicals	Accounting Office	Counselling Center
	Personnel Office	Student/Alum. Placement
	Admissions Office	
	Graduate Div. Office	Aux. Enterprises: Student housing & feeding
	Registrar's Office	Intercoll. Athletics Parking System
	Business Office	

	Academic Committees	Student Aid:
		  Fellowships/Scholarships
		  Loans

	Overhead	Services

Notice that the above figures include three primary programs and three supporting programs. The primary programs are directed to the three most commonly stated purposes of a university: instruction, research, and public service. Instruction is then broken down by disciplines (agriculture, biological sciences, engineering, etc.). Each discipline is divided into the following categories: departments, special programs like summer sessions, specialized libraries for specific fields, and overhead. The instruction in each department is further broken into lower division, upper division, graduate, and tutorial. Similarly, research and public service are disaggregated into their components. The three supporting programs are likewise divided into smaller subprograms and program elements.

The instructional program, thus analyzed for one program field on one campus of the university, prepared for PPB, is shown in the figure below. Multiyear extrapolation for ten years into the future derived from a complex model dealing with several organizational growth factors is also shown.[14]

Complex simulations enable management personnel to investigate many alternative programs in terms of cost-effectiveness once data like this have been gathered and stored in computer memory.[15]

5. *A state system of higher education.* There may be little difference between a state multicampus university and a state system of higher education. The latter may also embrace state colleges, community or junior colleges, and various sorts of technical institutes and specialized professional schools. The latter may be more decentralized in administration, each campus having more autonomy. But not necessarily so.

One Program Field (Engineering) on One Campus in the PPB of a Large University

Major Program   Instruction

Program   Engineering

Program Element Lower Division

	FISCAL YEARS									
	1968	1969	1970	1971	1972	1973	1974	1975	1976	1977
Number Of Students In Major	210.0	220.0	230.0	240.0	250.0	260.0	270.0	280.0	290.0	300.
Total Student Credit Hours	630.0	660.0	690.0	720.0	750.0	780.0	810.0	840.0	870.0	900.
Total Weekly Student Hours	683.0	716.0	749.0	782.0	815.0	848.0	881.0	914.0	947.0	980.
Total Faculty Contact Hours	29.0	33.0	37.0	41.0	45.0	49.0	53.0	57.0	61.0	65.
Mean Class Size	23.6	21.7	20.2	19.1	18.1	17.3	16.6	16.0	15.5	15.
Academic FTE										
Dean	0.3	0.3	0.3	0.3	0.3	0.4	0.4	0.4	0.4	0.
Professor	0.4	0.4	0.4	0.4	0.5	0.5	0.5	0.5	0.5	0.
Associate Professor	0.5	0.5	0.5	0.5	0.5	0.5	0.5	0.5	0.5	0.
Assistant Professor	0.5	0.5	0.5	0.5	0.5	0.5	0.5	0.5	0.5	0.
Instructor	0.5	0.5	0.5	0.5	0.5	0.5	0.6	0.6	0.6	0.
Lecturer	0.6	0.6	0.6	0.6	0.6	0.6	0.6	0.6	0.6	0.
Associate	0.6	0.6	0.6	0.6	0.6	0.6	0.6	0.6	0.6	0.
Teaching Assistants	0.6	0.6	0.6	0.6	0.6	0.6	0.6	0.6	0.7	0.
Professional Researcher	0.	0.	0.	0.	0.	0.	0.	0.	0.	0.
Librarian										
Other										
Total Academic FTE	4.7	4.7	4.8	4.9	4.9	5.0	5.1	5.1	5.2	5.
Non-Academic FTE										
Clerical, Technical & Agric.	2.2	2.4	2.6	2.8	3.0	3.2	3.4	3.6	3.8	4.
General Assistance	1.1	1.2	1.3	1.4	1.5	1.6	1.7	1.8	1.9	2.
Other										
Total Non-Academic FTE	3.3	3.6	3.9	4.2	4.5	4.8	5.1	5.4	5.7	6.
Total Instructional & Support Staff	8.0	8.3	8.7	9.1	9.4	9.8	10.2	10.5	10.9	11.

One Program Field (Engineering) on One Campus in the PPB of a Large University

Major Program   Instruction

Program   Engineering

Program Element Lower Division

	FISCAL YEARS									
	1968	1969	1970	1971	1972	1973	1974	1975	1976	1977
Research & Development Costs										
Initial Investment Costs										
Land										
Site Studies/Master Planning/ Site Clearance										
Utilities & Site Development										
Construction & Equipment										
Classrooms	7040	7080	7120	7160	7200	7240	7280	7320	7360	7400
Class Labs	1220	1240	1260	1280	1300	1320	1340	1360	1380	1400
Research & Office	2010	2020	2030	2040	2050	2060	2070	2080	2090	2100
Other										
Total Initial Investments	10270	10340	10410	10480	10550	10620	10690	10760	10830	10900
Annual Operating Costs										
Salaries & Benefits										
Academic Personnel										
Teaching Salaries	54000	56000	58000	60000	62000	64000	66000	68000	70000	72000
Benefits	2117	2137	2157	2177	2197	2218	2238	2258	2278	2298
Research Salaries	0	0	0	0	0	0	0	0	0	0
Benefits	0	0	0	0	0	0	0	0	0	0
Other Salaries										
Benefits										
Non-Academic										
Clerical, Technical & Agric.	12720	13483	14292	15150	16059	17022	18044	19126	20274	21490
Benefits	1056	1152	1248	1344	1440	1536	1632	1728	1824	1920
Other Salaries	4240	4494	4764	5050	5353	5674	6015	6375	6758	7163
Benefits	528	576	624	672	720	768	816	864	912	960
Total Salaries	70960	73978	77056	80200	83412	86696	90058	93502	97032	100654
Total Benefits	3701	3865	4029	4193	4357	4522	4886	4850	5014	5178

In recent months increased attention has been devoted to the establishment of management information systems and use of PPB in state systems of higher education. The following example is a brief description of such an aid to statewide management which is currently in operation.[16] This procedure deals with data concerning four major aspects of any statewide system of higher education: student enrollment, staffing, physical plant, and finances.

Information inputs in the form of regular, standard reports are introduced into the system by each of the state-assisted institutions of higher education. Computerized analytical routines manipulate these inputs for two purposes, public information and resource analysis by management personnel.

For public information data are analyzed as follows: In the student enrollment area, such facts are determined as the age, sex, and marital status of the students, where they come from, what student ranks they hold, what their major academic interests are, and what enrollment loads they carry. In the physical plant area, the facts concern how many buildings, rooms, and student stations each of the institutions has, how many hours each day these facilities are actually used, and the physical condition of each building. In the staffing and finances areas, selected operating facts are collected and comparisons among institutions made within each area.

Resource analysis is concerned with how all of the facts collected within the four major areas of operation relate to each other in the actual functioning of a given college or university. Just how do the staffing, physical plant, and financial resources actually contribute to the support of instructional activities in various academic program areas and at various levels of teaching?

As is illustrated in the figure on page 1055, resource analysis involves the establishment of a series of standard academic program categories, and within each category several standard levels of instructional courses. Through a sequence of allocation procedures, the various human, physical, and financial resources of the college or university are then "charged" against the program they support. By studying the relative rates at which various teaching programs and instructional course levels utilize an institution's resources, one should be able to learn a good deal about present and future needs of existing and yet-to-be founded institutions of higher education.

Data processing for resource analysis shows, for each institution in the state system: How many FTE students by rank were enrolled at each level of each program; how many FTE faculty members by rank were required at each level of each program; how all of the space available to the entire institution was used and how much instructional space was used by each level and each program; and the expenditures by the institution which related to the instructional process. It is necessary to allocate all expenditures in some meaningful way to each unit of instruction. By using enrollment, faculty staffing, and space data one can develop indices which serve to allocate certain expenditures. For instance, expenditures for maintaining various buildings constitute part of the cost of a given unit of instruction, the expense being roughly proportional to its use of available classroom space. Consequently an index of classroom utilization is developed, allocating a fraction of plant expenditures to each unit of instruction. Similarly all other expenditures (such as those for administration, public service, etc.) are allocated to specific units of instruction.

The first step in resource analysis is to load the data banks. For four academic programs [two fields (English and Music) at two levels, lower division (freshman-sophomore) and upper division (junior-senior)], the data bank would look like the example in the figure on page 1056.

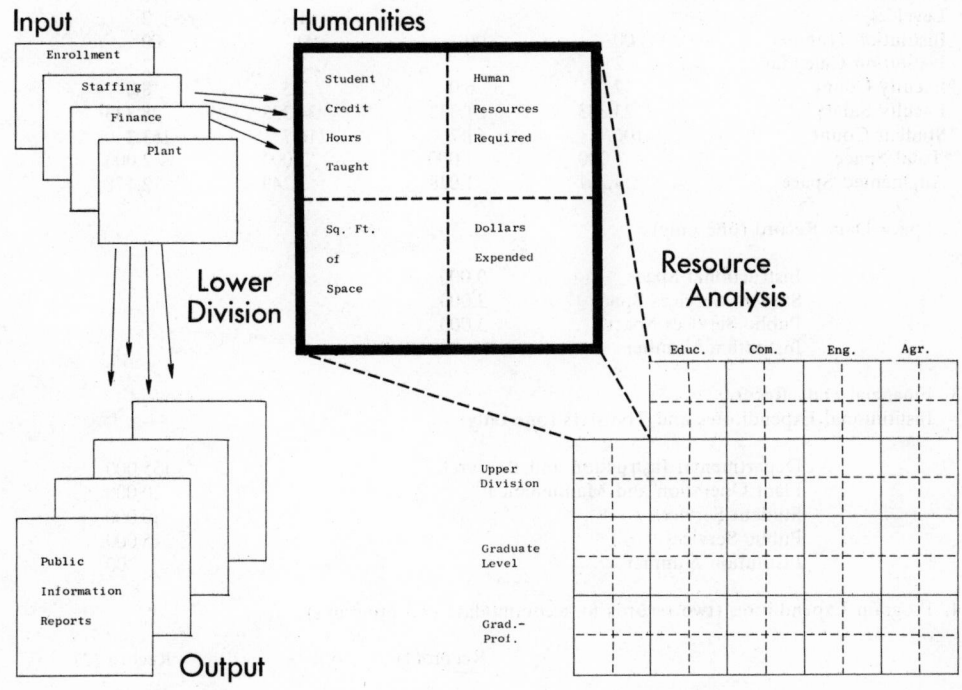

Contents of the Data Bank

1. Primary Data Bank (requires four records to accommodate two programs each at two levels)

	Record(1)	Record(2)	Record(3)	Record(4)
Program Number	14	14	10	10
Level	1	2	1	2
Institution Number	00	00	00	00
Institution Calendar	2	2	2	2
*Faculty Count	7.0	6.0	7.3	8.0
Faculty Salary	23,333	21,333	34,333	28,333
*Student Count	106.7	61.7	216.7	163.3
**Total Space	3,000	1,000	3,000	2,000
Augmented Space	3,201	1,028	3,249	2,178

2. Space Data Record (one only)

Instructional Space	9,000
Student Services Space	3,000
Public Services Space	3,000
Institution Number	00

3. Financial Data Record
   Institutional Expenditures and Transfers (one only)

Departmental Instruction and Research	155,000
Plant Operation and Maintenance	20,000
Student Services	10,000
Public Services	15,000
Institution Number	00

4. Program Expenditures (two records to accommodate two programs)

	Record(1)	Record (2)
Faculty Salaries	45,000	65,000
Other Salaries	10,000	15,000
Other Expenditures	10,000	10,000
Program Code	14	10
Institution Number	00	00

*Breakdown by rank is not shown in this example.

**Breakdown by classroom, laboratory and other space is not considered in this example.

Once information is stored in the data bank in the form in which it was summarized from institutional reports, the next step is to allocate all costs to specific units of instruction. Four indices are developed: enrollment, faculty, space, and the student services index. These indices represent the portion of total enrollment attributable to each level of each program, the portion of faculty salaries attributable to each level of each program, the portion of total instructional space used by each level of program, and, weighting graduate students one and undergraduate students two, the portion of total enrollment attributable to each level of each program. An example appears in the next figure.

Enrollment, Faculty, Space, and Student Services Indices

ENROLLMENT	STUDENTS	FRACTION
Lower Division English	106.7	.195
Upper Division English	61.7	.112
Lower Division Music	216.7	.395
Upper Division Music	163.3	.298
Total	548.4	1.000

FACULTY	SALARY	FRACTION
Lower Division English	23,333	.217
Upper Division English	21,333	.199
Lower Division Music	34,333	.320
Upper Division Music	28,333	.264
Total	107,332	1.000

SPACE	AREA	FRACTION
Lower Division English	3201	.331
Upper Division English	1028	.106
Lower Division Music	3249	.337
Upper Division Music	2178	.226
Total	9656	1.000

STUDENT SERVICES

Since no graduate students appear in this example, the index is the same as the enrollment index.

Expenditures of all sorts are then allocated to each program in proportion to the above indices. An example is given in the figure below.

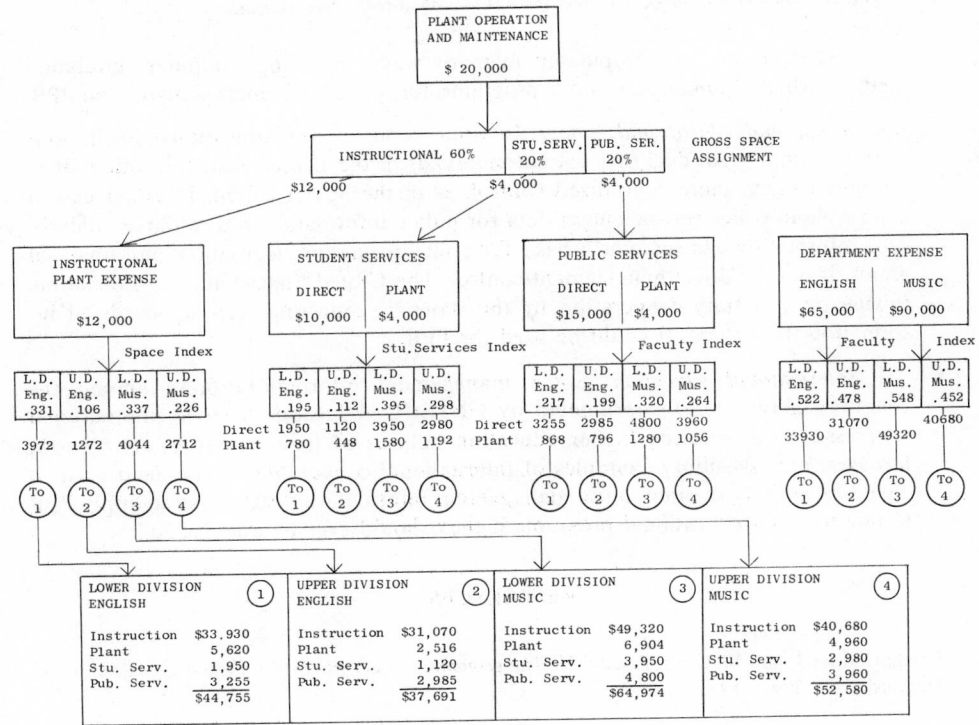

Example of Expenditure Allocation Procedure

When the allocation of expenditures is finished, the primary record in the data bank is complete (See figure below). Many reports can be developed from these data.

Example of Data in Data Bank Relevant to Four Programs

1. PRIMARY DATA BANK

	RECORD (1)	RECORD (2)	RECORD (3)	RECORD (4)
Program No.	14	14	10	10
Level	1	2	1	2
Institution	00	00	00	00
Inst. Cal.	2	2	2	2
*Faculty Count	7.0	6.0	7.3	8.0
Faculty Salary	23,333	21,333	34,333	28,333
*Student Count	106.7	61.7	216.7	163.3
**Total Space	3,000	1,000	3,000	2,000
Augmented Space	3,201	1,028	3,249	2,178
Enrollment Index	.195	.112	.395	.298
Faculty Index	.217	.199	.320	.264
Student Services Index	.195	.112	.395	.298
Space Index	.331	.106	.337	.226
Faculty Salaries	23,490	21,510	35,620	29,380
Other Salaries	5,220	4,780	8,220	6,780
Other Expenditures	5,220	4,780	5,480	4,520
Total Instruc. Cost	33,930	31,070	49,320	40,680
Public Services	3,255	2,985	4,800	3,960
Plant Operation	5,620	2,516	6,904	4,960
Student Services	1,950	1,120	3,950	2,980

Breakdown by rank is not shown in this example.

**Breakdown by classroom, laboratory, and other space is not considered in this example.*

These data can be manipulated in many ways, including computer simulation methods which examine alternative programs, for cost-effectiveness analyses and PPB.

6. *A national educational system.* In some countries the educational institutions operate with a great deal of local autonomy, as in the United States. In others they are under much more centralized control, as in the Soviet Union. In either case it is possible to collect management data for public information and resource analysis. This information can serve as a basis for policy formation, legislation, and financial grants, if not for direct management control. The United States Office of Education, relying on voluntary cooperation by the states, is collecting such standardized information from them. It could be used for PPB.

7. *International education.* Some management information flows among the countries of the world, coordinated by UNESCO. Educators meet in international congresses to discuss the higher education policies of their countries. As of now, however, only desultory examples of international cooperation in this field exist. It would be entirely feasible to use management information systems and to apply PPB to international educational programs if they should ever be established.

REFERENCES

1. Hitch, Charles J. and McKean, Roland N. *The economics of defense in the nuclear age.* Cambridge: Harvard Univ. Press, 1963, pp. 1-2.

2. The preceding four paragraphs contain quotations from Hitch, C. J. *Decision-making for defense.* Berkeley, Calif.: Univ. of Calif. Press, 1965, pp. 29-32.

3. *Ibid.,* p. 38.

4. *Ibid.,* p. 34.

5. *Ibid.,* p. 43.

6. *Ibid.,* pp. 43-44.

7. Research and Policy Committee, Committee for Economic Development. *Innovation in education: A new direction for the American school.* New York: Committee for Economic Development, July, 1968, pp. 18-19.

8. The preceding four paragraphs are based on Weathersby, G. *The development and applications of a university cost simulation model.* Berkeley, Calif.: Univ. of Calif., Graduate School of Business Administration and Office of Analytical Studies, 1967, pp. 68-69.

9. Struve, T. A. & G. J. Rath, "Planning—programming—budgeting in education." *Educational Technology,* June 15, 1966, pp. 5-6.

10. Research and Policy Committee, Committee for Economic Development. *op. cit.,* 18, pp. 60-61.

11. The preceding example of PPB for a school is based on Jungherr, J. A., *op. cit.,* pp. 134-140.

12. The preceding example of PPB for a school system is based on Rath, G. J. "PPBS is more than a budget: it's a total planning process" *Nation's Schools,* 1968, 82, No. 5, 51-60.

13. The preceding example of an automated management information system and PPB for a college is based on *College and university administrative applications,* IBM, Technical Publications Department, 1968.

14. The preceding example of an automated management information system and PPB, planned for the University of California, is based on Weathersby, G., *op. cit.*

15. Cf. also Judy, R. W. *Systems analysis for efficient resource allocation in higher education.* Institute for the Quantitative Analysis of Social and Economic Policy, University of Toronto, November, 1968.

16. Cf. Ohio Board of Regents. Uniform Information System. *Resource analysis procedures.* Columbus, 1968.

112.

The Costs of
Instructional Technology

by RICHARD E. SPEAGLE
Prof. of Finance
Drexel Institute
of Technology

Part I: An Overview

The potential of instructional technology to bring about a revolution in education can no longer be questioned, but anyone with the idea it might come cheap is in for a rude awakening. In the present state of the art, costs run from the high but affordable to the astronomical.

The general adoption of a sophisticated, multi-purpose computer configuration, and this on an introductory basis only, could easily double the annual $25 billion that the United

Table A
Cost Estimates of Major IT Media

16,000 school districts in larger populated states representing 75-80 percent of elementary and secondary school population in 1966.

MODE AND QUALITY	ANNUAL COST*
	(IN BILLIONS OF DOLLARS)
ITV	
Utility Model	$ .3
Intermediate Quality	.8
Top Quality	1.5
Computer Access	
Batch-Process	.9
Time Sharing	1.2
CAI	
Drill-and-Practice	9.0
Tutorial	24.0

*Current and amortized capital costs.

Source: C. N. Carter and M. J. Walker, Costs of Installing and Operating Instructional Television and Computer Assisted Instruction in the Public Schools, *Chicago, Ill.: Booz, Allen and Hamilton; General Learning Corporation, A Feasibility Study of a Central Computer Facility for an Educational System, Final Report, Washington, D.C.: U.S. Department of Health, Education and Welfare, Office of Education, February 1968; Academy for Educational Development.*

States spends today on the operation of public elementary and secondary schools. This does not include colleges and universities.

On the other hand, one billion dollars a year could bring the computer into every school district in the country for a limited teaching and administrative load.

In the more modest budget price range, instructional technology could be introduced into most schools as part of present programs for about a quarter of a billion dollars a year. The figures are shown in Table A. The number of options in between is legion.

Cost estimates here and now for instructional technology, which is as primitive in its development and limited in its application as the automobile was at the turn of the century, obviously do not do justice to the situation likely to exist at a more mature stage. Many factors will impinge on instructional television costs, and their collective impact is almost entirely in one direction—down. For a realistic appraisal of future costs . . .

THESE EIGHT FACTORS SHOULD BE STUDIED	BECAUSE
1. Heavy inherent overhead and fixed expenses	they are subject to economies of *scale* and of greater intensity of use.
2. Cost-saving technology	under which *smaller and cheaper* devices, like transistors and printed circuits, deliver a higher and more reliable performance as time goes on.
3. Geographic concentration of the student population	greater student *density* spells savings in transmission costs.
4. Cooperation among schools, districts, and systems	fosters the *sharing of central facilities* and the pooling of programs.
5. Machinery for evaluating the quality and effectiveness of teaching techniques and materials . . .	promotes *standardization* and multiple uses of hardware.
6. Level and type of teaching program desired . . .	the higher the demand for "quality" of instruction, the greater will be the required dollar input of software, hardware, and training.
7. Rate of learning under innovative techniques . . .	*faster learning* and fewer repeaters and drop-outs shorten the duration and therefore cost of instructional technology relative to student achievement.
8. Possibilities of replacing traditional teaching with instructional technology . . .	such *substitution* reduces demand for new faculty, and releases space.

One further observation is of vital importance: instructional technology in the sense of the most advanced media is almost entirely a matter of hardware costs. The expenses of producing and installing programs, once the media enjoy widespread adoption, are trivial on a per student basis—a dollar per year and less. Prior to such an adoption however higher research as well as development costs of software remain a serious hurdle, much like the River Jordan was in biblical time for the children of Israel. It had to be crossed before they could reach the Promised Land.

A Brief Buyer's Guide

Before pulling out his checkbook, the education buyer must ask himself three basic questions:

(1) How much does it cost?

(2) What am I getting for my money in the way of equipment, materials, and personnel?

(3) What is it going to do for me and members of my family in providing better and more effective education?

These are simple questions which have complex answers. The present Part I of this chapter as well as the more detailed Part II address themselves to the first two questions, the "price tag" and the "merchandise." The third question—about quality and effectiveness—leads to complications and is dealt with separately in a chapter on cost-benefit analysis.

The cost figures cited here are good enough for working purposes. They serve to give the reader something to go on while realizing that inflation and rapid changes in technology are making them obsolete and subject to reevaluation. Figures that give costs on a per student basis will be found in Part II below. Cost per student-hour is a term that, although familiar to economists, has not yet entered the working vocabulary of school officials. For that reason no direct use has been made of the concept in this presentation.

Part II: The Meaning of the Cost Figures

The Costs of Major Media

When people ask about the costs of IT they are not concerned with abstract definitions. They see children in a classroom using all sorts of modern equipment, from television sets to computers, while a teacher stands by monitoring the proceedings, giving advice or leading a discussion. Blackboards, chalk and inexpensive teaching aids are taken for granted by the average citizen and so they will be here.

This is not to downgrade the evident benefits of slide projectors, tape recorders, film strips and audio-visual devices in stimulating students and enriching the course content of the curriculum. Whatever the difficulties of these artifacts of IT they lie not in their cost of acquisition—it is modest—but in making full use of their potentialities.

In order to present the multi-faceted evidence about IT costs briefly and intelligibly, the analyst is forced to simplify. One way is to consider the new media serially, one at a time, and to make the question of combining or mixing them to a separate point.

The most exciting and talked-about possibilities of IT center around television and computers. Table B illustrates the cost structure of these media at several levels of "quality"—measured by the amount of care and elaboration that go into their application to the school system. At the bottom of the price range, the lowest-cost medium one could get away with and still transform the classroom situation in a technologically radical fashion is represented by instructional television (ITV); the most expensive plan calls for the full-fledged installation of a system approaching computer-managed instruction (CMI). These and intermediate options of ITV and CMI technologies are illustrated in Table B below.

There is still another alternative, bracketed in the medium-cost range and moderate in its technical demands, while of great possible importance to the development of an educational strategy towards IT. It is a type of installation that might be called a "computer access system." One of its virtues lies in getting the computer on to the school grounds while harnessing it to administrative tasks and, at the same time and at an increasing rate, to problem-solving by students.

Table B
Estimated Annual Costs of Major Instructional Technologies

MODE AND QUALITY	ANNUAL COSTS			
	PER 100,000 STUDENTS			
	HARDWARE	SOFTWARE	OTHER	TOTAL
	(IN MILLIONS OF DOLLARS)			
ITV				
Utility Model*	$ .8	b/	----	$ .8
Intermediate Quality*	.8	1.6	----	2.4
Top Quality*	2.2	2.4	----	4.6
Computer Access				
Batch Process	2.2	n.a.	.7a/	2.9
Time Sharing	2.9	n.a.	.9a/	3.8
CAI				
Drill-and-Practice*	20.0	.8	6.4	27.2
Tutorial*	50.0	4.6	17.2	71.8

n.a. = not applicable.
a/ Estimated at 30 percent of hardware.
b/ Less than $100,000.

Source: *C. N. Carter and M. J. Walker,* Costs of Installing and Operating Instructional Television and Computer Assisted Instruction in Public Schools, *Chicago: Booz, Allen and Hamilton, 1968. General Learning Corporation,* A Feasibility Study of a Central Computer Facility for an Educational System, Final Report, *Washington, D.C.: U.S. Department of Health, Education and Welfare, Office of Education, February, 1968. Academy for Educational Development.*

Cost Estimates through Model Building

Estimates of the cost of instructional technology should come with imaginary labels saying "Caution! Use at your own risk!" so as not to inspire unwarranted confidence in their precision. Cost projections in the complex education area depend on critical assumptions that must be identified and in a practical case changed to fit actual necessities.

In particular, the starred programs in Table B constitute a "family" of estimates derived from an example of typical model-building procedures. All assume the addition of ITV or CAI techniques to enrich conventional classroom teaching. Few if any elements of substitution or replacement of existing modes of instruction are contemplated, a premise of the model designers that will be subject to examination below.

Briefly, the postulated environment in which variations of the ITV and CAI modes are costed out has the following characteristics:

1. a school district with 100,000 students in grades 1 through 12;

2. 152 schools, half elementary and half secondary, containing respectively 720 students, 30 per classroom, and 600 students, 25 per classroom.

3. a typical six-hour instructional day in a 150 day school year;

4. one hour, or 16 percent, of each school-day taken up by *either* ITV or CAI.

Buyer's Options in the ITV Model

Investment in ITV divides into two major parts, software or live and film programs, and hardware or equipment. Programming labor and materials are estimated to run from $50 per hour for a simple televised lecture to $6,000 for an hourly presentation conducted by a TV professional with visual aids and props. Ultra-high quality spectaculars, say, of a reenactment of the Battle of Gettysburg, would carry a budget of perhaps $500,000 per hour of running time, but commercial video-tape copies might be rented at about $50. In all cases, the use of staff teachers avoids incurring additional personnel costs.

Hardware for this school-system module consists mainly of a central studio and transmitter plus peripheral receiving gear, inclusive of two 27″ black-and-white TV sets per classroom. Costs start at $600,000 annually for four-channel, closed circuit microwave—a standard component of all versions of the proposal—and run up to $2.2 million for an airborne transmission system. Estimates assume ten-year lives, and maintenance and power costs equal 11 percent of initial equipment expense.

The total annual outlay in the modular system depends on the particular software-hardware selection. Costs range from $800,000 for the simplest pattern, closed circuit and ordinary televised lessons, up to $4.6 million for airborne programs of professional caliber.

Buyer's Options in the CAI Model

Unlike ITV, the major CAI cost categories are three: instructional material, equipment, and a cadre of computer technicians. As to the first, the more comprehensive and ambitious the teaching approach taken, the more intricate becomes program design and installation.

Least expensive is drill-and-practice material, as used in mathematics or reading courses, where in-house production runs to about $5,000 per program-hour and rental of similar material from a commercial source to about $35. The more demanding tutorial mode of CAI raises the cost figures to $30,000 and $210 respectively.

Estimating the life of software at three years, the model specifies not more than one-third of annual programs content to be new, distributed in a ratio of 3:1 between rented and campus-produced courses. For the 100,000 student universe, the annual bill for software comes to $800,000 for the drill and $4.6 million for the tutorial approach.

Basic CAI hardware consists of a central data processing and storage facility (Central Processing Unit or CPU) linked with a set of student terminals which may range from simple typewriter-like devices to elaborate consoles with cathode ray tubes (CRT), light pens, keyboards, image projectors and audio gear.

A drill-and-practice hardware configuration would involve an annual rental of $2,400 per terminal, including the pro-rated cost of a CPU capable of handling up to 200 units. With 16,700 terminals needed to serve 100,000 students, total equipment costs would run to $40 million, although mass production of terminals might halve this figure to $20 million.

A tutorial mode of CAI runs the bill up sharply, based on the price tags of standard equipment now available. Here, each CPU accommodates no more than 32 student stations which boosts the pro-rate charge and the total cost per terminal to $6,000 a piece. Again, volume production might slash the $100 million outlay to an annual $50 million per system.

CAI occasions a third type of expense that puts an override of perhaps 30 percent on top of hardware costs—the expense of operating and administrative personnel, supplies, utilities, and the lease of telephone-computer transmission lines. Additional estimated disbursements amount to $6 million for the drill mode and $17 million annually for the tutorial mode. Still omitted are training costs and space costs, surely not negligible, but maintenance costs would be absorbed by the lessor of the equipment.

The Computer Access System

A different assignment for the computer, reflected in sharply lower costs, is represented by a "computer access system." It is not a pure teaching approach because administrative uses of computer facilities are expected to carry a large part of the expense burden. The design of a proposal for such a system to HEW was modular and hence turned out to be comparable with the rest of the instructional technology models presented here. Specifications called for:

1. a system of fifty educational institutions, within a 50 mile radius, having a total enrollment of 100,000 students;

2. grades from 9 to 16, but excluding major universities offering post-graduate work;

3. users of services including:

   a. students of computer programming;

   b. students and faculty performing teaching and research calculations;

   c. administrative personnel processing operating data.

The computer system design focused on two technical options: a time-sharing mode, which affords simultaneous access to multiple users; and batch-processing, which assigns multiple access according to a prearranged time schedule. The capability specifications for the two techniques were derived from a survey of actual rates of usage in selected currently operative computer installations around the country.

Because of the still scant use of digital computers in schools, that approach gave the projections a distinctly upward bias in estimating expenses. Annual hardware costs, based on production models and a conservative 40 month life, came to $2.2 million for the batch-process and $2.9 million for the time-sharing technique. Although personnel, utility, and other expenses were not specified, one may estimate them at roughly 30 percent of hardware costs. Software expenses, however, also left out of the picture, are probably trivial considering the simple nature of the tasks to be performed and the availability of standard programs from commercial sources.

It is not straying too far from the mark then to estimate the total annual costs per standard 100,000-student module at $3 million for a batch-processing and $4 million for a time-sharing installation. Transferred to the wider canvass of 16,000 public school systems, the nation-wide bill for adopting a "no-frills" computer access system, at the present state of the arts, would come to $900 million and $1.2 billion respectively.

Cost Reduction

Advanced versions of IT, leaving aside the issues of effectiveness and implied institutional change, face a formidable economic obstacle: they are too expensive in relation to what Americans are accustomed to pay for education. Any factor which can reduce costs to "realistic" proportions is bound to raise IT's competitive edge vis-a-vis traditional teaching methods, and make it financially more attractive to prospective backers. The same goes, to a lesser degree, for sophisticated "far-out" IT proposals.

As shown earlier in tabular form, eight key considerations are critical for the estimating procedures of IT costs, no matter what the underlying hypothetical model. Appropriate changes in these key variables—jointly if possible!—would do much to reduce the money hurdle. The vast potential impact in terms of lower future costs of IT makes a close inspection of these aspects well worth the trouble. What, in other words, must be done to make such potential savings a reality?

The Scale of Operations

Few principles are more fundamental to the practical application of instructional technology than the economics of overhead costs. When any cost is fixed for a given scale of operations—industrial, education, or whatever—a rise in the level of activity causes a reduction in the cost per unit. The fixed cost, a *constant*, becomes the enumerator of a fraction in which the denominator, units of output, is permitted to *expand*. In accounting language, overhead costs are being spread by the rise in volume, resulting in "economies of scale" that allow lowering the price for the good—or instructional technology service!

Five specific types of economies are achievable:

At the Factory level, those due to

1 mass production of equipment

2 a less than proportionate rise in the CPU's cost per unit of capacity (measured, say, in statements per second) as the size of equipment is increased.

3 the design of special-purpose educational computers.

At the school level, when

4 the number of students or tasks per installation expands.

5 the duration of equipment use is lengthened.

While interrelated, these factors lend themselves to separate discussion.

Quantity production of television sets, video tape, and audio tape units, to name only a few standard ITV components, is bound to reduce present price tags. The same holds true for computers and especially for student terminals in the various CAI modes. One informant, as noted earlier, projects a 50 per cent cut in cost, from $2,400 to $1,200 per terminal, once industry went into large-scale production of the drill configuration.

Larger models of computers require a larger initial investment or total annual lease cost, but they come cheaper in terms of unit of capacity—whether measured by data storage, output of statements per second, or student terminals serviced. The last-mentioned aspect is shown in Table C.

Table C
Size and Cost of Computer Installation:
Tutorial Mode of CAI

SIZE AND TYPE OF CPU	ANNUAL RENTAL	NUMBER OF TERMINALS	ANNUAL RENTAL PER TERMINAL
"Small"—IBM 1500	$180,000	32	$5,550
"Large"—PDP-10	650,000	448	1,450

Source: *F. F. Kopstein and F. J. Seidel, "Computer-Administered Instruction Versus Traditionally Administered Instruction: Economics,"* AV Communications Review, *Vol. 16, No. 2, Summer 1968, pp. 155-8.*

In ITV, cost per student may be expected to be cut similarly when more powerful transmitters—airborne or satellite—and larger receiving equipment are employed.

An increase in the number of students in the audience, ITV plainly demonstrates, need not occasion anything like a proportionate increase in unit costs. While the ratio of viewers per TV-set, or even per classroom screen, may be subject to a ceiling, so that more viewers means more purchases of sets, the cost of airborne equipment and communication satellites is fixed and largely independent of the size of the audience. The more viewers, the lower the potential "entrance fee."

In CAI, potential cost reductions from accommodating more students and hence putting in more student terminals, are considerable up to the maximum of CPU capacity. However economies of scale, once each CPU carries a full load, are less dramatic as the number of installations multiplies. At that point, it is the fixed software overhead that suggests the widest possible student participation in order to lower unit costs, as shown in Table D.

Mention should be made of an intriguing possibility, the "pairing" of two students to work simultaneously at one terminal, which promises virtually to halve per-student cost. Experiments point to little if any loss in learning efficiency—the use of the "buddy system" might even heighten learning motivation!

Table D
Size of Student Body and Instructional Television
Cost Per Student

NUMBER OF STUDENTS IN SYSTEM	ITV		CAI			
	MEDIUM QUALITY[a]		DRILL MODE		TUTORIAL MODE	
	HOURLY	ANNUAL[b]	HOURLY	ANNUAL[b]	HOURLY	ANNUAL[b]
10,000	$1.67	$250	$2.27	$340	$7.53	$1,130
100,000	.21	30	1.81	272	4.79	718
500,000	.08	12	1.77	265	4.27	640

[a]Based on CCTV and $6,000 per hour programs.
[b]Assumes 150 student hours of exposure per school year.

Source: *C. N. Carter and M. J. Walker,* Costs of Installing and Operating ITV and CAI in Public Schools. *Chicago: Booz, Allen and Hamilton, 1968.*

An obvious case of instructional cost reduction follows an expansion of the number and types of tasks assigned to one computer installation—say, accounting, record-keeping and research calculations. The situation is almost equivalent to a lengthening of the time period of computer use, discussed below.

Unused capabilities of computers engineered for industrial purposes but applied to instruction mean high costs. For example, the IBM 1500 system was designed for such tasks as process control of cracking towers in petroleum refineries and consequently has many expensive features not needed in elementary or secondary schools. Once an educational market of sufficient width is created it becomes feasible to design special purpose computers for education that will have lower price tags because of more limited data processing features.

Duration of equipment use becomes a factor wherever IT confronts substantial fixed costs. A longer use of the equipment during the day or over the calendar year brings obvious economies. In ITV, such restrictive initial assumptions as one hour's use per six-hour instructional day over a 150-day school year must be relaxed once the televised lesson is more widely accepted.

Similarly in CAI, running the computer round-the-clock means significant savings per student-hour. One could even visualize night shifts for students, now commonplace for scientific researchers working on expensive devices like the cyclotron. However, fairly continuous utilization of the computer could accrue simply from batch-processing administrative data during off-hours and at night—like posting accounting data and updating student records. Research problems of faculty and graduate students also could be scheduled to coincide with slack time on the input terminals. Such flexibility would not come cost-free because additional expenses are incurred in "marrying" the time-sharing and batch-processing modes within the same computer complex.

Cost-Saving Technology

The productivity of modern technology does not only rest on turning out more volume at a lower cost per piece by making the machine bigger. It rests increasingly on getting the same unit cost effect by making devices smaller and cheaper. The post-war history of the digital computer, a keystone of advanced IT, provides perhaps the most telling example, as shown in Table E.

Table E
Computer Progress:
Reduction in Cost of Computation

Costs are estimates based on reasonable assumptions
about computer configurations and use

EQUIPMENT	TECHNICAL INNOVATION INVOLVED	TIME TO DO ONE MULTI-PLICATION	COST OF MACHINE PER HOUR	COST OF 125 MILLION MULTIPLI-CATIONS
Desk Calculator	Mechanical	10 secs.	$ 0.20	$2,150,000
Harvard Mark I	Electro-mechanical	1 sec.	12.50	850,000
	Electronic	10 ms.	25.00	12,800
UNIVAC 1103 (type C)	Magnetic Core	500 mu's.[a]	70.00	1,420
Stretch (IBM 7030) (type A)	Parallel Circuits	2.5 mu's.[a]	320.00	29
IBM 360 (model 85)	Monolythic Buffer Storage	5.0 nsec[b]	550.00	5
CEC 7600	Remote Peripheral Process Units	1.4 nsec[b]	972.00	5

[a] mu = microseconds or one millionth of a second.
[b] nsec = nanoseconds or one billionth of a second.

Source: *President's Science Advisory Committee,* Computers in Higher Education, *Washington, D.C., 1967, p. 60;* Academy for Educational Development.

Cost Effects of Student Density

The concentration of students in a given geographic area has noticeable cost effects because under either ITV or CAI the leasing of the requisite communication cables and the transmission of signals is a function of distance. As Table F illustrates for the ITV mode, sparsely populated areas and rural sections of the country involve a considerable larger cost burden than, say, the Boston-Washington corridor. To the extent that the shift of population to the larger metropolitan areas will continue and smaller schools consolidate, transmission costs may well drift downward.

Table F
Population Density and Unit Cost of ITV

| | ITV COSTS PER STUDENT | |
	HOURLY	ANNUAL
Montana	$ .35	$52
Mid-Atlantic States		
(N.Y., N.J., Pa.)	.06	9
	INSTRUCTIONAL MATERIAL COSTS PER STUDENT [a]	
National Average	$ .02	$ 3

[a] Includes books and supplies.

Source: *C. N. Carter and M. J. Walker,* Costs of Installing and Operating Instructional Television and Computer Assisted Instruction in the Public Schools, *Chicago, Ill.: Booz, Allen and Hamilton; Academy for Educational Development.*

Cooperation Among Schools

Advances in computer capabilities have outstripped individual user requirements and are likely to keep on doing so in the future. Banking and industry have drawn the logical conclusion from this development by entering into mutual time-sharing arrangements to spread the overhead. There is no reason why the same efficient pattern might not be suitable in the schools. All that is needed is a spirit of cooperation and flexibility of follow the promptings of economic sense, whether this leads to a crossing of political boundaries or to a bridging of institutional differences in order to find appropriate partners for computer services.

Standardization

There is not only safety but economy in numbers through the widest possible participation of schools in a common pool of audio, television, and computer materials. The more schools can agree on the validity of a given program, as they now informally agree on the best-sellers on text book publishers' lists, the cheaper will be student costs.

But there is a difference. In the still underdeveloped IT area, agreement on competing teaching devices and materials presupposes a common ground on educational goals and techniques. This does not yet exist and awaits progress in the R and D of learning theory and teaching effectiveness. Here is one instance more, in the economics of overhead costs, where R and D turns out to be a critical factor in the adoption of advanced IT.

Eventually, some testing association may be created to evaluate new materials, and to "accredit" them with its stamp of approval. This does not require monolithic uniformity. The tremendous breadth of the education market, in the United States alone, would permit "many flowers to grow" in the program field at the same time that sufficient adoptions for a given mode could guarantee a tolerable cost burden.

Importance of Teaching Mode

Both the level and quality of instruction have a cost impact. For ITV as well as for CAI, the higher the quality specified, the greater the expense. This follows from three inputs:

1. more elaborate software.

2. more sophisticated hardware.

3. the need for more highly trained professionals to run the system.

In ITV, the cost difference between utility and high quality software is dramatic. However it tends to disappear when the student audience becomes very large—at that point the two unit cost curves converge at a very low level. Hardware costs similarly are sensitive to program quality—one need only note the difference between the price of color as against black-and-white television equipment and production. Whether the price gap will disappear is still questionable.

For CAI, a high-quality, audiovisual tutorial mode is sharply more capital-intensive, both in hardware and in the associated program pool, than is mere drill-and-practice. The resulting cost differential between these two modes is likely to persist, but advances in computer design, languages, and programming techniques are bound to lower costs at all levels of sophistication.

The Rate of Learning

The speed at which a student absorbs instructional material may turn out to be the most significant cost consideration of all. One management consultant asserts that the learning rate is the most important factor, on the basis of a carefully constructed accounting model.

Up to now, costs have been analyzed as if the learning achievement of the U.S. school population were a constant, distributed over a given time-span of faithful classroom attendance. This assumption puts ITV and CAI in the context of whether they might be able to match traditional levels of teaching performance at a comparable cost.

Once that hidden limitation is brought to light and relaxed, the way is open to think about a possible acceleration of "educational production"—the rate at which students acquire the skills and knowledge, at specified achievement levels, to qualify for a standard diploma or degree, society's measure of scholastic accomplishment. Should the average student aided by IT be able to master a given curriculum at, say, only three-quarters of the time imposed on him now by a fairly rigid schedule, his cost of education would automatically drop by a similar proportion.

A speeding up of the "learning process" could spell tremendous potential savings in public outlays and in human self-investment, and probably constitutes the greatest challenge facing instructional technology today. There is no good reason why some of these savings in certain situations could not be passed on to the student based on the speed at which he attained a given level of achievement, to reward him and spur him on to greater effort. Of course, the conventional tuition formula would have to be transformed into a variable dependent on the duration of school attendance.

Instructional Technology: Addition or Substitution?

Another and highly important part of the package of assumptions by which the models arrived at their respective cost figures was that ITV and CAI would simply be additions to the arsenal of educational tools, without disturbing existing patterns of student-teacher and student-administrator ratios. Such a premise may be prudent for making reasonable estimates in a practical world of established institutions, but it cannot be maintained in talking about the future of education and the longer-range leverage that instructional technology promises in the future.

The thrust of technology in the Western World is for machine inputs to be substituted for the human factor in the production process—whether of goods or services. That does not mean that teachers will be out of work any more than other people as long as national policies aim at full employment—it merely means that teachers will do new things and perform their special roles differently than they did before.

While model-builders generally have shied away from discussing substitution effects, some costing techniques that take account of them have been worked up. It is too early, however, to appraise these accounting techniques except in their theoretical aspects. Further discussion will be found under the heading of cost-benefit and systems analysis.

Cost of Improving Availability of Conventional Media

The traditional media have not been standing still, resigned to being displaced by more advanced teaching instruments. Organized and collected in a modern "media center," books, magazines, maps, film strips, slides, films, and recordings are clamoring for additional funds which a recent proposal by ALA and NEA targets at 6 percent of school operating costs. The price tag of this proposal nationwide for public elementary and secondary schools would come to $1.6 billion annually or about half a billion dollars more than is now being spent on instructional materials (Table G).

A Look at Annual Costs Per Student

One dimension of costs that needs emphasis because of its paramount practical interest to school administrators is the expense per student of the various innovative media. Such figures form the starting point for them in computing the costs per school on their home grounds.

This focus has additional advantages here because it allows the inclusion of a wider range of data, some not previously considered. It further illustrates an important proposition: *the significant costs are those of hardware,* because the costs of programmed materials shrink to insignificance once a new medium spreads across the nation.

Table G
Cost of Upgrading Traditional Instruction Media to ALA-NEA Standards
Public elementary and secondary schools

EXPENDITURES FOR INSTRUCTIONAL MATERIALS (1966 BASIS)	AMOUNTS (MILLIONS OF DOLLARS)
(1) Free textbooks	$221
(2) School library books	117
(3) Supplies and other	541
(4) Total	$879
(1968 basis)	
(5) ALA-NEA Target for "media centers"[1]	$1,596
(6) Total in (4) adjusted[2]	1,080
(7) Required additional cost to meet ALA-NEA Target	$516

[1] 6 percent of current operating expenditures of $26.6 billion.
[2] Raised by 23 percent, the rate of increase in current operating expenditures 1965-6 to projected 1968-9.

Source: *ALA-NEA Report (Draft)*, Standards for School Media Programs, *Washington, D.C.: 1968; U.S. Department of Health, Education and Welfare, Office of Education*, Projections of Educational Statistics to 1976-77, *p. 78; U.S. Department of Health, Education and Welfare, Office of Education*, Education in the Seventies, *Washington, D.C.: May, 1968, p. 28.*

Finally, it serves to put these costs side by side with average current expenditures per student today. If widely accepted, a low cost ITV mode could be installed for an extra 1 percent of current student outlays, as shown by Tables H and I below. The lowest cost CAI configuration now on the horizon would raise average current annual student costs in public schools by 13 percent and those in institutions of higher learning by 6 percent.

For hardware, what is new in Table H is the consideration of powerful computing equipment that may well lend itself to future educational use. If so, it promises to slice the hardware and eventually the total cost of a sophisticated tutorial CAI system by as much as three-quarters.

Confidence in this added group of cost projections is heightened by the fact that data on a tutorial IBM 1500 system, when suitably adjusted, closely match a second independent estimate for the same configuration.

The adjustment of all data to similar assumptions is of course crucial. One such assumption is the use of each television set and of each terminal by a typical student one hour a day, five days a week, for an annual 150 hours of exposure to the respective medium. For a six hour instructional day this works out to 900 hours of active used of the average TV set or terminal per year. Stepping up intensity of use by a second shift of students and adding some use on Saturday would cut the costs shown by more than one-half across the board.

Table H
Annual Hardware and Operations Costs of ITV and CAI Per Student
Each terminal shared by six students for a total use of 900 hours per year

SYSTEM AND INVESTIGATOR				ANNUAL SYSTEM COST PER STUDENT
ITV				Total
Booz, Allen & Hamilton				
Closed Circuit TV				$ 8
Airborne System				22
CAI	TERMINALS[a]	HARDWARE	OPERATIONS	TOTAL
Booz, Allen & Hamilton				
Drill-and-practice	200	$200	$ 64	$264
Tutorial	32	480	172	652
HumRRO[b]				
IBM 1500	32	480	172e	652e
PDP-10 (Teletype)	448	60	18e	78e
PDP-10 (CRT)	448	115	35e	150e

e Estimates based on 30 per cent of hardware costs.
[a] Per Central Processing Unit.
[b] Figures adjusted to reflect potential 50 per cent saving due to mass production for comparability with Booz, Allen data.

Source: *C. N. Carter* and *M. J. Walker*, Costs of Installing and Operating Instructional Television and Computer Assisted Instruction in Public Schools, *Chicago: Booz, Allen and Hamilton, 1968; F. F. Kopstein and F. J. Seidel,* "Computer-Administered Instruction Versus Traditionally Administered Instruction: Economics," AV Communications Review, *Vol. 16, No. 2, Summer 1968, pp. 153-9; Academy for Educational Development.*

Operating expenses are of special importance for computer systems but the degree varies according to the investigator. In one case, such costs were estimated at no more than 4 percent of hardware while in another case as much as 30 percent was estimated to be the true expense ratio. The difference seems to lie in the inclusiveness of this expense category as well as in the status assumed for the operation. The leasing of telephone lines to link remote terminals to central computers alone runs to 30 percent of equipment costs.

In the case of the low estimate the only operating cost mentioned was operator pay whereas the other study cited personnel, utilities, training, consultants and other related expense items. Furthermore, the low estimate was made on the basis of a going computer operation whereas the high estimate reflected actual school experience in what amounts to CAI experiments.

It would be wise to conclude that operating costs will start in the 30 percent-of-hardware range, and that only with the gain of operating experience would schools find costs descending along the so-called learning curve.

Software for CAI includes the outlays of instructing the computer in what to do and those of designing appropriate course materials. The programming costs run from $250 per student annually on the IBM 1500, if distributed over ten CAI installations, to about $18 for the PDP-10, since one system of the former can accommodate only 192 as against 2,688 students for the latter. Each stepwise addition of ten more installations would successively reduce these costs by one half.

Expanding the student body exposed to CAI to 100,000, the figure used in the original module, would bring computer programming costs, regardless of hardware used, down to only $0.48 annually per student. Further possible savings, as acceptance of CAI spreads, are easily extrapolated since costs drop proportionally with every rise in the number of students.

Instruction materials for CAI cost $29 per student annually if spread over a single IBM 1500 installation, and $2 annually for a PDP-10 configuration. Expanding the student population to 100,000 would distribute the investment in course materials over a far larger number of users and reduce costs per student to as little as $0.06 a year.

A second set of estimates of programming costs is far less optimistic but the eventual outcome is the same. Here the annual per-student cost of programmed materials would be $0.77 for drill-and-practice and as much as $4.60 for the tutorial mode. Since a further expansion of the student body would again reduce annual costs proportionally, it would not take long before instruction material expenses would become quite insignificant.

What is true for relatively expensive CAI course materials holds even more true for films and live presentations in ITV. No formal discussion of this point is needed since the mathematics of costs work in the same direction.

In sum, the analyst of the economics of the new media is back with hardware and operating costs. These may be compared with average annual current costs per student in the conventional classrooms and laboratories to evaluate their relative magnitude.

The $8 to $22 range of annual ITV hardware costs per student seem small indeed if it can be proven that the medium can "deliver" an at least proportionately higher rate of learning achievement.

It is also apparent that a $78 annual cost per student for a PDP-10 teletypewriter installation is not an outlandish figure when put next to the corresponding current outlay per student in the nation's schools today (Table I). The IBM 1500 system, by contrast, with a price tag of $652 a year per student, seems prohibitive.

The cost figures in the table further make clear that the logical entry path of the hardware-intensive media into the educational system is through colleges and universities where they will be cost-competitive much sooner than in public schools. Strategists planning to introduce instructional technology into the educational establishment would be well advised to give this factor their closest attention.

Table I
Projected Current Expenditures Per Student in the U.S.: 1968

ITEM	PUBLIC SCHOOLS K-12	HIGHER EDUCATION[1]
Fall enrollment	44.7 million	7.4 million
Current expenditures	$26.6 billion	$9.4 billion
Average current expenditure	$593	$1,270

[1]*Total resident and extension degree-credit and non-degree-credit institutions.*

Source: Projection of Educational Statistics to 1976-77 (1967 Edition), Washington, D.C.: U.S. Department of Health, Education and Welfare, Office of Education, 1968, pp. 9, 11, 77-78.

113.

Cost-Benefits:
A Buyers Guide
For Instructional Technology

by RICHARD E. SPEAGLE
Prof. of Finance
Drexel Institute
of Technology

Urgency of Efficiency Studies

Today's crisis in education, like that in medicine and other social services but greater in severity, is brought on very largely by production problems. If agriculture had as little expertise in how to produce and process its major crops as the educational establishment has with respect to teaching and learning, half the world would be starving.

But schools are different from farms. Any farmer who cannot raise grain or cattle economically will go broke. People would refuse to buy his substandard produce when he brought it to market.

The young student does not have that choice. His local school enjoys close to a monopoly on education. Moreover, bolstered by direct taxing powers, the school need not go bankrupt, no matter how inefficient. It can shift the spectre of bankruptcy to the hapless parent by assessing him to the hilt. No wonder taxpayers revolt.

To urge educators to apply businesslike methods is not advocating regimentation and the assembly line. The call is for a modern managerial approach to the school's basic production activity, the teaching-learning transaction. Whether mass lectures or individual tutorials are the indicated mode of instruction cannot be decided until one has analyzed, the way a successful manufacturer analyzes, the effectiveness and cost of each alternative.

Some visionaries dream about the advent of new technologies in education without being aware of the path by which technology, step by step, has conquered and continues to conquer other fields of Western culture. These steps are scientific and economic. Scientifically, technology has been the victor by virtue of a clear, research-based showing than it could perform old tasks better, and tackle new ones never before within the reach of man. Economically, technology has convinced the doubters by giving hard-headed, dollars-and-cents proof of its greater productivity, making use of increasingly sophisticated systems analysis, operations research, and cost-benefit techniques. To believe that technology can force its way into the school without a similar comprehensive effort is to close one's eyes to the evidence.

The sad truth is that managerial information and methods do not yet exist in education except in minute or experimental quantities. Education has been miserly in its research and development expenditures and, unlike health or medicine, has budgeted funds for R&D with an eyedropper. That a multibillion dollar industry like education should be lacking the fundamental data to conduct its affairs in an economical, cost-effective fashion is nothing less than an outrage and an underlying reason for campus rebellion.

This chapter sets out to do the following:

I. Explain the common sense meaning of cost-benefit (c-b) studies, advocated with increasing frequency as a powerful remedy for education's ills.

II. Outline the difficulties that exist in transferring the c-b techniques of business and defense to education.

III. Review specific pioneering c-b studies, particularly those aimed at evaluating new instructional media.

Before proceeding, it may be well to state the overall conclusion: meaningful c-b analysis in the most important areas of education is not feasible until a scientific data base on educational processes has been established. What can be done now are comparative cost studies, but they omit one-half of the equation, the benefit or output side. These benefits, in systems language, cover the primary mission of an educational enterprise: to improve the accuracy, speed and completeness of information flows to its student clientele for translation into learning.

I. Meaning of the Term Cost-Benefit

"Getting the most learning for the least money" is the way some pragmatists frame the basic problem of education in a world of scarce resources—a brief imperative that succinctly states what c-b analysis is trying to accomplish. On a simpler but familiar plane, a bargain-hunting housewife shopping in a supermarket, who reads the fine print on every box and compares the contents with the price, is a rudimentary type of c-b analyst.

Educators by contrast often herald some bright new idea and enthusiastically urge its universal adoption, without being able to measure the benefits or saying much about additional costs. An illustration is a scheme used in the Army, called "Instructional System Development Steps." It lists six stages in the design of courses such as Mechanical Principles, Electric Theory, or Applied Aerodynamics:

1. Collect job data and analyse

2. State training objectives

3. Design: content, method, media

4. Construct course

5. Field test (includes evaluation)

6. Implement

The first five steps actually comprise a feasibility study. They tell whether the proposed course can be taught effectively in the desired fashion, for instance through programmed instruction. From step five to step six however there is a jump—from "can do" to "let's do it"—without any specific analysis of costs. Military educators sometimes share a shortcoming with civilian school administrators, and overlook monetary constraints.

Some academicians draw a line between cost-*benefit* and cost-*effectiveness* analysis but this distinction is readily disposed of here. Benefit is the wider concept. It includes effectiveness, which may be measured concretely in dollars, bushels, or valid test scores. But, in addition, benefit also comprises aspects like enjoyment or recreation, deeply felt but defiant of precise quantification.

Since schooling aims at such intangible outcomes as art appreciation and civic consciousness, as well as at such "bread and butter" objectives as job training, the benefit terminology seems more appropriate. One may still talk freely and interchangeably about effectiveness whenever the discussion gets around to the "hard," measurable kinds of output.

Efficiency, despite its similar sound, is another concept: it is the relation between output and resource input. A given cost-benefit ratio is a practical measure of efficiency.

If indeed a semester of learning algebra were comparable to a box of cereal, and a course of English composition were as uncomplicated a product as a rib roast, c-b decisions in a school district would be a "breeze." Administrators would quickly reach for the instructional "package" promising, in combination, the largest quantity and the best quality per unit price. Even this would not relieve them, first, of having to define "quality" and, second, of balancing—in the jargon, "trading-off"—quality against quantity of instruction when the school budget was tight.

To add to the complexity, the school purchases not a standard product but a bundle of services, with multiple objectives in mind. The same complexity arises when a new health program is put into effect or when NASA tries to make a rational choice among multiple ways and practical means of putting a man on the moon.

C-b analysis as applied to productive processes is a feat of a far higher order of magnitude than is "comparison-shopping" at the meat counter, analogous in objectives though the two may be. To cope with this step-up in analytic difficulty resort has been had to systems theory and analysis, discussed in a separate chapter. Among the closely related operations research tools, formalized c-b analysis has proved to be one of the most prominent and useful.

The present discussion will concentrate on c-b analysis applied to the instructional phase of education, with particular emphasis on the evaluation of the new teaching media. However, the same general c-b techniques are perfectly adaptable to school administration and operating decisions where they are a lot simpler to apply.

Indeed the rationale of c-b analysis is most plausibly explained in a business setting. The following four central steps are typically involved in "cost-benefitting" a business project, such as opening a new branch office:

a. Defining the objectives, with profit expectations occupying a prominent place.

b. Costing out various alternatives, referring to size and type of store, location, market served, staffing, pattern of projected growth, and the like.

c. Determining the benefits of each alternative "bundle of options" analyzed in (b).

d. Relating the *benefits* of (c) to the *costs* of (b), and finally choosing the most efficient alternative—that with the highest ratio of benefits to cost.

This skeleton outline looks like a straight-forward business proposition of calculating the rate of return on a prospective investment. Actually it is still a rather simplistic version, such as one uses to initiate college undergraduates in the c-b approach. In real life, numerous important side conditions and constraints are at work, derivable from systems thinking, which color the businessman's branch decision:

Are there nonmonetary and indirect benefits, like larger market shares, personal prestige for owners and management, justification for higher staff salaries, a better image in the public mind?

Is executive and skilled manpower available for an expanded business?

Can funds be obtained on the terms desired?

How will competitors react and what will be their counter-moves?

Will there be new problems in organization, internal communication, warehousing and transportation?

Will the promise of growth motivate existing personnel and attract new employees of high caliber?

II. Cost-Benefit Analysis in Education

C-b based decisions obviously cannot be ground out mechanically by formula. Most factors moreover are not predictable with certainty, but must be weighed according to some estimated probabilities. Educators face all these hurdles of business and "then some," summarized under the previous four standard stages of c-b analysis:

1. *Objectives:* The taxonomy of educational objectives is exceedingly complex; measures and goals are difficult to define at all levels of the school—total curriculum, grade, course, lesson, and block of study.

2. *Costs:* Costs of instruction are crudely measurable in terms of teacher and materials inputs; the pricing of new media rests either on an experimental scale or on projections whose value is limited by highly restrictive assumptions.

3. *Benefits:* The pecuniary benefits of education are roughly measurable by future income differences but nonmonetary benefits resist measurement; the learning output of students is only imperfectly quantified by achievement tests.

4. *Rate of Return:* A monetary return on cost, or investment in education at any level is roughly measurable when compared with no education at all; c-b comparisons among instructional alternatives, as offered by the new media, remain feasible in theory only.

1. Objectives

The great commitment of society to education shows up in the wide spectrum of goals that schools are asked to pursue. Considerable progress has been made in identifying and categorizing these goals into such major breakdowns as the cognitive, affective and volitional domains. A wealth of subclassifications support this taxonomy.

Objectives may differ for each separate course of study to distinguish it from the others, but they all have a common denominator: to change the potentialities, proficiencies and attitudes of students who communicate in the instructional process.

It is important to stress the close connection between goals and measurement. The profession of a goal is meaningless unless one can at least tell whether one's distance from the goal has widened or narrowed. As a minimum, one must know "how well one is doing" in accomplishing an objective.

Successively more demanding requirements would be that one be able to sense one's direction of movement relative to the goal, be able to measure both distance and speed in moving toward or away from the goal, and be able to specify and rank means of reaching the goal.

The ultimate purpose of c-b analysis is to find an optimal solution through an appropriate ranking of alternative courses of action. Therefore the operationally most useful objectives are those whose attainment, expressed in outputs or realized benefits, may be measured cardinally, along a continuous scale. Considerably less useful are objectives that permit only an ordinal ranking of their benefits. No wonder that c-b analysis emphasizes objectives that are easily quantifiable over those that are "fuzzy."

Critics of "progressive" education sometimes charge it with a naive passion for testing and measurement. C-b analysts would answer that educators are prone to reject efforts at evaluating their activities. If a given course of study is designed to stimulate "creativity" or "intellectual curiosity" there must be a way to identify these qualities. Else one is merely talking in an echo chamber.

2. Costs

Perhaps the easiest phase of data collection for educational c-b analysis is the cost part. Conventional budget and accounting figures abound, even if administrators often mutter about the lack of management information. What they would like to have is: data properly classified to predict the impact of higher admissions on instructional space and faculty needs; further breakdowns by type of classroom, subject, and staff; and finally a propagation of definite patterns for future years, based on past attrition and transfer rates. Maintaining records in the necessary detail and categories costs money of course. Program accounting is different from conventional fiduciary accounting. While some institutions have adopted a program approach, most schools would rather spend any disposable funds on tangibles, like brick and mortar or scholarships.

Raw accounting data can lead the unwary analyst to simplistic ways of measuring school input. A smart factory superintendent knows not only the number but also the quality of his men and, with an eye on productivity, pays them accordingly. The major variable in teacher compensation seems to be not quality but seniority and passing through advanced courses organized mainly to produce automatic pay raises. The gifted teacher, measured admittedly by unscientific standards, is many times paid no more, and perhaps less, that the rest if he happens to be an innovator who "rocks the boat."

As for the materials input in the school, cost analysis is no better and probably worse. The annual bill for physical facilities, like science and language laboratories, gets folded into total costs without reference to degree and intensity of use. In industry, by contrast, inputs of plant and equipment are firmly controlled by a benchmark of performance, "standard costs." These shoot up sharply when the utilization rate falls below a desired percentage of capacity. Management is alerted and usually takes prompt action. At some levels of c-b analysis, like that concerning the economic benefits of higher education, the value of student income foregone through school attendance must be considered a cost input.

3. Benefits and Their Measurement

Measures of educational output or benefits—the two terms will be used here as stand-ins for one another—range from the global down to the minute and highly specific. At the top end of the scale, output may mean success in reaching a desired "capacity of reasoning" and "social sensitivity," and at the bottom end, ease of handling the multiplication table.

The difficulties of measuring output are mainly two:

1. An outright lack, or inadequacy of suitable yardsticks. In part this problem refers to the quality and validity of educational testing.

2. The joint-product nature of educational output. A prosaic analogy is ham,

tallow, and pork bellies, unobtainable in isolation and forthcoming solely in various mixes, depending on the individual hog.

Educational yardsticks come a cropper when they try to measure such ambiguous objectives as "acculturation to societal values." Are educators talking about opening up for students free choices within the framework of the Constitution and its supporting documents, or do they mean brainwashing them to promote conformance with endorsed community values? In either case, the learning output would consist of a change in attitudinal variables, which are notoriously nettlesome to define and measure. However, an attitudinal index scale, based on the expert judgement of psychologists and sociologists, could probably rate students before and after exposure to a given curriculum. Opinion polls too might find a useful niche. A successful test for output might show more positive attitudes toward books and learning among the underprivileged, "turned-off" students of the ghetto schools.

Undeniably, great progress has been made in refining test procedures and scores in national programs. The same cannot be said for "mini-tests" such as quizzes, midterms and final examinations, not to mention term-papers. Those do exceedingly well if they manage to establish a fair ranking of students that justifies a course grade. Such sloppy testing would never do in serious research on the output of particular instructional processes.

The joint-product aspect of the educational enterprise makes a general evaluation of effectiveness problematic. In principle, one would first test students for various subjects and attitudes. Second, one would weigh, and third combine the separate academic outcomes in some acceptable fashion—probably a composite index.

The hog butcher obtains the value of the animal by pricing each cut of meat, multiplying it by the quantity, and adding up the components. School procedures can never be that uncomplicated but conceivably a consensus could be reached on how to value good citizenship relative to a mastery of the differential calculus. The problem of finding an optimum mix of educational objectives and of allocating budget resources accordingly constitutes a Pandora's box that is best left unopened in the present context.

A word of caution must be added about the proper use of test scores in c-b analysis. Except perhaps in kindergarten, students do not enter a course totally ignorant of the prospective subject matter. What counts therefore is not their test performance on the final day of school but improvement over a pre-entrance test base—the before-and-after increment in test scores.

This idea is the equivalent, in industrial terms, of value-added in manufacturing: the difference between a firm's sale price of its product and the cost of raw and semi-finished materials purchased on the outside. Scholastically one could speak of "value-added" as the difference between "student output" over initial or pre-entrance "student input."

This approach is already used in evaluating education by student earning power. On an overall or "macro" level of analysis, a Cabinet official may want to know whether a given training program is worth its cost in dollar terms, apart from intangible cultural benefits. If the annual outlay for a specific Job Corps Center equaled the additional future earnings of participants for a reasonable number of years ahead, the project would at least break even from a national interest viewpoint. Alternatively, if the tax revenues generated by these additional earnings managed to match the budget cost of the annual program, the project would break even from a fiscal viewpoint. These statements abstract from such complications as discounted cash flows, opportunity costs and other technical aspects of capital budgeting.

C-b tools can be applied—some practically right now and others as yet only potentially —at various levels of an educational system. Consider a two-year nursing program in a junior college where the president may want to ask these critical questions:

LEVEL	C-B QUESTION
1. Overall program	What additional earning power do graduates enjoy over and above their expected income if they had only a high school diploma?
2. First-year curriculum	What measurable difference in learning achievement, relative to cost, would it make to add, drop or change a specific course?
3. Biology course	What differences in learning and cost would result from substituting programmed instruction for one quarter of the scheduled lectures?
4. Lesson in anatomy of frog	What difference in test scores, compared with the cost, would ITV make if substituted for the second hour of lecture?

Some analysts like to add such yardsticks as school attendance and drop-out rates to measure program output. Yet merely warming a seat in some lecture hall is not student-output but input. Student truancy and drop-out rates, if reflecting changes from some earlier base, might serve as proxies for changes in attitude and motivation. An improvement in attendance rates between senior and freshman year might be considered part of the educational output of the high school, indicating greater acceptance of achievement as a part of the American value system.

4. Rate of Return: Technical Cost-Benefit Ratios

The message of the foregoing is clear: in the absence of adequate cost and output figures no proper c-b ratio can be calculated. In some determinate areas, like skill training, it appears perfectly plausible to construct a ratio, by putting the new-learning output of a course in the numerator and its corresponding dollar cost in the denominator. But this ease of solution is deceptive. It fails to carry over into more complex, multi-purpose learning situations.

The practitioner of c-b techniques must solve two related problems in sequence:

1. How to properly match input and ouptut.

2. How to choose among competing alternatives available to do a job.

Up to this point, one major problem of c-b analysis in the educational enterprise has not been squarely faced: the prerequisite of appropriately matching the inputs and outputs of productive processes if useful results are to be obtained. One must know which resources cause what learning effects.

Take the example of a one-semester course, French I, upon completion of which the student is tested for language skills. Assume further that motivation is acknowledged to be a critical factor in learning; that appreciation of French literature, not ignoring its racier aspects, furnishes an excellent incentive to learning; and that certain classic and modern French writings are skillfully built into the content of the course. Obviously, facility with the language in this case is not the sum total of student learning. If a deep interest in French culture has been aroused, the motivation may carry over into advanced courses in French, into other languages, into history, and possibly into a course in poetry. Thus there are multiple outputs, spilling over from the supposedly limited learning objective of a foreign language, which must be caught by the evaluator.

On the input side, "direct labor and materials" expended on a course are easily identified. But assume an imaginative chairman of the romance languages department has ordered a special list of French books and magazines for the library. Further he has organized an exciting exhibition of French motion pictures, not restricted to Joan of Arc, the Bayeux tapestries and the production of Roquefort cheese. How are these costs to be allocated to French I?

The answer divides into several parts. To begin with, input and output do not match at the specific French I level. Rather outputs correspond to inputs only at a much higher educational plane, perhaps French studies or even liberal arts. Thus c-b analysis conducted for a small part of the curriculum makes little sense because output cannot be attributed simply and directly to the input processes.

This should not prevent the teacher from testing learning output in French I or in small segments of the course, like irregular verbs. But such partial testing constitutes something different, quality control. Industry makes extensive use of such controls all along the production line, without infringing on the managerial use of c-b techniques.

C-b analysis has an important time dimension that should not be lost sight of. Assume a school official wanted to know whether teaching French I with the aide of a new language laboratory was more "cost-beneficial" than conventional methods. A pertinent question he might ask would be how long it took the average student under either mode to reach a certain proficiency in reading and conversation. This would keep learning output constant and focus only the difference in cost. A cost reduction by one-half could then be interpreted as a doubling of teaching efficiency through the "language lab" medium.

The Place of C-B Techniques in a Systems Approach

In the logical sequence of systems-analytic steps, c-b techniques enter at a relatively late point. As a pre-condition they require that production alternatives be clearly identified and labelled feasible. They must be shown to "work" and to produce some measurable output, otherwise any costing exercise is futile.

In Greek mythology, Paris was confronted with three feasible choices in women: wisdom, power and beauty. On a benefit basis Helen looked like a winner until the cost was revealed in the Trojan war.

In industry, c-b routines are widely used in capital budgeting. Their basis is the process information furnished by the line departments—engineering, production, traffic, sales and the like—and the inputs of each process are costed out accordingly. If any vital details of the operation are insufficiently known—say the metallurgy of a particular ore deposit or the recovery of a catalyst in a chemical process—feasibility studies must be conducted to gather this information. Such studies are inputs for any complete c-b analysis of alternative mining or manufacturing opportunities.

In the school, the search for alternatives—for better ways of doing an education job—necessarily involves the design of experiments in the teaching-learning transaction. For example, as new media in instructional technology present themselves, they should be tested scientifically to see what they can do. Each medium should be given trials separately and in combination with others, discipline by discipline. The experiments should be based on carefully thought-out hypotheses on just how the medium enters into learning processes. Preliminary results should be fed back to formulate still more promising hypotheses for the next round of experimentation.

In this fashion the chain would run—apart from information feedbacks flowing "upstream"—from fundamental research in learning theory down to applied research and farther "downstream" to feasibility studies of new media. The latter should generate a large set of instructional possibilities, to serve as the basis for the final step in decision-making, a c-b based choice of an optimum learning pattern.

This system-inspired sequence of steps for progress in education plainly shows that c-b analysis is no panacea. A faddist clamor for greater employment of this technique as a cure-all confuses the issue and scrambles priorities. That is why responsible researchers confine their work to theoretical models while waiting for a valid base of useful data sometime in the future.

In the meantime, a workable technique is that of cost comparisons. It is less powerful because it deals only with the cost side on instruction. Educational outputs or benefits are treated as constants, under the tacit proviso that little is understood as yet about learning processes. Hopeful speculation about improvements in teaching performance through the use of new media is kept on a low key. Comparative cost analysis is the tool applied in this Study in the chapter on media costs.

III. Two Meanings of C-B Analysis:
A Review of Recent Work

Just as systems analysis taken as a whole has two meanings, as noted in the respective chapter, so logically do any of its parts like c-b techniques. One meaning would define c-b analysis as the writing of instructions in a prescriptive or "how-to-do-it" sense. This type of activity is also known as "model-building." It constructs a conceptual mock-up or scale model of the actual analysis to be performed at some later time.

In its second meaning, c-b analysis means going ahead and applying a particular prescription to a practical situation. An example would be formulating a decision whether to put library materials on miniature slides known as microfiche, or whether to keep the old system of books-on-shelves.

Up to now, and understandably in the absence of scientific information about what happens in "instruction," c-b analysis has confined itself to "recipe writing." Theoretical models of various kinds, but belonging to the same general family, have been elaborated. For one thing, they specify some of the data that an educational c-b analyst needs and how he is to use them if and when they become available.

As another characteristic, the models apply to whole institutions or general programs rather than the working classroom where instructional alternatives need to be tested. At that critical level yawns a vacuum even of theories of instruction so that c-b analysis is virtually out of the question.

The model-builders recognize their inability to tell:

> Who . . .
> Should teach what . . .
> To whom . . .
> Through what means . . .
> In what sort of environment . . .
> With what effects.

They know full well that in education the customer literally does not know what his dollar will buy and lacks a consumer's guide to tell him. Time and again authors explicitly disclaim any ability to choose among instructional patterns and disavow any attempt to measure instructional effectiveness. Regretfully they address their c-b studies to what *is* rather than what *should be.*

Model A

Some c-b models are preliminary blueprints that apply to particular skill training activities, like the Job Corps Centers organized by the Office of Economic Opportunity. One researcher limits his consideration of benefits to exactly eight possibilities which range from Outcome 1, a 30-day drop-out that spells failure, to Outcome 8, defined as graduation and successful job placement. He then compares various Centers, using for his purposes a set of symbolic equations that relate inputs and outputs. Finally he proposes mathematical rules that would enable a program director at least to rank various Centers and identify the most effective ones by their relation between "successes" and total costs.

The author also puts his ideas to work on accounting records covering four closed-down Men's Urban Training Centers, with promising results. It should be stressed, however, that his c-b analysis employs extremely crude measures of inputs and outputs. The study never descends to the critical level of the teaching-learning situation where the effectiveness of new media must be demonstrated. The reason again is obvious: adequate information does not exist.

Model B

Other models, besides providing more detailed specifications of benefits, aim for absolute rather than rank-order c-b ratios. That is, they want to measure costs and benefit directly rather than content themselves with saying that "Brand A" school is better than "Brand B." One such model, which attempts to evaluate Title I programs under the U.S. Elementary and Secondary Education Act, measures four educational inputs and four outputs as follows:

ELEMENT	MEASUREMENT
Inputs	
Quantity of instruction	Class duration;
Quality of instruction	Recency of curriculum materials;
Intensity of instruction	Teacher-student ratios; teaching materials per student;
Teacher quality	Education and degrees; teaching experience.
Outputs	
Student achievement	Course grades;
Learning attitudes	Drop-out and truancy rates;
Earning potential	Expected increase in life-time earnings;
Equality of educa- tional opportunity	Scholastic achievement becoming less dependent on socio-economic level of student.

These elements of an input-output matrix only faintly approach what a scientifically-designed experiment needs to compare a programmed text with a teacher-aided drill section, to name a typical example. Here too the author of the model is forced to accept the conventional classroom scenario as given, without delving into the basic question of what produces learning. This particular scheme, at the cost of some heroic simplications, ties its diverse elements into a complete package of equations, diagrammed and reasonably ready for the computer.

Model C

One large-scale type of c-b study has been proposed to determine the effectiveness of various conventional inputs at the school level against outputs measured by Iowa test scores. Statistical multiple-regression techniques would be applied to something like 500 schools to identify physical input-output relationships in education. For example, such a study would try to check the effects of higher teacher salaries, thought to imply a better quality of instructor, on average test scores.

A school system might use such results to conclude that raising salaries (after allowing for a lag of time) would raise teaching productivity at member institutions. A similar analysis would be performed on other causal variables representing school characteristics, like the pupil-teacher ratio or an index of academic quality. The massive data requirements of such a scheme, and the large and coarse input units to which it is scaled, make it unsuited for pilot studies let alone classroom experimentation in new teaching media. Even at its own level, on extensive study based on this model proved to be unwieldy and produced indifferent results.

Model D

Still another model design provides the cost accounting framework for a detailed comparison between computer-assisted and conventional instruction in a public school. This model comes equipped with elaborate flow charts and is based on highly flexible modular units. That last feature makes it adaptable to many different levels, instructional media and organizational situations. If actual accounting data were fitted into the slots prescribed by the model, a computer could analyze and rank any two or more teaching alternatives according to benefits gained and costs incurred.

In a concrete case, if it were desired to compare the present operation of a New York City high school with an innovative pattern whereby one-quarter of all lectures were presented on closed circuit television, the computer could scan the accounts and print out the benefit and cost differences.

The format of this model is sophisticated enough to deal directly with the hidden costs of unused capacity—known to economists as "opportunity costs"—as well as with the impact of a potential speeding up of the instruction cycle. For example, a simulation exercise involving the model shows that *time-to-learn is the single most critical factor in the general cost of education.* This highly significant finding is usually overlooked in time-honored, lock-step curriculum patterns. Further, the *scheduling of physical facilities for full utilization of capacity is the single most sensitive cost factor in instructional modes like CAI* which depend heavily on expensive hardware.

Once again the authors of this model reiterate the importance of knowing what makes a teaching medium learning-effective and of designing appropriate instruction processes. They note the long-standing unhappiness of the Department of Defense with premature and misdirected attempts to "cost-benefit" CAI. They apologize for the fact that their own model provides methodologies only for costing, leaving one-half of the c-b problem unresolved.

Model E

Finally one might mention the c-b models covering whole universities, although here the purpose is chiefly administrative and some eons away from the mundane task of defining teaching and learning. Inputs are taken to be personnel, space, and equipment. Output is identified by developed manpower, research, and public or technical services.

Broad academic goals of higher education, and the establishment of operational measures of "quality" are explicitly put outside the scope of the model. For example, raw student credit-hours are considered a product of the university, without further inquiry into learning as such.

"Super-models" of this type measure surface phenomena, and are highly useful at the top level of administration if one could only assume that submodels exist whose concern is the production and measurement of academic substance. In the absence of such submodels—that is, in the absence of effective academic production controls—such overall models of university operation may serve to institutionalize and computerize a mechanical, assembly-line type of instruction, and thus tend to dehumanize higher education.

Some Practical Considerations

The "hidden hand" that seems to push Western civilization from ritual towards reason may be perceived in an interaction between programmed instruction and c-b analysis. The latter's information problem is composed of two parts:

1. Getting hold of scientifically valid new data.

2. In the meantime, making maximum use of existing knowledge in redesigning courses for the employment and costing of diverse media.

A most salutary influence toward a rationalization of instruction, and one whose impact has only begun to make itself felt, is programmed instruction (PI). As one Army educational advisor put it, PI has caused a "cleansing" of the curriculum. What he meant was that PI required a systematic analysis of training objectives as well as materials and teaching procedures in the Army. The discipline of thinking through established teaching routines led to a sloughing off of the outmoded, the ineffective, and the redundant. As a special bonus, the content analysis of training courses at one particular Army installation sparked new thinking about required manpower skills and caused significant changes in Military Occupational Specialties (MOS) descriptions.

This observer also credited PI with a saving in time of 30 percent, citing this figure as typical of military experience. Without however knowing the additional costs incurred through PI, plus other relevant information on its advantages and disadvantages, time savings alone do not permit valid c-b interpretations.

Some of the newer instructional media have suffered from primitive cost-benefit thinking as educators have fastened on possible cost-savings over traditional modes of instruction.

Educational television for example has sometimes been hastily and narrowly conceived as a mere money saver. The usual lecture held by the usual instructor is put on closed circuit television without much change in style or format, while most or all student contact is assumed by low-paid graduate assistants. As a result, faculties in many institutions have come to look on educational television less as an opportunity than as an economy move to exploit them. Attitudes against the spread of ETV have hardened among faculty ranks and the medium itself has become discredited.

At the other extreme, educators have been called "stick-in-the muds" who refuse to accept new technology for selfish reasons. Administrators who jump on the bandwagon and eagerly embrace any new medium that comes along presumably are "progressives." This name-calling begs the issue. A dearth of data meets any question whether the new media justify their cost relative to their productiveness. A school principal's resistance to a sales pitch and refusal to buy a "pig in a poke" may be a healthy kind of conservatism. The strongest sales argument for any piece of equipment or new production process is a carefuly c-b study. That is the reason why industry and the military have increasingly adopted this approach and why it is now standard fare in the modern business administration curriculum. The school must also use this approach but it has a long way to go.

Index